PRINCE RUPERT

By the same author

Althorp: The Story of an English House
The Spencer Family
Blenheim: Battle for Europe

PRINCE RUPERT

THE LAST CAVALIER

CHARLES SPENCER

Weidenfeld & Nicolson

LONDON

TO LARA

First published in Great Britain in 2007
by Weidenfeld & Nicolson

3 5 7 9 10 8 6 4 2

A CIP catalogue record for this book
is available from the British Library.

ISBN 978 0 297 84610 9

Typeset by Deltatype Ltd, Birkenhead, Merseyside

Printed in Great Britain by Clays Ltd, St Ives plc

The Orion Publishing Group's policy is to use papers that
are natural, renewable and recyclable products and made
from wood grown in sustainable forests. The logging and
manufacturing processes are expected to conform to the
environmental regulations of the country of origin.

Weidenfeld & Nicolson

The Orion Publishing Group Ltd
Orion House
5 Upper Saint Martin's Lane
London, WC2H 9EA

www.orionbooks.co.uk

ACKNOWLEDGEMENTS

I would like to thank Her Majesty the Queen for allowing me access to the Royal Archives at Windsor Castle and for giving me permission to quote from them. At the same time I must thank the archivists and librarians there for their assistance.

Thanks are also due to the Trustees of the British Library, and especially to the staff of the Rare Books, Humanities and Manuscripts departments, during the nearly three years that I researched and wrote this biography. The Bodleian also provided important assistance, especially the staff in Duke Humfrey's Library.

I am similarly grateful to the Fellows of the Royal Society for access to their records. Other archivists – including those of the University of Oxford; of Magdalen College, Oxford; and of Belvoir Castle – also gave useful advice. A wide range of county archivists were similarly helpful.

Dr Tim Connor kindly read through my completed final draft and thankfully spotted a couple of 'howlers' (he was my tutor at school and is now a friend – but his terminology for my more monstrous mistakes has not changed in 25 years). Any mistakes that remain are entirely my responsibility.

I would also like to thank Ian Drury and Keith Lowe, from my publishers, for their enthusiasm and editorial input.

AUTHOR'S NOTE

SPELLING

I have applied modern spelling norms to all quotes incorporated in the body of the book, for the convenience of the general reader.

DATES

With regard to dates, the Julian Calendar (also known as 'Old Style') was in operation in Europe from 46 BC. In 1582 Pope Gregory XIII introduced the Gregorian Calendar ('New Style'). Although the Gregorian Calendar was embraced by much of Europe, it was not adopted by Britain (and its empire) until 1752. The two calendars were out of kilter during Prince Rupert's time by ten days (1 January 1642 in the Julian Calendar was 11 January 1642 in the Gregorian one). In order to achieve consistency, I have used the Gregorian Calendar throughout.

CONTENTS

LIST OF MAPS

LIST OF ILLUSTRATIONS

13. Rupert, the exhausted general. Contemporary engraving after William Dobson, *c.* 1646.
14. Rupert and his African page. Engraving after a portrait by Bouidon, 1654. AKG London.
15. The *Royal Prince* and Other Vessels at the Four Days Fight, 1–4 June 1666, by Abraham Storck. National Maritime Museum, London (acquired with the assistance of the National Art Collections Fund).
16. Trepanning. Contemporary engraving. Private Collection.
17. Rupert's mezzotint of the Execution of John the Baptist. British Museum.
18. Peg Hughes, Rupert's wife. Mezzotint by Robert Williams after Peter Lely. Mander and Mitchenson Theatre collection.
19. Ruperta; Rupert and Peg's daughter, by Godfrey Kneller. National Portrait Gallery, London.
20. Rupert and his son, Dudley, by Vignon, courtesy of www.knebworthhouse.com.
21. Prince Rupert of the Rhine. Stoneware bust made by John Wight at Fulham *c.* 1680. British Museum.
22. Old Guard Chamber in the Round Tower, Windsor Castle. Watercolour by J. Stephanoff, 1818. Royal Collection.
23. The Hudson's Bay Company's portrait of Rupert as first Governor of the Company, courtesy of the National Archives of Canada.

Images from the Royal Collection are the copyright of HM Queen Elizabeth II, 2007.

INTRODUCTION

Prince Rupert of the Rhine – it's a name touched in equal parts by glamour and glory, defeat and disappointment. The poster boy of the Royalist cause, Rupert attracted the unrestrained bile of Parliament's busy propagandists. They poured out pamphlets besmirching the aims and intentions of the king's talismanic nephew. His reputation has never fully recovered. However, he has never wanted for admirers: his many portraits show a good-looking and intelligent man, confident and focused. If opinions on the prince are divided, this has long been the case. He achieved his contentious status during some of the most divisive years in British history, which saw Charles I fighting Parliament in the English Civil War.

Those casually acquainted with the conflicts of the 1640s usually know something of the prince's military reputation – most likely that he was the leader of thundering cavalry charges, which overwhelmed opponents with the shock of their initial impetus, before spinning off the battlefield in woeful indiscipline. There is certainly truth in this popular image: at the first and last of the great Civil War battles, Rupert's troops sliced effortlessly through the enemy, then galloped after their foes instead of regrouping and re-engaging. At Edgehill, this unruliness robbed the king of victory. At Naseby, massively outnumbered, Royalist failure was probably inevitable, but the early absence of the prince and his squadrons made defeat certain and complete.

At 6 foot 4 inches tall, the sheer physical presence of Rupert was difficult to ignore. He attracted enormous attention from contemporaries. To his followers, he was a man 'whose very name was half a conquest'. The Marquess of Newcastle, a key Royalist grandee in northern England, wrote to the prince on this theme: 'Your name is grown so triumphant, and the world's expectations to look for more from you than man can do; but that is their fault, Sir, and not yours. Long may you live ... a terror to your uncle's enemies, and a preserver of his servants.'

The enemy viewed him in a more apocalyptic light: a Scottish observer, writing in 1644, summoned an awful image of the prince's approach of the city of York: 'The manner briefly was thus, Rupert, or the second Nimrod, the mighty Plunderer, the beginning of whose kingdom is confusion, comes in his hunting carrier, with his fellow hunters, and near 20,000 bloodhounds attending them, all more ravenous than wolves, and fiercer than tigers, thirsting for blood.' To Parliament, the prince was a figure of terror.

When examining Rupert's life, it is important to do so against a time line: the headline events frequently occurred when he was still very young. Born the son of a newly crowned king and queen, he embarked on a life of exile while still an infant. He gained a reputation as a notable soldier in his teens, exhibiting examples of the courage that marked his life and which frequently verged on the insane. Eventually he was taken prisoner of war. He endured years of incarceration, with periods of genuine deprivation and hardship. However, he used this time to develop his interests in art and science (which would remain dear to him throughout his life), and also experienced his first love – with his gaoler's daughter.

The prince was returned to freedom as the clouds of civil warfare settled over England. Aged 22, he arrived in time to take command of his uncle's 800 horsemen, and set about reinforcing and transforming them. They quickly became an eye-catching strike force. Dismissed by Parliament as demonic 'cavaliers', loose-living rapists and pillagers, Rupert moulded them into the most feared and effective part of the Royalist army.

The myth of the prince and his cavaliers evolved early in the conflict. On a warm day in the autumn of 1642, Rupert, his brother Maurice, and several of their comrades took time off from convoy duty to lie on the grass near Powick Bridge. Their breastplates lay beside them, while their horses grazed near by. Suddenly the princes spotted the Life Guard of the Earl of Essex, the enemy lord general, riding towards them at the head of a significant force.

Logic dictated a speedy retreat to the safety of nearby Worcester. Instead, Rupert shouted to his officers to follow him. He then sprung onto his horse and immediately galloped directly at the rebels. The rest of the Royalists went after their young general as quickly as they could: the first proper engagement of the Civil War was joined.

Perhaps only fifty rebels were slain at Powick Bridge, but the significance of the day lay beyond the body count. Parliament had anticipated a short campaign, with speedy victory over a king who was believed to be unpopular and poorly equipped for warfare, but this reverse caused a huge dent to morale at Westminster. Several prominent rebel officers were among the dead and Rupert had shown that his gallantry, and that of his devoted followers, stood between Parliament and victory.

The English Civil War was the backdrop to Rupert's most famous exploits. His flair on the battlefield led to hopes of finishing off Parliament, in 1643. However, Rupert found he faced enemies who were harder to defeat than those arrayed against him on the battlefield: his colleagues in the king's council of war were divided, several of them suspicious and resentful of the young, foreign princeling, who enjoyed Charles I's full favour. The Royalist cause was hamstrung by these internal divisions, which reduced Rupert to smouldering resentment. Meanwhile, Parliament refined its resources, and trained an army of a calibre that the king never possessed.

The prince became increasingly senior, militarily. Victories in the north were nullified by his humiliating defeat at Marston Moor. Naseby followed. His nadir came with the surrender of Bristol, then England's second city, which allowed Rupert's enemies to portray him, completely unfairly, as treacherous to the king. As Charles I spiralled towards ultimate defeat, he was ready to believe anything – even that his nephew was responsible for his key reverses. The weak monarch suspected his sister's son, who was one of his most loyal commanders, rather than question the conniving courtiers who hated the bloodied hero.

After the Civil War, Rupert found brief employment in Louis XIV's armies. However, he always had one ear cocked, waiting for the summons to serve his uncle's cause once more. When the call came, he ignored his lack of experience at sea to lead the Royalist navy. It was a difficult assignment, which nobody else wanted. Rupert's most heroic years followed, as he kept the Stuart banner flying while Parliament triumphed everywhere else. However, the effort of survival was enormous and exacted a heavy cost. The remainder of the prince's life betrayed the ravages to his health incurred on royal duty.

When tackling Rupert's life story, I was determined that only a third of the text should cover the key Civil War years of 1642–5: for a man who lived into his sixties, it seemed ridiculous to allot any more space to the four years that established his reputation. Fortunately, the rest of

Prince Rupert's days were filled with fascinating events, as his enquiring mind and his restless spirit took him in a variety of directions.

Every subject of a biography is, of course, to some extent, a product of his or her age. Of Rupert this is particularly so: his experiences, tastes, and interests were reflective of those preoccupying many European aristocrats and princes in the middle decades of the seventeenth century. He was enmeshed in one war after the other, hoping that battlefield success would lead to riches and glory. While he was a brilliant and charismatic cavalry general, he never progressed to successful overall command. However, soldiery – on land and sea – remained his vocation into late middle age.

His wider pursuits were typical of an active patrician with a good brain – many of his hobbies coincided with those of his first cousin, Charles II. Both men, predictably, enjoyed hunting and shooting, pursued actresses (although Rupert's conquests were paltry in comparison to the king's plenty), and played energetic tennis: Rupert was reputedly the finest player in England.

However, not all energies were expended in the bedroom and on the sports' field. Rupert, like Charles II, had a burning interest in science. The Restoration coincided with an expansion of knowledge in chemistry, 1661 seeing the appearance of Robert Boyle's *The Sceptical Chymist*, as well as the foundation of the Royal Society. Rupert was one of its first members. He was never afraid to dirty his own hands, spending happy, sweat-drenched, hours labouring in his laboratory and at his foundry. The Prince's inventions mainly had a military theme, but he also brought mezzotint engraving to Britain. Some believe that he devised the process.

Financial insecurity was Rupert's constant spur. It explains his never-ending pursuit of business schemes: he was determined to slough off the poverty bequeathed him as a younger son of a dispossessed royal family. The most enduring legacy of this search for wealth is the Hudson's Bay Company, which the prince established and championed. It opened up vast areas of what is now Canada. The town of Prince Rupert, just south of the Alaskan/Canadian border, is a reminder of Rupert's interest in North American trade and exploration.

Why write a biography of Prince Rupert now? There have been times when Rupert was better known than is currently the case. Eliot Warburton's three volumes in the 1840s brought to light much of the correspondence and commentary attached to the glory days of this

fascinating man. Subsequent biographies have also tended to concentrate on the Civil War years: there were three such works in 1976
alone. More recently, Frank Kitson has divided Rupert's military career
into two distinct phases – his years as a young general, and those as a
middle-aged admiral – and analysed both.

My book looks at the whole man, as well as the context of his life.
It does not claim to contain a definitive study of the Civil War, nor of
the later Anglo-Dutch Wars. I have instead endeavoured to tell the tale
of an intriguing individual, who frightened and inspired his contemporaries, and who was at the centre of a succession of fierce, personal
quarrels. His particular foes were George Digby, a foppish courtier, and
Samuel Pepys, the inspired naval bureaucrat most often remembered
for his diaries.

Rupert was not an easy man. He was a cavalier, but certainly not of
the laughing variety. At his best, he was serious, loyal, inspirational,
and incisive. At his worst, he was arrogant, inflexible, and irascible.
However, he lived life with passion and energy. He regarded himself
as a man who would always do the right thing, whatever the cost. His
lack of compromise was at once his greatest gift and his most significant
impediment.

Prince Rupert of the Rhine hails from a different era, but his conflicting complexities are recognisable to all today that have a broad and
compassionate view of the human condition. Writing his latest biography has left me an admirer of this fascinating man, accepting of his
shortcomings, and in awe of his extraordinary physical courage. Above
all, it is the range of his experiences that is most startling. It is hard to
believe that one man packed so much into a single lifetime.

CHAPTER ONE

BAPTISM OF FIRE

'Swaddled in Armour, Drums appeas'd thy Cries,
And the Shrill Trumpet sang thy Lullabies.'

Thomas Flatman, *On the Death of the Illustrious*
Prince Rupert, a Pindarique Ode

Rupert was born in Prague on 17 December 1619, at half past ten at night. He was the third son, and fourth child, of a union that exuded glamour and promised glory. His mother Elizabeth was a British princess famed as a romantic icon throughout the Continent. His father Frederick V was Count Palatine, one of the foremost Protestant princes of Europe. 'From thy noble Pedigree,' Rupert's eulogist would conclude, 'The Royal Blood ... sparked in thy veins.'[1] The princeling's royal heritage was of a north and middle European stamp: his grandmothers were princesses, one Danish, the other Dutch; his maternal grandfather was James I of England. When James heard that his only surviving daughter had produced a new grandson, he pressed a purse of gold coins into the messenger's hands, before ordering the drinking of toasts.

Frederick and Elizabeth invited their subjects to file past their baby. Rupert lay in an ebony cradle – a symbol of the rich luxury that they assumed would be his lifelong companion. Another of his gifts was a silver ship, a prophetic offering, for some of Rupert's most fascinating and challenging years would be at sea. Since he was native-born, unlike his two older brothers, there were calls for Rupert to be declared heir to his parents' new kingdom – a proposal that failed in the Bohemian parliament by one vote. However, the neighbouring territory of Lusatia proclaimed Rupert as its prince.

Rupert's christening took place on 31 March 1620, a contemporary recording: 'The solemnity of his baptism was very extraordinary, there being present the King himself, his brother, two princes of the House of Saxony, the Duke of Anhalt, Elector of Hohenloe, with many other

persons of eminent condition ....'[2] He was named after an ancestor who
had been Emperor between 1400 and 1410, Rupert the Clement. The
young prince inherited his forebear's Christian name, not his disposition.

Bethlem Gabor was chosen as godfather: he was a formidable,
Transylvanian, nobleman who claimed the throne of Hungary. Unable
to attend the christening in person, he sent Count Thurtzo to represent him. The count, in body armour, received the infant from the
priest and held him: a gesture that signalled his absent master's duty
of guardianship. Thurtzo then passed Rupert to the deputies of the
Bohemian dependencies, who were also encased in armour. The sight
of breastplates and swords in a cathedral was indicative of the close inter-
twining of the religious and the military in early seventeenth-century
Europe. This was a time when senior ecclesiastical figures were at the
centre of politics and lay princes were entrusted with spiritual duties.

Rupert's father had recently, by request, become King of Bohemia,
with Elizabeth his queen. The Bohemian nobility needed a Protestant
champion to replace, and then stand up to, the Catholic Habsburgs,
whom they had recently overthrown. Frederick, after much agonising,
had agreed to take on the role. Rarely can the acceptance of an invitation
have sparked such colossal devastation. Rupert's birth took place after
the fuse had been lit and just before the powder keg went up. Even as
the boy's arrival was celebrated, plans were forming in Catholic Europe
that would impact fatally on his parents' rule and set the newborn's life
on its helter-skelter course.

When Rupert's parents married, in 1613, it was the conclusion of his
mother's exhaustive search for a suitable husband. By the standards of
the age, Elizabeth's clean features and height marked her out as handsome. Her lineage and charm persuaded people, somewhat against
the evidence of her portraits, to declare her a great beauty. There was,
however, no doubting her personality. Elizabeth had a confidence and
sparkle inherited from her charismatic grandmother, Mary Queen of
Scots. Unfortunately, Elizabeth would also match her tragic ancestress
for heartbreak.

The princess was seven when her father left Scotland to assume the
English throne. It had been left vacant by the death of the girl's god-
mother, Elizabeth I. From the start young 'Lady Elizabeth' was hugely
popular, provoking delighted admiration and praise from all who met

her. James believed that royal children prospered better if kept away
from the distractions of court life, so Elizabeth was handed over to an
aristocratic couple, Lord and Lady Harington – 'persons eminent for
prudence and piety'[3] – for a strict education. The reports from their
residence at Combe Abbey, near Coventry, were consistently enthusiastic: 'With God's assistance', Lord Harington wrote, 'we hope to do
our Lady Elizabeth such service as is due to her princely endowments
and natural abilities; both which appear the sweet dawning of future
comfort to her royal father.'[4]

This princess of rare qualities was celebrated throughout the kingdom. If the Gunpowder Plot of 1605 had been successful in blowing up
James and his sons, the conspirators had intended to kidnap Elizabeth,
have her crowned, and bring her up a Catholic. 'What a queen should
I have been by this means!' she said when told of the plan, 'I had rather
have been with my Royal Father in the Parliament House, than wear
his Crown on such condition.'[5]

As womanhood approached Elizabeth's hand became much sought
after overseas. The French ambassador met the princess when she was
11 and was captivated by her poise. 'I assure you', he reported to Paris,
'that it will not be her fault if she is not dauphiness – and she might
have worse fancies – for she is not at all vexed when it is mentioned to
her.'[6] Sir Walter Raleigh thought Elizabeth 'by nature and education
endowed with such princely perfections, both of body and mind, as
may well deserve to be reputed a worthy spouse for the greatest monarch in Christendom'.[7] Her lengthy list of failed suitors included the
kings of Sweden and Spain, the Dauphin of France, and Maurice of
Nassau, the Dutch leader.

The collapse of the Spanish suit helps to explain Elizabeth's eventual
choice of husband. James I had hoped that such a union would under-
line the end of hostilities between England and Spain, and advertise
his wise and peace-loving kingship. However, his heir, Prince Henry,
spoke for the majority of Englishmen when loudly rejecting his sister's
sacrifice to Popery. 'The prince hath publicly said', the Spanish ambassador was shocked to note, 'that whosoever should counsel his father to
marry his sister to a Catholic prince, were a traitor, and that it cannot
be but to kill him and his brother, and make the succession theirs; he
is a great heretic!'[8]

The most obvious Protestant match was the gifted Swedish prince,
Gustavus Adolphus. However, Sweden was at war with Denmark,

and the Danish king was Elizabeth's maternal uncle, so this option fell away. Of the other choices, Frederick V, Count Palatine, was the candidate who stood out. He was the Palsgrave, or 'Palace Count', a role his family had filled since the tenth century. As such, he was the senior Protestant prince of the Holy Roman Empire – that hotchpotch of 300 Germanic, Bohemian, Lowland, and Italian lands, which was among the largest realms in Europe. The Count Palatine was one of the seven electors* charged by a fourteenth-century Papal Bull with the appointment of the Emperor. However, since the late Middle Ages, the throne – along with those of Hungary and Bohemia – had effectively become the possession of the Habsburg dynasty.

Frederick's upbringing had more breadth to it than Elizabeth's cloistered childhood. He had completed his education in Sedan, at the house of his uncle, the Duke of Bouillon. French was the main language spoken at Heidelberg, so this was an opportunity to progress to faultless fluency. His tutor was Tilenus, a Calvinist who stressed the need to guard against the evils of Catholicism. He planted in his pupil the lifelong conviction that the Pope, his Jesuit foot soldiers, and his Spanish Habsburg allies, were conspiring to undermine the rest of Europe for their own gain.

Religion was the cornerstone of a varied education. Frederick became a fine dancer, an adept swordsman, and an accomplished rider. By the time that he inherited the electorate, on his father's death in 1610, Frederick had the makings of the perfect prince: he was devout, polished, and manly. The following year, when James I took discreet soundings about Frederick's character and prospects from Bouillon, he received an enthusiastic critique: a perfect physique, a dark complexion and handsome face; a natural athleticism, particularly on horseback; a serious faith and pure morals; a wonderful portfolio of houses, including exquisite hunting lodges; and, when he came of age, arguably the most important electorate of the Holy Roman Empire. Eligibility was not a problem.

However, many in England had expected Elizabeth to marry a king. A prince, albeit one of Frederick's fine pedigree, was considered too humble a match for the 'Pearl of Britain'. Protestant supporters of the marriage felt it necessary to stress the importance of the Palatinate to

---

* The other six electors were the Archbishops of Cologne, Mainz, and Trier, and the King of Bohemia, the Duke of Saxony, and the Margrave of Brandenburg.

the disappointed: 'Now for his Highness's Country', wrote one of James I's chaplains, 'it is neither so small, unfruitful, or mean, as is by some supposed. It is in length about 200 English miles, the lower and the upper country. In the lower the Prince hath 26 walled towns, besides an infinite number of good and fair villages, 22 houses; and the land is very fruitful of wine, corn, and other comfortable fruits for man's use, having the Rhine and the Neckar running through it. The upper Country hath not so many walled towns and princely houses, but those that are, be generally fairer than in the lower, especially Amberg and Newmarket [*sic*].'⁹

It was Frederick's devotion to Protestantism, and his tolerance of all its forms, that ultimately secured Elizabeth's hand. Since 1555, the rulers of each part of the Holy Roman Empire had been permitted to choose their territory's official religion. This concession helped to defuse the tension between Roman Catholics and Protestants. Since 1562, with one short-lived aberration, the count's family had been solidly Calvinist, while its capital, Heidelberg, was known for its religious and intellectual enlightenment. 'We have to bless God', wrote an English translator of Palatine scriptures, in 1614, 'for the religious care of our dread sovereign, in matching his only daughter, a princess peerless, with a Prince of that soundness of religion as the Prince Elector is.'¹⁰

Although the princess's mother, Anne of Denmark, was a Catholic sympathiser, her father's succession to the English throne had been conditional on his promise to uphold Anglicanism. The English Establishment, which had so hurriedly welcomed James, already viewed him with concern. Nobles were appalled by his sale of hereditary titles, which introduced rich parvenus to the aristocracy. Furthermore, his rampant homosexuality was considered troubling in a king, partly on moral grounds, but more practically because his good-looking young favourites bypassed the conventional channels of patronage to gorge themselves on ill-deserved honours.

A sure way for James to regain some popularity was to play the religious card: in 1612 he took England into the Protestant Union, a defensive confederation of nine German principalities and seventeen imperial cities formed by Frederick's father, and which the young Palsgrave now led. The same year, he agreed that Elizabeth should wed Frederick. The public preacher in Bristol – England's second city and a place that was to play an important role in Rupert's adult life – welcomed the betrothal: 'Unto you happy Prince, and sent of

God to increase our happiness', he said in an open letter, 'Come in thou blessed of the Lord, for whom the choicest pearl in the Christian world is by God himself prepared. The Lord makes her like Leah and like Rahel [*sic*], which two builded the house of Israel. Let her grow into thousand thousands, and let her seed possess the gate of his enemies.'[11]

It was expected for princes and princesses to make dynastic marriages. Rupert's parents were unusual in that theirs was a genuine love match, whose romantic pulse never slowed. Frederick made a sublime impression, on arriving in England. His 'well-becoming confidence'[12] was noted, as was his 'wit, courage and judgement'.[13] Elizabeth was relieved to be marrying such a dashing young man: when Prince Maurice of Nassau had been presented as a possible mate, she had been repelled by the physical decay of his advanced middle age. By contrast, she fell quickly and completely in love with her handsome, youthful suitor.

The 16-year-old couple, only four days apart in age, married in Whitehall Chapel on St Valentine's Day, 1613. Elizabeth wore a gold crown, her white dress and loosely hanging hair advertising her virginity. Despite the bride's simplicity, James managed to spend nearly £100,000 on the celebrations, prompting one of his courtiers to offer a cheerless supplication: 'God grant money to pay debts.'[14] However, the revelry was not only about fleeting extravagance: William Shakespeare offered an enduring wedding gift, writing a play for the couple. *The Tempest* was performed fourteen times by the King's Men during the festivities, for which the players received £150. The Archbishop of Canterbury summed up the hopes of all who witnessed the match: 'The God of Abraham, of Isaac, and of Jacob bless these nuptials, and make them prosperous to these kingdoms and to his Church.'[15]

Frederick left for home ahead of his bride so that he could be in the Palatinate to receive her. Elizabeth travelled with a train of supporters that, by the time it reached the outskirts of Heidelberg, consisted of 12 princes, 30 earls, 1,000 gentlemen, and 2,000 soldiers. Her arrival was greeted with volleys of musket shot and salvoes of cannon fire from the Palatine army. 'Then they marched altogether orderly in good array,' wrote an eyewitness, 'conducting her to Heidelberg, where the citizens wanted no expressions of joy, love, and duty in hearty welcoming of her, & praying for her; all windows being replenished with people of all ages and degrees, and the streets thronged with multitudes of people, drawn thither from all parts, not so much to see the Pageants that were erected to further this honourable entertainment, as to have their eyes filled in beholding of her Highness, whom all honoured and admired.'[16]

Frederick and Elizabeth enjoyed six happy years in Heidelberg. The prince enlarged the pink, sandstone castle for his wife, adding a suite of ten rooms – 'the English wing' – to welcome her to her new home. The castle's floors were made of porphyry, while the cornices were inlaid with gems. Elizabeth's drawing room was hung with silver decorations, against a background of white marble. The library, with its priceless codices, housed one of the greatest book collections in Europe.

Outside, the Electress's passion for animals found expression in a monkey-house and a generously proportioned menagerie. The palace garden, the 'Hortus Palatinatus', was famous throughout the Continent, delighting visitors with its system of fountains, its fine statues, and its intricate network of flowerbeds. When an heir, Frederick Henry, was born, Frederick showed his delight by planting an extension to the garden under his wife's bedroom window: it was laid out with English flowers, to remind the princess of home. Two more children quickly appeared, Elizabeth and Charles Louis, before she fell pregnant with Rupert.

The Palatine shared a border with Bohemia. In July 1617, Ferdinand of Austria, a Habsburg prince, was appointed king-elect. The crown was supposedly decided by a vote of the Bohemian nobles, but they felt bypassed and believed that Ferdinand had been foisted on them through trickery. The intensity of Ferdinand's Catholic faith soon became clear: the new king's daily routine included several hours in religious meditation and attendance at two masses. Ferdinand reneged on previous assurances and brought in a raft of measures to root out Protestantism in Bohemia, including control of the printing presses. To English diplomats, this made him 'a silly Jesuited soul',[17] but his leading subjects declined to regard his actions with such lightness. Catholic fanaticism had no place in Prague: the city had produced the fifteenth-century martyr John Hus, burnt to death for questioning Roman orthodoxy. Hus had left behind a tradition of religious toler- ance, independence, and diversity: the Hussite majority harmoniously co-existed with Catholics, Calvinists, and even the extreme Church of the Bohemian Brethren.

In May 1618 Ferdinand went too far, ordering the destruction of two Protestant churches in the capital. This prompted a rebellion,

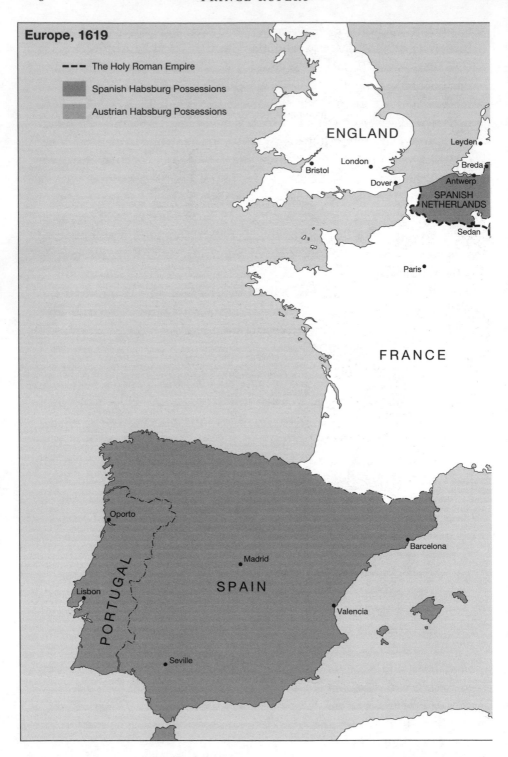

Europe, 1619

- - - - The Holy Roman Empire

Spanish Habsburg Possessions

Austrian Habsburg Possessions

ENGLAND

Leyden

London
Bristol

Breda
Antwerp
SPANISH
NETHERLANDS

Dover

Sedan

Paris

FRANCE

Oporto

Barcelona

Madrid

PORTUGAL

SPAIN

Lisbon

Valencia

Seville

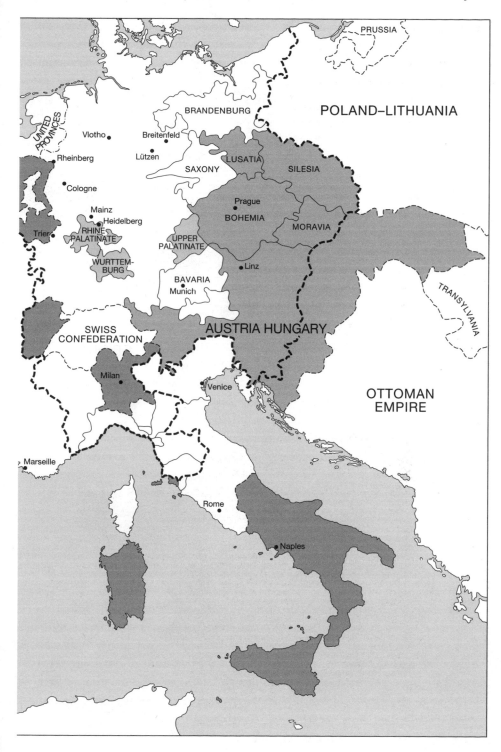

PRUSSIA

UNITED PROVINCES

BRANDENBURG

POLAND–LITHUANIA

Vlotho

Breitenfeld

LUSATIA

Rheinberg

Lützen

SAXONY

SILESIA

Cologne

Prague

Mainz

Heidelberg

BOHEMIA

MORAVIA

Trier

RHINE PALATINATE

UPPER PALATINATE

WURTTEM-BURG

Linz

BAVARIA

Munich

TRANSYLVANIA

SWISS CONFEDERATION

AUSTRIA HUNGARY

Milan

Venice

OTTOMAN EMPIRE

Marseille

Rome

Naples

led by the Bohemian nobility. Their representatives cornered the two Habsburg regents and their secretary in the council chamber of Hradcany Castle and hurled them from its upper windows. One of the victims, the hefty Jaraslas Martinitz, called out 'Jesu Maria! Help!' as he was ejected. The second, Vilem Slavata, clung onto the sill for his life, only loosening his grip when knocked unconscious. Their secretary, Philipus Fabricius, was so terrified by the violence he had witnessed that he put up barely a struggle.

Astonishingly, all three men survived the 80-foot drop, prompting Catholics to celebrate the miraculous intervention of the Blessed Virgin. In fact, salvation had arrived in a more humdrum form: the trio's billowing cloaks had acted as parachutes, and slowed their fall, before a slurry-pit had cushioned their landing. 'The Defenestration of Prague' was a suitably dramatic prelude to the horrors of the ensuing conflict, the Thirty Years' War.

As Ferdinand arranged avenging armies, the Bohemians sought a new king. After refusals from their first choices, they turned to Frederick to fill the void. He agonised about the decision: his Huguenot and Dutch uncles, his chancellor, as well as his spiritual sense of duty, all told him to consent, but his mother and his father-in-law strongly advised against. The Palsgrave's family motto was: 'Rule me, Lord, according to your word.' Frederick became convinced that God expected him to grasp the opportunity placed before him, for His sake. However, when he eventually agreed to accept the crown, he did so with a sense of deep foreboding. On a dull day in October 1619, waved off by his tearful mother, Frederick rode out with the heavily pregnant Elizabeth by his side, accompanied by young Frederick Henry. It was the last time any of them would see Heidelberg.

The omens were initially favourable: the people of Prague noted that the arrival of their new rulers coincided with several days when none of the capital's civil population died. However, it soon became apparent that Frederick had underestimated the risk he was taking by overestimating the level of support for his cause. Beside his Palatine army of 15,000 men, he had assumed he could also rely on the troops of the Protestant Union. This network of religious allies included several Germanic lands, England, the Dutch United Provinces, Venice, Denmark, and Sweden. But within days of the start of Frederick's rule, all his calculations were in disarray, for Ferdinand was elected Holy Roman Emperor. This altered everything. The Palsgrave, the Imperial right-hand man, now found himself in armed conflict with his feudal overlord. Many of his German allies found they could not draw their sword against their sovereign master.

Frederick had the opportunity to back down, but two months later he confirmed his acceptance of the crown. Ferdinand, initially unsure of his strength, persisted in urging Frederick to withdraw from Bohemia and return to Heidelberg. If he failed to do this by 1 June 1620, Ferdinand promised, he would attract an Imperial ban. This would place him, and anyone who assisted him, outside the law. Frederick could now be in no doubt: by accepting the throne that wiser men had rejected, and by challenging the orthodoxy of which he was supposed to be the champion, he had raised the possibility of losing everything.

The conduct of Frederick's allies ushered cataclysm closer. In July, French diplomats persuaded the Protestant Union to remain neutral, while Bohemia faced the consequences of its rebellion alone. Meanwhile, the timing of Frederick's call for help could not have reached the Dutch United Provinces at a worse time: after decades of fighting for their survival, they were now in the final stages of a truce with Spain, and were gearing up for renewed warfare with the old enemy on their borders. The United Provinces did little more than cheer Frederick on from the sidelines, hoping that his bid for power would succeed, while unable to lend adequate support: some money and 1,500 troops was all they could spare. Similarly, the Swedes and their warrior king, Gustavus Adolphus, were embroiled in a struggle with Poland: they sent Frederick just eight cannon; a pitiful contribution, but more than the Danes and the Venetians mustered between them. In the meantime Bethlem Gabor, Rupert's supposed protector and Frederick's sworn ally, chose to pursue his own campaign in Hungary, rather than redirect his forces to help in Bohemia.

The greatest disappointment was James I's response. He had discouraged his son-in-law from taking the crown of another monarch, and had underlined his disapproval by refusing to send an ambassador to either Frederick or Elizabeth's coronations. James remained adamant that, as a divinely appointed monarch, he could not raise an army to help a usurper – even if that usurper was his son-in-law. James's finances were so weak that the task of funding a foreign army was probably beyond him. However, the king's unhelpfulness was out of kilter with public sentiment: the English held collections for their popular princess and her handsome husband, seeing their cause as fundamentally important in blocking Papist aggression in Europe. These raised £80,000 and produced a small army of 2,250 men. For the Palsgrave, this was nothing like enough.

Emperor Ferdinand, meanwhile, received generous assistance from Catholic allies. Pope Paul V donated 380,000 florins to the Emperor's cause. Philip III of Spain gave 3 million ducats and sent an army from Flanders under Marquis Spinola. King Sigismund III of Poland, concerned that Frederick was prepared to negotiate with the hated Turks, despatched Cossacks to help suppress the Bohemian revolt.

In the meantime, Saxony, though Protestant, sided with the Emperor. The Elector, John George, was an alcoholic Lutheran who had turned down the Bohemian crown before it was offered to Frederick. He would not allow his Calvinist rival to profit from a gamble that he had declined. Ferdinand's election as Emperor gave the Saxon an excuse to turn against Frederick: in fighting defiant rebels, he claimed, he was upholding his princely duty to his sovereign lord.

A sizeable force also assembled under the banner of the Catholic League, an alliance of twenty princes sworn to counter the Protestant Union. Its founder was Maximilian, Duke of Bavaria – a Wittelsbach cousin of Frederick's, who was famed for his penny-pinching greed. He sent an army to assist under Count Tilly, a brilliant Walloon general. Maximilian extracted a secret promise from Ferdinand: if he achieved victory for the Emperor, his reward would be the Palatine electorate.

At the time of Rupert's birth, Frederick's enemies comprised a rich array of Imperialists, Catholic Leaguers, and Spaniards. There were 55,000 of them and they were converging on Prague.

Kings of Bohemia had a military tradition: one, blind predecessor of Frederick's had fought for France at the battle of Crecy, in 1346. When informed that the day belonged to the English, he ordered his men to lead his horse forward by the bridle, charging into the carnage of defeat. He and his son perished side by side, choosing death with honour over flight or imprisonment. Frederick, the new king, had no experience as a soldier, his military knowledge limited to the regulated tournaments that were a popular diversion at court. Yet now he was commander-in-chief of an army of 35,000 men, who were poorly fed and suffering from low morale. The civilian population was equally dispirited.

The king and queen had forfeited much of the good will that had greeted their arrival in Bohemia. Instead of providing tolerant rule, Frederick had allowed his chief adviser, Abraham Scultetus, to pursue a dogmatic, Calvinist agenda. When Scultetus secretly ordered the felling of an ancient crucifix on Prague's Charles Bridge, there was outrage. Elizabeth had already alienated many influential subjects because of her apparent frivolity, her revealing décolletage provoking indignation among the ladies, and her lack of punctuality causing consternation among courtiers and churchmen alike. Now she openly supported Scultetus against his critics and was seen to be contemptuous of her subjects' most dearly held customs and beliefs.

The decisive battle took place against this backcloth of discontent. On 8 November 1620 the two armies faced each other 5 miles to the west of the capital, on the broad summit of White Mountain. Despite his lesser numbers, Frederick's defensive position was strong: his men were deployed at the top of a ridge, protected by a stream and earthworks. However, the Protestants had failed to dig in as well as they might, complaining that their old spades were useless against the frozen ground.

Assured by his general, Prince Christian of Anhalt, that the enemy would not strike, Frederick returned to Prague for breakfast. Meanwhile, under a blanket of fog, Tilly pushed his army across the stream that separated the two armies and launched a surprise attack. It was not only the Protestants who were taken unawares: when Tilly's colleague, Carlos Bonaventura Bucquoy, learnt of this risky manoeuvre, he called for an immediate council of war. Here the two generals clashed furiously, their tactical deadlock threatening a paralysis that would play into the Bohemians' hands.

It was at this point that Father Dominicus, a Carmelite monk from Maximilian of Bavaria's retinue, stepped forward. He humbly asked permission to speak. Given the floor, Father Dominicus started his address calmly, before being transformed by religious fervour into an impassioned orator. He told the commanders it was God's undoubted will that they attack the rebel Bohemians: He would ensure victory against an heretical enemy; they need only be the instruments of divine retribution. The Father's inspired words put fire in the bellies of the Catholic high command. They resumed the action with unity, confidence, and energy.

It was all over in an hour. Four thousand of Frederick's men were killed or captured, including four of his generals. All his artillery and one hundred of his standards were also taken. The king only arrived at the battlefield in time to see his army utterly broken. He then rushed back to the city that had so briefly been his capital, to find pandemonium in the streets. Recognising his defeat, Frederick sent to Maximilian of Bavaria, requesting twenty-four hours' grace in which to gather his belongings and quit the city. Maximilian was not feeling generous: he granted his defeated cousin just eight hours to be gone. The royal family and its retinue frantically loaded up their carriages, ready for flight. In the panic, Frederick left behind the Bohemian crown, orb and sceptre.

Prince Rupert was also mislaid. His nurse had placed him on a sofa while she packed and then had either forgotten or deserted him. Christopher Dhona, an intellectual attached to the court from Heidelberg University, was conducting a final sweep of the palace when he was startled to hear the cries of a baby coming from the saloon. He discovered Rupert on the floor, screaming in protest after rolling off the sofa. Dhona scooped up the baby, wrapped him tight, and sprinted to the courtyard. Seeing the last Palatine coach departing, he ran alongside it and tossed the prince through its window. Rupert slipped into the boot where he bounced around among the fugitives' crammed belongings. Again, the strength of his lungs saved him: the coach's occupants heard his screams and pulled him to safety while the carriage sped out of Prague's gates. However, Rupert's mother was not at hand. Elizabeth was consoling Frederick, and comforting a lady-in-waiting. One of them had lost a kingdom that day, the other a husband.

The fugitives made for Silesia, a neighbouring Bohemian dependency. Elizabeth was in the final trimester of pregnancy and a halt was called at Glatz, so she might rest for a few days. The party then moved on to Breslau, the Silesian capital, where Frederick stayed to organise resistance. He sent his wife, Frederick Henry, and Rupert on to Brandenburg. Frederick was sure the Margrave of Brandenburg would help: he was a fellow Protestant Elector and the husband of Frederick's sister, Charlotte. However, the margrave proved a reluctant host, fearing Habsburg vengeance if he was seen to assist an Imperial enemy. He allowed the Palatine family to lodge in the castle at Küstrin. It was almost a ruin, half-roofed and crawling with rats. Here, at Christmas, two ladies-in-waiting helped Elizabeth to deliver her fifth child, a son. He was named Maurice after the Dutch stadtholder, Frederick V's uncle and a rare friend in an increasingly hostile world. All around him, Frederick's former supporters turned their back on his cause and begged for Habsburg mercy.

The rebel nobles of Prague capitulated a fortnight after the battle of White Mountain. For several months, it seemed that Emperor Ferdinand would forgo vengeance. However, he had not forgotten the rebellion, nor forgiven the rebels. Twenty-seven ringleaders were suddenly rounded up and a scaffold was erected. The condemned were publicly paraded, before torture and execution. Their remains were hacked up and left to decompose in key positions along the Charles Bridge. They stayed on view for several years, reminders of the reward for insurrection.

On 21 January 1621, the Emperor carried out his terrible threat: Frederick was issued with the Imperial ban, for 'the rupture of the public peace'. There were objections from the Elector's allies, criticising this 'so sudden, extraordinary, and most dangerous proceeding',[18] but Frederick was now an outlaw, who could be harmed by anyone with impunity. Young Frederick Henry chose this moment of imminent danger to report on his brothers and sisters to his grandfather in England: 'Sir, we are come from Sewnden to see the King and Queen and my little brother Rupert, who is now a little sick. But my brother Charles is now, God be thanked, very well, and my sister Elizabeth, and she is a little bigger and stronger than he.'[19]

Frederick's imperative was to withdraw himself and his family to a place where they would no longer be vulnerable to Habsburg vengeance. The United Provinces felt a moral duty to grant sanctuary to a man who they had encouraged to fight a common enemy, but who had failed. Frederick also had a significant blood link with the Dutch – his mother was the daughter of William the Silent. The republic took in its defeated ally, who was a grandson of their most revered warrior prince.

While baby Maurice, freshly weaned, was sent to live with his aunt in Brandenburg, and Charles Louis and young Elizabeth remained with their grandmother in Krossen, Rupert and Frederick Henry accompanied their parents to The Hague. Here they were housed and given a monthly pension of 10,000 guilders. Their residence was the Hof te Wassenaer, a large town house. Frederick immediately started plotting how best to reclaim his lands. In the summer, the Dutch lent him 150,000 guilders to raise an army.

*

Looking back, the risk of accepting the Bohemian crown had seemed reasonable. Frederick's formidable pedigree seemed to be matched by an extensive network of support: 'The great alliances which he had contracted, his high parentage; his mighty supportments, both within Germany, and without it; the considerable eminency of his House, his Estate, and the body of confederates, principally depending upon his directions; together with the hopefulness, that other Princes and Peoples had of him: these were the fair eminencies that differed him from other Princes; and these were the procurers of his election to the Crown of Bohemia.'[20] However, failure made Frederick a figure of ridicule across Europe.

Opponents of the couple gloated at their pitifully short rule, referring to them as the 'Winter King and Queen'. Such critics viewed their fall as the inevitable result of unreasonable ambition. There was a seventeenth-century proverb: 'They which take upon them more than of right belongeth, commiteth a great error, and seldom escape unpunished.'[21] Frederick and Elizabeth's fate seemed to embody this lesson. A 1621 book contains an illustration of Frederick clinging to the wheel of fortune. As it turns, he is spun from his throne into the sea. Friendly Dutch fishermen save him from the waves, hauling him, bedraggled, to safety. The text accompanying the image pulls no punches:

Whoever wishes to understand fortune and misfortune,
Let him observe this play of the Palatine.
Very happy was he in the Empire,
His like was not easy to be found.
He lacked neither people nor lands,
Ruled wisely and with judgement.
A wife of royal lineage,
Who multiplied his high name,
Was bringing happiness with young heirs.
His line would not soon die out.
By rich and poor, by young and old,
He was held in high esteem,
Which then was but just,
For he held the most important Electorate
Of the four lay Electors:
He was a jewel of the Holy Roman Empire.
In sum, he had everything, if only he had been satisfied . . .[22]

Frederick's doomed opportunism had huge ramifications. It acceler-ated a conflict that had ready combatants on both sides, and breathed life into the intricate alliances and bitter religious rivalries of Western Europe. During the ensuing Thirty Years' War, spiritual concerns would be frequently cited. However, the predominant issues confronting the German lands were political and secular.

For Rupert and his siblings, their father's miscalculation condemned them to a fragile future. Their childhood, instead of taking place in the glorious palace at Heidelberg, would be spent in exile.

CHAPTER TWO

CHILDHOOD

'The news is, that the Prince Palsgrave, with his lady and children, are come to The Hague in Holland, having made a long progress, or rather a pilgrimage, about Germany from Prague.'

Letter of James Howell, a gossip, 1620

Rupert's childhood was set against his family's constant expectation of restoration. The prince's youngest sister Sophie remembered her siblings' favourite game: a fantasy return journey to Heidelberg. The children would sit on chairs, pretending they were coaches, and then undertake the make-believe ride 'home'. There were stops, to rest the horses and refresh the travellers, before the longed for destination was reached. Whether this dream homecoming could ever become reality depended on their father and his ability to knit together an alliance strong enough to defeat a many-headed enemy.

By mid 1622, Frederick had lost not just his Bohemian kingdom, but also all his Palatine lands. Their reclamation remained his focus for the rest of his life. The Spaniards proposed that the Palsgrave's heir, Frederick Henry, be raised at Emperor Ferdinand's court, in Austria. He would then marry a Habsburg princess and, on coming of age, would be restored to his father's electorate. The compromise was clearly unacceptable: Frederick Henry would have to become Roman Catholic if he wanted a peaceful return of his ancestral lands. By rejecting this formula, Frederick elected to fight for his crowns, not bargain for them.

Though grateful for the sanctuary offered by the United Provinces, Frederick was keen to minimise his period as a Dutch pensioner: 'May it please God,' he wrote to Elizabeth, 'to give us a little corner of the world, to live there happily together, it is all the good fortune that I desire. But staying at The Hague hardly appeals to me.'[1] Despite his humiliating displacement, Frederick's marriage continued to be happy and bear fruit, the nursery receiving a new royal recruit on an almost annual basis: Louisa Hollandina was born in 1622 and was made a godchild of the States-General (which resulted in a useful, additional pension, of £200 per year); Louis, the seventh child, appeared in 1623; Edward followed, in 1625; Henrietta, in 1626; Philip, in 1627; Charlotte, in 1629; Sophie, in 1630; and Gustavus, in 1632. There were thirteen children in all: Rupert had seven brothers and five sisters.

Given the continuing expansion of their brood, Frederick and Elizabeth were thankful when, in 1623, the Prince of Orange offered the loan of one of his larger houses. The Prinsenhof had once been a convent dedicated to the memory of St Barbara. It was situated in Leyden, a town known for its learning and for its textile industry, and fronted onto a canal. A bridge over this waterway led to the town's famed university, which produced large numbers of Protestant priests, and which the Palatine princes attended. The Prinsenhof, long since demolished, was Rupert's family's principal home from when he was aged 3 until he turned 21.

Frederick also established a hunting lodge for the family at Rhenen. This was halfway between Arnhem and Utrecht, on the Lek, a tributary of the lower Rhine. The building had previously been a monastery and was a gift from the province of Utrecht, which also provided some of the house's furniture. It had none of the grandeur of the castle at Heidelberg, but Frederick oversaw renovations, determined to provide a retreat fit for his queen. The diarist John Evelyn visited Elizabeth there in the summer of 1641. He recalled Rhenen being 'a neat palace or country house, built after the Italian manner'.[2]

Queen Elizabeth retired to Rhenen for much of each summer: she loved the place for its tranquillity, beauty, and, above all, its lack of ceremony, which led to a welcome reduction in household expenditure. The exiles were living from hand to mouth, selling valuables to fund their lives. It was a family joke that they frequently dined on pearls and diamonds, since pawned jewels underwrote the domestic budget. Of the children, Rupert was the one who loved his time at Rhenen the most – from an early age he had a passion for hunting and the outdoors.

It was believed that upper-class children should be taught to read as soon as they could talk. Rupert had an early and easy facility with words: 'Rupert is here blithe and well,' Frederick Henry wrote to Charles Louis. 'He is beginning to talk, and his first words were "Praise the

Lord" in Bohemian.'³ By the age of 3, Rupert was able to speak some
English, Czech, and French. 'Little Rupert is very clever', his father
wrote to Elizabeth, in 1622, 'to understand so many languages.'⁴ While
still young, he mastered Dutch, but had no time for Latin and Greek.
He insisted that dead languages were no use to him, for he was going
to be a soldier.

Elizabeth and Frederick had both been brought up away from their
parents. Despite this, Frederick was a warm father: Sophie recalled in
middle age her father's 'tenderness for children, which was one of his
most lovely qualities'.⁵ However, Elizabeth's maternal instincts were
muted. The children remembered their mother 'preferring the antics
of her monkeys and lap-dogs to those of her babies'.⁶ Indeed, she even
seemed more enamoured of her guinea pigs than she was of her offspring.

The Palatine children were placed in the care of a middle-aged
couple, Monsieur and Madame de Plessen. 'Madame Ples' had been
Frederick's governess when he was a boy. Frederick wrote instructions,
outlining the upbringing he wanted for his heir, Frederick Henry: 'Be
careful to breed him in the love of English and of my people, for that
must be his best living; and, above all things, take heed he prove not
a Puritan, which is incompatible with Princes who live by order, but
they by confusion.'⁷ Rupert and the other princes and princesses were
brought up with similar guidelines in place.

Rupert was an inquisitive child, who particularly enjoyed natural
history, collecting objects of interest with his elder sister Elizabeth.
He had a scientific mind that found maths and calculations easy, and
chemical experiments fun. He was also artistic: he and his sister Louise
were extremely able painters and they received tuition from the Court
artist Gerard van Honthorst. With so many siblings, there was always
someone on hand who shared your tastes.

We do not know the exact routine of Rupert's schooldays. The
boys and the girls were educated separately, but female education
was in no way inferior to that of the males. The Netherlands at this
time was enjoying a flowering of intellectual life, and one of its stars
was Anna Maria van Schurmann, 'the Dutch Minerva', who lectured
at the universities of Leyden and Utrecht. Both sexes were given a
thorough grounding in logic and mathematics; writing and drawing;
singing and playing instruments. The school day was full and needed
structure. Princess Sophie remembered a demanding schedule, which

made the children greet minor illness as a fortunate release from drudgery.

Sophie and her sisters rose at seven each morning. They spent the first part of the morning praying, reading the Bible, and attending tutorials. Dancing lessons, from ten until eleven o'clock, provided a welcome break from religious and academic instruction. At eleven o'clock the princes would return from university for lunch. This took place around a long table and was conducted with all the formality of a functioning court. The children could easily forget that their royal family was in exile: 'When I entered', Sophie remembered, 'my brothers were ranged opposite with their Governor and Gentlemen-in-Waiting behind them. I had to make a deep curtsey to the Princes and a little one to the others; a very deep one on taking my place, and a little one to my Governess who with her daughters made a very deep one to me on entering ....'[8] There were further curtseys when the royal children handed their gloves to attendants, another on reaching forward to wash their hands in a bowl, and a final flurry of bobbing when taking their place at table.

Sophie's recollections betray a childhood of stultifying monotony. 'All was so regulated that one knew on each day of the week what one would eat, like in a Convent.'[9] Rigid Calvinism underpinned the time-table: on Sundays and Wednesdays a pair of priests or professors would eat with the children, their conversation always focused on religion. The girls would then have a rest until two o'clock in the afternoon, when another series of lessons would begin. Supper at six was only a brief respite in a day devoted to God. Bible readings and prayers aided the digestion, until the children's bedtime at half past eight. This was Sophie and her sisters' daily routine until they were 9 or 10 years old.

The linchpin of the children's instruction was the need to become 'Jesuit-proof'.[10] Frederick felt this could be more easily achieved through learning the Heidelberg Catechism, the embodiment of the Palatinate's Calvinist state religion, by heart. Upholding Protestantism against Catholicism had caused the family's displacement, and Frederick and Elizabeth were determined that the children should remember this and celebrate it as the honourable – if regrettable – consequence of virtuous devotion. Their sacrifice could never be viewed as being in vain, if it remained wrapped in the shroud of martyrdom.

The exiles were repeatedly touched by tragedy. Young Louis died of a fever while teething, prompting Elizabeth to write: 'He was the prettiest child I had, and the first I ever lost.'[11] An even heavier blow fell in January 1629. Frederick Henry, the eldest prince, had become the Elector's constant companion. Sir Henry Wotton, in his *Reliquiae*, called the boy 'a gentleman of very sweet hope'. We can glimpse exuberance and a boyish charm in a letter he wrote to his grandfather, James I, when aged 9:

> Sire,
> I kiss your hand. I would fain see your Majesty. I can say Nominativo hic, haec, hoc, and all five declensions, and a part of pronomen, and a part of verbum. I have two horses alive that can go up my stairs, a black horse and a chestnut horse.
> I pray God to bless your Majesty.
> Your Majesty's
> Obedient Grandchild
> Frederick Henry[12]

Frederick V had hoped to prosper by investing in a Dutch naval expedition. Its return was imminent and it was known to have several captured Spanish galleons in tow. The Palsgrave took 15-year-old Frederick Henry with him to Haarlem-Meere, to see the ships make harbour. However, in order to save time, or perhaps money, Frederick took his son aboard a packed public ferry. It was foggy and, in the confusion of a busy port, their vessel was rammed by a bigger boat and quickly sank. The Elector was thrown clear of the ferry and clung to a rope till pulled from the water. His son was not so fortunate: Frederick could hear him calling, 'Save me, father! Save me!' However, in the gloom it proved impossible to locate the boy, and soon his cries stopped. The next morning Frederick Henry was found, his lifeless body tangled in the ferry's rigging.

Frederick never recovered from the death of his favourite child. He wrote to inform Charles I of the loss, but found it impossible to describe the depth of his agony: 'It having pleased God to add to my preceding hardships a new affliction, the pain of which cannot be expressed with the pen.'[13] Charles reacted with sincere compassion. On a practical note, he transferred the £300 annual pension previously drawn by Frederick's second son (and his own godson), Charles Louis, to Rupert.

Charles Louis was now the Palatine heir. He was a more serious character than Frederick Henry. He had spent much of his childhood with his sister Elizabeth at their grandmother's house in Krossen. In

1627, they moved to Leyden. Charles Louis was reserved and prickly, and found it difficult to adjust to life with his fun-loving, energetic siblings. They called their earnest brother 'Timon', after the people-hating central figure of Shakespeare's *Timon of Athens*. It was a nickname Rupert used against his elder brother all his life.

Rupert was developing a strongly individual personality. In contrast to Timon's cold reserve, Rupert was fiery, mischievous, and passionate. His family called him 'Robert le Diable' – Rupert the Devil – and marvelled at his bravery and perseverance. A tale from Rupert's youth gives a snapshot of his energetic and uncompromising nature.

The Prince took part in a hunting party hosted by his mother. During the chase, the fox tried to escape the hounds by slipping down a hole. Rupert was in time to see one of his favourite dogs disappear after the fox, until it, too, was out of sight. The prince, worried when the hound failed to reappear, started to wriggle into the earth as well. A man called Billingsby, watching first fox, then hound, then prince, go underground, entered the hole himself, took hold of Rupert's heels, and pulled him out. The prince reappeared, still holding firmly onto the dogs' back legs. The hound shared its master's determination: in its jaws was the fox.

Although Elizabeth was happy to live away from her children during their nursery phase, she moved them from Leyden when they became adolescents. She kept her daughters by her side, at The Hague. The three elder girls, Elizabeth, Louisa Hollandina, and Henrietta, were physically very attractive, and were noted adornments at the Winter Queen's court. Sophie, who arrived in 1641, was less good-looking, yet she had a wonderful brain and a very quick wit, and became extremely popular. The boys, however, were not needed at court. Elizabeth wanted them to train for their life's purpose, the retrieval of their father's lost lands.

The Elector was dependent on the continued support of others. The United Provinces provided his home and a basic pension, but outside Protestant aid was needed, if the Palatine and Bohemia were ever to be regained. In 1625, Denmark, England, France, Sweden, Transylvania, and various German territories expressed their joint intention of assisting Frederick in his quest.

England's involvement seemed to promise much: James I had died in 1625 and had been succeeded by Elizabeth's brother, Charles. On his deathbed James regretted his stubborn refusal to help the Palatine cause and urged his heir to right the wrong. Charles I was sympathetic to Frederick's plight and the Elector played on his compassion: he sent Charles a portrait by Poelenberg of his seven elder children (Henrietta and Philip were considered too young for inclusion), with hunting trophies at their feet, in a classical landscape. The grand canvas was accompanied by a humble message: 'The great portrait in which your Majesty will see all your little servants and maidens whom you bring up.'[14] Frederick was determined that his brother-in-law should honour family obligations, in a way that his late father-in-law had repeatedly failed to do. Charles demonstrated his loyal intentions by declaring war on Spain in support of Frederick. When, in 1625, Charles sent the Duke of Buckingham to attack Cadiz, the royal favourite flew the Palatine flag as his battle standard. It brought him no luck: the attack was a disaster.

For the next four years, England remained at war with Spain. In 1627 Charles declared that: 'He had no other original quarrel with Spain but the cause of his dear sister, which he could no more distinguish from his own than nature had done their bloods, so would he never lend ear to any terms of composition, without her knowledge, consent and council.'[15] These were noble sentiments, sincerely meant. However, in 1629, Charles decided to dispense with Parliament for the foreseeable future, and soon found that the raft of questionable fundraising measures he relied on was incapable of supporting a costly foreign policy. The king made immediate peace with France, but found it harder to agree terms with Spain: the issue of the Palatinate could not be resolved to both sides' satisfaction. In the end it was simply left out of the peace treaty. From 1630, Frederick was once more left without English military aid.

Yet it was at this point that Frederick enjoyed his greatest hope of restoration. In the autumn of 1629, Sweden and Poland signed a six-year truce. This left the Swedish king, Gustavus Adolphus, free to enter the Thirty Years' War. The following year he landed in Germany with 10,000 men and in September 1631 he trounced the Imperial army at the battle of Breitenfeld. Frederick believed this was the first stepping-stone to ultimate victory. He was flattered by the compliments paid to him by the Swedish military genius. Gustavus Adolphus, meanwhile, appreciated that Germany could only find peace if the Palatine was returned to its electoral family.

Frederick spent much of his time away from home, on campaign, his sense of princely duty overriding his longing to be with his wife and children. In January 1632 he set off on what he anticipated would be the pivotal campaign – the one that would see him restored at last. Before he left, he wrote to Charles I asking him to look after his wife and children while he was gone. The fighting went well: in May, Frederick accompanied Gustavus Adolphus into Munich, the capital of enemy Bavaria. The Swedish king insisted that Frederick lodge in the abandoned palace of his great adversary, Maximilian. While there, Frederick found many of his cannon, captured at White Mountain a dozen years earlier. He dared to think that the tide had turned – that he would soon be back with his family, in the castle at Heidelberg.

Such thoughts fuelled Frederick's terrible homesickness. He and his wife kept up a passionate and constant correspondence, their letters accompanied by gifts, and miniatures of themselves and their children. Frederick wrote to Elizabeth from Munich: 'I am very pleased that Rupert is in your good books, and that Charles is doing so well ... God make me so happy as to be able to see you again soon!'[16] In fact, the Palsgrave would never be reunited with his wife and children again.

With ultimate victory in sight, the relationship with Gustavus Adolphus had begun to sour. The Swede insisted that, in return for his restoration, the Palsgrave must guarantee equal rights to his Lutheran and Calvinist subjects. Frederick took offence at this perceived meddling in his sovereignty. He decided to return to his family, rather than resolve the disagreement. Riding from Munich to Mentz, he was struck down by a serious fever, which left him delirious and short of breath. When it seemed that he was over the worst of it, news arrived of the battle of Lützen: his Swedish allies had narrowly won the day, but Gustavus Adolphus had perished in the thick of the fighting.

Frederick was consumed by depression: his hopes had rested on the continuing military success of the warrior king. Gustavus Adophus's death made everything desperate, once more. A few days later, to his doctor's surprise, Frederick died, meekly surrendering a life that had promised so much, but whose defining moment had been the risky acceptance of the Bohemian crown. Frederick was buried in a grave so anonymous that soon its whereabouts were forgotten.

The following month, on Christmas Eve, Elizabeth wrote to her brother Charles I that she was 'the most wretched creature that ever lived in this world, and this shall I ever be, having lost the best friend that I ever had, in whom was all my delight'.[17] She had genuinely adored her husband and wore mourning for the rest of her life. A decade later guests commented on how her receiving chamber was still hung with black velvet. Elizabeth remembered all the significant moments she had shared with Frederick and marked the anniversaries of his death by fasting.

The Winter Queen remained as loyal to her husband's aims as to his memory. 'The subjects of this good Prince', wrote two Englishmen who fought in Gustavus Adolphus's army, 'may have plentiful matter of consolation, from that most heroical, and masculine spirited princess, his Queen; and from that sweet and numerous issue, which he hath left behind him: which promises them an entire affranchisement, one day again; and the resettling of a family so many ways considerable, as is one of the first and ancientliest descended, of all Europe. An issue so fair; and for their numbers, such a blessing: as were not only prepared by God, for a present comfort to their widowed mother: but (which their own excellent towardliness, gives pregnant hopes of), for the raising of their own fair family again; and engrafting the Palatine branches, into most of the great Houses of the Empire.'[18] The widow focused her energy on helping Charles Louis reclaim his father's lost crown.

Elizabeth received an invitation from her brother Charles to return to England, where he could look after her and her fatherless children. She declined, claiming that she would rather travel home when not in mourning. Elizabeth also pointedly mentioned the military support that the United Provinces were offering Charles Louis for the 1633 campaigning season. She asked, though, that Charles offer his protection to her many children. Apart from God, she said, Charles was their 'sole resource'.[19]

CHAPTER THREE

BOY SOLDIER

*'The Low-countreys are (without all controversie) worthily stiled
the Academie of warre, where the art militarie (if any where) truly
flourisheth ...'*

Militarie Instructions for the Cavallrie, 1632

Tales of brave forefathers heightened Rupert's early appetite for warfare.
His most impressive fighting ancestor was Frederick the Victorious,
Count Palatine from 1425 until 1476. An inspirational leader, Frederick
was celebrated for his personal bravery and his penchant for the full
cavalry charge. In July 1460, at the battle of Pfeddersheim, Frederick
led his 2,000 horsemen in an assault against the combined forces of the
Archbishop of Mainz, the Count of Leiningen, and Ludwig the Black.
Frederick's battle cry was: 'Today Prince Elector, or no more!' This do
or die attitude brought total success: Frederick's enemies were shattered
by the Palatine horse and fled the field. The tactics remained the same
through the Palsgrave's subsequent years of triumph.

As Rupert contemplated a life in arms, the romance of ancestral glory
was tempered by the shocking reality of the Thirty Years' War. The conflict cost tens of thousands of civilian lives and was felt with particular
brutality in the Palatinate: located at the crossroads of destruction, its
population of 600,000 would be reduced by two-thirds by the conclusion of hostilities. Emperor Ferdinand II used his position as the shield-
bearer of Roman Catholicism to annihilate his opponents. Rupert grew
up hearing first-hand reports of outrageous Papist cruelty.

When the Catholic League under Tilly captured Magdeburg, in
1631, its excesses were broadcast round Europe. 'The church of St John
was full of womenfolk', wrote an eyewitness, Salvius, to the Riksrad of
Hamburg, 'whom they locked in from the outside, thereafter throwing burning torches through the windows. The Croats and Walloons
behaved mercilessly, throwing children into the fire and tying the more

beautiful and well-off women citizens to their stirrups, made off with
them behind their horses out of town. They spiked small children onto
their lances, waved them around and cast them into the flames. Turks,
Tartars and heathens could not have been more cruel.'[1]

William Crowne, a member of the Earl of Arundel's 1636 embassy to
the Emperor, wrote in his diary:

> On this same day, seven rebels, the leaders of an armed insurrection
> of 400 ignorant peasants against the Emperor, were beheaded. The
> ringleader of the revolt, a fellow who had persuaded himself that no
> bullet had power to harm him, was led to the scaffold with his face
> covered and with two men holding him firmly against the block. Here
> the executioners seized him firmly by the chest with a massive pair of
> red-hot pincers and, nailing his right hand to the block, chopped it
> off. Then, quickly drawing the sword he wore at his side, he cut off
> the wretched fellow's head which an assistant raised, shouting into the
> ears of the dead man: 'Jesus! Jesus!' At this juncture, the Jesuit, who
> had accompanied the criminal and had been admonishing him for his
> sins, asked those present to join in prayer for the soul of the dead man.
> Following this came the man's accomplices, including a young boy,
> all of whom bore crucifixes in their hands and made their individual
> confessions at the foot of the scaffold to priests, kissing their hands and
> feet at the end of every prayer.[2]

Their penitence was in vain: they were all beheaded and quartered.

Rupert was encouraged by his mother to take part in this war: 'He
cannot too soon be a soldier', Elizabeth declared, 'in these active times.'[3]
She knew it was Rupert's best hope of making his way in life, and of
helping his family to win back its lost lands. In 1632, aged 12, Rupert
was sent to Rheinberg to serve under his great-uncle Frederick Henry,
Prince of Orange. Soldiery was in his blood and he took to his new
profession well – a little too well, for his mother's liking. She heard
tales of camp life – of drinking, swearing, gambling, and womanising
– and feared for Rupert's morals. Elizabeth had been prepared to risk
her son's life, but not his soul, and ordered his recall.

The Prince busied himself honing his fighting skills. Over Christmas,
1633, the Prince of Orange arranged a Passage of Arms, a celebration of
military skill that harked back to the age of medieval chivalry. Rupert
had just turned 14, but he was tall and powerfully built for his age.

A contemporary recorded him 'carrying away the palm; with such a graceful air accompanying all his actions as drew the hearts and eyes of all the spectators towards him'.[4]

Rupert was, from the onset of puberty, viewed as highly eligible. His father had died a failure, in exile. However, the family's restoration to the Palatinate, if not Bohemia, remained feasible, and Rupert was still the nephew of the King of England. He was also charming and good-looking. Plans were first made for Rupert to be married in his early teens. He was not involved in the search for a bride: his mother and uncle masterminded the operation, looking for a girl who combined high birth with great wealth. The other prime consideration was religion – only a devout Protestant would be acceptable.

The favoured candidate was Marguerite de Rohan, daughter of a prominent French Huguenot duke. The union was first attempted in 1632 and Rupert's family anticipated a speedy conclusion. 'Concerning my brother Rupert', his brother Charles Louis wrote to their mother, 'M. de Soubise hath made overture that, with your Majesty and your brother's consent, he thinks M. de Rohan would not be unwilling to match him with his daughter. The King seemeth to like it, but he would have your advice and consent in it. I think it is no absurd proposition, for she is great both in means and birth, and of the Religion.'[5]

The negotiations foundered, largely because the Duc de Rohan, who supported the match, died before it could be completed. However, in Charles I's eyes, Marguerite remained the ideal wife for his nephew. Six years later the king was still pushing for the marriage, telling his ambassador in Paris to contact Cardinal Richelieu, to see if he could persuade Louis XIII to approve the union. 'This is a business of great weight,' he reminded the Earl of Leicester, 'and you know how much we take to heart any thing that concerns the good of our dearest sister, and her children, especially in so high a degree as this; which, if it speed, is to bring so fair an estate to the Prince our nephew.'[6]

Even in 1643, when immersed in Civil War, the king still hoped for Rupert and Marguerite's marriage. He wrote in his own hand to Prince Maurice, Rupert's younger brother and greatest confidant: 'Though Mars be now most in vogue, yet Hymen may be sometimes remembered. The matter is this, your mother and I have been somewhat engaged concerning a marriage between your brother Rupert and Mlle de Rohan, and now her friends press your brother to a positive answer, which I find him resolved to give negatively; therefore, I have thought fit to let you know if you will not by your engagement take your brother handsomely off. I have not time to argue this matter, but to show my judgement, I assure you that if my son James were of a fit age, I would want of my will but he should have her.'[7] However, Rupert resisted his uncle's advice – perhaps (as we shall see) because he was by then in love with another woman, the wife of a close friend.

In 1635, Rupert returned to the front line, serving as a lifeguard to Frederick Henry of Orange. The campaign against Spain, in the southern Netherlands, was bloody and tough. The Dutch, supported by the French, captured and pillaged Tirlemont, before approaching Louvain. The garrison there proved much more resilient, spurred on by their colleagues' fate. While the French returned home, the Dutch continued fighting. Rupert, despite his youth, repeatedly attracted praise for his fearlessness under fire. It was also noted that he never used his princely rank to shirk the most menial of military duties. He was determined to learn his chosen profession through a full and rigorous apprenticeship.

The following year, Rupert joined Charles Louis in England, as a guest of Charles I. Elizabeth of Bohemia wrote to Sir Henry Vane, a loyal admirer at court, urging: 'Give your good counsel to Rupert, for he is still a little giddy, though not as much as he has been. I pray tell him when he does ill, for he is good natured enough', she said, in a tone lacking maternal warmth, 'but does not always think of what he should do.'[8] To the king, however, his nephews' arrival added youthful vigour to his stately court. Sir Thomas Roe, who had served Elizabeth I and James I, was a trusted confidant of Elizabeth of Bohemia: she called him 'Honest Tom'. Roe had visited her in the Netherlands a decade earlier, and in 1630 had engineered the truce between Sweden and Poland that released Gustavus Adolphus to fight in Germany. Roe was now Elizabeth's eyes and ears in England, writing of Rupert: 'I have observed him of a rare condition, full of spirit and action, full of observation and judgement. Certainly he will *réussir un grand homme* [succeed in becoming a great man], for whatever he wills he wills vehemently: so that to what he bends he will be in it excellent.' Roe noticed Charles's appreciation of his nephew: 'His Majesty takes great pleasure in his unrestfulness, for he is never idle, and in his sports serious, in his conversation retired, but sharp and witty when occasion provokes him.'[9]

The brothers arrived to find their uncle's kingdom a haven of peace.

While much of Europe was absorbed in the physical and financial drain of the Thirty Years' War, England stood aloof and prosperous. The courtier-poet Thomas Carew celebrated the nation's blessings:

> Tourneys, masques, theatres better become
> Our halcyon days; what though the German drum
> Bellow for freedom and revenge, the noise
> Concerns not us, nor should divert our joys;
> Nor ought the thunder of their cabins
> Drown the sweet airs of our tun'd violins.[10]

'Let us be thankful for these times', wrote the balladeer Martin Parker in 1632, 'Of plenty, truth and peace.'[11] A reign that has, ever since, been synonymous with strife, started off so promisingly that the Earl of Clarendon later judged that England in the 1630s 'enjoyed the greatest calm, and the fullest measure of felicity, that any people in any age, for so long together, have been blessed with; to the wonder and envy of all other parts of Christendom'.[12] When, in 1637, Charles announced to his Palatine nephews that he counted himself the happiest king in Europe, he was not exaggerating.

This was a time of artistic excellence and royal acquisition, when a sensitive and knowledgeable king commissioned the portraiture of Rubens and Van Dyck, while buying the Vatican cartoons of Raphael and the canvases of Rembrandt. It was also an era in which medicine and science were valued and encouraged: William Harvey, who was to prove that blood circulated inside the body, and Sir Theodore de Mayerne, a brilliant clinician who saved Henrietta Maria's life during her first, complicated childbirth, were among the men of learning who enjoyed Charles's patronage.

There were cracks, but they were barely visible. Ironically, this was a period when popular support for the Palatine family was being used as a stick to beat the Crown. When, in 1636, the new Prayer Book appeared, shorn of its customary prayer for Elizabeth and her children, there was outrage among the more extreme Protestants. William Prynne, a Lincoln's Inn barrister, attacked the omission in *News from Ipswich*, claiming the omission proved that the king's advisers were Catholic sympathisers; charges that resulted in Prynne's prosecution. For this, and for further trouble three years earlier, Prynne and two other 'scandalous, seditious and infamous persons' were punished with the cropping of their ears. The trial of this agitator blew up into a wider protest against Charles I's rule without Parliament.

Rupert's first visit to England also coincided with the blossoming of resistance to Ship Money. In his determination to avoid parliamentary financial control, the king had taken this tax – designed to be paid by port towns for the wartime upkeep of the navy – and levied it in peacetime, across the country. Elizabeth I had done the same, in the 1590s, and had provoked uproar. Charles used most of the tax for its true purpose, strengthening the navy, but his opponents managed to present him as a gross abuser of royal power. The issue came to court in 1637, when John Hampden tried to have Ship Money declared illegal. He failed, but the controversy rumbled on, unresolved in the minds of the court's critics. People would only later realise that the seeds of civil conflict had taken root at this point.

Charles Louis and Rupert, meanwhile, were treated with all the solemnity accorded to the British royal family. They accompanied their aunt and uncle on a spectacular summer visit to Oxford University, whose chancellor was the controversial Archbishop of Canterbury, William Laud. Laud was a rigidly doctrinaire Arminian, who had overseen the punishment of dissenters (including William Prynne), in his drive to extinguish Calvinism from the Church of England.

The archbishop was a lonely bachelor, who enjoyed providing extravagant hospitality for his monarch and his family. Laud received the royal party at his college, St John's, and showed off the newly built library quadrangle, which was adorned with his coat of arms and mitre, and sculptures of angels. Statues of the king and queen dominated the space, while busts representing Grammar and Rhetoric assumed lesser positions.

As the royal party toured the magnificent buildings, Laud's choristers filled the air with anthems. The music had been calculated to perfection, every piece lasting as long as it took the group to mount each flight of steps. It was High Church theatre: the sort of practice that alienated Puritan England from the archbishop and fuelled the accusations that he was a Catholic stooge. Laud was unapologetic in his indulgence. 'I do not doubt but you have heard of the great entertainment my lord Archbishop of Canterbury gave the King and Queen at Oxford,' Charles Louis wrote to his mother in the Netherlands, 'and the honour he did me, at my request, to make a great number of Doctors, Bachelors, and Masters of Arts.'[13] Rupert was among those awarded an

honorary Master of Arts' degree on 30 August 1636. Laud insisted that
Charles Louis and Rupert's names be entered in St John's books, 'to do
that house honour'.[14]

Curiously, Laud thought Rupert a candidate for the church: he told
the king that his nephew would make a good bishop. Perhaps Laud was
impressed by Rupert's recall of his Protestant education and sensed his
leadership abilities? Perhaps he wanted to bolster his own position, by
having a royal lieutenant? Whatever the archbishop's calculation, it is
hard to think of a man less suited to the cloth than this single-minded
warrior.

The queen was equally intrigued by possibilities for Rupert. Henrietta
Maria was a distinctive-looking woman whose appearance had recently
shocked Rupert's youngest sister, Sophie: 'The beautiful portraits of
Van Dyck had given me such a fine idea of all the ladies of England,
that I was surprised to see that the queen, who I had seen as so beautiful
in paintings, was a woman well past her prime. Her arms were long
and lean, her shoulders uneven, and some of her teeth were coming
out of her mouth like tusks.'[15] Against these defects, she had lovely eyes,
a pretty nose, and an enviable complexion. She suspected that Rupert
was ripe for conversion to Roman Catholicism and worked on him
to join her faith. It is not clear where the queen saw the weakness in
her nephew's Protestantism. Rupert certainly enjoyed the rich tastes of
the court – the masques, the plays, the art, and the music. By contrast
Charles Louis's Calvinist devotion was much admired by Puritan onlookers.

During his visit, Rupert was tempted by a dramatic proposal, championed by Endymion Porter, a courtier who had introduced the works
of Anthony van Dyck to the king. Porter, a warm and sophisticated wit
in his late forties, liked the young prince very much and eased him into
a literary circle in London that included John Donne and Ben Jonson.
Porter was one of many at court seeking a short-cut to riches: he made
a decent income from hunting down abusers of commercial practice,
but allowed a fertile imagination to take him in increasingly eccentric
directions. He became involved in plans for a national treasure hunt
and was behind an unsuccessful attempt to foist an unpleasant soap on
an unwilling public.

For Rupert, Porter had altogether more ambitious designs: he proposed that the prince establish an English colony on Madagascar, which
he could rule as viceroy. It was suggested that Sir William Davenant,

who was one of Shakespeare's godsons (while falsely claiming to be his illegitimate son), would be the island's poet laureate; an idea that inspired Davenant to write a poem predicting Rupert's future conquests. At the same time, it was suggested that Charles Louis should be sent to the West Indies, to establish a kingdom. Charles I, who was very fond of Porter, thought these plausible ways of securing income and status for his nephews, and encouraged the schemes' further investigation by the East India Company.

The refined proposal had Rupert sailing to Madagascar with twelve warships and twenty-four merchantmen. A further twelve ships would be sent with supplies from England each year, before returning with the island's produce. Madagascar – known to Englishmen at this time as 'St Lawrence' – was thought to be fabulously wealthy. A bankrupt merchant called Boothby, eager to profit from the venture, exaggerated its worth, calling it: 'The chiefest place in the world to enrich men by trade to and from India, Persia, &c. He that is lord of Madagascar, may in good time be emperor of all India.' He enthused about: 'The plenty and cheapness of their food, flesh, fowl, and fish, oranges and lemons, sugar, amber-grease, turtle-shells, and drugs.'[16]

Despite Boothby's propaganda and Rupert's enthusiastic support, the Madagascar scheme stalled. The chief reason was Elizabeth of Bohemia's blunt dismissal of her boys' exotic ambitions: 'As for Rupert's conquest of Madagascar,' she wrote, 'it sounds like one of Don Quixote's conquests, where he promised his trusty squire to make him king of an island.'[17] Elizabeth doubted the project's feasibility, and thought it bound to compromise Rupert's safety and honour. She looked to her brother to stop filling her sons' minds with absurd flights of fancy and to offer more concrete assistance to her dispossessed boys.

Sir Thomas Roe, who as a younger man had explored the mouth of the Amazon and undertaken diplomatic missions to Hindustan, Persia, and Turkey, understood the need to find an outlet for Rupert's restless energy. He advised Elizabeth of Bohemia: 'It is an infinite pity that he is not employed according to his genius, for whatsoever he undertakes he doth it vigorously and seriously. His nature is active and spriteful, and may be compared to steel, which is the commanding metal if it be rightly tempered and disposed.'[18]

During his nephews' visit Charles sponsored a fundraising drive, to help equip an army that would regain the Palatinate for Charles Louis. The king wrote a letter, which was read out in every parish, requesting financial aid. Meanwhile, a general subscription was opened, with Lord Craven pledging £10,000 at the top of the list and Charles I signing off at the same rate. With a large sum in his fighting chest, Charles Louis departed for The Hague in June 1637 and set about raising an army.

Rupert accompanied his brother. His family had heard the rumours and become concerned that he was in danger of being won over by Catholics. 'My brother Rupert is still in great friendship with Porter,' Charles Louis reported from Whitehall to Elizabeth of Bohemia, 'yet I cannot but commend his carriage towards me, though when I ask him what he means to do, I find him very shy to tell me his opinion. I bid him take heed he do not meddle with points of religion amongst them, for fear some priest or other, that is too hard for him, may form an ill opinion in him. Besides, M. Condoth frequents that house very often, for Mrs Porter is a professed Roman Catholic. Which way to get my brother away, I do not know, except myself go over.'[19]

Rupert was forced to leave England, before he was compromised further. His mother gave a tactful reason for the prince's need to return to the Continent: 'Though it be a great honour and happiness to him to wait upon his uncle, yet, his youth considered, he will be better employed to see the wars.'[20] There was certainly something in his family's concerns: Henrietta Maria was sorry to see the prince go, for she felt sure his conversion was imminent. While Rupert was excited at the prospect of fighting for his family's rights, he was reluctant to bring to an end a thoroughly enjoyable time as his uncle's guest. The king and his nephew had grown extremely close, and Rupert had found a spiritual home in his kingdom. The prince expressed his love for England with typical enthusiasm while hunting with Charles I on the morning of his departure. He shouted out that he hoped to break his neck, so his bones could remain in England forever. When Rupert left for the Continent that day, his uncle awarded him a monthly pension of 800 crowns.

While Charles Louis went to seek Swedish assistance for his planned campaign, Rupert and Maurice returned to active service. They joined the Prince of Orange's army as it besieged Breda, the brothers again conspicuous because of their unquestioning bravery. Their most celebrated adventure occurred one night, when they stole up to the city walls and overheard the garrison preparing for a surprise attack on the Dutch. Rupert and Maurice slipped back to their lines and told their commanders what they had learnt. When the Spanish broke out, they were met by ordered ranks of musketeers, whose concerted fire scythed down their sortie and sent the survivors scrambling for safety.

On another occasion a Dutch assault was planned on Breda's defences. Among the attackers were Goring, Lucas, Monck, and Wilmot, all of whom would have important dealings with the prince in later years. While Frederick Henry of Orange was prepared to risk the lives of these British volunteers, he wanted to protect his great-nephew from the heat of the Spanish firepower and assigned him a secondary role in the operation. Rupert ignored the order, however, and joined the storming party: he was one of the first to breach the fort's walls. Goring and Wilmot were both wounded in the intense fighting – Goring was left lame for life – but Rupert was unscathed. The successful assault returned Breda to the Dutch after twelve years of Spanish occupation.

CHAPTER FOUR

PRISONER OF WAR

'Rupert's taking is all. I confess in my passion I did rather wish him killed. I pray God I have not more cause to wish it before he be gotten out.'

Elizabeth of Bohemia, 1638

Charles Louis felt ready to begin his campaign in Germany. While Maurice was sent to complete his education in France, Rupert rejoined his elder brother in Westphalia. At the age of 17, Rupert was given command of one of the three Palatine cavalry regiments. Count Conigsmark controlled the Swedish contingent; the Swedes were no longer the military Juggernaut of Gustavus Adolphus's time, but they were still highly respected troops. There was also a sizeable British unit, many of whom romantically believed themselves to be serving as knights errant for Elizabeth, the Winter Queen. Less altruistic was a Scottish general, James King, whose part in Rupert's life story was to be consistently disappointing. This polyglot army of Charles Louis's numbered just 4,000: 'too many for a raid, too few for a serious campaign',[1] as one of Rupert's military biographers has pointed out.

Setting off eastwards from Bentheim, the small force was soon in action. Rupert was riding with the advanced guard near Rheine when attacked by a unit twice the size of his detachment. The prince drew up his men and, for the first time, ordered the manoeuvre that would become his signature piece: the full-blooded cavalry charge. The enemy reacted, in a manner that would become familiar to Rupert, by breaking formation and fleeing in terror, pursued by his men's slashing blades all the way back to the town. 'We must not pass over one remarkable providence more upon this adventure', the prince's secretary later recalled, 'a soldier, with a screwed gun, snapped at the Prince within ten yards of his body, but happily missed fire.'[2]

Joy at the outcome of this skirmish was short-lived. The Imperialist high command now knew the exact position of Charles Louis's army and appreciated how small it was. A nearby force under General Hartzfeldt was despatched to annihilate it. Hartzfeldt realised that the Palatine army's only possible escape route through the surrounding high land lay via the Minden Gap. Charles Louis would have to approach this via Vlotho (also known as Flota), where he could cross the River Weser. When the Protestants arrived at the pass, however, an army as diverse as their own stood before them. The main body of the cavalry was Austrian, the infantry was mixed, and the dragoons, commanded by Colonel Devereux, were Irish. Devereux had gained lasting infamy by murdering Wallenstein, one of the Thirty Years' War's great mercenary commanders, in 1634.

The battle that took place at Vlotho on 17 October 1638 was a one-sided affair. This was largely owing to Conigsmark's inept leadership. He drew up his men in a narrow gorge in four rows, the third of which was commanded by Rupert, while he rode in the comparative safety of the fourth. The impact of the Imperial heavy cavalry against this static defence was devastating: the front two lines, comprised of Palatine cavalry, buckled and broke in the first moments of battle.

Rupert now found himself directing the front line of his brother's army. Clad in full armour, his visor down, and with Lords Grandison and Northampton by his side, he led his men forward at the charge. The enemy cuirassiers faltered, and then fled the field, pursued by Rupert's force. However, inexplicably, Conigsmark failed to reinforce the counterattack. Rupert suddenly found himself far from his own lines, surrounded by superior numbers of Imperialists under Marshal Götz. Lord Craven tried to come to the prince's assistance, leading forward two troops of Charles Louis's lifeguards. This brave intervention was too small to succeed: the Austrian cavalry rolled up Rupert and Craven's men, sending them back into the gorge where they had started the battle. As they milled around in confusion, they were caught in a flanking attack. The Imperialists charged down the hillside and joined in the massacre of the prince's men. Rupert was only spared from the slaughter because, by chance, he was wearing a white band in his helmet, similar to the one that the Austrians were sporting that day.

Finding himself alone among his fallen men, Rupert rode to help one of Craven's ensigns, who was defending Charles Louis's standard with the last of his troopers. Soon all these men were also slain. Rupert was cornered, the sole Palatine survivor in this pocket of the battlefield. He killed the soldier who was holding his brother's captured colours, then, in a desperate escape attempt, dug his spurs into his horse's flanks while pointing him at a wall. However, after the day's exertions, the height was too great for his mount and instead of jumping, it slowly sank to the ground, utterly exhausted. On foot now, Rupert killed the first enemy soldier who approached him. He refused to surrender, but his position was quite hopeless. He was quickly overpowered. Lippe, a veteran enemy colonel, pulled up the prince's visor, and demanded to know his prisoner's identity. 'A colonel!' replied Rupert. '*Sacre met!*' replied Lippe, 'You're a young 'un.'[3]

Rupert was recognised by Count Hartzfeldt, the Imperialist cavalry general, and was handed over to Colonel Devereux's care. The prince began furtive negotiations with the Irishman, giving him five gold coins, while promising more if he would allow him to escape. Devereux would probably have obliged, but Rupert was too valuable a prisoner to be left without a special guard, and Hartzfeldt returned with one before the bribe could take effect. The prince was sent for safekeeping at Warendorf.

What of Rupert's comrades? Conigsmark never committed his soldiers and fled from the battlefield without a scratch. Charles Louis took flight with him, nearly drowning in the chaos of retreat when his carriage overturned in the fast-running River Weser. He hauled himself out by a willow branch, while his coachmen and horses were swept to their death. King was suspected of treachery: it was later learnt that he had sent his baggage train, containing his silver and personal chattels, to safety, the night before the battle. Unless blessed with extraordinary foresight, he must have known of the enemy's plans. Captain Pyne, an eyewitness, was of the opinion 'that the wilfulness of the Elector and the treachery of King ... lost the day'.[4] The loyal Craven, by contrast, shared Rupert's fate, and was taken prisoner. He had been seriously wounded in the thigh and the hand, but would live. Craven was subsequently able to buy his freedom with the huge ransom of £20,000. When he offered to pay more to be allowed to stay with Rupert, he was refused.

Among the other prisoners was Sir Richard Crane, who Rupert was allowed to send to England with an account of the defeat. The scribbled message on a page torn from a notebook was the first confirmation that the prince's family had of his survival: early reports had counted him among the dead. Elizabeth of Bohemia reacted to the news of his capture with immense self-pity, declaring that it might have been better if Rupert had perished. As a prisoner, he would be vulnerable to Catholic conversion – a thought not worth contemplating. She had greeted the suggestion with horror, claiming: 'I would rather strangle my children with my own hands.'[5]

Rupert was defiant in the face of his enemies, the *London Post* recording: 'The Emperor that then was pitying his youth, and hearing that he had the face and physiognomy of a Soldier, did send unto him to change his Religion, assuring him, that he would restore him to the Electoral Dignity, and make him Generalissimo of his Army. Prince Rupert returned this answer to the Emperor: That he thanked him for his promised favours, but for matters of Religion, they were out of his element. If the Emperor had sent him a bale of dice (he said) he knew what answer to return him. This wild answer of his being brought unto the Emperor, the Emperor replied, that he might have the face of a soldier, but it appeared by his answer, he but had the condition of a fool, & in choler protested, that he would be troubled no longer with him.'[6]

Rupert was moved to the forbidding castle of Linz, overlooking the Danube. So important a captive was he, that 1,200 men accompanied him there. By contrast, as a prisoner he was allowed a skeleton retinue, comprising just a pageboy and two other servants. Ferdinand III, now Emperor in place of the dour bigot whose armies had triumphed at White Mountain, chose the prince's gaoler with care: Count von Kuffstein was a respected military veteran and an enthusiastic convert to Catholicism. The Emperor hoped Kuffstein would be able to win Rupert's respect and confidence, before laying siege to his soul. Kuffstein enjoyed discussing military theory with Rupert and soon grew to like his prisoner. He never forgot his mission, though, and soon suggested that the prince might enjoy the company of two Jesuit priests. Rupert flatly rejected the offer, unless he was also allowed the companionship of Protestant guests of his own choice. This was out of the question. The war of spiritual attrition continued.

Rupert busied himself with science and art. He worked on a variation of an instrument originally devised by Dürer, which helped in the drawing of perspective. The prince also drew: one of his etchings from this period shows a full-length mendicant friar in a landscape with a city, a river, and a handful of soldiers in the background. This is a precursor of his later, more celebrated, innovations with the mezzotint method of engraving. However, his ability to indulge in his favourite pursuits did not detract from the harshness of his confinement. Rupert would refer to it as 'a wretched close imprisonment', and point to his ability to endure it with pride. It was only his unshakeable Protestant faith that stopped him from accepting the Emperor's 'stately large promises',[7] which included not just freedom, but also generalship in the Imperial army and the grant of a small principality, which he would be able to call his own.

From time to time the prince joined the count's household for dinner and he was allowed occasional access to the castle's gardens. It is not recorded where he first met Kuffstein's daughter, Susan, but we know the two of them fell in love. Rupert recalled her much later as 'one of the brightest beauties of her age, no less excelling in the charms of her mind than of her fair body'.[8] 'He never mentioned her without admiration', remembered a contemporary, 'and expressing a devotion to serve her with his life.'[9] Given the strictness of his confinement, it seems unlikely that this relationship could ever have progressed beyond the platonic.

Rupert was an intriguing figure to his captors. Ferdinand III's brother, the Archduke Leopold, went to examine the prince during the second year of his imprisonment. Leopold felt that Kuffstein was keeping the prince on too tight a leash, and saw to it that Rupert be allowed to play 'ballon' – tennis – and practise military skills, including the use of a gun with a rifled barrel. He became an extremely accomplished tennis player, and a very accurate shot. Provided he gave his word not to escape, Leopold felt that Rupert should be granted greater physical freedom. He was given three-day passes that allowed him to join surrounding noblemen on hunting expeditions. His favourite host was Count Kevenhüller, whose residence was at Kamur, in Bavaria: 'It was', Rupert's manuscript biographer wrote, 'a most pleasant place, and the count received him with all the honour imaginable.'[10]

The prince's family seldom received news of his well-being, but Elizabeth of Bohemia never wavered in seeking Rupert's release. When the Earl of Essex visited The Hague, she urged him to go on to Austria and intercede with the Emperor on her son's behalf. When Essex declined, Charles Louis was disappointed. He felt that only somebody of the earl's stature could reasonably undertake such a mission, because any lesser figure would be vulnerable to the effects of Rupert's hot-headedness: 'Essex should have gone', Charles Louis wrote, 'because there was no one else would, neither could I force any to it, since there is no small danger in it, for any obstinacy of my brother Rupert's, or venture to escape, would put him in danger of hanging.'[11]

Charles I sent Sir Thomas Roe, Elizabeth of Bohemia's devotee, as an ambassador to reiterate English support for Rupert's release. Favourable reports reached The Hague of Roe's progress, the Countess of Löwenstein writing: 'I hope by the solicitation of Sir Thomas Roe we shall have our sweet Prince Rupert here: he hath been long a prisoner.'[12]

Ferdinand III eventually agreed to free Rupert, if he apologised for taking up arms against the Empire. The prince refused, saying that he had nothing to apologise for: he had only been doing his duty. This message reached Ferdinand when he was being visited by the Palatinate's greatest foe, the Duke of Bavaria. Maximilian persuaded his host that such impudence demanded severe punishment. Rupert's imprisonment now entered its toughest phase: his trips from the castle, his ability to play sports, and his contact with Kuffstein's daughter were all forbidden. A detachment of twelve musketeers and two halberdiers was ordered to keep the prince under 24-hour watch.

Rupert's only consolation lay in the company of pet animals. The Earl of Arundel was an eminent, cultured, English aristocrat who had joined the retinue accompanying the newly married Elizabeth to Heidelberg, after her marriage to Rupert's father. Arundel, permanently disabled after being thrown from his carriage in London, had subsequently been a benign presence in the life of the Palatines since 1632, when he was sent to the United Provinces in a futile attempt to persuade Elizabeth of Bohemia to bring her fatherless family to live in her brother's kingdom. Subsequently, the earl had greatly enjoyed Rupert and Charles Louis's company during their visit to England, commissioning Francois Dieussart, a French sculptor, to sculpt busts of the two princes.

Arundel was deeply upset by Rupert's protracted imprisonment and sent the prince a white dog, which seems to have been a rare strain of poodle. Rupert named him 'Boy' and made him his constant companion. The Grand Turk heard of the dog's beauty and ordered his ambassador to find him a puppy of the same breed. The prince also domesticated a hare, which followed him at heel. Rupert had inherited his mother's affinity for animals.

Once, the prince was nearly sprung from his cage. A Franco-Swedish force struck towards Linz, with Rupert's release its main aim. It was met and defeated by Imperialists under Archduke Leopold. Soon after the engagement, Leopold rode to visit the captive once more, and his friendship with Rupert resumed. Meanwhile, Ferdinand's Empress, who had been born a Spanish princess, began to advocate the prince's liberty. With domestic problems escalating dangerously in England, Charles I increased his pressure on the Emperor: he needed his nephew to help lead whatever army could be mustered, if hostilities broke out. The concerted efforts eventually persuaded Ferdinand to grant Rupert his freedom, provided he promise never to fight against the Empire again. This was a considerable undertaking from a prince who was keen to avenge his father's humiliations and whose vocation was the military. However, worn down by years of captivity, and eager to resume life as a free man, Rupert's stubbornness gave way. He reluctantly agreed to this far-reaching restriction.

A symbolic act was needed, to bring about the prince's release. When Ferdinand was hunting near Linz, it was arranged that Rupert would pretend to come across the hunting party and pay homage to the Emperor. This would be enough to trigger his freedom. Rupert arrived at the appointed time and place, to find a particularly ferocious wild boar holding hounds and hunters at bay. While everyone else hung back, Rupert rushed forward with a spear and slew the boar. The Emperor proffered a hand to the brave prince and Rupert kissed it. From that moment, he was free.

Ferdinand made a final offer to the prince of a senior command against the French and Swedes, and promised that he would be allowed to continue in the Protestant religion while serving. Rupert declined: he had compromised enough.

The prince was keen to surprise his family by reaching home before official messengers could bring them news of his release. He arrived back at the Prinsenhof in December 1641, just ahead of Sir Thomas Roe's letter announcing his freedom, and remained with his delighted mother for two months.

Rupert returned to find Elizabeth recovering from the loss of another child. Gustavus had died in agony on 9 January 1641, five days before his ninth birthday. Rupert's youngest brother had been in acute pain for much of his short life, but none of the many doctors the family had called on had been able to establish the cause of, or think of a cure for, his affliction. Gustavus's final days were so terrible that they left a lifelong impression on Sophie, Rupert's youngest sister. She later recalled that, 'on opening him stones were found in his bladder, one of which was the size of a pigeon's egg surrounded by four others that were pointed, and one in his kidneys in the shape of a large tooth that has been pulled out with its root.'[13] Only then did family members understand the full ghastliness of the ordeal that the little boy had endured for so long.

Rupert's return provided a fillip for the grieving, impoverished family-in-exile, most of whose financial reserves had been spent on the ill-fated expedition that had resulted in the prince's incarceration. That winter Rupert busied himself joining in scientific experiments with his sister Elizabeth. Active service soon reclaimed him, however. The uncle who had helped secure his freedom demanded Rupert's presence across the North Sea, for Charles's kingdom was facing the imminent prospect of civil war.

CHAPTER FIVE

TO HIS UNCLE'S AID

'Though I will never fight in any unrighteous quarrel, yet to defend the King, Religion and Laws of a Kingdom against subjects, who are up in arms against their Lord and Sovereign ... such a cause my conscience tells me is full of piety and justice: and if it please God to end my days in it, I shall think my last breath spent with as much honour and religion, as if I were taken off my knees at my prayers.'

Prince Rupert His Declaration, 1642

From 1629 until 1640 England experienced what royal opponents termed 'the Eleven Years' Tyranny', when Charles ruled without Parliament. The king managed to obtain funds through various controversial means, including the sale of commercial monopolies, the appropriation of tonnage and poundage customs dues, and by raising the naval war tax of Ship Money during peacetime. These methods helped to foment dissent, at a time when there was no national forum where it could be expressed. The king's personal rule polarised the political nation.

The tensions that led to civil war became discernible, with increasing vividness and frequency, from the late 1630s onwards. The problems were not new, as an intractable king and an ambitious Parliament clashed with escalating force. Two of James I's later Parliaments had been short-lived, as traditional monarchy failed to react with tact or understanding to strong social, economic, religious, and philosophical shifts.

Members of Parliament demanded a greater say in government, and a furthering of the Protestant cause at home and in Europe. Charles, though, was unresponsive. He had inherited his father's belief in the divine right of kings, which held the monarch to be God's anointed, with a right to rule as he saw fit. He expected his people's representatives to respect his sovereignty, while granting him revenue when required.

Four years into his reign, with three sessions already failed, Charles forewent the demanding politicians dominating Westminster and looked to fund his policies through the resurrection of ancient Crown privileges.

The religious sensibilities of seventeenth-century Europe compounded the discord. The atrocities of the Thirty Years' War demonstrated that the clash of different Christian sects could lead to carnage. Tales of Catholic brutalities in Germany found a ready audience in Protestant England: 'At the taking of Magdeburg,' it was reported in a pamphlet of 1641, 'a Preacher of great esteem was dragged out of the Church to his own house, that he might see his wife and children ravished, his tender infants snatched from the mother's breast, and stuck upon the top of a lance, and when his eyes and heart were glutted with so cruel a spectacle, they brought him forth bound into the street, and laid him in the midst of his own books, and setting fire thereto miserably burnt him, and thus have I given you a taste of the lamentations of Germany.'[1] The message was clear: the Papists would do the same to their religious foes in England, if they ever got the opportunity – a fear made more real by the threat of rebellion across the Irish Sea. Charles's marriage to Henrietta Maria, Henry IV of France's daughter, left him open to the Puritan fear that the queen's Catholicism would taint the monarch's soul. When the king failed to launch an armed crusade to restore Rupert's parents to the Palatine, critics claimed this showed a shameful lack of commitment to Protestantism abroad.

The king's promotion of the High Churchman William Laud to the Archbishopric of Canterbury was deeply unpopular. Laud's enemies claimed that: 'The Archbishop hath been a notable deceiver; for whilst he did always pretend to cast out Popery and faction, he endeavoured nothing more than to bring it in, and settle it among us.'[2] Charles's patronage of such a man seemed to confirm Puritan fears that the corrupt and ungodly, wilfully ignorant of the spiritual needs of the people, were favoured above true believers. This trend left the flock exposed to the wiles of Catholic predators, a theme John Milton angrily explored in his 1637 poem, 'Lycidas':

> Blind mouthes! that scarce themselves know how to hold
> A Sheep-hook, or have learn'd ought els the least
> That to the faithfull Herdmans art belongs! ...
> The hungry Sheep look up, and are not fed,

But swoln with wind, and the rank mist they draw,
Rot inwardly, and foul contagion spread:
Besides what the grim Woolf with privy paw
Daily devours apace, and nothing sed,
But that two-handed engine at the door,
Stands ready to smite once, and smite no more.

The Puritans believed the king to be dangerously out of kilter with the religious preferences of most of his subjects. This was, they believed, an abrogation of his duty to God. By logical extension, if Charles could not observe his obligations to the Lord, why should they offer unquestioning obedience to their monarch?

Charles was king not just of England, but also of Scotland and Ireland. It was his Scottish subjects that brought an end to his personal rule.

Presbyterianism was a radical form of Protestantism that flourished in Scotland, particularly in the Lowlands. In 1637, ignoring his advisers north of the border, Charles insisted on imposing Laud's English Prayer Book on the Scots. This attempt to achieve spiritual conformity in the two countries caused political as well as religious opposition. When Jenny Geddes, an Edinburgh servant girl, hurled her stool at a priest spouting Laudian offensiveness in St Giles's Cathedral, her aggression was symbolic of a people's fury. The Scots resented the highhandedness of a distant ruler who dared to meddle with their souls.

Two Anglo-Scottish conflicts, the Bishops' Wars, followed. The first, in 1639, was an inconclusive affair that did little more than reveal the feebleness of Charles's army. The second, a year later, ended in outright humiliation for the king: the Scots defeated the English in battle, and took orderly occupation of Durham and Northumberland. Charles, unable to finance a counterforce, was obliged to summon his first Parliament for more than a decade. Despite the national emergency of having a foreign force on English soil, the Members declined to grant funds unless the king first dealt with wider issues: 'No taxation without redress of grievances' was their uncompromising mantra. Their three prime grievances involved the liberty of Parliament, as well as questions of religion and civil government. Charles was not prepared to bargain on any point: 'the Short Parliament', so long in the gestation, perished after just three weeks.

The continuing Scottish crisis meant that Parliament had to be reconvened. November 1640 saw the start of what would come to be known as 'the Long Parliament'. During its first six months it used the foreign incursion to win concessions from the beleaguered king. Charles was forced to approve the Triennial Act, which obliged the Crown to summon Parliament at least once every three years. Members also dismantled the raft of revenue-raising methods that Charles had relied on during his personal rule.

Those favourites most closely associated with the Eleven Years' Tyranny were now exposed to vengeful fury. Archbishop Laud was imprisoned in the Tower of London. The equally controversial Earl of Strafford, who had ruled Ireland for Charles, suffered a humiliating impeachment. Extreme opponents then insisted on his execution. In a moment of weakness for which he never forgave himself, Charles signed the death warrant of his most loyal servant. Strafford's dignified acceptance of his fate added to the king's acute sense of guilt.

Constitutional surgery, combined with the removal of hated advisers, satisfied many in Parliament. However, the radicals, led by the Tavistock MP John Pym, wanted to push further. They sought the abolition of bishops, approval of the appointment of royal ministers, and control of the military. Charles's supporters were shocked by this broad attack on the royal prerogative, and presented the radicals as self-serving and greedy:

> ... The game they play for is so great,
> Vain is all hope them to intreat.
> The Crown is strong: the Church is rich,
> At these two things their fingers itch.[3]

But the Crown was not strong, and its weakness became ever more obvious. When Irish Catholics rebelled in October 1641, murdering thousands of Protestants, the king prepared to summon, and appoint, the commanders of the avenging English army. However, Parliament insisted on being party to such important matters of state. Meanwhile, critics of the court composed the Grand Remonstrance, an itemised list of the king's alleged misdemeanours. This was narrowly approved by Parliament. Pym and his acolytes were placing the king – a weak man prone to impulsiveness and stubbornness – under intense pressure. Eventually the strain told.

On 4 January 1642, Charles attempted to arrest six especially vocal Parliamentary critics. Five were Members of the Commons, while one sat in the Lords. However, all had fled before the arrival of the king and his party, which included Rupert's brother, Charles Louis. This clumsy lunge at the court's enemies was the brainchild of George, Lord Digby. Digby, heir to the earldom of Bristol, would become Rupert's greatest enemy in the Royalist camp. He had previously been a critic of the king's advisers, while always stressing his loyalty to the Crown. Digby had argued that the monarch could only function correctly with the cooperation of Parliament: 'The King out of Parliament hath a limited, a circumscribed Jurisdiction', he had told the Commons, 'But waited on by his Parliament, no Monarch of the East is so absolute in dispelling Grievances.'[4]

Digby had argued eloquently for Strafford's impeachment, but had been appalled when radical colleagues insisted on – and gained – the earl's head. The execution caused Digby to side with the king. His charm and eloquence had quickly earned Charles's forgiveness. The same gifts went on to win the king's highest favour. However, the armed intrusion was early evidence of Digby's poor judgement. The move backfired spectacularly, infuriating much of London and prompting the king to quit his capital. 'The Five Members' of the Commons sailed down the Thames in triumph, cheered by supporters celebrating their escape from a king whose key advisers were believed to have lured him into despotism. The failure of Digby's ill-considered plan greatly increased the likelihood of war.

Charles went first to Hampton Court, then to Windsor. To raise funds, he sold Windsor Castle's silver plate. In February, afraid that fighting was about to erupt, Charles took Henrietta Maria and the young princesses to Dover. Here the royal party met Prince Rupert, who had come to thank his uncle for his part in securing his release from prison. Although Charles was delighted to see Rupert again, he spent time closeted with the prince, explaining that it would be best if he returned to the Continent: there was still a hope of peace in England, but this would be diminished if the king was seen to have enlisted his warrior nephew. Rupert understood, and accompanied the queen and her daughter Mary to Holland, where the princess was to marry the Prince of Orange. Henrietta Maria took with her some of the Crown Jewels, which she intended to sell. She would invest the proceeds in forces and weapons, to aid her beleaguered husband. Meanwhile,

Charles headed for Greenwich for talks with Parliament. The dialogue was bitter and brief.

The king now made for York, keen to put distance between himself and his antagonists, and eager to seize arms that had been stockpiled in Hull since the Bishops' Wars: after the Tower of London, Hull was 'the chief magazine in the kingdom for arms and ammunition'.[5] However, Sir John Hotham, recently appointed Hull's garrison commander by Parliament, denied access to his king. Hotham flooded the surrounding fields with water from the Humber and promised to sacrifice his life, rather than surrender the town.

More important men than Hotham now declared against the king. Robert Devereux, Earl of Essex, was the 50-year-old son of the dashing Elizabethan courtier who had plunged from favouritism to armed rebellion and paid for his treachery with his life. James I had refused to visit the sins of the father on the son, and allowed Robert to revive the title and repossess the estates that his father had forfeited. Ironically, given his later clashes with Princes Rupert and Maurice, as a younger man Essex had fought against the Hasburgs for the restoration of the Palatinate.

Essex had spent much of the 1630s quietly enjoying his wealth and estates. A brief stint commanding a coastal naval squadron was followed by service as a lieutenant general in the First Bishops' War. The dispiriting campaign had been followed by a disappointing treaty that Charles I had insisted on brokering himself. The king then further alienated Essex, by failing to thank or reward the earl for his efforts. In January 1642, Charles tipped Essex irretrievably into the arms of Parliament. Egged on by the meddlesome Henrietta Maria, and ignoring the advice of his wisest councillors, Charles asked the earl to resign as Lord Chamberlain of the King's Household. Six months later Essex accepted his appointment as Lord General of the Parliamentary army. The royal couple had handed their enemies a cautious but competent commander.

Both sides in the Civil War claimed to be fighting for the king: it was the definition of kingship that separated them. For most Royalists, the thought of armed conflict against God's anointed was anathema – an aberration that challenged the cornerstone of their hierarchical beliefs. They saw matters as clearly and simply as Sir Francis Bacon, the Solicitor-General: 'Where a man doth levy war against the King

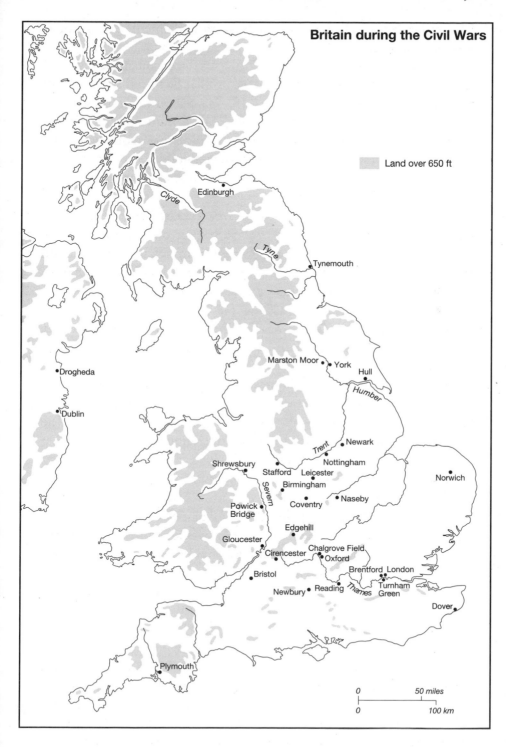

Britain during the Civil Wars

Land over 650 ft

Edinburgh

Clyde

Tyne

Tynemouth

Drogheda

Marston Moor · York

Hull

Humber

Dublin

Trent · Newark

Shrewsbury · Nottingham

Stafford · Leicester

Birmingham

Norwich

Powick Bridge

Coventry · Naseby

Severn

Edgehill

Gloucester

Chalgrove Field

Cirencester · Oxford

Bristol

Brentford London

Newbury · Reading Thames Turnham Green

Dover

Plymouth

0   50 miles

0   100 km

in the Realm, it is Treason. Where a man is adherent to the King's enemies, giving them aid and comfort, it is Treason.'[6] The Prince of Wales's chaplain echoed this sweeping condemnation of the Crown's opponents: 'Rebellion is a sin that strikes at God's own self, at the face of Majesty: there is no such express image of God in the world as a King is; every Christian is the Image of Christ as a man, every Minister of the Gospel is (or ought to be) the Image of Christ as Mediator, but a King is the Image of Christ as God, and to rebel against a King is to strike at the face of Christ as God; which was more than they that crucified him durst to do.'[7]

The Parliamentarians justified their armed opposition by making a delicate but precise distinction between the king as ruler, and the king as a man. It was quite possible, they believed, to support the king while attacking the evil advisers who were leading him astray. In July 1642, court critics in both Houses joined in a powerful declaration: 'It cannot be unknown to the World, how powerful and active the wicked councillors about his Majesty have been, both before and since this Parliament, in seeking to destroy and extinguish the true Protestant Religion, the liberty, and Laws of the Kingdom ...'[8] This subtle separation of loyalties was a common defence throughout Europe at this time and had been employed by rebels in England since the Middle Ages, when justifying resistance to absolute rule. Some critics of the king took their strand of logic past breaking point, openly calling the Royalists 'rebels'. Parliamentarians looked with disdain on those who offered unquestioning loyalty to the Crown: 'We found', a Parliamentarian wrote, when looking back on the start of the war, 'that the common people addicted to the King's service have come out of blind Wales, and other dark corners of the Land; but the more knowing are apt to contradict and question, and will not easily be brought to the bent.'[9]

The political certainty of both factions was fuelled by strong spiritual allegiances. Continental Europe gave compelling lessons in the importance of binding religious prejudices tight to military ambition. Contemporaries recognised the power of the blend: watching the fighting effectiveness of Gustavus Adolphus's troops, a British Protestant observed: 'It is not without a mystery, I suppose, that the old Israelites had an Armoury in their Temple: they would show us, that these two cannot well be parted. And truly, methinks, that a Temple in an Army, is none of the weakest parts of fortification.'[10] As the king and Parliament prepared for war, each claimed God's support.

If religion had been the sole consideration, the prince could have chosen to side with the Parliamentarians, as did his elder brother Charles Louis. Rupert's Calvinism was in tune with their Puritanism and his family had long benefited from parliamentary support for the Palatine restoration. However, his first loyalties were to the uncle he loved and to the basic principles of royal rule. Charles had been the generous patron of Rupert's family during its protracted exile, reassuring them of his best intentions even when failing to deliver much of substance. Meanwhile, the king helped to fund his impoverished relations – Rupert received an annual royal pension of £300 – and poured love on his sister and her hapless brood, after Frederick V's death. He wrote to Elizabeth of Bohemia in 1634:

My Only Dear Sister,
... I could not let this honest servant of yours go without these lines, to assure you of the impossibility of the least diminution of my love to you; the which, as I am certain you easily believe, so I desire you to be assured, that all my actions have and shall tend to your service; and that the counsels and resolutions that come from me, is and will prove, more for your good, than those of any body else: and so I rest
Your loving brother,
To serve you,
Charles R.[11]

It was now time to repay the family debt and Rupert did not hesitate in accepting Henrietta Maria's invitation, in August 1642, to cross once more to England, in support of King Charles. The prince made public his feeling of obligation to the king: 'And what a gracious supporter hath he been in particular to the Queen of Bohemia (my virtuous Royal mother) and to the Prince Elector, my Royal brother, no man can be ignorant of: if therefore in common gratitude I do my utmost in defence of His Majesty, and that Cause whereof he hath hitherto been so great and happy a patron; no ingenuous man but must think it most reasonable.' Rupert stressed the high regard in which Europe held his uncle, judging him 'the most faithful and best defender of the Protestant Religion of any Christian Prince in Europe, and is so accounted by all the Princes in Christendom.'

Rupert also countered those who painted him as a foreign mercenary, eager to ply his warrior trade whatever the cost to the native population:

'I would to God all Englishmen were at union amongst themselves, then with what alacrity would I venture my life to serve this Kingdom against those cruel Popish Rebels in Ireland.'[12] This last point was in response to enemy claims that Rupert and his men were secretly fighting for Catholicism.

In the same defence against his tormentors, Rupert revealed his views on the correct relationship between a monarch and his subjects. It was an uncompromising creed: 'Suppose that he [Charles] had swayed his Sceptre with a strict hand, reining in the bridle of Authority with harsh Taxation and Tyranny (which it is too well known he did ever abhor as infections to his Sacred Person) yet I say were it so, the Subjects are not thereupon to withdraw their Obedience and Duty neither by the Laws of God nor the Laws of Man, for they are however or at leastwise should be still his Subjects ...'[13] Such sentiments were succinct, traditional, and unburdened by profound analysis.

Rupert's first attempt to reach England failed. He set off across the North Sea on a 42-gun ship, the *Lyon*, with his brother Maurice. Accompanying them were Rupert's chief engineer, Bernard de Gomme, a Walloon; and his favourite explosives' expert, Bartholomew de la Roche, a Frenchman. Parliamentary sources reported: 'In this ship *Lyon*, Prince Rupert and Prince Maurice, with divers other commanders, came in her from Holland, but after three days and three nights storm at sea, not having eaten nor drunk in all that time, these two Princes were in a sick and weak condition, and the ships set to sea again for the North of England, leaving them sick in Holland.'[14] The Prince of Orange secured another vessel for Rupert and his party. They set off again, leading a lesser vessel – a galiot – containing weaponry for the coming campaign.

Rupert's passage was difficult. As his party approached Flamborough Head, on the Yorkshire coast, the Parliamentarian ship The *London* bore down on them. 'What are you doing?' the Parliamentarian captain hollered. 'We are cruising,' replied Colster, captain of Rupert's vessel, while the prince stood next to him in a mariner's cap. 'What is the galiot?' persisted the master of the *London*. 'It is a Dunkirk prize,' Colster lied. The suspicious Parliamentarians insisted that the galiot be searched. Rupert ordered Colster to sail on, prompting the *London* to summon assistance by firing her cannon. When two more enemy ships appeared on the horizon, Rupert told Colster to head directly for shore.

The prince and his men rowed to safety and landed at Tynemouth. That night the galiot set off again and took its much-needed contents to the Royalist haven of Scarborough.

Rupert wasted no time. He rode for Nottingham, which Charles had made his base, through fields rich with summer crops – the harvest of 1642 was to be especially bountiful. However, he was delayed when his horse lost its footing, throwing him to the ground and dislocating his shoulder. When he eventually reached Nottingham, he found that his uncle had departed for Coventry. Rupert set off south to join him. En route, the prince learnt that Coventry had closed its gates to Charles, its rebel garrison firing on his flag. The king, bewildered by this show of aggression, had moved on to Leicester. Rupert changed direction once more, arriving at Leicester Abbey, where he found his uncle with a tiny army. Its cavalrymen, under Henry Wilmot, had performed poorly in a skirmish. They were immediately entrusted to the prince's command.

The rank of General of Horse was much coveted. Military manuals of the time insisted that such a position be filled by a figure of rare qualities, reflecting the cavalry's pre-eminence on the battlefield: 'Cavalry, so called of Cavallo (which in the Italian and Spanish signifieth a horse) is worthily esteemed a most noble and necessary part of the military profession,'[15] recorded a military expert, in 1632. The same authority continued: 'The General of the Horse, as being one of the principal Chiefs of an army, must be a soldier of extraordinary experience and valour; having in charge the nerve of the principal forces, and on whom the good success of many designs and actions dependeth, as being most usually executed by the Cavalry, especially in battles: where the charging of the enemy in good order usually giveth victory; and contrariwise, the disorders of the Cavalry often disturb and disband the whole army.'[16]

The question for more seasoned veterans was whether the smooth-faced Rupert had either the experience essential to such a key position or the ability to transform the ragbag cavalry into a disciplined force. The German prince had bravery, they knew. He also possessed great charisma and style, his impressive figure topped with a plumed hat and ending in fine leather cavalry boots, while his back was swathed in the swish of a scarlet cloak. However, the sum total of his military experience was slight: the action at Rheinberg, four sieges, the cavalry charge at Rheine, and the defeat at Vlotho. Since then, he had been a prisoner of war. He had been absent during three years when some of them had been perfecting their skills on continental battlefields. They looked to

Rupert to prove his worth in the crucial, senior position allotted him by his uncle.

On 22 August 1642, when Charles raised the royal standard at Nottingham, it was less a declaration of war than an urgent call for supporters to rally to the Crown. The first night that it flew above the town, the royal standard was blown over. In a superstitious age, this was interpreted as an ill omen for the king's cause. Certainly, if the Royalists were to have a chance, reinforcements were direly needed: Sir Jacob Astley, the king's general of infantry, and a former military tutor of Rupert's, warned that without more men, he could not be sure that he could prevent Charles being 'taken out of his bed, if the rebels should make a brisk attempt to that purpose'.[17] Charles's army numbered about 2,000 men – a quarter of the size of Parliament's force, based in Northampton. Some of the king's men had seen service in the Thirty Years' War, but most of them were amateurs who were present because of a simple belief that it was their duty to support their monarch. Clarendon recalled the disparity between Rupert's cavalry and Parliament's, in the late summer of 1642: the prince's men 'were not at that time in number above eight hundred, few better arm'd than with swords; while the enemy had, within less than twenty miles of that place, double the number of horse excellently arm'd and appointed'.[18] In London there was optimism that the king's inability to raise a sizeable army would compel him to bow quickly to Parliament.

Rupert set about equipping and reinforcing his men. The training of horses for battle was as important as the schooling of their riders. John Vernon, who served in the Royalist cavalry, wrote of how best to prepare a horse for war:

> You must use him to the smell of gunpowder, a sight of fire and armour, hearing of drums and trumpets, and shooting of guns but by degrees. When he is eating of his oats you may fire a little train of gunpowder in the manger, at a little distance from him, and so nearer by degrees. In like manner you may fire a pistol at a little distance from him in the stable, and so nearer by degrees, and so likewise a drum, or trumpet may be used to him in the stable. The groom may sometimes dress him in armour, using him sometimes to eat his oats on the drum head. In the fields when you are on his back, cause a musket[-eer] and yourself to fire on each other at a convenient distance, thereupon riding up unto him with speed, making a sudden stand. Also you may use to ride him

up against a complete armour set on a stack on purpose, that he may overthrow it, and so trample it under his feet, so that by these means, the horse finding that he receiveth no harm, may become bold to approach any object.[19]

By the end of September, Rupert had 3,000 cavalry and dragoons (mounted infantry), most of whom had received some training. He had begun to establish that reputation for tireless energy that was to be his trademark: 'This Prince, like a perpetual motion', reported an agitated Parliamentarian historian, 'with those horse that he commanded, was in short time heard of in many places at great distances.'[20] With the myth came hostility and fear. Rupert and his younger brother Maurice were quickly made hate figures by their enemies: 'The two young Princes, Rupert especially, the elder and fiercer of the two, flew with great fury through divers counties, raising men for the King in a rigorous way ... whereupon the Parliament declared him and his brother "traitors".'[21]

Rupert relied on continental military practices, and in so doing revealed what the Earl of Clarendon, an ally but no friend, termed 'full inexperience of the customs and manners of England'.[22] On mainland Europe it was normal to force the local population to fund the army in the field, through levies and confiscations: the Thirty Years' War general, Wallenstein, invented the dictum, later borrowed by Napoleon, that 'war should support itself'. In early September Rupert wrote an ultimatum to the mayor of Leicester, demanding £2,000 for the king 'against the rebellious insurrection of the malignant party'. Although signed by 'Your friend, Rupert', there was nothing friendly about the PS: 'If any disaffected persons with you shall refuse themselves, or persuade you to neglect the command, I shall tomorrow appear before your town, in such a posture, with horse, foot, and cannon, as shall make you know it is more safe to obey than to resist his Majesty's command.'[23]

The startled mayor immediately referred this alien threat to the king, prompting an apology from Charles: Rupert's letter, he assured the people of Leicester, had been 'written without our privity or consent, so we do hereby absolutely free and discharge you from yielding any obedience to the same, and by our own letters to our said nephew, we have written to him to revoke the same, as being an act very displeasing to us'.[24] Charles was appalled by Rupert's misjudgement. At this delicate stage, before Leicester had even declared which side it would support, bullying extortion had no place.

Rupert's gaffe played into the hands of Parliamentary propagandists. From the moment the king's enemies learnt that Rupert was coming to Charles's aid, they portrayed him in the blackest light. He was condemned for being sinfully ungrateful for the efforts made on his family's behalf by England's Protestants. The prince would never be forgiven for siding against those who had so vociferously championed the Palatine cause.

It was not long before the propagandists presented him to a credulous public as the epitome of immoral soldiery. There was a determination that the most eye-catching of the Royalist leaders should be characterised as wild, dangerous, and even devilish. He was portrayed as a deviant, who enjoyed sex with his white poodle, Boy, and with a 'Malignant She Monkey'. A Parliamentary pamphleteer enjoyed imagining the creature's sexual repertoire:

> this monkey is a kind of movable body that can cringe and complement like a Venetian courtesan, though her face be not so handsome; yet all her gestures and postures are wanton and full of provocation, she being nothing else (as many others are) but a skin full of lust; her eyes are full of lascivious glances, and generally all her actions do administer some temptation or other; so that she cannot choose but work upon Prince Rupert's affections; and if he were any thing effeminate as it is not to be doubted but he is forward enough in expressions of love as well as valour; for as the Spanish painter wrote in a Church window *sunt* with a *C.* which was an abomination, so her name is an emblem of wanton-ness, *sunt* written in that manner being often called a Mon*k*ey, which is a *k*ind of prophanation, and thus you see what Prince *Ruperts* Mon*k*ey both nominally and figuratively signify, she being in all her posture the picture of a loose wanton, who is often figuratively called a Mon*k*ey.'[25]

It was not particularly subtle stuff.

His men suffered from similar slanders. Parliamentary printing presses began to use the term 'cavaliers' to demonise their enemies. It was an expression of contempt that had arisen from the excesses of the Spanish trooper, the *caballo*, during the Thirty Years' War. 'He's the only man of all memory', the author of *The Character of a Cavalier* stated, 'whose unworthy actions will perpetuate his memory to ensu-ing generations. His very name will be odious; and when Posterity ... shall find his name mentioned in our Annals, they will be inquisitive to know the Nature of the Beast: This *Skellum*, this *Nigro carbone notatus*, this *Monstrum horrendum*.'[26]

Parliamentary leaders encouraged people to give money and silver to their cause, rather than remain vulnerable to 'several sorts of malignant men, who were about the King; some whereof, under the name of Cavaliers, without having respect of the laws of the land, or any fear either of God or man, were ready to commit all manner of outrage and violence; which must needs tend to the dissolution of the Government; the destruction of their Religion, Laws, Liberties, Properties; all which would be exposed to the malice and violence of such desperate persons, as must be employed in so horrid and unnatural an act, as the overpowering [of] a Parliament by force.'[27] Violent, destructive, malicious, and overwhelmingly dangerous: Parliament's image of the cavalier had taken form before Rupert's arrival in England. However, he was presented as the quintessential example of this cursed phenomenon.

Meanwhile, the Royalists wanted Rupert – 'our most Gracious Prince' – to be seen as a positive influence on their admittedly undisciplined force. He was adamant, they argued, that his troopers 'should behave themselves fairly, not doing any harm, to man, woman, or child, giving them strict Command, that they should commit no Outrage whatsoever against any of His Majesty's loving Subjects, neither should they take any thing from them by violence'.[28] When any of his men's crimes were reported to him, it was claimed, Rupert dished out swift and decisive justice.

Among Parliamentary pamphleteers, there were occasional flashes of honesty about the shortcomings of some of their own: 'I answer that it is true indeed that some of the Parliament's army are as bad as the Cavaliers', one conceded, 'and such as are a very shame to the cause they pretend to stand for, & it were to be wished they were all cashiered, although there were but Gideon's army left behind.'[29]

A generation before the outbreak of war, Henry Peacham had written an unflattering description of the typical English gentleman: 'To be drunk, swear, wench, follow the fashion, and to do just nothing, are the attributes and marks nowadays of a great part of our Gentry.'[30] The Cavaliers were credited with all these debauched and dissolute ways. Fear of their capabilities was heightened as hostilities increased.

The recipients of this nickname, however, were keen to cast themselves in a more forgiving light. One writer in early 1643 talked of 'the

Cavaliers, whom now we see with our eyes to be the Flower of the Parliament, Nobility and Gentry of the Kingdom'.[31] An imaginary conversation in *The Cavaliers' Catechism* broadened the theme:

> *Question*: 'What is your name?'
> *Answer*: 'Cavalier.'
> *Question*: 'Who gave you that name?'
> *Answer*: 'They who understood not what they did when they gave it; for it was intended to my infamy, but it proves to my dignity, a Cavalier signifying a Gentleman who serves his King on horseback.'
> *Question*: 'I pray you tell me what Religion you are of, for it is generally reported of you Cavaliers that you are all most infamous livers, atheists, Epicures, swearers, blasphemers, drunkards, murderers, and ravishers, and (at the least) Papists.'
> *Answer*: 'To these and the like scandalous aspersions, I will only say thus, (in brief, Sir) that as I cannot excuse all of our Party (no more than you can all of yours) so I cannot but in Conscience (according to my ability) be bound to defend & vindicate the major part of us from such malicious, and fraudulent calumniations ...'[32]

The dark imagery of the rapacious Cavalier was an attempt to counter the reputation Rupert's horsemen had won in the public mind, in the early months of the conflict.

The personal myth of Prince Rupert began to blossom from the outset of the Civil War. It is so varied and rich that separation of fact from embellishment is often difficult. There were many eyewitnesses present, however, when Rupert, while passing through Stafford, stood in the garden of a Captain Richard Sneyd and fired his 'screw'd horseman's pistol' at a weathercock on top of St Mary's Church. He managed to hit it from a range of 60 yards – an astonishing achievement in an era when the handgun was notorious for its inaccuracy. Charles I dismissed the shot as a fluke, prompting Rupert to fire again. He repeated the feat. A visitor to Staffordshire two generations later could report 'the two holes through the weathercock tail (as an ample testimony of the thing) remaining there to this day'.[33]

Another credible episode was one the prince enjoyed recounting: when seeking food from a widow, Rupert asked her what her opinion was of the infamous royal nephew. 'A plague choke Prince Rupert,' she replied. 'He might have kept himself where he was born; this kingdom has been the worse ever since he landed.'

Less plausible are tales that were nonetheless believed at the time. These yarns endowed Rupert with almost supernatural powers. As part of his wizardry, it was said that he was a cunning master of disguise. One such story told how Rupert met an apple-seller, and bought 10 shillings' worth of apples from him, before a mischievous thought came to him:

'Hold thy hand,' said the Prince; 'there is a piece for thee: now hold my horse, change habit with me, and stay here while I sell thy apples – only for a merry humour that I have – and at my coming back I'll give thee a piece more.' The fellow willingly lent him his coat and hat, and away went the Prince, selling the apples through the [Parliamentary] army, at any rate; viewing their strength, and in what kind they lay; and, returning to the fellow gave him another piece, with this charge: 'Go to the Army and ask the commanders how they liked the fruit Prince Rupert, in his own person, did but this morning sell them.'[34]

The reader would be forgiven for expecting this merry tale to conclude with appearances by Little John and Will Scarlet. It is difficult to accept that even someone of Rupert's reckless courage would risk himself in such a perilous exploit. He was one of the most distinctive-looking of men, his great height of 6 foot 4 inches making him 9 inches taller than his average contemporary. However, the tale of the prince selling apples to the enemy in their own camp was accepted by many as fact, not just through gullibility, but because such yarns fitted an established pattern of story-telling.

The folklore surrounding Rupert's more improbable deeds stem from a cult thriving at this time – that of the gentleman outlaw. Robin Hood was the most popular mythological figure in this tradition: the yeoman bandit who first appeared in *Piers Plowman* in the 1370s had, by the late sixteenth century, been accorded noble status as Robin, Earl of Huntingdon. One of the best-known tales of his derring-do was 'Robin Hood and the Potter,' which celebrated Robin's ability to wrong-foot enemies by concealing his identity with brilliant cunning. Robin ventured into his enemies' camp, disguised in much the same way as Rupert was said to have been. It is an ancient, English story-telling device: the hero as daring chameleon. Over five hundred years before, Hereward the Wake, a Saxon rebel leader, was said to have played a similar trick on his Norman opponents, dressing as a fisherman to inspect his enemies' siege works, before returning to torch them later in the day. That Prince Rupert inspired similar tales shows the fear he provoked, but also the respect that was grudgingly given to a prominent foe who was considered formidable, dangerous, and resourceful.

The notion of a man of royal blood resorting to criminal subterfuge would not have surprised Caroline England: half a century earlier, Shakespeare had dramatised the youthful misdemeanours of Prince Hal, the future Henry V, when led astray by Falstaff and his guttersnipe band. John Taylor, the self-styled 'Water Poet', celebrated this irresponsibile phase in 1630, placing Hal, 'the Robber Prince', in the pantheon of famous English lawbreakers:

> Once the fifth Henry could rob excellent well,
> When he was Prince of Wales, as Stories tell.
> Then Friar Tuck, a tall stout thief indeed,
> Could better rob and steal, than preach or read.[35]

Rupert, like his princely predecessor two and a half centuries beforehand, was seen as a young warrior whose hot blood lured him into terrible transgressions. The young Palatine, though, was a foreigner, whose peccadilloes were harder to forgive. Furthermore, he had no credit to his name to touch that of Agincourt. His reputation could be blackened without fear; the greater his achievements, the more they must be presented as the sinister accomplishments of a high-born but devilish reprobate.

The image of the prince was coloured not just by outlaw romance, but also by the acts of real contemporaries. They joined high birth and personal courage to thrillingly daring, dastardly deeds. One such cad was John Clavell, a gentleman thief whose crimes were well known to Charles I's England: arrested in 1627, he attempted to justify and atone for his misdeeds with a series of pamphlets and plays detailing his exploits, many of which were greatly embellished. Clavell, from a good family that had fallen on hard times, was sole heir to a rich uncle. His unfortunate decision to become a highwayman – which he termed a 'knight of the roads' – saw him die impoverished, soon after the outbreak of the Civil War. His life of criminality showed that slyness and skulduggery were not the monopoly of the poor and the desperate, but could be attributed to those of gentler blood.

It was easy for Parliamentarian propagandists to seek to undermine Rupert's qualities and talents by tapping into this vein of popular story-telling. They presented the prince's legendary luck as the outrageous tricks of a highborn scoundrel. One of the many nicknames given to Rupert early in the Civil War was 'Prince Robber'.

The profile of the prince as foremost Royalist champion was reinforced when he openly challenged the Earl of Essex to fight. The prince, recently made a Knight of the Garter – England's highest chivalric honour – accused Essex of seeking the crown for himself, and invited him to bring his army to combat the Royalists at Dunsmore Heath on 10 October 1642. This, Rupert claimed, would settle the two sides' differences in a day: it would be ordeal by battle. 'And', offered Rupert, 'if you think it too much labour and expense to draw your forces thither, I shall as willingly, on my own part, expect private satisfaction as willingly at your hands for the same, and that performed by a single duel; which proffer, if you please to accept, you shall not find me backward in performing what I have said or promised. I know my cause to be so just that I need not fear; for what I do is agreeable both to the laws of God and man, in the defence of true religion, a King's prerogative, an Uncle's right, a Kingdom's safety; think it therefore not strange that a foreigner should take foot upon your English shore with intention to draw the sword, when the Law of Arms prompts him on to that Resolution.'[36] It was this sort of posturing – sincere, forthright, but overconfident – that allowed Rupert's enemies to represent him as hopelessly arrogant.

Yet Rupert's military worth was soon revealed. His ceaseless energy made one Parliamentarian write that the prince 'slashed through the land as the lightning that strikes from one quarter of the Heaven to the other'.[37] One of his tasks was escorting silver from Oxford University to the safety of Royalist Shrewsbury. Resting at Powick Bridge, 3 miles south of Worcester, he and his men were taken by surprise by 1,000 Parliamentarians in the first notable encounter of the war.

Rupert immediately leapt onto his mount, urged his men to follow him, and led the counter-charge. Unnerved, the Parliamentarians, discharging their firearms 'at too uncertain a distance, did no execution; but the front of Prince Robert's troops coming on, discharged just at their breasts, and quite cut off the front: Serjeant Major Byron shot a bullet into Douglas's belly; Prince Robert, his brother [Maurice], and Sir Lewis Dives slew each a man; Colonel Wilmot singled out Colonel Sandys, and gave him his death-wounds'.[38]

The rebels withstood another round of fire from Rupert's men, but the third time they were shot at, at point-blank range, they broke and fled. In the ferocious quarter of an hour of fighting, and in their subsequent flight across a river, dozens of Parliamentarians were slain or drowned, including some of their most promising officers. Their commander, Colonel Sandys, his life ebbing away, repented his disloyalty to the king: Dr Watts, Rupert's chaplain, received his dying words, which were full of regret. Only a handful of Royalists died at Powick Bridge, though several of the officers who had been at the forefront of the charge were wounded: 'Prince Maurice hath received two or three scars of honour in his head, but is abroad and merry,'[39] Lord Falkland wrote; while Lord Wilmot's back was slashed by an enemy sword and Sir Lewes Dives was shot in the arm. Rupert, though 'he ventured as far as any trooper of them all',[40] remained unharmed. He wrote to his uncle: 'Your Majesty will be pleased to accept this as a beginning of your Officers' and my Duty; and I doubt not, as (certainly) they behaved themselves very bravely and gallantly, that hereafter Your Majesty shall find the same behaviour against a more considerable number. Of this Your Majesty may be very confident.'[41]

'This victory', a Parliamentarian later conceded, 'was of great consequence to the Enemy, because [it was] the omen and first fruits of the war.'[42] Clarendon, in his chronicle of the Civil War agreed, recalling that the Parliamentary forces 'talked aloud of the incredible, and unresistible courage of Prince Rupert, and the King's Horse'.[43]

It remained to be seen how the charismatic young general and his spirited cavalry would fare in the more structured arena of set-piece battle.

CHAPTER SIX

EDGEHILL

'Thou wouldest think it strange if I should tell thee there was a time in England when brothers killed brothers, cousins cousins, and friends their friends. Nay, when they conceived it was no offence to commit murder.'

Sir John Oglander, *A Royalist's Notebook*

Both sides in the Civil War looked for past experience when raising their armies, but there were few in either army who could claim to be real soldiers: 'None was thought worthy of that name, but he that could show his Wounds, and talk aloud of his Exploits in the Low Countries,' recalled a contemporary, 'Whereas the whole Business of fighting, was afterwards chiefly performed by untravelled Gentlemen, raw Citizens, and Generals that had never seen a Battle.'[1]

Parliament found it easy to recruit in London and the southeast, but the intake in rural areas was often raw and easily shocked by the realities of war. The Earl of Bedford reported from Dorset, in the first month of fighting: 'The men we brought with us were all Trained-bands, so unskilful, from the colonel to the lowest officer, and withal so astonished, when they heard the bullets whistle about their ears ... and when the cannon began to play upon them, they run as if the Devil had been in them.'[2] Bedford estimated that the combination of being shot at and having to sleep rough in the field for two nights, resulted in the immediate desertion of more than half his men.

The Parliamentarians were short of junior officers and many sergeants suddenly found themselves commissioned. During the first year or more of the Civil War, partly as a result of this lack of leadership, Essex's troops were cited as pillagers as frequently as the infamous Cavaliers. A Parliamentarian pamphleteer writing from Ludlow in October 1642 was full of indignation about 'the barbarous and insolent actions of the blood thirsty party'[3] – the Cavaliers. Yet, en route to the first major battle, Edgehill, two Royalists who looted minor objects from an absent Parliamentarian's home were hanged for their crime. Meanwhile, Lord Clarendon noted with resentment, the rebels' propaganda was so effective that the many excesses of Essex's force were buried under the torrent of libels cascading from the printing presses.

Discipline was difficult to establish in either force, which largely comprised shilling-a-day agricultural labourers on foot and their supposed social superiors on horse. There were incidents of Essex's cavalry stealing from his infantry and of his officers being relieved of their possessions by their own men. Sir Thomas More's observation in *Utopia*, of 1516, seemed still to hold true in this, the fourth decade of Stuart rule: 'Robbers do not make spiritless soldiers, nor are soldiers the most cowardly of robbers, so well are the occupations in harmony with each other.'[4] Whichever side could bring its unruly forces under control first, and harness its aggression to its political cause, would enjoy a huge advantage.

To fill his ranks at the outbreak of war, the king drew heavily on the limited populations of Wales, Cornwall, and the northwest of England. The summer and early autumn of 1642 saw a scrambling to control areas with less clear-cut allegiances. Parliament quickly dominated East Anglia and Kent, and controlled the key Midland towns of Banbury, Coventry, Northampton, and Warwick. They also gained footholds in districts that had suffered from Royalist excesses. In September 1642, a large body of Nottinghamshire gentry approached the Earl of Essex and itemised 'the innumerable oppressions that they had suffered by the Cavaliers, who daily pillage men's houses, drive away their cattle, take away their arms and monies, cut and spoil their goods, taking away all means of living and subsisting, all their endeavours tending to the destruction of Religion, King and Kingdom'.[5] They resolved to live and die in Essex's service.

Most people, however, were unenthusiastic participants in a conflict that they felt sure was bound to bring them no good. The Recorder of Hereford, while declaring his loyalty to the Crown, begged the king to save his people from the impending apocalypse: 'O my dread Sovereign, let but your Servant put into your mind the dire effects of War, when flourishing Cities shall be turned to dust, nay this yet flourishing Kingdom shall become its own destroyer, buried in the tomb of blood and slaughter, when our young infants shall be rudely torn from the sad mother's breast whose shrieks and cries serve as sad music to the sacrifice, when our young virgins and our wives shall be subject to bloody cruelty, when death shall triumph'.[6]

A neutral pamphleteer, horrified at the 'great game' being played by king and Parliament, advised: 'That his Majesty would understand his Interest to be, to unite, not to divide his Subjects, and to remember with what manner of Trophies the magnanimous Princes of former times have adorned their Funerals and Fame. That he would choose rather to fight in the head of the British Armies, for restitution of his Nephews to their lost inheritance, than employ them here to pillage and destroy his own subjects.'[7] Parliament, meanwhile, should accept the king's concessions with humility and gratitude. But Charles and his opponents were too far down the warpath to heed the concerns of the common people; they carried on recruiting. When volunteers could not be found, men were pressed into service against their will.

The rebels had the edge in weaponry. They had taken quick possession of the armaments amassed for the campaigns in Scotland and Ireland. They also seized the royal arsenals and the ironworks of the Weald of Kent. As a result, Parliament never wanted for artillery throughout the war. The early defection of the navy to the rebels was another huge advantage, making it easy to supply their garrisons by sea and also to blockade the king's ports.

The Royalists had to work harder. Although they secured the weaponry of some of the county militias, it was the energy of a few key men that transformed the king's negligible support into a serviceable army. While Rupert's drive transformed the cavalry, in the regions grandees tried to raise men for the king and to create Royalist enclaves. This effort met with varying degrees of success. In south-central England the Marquess of Hertford, a descendant of Henry VII's, was frustrated in his efforts on Charles's behalf. In Yorkshire, though, the Earl of Newcastle successfully formed the Northern Army. He also held Newcastle, a crucial lifeline for aid and arms crossing from the Continent.

It was thanks to the arrival of the first of the earl's convoys of arms and ammunition that Charles was able to face Essex's army, when it moved into the Midlands in September, seeking to bring the king to heel. Parliament had instructed its lord general: 'You shall use your utmost endeavours by battle or otherwise to rescue his Majesty's person, and the persons of the Prince, and Duke of York out of the hands of those desperate persons who are now about them.'[8] Pym and his acolytes wanted the people to believe that the king was a reluctant captive of the Cavaliers and that Parliament was sending an army to rescue him.

In hoping that the king would be unable to raise a battle-strength army, Essex underestimated the strength and resolve of the Royalists. He had left London on 9 September, amid the crowds' calls of 'Hosanna!', cautiously stowing his coffin in his baggage train. News of Powick Bridge had stunned the earl, his own Lifeguard among the broken units. He was further surprised by intelligence that Rupert had sidestepped his force and hurried to unite with the king's main army at Meriden, between Coventry and Birmingham. With Essex a day's march behind them, it appeared that the Royalist target was London, a conclusion that Rupert's own recollections bear out: 'The King's purpose was all the while ... to bring them to a battle, and clear the way to London.'[9] Essex moved quickly southeastwards, hoping to overhaul the Royalists, while sending warnings to the capital to prepare itself for attack.

Reconnaissance during these fast-moving weeks was poor, and soon neither army was sure of the other's whereabouts. It was a shock to all when, on 22 October, the advance rebel units rode into the Warwickshire hamlet of Wormleighton and stumbled upon some of Rupert's troopers. The prince learnt from these prisoners that the main body of the enemy was near by and his scouts set out that evening to pinpoint its location. They discovered dozens of campfires twinkling round the village of Kineton and raced back with the news. Rupert ordered an immediate attack, but his senior officers restrained him, insisting that such a decision must be referred to the king.

Charles, after consultation with his other generals, agreed to turn back towards the enemy and offer battle on advantageous ground the next day. Before dawn Rupert received the following message: 'Nephew, I have given order as you have desired, so that I doubt not but all the foot and cannon will be at Edgehill betimes this morning, where you will also find, your loving uncle and faithful friend, Charles R.'[10]

Edgehill, near Kineton, was a 650-foot-high ridge whose defensive qualities promised to negate the king's disadvantage in numbers and weaponry: he had 12,500 men to Parliament's 14,500. Essex was so eager to accept the invitation to fight that he decided not to wait for straggling troops and artillery to catch up with his main field army. This left the earl with a slight deficit in cavalry.

There was pre-battle dissent among the Royalist high command, much of it sparked by Rupert. The prince insisted that he answer to no man except the king: he wanted to lead his cavalry in independent command. This has long been held up as an example of Rupert's arrogance and ambition, but this is to ignore context. It was normal for European royalty to have supreme power in the army – the wholesale reforms in Louis XIV's French armies, a generation later, left intact the premise that Princes of the Blood outranked marshals in the field.

The prince's preferred tactics were more controversial. There were two principal methods of fighting at this time: one the creation of Prince Maurice of Nassau, the other the legacy of Gustavus Adolphus. Rupert favoured the bolder tactics of the Swede. He believed that a bold strike at the rebels was more likely to succeed than the conservative and attritional methods of the Dutch. Lord Ruthven, a 70-year-old veteran who had fought for Adolphus and was now a Royalist general, was foremost among those who agreed with Rupert.

Charles was militarily ignorant and was easily persuaded by Rupert's passion. However, the Earl of Lindsey, the king's lord general and the leading advocate for Dutch tactics, felt humiliated: this was not the first time that uncle had turned to nephew and overruled his senior officer, who (Clarendon recalled) was 'a person of great honour and courage, and generally beloved; who many years before had good commands in Holland, and Germany, and had been Admiral at Sea in several expeditions'.[11] Apart from hurt feelings, though, Lindsey was also properly concerned that the Royalists' chances would be compromised by this last-minute change in battle-plan. An accomplished old soldier, who had served in the Lowlands alongside his enemy counterpart, Essex (whom he respected as a fighting man), Lindsey resigned a command that had been so publicly undermined. Demoting himself to the rank of colonel, he elected to lead his own regiment of Lincolnshire men into battle, telling friends that he hoped to meet an honourable death.

This falling-out over tactics was not so much the result of a young prince's petulance, as a clear and early example of the disunity in the upper reaches of the king's high command – a situation that was to hamstring the Royalist cause throughout the Civil War.

Further ripples came from the highly regarded Viscount Falkland, a supporter of Parliament against the king in the 1630s and an admirer of John Hampden – one of the 'Five Members' that Charles had failed to arrest in the Commons, and the most famous opponent of the imposition of Ship Money. Falkland's mansion at Tew, in Oxfordshire, formed a salon for men of learning in the years before the war. However, Falkland was essentially a cautious man and his radical colleagues' rush for wholesale constitutional change appalled him. Reluctantly appointed as one of Charles's secretaries of state, Falkland remained among the moderates on both sides who were sickened by the prospect of compatriots spilling each other's blood: his constant hope was for a negotiated peace. This aim conflicted with Rupert's view, that differences with Parliament could now only be settled by clear-cut military victory.

One of the secretary of state's key duties was the transmission of the king's will to others. However, when Falkland passed on Charles's instructions to Rupert, the prince declared that he would not receive orders from anyone but his uncle. Falkland, unruffled by the insult, replied with dignity: 'That it was his office to signify what the King bid him; which he should always do; and that his Highness, in neglecting it, neglected the King; who did neither the Prince, nor his own Service any good, by complying in the beginning with his rough Nature.'[12] Falkland quietly refused to serve in Rupert's division, choosing instead to ride with the Commissary General of the Horse, Wilmot, on the left wing.

There was further dissatisfaction in the King's Life Guard. Its 300 men were recruited from those aristocrats and gentry who had no independent command, together with their most senior servants. The rest of the cavalry had taken to mocking the Lifeguard for being a 'show troop', a pampered adornment rather than a serious fighting unit. To counter this slur its commander, Lord Bernard Stuart, persuaded Charles to place the Life Guard in the place of greatest honour, the extreme right of the front line of his army. Rupert reluctantly incorporated them in the first of his two lines of cavalry, alongside his regiment and those of his brother Maurice and of their cousin, the Prince of Wales. This forward deployment of the lifeguards – well armed with their long swords, pairs of pistols, and battleaxes – deprived the Royalists of a reserve force, if the battle started to go awry.

In the prelude to battle Charles rode among his units, his armour visible beneath a coat of black velvet, lined with royal ermine. He reminded his men of their noble purpose, while countering the enemies' verbal barbs:

'Friends and soldiers! You are called Cavaliers and Royalists in a disgraceful sense ... Now show yourselves no Malignants, but declare what
courage and fidelity is within you. Fight for the peace of the kingdom
and the Protestant religion. The value of Cavaliers hath honoured that
name both in France and other countries, and now let it be known in
England, as well as horseman or trooper. The name of Cavalier, which
our enemies have striven to make odious, signifies no more than a
gentleman serving his King on horseback. Show yourselves, therefore,
now courageous Cavaliers, and beat back all opprobrious aspersions cast
upon you.[13]

In the Parliamentary ranks Puritan ministers rode through the units,
leading prayers whose content was little different from those being
mouthed at the top of Edgehill. Churchmen on both sides convinced
their men that they would be doing the Lord's work later that day,
when the killing began. 'Such may the persons be,' one Royalist priest
was later to say, 'and such the cause they maintain, that in doing them
harm we shall do good, and sure then in wishing them harm we shall
do no ill. Such may the persons be, and such the cause they maintain,
that we may lawfully fight against them in the field ...'.[14]

An early afternoon exchange of artillery opened the battle of Edgehill,
with Parliament getting the better of the duel. Dragoons from both
sides then fought a series of preliminary skirmishes, a contest won by
the Royalists. Meanwhile, one of the King's Life Guard recalled, 'Prince
Rupert passed from one wing to the other, giving positive orders to
the Horse to march as close as possible keeping their ranks with sword
in hand, to receive the enemy's shot without firing either carbine or
pistol, till we broke in amongst the enemy and then make use of our
firearms as need should require.'[15] The prince then took his position at
the head of the right wing, whose 1,400 troopers he had deployed in
two lines. The second was to remain in reserve. Rupert led the front
line in an orderly advance that progressed from walk, to rising trot, to
full-blooded charge, swords drawn, firearms tucked away, spurs digging
into their horses' flanks. The battle cry was 'The King and the Cause!'

For the Parliamentarians, the enemy thundering towards them was
the same demonic force that had swept to bloody victory at Powick
Bridge. Colleagues eager to explain the shame of unexpected defeat
had boosted the Cavaliers' reputation, persuading Essex to place the
bulk of his horse in the wing facing Prince Rupert. There had been

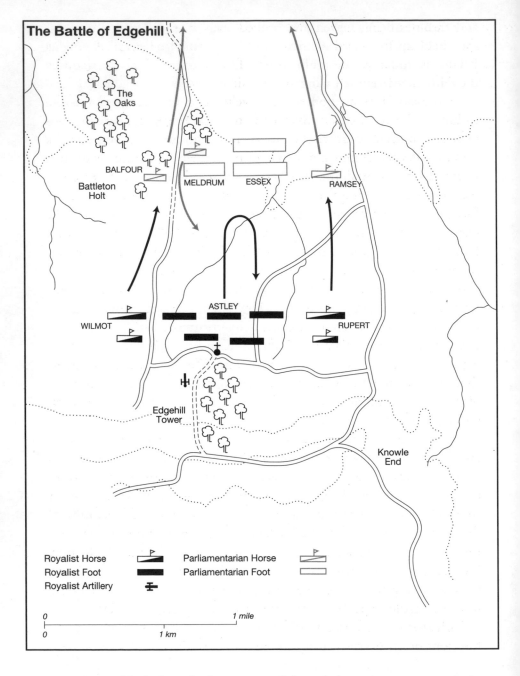

The Battle of Edgehill

The Oaks

BALFOUR

Battleton
Holt

MELDRUM   ESSEX

RAMSEY

ASTLEY

WILMOT   RUPERT

Edgehill
Tower

Knowle
End

Royalist Horse		Parliamentarian Horse	
Royalist Foot		Parliamentarian Foot	
Royalist Artillery			

0   1 mile

0   1 km

reports, readily believed, that many of the rebel survivors were seen in
Worcester, 'most woefully cut and mangled, some having their ears
cut off, some the flesh of their heads sliced off, some with their very
skulls hanging down, and they ready to fall down dead, their pistols

and carbines being hewed and hacked away in slices, which it seems they held up for guard of their heads'.[16] It was the legend of Powick Bridge, as much as the momentum of the charge, which condemned the Parliamentarian left wing at Edgehill.

As the Royalists hit home, they levelled and fired their pistols and carbines. The rebel cavalry had tried to meet the impetus with their own, half-hearted, counter-charge, but it was no use. They poured back into the infantry behind and then continued their flight, some with such panic that by nightfall they reached St Albans, 40 miles away. Rupert's men pushed on, annihilating the rebel musketeers on the ground before pursuing the broken enemy horse. Some Cavaliers headed for the baggage train, where the silver plate and personal possessions of senior Parliamentarians were seized. Others took the opportunity to pillage innocent civilians.

Wilmot's front line of Royalist cavalry on the left wing also rolled over their opponents. The terrain between them and the enemy was not suitable for a sweeping charge, being crisscrossed with ditches and containing pockets of Parliamentary musketeers, but Wilmot and his deputy, Sir Arthur Aston, led their men on. Met by a stuttering volley, they cut their way into Parliament's ranks before firing into the body of the enemy, with devastating effect. The Parliamentarians joined their colleagues in flight.

These twin successes tempted the second lines of the Royalist cavalry into fatal disobedience. Against Rupert's clear instructions, they charged forward, their commanders, Sir John Byron and Lord Digby, eager to be in at the kill. This waywardness left the infantry and artillery shorn of mounted protection in the face of superior numbers. One of the prince's colonels, Sir Charles Lucas – a colleague from the successful storming of Breda, several years earlier – rallied some of his men, intending to bring them immediately back to the battle's centre. But a wave of fleeing enemy blocked his men's return, and they plunged back into the headlong pursuit that Lucas had temporarily denied them.

Parliamentary propagandists later asserted that Rupert was at the forefront of his frenzied men, urging them on, the plunderer-in-chief*

---

* It was later claimed that Prince Rupert's conduct introduced the word 'plunder' to England: 'Many towns and villages he plundered', wrote May, 'which is to say robbed (for at that time was the word first used in England, being born in Germany when that stately country was so miserably wasted and pillaged by foreign armies), and

In truth, he took no part in the undisciplined rout. Instead, he rode among his men, imploring them to join him in a return to the battle-field. However, the adrenalin surge among his troopers, many of them fighting their first battle, was irresistible: the enemy's thrilling disinte-gration, so complete and so immediate, lured them on.

The social make-up of the Royalist cavalry in part explains their indiscipline: some were aristocrats and many were gentry – men who, in their own sphere, were used to giving, not receiving, orders. Besides, they were convinced that the day was already won. Now they saw their task, and their privilege, as being the mopping-up of a defeated enemy and the claiming of their just reward – plunder. Cavalrymen of all eras knew their role at such a moment in a battle. A manual for horse-borne troops advised 250 years later: 'To obtain the greatest results from a successful engagement it must be followed by a pursuit, which must be vigorous and unceasing.'[17] The unbroken, spirited amateurs of Rupert's squadrons felt compelled to pursue: it was what they had done on the hunting field since they could ride; it was part of their birthright; it was their entitlement.

A similar fiasco had occurred in 1264, during Henry III's reign, at the battle of Lewes. The king's son had led his over-excited cavalry off in a triumphant charge, leaving Henry and his infantry unprotected. When the prince returned, he found his father had been taken prisoner by Simon de Montfort's rebel barons. Edgehill, like Lewes, was far from won when the cavalry left the field. During the absence of so many at-tacking units, the Parliamentarians diligently achieved huge advantages of their own. 'When Prince Rupert return'd from the chase', Clarendon later recalled, 'he found a great alteration in the field, and his Majesty himself with few noblemen and a small retinue about him, and the hope of so glorious a day quite vanish'd.'[18] Fairfax's men had gradually regained on foot what Rupert's Cavaliers had claimed, then forfeited, on horseback.

The infantry battle formed its own distinctive part of the engagement, only starting once the main cavalry action had spun from the field under its own hectic energy. Sir Jacob Astley, the king's Major General

committed other outrages upon those who stood affected to the Parliament, executing some and hanging servants at their masters' doors for not discovering of their masters.' May, *History of the Long Parliament*, ed. 1854, p. 244

of Foot, had preceded the action by uttering his famous, soldier's prayer: 'Oh Lord, thou knowest how busy I must be this day; but if I forget thee, do not thou forget me!'[19] He had then risen from his knees and shouted, 'March on boys!' He led his men against an enemy that enjoyed superior numbers, strong artillery fire, and, crucially, some cavalry support.

Sir William Balfour was a Scots-born soldier who had served Charles as governor of the Tower of London. In this era of fluctuating loyalties, he was now Parliament's Lieutenant General of Horse. Balfour had rescued some of his troopers from the Royalist rout and now funnelled them through the gaps between Essex's three large brigades of foot. They bore down on, and broke, the Royalist centre. Lord Falkland, seeing this crisis unfold, tried to persuade Wilmot to regroup his cavalry and assist the infantry. Wilmot, however, dismissed the suggestion, replying: 'My Lord, we have got the day, and let us live to enjoy the fruit thereof.'[20] Balfour's squadrons rode on unchecked, reaching Charles's cannon, slashing their harnesses, and eliminating them from the battle. They then rode back, past Royalist musketeers who failed to fire on them, believing them to be their own: the cavalry of both sides looked similar and the orange scarves worn by Essex's men were difficult to see in the smoke-charged air of battle.

When the Royalist infantry on the left-hand flank appreciated the predicament of their colleagues in the centre, they attempted to come to their rescue. However, Essex, alive to the situation, now deployed a body of his infantry to block them. He then ordered his heavily armed Lifeguard to join Balfour's men in a three-pronged assault on Astley's beleaguered line. The strength of the Parliamentarian attack prompted many to flee the field, scrambling up Edgehill's slope in panic. In the confusion, a disaster of major proportions threatened Charles's army.

Sir Edmund Verney, knight marshal and hereditary bearer of the royal standard, was a reluctant Royalist. 'I do not like the quarrel', he remarked, when war became inevitable, 'and do heartily wish that the King would yield and consent to what they desire; so that my conscience is only concerned in honour and in gratitude to follow my master.'[21] Assuming his duties at Edgehill, he carried the royal standard as both a symbol of the king's military power, and as a rallying point for the Crown's cause. He was unarmed, apart from the speared point of the banner, and was dressed in civilian clothes. His avowed intent was to lay down his life in the king's service. Some Parliamentarians spied the standard fluttering invitingly among the king's wavering infantry and spurred their horses towards it. Frenzied fighting followed, which saw Verney's party whittled away by enemy swords. Sir Edmund battled on, using the point of the standard to good effect: he killed four rebels before being felled himself. So tight was his grip, even in death, that the rebel officer who captured the blood-splattered flag was forced to hack off Verney's fist in order to carry away the prize.

The infantry debacle claimed the life of that other fatalistic Royalist, The Earl of Lindsey. He strode out at the head of his regiment, before being felled by a shot high in the thigh. He was then taken prisoner and lay in some straw in a barn while bleeding heavily. Although the wound was not in itself life-threatening, he received no medical treatment. Lindsey died after several hours of blood loss, lying in the arms of his son, Lord Willoughby, another prisoner. If it had not been for his umbrage at Rupert's special commission from his uncle, he would most likely have been safely at the rear of the action, directing proceedings from the king's side.

When matters in the centre of the battlefield tilted further Essex's way, Charles's companions urged him to flee, but he would not. The king knew that his presence was essential to his hard-pressed forces and bravely insisted on remaining with his men. Rupert eventually returned to his side, realising that his efforts to organise a meaningful cavalry force late in the day were doomed.

As hopes of a great victory faded with the light, the only positive development was the recapture of the royal standard by John Smith, one of Rupert's cavalry captains. Smith earned a battlefield knighthood from Charles for his valour. However, the talisman would not have been forfeited in the first place, had the Royalist horse been on the battlefield to protect it instead of careering across the surrounding countryside.

Rupert was in time to see Essex prepare to close in on the right-hand side of the Royalist foot, the centre and left having already folded. But it was evening by this stage, and the lateness in the day and the reappearance of vestiges of Rupert's horse dissuaded the earl from trying to finish off the enemy infantry.

In the freezing night-time air, both sides reformed as best they could. Neither commander knew whose day it had been: by the standards of the time, which ever side left the field of battle was considered the loser, but Royalists and Parliamentarians both held their positions throughout a night remembered by survivors for its biting cold. Some

3,000 of Essex's stragglers, who had failed to reach Edgehill in time for the battle, now caught up with their lord general and urged him to resume the fight the following day. Across the valley, on the ridge of Edgehill, Rupert also advocated the battle's resumption at the earliest opportunity.

However, there was shock for many of the combatants as the reality of warfare hit home. The scale of the casualties has been debated ever since, but between 1,500 and 3,000 men probably died at Edgehill, with many others fatally wounded. Nothing similar had been seen in England for over a century and a half. The struggle between Crown and Parliament had developed from a political contest to a military engagement where large numbers of compatriots had killed one another in the name of opposing causes.

In the aftermath of battle, practical considerations came into play: Essex was reluctant to risk his forces in an attack on the Royalist position, since he would expose them to Rupert's cavalry which, for all its indiscipline, was recognised as a dangerously destructive force. For their part, the Royalist infantry was in no condition to fight again. Three of its five brigades had been routed.

Essex withdrew towards Warwick. When Rupert learned this, he persuaded his uncle to let him pursue the rebels with four mounted regiments. The prince attacked the enemy rearguard in Kineton, inflicting significant casualties and capturing prisoners, valuables, and correspondence. Among the letters addressed to the Earl of Essex were some from Blake, Rupert's secretary, giving details of Royalist manoeuvres and requesting greater financial reward for his espionage. Rupert had Blake hanged at Oxford, days later.

Parliamentarian sources accused the prince of murdering their wounded, but these claims were false. Thick fog stopped Rupert from pursuing further: the action in Kineton was the final episode of the battle of Edgehill.

The result of the battle was open to interpretation. While the Royalist cavalry had triumphed, the king's infantry had been utterly defeated. The Parliamentarians, meanwhile, had witnessed Rupert's destruction of their horse, while celebrating the success of their foot in the centre of the field. More rebels had been killed and captured than had Royalists, and forty of the former's regimental colours were taken, compared with a handful of Charles's. However, more prominent figures had fallen

in the king's cause than had died for Parliament. In the wider context
of the war, however, both sides had failed. Essex's priority had been
to close Charles's route to London. In this he had failed. Equally, the
Royalists had given battle at a time and place chosen by them, hopeful that they could decide the war in a day. They had seen their aims
evaporate in the cloud of Digby and Byron's indiscipline. Yet both sides
quickly claimed to have triumphed: it was important, at this early stage,
to be seen as the divinely-favoured party. Parliament rewarded Essex
with a victor's bounty of £5,000.

The Royalists knew that they had thrown away their great chance.
'Sometimes the good ordering of charging the Enemy causeth victory,'
wrote a Cavalier, later in the war, 'and the contrary sometimes causeth
the destruction of the whole body.'[22] Prince Rupert has to take ultimate
responsibility for his cavalry's failures, as well as its successes: at Edgehill,
his squadrons' order quickly unravelled. In mitigation, controlling
troopers after a successful charge demanded a level of discipline that
neither side possessed so early in the war, and which the Royalists were
never to attain. Eliot Warburton, Rupert's most partisan biographer,
also blamed the character flaws of the prince's men: 'They never could
be taught discipline; jealous and proud of their independence, and
fiercely chary of their fancied personal importance, control over these
wild and dashing troops was unattainable even by the stern Rupert.'[23]
After Edgehill, the prince admitted that his men 'shewed rather too
much valour'.[24]

One rebel observer, however, was impressed by the Royalist showing
at Edgehill. Comparing the confidence of the Cavaliers with the dif-
fidence of their own horsemen, Oliver Cromwell told his cousin John
Hampden: 'Your troopers are most of them old decayed serving men
and tapsters, their troopers are gentlemen's sons, younger sons, persons
of quality. Do you think that the spirits of such base and mean fellows
will ever be able to encounter gentlemen that have honour, courage
and resolution in them? You must get men of a spirit that is likely to go
as far as gentlemen will go, or you will be beaten still.'[25] If Parliament
failed in this, Cromwell was sure, it would be unable to better Rupert's
proud but wayward squadrons.

When Essex withdrew after the battle, he believed that the king
would look to make good his losses, and return towards his most productive recruiting grounds in Wales and the northwest. Instead Charles
led his army to the rebel stronghold of Banbury, which fell to him

without a fight, four days after Edgehill. At this point, with Royalist morale buoyant, Rupert urged his uncle to agree to a bold plan: he would hurry on to London with a flying army of cavalry, dragoons, and mounted musketeers, capture the members of the Lords and Commons in Westminster, and hold them at Whitehall until the king arrived with the rest of his troops. Edgehill had failed to end the rebellion, but the taking of the capital promised an immediate and successful conclusion to the war.

Charles's advisers were unconvinced. Some expressed serious reservations about the plausibility of Rupert's scheme. The Earl of Bristol, father of Lord Digby, revealed a distaste for Rupert's foreign ways, voicing concern that the prince would set London on fire. The German had shown his readiness to threaten unrestrained force against the citizens of Leicester. How could he be trusted with the safety of the capital, by far the biggest city in Britain – and, with 150,000 inhabitants, the most populous city in the world?

This has been seen as a defining moment in the Civil War. Charles was never to enjoy another opportunity to march on London. Rupert could, possibly, have succeeded in his Blitzkrieg, and such was the terror at his name that his numerical inferiority to the capital's militia, the London Trained Bands, might have been irrelevant. There was Royalist support in London, which may well have risen for Rupert. But it is hard to see the lightly armed force penetrating London's defences, decayed though many had become. To speed his progress, Rupert would have had to leave his artillery behind and this would have further reduced his chances of success. The Earl of Warwick had also begun to raise a second Parliamentary army; it was unproven and inexperienced, but it would have been a further impediment. Among all the hypotheses, there is one certainty: Rupert's aim of taking the Lords and Commons by surprise had absolutely no hope of success.

Charles sided with his more cautious advisers against his nephew's plan. From Banbury he turned to Oxford, which he made the Royalist headquarters. This was a town he knew well, since repeated bouts of the plague had forced him to move there from London with court and Parliament, earlier in his reign.

'After the famous Battle at Edge-hill', a Parliamentarian noted, 'the first large field of blood in these Civil Wars, though the King's Army was there much broken, yet his strength increased, and multitudes began to look towards him, as one at least wise possible not to be overcome, and in this strange confluence of men His Army seemed like that fabulous generation that sprung out of the teeth of the Cadmean Serpent buried in the earth.[26] After the embarrassing fiasco of the standard-raising at Nottingham, many had thought the king would struggle to form an army. Thanks to Rupert's energetic work with the cavalry, and Aston's efforts with the infantry, Charles had met Essex and at least achieved parity on the battlefield. Partial success helped attract waverers to the king's cause. If Charles were to have a hope of winning the war, Rupert and his colleagues needed to produce further success, quickly and consistently. If not, Parliament's advantages – in terms of recruitment, armament, and control of the navy – would surely tell.

CHAPTER SEVEN

THE CURSE OF PARLIAMENT

'Most Bloody Prince, and all your bloody Prelates and Cavaliers: I have as you may see by this ensuing Discourse, taken a little pains, to set that before your eyes in words, which by your actions you will not take notice of: namely, your unreasonable wickedness, and the doom that will follow: Advising you to take heed of persisting in such destructive ways, as now you are in; which counsel of mine, if you shall take, you will find it the best piece of work that ever you took in hand; but if you refuse and reject it, you will, I am sure, repent the day, when it is too late.'

Introduction to *The Bloody Prince, or a Declaration of the Most cruell Practises of Prince Rupert, and the rest of the Cavaliers*, London: 1643

The king marched triumphantly into Oxford, then sent a force on to take Reading. Rupert, meanwhile, pushed further down the Thames Valley towards Windsor. Most of the 1,500 townsfolk were Parliamentarians and, in the aftermath of Edgehill, they took control of the mighty Royalist castle – 'being a place of greatest strength in this part of the kingdom, by reason of the height and strength, the country lying under it so that the Castle can command it round about'.[1] The new governor was Colonel John Venn, a City merchant who was loathed by the Royalists: he was on a select list of eleven rebels (headed by Pym) ineligible for the king's pardon. If captured, he would be executed.

A fortnight after Edgehill, on 7 November, Rupert attacked Windsor from the Eton side of the Thames. The market town was almost defence-less and suffered badly during a seven-hour bombardment by Rupert's five field pieces. Many civilians fled for refuge into the surrounding woodland. Others sought shelter up the hill in the castle, where the prince's cannon made barely any impression on formidable defences. Rupert was told by his men that 'they would willingly attend him to fight against men but not against stone walls, rocks and inaccessible places, where a hundred men might keep out ten thousand, all valour being useless; and therefore desired the Prince that he would rise thence, and depart into other places where they might do the Cause better service'.[2] Rupert reluctantly agreed, leaving Windsor Castle in Parliament's hands. It would be its military headquarters throughout the Civil War, a counterbalance to Royalist Oxford 40 miles away.

Meanwhile, Charles and Parliament revisited possibilities for peace. But, when the king met the rebel commissioners near Slough, on the same day as his nephew was assaulting nearby Windsor, both sides believed the other to be insincere. Convinced that his enemies were deploying delaying tactics, Charles sanctioned Rupert's request to attack Parliamentary Brentford. The prince led a ruthless infantry assault, descending out of the mist at the head of Welsh troops to overwhelm the garrison and capture several hundred men and a dozen cannon. The king's opponents were outraged by this 'bloody and treacherous design'.[3] Their men had been caught off guard, they claimed, because of the truce accompanying the ongoing peace negotiations. The military success of the attack was countered by the claims of Charles's critics that he was 'environ'd by some such Councils, as do rather persuade a desperate division, than a joining and a good agreement with your Parliament and People'.[4] The drunken pillaging of the town by Rupert's men added credibility to the view that the prince, 'and all his followers, wheresoever they go, leave not a house in their way unplundered'.[5]

Londoners saw Brentford's fate as a foretaste of what they could expect, if Rupert breached the capital's defences. The prince became the target of increasingly vicious propaganda. Lord Wharton, returned after serving as a captain at Edgehill, claimed in a speech at the Guildhall that God's favour had spared Essex all but miniscule casualties in the battle. 'One great cause of the preservation, & of the success of that day', he continued, 'was that the troops under the command of Prince Robert, while we were a fighting, not only pillaged the baggage (which was a poor employment;) but killed countrymen that came in with their teams, and poor women, and children that were with them; this I think not amiss to tell you, because you may see what is the thing they aim at, which is pillage, and baggage, and plundering, and the way which they would come by it is murdering, and destroying, and therefore it will come in very properly, to encourage you to that work ... which is, the standing upon your defence.'[6]

Rupert reacted to Wharton's slanders with fury: 'If these abominable untruths (with many more like them in his Lordship's speech) be all true,' Rupert fumed, 'then shall he freely charge me with barbarousness and inhumanity; but if these be most gross falsities (as many thousand worthy Gentlemen will take their oaths they are) then I must profess I am sorry that any Baron of the English Nation should utter such foul untruths, to deceive the poor abused Citizens of London with false reports, and so slander us.'[7]

Many chose to believe Wharton. The capital's Puritan ministers harnessed fear at the prince's approach to persuade 20,000 Londoners to stiffen the city's defences. The citizens' unity of purpose, in the face of looming peril, was celebrated in verse:

> By hearsay our foes they are coming to town,
> And threaten to kill us and beat our works down;
> Which thing to prevent our tradesmen do strive,
> To build up new bulwarks to keep us alive ...
>
> The several tradesmen I to you will name,
> And tell you how orderly they to work came,
> With shovels and baskets, with pick-axe and spades
> Who laboured as hard as they did at their trades ...
>
> It do my heart good to see how fine wenches,
> Doth drive the wheelbarrows and work in the trenches,
> I dare undertake that they laboured so well,
> That all the whole kingdom will of the same tell ...
>
> Indeed they have cause for to do their endeavour,
> To work and take pains now at this time or never,
> To keep out Prince Robert and his Cavaliers,
> Which daily possesses the City with fears ...[8]

The entrances to London – at St James's, Hyde Park Corner, St Giles in the Fields, Pancras Fields, Gray's Inn Lane, Holloway Road, and Hoxton – were allotted artillery batteries, fortifications, and troops with which to hold back 'Prince Robber'. Warships were deployed along the Thames, their cannon standing sentinel over the Houses of Parliament.

Essex's troops rushed back to the capital and joined apprentice-boy volunteers and the London Trained Bands on Turnham Green, ready to block Rupert's approach from Brentford. The combined Parliamentary army numbered 24,000 men. An awkward stand-off ensued, both armies deployed for action but neither prepared to risk battle. Rupert saw that there was no open ground for his cavalry to exploit, and he could make out rebel muskets in the hedges and ditches before him. Essex's artillery was well entrenched, its exploratory shots claiming a few victims.

Rupert led his cavalry forward in some minor sallies, his enemies reporting seeing him 'charging like a Devil, rather than a man'. They were nervous of the prince's growing reputation and sought to portray his bravery in a sinister light: 'The prince, who without all doubt, is rather to be held desperate than truly valiant ... and though he was shot at a thousand times by our men, not any of them was to purpose; encouraging his horsemen, who were the flower of his garland, not to leave him nor the quarrel.'⁹ Despite Rupert's efforts, the skirmishes did not develop into the expected decisive battle.

It was enough for the Parliamentarians to have blocked the Royalist advance. In a humiliating end to the 1642 campaign, Charles led his men slowly away, eventually returning to Oxford. The king was not to see London again until returning as a prisoner, years later, on trial for his life.

The reality of war had been a shock for all but the few professional soldiers on either side. The violent clashes at Edgehill, and the extra-ordinary sight of an English king preparing to attack his capital, were events that many found bewildering. A third of Essex's army deserted during the first winter of the war, disillusioned and ill provided for. 'My hope was', Charles now admitted, 'that either by success on my part, or Repentance on theirs, God would have put a short end to this great storm.'¹⁰ However, he underestimated the passions unleashed by open conflict.

From January to April 1643, peace negotiations were conducted at Oxford. The concessions demanded of Charles remained unrealistic on many fronts: he would not contemplate surrendering his sovereign control of the militia; honour forbade him from handing over his key supporters to Parliament for punishment; his religious beliefs stopped him from abolishing the bishops; and common sense dictated that he should not disband an army that was showing encouraging growth.

While the talks dragged on, Rupert remained active and aggressive.

As a professional soldier, he was determined to win political advantage on the battlefield. As the son of a displaced ruler, he was eager to save his uncle's crown. The prince's military position was strengthened by the confirmation of Patrick Ruthven, the Earl of Forth, as commander of the Royalist army in succession to the dead Lindsey. Forth admired Rupert's exceptional drive and recognised his talismanic value to the king's cause. The prince was encouraged to strike into the enemy heartland: 1643 was to be the golden year of his military career.

Cirencester was the first to fall. A crucial stronghold in the Cotswolds, the town was home to a large Parliamentary garrison. Rupert attacked it with 6,000 men in February, after his summons to surrender had been declined, and took it in four hours. A well-aimed grenade ignited the key defences and when the enemy's musketeers fled, they were ruthlessly despatched by the prince's men. There were the customary rumblings from London, which followed in the wake of a Rupert spectacular: he was falsely accused of sanctioning the cold-blooded murder of women, children, and Puritan ministers. In truth, he took 1,000 prisoners, seized much-needed arms and provisions, and marched them all to Oxford, where the Royalists greeted his victory with a celebratory Evening Service. Sir Edward Nicholas, one of Charles's secretaries of state and a great admirer of the prince, wrote: 'The welcome news of your highness's taking of Cirencester by assault with admirable dexterity and courage, came this morning very seasonably and opportunely, as his Majesty was ready to give an answer to the Parliament Committee, and will, I believe, work better effects with them.'[11] Rupert's timely victory had narrowly saved his uncle from needless concessions to his enemies.

By taking Cirencester, Rupert gained the king a vital staging post between his Oxford headquarters and his key recruiting grounds in the northwest and Wales – the latter was referred to by the rebels as the 'feed-plot and nursery of Prince Rupert's soldiers'.[12] The new acquisition also threatened two significant Parliamentarian cities, Bristol and Gloucester. Rupert tried to sweet-talk the governors of both into switching allegiance, without success.

Rupert now swept through Hampshire, bettering a Parliamentary force at Alton in late February, before terrorizing enemy troops in Wiltshire. Speed and surprise were his hallmarks, and nowhere in southern or central England seemed to be beyond his reach; he spread round the country, his enemies complained, 'like wildfire'.

On 22 February, Henrietta Maria landed in Yorkshire with desperately

needed reinforcements and armaments from the Continent. Rupert
and 12,500 men – mainly mounted – were sent to escort the queen to
Oxford, through the hostile Midlands. The prince was encouraged to
attack enemy strongholds on his way northeast, to make the return of
his precious convoy easier.

Birmingham was the first victim; it prided itself on being the most
rebellious town in England, but its forces were unequal to its reputation. Rupert's papers recalled that: 'The Prince took Birmingham by
assault with little loss, only the Lord of Denbigh was unfortunately
slain.'[13] Denbigh had been one of the first to volunteer to serve the
prince, at the outbreak of war. His son, though, had opted to fight for
Parliament.

Rebel scribes accused Rupert's men of defiling the women of
Birmingham and of wilfully setting the town ablaze – their main pamphlet describing the assault was called *Prince Rupert's Burning Love for
England discovered in Birmingham's Flames*. Independent eyewitnesses
supported the prince's denial of both charges.

Lichfield was a tougher proposition. Its well-drilled garrison, under
a flinty professional called Colonel Rowsewell, made a stand inside the
moat and walls of the town's cathedral close. The rebel forces at Lichfield
behaved in an inflammatory manner, hunting a cat with hounds inside
the cathedral, and dressing up a calf as a bishop. Then, after capturing
several Royalists in a failed assault with ladders, they paraded one of
these prisoners, attached a noose around his neck, and goaded Rupert
to rescue his man, if he could, by shooting through the rope. They then
swung him over the wall from a gibbet, where he kicked his last in
view of the prince. Rules of war were rudimentary during this period,
and were frequently disregarded on the Continent, but in England the
cold-blooded murder of prisoners was still regarded as a heinous act.

Rupert vowed to slaughter the garrison. He was entitled to do this
because of the murder of his soldier and because his calls to surrender
had been rejected. However, he had insufficient artillery to breach the
walls. The prince now called on his experience in European warfare:
summoning fifty Staffordshire miners from Cannock Chase, he ordered
them to burrow a tunnel beneath the cathedral walls. It was a complex
operation, requiring the draining of the defensive moat and the penetration of an unforgiving stratum of rock, but eventually 'the first mine
sprung in England'[14] was complete, and five barrels of gunpowder were
detonated to good effect. Frenzied fighting took place in the resulting

breach, but the defenders, no doubt spurred on by fear of Rupert's reprisals, continued their resistance into the following day.

It was during his time outside Lichfield that Rupert received a stream of confusing and contradictory letters from the king. Initially, eager to be viewed as a magnanimous ruler, Charles wrote urging his nephew to 'have a care of spilling innocent blood'[15] when he took the city. This was an easy order for an inexperienced, absent commander to give, but a difficult one for Rupert to implement on the ground. Such interference risked compromising the effectiveness of an independent man of action.

Charles further complicated Rupert's task by dithering over how best to counter a serious threat to Reading. This important buffer between Parliamentary Windsor and Royalist Oxford was in peril, the full strength of Essex's army bearing down on its 3,000-strong garrison. However, if a rescue operation were to be mounted, Rupert's army would need to lead it. The choice for Charles was simple: either to urge Rupert on to hurry queen and convoy to Oxford's safety, while the garrison in Reading tried to hold out; or to call the prince back immediately, save Reading, and trust the queen would be safe until the Royalists could ride out to meet her again. Charles's inability to make this decision is betrayed in this muddled letter, which arrived at Lichfield during Rupert's siege:

Nephew,
I thought necessary to advertise you that the Rebels have attacked Reading, not to recall you (though I could be content you were here) but to desire you to hasten Northward. I write not this to make you raise your siege but that you lose no more time in it than you must needs. I suppose that this direction needs no ways retard my wife's coming ...[16]

Ambivalence was alien to a man of Rupert's uncompromising focus. The phrase in parentheses suggests that Charles wanted his nephew to decide for himself where he should be. The king's next letter was more decisive, probably because it resulted from his counsellors' deliberations:

Nephew,
Upon further debate this day I have resolved to desire you to come to me with what diligence you may and with as much force as you

can ... This I confess is somewhat differing from what I wrote to you yesterday.[17]

The postscript of Charles's letter, a personal addendum, revealed the king's wavering nature: 'I hope you will have done your work about Lichfield before this can come to you,' he added.

Rupert's papers recorded: 'The King sent for the Prince from Lichfield without delay to march to the relief of Reading.'[18] The urgency of the summons denied Rupert time to finish off the Lichfield rebels. He was forced to grant them generous terms of surrender, before setting off for the Royalist rendezvous at Wallingford. The next day the combined forces of king and prince tried to relieve Reading in an attempted push across Caversham Bridge. The Parliamentarians were strongly entrenched, however, and the besieged Royalists failed to help their would-be rescuers by striking out from Reading. Their commander, Sir Arthur Aston, had taken a serious blow to the skull from a falling brick. In his place stood Colonel Richard Feilding, who had already started negotiating Reading's surrender.

When Rupert heard of Feilding's defeatism, he took it upon himself to snuff it out. 'The Prince spoke to Feilding over the river by Reading to know if he wanted any thing,' the Prince's papers record, 'he said they wanted [gun-]powder, but that they were in treaty and were offered terms to march out of the town ... His Highness told him that there was no treating to be admitted, the king being there in person, and that for Powder he might be furnished when he pleased, passing over a quantity in a Boat for the present ...'[19] Yet Feilding, whether believing that he must honour the ongoing peace negotiations or out of fear of the enemy, disobeyed the prince and surrendered Reading. The terms of the treaty allowed Feilding's men to march unimpeded to Oxford, yet some Parliamentarians breached these terms, plundering the Royalists before they could reach safety. 'The soldiers were not only reviled', Clarendon wrote, 'and reproachfully used, but many of them disarmed, and most of the wagons plundered, in the presence of the Earl of Essex himself, and the Chief Officers; who seemed to be offended at it, and not to be able to prevent it.'[20]

Many viewed the capitulation of Reading as shameful and unnecessary, a treacherous betrayal by an inadequate colonel. Feilding was court-martialled, found guilty, and sentenced to death by beheading. However, Rupert helped secure a pardon, seeing Feilding's execution as an unnecessary additional casualty for the Royalist cause.

After Reading's fall Oxford was more vulnerable, prompting several of the king's counsellors to advise him to move his headquarters further north. But Rupert realised the strategic importance of maintaining a strong presence in the Thames Valley, within striking distance of London. He persuaded his uncle not to move.

By contemporary standards, Rupert possessed the key ingredient of a successful general: 'As one said that pronunciation was the first, second, and third part of a good orator,' said the Bishop of Derry, in a sermon to a Royalist congregation, 'so may I say that Courage is the first, second, and third part of a good commander.'[21] To valour, Rupert added versatility. *Militarie Instructions for the Cavallrie*, an influential tract published a decade before the Civil War, advised that: 'The Cavalry must principally be employed to travel and molest the enemy, sometime by hindering him from his victual, sometime by endamaging his foragers, sometime by sending some troops even up to his camp to take some booty, by that means to draw him forth, and to make him fall upon some embuscadoe disposed beforehand in some fitting place.'[22] The prince used all aspects of the cavalier's art to pull off one of his most famous successes.

Colonel John Urry was a Scottish mercenary whose Civil War record became a byword for disloyalty: he was to change sides four times. In mid June he slipped away from Essex's army, which was suffering from low morale and an epidemic of typhoid, and defected to Rupert. He brought with him tantalising news: Essex was awaiting the arrival of a convoy from London, bearing the pay for his entire army – a sum in excess of £20,000.

Rupert targeted this bonanza with his flying army. He had 1,800 men, three-quarters of whom were mounted. He was aware that this small force would be outnumbered, if cornered. However, he also knew the capabilities of his troops, who were commanded by his favourite lieutenants: Sir Richard Crane, a veteran of Vlotho, was in charge of Rupert's lifeguards; the Irishman Daniel O'Neill, an equally trusted comrade in arms, rode as lieutenant colonel of Prince Rupert's Regiment; and Will Legge, the son of one of Sir Walter Raleigh's naval officers – and who was to become closer to the prince than any other British Royalist, acted as brigade major. Legge rode ahead of the main body with 150 scouting skirmishers. On foot was Colonel Henry Lunsford, whose regiment of experienced Somerset men had seen action in the Bishops' Wars, at Edgehill, and at Reading. Rupert would soon show his admiration for their gritty professionalism by adopting them as 'Prince Rupert's Bluecoats'. This was the force that accompanied him as he departed Oxford, over Magdalen Bridge.

Rupert sent his handpicked men out in sweeping manoeuvres to disable Essex's outposts, so the rebels marching with the military chest would have no warning of the Cavaliers' approach. Early on 18 June, Parliament's detachments in the Chiltern villages of Postcomb and Chinnor were surprised and easily overcome. Many were killed and some were captured, but others escaped and fired shots into the air, raising the alarm and allowing the convoy to escape into nearby woodland. Rupert, disappointed that his plan had come to nothing, now looked for alternative action. He retreated slowly, luring on the superior numbers of the enemy, teasing them with the prospect of revenge for their recent reverses.

The prospect of bettering the infamous prince proved irresistible. Essex sent men from his main base at Thame to join in the pursuit. John Hampden, the leading Parliamentarian, learnt of Rupert's proximity while in bed at Warpsgrove House. Hampden was colonel of his own regiment, but now rode independently as a simple volunteer, so eager was he to join the fray. A rolling series of skirmishes took place throughout the morning near Chiselhampton. Rupert ordered his infantry to hold Chiselhampton Bridge, in case a speedy retreat became necessary, and then hid his dragoons in surrounding hedges, setting the ambush for the enemy.

When the Parliamentarian horse and dragoons bore down, charging through the ripening corn of Chalgrove Field, they expected the prince to gallop off in retreat. So did Rupert's officers, who could see they were outnumbered and thought flight their only option. Instead, to everyone's astonishment, Rupert turned to face the enemy and shouted: 'Yea, this insolency is not to be endured.' He then spurred on his horse and plunged over the hedge separating his force from the enemy. Without hesitation, one of Rupert's officers reported: 'The Captain and rest of his Troop of Lifeguards (every man as they could) jumped over after him, and as about 15 were gotten over, the Prince presently drew them up into a Front till the rest could recover up to him. At this, the rebels' Dragooners that lined the hedge fled: having hurt and slain some of ours with their first volley.'[23]

Rupert led his men in a fearless charge across flat and open country-side. Although the Royalist cavalry noted that the rebels resisted their first charge better than at any point since Powick Bridge, they were still quick to break and flee. Chalgrove Field was (like Powick Bridge) an action that had repercussions out of all proportion to its scale: it confirmed the already dread reputation of the prince and his Cavaliers. Rupert lost just twelve men. This slight cost had garnered huge psycho-logical advantages, as the Royalists left their enemy demoralised and disordered.

It also produced a significant enemy casualty: John Hampden had written an ode at the time of the marriage of Rupert's parents, wish-ing them many illustrious children. Now, while attacking one of the Palatine offspring, he was shot twice in the shoulder. After six days of ineffective medical treatment, he died of his wounds. Hugely respected in the Parliamentary camp, Hampden was regarded as a wise and calm-ing influence on his more extreme colleagues, particularly the radical Pym. At Chalgrove Field Rupert's Cavaliers silenced Westminster's clearest voice of reason.

This was one of several victories that turned the summer of 1643 into the season of greatest success for the king. In the north the rebels reeled from total defeat at Adwalton Moor. In May, in the southwest, Sir Ralph Hopton and his Cornishmen trounced Parliament's south-western army at Stratton, despite being outnumbered two to one. They then advanced through Devon to Somerset, looking to link up with the troops led by the Marquess of Hertford and by Rupert's brother, Prince Maurice.

Parliament had enjoyed a series of stunning successes in southern England early in the war, thanks to the inspired leadership of the Andover MP, Sir William Waller. Waller was a gifted opportunist, who revelled in his nickname of 'the Night Owl': he liked to move at night, then swoop on unsuspecting prey. In little over a month he took control of Farnham, Winchester, and Chichester. He then gained Hereford, Monmouth, and Chepstow in the west. London celebrated Waller's exploits by giving him the sobriquet 'William the Conqueror'.

Prince Maurice and Hertford were now approaching Waller's sphere of influence. The Parliamentarian was eager to keep the two Royalist armies apart, but he failed to stop them from joining at Chard. The combined force pulled off an astonishing, fast-paced victory over Waller at Lansdown Hill, outside Bath. This was followed by Prince

Maurice's greatest triumph, when he rode to Oxford, rounded up all available cavalry, took them towards Devizes, and led them with real intelligence at the battle of Roundway Down. That July day, Maurice helped in the destruction of Waller's army and the puncturing of his inflated reputation. As 'the Conqueror' scuttled off, vanquished, to Gloucester, with five or six hundred survivors from his army of several thousand, he left Bristol open to Rupert's long-planned assault.

In mid February 1643, partly in response to Rupert's success at Cirencester, Parliament promoted its own glamorous champion from colonel to major general. Waller was placed in charge of rebel troops in five western and southern counties, and was instructed to guard the Severn Valley. The newly vulnerable Bristol became his headquarters.

Bristol was, with Norwich, one of only two provincial cities in England to have a population in excess of 10,000. With its natural harbour, complemented by a thriving arms industry, Bristol was England's second city and a highly desirable prize for both causes. It started the war as Parliament's possession, but its population contained a sizeable Royalist contingent: 'So it was', a contemporary, rebel historian explained, 'that the King's cause and party were favoured by two extremes in that city; the one the wealthy and powerful men, the other of the basest and lowest sort, but disgusted by the middle rank, the true and best citizens.'[24]

Rupert had tried to take Bristol with his flying column of horse and dragoons in early March. Lacking sufficient infantry or artillery to attack, Rupert had instead resorted to subterfuge. Two prominent citizens – Robert Yeomans, a former sheriff, and George Bouchier, a merchant – agreed to open the gates to the waiting Royalists, which would be the prelude to Rupert's attack. But the two men were betrayed, their plans 'divulged by tattling women'.[25] They were arrested by Major Langrish, a fanatical Parliamentarian, just before their men attempted to overpower a guardhouse. The major had them chained to a dungeon's walls. During their imprisonment they were barely fed and were given unclean water to drink. Despite the pleas of the king, as well as the mayor and aldermen of Bristol, the men were condemned to death by hanging, the Commons insisting that an example be made of these dangerous conspirators.

On the day of their public execution the two men were taken to a scaffold, specially erected near the City Cross. On arrival the starving, terrified Yeomans collapsed and fainted. His executioners propped him up so that, when he came round, the first thing he saw was his home, along the street. As the pair huddled in final prayers, Major Langrish insulted and cursed them. Bouchier and Yeomans then summoned their final reserves of dignity and strength, and climbed the ladders to their death.

Parliament's harsh punishment had the desired effect: it deterred other Royalist sympathisers from acting on the king's behalf. Rupert realised that, if Bristol were to fall, it would have to be by conventional means: he must besiege the city.

Bristol was difficult to defend. Its perimeter walls were 4 miles long and were punctuated by infrequent fortifications, which left various approaches with vulnerable dead ground. Furthermore, the city's low-lying position (Warburton described it as 'situated in a hole') meant that an attacking commander enjoyed a panoramic view of proceedings.

Rupert arrived from Oxford with a sizeable army – fourteen infantry regiments, seven troops of dragoons, two wings of cavalry, and eight siege guns. Although his units were not at battle strength because of casualties, desertion, and sickness, they easily outnumbered the 1,800 Parliamentarian defenders. Sidelining the Marquess of Hertford, the prince took control of the siege. He made his camp at Clifton, appointed Maurice as his lieutenant general, and pressed for immediate action.

Rupert ordered the attack for before dawn on 26 July 1643. It was to be simultaneous, on all sides of the city: the prince wanted the defenders to be strung out along their perimeter, unable to concentrate their fire on his men. The assailants were drawn up in lines, each with a distinctive role. First went the dragoons, carrying bundles of faggots wrapped up in fascines and dragging carts: their job was to fill up any trenches and ditches that might slow down the Royalist advance. Next were the musketeers, under orders only to fire at close range. In the third line came pikemen, their weapons bearing blazing rags, designed to torch the rebel defences. Following these came a line of grenadiers and then more musketeers. The cavalry was kept in the rear, ready to support the attack when Rupert decided it was appropriate.

The fighting was intense, one eyewitness judging it 'the hottest service that ever was in this kingdom since the war began'.[26] Maurice's West Countrymen suffered horrendous casualties as they tried, but failed,

to scale the main fort on the south side of Bristol. They were beaten
back by volleys of musket-balls, and also by hurled rocks that knocked
them off their scaling ladders. After half an hour they slipped back to
the safety of some near-by hedges, from where they continued to fire
for several hours. 'In time of the retreat', wrote Rupert's engineering
expert, de Gomme, 'Prince Maurice went from regiment to regiment
encouraging the soldiers, desiring the officers to keep their companies
by their colours; telling them he believed his brother had already made
his entrance on the other side.'[27]

Maurice's optimism was premature. Rupert's infantry also suffered
initially, before finding some dead ground that allowed them to approach
within a stone's throw of the Parliamentary outer defences. From that
range, they were able to lob grenades into the exposed rebel lines. An
officer, Lieutenant Colonel Edward Littleton, then rode forward with a
fire-pike, swinging it menacingly and causing terror in the enemy lines.
The rebels screamed 'Wildfire!' as they fled in panic. The word went
through the Royalist ranks – 'They run! They run!' – and Rupert's men
surged forward in pursuit, hacking down and running through many
before they reached the safety of the city walls.

The struggle continued for several hours. One young Royalist lord
later recalled 'the noise and tintamarre of guns and drums, with the
horrid spectacles, and hideous cries, of dead and hurt men'.[28] Rupert,
in the thick of the action as ever, was thrown to the ground when his
horse was shot dead, a bullet piercing its eyeball. He joined his men
on foot until another mount could be found, screaming orders and
sustaining the assault in the cacophony of gunfire and grenade explosion. His soldiers pushed forward, through a breach made by Colonel
Henry Washington's dragoons. The fighting inside the city was confused and fierce as the men of both sides discharged their weapons,
before falling on one another with sword, musket butt, and gouging
hands. Eventually, the Royalists established a stronghold within sight of
the harbour, but Rupert forbade his men from using this as a position
from which to torch the ships or the city. In the heat of battle, with the
outcome still undecided, the prince's conduct was far from that of the
bloody destroyer of popular myth.

Indeed, at the storming of Bristol, Rupert showed himself the
model professional general, hectoring, encouraging, and controlling his
men so their impetus never wavered. He moved his cavalry through
Washington's breach, in support of the hard-pressed foot, who were

drawing heavy enemy fire in house-to-house fighting. Henry Lunsford, Rupert's favoured infantry colonel, already wounded in the arm, was now shot dead near the Frome Gate. The ferocity of the fighting was such that it became a question of which side could sustain the contest for the longest, in the face of terrible losses.

The Parliamentarian commander, Colonel Nathaniel Fiennes, had received his governorship of the city through nepotism. His military experience was limited to an extremely rapid retreat from Powick Bridge, and a minor role at Edgehill. However, he was the son and heir of Lord Saye and Sele, an eminent Westminster rebel. Over-promoted though Fiennes was, he had the sense to realise that his small force faced elimination. With the city and its shipping at the mercy of the prince, he offered to discuss terms of surrender. Rupert, eager to avoid time-wasting and now confident of taking Bristol by force, limited the ceasefire to a maximum of two hours: if Fiennes failed to agree terms in that period, his garrison would be annihilated. This proved enough time to reach a peaceful conclusion: Fiennes would be allowed to lead his vanquished men unmolested out of the city to a safe, Parliamentarian destination, but stores, weapons, and armaments must be left behind for the victors.

Many Royalists had been roughly treated in similar circumstances, after the surrender of Reading. 'Some of ours', Baron de Gomme reported, 'in requital, now plundered some of theirs.'[29] However, Rupert and Maurice were outraged, and Fiennes – despite facing criticism from London for losing Bristol – had the moral courage to testify on their behalf: 'I must do this right to the Princes', he said, 'contrary to what I find in a printed pamphlet, that they were so far from sitting on their horses, triumphing and rejoicing at these disorders, that they did ride among the plunderers with their swords, hacking and slashing them, and that Prince Rupert did excuse it to me in a very fair way, and with expressions as if he were much troubled at it.'[30] Rupert was furious: first, as a professional soldier, he was keen to adhere to honourable conduct; secondly, as a devout Christian, he was not prepared to have his solemn word made valueless by the dregs in his ranks.

The capture of Bristol was a major boost for the king's cause, paid for with 500 lives – most of them Cornish. One thousand of the defeated citizens joined the prince's victorious ranks. More importantly, the capture of hundreds of barrels of gunpowder, eighty pieces of artillery and 6,000 firearms was a welcome influx for a Royalist army short of key supplies. Charles wrote from Oxford: 'I know you do not expect compliments from me, yet I must not be so forgetful, as now that I have time, not only to congratulate with you for this last happy success of the taking of Bristol, but to acknowledge the chief thanks thereof to belong to you, which, I assure you, adds to my contentment.'[31]

There would be further triumphs, but the run of successes that culminated in Bristol was the zenith of Rupert's Civil War career. He was recognised as the most dynamic, effective, and flamboyant general in the land, the curse of Parliament and the darling of the Royalists. He had become a man 'whose very name was half a conquest'.[32] His military gifts were celebrated in verse:

> Thread the beads
> Of Caesar's acts, great Pompey's, and the Swede's,
> And 'tis a bracelet fit for Rupert's hand,
> By which that vast triumvirate is spanned.[33]

The Marquess of Newcastle, commander of the king's army in the north, wrote: 'Your name is grown so triumphant, and the world's expectations to look for more from you than man can do; but that is their fault, sir, and not yours. Long may you live ... a terror to your uncle's enemies, and a preserver of his servants.'[34] The problem, unrecognised by Newcastle, was that such clear-cut distinctions no longer applied: some of the king's most trusted servants were, in truth, becoming the prince's bitterest enemies.

CHAPTER EIGHT

FACTION FIGHTING

'Persuasion avails little at Court, where always the orator convinces
sooner than the argument.'

Arthur Trevor's advice to Prince Rupert, 1644

The arrival of Henrietta Maria in the Royalist camp changed everything. The queen was a powerful character who exercised huge
influence over an adoring husband. Charles was in thrall to his wife: a
conventional dynastic match between England and France had quickly
blossomed into deep and sincere love. The king looked to his consort
for strength, encouragement, and understanding. The queen understood her role, honoured it, but – insensitive and arrogant – frequently
exceeded it.

The king was shy. If his elder brother Henry had succeeded to the
throne, Charles may have become a respected churchman, pursuing his
modest hobbies: he enjoyed reading the Bible and Book of Common
Prayer, was a keen chess player, and was entertained by the gentle skills
of bowls. As a boy, his frame was so weak that his father wanted to cast
his legs in irons, hoping they would be strengthened and straightened.
To thicken Charles's feeble voice, James had ordered the cutting of
the membrane beneath his tongue. Only the protestations of a fiercely
protective guardian saved the boy from both interventions. However,
Charles's natural awkwardness, compounded by a stammer, made it
hard for him to form close relationships. When he broke through and
established a bond, he tended to do so unquestioningly. To the king's
critics, his choice of trusted confidants demonstrated a dangerous lack
of judgement.

Early in his reign Charles had forged a friendship with his late
father's catamite, the Duke of Buckingham, a man whose deep un-
popularity culminated in an assassin's blade. The equally controversial
Earl of Strafford had filled the void, providing loyalty, focus, and drive

during the difficult years of personal rule. In Scotland Charles relied on the Marquess of Hamilton, a moderate soldier and an extremely poor politician. While Buckingham and Strafford had undoubted talent, Hamilton was a mediocrity.

Thanks to his blood bond with the king and his military record on the Continent, Rupert was at the forefront of royal favour during the first year of warfare. The bumptious teenager had blossomed into 'that brave Prince and hopeful soldier',[1] whose devotion to the king's cause was unashamed and infectious. Rupert and his brother Maurice were alone, among the highest-born Royalists, in coming to the war as foreign, professional soldiers, untainted by the parochial concerns of British politics. However, they were soon drawn into the machinations of a Court that lacked a strong king and was out of control.

We have seen that Rupert would take orders from nobody other than his uncle. The prince was supremely confident in his abilities and also keenly aware of his royal status. To the modern eye, Rupert's insistence on his social superiority screams of snobbery. To contemporaries, however, it was the prince's lack of polish that rankled with the Royalist grandees. The Earl of Clarendon wrote: 'The reservedness of the Prince's nature, and the little education he then had in Courts, made him unapt to make acquaintance with any of the Lords, who were thereby likewise discouraged from applying themselves to him; while some officers of the Horse were well pleased to observe that strangeness, and fomented it; believing their credit would be the greater with the Prince, and desiring that no other person should have any credit with the King.'[2]

Rupert and his faction failed to anticipate how the queen's arrival in Oxford would impact on the prince's relationship with the king. Henrietta Maria expected that she would now be Charles's main counsellor on all matters relating to the war. She had long influenced him politically, but now she felt confident to advise on military matters, too: during her trek from Yorkshire, at the head of 4,000 men, she had dubbed herself the 'She Generalissima'. Although physically courageous, she was no strategist, but Henrietta Maria was determined to oust her nephew as chief family adviser to the king.

A coterie of noblemen appreciated the significance of the queen's arrival. They clung to her petticoats, eager for favour; they knew this was the route to power under an easily influenced monarch. George, Lord Digby, was one of the first to join the queen's party. Digby, born in 1612, had been a keen critic of the king during the 1640 Parliament and had argued eloquently for the punishment of Strafford. However, after the shock of Strafford's execution, Digby had entered into secret negotiations to change political sides. Promoted to the Lords, where he joined his father the Earl of Bristol, he cultivated a correspondence with Henrietta Maria that had regrettable consequences: letters between them had been intercepted by Parliament before the outbreak of war, convincing Henrietta Maria's enemies that she was a dangerous Catholic sympathiser.

Digby accompanied Rupert in his mission to shepherd the queen across the Midlands to Oxford. Digby wanted to renew links with the queen, before she was surrounded by Oxford's competing flatterers-in-exile. Rupert disliked and distrusted Digby, and was suspicious of the speedy conversion from anti-court agitator to avowed Royalist. After the fiasco of Digby's disobedient charge at Edgehill, he also judged him a poor soldier.

It is fascinating to see how Digby wheedled his way into royal favour. Van Dyck's portrait of the man reveals a weak-faced arrogance; a swagger without substance; a silken fop surrounded by flattering symbols of scholarship. Rupert's apologists have always presented Digby in a poor light: 'Digby was the last of the King's fatal list of evil advisers', Warburton wrote, 'and he united in himself almost all their gifts and errors; the grace and recklessness of Buckingham, the eloquence and imperiousness of Strafford, the love of intrigue and the military incompetence of Hamilton.'[3]

Clarendon, less one-eyed and no great admirer of Prince Rupert, was able to see what it was about Digby that entranced the king and queen: 'The Lord Digby was a man of very extraordinary parts by Nature and Art, and had surely as good and excellent an education as any man of that age in any country: a graceful and beautiful person; of great eloquence and becomingness in his discourse (save that sometimes he seemed a little affected) and of so universal a knowledge, that he never wanted subject for a discourse.' But there was an inherent danger in this most gifted of men: 'He was equal to a very good part in the greatest affair, but the unfittest man alive to conduct them, having an ambition and vanity superior to all his other parts, and a confidence in himself, which sometimes intoxicated, and transported, and exposed him.'[4]

Digby possessed the timeless attributes of the consummate political operator: a silky tongue, sly self-interest, and utter ruthlessness. It was fortunate for him, yet disastrous for his master, that he deployed his talents at a time of national discord, when an irresolute king was open to any ideas that promised a restoration of his former powers. As Clarendon concluded: 'The King himself was the unfittest person alive to be served by such a counsellor, being too easily inclined to sudden enterprises, and as easily startled when they were entered upon.'[5]

Rupert, meanwhile, was temperamentally unsuited to the conniving of court politics. 'And it may be', Clarendon was later to suggest, 'a better reason cannot be assign'd for the misfortunes that hopeful young Prince (who had great parts of mind, as well as vigour of body, and an incomparable personal courage) underwent, and the kingdom thereby, than that unpolish'd roughness of his Nature; whch render'd him less patient to hear, and consequently less skilful to judge of those things, which should have guided him in the discharge of his important trust: and making an unskilful judgment of the unusefulness of the Councils, by his observation of the infirmities and weakness of some particular councellors, he grew to a full disesteem of the acts of that board.'[6]

Rupert's style as a general revealed his character as a man: focused, straightforward, and uncompromising. The disappointments he was forced to endure in his soldiers – the lack of self-control of many, the greed and plundering of a few – were indicative of a wider malaise that reached to the very top of the Royalist hierarchy.

The prince sought an escape from such unpalatable truths by surrounding himself with like-minded acolytes, who joined him in openly despising their flawed comrades. Standing aloof, however, allowed enemies at court to continue unchecked in their quest for power. Their prime objective was to reduce Rupert's standing in his uncle's eyes.

The conflict between the cunning Digby and the uncomplicated but naive Rupert was symptomatic of a fault line that ran through the Royalist upper reaches. Clarendon put his finger on it when he identified 'the spirit of craft and subtlety in some, and the unpolished integrity of others, too much despising craft or art; all contributing jointly to this mass of confusion now before us'.[7] The Royalist Bishop of Derry, preaching in early 1644, believed such rifts to be among the greatest threats to the king's cause: 'Where there is Faction, Envy, and Emulation amongst great Officers,' he warned, 'it portends a Destruction, and Dissipation.'[8]

The first open rift between the prince's and the queen's parties appeared immediately after the capture of Bristol. Rupert believed that, since he had won the city, he was entitled to its governorship; this would have been normal procedure on the Continent. Charles, delighted with his nephew's triumph, quickly approved his request.

However, Rupert's opponents objected to a foreign prince being given control of England's second city. They pointed out that, whatever Rupert's military achievements during Bristol's capture, the Marquess of Hertford was nominal commander of the Royalists in the West. Hertford was an elderly man of little energy, who was happiest studying his books. Even Clarendon, who respected the marquess as a man of principle, conceded that Hertford had: 'contracted such a laziness of mind, that he had no delight in an open and liberal conversation'.[9] Rather than tackle this inertia, the two princes had bypassed it, taking matters into their own hands. Hertford, however, found their attitude disrespectful and hurtful. Although conscious of his considerable limitations as a soldier, he upheld an uncompromising standard of behaviour that had stood him in good stead when governor to the young Prince of Wales. He found Rupert and Maurice's highhandedness unforgivable. Besides, Hertford wanted to reward Sir Ralph Hopton for his doughty efforts: apart from his leadership, the Somerset man had demonstrated considerable personal bravery when badly scalded in an accidental gunpowder explosion. When Hertford's counter-recommendation arrived in Oxford, Rupert's court opponents saw an opportunity to cut the prince down to size. The queen encouraged her husband to recognise Hertford's seniority, elevate Hopton to the governorship, and rescind Rupert's commission.

Charles appreciated that this was a question of such sensitivity that it demanded his personal attention. The king sent a letter to Hopton, apologising for any unintended slight Hopton may have felt, while explaining that: 'We too much esteem our Nephew P. Rupert, to make him a means of putting any disrespect upon any Gentleman, especially one we so much esteem as you, than to give you any distaste.'[10] He then rode to Bristol, to broker a deal that would satisfy all parties. On arrival, Charles found Hopton embarrassed to be at the centre of a quarrel that had less to do with his promotion, than with the growing tensions between the Palatine princes and the queen's court. 'Besides that', Clarendon noted, 'he had always born an avow'd and declar'd reverence to the Queen of Bohemia and her children, whom he had personally and actively served in their wars, while they maintain'd any, and for whose honour and restitution he had been a zealous and known champion. And therefore he had no inclination to disoblige a hopeful prince of that house, upon whom our own hopes seem'd so much to depend.'[11]

Charles's solution, which revealed a diplomatic touch that he seldom matched during the rest of the war, had two faces – one public, one private. It was announced that Rupert would remain as governor of Bristol, with Hopton (now created a peer) as his deputy. In secret, Rupert agreed that Hopton should govern the city as he saw fit, with his position being purely titular. Charles could see that the hostility between Hertford and his nephews was irreparable. He persuaded the marquess to ride back to Oxford with him, cleverly removing him from the battlefield by making him a senior adviser. Maurice, so recently promoted to lieutenant general, was now created General of the Western Army: a fair reflection of the younger prince's military abilities and a move that delighted Rupert, who loved and trusted his devoted brother, who was also his greatest friend. Already, by this stage of the war, Rupert was not short of enemies.

Despite the adoration of his men, Rupert was, by the summer of 1643, perhaps the most hated man in England. He had earned the universal fear and odium of the Parliamentary cause, their vilification coursing through the kingdom via the printed word. They painted him as sexually incontinent and accused him repeatedly of having a love affair with Mary, Duchess of Richmond, the wife of one of his closest friends.

It is hard to establish if this accusation had substance. When Daniel O'Neill, an Irish follower of the prince's, talked to compatriots of 'the amours of Prince Rupert and the Duchess of Richmond',[12] he forfeited Rupert's friendship forever. This does not mean, however, that the relationship never took place. Indeed, it is hard to think why O'Neill would have invented a tale about a man who he clearly greatly admired.

Mary Richmond was the only daughter of the murdered Duke of Buckingham. As a girl, she had briefly been married to Lord Herbert, but her husband died when she was 11. She was spirited, good-looking, and highly entertaining. Her second marriage was to the king's cousin James, Duke of Richmond. Clarendon describes Richmond as a great favourite of Charles I's: the duke joined the Privy Council when only 21. 'He was a man of very good parts, and an excellent understanding', Clarendon judged, 'yet, which is no common infirmity, so diffident of himself, that he was sometimes led by men who judged much worse. He was of a great, and haughty spirit, and so punctual in point of honour, that he never swerved a tittle.'[13] Richmond's three brothers all perished in the Civil War, fighting for the king.

The duke and duchess liked Rupert enormously, and were constant in their support of their friend while he was away fighting, sticking up for him against his court enemies. Parliament assumed the worst about the three-way friendship and delighted in portraying it as yet another disgraceful Royalist scandal. In one pamphlet, *The Ladies Parliament*, the wives of Charles's grandees were presented as debating in a whore house as to which of the Cavaliers they should keep nearby, to fulfil their desires: 'The rattle-headed being assembled at Kate's in Covent Garden, and having spent some time in choosing their speaker, (it having been objected against the Lady Duchess, that she had used beating up of quarters, and other sports, too frequently with Prince Rupert,) they at last resolved upon the Lady Isabella Thynne, hoping thereby that the acts might have the great influence upon the King's majesty.' In this fanciful setting, Rupert was eventually chosen as the lead stallion, after 'the Duchess of Richmond assured them, that none was to be compared to Prince Rupert, against whom nothing could be urged, but that his labour was not always crowned with the desired and wished for success'.[14]

There seems little doubt that there was a very strong bond between Rupert and Mary – she sent him messages of support throughout the Civil War – but there is no evidence that their loving friendship progressed beyond the platonic. The duke's closeness to the prince never wavered, which strongly suggests that at no stage did he suspect that he was being cuckolded by his friend. When, in 1655, Richmond died, there was an expectation that his widow would quickly marry Rupert, but this never materialized.

The prince needed the Richmonds' unstinting support, as jealousy and resentment underpinned a burgeoning opposition to him within senior Royalist ranks. Although presented by enemies and posterity as tough and focused, we know from the effort Rupert put into refuting the more outrageous rebel claims that their libels cut him deep. It is also clear that his appetite for fighting for a cause that contained so many men – and one woman – whom he found increasingly unsympathetic, was taking its toll.

Rupert could accept the term 'cavalier' for himself, because his analytical mind separated the intended slur of the pamphleteers from his more rigid definition of the word: one who rode loyally in defence of the king. But even if he could claim such a chivalrous role for himself, for his brother, and for their closest military confidants, there was no denying that the more derogatory implications of the name described other prominent Royalists. Many of these, like Digby, and the roistering Wilmot and Goring, found favour at court. This was a situation that appalled and demoralised Rupert, sapping the inspiration and dampening the flair that were his greatest strengths as a military commander. It was difficult to give everything, to risk all, in a cause that was increasingly identified with individuals and creeds that the uncompromising prince loathed.

Rupert was soon openly at loggerheads with the queen. Three Parliamentarian peers, the earls of Bedford, Clare, and Holland, came to Oxford to seek the king's pardon, while offering to join his cause. The king was torn. He wanted their services, but he did not wish to show weakness to prominent enemies: Bedford had commanded the rebel cavalry at Edgehill, and Holland had been one of the Parliamentary commissioners whose demands the king had found so unpalatable earlier in the year. To Henrietta Maria, there could be no forgiveness for such traitors. She told Charles to reject the aristocrats' request and send them back to the enemy ranks.

Rupert took a more pragmatic approach: the Royalists had been successful, but he knew this could not continue indefinitely, because the rebels were well provided for, while his own men were short of supplies, especially gunpowder. To Rupert it was a case of simple arithmetic: every man that could be brought across from the enemy ranks counted twice over – depriving the rebels of a soldier while correspondingly boosting the king's army by one. Showing mercy to the three grandees, Rupert argued, might persuade others to change sides. Charles saw the strength of this argument and upset Henrietta Maria by agreeing to pardon the three earls. In winning this round, and getting his way in the Hopton affair, Rupert had used up much of his credit with his uncle: it was hard for Charles constantly to ignore his wife's advice.

Strategic differences between the king and the prince became increasingly evident. Gloucester was now, after Bristol's fall, the most important Parliamentarian stronghold in the west. Charles moved his army to Gloucester's walls and told Rupert to demand its surrender from the rebel commander, Colonel Edward Massey. Massey refused, declaring that he 'held the city for the King and Parliament, and would not surrender it to any foreign prince'.[15] Rupert was among the generals and nobles who urged Charles to march on, towards London, rather than expend valuable campaign time in besieging the city. But the king was not to be rushed. With memories of the terrible casualties suffered at Bristol fresh in his mind, he refused to storm the city. Sure that the generous terms he had offered would persuade the people of Gloucester to surrender, Charles settled down for what he expected to be a brief siege.

The king's optimism proved ill founded. Although his men, urged on by Rupert and Maurice, tried to bring the city to its knees, Gloucester held out. During one foray, Prince Rupert was nearly killed by a rebel grenade. Parliamentarians would look back on the determined defence of the city's garrison as a pivotal moment in the war:

> ... As Gloucester stood against the numerous Powers
> Of the besiegers, who with Thunder-showers
> Charg'd her old ribs, but vanisht like a storm
> With their own loss, and did no more perform
> Than squibs cast in the air, which throw about
> Some furious sparks, and so in smoke go out.
> 'Twas not her Trenches which their force withstood,
> Nor river purpled with Malignant blood,
> Canon, nor bulwarks rais'd with Martial art
> That did secure her, but Great Massey's Heart;
> That was the Fort no Engine could beat down,
> Nor mine blow up, more strong than was the Town.[16]

Eventually, with the defenders down to their last three barrels of gunpowder, the Royalist army learnt that the Earl of Essex was approaching with a relief force of 14,000 men. The order was given to retreat to Oxford, leading to widespread dissatisfaction in the king's upper ranks: 'I am afraid our setting down before Gloucester has hindered us from making an end of the war this year,' wrote the young Earl of Sunderland, 'which nothing could keep us from doing if we had a month's more time which we lost there, for we never were in a more prosperous condition.' Sunderland, in his letter to his wife, also commented on the worrying division in the king's counsel: 'How infinitely more happy I should esteem myself quietly to enjoy your company

... than to be troubled with the noises, and engaged in the factions of the Court, which I shall ever endeavour to avoid.'[17] The failure of the siege of Gloucester, and the delay that it had entailed, impacted immediately on the king's cause. The insidious workings of the factions were of longer-term significance.

While Essex disgorged arms and men into the relieved city, the Royalists belatedly marched towards London. However, Charles still failed to understand the need for speed and assumed that a day's head start was enough to leave Essex in his wake. But the earl, whose first year in command had been dogged by accusations of indecision, now showed real purpose. He cut across country, recapturing Rupert's prize of Cirencester on the way. When scouts reported that Essex's army was bearing towards Hungerford, the prince appreciated that the race for the capital was on.

Eager to regain the initiative, the prince sent for permission to attack the enemy with his cavalry as they crossed open ground. When the king's council of war refused his request, disbelieving the intelligence reports, Rupert set off in person with three retainers to press for immediate action. He eventually tracked the king down to a farmhouse and walked in to an astonishing scene. In this time of high urgency and drama, Charles was quietly playing cards with Lord Percy, his artillery general, under the lazy gaze of the Earl of Forth, the Royalist commander. Rupert blew into the room like a tornado, demanding that the army march that night. His physical presence managed to convince his uncle that Essex must be stopped from reaching London first.

Rupert's attacks over the next two days slowed the Parliamentarian progress. His cavalry and dragoons won the race with the enemy to secure the main bridge crossing the Kennet, at Newbury. The infantry and artillery then arrived, digging in to the southwest of the town, ready to meet Essex's army. However, the king's generals failed to utilise the advantage gained by the prince's dynamism: they left the higher ground before them unoccupied and failed to reconnoitre the likely battleground.

Rupert advocated a defensive battle. He pointed out that Essex had no option but to reach London, and this imperative would leave the rebels vulnerable when they crossed open ground. The prince had seen the patchwork of enclosures between the two armies and knew his cavalry would not be able to attack effectively over such terrain. But Charles's other advisers, including the meddlesome Henrietta Maria, persuaded the king to go on the offensive, negating the effectiveness of the horsemen who had brought him triumph over the preceding year. They marched into the teeth of Essex's infantry, which was superior in number and experience.

The Royalists fought bravely, but Rupert's advice had been correct: the lay of the land favoured the enemy. The king's forces were caught in withering artillery and musket fire, and their losses were terrible. Eleven of the twelve ensigns of Lieutenant Colonel Ned Villiers's foot regiment were wounded. 'Horse! Horse!', the infantry cried, desperate for mounted support, but this was not the ground for sweeping charges. Rupert lost 300 of his cavalry brigade, and thirty of the sixty men in his personal troop, as he repeatedly attacked the London Trained Bands. He could not break them, though he did see off the Parliamentary squadrons guarding their flanks. The prince was lucky to escape with his life: Sir Philip Stapleton, a Parliamentarian, had ridden up to him unhindered and discharged his pistol at Rupert. The bullet missed. In the confusion, Stapleton escaped.

Militarily, the First Battle of Newbury had been a stalemate. Lack of ammunition stopped the Royalists from pushing for victory: they could only afford to fire one round against every three of Parliament's. By the evening, the Royalists were reduced to just ten barrels of gunpowder, prompting Lord Percy to urge tactical retreat at the council of war. Rupert, aware of the imperative of blocking Essex's route to London at any cost, advised the king to hold his position. But Charles ordered his troops to return towards Oxford, allowing Rupert only to attack Essex's men as they passed near Aldermaston. This was a sop to a nephew whose influence was on the decline. In retrospect, Newbury was a battle that gave Parliament morale and momentum after the repeated pummelling they had received – mainly from Rupert – earlier in the year. Rebel commanders believed that: 'The Earl of Essex did break both the head and the heart of the King's army at Newbury.'[18]

The casualties were high among the Royalist nobility. In The Chequers coaching-house, in neighbouring Speenhamland, the bodies of the Earl of Sunderland, who had written of his disillusionment with faction fighting, and the Earl of Carnarvon, who had fought with distinction at Roundway Down, were laid out. The most notable loss, however, was of the respected, moderate Viscount Falkland, one of Charles's most influential advisers.

Some suspected that Falkland had thrown his life away, rather than

continue to participate in a conflict that he abhorred: Clarendon, in a
lyrical eulogy for his fallen friend, recalled that 'after the King's return
from Brentford, and the furious resolution of the two houses not to
admit any treaty for peace, those indispositions, which had before
touched him, grew into a perfect habit of uncheerfulness; and he …
became, on a sudden, less communicable; and thence, very sad, pale,
and exceedingly affected with the spleen'.[19] He had seemed upbeat
before the battle, confident and laughing as he took a lead position in
Sir John Byron's cavalry.

He rode close to hedges that were lined with enemy musketeers,
however, and 'more gallantly than advisedly spurred his horse through
the gap, where he and his horse were immediately shot'.[20] When he
failed to return from the charge, Falkland's friends hoped he had been
taken prisoner, but his body was recovered the following morning.

Falkland was much mourned by his colleagues, but the real loss was
his moderating influence on the more extreme Royalists. Although he
and Rupert had had their differences before Edgehill, there was little
further trouble between them. Both men, from different perspectives,
shared a deep dislike of the increasing influence of the queen's self-
interested warmongers: Falkland because he longed for peace; Rupert
because he distrusted their conniving. The prince believed their scheming undermined the prospects for the war, while also eroding his independent effectiveness as a general.

The real disaster for Rupert was the identity of the man chosen to
replace the dead Falkland as one of the king's two secretaries of state:
George Digby. The prince's *bête noire* was now, officially, one of his
uncle's inner coterie of confidants, on hand at all times to drip poison
into the King's ear. Digby, Clarendon wrote with regret, was 'one of
the chief promoters of the war: he advised the King worse, and acted
for him more zealously, than any of his councillors'.[21]

With Digby in the ascendant, and Henrietta Maria's other favourites
aware that hostility to the prince constituted a quick route to queenly
favour, Rupert busied himself away from the snake pit of Oxford.
The prince was able to distance himself from the disappointments of
Gloucester and Newbury, his reputation unaffected by setbacks not
of his own making. He now took command of Royalist forces in the
eastern counties of England. The principal action of the war had taken
place in the Midlands, the Cotswolds, the southwest, Yorkshire, and in
the Thames Valley. Rupert, the supreme cavalryman, was looking for an

exposed flank to exploit, and the bold plan he sent to the council of war involved a thrust into East Anglia. Parliament had quickly dominated this region at the outset of war, and it had since provided valuable recruits and supplies. However, localised uprisings showed that the eastern counties contained an untapped source of Royalist sympathisers. These were urgently needed to refresh ranks depleted by death, injury, and desertion.

But Rupert was overruled: the majority of Charles's advisers thought the project too risky. Certainly, it was a high stakes' strategy. However, by passing up his chance to make inroads into the east, the Royalists limited themselves to recruiting in areas of traditional support – Cornwall, Wales, and the northwest – which were already almost sucked dry. More worryingly, by gleaning Royalist sympathisers from these areas, the king was leaving them vulnerable to future enemy occupation.

Rupert took pride in his brother's successes in the southwest, although these were not without controversy: Maurice had brought the siege of Barnstaple to a successful conclusion by promising, 'on my Honour in the word of a Prince', that the inhabitants would be well treated. But his men had let him down with ugly plundering.

Maurice fell seriously ill, probably from typhus, while besieging Dartmouth. Rupert was in agonies at the prospect of losing the man who was closest to him in an increasingly hostile world. The prince sent the most eminent physician of the day, Sir William Harvey – the man who discovered that blood circulated through the body – to assist the three doctors already attending Maurice. Their combined efforts managed to save him.

Less happy was the news of another Palatine brother. Charles Louis appeared in London late in 1643, declaring his support for the Parliamentarians, who reinstated the generous pension that his uncle had previously granted him. There had been rumblings from the Continent, seized upon by enemy propagandists, that Rupert's family were furious and embarrassed by his fighting Parliament. Sir Thomas Roe had written to Elizabeth of Bohemia in September 1642, explaining how the Prince's Royalism was damaging the Palatine cause in England. A document, *The Best News That Ever was Printed*, was gleefully circulated, allegedly the words of Rupert's mother and elder brother, but in fact a fake: 'We do, in the presence of Almighty God, and of all the whole world, and in the sight of all good men, in no manner approve, give consent, or any way countenance the unjust and unruly actions of my son Prince Rupert, now in England; and so do I, the same with the Queen, my dear mother, by the same vow disrelish and hate all those outrages and cruelties of my brother, Prince Rupert. And it grieves us at our very souls for the inhuman cruelties we hear he commits; whose passion we cannot confine, and whose hot spirit we cannot calm ...'[22]

The composers of this fancy hoped to raise rebel morale by claiming that Rupert would soon be forced to return to the Continent. They also reflected a genuine belief that the prince, in striking out at Parliament, was betraying a loyal and generous ally that had repeatedly helped his family in its quest to reclaim the Palatine. 'Call Prince Rupert to the bar', the pamphleteers thundered, 'thou hast been a right-flying dragon prince, and hast flew strangely up and down in this island, and hast stung to death those that formerly preserved thy life. O, ungrateful viper ... Speedy vengeance on thy cursed head!'[23] 'The people's goodness alone made them give to the Queen of Bohemia so many great and free contributions', wrote another, 'and now you have not only taken away their wills but their means of ever doing the like; having brought us to so wretched a condition that we shall never hereafter have leisure to pity her, but rather condemn her as the mother of our calamity.'[24]

Before the war, Charles Louis had accompanied the king on his bungled attempt to arrest the Five Members of the House of Commons. However, unlike Rupert and the other Palatine siblings, the young Elector believed the duty of retrieving his father's squandered lands overrode his obligations as a dutiful nephew. In fairness, Charles I had made negligible efforts on his sister's behalf, while Parliament regarded Elizabeth's cause as a Protestant crusade. The majority of MPs agreed with Calybute Downing, Pastor of Hackney, who wrote to them in 1641 that: 'The present Prince Charles [Louis] hath a true title of right, to require the restitution, the investiture, and actual possession of all those Dominions and Dignities Electoral, in an individual, sole, and supreme way.'[25] Charles Louis believed that the Parliamentarians were his true allies in this aim. Rupert therefore found himself, at the end of 1643, fighting rebels, courtiers, and even his own brother.

CHAPTER NINE

RUSHING TO DEFEAT

'Courage, my Soul, now learn to wield
The weight of thine immortal shield.
Close on thy head thy helmet bright.
Balance thy sword against the fight.
See where an army, strong as fair,
With silken banners spreads the air.
Now, if thou be'st that thing divine,
In this day's combat let it shine.'

'A Dialogue, between the Resolved Soul and Created Pleasure'
by the poet and Republican Andrew Marvell (1621–1678)

The Civil War changed dramatically during the late summer and autumn of 1643. Parliament and the Scots signed the Solemn League and Covenant, a treaty that promised invasion from the north. Soon afterwards, a truce enabled Charles to bring back troops that had been fighting the Catholic rebels in Ireland. If the effect of Scotland's entry into the war were to be nullified, the Royalists would need to deploy the troops from Ireland as an efficient counterweight. In the meantime, Charles must juggle his resources to meet the challenge of five enemy armies operating in his kingdom.

Rupert pushed for command of the influx of troops from Ireland. For success, the prince would have to adapt his proven flair in attack to conditions that demanded defence. His instinct was for independence, with his favourite officers by his side. He longed to be far from the internal bickering of Oxford, where his presence seemed to act as a lightning rod for the disaffected. 'The army is much divided,' wrote Arthur Trevor, one of Rupert's sympathisers in the town, in November 1643, 'and the Prince at true distance with many of the officers of horse.'[1] The gulf was also growing between Rupert and the queen, although Charles demonstrated continuing trust in his nephew, giving him British peerages on 24 January 1644, so that he could sit in Oxford's

Royalist Parliament as Earl of Holderness and Duke of Cumberland. The Parliamentarians marked this last elevation with a new nickname for Rupert: 'Plunderland'.

The prince had no intention of attending the makeshift House of Lords while there was fighting to be done. He started 1644 by proposing a ruse to capture the important rebel stronghold of Northampton. This involved riding his cavalry into the town while posing as Parliamentarian reinforcements. Once inside the walls, the Royalists would reveal their true identity and overwhelm the garrison. However, this typically bold plan was – equally typically – rejected as unworkable and risky.

In the middle of January 1644, the Scots invaded England through thick snow. At the end of the month, Sir Thomas Fairfax trounced Byron's army outside Nantwich, in Cheshire. Rupert, convinced that the northwest was set to become a key battleground in the war, had secured a new command as captain general of the counties of Chester, Lancaster, Worcester, Salop, and the six northern counties of Wales. He set off for Shrewsbury on 6 February, while summoning reinforcements from Bristol.

Rupert's latest duties demanded a complex balancing act. Of real concern was the precarious situation of the Marquess of Newcastle's army to the east of the Pennines. Out on a limb, it was simultaneously awaiting one visit from the Scots and another from Parliament's northern forces. The prince could not allow the enemy to isolate and destroy Newcastle's men: he must do all he could to support it against the Allied armies. At the same time, Rupert needed to be on hand to assist Charles's headquarters at Oxford, which was under increasing pressure from Parliament's forces in the Thames Valley. Throughout the spring and early summer of 1644, the prince remained on the move, attempting to sustain the Royalist cause on its two most challenging fronts.

This was a critical time in the war, which led to a hardening of attitudes. The Royalist vicar of Barton upon Humber prayed that the king's enemies should suffer all manner of damnation: 'Let horror and amazement take hold on them, and keep them in a perpetual alarm ... Their sons and their daughters that were the joy of their hearts, let them be cut off in the flower of their days; and the wives of their bosoms, let them be given into the bosoms of those that hate them. And when they have seen all this, and a world of misery more than all this, let their last end be like the rest, let them go down to the grave with a tragic and disastrous death.'[2]

Meanwhile, Parliament met the arrival of Royalist troops from Ireland with a decree that they would be executed on capture. When the rebels took thirteen of Rupert's men near Nantwich – all English, but falsely classified by their captors as Irish Papists – they hanged the lot of them. The prince was furious. Soon afterwards he captured fourteen of the enemy. Thirteen of these he hanged in reprisal, releasing the fourteenth with a curt message for his superiors: if the Parliamentarians dared to repeat their outrage, two of their men would be executed for every Royalist prisoner hanged. Nobody thought the prince was bluffing – his stark threat 'stopped that efflux of blood ever after.'[3]

Rupert remained busy in the field, his difficult task complicated by a lack of support from the king's council of war. Of its members, lords Forth and Astley appreciated Rupert's talents and were broadly sympathetic, while the Duke of Richmond was a good personal friend to the prince. However, lords Digby, Percy, and Wilmot were all favourites of the queen, and Sir John Culpepper joined them in a cabal whose common enemy was Rupert. Charles increasingly listened to this vociferous clique despite Digby's negligible military record, Percy's poor showing at Newbury (he was blamed for the Royalists' crucial shortage of gunpowder), and the gifted Wilmot's legendary debauchery. Rupert's friend Arthur Trevor warned that influential enemies at court would succeed in isolating the prince from the king, unless he secured further military glory: 'For', Trevor observed, 'I find no court physic so present for the opening of obstructions as good news.'[4]

Such an opportunity soon presented itself. Newark was the key Royalist staging post between Newcastle's Northern Army and the headquarters of Oxford. In February, Sir John Meldrum began to besiege Newark with a 5,000-strong army. Charles ordered Rupert to march from Chester to Newark's relief. Summoning men from Shrewsbury, and recruiting en route, the prince organised horses for as many of his troops as possible, in order to speed his passage. The Royalists covered the ground fast, taking a cross-country route that avoided major roads. With the rebels unable to monitor the progress of this secret march, Rupert's sudden appearance outside the town took Meldrum completely by surprise. Although Rupert's men were exhausted by the speed of their advance, they had to fight immediately: their besieged colleagues were facing starvation.

The action, on 21 March 1644, was a triumph for Rupert, although not without its alarms. The Royalist cavalry led the attack, the right wing slicing through its opponents with ease. But Rupert's troop was caught in an awkward scuffle, the distinctive prince presenting an irresistible target: 'Three sturdy Roundheads at once assaulted him: one fell by his own sword, a second was pistolled by one of his own gentlemen, and a third, laying his hand on the Prince's collar, had it chopped off by O'Neal.'[5] Undaunted by his narrow escape, Rupert urged his cavalry on.

The Royalist infantry followed the horse with an aggressive advance, which convinced Meldrum that his position was hopeless. He surrendered on generous terms, which allowed him to march his survivors to another rebel stronghold. However, Meldrum was forced to leave behind valuable supplies: 4,000 muskets, 50 barrels of gunpowder, 11 cannon and 2 mortars. More importantly, against all expectations, Newark had been saved and the Marquess of Newcastle's army was spared dangerous isolation. 'Nephew,' wrote the king, 'I assure you that this (as all your victories) gives me as much contentment in that I owe you the thanks as for the importance of it, which in this particular believe me, is no less than the saving of all the north, nothing, for the presence being of more consequence; how to follow this (indeed beyond imaginable) success, I will not prescribe you ...'[6] The speed and secrecy of the march, the decisiveness of the attack, and the importance of the result mark the relief of Newark as one of Rupert's greatest military achievements. Clarendon called it: 'As unexpected a victory as happened throughout the war.'[7]

The breathing space won for Lord Newcastle was short lived. Rupert was forced to resume his balancing act, providing simultaneous support for the Royalist armies in the north and in the Thames Valley. Newcastle urged Rupert to remain in the northern Midlands, within range of his army, convinced that this was the sphere of the conflict where the war could be decided in a day. However, the vulnerability of the king's cause in the south demanded the prince's return to the Welsh borders, on a recruiting mission. In his absence the rebels quickly gnawed away at the advantages gained by the relief of Newark, recapturing Lincolnshire and then defeating Lord Bellasis's Royalists at Selby. Newcastle moved with his men from Durham to York, adding his infantry to the garrison there, while despatching his cavalry south to seek Rupert's renewed help. 'If your Highness do not please to come hither, and that nay very soon too,' the marquess implored, 'the great game of your uncle's will be endangered, if not lost; and with your

Highness being near, certainly won: so I doubt not but your Highness will come, and that very soon.'[8]

Taking stock of the Royalist situation across the nation in mid April 1644, Rupert proposed a bold plan to the council of war: the king should concentrate his infantry in Oxford and its four surrounding garrison towns, with enough cavalry to be able to sustain them through foraging. Charles would then depart for the west with the remainder of his horse and join up with Prince Maurice, recently appointed Lieutenant General of the Southern Counties. The king would help Maurice's army, which was having a difficult time besieging Lyme – one of the few remaining rebel strongholds in the southwest. Rupert, meanwhile, would take his army back north and repeat his recent heroics by lifting the siege of York. Provided the Thames Valley garrisons could hold out in the interim, the king and his two nephews would then return to Oxford to relieve the Royalist capital, their combined forces ready for a concerted assault on London. 'The great crisis of the North being expected', Prince Rupert's logbook recorded, 'a Council of War at Oxford resolved to put off fighting with Essex till that be over.'[9]

The prince headed northwards, buoyed up by unaccustomed support for one of his ambitious proposals. However, approval for Rupert's northern design had not been universal. As soon as he had departed, the king was persuaded to remain in Oxford, concentrating his forces nearby, while Reading's defences (the town had been recaptured after the battle of Newbury) were pulled down and abandoned. Soon afterwards the Royalists also quit Abingdon, Lord Digby taking the opportunity to blame this painful decision on Rupert's absence with so many troops.

Soon the consequences of ignoring Rupert's plan became apparent. With Abingdon and Reading no longer standing guard over Oxford, Waller joined Essex in an exercise of containment that threatened to isolate the town from the armies of the north and the west. It looked as though the king would be trapped in the town and, if he were forced to surrender, the Civil War would be abruptly concluded. In desperation, Charles slipped out of Oxford with an army of 7,000 men, managing to evade the enemy encirclement by using minor roads leading to the west. Waller and Essex pursued him, but their civilian masters, the members of the Committee of Both Kingdoms, sent the two rebel commanders in different directions, halving their effectiveness at a stroke. Essex was despatched to the southwest, while Waller continued his pursuit of the king alone, his mobile army rich in cavalry.

Charles's intentions after breaking out from Oxford are not known. He may have hoped to reach Prince Rupert's army in Lancashire or his plan may have been simply to remain at large until matters looked more favourable. However, the impetus was now with the enemy. Essex made successful inroads in the southwest, while Waller's troops stood menacingly between the king in Worcester and the prince further north. Hard pressed and demoralised, Charles wrote a letter from Tickenhill, in Bewdley – near Ashby de la Zouch – to Rupert.

Nephew,

First I must congratulate with you, for your good successes, assuring you that the things themselves are no more welcome to me, than that you are the means: I know the importance of the supplying you with powder for which I have taken all possible ways, having sent both to Ireland & Bristol, as from Oxford this bearer is well satisfied, that it is impossible to have at present, but if he tell you that I may spare them hence, I leave you to judge, having but 36 left; but what I can get from Bristol (of which there is not much certainty, it being threatened to be besieged) you shall have.

But now I must give you the true state of my affairs, which if their condition be such as enforces me to give you more peremptory commands than I would willingly do, you must not take it ill. If York be lost, I shall esteem my Crown little less, unless supported by your sudden march to me, & a miraculous conquest in the South, before the effects of the Northern power can be found here; but if York be relieved, & you beat the rebel armies of both Kingdoms, which are before it, then but otherwise not, I may possibly make a shift, (upon the defensive) to spin out time, until you come to assist me: wherefore I command and conjure you, by the duty & affection which I know you bear me, that (all new enterprises laid aside) you immediately march (according to your first intention) with all your force to the relief of York; but if that be either lost, or fried themselves from the besiegers, or that for want of powder you cannot undertake that work; that you immediately march, with your whole strength, to Worcester, to assist me & my Army, without which, or your having relieved York by beating the Scots, all the successes you can afterwards have, most infallibly, will be useless unto me: You may believe that nothing but an extreme necessity could make me write thus unto you, wherefore, in this case, I can no ways doubt of your punctual compliance with

Your loving Uncle and most faithful friend
Charles R.[10]

The king wrote this when his hopes were low, his council of war was divided, and defeat seemed imminent. He was unaware that Essex's army had departed for the southwest, and assumed that he would be caught and overwhelmed by the earl's and Waller's combined forces. Within a fortnight, though, the darkest clouds had lifted. Charles led his army to a handsome victory over Waller at Cropredy Bridge, near Edgehill – providing a glimpse of the 'miraculous conquest in the South' referred to in the middle of his letter. But Rupert was not to hear about this change in fortune until too late.

The correct interpretation of this letter exercised Rupert for the rest of his days. The prince read it and understood it to be a command to march directly to the relief of York, before attacking and defeating the Allied armies of Parliament and the Scots. The desperation of Charles's position, evident in the king's rambling and unhappy tone, seemed to Rupert to demand the immediate execution of these commands. The alternative, the prince surmised, was the sinking of the Royalist cause.

'The Tickenhill Letter' is a key document in Prince Rupert's life story. However, it would be wrong to see it in isolation: there were another half-dozen communications written in a similar vein, all urging the prince to ease the king's plight in the south by gaining speedy success in the north, before descending to his aid. An undated letter should be seen as a companion to the Tickenhill one: 'To what I wrote yesterday,' the king wrote, 'I can only add that the relief of York is that which is most absolutely best for my affairs whereof again I earnestly conjure you speedily to prosecute that if you have but the least hope to do good there but as I have told you my business can bear no delay for you must either march presently northwards or hitherward, and that without engaging yourself in any other action.'[11]

Rupert received these letters after further personal successes. He had invaded Lancashire in mid May, capturing Stockport before rescuing the Countess of Derby and her retainers from a three-month siege. Lathom House, her castellated mansion, was protected by a moat and high wall. Its garrison of 300 included the Derbys' gamekeepers, deployed as rooftop snipers, whose marksmanship 'shrewdly galled the enemy'. The countess, a granddaughter of William the Silent and a cousin of Rupert's, was undaunted by an enemy that outnumbered her force by ten to one. When their leader, Colonel Rigby, summoned her to surrender, she gave his messenger short shrift: 'Go back to your commander, and tell that insolent rebel, he shall have neither persons, goods, nor house. When our strength is spent, we shall find a fire more merciful than Rigby's, and then, if Providence of God prevent it not, my goods and house shall burn in his sight; myself, my children, and my soldiers, rather than fall into his hands, will seal our religion and our loyalty in the same flame.'[12] Rupert's intervention spared her from this futile martyrdom.

The prince marched on, at the end of the month, to Bolton – a bastion of Puritanism, known as 'the Geneva of the north'. It was while he was outside the town that he received the first of the stream of letters from the king demanding his urgent transfer from Lancashire to York. He immediately attacked Bolton. The outcome of the assault remained in the balance until Rupert, incensed by the public hanging of one of his Irishmen, led his infantry on foot in the decisive charge. The Parliamentary pamphleteers presented the ensuing bloodshed as 'the Bolton Massacre', claiming that civilians of both genders and all ages had been put to the sword by the Cavaliers. Evidence, however, points to the many casualties being military, and defeated soldiers being allowed safe surrender. We know that when 700 citizens sought sanctuary in the main church, they were spared.

Hearing of this latest gain, Sir John Meldrum, in Manchester, scoffed at the prince as 'that fierce thunderbolt which terrifies the ignorant'.[13] Less dismissive were Meldrum's colleagues in Liverpool, who were subject to Rupert's ferocious night attack. Here, civilian lives were most certainly lost and pillaging was rife. It was the capture of Bolton and Liverpool that Charles was appreciating, early in the Tickenhill Letter: Liverpool's port, with its easy access to Irish reinforcements, was a particularly valuable prize.

Yet Rupert's mood was more distracted than triumphant. Correspondence from Arthur Trevor to the Marquess of Ormonde states that news had reached the prince from Oxford, 'that the king grows daily more and more jealous of him and his army; and that it is the common discourse (at the openest places where men can discover themselves) of the Lord Digby, Lord Percy, Sir John Culpeper, and Wilmot, that it is indifferent whether the Parliament or Prince Rupert doth prevail; which did so highly jesuit Prince Rupert, that he was once more resolved to send the king his commission and get to France . . . This fury interrupted the march ten days; but at length time and a friend, the best coolers of the blood, spent the humour of travail in him, though not that of revenge; to which purpose he hath sent his letter to the king for the removal of them from his council; and if this be not done, he will leave this war and sit down.'[14]

The accuracy of Trevor's account is hard to ascertain. Certainly, Rupert was aware that his enemies at Court were at work, trying to drive a wedge between him and his uncle. However, their success to date must have been limited, given the loving and respectful tone of Charles's Tickenhill Letter. Equally, we know that Rupert was indeed delayed for ten days, but this was not spent sulking, but in trying to get the necessary supplies for his march to York. It appears that Lord Percy did not unduly exert himself in getting the Prince's requirements to him on time.

These delays infuriated Rupert. All the correspondence from Charles and his senior councillors emphasised the need for speed, and expected the quick completion of the prince's twin tasks in the north before he rode to the salvation of the king in the south. However, he had hoped to finish his own operations in Cheshire and Lancashire before being summoned elsewhere. The demands of the council of war meant this task must be left incomplete. Rupert appreciated how daunting the challenges before him would be: for a start, the three enemy armies around York totalled 30,000 men and were well supplied.

The prince needed more men and more weapons. The arrival of George Goring, General of the Northern Horse, gave Rupert an additional 1,000 cavalry. Goring also injected an even greater sense of urgency, bringing first-hand accounts of the extreme peril facing the York garrison. Although expecting the imminent arrival of Sir Robert Clavering and 1,000 fresh infantry, Rupert felt compelled to set off on his rescue mission without them. He was aware that he would be severely outnumbered when facing the allies. After a final rendezvous in Skipton, on 26 June, Rupert marched towards York with just 15,000 men.

En route, Rupert stayed a night at Denton House, a home of the Fairfaxes – two of whom were enemy commanders. The Civil War saw the destruction of many of the homes of prominent participants. Only three months earlier Rupert had dined with the widowed Lady Beeston, at Bridgenorth. He thanked his hostess for her hospitality, invited her to leave with her most precious belongings, then torched her home. A year before he had done the same to Wormleighton House, the main

residence of the Earl of Sunderland. The young earl had died fighting
for the king at Newbury, but his massive home could not be left vacant,
vulnerable to Parliamentarian occupation, so it was blown up. Now, the
prince's troops expected to be let loose on Denton House. However,
when walking round the interior, Rupert recognised a face in a family
portrait. It belonged to a Fairfax who had died in the Palatinate a generation earlier, fighting for the prince's father's cause. Out of respect for
this sacrifice, the prince ordered the property to be left intact.

Moving on to Knaresborough, a day's march short of York, the
prince gathered together his force and prepared for action. 'It hath
been daily reported this fortnight, that P. Rupert is coming to raise
the siege,' reported the chaplain to the Earl of Manchester, one of the
Parliamentary generals in the north. 'Now it's rumoured that he is upon
the borders of this county with a great Army. But our eyes are towards
Heaven, from where comes our help, and we will pray and wait upon
the God of our salvations and mercies.'[15] The Scots saw matters in a
more apocalyptic light: 'The manner briefly was thus, Rupert, or the
second Nimrod, the mighty Plunderer, the beginning of whose kingdom is confusion, come in his hunting carrier, with his fellow hunters,
and near 20,000 bloodhounds attending them, all more ravenous than
wolves, and fiercer than tigers, thirsting for blood.'[16]

Rupert was pleased to learn that the three enemy commanders
– Manchester, Fairfax, and Leven – had decided to advance to meet
him, rather than wait to be attacked. This lifted the siege of York, to
the joy of the garrison and inhabitants: they knew the allies were on the
point of completing mines that would have collapsed their defences. As
the Anglo-Scots departed for action against the prince, they could hear
triumphant hollering coming from within York's walls.

Rupert confused the enemy scouts by making a feint, which prompted
the allied generals to deploy on moorland 3 miles to the west of the city.
They were sure that they could intercept the prince there with their
massively superior forces. Rupert sidestepped them, though, sending
his men on a tortuous route that eventually brought them to the unprotected north gate of York. They relieved the city and overran the enemy
camp outside its walls. The Marquess of Newcastle was quick to praise
the prince: 'You are welcome, Sir, so many several ways, as it is beyond
my arithmetic to number, but this I know: you are the redeemer of the
North & the Saviour of the Crown. Your name, Sir, hath terrified the
great Generals and they fly before it.'[17]

The allied generals, however, had not gone far. That evening they marched their men to the nearby village of Long Marston, where they spent an uncomfortable night. 'Our soldiers did drink the wells dry,' remembered one of the Parliamentarians, 'and then were necessitated to make use of puddle water.'[18] As they suffered, they pictured the Royalists helping themselves to the provisions stockpiled in their abandoned camp outside York.

The allies expected the prince's forces to recuperate within York's walls, before returning south via Newark.

It was the logical move. But Rupert, having completed the first part of his mission, now looked to obey his interpretation of the Tickenhill Letter, and bring the enemy immediately to battle. He sent a brusque order to Newcastle to meet him the next day, 2 July, at four in the morning, with 10,000 men. The combined Royalist forces would then attack, catching the enemy off-guard in the early morning.

The marquess resented Rupert's tone: the young man was a prince, but he was a foreign one. Newcastle, on the other hand, was the king's commander in the north and enjoyed unofficial vice-regal status: Charles permitted him to confer knighthoods as he saw fit and to mint his own coins. As a general, the marquess was a mere figurehead – he was not a professional soldier, but an amateur man of letters. Newcastle was, in truth, a loyal dilettante. He was a friend of the philosopher Hobbes and of the poet William Davenant – indeed, he made Davenant his general of artillery. Parliamentarian pamphleteers found Newcastle an easy target: they claimed that he lay in bed until eleven, before combing his hair until noon. His chief military adviser was Lord Eythin – the Scotsman who, as James King, had let Rupert down so badly at the battle of Vlotho.

Rupert arrived in Newcastle's sphere of influence, convinced that he was the agent of the king's will. Social niceties had little importance to the prince in such urgent times. This attitude resulted from his misreading of Newcastle's character. Rupert had recently received a typically florid letter from the marquess, which seemed to show a willing subservience to the prince's superior military pedigree: 'Neither can I resolve anything since I am made of nothing but thankfulness and obedience to Your Highness's command.'[19] This fawning led Rupert to assume, wrongly, that he could take the lead. In doing so, he upset one of his most enthusiastic admirers, just when unity was most required. To be sent curt instructions by a man less than half his age was an affront to this proudest of grandees, a grandson of Bess of Hardwick and once the governor to the Prince of Wales.

Despite feeling affronted, Newcastle followed Rupert's commands and ordered his troops to assemble early the next day. However, the marquess's men were in no condition to obey: they had run wild after deliverance from the eleven-week siege, plundering the enemy camp and becoming riotously drunk. Furthermore, Eythin told the soldiers to stand down till they had received their salary (it was Friday – pay day) – a decision that sent the men back to their drinking and pillaging, when they should have been preparing for battle.

It was not until nine o'clock in the morning, five hours after the appointed time, that Newcastle joined Rupert. With him came just 2,500 men, a quarter of the force expected by Rupert. The prince's welcome was terse: 'My Lord, I wish you had come sooner with your forces, but I hope we shall yet have a glorious day.'[20] There were further delays while Newcastle insisted on rounding up his crack infantrymen. These soldiers, known as 'Newcastle's Lambs', wore white tunics (which gave rise to their other nickname, 'the Whitecoats') – they would, they promised, dye them scarlet in their enemies' blood. These were experienced warriors, but the wait for them was costly, finally extinguishing Rupert's hopes of launching a surprise attack. The prince set off for Marston Moor, intent on battle but unable to dictate its timing. When the Whitecoats joined the main Royalist body later in the afternoon, many of them were still sobering up after the previous night's excesses.

In the other camp, the allies' spirits were mixed. Soldiers were entitled to daily beer and bread, but the penny loaf each man had brought with him had long since been consumed and most of the beer had been left in the Anglo-Scottish camp outside York. They had expected a battle with the Royalists, then a swift return to their siege of the city, but Rupert's brilliance had left them detached in the field, with inadequate supplies.

There were jealousies between the Parliamentarians and the Scots, which had led to plans for the two units to separate. However, these were rescinded when the unexpected news arrived that Rupert was marching to engage their combined force. They were confident of their prospects in the imminent battle. Besides their numerical advantage – they were 28,000 men to Rupert's eventual 18,000 – the allies were sure that God was on their side: He would doubtless lead them to victory over the licentious hordes captained by the wicked 'Prince Robber'. Their password for the battle was 'God with us'. As they marched towards Marston Moor, they sang Psalms.

Even after two years, the fact that a civil war was being fought was not universally known. On reaching the moor, some soldiers discovered a farm worker going about his business and ordered him to be gone. The disgruntled labourer asked why he should move. When told that he was standing on a field that was about to host a battle between the king and Parliament, he said: 'Whaat! Has them two fallen out, then?'[21]

First occupation of the moor narrowed the odds slightly in the Royalists' favour. When the allies arrived in the early afternoon of 2 July, they found Rupert's men deployed along a 2-mile front, musketeers and artillery at the ready behind the moor's ditch and surrounding hedges. With summer showers falling, the Earl of Leven arranged his soldiers on a hilltop overlooking the moor. The surrounding fields were swathed in mature crops – rye, beans, and corn.

From mid afternoon the allied cannon fired intermittently. At a council of war with Newcastle and Eythin, the prince revealed his intention to attack. Eythin favoured defence, his opinion of Rupert evident in his inflammatory interjection: 'Sir, your forwardness lost us the day in Germany, where yourself was taken prisoner.'[22] The sharpness of this insult seems to have knocked Rupert back, for this most aggressive of soldiers agreed to stand in defence until the morning. Newcastle, meanwhile, expressed fear that the enemy might attack sooner – a thought that, curiously, the prince seems to have dismissed out of hand. The marquess retired to his carriage, reassured that Rupert had matters under control, and lit his pipe.

The Royalists had broken ranks to eat supper when, in the late evening, the enemy attacked in huge numbers. 'Our Army', reported a Parliamentarian, 'in its several parts moving down the hill, was like unto so many thick clouds, having divided themselves into Brigades.'[23] Rupert, the master of surprise, was taken completely unawares. His men were unable to re-form in time to defend the ditch, allowing Oliver Cromwell's cavalry to charge on, into the Royalist right wing. Rupert had been excited at the prospect of fighting this celebrated enemy, but now he witnessed at first hand the destructive horsemen – to whom he gave the nickname of 'Ironsides' – combine the impetus of his Cavaliers with a level of discipline that they had never approached.

Thunder and storming rain accompanied the allied attack, adding to

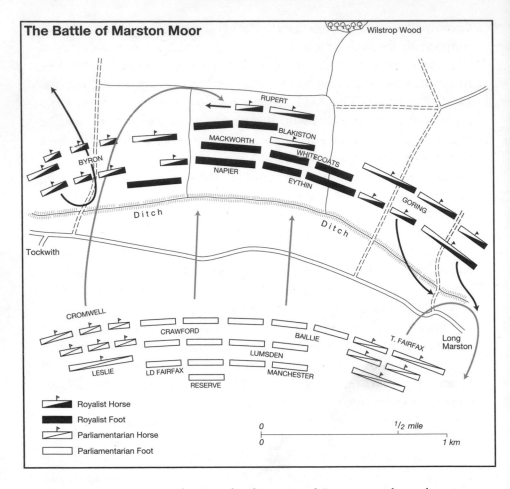

The Battle of Marston Moor

Wilstrop Wood

RUPERT
BLAKISTON
MACKWORTH
WHITECOATS
NAPIER
EYTHIN
BYRON
GORING

Ditch

Ditch

Tockwith

CROMWELL
CRAWFORD
BAILLIE
T. FAIRFAX
Long Marston
LUMSDEN
LESLIE   LD FAIRFAX   MANCHESTER
RESERVE

Royalist Horse
Royalist Foot
Parliamentarian Horse
Parliamentarian Foot

0   1/2 mile
0   1 km

the pandemonium in the Royalist lines. Lord Byron, on the right wing, had been commanded not to venture forwards, but the sight of enemy cavalry fast approaching was too tempting: he ordered the charge. The desperate result was that Rupert's musketeers were unable to fire, in case they also shot their own men. Meanwhile, Byron's two thousand troopers were no match for Cromwell's three or four thousand, and they retreated across difficult terrain, sustaining further casualties as they went, marshland and a rabbit warren slowing their flight. Cromwell pushed on, shrugging off a slight neck wound and pressing home his advantage.

Rupert arrived from the rear to take command of the right wing's second line of cavalry. He was just in time to stop his men from turning tail, their courage wilting at the sight of Byron's disarray. Through the broken ranks of their colleagues, they could make out the approach of

Cromwell's victorious squadrons, riding at a fast trot, knee to knee, purposeful, focused, and alarming. "Swounds, do you run?' Rupert shouted in disgust, as he saw his men faltering. 'Follow me!'[24] But, this time, there was to be no repetition of Powick Bridge or Chalgrove Field. Rupert's full-blooded charge was shattered by the unyielding ranks of the Ironsides. Half an hour of desperate struggle saw Cavalier and Roundhead hacking and slashing at each other with their swords, their pistols and carbines spent.

They fought each other to a standstill. The screams of the dying rang out above the dark, metallic rhythm of blade striking blade, which was punctuated by the whinnying of terrified, riderless horses and the bellowed exhortations of officers to their men. The outcome was already decided in the allies' favour when three regiments of Scottish lancers were let slip, to finish off their colleagues' handiwork. Marston Moor was the only large-scale battle of the English Civil War where such a force prospered. Generally, this was a conflict better suited to the heavier cavalry. Here, however, the lancers' nimble ponies, with their lightly armoured riders, caused havoc among a disordered enemy. Overwhelmed for the first time in a major battle, Rupert's Cavaliers fled, mostly for York. It was every man for himself, and the prince only escaped death or capture by setting his horse at a fence and leaping into a field of beans. From there, he played no further part in the battle.

The battle of Marston Moor was a see-saw affair. The allied infantry attacked in a running march, quickly breaching the Royalists' defensive ditch and capturing seven pieces of artillery, before dispersing Rupert's foot soldiers. The prince, however, had placed a cavalry brigade in reserve, which now fell on the Anglo-Scottish attackers with such ferocity that many of them fled the field. As they ran back through colleagues about to enter the fray, their evident terror persuaded others to join in the flight. 'It was a sad sight', wrote a rebel eyewitness, 'to behold many thousands posting away, being amazed with panic fears.'[25] This haemorrhaging of men convinced several of the senior allied officers that the day was lost. Leven was persuaded to save himself, and rode as fast as he could for the safety of Leeds. Lord Fairfax also quit the field with embarrassing haste. Of the principal commanders, only Manchester remained on hand, personally leading 500 deserters back into the fray.

On the Royalist left-hand cavalry wing, the mercurial George Goring performed with the dynamism and decisiveness usually associated with the prince. Goring's infantry support met Sir Thomas Fairfax's cavalry assault with intense musket volleys, which were followed up with a vigorous charge by the Northern Horse. Although Sir Thomas's own troop prospered, pursuing beaten opponents from the field, the rest of his men were routed. Returning to check what had happened to them, and bearing a cut to his cheek, Sir Thomas found himself surrounded by Goring's milling soldiers. Removing a white blaze in his hat, the mark that identified him as an ally, he trotted quietly back to his colleagues in the Earl of Manchester's ranks with news of his reversal.

Goring's efforts could not turn the course of the battle. His second line, commanded by Sir Charles Lucas, made some headway but, eventually, it became bogged down in the huge numbers of the enemy infantry and Lucas was captured. Cromwell now arced his cavalry round with extraordinary discipline, in the defining movement of the day. Using the full sweep of the battlefield, he fell on Goring's exposed flank from a position that had, at the start of the engagement, been Goring's own: the result of this brilliant manoeuvre was terrible carnage. Goring and the remnants of his Northern Horse were sidelined by the torrent of Allied troops that now possessed the field. The Anglo-Scottish cavalry, infantry, and dragoons worked in unison, mopping up the remaining pockets of Royalist foot soldiers with brutal efficiency. Cromwell's deft touch, after the hard graft of the early part of the encounter, had turned the day on its head: Manchester, Sir Thomas Fairfax, and the Scots' general David Leslie all made victory possible, but it was Cromwell who had seized the moment and made certain of the result.

Of these who perished at Marston Moor 3,200 of the 4,000 soldiers were Royalists. A further 1,500 of Rupert's men were taken prisoner. The Marquess of Newcastle's proud Whitecoats stood firm late in the evening, aware that the day was lost, but refusing to surrender. All but thirty of them perished, their pale tunics drenched in blood that was not, as they had intended, their enemies, but their own. Parliament's newspaper *Mercurius Britannicus* reported that, among the military bounty harvested that evening, was 'Prince Rupert's Standard, with the Ensigns of the Palatine, near five yards long, and broad, with a red cross in the middle'.[26] 'Besides all this,' announced *The Scottish Dove*, 'they took very good pillage, and some thousands of pounds in money, and Rupert's Sumpter [horse].'[27]

Under the moonlight, scavenging thieves picked over the bodies of the fallen, stripping them of clothes and possessions. 'In the morning, there was a mortifying object to behold', recalled Simon Ash, the Earl of Manchester's chaplain, 'when the naked bodies of thousands lay upon the ground, and many not altogether dead.'[28] Inspecting some of the casualties more carefully, Ash observed: 'The white, smooth, skins of many dead bodies in the field gives us occasion to think, that they were Gentlemen.'[29] Sir Charles Lucas, as senior prisoner of war, was obliged to identify these bodies. 'Unhappy King Charles!' he sobbed, on seeing so many familiar faces frozen in death.

A month later, despite local countrymen being ordered to bury the corpses, a traveller crossing near the battlefield reported that 'there was such a stench thereabouts that it almost poisoned them that passed over the Moor.'[30]

Rupert's beloved dog, Boy, was discovered among the casualties. This was the poodle that had been the prince's companion since his days as a prisoner of war in Austria. He had since become a lucky mascot to Charles I's troops. Boy had been left tied up in the Royalist camp, but he slipped his leash in the confusion of battle, running off to seek his master. Boy's death was celebrated by the Parliamentarians and featured in Ash's account of the battle: 'This is only mentioned by the way', he explained, 'because the Prince's Dog hath been much spoken of, and was more prized by his Master, than creatures of much more worth.'[31] Rebel propagandists had long portrayed the relationship between prince and hound as unnaturally close: perhaps, they had suggested, their bond had sinister, Satanic undertones:

> 'Twas like a dog, yet there was none did know
> Whether it Devil was, or dog or no.[32]

This, they claimed, would explain Rupert's unearthly run of success. Maybe the dog was the product of the prince's sexual encounter with a witch? If so, the death of this familiar must be a poor omen for the king's cause:

> Lament poor Cavaliers, cry, howl and yelp
> For the great loss of your Malignant whelp,
> He's dead! He's dead! No more alas can he
> Protect your dames, or get victory.

The effect of the dog's loss on his master was the cause of vivid conjecture:

> How sad that Son of Blood did look to hear
> One tell the death of this shagg'd Cavalier.
> He rav'd, he tore his Periwig and swore,
> Against the Roundheads that he'd ne'er fight more.[33]

Rupert made his way back from Marston Moor to York alone. On this sombre journey, it was said, he killed a handful of Parliamentarians who tried to block his way. The young general's aura of invincibility may have been destroyed in an evening, but the myth of the man endured for now.

CHAPTER TEN

COMMANDER OF THE KING'S FORCES

'The glories of our blood and state,
are shadows, not substantial things,
There is no armour against Fate.
Death lays his icy hand on Kings,
Sceptre and Crown,
Must tumble down,
And in the dust must be equal made,
With the poor crooked scythe and spade.'

The Contention of Ajax and Ulysses, James Shirley, 1596–1666.

First reports from Marston Moor spoke of a famous victory for the prince. Such assessments were based on news of the first hour of the battle, when thousands of the allies had been seen fleeing the field. Rupert's own account arrived with Charles at Evesham, ten days after the defeat. It was an honest appraisal of the situation, that looked to future opportunities rather than dwelling over-long on this devastating reverse. The prince knew he had been soundly beaten, but he also believed that the north was not lost: most of his casualties were in infantry, the bulk of his cavalry having been saved by the speed of their horses and the darkness of nightfall. He hoped to have a Royalist army back in action soon. In the meantime, his forces had inflicted heavy casualties on the Fairfaxes' troops, which would make it difficult for the other rebel commanders to move their men south without leaving the north vulnerable and undermanned. Allowing York to fall to the allies, Rupert set off to regroup his men and to gather recruits with 6,000 enemy horsemen snapping at his heels.

Rupert's fellow northern commanders did not share his optimism. Newcastle had fought bravely at Marston Moor, rushing into battle at the head of a troop of volunteers and killing three of the enemy with a sword borrowed from his page. However, the self-regarding marquess feared that the scale of defeat would lead to ridicule at court. He had threatened resignation twice before, but this time Newcastle meant it: he set sail from Scarborough for the Continent, with Eythin in his retinue. He was to remain in self-imposed exile for the remainder of the war.

Parliamentarians celebrated a glorious triumph over an enemy riven by dissent and lured to self-destruction – they maintained – by Rupert's fatal pride. They ordered a Day of Thanksgiving, their propagandists gloating, 'That when Prince Rupert had according to his own will relieved York, which (as was thought) was the greatest of his ambition, yet then he should so much glory in his own strength, as to give battle to our forces, though contrary to the advice and importunity of his own chiefest commanders.'[1] Thanks to God's intervention, they believed, Rupert had received his long overdue come-uppance. In the flush of victory colourful tales emerged, the Scots even claiming that Newcastle had tried to stab Rupert with a knife during their final, furious meeting.

The king was careful not to criticise his nephew, despite making it clear that it had never been his intention for Rupert to attack the enemy. The scale of the defeat shook Charles, but he could be philosophical about reverses, writing to Goring on another occasion: 'We must expect disasters in war.'[2] Marston Moor certainly fell into this category: the biggest cavalry engagement of the war – indeed, probably the largest battle ever fought on English soil – had ended in disaster. However, Charles was loyal to his own blood, and Rupert's past successes meant that even a debacle of this magnitude could be digested without censure.

The king's attitude denied Digby the opportunity to celebrate his rival's fiasco openly. Besides, the consequences of the defeat for the Royalist cause were too serious for obvious point-scoring. Digby's attacks had to be covert. He threw Rupert's failure into relief by emphasising others' heroics: 'Noble General,' he wrote to Goring, with a Classical flourish, 'As we owe you all the good of the day in the Northern battle, so we owe you all the good news from thence.'[3] Next, Digby fomented suspicion that Rupert was too pig-headed to be an effective general: 'It is given out here', a friend warned the prince from Oxford, 'that your commanders are unsatisfied, because you hear only private counsels, and never hear their opinions concerning your business.'[4]

Digby used the moment to settle other scores. The secretary of state had fallen out with Lord Wilmot – Rupert's Lieutenant General of

Horse had tired of Digby's slyness and was exasperated by his negative influence on the king. Wilmot was the epitome of the roistering,
drunken Cavalier, caricatured in Puritan propaganda, but he was also
a loyal and experienced general, not without talent, whose men loved
him. As Clarendon observed: 'He had, by his excessive good Fellowship
(in every part whereof he excelled, and was grateful to all the Company)
made himself so popular with all the Officers of the Army, especially of
the Horse, that he had, in truth, a very great Interest.'[5]

In the summer of 1644, disgruntled and drinking heavily, he allowed
his hatred for Digby to seep into the open: 'Wilmot continued still
sullen and perverse,' Clarendon wrote, 'and every day grew more insolent, and had contracted such an animosity against Lord Digby and
the Master of the Rolls, that he persuaded many officers of the army,
especially of the horse, where he was most entirely obeyed, to join in
a petition to the King, that those two councillors might be excluded,
and be no more present in councils of war, which they promised to
do.'[6] Wilmot had underestimated his enemy, however. By declaring his
hand, he left himself vulnerable to Machiavellian revenge.

As the summer progressed, Digby closely monitored this noisy threat
to his position. He made sure that Wilmot's increasingly outspoken
comments were relayed to the king, with the least generous interpretation attached. Wilmot's bravery at the battle of Cropredy Bridge
saved him for a while, but when it was reported that he was in secret
communication with the Earl of Essex, Digby encouraged the king to
strike.

On 8 August 1644, the knight marshal, Sir Edward Sydenham,
arrested Wilmot at the head of his men. The charge was high treason.
Wilmot was ordered to dismount his horse and follow Sydenham into
custody. Wilmot's loyal officers greeted this dramatic move with seeth-
ing disbelief – at one point, full-blooded mutiny seemed likely. Charles
felt compelled to ride up to each regiment to restore order in person,
offering an explanation for Wilmot's arrest that had been concocted
by Digby: Wilmot's detention was, the king assured the cavalry, only
temporary; George Goring would replace him for the time being.
Meanwhile, Charles lied, it was Prince Rupert who had recommended
the arrest.

It is hard to disagree with Warburton's view that: 'Digby must have
hugged himself on the contrivance of making his other great enemy,
Rupert, appear to be the mover in this transaction.'[7] Digby's removal

of Wilmot from his power base, and his blaming the prince for such an unpopular step, was a masterstroke.

By this stage, Rupert was making as little effort as Wilmot to hide his contempt for Digby. Charles, blind to his secretary of state's wiles, wrote pleading for a change of heart:

> Nephew,
> 'Digby, whom I must desire you (for my service's sake because he is a useful servant) so far to countenance as to show him a possibility to recover your favour, if he shall deserve it, which I hope he will; and if not he shall repent it too late. Not doubting that for my sake but ye will make this act a greater experiment; for I assure you that, as to me, you are and shall be capable to oblige any of my servants ...'[8]

Digby, for his part, hid his dislike for Rupert under a veneer of flattery. 'There is no occasion of my enlarging your Highness's trouble at this present,' he wrote to the prince, 'further than to assure you of the great comfort and new life, as it were, which it gives to those who have the honour to be trusted by your Highness, to think that our army shall shortly be again animated by your spirit.'[9]

Rupert greeted this obsequiousness with disdain. He wrote in cipher to his great friend and ally, Will Legge: 'Digby makes great professions and vows to Rupert; but it will do no good upon him. Great factions are breeding against Rupert, under a pretence of peace; he being, as they report, the only cause of war in the kingdom. This party is found out, but no particulars proved: they will be, and then the King did promise to punish, or there will be no staying; which else Rupert is resolved to do, since the King's friends are in no very good condition, and he hath promised me fair; it is well if half performed.'[10] Rupert knew that Digby was at the forefront of his Royalist enemies. He hoped that, once revealed in his true colours, Digby would lose the king's patronage.

The latter months of 1644 produced mixed fortunes for Charles I's cause. There had been a welcome victory at Lostwithiel, in Cornwall, when the king led his troops in a pincer movement that trapped the Earl of Essex's army on the west of the Fowey peninsula. The rebel infantry surrendered en masse, but Essex escaped to the waiting navy in a rowing boat, and his cavalry successfully broke out to freedom when they should have been taken. Charles misguidedly allowed the defeated foot soldiers to march away unharmed, rather than be imprisoned. He could ill afford to gift his enemies thousands of troops at such a time, but the desire to be seen as a magnanimous victor was too great to resist.

Rupert, worried that the king's success might breed overconfidence, made his uncle promise that he would immediately head back with his men to Oxford. However, to Rupert's intense annoyance, Charles was instead persuaded by Goring to attempt an attack on Waller, before trying to take two enemy strongholds. These delays gave the Parliamentarians the chance to catch up with the king and led to the Second Battle of Newbury – a messy and indecisive affair, fought at the end of October, at which the Royalist army was fortunate to escape serious casualties. Waller and Manchester expected too much from their artillery, an extended bombardment stopping their infantry and cavalry from joining in a concerted attack. Prince Maurice succeeded in drawing his battered infantry off into the safety of the night, while Charles rode with his lifeguards to join Rupert in Bath.

There were reports that, in the autumn, Rupert had sunk into a depressed state. Arthur Trevor infers in his letters that the prince indulged in the sort of loose living that he was frequently accused of by Parliament, but for which no other evidence exists. He seems to have finally succumbed to the constant assaults of his courtier enemies. He also appears to have reacted to his summer defeat, one Parliamentary commentator noting that Rupert: 'was grown dogged with the frowns he had for his miscarriage at Marston Moor, and would not come near his Majesty.'[11] Exhaustion no doubt played a part: he had been frenetically active for two years and even his famously robust constitution had reached its limits.

On 6 November 1644, Charles demonstrated that memories of Marston Moor were banished, by bestowing on his nephew his greatest show of favour to date. During a general rendezvous of the king's forces on Bullingdon Green: 'The Prince was declared General of the Army and Master of the Horse',[12] the author of Prince Rupert's diary recorded – a succinct sentence, but a mighty promotion. The 24-year-old Rupert replaced the doddery, alcoholic, and recently wounded Earl of Forth as commander of all the king's armies. However, Rupert was keen not to play into Digby's hands, by being seen to overreach himself. He cleverly insisted that his cousin the Prince of Wales bear the title of General of the Royal Army, while he settled for the rank of lieutenant general, his main task the coordination of the king's war plans.

Rupert's critics mourned Forth's replacement. 'The King's Army was less united than ever,' Clarendon gauged, 'the old General was left aside, and Prince Rupert put into the command, which was no popular change: for the other was known to be an officer of great experience, and had committed no oversights in his conduct; was willing to hear every thing debated, and always concurred with the most reasonable opinion: and though he was not of many words, and was not quick in hearing, yet upon any action he was sprightly, and commanded well. The Prince was rough, and passionate, and loved not debate; liked what was proposed, as he liked the persons who proposed it; and was so great an enemy to Digby and Culpepper, who were only present in debates of the War with the Officers, that he crossed all they proposed.'[13]

Rupert took advantage of his new powers to promote his most stalwart supporter, his brother Maurice, who took command of Wales and the Welsh Borders. Rupert also secured Goring's promotion to General of Horse. The king soon went further, entrusting Goring to lead all his forces in the southwest. To Rupert's fury, Goring managed to secure the dispensation that he had previously insisted upon for himself, receiving his orders directly from the king. When the Royalists most needed unified command, Charles gave them division.

The transfer of Rupert, Maurice, and Goring to new postings was the most significant change to take place on the Royalist side during the winter of 1644–5, a season that the rebels were to use to far greater effect.

Prince Rupert returned to Oxford in early November, going into winter quarters to prepare for the 1645 campaign. His priority was to claw provisions from every available recess in the kingdom, so the Royalists could supply their men in the field. Although Rupert approached these duties with purpose, he was unable to overcome a general breakdown in discipline. Charles could not afford to pay or feed his soldiers regularly and, in lieu of wages, he allowed his men to take matters into their own hands. Sometimes, this took a practical form: soldiers cut down a coppice in Brasenose, meeting a shortage of wood in Oxford, and kept the income for themselves. However, elsewhere pillaging became more frequent. A disgusted Parliamentarian wrote, in late November:

'The King's Party from Oxford have lately plundered Wantage, which is about ten miles from Oxford; and have taken all away from the poor inhabitants that was portable, leaving them poorer, and more miserable, than ever.'[14]

This disintegration of order was accompanied by war-weariness: the king's soldiers, under pressure throughout 1644, had marched from pillar to post in an effort to keep his cause alive. Now there was a growing sense, almost tangible in Oxford, that the conflict would be lost. A peace party emerged, led by Richmond, Clarendon, and Lord Southampton. Rupert found he increasingly sympathised with them: nobody had a greater appreciation of the Royalists' weaknesses than he, whose job was to paper over the ever widening cracks.

Rupert also saw that Charles's prospects were compromised by the poor quality of his closest advisers. This problem grew more serious when the king decided, for safety's sake, to send his eldest son to establish a secondary court in Bristol: Richmond, and many of the rest of Charles's wiser counsellors, accompanied the Prince of Wales to the southwest. Digby and John Ashburnham – the treasurer of the Royal army – were left behind, their self-interest undimmed and their guidance as flawed as ever.

Towards the end of the year, Rupert appeared to be in the ascendant over his rivals. Parliamentarians reported with optimism: 'Let me tell you, the power of Digby and the rest of the Irish [i.e., Roman Catholic] rebels faction is not so great with the King, at least, it is so given out, to the end we may think so, the more so sweeten them at Oxford in the opinion of us here: and none more forward to make peace, than Prince Rupert ...'.[15]

Rupert, as commander of the army, was asked by the king to write a letter inviting peace negotiations. He addressed Essex, on 5 December:

My Lord,
I am commanded by his Majesty to desire of your Lordship safe conduct for the Duke of Richmond, and the Earl of Southampton, with their attendants, coaches, and horses, and other accommodations fitting for their journey towards London, during their stay, and in their return, when they shall think fit, from the Lords and Commons Assembled in the Parliament of England at Westminster, to bring to the Lords and Commons assembled in the Parliament of England, and the Commissioners of the Kingdom of Scotland now at London, an answer

to the Propositions sent to his Majesty, for a safe and well grounded
peace.
Your Lordship's servant
Rupert[16]

It was far removed from his cocksure letter to Essex two years earlier,
challenging the lord general to a duel. Indeed, the prince's acknowledgement of Parliament as the legitimate assembly in England was an
act of unprecedented humility. This concession had been agreed on by
a majority of Charles's advisers (a vote from which Rupert abstained,
seeing himself as merely the communicator of his colleagues' will). It
was seen as a promising gesture in Westminster, the author of the rebel
news-sheet *Mercurius Britannicus* writing: 'This is so: we have Rupert's
hand for it, and the Duke [Richmond], and the Earl [Southampton],
are continually expected here: This acknowledging of a Parliament is a
good beginning, and gives great hope, that there may be a fair proceeding; whereas the want of this formal acknowledgement was a long time
as a great gulf betwixt us and Peace.'[17]

However, Richmond and Southampton were unable to persuade
Parliament to withdraw its more contentious demands. These were
contained in 'The Humble Desires and Propositions for a safe and
well-grounded Peace', the usual uneasy rebel blend of blind optimism,
sensible compromise, and wilful insult. The fourteenth clause specified:
'That the persons who shall expect no Pardon, be only these following:
...'. There then followed more than fifty names of prominent Royalist
generals, advisers, and priests. The first two were: 'Rupert and Maurice,
Count Palatines of the Rhine ...'. There were many other points that
Charles could not possibly accept, but leaving his most loyal followers
vulnerable to retribution was one of the more compelling reasons for
continuing the war.

Denied peace, singled out by Parliament as his uncle's chief 'malignant', and exhausted by the court's shenanigans, rumours circulated
that Rupert would look to continue his military career overseas. 'Nay,
it is affirmed by some (who seem to know much),' asserted the *London
Post*, in mid December, 'that Prince Rupert himself is now inclined to
peace, whether he is weary of war finding it to be carried on in no part
of Christendom, with greater violence, or whether England being now
sufficiently wasted, he would exchange the wants of England, for the
plenty and wealth of Venice: you heard that he hath been sent for by

the States of Venice to be one of their Generals in their wars. Indeed, he hath a name in arms beyond the seas.'[18]

Yet Rupert still had an important role to play at the head of his uncle's forces. His personal charisma was a potent weapon and wherever he travelled the Royalist cause prospered. However, the prince could not be everywhere at once, a fact bemoaned by colleagues reliant on the magic of his presence: 'Your highness's absence had cooled the affection of many,' Dudley Wyatt wrote from Shropshire, in January 1645, 'and consequently the hope of impunity raised many mutinous spirits.'[19] 'The want of your Highness's presence in these parts', echoed Sir John Byron, writing from Chester three months later, '(though occasioned by inevitable incidents) & the continuance of the Rebels' army so near unto us hath begot so much despair amongst all people here, that unless some speedy hopes of relief be given them, I much fear either a general revolt or neutrality . . .'.[20]

The continuation of war was a draining affair. Supplying armies was costly and complicated, and manning them was ever more difficult: years of armed conflict had taken their toll, not just in lives lost, but also in incapacitating many survivors. Lorentz Gamb bowed out of the contest with a wonderfully understated adieu to Prince Maurice, in which he made light of a skirmish that had cost him many men, as well as his health: 'For my part I hardly escaped with life having five deep wounds in my hand and right arm, whereof I doubt but I shall be lame forever . . . I, having so escaped, could get not as much as quarter for myself, nor surgeon for [my] maimed soldiers, but was forced to leave each one to seek his fortune. Wherefore I humbly desire that your highness may be pleased to give me your recommendation in writing to his Majesty for my three years service, having lost all, and nothing wherewithal to subsist, and that your princely brother (whom heavens preserve) be not ignorant of it, thus praying for your happiness, and continual success, I rest your highness's most humble servant during life.'[21]

Other avenues now had to be explored, to bring new recruits to the Royalist cause. Henrietta Maria secured an audience with Cardinal Mazarin, at which she hoped to persuade her native France to support her husband. However, Parliament knew of France's military distractions on the Continent: 'What reason have the French', enquired one rebel commentator, 'to pull an old house upon their heads in England, when with less money they may get new ones from Spain, and keep them when they have them without charge?'[22] Not even Henrietta

Maria's insistent pleas could divert France's troops from the Thirty Years' War.

Parliament faced similar problems with manpower and supply. At the end of 1644, Cromwell complained to his civilian masters that without more money to pay and feed his men, he would be unable to guarantee their future loyalty. He also became increasingly outspoken in his desire to push for victory, criticising those who failed to share his focus. There had been a suspicion earlier in the war that the Earl of Essex was reluctant to defeat his monarch: this would explain his failure to ram home advantages in the field. Now, Cromwell vented his distrust of the Earl of Manchester, whose reasonable weighing up of the odds facing the rebels – that one defeat could cost them their lives – was presented as defeatism. To the shock of many of his comrades, Cromwell declared that if he came across the king in battle, he would shoot him dead as happily as he would slay any lesser adversary.

Cromwell pushed for the transformation of the Parliamentary high command. He supported the Self-Denying Ordnance, which forbade Members of the Lords or Commons from serving as officers in the army. Cromwell was one of the few exceptions, receiving short-term commissions that recognised his indispensability in either sphere. However, the aristocratic generals who had failed to win the war thus far were jettisoned – their place was now in London, advising, rather than on the battlefield, fighting.

Parliament's military capability was reinforced by Christian probity. Cromwell had bemoaned the inferior quality of the rebel troopers at Edgehill. He now harnessed religious fervour to his cause, turning his fighting East Anglians into some of the finest, most disciplined regiments engaged in the Civil War. Twelve years earlier British observers felt they had identified the secret to King Gustavus Adolphus's success in war: 'Fighting and Praying, and Praying and Fighting: thus hath the King of Sweden learn'd to conquer.'[23] Strong Protestant ethics, insisted upon by an uncompromising leader, had proved an irresistible aid on the battlefield.

The correlation between godliness and military effectiveness was recognised by both sides: the Bishop of Derry, preaching to Royalists in York in early 1644, had chided the worldly excesses of some in his congregation, promising that more devotion would lead inevitably to battlefield success: 'It is a slander cast upon Religion,' he claimed, 'that it makes men cowards. The fear of God is the best armour against the fear of man. Religion is the root of Courage.'[24] Seven years later the Chief Justice of Munster was to expand on the same theme: 'For not only that knowledge which is divine is from God, but skill in arms and expertness in wars, which though it may in a great measure be acquired by natural valour and understanding, voluntary industry, and long experiences, yet considering how many veteran Commanders of noble extraction and education, famous in feats of chivalry; have been foiled, broken in pieces, and beaten at their own weapons by a few gentlemen (in comparison) and ... mechanics and honest tradesmen, whose hearts the Lord hath drawn forth and engaged to fight his battles; we must needs acknowledge, that their valour, prowess and dexterity hath either been infused by God, or improved by him to a miraculous proficiency.'[25]

Sir Thomas Fairfax, the rebel commander, shared this creed. He borrowed from rigid Puritanism to bring a level of order to his troops that the Royalists could not match. During the winter of 1644–5, while peace negotiations between the two sides played out with their customary futility, Parliament built on the foundations of tight order revealed at Marston Moor. The result was England's first truly professional fighting force, the New Model Army. It numbered 22,000 – a third of all rebel land forces.

The New Model Army's cavalry and dragoons were of high quality, many drawn from Cromwell's Eastern Association. The infantry was of less impressive heritage, many of them pressed men. However, once enlisted, they were obliged to observe 'The Articles of War', a rigid code of conduct with swingeing penalties for the disobedient: if a soldier swore, he was fined; if he blasphemed, he had his 'tongue bored with a red-hot iron'; if he indulged in 'rapes, ravishments and unnatural abuses', he was executed. In return for accepting these conditions, Fairfax promised his men 'coat and conduct money, wages and entertainments, and other necessary charges and allowances'.[26]

When the New Model Army marched out of Windsor, on 30 April 1645, Rupert had nothing to match it.

Fairfax was eager for action, but he found his enemy reluctant to fight. When he turned towards Taunton, the Royalists lifted their siege; when the New Model Army swivelled round to invest Oxford, Charles and his nephews marched quickly into the Midlands at the head of 11,000 men, leaving Will Legge to hold the town.

At the end of May the Royal field army proceeded to Leicester.

Rupert's demands of immediate surrender, coupled with threats of dire consequences if denied, were twice rejected. On the last day of the month he stormed the city, the charge led by the 500 infantrymen of Prince Rupert's Bluecoats, their battle cry 'God and the Prince!' The deterioration in discipline in the Royalist army was revealed in the performance of this crack unit: 'Rupert's regiment got in with the first', the Parliamentary journal *Mercurius Britannicus* recorded with disgust, 'that was for the plunder, else you should have seen them hang an arse, as if they were going to a sermon.'[27] In all, the pillaging Royalists amassed '140 cart loads of the best goods and wares in the shops'[28] and sent them off to Newark for safekeeping.

The capture of Leicester was a huge fillip to the Royalists. With Clarendon reporting excellent recruiting figures from the southwest and Montrose prospering in Scotland, the king wrote to Henrietta Maria that things had never looked so promising for his cause. It seemed that Prince Rupert's elevation to chief command had resulted in a sudden sea change in the king's fortunes. Charles looked forward to a decisive conclusion to the war – 'the last blow in the business'.

Parliament quit all its garrisons around Leicester and gloom spread among its supporters throughout the Midlands. 'I am most heartily sorry for the ill success of our forces in all parties,' wrote Sir Samuel Luke from Newport Pagnell, on 6 June, 'which hath caused a dead heartedness in all people, that they are struck with such a panic fear, that, if I am not deceived, the Parliament cause was never in so declining a condition as at present.'[29]

The Royalist council of war debated how to capitalise on their unexpected advantage. There were three choices: to head west, to Worcester, and join up with Sir Charles Gerard's army; to march north, to relieve Carlisle and fight the Scots; or to return to Oxford, and force Fairfax to lift the siege. Digby and his faction were for the Oxford option, playing on the king's sense of chivalry by emphasising the plight that the ladies would face if the town fell and the victorious attackers had their way with them. Rupert was eager to push northwards again: he wanted to avenge Marston Moor, but also to appease the Northern Horse, whose troopers were desperate to return home. The debate was heated, the civilian courtiers fighting hard to re-establish influence after a period when Rupert and his military allies had held sway.

To the prince's intense disappointment, Charles decided to march to the relief of Oxford. However, the Royal army had only reached

Daventry when news came that Fairfax had abandoned his siege. This prompted a jubilant letter from Prince Rupert to Will Legge: 'There was a plot to send the King to Oxford, but it is undone. The Chief of the Council was the fear some men [Digby and Ashburnham] had that the soldiers should take from the influence which now they possess with the King.'[30]

But, rather than push northwards as he had promised, Charles led his senior officers in a series of stag-hunts through the Northamptonshire countryside.

It was now that the Self-Denying Ordnance showed its worth: Essex, Manchester, and Waller were among those who pooled their combined battlefield experience in the Committee of Both Kingdoms in London, directing the generals in the field. There had been concern that Fairfax was hot-headed and would therefore be best deployed in the static business of siege warfare. But all appreciated that a crucial battle was now in the offing. The *Moderate Intelligencer* reported: 'The fighting at this time is a business of great hazard to both parties, and he that hath the victory will gain much by it.'[31] It was essential, in such circumstances, for the field commander to have strategic independence and to be given the lieutenants that he wanted: Fairfax was given the freedom to act on his own initiative; Cromwell was given temporary command of the horse, as lieutenant general. The two men were ordered to unite their forces and bring the king to battle at the earliest opportunity.

On 12 June patrols from the two armies stumbled on each other just outside Northampton. Charles ordered a hasty retreat towards Leicester. The following night, it was later claimed, the king had a dream in which the ghost of the Earl of Strafford appeared, advising him not to give battle. Charles was roused from his sleep with news that Fairfax was closing in on the Royalists faster than had been thought possible. He summoned a midnight council of war at which Digby, Ashburnham, and their acolytes urged the king to turn and fight – underestimating a force that they had contemptuously nicknamed 'the New Noddle'. They argued that it would be folly not to face the enemy so soon after it had failed in its siege of Oxford: the rebels must be demoralised by this failure and their own men would be dispirited if denied the chance of a great victory.

Rupert was equally insistent that it would be madness to risk all on the battlefield, while still at a numerical disadvantage. He advocated retreating to Leicester until reinforcements arrived. Gerard was expected at any moment, as was Goring, who had pleaded with the king to avoid battle until his return from the siege of Taunton. Goring's cavalry was the pick of the Royalist horse, containing squadrons that had triumphed at Cropredy Bridge and helped save the day at the Second Battle of Newbury. Leicester's walls had been quickly patched up, the weak points exploited by Rupert made strong, and the size of the Royalist army would make the speedy taking of the city impossible.

Charles, yet again, and this time disastrously, disregarded his nephew and opted to accept Digby's advice. It ranks alongside his order to Rupert the previous summer – to fight the Anglo-Scottish army outside York – as one of the greatest strategic mistakes that the king made during the Civil War.

The point chosen by Rupert to meet Fairfax and Cromwell was near to the village of Naseby. It was suited to his smaller numbers: only a mile wide, there were gorse bushes along the east side of the field and cramped enclosures to the west, ruling out rebel flanking attacks. Both armies would start the day by occupying opposing hills and the outcome would be decided at the dip of the parabola between them. This was a site that demanded victory: there was no hiding place for the defeated in the sweeping countryside beyond. The prince had been commanded to fight, so he had selected a killing zone where he would risk all.

In the early morning of Saturday, 14 June 1645, Rupert's scouts erroneously reported that Fairfax was in retreat. In fact, the rebels were simply rearranging their lines to take advantage of the wind. Believing this faulty intelligence, the prince despatched a messenger to find his uncle, so the Royalists could be immediately unleashed on a disordered enemy.

By nine o'clock the Royalists were ready for action. The prince, resplendent in a scarlet cape, opted to lead the charge of his right-hand cavalry wing. Astley again commanded the infantry centre and Marmaduke Langdale rode at the head of the Northern Horse, on the left-hand wing. To distinguish themselves from the rebels, they tied beanstalks to their helmets. They were given as their battle cry, 'Queen Mary'. The entire army was only 9,000 men.

Rupert dispensed with the traditional preliminaries of artillery bombardment. Cannon fire had reaped few benefits in previous battles

Rupert as a child, by Anthony van Dyck.

Frederick V, King of Bohemia,
Elector Palatine of the Rhine, Rupert's
father. By Willem Hondius.

(Left) Elizabeth, Queen of Bohemia,
Rupert's mother. Studio of Michiel
Jansz Miereveld.

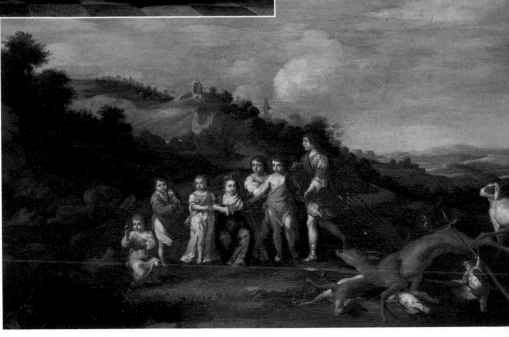

Seven children of the King and Queen of Bohemia, after Cornelius van Poelenburgh.

Rupert (right) and his brother Charles Louis,
by Anthony Van Dyck.

Prince Maurice,
Rupert's younger brother,
by Nathaniel Thache.

King Charles I of England, Rupert's uncle, by Anthony van Dyck.

Prince Rupert hides in a bean field after the Battle of Marston Moor. His dog 'Boy'
lies dead, while Parliamentarian soldiers capture his baggage horse.

Seventeenth-century painting of the Battle of Naseby. Rupert's cavalry made for the
baggage train, shown at the bottom left, leaving his infantry exposed.

Earle of Essex

Earle of Warwick

Englands
and the En
and Kingd

Though England
By Plotts of foes
yet to this day b
The Arks preserui

These boystrous waues do represent
Malignant foes to land & Parliment

Lo: Aubigny

L. Aubigny

Coms
Pray

House of Lord

ottington

Bishop

Greenui

P Rupert

B: Lorke

Hopton

Windebank

Sr Tho:
Fairfax

G: Forth

London printed and sould by Ro Walton

'England's Ark Secured and the Enemies to the Parliament and Kingdom Overwhelmed':
an engraving produced by the victorious Parliamentarians in 1645.
Rupert is seen drowning on the left.

William Legge, by J. Huysmans.

(Right) George Digby,
by Anthony Van Dyck.

Rupert, the exhausted general,
after William Dobson.

for either side and, besides, the prince had only twelve guns. He chose, instead, to close with the enemy along his entire front.

Fairfax commanded his infantry at the centre, with Cromwell to his right and Ireton to his left, opposite Rupert. Cromwell's recent arrival in the rebel camp with 4,000 men, meant that the Parliamentarians had 16,000 soldiers, outnumbering the Royalists by nearly two to one. They wore no distinguishing marks and their battle cry was 'God is our strength'.

Both sides had agreed to engage and on spying one another across the valley early in the morning, the armies had each signalled their thirst for action with gigantic roars. Everyone knew what was at stake: 'About eleven o'clock,' wrote an eyewitness, 'the trumpets began to sound, the drums to beat, the horses to neigh and prance, and now thought both sides, An afternoon for a Kingdom: *Caesar or nothing* was we suppose the voice of one army, *The Liberties of England* of the other: and thus they charged each other with all their might and equal courage.'[32]

Naseby was, in many ways, a fitting military climax to the Civil War, various episodes within its furious energy reminiscent of previous engagements. As at Edgehill and Marston Moor, Rupert's cavaliers were magnificent in attack, drawing admiration from enemy onlookers. Colonel Okey commanded Parliament's dragoons drawn up behind a hedge, who fired their muskets into the flank of Rupert's cavalry as they passed. Okey was moved to record the stirring sight of 'the Royalists moving on in a very stately and gallant style' as they galloped past him.[33] Another rebel conceded that Rupert's wing charged 'with such gallantry as few in the Army ever saw the like'.[34] Ireton's men were broken and their leader received two wounds.

With the rest of the Royalist army heavily outnumbered, it was essential that Rupert should now wheel his soldiers about and bring them swiftly back to the battlefield for further action. However, he instead led his men to the enemy baggage train. Colonel Bartlett, commander of its guard, was intrigued to see a red-caped cavalryman trot up to him and assumed that the man greeting him with such civility was Fairfax. Taking his hat off, Bartlett asked how the day was going. He did not receive the answer he was expecting: to his astonishment, a Parliamentary correspondent reported, 'The Cavalier whom we since heard was Rupert, asked him and the rest, if they would have quarter, and they cried no, gave fire and instantly beat them off.'[35] Bartlett's

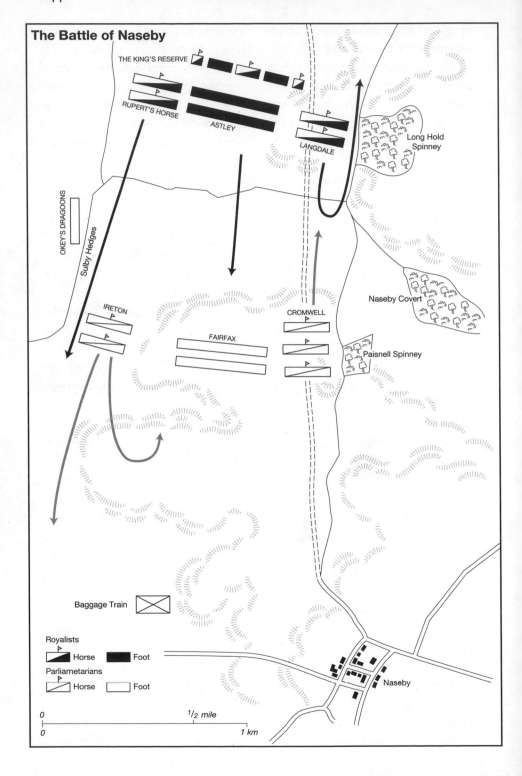

The Battle of Naseby

THE KING'S RESERVE

RUPERT'S HORSE

ASTLEY

LANGDALE

Long Hold
Spinney

OKEY'S DRAGOONS

Sulby Hedges

IRETON

FAIRFAX

CROMWELL

Naseby Covert

Paisnell Spinney

Baggage Train

Royalists

Horse   Foot

Parliametarians

Horse   Foot

Naseby

0   ½ mile

0   1 km

stubborn resistance detained the prince and his men for a crucial period, when their services were urgently needed elsewhere.

The Northern Horse, demoralised and tired, made up the left-hand cavalry wing. They had long wanted to return to their homes, to protect their lands and families. The king's refusal to honour his promise to head northwards, after the abortive lunge towards Oxford, had left them mutinous and distracted. Rupert ordered them to attack Parliament's right wing, led by Cromwell – a manoeuvre that involved leaving a strong defensive position and charging uphill at a powerful and confident enemy. Many on both sides were veterans of Marston Moor and although the fighting was unforgiving, the result was similar. Langdale's men were forced to retreat, at first in an orderly manner, picking their way through the gorse as they fell back. Eventually, though, the sheer weight of the Ironsides drove them from the field.

One of the broken Royalist cavalry regiments had embroidered their colours with the words, 'Come, Cuckolds', and had embellished this message with the image of a pair of horns. This flag was captured by the rebels, who then 'held the Horns and Motto towards the Enemy, and so charged them'.[36] Both sides shared a common nationality that revealed itself in an exuberant irreverence and a very Anglo-Saxon sense of humour.

Charles's infantry showed great courage, surprising the enemy with its resilience. It started the foot battle promisingly, locking with the first rebel brigades in the face of artillery and musket fire. The king's musketeers discharged their weapons before falling on Fairfax's troops, using their weapons as clubs, while the Royalist pikemen remained compact and focused, their points breaking their opponents' line, which fell back. However, on reaching the top of the hill, an awful sight confronted them: two more lines of enemy, until now hidden from view, were standing in battle order, ready to receive them. Astley's men faltered, knowing they could not hope to repeat their heroics once, let alone twice, more. At this moment, Cromwell's cavalry reserves ploughed into them and the fields around Naseby village became a place of slaughter.

As Newcastle's Whitecoats had done at Marston Moor, now Prince Rupert's Bluecoats became martyrs in a hopeless cause. While many other Royalist infantry units accepted the inevitable and surrendered to Fairfax, the Prince's infantry regiment levelled their pikes and chose to fight on. The arrival of rebel cavalry hastened their end, '... the right

wing of our Horse (wherein the General was in person),' remembered a
Parliamentarian eyewitness, 'charged in the flank of the blue regiment
of the enemy's Foot, who stood to it, till the last man, abundance of
them slain, and all the rest surrounded, wounded, and taken'.[37] Fairfax
called up his own regiment and a one-sided duel took place between the
two commanders' crack units, the rebels finishing off the Royalists by
staving in their skulls with the butt ends of their muskets.

The king still hoped that the day could be his. Wearing gilt armour,
he trotted round the beleaguered pockets of his remaining men shouting, 'One charge more, gentlemen! One charge more, and the day is
ours!'[38] But the sheer quantity of Cromwell and Fairfax's men smothered
any hopes Charles had of reconstituting his splintered force. The king
called for those around him to join him in a desperate charge. He was
about to gallop towards the enemy when one of his Scottish courtiers,
the Earl of Carnworth, seized Charles's bridle and chided the monarch
for his foolhardiness: 'Will you go upon your death in an instant?'[39]
He then led the king away from the field, snuffing out the last hope of
Royalist victory and precipitating the rout that saw the defeated break
for Leicester, Lichfield, and Newark.

At Naseby 800 Royalists lost their lives, 500 on the battlefield and
300 cut down by Cromwell's pursuing cavalry. Parliamentary pamphlets were abuzz with the scale of the victory, listing the officers taken
in this, the decisive battle of the Civil War. Five thousand Royalists
were captured, the majority infantry. Of these, 500 were officers: they
were sent to London, to be paraded through the streets like vanquished
barbarians, adding exotic colour to the scenes of triumph.

Savagery blossomed in the aftermath of the battle. The king's army
included female camp followers – officers' wives, cooks and servants,
whores – who were caught; many were killed, while others had their
features slashed in acts of deliberate disfigurement. The false justification for this outrage was that these women were Irish Papists of no
morality. The Irish were fair game in the minds of bigoted Puritans:
a Parliamentary naval officer expressed commonly held contempt for
them when he called them 'that ungodly crew of Revolters'[40] and one
of the propaganda sheets referred to them as 'unnatural Monsters'.[41]
The women's murder and brutalisation was a result of rampant religious
intolerance.

There was no shame at this bloodshed, an early battlefield report
merely mentioning in passing: 'The Irish women Prince Rupert brought

on the field (wives of the bloody Rebels in Ireland – his Majesty's dearly beloved subjects) our soldiers would grant no quarter to, about 100 slain of them, and most of the rest of the whores that attended that wicked Army are marked in the face or nose, with a slash or cut.'[42] Other pamphlets reckoned the number of women murdered between three and four hundred.

Early, excited reports that Prince Rupert had been taken alive proved to be unfounded: he slipped away, a commander who had suffered heavy battlefield defeat for the second time in a year. His sumpter horse was taken, as was his standard – along with those of his uncle, aunt, and brother. Two hundred wagons were filled by the victors with valuables and provisions – including, as one rebel recalled, 'great store of biscuit and cheese, a seasonable refreshment for our soldiers that had marched so hard, and the night before had not a bit of bread to a regiment for their refreshment'.[43]

Of huge embarrassment to Charles was the discovery of the cabinet containing his personal correspondence with Henrietta Maria. This revealed him to be negotiating with foreign, Catholic powers to aid him against Parliament. Politically, these letters were catastrophic for the king. They played into the hands of his bitterest enemies, whose message was hateful distrust of a monarch they held responsible for all the misery of the war. When the king learnt that his cabinet was lost, he ordered that those who had failed to guard it properly should be hung.

There were many reasons why the battle of Naseby ended in disaster for Charles: he should not have fought when at such a numerical disadvantage; he would have been wise to await the arrival of Goring's cavalry and Gerard's foot; and the Northern Horse had betrayed their flickering morale in the face of Cromwell's unblinking Ironsides. However, Rupert's inability to learn from previous experience made defeat more likely and more complete.

If the prince had been in a fixed command post at Marston Moor, it is less likely that he would have lost the battle. However, he had been wrong-footed by the sudden enemy charge and then was forced to flee for his life. At Naseby, though, he had a choice. He could have left the right cavalry wing to Maurice, while keeping a controlling overview of the battle. Instead, he decided to lead the cavaliers' assault.

Rupert's private papers show that he had hoped to annihilate the squadrons opposing him quickly, then lead his men back to the battle-field, surprising Cromwell's cavalry from the rear. But this was an ambitious plan that was always likely to fail. Even if Ireton's men had put up weaker resistance, the sheer number of rebel foot soldiers arrayed in the folds of the land between Rupert and the rear of Cromwell's position was always likely to be decisive. Attacking the baggage train was therefore probably not – as subsequent generations have been taught – yet another sign of hopeless, Cavalier, indiscipline. Rather, it was an attempt by Rupert to find an alternative route for his men, so they could swing round on the enemy's unprotected rear. Whatever the hypotheses, the absence of the prince's troopers from the centre of the battlefield proved catastrophic.

The Northern Horse's reputation suffered greatly at Naseby. Both sides saw its retreat as a major contribution to the Royalist defeat: 'Langdale's brigade ran away basely, and lost the King the day',[44] was the conclusion of one Parliamentarian. But blame for the misuse of a force low in morale, against the Puritan powerhouse of the New Model Army, must be laid at Rupert's feet. It would have been wiser to leave them to fight a defensive battle while the right wing sallied forth with its customary verve; indeed, the infantry would also have been better off receiving, rather than initiating, an attack. A more considered general – someone like Lindsey, in fact – would have served his king better that day.

The prince had belatedly taken command of an army whose discipline – never its strong point – had gently unravelled during the course of the war. 'Nothing could equal the gallantry of the Cavaliers,' Parliament acknowledged with relief, 'except their want of discipline.'[45] Rupert's role had increasingly become that of a commissar, trying desperately to keep his forces provisioned and armed so the military struggle could continue. These priorities left him with little time to drill his men or to hone their military skills: the Royalist army had some fine units, but the majority suffered from any combination of war-weariness, homesick-ness, disillusionment, or a penchant for plunder. In the face of Fairfax and Cromwell's New Model Army, aided by well-armed auxiliaries, they were shown up for the amateurs that many of them had always been.

To what extent one man can be blamed for a failure to deal with every aspect of a wide command, without committed support from the king or his council of war, is the yardstick against which Rupert should be judged as a commander. However, it is clear that Naseby was a mismatch, because Parliament's army was more numerous and more professional than Charles's force. The prince was left hoping for victory, in a battle that he did not want, as he tried to hold the Royalist cause together. Fairfax and Cromwell, meanwhile, had enjoyed the luxury of planning for a decisive engagement, and then had the calibre and weight of men to see their plans through.

Militarily, the commitment of his men to a battlefront advance against a superior enemy revealed Rupert's misplaced optimism. A pair of pragmatists called his bluff: their military nous, supported by a sincere and deep-seated religious fervour, proved to be an irresistible combination. Naseby was Rupert's last land battle as overall commander, fought when he was just 24 years old. It is as well to admit that, despite his startling bravery, his fighting skill, and his dynamic presence, he failed in this role.

The prince's inability to play at politics left him exposed after Naseby. Digby blamed the prince for the defeat, pointing in particular to the failure to use artillery before battle was joined. But Rupert's real crime had been allowing Digby to hold such sway over a malleable monarch. This time, the secretary of state could not resist the opportunity to kick his rival while he was down.

CHAPTER ELEVEN

NO HOPE OF BETTER THINGS

*'Sir, the Crown of England is and will be where it ought to be, we fight
to maintain it there; but the King, misled by evil counsellors or through
a seduced heart, hath left his Parliament and his people, under God
the best assurance of his Crown and family. The maintenance of this
schism is the ground of this unhappy war on your part, and what sad
effects it hath produced in the three kingdoms is visible to all men.'*

Sir Thomas Fairfax's Summons to Prince Rupert,
outside Bristol, 4 September 1645

Rupert was aware that the defeat at Naseby left him vulnerable to his
enemies at Court. A ciphered letter to his great friend Legge, the
governor of Oxford, reveals a wearied acceptance of his exposure:

Dear Will,
... Pray let me know what is said among you concerning our defeat.
Doubtless the fault of it will be put upon Rupert ... Since this business,
I find Digby hath omitted nothing which might prejudice Rupert, and
this day hath drawn a letter for the King to Prince Charles, in which he
crosses all things that hath befell here in Rupert's behalf. I have showed
this to the King, and in earnest; and if, thereupon, he should go and
send it, I shall be forced to quit generalship ...
Your faithful friend,
Rupert.[1]

Digby's servant, Felton, spread the slander that, on seeing the size of
the army arrayed against the Royalists, Lord Astley had tried to stop
Rupert from fighting. The prince had disregarded the veteran's advice,
Felton said, so must take full responsibility for the ensuing disaster; by
implication, Digby's insistence on fighting was not to blame.

Felton was lying, but in the aftermath of defeat, with scapegoats much sought after, the falsehood took root. Legge, eager to salvage the prince's reputation, asked Digby to explain whether he was behind the slander. He received a less than straightforward reply, from a man that – even his Parliamentary enemies acknowledged – had a way of producing, 'good lines, at which he is as good as the best'.[2]

> My dear Governor,
> ... I am sure that Prince Rupert hath so little kindness for me, as I daily find he hath, it imports both to me and mine to be much the more cautious not to speak anything that may be wrested to his prejudice. I can but lament my misfortune that Prince Rupert is neither gainable nor tenable by me, though I have endured it with all the industry and justness unto him in the world, and lament your absence from him ...
> But I conjure you, if you preserve that justice and kindness for me which I will not doubt, if you hear anything from Prince Rupert concerning me, suspend your judgement. As for the particular aspersion upon him which you mention, of fighting against advice, he is very much wronged in it, whether you mean in the general or in the particular of that day ...
> I shall only say this freely to you, that I think a principal occasion of our misfortune was the want of you with us; for had you been there, I am persuaded that when once we have come up so near them as they could not go from us, you would at least have asked some questions ...
> Well, let us look forward; give your Prince good advice as to caution, and value of counsel, and God will yet make him an instrument of much happiness to the King and kingdom, and that being, I will adore him as much as you love him, though he should hate as much.
> Your faithfullest friend and servant,
> George Digby[3]

Legge, usually so measured, started his reply with customary reserve. However, he could not hide his anger for long:

> My dear Lord,
> ... I do assure your Lordship it was out of great respect to you that your servant, Felton, did not feel a reward for his folly ... what I accused him of in my letter to you, were no more than what he confessed himself to me he reported; which was, that Prince Rupert did that day [at Naseby] fight contrary to the opinions of my Lord Astley ...

With people much distracted for the great loss, these words went far to the Prince's prejudice; and though he writes to your Secretary that this report was raised on him out of malice to you, he assures your Lordship it will not be beaten out of the heads of many that his report was out of malice to the Prince.

I am extremely afflicted to understand from you that Prince Rupert and yourself should be upon so unkindly terms, and I protest I have cordially endeavoured, with all my interest in his Highness, to incline him to a friendship with your Lordship conceiving it a matter of advantage to my master's service, to have good intelligence between persons so eminently employed in his affairs ... But, my Lord, I often found this a hard matter to hold between you; and truly, my Lord, your last letter to me gives me some cause to think your Lordship not altogether free from what he often accused you of as the reason of his jealousies; which was, that you did both say and do things to his prejudice contrary to your professions, not in an open and direct line, but obscurely and obliquely; and this way, under your Lordship's pardon, I find your letter, in my understanding, very full of. For, where your Lordship would excuse him of the particular and general aspersions, yet you come with such objections against the conduct of that business, as would, to men ignorant of the Prince, make him incapable of common sense in his profession.

For my part, my Lord, I am so well acquainted with the Prince's way, that I am confident all his General Officers and Commanders knew beforehand how or in what manner he intended to fight; and when, as you say, all mankind were of opinion to fight, his part was to put it in execution ... And, for the not calling of a Council for the instant, truly, the Prince having before laid his business, were there need of it, the blame must be as much yours as any man's ...

I cannot but conceive it the partiality of your Lordship's wonted favours towards me, that you impute the misfortune of the day to my absence ...

But your Lordship says, you write none of these things with reflection; yet, let me frankly tell your Lordship, no impartial man that reads your letters to me and others, will free you from that, nay, charge you with it in a very great measure: and this truth you must pardon me in declaring to you. And assure yourself you are not free from great blame towards Prince Rupert; and no man will give you this free language at a cheaper rate than myself, though many discourse of it.'[4]

*

Legge wanted Digby to understand that there were many in the Royalist camp who knew him for what he was and heartily despised him. Legge also needed Digby to appreciate that he was among those who preferred to look to Rupert for honest leadership, to rescue them from a rampant Parliament, and from the danger of sly, self-serving courtiers.

A surprising optimism pervaded the Royalist ranks immediately after the drubbing received at Naseby. The king and Rupert had made for Hereford, quickly linking up with Gerard's 2,000 men, who could have made such a difference in Northamptonshire, days before. Charles still believed he had enough men to form an effective force: 4,000 of his cavalry had escaped from Naseby and there was also Goring's army of 9,000 men in the southwest, as well as Montrose's Irish and Scots in the Highlands. An air of denial hung over the scattered Royalist forces, as they dreamt of a new dawn.

Small triumphs followed, fanning the flames of unreality. A further recruitment drive was ordered for Wales, in the hope that another infantry corps could be raised. In the general euphoria that followed the trauma of defeat, nobody wanted to acknowledge that Naseby had seen not just a haemorrhaging of men, but also a mass forfeiting of arms: the muskets required to arm the force had been left scattered on the battle-field, providing a bountiful harvest for the victorious Parliamentarians and leaving the Royalists woefully short of firepower.

Meanwhile, the prince had to move to the southwest, his dual mission a liaison with the Prince of Wales and the bolstering of Bristol's defences. The king was considering transferring there from Oxford and planned to ferry his new, Welsh recruits across the Bristol Channel as soon as they were ready. Further urgency was caused by fear that Fairfax might besiege the city – the general had quickly recaptured Leicester and was now moving southwestwards to tackle Goring outside Taunton.

Goring quickly lifted his siege and tried to avoid the approaching force, which outnumbered him two to one. However, on 10 July, he was taken by surprise at Langport: although few of his men were killed during the battle, half his cavalry was captured. Goring retreated into the southwest peninsula, leaving Fairfax with an empty stage. The New Model Army, its confidence boosted by a success it attributed to divine favour, now pushed on, quickly storming Barnstaple, and then taking Bath and Sherborne before July was out. Lord Digby lost Sherborne:

his Royalist enemies were suspicious of this defeat, wondering whether the secretary of state had treacherously brought about this reverse, in collusion with the Roundheads.

After Langport, Rupert recognised that his uncle's cause was lost. Charles had greeted the reversal of Naseby with his usual dilatoriness: he passed three weeks in Ragland Castle with 'sports and entertainment' in the morning, and engaging in 'controversies on questions of divinity in the evening'.[5] The prince wrote from Bristol to his friend the Duke of Richmond, on 28 July, urging him to let the king hear from a trusted mouth what was evident to so many. Rupert's advice was that 'His Majesty hath now no way left to preserve his posterity, kingdom and nobility but by a treaty. I believe it a more prudent way to retain something than to lose all.'[6] No doubt he was mindful of his father's fate, after accepting the throne of Bohemia.

The king took the advice in the right spirit, accepting the military reality of the situation while looking for salvation from a higher power: 'If I had any other quarrel but the defence of my religion, crown, and friends, you had full reason for your advice. For I confess that speaking as a mere soldier or statesman, I must say there is no probability but of my ruin. Yet as a Christian I must tell you that God will not suffer rebels and traitors to prosper, nor this cause to be overthrown, and whatever personal punishment it shall please him to inflict on me must not make me repine, let alone give over this quarrel.'[7] This letter was intercepted, the vulnerability of the monarch's lines of communication a symptom of Parliament's tightening net.

Rupert had expected the king to head for Bristol, where he hoped to provide his uncle with protection. However, to Rupert's consternation, he learnt that Charles was contemplating heading to Scotland with his cavalry – a 'strange undertaking', in Rupert's estimation, which seemed, at best, to have a slim chance of success. The prince also worried that the Royalist position in the south, already precarious, would be made desperate if deprived of its figurehead.

Rupert felt increasingly isolated from his uncle. Unaware that many letters from the king had gone astray, he wrongly concluded that Charles's apparent silence reflected anger at his frank advice. 'He did send me no commands,' Rupert grumbled to Will Legge, 'and, to say truth, my humour is to do no man service against his will. They say he is gone northward. I have had no answer to ten letters I wrote; but from the Duke of Richmond, to whom I wrote plainly, and bid be plain with the King, and desire him to consider of some way which might lead to a treaty, rather than undo his posterity. How this pleases I know not; but, rather than not do my duty, and speak my mind freely, I will take his unjust pleasure.'[8]

A week later the king wrote revealing his continuing affection for his nephew and his abiding optimism that the royal cause would prosper in the end: 'And now, because it is possible that it will be a long time before I see you, I earnestly desire you to have an implicit faith in my friendship and affection to you, for I assure you I hold myself interested equally to protect you as one of my children; so that you shall share largely with me, if ever it shall please God to send happy days unto Your loving Uncle and most faithful Friend, Charles R.'[9]

It seems strange, the king's acceptance of his military commander's absence from his side, when so hard-pressed by a rampant enemy. However, Rupert was happy to distance himself from his enemy, Digby, explaining in cipher to a curious Legge: 'You do well to wonder why Prince Rupert is not with the King, but when you know the Lord Digby's intentions to ruin him, you will then not find it strange. But all this shall not hinder me from doing my duty where I am.'[10] This was written from Bristol, scene of one of Rupert's greater triumphs earlier in the war, but now a city in peril: it was increasingly cut off from the rest of the Civil War by a naval blockade and encircling Roundhead land forces. The speedy capture of Bridgwater on 23 July, after concerted attacks, gave further evidence of the effectiveness of the New Model Army: the town had been expected to withstand a lengthy siege, despite Goring's defeat at nearby Langport. Its fall deprived the Royalists of a useful staging post for arms and supplies in the west and southwest.

Bristol was in a wretched state, impoverished by the continued warfare and afflicted by a summer outbreak of plague: 'They have few carts in the city,' a rebel wrote, 'but carry all upon their heads, for the most part. The sickness is still hot in the town, and it is also in the great fort, and in the castle; yet Sir Thomas Fairfax keeps Rupert and some others of note in Bristol, and draws out the line, and is in good hopes to take it, the citizens, for the most part, longing to be rid of the Cavaliers.'[11] Against this desperate backdrop, Rupert had to meet an imminent, full-blooded siege.

The prince reacted to the threat with his usual drive. He set his men to work, stiffening the city's flimsy defences and foraging for food. A rough census of the city informed him that 2,500 families – approximately

12,500 inhabitants – would need provisions. He told the citizens to prepare for a six-month siege. Those that were unable to afford extra supplies were assisted by 2,000 measures of corn, ordered by Rupert from Wales. Cattle from the surrounding area were driven into Bristol, to provide milk and beef during the coming blockade. However, despite the prince's efforts, the city could not be properly prepared for the rebels' arrival: 'The townsmen', Parliament was informed, 'being unprovided for a siege, have great scarcity of victuals, which, [it] is probable, may cause them to mutiny, but indeed the castle, and the Prince's fort, the great fort, where Rupert quarters, is well victualled.'[12] On 12 August the prince wrote to his uncle that, provided the citizens did not rise up, he hoped to be able to hold Bristol for four months. Given the lesson of Bridgwater, and the small size of the Bristol garrison, this assessment owed more to bravado than to realism.

Unsure of the citizens' support, Rupert tried to pacify the 'clubmen' of the southwest. These were civilian resistance fighters who, fed up with the abuses of Royalists and rebels, had taken to attacking both their tormentors. Their rudimentary weaponry was offset by their passionate desire to protect their property and families. By this stage of the war, with Parliament's forces increasingly disciplined, Charles's forces were more often seen as the clubmen's enemy. The Royalist Sir John Oglander conceded that some of his colleagues had brought their animosity on themselves: 'They imputed their failures to want of money, for they would idly spend it as fast as they had it, not caring how they burdened the country, thereby making of their friends their enemies.'[13] Rupert was unable to appease the clubmen: they had been too alienated by past Royalist excesses to be brought to heel now.

The Parliamentarian army continued to close in: Sherborne Castle (Sir Walter Raleigh's old home) was stormed, Bath was abandoned, and Frome was captured. Rupert was left to face the rebels with a garrison of just 1,500 men and a very limited supply of gunpowder – pleas to Sir Edward Nicholas for reinforcements and armaments had gone unheeded, and the one Royalist ship sent to help him was kept at bay by the rebel fleet. The prince found himself with the same problem that Nathaniel Fiennes had faced, the previous year, when Rupert had attacked Bristol: how to defend the city's 4 miles of perimeter walls, with their sporadic fortifications and with an inadequate force?

Rupert and his senior officers became increasingly despondent. Nothing had been heard from the king or his advisers for an age and there seemed to be no hope of relief. Meanwhile, irreplaceable provisions were being consumed quickly. The prince summoned his council of war – 'composed', in Warburton's words, 'of the most daring and gallant men that the war had spared'[14] – and examined the choices left open to them. Baron de Gomme, Rupert's Engineer-General, gave a grim account of the defences' shortcomings, concluding that the thin, low walls of the city would not be able to withstand a vigorous assault.

The council of war contemplated Rupert's breaking out from Bristol with the cavalry, leaving the infantry to fend for itself, but, it was later revealed, 'This, by all of us the Colonels of posts and Officers, was thought neither safe nor honourable.'[15] A second fighting option was for Rupert to pour his best troops into the castle and fort, and to hold these bastions for as long as possible. However, all present knew that everyone not chosen for this task would be at the mercy of the enemy. Besides, the castle and fort would not be able to hold out for long. 'Seeing that neither of the former ways could be taken,' the surviving members of the council were to recall, 'we were all resolved to fall upon the best general defence that could be made of the whole, wherein we might all share alike.'[16]

On 22 August, units of the New Model Army arrived outside Bristol, in advance of the main force under Fairfax and Cromwell. The prince sent Sir Richard Crane, recognised by rebel pamphleteers as a 'great favourer of Rupert's',[17] to skirmish with the approaching enemy. Crane's mission was short-lived: he was shot through the thighs – serious wounds that soon led to his death. This was one of several losses that further demoralised the prince: Sir Bernard Astley (son of Lord Astley, the erstwhile Royalist infantry commander) was ambushed, wounded in the shoulder and leg, and captured; and Colonel Daniell, who had been present at the attempted arrest of the Five Members, was shot seven times in the same action, ignorant surgery ensuring a speedy despatch. These casualties underlined the cost of pointless resistance.

Fairfax spent the following week laying the foundations for an armed assault. While rebel spies tried, unsuccessfully, to foment insurrection in the city, Fairfax pushed his cannon and his ships hard against the Royalist defences, 'and so hath made Bristol an in-land-town'.[18] Fairfax was aided by 2,000 clubmen, who beat a Royalist garrison out of Portishead.

Bristol's defenders experienced growing tension. They expected a

night attack each time that dusk fell, and their nerves and reserves of
gunpowder were worn down by dummy attacks on successive nights.
Rupert twice ordered his men to prepare to venture out against the
Roundhead encirclement, but he backed down on both occasions.
Fairfax's men grew in confidence: 'Rupert is resolved of a desperate sally,' one of his officers informed the Speaker of the House of
Commons from the front line. 'I hope he will be received, these two
nights past, he prepared but durst not come out: This morning at break
of the day, I never saw men take Horse and advance more cheerfully
than ours did, having an Alarum that he was coming.'[19] Rupert was no
longer the feared Royalist talisman of the early years of the war.

On 29 August the New Model Army erected a bridge across the
Avon: it now had a foothold on both sides of the river, completing the
city's isolation. Six days later, Fairfax sent a trumpeter into Bristol, formally summoning Rupert to surrender. Pamphleteers painted the scene
with relish: 'So soon as the Prince received the paper,' one propagandist
alleged, tapping into the caricature image of the Cavalier, 'he looking in
it, swore God damn him it was a summons, and called for a cup of sack
and sat down and read it and detained the trumpeter in Bristol.'[20]

The manner in which Fairfax addressed the prince shows regard for
a distinguished foe, whose lineage and character demanded respect: 'I
take into consideration your Royal birth, and relation to the Crown of
England, your honour, courage, and the virtue of your person', Fairfax
wrote. He then played on the well-known division between the prince's
and Digby's factions, claiming that, in the suppressing of the king's
'evil counsellors', Fairfax and Rupert shared a common cause: 'to bring
those wicked instruments to justice that have misled him, is a principal
ground of our fighting',[21] the rebel leader stated.

At the same time, Fairfax presented the surrender of Bristol as a
chance for Rupert to wash clean his bloodstained hands, and to repay
the Palatine debt to their doughty English allies: 'Let all England judge
whether the burning of its towns, ruining its cities, and destroying its
people be a good requital from a person of your family, which hath had
the prayers, tears, purses, and blood of its Parliament and people; and,
if you look on either as now divided, which hath ever had that same
party both in Parliament and amongst the people most zealous for their
assistance and restitution, which you now oppose and seek to destroy,
and whose constant grief has been that their desires to serve your family
have been ever hindered or made fruitless by that same party about his

Majesty, whose counsels you act, and whose interests you pursue in this unnatural war.'[22]

There was enough in Fairfax's clever construction to intrigue the prince. Surrender was a difficult concept for a former prisoner of war, whose proud reputation was to meet potential reversals with bold attack. The accusations cast against Digby and his clique resonated with Rupert. Similarly thought-provoking was the reminder of what would happen if the New Model Army were forced to attack. Prince Rupert and his senior officers, all seasoned fighters, knew the rules of war: a failure to surrender could expose not only their soldiers and the citizens of Bristol to the mercy of the Parliamentarians, but would also endanger the lives of the wives of Royalist officers who were in the city. Futile death and widespread destruction would be the only rewards for stubborn resistance.

Fairfax set about further undermining Royalist morale. He took to eating in the open, clearly confident of success and ready to deliver the final attack at any moment. He emphasised the point by inspecting his troops and Rupert's defensive lines in full view of the Royalists. 'And when the General had viewed all, he came to his own Cannon, and viewed them all to see how they were planted, and how levelled, particularly the great twisted piece . . .'[23]

Rupert stalled. He asked for permission to send to the king, to gain his approval for the surrender. Fairfax, who knew what the prince did not – that Charles was within 60 miles of the city and that Goring was also hoping to come to Bristol's relief – refused this request. Rupert then demanded that Sir Thomas have his Summons sanctioned by Parliament, in London. This attempt at time-wasting was dismissed out of hand: the prince had overplayed his extremely limited hand.

At 2 a.m. on 10 September 1645, the New Model Army began the storming of Bristol. Four great guns signalled an attack every bit as ferocious as Rupert's assault of the previous year. Major Price, a Royalist, held the fort for three hours, before being overwhelmed by rebels on scaling ladders: no quarter was offered – he and all his men were slain. Meanwhile, the clubmen caused terror around Bedminster, forcing Rupert's men back towards the city's centre. 'Ours being made masters of the most part of the Town,' recalled a Roundhead eyewitness, 'Rupert fled into the Castle; our men being about to plant Pieces [of artillery] against it, Rupert sent for a Parley to them: the Soldiers were unwilling, but the General, out of his noble resolutions to spare the Town, Rupert having fired it in three small places, condescended to it, which by six that night produced these Articles ...'[24]

It was agreed that Rupert could lead his men out of the city to any Royalist stronghold within 50 miles of Bristol, with colours flying, drums playing, and swords by their sides. The ordinary soldiers were to take with them all their personal possessions, without being searched or molested by Parliamentary troops. Rupert's officers and lifeguards were to be allowed to remain fully armed. The sick and wounded were to be permitted to follow when they could. The citizens of Bristol were not to be harmed in any way. Fairfax was to occupy the city and keep all remaining military accoutrements. These included 100 pieces of ordnance, 7,000 muskets, and 10 small ships. The really significant prize, however, was the city itself – the last major port held in Charles's name had fallen.

Rupert made as dignified an exit from Bristol as was possible. Oliver Cromwell, second-in-command of the New Model Army, accompanied the prince from the castle's gate to the outside of the city, where Fairfax greeted him. 'The Prince was clad in scarlet,' remarked an eyewitness, with reluctant admiration, 'very richly laid in silver lace, mounted upon a very gallant black Barbary horse; the General [Fairfax] and the Prince rode together, the General giving the Prince the right hand all the way.'[25] The great civility with which he was treated by the victors made a deep impression on Rupert. 'All fair respects between him and Sir Thomas Fairfax; much respect from the General Cromwell. He gave the gallant compliment to Major Harrison, "That he never received such satisfaction in such unhappiness, and that if ever in his power, he will recompense it".'[26]

Behind Rupert followed a mixed procession that comprised 1,100 soldiers, 40 of his noblemen's and senior officers' wives, 80 clergymen, and 450 horses. It was expected that this column would head for nearby Worcester, where Prince Maurice was dangerously ill with the plague, but when he arrived at the green outside Bristol, Rupert announced that his destination would be Oxford. Rupert asked for, and was given, muskets, to stave off attacks from the clubmen. These weapons were to be returned to the Parliamentary escort on reaching Woodstock.

Colonel John Butler was one of the senior New Model Army officers accompanying Rupert on this journey. On completion of his mission, he wrote to Sir William Waller, with his impressions of the prince: 'I had the honour to wait upon his Highness Prince Rupert with a convoy from Bristol to this place; and seriously I am glad I had the happiness to see him, for I am confident we are much mistaken in our intelligence concerning him. I find him a man much inclined to a happy peace, and will certainly employ his interest with his Majesty for the accomplishing of it. Therefore I make it my request to you, that you will use some means that no pamphlet be printed that may derogate from his worth for the delivery of Bristol. On my word he could not have held it, unless it had been better manned.'[27]

Rupert could not rely on such magnanimity from his own side. Marston Moor had punctured Rupert's aura of invincibility, while Naseby had further tarnished his reputation. With the fall of Bristol, Digby looked to administer the *coup de grâce* to an exquisitely vulnerable foe.

CHAPTER TWELVE

A MATTER OF HONOUR

'Tell my son, that I shall less grieve to hear that he is knocked on the head, than that he should do so mean an action as the rendering of Bristol Castle and Fort upon the terms it was.'

Charles I to Sir Edward Nicholas, chief adviser
to the Prince of Wales

'But is Bristol taken?' Parliament's *Moderate Intelligencer* taunted, pinching himself with delighted disbelief, 'And in less than three weeks? Fortified four times as well as when Colonel Fiennes was in it, and more men, and the cream of the Royal army. Poor Prince Rupert! "The sentence of death must surely pass on you!" Why not retreat to the castle; the King on one side and Goring on the other, within 60 miles of you!'[1]

In truth, there had been no chance of Charles's relieving Bristol: although he was, in theory, only five days' march from the city, he was closely shadowed by one of Parliament's finer generals, Sydenham Poyntz. Poyntz would have intercepted any attempt by the king to come to his nephew's aid. Besides, if scouts had reported Charles's approach, Fairfax would still have had time to storm the Royalist defences and eliminate the garrison before the main field army arrived. The king would then have been caught in a pincer movement, between his and Poyntz's armies, finishing off the task that Naseby and Langport had narrowly failed to complete.

Rupert knew that the war was lost, whether he held Bristol or not. He had been convinced of the inevitability of defeat since Naseby, if not before. His uncle's obstinate refusal to negotiate flew counter not only to Rupert's, but also to Henrietta Maria's, advice. Meanwhile, the prince felt responsible for men who had served him bravely and deserved better than certain death in a hopeless cause. Fairfax's clever letter had reminded him of the dubious colleagues for whom they would be laying down their lives. Surrender was the only responsible option left open to the prince.

Lord Digby saw things differently and he made sure that the king shared his perspective. It was Digby who started the rumour that Rupert had surrendered the city for 8,000 gold Jacobus coins. He was certainly behind the allegation that Rupert had been in treacherous correspondence with his Parliamentarian brother Charles Louis – 'though', Prince Rupert's diary refuted indignantly, 'he never wrote one letter to him'.[2] The king believed Digby's slanders. When Charles wrote from Hereford, on 14 September, his tone was one of shock and bewilderment at Rupert's betrayal:

Nephew,
Though the loss of Bristol be a great blow to me, yet your surrendering it as you did is of so much affliction to me, that it makes me forget not only the consideration of that place, but is likewise the greatest trial of my constancy that hath yet befallen me; for what is to be done? After one that is so near to me as you are, both in blood and friendship, submits himself to so mean an action (I give it the easiest term) such I have so much to say that I will say no more of it: only, lest rashness of judgement be laid to my charge, I must remember one of your letters of the 12 August, whereby you assured me, (that if no mutiny happened,) you would keep Bristol for four months. Did you keep it four days? Was there any thing like a Mutiny? More questions might be asked, but now, I confess, to little purpose. My conclusion is, to desire you to seek your subsistence (until it shall please God to determine of my condition) somewhere beyond seas, to which end I send you herewith a pass; and I pray God to make you sensible of your present condition, and give you means to redeem what you have lost; for I shall have no greater joy in a victory, than a just occasion without blushing to assure of my being
Your loving uncle and most faithful friend.[3]

Charles's position had further deteriorated, the day after Bristol's fall: Montrose's remarkable run of success ended at Philiphaugh, when defeat was followed by the cold-blooded murder of the duke's Irish troops and their families. They had surrendered in good faith. The king felt beleaguered, with Parliament closing in on him from every direction. He looked to those closest to him to reverse the inevitable slide

to total defeat. In this pressurised context, Rupert's surrender attracted
the harshest of interpretations. Meanwhile, Digby remained a source
of unrealistic hope, seeing salvation coming from Ireland, France, and
even Scotland. The meek capitulation of Bristol was set against this
wild optimism and seemed to substantiate all Digby's past attacks on
Rupert.

Digby now struck hard at his enemies. The prince's loyal friend Will
Legge was removed as Oxford's governor and imprisoned. His replacement was Sir Thomas Glemham, one of Digby's acolytes. Rupert was
now confined to his room, with musketeers posted outside his door.
'The Lord Digby hath drawn up articles of high treason against Rupert,'
a rebel pamphlet claimed, 'and swears he shall have his head, or it shall
cost him a fall. The substance of the articles of treason against Rupert:

1. That he hath, several times, traitorously undermined the designs
   of the King and his Council, to the hazard of his Majesty's person, and the loss of his army.
2. That he hath, several times, betrayed his Majesty's forces to the
   enemy ... by engaging them wilfully, to their destruction.
3. That he hath traitorously delivered the fort and castle of Bristol
   to Sir Thomas Fairfax.
4. That he himself declared, that he did worse in losing Bristol, than
   Colonel Fiennes did, in delivering it up to the King.
5. That he made promise to the enemy, to seduce his Majesty to
   come into the Parliament; promising never to fight more for the
   King against the Parliament ...[4]

Rupert countered Digby's attacks, writing to his uncle: 'I only say,
that if your Majesty had vouchsafed me so much patience as to hear me
inform you before you had made a final judgement – I will presume to
present this much – that you would not have censured me as it seems
you do: and that I should have given you as just satisfaction as in any
former occasions, though not so happy.'[5]

Charles now publicly disgraced Rupert. An open letter removed him
from his commands, and disbanded his infantry and cavalry lifeguards.
He was ordered to leave the kingdom. If the prince refused to go, or if
he tried to stir up a mutiny, then Sir Edward Nicholas was to imprison
him.

Digby manoeuvred to keep the king away from Oxford, in order
to deny Rupert access to his impressionable uncle. Clarendon wrote:

'The Lord Digby, who had then the chief influence upon his Majesty's Councils, and was generally believed to be the sole cause of revoking the Prince's Commission, and of the Order sent to him to leave the Kingdom, without being heard what He could say for himself, found that the odium of all this proceeding fell upon him.' Prince Maurice made it clear that he blamed Digby for Rupert's fall from grace, and Lord Gerard fell in with the brothers.

To avoid 'the breaking of that cloud upon him, which threatened his ruin',[6] Digby took Charles to Newark. This was the main Royalist stronghold left in the north and, in the diarist John Evelyn's estimation, 'a place of the best security'.[7] However, Digby underestimated the prince's determination: Rupert was not a man to leave false accusations unchallenged, as his printed rebuttals of Parliamentary lies had repeatedly demonstrated. Now, accused of the basest betrayal, he decided to ride to Newark to plead his case in person.

The journey was largely across enemy territory. His eighty companions included Prince Maurice – who joined his brother at Banbury – Lord Molyneux, Sir William Vavasour, and Lord Hawley. They managed to cross Parliamentarian Northamptonshire without incident, before arriving at Burghley. The mansion had become a Roundhead garrison, its governor one of Rupert's deserters. This turncoat raised the alarm and ordered his men to attack the prince. The opposing forces lined up, and then charged one another. 'The Governor came with the gross of his body', Prince Rupert's diary recorded, 'and knowing the Prince, he came up with his pistol and missed fire, and then cried for quarter, but the Prince shot him dead. And then in a short time the rest fled.'[8]

Enemies in both camps had now rumbled Rupert's objective. Digby, desperate to block any rapprochement between uncle and nephew, sent frantic messages in the king's name, forbidding the prince's approach. Meanwhile, Parliament committed 1,500 men to hunting down Rupert and his confederates, and commanded its forces in Lincolnshire and Leicestershire to be on the look out for this dangerous troop of Cavaliers. A Parliamentarian colonel filed a report from Grantham, his inflation of the Royalist numbers betraying his fear at the princes' names: 'On Tuesday morning we received intelligence that Prince Rupert & P. Maurice were at Banbury upon their march towards Newark, some reported them to be twelve hundred, others six hundred; upon which intelligence all the horse belonging to this garrison, being three hundred, and four hundred more which lay at Stamford, were drawn to Colonel

Rossiter, to interpose between the King and the Princes ... No sooner were we marching, but from Leicester we received intelligence that the Princes were upon their march towards Belvoir, [so] we pursued them with all speed.'⁹

Arriving at a bridge near Belvoir Castle, Rupert found 300 Roundhead troopers barring his way. 'The Prince stood first toward the horse,' Prince Rupert's diary recalled, 'as if he would charge them, and then upon a sudden turned, and the enemy followed him; the Prince turned and fought them, and beat them twice, by which the other forces of the enemy being alarmed they came up to the Prince. Says the Prince to his people, "We have beaten them twice, we must beat them once more, and then over the pass and away", which accordingly they did.'¹⁰ Rupert led his men off at a gallop, his route helped by memories of a boyhood visit to Belvoir. He had spent many hours shooting rabbits on the estate and he still remembered various little-known paths through the woods: by twisting down these tracks, Rupert kept ahead of his pursuers.

He was riding fast, with twenty of his men, when they were suddenly confronted by forty Parliamentarians on a hilltop. 'Will you have quarter?' their officer shouted down. Rupert quietly ordered his men to keep close to him and 'to turn when he turned'. The rebels careered down the hill out of formation, eager to kill or capture the retreating princes and their retinue. Rupert suddenly spun his smaller force round in a counter-charge, killing several of the enemy and forcing the rest to flee. Lord Molyneux despatched a rebel on a strong mare and gave the horse to the prince, who 'fair and softly went to Belvoir.'¹¹ The next day Rupert and his party approached Newark.

Digby was still in favour with the king, Parliament's *Mercurius Britannicus* commenting: 'It is remarkable that Prince Rupert, and all the Protestant leaders should be deposed for Popish Digby ...'.¹² Learning of Rupert's approach, Digby persuaded the king to move further north. However, he and Charles had only reached Rotherham when they learnt of Montrose's defeat of Philiphaugh.

Despite this disaster, Digby urged an advance into Scotland: it seemed preferable to returning to Newark, where Rupert's arrival was imminent. Digby was allowed to lead the remnants of the Northern Horse into Scotland as general of the King's forces North of the Trent, an impressive title for one with such a limited military record. This command came to an inglorious end at Annan Moor, in the Borders, at the beginning of November: 'Hath not God wrought wonderfully for us in destroying their powers', a Parliamentary newspaper asked, 'and crossing their designes; Digby himself routed and fled, nearly escaping with his life, of which he knoweth not how short a list he hath behind.'[13] Digby escaped to the Isle of Man on a fishing boat. From there he moved to Ireland, hopeful of raising an army that he would bring to the king's aid in England. In this, he failed. The same month, Goring fled to the Continent, with a considerable amount of money. Rupert's foremost Royalist enemies were overseas, but there were other hostile faces to take their place.

When the prince arrived at Newark, his retinue swollen to 120 men, he found that Charles had lost control of the town: with defeat hanging in the air, it had descended into dissolute chaos. Twenty-four generals had found sanctuary there, and they and their senior colleagues were hard to discipline. Sir John Oglander, a Royalist knight, witnessed similar debauchery elsewhere: 'Truly all, or the greatest part, of the King's commanders, were so debased by drinking, whoring and swearing that no man could expect God's blessing on their actions.'[14] When Charles tried to establish order, he was ignored.

A large welcoming party greeted Rupert outside the town walls, while the king skulked inside. Rupert rode into Newark, dismounted, and to the consternation of Sir Edward Walker, an eyewitness, 'comes straight into the [King's] presence, and without any usual ceremony, tells his Majesty that he has come to render an account of the loss of Bristol,'[15] Charles refused to acknowledge his nephew's presence and, appalled by his insolence, walked silently to his supper table. The two princes followed him, standing by his chair, Rupert eagerly trying to open a dialogue. The king started to eat and addressed only Maurice.

Rupert's persistence eventually won through, though, and Charles agreed to his request for a court martial. Sitting in judgement were seven Royalist grandees, including the Earl of Lindsey (son of the general slain at Edgehill), Lord Astley, Lord Gerard, Sir Richard Willis (governor of Newark), Lord Bellasis, and John Ashburnham. Bellasis and Ashburnham were Digby's men, but the court martial's verdict was unanimous: the prince was declared innocent of cowardice or treachery. The panel accepted that Rupert would have defended Bristol 'to the last man; though the tender regard he had to the preservation of so many officers and soldiers, was the chief reason that induced him to capitulate for the whole; they having so long and faithfully served us.'[16] Charles's counterclaim – that he would have saved the city if his nephew had held out for longer – was rejected.

On 21 October the king was obliged to sign the humiliating verdict. He then declared he would be leaving for Oxford. His parting shot was the dismissal of Willis as governor, and his replacement by Digby's acolyte, Bellasis. This was a provocative decision that intensified the faction fighting in the Royalist upper reaches. Charles's authority was no longer intact, having been eroded by continuous defeat, and the deposed Willis protested vociferously at his demotion. 'He consulted his friends, at the head of whom was Prince Rupert', Sir Edward Walker recorded, 'and they all agreed that he should demand a trial by a Council of War for the misdemeanour, of which ... he was guilty.'[17] The king's concession of a trial to his nephew had established a dangerous precedent.

Rupert sought an immediate redress of Willis's grievances. The prince, Maurice, Gerard, and more than twenty of their followers burst in on the king while he was dining with Bellasis and his supporters. Charles sprang to his feet, startled at the invasion of his private quarters. Willis demanded that the king justify the dishonour done to him, before Rupert explained that he would offer Willis every support, since it was Willis's friendship with the prince that had cost him the governorship. Gerard, encouraged by his comrades' candour, went further, claiming 'that the appointment of Lord Bellasis was Digby's doing, that Digby was a traitor, and that he could prove him so.'[18]

John Evelyn wrote about this charged encounter in his famous diary: 'Digby's character, however, was supported by Bellasis, the governor, and several others; but the Princes, Rupert and Maurice, sided with Gerard. At length swords were drawn, and the King rushed in to part them ...'.[19] With peace restored, Charles agreed to speak to Willis – but only privately. However, Willis insisted that his complaint be dealt with in public. The king, his shock turning to anger, ordered Willis, Rupert, and their entire party, to leave the room. He then summoned his other generals 'and it was debated what course to take with these wild Cavaliers.'[20]

On reflection, Rupert and his partisans accepted that they had behaved with ill-considered haste. The ruffling of Charles's dignity demanded, and received, an immediate apology:

May It Please Your Most Excellent Majesty,
Whereas in all humility, we came to present ourselves this day unto

your Majesty, to make our several grievances known, we find we have drawn upon us some misconstruction of the manner of that, by reason your Majesty thought it appeared as a mutiny. We shall therefore with all humbleness and clearness present unto Your Majesty, That we the persons subscribed, who from the beginning of this unhappy war, have given testimony to Your Majesty and the world, of our fidelity and zeal to Your Majesty's Person and Cause, do think ourselves as unhappy to lie under that censure, and as we know in our consciences, our selves innocent and free from it; We do in all humility therefore (lest we should hazard ourselves upon a second misinterpretation) present these Reasons of our humblest Desires unto Your Sacred Majesty rather in writing than personally, which are these:

That many of us, entrusted in high commands in Your Majesty's service, have not only our Commissions taken away, without any reasons or causes expressed, whereby our Honours are blemished to the World, our Fortunes ruined, and we rendered incapable of trust or command from any foreign Princes, but many others (as we have cause to fear) designed to suffer in the same manner.

Our Intentions in our addressing ourselves to Your Majesty were, and our submissive Desires now are, That Your Majesty will be graciously pleased, that such of us as now labour under the opinion of Unworthiness, and incapacity to serve Your Majesty, may at a Council of War receive knowledge of the causes of Your Majesty's displeasure, and have the Justice and Liberty of our Defences against what can be alleged against us, and in particular concerning this Government.

And if upon the severest Examination, our Integrity and Loyalty to Your Majesty shall appear, that then Your Majesty will be graciously pleased, to grant us either Reparation in Honour against the calumny of our Enemies, or liberty to pass into other parts ...'[21]

It was clear that Rupert, Maurice, and their twenty co-signatories – all senior Royalist figures – knew the king's cause to be lost. Before long, they would be obliged to seek military employment overseas and they needed to have their reputations cleared. Unless this happened, other rulers might shun their services.

Charles summoned Rupert and Maurice to an awkward meeting, where much was left unsaid. The king told his nephews that he welcomed their constant support, given the desperation of his position. He assured them of his continued trust, before contradicting himself by warning them that switching allegiance would lead to their eternal shame.

Rupert restated his loyalty to his uncle and asked the king to state openly that the princes' clique had not attempted mutiny. This Charles agreed to do – but it appears that Rupert was unconvinced by this assurance and remained concerned by his uncle's hesitancy. On leaving the king's presence, the two brothers went to consult Gerard. They concluded that Digby and his faction were too firmly in favour for the king to treat them fairly or honourably. With regret, they decided to quit Newark.

The king watched from a castle window as the princes led away 400 of their supporters. Eyewitnesses recalled seeing tears in Charles's eyes as the column rode off.

Rupert took his men to Worton House, 14 miles from Newark. They later moved to Belvoir Castle, from where the prince wrote to Parliament on 29 October:

> My Lords and Gentlemen,
> Having determined, with my brother Prince Maurice, my Lord Stanley, Lord Gerard, Sir Richard Willis, and many other Officers and Gentlemen, to leave this Kingdom, being altogether disengaged from the service we have been in, it hath given me the occasion to desire this favour from you, that you would grant a pass and safe convoy for me, my brother Prince Maurice and these Noblemen and Gentlemen that came along with me, together with their servants, horses, and all necessaries, to go beyond the seas or to retire to their houses, as shall be most convenient for them. And I engage my honour for myself and them, that no act of hostility shall be done by us, and that there is no other design in our journey, but to go wherever our particular occasion or design shall lead us ...
> Your Friend and Servant,
> Rupert[22]

Parliament reacted with suspicion, unable to accept Rupert's transformation from feared enemy to humble supplicant: 'To me it seems a mystery', wrote *The Scottish Dove*, 'that the two German Princes, and 400 officers so much spoken of five weeks since, should seem to go out of the King's Garrison from Newark in discontent, and send in such haste to desire the Parliament's Pass to go beyond Sea, &c.'[23] Members asked Rupert's emissary, Colonel Henry Osborne, to give them more details: what were the prince's true intentions? Osborne was blunt: if the Parliamentarians failed to agree to the terms spelt out in his master's letter, Rupert would return to serve the king. This clarification caused such consternation, Osborne writing to his master, 'that, to draw you from that, they will consent to anything'.

In the same letter Osborne relayed rumours circulating in London from overseas. There was little good to report: Henrietta Maria was said to have accused Rupert publicly of selling Bristol to the enemy; and Rupert's younger brother Prince Edward was alleged to have converted to Catholicism after falling in love with the Queen of Poland's sister, prompting the Pope and the Emperor to favour him as the next Elector Palatine. Princess Elizabeth, Rupert and Edward's eldest sister, summed up the family's shame in a letter to her friend René Descartes: 'If you take the trouble to read the gazette, you must be aware that he has fallen into the hands of a certain sort of people who have more hatred to our family than love of their own worship, and has allowed himself to be taken in their snares to change his religion and become a Roman Catholic, without making the least pretence which could impose on the most credulous that he was following his conscience. And I must see one whom I loved with as much tenderness as I know how to feel, abandoned to the scorn of the world and the loss of his own soul (according to my creed).'[24]

More promising was Osborne's news that: 'At the last fight of my Lord Digby, he lost all his letters, which the Parliament took, and three score ciphers, by which they have deciphered most of the letters, which, before, they could make nothing of. And, this afternoon, a committee hath been reading many of them. Amongst the letters they last took, there was one from the King to your Highness, being an answer to a letter of yours, of July last, where you advised him to peace, and not to trust the Irish. This letter hath done you a great deal of right, and gained much of their good opinion.'[25] Rupert's reputation as a blood-thirsty warmonger was gradually unravelling.

Osborne wrote the following week to warn that Parliament had decided to grant the prince a pass, but only if he promised never to serve the king again. Rupert had already waived his rights to fight one enemy, the Holy Roman Emperor. He was reluctant to make a similar commitment now, even though his uncle's cause was clearly lost.

Captain Pickering, a Roundhead officer with a reputation for trustworthiness, took the conditional pass to Rupert at Worcester. Pickering's mission was to discover the two princes' intentions and then return to London immediately with his findings. Rupert and Maurice did not want to be rushed: they stalled the talks with Pickering while opening up a line of communication with the king through the Duke of Richmond. Pickering became restless: 'When he had stayed some days,' The *Moderate Intelligencer* reported, 'he went to the Princes, to desire them to let him know if they would accept of the Parliament's offer, that so he might return with an affirmative, or negative.'[26] The princes said they could not reply to Parliament until Osborne was safely returned from London. This was a fatuous argument, since Osborne had been delayed by illness, not by restraint. However, it won Rupert time to move with his retinue to Woodstock, from where he began to explore his options with the king.

Charles had travelled from Newark to Oxford. Four days after his return, the king pardoned and freed Will Legge. The rapprochement was incomplete: Charles refused to reinstate Legge as governor of the town. However, with Digby absent and the king increasingly despondent, Legge took the opportunity to advance Rupert's cause. The first conversation he had with the king, on his release, involved Charles's sorry retelling of his quarrel with his nephew. Legge was genuinely distressed at the news, viewing Rupert's return to favour as the only, faint hope of Royalist success. 'I have not hitherto lost a day without moving his Majesty to recall you', Legge wrote to the prince on 21 November, 'and truly this very day he protested to me he would count it a great happiness to have you with him ... The King says, as he is your uncle, he is in the nature of a parent to you, and swears if Prince Charles had done as you did, he would never see him without the same he desires from you.'[27] Charles was seeking an unreserved apology from his nephew.

'My dearest Prince,' Legge continued, five days later, '... I am of opinion you should write to your uncle, seeing your stay hath been so long in his quarters in Woodstock – you ought to do it; and if you offered your service to him yet, and submitted yourself to his disposing and advice, many of your friends think it could not be a dishonour, but rather the contrary, seeing he is a king, your uncle, and in effect a parent to you.'[28] But Rupert was not to be rushed, while Parliament's offer of safe passage overseas remained an option. He tried to persuade the king to seek peace and insisted that he 'put from him Digby and other Machiavellians', but Charles countered that such requests were 'no more than the Parliament demanded.'[29]

Seeing that Legge had failed to reconcile the prince to his uncle, other ardent Royalists chimed in. 'If my prayers can prevail,' wrote the Earl of Dorset, on Christmas Day 1645, 'you shall not have the heart to leave us all in our saddest times; and if my advice were worthy of following, truly you should not abandon your uncle in the disastrous condition his evil stars have placed him. Let your resolution be as generous and great as is your birth and courage. Resolve, princely Sir, to sink or swim with the King; adjourn all particular respects or interests until the public may give way to such unlucky disputes.'[30]

During the winter of 1645–6, the prince remained at Woodstock. Troops joined him from the neighbouring Royalist garrisons of Wallingford, Banbury, and Oxford. While there, Rupert and Maurice considered serving the Venetian Republic, raising troops in Hamburg and marching them through Holland. However, they passed up this opportunity in favour of their younger brother, Philip, a teenager eager to rival his elder brothers' military exploits. 'I could wish,' Charles Louis wrote to Elizabeth of Bohemia, 'either my brother Rupert or Maurice would undertake the Venetian employment, my brother Philip being very young to undertake such a task.'[31]

Eventually the two princes elected to fight on, in their uncles' name. Rupert wrote to Charles, acknowledging his poor conduct at Newark and enclosing a blank sheet of paper with his signature at the bottom: he was prepared to confess to whatever the king believed him to be guilty of. Charles was moved by this show of humility. 'The Prince went to Oxford, and the King embraced him', Prince Rupert's diary recorded, 'and, as has been said, repented much the ill usage of his nephew.'[32] The princes brought with them relatively few men: some had already returned to Charles, in Oxford; others had slipped away to other Royalist garrisons; and yet more had secretly negotiated places in the Roundheads' ranks.

The brothers' motive for rejoining their uncle stemmed from family loyalty, for the hope of any personal advancement or financial rewards was by now long gone: 'The low, sad, despicable condition of the Royal party, confusion and despair, is spoken of very much among themselves,' The *Moderate Intelligencer* reported with satisfaction, 'that there is now no other means left in view, but the reward or encouragement of honour.'[33] 'Poor cavalier,' wrote another gloating rebel at the end of 1645, 'thy condition is lamentable; though thou have Antichrist, the Pope, the Devil and all to thy friends, thou must submit.'[34]

Surrender became the Royalists' theme. Chester, the last lifeline connecting Charles to his Irish recruiting ground, fell on 3 February 1646. Later in the month the southwestern army was defeated after a valiant display at Torrington. On 2 March the Prince of Wales sailed for the Scilly Isles. Lord Astley was forced to lay down the arms of Charles's last field army, at Stow on the Wold, on 21 March. Oxford remained defiant, one of a handful of garrisons still in the king's service.

Fairfax now closed in on the Royalist headquarters, arriving in front of the town on 22 April. 'You may prove to what condition want will bring men,' remembered Sir John Oglander. 'The Lords at the siege of Oxford, through want of power and money, were so undervalued that you could hear a common soldier cry out in their watches, "Roundhead, fling me up half a mutton and I will fling thee down a Lord."'[35]

The king realised that Digby's fanciful hopes of salvation had come to nothing: the Pope was not going to finance an Irish invasion; and agents in Denmark, France, and Holland had failed to engage potential allies. Charles requested a return to Westminster, but was rejected by Parliament. It was clear that Oxford would soon fall and then the king would have no negotiating position. Rebel spies confirmed that Charles was contemplating flight. 'The King is still in Oxford,' Commissary Henry Ireton wrote to Fairfax, 'but now (as it is thought) does again intend to get away if he can: we shall be as vigilant as we can to prevent it, & do our utmost duty if he attempt it.'[36]

'About this time,' noted Prince Rupert's diary, 'the King sent for the Prince, and desired him to go, with what force he could, to convoy him to the Scots; which the Prince undertook, but would have a command under his Majesty's hand, else not. The King was then in debate, whether to Ireland or Scotland.'[37] Rupert advised against relying on the Irish and said his uncle should only approach the Scots if sure of their loyalty. He asked the king to write a letter, confirming that Rupert had categorically advised against a risky journey to an uncertain Scottish reception. This Charles did, appreciative of his nephew's concern, but convinced by the French ambassador, Montreuil, that the Scots would rally to their monarch.

During the early hours of 27 April Charles woke Rupert to say that he was immediately leaving Oxford for his northern kingdom. He would ride disguised as a servant, attending his chaplain, Dr Hudson, and the loyal John Ashburnham. Rupert asked to accompany them, but the king pointed out that the prince's great height would compromise an already precarious mission. The two men parted, unaware that they would never meet again.

Charles handed himself over to the Scottish army as they besieged Newark. He was immediately forced to order Bellasis to surrender the garrison, which he did on 8 May 1646. Oxford, Pendennis, Ragland, and Harlech were now the only places in England and Wales still in the king's hands.

At Oxford, the confinement of the siege failed to curb Rupert's appetite for action. One day, accompanied by Maurice, Gerard, and twenty others, he was riding outside the town walls when, recalled Prince Rupert's diary: 'The Parliament forces sent three bodies of horse against him, and they fell upon the Prince, and pressed him. There was some skirmishing, and two pages, Lord Gerard and Prince Maurice's pages, were wounded by picketing; whereupon one of the enemy called, "Lord Gerard – capon-tail!" and challenged him; and a lieutenant of the enemy shot the Prince in the shoulder, and shook his hand, so that his pistol fell out of his hand, but it shot his enemy's horse.'[38] The Roundheads tried to cut off Rupert's retreat, but he managed to summon reinforcements. He then led his men in a brave charge that harked back to the glory days of the Cavaliers. The enemy reacted as their comrades had done in years gone by, opening fire prematurely, before buckling under the impact of the Royalists. Many of the rebels were driven into nearby marshland, allowing Rupert to lead his men back safely to Oxford.

It was clear to both sides that the siege could not continue for long. Fairfax sought Oxford's immediate surrender, addressing his summons to Prince Rupert. However, the Prince passed the communication to Glemham – Oxford's governor, and therefore the garrison commander. Glemham, obeying the king's parting instructions, summoned a council of war. There were two main questions: how generous would Fairfax be with his terms; and what treatment could the most eminent Royalists expect from him? There was particular concern about the fate awaiting the king's second son, the 12-year-old James, Duke of York. With the Prince of Wales overseas, the rebels insisted that he: 'be delivered into the hands of Parliament to be disposed of according to their pleasure'.[39]

Rupert and Maurice had spent much of the war on the list of Royalists who would be shown no mercy if captured. However, Parliament now knew of Rupert's efforts for peace, and sympathised with his hatred of Digby and the so-called Papist faction. Rupert had sounded out the enemy in May: 'Pray see if you can find Sir Thomas Fairfax will think me worthy to receive an obligation from him by setting his thought upon the means of providing for some place of liberty and safety for me.'[40] Now he would find out what the rebels intended to do with him.

The capitulation took place on 24 June 1646, a day of heavy summer rain. Rupert, for the second time in a year, headed the procession of the vanquished. Oxford still had six months of supplies and seventy barrels of gunpowder when it yielded to the enemy. However, with the king a prisoner and the field army repeatedly defeated, the Royalist wartime headquarters was redundant. Two thousand men followed Rupert out of the town, 'well armed, with colours flying and drums beating'.[41] Nine hundred of them chose to return peacefully to their homes, while the greater part sought service overseas: the Thirty Years' War was nearing its climax on the Continent, assuring ready employment.

Fairfax gave Rupert and Maurice more generous terms than their uncle had offered them after the fall of Bristol. After animated debate, Parliament was prepared to allow the princes to stay in England for six months, attended by a retinue that included grooms, footmen, an apothecary, a gunsmith, a tailor, and two washerwomen. Among the more exalted company permitted to remain with them were Lord Craven, de la Roche, de Gomme, and Dr Watts, Rupert's chaplain. In return, the princes had to promise not to approach within 20 miles of London. At the end of the six-month grace, they must go overseas, never to return: 'A pass is to be granted to Rupert as is desired in his letter, with Maurice, and other gentlemen to go with them beyond Sea,' reported a Parliamentary newspaper, 'and without doubt, they may do themselves more good, and us less hurt, to serve the State of France, than against the Parliament of England. Let them march, it is an old Proverb, "Lay an Enemy a bridge of gold".'[42]

Fairfax waived the exclusion zone so Rupert and Maurice could ride to Oatlands, on the outskirts of the capital, to meet their elder brother, Charles Louis. Now that it looked likely that the Palatine would be his, the two younger princes wanted to know if Charles Louis planned for them to benefit from the family's restoration. Meanwhile, the Holy Roman Emperor had asked Charles Louis to establish whether his two younger brothers would be bound by the peace terms he was offering.

However, Rupert and Maurice were early victims of the growing tension between Fairfax's Puritan New Model Army and the predominantly Presbyterian Westminster. Prince Rupert's papers recorded sourly: 'The House of Commons, taking advantage of their coming within 20 miles of London, notwithstanding the liberty granted them by General Fairfax so to do, declared, June 26th, that [they] had broken the articles agreed upon [and ordered their party] to repair to the seaside within 10 days, and forthwith to depart the kingdom.'[43]

The two brothers quit England in separate directions: Maurice sailed for Holland on 8 July, while Rupert left for France, three days earlier.

CHAPTER THIRTEEN

FRENCH GENERAL

*'Why hast not thou Prince Rupert and thou Prince Maurice obeyed
the voice of her good Parliament, what a Devil made you stay so long
in England? ... But you would stay volens nolens until you lost all,
and now you must be enforced to go, and carry your cruelties, your
plunderings and all the mischiefs you have done along with you, to
make you the more welcome into another country.'*

A true Copy of the Welch Sermon Preached Before
the two Princes, Prince Rupert and Prince Maurice
at Dover, September 1646

Rupert travelled directly from Calais to St Germain, the palace that
housed Queen Henrietta Maria and her displaced Royalist court.
The Prince of Wales had joined his mother there, after brief stays on
the Scilly Isles and Jersey, and gave his cousin an enthusiastic welcome.
Rupert recalled that the greeting he received from France's Queen
Regent, Anne of Austria, was more fulsome than the one accorded him
by his aunt, the hostile Henrietta Maria.

The prince arrived at a time of embarrassing family scandal. His hot-
headed 18-year-old brother Philip had been delayed in his posting to the
army of the Venetian Republic and had remained at The Hague during
the summer of 1646. As a result, he witnessed at first hand the posturing
of a young and charming Frenchman, Jacques d'Epinay, Sieur de Vaux.
D'Epinay was witty and good-looking, and had quickly become a popular figure at Elizabeth of Bohemia's court: indeed, he publicly hinted
that he had become extremely intimate with the widowed queen, who
was clearly dazzled by his attentions. Investigations by jealous onlookers
revealed that d'Epinay had been forced to leave the French court after
seducing the lover of his patron, the Duke of Orleans.

Elizabeth's children were humiliated by the rumours surrounding
their mother and her controversial admirer. One day, finding the queen

walking with d'Epinay in the rain, Charles Louis knocked the favourite's hat from his head and berated him for wearing it in the royal presence. Elizabeth angrily turned on her son, explaining that she had given d'Epinay permission to do so.

The scandal reached new heights when d'Epinay boasted of his 'bonnes fortunes' with not just the queen, but also her favourite daughter, Princess Louise. Prince Philip, furious at the insult to his family's honour, challenged d'Epinay to a duel. However, the contest was prevented at the last moment. The following day Philip encountered d'Epinay in the street and sprung on him in a furious attack. Before he could be restrained, he had plunged his hunting knife into the Frenchman's neck and killed him.

The queen was appalled by her son's violence and by the death of her devotee. She refused to hear Philip's words of explanation and told him that she would never see him again. Princess Elizabeth spoke in defence of her brother and was similarly banished: she travelled to Brandenburg, to stay with cousins, and never again lived with her mother. With the French in The Hague demanding that Philip pay for his crime, he rode for the coast and sailed to Denmark, before progressing to Hamburg. There he began to raise troops for his Venetian commission.

Rupert and Charles Louis wrote to their mother, begging her to forgive Philip. Rupert's letter does not survive, but Charles Louis's does:

Madam,
My brother Rupert sending this bearer to your Majesty about this business, I cannot omit to accompany him with my humble request in favour of the suit he hath to you in my brother's behalf; which, since he can more fully represent it to your Majesty, and that I have by the last post acquainted you with it, I will not be farther troublesome therein. Only, Madam, give me leave to beg your pardon in my brother Philip's behalf, which I should have done sooner if I had thought that he needed it.

The consideration of his youth, of the affront he received, of the blemish [that] had lain upon all of his lifetime if he had not resented it; but much more that of his blood, and of his nearness to you, and to him whose ashes you have ever professed more love and value than to anything upon earth, cannot be sufficient to efface any ill impression which the unworthy representation of the fact by those whose joy is in the divisions of our family, may have made in your mind against him.

But I hope I am deceived in what I hear of this, and that this precaution of mine will seem but impertinent, and will more justly deserve forgiving than my brother's action; so I will still be confident that the good of your children, the honour of your family, and your own will prevail with you against any other consideration: and thus I rest
Your Majesty's most humble and obedient servant,
Charles
This 10th of July, 1646.[1]

The siblings' unity of purpose seems eventually to have softened the queen's heart. Two years later, we hear of Prince Philip at The Hague, with Rupert and Maurice. However, Philip's tale had no happy ending: in 1650, while serving as a cavalry colonel in the Spanish army at the siege of Rethel, he was killed leading his men into action.

Rupert soon realised that the end of the war had not brought a close to the rivalries that had riven Charles's closest supporters during the conflict. Faction politics thrived at St Germain. Although one of Henrietta Maria's favourites, Henry Jermyn, was friendly towards Rupert, the malevolent Digby had also taken root in this disaffected environment. With the king detained by the Scots – they had effectively kidnapped the monarch, while claiming they were offering him 'protection' – and no hope of the court being brought under control, Rupert decided to move on. Anne of Austria offered him any role in her son Louis XIV's armies that he desired, and he accepted her invitation. His sole condition was that he must be at 'liberty of entering into the service of [King Charles] wheresoever the state of his affairs would permit it'.[2] This was agreed.

Rupert asked for and received the rank of *mareschal de camp*, the equivalent of an English brigadier general. He was given 'a Regiment of Foot, a Troop of Horse, and the command of all the English in France',[3] amounting to 1,400 men. His senior officers included Rokeby, Sandys, Tillier, Holles, Hawkins, and Lunsford – many of them familiar from the prince's Civil War campaigns.

It was an exciting time for a foreign mercenary to fight for France: its alliance with Sweden was proving vigorously successful against the ailing Spanish Habsburgs. The French army was in the initial stage of a transformation that would see it mature into the mightiest military Juggernaut that Europe had seen since the fall of the Roman Empire.

From the end of Louis XIII's reign, the French cavalry had developed into a decisive battlefield force. In 1639, plans for a military stud were first mooted: its role was to produce numbers of strong, fast horses, for use in the Thirty Years' War. Four years later such forward planning was vindicated by the success of Condé's squadrons at the battle of Rocroi – a startling and compelling victory over Spain. This marked the beginning of six decades of triumphs on land, uninterrupted until defeat at the hands of the Duke of Marlborough and Prince Eugène of Savoy, at Blenheim, in 1704. In 1646, the year of Rupert's arrival in France, Marshal Turenne was given command of the combined Franco-Swedish forces in Germany. It was the start of a career that spanned thirty years, during which time he was to become Louis's greatest general.

It was a relief for the prince to find a reasonably senior role in an army ably led, without the distraction of domestic or court politics: he could concentrate on military matters and leave Henrietta Maria's band of self-serving dependants far away, to stew in their own bile. 'Her Majesty of England's servants begin to look sad,' The *Moderate Intelligencer* gloated from across the Channel, 'wages hath been wanting 17 months, and few big boons are there to be had, wheels go round, that sometimes above, is anon below; every up hill, hath a down hill.'[4] Everything seemed to be going wrong for the court-in-exile: 'Prince Charles has the spice of a fever', *Mercurius Diutinus* reported, 'but is now very well again and merry, desiring rather to come to the Parliament of England than be anywhere: Provided it be with (the King) his Father's leave. But the English Lords, and Officers in France, their hearts are all broke to pieces in madness.'[5]

Free from this atmosphere of negativity, Rupert busied himself recruiting for the coming campaign. He sent old colleagues to Britain, to cajole former stalwarts into joining his ranks. 'Sir,' he wrote to Sir John Owen, a Welshman with a distinguished Civil War record, 'I have taken this opportunity of Colonel Donnell's coming into your country to make his levies, to invite you into the King of France's service, where I have taken conditions to command all the English, and should be glad that you would raise men for his service.' Rupert pointed at the generous rates of pay available in the French army: 'The particular condition you will receive from Colonel Donnell, which are much better than other Princes give.'[6] This element would have appealed greatly to Rupert: he had left England no richer than he had been on his arrival. Louis's liberal pay was extremely welcome.

*

For the prince, the 1647 campaign was busy and dangerous. Reports reached Paris that 20,000 Spaniards were besieging Armentières north-west of Lille: if reinforcements could not come quickly, the border town must fall. Mazarin ordered Rupert to help relieve it. He joined a small French force of 7,000 men, jointly commanded by two marshals, Gassion and Rantzau. They were both ten years Rupert's senior, and they were both remarkable men.

Count Gassion was a Calvinist from Pau, in the Pyrenees. He had seen extensive service during the 1630s, first in Bavaria and central Germany, then in Lorraine, Flanders, and the Artois. His portrait shows a handsome, dark-haired man with a fine moustache, a tightly clipped beard, and an air of disgruntled impatience: Gassion was committed to soldiery, to the exclusion of all else, including his personal safety. He had vowed always to remain single, since he foresaw that his life would end on the battlefield and he did not want to leave behind a widow.

The count had risen quickly to the pinnacle of the French army. A *mareschal de camp* at the battle of Rocroi, he had urged his commander, the Prince de Condé, to attempt a bold cavalry manoeuvre that owed much to Gustavus Adolphus's tactics. Condé accepted the advice and unleashed a sweeping attack against the Spanish *Tercios* – substantial infantry formations that had previously enjoyed a reputation for im-pregnability. The plan worked spectacularly: the Habsburg positions were cracked open and overwhelmed. Gassion's reward for his part in the victory was a marshal's baton – the last of the thirty-four gained during Louis XIII's three-decade reign.

Gassion's style of command relied on his personal bravery and ruth-lessness. In January 1646 The *Moderate Intelligencer* reported a doomed piece of Spanish skulduggery: 'The Enemy had formed an enterprise upon the Town of Armentières, by means of intelligence he held with some of the burghers; but it was discovered by the care of Marshal Gassion, who hanged a captain to whom the government of the place had been promised, six burghers, and five soldiers.' After beating up the surrounding Habsburg forces and capturing all the personal goods of its general, the Marquis of Caracone, Gassion returned to Armentières 'wherein he proceeds with Justice against all the rest that are discovered to have dipped their fingers in this foul treachery'.[7]

Gassion's fellow commander was also a Protestant – Josias Rantzau, a German from near Kiel. A dogged warrior who had twice been a prisoner of war, he had left various body parts across the battlegrounds of Europe. Fighting in turn for the Dutch, the Danes, the Swedes, the Imperialists, and then the French, he accumulated sixty wounds, his most notable losses being an arm, an ear, an eye, and a leg. When he finally died, his epitaph dwelt on his astonishing physical resilience:

> Of the body of Rantzau, this is only one of the parts,
> The other half remains in the place of Mars.
> It dispersed everywhere its members and its glory,
> Pruned though it was, it remained victorious
> Its blood was, in a hundred places, the price of victory
> And Mars did not leave him anything complete but his heart.

It was Rantzau's exemplary personal courage, rather than his strategic ability, that had secured his selection as one of Louis XIV's first marshals. He was also governor of Dunkirk.

Personal valour and religion apart, Gassion and Rantzau had little in common. They share the distinction, however, of being unwittingly responsible for a sartorial legacy that lives on today. The two marshals championed the use of Croatian hussars, which they deployed as nimble, ruthless auxiliaries. The Croats wore thin white scarves around their necks, those of the officers made of silk, while the men's were of coarser material. These garments were gifts from their wives – reminders to be faithful while far from home and valiant in battle.

The French noted the casual élan of this garment, which they called the '*Kravata*' – a bastardised version of their term for Croatia. They contrasted its all-round practicality with the chore of keeping their own lace ruffs stiff and brilliant, and adopted the cravat for themselves. The tie's popularity in western Europe can therefore be traced back to Gassion and Rantzau's reliance on exotic Croatian horsemen. This curious association aside, the two marshals were awkward colleagues: they were poor communicators, a fact that hindered the relief of Armentières.

Prince Rupert arrived in the French camp outside the town at nighttime and was greeted by Gassion with the ominous promise: 'You will see a brave action here tomorrow.'[8] The next day Gassion took Rupert and two others to reconnoitre the enemy lines on the far side of the River Lys. They used hedges as cover to approach the water's edge, before Gassion signalled to his companions to wait where they were until he called for them. Prince Rupert's Logbook recorded what

happened next: 'Gassion was got up to a little house upon the side of
the river, like a ferry-house, and the Prince in the meantime heard the
stroke of an oar, as if a boat were rowing over the river, but he durst not
give Gassion any notice of it for fear of being overheard, and discovering him to the enemy. The Marshal stayed there till the people out of
the boat were landed, who sent one before them to see if the house were
clear; but as Gassion was peeping at the army from behind the house
one way, this discoverer was just upon the back of him at the other end
of the house.'[9]

Gassion was wearing a cape in the Spanish style. This, together with
his quick-wittedness, saved his life. 'What the devil do you here?' he
bellowed at the enemy soldier, pretending that he was a Habsburg commander. 'Get you gone to your quarter!' The marshal took advantage of
the soldier's momentary confusion and sprinted back to where Rupert
was hiding. '*Mon Dieu!*' cursed Gassion, getting his breath back, 'this is
always happening to me!' The prince replied, dryly: 'I don't doubt that
at all, if you do things like that often.'[10] The men then galloped back to
the French camp.

The following day Gassion advanced towards the Spanish lines surrounding Armentières, before summoning his generals to a council of
war. Rantzau took the opportunity to ask Rupert quietly what 'that
mad man Gassion' intended to do: he hoped he would not be tempted
to order a mounted attack, since the enclosed fields around the town
would make it impossible for cavalry to manoeuvre effectively. Rupert's
reply to Rantzau is unrecorded, but we know what he said, when asked
to share his opinion with the council of war on the best way to proceed.
The prince spoke with the experience of one who had repeatedly been
forced to fight in numerically inferior armies against larger forces – he
advised against attacking such a powerful enemy. Others agreed with
Rupert's view and Armentières was left to its fate, falling softly into
Spanish hands later in the year.

After the capitulation of Armentières, the victorious Spaniards
marched on towards La Bassée, shadowed by Gassion and Rantzau.
Gassion's fearlessness soon led Rupert into fresh danger. He challenged
the prince to accompany him on a reconnaissance mission: 'Are you well
mounted, Sir?' he asked Rupert. 'Shall we go see the army?' Intrigued,
the prince accepted the invitation and while Rantzau stayed behind
with the army, Rupert and Gassion rode off, accompanied by a couple
of volunteers. The party had not ventured far when it ran into two or

three enemy, Croatian hussars. When these turned tail, Gassion could not resist pursuing them – straight into the teeth of an ambush. A dozen men fired at Gassion and Rupert from a hilltop, while a troop of horses appeared behind them, cutting off their escape.

Fortunately, some of Rupert's inner coterie were within sight when the trap was sprung. While the prince and Gassion struggled to safer ground through marshland, reinforcements rode to their rescue. Mortaigne, Rupert's Gentleman of the Horse, and Sir Robert Holmes, the prince's page, led a small but determined charge into the Habsburg troops. In the fury of the ensuing firefight, Prince Rupert's diary noted: 'Sir Robert Holmes's leg was shot in pieces just below the knee, and his horse killed under him where he lay upon the place, and Mortaigne also was shot in the hand.'

Rupert saw that Holmes was struggling on the ground, in agony and with nobody coming to his aid. He rode back into the heat of the action, 'with great danger and difficulty', Mortaigne by his side. The prince hauled Holmes onto the back of his horse – Mortaigne was unable to help, because of his wounded hand – 'and so carried him off; not a man of the French volunteers coming to his assistance'.[11] Such erratic behaviour, by Gassion and his compatriots, left Rupert increasingly disillusioned.

In a relentless campaign, the prince was next in action outside the besieged stronghold of Landrecy. Mazarin ordered one of his marshals to slip a body of reinforcements into the town by a little-known path. This plan failed because of the incompetence of a local guide. The French were forced to retreat and Rupert was ordered to cover the withdrawal. He commanded four regiments – three of German cavalry, the other of Croats – against a pursuing force of six thousand of Spain's best troops and their own Croat auxiliaries.

Rupert showed great skill, overseeing the retreat while keeping the enemy at bay. He was just leaving one pass, with the entire Habsburg force snapping at his heels, when Gassion rode up to him in a quandary: his cannon had become bogged down – should he continue to withdraw, and leave the guns behind, or should he risk serious casualties while trying to extract them from the mud? Rupert calmly took control of the situation. He asked Gassion to send back two of his best infantry regiments – that of Picardie and the Swiss Guards – to provide covering fire, while the prince's men extricated the artillery. Rupert managed to save the guns and to retire, without losing a single soldier.

Rupert had barely completed this task when, that same night, he was summoned with his troops to begin the siege of La Bassée. He led his cavalry off immediately, leaving the French infantry to follow. The prince set about the siege with vigorous energy, digging his men in as soon as they arrived. Rupert was alerted to an attempt by Lord Goring – who had thrown in his lot with the Spaniards – to reinforce the garrison with his own English division, which consisted of 1,000 infantry and 200 cavalry. Goring was ambushed: 200 of his men were killed, a similar number were captured, and the rest scattered. The French again claimed not to have lost a man. This was such a successful action that it demanded notice overseas: English, Puritan pamphleteers reported Goring's reverses with relish, but – reluctant to compliment an even more prominent old foe – omitted to mention that Rupert was the leading light on the French side. Instead, Gassion received the accolades in London: 'following his own course with his accustomed vigour, by finishing his trenches'.[12] It was the right compliment, awarded to the wrong general.

La Bassée was difficult to attack, 'the Spaniards having spent many years in the fortifying thereof'.[13] It had fallen to them in May 1642 after a month's bombardment by a mighty force under General Francisco de Melle. More than 10,000 cannon balls had pummelled its walls and 3,000 of the attackers had died in the assault. An equally bloody action was anticipated now but, after three weeks, the Spanish commander opened negotiations with Rupert and La Bassée was quietly surrendered to the prince.

This was a success that aroused Gassion's envy, and relations between him and Rupert were never to recover. The effect of this was felt immediately. When the French army moved quickly to Lens, Rupert urged an immediate attack on the town by the Picardie regiment. However, Gassion resisted this advice and as a result the opportunity to take the town evaporated. The marshal led his disappointed force back to La Bassée.

Once there, Gassion invited the prince to accomany him on a minor expedition. Rupert, grateful for the distraction, agreed. He found himself joining a troop of eighty horses in a ride to Eysters, where Gassion was to discuss provisions for the cavalry with a commissar. Learning the marshal and prince's intended route, a peasant farmer went to Armentières to present the opportunity of an ambush to the Spanish commander. The Spaniard despatched one hundred musketeers to intercept the convoy on its return.

Rupert rode at the head of the detachment. The road was heading towards some woodland when the alert prince noticed 'a dog sitting upon his breech, with his face towards the wood'. He passed his distinctive red cloak to his page, Sir William Reeves, and told him to continue as though nothing was out of the ordinary. Rupert then rode up to Gassion, 40 yards ahead of him, with the urgent warning: 'Have a care, sir, there is a party in the wood.' The prince had barely uttered these words of warning when the ambush was sprung: a volley of shots rang out and Reeves was among the prisoners taken during the initial confusion. Rupert, keeping his wits about him, pushed his men forward, and they fought their way through the enemy.

Gassion, however, found the dangerous thrill of the situation irresistible. He turned his horse back towards the Spaniards and shouted: '*Mon Dieu!* Let us break the necks of these rogues!' He then removed his feet from his stirrups and made to dismount. Rupert and his officers took this to be a signal that they were also to alight. They assumed they would join the marshal in an attack on foot, relying on their pistols and swords against the enemy's muskets. But Gassion either changed his mind or never intended engaging with the enemy in this way: he suddenly rode off, leaving Rupert's party dismounted and exposed.

The Spaniards closed in and Rupert received the most serious wound that his varied military career was to garner: he was shot in the head. The blood-spattered prince was dragged from the fray by his men, conscious but in a dangerous state. When he eventually rejoined Gassion's main body, the marshal said gravely: 'Monsieur, I am most annoyed that you are wounded.' 'And me also,' retorted Rupert, with wry understatement.

This was to be the last of Gassion's death-defying escapades. While Rupert's physicians tended his serious injury, the marshal rode off to renew the siege of Lens. Risking his life once too often, Gassion was shot dead, a Spanish musketeer hitting him in the head. His lasting legacy was a reputation for bravery that frequently crossed over into eccentricity. At least his premonition of doom meant that he left behind no widow.

Rupert was sent to convalesce. He made a brief trip to Paris, where he paid his compliments to the Court and received praise for his bold efforts on Louis XIV's behalf. He then repaired to St Germain in October. There he received a letter from his uncle, written from Hampton Court.

Charles's hopes of salvation at the hands of his northern subjects had come to nothing: his Scottish enemies had effectively sold him to his English ones. The king's progress south showed he still enjoyed widespread popular support: crowds came to cheer him as he passed. He was held under lenient house arrest at Holdenby, the vast royal palace 7 miles to the northwest of Northampton. Charles and Henrietta Maria had halted there a decade earlier, during a triumphal progress through the Midlands. Now his presence was low-key: he enjoyed walking round Holdenby's gardens, played chess, and visited surrounding mansions for games of bowls. Sundays he devoted to private prayer.

The queen, meanwhile, was deeply concerned by her husband's plight: 'From Paris letters say that the Queen is of late much discontented,' announced *Mercurius Diutinus*, 'and troubled at the hearing of his Majesty's propounding to come to London, as being out of hope (if he do go to Holdenby, or other of Parliament's quarters towards London) that his designs will then never be completed.'[14] The nearer that Charles was taken to the capital, the more Henrietta Maria feared for his well-being. Her concern was well placed: the king's fate was bound up in growing tensions between Parliament, the New Model Army, and extreme political and religious bodies.

The New Model Army removed Charles from Holdenby to Newmarket, where negotiations began to see if a new, modified role could be found for the king. He was asked to surrender control of the militia for ten years, to trim the power of the bishops, and to exempt five of his leading supporters from a general pardon. The king seemed to be open to these proposals, prompting his captors to restore him to his palace at Hampton Court. In truth, though, he was merely stalling for time, looking for a way out of his worsening predicament. His words to Rupert smack of increasing agitation and despair, tinged with regret for past mistakes:

Nephew,
Amongst many misfortunes, which are not my fault, one is, that you have missed those expressions of kindness I meant you, which, I believe, was occasioned by your being in the army. It being likewise the reason that made me write so few letters to you. Besides, the truth is, as my condition is yet, I cannot say anything to you as I would; not being able to second words in the deeds. Wherefore excuse me if I only say this to you now, that, since I saw you, all your actions have more than

confirmed the good opinion I have of you. Assuring you that, next my children (I say next) I shall have most care of you or have your company. And, be confident that this shall be really performed by
Your most loving Uncle, and constant faithful Friend,
Charles R.
PS – I heard not of your hurt before I was assured of your recovery; for which nobody, without compliment, is gladder than myself . . .'[15]

Charles would have been disappointed to learn that the animosity between his nephew and his favourite blazed anew. Digby was now at St Germain, after failing to raise a Royalist army in Ireland, and headed up the faction at court that was most disagreeable to the prince. The differences between the two men were now so dire that, in October 1647, Rupert challenged Digby to a duel, to take place at a crossroads in the Forest of Poissy. Only Henrietta Maria's personal intervention stopped Rupert and Digby from fighting: she sent Lord Jermyn to confine Digby to his quarters. Digby was so rude to Jermyn that he rode to Rupert and offered his services as a second. However, before the duel could begin, Prince Charles arrived with some guards and arrested Rupert and his other supporters, who included Lord Gerard. Henrietta Maria ordered Rupert and Digby to explain their grievances and brought the matter to a peaceful conclusion.

The queen was unable to stop a similar contest between the prince and Lord Percy, five months later. Percy's intimacy with Digby, and his inadequacy as General of Ordnance, had long marked him as one of Rupert's greater enemies. The prince fought and wounded Percy, 'the Prince being', a contemporary reported, 'as skilful with his weapon as valiant'.[16]

The duel was a symptom of Rupert's unhappiness in the court-in-exile. He chose to look for action away from St Germain.

CHAPTER FOURTEEN

GENERAL AT SEA

*'The Mariners of several of the Royal ships set forth in this last summer's
fleet, being by the cunning insinuation of men ill affected to the Peace
of this Kingdom seduced, have treacherously revolted from their duty,
and do still persist in their disobedience, by which horrid and detest-
able act in breach of their trust, they have much blemished the honour
and credit of the Navigation, and Mariners of this Kingdom.'*

'A Declaration of the Lords and Commons', 14 July 1648

A short-lived, uncoordinated reignition of Royalist resistance in parts
of England and Wales flared up in 1648. Despite its brevity, the
Second Civil War was an intense affair, whose repercussions were felt
across Britain. Parliamentarian propagandists had sensed the coming of
renewed warfare and lashed out at those behind it: 'Blush for shame ye
bastards of England,' fumed *The Lamentation of the Ruling Lay-Elders*,
in July 1647, '(for legitimate children ye cannot be) that prosecute such
horrid actions, and hatch such Crocodiles eggs of Rebellion and murder,
that the very Infidels, Pagans, Turks, Saracens, and no Nation though
never so barbarous and cruel but would shame to own.'[1]

Loyalty to the Crown remained, to many people, not so much a
matter of political choice, but rather a cornerstone of personal creed.
As long as the king lived, he would always have supporters. A contemporary pamphlet involved an imaginary interchange between an old
Cavalier and an interrogator:

Question: 'Then it seems you have been for the King?'
Answer: 'I have, Sir, and am still, with all my heart to wish his honour
and safety, and I hold it my duty to do so.'[2]

The Second Civil War began in the spring of 1648 with a rising in Kent
led by Goring's father, Lord Norwich. His force soon combined with

a similar one from Essex, commanded by Sir Charles Lucas – who had fought bravely at Powick Bridge and had helped identify the Royalist dead at Marston Moor. When the New Model Army appeared in strong numbers, the Royalists fell back to Colchester, whose sturdy defensive walls were accentuated by a hilltop position and the protective waters of the River Colne. The garrison prepared for a siege they were confident they could withstand until help arrived.

The king must have greeted news of the rising with hope and relief, for his position was extremely precarious. He had attempted to flee the country, getting as far as the Isle of Wight before being imprisoned there, in Carisbrooke Castle. By now his repeated untrustworthiness had eroded his enemies' patience and his confinement took on a more restrictive air: 'The King is now kept from destructive Councils,' the House of Commons heard in mid January. 'His Majesty is sad, and spends much time in writing, and at his books.'[3]

The *Moderate Intelligencer* gauged the tone and the scope of Charles's island captivity: 'Here is a melancholy Court. Walking the round is the daily recreation'.[4] The king was denied his choice of worship: Episcopalianism was not permitted, so he refused to take Communion. Charles was constantly at loggerheads with his chief gaoler, Colonel Hammond, a servant of Parliament and an enemy of monarchy.

In London, it was believed that the coming year would be a decisive one for the king, yielding up freedom or death. A ditty of the time went:

> Poor Charles pursu'd in forty-one,
> Un-king'd in forty-seven;
> The eighth will place him on his Throne,
> In Earth, or else in Heav'n.[5]

When, thanks to Digby's slanders, Charles had been most questioning of Rupert's integrity, the prince had concluded a letter to the king with a declaration of infinite loyalty:

> Wherever I am, or how unhappy soever, and by your will made so, yet I
> shall ever retain that duty to your Majesty which I have ever, as
> Your Majesty's most humble, and most obedient Nephew, and faithful
> humble servant,
> Rupert[6]

The outbreak of the Second Civil War gave the prince a chance to honour his word. He hoped to join Prince Charles as he set off for Scotland, but Lauderdale urged Charles not to bring over a man, 'against whom both kingdoms have so just cause of exceptions'.[7]

However, the disjointed rebellion against Parliament on land led to a spectacular result at sea: the majority of the navy, which had lent such important support to Parliament in the Great Civil War, now declared for the king and sailed for Holland. Its sailors had been alienated by the increasing political and religious extremism of the government, and of the army.

Parliament was rattled. The Lords and Commons condemned the defectors, while offering an amnesty to all who returned to their service within twenty days: 'But if they shall after the said time prefixed expired persist still in their disobedience, then the Houses will proceed to the reducing of them by force, and doubting not of a good success by the blessing of Almighty God.'[8] At the same time the two Houses offered a generous inducement to those seamen who had remained loyal: they would each receive two months' wages as a bonus, once the renegades were defeated.

In July, rumours circulated London that the Prince of Wales had left Calais in a Dutch ship of thirty-five guns. Charles was sailing at the head of five lesser vessels, which some feared were destined for the north of England. 'But those of better judgements', wrote one correspondent, 'suppose that he is rather gone towards Holland. And it is more likely because diverse English officers are gone by land towards Holland.'[9] Heading the list of those believed to be accompanying the heir to the throne was 'Prince Rupert, the Palsgrave's brother'.

Rupert, still recovering from his serious head wound, had quit Louis XIV's service to rejoin the Royalist cause. The prince had, in the words of his private papers, 'been plied over again with the repeated offer of any conditions in the French service, before his going for Holland'.[10] However, he had always insisted that, if the chance arose to serve his uncle once more, he would feel obliged to take it.

Arriving at The Hague, Rupert found that Charles had been re-united with his younger brother, James, Duke of York. The teenager had escaped house arrest in St James's Palace during a game of hide and seek. He had slipped away and disguised himself as a girl, wearing a wig and a lady's cloak. He had then succeeded in crossing from Gravesend to Holland, his arrival giving a fillip to the court-in-exile and embarrassing his former captors.

James bore the title of Lord High Admiral. He hoped that he would be called upon to lead the ships that, like him, had recently quit England. However, Prince Charles insisted on commanding the squadrons himself. The royal heir led the fleet into the Downs, off the southeastern English coast, eager for action. Princes Rupert and Maurice were by his side.

The expedition was not a success. The Prince of Wales's ships were poorly provided for: the English sailor of the mid seventeenth century endured harsh conditions, in return for limited but inalienable rights. Of prime importance to him was his daily food allowance. This comprised 1 lb of bread, ½ lb of cheese, and ¼ lb of butter. He also expected adequate clothing. Prince Charles had neither the money nor the logistical support to see that these basic needs were met, and the men became mutinous. They insisted in putting to shore near Deal, in the hope of finding food and booty, but the foray was a shambles and a detachment of Parliamentary cavalry saw off the raiders. 'Upon this repulse,' Rupert's papers recorded, with disappointment, 'disorders and discontents increasing in the fleet, and all disadvantages being artificially improved, it was thought ... best to return to Holland.'[11]

On their way back across the North Sea, the Royalists met Batten and Jordan, two enemy naval commanders who professed loyalty to the Crown. This was especially surprising of Batten, a figure of hate among the king's supporters since firing on Henrietta Maria as she landed on the Yorkshire coast at the start of the Civil War. Now, to Rupert's bewilderment, the queen's son chose to knight the rebel vice-admiral. Batten assured his new allies that, if they waited where they were, he would ensure that they received supplies from London. None came.

Some of the Royalists now suggested sailing to the relief of Colchester, while others advocated joining up with the Scots in the north. Rupert believed these plans to be of secondary importance when the chance remained of rescuing the king from the Isle of Wight. However, the seamen were less interested in strategy than in self-enrichment. They busied themselves taking prizes: picking off the colliers returning from London to the northeast was particularly lucrative, since they carried the money earned selling coal to the capital.

There were few opportunities to fight battles. When the Earl of Warwick emerged with Parliament's fleet, Rupert noticed that Batten was extremely nervous about the prospect of fighting his former comrades.

The prince's suspicions heightened when Batten took to carrying a large white napkin, which he claimed he needed for mopping sweat from his chin. Rupert felt sure that Batten was instead using the napkin to signal to the enemy, but Charles dismissed his cousin's concerns as the workings of an overactive imagination. Rupert conceded that he had no proof of Batten's treachery, 'But,' he vowed, 'if things go ill, by God, the first thing I will do is to shoot him.'[12]

The chance never arose: a storm broke when the two forces were about to engage, forcing all the ships to drop anchor. When the winds slackened, Warwick declined combat. The Prince of Wales, his crews' provisions and morale both running low, ordered a return to Holland. 'At night,' Prince Rupert's Logbook recalled, 'the Prince standing upon the deck in the *Constant Reformation*, Patison (the master of the ship) cried out to his Highness that he saw a light, and asked what he should do.'[13] Rupert was convinced that the light belonged to a ship from a Parliamentary fleet – a conclusion that Patison and the other officers endorsed. Batten revealed a suspicious reluctance to pursue this possible enemy sighting. 'Sir,' he said to the Prince of Wales, 'whither do we steer? Will your Majesty have him [Rupert] run out of the way for every collier that he sees?'[14] Prince Charles bowed to Batten's scepticism and ordered his ships to continue their course for the Netherlands.

However, Rupert had been correct. The light he had seen twinkling in the distance belonged to a vessel from Parliament's Portsmouth fleet, which had been looking to throw in its lot with the king. Batten's curious advice scuppered this plan and the fleet went back to Portsmouth, and to Parliament's service. Meanwhile, the Royalists returned to Holland with little to show for their efforts.

Disappointment and failure stoked the smouldering faction fighting in the Stuart court. Rupert's longstanding dislike of Culpepper was cleverly played on by Sir Edward Herbert, the manipulative attorney general. Herbert knew, as Clarendon put it, that Rupert: 'did not, upon many old contests in the late war, love the Lord Culpepper, who was not of a temper to court him'.[15] Culpepper's temper was, if anything, hotter than Rupert's. The two men clashed with increasing aggression in Prince Charles's council. One day, the council met at the lodgings in The Hague shared by the Lord Treasurer and the Chancellor of the Exchequer, to discuss who should dispose of the cargo of a recently taken prize ship. Clarendon recorded:

Prince Rupert proposed, 'That one Sir Robert Walsh (a person too well known to be trusted) might be employed in that affair': it was to sell a ship of sugar. No man present would ever have consented that he should have enjoyed; but the Lord Culpepper spoke against him with some warmth, so that it might be thought to reflect a little upon Prince Rupert, who had proposed him. Upon which, he asking 'What exceptions there were to Robert Walsh, why he might not be fit for it'; Culpepper answered with some quickness, 'That he was a known cheat'; which, though notoriously true, the Prince seemed to take very ill; and said, 'He was his friend, and a gentleman; and if he should come to hear of what had been said, he knew not how Lord Culpepper could avoid fighting with him'. Culpepper, whose courage no man doubted, presently replied, 'That he would not fight with Walsh, but he would fight with His Highness'; to which the Prince answered very quietly, 'That it was well'; and the Council rose in great perplexity.[16]

Prince Charles was determined to prevent a duel between his cousin and one of his family's most loyal servants. Clarendon took Culpepper for a walk outside and urged him to ask for Rupert's pardon. But Culpepper's temper was ablaze and he refused to back down, unless Rupert did so too. It took several days for Culpepper to calm himself and appreciate that nobody of influence was supporting him.

Culpepper went to Rupert's lodgings and apologised. Sir Edward Herbert had tried to dissuade him from forgiving the effrontery, but Rupert received Culpepper and his apology with grace. Herbert then worked on Sir Robert Walsh, telling him that, now Prince Rupert had given way, it was up to Walsh to defend his own honour. Herbert broke the confidentiality of the council, by quoting Culpepper's slurs word for word.

At ten o'clock on the morning after his reconciliation with the prince, Culpepper was intercepted by Walsh as he walked to the council. He spoke with quiet menace, leaving Culpepper in no doubt that he knew what he had said and that he would get his revenge. Culpepper replied that he would happily fight Walsh, but that he would not be drawn on what had or had not been said in council, since such matters were secret. At this, Walsh punched Culpepper powerfully in the face and then drew his sword. However, seeing that Culpepper was unarmed, he left him bleeding heavily and walked away.

Culpepper remained confined to his room, embarrassed and outraged by the wound to his face. Prince Charles, shocked at this violence against his confidant, asked the authorities in The Hague to take urgent action. They were not particularly interested in a spat among their royal guest's retinue, but eventually banned Walsh from their city. The whole business was unattractive and reflected poorly on the Royalist community-in-exile.

After a brief stay ashore, Rupert rejoined the fleet. There were rumours that Parliament was sending a force to occupy Helvoetsluys, a harbour that the Royalists planned to make their Dutch maritime headquarters. The two navies dashed for the port, Lord Warwick despatching his fastest frigate to secure its prime berth. Inside the harbour wall, the rebel frigate seemed sure to win a frantic rowing race with Rupert's vessel. However, when Warwick's men threw their rope to an apparently friendly figure on the shore, he turned out to be one of Rupert's officers, Captain Allen. Allen let the rope slip through his hands, into the water. He then assisted the prince's craft, tying it fast to the quay. The rest of the Royalist ships pulled in alongside, the race for Helvoetsluys narrowly won.

Warwick's fleet was forced to hover outside, waiting for the Royalists to reappear. The Dutch forbade any fighting in the harbour and posted a squadron of their own ships between the two enemy fleets, promising to open fire on whichever side breached the peace first. They could not, however, stop Warwick's men from infiltrating Helvoetsluys, where they mocked the harsh conditions endured by the Royalists and told them of the plentiful supplies that Parliament provided for its fighting men.

These claims left Rupert's crews 'mutinous and distracted', as well as vulnerable to 'flatteries and moneys from several of Warwick's agents that were dispersed there ashore'.[17] Morale was further undermined by reports from England. By September 1648, the Second Civil War was already effectively over. Cromwell had defeated the Scots in Lancashire in mid August. More shockingly, after Colchester had been starved into submission, Sir Charles Lucas and his deputy were 'in cold blood barbarously murdered',[18] victims of a hastily convened firing squad.

During the weeks that followed Rupert spread his most loyal officers equally among his ships, in an effort to control his increasingly disaffected men. The one vessel that gave particular, repeated problems was the *Antelope*, whose crew wanted an immediate return to England.

Rupert decided to confront the ringleaders in person. Gathering the ship's company together, he told them that anyone who was unhappy was free to go – he could easily find others, who would be proud to serve their king. The sailors were determined not to be intimidated by the prince's presence, but were unsure of how to react to this unexpected offer. In the event, apathy prevailed: most of the men stayed on in unhappy service.

Later in the year, trouble flared up on the *Antelope* once more. The prince had sent to them for twenty men, to help with the de-rigging of one of the larger ships before winter set in. When the sailors refused to obey his order, Rupert again elected to deal with the problem in person. The crew crowded menacingly round him, one of the seamen trying to spark a mutiny by shouting out, 'One and all!' Rupert seized him, pinned his arms back, and dangled him over the side of the ship, threatening to drop him into the sea. 'The suddenness of this action wrought such a terror upon the rest', the prince's private papers recorded, 'that they returned forthwith to their duty.'[19]

The Royal fleet was no use to the king cooped up in a Dutch port. Rupert hoped that poor winter weather would force Warwick to head home, allowing the Royalists to sail to Ireland, where the Marquess of Ormonde was struggling to keep Charles's cause alive. Warwick, though, had guessed Rupert's scheme and planned to stay outside the harbour for as long as possible. When the Dutch squadron left Helvoetsluys for other duties, its leaders extracted a promise from Warwick that his men would not violate the port's neutrality. However, Parliament's ships took advantage of the new space in the harbour and sailed in to berths that were near to their enemies.

Inevitably, brawls broke out between the rival crews. The discipline of Rupert's men continued to unravel, and the Royalists soon gained a reputation for aggression and wildness that drew protests from the Dutch authorities. The prince had so great a fear of the enemy, and so little control over his men, that he was forced to move artillery from his ships to form onshore batteries. The guns' muzzles were directed as much at his own ships as at Warwick's.

Despite his tough stance, Rupert was unable to stem the flow from his ranks to those of his opponents. Eventually, taking advantage of confusion in the harbour, the bulk of the Royalist ships sailed off to join Warwick. The earl now sailed back to England, sure that he had rendered the king's remaining naval force little more than an irrelevance. The prince was left with just eight ships. Four were frigates, while the other four – the *Constant Reformation, Convertine, Antelope,* and *Swallow* – were larger warships.

The exiled Royalists had, in the main, fled England with insufficient money and chattels to fund themselves. Their houses and estates had been confiscated by a Parliament eager for money to pay an increasingly uneasy New Model Army, whose salary was £1 million in arrears. The desire to keep the flag flying for the king was arguably secondary to this financial imperative. There was little hope of further military action in England; the Royalists there had been violently suppressed and there was an inability or unwillingness among Charles's fellow rulers to come to his aid. Even those with blood or marital ties to the Stuarts failed him.

Charles's daughter Mary was wed to the Prince of Orange, yet the republican politicians in the States-General, the Dutch parliament, stopped him from giving aid to his father-in-law. In France, Louis XIV was preoccupied with domestic ructions, while his war with Spain continued: he could give shelter and a small pension to his exiled cousins, but he had no troops or ships to spare. There was notional support for Charles in Russia, but it never amounted to practical assistance. The Duke of Lorraine offered help, but required the Channel Islands of Guernsey and Jersey as surety. The Duchess of Savoy had given the Prince of Wales 50,000 crowns on his arrival in France, but this had soon be spent. Scotland was unable to lend its forces overseas, or on the seas, though the Covenanters remained concerned by the rise of Puritanism in England, which oppressed their religious fellow travellers, the Presbyterians.

The exiled council of war persuaded Prince Charles to equip his ships for the taking of enemy prizes. Their contents could be sold, and the resulting funds could support the court. At the same time, the Royalist navy should inconvenience and attack Parliament's interests wherever possible. Parliament began to tarnish the enemy's fleet with negative propaganda, similar to that used so often and so effectively against the Cavaliers in the Great Civil War. It was to be expected, the two Houses warned merchants and ship owners, 'that the Revolters will endeavour to maintain their defection by rapine and violence'.[20]

There were no volunteers to be admiral of the miniscule, poorly equipped Royalist fleet. Batten and Jordan, the twin turncoats, had proved to be unreliable. The Prince of Wales asked Rupert if he would assume the role, with Maurice as his vice-admiral. Options for the two princes were limited. The Peace of Westphalia, signed in October 1648, marked the conclusion of the Thirty Years' War. Its provisions made dispiriting reading for Frederick V's children: they had hoped for a full restoration to their former titles, powers, and possessions, thanks to the support of Queen Christina of Sweden – Gustavus Adophus's only child and a Wittelsbach cousin. However, French diplomats were determined to block a Palatine restoration and they persuaded the Swedish mediators that Charles Louis should only receive a fraction of what he sought. His electorate was no longer to be viewed as more important than those of his peers. Furthermore, Charles Louis was to rule only the Rhenish Palatinate: the Upper Palatinate became Bavarian, while the Elector of Mainz received the Bergstrasse. Charles Louis's brothers and sisters had assumed they would be provided for, once harmony returned to Europe, but the Peace of Westphalia gave them next to nothing.

During the autumn of 1648, it looked as though there would be fewer siblings to provide for. The worrying news from Berlin was that Rupert's elder sister Princess Elizabeth was ill with smallpox. She had long suffered from depression and had been treated with the waters at Spa. However, now she battled a deadly disease that, even if she were lucky enough to survive it, threatened to ravage her features. As she recovered, she wrote to her brother Charles Louis, without vanity or self-pity: 'I have been persecuted by this wretched illness, and though the fever has left me and with it the peril of my life, I am still quite covered with it and can use neither my hands nor my eyes. They feed me like a little child, but the doctors would persuade me I shall not be disfigured, which I leave to their faith, since I have none of my own on the subject; but at the worse I console myself that the illness will only have the effect of three of four years, at the end of which age would have rendered me ugly enough without its aid.'[21]

With the Thirty Years' War concluded, and hopes of a reasonable inheritance dashed, Rupert had few alternatives but to continue as a warrior. He agreed to lead the Royalist navy, assuming all the responsibilities of supreme authority, while insisting that he remain nominally junior to the Prince of Wales and the Duke of York, out of respect for their superior social rank. A letter written by Prince Charles from The Hague, on 5 January, confirmed this arrangement and so began Rupert's career as an admiral.

The army and the navy, at this stage of their evolution, were not the distinct entities of later centuries: admirals were commonly referred to as 'generals at sea' and marines were frequently land troops occasionally deployed on ship. Naval tactics were essentially rudimentary, with battleships looking to close with each other before disgorging their firepower to maximum effect. Plans of battle were basic, with admirals struggling to control their fleets once an action was underway: the commander looked to win advantage of wind and tide, and then led his ships into actions that were brutal free-for-alls. The effect of cannon balls, musket fire, and splintering timber could be devastating.

Rupert was a professional soldier who had no experience as a sailor, although as a boy, he had enjoyed watching the activities of Dutch boatyards. The Earl of Arundel, sent by Charles I in 1633 to invite Elizabeth of Bohemia to England after Frederick's death, noted Rupert's excitement when aboard his uncle's vessels, 'and the gladness your Highness Prince Rupert showed when you took to help to row towards them'.[22] Likewise, Phineas Pett, from a dynasty that had overseen shipbuilding in England for a century, recalled Rupert and Charles Louis's great excitement as they witnessed the launch of two pinnaces in 1637, during their visit to Charles I. Youthful enthusiasm aside, his knowledge of the sea was limited to a few voyages shuttling back and forth across the Channel and North Sea.

Rupert, though, was temperamentally suited to seventeenth-century naval command. As Granger observed, in his *Biographical History of England*, the prince 'possessed, in a high degree, that kind of courage, which is better to attack than defend; and is less adapted to the land service than that of the sea, where precipitate valour is in its element'.[23] Only the bravest men could hope to prosper in a theatre of war so unforgiving, that it provided no hiding places.

Furthermore, naval service became Rupert because its isolation brought with it independence. Years later he shocked Samuel Pepys with his candid observation: 'God damn me, I can answer but for one ship, and in that I will do my part; for it is not in that as in an army, where a man can command everything.'[24] No courtiers could undermine his position, or obscure his focus, once he was under sail for communications were slow and unreliable. Whatever trepidation the prince may have felt as he set off on his first mission as admiral, the relief of autonomous command was rich compensation.

The prince's ships were in poor order, owing to the neglect of their previous Parliamentarian owners. 'I protest to God', Clarendon wrote, after seeing their condition, 'if I know anything, the Prince is in the most lamentable condition of want that any gentleman hath been acquainted with.'[25] Rupert paid for a thorough refit of his motley force by selling the brass cannon of the unreliable *Antelope*. When further money was needed to complete the task, he persuaded his mother to pawn her jewellery. He also maximised the few resources he had to hand: while the larger ships were being attended to, a pair of frigates was sent to forage in the North Sea. They returned with £800 taken from a collier and 'a ship from Hamburg richly laden, taken out of Yarmouth road, as she lay there at anchor'.[26]

There had been disquiet among the prince's critics, when he had first been mooted for naval command. A correspondent wrote from London to say that many Presbyterians were minded to support the king, but only in the interest of establishing lasting peace throughout the nation. 'Rupert's very name', he objected, 'hath a sound of war in it, and therefore it is hoped he may not be employed.'[27]

The prince, aware of this resistance, pushed his case with Charles, who confirmed his cousin's appointment. Many hoped that he would fail. Culpepper was foremost among the Prince of Wales's courtiers in undermining Rupert's efforts. However, Rupert's unstinting labours to prepare the navy for action won over the sceptics. From The Hague, Clarendon wrote on 21 January 1649:

> I presume the fleet will be with you before this comes to your hands; the preservation whereof must be entirely ascribed to Prince Rupert, who seriously hath expressed greater temper and discretion in it than you can imagine. I know there is, and will be, much prejudice to the service of his being engaged in command, you will believe me, and not be without that prospect, both by your own observation and the information we every day received from England. But, the truth is, there was an unavoidable necessity in it. Batten and Jordan played the rogues with us … In this distress Prince Rupert took the charge, and with unwearied pains and toil, put all things in reasonable order, it being then resolved that the Duke of York should go with the fleet to Ireland. But, to our amazement, his old Presbyterian counsellors wrought so on his Royal Highness, that in express terms he refused it. So you see the necessity of what is done, and really I believe the Prince will behave himself so well in it, that nobody will have cause to be sorry for it.[28]

Rupert's first action was in response to a letter brought to him by Will Legge from the king, on the Isle of Wight. Dated 28 October 1648, it was an abrupt and succinct call for help, which Legge was able to amplify in person: Charles needed to be removed from his increasingly perilous situation as soon as possible. Rupert immediately sent a ship, which remained off the Isle of Wight for nearly a week, waiting for a signal to land. But none came.

On 30 January 1649, William Juxon, Bishop of London, read Morning Service to Charles, before the two men walked to Whitehall. After a brief wait, the colonel of the guard came to escort the king to his death. He had been sentenced after a brief trial, the result of which was a foregone conclusion. Thomas Webb had written to Lord Craven, two weeks earlier: 'I have very little hope of the king's life, all seeming to be resolved.'[29] Charles had convinced Cromwell that he could not be trusted and that England's security lay in his death.

On the day of execution Juxon was prostrate with grief, while Charles remained composed, helping the bishop to his feet. The two men proceeded to the scaffold outside the Banqueting House, the king wearing an extra shirt to ward off shivers that might be misinterpreted as signs of fear. He was determined to remain a picture of dignity throughout his final ordeal, and in this he succeeded.

Reaching the scaffold, the king was disappointed to note Parliament's soldiers were holding the crowd at a distance from him. He was therefore forced to make his final, prepared address to those on the scaffold. He told them that he saw his fate as just reward for weakly agreeing to Stafford's execution – 'an unjust sentence that I suffered to take effect is punished now by an unjust sentence on me'.[30] The king's long hair was teased into a cap while he heard the bishop's assurances: 'There is but one stage more, which though turbulent and troublesome, is a very short one; you may consider, it will soon carry you a very great way, it will carry you from Earth to Heaven, and there you shall find to your great joy the prize you hasten to, a Crown of Glory.' Juxon's last words of comfort were: 'You are exchanged from a temporal to an eternal crown, a good exchange.' Charles's final comment to his priest was, 'Remember!'[31] He then knelt in prayer by the executioner's block, before lifting his arms as a signal of readiness.

Onlookers recalled that there was no cheering after the axe had fallen, but rather a shocked groan. The executioner raised his arm to the crowd, holding his dripping trophy for all to see, and astonishment greeted the uniquely disturbing sight of a king's severed head. They had witnessed the slaying of the man who, most still believed, was God's Anointed. All present knew the significance of the moment was so enormous as to be unfathomable.

CHAPTER FIFTEEN

PIRATE PRINCE

'Conceive him now in a Man-of-war, with his letters of mart, well armed, victualled, and appointed, and see how he acquits himself. The more power he hath, the more careful he is not to abuse it. Indeed, a Sea Captain is a King in the Island of a ship, supreme Judge, above appeal, in causes civil and criminal, and is seldom brought to an account in Courts of Justice on land for injuries done to his own men at sea.'

The Good Sea Captain, Thomas Fuller (1608–1661)

Prince Rupert set off for Ireland in December, his eight vessels severely undermanned. The prince had recruited in the Netherlands, securing the services of some Flemish sailors, although many more were needed. The *Constant Reformation*, the prince's flagship, was designed to have a complement of 300, but only 120 men could be found to man it at this stage of the voyage. The frigates were more generously provided for, so that they could fulfil their roving brief, scouring the seas in search of prizes.

Rupert's crews were worried that their course would take them through the Channel, and it was inconceivable that they would be able to navigate it without attracting enemy attention. However, when the Parliamentarians started to bear down on the Royalists, Rupert fell back on the tactics that had served him so well in his cavalry days: he turned and attacked, and the startled enemy dispersed and fled in the face of bold, Cavalier, aggression. Their new admiral's courage impressed the sailors and quelled many of the more disruptive voices on board. A fair wind followed, speeding the ships to Ireland.

Arriving in the Irish port of Kinsale, which had been a Spanish outpost during part of Elizabeth I's reign, Rupert learned of Charles I's beheading. The shocking news reverberated around Europe, causing thrilled revulsion and frenzied chatter: the execution of an anointed monarch was viewed by many as an insult to God and seemed to demand divine vengeance. The prince's feelings ran deeper. Whatever their spats towards the end of the Civil War, a pure love had existed between Charles and Rupert. The king had shown his nephew kindness and had partially filled the void caused by the early loss of his father, Frederick V. Differences over Marston Moor or the surrender of Bristol could not expunge the blood loyalty that bound the two men together.

The prince's siblings shared the sense of devastation. His elder sister, Elizabeth, was so horrified at the news that she became seriously ill. She wrote of her profound sorrow to her confidant, Descartes, who comforted the princess with soothing words: 'It is surely something to die in a way which commands universal pity – to leave the world, praised and mourned by whoever partakes of human sentiments. It is undeniable that without his last trial the gentleness and other virtues of the dead king would never have been so remarked and so esteemed as they will be in future by whoever shall read his history ... As to what regards his mere bodily sufferings, I do not account them as anything, for they are so short that, could assassins use a fever or any of the ills that Nature employs to snatch men from the world, they might with reason be considered much more cruel than when they destroy life with the short sharp blow of an axe.'[1]

Clarendon was less philosophical, stating that the king's execution was 'the most execrable murder that was ever committed since that of our Blessed Saviour'.[2] He wrote a letter of condolence to Rupert that was flecked with loathing for the Regicides and weighed down with sadness at the ghastliness of the execution:

Sir,
Though, when your Highness left this place, there was no reason to expect any good news from England, yet the horrid wickedness which hath been since acted there, with those dismal circumstances which attend it, was so far beyond the fears and apprehensions of all men, that it is no wonder we were all struck into that amazement with the deadly news of it, that we have not yet recovered our spirits to think or do as we ought.[3]

A sense of profound unease arose among many – even those who had been unsympathetic to Charles when he had been alive. They saw the king's slaying as a cause for national disgrace and mourning, prompting a flood of self-flagellating remorse from pamphleteers and poets:

> Come, come, let's mourn; all eyes, that see this day,
> Melt into shows, and weep yourselves away:
> O that each private head could yield a flood
> Of tears, whilst Britain's Head streams out His Blood;
> Could we pay that his sacred drops might claim,
> The World must needs be drowned once again.[4]

In defiance of his personal loss, and as an act of monarchical continuity, the Prince of Wales now proclaimed himself Charles II. However, he could afford few of the trappings of kingship: indeed, he was so impoverished, that he could not even find the money to send messengers to thank European rulers for their condolences. Rupert's task of providing for the Royalist exiles was now even more urgent, although his renewed instructions from the Court differed hardly at all from his original commission: 'There is no other alteration from the former', confirmed Charles's secretary, 'but what is necessary in regard to the change of condition in the person of the King, by the barbarous murder of his father by the bloody rebels in England.'[5] Rupert must raise funds to help free his cousin from financial embarrassment.

At the same time as the prince was coming to terms with his uncle's beheading, he had to comfort his mother who was confronting another family disaster: Princess Louise had converted to Catholicism, after being won over by the arguments of Jesuit priests. On 24 February, Rupert sent a letter to Elizabeth, telling her of his great sadness at his sister's change in faith. He also wrote angrily to the States-General, defending his mother's honour from scurrilous rumours doing the rounds in Holland, that she had encouraged Louise to become Papist. The princess's conversion had been so sudden and complete that she had left a short note one morning for Elizabeth stating that she was leaving for the true Church, and was leaving her mother and the outside world forever. She carried through this threat, later becoming the Abbess of Maubuisson.

Rupert's arrival in Ireland gave a huge fillip to Royalist morale. He was a talisman, a reminder of past glories, and a general whose dogged loyalty demanded respect. One correspondent greeted him with a warm tribute: 'I have been always ambitious to be esteemed your servant, and your unwearied labours for the King and gallant dangerous undertakings increase my desires therein; there are but few men, of your quality and fortune, that would expose himself to those difficulties you constantly are subject to, your ends therein having no particular relation to the interests of your own person, and seeing that the redemption of his sacred Majesty is that which your Highness proposes to make your actions glorious, I am sure you will accomplish it, and may he perish that contributes not thereto.'[6]

Rupert's time in Kinsale, far from the navy's prime bases in the Thames, was initially successful. He managed to supply the stubborn Royalists holding the Isles of Scilly. Privateers joined him, swelling his fleet to twenty-eight ships – considerably larger than Parliament's force in the Irish Sea. The prince suffered some losses – the frigate *Charles* became isolated in a storm, then lost in a fog, before being taken by two enemy vessels – but his tally of hostile ships was significant. Parliament decided to implement a convoy system, to protect its merchantmen from Royalist attacks. When losses in the west remained unacceptably high, it despatched the main fleet to deal with the problem. Flying the new 'cross and harp' jack as its flag, 'the State's Navy' had another task: to assist Cromwell's campaign on the Irish mainland. The roads in Ireland were terrible, so being able to supply the New Model Army by sea gave the invading English a huge advantage over Lord Lieutenant Ormonde's Royalists.

In May 1649 Parliament's fleet appeared outside Kinsale, blockading Rupert's men inside the harbour. 'We began to careen and fit for a summer voyage', Prince Rupert's papers recorded, 'but the fleet being ready to fall down to the mouth of the harbour, the enemy appeared with a very potent fleet before it, which caused us to stop our proceedings.'[7] Leading the enemy force was Robert Blake, a 50-year-old friend of Cromwell and Hampden, and a former MP. The princes knew Blake: he had distinguished himself during Rupert's capture of Bristol, holding out for a day and a night after the main Parliamentarian surrender. Blake had been even more successful when facing Rupert's brother. He had held Maurice's Western Army at bay for two months, with only 500 men, until the Earl of Essex's approach forced the Royalists to lift their unsuccessful siege.

Rupert organised batteries of artillery to protect the harbour entrance. He then summoned his council of war, whose members advised that the current fleet should be strengthened, while further craft were built as reinforcements. They also recommended that fire-ships be prepared: these were floating pyres that were set alight and directed at opposing ships, which they either scattered or burned. Once these additions had been made, the council members agreed that the prince could engage Parliament.

Rupert accepted these conditions, personally leading a recruiting drive along the coast, collecting soldiers and sailors to provide manpower for the tasks in hand. But, when Rupert had achieved the council of war's objectives, its members back-pedalled. They were concerned that the scanty Royalist fleet might be annihilated in a single action. Their strong advice now was that Rupert should ride at anchor, safe in his harbour, and wait for bad weather to drive Blake away.

The conditions, however, failed to deteriorate and Blake refused to budge. The Royalists remained so tightly cooped up that not even merchantmen were able to enter or leave Kinsale. With supplies failing, and morale wavering, the *Perfect Weekly Account* reported to Westminster: 'Letters from the West gave us some particulars of the State of the Prince his Fleet at Kinsale representing of it thus. The English seamen, will not endure to have received aboard with them the Irish Rebels, provisions also becomes scarce amongst them, and therefore time is thought will be necessitated to fight if the Parliament ships are able to lie but some few days longer before it.'[8]

Rupert's situation deteriorated further when he lost the man who, after his brother Maurice, was his most trusted ally. The Parliamentarians swooped on a frigate just outside the harbour, taking the ship and sixty prisoners: 'In this frigate', a Parliamentary pamphleteer reported, 'we found Colonel William Legge, which was once at Oxford.'[9] Legge was sent for imprisonment at Bristol Gaol (one of a remarkable eleven prison sentences that Legge suffered for his loyalty to Rupert or the Crown), an accusation of high treason hanging over him. With execution of defeated Royalists now quite common – the Duke of Hamilton and Lord Capel had followed their king to the block – it seemed likely that Legge would also be killed. Meanwhile, there were further erosions of Rupert's manpower and resources. 'Letters from the Navy say, that there have happened some dispute and action between the Parliament's Fleet and the Princes near Kinsale, and after several volleys, the Parliamentary Navigators became victors.'[10] Two ships and one hundred prisoners were taken.

While Rupert remained inside the harbour, the self-proclaimed Charles II and his court moved to Jersey, landing at St Helier in mid September. The plan was to move on to Ireland at the earliest opportunity, but Charles's advisers were hampered by their own faction fighting, their lack of funds, and their leader's innate laziness. As they lingered in the Channel Islands, news arrived of savage Parliamentary victories at Wexford and Drogheda in September and October. Drogheda, just north of Dublin, held out until Cromwell led his men in a ferocious charge. When the defensive walls were breached, Cromwell ordered his men to spare nobody: 2,500 defending troops and up to 1,000 civilians perished. Those seeking sanctuary in the church were smoked out to waiting executioners, or chose to burn alive. Aston, the Royalist commander, was held down and his skull was staved in with his own wooden leg. All other captured officers were summarily shot, while their soldiers were lined up and decimated: one in ten was hauled out and clubbed to death in front of his comrades. The rest were sent to toil in servitude, in the sugar-cane fields of Barbados. News of the brutality that followed futile resistance led to many of the new king's remaining garrisons quickly surrendering.

It was clear that Cromwell's advance was unstoppable and that he would eventually reach Kinsale by land. Rupert heard rumours of discontent in the town's garrison and judged that the safety of his fleet demanded decisive action: he overpowered the governor and took command of the fortress. This persuaded the governor of nearby Cork, who had already made up his mind to betray his town, to attempt a small place in history as the man who killed Prince Rupert of the Rhine.

Rupert's passion for stag-hunting being well known, the governor invited him to join a hunt outside his town. Rupert accepted, before urgent business prevented his going. When the invitation was reissued, with rather too much haste and enthusiasm, Rupert's suspicions were aroused. He confronted the governor, who confessed his true intentions and then surrendered Cork to the prince. There was a further plot, involving one of Rupert's ensigns who had been compromised by the enemy. The plan was for this traitor to overrun one of the guard-posts at the entrance of Kinsale, allowing the Parliamentarians to sail into the harbour. But he and his colleagues were rumbled before they could attempt their treachery and were executed after a summary trial.

Although these intrigues and plots on land were worrying for Rupert, a far greater challenge lay outside Kinsale harbour. Robert Blake shared the prince's lack of naval experience. However, he fully understood the meaning of his orders: Parliament had told him to 'pursue, seize, scatter, fight with and destroy'[11] the Royalist fleet. Both princes were already aware of his military tenacity and skill. They were to be unsettled, though, by the ease with which he transferred these gifts to maritime warfare. It was Rupert's grave misfortune to be pursued by such a fierce and determined terrier, whose career drew the admiration of Nelson who, in a rare moment of modesty, said: 'I do not reckon myself equal to Blake.'[12] It was Rupert's ill luck to be faced with Blake at his most able and focused.

Eventually the weather came to Rupert's aid, strong northeasterly winds dispersing Blake's blockade. 'The seas thus cleared,' Prince Rupert's papers recalled, 'we set sail for Portugal.'[13] The prince began his expedition on 17 October 1649 with seven ships. He was forced to leave several others behind: they were in good condition, but there were not enough men to crew them.

The small Royalist fleet was buffeted by the same storm that had driven away its enemy. However, there were immediate rewards for braving the gales: Prince Maurice took the first prize of the voyage and this was quickly followed by a brief engagement, which yielded up two more trophies. Maurice then took a fourth ship. At this point King John IV of Portugal, who in 1640 had secured his nation's independence from Spain, invited the princes to Lisbon as his guests.

Rupert sought and received the king's assurance that he and his flotilla would be subject to the Law of Nations, which guaranteed the Royalists' safety while in Portuguese waters. If the prince was nervous about how he would be received, he need not have worried: his and Maurice's welcome was warm, the gun emplacements along the River Tagus saluting them as they passed. Anchoring in the Bay of San Katherina, Rupert organised supplies for his fleet and discussed the disposal of his plunder with local merchants. The princes were then invited ashore, 'where they were received by many of the nobles, and treated in very great state for some days, until preparation was made for their reception at Court; which being ready, the King sent his nobles with a great train to attend them to his palace, where he received them with great kindness'.[14]

With the formalities completed, Rupert oversaw the sale of his goods, which raised £40,000. He then prepared his ships for the next leg of their voyage. The seven, original vessels were careened and filled with fresh provisions, while the captured merchantmen were adapted for warfare. It was clear the prince was not planning to indulge the King of Portugal's hospitality for long: he wanted action and booty. However, his plans were undone by the appearance, on 10 March 1650, of Blake. He was in his customary role, menacingly patrolling the harbour mouth, waiting to pounce.

Parliament looked to Blake to rid the seas of the threat of the Royalist privateers: 'The clearing of the coasts of such implacable enemies, would be a great encouragement to merchants, and therefore we are very joyful to hear there is a gallant fleet prepared by the Parliament', London learnt from its pamphlets, 'the knowledge whereof, strikes a terror into the enemy, who having persisted in their obstinacy, deserve not the least favour; for how can it be safe for the Commonwealth not to revenge such injuries done to the State?'[15]

Blake carried an ambassador with him from England, who demanded that Rupert, Maurice, and their ships either be immediately handed over or forced to sail for open waters. The ambassador pointed out that the princes had been capturing neutral ships to add to their fleet and that this was an unacceptable threat to peaceful commerce. The king refused to yield to these demands, stating that he would, as he had promised to do, observe the Laws of Nations: this meant that Rupert's fleet would have three days to leave Lisbon. The ambassador replied that such a delay was unacceptable. If King John persisted in harbouring its enemies, he explained, then the Commonwealth's navy would feel free to attack Portuguese shipping.

In the meantime the weather deteriorated and Blake looked for protection in Weyes Bay. Blake's proximity encouraged some Portuguese merchants to express their unhappiness at the Palatine princes' presence. One of John IV's chief advisers, the Conde de Miro, strongly sympathised with Parliament and urged the king to expel his guests. The matter proved divisive at a heated meeting of the Royal Council: strong support was expressed for both of the English navies, with de Miro fanning opposition to the princes' continued presence. The king proposed that the Portuguese were duty bound to escort the vestiges of Charles I's navy out of the harbour, to prevent their annihilation by a superior force. However, his merchants wanted to be rid of the princes and of the unsettling effect their visit was having on their peaceful dealings: England was a very important export market for Portuguese wines, figs, oranges, and lemons, while King John's dependencies (especially Brazil) sold their sugar to London via Lisbon. The merchants' greatest fear was Blake's threat to interfere with their shipping.

Rupert skilfully exploited the rift among the Portuguese. He concentrated his attention on the clergy, who were sympathetic to his plight, and who: 'began to fill the pulpits with how shameful a thing it was for a Christian King to treat with the rebels'.[16] At the same time the prince made sure the people saw him in the flesh, rather than merely hearing about him as a faceless troublemaker in their midst. While secretly preparing his fleet for departure, Rupert rode to hounds each day, a glamorous, energetic prince, seemingly unconcerned by the furore engulfing his hosts. Rupert's ease with people of all backgrounds, which had so shocked the aloof Royalist grandees early in the Civil War, charmed a populace accustomed to a snobbish aristocracy. This clever public relations' exercise paid off, the groundswell of opinion siding with the put-upon prince. For the time being, it was impossible for de Miro to toss Rupert into the waiting, open jaws of the enemy.

The Parliamentarians now resorted to skulduggery. A small force was put ashore to ambush and kidnap the princes on one of their hunting expeditions. The trap was sprung, but Rupert and Maurice reacted quickly, galloping to safety. Rupert then plotted his revenge, his love of science leading to the creation of an ingenious booby-trap: he 'fitted a bomb-ball in a double-headed barrel, with a lock in the bowels to give fire to a quick-match, [and he then] sent it aboard their Vice-Admiral in a town-boat with one of his soldiers clad in a Portugal habit, to put into the stern-boat as a barrel of oil'.[17] But the would-be assassin gave himself away, undermining his foreign disguise by swearing in remarkably fluent English. Blake's men dismantled his device and arrested him. Rupert, always loyal to his bravest men, later managed to secure his release.

The prince looked for an escape from Portugal with increasing anxiety. A letter arrived from Charles candidly revealing his appalling financial position and urging his cousin to place him in funds through privateering. But Rupert's task was made more awkward when Parliament reinforced its blockading fleet: not only did this complicate his escape plans, it also endangered the Portuguese fleet whose trade with Brazil was so extraordinarily profitable. The prince realised that this threat would make the Lisbon merchants even keener to see the back of him. It was best if he went quickly, and voluntarily.

John IV persisted in his support of the Royalists, but his influence was waning. Meanwhile de Miro's supporters ensured that the dock-workers performed slowly, so delaying Rupert's plans. However, organising provisions was one of the prince's strengths: through hectoring and bullying he prepared his flotilla for a dash for the open seas. The king told his admirals to assist the Royalists' flight, when it came, by sailing out with them.

On 16 July the perfect opportunity arose for Rupert to slip the block-ade: news came that Blake had taken the majority of his ships to find fresh water in Cadiz. However, to Rupert's annoyance, the promised Portuguese escort failed to materialise, its admiral delayed so long that eventually Rupert's men were forced to sail alone. Despite Blake's temporary absence, there were still enough Commonwealth ships patrolling outside the Tagus to contest Rupert's escape, especially now that he had forfeited the advantage of surprise. In the ensuing action the prince's fore-top mast was destroyed by a cannonball, leaving his ship temporarily immobile. He limped on, but after a fortnight, with his provisions running low, Rupert returned to Portugal. He remained there for the rest of the summer. Another attempt to break out, in the fog of early September, was also a failure because one of de Miro's men betrayed the plan.

A week after this second fiasco, Parliament carried out its threat to fall upon the Brazil fleet: Blake captured nine Portuguese ships, adding them to his force. The king was so disturbed by news of this aggression that he went directly to Rupert's ship and asked him to attack Blake. Even though his vessels were unprepared for such a venture, Rupert felt obliged to assist, but the enemy steered clear of the Royalists. Eventually, his supplies exhausted, Rupert was forced to return once more to Lisbon.

In October, Blake summoned all his ships to regroup and refit in Cadiz. 'The King, having no more use of our ships,' recorded Prince Rupert's papers, with mild resentment, 'victualled our fleet, and fitted us with such other stores as were necessary for us, giving the Princes many thanks for their endeavours to preserve the fleet, and assured them of his friendship.'[18] The stress of hosting unpopular guests for so long had sapped John IV of his loyalty to their faltering cause. Soon after the Royalists quit his kingdom, he gave in to de Miro: Portugal made peace with England's Parliament and agreed that the princes would receive no further protection in any of its territories.

The outlook for Rupert's expedition was bleak. Under-resourced and with ill-defined aims, Prince Rupert's papers recalled, 'Poverty and despair [were our] companions, and revenge our guide.'[19] Blake allowed no breathing space, his eagerness in pursuit fuelled by concern at Royalist attacks on Commonwealth shipping along the Portuguese and Andalusian coastline. Fearing that the superior enemy fleet would pick off his ships one by one, the prince ordered his captains to meet at Formentera in the Balearic Islands. His commanders, however, were eager for booty and dangerously delayed their rendezvous. When they suddenly saw the enemy on the horizon, they dashed for the harbour of Carthagena, where they expected to be granted sanctuary.

The Spaniards, however, did nothing to stop Blake as he sailed into Carthagena, firing at Rupert's ships. One Royalist vessel, the *Henry*, was overrun by its crew and joined the enemy. The rest realised that they were in a hopeless position: 'Our officers not being able to defend themselves', the prince's papers revealed, 'ran their ships ashore, making them unserviceable; another having landed his ammunition, set fire on his ship, so as they were no ways profitable to the enemy.'[20] Blake destroyed or captured nearly all the Royalist fleet in a day. The only two ships to escape were those commanded by Rupert and Maurice.

Unaware of his comrades' fate, Rupert waited by Formentera with mounting concern. The island was uninhabited, so when he quit it he left letters for his men, urging them to meet him in Toulon as quickly as possible. His instructions were rolled up in a bundle and placed under a rock. This he draped with a white flag, to attract attention. Rupert then set sail for Toulon, where he hoped to meet up with Maurice immediately, and to see his captains soon afterwards.

CHAPTER SIXTEEN

SUFFERING FOR THE CAUSE

*'Prince Rupert being not ashamed of openly to declare that, provid-
ing he might but ruin and destroy the English interest, especially the
estates of the merchants and mariners of London, and the owners and
proprietors of all ships belonging to the same, he cared not whether he
got a farthing more while he lived, than only what would maintain
himself, confederates and fleet.'*

William Coxon, a prisoner of Prince Rupert

The position for Prince Rupert was now as forlorn as any he had
experienced in his fighting career. He was admiral of a group of
ships so slight that it barely merited the description of 'flotilla', let alone
'fleet'. However, the destruction and capture of most of his force failed
to distract him from his duty: he remained committed to gathering
prizes to pay for his exiled cousin's court, as well as to continuing the
struggle on behalf of his late uncle. To achieve these aims, he needed to
outwit a vastly more powerful enemy.

The reserves of the Commonwealth's navy were formidable and
increasing, for Cromwell realised that continuing naval dominance was
crucial to his grip on power. He was at the head of a political structure
that needed military muscle to control the extreme forces unleashed by
the Civil War. Out of the ashes of conflict had sprung spiritual zealots,
who wanted to sweep away all religious hierarchies, and Levellers, who
sought a communist political structure. Although the New Model
Army contained elements from both sets of fanatics, it was control of
the army that ensured the Commonwealth's continuation.

The navy was essential for funding the army. Customs and excise
underpinned a structure that was, by any other name, a military dic-
tatorship. After the mutiny that had taken the fleet to Helvoetsluys in
1648, a drastic purge rid the navy of two-thirds of its officers, who were
judged political defectives. Their replacements were God-fearing men,

either drawn from the army or promoted after long service in merchant ships. The latter were known as 'tarpaulins', to distinguish their hardy professionalism from the dilettantism of the previous, gentlemanly, officer class.

The Commonwealth fleet doubled in size between 1649 and 1651, and its vessels were made more robust, the key vessels named after Parliament's military victories. The *Naseby* was the flagship, its figure-head a representation of the all-conquering Cromwell trampling his foes. Lighter, faster escorts were also built, to protect England's ships from Royalist and French raiders, and to help merchantmen to trade in distant markets. A convoy system was introduced in 1649 to guard against privateers. The end of the Thirty Years' War had also intensified mercantile rivalries: the Dutch, in particular, were keen to regain their global pre-eminence in trade, while Britain was eager to keep the profitable business it had built up while its competitors were distracted. Cromwell judged a strong navy essential, for reasons of politics and commerce.

Commonwealth apologists celebrated the growing muscularity of their regime. 'Methinks I see in my mind a noble and puissant Nation rousing herself like a strong man after sleep, and shaking her invincible locks,' John Milton wrote in *Areopagitica*. 'Methinks I see her as an Eagle mewing her mighty youth, and kindling her undazzled eyes at the full midday beam, purging and unscaling her long abused sight at the fountain itself of heavenly radiance, while the whole noise of timorous and flocking birds, with those also that love the twilight, flutter about, amazed at what she means, and in their envious gabble would prognosticate a year of sects and schisms.' If the Republic were to achieve its aims of maturity and permanence, then there could be no place for reactionary Royalists, such as Prince Rupert. They must be obliterated.

1650 seduced Charles Stuart with a false dawn. The would-be king left Jersey in February to inform his mother of plans to fight with the Scots against the Commonwealth. Despite Henrietta Maria's entreaties not to betray his father's legacy, he went to Breda to broker a deal with the Covenanters – when he promised to establish Presbyterianism in his northern kingdom, he stooped to a religious compromise that his father had rejected in favour of execution.

Charles's desperation for the throne led him to sever relations with the Marquess of Montrose, who had given his all for the Royalist cause. The marquess, an open admirer of Rupert's military style, was the enemy of Charles's new allies. He was captured soon afterwards. Montrose showed astonishing bravery at his May execution, before his body was quartered and its parts despatched to hang above the gates of various cities. Charles's betrayal of his loyal supporter was a cowardly, vile disgrace, which echoed his father's feeble sacrifice of the Earl of Strafford.

Days later Charles sailed for Scotland. However, in September his supporters were trounced at the battle of Dunbar, perhaps Cromwell's most brilliant victory. Charles remained in Scotland throughout the winter and was proclaimed the nation's king on 1 January 1651. There were plans to invade England but, although the Scottish army contained able and experienced soldiers, only a fraction of its troops was fully behind its new monarch. The Commonwealth, meanwhile, could call upon 70,000 men under Cromwell's dynamic leadership.

The year 1651 also marked an expansion in the Commonwealth's commitments at sea: in reaction to the slump in trade, and in an effort to make inroads into Dutch commerce, Parliament passed the Navigation Act. This was an attempt to bypass the Dutch merchant system to the benefit of British business. From now on trade would have to be direct, between the goods' port of origin and England. At the same time, the ships employed had to be English, with English crews. There was no realistic chance that the Netherlands would agree to these strict stipulations. Hostilities between the two naval powers were inevitable, once Cromwell felt his fleet strong enough to enforce this inflammatory legislation.

France, although experiencing its own civil wars, offered Rupert a rare safe haven in an increasingly hostile Mediterranean: Blake's successes had impressed the Spaniards, persuading them officially to recognise the English Republic at the end of 1650. Yet the Commonwealth was in a state of undeclared war with France, after suffering numerous losses from privateers. Some of these privateers were Royalist and others were French.

At Toulon, Rupert and Maurice enjoyed an excited reunion. Maurice had arrived there first, convinced his brother had died in a recent dramatic storm. Mourning his loss, Maurice initially refused to leave his ship. Eventually the senior French admiral in the harbour, Chevalier Paul, coaxed him ashore. 'The day appointed for his landing being come, and all things in readiness for his reception, it pleased Heaven to remove all obstacles of sorrow by the happy tidings of his brother's safety, who came that day to an anchor, and went ashore together.'[1] The French greeted the princes with marks of respect, cannon saluting them from land and sea. Maurice had arrived with a prize in tow and its contents were sold to merchants from Leghorn. With the proceeds, Rupert paid for the careening of his two remaining fighting ships and began to convert the prize into a man-of-war. He intended to put to sea again that summer.

Gradually, the captains of the ships taken at Carthagena drifted into Toulon, with news of the debacle. There was much squabbling among the defeated as to who should bear the most blame. Captain Allen Elding, who had previously been given a prize to skipper, was blamed by many for putting the safety of his vessel above the imperative of aiding his comrades. Meanwhile, others accused Burleigh, captain of the *Henry*, of treachery, 'by giving [Blake] intelligence of our rendezvous'.[2] Burleigh insisted that his men had detained him, before handing his papers to the enemy. Although Rupert suspected the worst of both captains, he refused to conduct a court martial in another king's port. Burleigh, though, he could no longer trust: he was permanently dismissed from the fleet.

The rest of the Carthagena captains were received back into Royalist service, to oversee Rupert's burgeoning crews. 'Seeing himself reduced to three sail', the prince, 'strained the utmost of his treasure, and bought another, which was named the *Honest Seaman*; and, being but weak in ships, endeavoured to be strong in men.'[3] When an Englishman, Captain Craven, asked if his ship could join the flotilla, he was welcomed. His vessel, the *Speedwell*, was renamed the *Loyal Subject*.

Aware that Toulon contained enemy spies, Rupert fanned false rumours that he was taking his flotilla 'for the Archipelago'. Falling for the bluff, the Commonwealth despatched its fleet to intercept him at Cape Corsica. In fact, Rupert had decided to head west: when he left the French port in May 1651, he made for the Straits of Gibraltar, 'to take revenge on the Spaniard'[4] in the West Indies.

Rupert was fortunate that the Commonwealth now recalled Blake: London believed that the threat of the prince had been neutralised after twenty months of dogged pursuit. Blake returned to England and received the thanks of Parliament, a gift of £1,000, and the eminent position of Lord Warden of the Cinque Ports. He was now deployed closer to home – taking the Scilly Isles, before subduing the Royalists on Guernsey and Jersey.

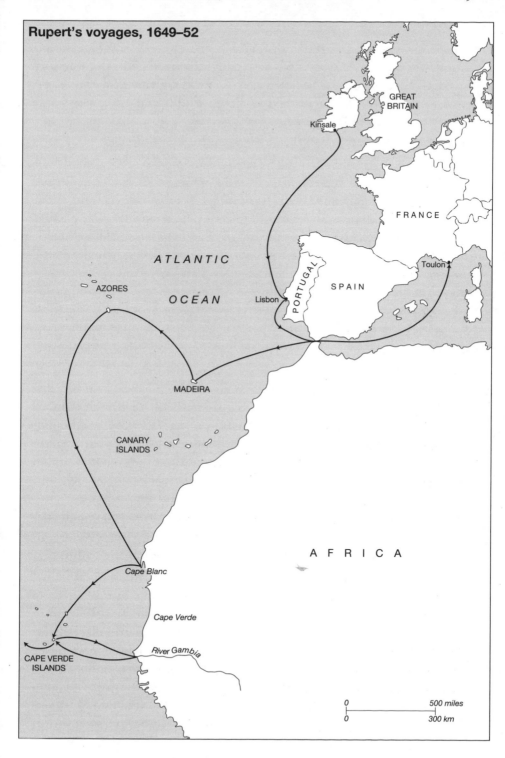

Rupert's voyages, 1649–52

GREAT
BRITAIN

Kinsale

ATLANTIC

OCEAN

FRANCE

Toulon

AZORES

PORTUGAL

Lisbon

SPAIN

MADEIRA

CANARY
ISLANDS

AFRICA

Cape Blanc

Cape Verde

CAPE VERDE
ISLANDS

River Gambia

0   500 miles

0   300 km

*

Rupert was not to reach the Caribbean for a year. The flotilla had barely set off when the sailors insisted on taking a Genoese ship heading for Lisbon. This episode was indicative of the problem the prince faced in concentrating on military matters, while most of his sailors were preoccupied by a thirst for booty. However, there were scant prizes to be had along the Andalusian coast: the Genoese ship's main cargo was not – as hoped – spices or treasure, but rice and corn. When a more promising victim was eventually spotted, Rupert resorted to trickery to lure in his prey: he flew the Commonwealth flag. The Spanish galleon came alongside its supposed friend and, when her officers came aboard, the Royalist buccaneers revealed their true identity and overwhelmed her.

At the end of June Rupert and Maurice stopped at Madeira to sell the perishable grain from the Genoese ship and to take on fresh supplies. Although Madeira's merchants were too poor to give a good price for the corn, the brothers were greeted with the respect and hospitality due to visiting foreign royalty: 'The Princes were received with much kindness, and assisted with anything the island afforded for refreshment.' The governor entertained them in his fort, mounting a military tattoo for the brothers' appreciation, before taking them on a tour of the island's monasteries, 'and having accompanied them to the sight of what was worthy seeing on the island, returned with them to the seaside, where at setting off saluted us with all the artillery'.[5]

On board ship, Rupert could not count on the same deference. His crews were men who, either through choice or force, were risking their lives in a dangerous voyage, where everyday conditions were tough and military encounters could be brutal. They knew that they were fighting in a force that was likely to face a superior enemy. Theirs was, essentially, a defeated unit whose continued existence was a result of their admiral's cussedness, grafted uneasily onto their own hopes of self-enrichment.

Rupert preferred to take his war away from Europe, where he realised he could be no more than an irritant. He also sought to distance his flotilla from the enemy ships combing the seas, seeking him out for destruction. In choosing discretion over valour, he was in tune with the advice offered to 'The Good Sea Captain', in Thomas Fuller's contemporary book, *The Holy State and the Profane State*: 'Escaping many dangers makes him not presumptuous to run into them.'[6]

However, there was no escaping the weather. A massive storm near Madeira gave a foretaste of what was to come. Rupert's ship, the *Constant*

Reformation, took in so much water that it was clear that she had a leak, but not even the governor's personal diver could locate the hole. Rupert ordered bonnets to be stitched together, which were compressed into parts of the vessel that might be concealing the fissure. It was to no avail. Since the ship could not be docked for a proper investigation, she continued at sea, the unplugged leak a source of constant worry.

Rupert wanted reinforcements. He proposed that the ships go to the Canary Islands to persuade passing English ships to join his expedition. More experienced sailors told Rupert that stopping at the Canaries would be of no use: it was too early in the year for vessels to be there in any number. The prince accepted this advice and led the fleet past the Canaries without alerting their inhabitants to his presence.

Rupert now let it be known via the unpopular commander of his ship, Captain Fearnes, that his intention was to sail for the Caribbean. His projected route was via Cape Verde, a cluster of tropical islands 1,000 miles southwest of the Canaries. This was a good plan: the archipelago had been a crucial stopping off point for Portuguese explorers since its discovery in 1456. 'Yet,' recalled an officer called Pitts, when writing about this troubled voyage, 'his Highness was prevented by a party that opposed going to the West Indies, merely because Capt. Fearnes proposed it; and strengthened their party by alleging the leak ... in the Admiral [that is, the *Constant Reformation*] made the ship in too bad a condition to be carried [on] so long a voyage.'[7] Rupert, concerned at the strength of opposition to his plan, called a council of war, to which all captains, lieutenants, and masters were summoned.

Rupert was more vulnerable to dissent than most commanders, since his authority lacked effective support. His king was dead, while his heir was merely an exiled pretender, and there was no forceful body able to underwrite Rupert's power. Besides, if pushed too far, mutiny remained a realistic threat: it would be simple for any ship to sail away and transfer allegiance to the Commonwealth. The prince needed the diplomacy to absorb or deflect his officers' antagonism, while not losing control of an increasingly fractious force.

Rupert had Fearnes present his plan to the council of war: he proposed that the ships should head for the islands of Cape Verde, where supplies of dead and living goats would be readily available. From there they could progress to the West Indies, where cassava and meat were in abundance. But only one other captain, Goulding, agreed with this plan: the rest insisted that Fearnes was dangerously exaggerating the availability of meat in Cape Verde and that, because the men refused to eat cassava, 'we must expect no more than starving in the West Indies'.[8]

The majority wanted the flotilla to sail to the Western Islands, the Azores. Here all their needs could be met: supplies could be taken on board, bounty sold, and further prizes would be on tap, since the English East Indies' fleet used the islands as a staging post. Some of the officers also pointed to the harbours of the Azores, which would be ideal for the refitting of the *Constant Reformation*.

Rupert adjourned the council to consider his decision. The following day, with the wind blowing away from his favoured West Indies course, and with the *Constant Reformation* riding higher in the water than she had for some time, he reluctantly gave way to the majority's resolution. Those who had won the argument 'neither considered the extremity of the weather,' Rupert's papers ruefully acknowledged, 'nor the time we were to consume in victualling ... Yet to avoid the censure of self-will and rashness, he stood for those Islands, although he foresaw part of his ensuing disasters.'[9]

The disagreements in the council of war fomented the divisions among the Royalist officers, leading to the most vituperative passage in Prince Rupert's diary:

> But they whose souls were seized with a fatal cancer, suffered their undigested venom to overflow like a raging billow, to the destruction of us all. So high was their insolence, that they infested [Rupert's] very domestics, and so public their improvidence, that they concealed not their intentions in their cups, making private meetings in their cabins where they conceived it convenient to engage any man to their faction, until his Highness, full freighted with such contempt of their audacious proceedings and actions, commanded some of the cabins to be pulled down, with further order to the captain of his guards not to suffer any meetings after setting the watch, nor candle to be lighted betwixt decks, but in such places as were appointed for the ship's use. So great and violent was their distemper that he feared the private communication of his men.[10]

The discontented flotilla reached the Azores on 15 July. It was immediately evident that those who had opposed Fearnes had grossly exaggerated the islands' facilities: there were few supplies to be had; there was no sign of the promised East Indiamen; and there was nowhere to fix the leaks of the *Constant Reformation*, since all the approaches to the coastline were treacherous – especially so during the many days when the weather was poor. 'By this relation,' Pitts reported home, 'you may perceive how miserably we have been misguided and ruined, more by these Islands than possibly we could have been by any strength that ever the Rebels could have sent against us.'[11]

Rupert, regretting having acted against his better judgement, decided to bypass another heated council of war. On 3 September he ordered Pitts to go to each ship in turn, bearing his warrant as admiral, insisting that each captain and master give his individual written judgment whether the fleet should stay where it was, or go to the West Indies. In this way Rupert not only put each of his officers on the spot, he also extracted from them tangible proof of their opinion, which could be referred to in future. The majority, this time, elected to head for the West Indies. The ringleader of the opposition, 'finding himself outwitted, took occasion to pick a quarrel with the master of the Admiral [the *Constant Reformation*], whereby to have more pretence to leave the fleet'.[12] Rupert was happy to be rid of him. From now on, he made it clear that he would make all the decisions: the council of war would not be summoned again.

Before the flotilla could be prepared for the voyage, however, it was struck by a spectacular storm. The *Constant Reformation*'s leak grew, as the waves pummelled its timbers. Rupert, on board the ailing flagship, ordered the crew to man the pumps. This kept the ship afloat. He then manoeuvred the *Constant Reformation* 'to bear up before the wind', but this exposed her holdings, which was where the invisible tear had begun. The weather continued to deteriorate over the ensuing three days, during which the *Constant Reformation*'s pinnace was whipped away by the wind. On the third day, 20 September 1651, it was clear that the ship was in mortal danger. Rupert ordered his gunners to fire their cannon at regular intervals, so the other ships were aware of the *Constant Reformation*'s location: he wanted his comrades close at hand, to pluck survivors from the sea when his ship could take no more.

The desperation of the crew galvanised frantic energy on board: the pumps were operated at full capacity and the sailors used everything that came to hand to bale out the water. When the battle seemed to be won, Rupert ordered 120 pieces of raw beef to be taken from storage down into the bowels of the ship, to plug the leak. This staunching of the wound failed to hold: the force of the sea blew in the meat, as well as the barrier of bonnets and planks that had been formed around the leak. Staving off the inevitable, the crew now jettisoned the ship's cannon. The doomed sailors then signalled to the other crews that they were about to go down. They stopped pumping and baling, because there was no longer room for a man to stand up in the hold. Besides, the ship's barrels had come loose and were rolling around dangerously: anyone who ventured below decks would most likely be crushed.

There was no hope of other ships coming alongside to take the crew off: the sea was so rough that this would have resulted in the loss of the rescue vessel, too. The *Constant Reformation*'s men knew they were about to perish. The chaplain told those who required the sacrament to meet him at a pre-assigned point, when the end was inescapable, and they would all die together. When the main mast was felled by the tempest, the *Honest Seaman* strained to reach it, expecting to find some of the *Constant Reformation*'s men latched onto it, waiting for rescue. But the resolution to die together had held: not one chose to desert his comrades.

Rupert waved to Maurice to come as near as he could, so that he could say a final goodbye to his favourite sibling and his dearest friend. The younger prince raged against the imminent loss of his brother and ordered his men to take their ship alongside the *Constant Reformation*, so he could attempt to rescue Rupert. But Maurice's officers declined to let emotion affect their judgement: they refused to obey an order that promised to add their own destruction to that of the condemned crew of the *Constant Reformation*. Maurice then insisted that a small boat be prepared, which he would take across to bring his brother off. But volunteers to row through the towering waves were slow in coming forward and the rescue launch was prepared with a marked lack of haste.

Rupert's men urged him to attempt to save himself. There was one remaining lifeboat and they insisted he take his chance in it, rather than join them in certain death. Rupert, brought up in a strict military code, refused to desert his men as their collective fate approached. He thanked them for their loyalty, but told them that it would be an honour to die with his brothers-in-arms. The sailors persisted: they knew they were to drown; let them, though, preserve their leader as a final act of heroism, by which history would remember them. The prince again declined. 'His men,' Prince Rupert's papers note, 'seeing supplications would not prevail, having selected a crew of undaunted lads, hoisted out their boat, and by force put him into it, desiring him at parting to remember they died his true servants.'[13]

The skiff somehow made it from the sinking *Constant Reformation* to the nearest vessel, the *Honest Seaman*. Rupert, hauled aboard, insisted that the lifeboat return immediately, to save as many others as was possible. He nominated three men who must be given priority during the second rescue mission: Captain Fearnes; Captain Billingsley, one of the prince's army officers; and Monsieur Mortaigne, Rupert's Gentleman of the Horse, who had helped save his life during one of Marshal Gassion's madder escapades. The skiff managed to shuttle back and forth, through mountainous seas, but Mortaigne and Billingsley were not aboard when it reached the *Constant Reformation*: they had insisted on sharing their soldiers' lot. Fearnes, though, had accepted his chance of salvation. He was accompanied by Galloway, one of Rupert's servants.

Maurice continued to agitate for the *Honest Seaman* to move nearer to the *Constant Reformation*. He wanted to launch its lifeboat, which was of a stronger design than the flagship's little skiff. But Captain Chester, the *Honest Seaman's* commander, refused to help his comrades. Pitts noted with disgust that when Chester 'saw the ship perishing he made no action at all for their boat to help to save the men, but walked upon the deck, and said, "Gentlemen, it is a great mischance; who can help it!" And the Master never brought the ship near the perishing ship, notwithstanding Prince Maurice's command for it.'[14]

The sailors on the *Honest Seaman* could make out their colleagues' final moments through the storm. The condemned men were seen: 'Taking a sad farewell of their friends, by making sorrowful signs one to another.' But the *Honest Seaman's* crew still refused to risk their lives attempting to save their comrades: the lifeboat was not even put in the water, 'which savoured more of malice than excusable judgement', according to the author of Prince Rupert's papers. 'Thus these distressed persons kept the ship above water until nine at night, and then, burning two fire-pikes, to give us notice of their departure, took leave of the world, being at that instant 100 leagues south and east from the island of Terceira.'[15]

When the *Constant Reformation* sank 333 men died. These were not the only casualties: soon after the storm abated, the wreck of the *Loyal Subject* was also found. Craven's ship had been driven from its anchor and shattered against some rocks. Rupert was extremely fortunate not to have joined the casualties: Pitts believed that 'God almighty had ... miraculously preserved his person.'[16] It remained to be seen how long he and his brother's luck could hold, during such a perilous voyage.

CHAPTER SEVENTEEN

MAURICE

'He that like Thunder still his Passage wrought,
who led like Caesar, and like Sceva fought,
Is stoop'd unto the Grave (be proud thou Earth)
More splendid than that Queen that gave him birth.'

'An Elegy on the Report of the Death of the most renowned
Prince, Prince Maurice'

Rupert was shaken by the loss of his men and deflated by the sinking of his cargo: much of the 'treasure and rich goods' harvested from enemy ships was in the *Constant Reformation* when she went down. The rest of his vessels were in a ragged state, blasted by the severity of the storm. The prince decided to head back for the Canaries, looking for new rigging for his masts and hoping for fresh plunder for his buccaneers. But when news arrived that the Commonwealth had sent a strong fleet to hunt him down, Rupert was forced to plot a new course. He headed for West Africa, to prepare his ships for the crossing to the Caribbean.

They sailed first to Cape des Barbas, before making their way along the coast to 'a harbour near Cape Blanc, in the kingdom of Argen [Arguin], in the Barbary Coast, towards Guinea'. This was an Islamic, Moorish island, off modern-day Mauritania, controlled by the Santon of Sale. Cape Blanc was a safe distance from the Commonwealth force and it possessed a good, secure harbour. Here, Rupert personally oversaw repairs.

Locating provisions was more problematic than the prince had anticipated. Although fish – especially mullet – were plentiful, water and meat were not, and the Royalists needed plenty of both, for their ocean crossing. Fortunately the Netherlands had established a castle near by, to help its merchants trade along the coast. When the Dutch commander learnt of Rupert's arrival, he sent him many barrels of fresh water: any enemy of the increasingly aggressive English Commonwealth deserved support.

The indigenous people were less forthcoming: 'The inhabitants were a kind of *banditti*,' the author of Prince Rupert's diary observed, 'who, refusing to pay tribute to the Santon of Sale, secure themselves in that sandy desert. They observed the Mahometan law, and are governed by the eldest of their family, whom they obey as Prince. They are tawny of complexion, habited in vests, after the Turkish manner. Their arms are darts and lances, which they use with great dexterity and skill.'[1] Because of the scarcity of fresh water, their staple drink was cows' milk. Theirs was a nomadic existence, living in tents, their daily priority the care of their livestock.

Rupert wanted to meet these people – to explore trading opportunities and to assure them of his peaceful intentions. On 1 January 1652 he led one hundred men in an expedition inland, to establish contact with them. The Royalists had ventured nearly 20 miles when they discovered a track. This they followed through morning mists, until they suddenly found they had walked directly into the middle of the aboriginal settlement. The Moors scattered at the sudden appearance of armed and armoured Europeans, leaving behind their tents, their sheep, and their goats.

Prince Rupert tried to calm their fears. But the terrified Moors were understandably reluctant to listen to this massively tall figure who had appeared in their midst, surrounded by men carrying muskets. The prince attempted to stop one man from deserting the scene. However, when he continued to flee, Rupert lost patience and shot his mount – a camel. The Moor ran to another camel, hauled his wife up behind him, and lumbered off into the mist. The couple left behind a young boy, who looked to the prince for comfort, clinging to his legs for security. Rupert returned to the harbour with the boy beside him and the livestock in tow. The Royalists could see the Moors shadowing them, just out of range of their muskets.

Two days after the commotion in their camp, the Moors sent a hostage while they negotiated for the restoration of their belongings. Rupert anticipated spirited haggling for the beasts, but was surprised that the Moors' only stated concern was the return of the boy. Suspecting that this was the prelude to something underhand, the prince forbade any of his men to leave camp. Soon afterwards, one of his men paid the price of disobedience: he was mutilated and his body was found bobbing in the sea.

Fearing his life would be taken in vengeance, the Moorish hostage bolted for safety. He zigzagged like a snipe as Rupert's soldiers fired at him and escaped uninjured. The Moors then disappeared into the desert, leaving the boy behind. Although the prince and one of his braver officers, Captain Robert Holmes, tried to re-establish contact with the nomads, they were not found again. The boy remained in Rupert's company, an exotic servant who was later included in one of the prince's better-known portraits.

Hurrying to complete preparations for the next, demanding leg of their voyage, the Royalist vessels were soon ready: 'Now, having cleansed, fitted, and new-rigged our 3 ships, viz., the *Swallow*, of 42 guns; the *Revenge* of 40 guns; and the *Honest Seaman*, of 40 guns,' Pitts recorded, with optimism, 'we are this instance setting sail from hence. In this intended voyage God Almighty guide us for the best, and send us better fortune than we had for the last, to his Highness's content, he being resolved not to make any part until he shall get somewhat considerable to bring with him to serve his Majesty, and to make his fleet subsist.'[2]

Before leaving Arguin, Rupert sent gifts of ginger and sugar back to his cousin Charles in Europe, together with a letter that was at once proud and wistful: 'Your Majesty be pleased to look upon us as having undergone some hazards equal with others, had it pleased God to preserve the *Constant Reformation*, I had loaded that vessel with better goods.'[3]

Rupert sailed for the Portuguese islands of Cape Verde, arriving at Sal, its most northeasterly isle. He had hoped to link up with the Newfoundland fleet, so he could barter for rigging and water, but he found neither shipping nor fresh water there – just a flat terrain, whose most remarkable features were a volcanic crater and the 40-acre saltpan that gave the island its name.

The larger island of Boa Vista, to the south, replenished the Royalists' water supplies. The island's population was tiny – 'about 100 in number, of a mulatto kind',[4] the descendants of Portuguese sailors and African slaves – but they were able to supply Rupert with goats. These were taken aboard, some live and 'near 1,000 dried'[5]: apart from their meat and milk, goats were valued for their skins, which provided seafarers with prized waterproof clothing.

The prince next reached Santiago, the largest landmass in the Cape Verde chain with two mountain ranges, dominated by the 1,400-metre

Pico d'Antonia, and surrounded by black reefs and white beaches. It was a stopping-off point for the East Indies fleet on its voyages between Lisbon and Brazil. The Portuguese governor seemed to be friendly, but the baskets of watermelons, plantains, oranges, lemons, and bananas that greeted Rupert were the gifts of an embarrassed host, burdened with an unwanted guest. His master, King John, was allied with Cromwell's Commonwealth.

Eager to move the princes on at the earliest opportunity, the govern-or reported sightings of English vessels high up the River Gambia. He encouraged Rupert to pursue them and offered to lend some of his own forces to join in the hunt. The prince agreed and set off for the African coast 280 miles to the east, but his Portuguese companions disappeared at the earliest opportunity, leaving the Royalists unsupported in alien waters.

There were some reasonable pickings in the river. Prince Maurice took the most substantial prizes, a Spanish merchant vessel and her smaller sister ship. After surrendering, the Spaniards complained that they had been tricked: 'There was some dispute made by them,' recalled Prince Rupert's diary, '. . . by reason their merchant was not included in the conditions. The Prince, to avoid censure, offered them their ship in her former freedom, and so dispute it by force; but they rather obeyed the first conditions than hazard their lives.'[6] Maurice had an intimidat-ing presence, being every bit as ferocious a warrior as his elder brother. Few risked crossing him.

Some of the Royalists penetrated 150 miles up the River Gambia, before the flotilla was ordered to regroup around the island of Tulfrey. The islanders proved fascinating to the visiting Britons, one recording that: 'They are very severe in punishing such as transgress the rules of morality, which I observed by a law among them, that if any man made a lie which tended to the prejudice of the commonwealth, he is presently made a captive, and sold to the next Christians that trade with them. This makes them keep their words inviolable . . .'.[7]

Rupert realised that the summer hurricane season was approaching. He did not want to leave his ships vulnerable to a storm as terrible as the one that had claimed the *Constant Reformation*. The main Spanish ship was broken up, its parts cannibalised by the other vessels. Prince Maurice moved to the second of his prizes, judging her a superior sail-ing craft. She was named the *Defiance*.

Sailing for Cape Verde, the flotilla stopped at Reback, a town to the south of Cape Mastre. Here, relationships with the indigenous people proved fraught and one of Maurice's sailors was kidnapped. As a reprisal, Maurice ordered a canoe to be seized and the two natives on board it to be held until his man was released. When this demand was ignored, Rupert led one hundred men ashore, determined to settle the matter by force. As soon as his unit landed, however, it was surrounded by irate hordes. Captain Holmes recognised the danger the prince was in and quickly organised a second force, which he took to reinforce Rupert's beleaguered men.

A West African, known as 'Captain Jacus', now stepped forward. He vouched for Rupert, saying that he had been well treated by the prince on a previous occasion. This endorsement momentarily calmed his compatriots' mood. However, soon afterwards, trouble erupted further down the shore: a native was killed in the commotion and, in revenge, the Africans took two Royalists prisoner – Captain Holmes and Mr Hall.

Rupert ordered his men to make for the safety of their ships, while he spent a day plotting the best way to recover his captured men. The prince eventually decided to negotiate their release in person and ordered some of his crew to row him near to the shore. He then opened negotiations, employing Captain Jacus – who was on land – as interpreter. Jacus told the prince that the natives promised to release the prisoners as soon as their canoe and its occupants were returned. However, when Rupert ordered his men to set the canoeists and their craft loose, Jacus ran forward into the waves and shouted to Rupert that it was all a trick: his people had no intention of releasing Holmes or Hall, and the prince should recapture the canoeists while he could.

Rupert ordered his men to open fire on the tightly packed crowd on the shore, while he summoned his pinnaces to bring reinforcements. As these small craft approached land, though, they were impeded by natives who were standing up to their necks in the water. They obstructed the Royalist landing by pushing their boats away. When the Europeans levelled their muskets at the Africans, they dived under the waves, firing darts and arrows on resurfacing. 'Thus we exchanged shot in expectation of our pinnaces,' noted the author of Prince Rupert's diary, 'until one of their arrows unfortunately struck his Highness Prince Rupert above the left pap, a great depth into the flesh.'[8] Rupert called for a knife and used it to prise the arrow from his chest. Fortunately, although the wound was deep, it was also clean.

During this tussle in the shallows, Captain Jacus gathered some of his friends together and managed to get Holmes and Hall away – 'which act being both an example of gratitude and fidelity, may teach us that heathens are not void of moral honesty',[9] the diarist recorded with surprised condescension. Captain Jacus, offered a safe place on board ship by Rupert, chose instead to stay with his people.

The Royalists returned to Santiago, the principal island of Cape Verde. They captured an English ship there, but this good luck was counterbalanced by the loss of the *Revenge*: unconvinced by the prince's plan to head for the West Indies, her crew mutinied and sailed away to join Cromwell's fleet.

The crossing to the 'Caribbee Islands', much delayed and much debated, proved uneventful. The navigators missed the first planned landfall, of Barbados – the flotilla passed it by mistake, in the night. This turned out to be a fortunate error for, unknown to Prince Rupert, the island had been taken by Sir George Ayscue's Commonwealth squadron at the beginning of the year.

Rupert ordered his men on to St Lucia, which the author of Prince Rupert's diary found: 'Spacious and fertile, well stored with wood and water, and having divers fresh rivers in it; and on the leeward side two very good harbours. It hath also great store of wild hogs, goats, and other provisions.'[10] The Royalists anchored at Point Comfort, where Rupert successfully plugged a leak in his vessel with the help of some sewn-together bonnets. The island had been English, but the few settlers were slain by the indigenous 'Indians' and their houses destroyed. The French now claimed ownership of St Lucia. Their governor in Martinique, a snake-infested island to the north, invited Rupert to visit. On his arrival, Dutch ships greeted the prince, firing a salute for their fellow enemy of the Commonwealth. The prince now received disappointing news: all the English lands in the Caribbean were Parliament's. Rupert decided that he would therefore 'visit them as enemies'. His targets would be English and Spanish possessions, on land and sea.

Rupert also began to trade. 'Our commodities for traffic were beads, glass, coral, crystal and amber, penknives, looking-glasses, bills, hatchets, saws, and strong liquors, for which they exchange tortoiseshells, fine cotton yarn, and green stones, which they bring from the mainland, having many virtues in them, as curing the falling sickness, and easing women in labour.'[11] On Dominica, the Royalists swapped a few of their glass beads for fruit, before bartering for goods prized in European markets.

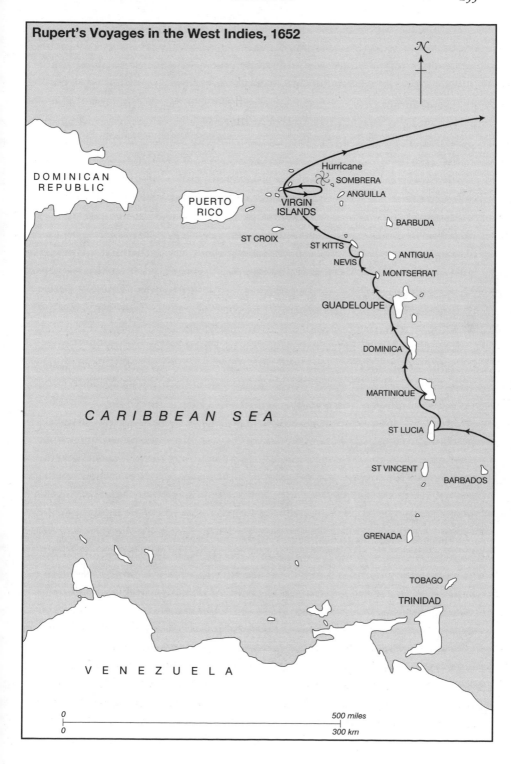

Rupert's Voyages in the West Indies, 1652

𝒩

Hurricane
SOMBRERA
ANGUILLA

DOMINICAN
REPUBLIC

PUERTO
RICO

VIRGIN
ISLANDS

ST CROIX

BARBUDA

ST KITTS

ANTIGUA

NEVIS

MONTSERRAT

GUADELOUPE

DOMINICA

MARTINIQUE

CARIBBEAN SEA

ST LUCIA

ST VINCENT

BARBADOS

GRENADA

TOBAGO

TRINIDAD

VENEZUELA

0   500 miles
0   300 km

Progressing northwards, in early June, Rupert's flotilla sailed via
Guadeloupe to Montserrat, taking two Commonwealth ships en route.
Montserrat had a small English population and a reputation for producing the finest sugar in the Caribbean. It was an area ideally suited to
privateering: there were many merchant ships to pursue and the inhabitants of the surrounding islands were used to supplying, and trading
with, vessels passing through.

Continuing in a northwesterly arc, Rupert's ships cruised towards
Nevis. They sailed into the bay behind Pelican Point, scattering ships
that had been sheltering there. Some made for the open sea, while others beached themselves on land. A lively encounter saw Rupert board
one ship and take it, while sporadic gunfire claimed a few casualties,
some of them notable: the prince's secretary was killed and Maurice lost
the master of his ship. The princes captured two ships, which contained
large quantities of sugar, but five other merchantmen escaped. The
vessels that had been run aground proved impossible to refloat and had
to be left behind. Rupert's aggression forfeited much of the goodwill
that had previously greeted his approach of the islands.

Arriving off St Kitts, the Royalists anchored alongside twenty-four
Dutch and French ships. There were some Commonwealth vessels
there, too, stationed to provide extra defences for the Parliamentarian
troops holding the island. The two English forces fired at one another
in a show of antagonism, but failed to engage. Rupert contemplated an
attempt on his enemies, but judged them to be in too strong a position
to attack. The prince took his flotilla round to Sandy Point Road
– a good anchorage that was controlled by the French. Although the
Royalists were given fresh water, no further supplies were forthcoming,
for the French were in cahoots with the Commonwealth garrison.

After twelve days anchored off St Kitts, Rupert set sail for the Virgin
Islands, where he intended to prepare his craft for the promised hurricanes and to rationalize his ragbag fleet of warships and prizes. On 2
July his men anchored at Dixon's Hole. This was the start of a stay that
was to last nearly two months, after which the cove was known first as
'Cavaliers' Harbour', and subsequently as 'Rupert's Bay'. Despite their
nominal link with this anchorage, the prince and his men's association
with it was neither easy nor pleasurable.

Essential provisions were hard to find and it took three days to discover water. The staple food was cassava – unpopular with the men,
it also proved difficult to locate, since it was a root and the island was

covered in dense undergrowth. The men ate it reluctantly, making a bitter bread from its flour. But it was found in such sparse quantities that Rupert was forced 'to retrench our provisions, allowing to each man four ounces of bread *per diem*; and the like of all other viands, and himself no more; which abstinence of his made every one undergo their hardship with alacrity'.[12] But not everyone was prepared to endure such miserable conditions: when the prince sent carpenters ashore to cut timber, some of them took the opportunity to desert, sailing off in their pinnace towards the Spanish stronghold of Puerto Rico. Rupert appreciated that his fleet's safety was compromised; the enemy would soon be aware of its position and would come after him. He had to move from his safe harbour just as the worst of the hurricanes were expected.

Rupert ordered his three weakest vessels to be burnt, before setting course for Anguilla. A terrible hurricane hit the Royalists on 13 and 14 September, almost as soon as they were in the open seas. Rupert's ship was the sturdiest, but it barely survived this intimate examination by furious elements. A survivor recalled the storm being so intense that it was impossible to see from one end of the ship to the other.

The master ordered all sails to be brought in apart from the mainsail, 'but then the storm increasing,' recalled the author of Prince Rupert's diary with horror, 'tore our sail from the yard, though of new double canvas. Rolling now in the trough of the sea, we strove to set our mizzen to keep her up, but ... the sails blew quite away, so that being destitute of all human help, we lay at the mercy of God.'[13] Rupert's men later calculated that they had unknowingly been tossed between a high rock, called Sombrero, and the island of Anguilita – a stretch of water that was considered impossible to navigate, because of its treacherous shallows.

At 3 a.m. the storm reached a violent crescendo. Rupert and his crew watched with terror as their ship was taken towards a ledge of jagged rocks between Anagadas and the Virgins. They were approaching their doom at speed, when the wind suddenly changed direction and threw the ship eastward. The crew's great luck continued: it was washed into a harbour in the uninhabited island of St Anne's, where the anchors held in 12 fathoms of water. The hurricane blew itself out the following day.

After the passing of the storm, Rupert's ship was alone and in a terrible condition, 'both our topmasts being spent, and our ships left like a wreck, without rigging or sails'.[14] She limped back into the harbour at Dixon's Hole, with the prince keen to repair the damage and hopeful that the rest of the fleet would soon find its way back. But the *Honest Seaman* was unable to return: she had been carried by the storm as far as Hispaniola and bad seamanship later drove her on to the coast at Porto Pina.

More disastrously, Maurice's ship the *Defiance*, and its fly-boat, were lost with all hands. Nobody witnessed the sinking, which allowed hopes of the younger prince's survival to continue for many years. It seems likely that Maurice was denied his brother's extraordinary good luck: his ships probably splintered on the rocks that had so nearly claimed Rupert.

The author of Prince Rupert's diary struggled to quantify the shock felt at Maurice's loss: 'In this fatal wreck – besides a great many brave gentlemen, and others – the sea, to glut itself, swallowed the Prince Maurice, whose fame the mouth of detraction cannot blast, his very enemies bewailing his loss. Many had more power, few more merit: he was snatched from us in obscurity, lest, beholding his loss would have prevented some from endangering their own safety: – so much he lived beloved, and died bewailed.'[15] Rupert was devastated at the loss of a man who was not only his brother, but also his treasured friend.

Maurice has received little attention from History. Clarendon, while acknowledging the young man's 'great courage and vigilance'[16] wrote him off as boorish – a soldier's soldier, incapable of sensitivity, civility, or diplomacy: 'The prince had never sacrificed to the Graces, nor conversed amongst men of quality, but had most used the company of ordinary and inferior men, with whom he loved to be very familiar. He was not qualified with parts of nature, and less with any acquired; and towards men of the best condition, with whom he might very well have justified a familiarity, he maintained at least the full state of his birth, and understood very little more of the war than to fight very stoutly when there was occasion.'[17] This harsh judgement owes much to the earl's difficult relationship with Rupert. The Earl of Leicester was more generous in his assessment of a promising youth: 'For besides that he hath a body well-made, strong and able to endure hardships, he hath a mind that will not let it be idle if he can have employment. He is very temperate, of a grave and settled disposition, but would very fain be in action, which with God's blessing and his own endeavours will make him a brave man.'[18]

Maurice displayed constant loyalty to his controversial brother and it is this steadfastness that makes him so admirable. The brothers had been born a year apart, and although they endured forced separations, they were at their happiest when united. It was a fraternal love so strong that it overrode everything put in its way. They had both been bred for fighting. Together they had served their apprenticeship with the Dutch army of their uncle. While Rupert languished as a prisoner of war, Maurice fought hard for the Swedes, eager to inconvenience his brother's captors.

Maurice was content to play the secondary role in their relationship – lieutenant general to Rupert's commander; vice-admiral to his admiral. He did so without resentment and with admirable devotion. When Rupert's duties took him eastwards, in the spring of 1644, the Chester commander Sir John (later Lord) Byron greeted news that Maurice was to replace his elder brother with relief: 'Since these countries can not be terribly happy with your Highness's return to your former command; nothing could be more welcome to them than to hear that Prince Maurice is to succeed your Highness; in that charge, & certainly the sooner he take it upon him, the more advantageous it will be for his Majesty's Service.'[19] The chaplain of the Prince of Wales's Life Guard called the two brothers, 'the two great Instruments of our supportation'.[20]

Maurice's Civil War record was as mixed as Rupert's. He, like his elder brother, had immediately rallied to his uncle's cause, fighting hard as a Colonel of Horse. His greatest moment came at Roundway Down, when he bettered the highly able Waller. Maurice was promoted to lieutenant general of the Marquess of Hertford's army, in the west and southwest. He quickly assumed a senior role over the well-meaning but inadequate Hertford, overseeing the capture of Exeter and gathering together an army of 7,000 men. However, Maurice failed to take Plymouth when it was vulnerable: 'But', wrote Clarendon, 'when I say it was an error that he did not, I intend it rather as a misfortune than a fault; for his Highness was an utter stranger in those parts ...'[21] The foreign prince was persuaded to attack the lesser port of Dartmouth, giving Plymouth time to prepare its defences, while his army lost impetus and manpower. Indeed, Maurice's powers unravelled so quickly that he failed to take the fishing town of Lyme, which Blake had transformed into a bastion of Parliamentary resistance.

At the Second Battle of Newbury, Maurice's cool professionalism
ensured the safe retreat of the Royalist infantry, preventing an unwise
engagement from descending into catastrophe. When Maurice took
control of Wales, in early 1645, he found his effectiveness was compromised by a lack of real power: 'Dear Brother,' he pleaded with Rupert, 'I
shall not need to mention any other particular than that which concerns
the enlargement of my commission, and therein I desire no further
latitude than the same from you which you had from the King, which
is absolutely necessary for the performance of what is expected from
me.'[22] But this commission never came and Maurice, surrounded by
inexperienced lieutenants and suffering from high desertion rates, had
an unsuccessful and unpopular time in Wales, trying to make up for his
impotence with flashes of ruthlessness. 'And for you Prince Maurice,'
scolded a pamphleteer, when the brothers were exiled from Britain,
'[we] pray never think of coming into Wales again, for if you do, all the
plundered cows-bobby, all the onions, leeks, and oat-cakes in Wales will
muster themselves together, and rise up in judgement against you.'[23]

Maurice remained committed to his brother, as the war spiralled
towards Royalist defeat. He was, however, prepared to criticise Rupert's
instructions when he believed them inappropriate: summoned from
hard-pressed Worcester to help in the defence of Bristol, Maurice
scrawled a covering note on his reply: 'For his Majesty's special service.
To my dear brother Prince Rupert, Prince Palatine, &c. Haste, haste,
post haste!' Inside, Maurice wrote: 'The Scots being advanced very near
to us, with an intention, as is conceived, to besiege this place, I could
not remove from hence without putting this town into a great distraction; besides the dishonour that would thereby reflect on me.'[24]

When Rupert was so out of favour after surrendering Bristol, Charles
actively encouraged a rift between the brothers, writing to Maurice of
Rupert's 'unhandsome quitting the castle and fort of Bristol ... So much
for him. Now for yourself. I know you to be so free from his present
misfortune, that it no ways staggers [me] in that good opinion I have
ever had of you; and so long as you be not weary of your employments
under me, I will give you all the encouragement and contentment in my
power.'[25] Maurice, however, ignored the flattery and the inducement,
and remained loyal to his disgraced brother. Still recovering slowly
from a vicious dose of the plague, which had nearly killed him, he
rode to Newark through largely enemy territory, in support of Rupert's
demand for a court martial.

After expulsion from England, Maurice's performance as Royalist vice-admiral had been committed and successful: he was frequently at the forefront of the fleet, taking the most prizes, and fighting with unrivalled bravery and muscularity. Whenever there was dissent among the officers, Maurice provided Rupert with unequivocal support. He had endured the hardships of a demanding voyage, content to serve with his brother in a cause that was otherwise dormant and seemingly headed for extinction.

Granger, in his *Biographical History of England*, gives a fair evaluation of Maurice: 'He was not of so active and fierce a nature as Rupert; but knew better how to pursue any advantages gained over the enemy. He wanted a little of his brother's fire, and Rupert, a good deal of his phlegm.'[26]

Rupert refused to accept that Maurice was dead: previous reports of his loss – most notably after the Second Battle of Newbury, and during the siege of Worcester, from the plague – had happily proved incorrect. Rupert prayed that this was another such mistake. He ordered his ships to search for his brother's vessel, but they found nothing. The following year the princes' mother, Elizabeth, wrote excitedly to her devotee Lord Craven of reports from the Caribbean that Maurice had survived the hurricane and was on Lomnema Island. This was not so.

Outlandish theories continued to entertain those who deemed drowning too mundane an end for a glamorous prince. On 19 June 1654, a Dutchman wrote: 'Here is news of Prince Maurice, who was thought and believed to be drowned and perished, that he is a slave at Africa. For being constrained, at that time that he parted from Prince Rupert, to run as far as Hispaniola in the West Indies, he was coming back thence towards Spain in a barque laden with a great quantity of silver, and was taken by a pirate of Algiers. The Queen, his mother, hath spoken to the Ambassador of France, to the end he may write in his behalf to the Great Turk, for it is pre-supposed this State dare not speak for him for fear of offending the Protector.'[27] This was a complete fabrication.

Later, there was even a rumour that Prince Maurice was being held at a castle called 'The More at Porto Rico': 'Some would have it that he was taken up at the Island of Porto Rico, and carried into the Castle, and there detained and concealed,' Prince Rupert's Logbook reported, 'which seems improbable in regard that of 200 men in the ship with him, never any one man of them was heard of after.'[28] This proved to be yet another false hope.

Rupert continued to hope that his brother would reappear, alive. Eleven years after the shipwreck, he sent a ship to look for Maurice once more. It returned empty, unable to fill a void that ached throughout the remainder of Rupert's life. Without Maurice, Rupert was incomplete.

CHAPTER EIGHTEEN

WILDERNESS YEARS

'Prince Rupert is in some measure recovered of his bloody flux, but goes little abroad out of the Palace Royal, because he wants a princely retinue, which I see no probability for him to have in France yet a while. Charles Stuart is at a non plus what to do; things do not answer his expectations; his designs fail him.'

A Letter from Paris, April 1653

Rupert returned to Europe with a handful of ships. The goods he carried, including precious tobacco, were scant reward for an excruciating, four-year voyage. His odyssey had been punctuated by many causes for regret, of which the loss of Maurice was by far the greatest. While the continued existence of Rupert's tiny fleet had kept the Royalist cause afloat, its significance had been largely talismanic: after Blake's clinical destruction of many of Rupert's best ships, the small remnant had been, at best, a distant irritant to the Commonwealth. However, the determination, stamina, and inventiveness the prince had displayed during his independent command were truly heroic. He had underlined the reputation for bravery and perseverance won in boyhood and reinforced during the Civil War.

Rupert was soon reminded that his foes had not forgotten him. When he approached Fayal, and then St Michael's, he was turned away, direct artillery fire confirming the warmth of Portugal's friendship with Cromwell. Rupert was keen to reach land: he had been ill with a bloody flux – a vicious form of dysentery – since leaving the Caribbean. His health was further undermined by the lack of fresh provisions on board. The prince was grateful when the master of one of his prize ships gave him two hens, whose eggs provided welcome nutrition, but he urgently needed to find a harbour where he, his crews, and his battered flotilla could receive proper care. He sailed for northwest France, with all possible speed.

It was a slightly recovered Rupert who reached Brittany, sailing up river at Nantes to Paimboeuf. The French greeted Rupert warmly, granting him a hero's welcome, even though their king had recognised the Commonwealth's legitimacy a few months before. On 3 March 1653, 'After many storms and tempests, his Highness, with his little fleet of five ships, arrived in sight of Belle Ile, and next day came to an anchor at St-Nazaire, near the castle, from which, as also from a fleet of Dutch ships, his Highness received and returned salutes.'[1]

Rupert's appearance provided a welcome fillip to the Royalist exiles based in France. Prince Charles sent his own coach to meet his cousin, together with a delighted letter: 'I am so surprised with joy at your safe arrival in these parts, that I cannot tell you how great it is, nor can I consider any misfortunes or accidents which have happened now I know your person is in safety.'[2]

'I am sure it can be no news to you,' Clarendon wrote to Sir Richard Browne, from Paris, with equal excitement, 'that Prince Rupert is safe at Nantes, and therefore it is very probable this letter may not find you at Brest, but that you may have thought it fit to attend his Highness, and offer him your service.'[3] There was an assumption that the prince was returning with enormous bounty, which would cause Charles's empty Privy Purse to overflow. Stuart loyalists rushed to attend their returning champion and to marvel at the magnificent trophies he would surely lay at their master's feet.

Their hopes were soon snuffed out when some seamen from Rupert's fleet deserted for England. Arriving at Weymouth, they publicly estimated that the prince had accumulated just £10,000 worth of prizes from his four years of privateering – a mere quarter of what he had raised from the sale of captured goods when arriving at Lisbon, early in his travels. The true figure was £14,000, still an extremely poor tally for such an arduous and costly voyage, explained by the sinking of his most richly laden ships. On 29 March, with his colleagues coming to terms with their disappointment, Rupert, still very weak from dysentery, travelled to Paris. There, Louis XIV received him with warmth and concern.

Disillusionment at Rupert's poor yield quickly turned to resentment. Three weeks after his excited letter to Browne, Clarendon's tone had become cynical: 'The Prince ... no doubt will have occasion to use all and more than he can have brought home, to repair and fit out his ships.'[4] Faction fighting among the exiled Royalists fanned the controversy over Rupert's inadequate return. Clarendon, who loathed Lord Keeper Herbert, complained to Nicholas: 'You must never expect information from me of any of the business of the Prize, or any thing that is managed by Prince Rupert, who consults only with the Lord Keeper; and I much doubt very little of that money will come to the King. I shall be satisfied if what is raised on the guns and the ship (for all is to be sold) come justly to his hands.' [5] There was a suspicion that Rupert's financial accounts of his spoils were less than honest. Royalists talked of sending Rupert to sea again, to attack English ships distracted by naval war with the Dutch. But his vessels were in a terrible state and there were no funds to pay for refitting.

The ill feeling towards Rupert reached its peak when he refused to hand over all the proceeds of his voyage to Charles. Indeed, Rupert seemed determined to make his cousin meet the expenses of the voyage. Rupert insisted that his men should be paid first, with second call on the prize money going to those Toulon merchants who had helped to furnish the fleet in the first place. A failure to settle these debts would reflect terribly on Rupert's reputation: they were both matters of fairness and of honour. Meanwhile, the French interfered, impeding the sale of the captured cargo and insisting on acquiring the *Swallow*'s artillery at a knock-down price.

Charles, desperate for money and unconcerned by what he regarded as lesser claims, wanted to seize everything for himself. Rupert refused to give way, prompting Clarendon to write with exasperation to Nicholas: 'You talk of money the King should have upon the prizes at Nantes; alas! He hath not only not had one penny from these, but Prince Rupert pretends the King owes him more money than ever I was worth.' [6]

Rupert expected to be rewarded for his exertions. He was no richer now than he had been when embarking on his voyage. Indeed, a decade of devoted service to the Royalist cause had failed to advance his personal fortune one jot. Whereas he had tolerated relative poverty in further-ance of his uncle's aims, he now returned from a series of death-defying adventures eager to live in a style that befitted his princely birth.

After much bad feeling on both sides, Charles and Rupert reached a compromise, dividing the limited spoils between them. Rupert saw that his men and the creditors in Toulon were properly repaid. To com-pensate for the poor return he had received from his exertions, Rupert accepted one commodity that his impoverished kinsman could confer: status. An observer reported to London: 'Prince Rupert flourishes with his Blackamoors and new liveries, and so doth his cousin Charles, they having shared the monies made of the prize goods at Nantes; and in recompense Rupert is made Master of the Horse.'[7]

The prince stayed in France, slowly recovering from the hardships of his voyage, his famed reserves of energy sapped. In June 1653, while in this weakened condition, he went to swim in the Seine and nearly drowned. This incident is indicative of a general change that had overtaken Rupert during his extreme exertions at sea: the fiery, confident, athletic young man who had set off for Kinsale had returned an altogether more sombre and muted figure. A series of lucky escapes, compounded by the loss of Maurice, had made him aware of his own mortality. Rupert's changed outlook betrayed the fact that he had reached middle age prematurely, after a youth of repeated hard knocks. There was, from now on, a hardness about him. It had formed, like the barnacles on his ships' keels, during his protracted sea quest. It was never to leave him.

Rupert ended his marathon voyage at the age of 33. He was keen to find a wife, but his financial means failed to match his princely rank: he could not wed while unable to provide his spouse with the means to live, entertain, and dress like a princess. After the disruption of the Civil War, the aristocracy found a satisfactory balance between status and fortune difficult to find. The Duke (previously Marquess) of Ormonde, the Royalist figurehead in Ireland, later wrote about his struggle to find a suitable bride for his son: 'Where there is birth and an unblemished family there is but little money to be had; £10,000 is the most that can be expected in such cases: where money is to be had there is neither birth nor alliance to be expected, and none of those that I can hear of have such surety as to counterweight the defect of quality.'[8]

Rupert epitomised this conundrum: he was a man of the highest birth, but impoverished. It was easier for his sisters to attract the attentions of eligible men. Elizabeth of Bohemia wrote to Secretary Nicholas in October 1654, 'about a match betwixt Prince Adolphus the King of Sweden's brother and Sophie; he has desired it very handsome'.[9] When this proposal failed, Sophie married the Bishop of Osnaburg, who would succeed his brother as the Elector of Hanover. Princess Elizabeth, who Descartes described as having 'angelic looks' and an 'incomparable' mind, found a serious suitor in Ladislaw, the young King of Poland, but Ladislaw expected his bride to become a Roman

Catholic, a transfer of religious loyalties that she refused to contemplate. After this disappointment, Elizabeth moved to the Lutheran Abbey of Herford, rising to become its abbess. The strawberry blonde Princess Henrietta, whose oval face had a lilies and roses complexion, was the beauty of the family. She married Prince Ragotski in 1651, but died the same year. Rupert's career as soldier and sailor had provided him with more fame and respect than any of his sisters. However, his poverty undermined his marital prospects.

The end of the Thirty Years' War restored part of the Palatine lands to the prince's elder brother, Charles Louis. The Holy Roman Emperor had also agreed to make provision for the Elector's siblings, but Rupert was still a younger son. In England, at this time, a petition to Parliament challenged the concept and custom of primogeniture. 'I do not deny but that there is a priority, a precedency of place, a civil respect due to the elder from the younger,' wrote Champianus Northtonus in a pamphlet accompanying his request, 'and before the Law, a blessing and special privilege and prerogative annexed to their birth, but I have not read that by virtue of that birthright, that then they had power to detain all the inheritance from the younger'.[10] This was the thinking of some of the aggrieved younger brothers of London, in 1654.

Similar thoughts exercised Rupert as he prepared to leave for Heidelberg that same year, intending to secure his patrimony. The Palatinate had no history of everything going to the firstborn son: Rupert's uncle – Frederick V's brother – had been included in his father's Will, with a bequest of 'a domain in the low Palatinate worth about 100,000 florins'.[11]

Rupert found life in the Stuart court-in-exile as frustrating as ever. He had maintained his close association with Sir Edward Herbert, and joined with lords Jermyn and Gerard in the faction opposed to the dominance of Clarendon in the council. However, Charles stood by his favourite and Rupert eventually threw in the towel, resigning the Mastership of the Horse and informing his cousin: 'that he was resolved to look after his own affairs in Germany, and first to visit his brother in the Palatinate, and require what was due from him for his appanage, and then to go to the Emperor to receive the money that was due to him upon the treaty of Munster.'[12] He quit Paris in June 1654.

Rupert's visit with his brother was a disaster. Charles Louis has been portrayed by Rupert's more partisan biographers as cold, calculating, and mean; whereas Rupert and Maurice had been prepared to sacrifice all for the Royalist cause, Charles Louis had collaborated with their enemies, hoping they might help him reclaim the Palatinate. However, it was Charles Louis's duty to seek such a restoration: his father, Frederick V, had died heartbroken after his similar aims had been frustrated. Charles Louis would have been failing his hereditary duty if he had not made this task his priority.

After the Thirty Years' War, the Palatinate was ruined, its population either displaced or dead. Charles Louis was summoned to the Electors' Diet in Prague in 1653, to discuss his future role with the Emperor, Ferdinand III. The two men met on White Mountain, where Frederick V's army had been defeated in an hour a generation earlier. This meeting was so successful that it was assumed Charles Louis would soon be given back his father's forfeited lands. The Emperor gave him a new title – Imperial Arch Treasurer – and Charles Louis looked forward with optimism to the next Diet at Ratisbon. There, Charles Louis was given a new, eighth electorate. His ancestors had been the senior electors. He was now the junior one. However, he had at least regained a seat round the table of Imperial influence.

Charles Louis faced a daunting task, trying to make good the ravages of war and patch up his broken lands. As he embarked on this great challenge, Rupert appeared in Heidelberg, for a short stay en route for the Emperor's Court. The younger prince arrived with a flourish at the end of June: his entourage had an African theme, with three black servants, the black boy brought back from his voyages, and a menagerie of parrots and monkeys. His reception was warm, a Commonwealth pamphlet recording that the prince was 'met without the city by the Prince Elector his brother, accompanied of much Nobility and Gentry', before adding, 'but as for his brother Maurice, you are not like to hear any more news of him.'[13]

Rupert was clear that he wanted part of the restored lands for himself. He asked for the county of Simmern, which his uncle had surrendered, before returning to Heidelberg. However, since this was the area from which Charles Louis and his heirs took their family name, it was an unrealistic demand. When Charles Louis tried to explain that he would grant his brother lands, but that reduced circumstances meant he could not meet Rupert's ambitions, the younger brother sulked. He refused to accept the offer of Laubach, claiming its terrain was wet and unhealthy. The alternative, Umstadt, was also rejected: it was a border territory, whose ownership was constantly disputed by neighbours. Rupert did not want to become his brother's border guard, his life a constant fight against marauding Hessians.

During the summer of 1654, the brothers' relationship worsened. They had never been close, but now the gorge between them broadened. Both were stubborn and each struck the other as totally unreasonable. It seemed to Rupert that he was destined to be treated like Orlando, in Shakespeare's *As You Like It*: a third son, due a slice of the family's inheritance, but denied his birthright by a selfish and greedy elder brother.

Rupert's stay with his brother lasted three weeks. It was extended, after word arrived that the Imperial heir, the King of the Romans, had died of smallpox in Vienna. The superstitious citizens had been hit by an earthquake just before the death, and then witnessed a comet in the sky, before hearing the cathedral bells ringing by themselves. Now the Emperor was extremely ill. It seemed wise to avoid such a God-forsaken place, so Rupert chose instead to accompany Charles Louis on a tour of his dependencies. Parliamentarians, always eager for news of the prince, read that: 'The Prince Elector, with his brother Prince Rupert, are returned to Heidelberg from their journey into the Duchy of Lautren, and the Counties of Strembergh and Creutznach, and there have taken throughout the new oath of allegiance.'[14] All the local nobility turned out to welcome Rupert home.

However, even when the brothers tried to relax together, problems arose. The country sports they both enjoyed were poorly executed and intensified Rupert's brooding resentment. He found his brother's gamekeepers and huntsmen hopelessly amateur and offered to bring his English hounds, at his own expense, to replace the Elector's pack. When the brothers went shooting, Rupert complained that the beaters gave him little warning when birds were approaching. Charles Louis, perhaps made jittery by his brother's constant complaints, at one point accidentally let his gun off, singeing Rupert's wig in the process. He was lucky not to be killed.

To complicate matters further Rupert unwittingly became a participant in his brother's unhappy love life. Charles Louis and his wife Charlotte had a terrible marriage: the Elector believed himself the victim of constant nagging, while the Electress felt her husband to be dismissive and cold. When Rupert arrived, Charlotte began to think of this dashing, unmarried, younger brother as a possible lover, to distract her from conjugal misery. The same thought does not appear to have crossed Rupert's mind. Although the prince was glad to have an ally who shared his low opinion of his brother, Rupert seems to have ignored the increasingly obvious advances of his sister-in-law. In fact, Rupert had noticed a tall and striking 17-year-old, Louise von Degenfeld, who served as one of Charlotte's ladies-in-waiting. Unfortunately, Charles Louis had also spotted her charms and had started sending her love notes in Italian, in which he apologised for being old, while encouraging her to become his mistress. Louise declined, refusing to compromise her honour. This made Charles Louis even keener and he contemplated making the virtuous girl his wife. Eager to scupper this plan, Charlotte insisted on remaining married, and looked to make any contact between her husband and Louise extremely difficult.

All of these elements – the tortured marriage, the secret passions, the misdirected love, the jealous suspicion – led to a farcical climax, recounted by the princes' youngest sister Sophie in her memoirs:

> The Elector had at last become fed up with the bad moods of his wife ... and had chosen as a mistress one of the ladies-in-waiting, named la baronne de Degenfeld, that the Electress was making for some time sleep in her bedroom. The business had gone on for quite a long time without the electress being aware of it, because she had not noticed the love that my brother Rupert had for this girl, in whose eyes she wanted to appear the most beautiful girl in her court. She discovered this love by a note that the prince wrote to this girl, which she believed to be for the electress, and which she passed to her [mistress] in closed hands. The electress believed it [was] also [intended for her], which made her say to the prince: 'I do not know why you complain of me, nor what reason I have ever given you to doubt my affection.'[15]

This conversation made the prince blush violently and the Electress realised by his confusion that the note had not been intended for her. She vented her embarrassment and anger on Louise, accusing her of being a slut.

A few nights later, the Electress was woken by a noise, which turned out to be the Elector getting into Louise's bed. Charlotte attacked the young girl viciously, biting deep into her little finger. The damage would have been much worse, but the Elector pushed himself between the two women and shouted for guards to come to his assistance. A truce between the women was arranged, but combusted spectacularly when the Electress discovered a hidden cache of love notes and jewels sent by her husband to his young love.

Charles Louis's sisters Elizabeth and Sophie walked in on the quarrel. They found Louise cowering behind her admirer, while Charlotte screamed abuse at them both, the jewels in her hand. Charlotte turned to her sisters-in-law and asked through her tears: 'Princesses, this is the whore's reward. Should it not be mine?' Sophie thought this a wonderfully absurd question and got an attack of the giggles. Charlotte, hysterical, started to laugh and cry at the same time. However, when Charles Louis ventured that the gems should really be returned to Louise, Charlotte hurled the jewels round the room and screamed: 'If they can not be mine, then there they are!'[16]

Charles Louis locked Louise in a room for safety. When his wife went for supper, he let her out and moved her to a room above his bedroom. He then had a hole cut in his ceiling, so he could access his mistress by ladder. The ever-vigilant Charlotte discovered this route and was about to mount the ladder with a knife in her hand when her ladies-in-waiting forcibly restrained her.

Charlotte would not allow a divorce, so Louise became Charles Louis's morganatic wife. She bore him thirteen children and died during her fourteenth pregnancy.

The Thirty Years' War had left much of mainland Europe in a dire state: the battlefield had claimed tens of thousands of victims, but the civilian population had also suffered from the devastation, rape, and pillage that came in the wake of warfare. The result was a pestilential landscape that had heaped repeated horrors on communities across the Continent: 'In some of the villages', Rupert's sister Princess Elizabeth wrote to the philosopher Descartes, 'there has been such a plague of the flies they call *cousins* that many men and animals have been stifled and rendered deaf and blind; they come in a cloud and go away in the same manner. The inhabitants attribute it to sorcery, but I account for it by the unusual floods from the river, lasting until April, when it was very warm'.[17] There were few opportunities for Rupert to ply his warrior trade in lands preoccupied with recovery, after the ravages of the three previous decades. He flirted with the idea of fighting for the Duke of Modena in 1655, but the plan was sabotaged by the French. In 1657 he briefly served the King of Hungary, 'who they say will owe his Empirate to his sword'.[18]

Meanwhile, Charles Louis was having trouble re-establishing himself in his returned lands. He had been given back Galsheim, a town near Bingen. Yet the Elector of Mainz claimed that one of his dependants, the Baron of Bremble, had a lifelong interest in the property, which produced useful revenue. Mainz turned out Charles Louis's officers, ordered new fortifications to be built, and had the Palatine coat of arms pulled down and thrown into the Rhine. Both Electors prepared to fight. Later in 1654, the Bishop of Speyer twice refused to let one of the Palsgrave's convoys pass through Deidesheim, even though it belonged to Charles Louis. He despatched 1,000 musketeers, backed up by a small cavalry force, which broke down the town's main gates and made the bishop's men flee to the safety of the castle. The Duke of Neuburg was also keeping lands in the county of Gulick from Charles Louis.

Rupert could have been a useful military ally for his brother. However, his relationship with Charles Louis was sour enough for him not to want to help. Rupert decided to retire to a quieter life, where he could immerse himself in his great passion, scientific experimentation. 'Prince Rupert was fond of those sciences which soften and adorn a hero's private hours; and knew how to mix them with his minutes of amusement, without dedicating his life to their pursuit,' wrote an admiring Lord Orford, a significant naval and political figure in the late seventeenth century, 'like us who, wanting capacity for momentous views, make serious study of what is only the transitory occupation of a genius.' Orford believed that, with Rupert's artistic abilities, if Charles I's reign had been peaceful: 'How agreeably had the prince's congenial propensity flattered and confirmed the inclination of his uncle! How the muse of arts would have repaid the patronage of the monarch, when, for his first artist, she would have presented him with his nephew!'[19]

Art and science combined in one of his more famous contributions to English life. While in Germany in the mid 1650s, Rupert was walking among some soldiers early one morning when he spotted a guard fiddling with his musket. The prince asked him what he was doing. The guard replied that the dew had rusted his gun and so he was scraping it clean. Rupert checked the soldier's progress: 'The Prince looking at it, was struck with something like a figure eaten into the barrel, with innumerable little holes closed together, like friezed work on gold or silver, part of which the soldier had scraped away ... He concluded, that some contrivance might be found to cover a brass plate with such a grained ground of fine pressed holes, which would undoubtedly give an impression all black, and that by scraping away proper parts, the smooth superficies would leave the rest of the paper white.'[20] This was the beginning of Rupert's association with mezzotint engraving.

Some have credited the Prince with being mezzotint's creator, but it seems more likely that '*mezzotinto*' was the invention of Colonel Ludwig von Sielen. Sielen's family was from Cologne, but he spent many years in the United Provinces. In August 1642, when Prince Rupert was rallying to Charles I's standard at Nottingham, Sielen proudly showed his patron, Amelia Elizabeth of Hesse-Cassel, an engraving the likes of which, he claimed, had never been seen before: 'There is not a single engraver, a single artist of any kind, who can account for, or guess how this work is done, for, as Your Highness well knows, only three methods of work are recognised in engraving, viz: 1st, engraving or cutting; 2nd, biting with acid or etching; 3rd, a method very little used, executed in small dots made with punches, but which is difficult and so arduous that it is seldom practised. My method of operation is quite different from any of these although one only notices small dots and not a single line; and if in some parts this work seems to be done in hatching, it is notwithstanding, entirely dotted ...'[21]

This effect was achieved using roulettes – wheels with sharp revolving teeth that left small indentations as it passed over metal. The roulettes, and their teeth, were of varying sizes, allowing the artist a range of effects that rival engravers could only envy. Mezzotint engraving worked in a different way from the conventional processes, for it was a 'deductive', as opposed to an 'additive' process – like photography, it worked first with the negative image, before progressing into the positive.

Rupert was a very close friend (and cousin) of William IV, the Landgrave of Hesse-Cassel, and it may have been while staying with him in 1655 that the prince first came across the mezzotint process. Another possibility is that Sielen, also a soldier, met Rupert on campaign. Sielen's duties took him on many journeys through the German states and he may have come across the prince in Heidelberg, Mainz, or Cologne, cities where Rupert spent much of the mid to late 1650s. Whatever the two men's connection, the prince took credit for improving the process after a variety of experiments in 1657 and 1658: his first known work, *Head of Titian*, dates from 1657. Whereas Sielen used the roulette solely to tidy up mistakes, Rupert employed it as part of the creative process, adding texture to his finished images. He took mezzotint to a level of refinement that Sielen's first efforts, in the early 1640s, could not rival.

John Evelyn, a keen collector of prints, was intrigued by the prince's innovations: 'This invention, or new manner of Chalcography his Highness Prince Rupert was pleased to show me with his own hands in the year 1661. He told me it was the device of a common soldier in Germany, by observing something which had scraz'd his musket, upon which (being an ingenious fellow) he refined, and he has brought it to that perfection in copper, as to exceed all the sorts of graving.'[22] Evelyn used a copy of the prince's *The Great Executioner* as a frontispiece for his book *Sculptura* in 1662. Rupert's most accomplished work, it was inspired by Juseppe de Ribera's painting of the man who beheaded John the Baptist.

Rupert's form of mezzotint was much admired: the prints of Jan Thomas of Ypres, the court painter to the Holy Roman Emperor in the mid seventeenth century, betray a style that seems to be directly drawn from the prince's methods. William Sherwin, court engraver to Charles II, asked Rupert to instruct him in his art. By way of thanks, Sherwin dedicated his 1669 print of the king to Prince Rupert.

Twenty of Rupert's mezzotint engravings survive. The majority have a classical theme, including *The Standard Bearer*, based on Pietro della Vecchia's painting of the same name. An altogether more modern feel is to be found in his informal portrait of Queen Christina of Sweden: hand on hip, braced four square on her parted legs, her hair hanging in a thick parting, she looks portly and uneasy. The prince's ability to capture everything from military posturing to Biblical tragedy, as well as contemporary caricature, display a skill that persuaded one twentieth-century expert to declare: 'The best of his mezzotints are among the finest ever produced.'[23] John Evelyn thought Rupert's work 'comparable to the greatest masters, such a spirit and address there appears in all he touches'.[24]

Rupert left his brother in mid August 1654, with a large and costly retinue of eighteen attendants, including two blackamoors. On arriving in Vienna, the prince went to see the Emperor at Ebersdorf, having been assured of a warm welcome. The Emperor was still recovering from the death of his son, the King of the Romans, whose body had been laid out in the Imperial mausoleum in a black cloak, adorned with gold and silver. Rupert was accompanied by one of Charles Louis's courtiers, who brought his master's condolences.

The Emperor was recovering from serious illness, as well as his loss, but he was determined to show how much he appreciated the prince's visit: 'Prince Rupert hath been very nobly received by his Imperial Majesty', noted a London observer, 'and had this honour, that many ambassadors attending there expecting audience, were delayed for a time, by reason the Emperor was not in health; but as soon as he went abroad Prince Rupert had the first honour of kissing his hand, and had audience with the usual ceremonies.'[25]

There was much speculation about Rupert's intentions in seeking the audience. Most thought that the prince came seeking Imperial aid for Charles Stuart. Others assumed that Rupert would also take the opportunity to press his personal interests – asking for assistance in finding Maurice's shipwreck, securing his financial dues, and exploring his marriage options. It was noted by all present that the Emperor and the prince enjoyed each other's company enormously. Rupert stayed for several weeks as an Imperial guest. In late September, it was reported in London: 'Prince Rupert doth daily receive new tokens of the Emperor's love to him, who hath promised to give him satisfaction upon his demand of payment of what hath been granted him by the treaty of Munster.'[26]

More intriguingly, separate accounts claimed: 'Letters from Regensburg do make mention, that a great match is propounded to Prince Rupert, to which the Emperor seems very much inclined, and gives all the assistance and encouragement that can be desired; Prince Rupert himself seemeth not to be very forward in it, peradventure he remembers what was told him the last spring by the fortune-teller at Paris, who advised him not to marry this year, for he found by the disordered and preposterous resolution of the Planets, that when his Lady was in Gemini, he should be no further than in Aries.'[27]

During his stay, a Turkish ambassador from Budapest arrived for an audience with the Emperor. His mission had two purposes: first, to express his dismay at the reported poisoning of twelve of his countrymen, held captive by the governor of Baab; second, 'He solicits likewise for the liberty of a young Turk, son to one of the chiefest of the Ottoman Court, lately taken at sea by Prince Rupert.'[28] It is not known if the prince was able to help.

Rupert took leave of the Emperor and his senior ministers on 23

November 1654 and headed back to Heidelberg via Nuremberg, accompanied by a large retinue. 'Prince Rupert is returned satisfied from the Emperor's Court', reported the *Faithful Scout* that Christmas, 'and hath presented the King of Scots [Charles] with two delicate Turkish horses.'[29]

Charles Stuart made a pitiful sight, during his exile on the Continent. Louis XIV's alliance with the Commonwealth had been conditional on the Royalists being expelled from France. Charles therefore spent time in Germany, the United Provinces, and the Spanish Netherlands, while the people that he hoped to rule one day watched his progress, furnishing him with some dignity by referring to him as the King of Scotland. 'A Messenger came to Whitehall with Letters from Sweden', recorded a London pamphlet, 'and saith, that he came by the way of Collen, and as he was passing Post through the City, he met the King of Scots with a great train going to dine with the Duke of Newburgh, the Duke of Brandenburgh, his Nephew [sic] Prince Rupert and some other Princes; and when the Scots King perceived that a Post was passing by, he beckoned him to him, and demanded of him whither he was bound, and answer was returned, that he was going with Letters for England; at which the titular King shook his head, and went on his way. The party saith, that he was in a sad coloured cloth Suit, a Hatband of Pearl, and a very rich Silver Belt and Sword.'[30] Charles was so poor, that throughout his long stay in the city he lodged with a widow and could not afford to maintain a coach.

Although his circumstances were humble, Charles enjoyed life in Cologne: he later remembered it being his most hospitable sanctuary. His court overseas found everyday life more difficult: 'All those who were either great on account of their birth or their loyalty, had followed him into exile; and all the young persons of the greatest distinction, having afterwards joined him, composed a court worthy of a better fate. Plenty and prosperity, which are thought to tend only to corrupt manners, found nothing to spoil in an indigent and wandering court.'[31] Sir Stephen Fox, who had made a fortune from banking, was charged with overseeing the court's finances: he set the ceiling for expenditure at a miserly 600 pistoles per month.

Since Charles I's execution, the political climate in England had intensified. The Commonwealth had moved towards more extreme republicanism, which made the restoration of the monarchy seem only a distant possibility. In April 1653 Oliver Cromwell expelled the 'Rump' Parliament. At the end of the year, he assumed the title of Lord Protector, his rule marked by God-fearing austerity. He goverened England through a network of senior army officers – major generals – whose power was as unpopular as it was undemocratic.

Throughout the mid 1650s Rupert's name continued to inspire fear in Protectorate ranks. In the summer of 1654 three conspirators stood trial in London for the planned assassination of Oliver Cromwell. They had aimed to strike at the Lord Protector on his weekly ride to Hampton Court – a journey he undertook with lightly armed bodyguards on Saturdays. Their intention was then to overwhelm the guards at the Tower of London, Whitehall, and St James's, seize the Lord Mayor of London, and proclaim Charles king. The prosecution's case against this 'base, bloody, unworthy, murderous design'[32] was strong: Somerset Fox admitted his involvement, while John Gerrard's and Peter Vowell's claims of innocence were undone by the sworn testimony of former friends (and Gerrard's brother), prepared to give evidence against them.

As the trial progressed, it was revealed that Rupert had proposed this plot to Charles. The would-be assassins had reached the prince first and explained their plan, which Rupert liked enough to organise an audience with his cousin. However, Charles poured cold water on the plot, believing assassination dishonourable conduct for a prince and calculating that the plan had little chance of success. The court heard, 'Prince Rupert afterwards did much encourage and persuade, that the design might be carried on, and promised all assistance.'[33] Rupert had no qualms about murdering the man who had engineered his uncle's execution: he was convinced that only a bold strike could overturn the Protectorate. He promised to arrange an army of 10,000 English, Scottish, and French troops to land in Sussex after Cromwell's death.

The conspiracy ended in failure and the three prisoners were found guilty. The honest and repentant Fox was reprieved. Gerrard, terrified of the rope, was granted permission to be beheaded. Vowell, stubborn to the end, refused to admit his guilt and spoke at length from the ladder, before being hanged. Both condemned men warned their audiences that, one day, the true king would return.

While Rupert agitated for armed intervention, other Stuart stalwarts saw the prince's presence as one of the main impediments to restoration. The Earl of Clarendon advised Charles to dissociate himself from

his controversial cousin, if he wanted to regain the Crown. Hurt by
Charles's growing coldness towards him, Rupert left the court-in-exile
in the late spring of 1655 – almost exactly a year after his last heated departure in protest at Clarendon's influence: 'I need not tell you by whom
Prince Rupert was turned from Court', a Protectorate spy reported to
London, 'yet perhaps you have not known that Hyde [Clarendon] then
offered Charles Stuart, that 50,000 men should be in arms in England,
before a year went about, if he would quit the Queen's Court and the
Prince's party.'[34]

This outcome remained improbable until Cromwell suddenly died at
the beginning of September 1658, leaving a vacuum that his son Richard
proved unable to fill. For sixteen months the Protectorate struggled
to survive. It eventually foundered, weighed down by vicious faction
fighting, whose main protagonists' extremism was out of kilter with the
general populace's yearning for calm and order.

General George Monck, a favourite of Cromwell's, betrayed his
patron's legacy. Marching from Scotland into England, Monck
approached London. His army of Scots and Coldstreamers stood in the
wings while Parliament received 'the secluded Members' – those who
had been elected before the Civil War, but had since been purged by
Cromwell. The House of Commons was reconstituted in mid February
1660, more sympathetic to monarchy than its predecessors had been
for a generation. It was a foregone conclusion that it would vote for
the restoration of the Crown. Three months later, England excitedly
awaited the return of Charles Stuart, so that he could become king.

CHAPTER NINETEEN

RESTORATION

'Dread Sovereign! I offer no flattering titles, but speak the words of truth: you are the desire of three kingdoms, the strength and the stay of the tribes of the people, for the moderating of extremities, the reconciling of differences, the satisfying of all interests, and for the restoring of the collapsed honour of these nations. Their eyes are toward your Majesty, their tongues with loud acclamations of joy, speak the thoughts and loyal intentions of their hearts, their hands are lift up to Heaven with Prayers and Praises; and what oral triumph can equal this your Pomp and Glory?'

The Earl of Manchester's speech to Charles II, 1 June 1660

The restoration of the Stuart line to the English throne was greeted with an almost childish enthusiasm and optimism. The majority refused to look back beyond the previous decade, deciding to draw a discreet veil of denial over the causes, course, and aftermath of the Civil War. Parliament, not without self-interest, urgently set about drafting a bill of General Pardon. Meanwhile, the people declined a close examination of their new king's character. People wanted to believe in the return of a system of government that was familiar and comforting. They chose to assume that Charles possessed the kingly qualities that neither of his Stuart predecessors had displayed.

The flirtation with republicanism had utterly failed. Most people welcomed the break with extreme Puritanism and the end of martial law. James, Duke of York, looked back with patrician contempt on a period when England was: 'Governed by an army; officers of the meanest sort of men, brewers, colliers, mechanics. Oliver Cromwell was more arbitrary than any king.'[1] The duke was confident that the joyful welcome extended to his elder brother marked the return of the correct system of government – monarchy, to its natural custodians – his family.

Those who had previously opposed the Royalist cause, in battle or in heart, now hoped to expunge their disloyalty through energetic celebrations of Charles's return. Dryden, formerly a secretary in Cromwell's regime, captured the vibrant hopefulness of the moment in verse:

> Oh Happy Age! Oh times like those alone
> By fate reserv'd for great Augustus Throne!
> When the joint growth of Arms and Arts foreshew
> The World and Monarch, and that Monarch You.[2]

Charles appeared in London on 29 May 1660, his thirtieth birthday, flanked by his two younger brothers, the dukes of York and Gloucester. All three of Charles I's sons wore silver doublets. John Evelyn watched the procession pass through the Strand, 'with a triumph of above 20,000 horse and foot, brandishing their swords and shouting with inexpressible joy; the ways strewed with flowers, the bells ringing, the streets hung with tapestry, fountains running with wine'.[3] The first days of Charles II's reign saw representatives from across his kingdoms hurry to pay homage to the new sovereign.

There were dissenters, who had hoped that the days of monarchy were gone forever. However, they were wooed in a sophisticated public relations' exercise that began the day before the Coronation. Charles processed through London in a pageant choreographed by John Ogilby, a Royalist who wanted to reconnect his contemporaries with the ways of 'the ancient Romans, who at the return of their Emperors, erected Arches of Marble'.[4] Four triumphal arches – albeit of wood – were erected in different parts of the capital.

Despite the delirious outpourings and the effusive professions of loyalty, the new king was insecure. He knew that the spirit of revolution that had undone his father could quickly reappear, if he failed to unite his people. He appreciated the need for sensitivity and generosity of spirit. To the disappointment of those supporters who had suffered so much during the previous eighteen years, he declined to punish all who had, in the words of one of his closest advisers, been 'on ye wrong side'.[5] Even Rupert's great enemy Digby understood that Charles had no choice but to offer an olive branch:

> My Lords, I profess unto you I find myself set on fire, when I think
> that the blood of so many virtuous and meritorious persons, peers, and

others of all ranks, so cruelly and so impiously shed, should cry so loud for vengeance, and not find it from us.

That many of the wickedest and meanest of the people should remain, as it were, rewarded for their treasons, rich and triumphant in the spoils of the most eminent in virtue and loyalty of all the nobility and gentry of the Kingdom. What generous spirit can make reflection on these things, and not find his heart burn into rage within him? Here it is, my Lords, that we sufferers have need of all our philosophy.

But when I consider that these are mischiefs only to the sufferers, and that to insist on a remedy might perhaps expose the public to an irreparable inconvenience, I thank God I had in an instant all my resentments calmed and submitted to my primary duty.

My Lords, we have here in our view a kingdom tossed and rolling still with the effects of past tempests; and though, God be thanked, the storm be miraculously ceased, we cannot say that the danger is, until we get into still water: that still, that smooth water, is only to be found in the generality's security from their guilty fears, and in the two Houses' union between themselves, and with their sovereign.[6]

Digby's mature eloquence echoed the general yearning for peaceful reconciliation. The executioner was employed not in the snapping of spines or the severing of heads, but in the public burning of John Milton's republican books. Only those whose hands were indelibly stained with Charles I's blood could expect no pardon. Royalists had warned during their years of impotence that: 'Natural men ... upon the violent death of their King (even after a good successor was possessed) have never rested till the doers were punished.'[7] Now they were, at last and unexpectedly, in a position to administer vengeance. Twelve of the surviving forty-one Regicides were hanged, drawn, and quartered. 'I saw not their executions,' John Evelyn wrote on 17 October, when four were despatched at Charing Cross, 'but met their quarters mangled and cut and reeking as they were brought from the gallows in baskets on the hurdle. Oh the miraculous providence of God!'[8]

One of the executed was Hugh Peters. The jury had heard sworn evidence of his extreme hatred of Royalists in general, and of three figures in particular: Charles I, Charles II, and Prince Rupert. Peters was exceptionally unpopular: the noise from the crowd was so loud and so gleeful as he mounted the ladder, as the halter was placed around his neck, and after his head was cut off, that one onlooker wrote that it sounded like the nation was celebrating a great military victory.

Not even death could spare Charles I's tormentors from the settling of scores. The coffins of Cromwell, Ireton, and Bradshaw – president at the king's trial – were prised open and their carrion hauled off to Tyburn, the place of execution for London's common criminals. There the corpses were suspended for a day, their decomposed rankness a source of lurid fascination to those who had witnessed the trio in their prime. At sunset the three cadavers were beheaded, their skulls stuck on poles on top of Westminster Hall – the building where they had tried and sentenced the king. The rest of their remains were thrown into a deep hole under the gallows. In Cambridge, eighteen years earlier, Cromwell had first declared his armed opposition to the Crown. His horse had thrown him off, depositing him beneath the town's gallows. The superstitious had claimed at the time that this was a sign that Cromwell's final resting place would be under the noose. Now, they were finally proved right.

The bones of Rupert's naval nemesis, Robert Blake, were treated with greater respect. Blake had been given a hero's burial in Henry VII's Chapel, after his death in August 1657. His coffin was now removed from this select resting place and interred in the churchyard outside – still a site of great honour.

Rupert had visited England as a restlessly energetic teenager, before returning to serve as a cavalry commander in his uncle's wars. He had intended to return after the Coronation – in order, his family suspected, to avoid the huge expense of taking part in the ceremony and its attendant celebrations. However, he had merely got his timing wrong, a news-sheet in The Hague reporting on 11 June that: 'Prince Palatine Rupert came hither lately, thinking to have met the King of England, but he was gone before, therefore he went back to his Quarters, having had leave to be absent for only twelve days.'[9] Rupert had briefly found service in the Imperial army. In March 1660 he led the successful assault on a Swedish position at Warnemunde. The prince's allegiance to the army that had defeated and imprisoned him as a young man, against the one that had given his father his brightest hope of restoration, underlined the profound reordering of European politics after the conclusion of the Thirty Years' War.

Rupert eventually arrived four months into Charles II's reign. Samuel Pepys, the 27-year-old Clerk of the Acts on the Navy Board, wrote in his

diary for 23 September 1660: 'Prince Rupert came to Court, welcome
to nobody.'[10] This was not entirely true: Charles II was delighted to see
Rupert again, awarding him a generous sum from the annual pensions
allotted his most loyal followers. There were 217 such grants, totalling
just under £80,000 per annum. Of this, Rupert received £4,000. James,
Duke of York, was similarly well disposed to the prince. The three royal
relatives shared many tastes, in particular a passion for tennis, country
sports, and scientific innovation. Charles and Rupert played tennis
against each other with huge energy: the king would weigh himself
before and after each contest, and once lost 4½ lb during a particularly
punishing match.

While Grammont and Pepys were critical of Rupert at this time,
others still noticed his charm. In October 1660, a friend of his mother
Elizabeth wrote to assure her that: 'I have had the honour to receive
your Majesty's letter by Prince Rupert: me thinks his Highness looks
very well; every body here seems to look very graciously on him.'[11]
This was heartening news for the queen, for Rupert had vowed to help
put right her financial problems while in London. She had attempted
to look after them herself, but one of her devotees had written from
London: 'Sir Thomas Treners soon will come to me and I shall not
fail to inform your Majesty what his opinion is of what concerns your
Majesty's affairs, but I think the way to effect it is to get the Prince to
speak with him for certain.'[12]

Elizabeth returned to England in May 1661, nearly half a century
after departing with girlish optimism for married life with Frederick V
in Heidelberg. She had been bitterly disappointed by Charles Louis's
attitude to her: the queen had amassed heavy debts during her decades in exile and had hoped that he would mark his restoration to the
Palatine by meeting her dues. He declined to do so, even refusing to
help her retrieve her jewels from pawnbrokers when she left Rotterdam
for England. Elizabeth felt sure that Charles Louis was unwilling to
help, because 'he does not think he deserves well enough of me to have
them after my death. But I will leave him my debts and that will trouble
him more.'[13]

Her revenge came quicker than she could have expected: Elizabeth
died of smallpox in February 1662 while staying at Leicester House, Lord
Craven's London home. Rupert was by her side when she expired and
was chief mourner at her funeral. She bequeathed her debts to Charles
Louis, trinkets to her other children (apart from Louise, who had been

Elizabeth's favourite daughter, but whose conversion to Catholicism could never be forgiven: she was not mentioned in the Will), and all her remaining assets to Rupert. This included her jewels and the hunting lodge at Rhenen, which Charles Louis had recently claimed as his own. Elizabeth had seen off this contention by reminding Charles Louis that Frederick V had bought the property for her. No son could withdraw his father's gift.

The Elector tried to minimise his losses, sending assessors to see what could be seized from his mother's apartments to please her creditors. Rupert was quicker off the mark, though, and ordered Elizabeth's rooms to be sealed. When Charles Louis insisted that his man be allowed to enter, Rupert denied him access. Having been left as his mother's executor, Rupert for once had power over Charles Louis and he was not afraid to use it. Elizabeth's Will took the brothers' relationship past breaking point.

With a king reinstated, the nation required a queen. Charles was already a proven breeder, his time in exile on the Continent resulting in numerous affairs, some of which produced children. The monarch now needed a wife of royal blood, who could legitimise his fertility and provide an heir.

Such a question was very much bound up in the nation's foreign policy requirements. Although France had sided with Cromwell during the latter's Protectorate, this unhappy decision was blamed on Cardinal Mazarin. Louis XIV, Charles's first cousin, was keen to establish good relations with Britain and keep her out of Spain's orbit. When Catharine of Braganza, daughter of Rupert's erstwhile protector, John IV of Portugal, was proposed as a bride, Louis XIV endorsed the choice, seeing it as an insult to the Spanish Habsburgs, who were still smarting from the loss of Portugal. Parliament was unhappy about a match with a Catholic, but the lure of a superb dowry persuaded Charles to override their objections: Catharine brought £360,000 in cash, as well as the exotic outposts of Bombay and Tangier. Tangier was especially attractive, providing an alternative Mediterranean staging post for British merchantmen to Cadiz or Lisbon, and Rupert was appointed one of the commissioners for its government.

Rupert, who had become one of the forty or so Privy Councillors the previous month, rode with Charles to meet the new arrival as she alighted at Portsmouth, in May 1662. The impression made by the

Infanta and her retinue was deeply unfortunate: the girl had a temperature and a cough, and on setting foot on English soil requested a cup
of tea, which, up until this point, was an extremely rare drink (the new
queen helped to put tea on its path to national popularity). Moreover,
her ladies-in-waiting were of a mesmerising plainness. They were in the
charge of the Countess of Panetra, and Count Grammont judged them:
'six frights, who called themselves maids of honour, and a Duenna,
another monster, who took the title of governess to those extraordinary
beauties'.[14] To a nation in thrall to the latest fashions, the Portuguese
women's attire was comically dowdy: they wore *guardenfantos,* dresses
whose boxlike structure neutralised the feminine form, leaving the
wearer sexless.

The Infanta's illness slightly worsened over the following weeks:
'Many impute this indisposition of the Queen's to the cough she got
on shipboard,' a correspondent informed the Duchess of Beaufort, 'but
more to her ill diet, which, I believe, is the strangest you ever heard of,
and she cannot yet bring herself to eat English meat; it is either eggs
and sugar, or eggs and lard, and now and then a burnt lean pullet (for
the Portuguese complain that all our meat is too fat), and she eats so
little of all this, that it is almost impossible she can receive any nourishment by it.'[15]

Equally remarkable to a court quickly infected by its king's love of
lightness and pleasure, was Catharine's religious devotion. Her retinue
contained six priests, and she professed astonishment at the amount of
time the English ladies took to dress and beautify themselves, wondering innocently how they were left with enough time to complete their
duties to God.

All of these foreign, Catholic, ways would have been acceptable, if
Catharine had succeeded in her principal role of procreating. There were
pregnancies, but they all miscarried. Even if they had succeeded, it is
most unlikely that she would have succeeded in breaking her husband's
addiction to the many beauties that attended his court.

The barrenness of the marriage, and the death to smallpox in
September 1660 of 'that incomparable Prince', the 21-year-old Duke
of Gloucester, left Rupert the third most important man in the royal
family. The Duke of York had a son, Charles, late in 1660, whose
christening Rupert attended, but the baby's life was brief. Records of
royal occasions and meetings always place Rupert after Charles and the
Duke of York in seniority, and ahead of every other attendant.

It was clear that Rupert would be rewarded for past loyalty, as and when the possibility arose. His move to London coincided with Parliament paying off most of the army and part of the navy, to stop 'the vast expense of the nation.' The king approved the disbandment of 15 garrisons, 21 infantry regiments, 15 cavalry regiments, and 22 warships in England, with further cuts in Scotland.

Despite there being no military position for him in England, the prince had no incentive to stay on the Continent. He had hoped to serve the Emperor against the Turks and had travelled to Vienna in April 1661, to explore possibilities. Two months later, he wrote optimistically to Will Legge: 'A friend of mine, at my coming, assured me that there were but two difficulties which hindered my advancement to the generalship of the Horse: the one was my being no Roman [Catholic]; the other, that the Marquis [Margrave] of Baden and General Zelzingmaister de Sancha had taken ill, if I was advanced before them; and as he thought both these small impediments might easily be come over, especially the first, on which he was afraid most did depend. I can see so small preparations for a war against the Turks, otherwise than for a defencing one, in which, roasting in the sun and getting sickness will be the greatest danger.'[16]

Although the Emperor and his heir encouraged Rupert to apply for the Generalship of Horse, the Imperial ministers refused to pay the prince what he was owed from the Peace of Munster. They were also extremely reluctant to offer the level of remuneration that Rupert expected for holding such a senior rank. The prince was disappointed, while acknowledging: 'It is true that money is a scarce commodity in great request in this Court.'[17] In September 1661 the Prince's youngest sister, Sophie, wrote to Charles Louis from Hanover: 'Mr Blum who is here told us this news, that Prince Rupert is returned to England dissatisfied with the Imperial Court because of a dispute over an army rank.'[18]

Rupert's mood darkened further when he was sent a copy of a book, *The Frondage,* which contained harsh criticism of his Civil War record, while strongly praising Cromwell's. 'One Harris translated it,' Rupert complained to Will Legge. 'Pray, enquire after the book, and judge if it were not a Scotch trick to send it ... I am confident if Honest Will had read the book, he had broken the translator's head.'[19]

The prince decided to move to England, lock, stock, and barrel. An inveterate country sportsman, he planned to bring over his illustrious pack of hunting dogs. Tidying up his affairs in Vienna in the autumn of

1661, Rupert boasted to Will Legge: 'The Emperor is gone to Ebersdorf, nine leagues off, where he expects my greyhounds, to course a stag.'[20] Rupert knew each of his dogs individually. When his lead hound was waning, he asked a favour of Legge: 'If my Lord Lindsay be at Court, [please remember my service to] him, with the doleful news that poor Rayall at this time is dying, after being the cause of the death of many a stag. By Heaven', he continued, 'I had rather lose the best horse in my stable!'[21] He also loved his horses: all his best mounts crossed the Channel via Dunkirk, while the prince made his way to England once more from Rotterdam. With him came large quantities of his preferred, German, Moselle wines. The transport of so many favourite things indicates that Rupert's move from the Continent to England was always intended to be permanent. He arrived in England in November 1661. From that point until his death, it was home.

The prince was quick to find outlets for his key interests in his adoptive land. Rupert's name appears as the third entry, after his two royal cousins, in the list of founding members of the Royal Society. Lord Orford referred to the prince as a 'philosophic warrior'[22], but Rupert's fascination with science and the advancement of knowledge was not unusual among the upper echelons of English society. In dedicating much of his time to such pursuits, he was very much the product of a questioning age. It was the Restoration that led to the formalisation of a system of enquiry that had been growing in England since the beginning of the century.

Sir Francis Bacon had been an influential champion in this field during the reign of Rupert's grandfather, James I. In 1603 he wrote *Of the Interpretation of Nature,* which can be viewed as the blueprint for his later intellectual pursuits. In the four years before he became Lord Chancellor, between 1614 and 1618, he produced the *New Atlantis,* which proposed the foundation of a scientific body of twenty-four members: half of these were to travel, collecting foreign literature; three were to digest and dissect the thoughts contained in these books; a further three were to look for foreign mechanisms that could be adapted for use in England; another trio was to process experimental data from such machinery and look for leads towards further invention; and the remaining three were to be wise men, charged with taking an overview of all these elements of advancement, to the betterment of mankind's day-to-day existence.

Bacon sought a system of knowledge that was logical, useful, and proof-based, governed by a troop of wise men occupying what he called a 'house of Salomon': 'Those, therefore, who determine not to conjecture and guess,' urged Bacon, 'but to find out and know; not to invent fables and romances of worlds, but to look into and to dissect the nature of this real world, must consult only things themselves,'[23] Bacon's insistence on conducting his own experiments cost him his life: while testing his theory that ice could delay putrefaction, he packed a dead chicken with snow, catching a fatal chill in the process. By the time of his death this doyen of the Elizabethan and Jacobean courts had helped to popularise a brand of experimental science known as the 'new philosophy'.

Bacon's core belief, that the quest for learning should be fostered by noble men with superior minds, survived the strife of the Civil War. By the time of the battle of Naseby, a group of a dozen Parliamentarian intellectuals was regularly meeting in London, to discuss experiments and theories over lunch. Among them was Dr Wilkins, Puritan chaplain to Rupert's brother Charles Louis, and Robert Boyle, whose innovative work with air pumps and gases led him to formulate 'Boyle's Law'. After the war, the Philosophical Society began to flourish in Oxford – again with Parliamentary champions. Wilkins was once more to the fore, hosting meetings in his room at Wadham College – 'then the place of resort for virtuous and learned men'.[24] The Wadham conversations were recorded and published for wider circulation.

Theodore Haak was another influential man of learning with a connection to Rupert's family. Haak was a Palatine subject who had helped raise funds in England during James I's reign, in the hope of restoring his elector by force of arms. Haak was a keen student of Bacon's texts and also of the teachings of John Amos Comenius. Comenius was a philosopher exasperated by the arcane approach to education of the two universities. Oxford and Cambridge refused to teach mathematics, or to break free from the Classical texts and medieval customs that had dominated learning for so long. John Milton was swayed by Comenius's advocacy of modern, inclusive scholarship and it influenced his writings on education.

The diarist John Evelyn, a keen champion of learning and the author or interpreter of twenty-five books, was another enthusiast for the new philosophy. He wanted its different strands brought together in a cohesive way. Frustrated by the Protectorate's refusal to help the march of intellectual progress, Evelyn wrote to Boyle in 1659 with plans for a system based on benevolent paternalism: 'Since we are not to hope for a Mathematical College, much less a Salomon's House ... why might not some gentlemen, whose geniuses are greatly suitable, and who desire nothing more than to give a good example, preserve science, and cultivate themselves, join together in a society and resolve upon some orders and economy, to be mutually observed, such as shall best become the end of their union?'[25]

The Stuart Restoration gave form to Evelyn's fantasy. Charles II was fascinated by scientific instruments: his bedroom contained seven clocks, while an eighth, in his ante-room, showed the direction in which the wind was blowing. The king conducted experiments in alchemy with his friend the Duke of Buckingham, an amateur chemist. Later in his reign, he encouraged the work of John Flamsteed, appointing him the first Astronomer Royal in 1675, when the foundation stone of the Royal Observatory was laid at Greenwich. Charles also had a passion – and genuine gift – for the science of naval design.

When the Philosophical Society approached him, soon after his Coronation, the king was happy to give it his enthusiastic encouragement. In 1662 it was rebranded as 'the Royal Society' and its charter was sealed. The following year, in April, a second charter was incorporated, with Charles proclaiming himself 'Fundator' (founder) and patron. As a sign of his special attachment to the new body, Charles gave a large silver mace, embossed with the symbols of his kingdoms on its head, with instructions that it be present at all subsequent meetings of the Royal Society.

In return for his patronage, Charles received a glowing commendation from the Society's Fellows: 'Sir, Of all the Kings of Europe, Your Majesty was the first, who confirmed this noble design of experiments, by your own example, and by a public establishment. An enterprise equal to the most renowned actions of the best princes. For, to increase the powers of all mankind, and to free them from the bondage of errors, is greater glory than to enlarge Empire, or to put chains on the necks of conquered nations.'[26] The Fellows decided to match the king's enlightened mindset and forbade the discussion of religion or politics at their meetings.

Prince Rupert was one of the twenty-one councillors who oversaw the workings of the Royal Society, after its inception. There were a further 119 original Fellows, who included Boyle, Evelyn and Robert Hooke.

'Their purpose is', recorded the Royal Society's first historian, 'in short, to make faithful Records of all the works of Nature, or Art, which can come within their reach; that so the present Age, and Posterity, may be able to put a mark on the errors, which have been strengthened by long prescription; to restore the truths, that have lain neglected; to push on those, which are already known, to more various uses; and to make the way more passable, to what remains unravelled. This is the compass of their design.'[27]

So envious were the French of this prestigious body that they soon attempted to copy it. In 1666, Colbert founded the Académie des Sciences. However, Louis XIV's imitation was not the construction of like-minded amateurs advocated by Evelyn. It was, rather, a state-controlled entity with a penchant for pretentiousness that the Anglo-Saxon original found ludicrous: 'I know indeed,' wrote the Bishop of Rochester in 1680, 'that the English Genius is not so airy and discursive, as that of some of our neighbours, but that we generally love to have reason set out in plain undeceiving expressions; as much as they to have it delivered with colour and beauty.'[28]

Rupert's nature was perfectly suited to the straightforward, English model. He was a respected scientist and inventor, whose combination of high birth and inquisitiveness were topped off by a determination to dirty his hands in the laboratory and to sweat in the foundry. One poet paid tribute to Rupert's efforts in verse:

> Thou prideless thunderer, that stooped so low
> To forge the very bolts thy arm should throw,
> Whilst the same eyes great Rupert did admire,
> Shining in fields and sooty at the fire:
> At once the Mars and Vulcan of the war.[29]

One of the first demonstrations that the Royal Society witnessed, at the command of Charles II, was of the extraordinary qualities of 'Prince Rupert's Drops'. These were globules of green glass that had been dropped into cold water while still molten. They solidified on impact, forming elongated bubbles. On 14 August 1661, the records of the Royal Society noted that: 'A blow with a small hammer ... will not break one of the glass drops made in water, if it be touched no where but upon the body. Break off the top of it and it will fly immediately into very minute parts with a smart force and noise; and these parts will

easily crumble into a coarse dust.'³⁰ At the time the 'Drops' were seen
as puzzling creations – even Pepys conceded that the 'chymicall glasses'
were 'a great mystery to me'– whose properties became part of everyday
language. In *Hudibras* we read:

> Honour is like that glass bubble
> That finds philosophers such trouble,
> Whose least part crack'd, the whole does fly
> And wits are crack'd to find out why.³¹

The Royal Society contained a rich crop of enquiring minds, not all
of them from the gentlemanly stock that Evelyn had envisaged. These
academics sometimes looked down on their aristocratic colleagues: the
astronomer Thomas Streete once told Rupert that he was 'no mathematician'. The prince was indignant and Streete was ever after referred to
as: 'the man that huffed Prince Rupert.'³²

Among Rupert's abler Fellows was William Petty, the son of a
clothier, who was to become one of the most respected and influential
statisticians of his age. Petty had studied on the Continent during the
Civil War, mastering the Classical languages and mathematics at an
early age. In France he learnt about anatomy. He also read philosophy
with a young Thomas Hobbes. Petty never allowed his poverty to hinder
his studies: once, his money spent, he staved off starvation for a week by
living off a diet of walnuts, foraged in the wild.

Petty attracted public attention in London after the execution of a
woman called Anne Green. She was found guilty of murdering her illegitimate child, and hanged. While she was lying in a mortuary, somebody noticed that she was still breathing: in a superstitious age, such
an escape from death was seen to be the work of God, intervening to
spare a wrongly convicted innocent. After an onlooker had pummelled
her rib cage and stomach, Petty was one of two doctors summoned to
administer gentler restorative measures. They 'gave her cordial spirits,
took off five ounces of blood, tickled her throat with a feather, and
put her to bed with a warm woman'.³³ A complete – and seemingly
miraculous – cure followed.

Petty's scientific studies were of a broad range and his famed brilliance secured him a founding Fellowship of the Royal Society, as well
as a knighthood. His debut as a lecturer was a talk on the history of
shipbuilding. Many of the early talks had a military or naval focus,

demonstrating that Rupert was not the only man of war intrigued by science: indeed, even the peace-loving Petty was to serve as Physician General to the army in Ireland. 'Our greatest captains and commanders have enrolled their names', boasted the Bishop of Rochester in his 1680 history of the Royal Society, 'and have regarded these studies: which are not, as other parts of learning, to be called the studies of the gown; for they do as well become the profession of a soldier, or any other way of life.'[34] Rochester must have had Rupert very much in mind when he wrote that: the prince was the archetypal soldier-scientist.

There were others of a similar bent: Lord Brouncker, the first president and (in Evelyn's words) 'that excellent mathematician', gave a popular talk on 'Experiments of the Recoiling of Guns'. His practical demonstration involved the firing of a full charge (that is, 'about a four-penny weight') of gunpowder in the Society's courtyard at Gresham College. 'The History of Making Gunpowder' was another talk that would have appealed to the prince. The Register of the Royal Society records Rupert's 'mode of fabricating a gunpowder of ten times the ordinary strength at that time used'.[35] There were also examinations of the effect of rust on metal weapons and attempts to measure the different volume of artillery fire from the top and bottom of hills.

The prince harnessed the burgeoning scientific knowledge of the day in order to assist him in mechanical advances. His interest in art led to the introduction of a device that helped the onlooker to judge perspective, but the majority of his studies had a military focus. In March 1663, he wrote of the best way 'To make small shot of different sizes', the handwritten record of which remains in the Royal Society's archives today. It is clear that the experiment was well practised by the prince and he advised those following his directions to be careful throughout the process: 'When it is done, take your shot out of the pale of water and put them in a frying pan over the fire to dry them, which must be done warily, still shaking them that they melt not, and when they are dry you may separate [them].'[36] From this level of detail, it seems evident that the prince had suffered a few setbacks late in the process in his own laboratory.

Similarly, he shared with the Royal Society 'A Description of the Way of Making Good Gunpowder', in July 1663. He gave directions on the optimum blend of saltpetre, brimstone, and coal, ending with the warning: 'Note only, because this powder is pretty strong, you must make your charge somewhat less, in all small guns; and especially in

Rupert and his African page, after a portrait by Bouidon.

The *Royal Prince* and other vessels at the Four Days Fight, 1–4 June 1666,
by Abraham Storck.

Contemporary engraving of a trepanning. Rupert had to undergo this procedure twice.

Rupert's mezzotint of the Execution of John the Baptist.

Peg Hughes, by Robert Williams after Peter Lely.

Ruperta; Rupert and Peg's daughter,
by Godfrey Kneller.

(Top right) Rupert and his son, Dudley,
by Vignon.

Stoneware bust of Prince Rupert,
by John Wight.

Old Guard Chamber in the
Round Tower, Windsor Castle,
by J. Stephanoff.

The Hudson's Bay Company's
portrait of Rupert as first
Governor of the Company.

pistols, for else they will break.'[37] The prince's powder was reckoned to have ten times the strength of regular gunpowder.

Rupert also improved the technique of laying and detonating mines, both for blowing up rocks and for use underwater. His list of discoveries and experiments is impressive because of its range, rather than being glamorous in its content. He improved the locks on firearms and developed a form of grape shot (referred to as 'hail shot') for use by artillery at close range. He also presented a gun that fired repeated rounds at high speed; a handgun with rotating barrels; as well as an explosive charge that could be powered through water towards its target. These last three innovations were extremely primitive ancestors of, in turn, the machine gun, the revolver, and the torpedo.

Rupert's experiences – and frustrations – during his marathon sea voyage encouraged him to make naval experiments. He developed a 'diving engine', designed to retrieve sunken objects (treasure or lost cargo) from below the surface. Similarly, he remembered the long days he and his captains had spent during their voyage, unsure of where they and their colleagues were. The prince's naval quadrant was a mildly successful attempt to find bearings in the ocean's water wilderness.

Rupert was less interested in the biological experiments of the Royal Society. Hooke talked on 'A Method For Making a History of the Weather'. He also gave an 'Account of a Dog Dissected': 'In prosecution of some inquiries into the nature of respiration in several animals', the Royal Society recorded, 'a dog was dissected, and by means of a pair of bellows, and a certain pipe thrust into the wind-pipe of the creature, the heart continued beating for a very long time while after all the thorax and belly had been opened.'[38]

By 1671, when Sir Isaac Newton was elected to its ranks, the Royal Society consisted of 187 ordinary Fellows, as well as its royal ones. Rupert, by that stage, was experimenting with a new substance, to improve the effectiveness of naval artillery. Known as 'Prince's metal', it contained a higher proportion of zinc than that found in brass. This followed a stint as an admiral: a period when, instead of attacking British shipping as a buccaneer, as he had done in the Interregnum, he helped to lead it with distinction.

CHAPTER TWENTY

MAN OF WAR

*'It was that memorable day, in the first summer of the late War, when
our Navy engaged the Dutch: a day wherein the two most mighty
and best-appointed Fleets which any age had ever seen, disputed the
command of the greater half of the Globe, the commerce of nations,
and the riches of the Universe.'*

John Dryden, 3 June 1665

Greedy for the same trade, the merchants of England and the
Netherlands were bound to collide overseas. The Dutch began
their expeditions to the East in 1590 and became the first European
power since Spain and Portugal to construct a sizeable commercial network abroad. The English followed in their wake, their activities soon
cutting into the United Provinces' profits. The Dutch saw off foreign
competition in Java and Ceylon through the threat of military force.
In 1622, though, they showed how far they would go, if their business
interests were threatened.

The Dutch had become deeply irritated by English incursions into
their spice business (predominantly in cloves) in Amboyna, in the
Molucca Islands. The English even erected five factories there, which
profited from their merchants' easy relations with the native inhabitants.
Pretending that they had learnt of a plot to overrun their castle on the
island, the Dutch garrison rounded up the Englishmen, torturing and
then murdering them – 'An act so horrid!', a London writer claimed,
fifty years later, 'That the Hollanders are infamous to this very day
among the rude and savage Indians, for their barbarous inhumanity.'[1]
James I chose to treat 'the Amboyna Massacre' as a terrible accident,
rather than let it develop into a cause for war. It was said, though, that
he prophesied that his grandson would one day seek vengeance from
the Dutch for the atrocity.

In fact, the first full-blown war between the maritime nations involved
no King of England, Stuart or otherwise: it was fought during the brief

period when both countries were simultaneously republics. Given the constitutional and religious similarities on both sides of the North Sea, some in Parliament had hoped to join with the States-General, in a Protestant crusade against European Catholicism, to form 'the New Jerusalem'. However, the United Provinces dismissed this notion, having had a surfeit of warfare in the preceding centuries. This placing of materialism over religion disappointed many in London and convinced them that the United Provinces were insufficiently godly. Such insincerity invited correction.

The Dutch were unconcerned by the hostility brewing in London. They underestimated England's naval power, while overestimating their own: the United Provinces' last significant engagement had been the utter destruction of the Spanish fleet in 1639. Since that glorious victory, however, Cromwell had expanded Charles I's ambitious shipbuilding programme to create a mighty fleet. Dutch reinforcements had been constructed, but at a gentler pace.

The Lord Protector had planned to unleash his squadrons against Catholic France. However, economic considerations soon eclipsed religious ones. The Commonwealth's finances were depleted by a succession of blighted harvests and repeated visits by the plague. Meanwhile, the rapid expansion of Dutch shipping in the Baltic, Mediterranean, and Spanish arenas made matters even more desperate: the trade built up by England while much of Europe was convulsed by warfare was rapidly reclaimed by the United Provinces, when peace returned. Dutch ships contained leaner, tougher crews who could undercut their rivals' costs. As the Duke of Buckingham observed: 'The Power of Holland depends upon two things, their Parsimony, and their Liberty. By their Liberty, they are encouraged to trade, and by their Parsimony, they are encouraged to do it cheaper than any other people.'[2]

In an attempt to see off its financial woes, Parliament reached for the blunderbuss. It approved the Navigation Act, which insisted that all goods bound for English colonies should only be transported in English ships. For the States-General this was a highly unwelcome development. However, Parliament's assertion that all foreigners should acknowledge England's maritime pre-eminence by saluting her shipping in 'British Seas' was insufferable. The definition of these seas was open to interpretation. London's version was, in Dutch eyes, unacceptably greedy.

The First Anglo-Dutch War began in 1652. Blake, his reputation made by his successes against Prince Rupert, again commanded the

English fleet with distinction. The United Provinces' colonies were infiltrated and their ships – so numerous, that they could not all receive adequate protection – were captured in droves. There were three major naval engagements in 1653. At the battle of Portland, fought over three days, nine Dutch ships were sunk, thanks largely to the fighting skill of George Monck, recently moved from his land command to become one of the three 'generals at sea'. Monck was also to the fore later in the year, when twenty Dutch vessels were destroyed off the Gabbard shoal. When peace came, the English emerged as victors from a war the United Provinces had assumed would be theirs.

By the time Charles II was restored to the throne, the navy, which had grown from 39 ships in 1649 to 156 in 1660, had amassed debts of £1.3 million. The army, also expensive, but deeply mistrusted, was quickly whittled down from its Commonwealth and Protectorate head count of 50,000 to a token force of a few thousand. But the new monarch had a pride in his fleet that was shared by many of his subjects and he kept the pruning of the navy to a minimum. Not only the Anglo-Dutch war but also the triumphs of the Elizabethan age (which were viewed in a particularly rosy hue) gave the navy a romance and glamour that rendered its massive cost acceptable. It was seen as the one sure defence against Catholic aggression. The Earl of Essex, early in the Civil War, had received instructions from Parliament for England's safety, of which one of the most fundamental was: 'That the safest and surest defence of this Kingdom is our Navy, and that we can never be hurt by land by a foreign Enemy, unless we are first beaten at sea.'[3]

Indeed, huge bounty from recent attacks on the Spanish Main, the South American coast that is now Colombian and Venezuelan, convinced many that building up the navy, and letting it loose on weaker foes, made sound financial sense. The navy became the linchpin of English colonial growth – a combined legacy of Cromwell and the two kings whose rules sandwiched his Lord Protectorship.

In 1660, Charles II tightened up the Commonwealth's Navigation Act, insisting that key commercial products be transported only by English ships. The commodities listed included timber, grain, salt, and wine from the Baltic and the Mediterranean. Foreign merchants were also forbidden from importing tobacco, sugar, and dyes from England's North American colonies. Further Acts, in 1662 and 1663, tightened England's hold over foreign shipping and the right to trade with its American possessions. At the same time it was stipulated that at least two-thirds of the ships' crews must be English-born. This was extreme and aggressive protectionism, conjured up by a nation confident in its maritime muscle.

Although the navy was a brutal place for the average seaman, with press-gangs having to top up the ships' complements, it still attracted many volunteer officers. In particular, impoverished Royalists, their fortunes devoured by Civil War defeat, saw the sea as the quickest available route to riches. James, Duke of York, provided a rallying point for those who hoped for war. A brave soldier, who had fought for Louis XIV under Marshal Turenne, James now sought to find a meaningful role for himself while his brother ruled. The duke had been appointed Lord High Admiral as a boy. Now he was in his prime, he looked to find purpose in his courtesy title. His secretary Sir William Coventry, when looking back on the causes of this war, wrote: 'I must not forget to add his Royal Highness's own vigour, who, having been bred to arms, was willing to have an occasion to show his courage on sea as on land.'[4]

One of the most able and ruthless of the Duke of York's warmongers was Sir Robert Holmes, a stalwart companion of Rupert's on land and sea. In the summer of 1661, a correspondent wrote from The Hague to Rupert's mother, Elizabeth, expressing Dutch concern at Holmes's presence off West Africa: 'It is believed that in England a design has been hatched on the river Guaiana, following on information given by His Highness Prince Rupert.'[5] Holmes returned to the territory he had first visited with the prince, relishing the opportunity for friction and sure of action. Conflict was inevitable, since the Dutch West India Company claimed a commercial monopoly in the area.

At the same time, the English were intolerant of Dutch intrusion into their North American commerce. They captured New Amsterdam from its Dutch governor, Peter Stuyvesant, in April 1663. The English renamed the port New York, in honour of their Lord High Admiral. Just before Christmas the same year, the English waylaid the Dutch Smyrna Convoy outside Cadiz.

In January 1663, a joint stock company was formed in London, called the Royal African (or Guinea) Company. The Duke of York became its governor and Prince Rupert was one of the company's patentees, as well as one of its councillors. Gold ore and slaves were the principal goals of the investors: Jamaica had become English during Cromwell's time and slave labour was required to suffer the harsh conditions of the sugar and tobacco plantations. Planters would pay £18 for a 'negro'.

In 1664 the company sent Holmes to West Africa with two warships and orders to protect English commercial interests there. He exceeded his brief, overrunning Dutch trading stations, including Cormantine Castle, and bringing havoc in his wake: at Aga his African mercenaries fell on surrendered Dutchmen, hacking off their heads for trophies. Open hostilities were now inescapable, with avenging attacks ordered by the States-General on Holmes, as well as against English shipping in the West Indies.

The Zeeland admiral, Michiel Adrians zoon de Ruyter, had been summoned out of retirement as a merchant captain to lead the United Provinces' fleet during the previous war. He was now sent with twelve ships to deal with six English vessels that were causing trouble off Cape Verde. News reached London that de Ruyter had captured Cape Verde and was now heading for the African coast, his intention the recapture of Cormantine Castle.

Because of his familiarity with West Africa, because he was a member of the council of the Royal African Company, and because of his fighting reputation, 'Prince Rupert was ordered, with twelve men of war and six company's ships of, at least, forty guns each; and the fleet sailed about the middle of October.'[6] The Duke of York felt the Dutch had underestimated England's resolve: 'Whereas they think us in jest', Pepys recalled the duke's secretary saying about his master, 'he believes that the Prince (Rupert) which goes in this fleet to Guinny will soon tell them that we are in earnest.'[7] The United Provinces had provided Rupert with a childhood refuge and had consistently shown him kindness since. In 1649 he had recognised his debt to the States-General with a fulsome tribute:

> I beg you, Sirs ... to believe that in my case I will never forget to bear witness to your lordships' friendship and protection on all occasions by my very humble service, protesting to you, that I am passionately,
> High and mighty lords, your very humble servant,
> Rupert[8]

Now the Prince was riding out in his flagship, the *Henrietta*, at the head of a squadron looking for action against the Dutch. As always, his loyalty to the English Crown overrode all other considerations. Rupert was excited not only by the prospect of taking prize ships, but also by the scientific experiments entrusted to him by the Royal Society: during the voyage, he was to test out a new sounding device without the use of a line and to obtain samples of water from the depths of the sea. Pepys recorded the sense of optimism surrounding Rupert's assignment: 'This morning, by three o'clock, the Prince and King, and Duke with him, went down the River, and the Prince under sail the next tide after, and so is gone from the Hope. God give him better success than he used to have!'[9]

It was a short command, terminating when Rupert had got no further than Portsmouth: news that a larger Dutch fleet was being fitted out encouraged James to take over active control of the navy. Full-scale war was in sight.

Rupert fell severely ill, soon after his recall from the expedition. His enemies claimed he had fallen victim to the effects of dissolute living, but he was almost certainly suffering from an inflammation of the head wound received when serving under Marshal Gassion. He recuperated slowly in London. Late in 1664 the prince was sufficiently recovered to accompany the Duke of York as he spent four days in the Channel, assessing the fleet. These sea trials convinced James that the English had a fleet so powerful that they would quickly overcome an overawed enemy. However, James had no experience of war at sea, and he was forgetting the hardiness and pride of the Dutch, which had ensured their survival against Spain in her pomp. He also appears to have been unaware that Johan de Witt, the *Raadpensionaris* (Grand Pensionary) of Holland, had spent the years since the previous war building up a significant fleet of warships.

On 4 March 1665, war was declared. Both Houses of Parliament urged Charles II on, granting the navy £2.5 million to prosecute the contest. The Earl of Clarendon, the king's senior councillor, was chief among 'those ministers who should otherwise have preserved peace at any price',[10] but his words of caution were ignored. Both the Dutch and the English were confident that they would win the Second Anglo-Dutch War.

The Duke of York commanded the English navy. It was divided into three squadrons, which bore the names of colours – the Red, the White, and the Blue. James was admiral of the senior unit, the Red, which comprised the centre of the combined force. Rupert was vice-admiral of the fleet and admiral of the second squadron, the White, whose place was at the front of the fleet. Admiral of the junior detachment, the Blue, was a former Cromwellian, the Earl of Sandwich. Each squadron had its own vice-admiral and rear-admiral: in all there were seventeen flag officers, eleven of whom had served the Commonwealth and Protectorate.

York's plan in 1665 was simple: to sail to the Dutch coast and block-ade the enemy ports until the 'Hogen-Mogen Hollanders' were forced to make a dash for the open seas. It was clear, after all, that the United Provinces' survival depended on trade. When they were out in the open, the English were confident that they would make short work of the Dutch. Unfortunately, the logistics and expense of supplying a sizeable fleet at sea was beyond the navy. James had to cease the blockade and lead his ships back to the Gunfleet, where food and fresh water were readily available.

While there, he learnt that the Dutch were approaching, looking for battle. James sailed the fleet to Southwold Bay, near Lowestoft: on 3 June, a cloudless day with a strong southwesterly wind, the Dutch attacked York's fleet with 113 men-of-war. The English had 98 warships of a size and firepower that, the Duke of York boasted, made his fleet 'the greatest England had ever seen'.[11]

Seventeenth-century naval encounters were brutal affairs, the ship's decks awash with blood as cannon fired at close range, scything through flesh, while splinters tore round decks crammed with sailors, marines, and gentlemen volunteers. Medical knowledge was minimal, and what was practised was often life-threatening. There was no dedicated hospital for wounded sailors and the compensation available for men disabled in action would have been familiar to Elizabeth I's men. Each injury received a set amount: £6 13 s. 4 d. for the loss of each leg; £4 per eye; and £15 for being deprived of both arms.

The battle of Solebay began at dawn, although the main forces were not fully engaged until ten in the morning. From that moment, it was a desperately hard-fought encounter. The poet John Dryden recalled being able to hear the gunfire in London, 'like the noise of distant thun-der, or of swallows in a chimney'. The capital's audience was gripped by the distant drama. Passengers on the Thames urged the watermen to pull more softly on their oars, the better to catch the far-away sound of rumbling death: 'The noise of the cannon from both Navies reached our ears about the City', Dryden continued, 'so that all men being alarmed with it, and in a dreadful suspense of the event which we knew was then deciding, every one went following the sound as his fancy led him; and leaving the Town almost empty, some took towards the Park, some cross the River, others down it; all seeking the noise in the depth of silence.'[12]

Rupert led the English formation, although he was suffering from health so poor that he could barely stand. His old head injury had flared up dangerously, causing him agony. A poet described the sight of the ailing prince stoically fulfilling his duty while in real pain:

> Rupert that knew no fear, but Health did want,
> Kept State suspended in a Chair Volant;
> All save his Head shut in that wooden Case,
> He shew'd but like a broken weather glass;
> But arm'd with the whole Lyon Cap-a-Chin,
> Did represent the Hercules within.[13]

Eyewitnesses present a less florid, but equally admiring, view of the prince's conduct during the battle. An official account recorded that he 'received the charge of their fleet, not discharging again till close to, and then firing through and through the enemy with great success'[14] — a description that could have applied as well to the prince on horseback, two decades earlier, when he forbade his men from firing before they were into the enemy lines.

Over the preceding weeks the Duke of York, with his flag officers, had painstakingly planned to fight the Dutch in line: his ships would sandwich each other, creating a column of blazing guns, against which the Dutch would flail without form or plan. However, in the Titanic clash, it was impossible to preserve such order for long. The general mêlée that ensued was much more to Rupert's liking. He preferred to let his men loose, confident that the superior spirit of his officers would win the day.

The Dutch commander was Jacob van Wassenaer, Heer van Opdam, a gallant old soldier with little experience of sea warfare. He owed his command to compromise: there was fierce competition among the five fleets of the United Provinces for precedence, underpinned by ancient rivalries. Opdam – being a cavalry officer, not a naval one – was a choice designed to sidestep these problems, but choosing a man of such inexperience was a risk.

Even Opdam was alive to the danger of attacking the English in their lair, but the States-General's delegates rebuffed his concerns. When his senior officers heard the command to strike the enemy in Solebay, they

were quick to voice their consternation: 'I am entirely in your sentiments', Opdam said, 'but here are *my orders*, tomorrow my head shall
be bound with laurel, or with cypress.'[15]

In the early afternoon Opdam, on the *Eendracht*, led a fierce attack
by several Dutch ships on the Duke of York's flagship, the *Royal Charles*.
The exchange of gunfire was relentless and claimed Opdam's life. Soon
afterwards, a cannonball from the Duke of York's ship pierced the
Eendracht's powder store, causing her to erupt in splinters: all but a
handful of the 400 men on board perished. An English poet saw this
as suitable repayment for the Dutchman's arrogance in attacking the
Duke of York:

> Let Opdam speak, that now with Neptune dwells,
> Condemn'd to sword fish in his watery cells,
> For daring to attack your Royal Ship,
> With his unequal and confounded skip:
> See where he flew in Sulphorous atoms, sent
> To th' Prince of Flames, for his most bold attempt ...[16]

The watching Netherlanders fought on briefly after the loss of their
commander and his flagship, but eventually broke and fled. James
ordered an all-out pursuit of the defeated Dutch, before retiring to his
cabin at 11 p.m., to recover from an exhausting, terrifying, and exhilarat-
ing day. However, while James slept on a quilt with his clothes on,
one of his courtiers, Henry Brouncker (brother of the first president of
the Royal Society) intervened. Possibly he was worried about his own
safety or was carrying out a request from the Duchess of York to keep
her husband safe. Whatever the reason, Brouncker persuaded James's
captain to slacken his sails. The rest of the fleet followed the flagship's
lead. In the morning, James awoke fresh, ready to resume the previous
day's engagement. To his fury, the Dutch were nowhere to be seen:
they were over the horizon, almost home, the opportunity to catch up
with them gone.

James had won a battle, sinking twenty Dutch warships, slaying
four enemy admirals, and taking, killing, or wounding 10,000 of their
men. His own casualties numbered just 800. But the main job was left
undone by Brouncker's untimely meddling. As Rupert later reported
to Parliament: 'I shall only say, in short, if the Duke's orders, as they
ought, had been strictly observed, the victory which was then obtained

had been much greater, nay, in all probability the whole fleet of the enemy had been destroyed.'[17]

Returning disconsolate to land, James and Rupert were summoned by a king grateful for his fleet's success. However, their supporters complained that reports of the victory failed to honour the personal contributions of the commanders. A civil servant called Hickes thought more should have been made of the duke's bravery when slogging it out with Opdam and his posse of warships. 'Nor is a word said of Prince Rupert', Hickes continued, 'though the seamen said none excelled him in valour and success.'[18] When some claimed that the Earl of Sandwich deserved more credit for the victory than Rupert, a few of the prince's supporters in Parliament mischievously proposed that Rupert receive a £10,000 reward from a grateful nation, while Sandwich be given half a crown for his inferior efforts.

Charles was shocked at the bloodiness of an engagement that had claimed so many of his senior officers and noblemen, including James's vice-admiral, Sir John Lawson; Rupert's rear-admiral, Robert Sansum; and the earls of Marlborough and Portland. The Queen Mother intensified Charles's anxiety: Henrietta Maria visited England that summer, and she learnt that James had nearly been the victim of a costly Dutch cannonball, which had carried away his friend the Earl of Falmouth, Lord Muskerry, and Richard Boyle, the second son of the Earl of Burlington. James had been standing close to them, 'their blood and brains flying in the Duke's face',[19] according to Pepys: indeed, Boyle's severed head had knocked James off his feet. Henrietta Maria pointed out that, with the Duke of Gloucester dead and Catharine of Braganza having yet to produce an heir, James's preservation was essential to the future of the Stuart dynasty. Egged on by his mother, Charles called a council of war attended by James, Rupert, and all the flag officers. Here, according to John Evelyn, an onlooker, the king 'determined that his Royal Highness should adventure himself no more this summer'.[20]

With James confined to shore, the king offered control of the fleet at sea to Rupert and the Earl of Sandwich. However, Rupert refused to accept divided command with an old adversary and Sandwich therefore assumed overall authority. But Sandwich was disgraced soon afterwards – accused of pocketing bounty from captured Dutch merchantmen, he was bundled off to serve as ambassador to Spain, to avoid impeachment at home. In early 1666, command of the navy was divided between George Monck (who had been created Duke of Albermarle and

Lord General, as rewards for his role in the Restoration) and Prince Rupert.

Albermarle and Rupert were old acquaintances. Albermarle's record extended back to the unsuccessful expeditions to Cadiz and La Rochelle, in the 1620s. He had fought for Charles I in the Civil War until captured at the battle of Nantwich in 1644. Rupert had personally tried to broker his release, without success. During Albermarle's captivity in the Tower of London, he was persuaded to switch allegiance to Parliament. He then fought well for Cromwell, impressing particularly at the battle of Dunbar in 1650, before showing he had a real gift for naval combat in the First Anglo-Dutch War: he was seen as the principal victor at the 1653 battle of Portland, when the English sank thirty-three enemy ships, including nine men-of-war.

Albermarle accepted the offer of joint command, while making it clear he would happily serve under Prince Rupert. Yet the king, perhaps out of concern for Rupert's health, perhaps because of his high regard for Albermarle, and perhaps, too, because he was worried that his cousin was too headstrong for ultimate control, insisted that command of the fleet be divided in two. This was not, however, the Wisdom of Solomon.

CHAPTER TWENTY-ONE

JOINT COMMAND

'Whereas the King my Sovereign Lord and Brother, hath thought fit and expedient for his service, that the chief command of his Majesty's Fleet should be exercised by joint Commission, that so the affairs thereof may be carried on by joint council and advice, and also in regard of the accident of war, and the distraction which many times happened by the loss of the chief commander, when the same is entrusted on a single person, and whereas through long experience which his Majesty as well as myself, hath had of your affections, courage, and knowledge in maritime affairs, his Majesty hath been pleased to approve of the choice of you for the chief Command of his Majesty's Fleet for the present expedition.'

James, Duke of York, to Prince Rupert and the
Duke of Albermarle, 22 February 1666

In 1666 Louis XIV entered the Second Anglo-Dutch War on the side of the United Provinces: his written declaration was announced to a fanfare of trumpets. The three greatest military fleets in the world were now engaged in a conflict whose victors stood to make very real commercial gains. When Denmark also declared against Charles II, England faced an imposing trinity of enemies.

Rupert and Albermarle were undaunted by the combined strength of their foes: they were both men of action, eager to secure the decisive defeat that had slipped tantalisingly from James's grasp the previous year. Their joint command began on St George's Day, 1666. They immediately set about tightening naval discipline. One of their first orders was to: 'Turn all the women to shore and suffer none to come aboard.'[1] This was in response to the suspicion that a whore had transmitted the plague to a ship, the *Princess*. She and her colleagues were no longer to be allowed to ply their trade and any captain who failed to see to this was to be replaced immediately.

Dennis Gauden, Victualler to His Majesty's Navy, received one of

the earliest joint orders from the prince and the duke: 'We understand by the Flag Officers,' they wrote during that first April, 'that many of the ships do spend in vain their sea provisions of beer and bread, we desire you will take care to supply them with such victuals as have been spent of the sea, which we expect should be done, and that you will be blamed very much if you do not keep the ships to this rule of victualling of them, for his Majesty and his Royal Highness expects it, and so do we.'[2]

The two admirals were also quick to put the Commissioners of the Ordnance on notice, insisting that adequate and appropriate ammunition be provided for the fleet. In particular, Rupert and Albermarle wanted more cannonballs and better waterproofing for the paper cartridges that helped propel them:

We perceive generally the Fleet is furnished but with 40 rounds of powder and shot. The officers complain much of the small proportion of canvas they have ... for we find that if we fill paper cartridges with powder, that the saltpetre will make them moist, and so, when we come to charge our guns, they will be apt to break and be something dangerous at such a time when there are so many lighted matches about the ships, besides the disappointment if they should break in the gunner's hands, when they are to charge the guns, and therefore we think it necessary for his Majesty's service that there be as much canvas again sent down, as is already, and if you please to send 50 rounds to each ship, the same cannot carry it, yet there will be other ships that will be able to take it in for the use of that squadron they sail with, and then it will be ready at hand. We shall earnestly desire, that you will please to grant us our desire in this thing, for there is nothing that can endanger the losing of the victory more than the want of powder and shot.[3]

Confidence was high: two seasoned veterans were in command of the navy and they were using their battlefield experience to prepare for a campaign that invited optimism. As the squadrons assembled, they provoked admiration from all who saw them. The diarist John Evelyn had responsibility for sick and wounded prisoners of war. These duties took him at this time: 'To the Buoy of the Nore to my Lord General and Prince Rupert, where was the rendezvous of the most glorious Fleet in the world, now preparing to meet ye Hollander.'[4]

At the end of May, reports reached the English fleet in the Downs that thirty-six French ships under the Duc de Beaufort had been spotted assembling at Belle Ile, off Brittany. Others were expected to join them from Brest. Rupert was instructed by the king to take thirty 'good ships' and prevent either a Franco-Dutch rendezvous or a possible landing of enemy troops in Ireland. Meanwhile, spies in the United Provinces assured Albemarle that de Ruyter's force would not leave harbour for several weeks. This gave Rupert plenty of time to complete his mission and return, before Albemarle was exposed to the enemy's superior numbers. Furthermore, in the unlikely event that the Dutch did set sail, Rupert and Albemarle calculated that it would be on a wind that would speed Rupert's return to the Downs. Albemarle, full of bravado, said: 'Leave us 60 sail, and we shall do well enough.'[5]

The division of the fleet was reasonable, provided – as Lord Arlington assumed – 'our intelligence do not deceive us'.[6] But, in fact, every detail of the information was wrong: the French were far away, near Lisbon (Louis XIV was in no rush to expend French lives when his Dutch allies could take the brunt of English attacks); the ships that had been spotted to the west were Spanish and neutral; and the Dutch fleet was on the point of leaving port, its intention to attack.

Three days into his voyage, on 1 June, Rupert was forced by bad weather to drop anchor in St Helen's Road. There he received an urgent despatch from the Duke of York, carried by a ketch, which ordered his immediate return to the Downs: the Dutch were closing in on Albermarle, who would be severely outnumbered.

Albermarle had been commanded to withdraw to the Gunfleet – an anchorage off the Essex coast, south of Harwich – and to meet the Dutch if they encroached. He decided to take a bolder stance: ignoring his captains' advice, he attacked de Ruyter's fleet of ninety ships with his sixty. 'And then began', wrote Lieutenant Jeremy Roch of the *Antelope*, without exaggeration, 'the most terrible, obstinate and bloodiest battle that ever was fought on the seas.'[7] This was not a brief and decisive action, like Trafalgar, the Nile, or Navarino, but a lengthy and gory engagement, its duration reflected in its momentous name: the Four Days' Fight.

On the first day, Roch's ship led the English fleet's surprise attack against the densest part of the enemy fleet. The Dutch captains cut their ships' cables as they scrambled to prepare for Albermarle's second approach. The duke's fleet was caught between two lines of enemy cannon and remained in this crossfire until ten that night. This, the opening period of the Four Days' Fight, claimed several English ships, leaving Albermarle with fifty vessels against de Ruyter's seventy-seven.

The second day was even more punishing for the English and by nightfall they were left with only twenty-eight battleworthy ships. If it had not been for Albermarle's disciplined withdrawal, casualties would have been greater: he employed a rolling manoeuvre, protecting his damaged and smaller vessels with the guns of his sixteen most powerful ships. But the outlook was grim and morale was low, one officer report-ing: 'There was nothing to be heard among the common seamen but complaints against deciding our fleet sending away Prince Rupert.'[8] His presence was urgently required or annihilation beckoned.

Meanwhile, Rupert's ships had returned to the Downs, expecting to find Albermarle and the Dutch locked in combat. Instead, they found empty seas. 'The Duke of Albermarle,' Rupert later reported, 'it seems by order he had received after my parting from him, was gone thence for the Gunfleet; and in passing met the Dutch upon the said 1st of June, and I, meeting no intelligence in the Downs, steered my course on towards the Gunfleet also; and on Sunday the 3rd of June met the English and Dutch, who had then been some days engaged.'[9]

It was Whit Sunday, and Rupert's arrival answered the prayers of Albermarle's exhausted sailors. 'When from topmast-head we made a fleet coming towards us', Sir Thomas Clifford, one of Charles II's ministers, wrote to the Duke of Ormonde, 'which we supposed to be (as it was) Prince Rupert and his squadron, there was such shouting in our whole fleet and the English hollow that the Dutch that were all along firing at us made a little pause.'[10] The surge of excitement at the prince's arrival even touched London. John Evelyn was among those in the capital anxiously following the progress of the battle. He received a letter that contained the thrilling news, 'that Prince Rupert was come up with his squadron ... and put new courage into our Fleet, now in a manner yielding ground, so that now we were chasing the chaser.'[11]

The poet Dryden captured English euphoria at the appearance of the prince:

> But now brave Rupert from afar appears,
> Whose waving streamers the glad general knows;
> With full-spread sails his eager navy steers,
> And every ship in swift proportion grows...
>
> Thus reinforced, against the adverse fleet,
> Still doubling ours, brave Rupert leads the way;
> With the first blushes of the morn they meet,
> And bring night back upon the new-born day.
>
> His presence soon blows up the kindling fight,
> And his loud guns speak thick like angry men;
> It seem'd as slaughter had been breath'd all night,
> And Death new-pointed his dull dart again.
>
> Thousands were there, in darker fame that dwell,
> Whose deeds some nobler poem shall adorn;
> And though to me unknown, they sure fought well
> Whom Rupert led, and who were British born.[12]

However, Rupert could not stop further losses, the most shocking of which was the torching of the stranded *Royal Prince*, the second best ship in the navy: 'The sight of which', Sir Thomas Clifford wrote, 'was a sensible touch to every man's heart in our fleet ... She was like a Castle in the Sea.'[13] Her admiral, Sir George Ayscue, was taken prisoner and was later humiliatingly paraded in the street by his captors, the most senior English naval officer ever captured in battle.

Rupert first joined with Albermarle, before leading his squadron – which included a ship commanded by his disciple in destruction, Sir Robert Holmes – into the teeth of the enemy. For two hours the prince attacked, until he managed to prise open the Dutch line. His vessel only narrowly avoided being clapped between two fire-ships. Meanwhile, she took hits from both sides, causing masts and rigging to tumble: 'Yet,' said an eyewitness, 'he answered the shot they poured on him, with as many close returns, which the Enemy felt and carried away with them; and in that whole day, to say no more, the Prince did manifest a Courage and Conduct answerable to the other great Actions, which belong to the story of his Life, whereby he gave spirit to his friends and terror to the Enemy.'[14]

This sounds like the brave and impetuous prince of old, but experience had added refinement to Rupert's natural aggression. Sir Thomas Clifford was struck by the maturity of Rupert's leadership: 'Prince Rupert behaved himself in the whole action with such conduct that it is hard to say which was most remarkable, either his prudence or courage.'[15]

The Four Days' Fight has been recognised as: 'the greatest naval battle of the age of sail'.[16] Despite Rupert's belated intervention, it ended in Dutch victory. There were 6,000 English casualties, some the victims of enemy fire-ships: many of those who escaped incineration were drowned. Johan de Witt, leader of the States-General was generous in victory: 'If the English were beat, their defeat did them more honour than all their former victories; our own fleet could never have been brought [back into the battle] after the first day's fight, if they had been in the other's place; and I believe none but the English could. All that we discovered was, that Englishmen might be killed, and English ships burnt, but that English courage was invincible.'[17] Establishing this fact cost de Witt 2,000 Dutchmen.

There had been real hope in England that Albermarle and Prince Rupert would finish off an enemy so badly mauled the previous year.

Indeed, Charles had misinterpreted messages from the fleet as reporting victory and had ordered a Day of Thanksgiving. It was soon clear that this was inappropriate: 'There was however,' Evelyn recalled, 'order given for bonfires and bells; but God knows it was rather a deliverance than a triumph. So much it pleased God to humble our late over-confidence.'[18] News arrived that the body of one of the slain English admirals, Sir William Berkeley, was being displayed in The Hague in a sugar chest. Ten days later, Evelyn mourned the 'sad spectacle, namely more than half of the gallant bulwark of the kingdom miserably shattered, hardly a vessel entire, but appearing rather so many wracks and hulls, so cruelly had the Dutch mangled us.'[19] Samuel Pepys recorded the pervading disappointment at the defeat. This centred on Albermarle's decision to fight when severely outnumbered and advised not to do so by his senior officers. At the same time Pepys criticised the prince, although he tempered his attack by recording that Rupert, 'was counted always unlucky.'[20]

Just as typical as his bad luck was Rupert's ability to bounce back quickly from defeat. He and Albermarle understood that, however bad the result, things could have been substantially worse. They had both been on the losing side before – indeed, both had been prisoners of war – and they knew the narrow margin between defeat and victory. They immediately set about repairing their squadrons for further action and sent an urgent request for more fire-ships, having been impressed by the effectiveness of the enemy's during the recent battle: there was still plenty left of the fighting season.

Two weeks after the Four Days' Fight, Arlington wrote of a royal meeting, presided over by Charles II: 'His Majesty returned last night from the fleet very well satisfied with the diligence employed to fit it to sea again, towards which assisted with his R. H. [the Duke of York] he did take all the other necessary resolutions with Prince Robert & my Lord General who are very well together now in one ship with a purpose to continue so, having observed the disadvantage of being separated in this last fight.'[21]

The folly of dividing the fleet was one of many lessons learnt. In the aftermath of defeat, Rupert's analytical mind helped construct a series of new orders for the navy, which would not be significantly modified or improved till 1749. Building on the *Instructions for the Better Ordering of the Fleet in Fighting* that had evolved during the First Anglo-Dutch War, Rupert and Albermarle established the following clear set of

principles: that the commander of every ship was to fight for the common good; that the flagship would give the signal for attack, which all
must follow as soon as they saw it; that if a flagship should be damaged,
then all ships in that squadron should look to the admiral of the fleet
for their subsequent orders; and that the flag officer should move to
another vessel if his ship was disabled making that his new command
centre. Rupert was seeking a clarity and continuity of command, even
in the maelstrom of battle. He believed a concerted thrust at the enemy
with the bulk of his vessels was the best way of tearing through the
protracted enemy line.

Although now an admiral, the prince remained at heart a Cavalier.
He trusted that courageous men, bravely led, could win any battle,
regardless of the odds.

Both fleets were quickly refitted after the Four Days' Fight. There were
rumours at the end of June that the Dutch were at sea again, off the
North Foreland coast. Rupert and Albermarle were overseeing the
repair of their damaged vessels in Chatham, Harwich, and Sheerness.
At the same time, they were finding it extremely difficult to man their
ships and had to deploy soldiers around the ports to prevent desertion.
They also enforced 'a severe press' to try to replenish their crews, but
the quality of the men gleaned by the press-gangs was disappointing.
The prince complained that suitable seamen would much prefer to
work on merchantmen or colliers, rather than risk all in naval warfare.
Meanwhile, the trained bands of the coastal counties were placed on
alert, in case of invasion.

On 19 July, Rupert and Albermarle weighed anchor and left to meet
the enemy: the English fleet, sailing in a single line, was nearly 10 miles
long. 'Our last news from the coast', Arlington informed Ormonde,
'assuring us that the Dutch continued in their station when they saw
ours move, we conclude they will stay to fight us. God give us good success for we play for a great stake.'[22] Three days later de Ruyter was spotted near the Gunfleet, and Albermarle and Rupert scrambled to meet
him. They cussed as foul weather hid the enemy from view. However,
the foes eventually hunted one another down and on 25 July – the Feast
of St James the Apostle – they closed on each other.

The combined fleets numbered 160 ships, promising another day of
extravagant carnage. 'As soon, however, as the bloody flag was set up ...',
an eyewitness recalled of the prince in the prelude to battle, 'Mr Saville

and another gentleman-volunteer, being on the quarter-deck, observed him charging a very small pocket-pistol and putting it in his pocket, which was so odd a sort of weapon on such an occasion, that they could imagine no other reason for it except his having taken a resolution of going into the powder-room to blow up the ship, in case at any time she should be in danger of being taken; for his Grace had often been heard to say that he would answer for nothing but that they should never be carried into Holland. Therefore, Saville and his companions, in a laughing way, most mutinously resolved to throw him overboard in case they should catch him going down to the powder-room.'[23] Rupert had no intention of following Sir George Ayscue's humiliation after the Four Days' Fight: he would not be paraded like a slave through Ancient Rome.

The St James's Day Fight took place about 35 miles east of Orfordness. The English formation was solid, in accordance with Rupert's recent instructions, while the Dutch deployment was less tidy, snaking vulnerably across a long front. Such weaknesses were compounded by the disobedience of Cornelis van Tromp, the headstrong admiral of the Dutch rear squadron. Son of the great maritime commander Martin van Tromp (who had been knighted by Charles I in 1642, when Anglo-Dutch relationships were more cordial), Cornelis strayed from de Ruyter's battle-plan. He botched a difficult manoeuvre in unfriendly seas and ended up far from the main action. When he tried to return, he found his route blocked by Sir Jeremiah Smith's Blue squadron, and the two admirals began their own private battle.

This separation of enemy forces allowed Rupert and Albermarle to concentrate on de Ruyter in the centre without distraction. The Dutch commander had seen van Tromp disappear in one direction. In the other he could make out his third squadron, sailing away from the battle, defeated – and, unbeknown to de Ruyter, with its admiral slain. De Ruyter fought on with typical resolve, until his 80-gun flagship, the *Seven Provinces*, had its mast blown away. It was only when the *Royal Charles* was similarly disabled that de Ruyter was able to limp towards Dutch waters, mustering his remaining vessels around him.

Lack of wind slowed the English pursuit. As de Ruyter turned for home, he fired on Rupert's sloop, the tiny *Fan Fan*, which was assisting repairs to the *Royal Charles*. One of the *Fan Fan*'s crew was killed. Although this was a single casualty among the 1,000 suffered by the English that day, it infuriated the prince. He ordered the sloop to row

after the *Seven Provinces* in search of a modicum of revenge. Sir Thomas
Clifford recorded the comedy after the carnage, as the diminutive cutter
snapped at the heels of the huge, lumbering, Dutch flagship: 'The little
Fan Fan made up with her oars to de Ruyter and brought her two little
guns on one side, and for near an hour continued plying broadside
and broadside which was so pleasant a sight when no ship of either
side could come near. There was so little wind that all ours fell into a
laughter, and I believe the Dutch into indignation to see their Admiral
so chased.'[24]

The Dutch made it home, licking their wounds behind harbour
defences as the English processed triumphantly up and down the coastline: although they had lost only two ships, four Dutch admirals had
been killed during the defeat. Rupert and Albermarle were determined
to capitalise on their victory before returning home. A Dutch deserter
told them of a fleet of enemy merchantmen lying behind the Frisian
islands of Terschelling and Vlieland. They unleashed Sir Robert Holmes
on this unsuspecting prey. His orders were to destroy the enemy ships,
but not to take civilian life.

The result was spectacular: Holmes took the Dutch completely by
surprise and succeeded in torching 150 of their merchantmen, before
escaping the devastation with only a foot of water under his keel. Two
enemy men-of-war also went up, in a conflagration known as 'Holmes's
Bonfire'. 'I received a letter from Sir Robert Holmes, giving an account
of the exploit he had done at the Ulie [Vlieland],' Arlington reported
to Ormonde, '... & I persuade myself we are not deceived in thinking it the greatest loss the Dutch have received since the War began.'[25]
Amsterdam went into mourning, its merchants calculating that Holmes
had cost them £1 million.

Success against the Dutch on St James's Day and at Vlieland won
Rupert and Albermarle great popularity. Charles ordered a national Day
of Thanksgiving, led by services in St Paul's and Westminster Abbey. At
the end of this summer of brutal maritime combat, one poet celebrated
the heroics of the prince and the Lord General, who he compared to
the Classical heroes, Castor and Pollux:

> Look up, and view in tail o'th' Waine of *Charles*
> Two new-found lights, *Rupert's* and *Albermarle's.*
> Did ever *Fortune* before loss of eyes
> More justly temper these great Deities

Unto a *pondus* valiant? A rare rate,
Of which Physicians do but fondly prate.

He placed Rupert's latest exertions in the context of a quarter of a century of astonishing personal bravery:

That Valour and Success, which on *Edgehill*
Enter'd the Camp, doth rest upon Thee still,
It is the same with Thee (Nephew of Kings)
To baffle Squadrons, as thou once didst Wings.[26]

Rupert spent the autumn vainly attempting to re-engage the Dutch in battle. He was frustrated by the enemy's reluctance to leave harbour, repeated gales, and the inadequacy of the supplies given his men at sea. 'From that expedition where we commanded,' the prince told Parliament, 'I returned home in the beginning of October; but before I came in with the fleet, I sent it as my humble advice to the King, amongst other things which I thought for his Majesty's service, that care should be taken to prevent an attempt upon Harwich, which was to be apprehended some time or other from the enemy, after the fleet should be come in, and his Majesty's commands were accordingly afterwards issued forth for the fortifying [of] both Harwich and Sheerness, which should have prevented any such design.'[27]

The Duke of York was responsible for naval defences. He increased the number of ships guarding the River Medway, which led to Chatham Docks. He also ordered a platform to be constructed off Sheerness, solid enough to hold twelve heavy cannon. The ships materialised, but the platform was only tackled in a half-hearted manner and was not completed by the following summer. In hearing Rupert's advice, but failing to act on it, the Lord High Admiral left his prime ships vulnerable to disaster.

CHAPTER TWENTY-TWO

'SAD & TROUBLESOME TIMES'

'My Lord,
'The letters of this night will paint our misfortunes in black colours, &
the truth is we have received a great affront which we shall not quickly
be able to wash off ...'

The Earl of Arlington to the Duke of Ormonde,
from Whitehall, 15 June 1667

The Second Anglo-Dutch War played out between 1665 and 1667. During each of the three years of conflict London suffered a catastrophe of a scale that might be expected, at worst, once in a century. The first calamity struck in 1665, the Great Plague killing a fifth of the capital's half a million population. The disease, borne by fleas nestling in the fur of black rats, had as its symptoms swollen lymph glands in the groin or armpit. If these burst, and progressed to suppurating sores, the patient could survive. If not, death would occur within a week, the corpse erupting in a welter of black spots.

The Black Death, a distant ancestor of this scourge, first appeared in 1348, killing one in three Englishmen. Similar pestilence had flared up sporadically thereafter. Throughout the seventeenth century, London's filthy streets provided a fertile habitat for the black rat: in 1603, 30,000 people had died from the bubonic plague and the Coronation of Rupert's grandfather, James I, had been postponed as a result. But 1665's outbreak was of a different magnitude to anything that had been suffered for more than 300 years: abetted by an unusually hot summer, it ripped through the capital, choked the cemeteries, caused mass graves to be dug, and spread panic and terror.

There were few effective countermeasures to the plague. The 1646 Anti-Plague Laws instructed communities to seal up households where the disease struck, leaving the occupants to battle through it or to die in isolation. Those who could afford to do so, fled, while the poor awaited their fate. John Evelyn was wealthy enough to send his family away from London, while he chose to stay in the capital. On 7 September he recorded: 'Came home, there perishing now near ten thousand poor creatures weekly: however I went all along the City & suburbs from Kent Street to St James's, a dismal passage & dangerous, to see so many coffins exposed in the streets & the street thin of people, the shops shut up, & all in mournful silence, as not knowing whose turn might be next.'[1]

The restored monarchy struggled to control a situation that threatened to incubate anarchy and aid the enemy: Charles II went to Salisbury, then Oxford, with the Court; his brother James repaired to York, in order to keep the northern counties under control; while Albermarle and the Earl of Craven – the Palatines' oldest and most loyal supporter – were given command of half the army's Footguards and a detachment of cavalry, 'to take care of London,' the Duke of York recalled, 'lest the Republicans and fanatics, encouraged by the Dutch, should rise'.[2] Together with the Archbishop of Canterbury, Sheldon, they did an admirable job, seeing that victims' clothes were burnt and their remains interred in lime. Only doctors and nurses were allowed to venture into houses containing the sick.

Rupert might have undertaken such duties, but his health was poor. His various wounds refused to heal, especially the serious blow to his head, which caused him real and repeated pain. He also was prone to malaria, another souvenir of a youth spent fighting hard, sometimes in exotic climes. Keen to encourage his cousin's convalescence, the king instructed the prince to join the court in Salisbury, before spending three months at Windsor Castle.

The Great Plague started to abate in the autumn, but it remained a serious threat to health until cauterised by the great disaster of 1666 – the Great Fire of London. What started as an accidental blaze in a Pudding Lane bakery was quickly whipped up into an inferno that cost the nation £10 million. The City suffered particularly badly, the commercial heart of the nation losing the livery halls of forty-four merchant bodies, as well as the Custom House, the Guildhall, and the Royal Exchange. The flames spread under a strong east wind – unchecked, until too late, thanks to the stupidity of the Lord Mayor. The messenger who woke Sir Thomas Bludworth with breathless news of the disaster must have realised that he had failed to transmit its true scale when dismissed with the words: 'Go and piss on it'. Even when it became clear that more drastic countermeasures were necessary, Bludworth hesitated: 'The Lord Mayor declined soldiers, and scrupled blowing up houses', recalled the Duke of York. 'The fire spread; and, about noon, he sent for the troops.'[3] It was too late.

Besides the commercial devastation, the Great Fire destroyed more than 13,000 houses as well as eighty-nine churches – including St Paul's Cathedral. Shock at London's fate resonated abroad. The Lord Lieutenant of Ireland wrote to the Earl of Anglesey: 'You will herewith receive a letter from me and the council to the Lord Mayor of London and the Court of Aldermen, expressing in the style of the board the deep sense we have of the calamity befallen that city by the late fire, and informing them that we have thought of by way of contribution from this Kingdom for the relief of such as are most impoverished by that judgement.'[4]

It seemed to the superstitious that God was launching thunderbolts at England in order to castigate an indolent, hedonistic king and his debauched court. Although charming, Charles II appeared to his critics to have a fatal lack of 'gravitas'. The tales of innumerable mistresses and other worldly indulgences played badly with a population at war – particularly because it was a disappointing war. The failure of the much-vaunted navy to finish off the Dutch – a people popularly derided as greedy, cheese-eating misers and 'Hogen Mogen Ninnies' married to 'brawny wenches fat as does'[5] – increased the dissatisfaction of a hard-pressed, disenchanted people.

The navy in the 1660s provides, in some respects, a microcosm of the fault lines running through the Restoration monarchy in its first years: much was expected of it, but its ability to perform was compromised by a dire lack of funds. At the same time there remained very real tensions between those in positions of authority, for they came from the two creeds that had clashed so fiercely two decades earlier.

The easy cooperation at the head of the navy between Rupert and Albermarle – a Royalist and a Parliamentarian – could not prevent an uneasy tussle between former enemies further down the chain of command. Most of the leading naval officers in the Second Anglo-Dutch War were formerly Commonwealth or Protectorate men: Charles II inherited them with his Crown. Of these, the majority were professional sailors, who had been at sea all their working life. Christopher Myngs, son of a cobbler, had joined as a boy and rose to become a knighted admiral, adored and respected by his men. They were known as 'tarpaulins', after the rough protective clothing they wore in stormy seas. A small minority refused to serve the king after the Protectorate's implosion, but many others were welcomed back into the service at the outbreak of war. As Sir William Coventry, the Duke of York's secretary, told Pepys: 'Why ... in the sea service it is impossible to do anything without them, there being not more than three men of the whole King's side that are fit to command almost.'[6]

The Stuarts' return injected a stream of men of nobler birth into the upper echelons of the navy. Those that had accompanied Rupert on his 1650s' odyssey – such as Sir John Mennes, who became one of Charles II's admirals and comptroller of the new Navy Board, and Sir Robert Holmes, the fearless captain – came to their posts with useful nautical experience. Many others had none. They were attracted to the navy because of the promise of action, because the army had no place in a sea war, and because they hoped for financial reward.

Ill feeling existed between two groups of men who, until recently, had been active foes. The situation was not helped by the rigid loyalty of patrons such as Monck, Sandwich, Penn, and Lawson on the Commonwealth side, and Prince Rupert on that of the Royalists. These leaders saw it as their duty to reward their 'following' of men, over the heads of officers drawn from the opposing faction. Monck's main recruiting agent was Sir Jeremiah Smith, whose importance was increased after saving the Duke of York from a Dutch fire-ship. Rupert's man was the redoubtable Holmes.

Among those eager to promote the professional, seasoned naval officer over the opportunist, fighting gentleman was the naval bureaucrat Samuel Pepys. He strongly approved of the Duke of York's determination to improve the service and forget the differing allegiances of the past. James, pragmatic and professional, was happy to employ Cromwellians in his fleet: at the outbreak of war, he had selected Sir John Lawson, a Commonwealth stalwart, to be vice-admiral of his squadron. James regarded his former foes as generally superior to the amateurs who had fought with brave indiscipline for his father's cause. This philosophy clashed directly with Rupert's unquestioning loyalty to those who had suffered for the king, regardless of their individual shortcomings. During a meeting, the duke proposed that any captain found drunk aboard ship should face dismissal. This suggestion astonished the prince: 'God damn me', he spluttered, 'if they will turn out every man that will be drunk, he must out all the commanders in the fleet. What is the matter if [he] be drunk, so when he comes to fight he doth his work?'[7] Rupert believed in the power of personality and daring, over the confines of uniformity and regulation.

Pepys's diaries resound with contempt for the prince. His Rupert is a foul-mouthed, foul-tempered, cantankerous menace. While Pepys was also vicious in his written attacks on Albermarle and Sir William Penn – both senior Cromwellians – he reserved his strongest criticism for the gentlemen-officers whose increasing influence in the navy he resented. As the most prominent example of this creeping infestation, Rupert attracted the diarist's most pungent bile.

Pepys's attitude to the prince betrays his strongly Parliamentarian roots. Pepys's route to office had started via his kinship with Edward Montagu, the Cromwellian sailor who served the Restoration monarchy as Earl of Sandwich. Pepys had been anti-Royalist as a youth: he claimed to have witnessed Charles I's execution as a schoolboy and seems to have been thrilled by its spectacle and significance. Although later convinced of the need to return the Stuarts to power, Pepys's prejudices were never expunged and he appears to have found it impossible to overcome the chauvinism of his formative years. In early 1666, he wrote about a duchess whose views he found odious: 'But one good thing she said, she cried mightily out against the having of gentlemen Captains with feathers and ribbands, and wished the King would send her husband to sea with the old plain sea Captains, that he served with formerly, that would make their ships swim with blood.'[8] The prince epitomised the amateur, dilettante culture that Pepys sought to erase.

The dark image of Rupert, perpetrated by the Puritan pamphleteers of the 1640s, must have affected Pepys as a boy. Now he found himself working alongside the ageing, irascible 'Prince Robber'. Although other contemporaries, including the king, joked about Rupert's sombreness and commented on his brooding energy, nobody else wrote as critically of the prince as Pepys.

Pepys lapped up the slander that Rupert's high profile and controversial character attracted. He recorded with relish a highly partisan recollection of Rupert and Maurice's 'mutiny' at Newark, in 1644: 'My Lord Bellasis told us how the King having newly put out Prince Rupert of his generalship, upon some miscarriage at Bristol, and Sir Richard Willis from his governorship of Newark, at the entreaty of the gentry of the county, and put in my Lord Bellasis; the great officers of the

King's armies mutinied, and came in that manner with swords drawn into the market-place of the town where the King was; whereupon the King says, "I must horse". And there himself personally, when everyone expected they should be opposed, the King came, and cried to the head of the mutineers, which was Prince Rupert, "Nephew, I command you be gone." So the Prince, in all his fury and discontent, withdrew, and his company scattered.'⁹

This incident, as we have seen, involved a much richer, deeper context than Pepys allows. There is no mention of Digby's malice, of Rupert's justifiable anger at his mistreatment by the king, of his understandable wish to be exonerated of the charge of disloyalty, or of Charles I's subsequent full forgiveness of his nephews. Neither does Pepys give a balanced assessment of Bellasis – a man of questionable integrity, who wished to place himself in a flattering light, in an episode that, in fairness, reflected well on none of its participants. Pepys swallowed Bellasis's tale whole, because it dovetailed with his dislike of everything the prince stood for. He wrote it down as fact, without hesitation or balance.

The personality clash between the glamorous, experienced but grizzled prince and the physically unattractive, self-made, insecure bureaucrat was complicated by professional tensions. As the conflict with the Dutch garnered more disappointments than triumphs, heated recriminations flew between the forces at sea and the naval suppliers on land. Pepys was quick to defend his fellow administrators, while Rupert, in his mid forties, had become increasingly outspoken: he would brook no criticism of his men or of his leadership. He remained confident in his abilities and contemptuous of his denigrators. Two proud men, with different hinterlands, labouring to maintain very high standards in their separate spheres, were bound to clash – especially when both were labouring under conditions that made their tasks impossibly hard and which neither could control.

The rush to war with the Dutch had exacerbated the huge naval debts inherited from Cromwell. The £2.5 million subsidy voted by Parliament to fund the conflict, although a huge sum, was insufficient for anything but a short struggle: indeed, creditors absorbed half this grant immediately. In 1666, the king ordered ten ships to be built, but financial constraints meant only three were completed. By the end of the year, all the money was spent. Charles was now unable to afford to pay for the repairs to, or replacement of, his key ships.

The financial crisis had become evident earlier in the year. Provision for the fleet was so poor that Rupert was forced three times in as many months to place his men on short rations. False economies had been made. It was, for example, known that three tons of fresh water were needed per week for every one hundred men on a ship. However, supplies had foundered when poor quality barrels (with wooden instead of iron-bound casks) had cracked open, spilling some of their contents and leaving the remainder open to contamination. Dysentery stalked the fleet throughout the summer.

Beer was the navy's other great liquid sustenance. Alcoholic fermented grain was less prone to go sour, but Pepys argued that its value made it more susceptible to the cheating ways of profiteering suppliers: giant barrels of it were received with up to 20 gallons missing from each. But the joint commanders were not prepared to accept Pepys's excuses: 'If any thing which hath been sent us hath been miscarried', they wrote to the Duke of York, who was still their Lord Admiral, 'or if there hath been a fault or neglect of duty anywhere, it will be better examined, when the fleet comes in, than now when his Majesty's service is so much concerned in our speedy supplies. In the meantime since Mr Pepys takes the liberty to say, that we are abused wholly by the Pursers, we must take the like humbly to assure your Highness that we do not content ourselves with the brave affirmation of the Pursers, but have made our enquiries by the captains of several ships, and have found the cask to be, as we have represented them unto you, that is to say, that the much greater part of the lower part is of wood-bound case.'[10] Albermarle and the prince also complained that the ships bringing supplies to the fleet dawdled en route: their commanders were paid for their time at sea – a disincentive to rush the delivery. 'This want of provisions', Rupert told Parliament, 'did manifestly tend to the extraordinary prejudice of his Majesty's service in that whole summer, but most especially after the victory obtained in July fight, when we had carried the fleet on the enemies' coast, and lay there before the Uly [Vlieland], in the way of all their merchant ships, we were enforced, merely for want of provisions, to quit out of Swold Bay.'[11]

Rupert's frustration was understandable, his points well made. However, the crisis confronting the navy was not just a question of incompetent or dishonest victuallers, as he suspected, but was more the consequence of insufficient revenue. Partly because public receipts had been halved by disease and fire, the navy's accumulated debts were nearing £1 million in the autumn of 1666. Pepys was realistic about the shortfall: summoned in his capacity as Surveyor-General of Victualling for the Navy to attend a council containing Charles, James, Rupert, and Albermarle, Pepys insisted that £100,000 was immediately required to keep the fleet afloat. The king, however, could only offer £5,000.

At the same meeting, Rupert was incensed by Pepys's assertion that, 'the fleet was come in, the greatest fleet that ever his Majesty had yet together, and that in as bad a condition as the enemy or weather could put it'. Pepys recorded in his diary: 'I . . . made a current and, I thought, a good speech, laying open the ill state of the Navy – by the greatness of the debt – greatness of work to do against next year – the time and materials it would take – and our incapacity, through a total lack of money. I had no sooner done, but Prince Rupert rose up and told the King in a heat that whatever the gentleman had said, he had brought home his fleet in as good a condition as ever any fleet was brought home – the twenty boats would be as many as the fleet would want – and all the anchors and cables left in the storm might be taken up again.'

The force of Rupert's blast stunned all present, Pepys recalling that: 'I therefore did only answer that I was sorry for his Highness's offence, but that what I said was but the report we received from those entrusted in the fleet to inform us. He muttered, and repeated what he had said, and so after a long silence on all hands, nobody, not so much as the Duke of Albermarle, seconding the Prince, nor taking notice of what he said, we withdrew.'[12]

In fact, the prince and the diarist had both made fair points. Rupert had done his best at sea in very difficult circumstances, against an able enemy and in often treacherous seas. Pepys, meanwhile, had pointed out the impossibility of providing adequate supplies while being denied funds. Although corruption and incompetence undoubtedly deprived the navy of much needed resources, the key problem for the Crown was the primitive mechanism available to it for raising extraordinary revenue in times of war. This was in cruel contrast to the enemy.

The States-General had an understanding relationship with their bankers, which made it possible for the Dutch to fund their battle fleet with relative ease. Politicians and traders could see where their priorities coincided, and merchants lent their ships for fighting. Citizens also understood where their best interests lay and this partly explains why the Dutch were able at all times to rely on volunteer, rather than pressed, sailors.

In England, however, the Royalist inner circle and the merchant class shared little common ground. The two interest groups were still largely attached to the differing beliefs that had left them as opponents in the Civil War. Although both factions had wanted the fight with the Dutch, the merchants – with their strong representation in Parliament – were wary of supplying a king of questionable trustworthiness with more than the bare minimum of funds. Even Royalists were despairing of their feckless monarch, John Evelyn comparing Charles's lazy self-indulgence with Cromwell's dynamism: 'so much reputation got and preserved by a rebel that went before him',[13] he lamented in his diary.

As a result, when the king sought a permanent excise tax from Parliament, the Commons refused. Members declined to grant a source of income that would outlive the war and which might give the Crown dangerous independence. For their part, MPs tried to take advantage of the monarch's financial hiatus, offering to buy out one of his constant revenue streams, the deeply unpopular Hearth Tax. The king refused. Next, Members established a special committee to investigate whether the king had used any of the funds granted him for the prosecution of the war for other purposes. Charles I would have recognised the insult and concern felt by his son, at this squeezing of the royal prerogative. The upshot of this political wrangling was simple: Parliament in the autumn of 1666 would grant no more money for the following year.

By 1667 the situation was desperate. In the spring, crews of two of the few vessels that reported for duty, the *Pearl* and the *Little Victory*, refused to go to sea because they had not been paid for more than two years. The men's wages were met in the form of written 'tickets' – paper vouchers that were extremely hard to redeem for cash, and which were often available at a discounted rate to officers and others with access to ready money.

Conditions for harbour workers were similarly dire. The dockyards at Chatham, Deptford, and Woolwich employed 1,400 men, who were charged with replacing, repairing, and maintaining the fleet, on an evaporating budget. The importance of their job was matched only by the shoddiness of their treatment. Rupert drew Parliament's attention to this national disgrace: 'I must remember', he told the Members, 'the horrible neglect of his Majesty's officers, and the work-men of his yards.'[14] Desperately impoverished artisans struggled to find food. Sometimes, though, relief arrived too late: 'I am more sorry to see men really perish for want of wherewithal to get nourishment,' a commissioner reported to Pepys. 'One yesterday came to me crying to get something to relieve him. I ordered him 10 shillings. He went and got hot drink and something to help him, and so drank it, and died within two hours'.[15] Faced with such deprivation, the workforce felt the bond of loyalty had been cut and became mutinous. At the same time, it became ever more difficult to recruit sailors: press-gangs roved around England's coastal towns and then turned inland, trawling for men to serve in a dangerous, brutal, and bankrupt navy.

In March 1667, with dockyard employees starving to death, Parliament unwilling to grant more money, and the king's reserves gone, a truly astonishing decision was made: the navy would not put to sea, but would be placed in mothballs. Only frigates were to sail, to distract the enemy's warships and harry her merchantmen while the English first rates, the pride of the fleet, remained in harbour. Rupert was not party to this decision because he was busy battling his dangerously declining health.

The prince had a lifelong aversion to doctors and surgery, but he was obliged to look to both when his old head wound violently erupted during the winter of 1666–7. It had been in a dangerous condition for two years, Pepys writing in early 1665 of a friend's tales of 'Prince Rupert's disease telling the horrible degree of its breaking out on his head'. It seems likely that a fragment of bone had detached from his damaged skull, causing a dangerous inflammation that was agonising and stopped him from sleeping. Rupert had been convinced that he would die, but then suddenly his condition improved. 'Since we told him that we believe he would overcome his disease', Pepys wrote, 'he is as merry and swears and laughs and curses, and do all the things of a man in health, as ever he did in his life.'[16] Now, though, the infection had returned, in an even more vicious form. So serious was the prince's condition that gossips on the Royal Exchange erroneously reported him dead. Since the treatment recommended to him was trepanning, it would be understandable if the prince had wished himself so.

Trepanning has been performed on human skulls since at least 2000 BC: we know that the Incas trepanned and there is evidence of it in Neolithic remains. By the mid seventeenth century in England, the procedure had progressed little from its roots. The treatment of head wounds was largely a mystery to Rupert's contemporaries, a learned surgeon writing in 1678: 'Wounds of the head being received in the

winter do suffer the patient to live longer than those made in the summer, for herein the native heat is ... most copious and strong ... in
summer, the natural heat is expanded and exploded to the external
parts, and as it were there dissolved and dissipated, the which in winter
is contracted and cohabited.'[17] This was a theory based on Classical
sources and flawed logic. Similar Restoration medical manuals help to
build up a picture of Rupert's ordeal.

The area around Rupert's wound was shaved and then the skin cut
in a vertical and a horizontal incision, to form the shape of a cross. His
ears were stopped with cotton, both to deaden the sound of the surgeon's drilling and to soak up excess blood. Assistants held the prince's
head still and his arms back. His wound was infected and raw, but the
surgeon's point of attack would have been close to its centre. There was
no anaesthetic, no antiseptic, and little understanding of the need for
hygiene. The surgeon sliced through the rotten flesh, scooping it out in
order to have a clear run at the exposed skull beneath.

A pin was then inserted where the drill was to go and the surgeon
gently twisted it into the bone, until it was fixed at some depth. It
was then unscrewed and the opening was used as the starting point
for the invasion of the skull. The drilling was the job of the trepan, an
instrument that looked and acted like a corkscrew – except, instead of a
twisting piece of thin and tapering metal, it had a solid and cylindrical
stem with a circular, serrated blade at its base. While the surgeon held
the shaft firm in his left hand, he turned the blade with his right, boring
the trepan's teeth into the bone.

At this stage he may have used a Hey saw or a bone file – the former
like a small tomahawk, the latter more like a package cutting knife – to
tidy up the bone. Then he would have bored deeper with the trepan,
using a brush to remove dry bone flakes from around the widening,
deepening cavity. Splinters that were sodden with blood or pus were
swabbed away with a cloth.

The trepan was removed occasionally and doused in oil or water: oil
eased the rotation of the blade; water helped to cool the overheated metal
after prolonged friction. John Brown, a Restoration surgeon, wrote of
the extra caution needed once the trepan had penetrated the skull: 'If
any blood appear', he advised, 'it is a certain sign that it hath penetrated
the first table, and this directs you to be very careful how you proceed,
lest you hurt and wound the Meninges by an unhappy slip, being a very
great cause of Death. When you perceive the piece of bone is loosed

by the trepan, you may with a fine lavatory or small instrument free it by degrees from the other parts of the cranium, so as you may without danger take it up with your forcipes, if any ragged pieces appear, which may hurt the Meninges, you are to remove them.'[18]

The operation was slow and agonising. Rupert would have indicated when he could take no more and would have been allowed recovery time before the drilling restarted. At the trepanning's conclusion, a piece of taffeta or satin was dipped in Mel Rosarum and Oleum Rosarum, and used to swab the wound. The prince would probably not have noticed this, because of the shock of the pain. He would have been laid out on a bed while he and his surgeon waited anxiously to see how the head reacted to the trepan's assault: as John Evelyn recorded, after watching five contemporaries being operated on for another invasive procedure, 'The danger is fever, and gangrene, some wounds never closing.'[19] These were common dangers during an era of ignorant surgery. The surgeon's powders and potions often did more harm than good.

Rupert reacted badly to the trepanning. He had to return for a second operation, the surgeon going wider and deeper in a bid to complete the job he had previously botched. 'Prince Rupert has again been trepanned,' wrote a pamphleteer, 'the former [operation] not having gone down deep enough; this gave him present ease, by letting out a great quantity of corrupt matter, since when he has slept better, and is amending.' The second trepanning had worked.

Relieved of constant pain and granted rest, Rupert's inquisitive mind sprang into action. He was intrigued by medical gadgetry and it was noted that, during his recuperation, 'he often diverts himself in his work house [laboratory], where, among other curiosities, he had made instruments which the surgeons use in dressing him, which do it with more ease than any formerly used'.[20]

Rupert's recovery took many weeks, his steady improvement occasionally commented on by Pepys. In the spring of 1667, after the decision had been made not to put the fleet to water, the diarist spotted a peculiar-looking convalescent: 'This day I saw Prince Rupert abroad in the Vane-room, pretty well as he used to be, and looks as well, only something appears to be under his periwig on the crown of his head.'[21] Perhaps this was a thick medical dressing, or possibly the prince had invented a device to keep the weight of the wig from the tender scars of his successful second operation.

*

Although Clarendon wrote otherwise, it seems impossible that the incapacitated prince was party to the decision to lay up the fleet. 'In the beginning of 1667', his nineteenth-century biographer Warburton wrote, 'the Dutch determined to make reprisals on our commerce in the very face of London. The imbecile ministry of Charles was easily blinded.' Indeed, it was Clarendon and his political allies who selected this option, because they were convinced that the end of the war was near: the dramatic clashes of the previous two years persuaded them that the peace explorations taking place in Breda would lead to terms. Surely the States-General would opt for profitable peace over costly war?

Warburton also pointed the finger at Rupert's old adversary, whose meddling had troubled him before: 'The Queen Mother, Henrietta Maria, lent her fatal assistance to deceive her son. On the strength of her information and advice, England was left almost defenceless; ... the Navy remained cradled in winter quarters, and two small squadrons alone were left at sea.'[22]

The English severely underestimated a resourceful and stubborn enemy. Dutch knowledge of the Thames Estuary matched that of the English due to the amount of peacetime trade between the United Provinces and London. The president of the States-General, Grand Pensionary Johan de Witt, was aware of the vulnerability of his enemies' dockyards. In 1664 he sent a spy to see if an attack on the dry docks at Chatham was feasible. Three years later, with the English ships laid up, he unleashed his ships on a sleeping enemy.

Cornelis de Witt, Johan's brother, stood with de Ruyter in a longboat, directing operations. The Dutch were assisted by the terrible morale of the defenders: as they made their way up river, English seamen's wives screamed at those in authority that this disaster was the consequence of failing to pay their husbands. The invading vessels – some piloted by British navigators, happy to serve masters who remunerated them – proceeded from Gravesend to Sheerness. The English fled before them and the partially built fort at Sheerness was overrun. The ship stationed at the entrance to the river, the *Unity*, failed to pull tight the heavy protective chain that guarded the Medway and although the first Dutch ship was snagged on it, the second cut through, allowing its colleagues a free punch at the exposed English solar plexus. Fire-ships destroyed three of the navy's great ships, the *Loyal London*, the *Royal Oak*, and the *Royal James*. The true catastrophe, however, was the overpowering of the small force guarding the *Royal Charles*. This mighty ship, which had carried the restored monarch back to England and bore his name, was soon sailed to the United Provinces, the finest imaginable reward for de Witt's daring.

Rupert was summoned to help meet the Dutch encroachment. His skull was barely recovered from the double trepanning, but he joined the dukes of York and Albermarle as they summoned troops and took them to Upnor Castle. Pepys sneered at the sight of gentlemen volunteers – 'young Hectors' – assembling to meet the expected Dutch invasion. While these men rushed to the front line, the diarist enjoyed (in turn) a fine dinner, his mistress, and a good book. The next day Pepys gave further vent to his inferiority complex, mocking Albermarle for riding 'with a great many idle lords and gentlemen, with their pistols and fooleries'.[23] As these men were fighting the Dutch, Pepys was planning how to get his personal savings out of London to a safe place. Meanwhile, Prince Rupert, who Pepys so despised, deployed a battery of artillery at Woolwich, covering a point in the river where he knew the enemy must pass. 'On Thursday they came on again with 6 men of war and 5 fire ships', Arlington wrote on 15 June, '... but were so warmly received by Upper [sic] Castle and battery on the shore that they were forced to retire, with great damage beside the burning of their 5 fire ships.'[24]

Although the Dutch hovered at the entrance to the Thames for several days, and controlled the Channel for the next few weeks, they chose not to run the gauntlet of the Upnor and Woolwich gunners again. Warburton wrote that the Dutch were within point-blank range when the prince gave his first order to discharge at the enemy: 'The sudden fire was maintained so fiercely, that there was no thought of resistance for a moment; as soon as the ships could be got about, they fled.'[25] John Evelyn recorded the aftermath of Rupert's bombardment: 'I went to see the Work at Woolwich, a battery to prevent them from coming up to London which Prince Rupert commanded, & [which] sunk some ships in the river.'[26]

There were few consolations to accompany this humiliation. Because she was in Portsmouth, the *Royal Sovereign* was the only one of the navy's five great ships to survive. And, thanks to the land-based defences commanded by James, Albermarle, and Rupert, Chatham dockyard was saved from destruction. However, following hard on the heels of the Great Plague and the Fire of London, the Dutch incursion up the Medway made a grim trinity of reversals for Restoration England.

Feeling 'dismally melancholy', Ormonde expressed a commonly held
sentiment when he wrote to the Earl of Anglesey: 'God give us time and
understanding to see and mend our faults of all sorts.'[27]

The Second Anglo-Dutch War ended the following month, with
both sides winning trading concessions, and most crucially, New York
remained British. 'Thus in all things,' Pepys wrote, exaggerating the
enemy's overall ascendancy, 'in wisdom – courage – force – knowledge
of our own streams – and success – the Dutch have the best of us,
and do end the war with victory on their side.'[28] While England's
Parliament and the United Provinces' States-General signed the treaty
with sincerity, the Duke of York and his following of warmongers saw
this peace as an unwanted but inevitable interlude. They planned to
resume hostilities as soon as a favourable opportunity presented itself.

CHAPTER TWENTY-THREE

THE HAPPIEST OLD CUR IN THE NATION

'Scorn me not Fair because you see
My hairs are white; what if they be?
Think not 'cause in your Cheeks appear
Fresh springs of Roses all the year,
And mine, like Winter, wan and old,
My love like Winter should be cold:
See in the Garland which you wear
How the sweet blushing Roses there
With pale-hu'd Lillies do combine?
Be taught by them; so let us join.'

'An Old Shepherd to a Young Nymph', Edward Sherburne (1659)

Rupert's romantic history is one of the most frustrating strands of his life to unravel, because he was extremely discreet and was a very lazy letter writer. It is hard to imagine that a tall, handsome, dashing prince would ever have wanted for female admirers: Sir John Southcote, who served under Rupert in the Civil War, told his son that the prince was: 'the greatest beau' and 'the greatest hero'.[1] Rupert never espoused celibacy and lifelong bachelorhood provided a succession of relationships, many of whose details remain obscure. In attempting to construct a true picture of Rupert's love life, we have to rely to a large extent on the observations of his contemporaries.

Samuel Pepys, Rupert's great critic, assumed the prince to have been promiscuous into middle age. In 1666, before the two trepanning operations brought relief, Pepys wrote with relish of discharge from the prince's head wound and speculated on its causes: 'It seems, as Dr Clerke also tells me, it is a clap of the pox which he got about twelve years ago, and hath eaten to his head and come up through his skull.'[2] Although we know Pepys's diagnosis to be flawed, this regurgitated gossip suggests Rupert had a reputation as a ladies' man. However, we are aware of few of his lovers' identities.

We know of the gaoler's daughter, during his imprisonment after Vlotho. There is also the possible union with the Duc de Rohan's daughter – 'The Mirror of Virtue'. Then there is the alleged affair with the Duchess of Richmond, during the Civil War. Otherwise, there are hints of flirtations, some of which may have become sexual encounters: John Evelyn recorded in his diary, in 1663, 'Sir George Carteret, Treasurer of the Navy, had now married his daughter Caroline to Sir Thomas Scot, of Scottshall, in Kent. This gent: was thought to be the son of Prince Rupert.'[3] If Scot was Rupert's illegitimate child, he was never acknowledged as such by the prince.

Dudley Bard was openly recognised as Rupert's son. He was born during the Second Anglo-Dutch War – probably in 1666 – and educated at Eton, across the Thames from his father's quarters in Windsor Castle. He was commonly referred to as 'Dudley Rupert' and, after he followed his father into the military, as 'Captain Rupert'. His mother was Frances Bard, the daughter of one of Charles I's most loyal and exotic supporters.

Frances's father, Henry Bard, was the academically gifted son of a priest. A Fellow of King's College, Cambridge, Henry's passion was foreign travel: as a young man he walked through France, Germany, Italy, Turkey, and Palestine, before reaching Egypt, where he stole a copy of the Koran from a mosque. At the outbreak of the Civil War, Henrietta Maria secured his appointment as a lieutenant colonel of infantry. Bard justified this patronage: he proved an effective recruiting officer in Ireland and performed with initiative and courage at the battle of Cheriton Down, in March 1644, before his men were cut to ribbons in a powerful Parliamentary cavalry charge. He lost an arm there and was taken prisoner. On his release, he rejoined the Royalist army and was given the Irish title of Viscount Bellamont. When Rupert stormed Leicester in 1645, the one-armed peer was the first Royalist up the scaling ladders. He was next seen with the prince at Naseby.

Towards the end of the Civil War, Henry was captured once more and was given the choice of an indefinite spell in gaol or permanent exile. He joined the Prince of Wales's court on the Continent and continued to make waves: he was arrested as a suspect in the murder of Isaac Dorislaus, a Dutchman who had coordinated the prosecution at Charles I's trial. For want of evidence, the case against Bellamont was dropped and he was released.

In 1656, Bellamont was sent as ambassador to Persia (a country he loved – he named one of his daughters Persiana) and India, to trawl for funds for the Royalist cause. His mission failed and, soon after seeing the Taj Mahal nearing completion, he died – accounts say either of heat stroke or in a sandstorm. He left behind a penniless wife and four children. His only son was called Charles Rupert: he was a godson of Charles I, which explains the first name, while the second is testimony to his close friendship with the prince. Certainly, Rupert remained in contact with Bellamont's children after their father's death: he began his affair with Frances, the eldest of the three daughters, soon after she reached womanhood.

Frances has left only a faint historical footprint – a great frustration, since we know she was one of Rupert's two great loves. Indeed, she claimed to be his wife. This is certainly possible, but since the prince continuously and vigorously denied the union, one of them was lying. Supporters of Frances's claim point to a scrap of paper that reads:

> July the 30th 1664
> These are to certifie whom it may concerne that Prince Rupert and the Lady ffrances Bard were Lawfully married at petersham in Surry by me Henry Bignell
> minister [4]

Bignell was not Petersham's priest in 1664, but served there both before-hand and afterwards. It therefore seems probable that – if genuine – this affidavit was written at a later date, perhaps at the request of Frances or of one of her supporters, to give retrospective evidence of the event. The parish's official register of births, deaths, and marriages is unfortunately incomplete, the relevant pages for 1664 among several passages that have been torn out and lost.

It is equally plausible that Frances was never married to Rupert. Perhaps she was embarrassed by her years as a mistress and chose to deny them by falsely claiming a more respectable status. She had a reputation for integrity later in life, which Rupert's sister Sophie thought excep-tional: 'She is an upright, good and virtuous woman. There are few like her; we all love her!'[5] It is impossible to judge whether this uprightness was a feature throughout Frances's life or whether it developed after a spell as a prince's paramour.

The piece of paper allegedly signed by the priest is the only tangible evidence to suggest that Rupert and Frances were married. If they were,

it must have been secretly, for there are no contemporary references
to their wedding. The couple spent three years together, before their
relationship ended in bitterness. 'She cannot be very good-natured,'
Sophie consoled her brother at the time of the break-up, 'if she has
offended you.'[6] However, Frances had every right to feel bitter, for it
seems likely that she was spurned by Rupert for another woman, and a
glamorous one, at that.

In the autumn of 1667, Rupert suffered further complications to his
unrelenting head wound. The Duke of York immediately despatched
his French surgeon to assist, before writing with concern:

> My dear Cousin,
> As soon as Will Legge showed me your letter of the accident in your
> head, I immediately sent Choqueux to you in so much haste as I had
> not time to write by him; but now I conjure you, if you have any kind-
> ness for me, have a care of your health, and do not neglect yourself, for
> which I am not so much concerned ... I write to you without ceremony,
> and pray do the like to me, for we are too good friends to use any. I
> must again beg of you to have a care of your health; and assure you that
> I am yours,
> J.Y.[7]

The following summer Rupert was persuaded to accompany Catharine
of Braganza and the court on their annual descent on Tunbridge Wells.
The queen had first taken the waters there in 1664, to convalesce from
a life-threatening illness. She found it a comfortable summer retreat – a
rural escape from the heat and dirt of the capital: it was to London what
Fontainebleau was to Paris. Writing in 1771, Richard Oneley described
a landscape that would have altered little since Rupert's visit a century
before: 'The town and castle of Tunbridge, the navigable river Medway,
and the rich meadows, through which it runs, finely diversified with
corn-fields, pasturage, hop-gardens and orchards ... form a most beautiful scene.'[8]

   The town was famed for its spa water, which was viewed as a cure-all.
While Rupert drank it to purge his blood, the queen hoped it might
boost her fertility: she remained childless and was desperate for a remedy.
The seasonal influx included many aristocrats whose only maladies were
chronic sycophancy and rampant hedonism, and who wanted to be

near the royal family at play. The queen insisted that Tunbridge relax the formalities that were her everyday lot elsewhere. Grandees played at the simple life, renting small houses and relying on skeleton staffs. Each day began with a general congregation around the wells. Cups of water were consumed before strolls in the shade of the trees, games of bowls, or dancing in the queen's apartments. Catharine's physician encouraged dancing, believing it would jiggle the queen's reproductive system and help her to conceive. Fruit, game, and flowers were available from market stalls run by 'young, fair, fresh-coloured country girls, with clean linen, small straw hats, and neat shoes and stockings.'[9]

The gentle, rural idyll gave way to more sophisticated evening entertainment. Al fresco dancing took place on the bowling green, 'a turf more soft and smooth than the finest carpet in the world'.[10] In the holiday atmosphere, flirtation was common and affairs were rife. The prince, renowned for his sternness and eccentricity, must have cut a strange figure in such heady, frivolous company. Lord Orford, a great admirer of Rupert's scientific abilities, wrote that the Prince 'could relax himself into the ornament of a refined court, [but] was thought a savage mechanic, when courtiers were only voluptuous wits'.[11]

These 'wits' were a new generation, who entertained the king and helped shape history's perception of his rule as a time of loose living and superficial pleasure-seeking. Their time had come, now Clarendon and his sensible, disapproving manner had been condemned to exile. They viewed Rupert as a curmudgeon, a relic from a distant age: 'He was brave and courageous, even to rashness,' Count Grammont conceded, 'but cross-grained and incorrigibly obstinate: his genius was fertile in mathematical experiments, and he possessed some knowledge of chemistry: he was polite, even to excess, unseasonably; but haughty, and even brutal, when he ought to have been gentle and courteous: he was tall, and his manners were ungracious: he had a dry hard-favoured visage, and a stern look, even when he wished to please; but, when he was out of humour, he was the true picture of reproof.'[12] It is a sharp but cruel portrait of a bruised old warrior. The prince was not yet 50, but he appeared older, his manner and appearance prematurely aged by the demands and exertions of a life in the front line. Prince Rupert seemed to have been around forever, and to have no place in the new, lax atmosphere of Charles II's court.

The talk of Tunbridge Wells in 1668 was Charles II's lust for the ravishing but chaste Frances Stewart. The more she denied him, the more vigorously he pursued her. Catharine of Braganza, seeing the state into which 'la belle Stewart' had whipped her husband, decided to unsettle her rival by importing further competition. She summoned a company of actors to Tunbridge Wells, one of whom was Nell Gwynn, the daughter of a brothel-keeper who had drowned in a ditch while drunk. Nell had progressed from selling herring in the street and then oranges in the theatre, to becoming one of the liveliest and best-known actresses in the land. Bawdy, sexy, and witty, she was to be Charles II's most famous mistress. Within two years she had added to the king's illegitimate tribe, producing a boy who was called Charles, Duke of St Albans – living proof of her light-hearted boast that she was a 'sleeping partner in the ship of state'.[13] Rupert's eyes, however, were not on the captivating Nell. As Count Grammont recorded with glee, they were fixed elsewhere:

> The Queen had sent for the players, either that there might be no inter-mission in the diversions of the place, or, perhaps, to retort upon Miss Stewart, by the presence of Miss Gwynn, part of the uneasiness she felt from her's: Prince Rupert found charms in the person of another player, called Hughes, who brought down, and greatly subdued his natural fierceness. From this time, adieu alembics, crucibles, furnaces, and all the black furniture of the forges: a complete farewell to all mathematical instruments and chemical speculations: sweet powder and essences were now the only ingredients that occupied any share of his attention. The impertinent gypsy chose to be attacked in form; and proudly refusing money, that, in the end, she might sell her favours at a dearer rate, she caused the poor prince to act a part so unnatural, that he no longer appeared like the same person. The King was greatly pleased with this event, for which great rejoicings were made at Tunbridge; but nobody was bold enough to make it the subject of satire, though the same con-straint was not observed with other ridiculous personages.[14]

Margaret Hughes, known as 'Peg', was from a thespian family and was one of the first generation of professional English actresses. Stage plays had been banned by Parliament in 1642. However, Charles II greatly enjoyed the theatre – he had been weaned on it, receiving his own troupe ('Prince Charles's Players') at the age of one – and three months after the Restoration he granted patents to two playwrights, Sir Thomas Killigrew and Sir William Davenant, which permitted them to open theatres and to put on plays for profit. These were coveted awards, given to two Royalists, in the face of intense competition. Killigrew had served as a page to Charles I and had followed the court into continental exile. He founded the King's Company, which was initially more prestigious than its rival, gleaning the more accomplished actors and specialising in the established texts. Killigrew's troupe was based at the Royal Theatre, Drury Lane, from 1663. Davenant had been the Marquess of Newcastle's senior artillery officer at Marston Moor. He later spent two years imprisoned in the Tower of London. Now, in happier times, he formed the Duke's Company and began to build a theatre in a converted real tennis court at Lincoln's Inn Fields, which was noted for its innovative use of moving scenery. Both men were to benefit from a revolution to their art, which sprung from the monarch's permissiveness.

Charles had seen his mother and her ladies-in-waiting act in the privacy of the court from an early age – indeed, the first time the word 'actress' was used in its modern context, to describe a female stage performer, was when it was applied to the queen by the pen of an admiring courtier. During his travels on the Continent, Charles had seen the ready acceptance of actresses: they had been permitted in France, Italy, and Spain in the late sixteenth century, and in parts of Germany in the early seventeenth.

Out of Protestant prudery, which held that flaunted female flesh would corrupt morals, women's roles on the English stage were played by boys and effeminate men – the most famous of whom, Ned Kynaston, was judged by Pepys, during one performance, to be 'the prettiest woman in the whole house'.[15] The king – sexually adventurous and a keen appreciator of all things feminine – did away with gender discrimination. From 1660, both Killigrew's and Davenant's companies employed women. In 1662 Charles issued a royal warrant that declared that women were to play all female parts: this, he was sure, would guard against 'unnatural vice'.

Actresses in late seventeenth- and early eighteenth-century England were a source of prurient fascination: they were, in a sense, the nation's first celebrities. Playwrights titillated theatre-goers with plotlines that included blatant flirtation, feminine guiles, and rough sexual domination. The women were similarly used backstage: deprived of privacy, members of the public could access them there. Samuel Pepys enjoyed watching them in various stages of preparation, particularly undressing.

He recalled, with a frisson, a visit 'into the [at-]tiring rooms and to the women's shift where Nell [Gwynn] was dressing herself and was all unready'.[16] The playwright Shadwell suggested that a few guineas would ease a man's admittance to the actresses when off duty, while some of them might grant 'free ingress and egress too'. In popular culture, actresses were viewed as little better than whores.

To the wealthy male, theatre-going provided an opportunity to scout for a mistress. Given the insecurity of their jobs and the inferiority of pay (experienced actresses would receive 30 shillings per week; an actor 50 shillings), there was a financial vulnerability to exploit. In general, these were women who had only escaped domestic service because of their looks. ''Tis as hard a matter for a pretty woman to keep herself honest in a theatre,' one observer wrote, 'as 'tis for an apothecary to keep his treacle from the flies in hot weather; for every libertine in the audience will be buzzing about her honey-pot.'[17]

The first time a woman took a major role in a play in England was 8 December 1660, when the King's Company employed a female as Desdemona. This was such a novelty that Killigrew thought an explanation necessary. He commissioned the poet Thomas Jordan to write a special introduction, which included the advice:

> The Woman plays today, mistake me not.
> No Man in gown, or Page in petticoat.

Jordan stressed that this innovation must be greeted with an open mind:

> Do you not twitter, Gentlemen? I know
> You will be censuring, do't fairly though;
> 'Tis possible a virtuous woman may
> Abhor all sorts of looseness, and yet play;
> Play on the stage, where all eyes are upon her,
> Shall we count that a crime France calls an honour?[18]

Peg Hughes's name was long associated with this groundbreaking performance, but more recent research points to the distinction being Anne Marshall's. It seems likely, rather, that Peg was with the King's Company from soon after its 1663 beginnings: the prompter John Downes, writing forty-five years later, remembered Hughes as one of the first women employed by Killigrew. There is also a reference to 'Hews' in a 1661 or 1662 cast-list for *The Royal King*, which suggests Peg's earlier involvement. She was certainly one of the first women to play Desdemona and was the first Theodosia in *Evening Love*, Dryden's play of 1668. Also in the 1668–9 season, she played Angellina in *The Sisters*. It is possible that she was playing one of these roles when she captivated the prince.

Rupert had slept with actresses before, his name appearing in a list of shame composed by the pious John Evelyn in October 1666: 'This night was acted my Lord Brahal's tragedy called *Mustapha* before their Majesties &c. at Court: at which I was present, very seldom at any time, going to the public theatres, for many reasons, now as they were abused, to an atheistical liberty, foul and indecent; women now (& never 'til now) permitted to appear & act, which inflaming several young noblemen & gallants, became their whores, & to some their wives, witness the Earl of Oxford, Sir R. Howard, Pr: Rupert, the E[arl] of Dorset, & another greater person than any of these [the King], who fell into their snares, to the reproach of their noble families, & ruin both of body and soul.'[19] However, no other actress had an effect on Rupert to match that of Miss Hughes.

Although Peg's name is not as famous as those of half a dozen Restoration leading ladies, she caused a stir during the mid 1660s. An anonymous admirer found her in many ways more captivating than her more celebrated contemporaries:

> Who must not be partial
> To pretty Nan Marshall?
> Though I think, be it known,
> She too much doth de-moan,
> But that in the Moor
> May be right, to be sure,
> Since her part & her name
> Do tell her the same
> But none can refuse
> To say Mistress Hughes
> Her rival out-does.[20]

Rupert's transformation from lugubrious, frightening, bloodied warrior to skittish lover caused hilarity among Charles's court. Peg Hughes was a great beauty, with dark ringletted hair, a fine figure, and particularly good legs. However, she had a past: when Pepys met her, he wrote that she was 'a mighty pretty woman, and seems, but is not, modest'.[21] The diarist recorded that she had been the mistress of the poet and play-wright Sir Charles Sedley. Sedley, twenty years Rupert's junior, was a favourite of Charles II and one of his 'wits'. It also seems likely that Peg had a child with an earlier lover, a boy called Arthur who would write a play called *The Frolics* in 1681. For a man as feared and respected as Rupert to fall so hopelessly in love with a common actress, the cast-off of one of the court wags and the former plaything of others, somewhat reduced his stature.

However, Rupert was sincere in his love and Peg proved not to be the passing fancy of an older man hankering after young flesh. Even if Grammont was right and Peg initially resisted the prince's advances in order to up her price, the couple seems to have come quickly to a happy accommodation. She continued to act for a while and in October 1669 was listed by the Lord Chamberlain as a member of the King's Company. This provided her with some status: actresses regis-tered with the Lord Chamberlain were considered to be servants of the monarch and enjoyed privileges, such as being immune from arrest for debt.

Being the mistress of the third most important man in the royal family brought Peg immediate and dramatic social elevation. Sir Peter Lely, Charles II's principal painter, completed her portrait soon after-wards, and it is as a lady rather than an actress or mistress that she is shown. She holds a lemon in one hand and a scallop shell in the other. The lemon symbolises purification and love, while the shell represents resurrection, a reference to how Peg has been rescued from a life of im-morality by Rupert's love. Behind her, water cascades from a dolphin's mouth, while two cherubs attend the dolphin: the theme remains love, purity, and deliverance from a dark alternative.

In the potrait, Peg wears a rich silk nightdress, common to the court's tastes at the time, together with a fine pearl necklace and bulbous pearl earrings. The prince gave generously to his lover: he was in his late mid-dle age, besotted by a young beauty who made him genuinely happy. 'I am obliged to her for many things,'[22] he acknowledged to his youngest sister. In turn, Sophie wrote to Charles Louis in January 1674: 'George William [of Brunswick-Luneburg – Sophie's brother-in-law] said, that Prince Rupert ought to get married.'[23]

Peg had given birth the previous year, causing Rupert's affection and generosity to redouble. He proudly claimed the illegitimate girl as his daughter: her name was Ruperta. Ruperta inherited feistiness from both sides, which was soon evident, her father delightedly writing to his sister Sophie: 'She already rules the whole house and sometimes argues with her mother, which makes us all laugh.'[24]

Never a wealthy man, the prince denied his small family nothing. Peg proved expensive: in particular, she liked to gamble and she loved jewels. It has been estimated that Rupert gave his lover £20,000 worth of jewellery in a decade. Some have claimed the real figure was ten times that. It was probably somewhere in between.

Her love of the stage persisted. In 1676, six years after retiring, she briefly resurrected her career, this time for the Duke's Company, which was by then considered superior to its rival. She appeared in at least eight plays that season, her credits ranging from Octavia in *The Wrangling Lovers* to Charmion in Sedley's *Antony and Cleopatra*. These were her last performances, for in 1677 Rupert built a home for her and Ruperta in Hammersmith, on the site of a house he bought from Sir Nicholas Crispe. It was a grand building, which cost £25,000 to construct. Those who remembered Peg's humble beginnings were jealous of her ever-increasing grandeur. Captain Alexander Radcliff mocked her in a ditty:

> Had I been hang'd I could not choose
> But laugh at whores that drop't from slues
> Seeing that Mrs Margaret Hughes so fine is.[25]

Rupert's generosity was a reflection of his happiness and gratitude for this late chance to sample the pleasures of family life. However, relationships such as his were increasingly satirised on stage. Lustful, rich, old men falling in love with pretty, scheming, young women became a favourite theme of Restoration comedy. Crown's *The Countrey Wit*, of 1675, even seems to contain references to Rupert's various trading ventures and to his past battles with the Dutch. The prince may well have been in the playwright's mind when constructing the character Lord Drybone and Peg could have been the prototype of his greedy mistress, Betty Frisque:

DRYBONE: Go, go, hussey, you are an unkind naughty girl, to make me pay thus dear for every smile and smirk I get from you; I dare safely say, not a dimple you make, when you smile, that does not cost me, one with another, forty pounds a dimple.

BETTY: 'Tis your own fault, my dear Lord, you will be chiding o'one, and quarrelling with one.

DRYBONE: Chiding o'one, and quarrelling with one; ay, and I had better quarrel on, I am a fool to buy Peace so dear, considering what a poor trade I have, and how little I get by it.

BETTY: People that cannot barter commodity for commodity, must spend money in *specie*, you know they do it all the world over.

DRYBONE: But that's a very ruinous trade, one had better war with such a country, and forbid all traffic with it, my dear Frisky.[26]

There is also an echo of Rupert in Squire Oldsapp, the lascivious old dupe in Thomas Durfey's *The Night-Adventurers*, a romantic farce of 1678. Rupert was famous for his love of science, and some of his experiments were popularly believed to be attempts at alchemy and other scientific trickery. Before meeting the pert Madam Tricklove, the aged Oldsapp engages in crude magic spells:

> Draw near ye Spirits, that dispense
> Your Pow'rs o'er Concupiscence;
> Bring all your Spells and come along,
> To make an amorous Old Man young!
> Whose frozen joints, long since have cool'd his passion,
> But now he sighs, and blows, and puffs, for generation;
> Come, come away; your assistance confer,
> And then I shall be the happiest Old Cur,
> The happiest Old Cur in the Nation.[27]

The relationship between the prince and the showgirl was touched by tragedy in the summer of 1670. Peg's brother, who was employed in Rupert's household, was furious to hear one of Charles II's retinue belittle his sister's beauty and claim Nell Gwynn the prettier of the two actresses. On 20 June, six weeks after Nell had given birth to her royal bastard, Lady Chaworth wrote to Lord Roos that 'one of the K[ing]'s servants hath killed Mr Hues, Peg Hue's brother, servant to P. Robert upon a dispute whether Miss Nelly or she was the handsomer now at Windsor.'[28]

The duel happened at Windsor, because the castle was now one of Rupert's homes.

CHAPTER TWENTY-FOUR

WINDSOR CASTLE

'The Constable of Windsor Castle is Keeper and Governor of the Castle, and is to Command any Garrison, or under Officers there ... The Constable of Windsor Castle is likewise Chief Forester and Keeper of the Forest of Windsor, which is a great command, especially to such as delight in Pleasures.'

Sir Bulstrode Whitlock's advice, contained in the 'Windsor Castle Governor's Book, 1668–1671'

Windsor Castle, the Parliamentary acquisition that Rupert failed to retrieve early in the Civil War, was the rebels' military headquarters for the remainder of the conflict. In this impregnable bastion the Royalists' nemesis was spawned, its parade ground honing mastery of pike, musket, and sword. In the spring of 1645, the freshly hatched New Model Army disgorged from its gates, clad in scarlet and looking for action, certain that God would hand it victory. Naseby followed within seven weeks.

Some of the rich crop of Royalist prisoners harvested that summer and autumn was stored in the castle. It had a history of incarcerating the highest born: Edward III had detained the kings of France and Scotland there. Eventually, Windsor held an English monarch captive. After his various false hopes had ended in disappointment, Charles I spent his last Christmas at the castle before moving to London for trial and execution. Parliament refused to allow the king's head and trunk to be laid to rest in Henry VII's Chapel at Westminster Abbey: its leading members, keen to fashion a workable national reconciliation, could not permit the creation of a shrine to their enemy in the capital.

Loyal Bishop Juxon accompanied the royal coffin back to the castle through snowdrifts and presided over the night-time burial of his master's remains. They were committed to a vault occupied by the coffins of Henry VIII and Jane Seymour, beneath the choir of St George's Chapel. The king had cherished the Prayer Book, but the governor of the castle 'positively and roughly'[1] refused to allow its use at the funeral: it was a forbidden religious text and he would brook no exception to the ban. The service therefore took place in silence, punctuated by the sobs and sighs of the tiny congregation. Present on this dismal occasion was Rupert's friend the Duke of Richmond, who had offered to forfeit his head in place of his monarch's.

After the king's death, Parliament initially decided that 'the Castle of Windsor, with all the Houses, Parks and Lands there, belonging to the State, be sold for ready money'.[2] The stronghold was stripped of its magnificent decorations at the end of 1651, including 'five pieces of hanging of Triumphs, 6 pieces of David, Nathan, Abigail and Solomon, 7 of the siege of Jerusalem, 5 of Goddesses.'[3] Such vanities were an affront to Puritans. They were also valuable works of art, their disposal providing extremely welcome revenue for a regime struggling to pay its soldiers' wages. When John Evelyn visited the castle after its despoliation, his impressions were of 'rooms melancholy and of ancient magnificence'.[4]

When no buyer could be found for the castle, Cromwell planned to turn over the parks and woodlands to his soldiers, so they could lay down smallholdings for themselves, in the manner of Ancient Rome's legionnaries. But the Constable, Sir Bulstrode Whitlock, juggled his devout Puritanism with a passion for hunting and he dissuaded his leader from a course that would have ruined his sport. Parliament instead resolved that Windsor should be one of eight prestigious properties – which included Whitehall, Greenwich, and Somerset House – 'to be kept for the Lord Protector, and for succeeding Lord Protectors, for the honour of the Commonwealth'.[5] However, Cromwell found Hampton Court suited his needs and tastes better, and spent little time at Windsor.

During the remainder of the Interregnum the castle was used, rather than enjoyed. It was on the roster of southern and Midland fortresses that took it in turns to be the administration's military headquarters. The soldiers' barracks were the fulcrum of activity, while the remaining quarters were turned over to the widows, wives, and children of those who had died or been wounded, fighting for the cause.

The Stuart Restoration marked the castle's return to royal favour. Charles II appreciated its military value and, concerned that he might follow his father as a victim of revolution, set about restoring it to its true purpose: a bastion of royal martial strength. It was essential to find a strong and able constable to command the garrison.

Of secondary importance was the desire to have a place of enjoyment, outside London but within distance of it, where the king could
retire and live in great style, free from the burden of his day-to-day
responsibilities. Windsor had long been a royal pleasure-dome. William
the Conqueror acquired it from monks, partly because its abundant
woodlands provided excellent deer-hunting. Such sport had since entertained generations of kings: the constable's seal of office showed a castle
between a stag's antlers. But the stock of quarry had evaporated in a
welter of poaching during the Interregnum, and the woods had also
suffered from uncontrolled scavenging for firewood.

Charles wanted his coverts replanted and his herds fostered.
Somebody strong, determined, and trustworthy was needed to oversee
this aspect of the governorship of the castle, administering the vast territory of 'Windsor Forest', whose twenty separate parks had a combined
perimeter of 120 miles. They spread far beyond the town itself: 'This
forest lyeth in Berkshire,' a contemporary recorded, '[and] also extends
into it: It consisteth – Surrey, Hampshire, Berkshire, Oxfordshire,
Buckinghamshire, and Middlesex, The Thames bounding it North, The
Lodden [river] west, Bradford River, and Gulddowne South. And the
Way river East.'[6]

From 1661, the constable was Viscount Mordaunt. His commission
was terminated seven years later, after royal auditors unearthed financial irregularities. In the autumn of 1668, Charles II announced his
replacement: 'And know ye farther, that we reposing especial Trust &
Confidence in the care, fidelity, and circumspection of our dear and
entirely beloved cousin and counsellor Prince Rupert, Count Palatine
of the Rhine, Duke of Bavaria and Cumberland, &c of our especial
Grace, certain knowledge, and mere motion, have given & granted,
and by these patents, for Us our Heirs & Successors, Do give & grant
unto the said Prince, the Office & Place of Governor and Captain of
our Castle of Windsor ...'.[7]

The generous public endorsement was a standard formula for the
gazetting of such appointments. In truth, though, Charles was offering little more than a sop to his cousin. Rupert had long wanted
to become Master of the Horse, a position of great honour given to
the Duke of Albermarle as one of many rewards for his pivotal role
in the Restoration. During the early 1660s, Rupert began negotiating
the purchase of the post from the duke: 'And they had almost agreed,'
James II later recorded, 'But the King refused his consent, because the

general's [Albermarle's] quitting it would be prejudicial to his affairs.'[8] This was a bitter blow for the prince. It is hard to think of a more suitable incumbent for the position than the man who had led the Cavaliers into military mythology. Certainly, Rupert believed the title to be his by rights.

The prince was obliged to accept the king's insistence that Albermarle retain the post. But he was reduced to anguished fury when, in the spring of 1668, it was revealed that the Duke of Buckingham had secretly been permitted to buy the Mastership from Albermarle for £1,000 a year. The insensitivity of the king was particularly galling, for the new Master of the Horse was, in everyone except Charles's eyes, a sycophantic fraud.

Buckingham was the son of the royal favourite assassinated early in Charles I's reign. He had subsequently been brought up with the royal princes, at Richmond. After the Civil War, Buckingham had accompanied Charles abroad, before joining him on his ill-fated foray from Scotland into England. There, his veneer of loyalty began to crack, before he deserted the Prince of Wales at his time of greatest need. Charles chose to ignore this wobble and later welcomed the duke back into his court-in-exile in France.

Buckingham, however, spurned his second chance. Bored of life abroad and convinced that the Stuarts were a spent force, he persuaded Charles to let him return to England, supposedly in a mission to help the royal cause. But instead, in an astonishing turnaround, he suggested to Oliver Cromwell that he marry one of the Lord Protector's daughters. To press his suit, Buckingham publicly expressed his contempt for 'Charles Stuart' and claimed to relish the prospect of drawing his sword against the man whose family had looked after him as one of their own. Cromwell, made of sterner moral fibre, was less than impressed: he would not contemplate accepting such a snake in the grass as a son-in-law. Lord Fairfax proved a softer touch: Buckingham succeeded in winning his daughter. He married into the family that had done more than any other to tame the Stuarts on the battlefield.

After the Restoration, Buckingham was at first ostracised for his treachery: he remained on the sidelines, an outcast, while the Royalist world triumphantly reordered itself. However, the duke's charms were undimmed and could not long be ignored by an impressionable king. Buckingham soon wheedled his way into the Privy Council and then retrieved his estate, which was worth £20,000 per year. Such advances allowed the duke to dream of further promotion. Yet Buckingham remained incapable of straight dealing and was destined to fail: he would squander his money and conspire against the king. But, before he revealed his treachery once more, he was allowed to become Master of the Horse. In the circumstances, giving Prince Rupert the Constabulary of Windsor Castle was the least that Charles could do: his loyal, long-suffering cousin had stood by his cause throughout its darkest days, losing his brother while keeping the royal banner flying.

Rupert was the ideal candidate for the position: he was one of the most famous old soldiers in the land, his record well matched to the castle's martial significance. Furthermore, he had long been one of the select Knights of the Garter, whose Camelot Windsor was. Charles needed a respected and accomplished champion to head up one of his key garrisons, at a time of increasing political tension: the Earl of Clarendon, omnipotent in the first years of the Restoration had fallen spectacularly from favour and was now in exile, all the failures of the Anglo-Dutch War unfairly laid at his feet. The vigorous attention of Clarendon's enemies was now concentrated on the king's brother and heir, James. Soon after his return to England, on reading accounts of the Reformation, the Duke of York had become a Roman Catholic. Although he forced himself to take Anglican Communion until 1672, his faith was sincere and intense, and increasingly difficult to conceal. Catharine of Braganza's apparent inability to provide an heir brought closer the prospect of the next king being a Papist.

In 1668, there were the first rumblings that Charles must address this matter urgently: if the current queen could not provide an heir, Anglican opponents insisted, Charles must divorce and remarry. Rupert's old enemy George Digby, now Earl of Bristol, even took it upon himself to go to Italy, in search of a fertile replacement bride. Meanwhile, Rupert's friend and business partner Anthony Ashley Cooper (the future Earl of Shaftesbury) led the calls for James to be removed from the succession and from command of the fleet. His acolytes began to talk openly of the need for a Protestant heir, the illegitimate Duke of Monmouth their favoured candidate. This tall, handsome, but dim young man was the result of Charles's affair with Lucy Walter, a promiscuous Welsh woman who died of venereal disease, and one of the seventeen or so mistresses attained during his European exile. With his brother under sustained attack, Charles was wise to promote his dependable cousin to a meaningful military position, having denied him the honorific post he so desired. Rupert offered solidity in a fickle, increasingly menacing, world.

From the prince's point of view, the appointment was a good one. He needed somewhere to drop anchor after nearly five decades of wandering. Since the age of one, he had roamed northern Europe, criss-crossed the seas, and never found a place to settle. Since his teens, he had felt a spiritual connection with his mother's homeland. Yet, despite his royal blood and his many labours on behalf of the Stuart dynasty, he still had no fortune, no mansion, and no estate.

In his late forties, the governorship of Windsor Castle answered many of his needs and, most importantly, it gave him a home. Although it could never be his to possess, as constable he enjoyed the run of the place. One of the perks of the job, a previous incumbent recalled, was being able to 'use any of [the] lodgings or rooms in the Castle, whereof the King hath not present use'.[9] He appointed his own men to key offices: Anthony Choqueux, the doctor who had helped cure his nasty head wound in 1667, was appointed the castle's 'chirurgeon' (surgeon); and Sir William Reeves, Rupert's page at the time of the near-fatal ambush precipitated by Marshal Gassion's madcap streak, was made 'Rider of the Forest of Windsor'. Reeves was given powers to act as Rupert's lieutenant when necessary.

The prince was now able to repay some of the hospitality that he had received from friends on the Continent: in late July 1670, he marked the arrival of the Landgrave of Hesse with a salute from the castle's thirty-one great guns.

At last, stability, position, and purpose coincided, to promise security and contentment in middle and old age. Apart from when fighting for his adopted country at sea, Rupert would never leave England again.

The passing years failed to dull the prince's keen energy. In a general reordering of the castle's defences, he had the real tennis court pulled down and resurrected elsewhere. He also levelled the nearby soldiers' houses, with wooden huts providing temporary shelter for the men. These contained 'forty double beds for two soldiers to lie in,' according to a letter from the Duke of Monmouth to Colonel Will Legge, 'each bed, with bedding and bedclothes for them accordingly to be provided & furnished for the use of his Highness Prince Rupert's Company at Windsor Castle.'[10]

Rupert then repaired the neglected Devil's Tower and moved the garrison's gunpowder there from the keep, where he now installed his company of soldiers. Finding the proportions of this part of the castle too constrained for the efficient use of pikes, he ordered halberds for his men: these were shorter and better suited to action in confined spaces. Each of the changes dovetailed with one another – making sense individually, while collectively bringing real improvements to the king's Thames Valley stronghold.

Finding the procedures inherited from his predecessor unacceptably slack, Rupert issued a set of twelve clear instructions through his secretary, James Hayes: Orders Established by his Highness Prince Rupert, Constable of the Royal Castle of Windsor, for the better Government of the Garrison there.

1. That Fifteen Soldiers of each Company within the said Garrison are to be upon the Watch every night, Viz. forty-five in ye Whole, and one Lieutenant, one Ensign, and a Sergeant with them.

2. That every one of the said Officers who are upon the Watch take their Round every night: The Lieutenant, the Grand Round, and the other Officers once apiece at least.

3. That there be a Corporal, and Six men, upon the Watch at the outward Gate of the Castle; and the key of the Said Gate be left with the said Corporal, to use upon necessity.

4. The Sentinels shall be placed at the several Posts where they now are; and when they are Relieved, it shall be done in a Troop.

5. That the Keys be always fetched by the Major of the Castle from the Constable, or other Superior Officer in his absence, with a Guard.

6. That the Major of the Castle do see the Gates shut and opened, and bring the Keys to the Constable, or other Superior Officer, and take the Word; and that the Sergeants attend him for the same.

7. That in Winter, at the shutting in of the Day, the Gates shall be put together, & latched.

8. That the Taptou be at nine a Clock in the Winter, and at Ten in the Summer; and the Reveal always at Break of day.

9. The Watch shall always be Relieved at nine a Clock in the morning.

10. Before the Gates are open, some Soldiers shall be first sent out at the Wicket for discovery; and all the time the Gates are opening, the Soldiers are to stand to their Arms.

11. The Officer that hath the Guard is to take notice of any Stranger that

comes into the inner Castle, or lies there, and to give an account thereof: And if any thing belonging to the King be embezzled from thence, The Officer that hath the Guard shall be responsible for the same.

12. The Sentinels who are placed upon the Batteries & Magazines, are not to permit any Stranger to come near them, but to Command them to keep at a Distance.

Signed

Rupert[11]

The tone of these words – assured, direct, and clear – could have emanated from the prince at any stage of his adult life: they expected – indeed, demanded – obedience. Their detailed contents also reveal a new, mature understanding of the task required of him: behind them lay more than three decades of military experience, which had seen the capture and the forfeit of important military bastions. Rupert's new orders demonstrated a refusal to risk his latest charge. If obeyed, they would keep Windsor safe for the Crown in a way that had been beyond him when defending Bristol.

His credentials as a man of war aside, Rupert's passion for the chase made him the ideal custodian of the castle's great sporting estate. With political conflict raging in the capital, it was even more important that the king could get away to enjoy his favourite pastimes. Charles had a restless physical energy that contrasted with his easygoing, often indolent, style of rule. He liked to exercise, particularly enjoying real tennis, which he played daily, referring to it as his 'usual physic'. He swam and sculled in the Thames, generally at dawn. He inherited his father's enjoyment of bowls, and also participated in falconry and cockfighting. Charles was a fine, natural horseman, but he gained equal pleasure covering his kingdom on foot: companions complained of the pace set by their fiercely fit monarch. John Evelyn, who enjoyed more sedentary pursuits, wrote during his visit to Windsor Castle in the summer of 1670 of how: 'The King passed most of his time in hunting the stag, and walking in the parks, which he was now planting with rows of trees.'[12] In fact, the landscaping around Windsor was relatively minor, compared to the changes implemented at other royal residences: the monarch planted swathes of trees in Greenwich, including 6,000 elm saplings, and the surrounds of Hampton Court were studded with lime trees.

Charles took direct control of restocking and replanting the New Forest and Sherwood Forest, and delegated much of the restorative work at Windsor to his cousin, one of whose titles was 'Keeper of the Forest'. The prince knew what was necessary to bolster the numbers of wild game: he stamped out poaching and protected the natural habitat. Rupert set about his task with enthusiasm. He ordered racks to be built in the clearings, where fodder could be placed during the winter months when natural food was scarce. Not just red and fallow deer but all game – including 'hares, coneys [rabbits], pheasants, partridges [and] heathpoults' – fell under the protection of the prince. He monitored the increase in numbers of the deer, sending 'Regardors' to take regular head counts which were kept in accounting books. Rupert's personal responsibility was Cranborne Walk, which, within a year of his taking it on, boasted 175 fallow deer. Only one other walk contained more than fifty-five deer.

The prince was impatient with officers who allowed poachers to prosper. Sir Thomas Foster and his fellow JPs in Chertsey received a forceful reprimand:

Gentlemen,
I have been informed, That his Majesty's Game of all sorts hath been of late, and is daily destroyed, in the Forest of Windsor; but especially in the Perambulation of Chertsey, there by some disorderly persons, who, without authority or permission, carry guns, and also use greyhounds, mongrels, setting-dogs, trammels, tunnels, nets, and other engines, wherewith they destroy his Majesty's game ...

The prince added: 'I shall not need to say more to you on this matter'.[13] He expected the poachers' speedy apprehension and conviction. Suspects were tried in Rupert's courts and offenders were kept in 'the Coale house', a prison in the castle.

Rupert was a popular figure with the law-abiding people of Windsor and its surrounds. The terrible aggressor of Civil War propaganda seemed far removed from this honourable and conscientious man, who exercised his duties fairly, and seemed content in his position both as constable and as lord lieutenant for the county: we hear of him being 'much beloved by all the country gentlemen of Berkshire'.[14]

The prince had plenty of time for his active pleasures: he was excellent at real tennis and was rated by Pepys as one of the four finest players in England. He sailed as well, keeping a private yacht on the Thames. He also took full toll of the deer whose numbers were boosted by his careful husbandry. Choosing to remain aloof from the turmoil of politics at court and in Westminster, Rupert had time for what truly interested him, particularly his scientific experiments. He established a suite of apartments in one of the castle's towers where, according to Warburton, 'forges, laboratory instruments, retorts and crucibles, with all sorts of metals, fluids, and crude ores, lay strewn around in the luxurious confines of a bachelor's domain'.[15]

His unreconstructed bachelorhood was evident in his masculine tastes in interior design. Swathes of swords, spears, and shields were displayed on the walls in a heavy hang, the tools of war taking the place of conventional tapestries and canvases. John Evelyn was intrigued by the effect, recording in August 1670: 'Windsor was now going to be repaired, being exceedingly ragged and ruinous. Prince Rupert, the Constable, had begun to trim up the keep or high round tower, and handsomely adorned his hall with furniture of arms, which was very singular, by so disposing ye pikes, muskets, pistols, bandoliers, holsters, drums, back, breast, and head pieces as was very extraordinary. Thus those huge steep stairs ascending to it had the walls invested with this martial furniture all new and bright, so disposing the bandoliers, holsters, and drums as to represent festoons, and that without any confusion, trophy-like.'

But Rupert, the renowned warrior, also possessed a softer side – the part of his character that made him capable of producing accomplished works of art with his own hands. Evelyn, aware of the Cavalier legend but ignorant of the gentler creativity within, was amazed by the contrast between the arrangements of weaponry in the public spaces and the subtle touch evident in the prince's private quarters: 'From the hall we went into his bedchamber, and ample rooms hung with tapisserie, curious and effeminate pictures; so extremely different from the other, which presented nothing but war and horror.'[16]

Rupert believed it his prime duty to make the king love his time at Windsor. This was not a difficult task, for Charles shared many of his cousin's tastes. Like Rupert, he devoted increasing time to experiments and science. One of his chief delights when at Windsor was watching an extraordinary contraption made by Sir Samuel Morland, which pumped drinking water up to the higher reaches of the castle, for the court's consumption. One contemporary judged Morland's device: 'the boldest and most extraordinary experiment ever performed by water in any part of the world'.[17] The king would stand beside it, timing the upward flow to check that it was working correctly, delivering a barrel a minute to the top of the building.

Charles enyoyed spending time at Windsor and the evenings offered scant respite. When there were no plays or concerts, he would visit his women. Although most of his mistresses were left in London, Catharine of Braganza was rarely without competition for her husband's attentions. Louise de Kéroualle was a beauty from Brittany who captivated the king. She was created Duchess of Portsmouth and transcended her mistress status to become Charles's true friend and confidante. He granted her use of a suite of apartments at Windsor Castle. Nell Gwynn, who was also good company outside the bedroom, was similarly housed in the grounds: her lodgings, Burford House, took its name from the title given to her and Charles's illegitimate son, the Earl of Burford.

It was during Rupert's tenure of the castle that the king ordered the modification of the State Apartments, so they could accommodate his retinue in style. St George's Hall, built by Edward III 300 years before, was remodelled during the mid to late 1670s in the Baroque style (which Louis XIV had favoured when building the Louvre, a decade earlier). Charles commissioned Antonio Verrio, the great Neapolitan artist, to paint bold frescoes of scenes from the lives of Edward III and the Black Prince. He also included representations of Charles's martial exploits, even though he had none to be proud of. With a similar touch of flattery, Verrio portrayed his patron accompanied not only by Fortitude but also by Prudence and Temperance. Rather more justifiably, the queen's Audience Chamber and the queen's Presence Chamber were adorned with images of Catharine of Braganza surrounded by symbols of virtue, one of which showed the long-suffering consort in a chariot drawn by swans. Grinling Gibbons added to the lustre of the display, with ornate cornices and frames. John Evelyn, witnessing these achievements months after Rupert's death, wrote that Gibbons must now be considered: 'without controversy, the greatest master both for invention and rareness of work, that the world ever had in any age'.[18]

The king transformed the castle from a mishmash of dark medieval spaces into a modern palace: interlocking corridors led to rooms given large windows. His architect during Rupert's Constabulary was Hugh May (Sir Christopher Wren was subsequently to take on the project), whose greatest success was a new structure near the North Terrace – the Star Building, emblazoned with the Garter Star. This was the fulcrum of many of the other improvements. From this point May established a gradation of rooms that progressed from the universally accessible Guard Room, through increasingly exclusive salons, culminating in the King's Bedchamber.

As well as overseeing Charles II's refurbishments, Rupert was also charged with maintaining the castle's rich ceremonial tradition. Edward III had linked Windsor inextricably with St George, and every 23 April his Saint's Day was acknowledged with a salute from the garrison's thirteen great guns, which consumed over 30lb of gunpowder. The number of Knights of the Garter had declined significantly during the Interregnum, but the new king replenished their ranks within a year of the Restoration. Indeed, he made a greater fuss of the Garter Knights than any monarch since Henry VIII: Edward VI had disapproved of their 'Papist' ceremonies and his successors had done little to return them to prominence. Charles, conversely, celebrated the chivalry, tradition, and pomp of the order, restoring St George's Chapel as their place of worship.

St George's Hall, another of May's Baroque creations, was normally the setting for plays and other entertainments. The Knights, however, were allowed to use it for their annual celebrations. Over three days, they feasted on English fare, the food 'most costly and delicate, completely royal and set forth with all befitting state and grandeur.'[19] Prince Rupert took his place at these glittering occasions, along with his fellow Knights.

The position of Constable of Windsor Castle was part military, part civil, and entirely in tune with the prince's tastes and capabilities. Although it suited Rupert on so many levels, it did not answer his perpetual problem: lack of funds. The stipend was meagre and rarely paid on time: in January 1673, Rupert was forced to apply for a backlog of eighteen months' allowance, a feat repeated in May, 1675, when an official memorandum recorded: 'Charles Bertie to the Auditor of the Receipt to pay Prince Rupert 1½ years of his allowance of 10s. a day as Governor of Windsor Castle.'[20] Only the constable's traditional perk from the forest could be relied upon to arrive in good time, but Rupert would happily have forfeited the provision of twenty free loads of firewood in return for more money. He looked at various enterprises for increasing his wealth, including a scheme for minting farthings, but they all failed to alleviate his financial woes. As Sir Bulstrode Whitlock noted, after holding the post throughout the 1650s: 'The Office of

Constable of Windsor Castle is of very great Antiquity, Honour, Power
& Pleasure; but of very little profit.'[21] If Rupert were at last to make
money, it would have to be elsewhere.

CHAPTER TWENTY-FIVE

HUDSON'S BAY

'We were Caesars, being nobody to contradict us.'

Médard Chouart, Sieur des Groseilliers

Before he became constable of the castle, Rupert was a frequent guest at Windsor, with regular use of a set of apartments there. In the winter of 1665–6, with the Plague still raging throughout London, his stay there was a prolonged one. It overlapped with the three-month visit of a pair of fascinating Frenchmen.

Pierre-Esprit Radisson and Médard Chouart were brothers-in-law who arrived with tales of unimaginable wealth and the tantalising possibility of finding the mariner's Holy Grail, the Northwest Passage leading from the Atlantic Ocean to the Pacific. Rupert found their extraordinary story credible and enthralling.

The two men were very different. The bumptious Radisson was nearly 30 and had left the family's smallholding in the Rhone Valley to seek his fortune in New France. This colony, part of modern-day Canada, had its centre in Quebec and an overall population of 5,000 Frenchmen. Most were involved in the fur trade, especially the acquiring and selling of beaver pelts, which were made into warm, waterproof headgear for Europeans in the era before umbrellas. Because of its special properties, beaver was then the most valuable fur in the world.

Radisson settled in Trois Rivières, a farming community midway between Quebec and Montreal, deep in Mohawk territory. One day, ignoring warnings that the indigenous tribe was on the warpath, he and two companions left the settlement to go wildfowling. Radisson, never an easy man, fell out with his friends and ventured off by himself. It is extremely likely that Radisson's tricky nature saved his life: for, heading home that evening, he stumbled across his colleagues' remains, horribly mutilated. The Mohawks had killed them and they now took Radisson prisoner. For some reason, they spared Radisson's life and

made a great fuss of him. One of the Mohawk families was headed by
a fearsome figure, a bloodthirsty warrior who was proud of his tally of
nineteen white scalps. This man took Radisson to live in his village on
Lake Champlain.

Over the following months, the young Frenchman absorbed the
ways and the psychology of his captors. He learnt their language, their
songs, and their hunting methods, and he joined them in their skirmishes against neighbouring tribes. There is no record of his trying to
escape, until a fellow prisoner – an Algonquin tribesman – suggested
running away during a hunting expedition. The two men murdered
the Mohawks in their sleep, staving in their skulls, before making a
dash for Trois Rivières, and freedom. But, terrified that they would
be recaptured, the pair made too much haste: trying to cross a river in
daylight, they were captured by Iroqois. The Algonquin was tortured to
death, while Radisson was forced to look on.

This was not the only grim spectacle that Radisson witnessed. He was
placed with a larger group of prisoners, among them the wives and children of fellow settlers, taken from their homes by raiding parties. They,
too, were all slain, their executions public, protracted affairs, involving
the singeing and slashing of flesh, and the tearing out of finger- and
toenails. They were finished off with a sadistic flourish: sheaths of birch-
tree bark were forced over the torsos of the condemned, then set alight.
Death was the postscript to final, screaming agony.

Radisson's astonishing grip on life continued. He was forced to
endure preliminary tortures of such savage intensity that they left physical and mental scars that could never heal. His tormentors branded the
soles of both feet with iron instruments, fresh from the fire. They then
punched a sizzling blade through one of his feet. Turning to his upper
limbs, they ripped out his fingernails, then forced his bloodied hands
into pails of hot coals, whose contents seared, then charred, his wounds.
But, compared to his fellow captives, who were all killed, Radisson was
extremely lucky. As the village children began to gnaw on the blackened
flesh of his hands and the adults prepared his suit of burning bark,
members of his adoptive family suddenly appeared. They reclaimed him
and he returned to captivity.

Radisson finally escaped to a Dutch outpost in late 1653, from
where he went to New Amsterdam (New York) and then to France.
Remarkably, though, given his earlier cruel treatment, Radisson returned
to Trois Rivières the following spring. He had come to profit from the

knowledge garnered as both freeman and prisoner. Accompanying him on this trip was Médard Chouart, twenty years his senior, who had recently married Radisson's widowed half-sister.

Chouart was known as the *Sieur des Groseilliers* – the Master of Gooseberries – after his family's landholding in the Marne country. English contemporaries, failing to grasp the subtlety of the honorary, French title, frequently referred to him in good faith as 'Mr Gooseberry'. This naming after a soft fruit is a good joke, but such an impressive figure – physically and mentally strong, resourceful and brave – deserves a more robust sobriquet.

Des Groseilliers had spent the 1640s in New France, part of the time as a disciple and lay assistant to the Jesuits of the local mission. But religion was not his vocation; the fur trade was. Trapping animals was a tough and dangerous business, which took the hunters ever further northwards and westwards, as each colony of beavers was annihilated in turn, its lodges torn open and all its occupants killed. Des Groseilliers noted that the further northwest he progressed, the thicker (and therefore more valuable) the furs became – Nature's answer to the escalating cold. His work in the woods helped him to build up an impressive knowledge of a primitive, largely uncharted, land.

Between 1654 and 1660 des Groseilliers and Radisson made three journeys deep into the northwest, the first two separately, with other companions, and the third together. Groseilliers's initial exploration, in 1654, opened up a swathe of territory almost unknown to Europeans. He crossed lakes Huron, St Clair, and Michigan, eventually arriving at Green Bay, where his beard startled the indigenous Pottowatami people – it was the first time they had seen facial hair on a man.

Des Groseilliers also experienced the shock of the new. When he witnessed herds of bison pounding across the Great Plains and spotted beavers living in huge numbers in a largely undisturbed state, he realised the rewards on offer to the hunter bold enough to venture north of Lake Superior. Of still greater interest, he heard Cree tribesmen talk about 'the Bay of the North', which Groseilliers realised must be Hudson's Bay, whose reputation was known to all trappers: a generation earlier, Henry Hudson, an English explorer, had written of this gigantic inlet that it was 'the home of many of the choicest fur-bearing animals in the world'.[1] Groseilliers returned from this initial foray wiser and richer: he and his companion brought furs to market that fetched 15,000 livres. But he knew that greater prizes beckoned.

Des Groseilliers returned the following summer with Huron guides, accompanied by two compatriots, who were Jesuit missionaries. He now encountered the savage disregard for life that Radisson had also witnessed. The party was overwhelmed by an Iroquois war party, which slaughtered most of the Hurons as part of an ongoing feud. The three Frenchmen were spared, though they were in the thick of the slaughter: des Groseilliers was drenched in the blood of one of the butchered guides and was not allowed to change his clothes.

Understanding that the Iroquois intended to kill them as well, des Groseilliers and the priests offered to prepare their captors a rich feast. The hunter-gatherers' finely tuned metabolisms were overwhelmed by the surfeit of rich food, and after eating they began to doze off. The prisoners made a speedy escape by water.

In 1659, Radisson and des Groseilliers mounted a joint expedition, pooling their differing expertise. Radisson was a convincing communicator, with a keen appreciation of the ways of the indigenous people. Des Groseilliers was more adept at logistics and organisation. Together they had a clear understanding of the realities of life in the wilderness and an eagerness to profit from its natural wealth. Above all, they celebrated the freedom and power they felt, as they headed into ungoverned territories.

They were hampered in their goal, however, by the unhelpfulness of their fellow countrymen: in particular, the governor, the Marquis d'Argenson, forbade their expedition unless it contained a high proportion of his staff and dependants. The two traders reluctantly agreed to this condition, because they were compelled to do so. However, early in the journey, they gave their unwanted companions the slip. Their subsequent, independent trek confirmed the two men in their optimism. The northern lands were teeming with thickly coated wild animals, so it was logical that further north, in Hudson's Bay, the potential crop would be even more fertile.

Radisson and des Groseilliers took care to examine the topography of the wilderness. Their experiences convinced them that the best way to access Hudson's Bay was by sea: traversing the inland waterways was simply too laborious. In the meantime, they enjoyed an extremely fruitful time, hunting and trapping. On their return to Montreal, with sixty canoes laden with pelts, their hopes were similarly brimming over – surely now they would receive unequivocal official backing for the next phase of their venture. They had failed to anticipate the stifling hand of small-minded officialdom, however. The Marquis d'Argenson, in the most regrettable and far-reaching decision of his governorship, was deaf to the men's excitement. He chose instead to focus on their disobedience, imprisoning des Groseilliers for trading without a licence and confiscating much of the pair's harvest of furs.

On his release, determined to sidestep such suffocating pettiness, des Groseilliers sailed to France. But he found no backers there, either: the common view was that the North American colony was a brutish place, whose savagery was best avoided. If there were Frenchmen who chose to inhabit such a heartless, godless, environment, their material greed exceeding their better judgement, then that was their look-out. Besides, many suspected des Groseilliers's tales were mere fancy and they would not subsidise his further ventures.

Deflated, des Groseilliers rejoined his brother-in-law in New France. After further disappointments, they decided on a different course. Pretending to set off for Hudson's Bay, they in fact moved to New England, hoping that the merchants there would be more accepting of their vision. They eventually spent three years in Boston, where their accounts of fabulous, untapped natural riches aroused interest, but failed to attract a sponsor.

Eventually the Frenchmen's tale came to the attention of two commissioners. These officers had been sent by Charles II to begin English rule in the freshly captured prize of New York. One of these, Colonel George Cartwright, persuaded the duo to go with him to England. When they agreed, Cartwright was confident that he had pulled off a coup, boasting to Lord Arlington that Radisson and des Groseilliers were: 'the best present I could possibly make to his sacred Majesty'.[2]

Charles took the men seriously. He accepted their estimation of the possibilities from the fur trade. He believed their sightings of copper, glistening in rocky outcrops. He also dared to hope that Hudson's Bay might offer the longed for Northwest Passage: the Frenchmen claimed this could be reached in a canoe from Hudson's Bay in two weeks, via Lake Winnipeg. Two English expeditions in 1631 had independently concluded that no such route existed. But, in an age when science was regularly causing the surrender of long-held preconceptions, anything seemed possible. Even the Royal Society's Robert Boyle deviated from his analytical norm, writing excitedly of the discovery of a navigable path to the 'South Sea'. It seemed as though the king had found an outlet for the energies of courtiers eager to enrich themselves, as well as the possibility of a new income stream. This would be particularly welcome if it could make him less dependent on Parliament, or on the handouts secretly negotiated with Louis XIV.

Rupert proved a clever choice to follow through the hopes of an adventurous, intelligent, but impecunious monarch. The prince's youthful hopes of sailing to Madagascar and ruling it, while opening up its trading possibilities, had come to nothing. In early 1662, Charles had permitted him to form the 'Company of the Royal Adventurers of England trading into Africa', with 'the privilege of exclusive trade from Sallee to the Cape of Good Hope'.[3] This was an investment with huge potential: when one of its convoys was waylaid by the Dutch in 1664, it was found to contain 1,420 ivory tusks, 1,000 copper kettles and bowls, and three tons of pepper.

However, this venture led to the prince's direct involvement in the slave trade of West Africa. It would be harsh to judge Rupert by modern standards, for participating in a trade we find utterly obnoxious. During most of his lifetime, slavery was rarely criticised on moral grounds. It was not until 1671 that the Quakers began publicly to condemn the market's cruel inhumanity, but few thought such objections worth listening to: they were seen as the rantings of an eccentric minority. The Royal Society invested in the Royal Africa Company, as did the king and the Duke of York.

Yet not even the enthusiastic trading of human flesh could bring the Royal Adventurers success: the Anglo-Dutch War and poor financial control both played a part in stymieing its prospects. It slowly unravelled, under the governorship of the Duke of York, eventually folding in 1670, its existence brief and undistinguished. Now, thanks to Radisson and des Groseilliers, a further opportunity to arrange a successful overseas trading empire beckoned. Rupert was not prepared to let it fail and invested £270 of his own money at the outset of the scheme, remaining enthused by the project for the rest of his life.

The first years were frustrating. In 1666 the French, suddenly scared that their lack of enterprise had handed England a very valuable prize, sent secret agents to try to entice des Groseilliers back to the Continent. That same year, much of the City of London was destroyed in the Great Fire, impeding Rupert's organisation of investors – this was an exciting but dangerous venture that, despite its royal patronage, required private finance. The following year, the Anglo-Dutch War provided a further stumbling block: ships were needed for fighting, not for speculative voyages. But still the prince persevered, keeping the project in focus despite the distractions.

By the end of 1667 he secured his first investor when Sir George Carteret bought £20 worth of stock. Others followed, including one woman, Lady Margaret Drax. Early the next year, Rupert had formed a private syndicate with enough credibility to persuade Charles II to lease it a small ship, the 54-ton *Eaglet*. She was to make an exploratory voyage to Hudson's Bay with the *Nonsuch* – which, at 43 tons, was an even more diminutive vessel, bought by the company for £290. Crews were found for the Atlantic crossing, and the mixed list of passengers included an array of artisans capable of building a base in the bay: it was clear from the outset that Rupert intended the company to be a long-term concept.

On the eve of the voyage the prince invited his fellow syndicate members to dinner at his townhouse in Spring Gardens. These not only included grandees – the 2nd Duke of Albermarle, the ever-dependable Earl of Craven, and the Earl of Arlington – but also self-made men – John Portman and Sir Robert Vyner, bankers both, as well as John Fenn and Francis Millington, civil servants. They toasted the success of their joint venture and congratulated themselves on their bold involvement in a business with such potential: they were the original eighteen who had 'at their own great cost and charge undertaken an Expedition for Hudson's Bay in the Northwest part of America for the discovery of a new Passage into the South Sea and for the finding some Trade for Furs, Minerals and other considerable Commodities'.[4]

The next morning they excitedly boarded a barge, which rowed them to a point off Gravesend. From here they witnessed the company's ships disappear over the horizon. The vessels' captains took with them orders, signed by Prince Rupert, that confirmed the purposes of their mission, and a reminder to 'use the said Mr Gooseberry and Mr Radisson with all manner of civility and courtesy and to take care that all your company do bear a particular respect unto them, they being the persons upon whose credit we have undertaken this expedition'.[5]

Radisson's participation in the voyage was short-lived: the *Eaglet* was too flimsy for the Atlantic gales and lost its mast before limping back to Plymouth. The Frenchman used his unexpected free time to write a report of his former travels. Meanwhile, the *Nonsuch*, a hardy veteran of the navy, successfully handled the waves. After nearly four months at sea, she dropped anchor in James Bay. In recognition of the prince's importance to the venture, the nearest freshwater source was immediately named Rupert River.

Trading was brisk and peaceful. The Indians of James Bay traded their furs for the Englishmen's assorted cargo of weapons, tools, and baubles. Des Groseilliers also provided – at a cost – wampum, the shells used by Indians as currency. This oiled the wheels of commerce. As winter approached, the *Nonsuch* was beached, in order to stop it being crushed by the ice. The expedition's artisans then constructed the first of five forts, which were to provide shelter from the snow and to deter other nations – essentially, France – from seeking to profit from the local trade. This first building, made of spruce trees, was initially called 'Fort Charles', but to later generations it was known as 'Rupert's House'.

Winter was long that year and the *Nonsuch* was only able to penetrate the thawing ice of Hudson Strait in mid August, 1669. The ship returned to London two months later with a consignment of furs worth £1,400. Although there was nothing by way of profit, the expedition had been a success, offering real hope that this was the start of a lucrative business. The king, sniffing a potential bonanza, acted decisively. He ordered the preparation of 'The Charter of the Governor and Company of Adventurers'. It was formally signed in Whitehall on 2 May 1670 and Rupert was appointed governor. His 'Adventurers' – all British – were eleven aristocrats and six gentlemen. Of these, seven formed a board with the prince, overseeing the running of the corporation. Rupert's committee was drawn entirely from the business-minded section of his colleagues as this was to be a professional outfit, not an aristocratic caper. To ensure openness and effectiveness, all eighteen Adventurers were answerable to an annual shareholders' meeting, where elections for the coming year were held.

Charles's ignorance of the potential scale of the operation led to the governor and company being granted an extraordinarily generous commission. 'We do grant,' he proclaimed, on the sheepskin parchment of the founding document, 'unto the said Governor and Company and their successors the sole Trade and Commerce of all those Seas, Straits, Bays, Rivers, Lakes, Creeks, and Sounds that lie within the entrance of Hudson's Straits – and make, create, and constitute [them] the true and absolute Lords and Proprietors of the same Territory.'[6]

Not only Hudson's Bay, but also all the drainage area of its myriad tributaries, was entrusted to the entrepreneurs. A strict interpretation of the terms of the founding document meant that Rupert and his colleagues were 'true and absolute Lords and Proprietors' of a territory covering 1.5 million square miles: what was now known as 'Rupert's Land' comprised roughly half of America north of the Rio Grande. (If the Northwest Passage *had* existed, Rupert would have been nominal governor of the largest empire known to man.) In return for his largesse, Charles accepted meagre payment: he was to receive two elks and two black beavers per year. Rupert, eager to keep his cousin sweet, occasionally added extra small gifts from the company: the king was reported to be delighted with a pair of beaver stockings.

From its true inception, the Hudson's Bay Company promised success, which the shareholders backed with continuing investment. A three-masted, 75-ton frigate was built, her storage areas designed to transport beaver pelts with the maximum of care and efficiency. She was named the *Prince Rupert*. At the end of May 1670, less than a month since the king signed the company's charter, the *Prince Rupert* and the *Wivenhoe* (loaned by the king) began a voyage to the bay with not just Radisson and des Groseilliers aboard, but also a jailbird called Charles Bayley.

Bayley's most recent detention had been in the Tower of London, on charges of sedition, but he had also spent time in various European prisons. A Quaker with a long beard, Bayley certainly did not want for optimism: he had once tried to convert the Pope to Protestantism. Despite his eccentricity, Bayley was selected by Rupert and his colleagues to protect the corporation's interests in North America. He proved to be an inspired choice.

Bayley remained at his post for nearly a decade, during which time the company progressed from promising much, to delivering plenty. He had a clear understanding of what was needed: he concentrated his efforts on the most important points in the forbidding landscape, erecting factories to process and receive the animal furs, and ensuring that nobody else controlled the waterways that drained into the bay. He had a hands-on style of leadership, physically helping to erect buildings and assisting in their thatching. Bayley also maintained good relations with the indigenous people. This peaceful co-existence – a result of his Quaker beliefs – meant his men were never short of game and fish to eat: either they shot or caught for the pot themselves or they bought fresh flesh from native hunters.

So successful was Bayley in his empire-building that he put Radisson's and des Groseilliers's noses out of joint. In 1674 they were lured back into the service of their motherland, their passage eased by the payment of lavish inducements and made easier by the encouragement of a Jesuit priest. However, the efforts of Prince Rupert in England, and Bayley in America, meant that the English had scooped the prize from under French noses.

The expansion was steady to start with. The *Prince Rupert* and the *Wivenhoe* returned from the bay in 1671 with enough furs to attract more, eager investors. The following January, 11,000lb of beaver furs were disposed of in twenty-seven lots, at a public auction in Garraway's Coffee House, for nearly £4,000. (In its first dozen years, the company had no permanent offices: its business took place in taverns and coffee houses.) Slightly larger returns were recorded the following year, when three ships returned from the burgeoning outpost.

Prince Rupert's efforts on behalf of commerce were publicly recognised when he was granted the honour of laying the cornerstone of the Royal Exchange. In August 1670 he was one of the first men appointed councillors for trade and plantations.

By 1676, the company was making a profit of £19,000 against costs of £650. However, during Rupert's governorship, the Hudson's Bay Company never paid its investors a dividend: this was to be a long-term investment and one that its founders were determined should have every chance of success. There were also disappointments: in 1678 the company's ship the *Shaftesbury* was sunk on its return journey, with the loss of all of that year's furs.

The prince remained fully involved with the promotion of the company. Minutes show his tireless energy and his appreciation of contemporary business practices: bribes – pieces of silver and hogsheads of claret – found their way to those able to progress the investors' fortunes. Rupert's Land was a significant territory by the time of the prince's death. Out of its ashes rose an important part of modern Canada: without the company's presence, it is probable that American settlers would have claimed the land for themselves. Furthermore, three of today's provincial capitals – Winnipeg, Edmonton, and Victoria – started life as trading outposts for the Hudson's Bay Company.

CHAPTER TWENTY-SIX

THE WRONG ENEMY

'I saw the chirurgeon cut off ye leg of a wounded sailor, the stout and gallant man enduring it with incredible patience, without being bound to his chair as usual on such painful occasions. I had hardly courage enough to be present. Not being cut off high enough, the gangrene prevail'd, and the second operation cost the poor creature his life. Lord! What miseries are mortal men subjected to, and what confusion and mischief do the avarice, anger, and ambition of Princes cause in the world!'

John Evelyn's Diary, 24 March 1672

The Second Anglo-Dutch War had been expensive for both of the main protagonists: it cost England £5 million, but the United Provinces had spent £11 million scrapping their way to a narrow overall victory. When fighting was concluded, in the summer of 1667, both the States-General and Parliament hoped for a long and prosperous peace. However, the Duke of York secretly planned to resume hostilities. He hoped that, with better preparation and more resources, a third war against the Dutch might secure sufficient bounty to free the Crown from the Commons's financial control, forever. James waited for the right moment to strike again.

The stain of shame emanating from the Medway debacle gave useful cover to his aggressive intent. Sir Bernard de Gomme, brought over by Rupert from the Continent at the outbreak of the Civil War as his chief engineer, was commissioned to make English harbours safe. In 1668 he erected 'A new fortification at the old Block House of Tilbury Fort',[1] with a circumference of two-thirds of a mile. The following year de Gomme strengthened three gunnery platforms around Portsmouth and added a fourth, screening them all with mortar made from Isle of Wight stone. De Gomme later improved the sea protection of Gosport and Dublin.

Many in Parliament thought such new defences necessary – but not against the United Provinces. Louis XIV of France was constructing a huge and frightening military machine across the Channel, and it was feared that he intended to use this to export his absolutist, Roman Catholic brand of government overseas. The growing French menace persuaded England, the United Provinces, and Sweden to form the Triple Alliance, in 1668. With the sickly young Carlos II of Spain reportedly near to death, and with France a possible heir to his Spanish Empire, it seemed sensible to form a Protestant shield in case of future Catholic aggression.

Rupert's sister Sophie had long viewed the enmity of England and the United Provinces as madness. While the Protestant trade rivals exhausted each other in combat, she saw that France was the real bene-ficiary, quietly stockpiling power on the sidelines. At the conclusion of the second war she wrote to the Earl of Craven: 'Peace is at last made between England and Holland. I would wish for the honour of your country that it had been made after the death of poor Opdam because then it would have been more glorious, but better late than never, and I am sure that the King will find it preferable to live in peace with Holland than at war, because on sea they [the United Provinces] will always be invincible as long as they hold together; I wish with all my heart both that the arms of the king of France be opposed, and that the Empire might also perform better than it has done, so far.'[2]

The French failed to alarm Charles II. He knew Louis XIV well from his time in France after the Civil War and judged that there was nothing to fear, and much to gain, from the increasing power of his cousin. This set him at odds with the majority of his people. 'The French indeed', said John Doddington, an English diplomat, in 1670, '[are] generally hated to the devil by all the English except the King in the first place & the gentry or noblesse who had seen the world and travelled abroad.'[3]

Charles's relaxed attitude towards France was reinforced by a clan-destine annual pension from Louis of £225,000. This sum eased the shackles imposed by a Parliament that, it seemed, would only make extraordinary payments to the Crown in return for political concessions. In 1670, Charles signed the Treaty of Dover, whose secret provisions formalised the Anglo-French union against the United Provinces.

The Duke of York advised against the alliance. Although he remained eager for a profitable war against the Dutch, James appreciated the inten-sity of Parliament's anti-Catholic bias better than his brother. He feared that a coalition with Louis would stop Parliament granting the navy the funds necessary for victory. Without them the problems of the previous war would recur: a lack of cash would pull the English fleet up short, when success was within its grasp. James put these concerns to the king and noted Charles's reply: 'His Majesty answered, that 50 of his own ships, and 30 from France, would serve for the war. So that there was no danger of running in debt. The charge might easily be supported by the Customs, estimated at £600,000, yet he could not look the Dutch in the face with 80 ships, such as proposed, and fire-ships proportionable; and keep convoys for trade and the preservation of plantations ...'.[4] When James realised that his brother was going to proceed with the alliance, he made Charles insist that an English admiral be placed in command of the combined fleet. James had himself in mind for the position. Charles would then provide 6,000 soldiers, to serve under Louis's marshals.

Charles was convinced that, with French support, the two kingdoms' troops would quickly overwhelm the 25,000 soldiers of the United Provinces. Louis XIV's rampant armies would attack from the east, while the English would land a second force on the North Sea coast. Once the republican Dutch were defeated, Charles's 22-year-old nephew (and Rupert's godson), Prince William of Orange, could be installed as a client ruler: William's parents were both long dead and Charles had been left as the orphan's guardian. The plan seemed feasible after a one-off Parliamentary grant of £1.3 million, in January 1672. This was enough to fund a short conflict – all that Charles thought would be required.

To help justify this third war, the king combined the sense of effrontery that had ignited the first conflict with the trade grievances that had led to the second. 'The Hollanders therefore refusing to strike sail, do deny his Majesty's Sovereignty in the Seas (one of the most precious Jewels of the Crown)', complained William de Britaine, in 1672, 'and the principal means of the Trade, Wealth and Safety of this Nation; and which all true English men, with the hazard of their lives and fortunes, are obliged to preserve and maintain.'[5] This was enough to spark a conflict that, unlike its predecessors, had little backing from England's merchant classes: the Third Anglo-Dutch War was about royal greed and opportunism, not the national interest.

Rupert's champion, Sir Robert Holmes, was first into action, attacking the 60-strong Dutch Smyrna convoy in the Channel on 13 March

1672. Four days later, on the pretext that Dutch ships had fired on Holmes, Charles declared war on the United Provinces. In late May, de Ruyter replied, surprising the Duke of York's fleet in Southwold Bay. The battle mirrored the titanic clashes of the previous wars, with many casualties from all ranks: 2,500 men were killed on each side. James was extremely lucky to survive the sinking of two of his flagships. Less fortunately, the Earl of Sandwich, recalled from his diplomatic exile, was drowned. The result was a narrow English victory, but the damage inflicted on James's ships was sufficient to rule out an invasion of Holland during the remainder of the year.

With their religious sensitivities heightened by war, Anglican politicians in London looked to create safeguards against Catholicism. They succeeded in passing the Test Act in the spring of 1673, which allowed only Protestants to hold public office. The next day, Easter Sunday, James declined to take Anglican Communion. This was, according to Evelyn, a decision that caused 'exceeding grief and scandal to the whole nation, that the heir to the throne and son of a martyr to the Protestant religion should apostasise'.[6] The duke was obliged to relinquish his naval command in June. Charles decided that the fleet was now to be run by a commission, which he would chair. A substantial figure was required to lead the forces at sea.

With Sandwich drowned, and Albermarle having died between the wars, the king announced that the senior commissioner would be Prince Rupert. He was promoted from the rank of Vice-admiral of England, to General at Sea and Land: 'And with this his Majesty's purpose,' a contemporary wrote, 'there immediately ensued a marvellous concurrence of the people's affection in city and country, all over the kingdom, as well in regard of the Royal stock from whence his Highness sprang, as of his high courage, conduct, and long experience in affairs military by sea and land, in this, and many other nations; but yet more in respect of his tried constancy to, and zeal for, the Reformed Protestant profession of religion, and all the interests thereof, for the sake whereof he and his Royal family had long suffered the utmost extremity.'[7]

It was a shrewd appointment. At a time of insecurity, many found Rupert's religious and military pedigree deeply reassuring: he would be in charge not only of the English fleet, but also of the auxiliary French squadron. The king and duke used their cousin's respectability to bolster their own public relations with Charles's increasingly jittery subjects. At the Lord Mayor's Day Show in London at the end of 1672, six months into the third war, the royal brothers took pains to appear at the Guildhall accompanied by 'the duke of Monmouth, Prince Rupert, the Archbishop of Canterbury, [and] all the bishops present in London'.[8]

These shows were blatant propaganda exercises by the Court, when messages of policy and belief were transmitted to the masses through easily digestible poetry and pageantry. By associating so visibly with the Anglican elite, Charles and James wished to portray themselves as key participants in, and supporters of, the Protestant hierarchy. This was meant to counter the concerns of a people who watched their king cavorting with a French mistress, Louise de Kéroualle – '*la Belle Bretonne*' – from the end of 1671 (she provided him with a son nine months later); and an heir to the throne who was betrothed to an Italian, Catholic princess, Mary of Modena. James and Mary married by proxy, in September 1672. Modena was pro-French: Mary's mother was a niece of Louis XIII's and Louis XIV's chief minister, Cardinal Mazarin. By entrusting Monmouth with the English brigade fighting alongside French troops against the Dutch, and by choosing Rupert to command the Anglo-French fleet, the Stuarts hoped to distance themselves from the accusation of having secret, Catholic designs.

The prince was 53, an old hand who might have thought he had seen it all. However, his new position of authority was to test his patience to the full. Rupert's time as a brigade commander in Louis XIV's army immediately after the Civil War had left him baffled: at times it had seemed as though Marshal Gassion had wanted him dead. The prince's command of the combined Anglo-French fleet would leave him similarly mystified. Furthermore, despite the widespread relief expressed at his new appointment, Rupert faced powerful enemies at home.

Throughout his adulthood Rupert had hankered after independent military command. On joining the Royalists in 1642, the king had given his nephew a surprising degree of autonomy. This led to the regrettable clash with Lindsey before Edgehill, which prompted the earl's resignation. Many of Rupert's later problems with Henrietta Maria and Digby stemmed from a belief that they were undermining his authority. Then, at Marston Moor, he insisted on precedence over the head of the affronted Marquess of Newcastle. By the time he received supreme command of the Royalist forces, it was hamstrung by looming defeat and the continuing interference of his enemy Digby.

After the Civil War, during his campaigns at sea, his forces may often have amounted only to a small flotilla, but at least it was *his* flotilla. The Second Anglo-Dutch War saw Rupert refuse to share control of the fleet with the Earl of Sandwich. He had only accepted the subsequent divided command with Albermarle out of a long-held respect for the duke. Now, in very late middle age, it seemed that Rupert had finally secured his ambition – supreme effective command of the navy. However, he was soon to experience the familiar deflation of disappointment.

Rupert intended to equip the fleet and then seek battle with the Dutch at the earliest opportunity: his every instinct remained aggressive and he wanted to deny the enemy a head start in the campaign. However, it was now that opponents of his appointment made themselves known. Faction fighting had compromised the effectiveness of the fleet during the Second Anglo-Dutch War and it was to prove equally disruptive during the Third.

Rupert was the leading figure in the navy's Royalist clique. As ever, he was eager to have men serve him whose loyalty was undoubted: 'If the officers of *my* fleet have any other way to apply themselves than to me,' the prince asked, 'I beseech you to consider how it can be possible for me to bear any command amongst them.'[9] However, critics resented his favouring men from his own following over those from rival factions, regardless of merit. They seized on the prince's promotion of Sir William Reeves, his long-term fighting companion and deputy at Windsor Castle, as an act of irresponsible patronage. Rewarding dilettante adventurers instead of professional naval officers outraged Rupert's enemies – men identified by one of the prince's following as: 'a generation of men of another mind, who, having found all their arts and endeavours of diverting his Majesty from this choice to be in vain, tacked about to the old trick of State, of devising how to take off the chariot-wheels of the Prince's expedition, and to clap a dead weight to retard him'.[10]

The Duke of York resented having to resign his command of the fleet and so made life difficult for his successor. Rupert suspected that Sir John Werden had been recently appointed a commissioner by James to complicate his job, by fermenting dissent. The prince reacted predictably, seeking the removal of officers he felt unable to trust and surrounding himself more tightly with his own men. This led to increasing tensions, which fed the faction fighting in the fleet.

The prince found that his orders were met with delay and obstruction.

When he asked for supplies for his ships, they were unavailable. When they finally arrived, they did so in inadequate quantities. The prince's instructions to press men into service were greeted with a similar lack of urgency: an operation that usually, in time of war, took place in November, was delayed until March. When the press finally took place, thousands of those who would have been most useful to the navy – fishermen, watermen and merchant seamen – were granted dispensation from their duties. Meanwhile, the prince's enemies deprived him of a commander's right to appoint officers: he must rather submit his recommendations to the commission, for approval. The slights seemed endless. When Rupert proposed raising a regiment of marines in Ireland – a fertile recruiting ground for him during the Civil War – the idea was rejected.

The prince's ambitions were also blocked by budgetary constraints. In his foundry in Windsor he had invented a new gun, the 'Rupertinoe', which he was convinced would give the navy the edge over the Dutch. 'This was a pattern of gun which was first cast, then annealed in a furnace and machined on a lathe to finish it, giving a piece of very high quality.'[11] The intricacy of the process meant that each gun cost more than twice the rate of the ordinary, iron gun: indeed, Pepys investigated the prince's bills, in the hope that he could expose fraud. Because of the expense, only three of the first rate ships used in the Third Anglo-Dutch War – the *Royal Charles, Royal James,* and *Royal Oak* – were fitted with Rupert's guns.

The Dutch fleet arrived off the English coast before Rupert's ships were properly equipped with provisions or crews. De Ruyter began to sink obstructions in the mouth of the Thames, hoping to keep the main English force hemmed in so he could deal with the French and the navy's Portsmouth squadron, at a numerical advantage. However, the prince interrupted de Ruyter, boldly sending a force of frigates and fire-ships through shoal waters that were only passable on a spring tide. The Dutch were dispersed, leaving the channels clear for Rupert's great ships.

Fearing de Ruyter's return, Rupert felt compelled to leave port immediately. He took with him marines, soldiers, and artillery, which he intended to land on the Dutch coast. Six of his larger ships were laden with 'great stores of War, viz. of granadoes [grenades] for mortar-pieces and hand, firearms, pikes, powder, shot, scaling ladders, turnpikes, and many other chargeable stores for land service'.[12] However, everyday supplies for the fleet were inadequate for a summer at sea. In May the prince led out his amphibious force, reluctantly relying on his naval commissioners' assurances that more provisions and men would be forwarded to him as soon as they became available.

The prince found the enemy unwilling to fight: the French successes on land meant de Ruyter's marines were sent to reinforce the army, so his weakened force was now obliged to employ defensive, guerrilla tactics at sea. The Dutch watched the English from behind the supposed safety of the Schooneveld's sandbanks, on the Zeeland coast. But Rupert was not to be denied: fearing a summer of frustrating watching and waiting, he sent scouts to sound out the enemy water. He then presented a plan for an audacious attack to Charles II, which the king approved.

On the morning of 28 May, the Dutch were riding at anchor when they heard a distant cannon shot. It was from Rupert's flagship, the *Royal Charles* – newly built, to replace the vessel carried off from the Medway, and untried in battle. The prince then raised the Union Flag, the signal to bear down on the enemy. Rupert's attack force was comprised of thirty-five shallow-bottomed frigates, assisted by thirteen fire-ships. It approached the Dutch with loosened fore-top sails, easing past Stony Bank in a stiff south-southwest breeze. A French squadron, commanded by one of Louis XIV's court favourites, the Comte d'Estrée, also dropped its sails and followed the English advance. When Rupert was through the initial shallows, he raised the red flag, which was the sign for the assault to start in earnest.

The fleets closed at noon, the Dutch startled by this unprecedented attack: they had always viewed these waters as their sanctuary. Van Tromp faced Rupert, while de Ruyter greeted d'Estrée. The prince got the upper hand in his sector of the battle, driving his opponents close to the shore, where some ran aground. However, the French were less successful, their disarray allowing de Ruyter to come to van Tromp's aid. Rupert had to fight both enemy formations simultaneously, his efforts hampered by 'his Highness's own ship,' an eyewitness recalled, 'which proved so crank-sided, and fetched so much water in at the ports, that her lower tier of guns could not be made use of, though it was a very easy gale we had'.[13] Despite this handicap, Rupert and his frigates lost few men and no ships, while the United Provinces had two ships sunk, one burnt, two disabled, and three run aground. The prince had the pleasure of seeing de Ruyter and van Tromp flee for safety, in the face of his blazing fire-ships.

Although this was a minor victory, it gave Rupert the satisfaction of justifying his suitability for supreme, independent command. Charles acknowledged this soon afterwards, when appointing him Admiral of the Fleet. Rupert had done what no English admiral had managed in the previous maritime wars: he had shown the United Provinces that no place was safe, outside their harbours, in the face of determination and bold piloting.

Rupert led the fleet in a further engagement a few days later, which followed an ambush by de Ruyter. This was a scrappy affair, which neither side could claim to have won. The prince's conduct during this battle was subsequently criticised by one of his admirals, Sir Edward Spragge – like Holmes, an Irish Protestant who had spent time as a Royalist privateer. De Ruyter had caught the Anglo-French off guard and Spragge was aboard Rupert's ship when the attack began. The prince ordered Spragge back to his flagship, with instructions to lead the counterattack as soon as he could: Spragge's squadron was to be in the van, with Rupert's in the middle of the formation. But Spragge took an age to reach his vessel and Rupert could wait no longer. Without being able to communicate his change of plan, he chose to lead the fleet with his own squadron to the fore.

Spragge was incensed. 'The Prince placing himself in the van', he recorded, in his journal, 'the French in the middle, the line-of-battle, being of 89 men-of-war and small frigates, fire-ships and tenders, is so very long that I cannot see any sign the general admiral makes, being quite contrary to any custom ever used at sea before, and may prove of ill consequence to us. I know not any reason he has for it except being singular and positive.'[14] Although Rupert had strayed from the diktats of the training manual, Spragge's critique made no allowances for de Ruyter's exceptional skills in his home waters, which had cleverly hurried the prince into action earlier than he had planned.

For Rupert, the most worrying aspect of these engagements was the behaviour of the French: they had been little more than onlookers throughout. The suspicion was beginning to form that Louis wanted the two maritime powers to damage each other, while not exposing his ships in battle. Unhappy with his allies, disappointed that his new flagship was like 'a mere table'[15] in the wind, and angered by the promised supplies failing to appear, Rupert returned to England and demanded an audience with the king. Charles felt obliged to accompany his cousin

to the coast, where the prince showed him the pitiful condition of his
ships. Rupert suggested that those responsible for the inadequate provisions should be forced to sail with the fleet and suffer the consequences
of their incompetence and corruption. The prince also told the king of
the unacceptable conduct of the French.

Rupert's opinion of his coalition partners continued to decline. On
land, the French had performed magnificently in 1672: marshals Condé,
Luxembourg, and Turenne had made quick and decisive inroads against
the Dutch defences, overwhelming the tiny army and committing
atrocities against civilians. While one of Charles II's natural sons, the
Duke of Monmouth, commanded a British brigade on land, England's
role in the coalition was primarily at sea, although the French navy was
expected to play its part, too. Louis's navy had grown from fourteen
ships of the line in 1663 to seventy-three in 1671. The prince expected
it to pull its weight.

Rupert was further disappointed when Charles II appointed one of
Louis XIV's marshals as captain general of English land forces. Marshal
de Schomberg was a Palatine German whose family had served Rupert's
father, Frederick, in Heidelberg. Schomberg had, like Rupert, found
military employment abroad after the electorate was overrun. However,
to many, he was a French appointment foisted on their king by an
overseas tyrant. To the prince, he was an inferior who was now assuming equality.

Waiting to embark on Rupert's ships for the planned invasion of
the United Provinces, Schomberg and his men camped at Blackheath.
Preferring to be at sea, Schomberg transferred to the frigate *Greyhound*.
His senior officers advised him that, from the land, they could not tell
which was their commander's vessel. Schomberg therefore decided to
fly his family's standard from the main mast, to assist identification. To
Rupert, this was an intolerable insolence: only admirals were allowed
to hoist their own flags. He fired two of his cannon, as a signal that
the marshal should lower the flag immediately. At the same time, he
dispatched an officer to confiscate the standard and to insist that it
never again be raised aboard one of his Majesty's ships. Now it was
Schomberg's turn to be outraged: as captain general he was Rupert's
equal in rank (the prince was Lord Admiral) and was not prepared
to obey orders from his peer. Schomberg sent his frigate's captain to
protest at Rupert's highhandedness and ordered that the offending flag
remain in place.

This was a clash of two proud and passionate leaders, which soon escalated from the bad tempered to the absurd. The prince was in a rage: Schomberg was aboard one of his ships and he was the overall commander of every vessel. The marshal had, in Rupert's eyes, compounded his arrogance with disobedience. He ordered that the marshal's messenger be arrested as soon as he came aboard. Rupert then sailed his flagship towards the *Greyhound* and threatened to sink her unless the flag was immediately taken down. Schomberg realised that Rupert was not bluffing and ordered his standard to be lowered. Both commanders then sent their version of events to Charles II, who chose not to side with either man. No doubt he found the whole affair remarkably childish.

This spat aside, Rupert's overall concern about his allies coincided with a growing anxiety in England about the coalition with France. As early as the summer of 1672, the Bishop of Lincoln had written of the marshals' Blitzkrieg through the United Provinces: 'Holland deservedly suffers all the miseries it now lies under ... [but] if it submits to France, where are we? I am persuaded France will treat and conquer on, till there be little left to treat for.'[16] The conduct of the French navy in 1673 added to this fear and suspicion.

After the two small June engagements, Rupert was obliged to return to the Thames for provisioning. On returning to duty, he wanted to attack the Dutch behind their sandbanks. However, Charles – probably as a result of his brother's continuing meddling – insisted that all initiatives be passed by James, for approval: the Duke of York had been relieved of his command, but could not resist covert involvement in the workings of the fleet. The king, though, failed to appreciate the urgency of the situation. Rupert must now have felt the same disappointment that Sir William Coventry had expressed so poignantly, when resigning from the Navy Board at the end of 1667: 'The serving a prince that minds not his business is most unhappy for them that serve him well.'[17]

The result was everything that Rupert detested about subordination: he saw opportunities of sudden and decisive action disappear, during the last days of July and the first week of August, because he was forced to await the king's instructions from England. The prince, meanwhile, concentrated on trying to lure de Ruyter out of the Schooneveld, which English officers now referred to as de Ruyter's 'hole'. The prince led his Anglo-French fleet off the Texel, an island whose main channel, the Marsdiep, was the route for the ships of three of the United

Provinces' five admiralties – those of Amsterdam, Friesland, and the 'North Quarter' (the latter's command centre alternating between Enkhuizen and Hoorn) – to reach the North Sea. Rupert sailed up and down the coastline between this, the principal Dutch naval base, and Camperdown, hoping to tempt the enemy to attack.

On the late afternoon of 10 August, the opportunity to fight arose. However, despite having the advantage of the wind, the prince decided to wait until morning, since he wanted a full day at the Dutch to make sure of total victory. By waiting, he risked losing the enemy altogether. However, by the next morning, the wind had changed, which persuaded the Dutch to use their advantage and fight, even though Rupert had eighty-six ships to the United Provinces' sixty.

The battle of Texel was one of the most disappointing encounters of Rupert's life. At last, after all the squabbles over supplies and the interference of the Duke of York, he had the opportunity to better the Dutch. This would surely have hastened the end of the war, for victory at sea would have left the way open for land invasion. With his troops landing on the western coast, and the French advancing from the east, the States-General would be compelled to yield. All that the prince required was a unity of purpose from his three squadrons – two English and one French.

The engagement split into two contests between familiar opponents. Van Tromp and Spragge clashed in a ferocious duel, which resulted in the total destruction of both flagships' masts and rigging. While Spragge was transferring to a new ship, his pinnace was sunk and he drowned. Meanwhile, Rupert and de Ruyter locked horns in the battle's midst, the prince and his men displaying 'an incomparable resolution',[18] according to an eyewitness, against two enemy squadrons. Their fight was brief, however, both commanders breaking off to link up with the rest of their forces.

What transformed the battle of Texel from a crucial battle into a virtual irrelevance was the performance of d'Estrée's Frenchmen. By twice slackening their sails at the start of the engagement, they managed to put a considerable distance between themselves and the main action. Despite Rupert's clear and constant signalling for them to join in the fight, the French stayed aloof from the bloodshed, watching from 6 miles away 'instead', wrote an eyewitness, 'of falling with the fair wind they had upon de Ruyter or Tromp, who were going to attack the English squadrons with a far greater force than theirs; which would have been the entire defeat of the enemy had they been enclosed between his Highness Prince Rupert, & Mons. d'Estrée'.[19] The French decision to become bystanders eliminated Rupert's numerical advantage at a stroke and enabled de Ruyter to slip away virtually unscathed: he lost just one man-of-war, although two of his vice-admirals were slain.

The Texel was Rupert's last battle as admiral or general. As the conclusion of a pulsating fighting career, it was a miserable anti-climax. Despite both sides suffering the same level of casualties, the stalemate ended Rupert's hopes of a successful invasion in 1673. The prince bewailed the squandering of 'the plainest and best opportunity'[20] the alliance had had of winning the war. Returning to England, he oversaw the sale of the supplies taken with him to feed his land forces, including cheese for the men and oats for their horses. Fearing criticism, he lashed out at those he believed to be to blame for the failure. He found he was preaching to the converted: nobody in London wanted to hear about de Ruyter's brilliant cunning; they longed, instead, to learn more about dastardly French treachery.

Rupert had no respect for the dead and repaid Spragge's past criticisms by accusing him of having been in cahoots with the French. It seems likely that the cause of Spragge's unreliability lay closer to home: he was one of the Duke of York's creatures and such men were apt to cause Rupert great mischief, undermining his command out of loyalty to their master. The prince also revealed that d'Estrée had sent a messenger at the end of the battle to ask the meaning of the flag raised on his mizzen. This proved to Rupert, and to the conspiracy theorists, that the French had seen the signal to attack and chosen to ignore it. Their ignorance was feigned and their guilt surely established.

Charles's ministers tried to censor accounts of the battle of the Texel, to spare their controversial alliance from further condemnation. However, English sailors returning home were quick to vent their disgust, and an observer noted that: 'the citizens of London looked more disconsolate than when their city lay in ashes'[21] on hearing of d'Estrée's reluctance to fight. 'All men cried out', wrote Bishop Burnet, 'and said, we are engaged in a war by the French, that they might have the pleasure to see the Dutch and us destroy one another, while they knew our seas and ports, and learned all our methods, but took care to preserve themselves.'[22]

The scandal was given fresh impetus when the Marquis de Martell, d'Estrée's second-in-command, wrote his account of the battle. William

Bridgeman, a correspondent of the Earl of Essex, wrote: 'The discourse about the behaviour of the French in the last fight continues still, the generality being no ways satisfied with it, which is much augmented by Mons. Martell's relation, a copy of which I have enclosed here.'[23] This confirmed English suspicions that the French were under instructions not to engage: after a gentle brush with the Dutch, during which he fired only one broadside, d'Estrée ordered his squadron to regroup round his flagship. Martell revealed:

> This being all finished in our station by eleven of the clock in the morning the whole squadron united again, & with a fair wind made toward the place where we left his Highness Prince Rupert, who was above three leagues from us, engaged in a fight with a considerable body of the Enemy's. His Highness Prince Rupert seeing us come with that fair wind, gave us the signal to bear into his wake, Mons. de Martell laid his sails to the masts expecting that Mons. d'Estrée would advance with his whole squadron & fall all together with this fair wind upon the body of the Enemy & send in fire ships among them; but instead of that he kept the wind and contented himself to give his ships leave to shoot at more than [a] cannon and [a] half distance from the enemy. Mons. de Martell saw very well how shameful this was. But having received an express order to attempt nothing without the particular orders of Mons. d'Estrée, & besides having been so ill attended that morning by the ships of his division that he could have no assurance they would follow him, he shrugged up his shoulders, and only forbid any shooting from his ships, and this hath been all that was acted that day in relation to us.'[24]

Martell was sent to the Bastille for his indiscretion, but his testimony, added to Rupert's disgust, brought to an end Charles II's attempts to link England militarily with France. English sailors, who were expected to cheer their allies' ships as they passed, refused to do so. The Venetian ambassador reported that dummies dressed as Frenchmen were shot on Guy Fawkes' Night, before being thrown onto bonfires.

In January 1674, Charles was obliged to summon Parliament. Fumbling his notes, he countered suspicions of a secret agreement with Louis with a lie, claiming that no such arrangement was in place. However, a paper circulated through Westminster claiming that: 'All the mischiefs we have felt or may hereafter fear from the Hollanders, though ten times greater than what are falsely pretended, cannot possibly be of half that dangerous consequence to us, as the advantages now given to the growth of French power, by this pernicious league.'[25] Parliament refused to grant the king revenue for the continuation of the war. The following month England made unilateral peace with the Dutch: it was agreed to cease hostilities on 20 February. On 11 February, learning that a Dutch ship was harbouring in the Shetlands en route for the West Indies, Rupert ordered that she be seized before the war's end.

This piece of cheeky opportunism was the final act in the prince's long and varied military record. Rupert relinquished command of the fleet and returned to Windsor with unprecedented popularity: he had blown the whistle on an alliance that, many believed, had threatened their religion and their freedom. The prince and his friend Lord Shaftesbury were now, reported a contemporary, 'looked upon to be the great Parliament men, and for the interest of Old England'.[26] Thirty years earlier, people would have laughed at such a notion, but Rupert was now believed to be much changed from the man who had terrorised the Parliamentary cause a generation before.

Rupert's mistrust and suspicion of France were proved correct in time. Sir William Coventry told the Commons, in May 1678: 'If you stay till all Flanders be gone, you will do as King James did in the Palatinate War, treat, and treat, till all was gone, and nobody to treat with him.'[27] This was the platform that William of Orange was able to build on when he stole the English throne in 1688 to become William III. He led the Grand Alliance against Louis XIV's aggressive expansionism in the 1690s and prepared his adoptive kingdom for the gruelling necessity of standing up to France in the War of the Spanish Succession.

CHAPTER TWENTY-SEVEN

DEATH OF A CAVALIER

'All my past Life is mine noe more,
The flying hours are gone;
Like transitory Dreams giv'n o'er,
Whose images are kept in store,
By Memory alone.'

'Love and Life: A Song', John Wilmot,
Earl of Rochester (1647–80)

Relative to the frenetic pace of the rest of his life, Rupert's latter years were quiet: Windsor Castle provided his principal residence, its laboratories and foundries, together with his collection of old books, stimulating his mind. The reputation of Rupert's original thought continued to the end. When, aged 60, nobody could break a French cipher that had fallen into English hands, it was sent to the prince. Although he failed to crack the code, he made out the words, 'Strike, strike, strike'.

Rupert enjoyed greater popularity during his final, settled years at Windsor than at any other time of his life. 'In respect of his private life,' Dr Campbell wrote, half a century after Rupert's death, 'he was so just, so beneficent, so courteous that his memory remained dear to all who knew him. This I say of my own knowledge, having often heard old people in Berkshire speak in raptures of Prince Rupert.'[1] The prince's eulogist was to write of Rupert's 'easy good old age, Remov'd from [the] tumultuous stage'.[2]

We find the punctilious prince of the past now more relaxed, prepared to enjoy the privileges of high rank. He was still an admiral and regularly sent ships to Germany to bring back supplies of his favourite Rhenish wines. These would be shuttled up the Thames in his private yacht, the *Rupert*. Since some of the shipment was used for the king's cellar, Rupert charged all of the crews' wages against the Admiralty. Once the prince went further, diverting a man-of-war to collect some Spanish onions from the Continent.

The king was also slowing up in middle age. The Yorkshire squire Sir John Reresby, who had glimpsed Charles, James, and Rupert boisterously playing billiards in France during the heyday of the Commonwealth, was struck by the monarch's quiet life, thirty years on: 'There was little resort to him, and he passed his day in fishing or walking in the parks which indeed he naturally loved more than to be in a crowd or in business.'³

There was certainly plenty of 'business' for the king to attend to. From behind the castle's walls, Rupert could see that the divisions that had led to the Civil War were still alive and dominated the public life of the nation. The tensions between James, Duke of York, and his increasingly bold critics, became more pronounced as Charles aged, his many offspring illegitimate, his heir an increasingly intractable Catholic. Over the Channel, Louis XIV's increasing military aggression intensified Anglican paranoia.

Those who wanted James's claims to the crown annulled – the 'Exclusionists' – dreamed up increasingly wild reasons for meddling in the rightful order of succession. In 1678 an eccentric priest, Israel Tonge, and a bogus doctor of Divinity, Titus Oates, whipped up a hysterical storm by claiming knowledge of a plot to murder the king. This, they insisted, would be followed by an invasion of Jesuits, assisted by Catholic armies from Ireland and Scotland. The 'Popish Plot' was fanciful nonsense – Tonge's and Oates's evidence differed wildly – but it was believed by the fearful and gullible, until Oates was discredited.

Oates said that incriminating letters, to be found at Windsor post office, would prove his assertions. But, as soon as they were seen, they were suspected of being forged. The Duke of York insisted that the Committee for Foreign Affairs be allowed to examine them further. 'The whole committee was then present,' James recalled, 'the duke of York, Prince Rupert, Chancellor, Treasurer, Lauderdale, Arlington, Coventry, and Williamson ... After all were delivered to Sir W. Jones, attorney-general, and Sir Robert Southwell, clerk of the council, they compared some of Oates's writing with these letters, they verily believed one of them was in his handwriting ... The letters sent by post were so ill-worded, that none, but such an illiterate dunce as Oates, could have written them.'⁴

In September 1679, the king fell worryingly ill with a malarial fever while at Windsor Castle. The Earl of Sunderland – son of Rupert's comrade, killed at the First Battle of Newbury – was the most devious and canny of politicians. Eager to perpetuate his power into the next reign, he wrote advising James to return from exile in Brussels, in case the throne should suddenly fall vacant. A handful of Charles's closest allies knew of this invitation, as did the king himself, but it is testimony to Rupert's political irrelevance by this stage that he was kept in the dark. He was genuinely surprised, one autumn morning, to find James in the castle, accompanied by his right-hand man, John Churchill.

Doses of 'the Jesuit's powder' – quinine – saved the king on this occasion and James slunk back to Ostend early in October, reluctantly resuming his pariah status. Charles, however, had enjoyed being reunited with his brother and in early 1680 insisted that he return to England. This development brought the differences between the Court and 'the faction' into sharp relief. In his memoirs, James recalled the very different reactions to his reinstatement: 'An address from Norfolk thanking the King for recalling the duke of York. The faction alarmed at his return. Rumours of plots.'[5] James, ever mindful of his friends and foes, noted who supported his return with loyal petitions. 'In Berkshire,' he remarked, 'the petition was presented by Sir J. Stonehouse, Mr Barker, Wood, &c., most of them honest gentlemen; though Prince Rupert was lord lieutenant, and constable of Windsor Castle and Forest.'[6] James was disappointed at his cousin's reticence: he expected Rupert to be at the forefront of his cause, but in that he was disappointed.

Although Rupert was a close friend and business partner of James's most persistent critic, the Earl of Shaftesbury, it stretches credulity to think that, after a lifetime of loyalty to the Crown, Rupert flirted with Shaftesbury's republicanism. However, the prince remained a devoted Calvinist and had not expended so much of his adult energy supporting a dynasty to see it now threaten to foist Catholicism on a reluctant, Protestant nation. When Charles dismissed Shaftesbury, Rupert displayed solidarity with a very public visit to the former chancellor.

Rupert, in old age, felt able to behave as he wished and certainly had no fear of Charles II. It was Rupert, in 1679, who headed the petition to the king to dissolve the Cavalier Parliament. It had sat since 1660 and no longer reflected the will of the electorate. When one of the Members of the Cavalier Parliament, Speke – a Somerset man – was arrested on false charges of disloyalty and faced possible execution, Rupert spoke on his behalf. The prince told of a loan of 1,000 crowns that Speke had given him for the defence of Bridgwater, late in the Civil War. Speke, Rupert pointed out, had never publicised his generosity, nor sought repayment: far from being disloyal, the prince concluded, this was a man of noble dependability. Speke was released and that evening Rupert invited him to dinner as his guest of honour.

The question of James, his Catholicism, and his right to succeed his brother, remained the burning issue in English politics during the remainder of Rupert's life and beyond. By the end of 1680, Charles II was forced to place his brother in exile once more, rather than risk the duke's impeachment. James's more radical critics wanted him 'banned for the King's life to some place five hundred miles from England; to forfeit his revenues if he came nearer, and his life if he returned to any of the King's dominions'.[7] Charles rejected these extreme demands, allowing James to reside in Scotland.

The year 1681 saw the Exclusionists push further. They concocted another in a line of false conspiracy theories, this time claiming that an Italian envoy had tried to arrange the murder of the king with James's compliance. The Duke of York was falsely alleged to have claimed that a French army would then come to his aid, so he could boil his Parliamentary enemies alive, setting aside the tallow from their bones for use as anointment oil at his and his descendants' coronations.

Charles felt compelled to summon Parliament in Oxford, rather than risk unrest in London. At the opening session, the Commons pressed forward their Exclusion Bill. The king, determined to deal decisively with dangerous opposition, summoned the Commons to the House of Lords. They found him seated in his robes, and were astonished and enraged to hear him dissolve Parliament. Immediately afterwards, the king got into his coach and headed for Windsor Castle.

The backdrop of Rupert's final year saw James return to England in March – he spent part of the spring at Windsor – but his rival Monmouth gaining popularity locally, as he progressed towards Cheshire. 'A Monmouth and no York'[8] was the Exclusionists' mantra. Soon, this would lead to Monmouth's Rebellion – the 1685 attempt to overthrow the main Stuart line.

Largely sidelined from politics, Rupert busied himself with matters that intrigued him. His efforts on behalf of the Hudson's Bay Company were unstinting. The year before his death, he negotiated sweeping customs' privileges to give his enterprise an edge over its rivals. And, in his final year, the company sent its largest flotilla to date – five ships, including the *Prince Rupert* – to trade in the bay. By this stage the traders had established their own permanent office, in Scrivener's Hall. Sir George Clark concluded that: 'The old hero of so many fights on land and sea, with his high station, his many interests, and his chequered, adventurous memories, had stood up for the Company well.'⁹

If proof were needed of his key role in the eventual success of this venture, it can be found in the near-fatal result of his successor's indolence: during a mercifully brief tenure of the governorship of the company, James, Duke of York, failed to champion his shareholders' or his people's interests. He was worried that denying French access to Hudson's Bay's trade would upset Louis XIV. His timidity saw the loss of four of the company's five forts to France. It was the third governor, John Churchill, later Duke of Marlborough, who from 1685 retrieved the situation. In the process he honoured the enterprising and daring legacy of the prince. At its peak, the Hudson's Bay Company covered an expanse of land ten times the size of the Holy Roman Empire, from which Prince Rupert had sprung.

The Hudson's Bay Company remained true to its original business intentions until 1991, when it stopped trading in fur and continued as a chain of department stores. The company remains the world's oldest surviving commercial enterprise.

Rupert was effectively in semi-retirement from the end of the Third Anglo-Dutch War. He remained First Lord of the Admiralty until 1679, but his influence in the navy lessened as the years passed. James, Duke of York, recorded in 1677: 'On the tenth of April, Prince Rupert told the King, that he had opposed a design, in the House of Commons, for his being High Admiral; but hoped he would make him so, in case of a war. The King said, it was time enough yet to consider what was to be done in that case.'¹⁰

If further evidence was needed that Rupert's era was over, it was provided by Samuel Pepys, who was now a Norfolk MP as well as Secretary of the Admiralty. In December 1677, Pepys advocated the professionalisation of the officer class on sea: nobody could be appointed lieutenant without at least three years' service, an endorsement from his captain, and a pass in navigation and seamanship exams. Rupert objected that this would excuse good men – amateurs who could switch their expertise from land to sea with ease, thanks to their natural fighting spirit. The prince was ignored and the battle between 'tarpaulin' and gentlemen captains, which had divided the fleet since the Restoration, was over.

The meritocratic Pepys had won an impressive and far-reaching victory over the aristocratic prince.

Rupert's presidency of the Admiralty Board ended in May 1679. He went, as a concession to Parliamentary suspicion that Charles or James might attempt to rule arbitrarily. In another bold footstep towards modernity, the king relieved his cousin of control of the navy and handed it to a body of MPs. At times, Rupert must have seen his final years as a time of bewildering change.

As he entered late middle age, his contemporaries began to fall away. His old enemy George Digby died in March 1676, 'neither loved nor regretted by any party'. Lord Orford wrote of him: 'His life was one contradiction. He wrote against popery, and embraced it; he was a zealous opposer of the Court, and a sacrifice to it; was conscientiously converted in the midst of his prosecution of Lord Strafford, and was most unconscientiously a prosecutor of Lord Clarendon. With great parts, he always hurt himself and his friends; with romantic bravery, he was always an unsuccessful commander. He spoke for the Test Act though a Roman Catholic, and addicted himself to astrology on the birthday of true philosophy.'[11]

Writing to Charles Louis in January 1678, Princess Sophie congratulated her elder brother on his health and spirit as he entered his sixtieth year. 'Bodily health is an inheritance from the late queen our mother', she said, 'that nobody will be able to dispute with you, and the better that we have had of it, of which Prince Rupert has been very well provided too; without which he would not have been able to resist some terrible accidents, from which he is still escaping. Everyone believed that he ought to die; however he escaped it by an effort of nature.'[12]

Late middle age gave way to old age and Electress Sophie – ten years Rupert's junior – wrote to Charles Louis, in June 1679: 'It seems, when one begins to grow old, that it is necessary always to feel some sickness. If I didn't have the fever, I would have had something else – perhaps also a bad leg like you, Prince Rupert and the Abbess of Herfort. It is human misery, to see oneself perish and others be born who will outlive us and who are so passionately attached to us, that we would not want to leave them before seeing them well established in life.'[13]

On 11 February 1680, Princess Elizabeth died after a terrible battle with cancer: Sophie had visited her during her final days and had been shocked to see the skeletal form lying in bed, with three huge growths visible under her skin, the largest swelling ravaging her stomach. 'She was in such a pitiful state', Sophie wrote to Charles Louis, 'that we ought to be very relieved that she has been delivered from it.'[14] The same year, Will Legge died.

The Palatines had contempt for doctors, Sophie calling them charlatans. Rupert had always had a deep fear of blood-letting and appears to have kept his worsening health secret till near the end. He died from a fever and pleurisy on 29 November 1682, at his house in Spring Gardens, close to where Pall Mall runs into Trafalgar Square. His funeral was a grand affair, made more personal by the procession that surrounded the coffin. The Earl of Craven, a very old man now, was chief mourner. Behind, betraying the varied tastes of the deceased, followed Rupert's tennis coach, his huntsman, his gunsmith, and his butler. He was buried in Henry VII's Chapel, Westminster Abbey, on 6 December.

In his Will, Rupert left most of his possessions in trust to 'Margaret Hewes and ... Ruperta, my natural daughter begotten on the body of the said Margaret Hewes, in equal moieties'. Craven was the executor of the Will: by tidying up the prince's affairs, he managed to procure £6,000 for each of the beneficiaries. In Rupert's private, iron box he found 1,694 guineas and £1,000 in silver. The prince's other possessions were, in the main, sold: his silver raised £2,070; his pack of hounds £120; his books £100; his yacht £46; his best hunter £40; his carriage horses £6 10 s. each. Colonel Oglethorpe bought Rupert's guns and Sir James Hayes his shares in the Hudson's Bay Company. Craven settled a variety of debts – with the jeweller, the apothecary, the periwig-maker, the Gentleman of the Horse, the secretary, and the undertaker.

Rupert's instructions to 9-year-old Ruperta were to be 'dutiful and obedient to her mother, and not to dispose of herself in marriage without her consent, and the advice of the said Earl of Craven, if they, or either of them, shall be then living'.[15] She eventually married Emanuel Scrope Howe, who became a lieutenant general in William III's armies. He died in 1709. Ruperta survived until 1740, dying at Somerset House.

Peg's was an uncomfortable widowhood. She had lived long and hard at the prince's expense and was forced to sell much of her jewellery to meet accumulating debts. Elizabeth of Bohemia's earrings had to go, sold to Sarah, the wife of John Churchill. Nell Gwynn paid £4,250 for a pearl necklace Peg had received from Rupert – the wedding gift of the prince's father to his mother. Peg also disposed of the grand house that Rupert had given her: it became known as Brandenburg House after its new owner, the Margrave of Brandenburg. Peg eventually died in Eltham, Kent, on 1 October 1719, thirty-seven years after Rupert.

The prince's son by Frances Bard, Dudley, was well liked at Eton, where he was, according to Warburton, 'distinguished for gentleness of temper, as well as for his father's courage, honesty of character, and love of truth'.[16] His passion was soldiery. Rupert gave him a tutor from the Tower of London, Sir Jonas Moore, who taught Dudley military theory, mathematics, and engineering.

On his death, Rupert left his son the hunting lodge at Rhenen and his various claims to German lands and money, still not received in full from Charles Louis and the Emperor. 'Captain Rupert' served in the Royal army that helped to quash Monmouth's 1685 rebellion: at a skirmish at Norton St Philip, he commanded the musketeers. The following year, on 13 June 1686, he joined in the final Christian assault against the Turks at Buda. Whereas his father survived many such actions, Dudley was less fortunate: he perished, aged just 19 or 20.

If Dudley had been legitimate, and had he outlived Queen Anne, his claim to the English throne would theoretically have been superior to that of Rupert's nephew, George of Hanover. Just before his death, Rupert had offered George's mother Sophie £1,000, to pay for the boy's stay in England: Rupert wanted him to learn the English language and the people's ways. Sadly, the offer was not accepted and George I remained, to his subjects, a disappointingly German monarch.

Prince Rupert's life story has always focused on his Civil War years, when he was the most glamorous general on either side. He joined his uncle's cause when it seemed improbable that the king could raise an army capable of facing Parliament. Rupert's energy and flair helped to transform this desperate position, giving hope of ultimate victory to the Royalists, and forcing the rebels to paint the prince and his horsemen as demonic Cavaliers. By the end of 1643, after a succession of triumphs, Rupert had helped to give his side a genuine expectation of victory. However, he was hamstrung by his colleagues' inability to secure sufficient manpower and arms to counter an increasingly numerous and well-trained enemy. The prince's reliance on the impact of his horsemen's charge, a tactic that made subsequent control extraordinarily difficult, was probably the only way in which he could seek to defeat an ever more powerful foe.

Thereafter, Rupert's suitability for high command was rigorously examined. As Parliament called on stronger reserves, and the assistance of Scottish allies, so the prince's priority became the propping up of the Royalist cause in the south and north. The rescue of Newark was the high point of his military achievements. His determination to fulfil his uncle's commands to the letter, against unrealistic odds, led to his nadir almost immediately afterwards: Marston Moor was a humbling and catastrophic defeat.

By the following summer, Rupert knew that his uncle's chance of victory had gone. Frequently at odds with Digby and his courtier faction, the prince's performance at Naseby was personally brave, but tactically naive. Defeat was all but guaranteed, once he decided to lead a cavalry wing, rather than direct the battle. The subsequent loss of Bristol was inevitable, but sounded the death knell for Charles I's cause.

Temperamentally, Rupert in his early twenties would have been better deployed as a commando leader, or a cavalry general, than as overall military supremo. He was too immature to appreciate the importance of politics and diplomacy to high command, and too short-tempered to disguise his contempt for colleagues who opposed his plans.

Rupert had many faults: he was impetuous, dismissive, and blunt. However, he always tried to adhere to the highest standards, both military and personal: he was a professional fighting man and a devout Calvinist. The sorry record of his ineffectual father – whose ambition and sense of duty had led to disaster for his family, his peoples, and his inheritance – may have left Rupert with an exaggerated desire to prove himself and to restore pride to his line.

His neglectful, narcissistic mother, fêted since girlhood with extraordinary adulation, may also have contributed to Rupert's unyielding nature. Even in extended, impoverished exile, she never lost the need to be worshipped. She fostered a court that welcomed knight-errants, while banishing her young children to an upbringing away from her view: the emotional needs of others were unwelcome drains on Elizabeth's love of self. Irresponsible and inappropriate parenting may have accentuated Rupert's need for praise and applause. Soldiery was the prince's chosen path to glory: anyone who compromised his dream of battlefield success therefore attracted his withering hostility.

Contemporaries were used to gruff soldiers, but Rupert's black and white views of life, and of people, were startling. He was particularly distrustful of the machinations of politicians and courtiers, because they clouded matters that he needed to remain clear. He did not understand how men could morally compromise themselves in order to further their personal agenda. It was easier for Rupert to dismiss such people as underhand and undesirable, than to accept them as an inevitable component of the politics of war. As Sir Philip Warwick, one of the prince's admirers, remarked with sadness, Rupert's 'sharpness of temper of body, and uncommunicableness in society or council, (by seeming with a pish to neglect all another said, and he approved not) made him less grateful, than his friends wished; and this humour soured him towards the Councillors of Civil affairs, who were necessary to intermix with him in Martial Councils'.[17]

While accepting that Rupert's achievements on the battlefield fail to gain him a place in the first rank of generals, his huge charisma is undeniable. The rest of his life story shows an unusual range of talents and interests. He was a gifted artist and an intelligent, conscientious, and committed scientist. His championing of the Hudson's Bay Company showed a clear ability to spot an opportunity and to act decisively on it. The same talent made him a respected adversary at sea, both as admiral and pirate. To have kept the Royalist flag flying in the Caribbean, while it had been trampled underfoot everywhere else, was a feat of heroic endurance that exacted a terrible cost: the loss of his brother Maurice was the greatest body blow of his life and the compromises to his own health were felt throughout his subsequent three decades.

Parliamentary propagandists liked to portray the prince in the poorest possible light. However, the amount of attention they gave to the Cavalier Prince, and the number of lies they weaved into their portrayal of him, demonstrate their fear of a man that they knew to have exceptional potential, which could be extraordinarily dangerous to their cause. To few historical figures can the cliché more aptly be applied, that you can judge a man by the strength of his enemies.

Set on a lifetime of wandering adventure by his father's misfortune and misjudgements, it was only when he came to live in England that he found a home. As a boy, he had shouted out from his galloping hunter that he wanted his bones buried in his uncle's land. In a life punctuated by painful disappointment, this was one wish that came true.

NOTES

CHAPTER ONE:

1 Thomas Flatman, *On the Death of the Illustrious Prince Rupert, A Pindarique Ode*, (London: 1683) p. 2

2 Prince Rupert's life story, probably written by his secretary, Colonel Bennet, quoted in Eliot Warburton, *Memoirs of Prince Rupert and the Cavaliers*, vol.I (London: 1849) p. 447

3 Sir John Harington, *Nugae Antiquae*, vol. III (London: 1779) p. 156

4 Ibid., vol. II, p. 237

5 Ibid., pp. 239–40

6 A. Le Fere de la Boderie, *Ambassades* (Paris: 1750), quoted in Carola Oman, *The Winter Queen* (London: 1938) p. 36

7 Sir Walter Raleigh, *Works* vol.VIII, p. 234, quoted in Oman, *The Winter Queen*, p. 51

8 The Spanish ambassador, Don Pedro Zuniga, to the King of Spain, 2 August 1612, quoted in M. A. Everett-Green, *Elizabeth, Queen of Bohemia*, (London: 1909) p. 28

9 James Medlus, 'and one of his Majesties Chaplaines', *A Sermon, Preached before the two high borne and illustrious Princes, Fredericke the 5 Prince Elector Palatine, Duke of Bavaria, &c. And the Princesse Lady Elizabeth ... Together with a short narration of the Prince Elector's greatness, his Country ...*, (London: 1613) pp. 57–8

10 From p. 3 of 'The Epistle to the Reader' introducing *A Full Declaration of the Faith and Ceremonies professed in the Dominions of the most Illustrious and noble Prince Fredericke 5, Prince, Elector Palatine*, trans. John Rolte (London: 1614)

11 *A Vow of Teares, For the losse of Prince Henry*, pp. iv–v of the Epistle Dedicatory by E. C., 'publike Preacher' to Bristol (London: 1612)

12 Nichols, *The Progresses*, p. 464, quoted in Brennan C. Pursell, *The Winter King* (London: 2003) p. 18

13 Quoted in Pursell, *The Winter King*, p. 18

14 Journal of Sir Roger Wilbraham, quoted in *The Camden Miscellany*, vol. 10 (London: 1902) p. 110

15 Gardiner *History*, vol. II, p. 160 [quoted in 'The Camden Miscellany', vol. 10, p. 110 (London: 1902)]

16 John Beale, *A Sermon ... Together with a short narration of the Prince Elector's greatness, his Country, his receiving of her Highnesse*, (London: 1613) pp. 65–6

17 Letter of Doncaster to Naunton, 30 May/9 June 1619, in S. R. Gardiner, *Letters and other Documents*, vol. I, (London: 1865) p. 107

18 *A Briefe Description of the reasons that make the Declaration of the Ban made against the King of Bohemia, as being Elector Palataine, Dated the 22 of Januarie last past, of no value nor worth ...*, published by Arthur Meuris (London: 1621) p. 13

19 Letter from Prince Frederick Henry to James I, quoted in Elizabeth Godfrey, *A Sister of Prince Rupert*, (London: 1909) p. 35

20 Nathaniel Butter and Nicholas Bourne, *The Swedish Intelligencer*, 'the third and fourth parts', (London: 1633) p. 171

21 *Newes from Sea, concerning Prince Rupert, Capt. Plunket, Capt. Munckel, And Others*, printed by J. C. (London: 1650)

22 *Caricatures of the Winter King* (Oxford: 1928), quoted in Gerhard Benecke, *Germany in the Thirty Years' War* (London: 1978)

CHAPTER TWO:

1 Frederick to Elizabeth, 20/30 August 1622, in *A Collection of Original Royal Letters*, ed. Sir George Bromley (London: 1787) p. 16

2 John Evelyn's Diary, 29 July 1641

3 Frederick Henry to Charles Louis, quoted in Godfrey, *A Sister of Prince Rupert*, p. 30

4 Frederick to Elizabeth, from The Hague, 30 September 1622, in *A Collection of Original Royal Letters*, p. 21

5 Sophie, Electress of Hanover to Charles Louis, Elector Palatine, 13 July 1667, in the French translation of *Briefwechsel der Herzogin Sophie von Hannover mit ihrem Bruder, dem Kurfuersten Karl Ludwig von der Pfalz*, ed. Eduard Bodemann (Leipzig: 1885) p. 121

6 Electress Sophie, quoted in Godfrey, *A Sister of Prince Rupert*, p. 42

7 Elector Frederick V's instruction to Madame de Plessen, quoted in Godfrey, *A Sister of Prince Rupert*, p. 44

8 Princess Sophie's recollections, quoted in Godfrey, *A Sister of Prince Rupert*, p. 55

9 Ibid.

10 Quoted in Warburton, *Memoirs of Prince Rupert* vol. I, p. 44

11 Elizabeth of Bohemia to Sir Thomas Rowe, quoted in Godfrey, *A Sister of Prince Rupert*, p. 49

12 Frederick Henry to James I, quoted in Godfrey, *A Sister of Prince Rupert*, p. 44

13 Frederick V to Charles I, 10/20 January 1629, PRO, SP, 81/35, f. 125, quoted in Pursell, *The Winter King*, p. 261

14 Frederick V to Charles I, quoted in Godfrey, *A Sister of Prince Rupert*, p. 49

15 Carlisle to Nethersole, 6/16 March 1627, Bayerisches Hauptstaatsarchiv, Munich, Kasten Blau, 122/21, quoted in Pursell, *The Winter King*, p. 257

16 Frederick to Elizabeth, Queen of Bohemia, 7/17 May 1632, in *A Collection of Original Royal Letters*, p. 38

17 Elizabeth, Queen of Bohemia, to Charles I, 24 December 1624, in L. M. Baker (ed.), *Letters of Elizabeth, Queen of Bohemia*, (London: 1953) p. 86

18 Nathaniel Butter and Nicholas Bourne, *The Swedish Intelligencer*, 'the third and fourth parts', pp. 173–4

19 Elizabeth, Queen of Bohemia, to Charles I, 24 December 1624, in Baker, *Letters of Elizabeth, Queen of Bohemia*, p. 86

CHAPTER THREE:

1 Letter of Salvius to the Riksrad of Hamburg, May 1631, in Benecke, *Germany in the Thirty Years' War*, p. 35

2 Diary of William Crowne, Gent., quoted in Benecke, *Germany in the Thirty Years' War*, p. 99

3 Elizabeth of Bohemia, quoted in Maurice Ashley, *Rupert of the Rhine*, (London: 1976) p. 10

4 Lansdowne MSS 817, f.157, quoted in Warburton, *Memoirs of Prince Rupert*, vol. I, p. 50

5 Charles Louis to Elizabeth, Queen of Bohemia, 16/26 September 1632, quoted in Warburton, vol. I, p. 62

6 Charles I to Robert, Earl of Leicester, April 1638, quoted in Warburton, vol. I, p. 65

7 Harl. MSS 6988.88: Charles I to Prince Maurice, 4 July 1643, quoted in Warburton, vol. I, p. 68

8 Elizabeth of Bohemia to Sir Henry Vane, *Calendar of State Papers*, Domestic Series, Charles I, 1635–6, pp. 206–7

9 Sir Thomas Roe to Elizabeth of Bohemia, *Calendar of State Papers*, Domestic Series, Charles I, 1636–7, p. 71

10 Thomas Carew's poem, in *Poems* (Oxford: 1949) p. 77; quoted in C. V. Wedgwood, *The King's Peace*, (London: 1955)

11 Martin Parker, *A True Tale of Robin Hood*, stanza 116 (London: 1632)

12 Earl of Clarendon, *History of the Rebellion*, vol. I (of VI) (Oxford: 1732) p. 74

13 Prince Charles Louis to Elizabeth of Bohemia, from Oatlands, 22 September 1636, in *A Collection of Original Royal Letters*, p. 83

14 Archbishop Laud, *Works*, vol. V, p. 150

15 Sophie, Electress of Hanover, *Mémoires et Lettres de Voyage*, ed. Dirk Van der Cruysse (Paris: 1990) p. 43

16 Mr Boothby, *King's Collection of Pamphlets*, BL 266.17, quoted in Warburton, vol. I, pp. 59–60

17 Elizabeth of Bohemia, quoted in W. G. Perrin, *The Autobiography of Phineas Pett*, (1918) pp. 162–3

18 Sir Thomas Roe to Elizabeth of Bohemia, *Calendar of State Papers*, Domestic Series, Charles I, 1637, p. xxvi

19 Prince Charles Louis to Elizabeth of Bohemia, from Whitehall, 24 May 1637, in *A Collection of Original Royal Letters*, p. 86

20 *Calendar of State Papers* Domestic Series, Charles I, 1637, p. 82

CHAPTER FOUR:

1 Bernard Fergusson, *Rupert of the Rhine*, (London: 1953) p. 19

2 Prince Rupert's life story, probably written by Colonel Bennet, the prince's secretary, quoted in Warburton, *Memoirs of Prince Rupert*, vol. I, p. 453

3 Quoted in Warburton, vol. I, p. 90

4 Pyne's MS, quoted in Warburton, vol. I, p. 90

5 Elizabeth of Bohemia, quoted in Warburton, vol. I, p. 91

6 BL E 21 (24): *London Post*, No. 16, (London: 17 December 1644) pp. 2–3

7 *Prince Rupert His Declaration*, (Oxford: 1642) p. 5

8 Bennet MSS, quoted in Warburton, vol. I, p. 93

9 Quoted in Warburton, vol. I, p. 96

10 Bennet MSS, quoted in Warburton, vol. I, p. 97

11 Charles Louis to Elizabeth of Bohemia, 17 December 1638, quoted in *A Collection of Original Royal Letters*, p. 103

12 Letter of Countess de Löwenstein, from *The Fairfax Correspondence*, vol. I, p. 322, quoted in Warburton, vol. I, p. 98

13 Sophie, Electress of Hanover, *Mémoires et Lettres de Voyage*, p. 40

CHAPTER FIVE:

1 BL E 164 (11): *A Revelation of Mr Brigtmans Revelation* anon., 1641, p. 11

2 BL E 18 (8): *A Prophecie of the Life, Reigne, and Death of William Laud*, printed for R. A. (London: 1644) p. 2

3 *The Holy Rebell*, printed by Stephen Bulkeley (York: 1642)

4 BL E 196 (7): *The Lord Digbyes Speech In The House of Commons*, (London: January 1641) p. 24

5 *Memoirs of Prince Rupert*, Warburton, vol. I, p. 241

6 BL E 60 (1): Sir Francis Bacon, *Cases of Treason* (London: 1641)

7 Edward Symmons, *A Military Sermon, preached at Shrewsbury, March 1644* (Oxford: 1644) p. 33

8 BL E 238 (24): *Two Declarations of the Lords and Commons assembled in Parliament*, printed by R. O. and G. D. for Joseph Hunscott (London: 1642) p. 3

9 BL E 402: John Corbet, *A true and impartial History of the Military Government of the City of Gloucester* (London: 1647)

10 *The Devotions and Formes of Prayer, Daily Used in the King of Sweden's Army*, printed for Nathaniel Butter and Nicholas Bourne (London: 1632) p. 1

11 *A Collection of Original Royal Letters*, p. 67

12 *Prince Rupert His Declaration*, p. 5

13 BL E 121 (10): *Prince Robert's Message to my Lord of Essex*, printed for Thomas Banks (London: 6 October 1642) p. 5

14 BL E 238 (22): *Some Speciall Passages from Westminster, London, Yorke, and other parts*, No. 7, anon. (London: July 1642) p. 8

15 John Cruso, *Militarie Instructions for the Cavallrie: or Rules and Directions for the Service of Horse, Rectified and Supplied, According to the Present Practice of the Low-Country Wars*, (Cambridge: 1632) p. 1

16 Ibid., pp. 3–4

17 Clarendon, *The History of the Rebellion*, vol. III (of VI), p. 2

18 Ibid.

19 BL E 48 (8): John Vernon, *The Young Horse-man, or The Honest Plain-dealing Cavalier*, (London: 1644) p. 10

20 Quoted in Warburton, vol. I, p. 383

21 Mas. 52, quoted in Warburton, vol. I, p. 389

22 Clarendon, quoted in Mark Bence-Jones, *The Cavaliers* (London: 1976)

23 Rupert to the Mayor of Leicester, 6 September 1642, quoted in Warburton, vol. I, p. 394

24 Charles to the Mayor and Aldermen of Leicester, written from Nottingham, 8 September 1642, quoted in Warburton, vol. I, p. 395

25 *An exact description of Prince Rupert's Malignant She-Monkey, a great Delinquent ...*, quoted in Patrick Morrah, *Prince Rupert of the Rhine*, (London: 1976) p. 406

26 BL E 383 (5): *The Character of a Cavalier, with his Brother Separatist*, printed for W. H. (London: 1647) p. 3

27 'Propositions and Orders of both Houses for bringing in Money and Plate for maintaining Horse, &c.', quoted in Clarendon, *The History of the Rebellion*, vol. II (of VI), p. 649

28 BL E 112 (39): *Being Comfortable Tydings for Both Houses of Parliament: Exceeding Joyful Newes from the Prince*, anon. (London: 19 August 1642)

29 BL E 99 (14): *The Bloody Prince, or a Declaration of the Most Cruell Practises of Prince Rupert*, I. W. (London: 1643) pp. 26–7

30 Henry Peacham, *The Compleat Gentleman* (London: 1622) p. 10

31 BL E 90 (4): *A Warning-Piece To all His Majesties Subjects of England*, anon. (Oxford: February 1643) p. 4

32 BL E 1186 (7): *The Cavaliers Catechism*, printed for Richard Burton (London: 1647) p. 3

33 Robert Plot, *The Natural History of Staffordshire*, (Oxford: 1686)

34 *Prince Rupert's Disguises*, anon. (London: 1643)

35 John Taylor the Water Poet, *All the Workes* (London: 1630)

36 BL E 121 (10): *Prince Robert's Message to My Lord of Essex*, pp. 4–5

37 BL E 402: John Corbet, *A True and Impartial History of the Military Government of the City of Gloucester*, p. 12

38 BL E 121 (26): *True, But Sad and Dolefull Newes from Shrewsbury …* anon. (London: 10 October 1642) p. 4

39 BL E 121 (22): *A Letter Sent from the Lord Falkland unto the Rt Hon Henry, Earl of Cumberland* (London: 7 October 1642)

40 BL E 121 (26): op. cit., p. 5

41 Ibid., p. 7

42 BL E 402: op. cit., (London: 1647) p. 13

43 Clarendon, *The History of the Rebellion*, vol. III (of VI), p. 26

CHAPTER SIX:

1 Thomas Sprat, Lord Bishop of Rochester, *The History of the Royal Society of London, For the Improving of Natural Knowledge* (London: 1680) p. 73

2 BL E 117 (6): *A Letter written from the Right Honorable the Earle of Bedford, to a Lord of the House of Peeres*, printed for Hugh Perry (London: 15 September 1642) p. 2

3 BL E 121 (12): *True Intelligence and Joyfull Newes from Ludlow*, printed for Thomas Rider (London: 6 October 1642) p. 2

4 Thomas More, *Utopia*, from *Complete Works*, vol. 4, ed. Edward Surtz (New Haven: 1965) p. 64

5 BL E 117 (7): *The Resolution of the Gentry and Commonalty in the County of Nottingham …*, printed for Henry Fowler (15 September 1642) p. 3

6 BL E 121 (19): *A Worthy Speech Spoken to the King's most Excellent Majesty by the Recorder of Hereford*, printed for Henry Hutton (London: 7 October 1642)

7 BL E 117 (8): *A Discourse upon the Questions in Debate between the King and Parliament*, anon. (September 1642) p. 19

8   BL E 121 (16): *A true Coppy of the Instructions agreed upon by the Lords and Commons assembled in Parliament and sent to his Excellency the Earl of Essex*, printed for Fr. Coles (London: 4 October 1642)

9   BL ADD MS 62085A: Prince Rupert's Logbook, aka Pythouse Papers, vol. V, p. 121

10 Quoted in Warburton, *Memoirs of Prince Rupert*, vol. II, p. 12

11 Clarendon, *The History of the Rebellion*, vol. II (of VI), p. 673

12 Ibid., vol. III (of VI), p. 43

13 Quoted in Warburton, vol. II, p. 20

14 William Ranson, vicar of Barton, *A Sermon preached in the Metropoliticall Church of York, upon the 19 Day of May ...*, (York: May 1644) p. 7

15 Sir Richard Bulstrode, *Memoirs and Reflections upon the Reign and Government of Charles I and Charles II* (London: 1721) p. 81

16 J. Vicars, *Jehovah Jireh, God in the Mount* (1644), p. 166, quoted in C. Scott, A. Turton, and Dr E. G. von Arni, *Edgehill: The Battle Reinterpreted*, p. 30

17 A Cavalry Officer, *Cavalry Tactics* (London: 1897) p. 31

18 Clarendon, vol. III (of VI), p. 48

19 Quoted in Warburton, vol. II, p. 21

20 Quoted in Bence-Jones, *The Cavaliers*, p. 40

21 J. Adair, *By the Sword Divided* (London: 2001) p. 15, quoted in Scott et al, *Edgehill: The Battle Reinterpreted*, p. 44

22 BL E 48 (8): Vernon, *The Young Horse-man, or The Honest Plain-dealing Cavalier* p. 3

23 Quoted in Warburton, vol. I, p. 426

24 'Prince Rupert His Declaration', p. 2

25 Quoted in Christopher Hill, *God's Englishman* (London: 1970); pp. 64–5 and in Raymond South, '*Royal Castle, Rebel Town*' (Birmingham: 1981) p. 47

26 BL E 402: Corbet, *A true and impartial History of the Military Government of the City of Gloucester*, p. 13

CHAPTER SEVEN:

1   BL E 123 (20): quoted in South, *Royal Castle, Rebel Town*, p. 31

2   BL E 127 (10): *Exceeding Joyful News out of Surrey, Shewing the proceedings of Prince Robert and his mischievous Cavalliers*, printed for John Johnson (London: 1642) p. 4

3   BL E 127 (12): *Special Passages*, anon. (November 1642) p. 119

4   Clarendon, *The History of the Rebellion*, vol. III (of VI), p. 80

5   BL E 121 (10): *Prince Robert's Message to my Lord of Essex*, p. 6

6   BL E 127 (27): *The Two Speeches of the Lord Wharton, Spoken in Guild-*

Hall, October 27 1642, printed for Samuel Gellibrand (London: 1642) final page

7 *Prince Rupert His Declaration*, p. 2

8 *London's Alacritie*, printed for Thomas Lambert (London: 1643). Pamphlet on p. 8 of 'Collection of Broadsides', BL 74/1870 D 1 No. 8

9 BL E 127 (15): *A true and perfect Relation of the chief Passages in Middlesex*, printed for John Johnson (London: November 1642) pp. 4–6

10 *His Majestie's Speech Delivered the Twenty second of January 1643, at Oxford* (Oxford: 1643) p. 3

11 Secretary Nicholas to Prince Rupert, quoted in Warburton, *Memoirs of Prince Rupert*, vol. II, p. 115

12 BL E 288.1 (3): *Exchange Intelligencer*, No. 4 anon. (London: June 1645) p. 28

13 BL ADD MS 62085A: Prince Rupert's Logbook, aka Pythouse Papers, vol. V, p. 25

14 Prince Rupert's Diary, quoted in Warburton, vol. II, p. 169

15 King Charles to Prince Rupert, quoted in Warburton, vol. II. p. 168

16 BL ADD MS 18982: Rupert Correspondence, quoted in Morrah, *Prince Rupert of the Rhine*, p. 113

17 Ibid. pp. 113–4

18 BL ADD MS 62085A: Prince Rupert's Logbook, aka Pythouse Papers, vol. V, p. 25 (obverse)

19 Ibid.

20 Clarendon, *The History of the Rebellion*, vol. III (of VI), p. 237

21 Bishop of Derry, *A Sermon, preached in Yorke Minster, Before his Excellence the Marquess of Newcastle, Being then ready to meet the Scotch Army* (York: 1643) p. 9

22 Cruso, *Militarie Instructions for the Cavallrie*, p. 89

23 *His Highness Prince Rupert's late beating up the Rebels' quarters at Postcomb and Chinnor*, p. 7, quoted in Morrah, pp. 117–8

24 BL E 402: Corbet, *History of the Military Government of the City of Gloucester*, p. 14

25 'Quip' (aka Phil Barnes), 'Unbeaten Tracks of the West', 25 January 1938 (unpublished), quoted in 'Forgotten Tales', *West Country Life*, 2 July 2005, pp. 18–19

26 *A True Relation of the Taking of Bristol, the Several Circumstances as it was sent in a letter by an eye-witness to the Governor at Oxford, July 30*, quoted in Warburton, vol. II, p. 264

27 Baron de Gomme, quoted in Warburton, vol. II, pp. 258–9

28 The Earl of Sunderland to his wife, 25 August 1643, from Gloucester, quoted in Charles Spencer, *The Spencer Family* (London: 1999), p. 44

29 Baron de Gomme, quoted in Warburton, vol. II, p. 262

30 Colonel Nathaniel Fiennes, *A Relation made to the House of Commons*, 5 August 1643, quoted in Warburton, vol. II, p. 267

31 BL ADD MS 62085A: Prince Rupert's Logbook, aka Pythouse Papers, p. 7 [obverse]: King Charles to Prince Rupert, from Oxford, 28 July 1643

32 'Memoirs of Richard Atkyns' in *Military Memoirs: The Civil War*, ed. Peter Young (1967), p. 28

33 Cleveland, 'Rupertismus', from *Poems*, ed. 1681, p. 51

34 The Earl of Newcastle to Prince Rupert, from Lincoln, 7 August 1643

CHAPTER EIGHT:

1 Memoirs of Sir Philip Warwick, p. 227, quoted in Warburton, *Memoirs of Prince Rupert*, vol. I, p. 367

2 Clarendon, *The History of the Rebellion*, vol. III (of VI), p. 43

3 Warburton, vol. II, p. 307

4 Clarendon, vol. II (of VI), p. 311

5 Ibid., p. 344

6 Ibid., vol. III (of VI), p. 385

7 Ibid., vol. I (of VI), p. 3

8 Bishop of Derry, *A Sermon, preached in Yorke Minster, Before his Excellence the Marquess of Newcastle*, p. 8

9 Clarendon, op. cit., vol. II (of VI), p. 426

10 *Bellum Civile: Hopton's Narrative of the Campaign in the West*, p. 59, quoted in Morrah, *Prince Rupert of the Rhine*, p. 125

11 Clarendon, op. cit., vol. III (of VI), p. 309

12 Thomas Carte, *An History of the Life of James, Duke of Ormonde*, vol. VI, p. 277, quoted in Morrah, p. 404

13 Clarendon, op. cit., vol. III (of VI), pp. 198–9

14 *The Ladies Parliament*, quoted in Morrah, p. 403

15 Saunderson's *Charles the First*, quoted in Warburton, vol. II, p. 110

16 BL E 402 (4): *Verses on the Siege of Gloucester and Colonel Massey* (London: August 1647)

17 Earl of Sunderland to his wife, 25 August 1643, from Gloucester, quoted in Spencer, *The Spencer Family*, p. 44

18 BL E 401 (12): *The Declaration of General Massey and Colonel General Poyntz*, (London: 1647) p. 2

19 *Clarendon: Selections from 'The History of the Rebellion' and 'The Life by Himself'*, ed. Gertrude Huehns, (Oxford: 1978) pp. 58–9

20 BL Clarendon MS: 1738, quoted in John Barratt, *Cavalier Generals*, (Barnsley: 2004) p. 125

21 Clarendon, quoted in Warburton, vol. II, p. 306

22 *The Best News That Ever Was Printed – Prince Rupert's resolution to be*

gone to his Mother, who has sent for him, printed for I. A. (London: 1643), Thomason Tracts, quoted in Warburton, vol. II, p. 148

23 *A Nest of Perfidious Vipers*, printed for G. Bishop, September 1644, quoted in Warburton, vol. II, p. 118

24 *An Answer to 'Prince Rupert's Declaration'*, 16 February 1643, quoted in Warburton, vol. II, p. 125

25 BL E 160 (8): Calybute Downing, *A Discoverie of the false Grounds the Bavarian party have layd, to settle their own Faction, and shake the Peace of the Empire*, (London: 1641) p. 7

CHAPTER NINE:

1 Carte, *An History of the Life of James Duke of Ormonde*, vol. V, pp. 520–1, quoted in Morrah, *Prince Rupert of the Rhine*, p. 133

2 Ranson, *A Sermon preached in the Metropoliticall Church of York, upon the 19 Day of May . . .*, p. 8

3 Prince Rupert's Diary, quoted in Morrah, p. 136

4 Carte, *An History of the Life of James Duke of Ormonde*, vol. V, pp. 337–8, quoted in Barratt, *Cavalier Generals*, pp. 32–3

5 Baker's Chronicle, 551, quoted in Warburton, *Memoirs of Prince Rupert*, vol. II, p. 395

6 The king to Prince Rupert, from Oxford, 25 March 1644, quoted in Warburton, vol. II, pp. 397–8

7 Clarendon, *History of the Rebellion*, vol. III (of VI), p. 466

8 The Marquess of Newcastle to Prince Rupert, quoted in Warburton, vol. II, p. 397

9 BL ADD MS 62085A: Prince Rupert's Logbook, aka Pythouse Papers, p. 11 (a)

10 'The Tickenhill Letter', Charles I to Prince Rupert, 15 June 1644

11 The king to Prince Rupert, probably 16 June 1644, quoted in Malcolm Wanklyn and Frank Jones, *A Military History of the English Civil War* (London: 2005) p. 179

12 The Countess of Derby, quoted in Warburton, vol. II, p. 429

13 Sir John Meldrum, quoted in Barratt, *Cavalier Generals*

14 Carte, *An History of the Life of James Duke of Ormonde*, vol. V, p. 151, quoted in Morrah, p. 149

15 BL E 2: Simon Ash, *A Continuation of True Intelligence from the English and Scottish Forces, in the North for the service of King and Parliament, and now beleaguering York*, 16 June–10 July 1644, p. 2

16 *Scottish Dove*, No. 39, 5–13 July 1644, p. 306

17 The Marquess of Newcastle to Prince Rupert, from York, 1 July 1644, Pythouse Papers, p. 19

18 BL E 2: op. cit., p. 3
19 Newcastle to Prince Rupert, quoted in Bence-Jones, *The Cavaliers*, p. 30
20 Cholmley's Narrative: *English Historical Review*, vol. V, p. 348
21 Quoted in Maurice Ashley, *England in the Seventeenth Century* (London: 1952) p. 81
22 Cholmley's Narrative: *English Historical Review*, vol. V, p. 348
23 BL E 2: op. cit., p. 5
24 Cholmley's Narrative: *English Historical Review*, vol. V, p. 348
25 BL E 2: op. cit., p. 6
26 *Mercurius Britannicus*, Mon. 8 – Mon. 15 July 1644, p. 339
27 *Scottish Dove*, No. 39, 5–13 July 1644, p. 308
28 BL E 2: op. cit., p. 7
29 Ibid. p. 8
30 Ibid. p. 7
31 Quoted in Bence-Jones, *The Cavaliers*, p. 59
32 BL E 3 (17): *A Dogge's Elegie, or Rupert's Tears* anon. (London: 27 July 1644) p. 5
33 Ibid., p. 3

CHAPTER TEN:

1 *True Informer*, No. 38, 6–13 July 1644, p. 275
2 BL SLOANE MS 1519, Plut. XC.G: f.25, Charles I to George Goring (3 March 1644)
3 Quoted in Warburton, *Memoirs of Prince Rupert*, vol. II, p. 475
4 Ibid. vol. III, p. 8
5 Clarendon, *The History of the Rebellion*, vol. IV (of VI), p. 482
6 Ibid.
7 Warburton, vol. III, p. 10 (fn)
8 Charles I to Prince Rupert, from Boconnock, 30 August 1644, quoted in Warburton, vol. III, p. 23
9 Lord Digby to Prince Rupert, from Exeter, 23 September 1644, quoted in Warburton, vol. III, p. 26
10 Prince Rupert to Colonel Will Legge, from Bristol, 16 October 1644, quoted in Warburton, vol. III, p. 28
11 BL E 18 (6): *Parliament Scout*, No. 73 (London: November 1644) p. 590
12 Prince Rupert's Diary, 6 November 1644, quoted in Warburton, vol. III, p. 31
13 Clarendon, vol. IV (of VI), p. 554
14 BL E 18 (7): *Scottish Dove*, No. 57, (November, 1644), p. 448
15 BL E 21 (25): *Kingdomes Weekly Intelligencer*, No. 85 (London: 17 December 1644)

16 BL E 21 (23): *Mercurius Britannicus*, No. 61 (London: December 1644) p. 480

17 Ibid., p. 481

18 BL E 21 (24): *London Post*, No. 16, printed for G. B. (London: 17 December, 1644) p. 2

19 BL ADD MS 18982: Rupert Correspondence, 1645–1658, f. 386: Letter from Dudley Wyatt to Prince Rupert, from Shropshire, 5 January 1645

20 BL SLOANE MS 1519, Plut. XC.G: Original Letters, 1574–1667, f. 34: Sir John Byron to Prince Rupert, 3 April 1645, written from Chester

21 BL ADD MS 18982: Rupert Correspondence, 1645–1658, f. 706: Letter from Lorentz Gamb to Prince Maurice, 9 March 1645

22 BL E 21 (15): *Parliament Scout*, No. 77, London: December 1640) p. 620

23 *The Devotions and Formes of Prayer, Daily Used in the King of Sweden's Army* printed for Nathaniel Butter and Nicholas Bourne

24 Bishop of Derry, *A Sermon, preached in York Minster, Before his Excellence the Marquess of Newcastle, Being then ready to meet the Scotch Army* p. 9

25 BL E 1238 (572): John Cook, Chief Justice of the Province of Munster, *Monarchy No Creature of Gods Making, &c.,* (Westminster: February 1651) p. 115

26 'Articles of War', quoted in South, *Royal Castle, Rebel Town*, p. 52

27 BL E 288.2 (49): *A Perfect Relation of the Taking of Leicester, Mercurius Britannicus*, 16–23 June 1645) p. 11

28 BL E 288.1 (4): *A Perfect Relation of the Taking of Leicester* pp. 2–3 printed for John Wright (London: 1645) pp. 2–3

29 *Ellis's Collection*, vol. IV, p. 243, quoted in Warburton, vol. III, p. 90

30 Prince Rupert to Will Legge, from Daventry, 8 June 1645, quoted in Warburton, vol. III, p. 100

31 BL E 288.1 (7) *Moderate Intelligencer*, No. 15, anon. (London: June 1645), p. 118

32 BL E 288.2 (22): *A True Relation of a Victory obtained over the Kings Forces …,* printed for Robert White (London: June 1645) p. 3

33 *King's Collection* (E) No. 212, quoted in Warburton, vol. III, p. 106

34 BL E 288.2 (33): *Weekly Account*, anon. (London: 18 June 1645) p. 2

35 BL E 288.2 (26): *An Ordinance of the Lords and Commons*, printed for Edward Husband (London: 17 June 1645) p. 4

36 Ibid., p. 5

37 Ibid., p. 2

38 Vicars, *Jehovah Jireh*, quoted in Warburton, vol. III, pp. 108–9

39 Quoted in Bence-Jones *The Cavaliers*, p. 17

40 BL E 838 (19): *A Modest Narrative of Intelligence*, No. 16, (London: July 1649) p. 125

41 BL E 353 (3): *Kingdomes Weekly Intelligencer*, No. 163 (London: 1 September 1646) p. 220
42 BL E 288.2 (26): op. cit., p. 4
43 Ibid., p. 3
44 Ibid., p. 5
45 Quoted in Warburton, vol. III, p. 111

CHAPTER ELEVEN:

1 Prince Rupert to Colonel Legge, from Bewdley, 18 June 1645, quoted in Warburton, *Memoirs of Prince Rupert*, vol. III, pp. 119–21
2 BL E 21 (15): *Parliament Scout*, No. 77 (London: December 1644) p. 620
3 Lord Digby to Colonel Legge, quoted in Warburton, vol. III, pp. 125–8
4 Colonel Legge to Lord Digby, 30 June 1645, quoted in Warburton, vol. III. pp. 128–31
5 Quoted in Warburton, vol. III, p. 114
6 Quoted in Warburton, vol. III, p. 149; and in Wanklyn and Jones, *A Military History of the English Civil War*, p. 259
7 Charles I to Prince Rupert, *Historical Collections*, vol. VI, p. 132, ed. J. Rushworth (1721). Also: *Parl. History*, p. 95, quoted in Wanklyn and Jones, op. cit., p. 260
8 Prince Rupert to Colonel Legge, from Bristol, 28 July 1645, quoted in Warburton, vol. III, p. 151
9 Charles I to Prince Rupert, from Cardiff, 4 August 1645, quoted in Warburton, vol. III, p. 152
10 Prince Rupert to Colonel Legge, from Bristol, 29 July 1645, quoted in Warburton, vol. III, p. 156
11 BL E 264 (3): *Perfect Occurrences of Parliament*, No. 37, printed by Jane Coe (London: August 1645) p. 4
12 Ibid.
13 Sir John Oglander, *A Royalist's Notebook*, ed. Francis Bamford (London: 1936) p. 118
14 Warburton, vol. III, p. 63
15 *A Declaration of His Highness Prince Rupert*, quoted in Warburton, vol. III, p. 169
16 Ibid.
17 BL E 264 (8): *A Diary, or an Exact Journall, Faithfully communicating the most remarkable proceedings of both Houses of Parliament*, No. 68, printed for Mathew Walbancke (London: September 1645) p.5
18 BL E 264 (7): *Perfect Passages of Each Dayes Proceedings in Parliament*, (London: September 1645) p. 358

19 BL E 264 (8): op. cit., p. 4
20 BL E 264 (13): *Perfect Occurrences of Parliament*, No. 38, (London: 1645) 'A Letter from Sir Thomas Fairfax's Quarters', p. 6
21 Sir Thomas Fairfax's Summons, 4 September 1645, quoted in Warburton, vol. III, p. 173
22 Ibid., p. 174
23 BL E 264 (13): op. cit, pp. 6–7
24 BL E 264 (16): *A Diary, or an Exact Journall, Faithfully communicating the most remarkable proceedings of both Houses of Parliament*, No. 69, printed for Mathew Walbancke (London: September 1645) p. 4
25 BL E (King's College Pamphlet 226, No. 3), quoted in Warburton, vol. III, p. 181
26 *Moderate Intelligencer*, 12 September 1645, quoted in Warburton, vol. III, pp. 182–3
27 Nicholas Papers, vol. I, p. 65, quoted in Morrah, *Prince Rupert of the Rhine*, pp. 195–6

CHAPTER TWELVE:

1 *Moderate Intelligencer*, 12 September 1645, quoted in Warburton, *Memoirs of Prince Rupert*, vol. III, p. 182
2 Notes to Prince Rupert's Diary quoted in Warburton, vol. III, pp. 193–4
3 Clarendon, *The History of the Rebellion*, vol. IV (of VI), pp. 694–5
4 *Perfect Passages of Each Dayes Proceedings in Parliament*, 22 September 1645, quoted in Warburton, vol. III, pp. 183–4
5 Prince Rupert to Charles I, September 1645, quoted in Warburton, vol. III, p. 187
6 Clarendon, vol. IV (of VI), p. 715
7 *Memoirs of John Evelyn*, 1641 to 1705–6, vol. II ed. William Bray (London: 1819) p. 169
8 Prince Rupert's Diary quoted in Warburton, vol. III, p. 194
9 BL E 307 (3): Colonel Rossiter, *A Letter Concerning a great Victory obtained by Colonel Rossiter, against Prince Rupert and Prince Maurice, neer Belvoyr Castle in Leicestershire*, (London: October 1645) p. 6
10 Prince Rupert's Diary, quoted in Warburton, vol. III, p. 194
11 Ibid. p. 195
12 *Mercurius Britannicus*, 10 November 1645, quoted in Warburton, vol. III, p. 200
13 BL E 266 1 (17): *Perfect Occurrences of Parliament* (14 November 1645) p. 2
14 Oglander, *A Royalist's Notebook*, p. 117
15 Quoted in Warburton, vol. III, p. 201

16 Newark Court Martial's verdict, 21 October 1645, quoted in Warburton, vol. III, p. 202

17 Sir Edward Walker, p. 149, quoted in Warburton, vol. III, p. 204

18 Ibid.

19 *Memoirs of John Evelyn*, vol. II, p. 110

20 Quoted in Warburton, vol. III, p. 205

21 BL E 313 (29): *The Humble Desires of Prince Rupert, Prince Maurice, and others their Adherents, To the Kings most Excellent Majestie; To Be tried at a Counsell of War*, printed for Edward Husband, Printer to the Honourable House of Commons (London: December 1645) pp. 3–5

22 Clarendon State Papers MSS, Bodlcian, quoted in Warburton, vol. III, p. 207

23 BL E 313 (1): *Scottish Dove*, No. 113 (10–17 December 1645) p. 891

24 Princess Elizabeth to René Descartes, winter of 1645, quoted in Godfrey, *A Sister of Prince Rupert*, p. 151

25 Colonel Henry Osborne to Prince Rupert, 1 November 1645, quoted in Warburton, vol. III, p. 209

26 BL E 313 (3): *Moderate Intelligencer*, No. 41 (London: 11–18 December 1645) p. 224

27 Colonel Will Legge to Prince Rupert, 21 November 1645, quoted in Warburton, vol. III, pp. 211–2

28 Colonel Will Legge to Prince Rupert, 26 November 1645, quoted in Warburton, vol. III, p. 212

29 BL E 313 (3): op. cit.

30 The Earl of Dorset to Prince Rupert, 25 December 1645, quoted in Warburton, vol. III, p. 213

31 The Elector Palatine to Elizabeth of Bohemia, 9 January 1646, in *A Collection of Original Royal Letters*, p. 136

32 Prince Rupert's Diary, quoted in Warburton, vol. III, p. 196

33 BL E 313 (3): op. cit. p. 225

34 BL E 307 (2): *A Looking-Glasse for the Popish Garrisons*, W. W. (London: 24 October 1645) p. 2

35 Oglander, *A Royalist's Notebook*, p. 117

36 BL SLOANE MS 1519, Plut. XC.G: Original Letters, 1574–1667, f. 64, Commissary Henry Ireton to Sir Thomas Fairfax, 25 April 1645

37 Prince Rupert's Diary, quoted in Warburton, vol. III, p. 196

38 Ibid. pp. 196–7

39 John Rushworth, *Historical Collections*, Part iv, vol. I, (1659–1701) pp. 280–1

40 BL SLOANE MS 1519, Plut. XC.G: Original Letters, 1574–1667, f. 64, Prince Rupert to Sir Thomas Fairfax, 9 May 1645

41 *Scottish Dove*, July 1646, quoted in Warburton, vol. III, p. 230

42 BL E 266 (1): *Perfect Occurrences of Parliament* (14 November 1645) p. 3

43 BL ADD MS 62085A: Prince Rupert's Logbook, aka Pythouse Papers, vol. V, p. 120 (over page)

CHAPTER THIRTEEN:

1 Charles Louis to Elizabeth of Bohemia, 10 July 1646, quoted in Godfrey, *A Sister of Prince Rupert*, pp. 158–9

2 BL ADD MS 62085A: Prince Rupert's Logbook, aka Pythouse Papers, vol. V, p. 120 (over page)

3 Ibid.

4 BL E 383 (8): *Moderate Intelligencer* (London: April 1647) p. 994

5 BL E 372: *Mercurius Diutinus* (London: 27 January 1647) p. 67

6 Prince Rupert to Sir John Owen, from Paris, 10 April 1647, quoted in Warburton, *Memoirs of Prince Rupert*, vol. III, p. 237

7 BL E 372 (15): *Moderate Intelligencer* (London: January 1646) pp. 875–6

8 BL ADD MS 62085A: Prince Rupert's Logbook, aka Pythouse Papers, vol. V, quoted in Warburton, vol. III, p. 238

9 Ibid.

10 Ibid., p. 239

11 Prince Rupert's Diary, quoted in Warburton, vol. III, pp. 240–1

12 BL E 401 (34): *Moderate Intelligencer* (London: August 1647) p. 1209

13 Ibid.

14 BL E 372: *Mercurius Diutinus*, (London: January 1647) p. 67

15 BL E 401 (34): *Moderate Intelligencer* (London: August 1647) p. 1208

16 Hamilton Papers, p. 178

CHAPTER FOURTEEN:

1 BL E 400 (14): *The Lamentation of the Ruling Lay-Elders* (July 1647) p. 7

2 BL E 1186 (7): *The Cavaliers Catechism*, printed for Richard Burton (London: January 1647)

3 BL E 423 (11): *Heads of Chiefe Passages in Parliament*, anon. (London: January 1648) p. 9

4 BL E 423 (12): *Moderate Intelligencer*, No. 148 (London: January 1648)

5 BL E 423 (21): *Mercurius Pragmaticus*, No. 19, verse 4

6 Prince Rupert to Charles I, September 1645, quoted in Warburton, *Memoirs of Prince Rupert*, vol. III, p. 188

7 Hamilton Papers, p. 234

8 BL E 452 (33): *A Declaration of the Lords and Commons Assembled in Parliament: Concerning the reducing of the late Revolted Ships to the obedience*

of Parliament, printed for John Wright (London: 14 July 1648) pp. 3–4

9 BL E 452 (32): *Prince Charles Sailing from Callice, towards the North of England* (London: July 1648) p. 2

10 Prince Rupert's Papers, quoted in Warburton, vol. III, p. 250

11 Ibid.

12 Warburton, vol. III, p. 468

13 BL ADD MS 62085A: Prince Rupert's Logbook, aka Pythouse Papers, vol. V, p. 114

14 Prince Rupert's Papers, quoted in Warburton, vol. III, p. 252

15 Clarendon, *History of the Rebellion*, vol. VI (of VI), p. 155

16 Ibid., p. 193

17 Prince Rupert's Papers, quoted in Warburton, vol. III, p. 261

18 Quoted in Bence-Jones, *The Cavaliers*, p. 183

19 Prince Rupert's Papers, quoted in Warburton, vol. III, p. 264

20 BL E 452 (33): op. cit., p. 4

21 Princess Elizabeth to Charles Louis, autumn of 1648, quoted in Godfrey, *A Sister of Prince Rupert*, pp. 194–5

22 The Earl of Arundel to Prince Charles Louis and Prince Rupert, 6 February 1633, quoted in David Howarth, *Lord Arundel and His Circle* (New Haven and London: 1985) p. 201

23 *A Collection of Original Royal Letters*, p. xiii, quoting Granger, *Biographical History of England*, vol. II, p. 106

24 Samuel Pepys's Diary, 5 September 1664

25 Quoted in Bence-Jones, *The Cavaliers*, p. 70

26 Ibid.

27 Prince Rupert's Papers, quoted in Warburton, vol. III, p. 274

28 Sir Edward Hyde (Clarendon) to Sir R. Fanshaw, 21 January 1649, quoted in Warburton, vol. III, pp. 279–80

29 BL ADD MS 63743 (unbound): Thomas Webb to Lord Craven (12 January 1649) p. 1

30 Quoted in Warburton, vol. III, p. 258

31 Ibid. p. 275

CHAPTER FIFTEEN:

1 Descartes to Princess Elizabeth of the Rhine, quoted in Godfrey, *A Sister of Prince Rupert*, pp. 197–8

2 Clarendon, *The History of the Rebellion*, vol. V (of VI), p. 256

3 Sir Edward Hyde (Clarendon) to Prince Rupert, 28 February 1649, quoted in Warburton, *Memoirs of Prince Rupert*, vol. III, p. 283

4 BL E 1217: *On the Martyrdom of his late Majesty* (March 1649)

5 R. Long to Prince Rupert, 1649, quoted in Warburton, vol. III, p. 286

6 'Taafe' to Prince Rupert, 2 February 1649, quoted in Warburton, vol. III, p. 291

7 Prince Rupert's Diary, quoted in Warburton, vol. III, p. 293

8 BL E 565 (12): *Perfect Weekly Account* (London: July 1649) p. 545

9 BL E 838 (19): *A Modest Narrative of Intelligence: For the Republique of England & Ireland*, No. 16 (July 1649) p. 124

10 BL E 565 (13): *A Bloudy Fight in Hartfordshire*, printed for R. W. (1649)

11 Quoted in E. T. Page, *Robert Blake, Admiral and General At Sea* (London: 1900) p. 19

12 Ibid., p. 26

13 Prince Rupert's Diary, 'The Voyage from Ireland', quoted in Warburton, vol. III, p. 299

14 Prince Rupert's Diary, 'The Proceedings in Portugal', quoted in Warburton, vol. III, p. 301

15 *Newes from Sea, concerning Prince Rupert, Capt. Pluncket, Capt. Munckel. And others: with some Transactions betwixt the King of Portingal, And Them*; printed for J. C. (London: 1650) p. 2

16 Prince Rupert's Diary, 'The Proceedings in Portugal', quoted in Warburton, vol. III, p. 303

17 Ibid. p. 305

18 Ibid. p. 313

19 Ibid.

20 Prince Rupert's Diary, 'The Voyage Into the Straits (Michaelmas-Day, 1650)', quoted in Warburton, vol. III, pp. 317–8

CHAPTER SIXTEEN:

1 Prince Rupert's Diary, 'The Proceedings at Toulon', quoted in Warburton, *Memoirs of Prince Rupert*, vol. III, p. 320

2 Ibid., p. 322

3 Ibid., p. 323

4 Ibid., p. 324

5 Prince Rupert's Diary, 'The Voyage out of the Straits', quoted in Warburton, vol. III, p. 325

6 'The Good Sea Captain', in Thomas Fuller, *The Holy State and the Profane State* (1642)

7 Letter of Pitts to 'Sir' [Mr Carteret?], undated, quoted in Warburton, vol. III, p. 532

8 Ibid.

9 Prince Rupert's Diary, 'The Voyage out of the Straits', quoted in Warburton, vol. III, p. 327

10 Ibid., p. 331

11 Letter of Pitts to 'Sir' [Mr Carteret?], undated, quoted in Warburton, vol. III, p. 533

12 Prince Rupert's Diary, 'The Voyage out of the Straits', quoted in Warburton, vol. III, p. 341

13 Ibid., p. 335

14 Letter of Pitts to 'Sir' [Mr Carteret?], undated, quoted in Warburton, vol. III, pp. 534–5

15 Prince Rupert's Diary, 'The Voyage out of the Straits', quoted in Warburton, vol. III, pp. 335–6

16 Letter of Pitts to 'Sir' [Mr Carteret?], undated, quoted in Warburton, vol. III, p. 534

CHAPTER SEVENTEEN:

1 Prince Rupert's Diary, 'The Proceedings at Cape Blanco in Argin', Warburton, *Memoirs of Prince Rupert*, vol. III, p. 344

2 Letter of Pitts to 'Sir' [Mr Carteret?], undated, quoted in Warburton, vol. III, p. 537

3 Prince Rupert's Diary, 'The Proceedings at Cape Blanco in Argin', Warburton, vol. III, pp. 348–9

4 Prince Rupert's Diary, 'From Cape Blanc to the Islands of Cape de Verd', Warburton, vol. III, p. 353

5 'Extracted out of a Journal Kept of the Prince's Own Ship', 1 February 1652, quoted in Warburton, vol. III, p. 541

6 Prince Rupert's Diary, 'From Cape Blanc to the Islands of Cape de Verd', Warburton, vol. III, p. 360

7 Ibid., p. 362

8 Ibid., p. 366

9 Ibid., pp. 366–7

10 Prince Rupert's Diary, 'The Voyage to the Indies', Warburton, vol. III, p. 371

11 Ibid., pp. 374–5

12 Ibid., p. 379

13 Ibid., pp. 380–1

14 Ibid., p. 382

15 Ibid.

16 Clarendon, *The History of the Rebellion*, vol. III (of VI), p. 274

17 Ibid., vol. VII, p. 16

18 The Earl of Leicester, quoted in Godfrey, *A Sister of Prince Rupert*, p. 149

19 BL ADD MS 18982: Rupert Correspondence, 1645–1658, Letter from John Byron to Prince Rupert, from Chester, 9 April 1644

20 BL: Edward Symmons *A Military Sermon, Preached at Shrewsbury, March 3 1643* (Oxford: 1644) p. 43

21 Clarendon, vol. III (of VI), p. 396

22 Prince Maurice to Prince Rupert, 29 January 1645, quoted in Warburton, vol. III, p. 54

23 BL E 353 (13): Anon., *A true Copy of the Welch Sermon Preached Before the two Princes, Prince Rupert and Prince Maurice at Dover* (London: 1646) p. 6

24 Prince Maurice to Prince Rupert, 7 July 1645, from Worcester, quoted in Warburton, vol. III, p. 133

25 Charles I to Prince Maurice, 20 September 1645, quoted in Warburton, vol. III, p. 189

26 Granger, *Biographical History of England*, vol. II, pp. 106–7

27 J. Thurloe, *State Papers*, (London: 1742), quoted in Oman, *The Winter Queen*, p. 392

28 BL ADD MS 62085A: Prince Rupert's Logbook, aka Pythouse Papers, p. 110

CHAPTER EIGHTEEN:

1 'Extracted out of a Journal kept on the Prince's own Ship', quoted in Warburton, *Memoirs of Prince Rupert*, vol. III, p. 546

2 Prince Charles to Prince Rupert, quoted in Warburton, vol. III, p. 419

3 Sir Edward Hyde (later the Earl of Clarendon) to Sir Richard Browne, 22 March 1653, quoted in *Memoirs of John Evelyn*, pp. 207–8

4 Ibid., 12 April 1653, p. 209

5 Sir Edward Hyde (later the Earl of Clarendon) to Sir Edward Nicholas, quoted in *Memoirs of John Evelyn*, pp. 210–211

6 Ibid., p. 211

7 Quoted in *Memoirs of John Evelyn*

8 CARTE MS 50: Ormonde to Captain Mathew, 10 June 1682

9 Elizabeth of Bohemia to Mr Secretary Nicholas, from The Hague, 2 October 1654, quoted in *Memoirs of John Evelyn*, vol. II (of II), p. 150

10 BL E 234 (5): Champianus Northtonus *The Younger Brother's Advocate*, (London: 1654) p. 10

11 S. P. German States, endorsed 'Feb. 1610 [-11] a memorial delivered by the Duke of Bouillon of the state of the Elector Palatine', quoted in Everett-Green, *Elizabeth, Queen of Bohemia*, p. 31

12 Clarendon State Papers, vol. III, p. 245

13 BL E 230 (8): *Perfect Diurnall*, printed by Francis Leach (London: July 1654) p. 3661

14 BL E 230 (32): *Perfect Diurnall*, No. 243, printed by Francis Leach (London: August 1654) p. 3726

15 Sophie, Electress of Hanover, *Mémoires et Lettres de Voyage*, p. 67

16 Ibid., p.68

17 Princess Elizabeth Palatine to Descartes, quoted in Godfrey, *A Sister of Prince Rupert*, p. 194

18 Quoted in Fergusson, *Rupert of the Rhine*, p. 120

19 Count A. Hamilton, *Memoirs of Count Grammont*, (London: 1965) p. lxviii

20 *A Collection of Original Royal Letters*, pp. xviii–xix

21 Orovida C. Pissarro, *Prince Rupert and the Invention of Mezzotint*, The Walpole Society (1956–8)

22 The Evelyn Papers, MSS 52, p. 308

23 P. H. Hulton, *Prince Rupert: Artist and Patron of the Arts* (1960) p. 9

24 John Evelyn, quoted in Warburton, vol. III, p. 435

25 BL E 233.1: *Perfect Diurnall*, No. 18, printed for F. Coles, (London: September 1654) p. 140

26 BL E 236 (1): *Severall Proceedings in Parliament*, No. 265, printed for Robert Ibbitson (London: October 1654) p. 4197

27 BL E 233.2 (42): *Certain Passages of Every dayes Intelligence*, anon., (London: September 1654) p. 2

28 BL E 236 (9): *Severall Proceedings in Parliament*, No. 266, printed for Robert Ibbitson (London: November 1654) p. 4199

29 BL E 237 (9): *The Faithful Scout*, No. 206, printed by Robert Wood (London: December 1654) p. 1688

30 BL E 838 (17): *A Perfect Account of the daily Intelligence from the Armies in England, Scotland, and Ireland, and the Navy at Sea*, No. 227, printed by E. Alsop (London: 16 May 1655) p. 1816

31 Hamilton, *Memoirs of Count Grammont*, p. 90

32 BL E 230 (1) *Perfect Diurnall*, No. 238, printed by Francis Leach (London: July 1654) p. 3653

33 BL E 230 (4): *Severall Proceedings of State Affairs*, printed for Robert Ibbitson (London: July 1654) p. 3

34 Thurloe Papers, vol. III, p. 459: Mr Manning to Thurloe, 1 June 1655

CHAPTER NINETEEN:

1 *The Life of James II, Written by Himself*, prefixed to James Macpherson, *Original Papers, containing The Secret History of Great Britain, From the Restoration to the Accession of the House of Hanover*, vol. I (London: 1775) p. 16

2 Dryden, *Poems*, I, 24

3 John Evelyn's Diary, 29 May 1660

4 John Ogilby, *Relation of His Majestie's Entertainment Passing … To His Coronation* (1661)

5 CARTE MS 50, f. 303: The Duke of Ormonde to the Earl of Arran, from Whitehall, 2 December 1682

6 BL E 765 (15): *The Earle of Bristoll His Speech in the House of Lords* (London: July 1660)

7 *A Sermon Preached before Sir Marmaduke Langdale At his entrance into Barwick*, I. K. (1648) p. 22

8 John Evelyn's Diary, 17 October 1660

9 BL E 192 (18): *Kingdom's Weekly Intelligencer* (London: February 1661) p. 72

10 Samuel Pepys's Diary: 23 September 1660

11 BL ADD MS 63744, fl. 85: Letter to Elizabeth, Queen of Bohemia, 5 October 1660

12 BL ADD MS 63744, fl. 9: Letter to Elizabeth, Queen of Bohemia, 9 November 1660

13 Quoted in Maria Kroll, *Sophie, Electress of Hanover* (London: 1973) p. 103

14 Hamilton, *Memoirs of Count Grammont*, p 96

15 Lord Cornbury to the Duchess of Beaufort, 10 June 1662, quoted in Warburton, *Memoirs of Prince Rupert*, vol. III, p. 462

16 Prince Rupert to Will Legge, from Vienna, 22 June 1661, quoted in Warburton, vol. III, pp. 450–1

17 Prince Rupert to Will Legge, from Vienna, 6 August 1661, quoted in Warburton, vol. III, p. 453

18 Electress Sophie of Hanover to Charles Louis, Elector Palatine, 26 September 1661, in the French translation of *Briefwechsel der Herzogin Sophie von Hannover mit ihrem Bruder, dem Kurfuerstin Karl Ludwig von der Pfalz*, p. 45

19 Prince Rupert to Will Legge, from Vienna, 22 June 1661, quoted in Warburton, vol. III, p. 451

20 Prince Rupert to Will Legge, from Vienna, 9 September 1661, quoted in Warburton, vol. III, p. 456

21 Prince Rupert to Will Legge, from Vienna, 24 September 1661, quoted in Warburton, vol. III, p. 457

22 Lord Orford's 'Catalogue of Engravers', quoted in Warburton, vol. III, p. 491

23 Quoted in Sir Henry Lyons, *Royal Society, 1660–1940* (Cambridge: 1944) p. 4

24 Thomas Sprat, Lord Bishop of Rochester, *The History of the Royal Society of London, For the Improving of Natural Knowledge* (London: 1680) p. 53

25 Quoted in Dorothy Stimson, *Scientists and Amateurs: A History of the Royal Society* (New York: 1948) p. 20

26 'The Epistle Dedicatory' of the Royal Society, quoted in Sprat, *The History of the Royal Society of London*

27 Sprat, *The History of the Royal Society of London* p. 61

28 Ibid., p. 40

29 *Memoirs of the Life and Death of Prince Rupert*, anon. (1683) p. 80

30 Royal Society minutes for 14 August 1661, quoted in Stimson, *Scientists and Amateurs: A History of the Royal Society*, p. 81

31 Samuel Butler, *Hudibras*, part II, canto 2, quoted in Warburton, vol. III, p. 444

32 Thomas Streete, quoted in Bence-Jones, *The Cavaliers*, p. 63

33 Richard Nichols, *Robert Hooke and the Royal Society* (Chippenham: 1999) p. 19, quoting from a biography of Thomas Sydenham

34 Sprat, *The History of the Royal Society of London* p. 132

35 Quoted in Warburton, vol. III, p. 432

36 CLP/3i/11: Prince Rupert (2 March: 1663), Manuscripts of the Royal Society

37 RBO/2i/64: Prince Rupert (22 July 1663), Manuscripts of the Royal Society

38 Lectures of the Royal Society, quoted in Sprat, *The History of the Royal Society of London*, pp. 173–305

CHAPTER TWENTY:

1 William de Britaine, *The Dutch Usurpation* (London: 1672) p. 15

2 Duke of Buckingham, *A Letter to Sir Thomas Osborn, One of His Majesties Privy Council, Upon the reading of a Book, called 'The present Interest of England Stated'* (London: 1672) p. 15

3 BL E 121 (30): *A Letter Sent from Both Houses of Parliament, to his Excellence, the Earl of Essex, Lord generall of the Army for the King and Parliament* printed by John Franc (London: 11 October 1642)

4 Coventry MSS vol. 102, f. 12: N. A. M. Rodger, quoted in Sir William Coventry, from Longleat, *The Command of the Ocean: A Naval History of Britain, 1649–1815* (London: 2004) p. 66

5 BL ADD MS 63744: Letter from The Hague to Elizabeth of Bohemia, 12/22 July 1661

6 *The Life of James II, Written by Himself*, in Macpherson, *The Secret History of Great Britain*, vol. I, p. 25

7 Samuel Pepys's Diary, 6 September 1664

8 Prince Rupert to the States-General, February 1649, quoted in Warburton, *Memoirs of Prince Rupert*, vol. III, p. 288

9 Samuel Pepys's Diary, 5 October 1664

10 Coventry MSS vol. 102, f.12: op.cit, p. 67

11 *The Life of James II, Written by Himself* in Macpherson, vol. I, p. 28

12 John Dryden, *Essay of Dramatic Poesy*: account of 3 June 1665

13 Sir John Denham, *Poems on Affairs of State*, p. 26, quoted in Morrah, *Prince Rupert of the Rhine*, p. 328

14 *Calendar of State Papers*, Domestic Series, 1664–5, p. 420, quoted in Morrah, p. 325

15 Quoted in Warburton, vol. III, p. 472

16 Edmund Gayton, *The Glorious and Living Cinque-Ports of Our Fortunate Island* (Oxford: 1666) p. 3

17 Prince Rupert's Narrative (1666), quoted in Warburton, vol. III, pp. 480–1

18 *Calendar of State Papers*, Domestic Series, 1664–5, p. 420, letter of James Hickes to Joseph Williamson

19 Samuel Pepys's Diary, 3 June 1665

20 John Evelyn's Diary, 1 July 1666

CHAPTER TWENTY-ONE:

1 Prince Rupert and the Duke of Albermarle to Sir Thomas Allen, 24 April 1666, quoted in *The Rupert and Monck Letter Book, 1666*, eds. Rev. J. R. Powell and E. K. Timings (London: 1969) p. 11

2 Prince Rupert and the Duke of Albermarle to Dennis Gauden, 5 April 1666, quoted in *The Rupert and Monck Letter Book, 1666*, p. 20

3 Prince Rupert and the Duke of Albermarle to the Commissioners of the Ordnance, 28 April 1666, quoted in *The Rupert and Monck Letter Book, 1666*, p. 27

4 John Evelyn's Diary, 8 May 1666

5 'The Division of the English Fleet in 1666', in Roland J. A. Shelley, *Mariner's Mirror* (1939) p. 182, quoted in Morrah, *Prince Rupert of the Rhine*, p. 334

6 CARTE MS 46 (311): Arlington to Ormonde, from Whitehall, 29 May 1666

7 Bruce Ingram, *Three Sea Journals* (London: 1936) p. 48, quoted in Rodger, *The Command of the Ocean*

8 CARTE MS 46 (317): Thomas Clifford to Ormonde, from on board the *Royal Charles*, 5 June 1666

9 Prince Rupert's Narrative (1666), quoted in Warburton, vol. III, p. 482

10 CARTE MS 46 (315): Thomas Clifford to Ormonde, from on board the *Royal Charles*, 5 June 1666

11 John Evelyn's Diary, 3 June 1666

12 John Dryden, quoted in Warburton, *Memoirs of Prince Rupert*, vol. III, p. 476 and p. 478

13 CARTE MS 46 (317): Sir Thomas Clifford to Ormonde, from on board the *Royal Charles*, 9 June 1666

14 'A True Narrative of the Engagement between His Majesties Fleet and that of Holland' in A. W. H. Pearsall, *The Second Dutch War, Described in Pictures and Manuscripts* (1967) p. 22, quoted in Morrah, p. 338

15 CARTE MS 46 (318): Sir Thomas Clifford to Ormonde, from on board the *Royal Charles*, 5 June 1666

16 Rodger, *The Command of the Ocean*, p. 72

17 Wiquefort, *Histoire de Provinces Unies*, vol. XIV, quoted in Dr John Campbell, *Admirals*, vol. II (London: 1818) p. 110

18 John Evelyn's Diary, 6 June 1666

19 John Evelyn's Diary, 17 June 1666

20 Quoted in Warburton, vol. III, pp. 478–9

21 CARTE MS 46 (321): Arlington to Ormonde, from Whitehall, 19 June 1666

22 CARTE MS 46 (337): Arlington to Ormonde, from Whitehall, 21 July 1666

23 *The Tell-Tale*, 2 vols (London: 1776), quoted in Warburton, vol. III, p. 469

24 *The Rupert and Monck Letter Book, 1666*, p. 277

25 CARTE MS 46 (355): Arlington to Ormonde, from Whitehall, 18 August 1666

26 Gayton, *The Glorious and Living Cinque-Ports of our fortunate Island*, pp. 5–6

27 Prince Rupert's Narrative, quoted in Warburton, vol. III, pp. 484–5

CHAPTER TWENTY-TWO:

1 John Evelyn's Diary, 7 September 1665

2 *The Life of James II, Written by Himself* in Macpherson, *The Secret History of Great Britain*, vol. I, p. 36

3 Ibid.

4 CARTE MS 51 (4): The Marquess of Ormonde to the Earl of Anglesey, 1 October 1666

5 Gayton, *The Glorious and Living Cinque-Ports of our fortunate Island*, p. 11

6 Samuel Pepys's Diary, 24 June 1663

7 Ibid. 2 January 1668

8 Ibid. 11 January 1666

9 Ibid. 4 February 1665

10 Prince Rupert and the Duke of Albermarle to the Duke of York, 22 August 1666, quoted in *The Rupert and Monck Letter Book, 1666*, p. 138

11 Prince Rupert's Narrative, quoted in Warburton, *Memoirs of Prince Rupert*, vol. III, p. 483

12 Henry B. Wheatley (ed.), *Diary of Samuel Pepys*, vol. VII, pp. 311–12, quoted in Morrah, *Prince Rupert of the Rhine*, p. 347

13 John Evelyn's Diary, 3 June 1667

14 Prince Rupert's Narrative (1667), quoted in Warburton, vol. III, pp. 483–4

15 Commissioner Captain John Taylor to Samuel Pepys, 4 April 1667, in *Further Correspondence of Samuel Pepys, 1662–1679*, ed. J. R. Tanner (London: 1929) p. 172; quoted in Rodger, *The Command of the Ocean*, pp. 100–1

16 Samuel Pepys's Diary, 15 January 1665

17 John Brown, *A Compleat Discourse of Wounds* (London: 1678) p. 132

18 Ibid., pp. 142–3

19 John Evelyn's Diary, 3 May 1650

20 Newsletter of Henry Muddiman, in *Calendar of State Papers*, Domestic Series 1665–6, p. 523

21 Samuel Pepys's Diary, 3 April 1667

22 Warburton, vol. III, p. 492

23 Samuel Pepys's Diary, 10 June 1667

24 CARTE MS 46 (490): Arlington to Ormonde, from Whitehall, 15 June 1667

25 Warburton, vol. III, p. 493

26 John Evelyn's Diary, 14 June 1667

27 CARTE MS 51 (52): Ormonde to the Earl of Anglesey, from Dublin, 22 June 1667

28 Samuel Pepys's Diary, July 1667, quoted in Rodger, *The Command of the Ocean*, p. 78

CHAPTER TWENTY-THREE:

1 John Morris, *Troubles of our Catholic Forefathers* 1872–77, vol. I, p. 392

2 *Diary of Samuel Pepys*, ed. Wheatley, vol. VI, p. 151

3 *Memoirs of John Evelyn*, vol. I, p. 359

4 Quoted in Morrah, p. 411 (Was in Surrey County Archives.)

5 Eva Scott, *Rupert, Prince Palatine*, p. 361, quoted in Morrah, p. 411

6 Original letter from Sophie, Electress of Hanover, to Prince Rupert, quoted in Morrah, *Prince Rupert of the Rhine* p. 411

7 James, Duke of York to Prince Rupert, from Whitehall, 27 October 1667, in 'Bromley Collections', p. 486

8 Richard Oneley, *General Account of Tunbridge Wells and its Environs* (1771) p. 37, quoted in Hamilton, *Memoirs of Count Grammont*, p. lxviii

9 Hamilton, *Memoirs of Count Grammont*, p. 296

10 Ibid.

11 Ibid., p. lxviii

12 Ibid., pp. 297–8

13 Philip H. Highfill et al. (eds.), *A Biographical Dictionary of Actors, Actresses, Musicians, Dancers, Managers and Other Stage Personnel in London, 1660–1800*, vol. 6 (Southern Illinois University Press: 1978) p. 462

14 Hamilton, *Memoirs of Count Grammont*, p. 298

15 Samuel Pepys's Diary, vol. VII, p. 7

16 Ibid., vol. VIII, p. 463

17 Tom Brown, *Second Part of the Letters from the Dead to the Living* (1708) p. 166, quoted in Elizabeth Howe, *The first English Actresses* (Cambridge: 1992) p. 32

18 'A Prologue to introduce the first Woman that came to Act on the Stage in the Tragedy, call'd the Moor of Venice', in Thomas Jordan, *A Royal Arbor of Loyal Poesie*, (1664) pp. 21–2

19 John Evelyn's Diary, 18 October 1666

20 A poem found in Bridgewater House by John Payne Collier, quoted in Highfill, *A Biographical Dictionary of Actors, Actresses …*, vol. 8, p. 24

21 Samuel Pepys's Diary, quoted in Highfill, *A Biographical Dictionary of Actors, Actresses …*, vol. 8, p. 24

22 K. Hauk, *Die Briefer der Kinder des Winterkoenigs* (Heidelberg: 1908) p. 302

23 Sophie, Electress of Hanover to Charles Louis, Elector Palatine, 24 January 1674, in the French translation of *Briefwechsel der Herzogin Sophie von Hannover mit ihrem Bruder, dem Kurfuersten Karl Ludwig von der Pfalz*, p. 175

24 Hauk, *Die Briefer der Kinder des Winterkoenigs*, p. 346

25 Highfill, *A Biographical Dictionary of Actors, Actresses …*, vol. 8

26 Mr Crown, *The Countrey Wit* (London: 1675) p. 58

27 Thomas Durfey, *Squire Oldsapp or, The Night-Adventurers* (London: 1679) p. 11

28 Lady Chaworth to Lord Roos, quoted in Highfill, *A Biographical Dictionary of Actors, Actresses …*, vol. 8, p. 24

CHAPTER TWENTY-FOUR:

1 Clarendon, *The History of the Rebellion*, vol. VI (of VI), p. 260

2 Quoted in Christopher Hibbert, *The Court at Windsor: A Domestic History* (London: 1964) p. 66

3 *Calendar of State Papers*, Domestic Series, 1651–2, p. 546

4 John Evelyn's Diary, 8 June 1654

5 BL E 237 (10): *Perfect Diurnall*, No. 263, printed by Francis Leach (London: December 1654)

6 BL ADD MS 16370: Plans of the Fortified Towns of England, p. 54
7 MS RA GEO/Add 52/1: Windsor Castle Governor's Book, 1668–1671, 'His Majesty's Patent to his Highness Prince Rupert, 19 October 1668'
8 *The Life of James II, Written by Himself* in Macpherson, *The Secret History of Great Britain*, vol. I, p. 49
9 MS RA GEO/Add 52/1: Windsor Castle Governor's Book, 1668–1671, 'Certain Particulars Relating to the Office of Constable of Windsor', Sir Bulstrode Whitlock, (*c.* 1661) p. 1
10 MS RA GEO/Add 52/1: loose-leaf letter from the Duke of Monmouth and Thomas Chicheley to Colonel William Legge, 8 December 1669
11 MS RA GEO/Add 52/1: Windsor Castle Governor's Book, 1668–1671, p. 59, 'Orders Established by his Highness, Prince Rupert' (1668)
12 John Evelyn's Diary, 28 August 1670
13 MS RA GEO/Add 52/1: Windsor Castle Governor's Book, 1668–1671, p. 59, 'Letter from Prince Rupert to Sir Thomas Foster and other JPs in the Chertsey area'. Date unknown
14 Quoted in Warburton, *Memoirs Prince Rupert*, vol. III, p. 495
15 Warburton, vol. III, p. 460
16 John Evelyn's Diary, 28 August 1670
17 Quoted in Hibbert, *The Court at Windsor: A Domestic History*, p. 73
18 John Evelyn's Diary, the summer of 1683, quoted in Hibbert, *The Court at Windsor: A Domestic History'*, p. 71
19 Quoted in Hibbert, *The Court at Windsor: A Domestic History*, p. 75
20 *Calendar of State Papers*, 1672–1675, 20 May 1675, p. 744
21 MS RA GEO/Add 52/1: Windsor Castle Governor's Book, 1668–1671, 'Certain Particulars Relating to the Office of Constable of Windsor', Sir Bulstrode Whitlock (*c.* 1661) p. 7

CHAPTER TWENTY-FIVE:

1 'The Strange and Dangerous Voyage of Captain Thomas James', quoted in Peter C. Newman, *Empire of the Bay* (Toronto: 1989) p. 30
2 Quoted in George Woodcock, *The Hudson's Bay Company* (New York: 1970) p. 20
3 W. R. Scott, *Constitution and Finance of English, Scottish and Irish Joint-Stock Companies to 1730* (1910) p. 17
4 Sir John Clapham, *Minutes of the Hudson's Bay Company, 1671–1674*, p. 131, quoted in Morrah, *Prince Rupert of the Rhine*, p. 385
5 Quoted in Woodcock, *The Hudson's Bay Company*, p. 23
6 Founding document, quoted in Newman, *Empire of the Bay* p. 41

CHAPTER TWENTY-SIX:

1 BL ADD MS 16370: Plans of the Fortified Towns of England, p. 7
2 BL ADD 63743, f. 56: Princess Sophie, Prince Rupert's sister, to the Earl of Craven, from Heidelberg, July 1667
3 MSS STT 625: John Doddington to Joseph Williamson, 27 June 1670, Huntingdon Library, quoted in Steven Pincus, 'Republicanism, Absolutism and Universal Monarchy: English Popular Sentiment During the Third Dutch War', Ch. 12 of *Culture and Society in the Stuart Restoration*, ed. Gerald Maclean (CUP: 1995) p. 25
4 *The Life of James II, Written by Himself*, in Macpherson, *The Secret History of Great Britain*, vol. I, p. 55
5 William de Britaine, *The Dutch Usurpation*, p. 31
6 John Evelyn, Easter 1673, quoted in Maurice Ashley, *James II*, (London: 1977) p. 110
7 *An exact relation of the several Engagements and Actions of his Majesty's fleet, under the command of his Highness Prince Rupert* (1673), quoted in Warburton, *Memoirs of Prince Rupert*, vol. III, p. 497
8 Thomas Jordan, *London Triumphant, or the City in Jollity and Splendour*, (London: 1672) p. 12
9 Prince Rupert, quoted in J. R. Jones, *The Anglo-Dutch Wars of the Seventeenth Century* (New York: 1996) p. 203
10 *An exact relation of the several Engagements and Actions of his Majesty's fleet, under the command of His Highness Prince Rupert* (1673), quoted in Warburton, vol. III, p. 498
11 Rodger, *The Command of the Ocean*, p. 224
12 Nathaniel Brooke, *A Just Vindication of the Principal Officers of His Majesties Ordnance*, (London: 1674) p. 4
13 *An exact relation of the several Engagements and Actions of his Majesty's fleet, under the command of His Highness Prince Rupert* (1673), quoted in Warburton, vol. III, p. 502
14 Spragge's Journal, *Journals and Narratives of The Third Dutch War*, ed. R. C. Anderson, NRS, vol. 86, 1946, quoted in Rodger, *The Command of the Ocean*, p. 83
15 Prince Rupert, quoted in Rodger, *The Command of the Ocean*, p. 219
16 *Calendar of State Papers*, Domestic Series, 22 June 1672, p. 264: William, Bishop of Lincoln, to Williamson, 22 June 1672
17 Sir William Coventry (1667), quoted in Claire Tomalin, *Pepys: The Unequalled Self* (London: 2002) p. 193
18 STOWE MS 203: *A Relation of the French Squadron sent to his Highness Pr. Rupert by Mons. de Martell their Vice-Admirall* (1673) p. 16
19 Ibid.

20 Prince Rupert, quoted in Jones, *The Anglo-Dutch Wars of the Seventeenth Century*, p. 209

21 Sir Thomas Player to Williamson, 9 September 1673, Christie, ed., *Letters*, volume II, p. 16, quoted in Pincus, 'Republicanism, Absolutism and Universal Monarchy: English Popular Sentiment During the Third Dutch War', p. 265 in Maclean (ed.), *Culture and Society in the Stuart Restoration*

22 Bishop Burnet, *History*, vol. 2, page 15, quoted in ibid., p. 265

23 MS STOWE 203: vol. IV, September–December 1673: William Bridgeman to the Earl of Essex, from Whitehall, 6 September 1673, in *Correspondence of Arthur Capel, Earl of Essex, 1672–1679.*, p. 7a

24 STOWE MS 203: vol. IV, September–December 1673, p. 15a: *A Relation of the French Squadron sent to his Highness Pr. Rupert by Mons. de Martell their Vice-Admirall*, (1673)

25 '*Verbum Sapienti*' (January 1674), quoted in Pincus, 'Republicanism, Absolutism and Universal Monarchy: English Popular Sentiment during the Third Dutch war', p. 253

26 Henry Ball to Williamson, 19 September 1673, quoted in Pincus, 'Republicanism, Absolutism and Universal monarchy: English Popular Sentiment During the Third Dutch War' p. 265

27 William Coventry, 11 May 1678, from Grey 'Debates', vol. 5, p. 387, quoted in Pincus, 'Republicanism, Absolutism and Universal monarchy: English Popular Sentiment During the Third Dutch War', p. 256

CHAPTER TWENTY-SEVEN:

1 Dr John Campbell, *The Naval History of Great Britain*, (London: 1818) pp. 310–311

2 Thomas Flatman, *On the Death of the Illustrious Prince Rupert, A Pindarique Ode*, p. 5

3 Quoted in Hibbert, *The Court at Windsor: A Domestic History*, p. 73

4 *The Life of James II, Written by Himself* in Macpherson, *The Secret History of Great Britain*, vol. I. pp. 139–140

5 Ibid., vol. I, pp. 100–1

6 Ibid., vol. I, p. 101

7 Ibid., vol. I, p. 10

8 Ibid., vol. I, p. 136

9 Sir John Clapham, *Minutes of the Hudson's Bay Company*, 1679–1684, p. xxiii, quoted in Morrah, *Prince Rupert of the Rhine*, p. 386

10 *The Life of James II, Written by Himself*, vol. I, pp. 83–4

11 *Catalogue of Royal and Noble Authors*, vol. II, p. 25, quoted in Hamilton, *Memoirs of Count Grammont*, p. xlvii

12 Sophie, Electress of Hanover to Charles Louis, Elector Palatine, 5 January

1678, in the French translation of *'Briefwechsel der Herzögin Sophie von Hannover mit ihrem Bruder, dem Kurfuersten Karl Ludwig von der Pfalz'*, p. 309

13 Electress Sophie to Charles Louis, 20 June 1679, ibid., p. 361

14 Electress Sophie to Charles Louis, 12 February 1680, ibid., p. 408

15 J. Gough Nichols and J. Bruce, *Wills from Doctors' Commons* (London: 1863) pp. 143–4

16 Quoted in Warburton, *Memoirs of Prince Rupert*

17 Sir Philip Warwick, *Memoires of the reigne of King Charles I* (London: 1701) pp. 227–8

BIBLIOGRAPHY

PRIMARY SOURCES (MANUSCRIPT)

BRITISH LIBRARY
ADD MS 62085A: Prince Rupert's Logbook, aka Pythouse Papers
ADD MS 18982: Rupert Correspondence, 1645–1658
ADD MS 63743
ADD MS 63744
ADD MS 18738: Autograph Letters, 1433–1817
ADD MS 16370: Plans of the Fortified Towns of England
ADD 72895
ADD MS 38091: Miscellaneous Letters and Papers
EGERTON 785: Letter Book of Sir S. Luke, 1643–1645
HARLEY 166: Sir S. D'Ewes's Journal of the House of Commons
SLOANE 1519, Plut. XC.G: Original Letters, 1574–1667
SLOANE 1983.B
STOWE 203

BODLEIAN
CARTE MS 46, 49, 50, 51
MS Eng. C. 7019: Clarendon to the Duke of York
MS Eng. C. 5237: Letters of James, Duke of York

THE ROYAL SOCIETY
CLP/3i/11
RBO/2i/64

WINDSOR CASTLE
MS RA GEO/Add 52/1: Windsor Castle Governor's Book, 1668–1671.

PRIMARY SOURCES (PRINTED)

Calendar of State Papers, Domestic Series

Clarendon State Papers

The Evelyn Papers, MSS 52

The Hamilton Papers

Thurloe Papers

Anon., *A Revelation of Mr Brigtmans Revelation*, 1641

Anon., *Exceeding Joyful Newes from the Prince*, 1642

Anon., *Some Speciall Passages from Westminster, London, Yorke, and other parts*, 1642

Anon., *True, But Sad and Dolefull Newes from Shrewsbury*, 1642

Anon., *A Discourse upon the Questions in debate between the King and Parliament*, 1642

Anon., *His Majesty's Speech Delivered the Twenty second of January 1643, at Oxford*, 1643

Anon., *Prince Rupert's Disguises*, 1643

Anon., *A Warning-Piece To all His Majesties subjects of England*, 1643

Anon., *A Dogge's Elegie, or Rupert's Tears*, 1644

Anon., *A true Copy of the Welch Sermon Preached Before the two Princes, Prince Rupert and Prince Maurice at Dover*, 1646

Anon., *Verses on the Siege of Gloucester and Colonel Massey*, 1647

Anon., *The Declaration of General Massey and Colonel General Poyntz*, 1647

Anon., *The Lamentation of the Ruling Lay-Elders*, 1647

Anon., *Heads of Chiefe Passages in Parliament*, 1648

Anon., *Prince Charles Sailing from Callice, towards the North of England*, 1648

Anon., *On the Martyrdom of his late Majesty*, 1649

Anon., *Certain Passages of Every dayes Intelligence*, 1654

Anon., *Memoirs of the Life and Death of Prince Rupert*, 1683

Ash, Simon, *A Continuation of True Intelligence from the English and Scottish Forces, in the North ...*, 1644

Bacon, Francis, *Cases of Treason*, 1641

Banks, Thomas, *Prince Robert's Message to my Lord of Essex*, 1642

Beale, John, *A Sermon ... Together with a short narration of the Prince Elector's greatness ...*, 1613

Best, Richard, *A Declaration of the Lords and Commons of the Parliament of England to ... the United Provinces*, 1642

Bishop, G., *A nest of Perfidious Vipers*, 1644

Bodemann, Eduard (ed.), *Briefwechsel der Herzogin Sophie von Hannover mit ihrem Bruder, dem Kurfuersten Karl Ludwig von der Pfalz* (French trans.), 1885

Bray William (ed.), *Memoires of John Evelyn, 1641 to 1705–6*, 1819

Bowman, Seymour, *Diary of the Proceedings of the House of Commons*, 1660

Bromley, Sir George (ed.), *A Collection of Original Royal Letters*, 1787

Brooke, Nathaniel, *A Just Vindication of the Principal Officers of His Majesties Ordnance*, 1674

Brown, John, *A Compleat Discourse of Wounds*, 1678

Buckingham, Duke of, *A Letter to Sir Thomas Osborn, One of His Majesties Privy Council, Upon the reading of a Book* ..., 1672

Bulkeley, Stephen, *The Holy Rebell*, 1642

Bulstrode, Sir Richard, *Memoirs and Reflections upon the Reign and Government of Charles I and Charles II*, 1721

Burton, Richard, *The Cavaliers Catechism*, 1647

Butter, Nathaniel, and Bourne, Nicholas, *The Swedish Intelligencer*, 1633

Butter, Nathaniel, and Bourne, Nicholas, *The Devotion and Formes of Prayer, Daily Used in the King of Sweden's Army*, 1632

Carte, T., *A Collection of Original Documents and Papers*, 1641–60, 1739

Clarendon, Earl of, *History of the Rebellion*, 1731–2

Coles, Fr., *A true Coppy of the Instructions agreed upon by the Lords and Commons assembled in Parliament and sent to his Excellency the Earl of Essex*, 1642

Cook, John, *Monarchy No Creature of God's Making*, 1651

Corbet, John, *A true and impartial History of the Military Government of the City of Gloucester*, 1647

Crown, Mr, *The Countrey Wit*, 1675

Cruso, John, *Militarie Instructions for the Cavallrie*, 1632

de Britaine, William, *The Dutch Usurpation*, 1672

Derry, Bishop of, *A Sermon Preached in Yorke Minister*, 1643

Digby, Lord (later 2nd Earl of Bristol), *The Lord Digbyes Speech In The House of Commons*, 1641

Digby, Lord (later 2nd Earl of Bristol), *The Earle of Bristol His Speech in the House of Lords*, 1660

Downing, Calybute, *A Discourse Upon the Interest of England* ..., 1641

Downing, Calybute, *A Discoverie of the false Grounds the Bavarian party have layd, to settle their own Faction, and shake the Peace of the Empire*, 1641

Dryden, John, *Essay of Dramatic Poesy*, 1665

Durfey, Thomas, *Squire Oldsapp*, 1679

E. C., *A Vow of Teares, for the losse of Prince Henry*, 1612

Evelyn, John, *The Diary of John Evelyn*, ed. E. S. de Beer, 1959

Falkland, Viscount, *A Letter Sent from the Lord Falkland unto the Rt Hon Henry, Earl of Cumberland*, 1642

Fiennes, Nathaniel, *A Relation made to the House of Commons*, 1643

Flatman, Thomas, *On the Death of the Illustrious Prince Rupert, A Pindarique Ode*, 1683

Fowler, Henry, *The Resolution of the Gentry and Commonalty in the County of Nottingham* ..., 1642

Franc, John, *A Letter Sent from Both Houses of Parliament, to his Excellence, the Earl of Essex* ..., 1642

Fuller, Thomas, *The Holy State and the Profane State*, 1642

Gardiner, S. R., *Letters and other Documents*, 1865

Gayton, Edmund, *The Glorious and Living Cinque-Ports of our fortunate Island*, 1666

Gellibrand, Samuel, *The Two Speeches of the Lord Wharton, Spoken in Guild-Hall*, 1642

Harington, Sir John, *Nugae Antiquae*, 1779

Holland, John, *Mr Holland, His First Discourse of the Navy*, 1638

Husband, Edward, *An Ordinance of the Lords and Commons*, 1645

Husband, Edward, *The Humble Desires of Prince Rupert, Prince Maurice and others their Adherents, To the Kings most Excellent Majestie* ..., 1645

Hutton, Henry, *A Worthy Speech spoken to the King's most Excellent Majesty by the Recorder of Hereford*, 1642

I. A., *The Best News That Ever Was Printed – Prince Rupert's resolution to be gone to his Mother* ..., 1643

I. K., *A Sermon Preached before Sir Marmaduke Langdale* ..., 1648

I. W., *The Bloody Prince*, 1643

James II, *Life of James II collected out of memoirs written by his own hand*, ed. J. Clarke, 1816

J. C., *Newes from Sea, concerning Prince Rupert, Capt. Plunket, Capt. Munckel, and Others'*, 1650

Johnson, John, *Exceeding Joyful Newes out of Surrey, Shewing the proceedings of Prince Robert and his mischievous Cavalliers*, 1642

Johnson, John, *A true and perfect Relation of the chief Passages in Middlesex*, 1642

Jordan, Thomas, *London Triumphant, or the City in Jollity and Splendour*, 1672

Lambert, Thomas, *London's Alacritie*, 1643

Macpherson, James, *Original Papers, containing the Secret History of Great Britain, From the Restoration to the Accession of the House of Hanover*, 1775

Medlus, James, *A Sermon, Preached before the two high borne and illustrious Princes* ..., 1613

Meuris, Arthur, *A Briefe Description of the reasons that make the Declaration of the Ban against the King of Bohemia ... of no value nor worth* ..., 1621

Northtonus, Champianus, *The Younger Brother's Advocate*, 1654

Ogilby, John, *Relation of the Majestie's Entertainment Passing ... To His Coronation*, 1661

Oglander, Sir John, *A Royalist's Notebook*, ed. Francis Bamford, 1936

Parker, Martin, *A True Tale of Robin Hood*, 1632

Peacham, Henry, *The Compleat Gentleman*, 1622

Pepys, Samuel, *Diary of Samuel Pepys*, ed. Henry B. Wheatley, 1893–9

Perry, Hugh, *A Letter written from the Right Honorable the Earle of Bedford, to a Lord of the House of Peeres*, 1642

Plot, Robert, *The Natural History of Staffordshire*, 1686

R. A., *A Prophecie of the Life, Reigne, and Death of William Laud*, 1644

Ranson, William, *A Sermon Preached in the Metropoliticall Church of York*, 1644

Rider, Thomas, *True Intelligence and Joyfull Newes from Ludlow*, 1642

R. O., *Two Declarations of the Lords and Commons assembled in Parliament*, 1642

Rolt, John (trans.), *A Full Declaration of the Faith and Ceremonies professed in the Dominions of the most Illustrious and noble Prince Frederick …*, 1614

Rupert, Prince, *Prince Rupert His Declaration*, 1642

Rossiter, Colonel, *A Letter Concerning a great Victory obtained by Colonel Rossiter, against Prince Rupert and Prince Maurice, near Belvoyr Castle …*, 1645

R. W., *A Bloudy Fight in Hartfordshire*, 1649

Sprat, Thomas, *The History of the Royal Society of London*, 1680

Symmons, Edward, *A Military Sermon, preached at Shrewsbury …*, 1644

Taylor, John, *All the Workes*, 1630

Vernon, John, *The Young Horseman or the Honest Plain-dealing Cavalier*, 1644

Walbancke, Mathew, *A Diary communicating the most remarkable proceedings of both Houses of Parliament*, 1645

Warwick, Sir Philip, *Memoires of the reigne of King Charles I*, 1701

White, Robert, *A True Relation of a Victory obtained over the Kings forces …*, 1645

W. H., *The Character of a Cavalier, with his Brother Separatist*, 1647

Wilbraham, Sir Roger, *Journal of Sir Roger Wilbraham*, quoted in *The Camden Miscellany*, vol. 10, 1902

Wortley, Sir Francis, *Characters and Elegies*, 1646

Wright, John, *A Perfect Relation of the Taking of Leicester*, 1645

Wright, John, *A Declaration of the Lords and Commons … Concerning the reducing of the late Revolted Ships to the obedience of Parliament*, 1648

W. W., *A Looking-Glasse for the Popish Garrisons*, 1645

CIVIL WAR PERIODICALS

A Modest Narrative of Intelligence
A Perfect Account of the daily Intelligence from the Armies in England, Scotland, and Ireland, and the Navy at Sea
Exchange Intelligencer
Faithful Scout
Kingdomes Weekly Intelligencer
London Post
Mercurius Britannicus
Mercurius Diutinus
Mercurius Pragmaticus
Moderate Intelligencer
Parliament Scout
Perfect Diurnall
Perfect Occurrences of Parliament
Perfect Passages of Each Dayes Proceedings in Parliament
Perfect Weekly Account
Scottish Dove
Severall Proceedings in Parliament
Severall Proceedings of State Affairs
True Informer
Weekly Account

OTHER SOURCES

A Cavalry Officer, *Cavalry Tactics*, 1897
Adair, J., *By the Sword Divided*, 2001
Adams, John Lawrence, *Friedrich the Victorious, 1425–1476*, 1993
Anderson, R. C. (ed.), *Journals and Narratives of The Third Dutch War*, 1946
Asch, Ronald G., *The Thirty Years' War, the Holy Roman Empire and Europe, 1618–1648*, 1997
Ashley, Maurice, *England in the Seventeenth Century*, 1952
Ashley, Maurice, *Rupert of the Rhine*, 1976
Ashley, Maurice, *James II*, 1977
Baker, L. M. (ed.), *Letters of Elizabeth, Queen of Bohemia*, 1953
Barnes, Phil, 'Unbeaten Tracks of the West', 1938
Barratt, John, *Cavalier Generals*, 2004
Bence-Jones, Mark, *The Cavaliers*, 1976
Benecke, Gerhard, *Germany in the Thirty Years' War*, 1978
Campbell, John, *Histoire des Provinces Unies*, 1818

Campbell, John, *The Naval History of Great Britain*, 1818

Chotebor, Petr, *Prague Castle*, 1991

Everett-Green, M. A., *Elizabeth, Queen of Bohemia*, 1855 and 1909

Fergusson, Bernard, *Rupert of the Rhine*, 1953

Gardiner, Juliet (ed.), *The History Today Who's Who in British History*, 2002

Glete, Jan, *War and the State in Early Modern Europe*, 2002

Godfrey, Elizabeth, *A Sister of Prince Rupert*, 1909

Guthrie, William P., *Battles of the Thirty Years' War*, 2002

Hamilton, Count A., *Memoirs of Count Grammont*, 1965

Hauk, K., *Die Briefer der Kinder des Winterkoenigs*, 1908

Hibbert, Christopher, *The Court at Windsor: A Domestic History*, 1964

Highfill, Philip H., et al. (eds.), *A Biographical Dictionary of Actors, Actresses, Musicians, Dancers, Managers and other Stage Personnel in London, 1660–1800*, vols. 2, 4, 6, and 8, 1982

Hill, Christopher, *God's Englishman*, 1970

Hindle, John, *Prince Rupert's Drops*, 1993

Hornstein, Sari R., *The Restoration Navy and English Foreign Trade, 1674–1688*, 1991

Howarth, David, *Lord Arundel and his Circle*, 1985

Howe, Elizabeth, *The First English Actresses*, 1992

Huehns, G. (ed.), *Clarendon: Selections from 'The History of the Rebellion' and 'The Life by Himself'*, 1978

Hulton, P. H., *Prince Rupert, Artist and Patron of the Arts*, 1960

Hutton, R., *The Royalist War Effort, 1642–1646*, 1982

Ingrao, Charles W., *The Habsburg Monarchy, 1618–1815*, 2000

Jones, J. R., *The Anglo-Dutch Wars of the Seventeenth Century*, 1996

Kitson, Frank, *Prince Rupert: Portrait of a Soldier*, 1994

Kitson, Frank, *Prince Rupert: Admiral and General at Sea*, 1998

Klima, Arnost, *Economy, Industry and Society in Bohemia in the 17th to 19th Centuries*, 1991

Kroll, Maria, *Sophie, Electress of Hanover*, 1973

Lewis, John, *May It Please Your Majesty*, 1996

Lyons, Sir Henry, *Royal Society, 1660–1940*, 1944

Mackworth-Young, Robin, *Windsor Castle*, 1983

Maclean, Gerald (ed.), *Culture and Society in the Stuart Restoration*, 1995

MacLeod, Catharine, *Painted Ladies: Women at the Court of Charles II*, 2001

Marshall, Sherrin, *The Dutch Century, 1500–1650*, 1987

Martin, Henri, *Histoire de France*, vol. 12, 1860

Morrah, Patrick, *Prince Rupert of the Rhine*, 1976

Morris, John, *Troubles of our Catholic Forefathers*, 1872–7

Nagel, Lawson C., *Prince Rupert's Bluecoats*, 1973

Newman, Peter C., *Empire of the Bay*, 1989

Newman, P. R., *The Old Service*, 1993

Nichols, J. Gough, and Bruce, J., *Wills from Doctors' Commons*, 1863

Nichols, Richard, *Robert Hooke and the Royal Society*, 1999

Oman, Carola, *The Winter Queen*, 1938 and 2000

Page, E. T., *Robert Blake, Admiral and General At Sea*, 1900

Payne Fisk, Deborah (ed.), *The Cambridge Companion to English Restoration Theatre*, 2000

Pearsall, A. W. H., *The Second Dutch War, Described in Pictures and Manuscripts*, 1967

Perrin, W. G. (ed.), *The Autobiography of Phineas Pett*, 1918

Pissarro, Orovida C, *Prince Rupert and the Invention of Mezzotint*, 1958

Polisensky, J. V., *War and Society in Europe*, 1978

Porter, Tim, *Prague: Art and History*, 1991

Powell, J. R., and Timings, E. K. (eds.), *The Rupert and Monck Letter Book, 1666*, 1969

Price, J. L., *The Dutch Republic in the Seventeenth Century*, 1988

Pursell, Brennan C., *The Winter King*, 2003

Robinson, H. M., *The Remarkable Activities of the Gentlemen Adventurers of the Hudson's Bay Company*, 1977

Rodger, N. A. M., *The Command of the Ocean: A Naval History of Britain, 1649–1815*, 2004

Rowlands, Guy, *The Dynastic State and the Army under Louis XIV*, 2002

Rushworth, J. (ed.), *Historical Collections*, 1721

Russell, Conrad, *The Causes of the English Civil War*, 1990

Scott, C., Turton, A., and von Arni, E. Gruber, *Edgehill: the Battle Reinterpreted*, 2004

Scott, W., *Constitution and Finance of English, Scottish and Irish Joint-Stock Companies to 1730*, 1910

Shelley, Roland J. A., *Mariner's Mirror*, 1939

Sophie, Electress of Hanover, *Mémoires et Lettres de Voyage*, ed. Dirk Van der Cruysse, 1990

South, Raymond, *Royal Castle, Rebel Town*, 1981

Spencer, Charles, *The Spencer Family*, 1999

Stimson, Dorothy, *Scientists and Amateurs: A History of the Royal Society*, 1948

Surtz, Edward (ed.), *Complete Works of Thomas More*, 1965

Tomalin, Claire, *Samuel Pepys: The Unequalled Self*, 2002

Trevelyan, G.M., *England Under the Stuarts*, 1938

Wagner, Eduard, *European Weapons and Warfare, 1618–1648*, 1979

Wanklyn, Malcolm, and Jones, Frank, *A Military History of the English Civil War*, 2005

Warburton, Eliot, *Memoirs of Prince Rupert and the Cavaliers*, 3 volumes, 1849

Wax, Carol, *The Mezzotint – History and Technique*, 1990
Weber, Kurt, *Lucius Gray, Second Viscount Falkland*, 1940
Wedgwood, C. V., *The Thirty Years' War*, 1938
Wedgwood, C. V., *The King's Peace*, 1955
Weld, Charles Richard, *History of the Mace given to the Royal Society*, 1846
Woodcock, George, *The Hudson's Bay Company*, 1970
Woolrych, Austin, *Battles of the English Civil War*, 1961
Young, G. M., *Charles I and Cromwell*, 1950
Young, Peter (ed.), *Military Memoirs: The Civil War*, 1967
Young, Peter, and Holmes, Richard, *The English Civil War*, 1974

INDEX

The index is arranged alphabetically on a word-by-word basis. Sub-headings are arranged in approximate chronological order where appropriate.

D0850695

A Practical Handbook for Ministry

A Practical Handbook for Ministry

From the Writings of Wayne E. Oates

THOMAS W. CHAPMAN, *Editor*

WESTMINSTER/JOHN KNOX PRESS
Louisville, Kentucky

Scripture quotations from the Revised Standard Version of the Bible are copyright 1946, 1952, © 1971, 1973 by the Division of Christian Education of the National Council of the Churches of Christ in the U.S.A. and are used by permission.

Scripture quotations marked NEB are taken from *The New English Bible,* © The Delegates of the Oxford University Press and The Syndics of the Cambridge University Press, 1961, 1970. Used by permission.

Book design by Publishers' WorkGroup

First edition

Published by Westminster/John Knox Press
Louisville, Kentucky

This book is printed on acid-free paper that meets the American National Standards Institute Z39.48 standard. ∞

PRINTED IN THE UNITED STATES OF AMERICA

2 4 6 8 9 7 5 3 1

Library of Congress Cataloging-in-Publication Data

Oates, Wayne Edward, 1917–
   A practical handbook for ministry: from the writings of Wayne E. Oates / edited by Thomas W. Chapman. — 1st ed.
      p.   cm.
   Includes bibliographical references and index.
   ISBN 0-664-21975-6 (alk. paper)

   1. Pastoral theology—Handbooks, manuals, etc.   2. Pastoral counseling—Handbooks, manuals, etc.   I. Chapman, Thomas W. (Thomas William), 1946–   .   II. Title.
BV4016.0173   1992
253—dc20   92–2317

Contents

Acknowledgments

Grateful acknowledgment is made for permission to reprint copyrighted material:

Chapter 1, from *Spiritual Dimensions of Pastoral Care,* edited by Gerald L. Borchert and Andrew D. Lester (Philadelphia: Westminster Press, 1985). Copyright © 1985 Gerald Leo Borchert and Andrew Douglas Lester.

Acknowledgment is made for permission to reprint material from the following copyrighted works by Wayne E. Oates:

Chapters 2, 3, 26, from *The Christian Pastor,* 3rd edition, revised (Philadelphia: Westminster Press, 1982). Copyright © MCMLI, MCMLXIV, W. L. Jenkins. Copyright © 1982 Wayne E. Oates.

Chapters 4, 5, 14, 22, 23, from *Pastoral Counseling* (Philadelphia: Westminster Press, 1974). Copyright © 1974 The Westminster Press.

Chapters 6, 29, 31, from *When Religion Gets Sick* (Philadelphia: Westminster Press, 1970). Copyright © MCMLXX The Westminster Press.

Chapter 7, from *Anxiety in Christian Experience* (Philadelphia: Westminster Press, 1955; Waco, Tex.: Word Books, 1971). Copyright, MCMLV, by W. L. Jenkins.

Chapters 8, 35, from *Your Right to Rest* (Philadelphia: Westminster Press, 1984). Copyright © 1984 Wayne E. Oates.

ACKNOWLEDGMENTS

Chapters 15, 16, 17, from *Confessions of a Workaholic* (New York: World Publishing Company, 1971). Copyright © 1971 by Wayne Oates.

Chapters 9, 32, from *Your Particular Grief* (Philadelphia: Westminster Press, 1981). Copyright © 1981 The Westminster Press.

Chapter 10, from *Convictions That Give You Confidence* (Philadelphia: Westminster Press, 1984). Copyright © 1984 Wayne E. Oates.

Chapters 11, 12, from *On Becoming Children of God* (Philadelphia: Westminster Press, 1969). Copyright © MCMLXIX The Westminster Press.

Chapters 13, 18, from *The Bible in Pastoral Care* (Philadelphia: Westminster Press, 1953; Grand Rapids: Baker Book House, 1971). Copyright, MCMLIII, by W. L. Jenkins.

Chapters 19, 20, 21, from *The Revelation of God in Human Suffering* (Philadelphia: Westminster Press, 1959). © W. L. Jenkins MCMLIX.

Chapters 22, 24, 25, from *Protestant Pastoral Counseling* (Philadelphia: Westminster Press, 1962). Copyright © MCMLXII W. L. Jenkins.

Chapters 27, 28, from *The Religious Care of the Psychiatric Patient* (Philadelphia: Westminster Press, 1978). Copyright © 1978 The Westminster Press.

Chapter 30, from *Pastoral Counseling in Social Problems: Extremism, Race, Sex, Divorce* (Philadelphia: Westminster Press, 1966). Copyright © MCMLXVI W. L. Jenkins.

Chapter 33, from *People in Pain,* by Wayne E. Oates and Charles E. Oates (Philadelphia: Westminster Press, 1985). Copyright © 1985 Wayne E. Oates and Charles E. Oates.

Chapters 34, 36, from *The Struggle to Be Free* (Philadelphia: Westminster Press, 1983). Copyright © 1983 Wayne E. Oates.

A Note from the Publisher

We at Westminster/John Knox Press have had a long and pleasant and fruitful relationship with Wayne Oates. In 1951 we published *The Christian Pastor,* his first book with The Westminster Press. Forty-one years later, and now in its revised third edition, it remains in the active booklist of Westminster/John Knox Press. Through the years since that first book, Wayne has remained steadfastly a good friend, valued author, and trusted adviser for us. We are delighted to recognize in this special way the vital contribution that he has made to the life and ministry of many others through his writings.

It is particularly fitting that this book grew out of the Rev. Thomas Chapman's desire to share with others the valuable help he had found in the works of his former teacher. That desire to share is itself in keeping with the spirit that has informed Wayne Oates's writing and teaching. The selections here are chapters from his books that sound to Tom Chapman "as if written for today." We hope that making them available in this collection will be both a tribute to Wayne Oates and a new channel for his continuing support of the ministry of others.

Foreword

I am indebted beyond my ability to express my gratitude to Thomas Chapman for the prodigious amount of work he has done to produce this edition of some of my writings. I have had the privilege of knowing Thomas and Brenda Chapman for over a quarter of a century. We have stayed in close communication over these years. They know me in all my limitations and strengths, and he is uniquely qualified to edit this volume.

I have a strong need to introduce Thomas and Brenda to you as I know them. They are authentic products of the genius of Appalachian and rural culture. Thomas is from West Virginia and has faithfully not let the sophistication of colleges, seminaries, and clinical pastoral education obscure or obliterate this genius. After finishing Southern Baptist Theological Seminary with his Master of Divinity, Thomas did two years of residency in Columbia, South Carolina, one at the Baptist Medical Center and one at the Hall Psychiatric Institute. His and Brenda's mission was and is to extend a ministry of pastoral care to the people of Appalachia and rural Kentucky in terms of the unique genius of the people themselves. They have over these twenty years steadfastly refused to try to superimpose a whole alien culture on the people to whom they minister. They work within the idiom and valid customs of the territory itself.

For several years they worked with a psychologically sophisticated lay couple, Bill and Martha Wiglesworth of Cynthiana, Kentucky, in establishing a retreat center called Quiet Trails. Once they completed this, Thomas became the director of a program for the aging in Cynthiana. All the while, Brenda was carrying on her own ministry in early childhood education. She is an authority in her own right in this work.

From there they moved to a formal counseling service to the south of

Berea, Kentucky. The bureaucratic process involved in this was too much for these free spirits to abide. They set up a shoppe in the center of Berea where they served outstanding cookies and pastries along with tea and coffee. In this informal setting they met people and it became easy for people to converse with them about the happenings in their lives. This worked like a charm, but the sheer mechanics and labor problems of keeping a business going prompted them to sell the building and try something else.

At the present time Thomas serves in the role of Executive Director of the Association of Older Kentuckians and sees counsclees in the context of his deep relationships with churches and the people in the community around Berea.

During all this time Thomas and Brenda have lived disciplined lives of simplicity. They do not have their lives cluttered with a lot of this world's goods and the pride and circumstance of the prestige systems of life. When you meet them, you will sense immediately their depth, substance, and close touch with reality. They practice a prudent poverty in order to have time for each other and for those to whom they minister. They are devout in the faith in Jesus Christ but fit none of the stereotypes of conventional church life.

They are affectionately related to people within the gates of the churches. However, the focus of their ministry is "outside the camp," where Jesus suffered and endured (Heb. 13:13). If you are ever in the enchanting village of Berea, Kentucky, the home of Berea College, I hope you can meet them. They seem not to be in a hurry but are always eager for substantive conversation.

The selection and the arrangement of chapters from many of my books have a stamp of originality that supplies new meaning to materials I have written in the past. In 1974 I began writing in inclusive language. At the same time, I began writing in basic English rather than in the technical terms of academia. If any noninclusive language appears, please overlook it and say, "He's changed!" With a few exceptions, the wording of these chapters is substantially intact and as it was when first published.

I am especially grateful for the inspiration and encouragement of Westminster/John Knox Press in the production of this reader. This marks the forty-first year of my publishing adventure with this outstanding press and its staff.

Wayne E. Oates
Professor of Psychiatry Emeritus,
    University of Louisville School of Medicine
Senior Professor of Psychology of Religion,
    Southern Baptist Theological Seminary

Introduction

This volume has come about chiefly by the means most common to events and things happening around Dr. Oates: through the gifts of his hard work, faithful discipline, and keen insight. My contribution to this product has been minimal, but maximal has been the honor of being allowed to offer small points of suggestion for the selection of these writings for their contemporary message and timeless wisdom that Dr. Oates has tempered on the anvils of clinical experience, sound biblical evaluation, and personal integrity.

The conscious happenings that started the process leading to this publication began one night in April 1990 as Dr. and Mrs. Oates, and I and my wife, Brenda, sat in a reverie of comfort in a small inn in our town following a meal filled with laughter and hope. In that evening of discussion I expressed my concern about my inability to successfully ransack used bookstores to find secondhand copies of his books that were out of print. It was my intent to request him to encourage a publisher to reissue some of his writings. I had come to depend on many of them for my ministry among persons who have not had access to the halls of academic endeavors for the training of ministry and also with those persons who have such advantages but have not had sound counsel on the matters of pastoral care and counseling.

During that evening the concern expressed by Dr. Oates was that his writing has always been geared to a particular time, setting, or issue that may not serve the present needs of Christian caregivers, whether they be in formal expressions of ministry or simply providing a cup of cold water in Christ's name.

I challenged him that, while whole works may indeed have served as a specific reference for a well-defined area, there were selected readings of individual chapters that read as if written today for persons seeking concrete advice about ministry in the trenches. An immediate thought was of my recent use of a chapter from *Pastoral Counseling in Social Problems: Extremism, Race, Sex, Divorce.* I had pointed out the chapter to a minister who came to me to unburden himself about his involvement in a racially tense situation in his town. He was seeking to find guidance for what his role should be as a minister who also was dependent on his congregation's support. He was worried that taking the stand he believed in would bring a slow, but effective, campaign to remove him from his church. It was a chapter that is now in this volume, "Pastoral Counseling and the Prophetic Task," in which he discovered a keen sense of direction and purpose for facing the challenge of the moment.

Over the past twenty years there have been hundreds of situations like this, where the answer to persons' struggles in ministry was met with my response of—in good Kentucky language—"reaching" them a copy of one of Dr. Oates's books for their library or home. In doing so, I knew that the readers, whatever their educational level, would neither be "spoken down to" nor "spoken up to" but would be led to discover the power of their own skills and encouraged in their battles for hope and identity.

I was also unable to shake from my mind the belief that it was important to have my college class read and evaluate *The Christian Pastor,* as I knew seven of the students in that class were to go directly into the ministry from college. I knew they would need the straight advice of someone like Dr. Oates for surviving their first years of ministry.

In that particular evening in Berea we moved on to other things our souls needed to say, but the thought kept returning to me that someone, preferably Dr. Oates, should take the time and effort necessary to select, edit, and publish at least a few selections of the out-of-print writings of Dr. Oates so that I might once again be able to place in the hands of the student, the minister, or the layperson a foundational practical reference for ministry. Of greatest presence in my mind were those many ministers in rural areas who may, or may not, be of a less educated background than their urban counterparts but for whom the desire to learn, grow, and serve Christ is equally strong.

Later in the summer of 1990 I wrote to Dr. Oates on another matter but included once again my belief in the need for the publication of several of his earlier works. In my thinking on this subject I knew of Dr. Oates's long association with, and long appreciation of, The Westminster Press, which is now Westminster/John Knox Press. In my letter I offered the idea that it might be a good place of beginning to select chapters from works published by Westminster/John Knox. I knew that this would eliminate such important and influential works as *The Psychology of Religion, Nurtur-*

ing Silence in a Noisy Heart, and over twenty other volumes, but it was the books presented by Westminster/John Knox to which I most often turned for guidance for myself and others.

In response to my letter, Dr. Oates wondered with me what such a volume would look like and indicated that he would welcome the chance to look over what I had in mind. With great joy I threw myself into the task of reading all of his books published by this press. From this process I felt as if certain chapters presented themselves to me, rather than that I selected them. The problem was not finding key chapters to include but knowing which ones to eliminate.

At the time of this initial selection it seemed that these chosen chapters were in natural groups of subject matter, so I let them lie where they fell. I finally gathered up the whole bunch, put them in a binder, and shipped them to Dr. Oates. It was my desire for this to serve only as an example of what *could* be done, not what should be done.

Dr. Oates then sought the advice of his editors and friends at Westminster/John Knox Press. They were supportive of this idea and recognized the need for such a work on merits far beyond my personal desire for a handy tool in my own ministry.

The overwhelming matter for me is that, except for minor changes in language, what has come forth as A PRACTICAL HANDBOOK FOR MINISTRY is essentially in the form of that bulky binder I sent through the mail to Dr. Oates. He suggested the inclusion of the chapter entitled "Pastoral Counseling as Self-Encounter" from *Protestant Pastoral Counseling.* It is a piece about which he has received a large number of responses from ministers as a significant aid to their work.

It was the insightful wisdom of Walter Sutton of Westminster/John Knox Press that it was essential to include Dr. Oates's groundbreaking contributions in introducing the concept of the "workaholic" in his *Confessions of a Workaholic.* It is also the fine hand of Mr. Sutton that guided this whole endeavor to completion, so that now it has been placed in the hands of the reader.

This work is but one small piece of joyful history for me since I first encountered Dr. Oates while I was a student at the Southern Baptist Theological Seminary in Louisville, Kentucky. I first found myself talking to him as my teacher in the context of dealing with the death of our only child. It had been a practical conversation in regard to the difficulties created by this grief in the midst of a finals period. That conversation, however, gave change to my sense of direction in life. Dr. Oates did not become my guru, a saint, my counselor, or anyone beyond an intriguing person who was unusual to me in his speaking to the real world in which I lived.

Over the years he has been there in places and times where his presence has meant much to me. Wayne Oates doesn't impose himself on others, but he does allow them into his own world when he can. He has sustained me in letters that have come in those moments when a letter was needed. Maybe it was simply an article from a journal, a story he had heard, or something quickly written on the corner of a memo. In this ministry of letters I am only one of thousands who have shaken with anticipation on finding one of his envelopes stuffed among other mail in the mailbox.

It is this power that comes through to the reader of the writings of Dr. Oates. A more proper title for this work may be, "Letters to Those on the Frontlines of Ministry." Many times I have wished that persons in ministry whom I knew could correspond with Dr. Oates on a matter of ministry with which they were struggling. In this volume these persons now have some of his letters and they speak to the heart of his work.

Brenda and I will never get around to communicating to him effectively what he has meant to us, and I guess that is okay. Those of us who are of certain religious persuasion know that God is the only one who can do this for us, so we tell God as often as we can to keep an eye on him and those whom he loves.

I do have a small understanding of what it is that is the *essence* of Wayne Oates for me. It is fine that he is a world teacher and significant contributor to the great psychological and spiritual repair of the human spirit, but for a long time I wondered why he should remain of interest to me out here as I wandered around in the wilderness trying to stumble through this life without doing too much harm to those into whom I bump while on my way.

A small answer has been with me for a few years. While ferreting out a used copy of Dr. Oates's *When Religion Gets Sick* from the back shelves of an old bookstore, I picked up a copy of *The Death of the Great Spirit: An Elegy for the American Indian,* which was written by Earl Shorris and published by Simon & Schuster in 1971. When I reached page 9 of the volume, I discovered a great smile making its way from somewhere inside me toward my face for having found an explanation of what I had known affectively for many years.

In this book, Mr. Shorris writes of a period in which he was living among the Oglala Sioux in South Dakota. During this period of research and writing, he had taken along his eight-year-old son to live with him for a week. In his preface, Mr. Shorris closed an observation with words that spoke for me the substance of the ministry of Wayne Oates.

In part, what the author wrote was this:

> I was prepared for something quite different [in how he and his son should be treated]. We were strangers, representatives of the people

who had made war on the Indians for three hundred years and now hold them in poverty and subjugation. I could not imagine either their capacity to forgive or their fondness for children. Nor was their warmth for him shown in an expected way. He was not physically embraced, as in the academies of group joy and therapy. *They let him be a human being; they gave him his dignity. And he basked in the safety and comfort of it.* (Italics added.)

The gentle touch of Wayne Oates in my own life has been his allowing me to be a human being with him. He has allowed me dignity when I had little of it. When I was fearful, he pointed out to me courage I did not know I had. I believe that in these selected writings you too will experience the discovery, not of the wisdom of Wayne Oates, but of the joy and comfort of being pointed the way to your own dignity and life where you will bask in the safety and comfort of your own identity in the service of Jesus Christ.

Thomas W. Chapman

Berea, Kentucky

Part One

THE MINISTRY OF THE CHRISTIAN PASTOR

1

The Power of
Spiritual Language
in Self-Understanding

In the Yahwist's earthy and unblushing account of the creation we do not have to rack our brains to grasp what the author is getting at. We are shown a simple but exquisitely tender picture of God personally leading animals to the man and waiting expectantly to see what he would name them (Gen. 2:19). The gift of the *ability* to speak, to use language to *name* the animals, symbolized the man's power over them. The power to name the animals is only the beginning. We are given the ability to name actions and thoughts with verbs and ideas, to put our feelings into words and pictures. In the process of doing so, we make decisions as to who we are, to whom we belong, what we are doing, and where we are going in life. We make covenants, we break covenants, and we remember covenants with the words we have used to describe them.

Language therefore is powerful as we walk in the garden of life in the cool of the day and try to hide from God or as we confess our sins to each other and to God in order that we may be healed (Gen. 3:8). Language is also the mechanism of confusion as we compete with each other in building towers of ambition, destroying the unity of a "whole earth" with "one language and few words" (Gen. 11:1). The Lord God confuses the language given to us. God scatters us over the face of the earth. We leave off building because we do not understand each other's speech (Gen. 11:7–8).

In this volume devoted to the state of the art of the pastoral care of the sick and the well, the broken and the whole, those who mourn and those who celebrate, I want to focus on the power of language—both verbal and nonverbal—to heal and to hurt, to break apart and to bind together, to comfort and to condemn, to celebrate and to make jealous. Language energizes our self-understanding. We do these ministries in a

3

world that is confused. Strident rhetoric struts in its masquerade of understanding. We do not have a common international language, a common interchurch language, or a common interprofessional and interdisciplinary language. We are not a world with "one language and few words" (Gen. 11:1).

Historically, our task as pastors therefore has been and will continue to be one of translation and interpretation as we help persons, as Charles Gerkin says, to grasp and put into effect the intention of God in the long sweeps of persons' life stories. We are, Gerkin says, "listeners and interpreters of stories."[1] This requires language, a common language at that. Consensual validation in speech calls for a meeting in words. John Wycliffe (1320?–1384) determined to translate the Latin Vulgate into the English tongue for use by the common people. He began the process of providing a common language for the English people. Before his time they spoke a far larger number of different dialects than afterward. William Caxton (1422?–1491) translated French stories about Troy, Aesop's fables, and Cicero. He set up his own press and published Chaucer's *Canterbury Tales.* Before he could do so, however, he decided for himself what precisely "he meant by the 'English' language," for there were "almost as many dialects as there were counties in England."[2] Then came the King James Version of the Bible, which, as Daniel Boorstin, the Librarian of Congress, says, shaped and invigorated the English language. He also says the King James Version is perhaps the only literary masterpiece ever written by a committee. Shakespeare (1564–1616) wrote his major works in the same period. The powerful spirituality of these shapers of the English language gave English-speaking persons a common identity, an awareness of selfhood, and a means of communion and commerce with and concern for each other.

This heritage has been ours as Americans. The power of biblical and Shakespearean English has been our means of understanding ourselves and each other until the middle of this century. The wholesale branding of spiritual language as unintelligible God talk, the increasing secularization of American education, the severing of technological education from the humanities, and the intensive specialization of professional education—particularly theological, medical, and legal education—however, have shattered the English language itself into as many dialects of sophistication in the helping professions as there were dialects in England before Wycliffe's translation, Caxton's work, the King James Bible, and Shakespeare's writings. We are a people "without one language and few words." We leave off building a common self-understanding of our spiritual selfhood, of our healing in time of suffering, and our redemption in the face of our mortality and death.

Therefore you and I as theologian-pastors once again face the responsibility of translating the dialects of the secularized value systems of the behavioral sciences into the wisdom, words, and power of the good news of God in Jesus Christ. This translation is not quid pro quo, tit-for-tat rendering. For example, psychologists and psychiatrists, such as Erich Fromm, make much of self-love as the measure of love for others. They occasionally think to quote Jesus as a teacher of this idea. So he was. But that is not the highest measure of the love of others that Jesus taught. He said, "Greater love has no [person] than this, that a [person] lay down his [or her] life for his [or her] friends" (John 15:13). Furthermore, he said, "A new commandment I give to you, . . . even as I have loved you, that you also love one another" (John 13:34). Every good translation has a built-in interpretation that is true to the thing-in-themselves being translated. Therefore the Christian pastor who disciplines himself or herself has as much to share with as to receive from the psychologist and the psychiatrist.

In order to make concrete what I have said thus far I want to take the concepts of temptation and sin, as we perceive them in the Judeo-Christian scriptures, and translate them back and forth with psychological and psychiatric concepts of unacceptable and socially maladaptive behavior. Doing so has specific rewards for you and me as pastors of persons who disburden to us their complaints before God.

For as Luther said, one reason why Protestants are opposed to the Catholic confessional is that they don't *want* to make confession. But as Calvin commented, "Let every believer, therefore, remember that if in private he is so agonised and afflicted by a sense of his sins that he cannot obtain relief without the aid of others, it is his duty not to neglect the remedy which God provides for him—viz. to have recourse for relief to a private confession to his own pastor." He further says that "confession of this nature ought to be free so as not to be exacted of all, but only recommended to those who feel that they have need of it."[3] Such translation gives us a larger repertoire of responses to persons for whom the "shorthand of grace" is a closed book, as Scott Peck calls the great Christian words of reconciliation, redemption, and sanctification. For many respond to these words as the "same old stuff," as clichés that we say because we are supposed to say them. A wider choice of idiom has more chances of being heard.

Furthermore, such translation helps us to work more effectively with other professionals in our mutual care of persons. At the same time, we can establish a spiritual community with them, many of whom were reared in the Judeo-Christian faith but have been amputated from it by the confined straitlacedness of family, home churches, and synagogues, and by the secular humanism of their educations. The choicest reward, however, is that

5

pastor, parishioner, psychologist, and psychiatrist have new access to the power of spiritual language in our understanding of ourselves and each other. Thus, we can more faithfully do the works of love toward each other in a common language of the grace of God in Christ.

TEMPTATION

First, let us attempt a translation of the Christian understanding of temptation. We of the free-church tradition—Baptists, Methodists, Disciples, for example—have equated temptation with sin. However, Jesus was tempted in all points as we are, yet without sin. So—there must be a difference between the two. Yet in conventional wisdom the thoughts of anger, lust, or envy are the same as the acts. Dietrich Bonhoeffer says that "temptation is a concrete happening that juts out in the course of life."[4] Temptation, however, is a universally human experience either ignored or misinterpreted.

Temptation as Defense Mechanism

The psychologist and the psychiatrist have largely secularized the modern interpretation of temptation with their elaborate descriptions of the defense mechanisms of projection, reaction formation, and fantasy formation. Projection is seeing our own faults in others rather than in ourselves. It is overtaking a brother or a sister in fault *without* looking to ourselves lest we are also being tempted. Reaction formation is the "Mr. or Ms. Clean" syndrome of vigorously acting one way in order to keep from doing just the opposite. Nietzsche described it when he said our contempt is the sidelong glance of our envy. Shakespeare put it well when he said, "[He] doth protest too much, methinks." Jesus put it best when he spoke of blind guides who strain at gnats and swallow camels (Matt. 23:24).

Fantasy formations get at one of the major themes of temptation in Christian teaching. Fantasy formation, psychiatrically speaking, is a mental substitute for action, a dreaming state while awake, the high imagination, for example, that one is now a king and then a slave, that one is exempt from death, that one is an exception to all rules of life, both old and new. These childish feelings of omnipotence "sicklied o'er" the path of action "with the pale cast of thought," as Shakespeare described it. One does not actually sin but only thinks about what it would be like to do so. Thus he becomes what Nietzsche called the "pale criminals" who, he said, "possess their virtue in order to live long in a miserable ease."[5]

Jesus' word "blind" describes precisely these thought processes of projection, reaction formation, and fantasy formation. The person does not know consciously what he or she is up to. Yet these processes use up energy just the same and can "burst open," as Kierkegaard was fond of saying, into mindless and bizarre actions which only lamely deserve the name of being good, clean, honest sin. They are blind and unconsciously driven actions. They are the state of sin "couching at the door," as God said to Cain. "Why are you angry, and why has your countenance fallen? If you do well, will you not be accepted? And if you do not do well, sin is couching at the door; its desire is for you, but you must master it" (Gen. 4:6–7). Self-understanding comes from *knowing* what you are thinking and doing what you purpose to do under God, not being drawn blindly by your unknown fantasies. As Socrates prayed, "O Lord, give me beauty in the inner person, and may the outward person and the inward person be at one." Only God can really bring this to pass. The psalmist's prayer says it best: "I hate them with perfect hatred; I count them my enemies. Search me, O God, and know my heart! Try me and know my thoughts! And see if there be any wicked way in me, and lead me in the way everlasting!" (Ps. 139:22–24).

Temptation as Response to Abandonment

Yet these are not the most life-threatening conceptions of temptation shared in the different languages of the Christian faith and contemporary psychiatry. The most lethal disorder with which psychiatrists deal is clinical depression. The person so afflicted often dies by suicide. The person is clutched by dreadful unspeakableness, an overpowering sense of being helpless in the face of the terror of his or her desolate orphanhood in a cold, gray, relentless world of no options for living. Often such persons will tell us that God has forsaken them, that the spirit has left them, and that they have committed or are about to commit the unpardonable sin. One such man, when I asked him what his greatest temptation was, said, "To kill my whole family and myself."

Dietrich Bonhoeffer is the great translator of this understanding of temptation into the language of the Christian faith. He says:

> This is the decisive fact in the temptation of the Christian, that he is *abandoned*, abandoned by all his powers—indeed, attacked by them— abandoned by everybody, abandoned by God himself. His heart shakes, and has fallen into complete darkness. He himself is nothing. The enemy is everything.[6]

Bonhoeffer quotes Ps. 38:10: "My heart throbs, my strength fails me; and the light of my eyes—it also has gone from me." Yet the saving insight he quotes from Isaiah:

> For a brief moment I forsook you, but with great compassion I will gather you. In overflowing wrath for a moment I hid my face from you,

but with everlasting love I will have compassion on you, says the LORD, your Redeemer. . . . For the mountains may depart and the hills be removed, but my steadfast love shall not depart from you, and my covenant of peace shall not be removed, says the Lord, who has compassion on you. (Isa. 54:7–8, 10)

You and I are on pilgrimages of self-understanding as we exist before God; we seek to know ourselves even as we are known to God. This knowing we can best achieve by turning whatever cleverness we have inward upon ourselves. Along with the sense of humor that can laugh at ourselves, this cleverness helps us to face with courage our own fantasies and dark feelings of having been abandoned. Our own temptations are the obstacle course and drill field in which we learn, both biblically and psychologically, terms to discern reality, to represent reality, and to bring an inseparable comradeship to those who feel abandoned by people and by God. Thus God becomes good news to us and makes us good news to others.

SIN

Most of what psychiatrists and psychologists have to say about guilt refers to the experience of temptation, not sin. Sin is a relational and not just an intrapsychic experience. Sin is estrangement from God and from our neighbor, for whom we are responsible before God. David had sinned against Uriah, Bathsheba, and his child by Bathsheba who died at its seventh day. Yet he prayed to God: "Against thee and thee only have I sinned." His primary separation was from God. Yet, for the sin against Uriah, Bathsheba, and his son he felt acutely responsible to God. Karl Menninger asks, Whatever happened to sin? One thing that happened was the exclusion of God from our sense of responsibility for our actions. Secularization does just that. The secular sciences, however, still have humanistic assessments of human behavior which, when put into relationship to God, become translatable into Judeo-Christian concepts of sin. Let us examine several, not all, of these psychiatric and psychological assessments.

Complexes
Carl Jung speaks of this independent action of a part of the psyche against the total person as complexes. He says, "The . . . complexes . . . come and go as they please. . . . They have split off from consciousness and lead a separate existence, . . . being at all times ready to hinder or reinforce the conscious intentions."[7] András Angyal calls these "part processes" of the human spirit. They are to him "bionegativities" with the power to rule the whole life.

8

Plato said that sin is a rising up of a part of the soul against the whole. Treating the total person was Hippocrates' way of being a physician. The Judeo-Christian tradition teaches that the life is in the blood, that revelation comes through the normal processes of the human body, and truth is incarnated in human flesh of prophets and ultimately of Jesus of Nazareth. Illness results when any part of the whole organism begins to eat away at all the rest of the organism with no regard to its own place in the totality of the person's being. Plato did not call it illness. He called it sin, the violation of the whole by the part.

Jesus used a surgical metaphor to drive home the truth of the part against the whole of our beings. In one of the most difficult passages in Jesus' teachings, he said:

> If your right eye is your undoing, tear it out and fling it away; it is better for you to lose one part of your body than for the whole of it to be thrown into hell. And if your right hand is your undoing, cut it off and fling it away; it is better for you to lose one part of your body than for the whole of it to go to hell. (Matt. 5:29–30, NEB)

This metaphor is essentially a surgical figure of speech referring to the domination of the whole life by a sexual mania. Surgery is recommended. It is better to cut out sex than to be a sexual maniac. Anyone working in a rape relief center will nod her head yes. Some even justify male castration as a treatment. The psychotic patient likewise reads this text concretely, literally. He or she actually does pluck out the eyes or cut off the hand. One psychiatric contribution to the Christian perception of sin is the way persons avoid the larger issue of consecrating our sexual energies to God and the responsible care of the sexual partner by becoming overconcrete and literal about figures of speech. Jesus did mention straining gnats and swallowing camels. Paul did say that the letter kills but the Spirit gives life (2 Cor. 3:6). Hence, sheer peril accompanies being too allegorical, metaphorical, or symbolic with psychiatric patients. This particular passage from the New Testament can be deadly to some. When I hear a psychotic patient quoting it, I know the person will literally gouge out the eyes or cut off the hands if given a chance.

Sin as That Which Is Unfitting

In the classical Greek world, people had a verb (*dikaioō*) that indicated an attachment to what is fitting, right, fair, or orderly. The opposite was *adikeō,* which meant to do wrong. The adjective *dikaios* meant observant of customs, well ordered, and civilized. The Greeks' almost inerrant sense of line, proportion, symmetry, and beauty inheres in this concept. Psychiatric assessment today uses it regularly to identify what is appropriate and inappropriate, fitting and unfitting, in place and out of place. The common populace is much more harsh on inappropriate behavior than on infractions of the Ten Commandments.

The apostle Paul uses this concept of observing customs, of acting appropriately about the eating of meat offered to idols. In Rom. 14:14 he says, "I know and am persuaded in the Lord Jesus that nothing is unclean in itself; but it is unclean for any one who thinks it unclean." In 1 Cor. 10:23 he says, " 'All things are lawful,' but not all things are helpful . . . not all things build up." He put the principle of appropriateness into the larger ethical context of "building up" one's neighbor, being empathetic toward his or her sensibilities. Thereby he made simple, appropriate behavior an exercise in reverence for one's neighbor and for God.

Sin as Cowardice, Shrinking Back, Refusing to Grow

The developmental perspective of redemption and sin is both corporately and individually evident in the history of the Old and New Testament peoples. The psychological and psychiatric interpretations of health and illness stand on the understanding of persons either growing or regressing. These interpretations are translated to give a fresh approach to the life of love and faith before God.

The process of growth in different levels of maturity being put away in behalf of a higher one is the meaning of love in the Old and the New Testament. Children drink milk; adults eat meat (Heb. 5:11–14). When you are a child, you think and act as a child; when you are an adult, you put away childish things (1 Cor. 13:11). You are to put away the elementary things of the faith and "go on to maturity." Not to do so is sin. To do so takes faith. "Whatever does not proceed from faith is sin" (Rom. 14:23). The opposite of sin is not purity, perfection, or "compulsive, obsessional, nasty niceness," as Paul Adams so vividly puts it. The essence of sin is shrinking back, losing one's nerve, refusing to grow. These picture phrases are nonlegalistic conceptions of sin as the failure of nerve in the face of the demands of maturity. Faith is the courage to grow. As the writer to the Hebrews says, "Do not throw away your confidence, which has a great reward. . . . We are not of those who shrink back and are destroyed, but of those who have faith and keep their souls" (Heb. 10:35, 39).

Sin as Impaired Judgment

One of the concerns of the psychiatrist in assessing a patient's mental status is the quality of judgment the patient demonstrates. Is it impulsive, with no regard for time? Is it grandiose? Is it self-derogatory, resulting in self-immolating behaviors?

10

The conception of sin from classical Judaism and Christianity that is relevant here is that of "the fool." *Nabal* is the empty person. *Saral* is the thickheaded person. *Kesil* is the boastful, overconfident person most mentioned in Ecclesiastes and Proverbs. In the New Testament the *anoëtos* is the thoughtless person. The unwise person is the *asophos*. The *aphrōn* is the headless person (Thou fool . . .). The *mōros* is the slow of heart and dull-witted. These are all persons who are presumed to have average or above-average intelligence that they are not using. The feebleminded, the mentally retarded, are called *oligopsychos* and are to be treated tenderly and with compassion.

The Judeo-Christian classical tradition of sin lays great emphasis upon the use of the intelligence, for the mind of man is the candle of the Lord to be used with diligence, reverence, teachableness, and care. In pastoral care you may be asked, "Do you think what I am about to do is good or bad?" You can say, "I would prefer to ask, 'Is it wise or unwise? What kind of wisdom does each alternative have? In short, is this or that action foolish? Which has the most sense? God gave you a good intelligence and foresight: how do you use these gifts in this situation?' "

Sin as the Bondage of the Law

The revolt of the New Testament era, led by Jesus of Nazareth, was sparked by the excessive weight of the bondage of religious control, ritual, and ethical hypocrisy. The law of Moses was initially devised for the health, ordering, and well-being of persons. Much of it was built around sheer survival needs in the austere desert country of Palestine and the Sinai Peninsula. Contrary to eras of the past, such as those of Josiah, Isaiah, Jeremiah, Ezekiel, and others, no real internal reform was even in the distant future. Religion became a compulsive binding force that was rigidly enforced by a theocratic hierarchy. Some religious authorities exercised both religious and political force in the lives of people. The kind of ritual blindness of which Freud spoke in the late nineteenth- and early twentieth-century Vienna was mild in contrast to it. Little wonder is it that Harry Emerson Fosdick said that what Freud called religion Jesus called sin.

This weight was bound upon the people by the ecclesiastical power figures. Jesus said these power figures lived in kings' houses and wore soft raiment. They bound heavy burdens and did not lift a finger to help people bear them. Religion was a business, not even a form of entertainment, as, for the same reasons, it often is today. Jesus invited people who were outcasts to come to him. He extended forgiveness, love, acceptance, and healing to them. He said, "Come to me, all whose work is hard, whose load is heavy; and I will give you relief. Bend your necks to my yoke, and learn from me. . . . For my yoke is good to bear, my load is light" (Matt. 11:28–30, NEB).

11

The yoke of which Jesus spoke was not a day's work for bread to eat. It was the demand of the professional religionists that was destroying their lives. It was the same yoke of which Paul spoke to the Galatians. He taught them a way of life that revealed God as a God of unconditional acceptance, love, and forgiveness. He had taught them that redemption which comes from faith of a person who is willing to learn, to grow, to change into a mature person. They wanted to go back to the new moons, sabbaths, the rules, the regulations, the compulsive security operations of their past. He said, "For freedom Christ has set us free; stand fast therefore, and do not submit again to a yoke of slavery" (Gal. 5:1).

Yet the raison d'être for having a serious rather than a perfunctory approach to pastoral counseling in the care of the psychiatric patient today is that about 17 percent of our patient population suffers from this kind of bondage to a life-threatening kind of religious burden. Our task is to use things both old and new from our good treasure to make faith in Christ a source of power, not a legalistic reinforcement of the sick religion on which they have been reared. Psychiatrists and ministers are at the point now of ceasing to write about whatever became of sin and starting to ask whatever became of forgiveness and creative refusal to give up on people.

Sin as Idolatry

Another classical conception of sin relevant to the care of psychiatric patients is that of sin as idolatry. Psychiatry, however, has no valid equivalent for the translation of idolatry into a therapeutic sense. The very idea of idols implies the criterion of the one true God. A purely secular professional represses the idea of the Transcendent into his or her unconscious. This is not to say that all professionals are purely secular. Many are highly informed religious believers. Here, however, is where the Judeo-Christian faith has a basic contribution to make. A patient or a physician does not believe in God, let us say. Then we must ask, "What *kind* of God is it that you do not trust or believe?"

Paul Tillich defined idolatry well when he called it absolutizing the relative. Any relative value, person, cause, possession, or such can take on absolute value to a person. Such people feel that without this particular value their world ends, they cease to be a person, they are a "zero," they do not exist. Persons who have invested all their emotional resources in a spouse fall apart when death, divorce, or defection takes that person from them. Persons whose work is the sum total of their existence tend toward suicide when they find themselves in an unbearable cul-de-sac on that particular job. Parents whose world orbits around a particular son or daughter soon find that they themselves are a vital part of the son's or daughter's real pathology. In such instances they, for all practical purposes, are idolaters.

12

I spoke several years ago with a woman whose marriage had collapsed in divorce. I asked her whether her husband had been an idol to her. Her reply the next day was that her husband had not become an idol but that the institution of marriage had, and without the status of being married, she was a nonperson, her life had no validity, she did not want to live. One can see a tiny shaft of light as to what was wrong with the marriage. A husband is more than a means to keep an institution of marriage intact; certainly a wife is. Marriage, like the Sabbath, was made for persons and not persons for the marriage.

Therefore pastoral counseling is somewhat iconoclastic, especially when psychiatric categories become burdens laid upon the backs of persons, with no one to lift a finger to help them bear them. These categories we use can easily become a yoke of bondage, just as other religious rituals and prescriptions. They can become vested interests of power, idols in themselves. They can prompt the necessity for a return again and again of a Spirit that offers a yoke that is easy and a burden that is light, a faith imbued with joy.

Sin as Self-Elevation and the Destruction of Creation

Another profound concept of sin is self-elevation, or hubris, and its consequent assumption that you or I am to take God's place. It, too, finds little conceptual base in the behavioral sciences. Here again the Christian can make contributions to the behavioral sciences. The alienation of persons from God comes by their intention to put themselves in God's place. Erich Fromm provides us with a historical study of this in his book *You Shall Be as Gods*. The philosophical grasp of the demonic is right here. In the Promethean will, man steals fire from heaven and is excommunicated. Lucifer pulls a power play in heaven and is thrown from among the gods. Nietzsche was most honest about it: "There is no God! If there were, how could I stand it if I were not he?"

The critical issue in this concept of sin, however, is not that an individual tries to be God, although unwillingness to live within, understand, and enjoy the limits of being human is one way to go mad. The critical issue is when ways of life are developed that assume that we as creatures know better how our bodies personally and corporately can live than does the Creator. Thus we put pollutants into our bodies that shorten our lives. We use time, energy, and relationships in ways that doom us to failure. We develop an energy policy and insist on selling multimillions of cars to use more gasoline. The creation is diverted, perverted, converted, and reverted away from its original aim. Such is our self-elevation.

13

Sin as Missing the Mark

A most common meaning of sin is simply that of missing the mark—bad aim, low shot, cheap shot, poor shot, missing the mark. Behavioral sciences give little attention to psychological equivalents for this idea. "The mark" here has a backward and a forward meaning. We miss the mark of the intention of God in creation and therefore are alienated from ourselves and others as well as from God. We miss the mark of our own sense of calling and destiny and therefore lose our way and sense of direction in life. Helen Merrell Lynd calls this kind of feeling "shame" in her book *Shame and Identity*. Therefore we as therapeutic agents of healing find that the forgiveness of sins and the restitution of creation join hands with the healing of the total being of the person.

Thomas Merton describes missing the mark and hitting the mark well in his metaphor: "A tree gives glory to God by being a tree. For being what God means it to be, it is obeying God. It consents, so to speak, to God's creative love. It is expressing an idea which is God's and which is not distinct in essence from God, and therefore imitates God by being a tree."

Sin as Violation of a Covenant with God

One biblical understanding of sin has no translatable equivalent in the behavioral science that I can find; that is the transgression of an individual or small group within a fellowship of persons against the covenant that binds them together. A covenant is the spiritual vision and shared responsibility of a community for and to one another and to God. A covenant is a solemn promise before God made binding by a commitment in words and ritual symbolic acts. Christians are bound together by the new covenant of Christ's blood. The Lord's Supper is the ethical threshing floor for our motives either in tune with the covenant or in violation of the covenant.

Christian marriage is built on such a covenant, and this covenant is not to be a nonverbal covenant and certainly not a set of blind assumptions. To develop a shared wording of this covenant is the purpose of premarital counseling, wedding ceremonies, and marital counseling. Trust is vested in the keeping of these covenants. Distrust, suspicion, and alienation arise when they are broken. The covenant itself has a separate existence of its own as a regulator and interpreter of behavior. Sin is a violation of the substance and intent of these covenants. Keeping faith becomes the criterion of integrity, health, hope, and growth. Breaking the covenant becomes the measure of sin.

For this conception of sin, only the anthropologists and the experts in primitive psychiatry give us any inkling. Yet their discussions are, it seems to me, "arms distance" discussions. The scientist *studies* these things but does not include them in their own treatment plans. They are more or less

14

curios and museum pieces that pique the curiosity but do not affect the practice of therapy.

In this sense, the Christian community can be admonished to take itself more seriously and to be more articulate and redemptive in the exercise of its covenantal nature. Even among us as Christians, however, we ourselves have become so fragmented and secularized that we too are unconscious of our covenantal nature as we address the sins of the world.

Secular and sacred believers alike, we and the behavioral scientists stand together as sinners before whatever God we perceive as our ultimate concern in our loss of awareness of our essential covenantal nature as human beings in relation to each other. Alan Paton, in his poignant novel about South Africa, has a way to describe us. Writing about a dramatic moment in the life of a South African tribe, he says:

> Kumalo began to pray regularly in his church for the restoration of Ndotsheni. But he knew that was not enough. Somewhere down here upon the earth men must come together, think something, do something. . . . For who would be chief over this desolation? It was a thing the white man had done, knocked these chiefs down, and put them up again, to hold the pieces together. But the white men had taken most of the pieces away. . . . He looked at the counsellors, . . . and he saw too that they were frowning and perplexed, and that for this matter there was no counsel that they could give at all. For the counsellors of a broken tribe have counsel for many things, but none for the matter of a broken tribe.[8]

And neither do we.

NOTES

1. Charles V. Gerkin, *The Living Human Document: Re-Visioning Pastoral Counseling in a Hermeneutical Mode* (Nashville: Abingdon Press, 1984), p. 26.

2. Daniel J. Boorstin, *The Discoverers* (New York: Random House, 1983), pp. 521–523, quote on p. 522.

3. John Calvin, *Institutes of the Christian Religion,* trans. Henry Beveridge (Grand Rapids: Wm. B. Eerdmans Publishing Co., 1953), 3.4.12, pp. 544–545.

4. Dietrich Bonhoeffer, *Creation and Fall: A Theological Interpretation of Genesis 1–3,* trans. John C. Fletcher; and *Temptation,* trans. Eberhard Bethge; 2 vols. in 1 (New York: Macmillan Co., 1959), p. 98.

5. Friedrich Nietzsche, *Thus Spoke Zarathustra,* trans. R. J. Hollingdale (Baltimore: Penguin Books, 1961), p. 67.

6. Bonhoeffer, *Creation,* p. 98.

7. Carl Jung, *Modern Man in Search of a Soul* (New York: Harcourt, Brace & Co., 1955), p. 91.

8. Alan Paton, *Cry, the Beloved Country* (New York: Charles Scribner's Sons, 1948), pp. 229–232.

2

The Identity and Integrity of the Pastor

You as a pastor are justified by your faith relationship to God in Christ, to yourself, and to your faith community, not by the tasks you perform. Therefore this is a shift from the task-oriented, work-centered meaning of your existence as a Christian pastor to an identity-centered integrity.

The overall shift of emphasis between the Niebuhr, Williams, and Gustafson study of the ministry done in the middle 1950s[1] and that of Schuller, Strommen, and Brekke in 1980[2] reflects a shift both in the expectations that the laity have of ministers and in the ministers' own expectations of themselves. That shift is from a task-oriented group of functions and "doings" by the pastor to the integrity, personal commitment, and faith of the minister. They center upon you as a priest and a person. This study, *Ministry in America*,[3] places personal integrity as the second agreed-upon expectation of ministers across forty-seven denominations.

With clarity of identity and integrity of being, you as a Christian pastor do and do not do many things. *What* you do is not determined by the other-direction of the most recent demand laid upon you. Your functions are determined by your inner sense of identity and integrity or lack of it. The major thrust of your dialogue in prayer with God, in conversation with yourself and your family, and in interaction with your faith community of the church is, then, the clarification of your identity and the focus of your "personhood" under God. From this you draw your guidance as to the nature of your task. By means of this you resolve conflicting expectations of yourself by others.

You search for a unified perspective of your calling under God that issues in a joyous participation with the people whom you serve. If you are able to do your work well, refreshing strength must be afforded you from a

16

coherent vision of your identity. Instead, Christian pastors are often confused in identity. They seek to find the way between the divided camp of the contradictory social demands and personal ambitions that beset them, knowing neither who they are nor where they are going. A vision of his identity both challenged Jesus to lay down his life and at the same time gave him satisfaction that "the world knew not of." The vision must have been renewed daily in our Lord Jesus Christ through his worship in intimate communion with the Father, through his powerful interchanges with the expectations of his disciples, and through his responses to the shepherdless multitudes who sought his ministry. It can hardly be different for the Christian pastor today who, as undershepherd of the Good Shepherd, is an authentic person under God, not just a walking job description.

In 1956, Samuel Blizzard[4] consulted six hundred active Protestant ministers. They were asked to describe, from three different vantage points, their own self-image concerning whom they considered themselves to be. First, they were asked what they thought was *most important* in their calling; second, they were asked in which identity they considered themselves *most effective;* and, third, they were asked in which identity they were happiest and from which they received the *most enjoyment.* The following ranking of the six functional identities of the minister was found:

Importance	*Effectiveness*	*Enjoyment*
1. Preacher	1. Preacher	1. Pastor
2. Pastor	2. Pastor	2. Preacher
3. Priest	3. Teacher	3. Teacher
4. Teacher	4. Priest	4. Priest
5. Organizer	5. Administrator	5. Organizer
6. Administrator	6. Organizer	6. Administrator

Considerable internal contradiction prevailed in the self-images of these ministers. They felt that preaching was their most important function and that they were most effective at preaching. But they received more satisfaction from their work as a pastor, which they ranked next in importance and in personal effectiveness. Thus they probably allowed less time for preparation of sermons and neglected that which they, for one reason or another, felt was more important than pastoral care. On the other hand, their sense of effectiveness as pastors was less than that of preachers. Ranking fourth in importance and third in effectiveness and enjoyment was the work of teaching. The pastor's identity as a person of prayer and worship was third in importance but fourth in effectiveness and enjoyment. At the very bottom of the scale in importance, effectiveness, and enjoyment were organizing and administering the life of the church. The internal integrity of the pastor at that time was perplexed, confused, and frustrated, according to Blizzard's initial findings.[5] Though these findings are somewhat dated, they still are a helpful schema for assessing your identity in relation to your multiple tasks. A valuable and imaginative discussion is to be found in Seward Hiltner's *Ferment in the Ministry*.[6]

Blizzard sought some objective basis for measuring the actual decisions of the same group of ministers regarding what their identity is in fact and function as well as in their idealizations. He asked these ministers to analyze their use of time, as ministers, on ordinary working days. The use of time is one candid criterion of a person's internal sense of identity. In the same article cited with reference to the previous data, Blizzard published the following information on the ministers' use of their time. He combined the priest and preacher categories because of their close affiliation in the preparation and participation phases of ministerial work.

THE MINISTER'S WORKDAY

Rural: 9 hours, 17 minutes
Urban: 10 hours, 32 minutes

Administrator	8/20
Pastor	5/20
Priest	
Preacher	4/20
Organizer	2/20
Teacher	1/20

Average time per day spent in sermon preparation:
34 minutes (rural), 38 minutes (urban)
Stenographic tasks: 1 hour, 4 minutes

Blizzard's study revealed that the particular tasks the ministers in their own self-concepts valued least, felt least effective in performing, and received the least satisfaction from—that is, administration and organizing—occupied half of their time. Their identity as a pastor came more nearly to having the same place in their output of time that it did in their personal values, taking one fourth (five twentieths) of their time. The priestly, preaching, and teaching functions consumed the other fourth of their time. Teaching, as such, was the most neglected dimension, receiving only one twentieth of their time. Stenographic tasks occupied more time than did the teaching ministry of the pastors.

Blizzard was careful to note in his studies that these impressions were derived from the ministers themselves, not from their parishioners.

Charles Glock and Philip Roos of the University of California studied twelve Lutheran congregations in order to get the parishioners' view of how their ministers spent their time and what kinds of performance on the part of the minister received the greatest and least approval from the congregation.[7] Their study was based on 2,729 questionnaires received from a sample of the memberships of twelve churches. The persons were asked what two kinds of work they thought their pastor spent the most time on and what two kinds of work the pastor spent the least time on. The following table represents their replies.

PARISHIONERS' RANKING* OF TIME SPENT
ON EIGHT ACTIVITIES BY MINISTERS IN
TWELVE LUTHERAN CONGREGATIONS

| | Ranking | | | | | | | | |
| | Most Time | | | | | Least Time | | | Mean |
Activity	1	2	3	4	5	6	7	8	Rank
Sermon preparation	8	2	2	–	–	–	–	–	1.5
Work for church at large	2	5	3	1	–	1	–	–	2.6
Attending church meetings	2	2	5	2	1	–	–	–	2.8
Office work	–	–	–	5	2	2	3	–	5.2
Giving people advice	–	–	1	2	6	2	1	–	5.0
Visiting nonmembers	–	1	1	1	1	5	3	–	5.4
Visiting members	–	2	–	1	2	2	5	–	5.4
His own recreation	–	–	–	–	–	–	–	12	8.0

*Ranks were based on scores for each activity computed by subtracting the number of "least" responses from the number of "most" responses and dividing by the total number of responses, "n." "Don't know" responses, which ranged from 27 percent to 52 percent of the parishioners in the twelve congregations, were omitted in the computation of this table.

Glock and Roos concluded that parishioners formed their opinions on the basis of *visibility,* that is, the importance of an activity was determined by the number of members who directly saw the minister in action at this particular kind of work. As a result, the parishioners felt that pastors spent most of their time at (1) sermon preparation, (2) work for the church at large, (3) attending church meetings, and (4) office work, in that order. They felt that the pastors spent the least amount of time in (1) personal recreation, (2) visitation of members, (3) visitation of nonmembers, and (4) giving advice and counsel to individuals, in that order. Glock and Roos compared this information with Blizzard's studies. They concluded that the wide margins of difference between the ministers' self-images and their actual reports of time use, on the one hand, and the parishioners' perceptions of the same things, on the other, reflect a serious failure of communication on the part of the church and its ministry to interpret to its membership "just what the ministerial role entails in practice."

Although Glock and Roos do not say so, the main avenue of communication between the leadership and the membership of the church, namely, effective teaching, occupies only one twentieth of the pastor's time. From these data the hypothesis can be drawn that the failure of communication may lie in the devaluation of a teaching ministry by both pastor and congregation. If pastors were involved in more give-and-take discussion with small groups of their church, possibly the level of communication could be effectually improved. Apart from some such face-to-face encounters in which minister and people can communicate on a common ground with two-way interchange, the hypothesis of Glock and Roos will hold unchanged: "The image of a profession will be largely informed by what is visible in the professional activity."

Glock and Roos then asked additional questions of the parishioners as to their evaluations of what their ministers ought to be doing with their time. The parishioners were asked whether they felt their pastor spent too much, too little, or about the right amount of time on each of eight functions. The study revealed that the majority of the parishioners were uncritical of their ministers. The following table represents the opinions of those who did express an evaluation:

INDEX OF PARISHIONER APPROVAL
OF EIGHT MINISTERIAL ACTIVITIES ACCORDING TO
PARISHIONER CONCEPTIONS OF TIME SPENT ON THEM

	Approval Score* for Parishioners Who Perceive Their Ministers as Spending:		
Activity	Most of their time on an activity	Least of their time on an activity	Neither most nor least of their time on an activity
Sermon preparation	.65	.05	.80
Work for church at large	.25	.55	.70
Attending church meetings	.45	.50	.55
Office work	.00	.85	.65
Giving people advice	.60	.10	.80
Visiting nonmembers	.80	.10	.65
Visiting members	.85	.00	.65

*Scores should not be interpreted as representing proportion of parishioners approving an activity. In fact, a majority of parishioners were uncritical of their minister. ["His own recreation" omitted by the authors of this article.]

Two activities—visiting members and visiting nonmembers—were most approved by the members. Although the members perceived their ministers as spending most of their time on sermon preparation, the members believed this to be of only moderate importance. These members considered attending church meetings and doing office work as of minimal importance or insignificant in their approval of their minister. When we compare these parishioner expectations with Blizzard's estimates of what ministers themselves consider to be most important, the expectations are almost identical. The preaching and pastoral functions take precedence in the minds of both the pastor and the parishioner. A positive conclusion can be drawn from these two studies: Delegate some of your clerical tasks. Reject the compulsion to attend *all* the meetings both in and out of the church. In turn, concentrate the time saved in this way upon a more effective teaching ministry of your own. Thus, you can create a situation in which the basic truths of the Christian faith can be communicated in depth and detail. Some of the failures of communication between you and your congregation could thus be overcome. At the same time, you would have natural group situations for developing lay ministers for preventing and remedying some of the problems that consume your energies in individual counseling work.

When you draw such a conclusion, however, your defenses begin to mobilize. You perceive yourself predominantly as a preacher. You think of yourself as most effective here, and, next to your pastoral work, you actually enjoy the pulpit ministry most. In your education and in the church at large, you have been both taught and encouraged to think of your ministry of teaching as something any willing layperson can do. You feel, therefore, unfaithful to your call to be a prophet if you do not strictly define your ministry to groups in the formal preaching situation.

These data suggest several pertinent ideas concerning the diffusion of your identity. The task of administration takes far more time than you feel is important, uses you most effectively, or provides you with the most meaning and satisfaction. Niebuhr's attempt to enrich this focus of the minister's identity by calling the minister a pastoral director really has not taken root since he first presented the concept in the middle 1950s. You as a minister are an "overseer" of a particular congregation. You are a shepherd and cannot divorce your pastoral ministry, in which you do get such real satisfaction, from your creative oversight of the fellowship of believers as a community. Contemporary systems analyses on concepts have much more to offer you than simply giving the task the name of pastoral director.

Again, your best strategy is to assert and activate your own identity as a teacher. If you are fortunate enough to have the additional services of an educational director, the duties of this person can be reshaped to include more actual teaching and less administrative and clerical work.

However, if your *pastoral* instruction as a Christian shepherd is activated, you can equip many laypersons to be pastors to one another. An effective perception of yourself as a teaching pastor enables you to develop an appropriate background for any of the things you preach from the pulpit. Two-way communication in teaching groups creates a healthy dialogue between the person in the pew and the message being preached.

A mistaken sense of prophecy pervades much of the contemporary ministers' conception of themselves as preachers. Many pastors directly identify themselves with Old and New Testament prophets and apostles in their forthrightness of utterance. However, pastors neglect to note that the system in which these prophets and apostles preached was an open, not a closed one. Rarely did they preach under the highly formal circumstances of the typical Sunday morning audience of today. They could be interrupted, asked questions, and disagreed with by their hearers. The conditions of prophetic and apostolic preaching were much more akin to the two-way group teaching situations of today. The pastors of today have neglected these opportunities and ruled them out of their working day to such an extent that little of their time is spent in this way. As a result, pastors attempt to prophesy in a preaching situation in which response, retort, and resonance are improbable, if not impossible. The members of the audience have no way of expressing their feelings except by compliments or by personal hostility, withdrawal from attendance of church, the use of the telephone at home, and personal head-knockings with the pastor. These reactions must, then, be dealt with through personal diplomacy. This consumes the time of pastors and leaves them with the feeling that they dare not speak their minds fully in the pulpit. The end result is insipid preaching and bored listeners who endure silently while the pastors have their say.

The point of suggestion here, then, is that the identity of yourself as a pastor can be integrated most effectively around your sense of being a teacher. The *Ministry in America* study indicates a high expectation of you that you have "clarity of thought and communication," that you be alert to the world around you, sensitively using a broad base of information to stimulate people to become thinking Christians, and to do so as a "service in humility, relying on God's grace," without seeking personal fame or deliberately agitating controversy. Teaching is a situation in which this can happen. You do not do all the talking, as in preaching, or most of the listening, as in counseling. Rather, teaching is a communication "halfway house" between preaching and counseling, providing background for and entrée into either preaching or counseling. Yet in Blizzard's earlier findings he discovered that only one in twenty-five ministers perceived himself or herself as being an educator, an identity around which all the other dimensions of the calling were integrated. Let us see how pastoral care as practiced by parish ministers can be focused in their identity as a teacher; also, how their work as a preacher and as a leader of worship can be similarly focused in their function as a "teacher come from God"; and finally, how their identity as an administrator and organizer can be focused in their identity as a teacher.

PASTORAL TEACHING AND THE
CARING FELLOWSHIP

The group life of the church as a teaching agency of the community is intimately related to the pastoral care and personal counseling that the pastor does. You as a pastor cannot relegate the teaching ministry of your church to assistants without doing violence to both your preaching and your pastoral relationship. The education that a congregation receives through the church school provides the background of understanding with which the people hear a pastor preach. This education serves as a front line of preventive defense against those conflicts which cause people to seek pastoral counseling. The reasons for this are not so evident and need clarification, however.

When you as a pastor take the personal problems of your parishioners seriously, you find yourself overwhelmed by the many individuals both within and without your congregation who seek help. You cannot possibly get to them all. You find yourself in need of arranging persons with similar difficulties and needs together in groups in order that you may serve them more adequately in those needs which can be dealt with on a group level. Also, they need to know and learn from one another. A large measure of their distress is caused by their isolation and loneliness in suffering. For instance, many pastors have discovered that a wholesome group life cushions the shock of retirement for older people and keeps them from becoming ingrown in their later years. Group work with and pastoral care of older people are complementary ways by which the church and you as a pastor minister to persons in later maturity. You need not choose between these two methods. You use both. This could be said also of the other age groups and interest groups of the church.

Again, the teaching ministry of the church gives you access to the families of the individuals who seek your counsel. The taproot of the unhappiness of the individuals with whom a pastor counsels is in their family relationships. A pastor spends great parts of each week in marriage and family counseling. To conduct such a program of pastoral care and personal counseling without an adequate curriculum in family life education, with which to prevent such difficulties and to do away with some of the need for counseling, is pastoral nearsightedness. The training of young people, not only in the dramatic story and ethical imperatives of the Bible but also in the preparation for and participation in Christian marriage, is an indispensable part of the pastoral care and personal counseling of a pastor.

Furthermore, an adequate teaching ministry provides both an inlet and an outlet for pastoral care and personal counseling. For instance, from two contacts with a discussion group on the subject "Learning Spiritual Values in Family Living" a pastor received three requests from individuals attending the group for counsel concerning their family problems. One was an impending divorce situation, another a case in which a marriage had been consummated under false pretenses, and another a family in which the presence of the parents of both the husband and the wife in the home was stifling the growth of the children. Likewise, in the same group were several couples with whom the pastor had already counseled in premarital guidance, two of whom had invited the pastor to perform their wedding ceremony. The fact that instructional groups serve as an inlet through which people may come to you the pastor for individual help and an outlet with which you can conserve the results of your personal counseling makes your own teaching ministry of primary concern to you. To neglect this center of your calling in the church or to relegate it to others without concern is to lose touch with one of the main sources of counseling opportunities.

Furthermore, you are largely responsible for the selection and equipping of lay leadership in the teaching ministry of the church. At this point your counseling function and your work as an educator converge most meaningfully. Whatever methods the churches of various denominations have for recruiting lay workers in the educational life of the church, one need remains constant: *these persons should be emotionally healthy and carefully instructed in addition to being willing to serve.* Religious work meets many inner needs of persons; relief from guilt, escape from home tensions and conflicts, relief from boredom, and other security needs. These needs, however, should be secondary to the welfare of the persons whom a Sunday school teacher seeks to guide. Quite often the parishioner who is most eager to gain or to retain a church office is the one least competent to do the work.

Therefore, choose leaders carefully and give close attention to the personal adequacy, emotional stability, and basic construction of persons who volunteer for a given task. This can be done tactfully through home visitation, personal counseling, and specialized groups taught by professionally skilled persons. I know of one church that consistently follows this practice, and the result has been a healthy church with a minimum of inner conflict and friction among its organizations.

Finally, the family life of parishioners and their group life in the church are psychologically and educationally separate facets of the same experience. The marital and parental happiness of the leaders of the church becomes a contagion for good and evil in the younger members who follow their patterns of living. Therefore you as a pastor need to work for the selection and training of leaders who have adequately succeeded as parents and as participating members of families. Such leaders can sponsor a strong curriculum in family life education. Healthy leadership and an adequate church school curriculum become bonds that tie the pastoral task and the educational work of a minister together in an inseparable union. You can bring new life and disciplined instruction into the whole life of the church if you use the time you spend in attending meetings and doing clerical tasks for preparation for and leadership of "equipping sessions" in which you yourself are the teacher.

However, one of the reasons why pastors do not do this is that they are ill at ease in small groups. They want a crowd. They are defensive about groups in which they do not do all the talking but are open to being challenged by varieties of opinions. They are more secure in the lecture-sermon situation than in a workshop group. But you can overcome these inhibitions. You can develop your skills and insights for small-group teaching ministries. When you do so, you have the instruments for releasing the powers of a congregational fellowship that the monotones of one-way preaching and the isolation of private counseling with individuals cannot touch.

PASTORAL TEACHING,
THE PREACHING MINISTRY, AND
PASTORAL CARE

The vitality of the small-group ministry provides a fellowship of people who know one another. You teach them how to care for one another and for those on the outside of their fellowship. The atmosphere created by these two-way communication groups makes your preaching ministry more than mere speechmaking. You become an articulator for the single-heartedness that the Holy Spirit has produced in the small groups. You have already dealt with heavily controversial subjects in situations where listeners can have their say. In the interaction between the members of the group and between the group and the leader, definite understandings and new insights have been developed. The combined witness and wisdom of the group as a whole can become the basis for your development of sermons. In turn, the sermons can be starters for new directions of thinking in the groups that you teach and lead. This gives you more freedom in dealing with controversial subjects. It provides a medium for the expression of feeling and opinion that may be contrary to your own. Such teaching groups are in themselves preaching opportunities in the sense of dialogue as over against the monologue of formal pulpit situations of preaching. On the other hand, the group members who listen to the formal pulpit sermon feel they have had a part in "the making of the sermons."

Contemporary preachers often find themselves in a complaining mood because, for instance, "they cannot preach what they know about the Bible" in the pulpit. They look upon their technical training in the historical method of biblical study, the literary approach to biblical interpretation, and the results of modern scholarship concerning the Bible as something they cannot communicate to lay people. They convey just enough of this knowledge to make both the congregation and themselves anxious, indecisive, and suspicious of one another. The pulpit situation provides them only twenty to thirty minutes a week in which to preach to the majority of the congregation. The lay-taught church school provides another thirty to forty minutes a week of instruction in the dramatic and moral truths of the Bible, with all too little attention to the context and basis for biblical interpretation.

Furthermore, as I have indicated in my small volume *The Bible in Pastoral Care,*[8] many of the personal problems of family conflict, sexual temptation and deviation, hostility, and community distress presented to the pastor in personal counseling reflect distinct misinterpretations of the Bible at one or more significant turning points in the counseling relationship. These misinterpretations amount to gross superstition at times. They represent the failure of the teaching ministry of the church in the clear communication of the word of God. Similarly, William Oglesby, in his book *Biblical Themes for Pastoral Care,*[9] has related the Bible to the broken relationships, wounds of loneliness and grief, and the need for forgiving and being forgiven that pastors meet in their pastoral care.

Thus the absence of an effective teaching ministry of the church and its pastor actually creates hindrances to preaching. On the other hand, some of the need for counseling grows out of the sheer ignorance and misinterpretation of the scriptures. The falling away of young people from the church and from the stability of the scriptures is just one of the many results of this lack of effective teaching. Therefore pastors who activate their identity as teachers of small, face-to-face groups where they "leap the gap" between their own education and that of their congregation in the Bible, theology, church history, Christian ethics, and pastoral care find a coherent center for both their preaching and their pastoral care. They will find a fresh, new kind of preaching in which they can be open, candid, and spontaneous with people. They will cease to curse the darkness of their people about the Bible. They light the candles of a teaching ministry. Even if at first they can get only two or three persons to take the time to be with them, these pastors have the leaven that may spread to the whole congregation.

More specific attention, however, must be given here to the interaction of formal preaching with the pastoral ministry to individuals and families. Historically, the renascence of concern with the intimate, personal ministry of a pastor to individuals in distress began with the emergence of a kind of preaching which Charles Kemp has rightly called "life-situation preaching." As early as the ministry of Horace Bushnell, there was a studied effort of ministers to begin with the human situation and derive the message of the pulpit from the dilemmas of their hearers. Bushnell preached such sermons as "Unconscious Influence" and "The Moral Use of Dark Things," which even now are used as models in homiletics classes. Later, Harry Emerson Fosdick became the main exponent of this kind of preaching and is said to have measured the effectiveness of his sermons by the number of persons who sought his personal guidance in the following week. Of course this was not new with Fosdick, for Jonathan Edwards had himself done much of his most effective work with individuals who sought him out after his sermons. This indicates clearly that this approach to preaching does not necessarily presuppose a particular kind of theology.

Vital contrasts distinguish the preaching ministry from the pastoral task. Elaboration of each of these distinctives will add strength to this meaning. The preaching ministry is a public one; the pastor's access to the crowd is emphasized. But the pastoral task is ordinarily a private and personal ministry, and the relative anonymity of the service is emphasized. This difference is accentuated when a parishioner fears that what has been said to a minister in private may become topics and illustrations for the minister's preaching in public. You may discover as you counsel with a parishioner that the person feels singled out in certain statements you may have made in a sermon.

Therefore, as preacher-counselor you do well to ask for the permission of a given individual before you refer in a public address of any kind to the person or to what the person has said. When you do refer to the person, it is better to do so in a two-way communication group where the person can respond if need be. But if the reference does happen to be in a formal, pulpit situation, then let it be done in such a way that the integrity and dignity of the person are enriched, not destroyed. For you to hold individual persons up for ridicule, disdain, or as "horrible examples" should be strictly forbidden, *tabu, verboten, interdict*—that is, unlawful in any language! The Bible and classical literature are replete with such bad examples. Use of acquaintances of your personal ministry in this way indicates laziness in preparation and ad-libbing in delivery. Therefore, before you make any reference to individuals, observe the rules of advance preparation, ask for their permission, and make reference in a way that will edify them, not ridicule them.

Furthermore, many people prefer to talk with a minister whom they do not see every Sunday and who does not know all their friends, rather than with their own pastor. This may be true even though these persons have no fear of or lack of confidence in their own pastor. The chaplain in the hospital observes this in remarks that patients make about their pastors. As one woman said, "I could never tell my pastor these things. He knows me too well. But I can tell them to a chaplain, because he is detached." The pastoral relationship, in its deeper reaches, requires a considerable degree of anonymity in order that the persons may be aided in the difficulties that matter most to them.

This calls for extensive cooperation among ministers of the same community in referring persons who are too close to them to other pastors who can maintain a more detached and objective relationship. It also necessitates a close cooperation between the parish pastor, physicians, and specialized pastoral counselors. In larger communities, pastoral referral centers and pastoral counseling centers have been and will continue to be established. Specialized help of skilled psychologists of religion and pastoral counseling is becoming a felt need in an exceptional number of communities. You can locate these by writing or calling the American Association of Pastoral Counselors: 9508A Lee Highway, Fairfax, VA 22031. The telephone number is (703) 385-6967.

The second distinction between the pastoral and the preaching situations is the time element. Pastoral work is difficult to control in terms of the extent of time needed for each individual and the number of persons who seek the pastor's help. Your pastoral care and personal counseling ministry can so encroach upon your time that you will have none left for anything else. This overloading becomes in turn a barrier to effective pastoral counseling. People will feel so guilty about taking your time that their qualms of conscience will prevent them from using wisely the time you do give them. Conversely, the time element enters again when you, pressed for the preparation of the sermon for Sunday, are interrupted by a person who needs immediate attention. You may have difficulty listening to the person's story. You may be tempted to preach to the parishioner what little of the sermon you have prepared.

Again, the preaching-pastoral relationship proposes a paradox in the approach you use to meet the needs of the same people. As a preacher, you approach their lives in terms of goals, ideals, objectives, and purposes for living in the kingdom of God. But in pastoral care and personal counseling, you approach each person not merely as one who is unswervingly loyal to the absolute ideals of Jesus but also as one who understands when people miss the mark of the ideals of Jesus. As a pastor, you have the wisdom of the serpents concerning the frailties of human nature and an affectionate tenderness that will "lift up the fallen." This gentleness grows out of the forgiveness you have received for having missed the mark yourself. Pastoral leadership casts its light in the arc of these two poles of influence: the devotion of a pastor to the absolute ideals of Jesus and the patience of a pastor with human imperfection. The preaching task is primarily that of challenging people with the distant and flickering but unquenchable lights of the City of God. The pastoral task is primarily that of being able to identify with people just as they are, "to sit where they sit," even in their "haunts of wretchedness" in the cities of persons "where cross the crowded ways of life." The two functions are coalesced in the worship of God as you learn to participate with your congregation in the processes of growth in the covenant of the loving ideals of Jesus.

Enough of the distinctions between your preaching function and your pastoral task have been named. However, some startling parallels between the two relationships ease the adjustment of these functions to each other. The similarities outweigh the difficulties.

The good preacher depends on the same laws of personality as does the good pastor for effectiveness. The dynamics of preaching, teaching, and healing are much the same as far as the pastor's relationship is concerned. For instance, in pastoral care and personal counseling, you must establish a "relationship of a trusted motive," before you can help the person. You must be able to put yourself in the place of the individual with whom you are counseling. In turn, that person must be able to identify with you as a pastor, that is, to trust your motives, appreciate your way of life, and even desire to be like you. The establishment of this rapport takes time and patient relaxation of suspicions and defenses of all kinds.

This is equally true of the relationship of a preacher to a congregation. A bond of honor and shared feeling transmits the message of a preacher to a people. Some pastors can establish this more quickly than others, but the sense of togetherness must be there before the sermon becomes a reality to the hearers. The congregation tests the reality of a person's utterance without planning to do so, and the sermon becomes an "I-Thou" relationship, a personal encounter involving both candor and comfort.

Preaching as a personal encounter becomes the careful and devoted management of a growing understanding between you and your congregation rather than merely an oratorical demonstration. The theology professor who has been a pastor and blended with a congregation finds occasional preaching in first one pulpit and then another to a group of total strangers to be a tasteless experience in comparison. Pastoral care and counseling lend feeling and meaning to preaching. Preaching becomes the spiritual preparation for counseling.

As such, the preaching of a sermon becomes an inlet into counseling with individuals, an important source of precounseling contacts. Also, the ministry of comfort and reassurance, instruction and interpretation, can often be done more powerfully through preaching than through individual counseling, because it is done in the presence of the larger community of worshipers. Furthermore, individuals can more easily accept or reject a given interpretation when they are in a group or crowd. On the other side of the pulpit, too, you can give guidance that applies to "all mankind" and carefully avoid being too stringent on a given individual. Having done this, you, in private conference with parishioners, can spend your time listening to their side of the story. Such a reciprocal relationship between pastoral care and preaching will go far in alleviating the feeling that many lay people express when they object to not being allowed to answer the preacher back or to ask a question. A listening pastor makes an understanding preacher.

The pastor who maintains a consistent counseling ministry will move in the direction of life-situation preaching. By definition, life-situation preaching "begins with life situations and is aimed at them. . . . It starts where people live. Such preaching must, of necessity, have a close relationship to pastoral work."[10] The characteristics of such preaching are fourfold: (1) the *interpretation* of human experience in the light of biblical truth rather than the exhortation of the people to the observance of certain moral precepts, as such; (2) the development of personal *insight into the motives of personal and group action* rather than the condemnation of this or that kind of behavior; (3) the *encouragement* of the congregation toward faith in God, in one another, and in themselves as means of gaining control over behavior that they themselves discover to be alien to the mind of Christ; and (4) the growth of a *sense of comradeship with God in Christ* and the changing of personality through this "transforming friendship."

Contrary to some opinion, life-situation preaching may be thoroughly biblical and even exegetical. However, the approach to the Bible itself is a life-situation approach. The studied effort of the exegesis is to reconstruct the "situation that was" at the time of the writing. The interpretation, however, is not simply paralleled with a similar contemporary situation-in-life. Instead, the timeless elements of both situations are identified and become the outline of the sermon. The end result is a meditative interpretation of scripture in the present tense. This was my intention when I wrote the book of sermons *The Revelation of God in Human Suffering*,[11] which was published in 1959. Similarly, Charles Kemp has edited a book of life-situation sermons entitled *Pastoral Preaching* (1963).[12] A more recent thesaurus of such sermons is *The Twentieth-Century Pulpit*, edited by James W. Cox (1978).[13]

Of course, certain aspects of the life-situation approach are immediately identifiable as "the psychological approach" to homiletics. Such an approach implies a *conversational, eye-contact, extemporaneous delivery* rather than a more impersonal, formal, and oratorical delivery. It rules out the histrionics and other appeals to the more superficial emotions. Yet, being united to the sense of touch, to sound, and to rhythm makes the message more concrete. It calls for personal inventory, a confrontation of the self, and a reordering of the deep emotions of family love and hate, vocational intention, and the fundamental desires that drive human action.

You as a preacher, through the processes of sympathetic imagination, empty yourself of your own frame of reference and take upon yourself the condition and cries of the people's inner lives. You seek to articulate their prayers for them. In so doing, you are their spokesperson before God as well as God's spokesperson before them. In this kind of preaching, prophetic and priestly functions are blended into one act of preaching. No artificial dichotomy separates these. For as a prophet at one and the same time you declare yourself to be a person of unclean lips and a person dwelling in the midst of a people of unclean lips. Therefore you can sit where they sit.

Naturally, life-situation preaching produces relief from a sense of guilt and rest from tension through the resolution of conflict. It stands over against the type of preaching that creates unrest through the introduction of conflict into the complacent mind and the development of a sense of guilt in people who are "past feeling" a given moral or spiritual value. As such, a sermon based on life itself qualifies as an act of worship in itself. As Seward Hiltner puts it:

> The preacher is a living human organism, as are the other people to whom the Word is also life and salvation. Preacher—Word—people: these are all alive. Discourse—Book—behavior: these are all, in a significant sense, dead because they are nonorganic. But life, the image suggests to us, is never to be apprehended with simple directness, alone and in itself. The order of the Word is "no angel visitants, no opening skies." It is, instead, through death to life, through the nonorganic to the organic, through the Book to the Living Word, through the three dead homiletical points to just possibly a receptive heart or two. Homiletically speaking, in the midst of life we are in death; and

only if we learn to tolerate death—a Book and not an angel, an idea and not just a feeling, a conviction and not merely a charitable impulse—can we approach life.[14]

WORSHIP: THE LIFEBLOOD
OF THE PASTOR

The relationship of a pastor to individuals, groups, and congregations undergoes a metamorphosis in the act of worship. Consciousness of the pastor's presence fades out and awareness of the real presence of God reaches its zenith. The quantitative differences of character between the pastor and those to whom the pastor ministers become as nothing as the eternal qualitative difference between all persons and God becomes more evident.

Worship, as Gaines S. Dobbins has said, is the "interruption of our daily routine" and our involvement in the transitory things of life "to recognize the supreme worth of God, to praise him for his goodness, to meditate on his holiness, to renew devotion to his service," and to sever our idolatries.[15] The act of worship therefore has a wealth of connotations for the pastoral task of the minister.

Informal worship, where two or three are gathered together in the spontaneity of the shared knowledge of the presence of God, is the true atmosphere of the face-to-face relationship of a minister to an individual. The reverent care of living persons is a type of worship in its own right. This has been the primitive foundation of many religions and, with all its limitations, is the extent of the worship of the vast majority of the people of the world. However, even in the Christian experience of worship, the reverence for God and the reverence for human personality are inseparable. The acute appeal of a suffering person is the medium of revelation most often promised by Jesus. "When did we see thee?" is the question of both true and insincere worshipers. "As you did it to one of the least of these my brethren, you did it to me" (Matt. 25:40).

Although the face-to-face ministry of a pastor to individuals should be, and often is, an Emmaus road form of prayer, it does not become such without personal discipline on the part of the pastor. The question regularly comes to a pastor: "To whom do you go when the worries of other people become too heavy for you?" The answer to this question in a pastor's private worship life is the beginning of your own response to "a serious call to a devout and holy life." As Thomas à Kempis said, "No man doth safely speak, but he that is willing to hold his peace. No man doth safely appear abroad, but he who can gladly abide at home, out of sight. No man can safely command others but that he hath learned to willingly obey." The transforming power of Jesus came through prayer and self-discipline, and you and I cannot expect it to be otherwise with us.

When you consider your interpersonal work of caring for people as a form of prayer itself, you find personal resources that keep your confidence in people strong, prevent you from losing patience with them, and undergird you with a steady calmness in the presence of acute pain and unhappiness. Without this sense of worship, you become threadbare in the wear and tear of the emotional tension in your task. Fatigue sets in, irritability increases, aggressiveness and defensiveness are the next to follow. In order to allay your own sense of guilt, you then become overconcerned and overprotective toward those to whom you minister. Consequently, you will spend more and more time with fewer and fewer people and lose your perspective of even their needs.

Another connection between informal worship and pastoral work is apparent. Your capacity to listen to people is dependent upon your reverence for them and your own teachableness. You cannot give such concern unless you have received it yourself as an act of grace from God and those persons who nurtured you. The surplus of God's grace abounds to meet the needs of others. You as a Christian shepherd are one whose "cup runneth over." Without this awesome sense of gratitude, without this sense of the abundance of the fullness of God in the satisfaction of your own needs, you yourself become demanding. You feel misunderstood and imposed upon. You feel like telling your own troubles to the person who is seeking your help. You become more talkative, and, with this, your capacity to listen has failed you. You become inattentive and insensitive to the subtle feelings of the person who seeks your help.

The third tie that binds worship to pastoral calling and counseling is the expectancy and need of people. If you do not share in worship with those with whom you work, you soon begin to lose their respect. They begin to suspect your motives and to doubt your sincerity. A prayerless relationship between you and your parishioners gradually relegates you either to the familiarity of all of the rest of their social companions or to the atmosphere of an interviewer-client relationship. Both of these latter relationships have their intrinsic values, but they are peripheral to the central function of the minister as a representative of God.

Public worship, as indeed is true of private worship, likewise affords necessary resources for the conservation and multiplication of your pastoral effectiveness. One of the main distinctives of your role and function as a Christian pastor is that you are related to the persons whom you help both individually and socially, both privately and publicly, both on horizontal planes of fellowship between persons and on a vertical plane of communion between persons and God. The place of public worship is where all these lines of influence and relationship meet. Therefore you have at your disposal the resources of the community of worship to meet the needs of the individual for worship and relief from isolation. The resources of the individual are at your disposal, also, to guide you toward the beautification of worship and the strengthening of the moral fiber of the community.

The chief end of worship is "to glorify God, and to enjoy him forever." The church at worship is celebrating the joy of the resurrection of Jesus Christ. The people are jubilant over the redemption of their lives from destruction, the steadfastness of their relationship to God, and the inseparableness of the fellowship they have in Jesus Christ.

The results of public worship are by-products of this fellowship. In these results, the fruits of teaching, preaching, and caring are multiplied. *Rest, the renewal of strength and energy through relaxation, is one of the shared objectives of both pastoral work and public worship.* The release from nervous tension and the discovery of new reserves of power for living through worship is a neglected emphasis in the activism of many Protestant churches. "Even youths shall faint and be weary, and young men shall fall exhausted; but they who wait for the LORD shall renew their strength, they shall mount up with wings like eagles, they shall run and not be weary, they shall walk and not faint" (Isa. 40:30–31). This need for rest prompted the institution of the Sabbath, sustains the continued practice of public worship, and vitally relates that practice to your caring ministry as a pastor.

The quest for community in a sense of the shared meaning of life with others is also a common venture that prompts people both to participate in public worship and to seek your understanding counsel as their pastor. You are the chosen representative of that specific community. To converse with you personally is a private way of approaching that community. The relief from isolation through public worship with the people in Christ is the heart of the worshiper's motive.

Sin and guilt isolate people from those of their own community. They are accompanied by a longing for restoration "by those who are spiritual," for a sense of belonging again to the group whose approval is most important to the sinner, as well as for restoration to God, who insists upon clean hands and a pure heart in those who "worship him in spirit and in truth."

The private confession of sin has very little meaning apart from the corporate worship between imperfect people and the God and Father of the Lord Jesus Christ. These persons in turn are people of unclean lips also, and the individual lives "in the midst of a people of unclean lips." All sin is shared guilt as well as being an individual responsibility before God. Corporate worship is God's remedy for corporate sin. Here a person realizes that one is not alone in sinfulness or in dependence upon the forgiveness of God. "All we like sheep have gone astray; we have turned every one to his own way" (Isa. 53:6) is an accurate description of the path toward isolation, self-centeredness, and loneliness in a person who is burdened with sin. The ingathering of corporate worship leads to the unification of persons who have a common experience of the forgiving grace of God. The outgoing of the worshiping community is a witness of the joy of fellowship. This witness is the most convincing form of evangelical outreach. "That which was from the beginning, which we have heard, which we have seen with our eyes, which we have looked upon and touched with our hands, concerning the word of life— . . . that which we have seen and heard we proclaim also to you, so that you may have fellowship with us; and our fellowship is with the Father and with his Son Jesus Christ" (1 John 1:1, 3).

Thus the values of personal insight and the beginning of lasting community are created, conserved, and then multiplied in public worship. The radiation of gratitude and self-acceptance lays the foundations upon which Christian worshipers can agree as to common goals and objectives for concerted Christian action. At this point, the work of a pastor, in the secret places of personal counseling to change people's attitudes privately, becomes manifest in public work and social action as these individuals set about righting glaring social wrongs in the community.

THE PASTOR'S INTEGRITY AS A SPIRITUAL OVERSEER

The center of your integrity rests in your own faith in God and your identity as "a teacher come from God." The circumference of your identity is the body of Christ with which you live in worshipful fellowship. This parish of yours is not an "administrative fiction," but, as Georges Bernanos called "the face of his parish," the church is "a living cell of the everlasting church." In your perspective of yourself as a "spiritual overseer," you find that integrity to sustain yourself in your identity as "a teacher come from God." Some ministers who read this description will feel that it is not in keeping with the realistic problems of time and quantities of work with which the average pastor must grapple. Such a concept of pastoral work in the context of the identity and integrity of the minister, however, implies radical departures in the underlying philosophy of the oversight of the church.

American churches have been schematized according to two secular patterns of administration: (1) mass production in business, which depends primarily upon volume rather than discipline of quality for profit, and (2) promotional advertising techniques, which depend upon the unpersonal media of publicity, correspondence, telephone, and bulletins for results. Churches and denominations have more or less unconsciously fallen into these same patterns by insisting upon the largest congregations possible and relying on the cleverest techniques of propaganda possible for the recruitment of members. All this moves preaching and the sacraments to the center of the church life. It insulates you as a pastor from personal contact with people, making of you an executive and administrator of a corporation rather than a shepherd of a flock.

The end result of this has been that the participation of the individual church members has decreased in proportion to the increase in the size of the congregation. The church members accept less and less personal responsibility for participation in the kingdom of God. They shift more and more of it to paid workers. They give less and less money to the causes of the church, and the paid workers must depend more and more upon small gifts from larger and larger numbers of people. The early churches were in a reversed position. They were disciplined rather than inclusive in their membership. They emphasized personal discipline rather than promotional values. They exerted influence and gave gifts all out of proportion to their numbers and wealth, because they "first . . . gave themselves."

Consequently, the position taken here is that numbers, whether large or small, are not the criterion for effective church life, pastoral ministry, and Christian outreach. The mere fact of largeness does not predestine a church and its minister to carelessness in the oversight of the flock. In fact, the church may have by reason of its larger numbers a wider variety of services, potential leadership, and professionally trained ministers to perform the work of ministry. Yet, maintaining a disciplined fellowship presupposes face-to-face relationships of people who know each other, regardless of the numerical size of the church.

A large church, however, must have a conception of the ministry as a group effort in which the pastor is not a soloist, assisted and accompanied by others. Rather, the pastor is a more experienced person with more seniority and historical wisdom in the given parish. Such a pastor functions as a quarterback of a working team the members of which stay in close and unbroken communication with each other. A multiple ministry of four pastors served on an equal basis in a certain church—equal in status, salary, preaching, and so forth. The experiment was a gratifying success in terms of what the ministers learned about human nature and their interactions with each other. The experiment ended abruptly when the four ministers, it was reported by one of them, were unable to work out their differences at one point. The reasons for this were listed: No two, much less four, ministers are equal! Decisive action should be taken by one member of the team, especially in time of crisis. The decision as to who does this should be based upon experience, seniority, and historical wisdom of the person so designated, and determined by the congregation itself. Plenty of theological reason underlies the importance of taking into account both diversity of talents and proneness to self-regard, pride, and hidden motives in ministers themselves and the importance of realizing that no one member of the team is free but each is bound to Jesus Christ to act in behalf of the church as a whole and not for themselves alone. More positively, I would recommend that ministers who work together on a large church staff build a covenant of communication with one another and consider a part of each week as a time to share their faith and theology in freedom, acceptance, and trust. The objective would be to deepen their relationship with Christ and with one another. Such an approach has possibilities for transmuting the organization of the large church into an organism of fellowship of the staff members with one another with concern for people other than themselves, either individually or corporately.

On the other hand, the mere fact of smallness in numbers is not a guarantee of effective pastoral care and personal concern on the part of members for one another, much less for those on the outside. Many small churches expect only that the minister be the "preacher" in the strict sense of the word. The church members will assume that they must handle their personal problems with no regard either for the church or for the minister. The exceptions to this would be socially acceptable problems such as acute illness, death, and bereavement. Then, too, a small church can be a mere extension of two or three families and their employees, tenants, or servants. As such, the patriarchs and/or matriarchs of these families exercise the overseeing functions. The pastor serves only in the strictest formal sense as an "overseer of the flock," responsible primarily for preaching at formal services, officiating at funerals, and occasionally performing a wedding ceremony. The family "ingroup" may exclude by silence anyone who is "outside" and almost automatically "rank" those who are on the "inside." A small church therefore can become a colony of hell much more easily than it can become a colony of heaven in which the church is a self-transcending fellowship, disciplined by obedience to God. Lewis J. Sherrill has said that in a spiritual community every other dimension of the community—cultural, family, personal—is transcended in that "God is present in this community; . . . the Spirit of God is forthgoing into, and present in, every relationship within the community."[16]

Therefore the conclusions and hypotheses that have been reached here are simply stated: whether the church is large or small numerically, it should be a *disciplined church*. By "disciplined" I mean an *instructed, committed, self-aware, self-transcending, and self-forgetting church*.

These five dimensions of the disciplined church all center upon the first one, *instruction*. The minister and the church place primary value upon *openness and teachability* as a prerequisite for membership in the church.

Granted that the person has either been brought up in the church or comes new to the church seeking membership as an adult, the point of discipline at which to begin is the willingness of the person to enter upon a thorough program of instruction and guidance as to the meaning and direction of the individual's own history, calling, and destiny as a Christian.

In the second place, the disciplined church is a *committed* fellowship. Commitment involves an explicit and definite covenant of faith based upon the knowledge of the biblical account of the revelation of God in Jesus Christ, the witness of the church throughout Christian history, the bond of ethics that holds Christians together with one another and makes their witness distinctive among others, and the kinds of responsibilities that Christians have for caring for distressed and broken persons about them. For example, when the Christian fellowship participates in the joyful celebration of a wedding, this is an act of worship and commitment of two persons to each other and also to the church. They disavow their previous sins and commit themselves to Jesus Christ as Lord of the home they are about to establish. Becoming Christians is not just in order to keep the marriage together in the same social group. It is a commitment to the fellowship of faith that will sustain the couple in the same way of life in Jesus Christ as Lord. When, by whatever means a church does so, the fellowship baptizes a person, this is done with explicit knowledge, previously arrived at by the individual and observed by the fellowship of believers, of the meaning of the Christian faith. The church becomes an instrument of confrontation for the prospective marital partners, new parents, and new Christians. These people are confronted as to what they know of the Christian faith and whether they are genuinely committed to what they know. The church is a "company of the committed," as Elton Trueblood has eloquently said.

In the third place, the disciplined church is the *self-aware* fellowship. Members do not worship in isolation from one another. They are aware of the nature of their relationships to each other. For example, students in theological seminary classes often attend them as "courses to be passed," "requirements to be met," and "notes to be taken." They are often rudely awakened to the fact that a professor expects them to become aware of the other members of the class around them, to become acquainted with them, and actually learn from them. Only slowly do they take hold of the awareness that they have a responsibility to one another in the learning process. In turn, members of their churches are similarly individualistic in their relation to the church and its minister. Church members are startled to become aware of the church as a powerful, interacting field of varied and exciting human relationships. The disciplined church has a "we consciousness" in Christ and among the separate members. I saw this most vividly when I thanked a widow for her ministry to an unwed mother in New York City, a girl about whom my wife and I had been concerned and to whom we committed ourselves to minister. This widow had provided a room in her apartment for the girl. When I thanked her, she said, "Oh, I haven't done anything. You see, I'm a member of Riverside Church!" She saw herself as part of the living organism of Riverside. She saw what was done as the ministry of the church. This self-awareness of a group and its members is what Anton Boisen has called "the group whose approval one considers most worthwhile." The disciplined church is the one that has made its approval that which its members consider most worthwhile among persons.

Again, the disciplined church is the *self-transcending* church. This is not just a mutual admiration society. The community judges itself not by itself but transcends itself in the worship of God. It is not religiously shy about mentioning God. On the contrary, the transcendent light of the Father beams brightly upon this fellowship, and the members are aware of both the light of God's love and the shadow they cast when that light falls upon them as a people of God and as individuals within the "we conscious" group. The petty idolatries of family, causes, programs, pressure groups, trivial ambitions, and so forth, are brought into serious confrontation with the Lordship of Christ. This is the heart of the meaning of worship.

The disciplined church comes to the pinpoint of the caring ministry in its *self-forgetfulness.* The church has to lose its life if it is to keep it. The pastor who represents the church becomes weary, for example, of "badgering" people into coming to church, being more active in the church, giving more money to the church. A pastor must discover deeper and richer reasons for visitation than these. If not, visitation will be a chore to which you as a pastor go "like a quarry-slave" and from which you return as if "scourged to [a] dungeon." Sooner or later you forsake visitation of this kind as sheer boredom. Conversely, the perception of the church as an organization that is in the world to be ministered unto provides most of the excuses for those who are opposed to, indifferent to, and suspicious toward the church. Those people are completely disarmed when the church and its ministry forgets itself, ceases to devise ready-made answers for criticisms, and becomes genuinely interested in the persons themselves for their own sakes.

The discipline of the church to outsiders, then, becomes the intention to build a durable, trustworthy relationship to them and their families as persons, quite apart from whether they attend all the meetings, listen to all the sermons, or give money. The church must in this way seek first the kingdom of God and his righteousness, and all these things will be added by God. To be self-forgetful in this way requires an act of faith on the part of the church itself, for faith is not just an individual matter. Groups of people have a corporate faith, too. It must be something rooted in God, not in the human desire to get prospective members in the community before some other denomination—or, God forbid, before some other church of your own denomination—does.

One may rightly ask, Where has this call to instruction, commitment, self-awareness as a people of God, self-transcendence, and self-forgetfulness been tried recently? Gordon Cosby returned from World War II, in which he had served as a paratroop chaplain. In the unrelenting stress of battle, he saw even active church members torn away from their spiritual resources. After the war, he returned to Washington, D.C., and established the Church of the Saviour. The fellowship of this group extends to people of all races, denominations, and creeds or creedlessness. The requirements for membership are stringent. Those who want to join must have completed satisfactorily an extensive program of instruction in biblical studies, church history, the study of great devotional literature, the arts of caring for distressed people, and so forth, before they are considered for membership in the church. Members are pledged to tithing and to giving time to specific tasks in the service of the church. Each member belongs to a small group dedicated to vital Christian outreach. The whole exciting story of this church has been written by one of the original members of the staff of the church. With anecdotes, specific program descriptions, and her own gift of the Holy Spirit, Elizabeth O'Connor challenges most of our major presuppositions about church life and the Christian life in her book *The Call to Commitment*.[17] When you read this story, you will be convinced that one positive example of a disciplined church outweighs all the negative evidence.

Finally, these conclusions imply that the church must have an aggressive missionary strategy for its own community. New churches must be formed in order to localize and personalize the ministry of both the pastor and the churches themselves. Individual churches cannot live on a competitive basis in relation to one another, therefore, but must devise plans for a cooperative missionary strategy in which the total life of the community as a whole is the primary concern of each group. This implies a cooperative rather than organic relationship, in order that the autonomy of each face-to-face group may be conserved. At the same time, the effectiveness of the social outreach of the whole Christian community can be increased.

NOTES

1. H. Richard Niebuhr; Daniel Day Williams; and James M. Gustafson, *The Advancement of Theological Education* (New York: Harper & Brothers, 1957).

2. David S. Schuller, "Identifying the Criteria for Ministry," in *Ministry in America*, ed. David S. Schuller, Merton P. Strommen, and Milo L. Brekke (San Francisco: Harper & Row, 1980).

3. Schuller, Strommen, and Brekke, *Ministry in America*.

4. Samuel Blizzard, "The Minister's Dilemma," *The Christian Century*, April 25, 1956.

5. The original text by Wayne Oates read: "Though these findings are twenty-five years old." It has been edited to read according to the present text.

6. Seward Hiltner, *Ferment in the Ministry* (Nashville: Abingdon Press, 1969).

7. Charles Y. Glock and Phillip Roos, "Parishioners' Views of How Ministers Spend Their Time," *Review of Religious Research*, Spring 1961, pp. 170–175.

8. Wayne E. Oates, *The Bible in Pastoral Care* (1953; Grand Rapids: Baker Book House, 1971).

9. William B. Oglesby, Jr., *Biblical Themes for Pastoral Care* (Nashville: Abingdon Press, 1980).

10. Charles F. Kemp, ed., *Life-Situation Preaching* (St. Louis: Bethany Press, 1956), p. 16.

11. Wayne E. Oates, *The Revelation of God in Human Suffering* (Philadelphia: Westminster Press, 1959).

12. Charles F. Kemp, ed., *Pastoral Preaching* (St. Louis: Bethany Press, 1963).

13. James W. Cox, ed., *The Twentieth-Century Pulpit* (Nashville: Abingdon Press, 1978).

14. Hiltner, *Ferment in the Ministry*, p. 56.

15. Gaines S. Dobbins, *The Church at Worship* (Nashville: Broadman Press, 1963).

16. Lewis J. Sherrill, *The Gift of Power* (New York: Macmillan Co., 1955), p. 50.

17. Elizabeth O'Connor, *The Call to Commitment: The Story of the Church of the Savior, Washington, D.C.* (1963; paper, New York: Harper & Row, 1975).

3

The Levels of Pastoral Care

Christian pastors care for people on many different levels of relationship. At one and the same time, you may be the personal friend, next-door neighbor, pastor-preacher, pastor-counselor, and golf or fishing companion of the person to whom you minister. Furthermore, you do not, unless you are a pastor in an unusually large city, spend much time with people whom you will never see again after finishing a series of three or four interviews. You are related to the same persons over a period of years, during which your relationship moves from one level of formality and informality to another and back again, depending upon the variety of crises endured.

These are the facts that make it unwise for you to carry over in toto the office techniques of professional counselors of any kind. It is true that hospital chaplains, professors of pastoral psychology in seminaries, specialist pastors in pastoral counseling centers, and other persons do very much formal counseling. Some exceptionally large churches have placed clinically trained pastors on their staffs to do mostly formal counseling of people who are referred to them. Churches, associations of churches, and councils of churches have developed counseling services in which exceptionally well trained ministers have a full-time responsibility as counselors. They are increasing rapidly. Every pastor needs to know what to do when called upon for more complex and detailed pastoral counseling which might be characterized as one of the "nonmedical forms of psychotherapy." At the time of this writing there are well over two hundred different kinds of psychotherapy. Pastoral counseling, in this book, refers to the multiple-interview counseling done by a parish pastor, a teacher in a college or seminary, a service chaplain, and others—a *generalist*. Pastoral psychotherapy refers to specialized and controlled therapy done by exception rather than the rule in the pastorate. Today this is a highly disciplined sub-specialty of the ministry. These ministers are thoroughly educated in both theology and psychotherapy. They have paid the price in time, energy, money, and personal discipline to do so. They are competent in nonmedi-cal forms of psychotherapy. An increasing number of them are educated, ordained, and certified in medicine. Their consecration must be incorpo-rated into any full-fledged understanding of the ministry of the gospel. I myself am one of these. However, my primary commitment in counseling, teaching, and writing is to equip *generalist,* nonspecialized pastors to do well their daily care of the flock of God. Yet, at the Ph.D. levels of my work, I seek to equip a pastor to be either a generalist or a specialist or both. Nor do I as a specialist feel that the intrinsic tasks of preaching, leading public worship, performing weddings, conducting funerals, and consistent pas-toral visitation in homes should ever be deleted from even the specialist's day's work.

Furthermore, the research findings, the proven data base, and some of the demonstrated methods of the specialist minister go far in making the work of the generalist pastor more skillful and application of the gospel more prescriptively exact and specific.

One basic principle, however, operates in the work of both the pastor and the pastoral psychotherapy specialist. One of the major difficulties un-derlying the problems of both parishioners and patients is the individual's inability to establish and maintain durable relationships with significant people. Whether it is a physician suggesting long-term, multiple-interview psychotherapy, a full-time pastoral counselor initiating a formal, multiple-interview kind of counseling, or the generalist pastor seeking to get this person to be a faithful, regular churchgoer, the issue tends to stand or fall on the individual's ability and willingness to link a covenant with a signi-ficant person and carry through with it on a sustained basis over a period of time.

You, therefore, do best to study and to evaluate the specific level on which you have access to personal encounter with people to whom you are related in a helpful way. On what basis *is* this person able to sustain a durable relationship? On that level you can begin work where you find yourself. You must be flexible enough to adapt yourself to a person on *that level of relation-ship at which you can best serve the person.* When you do this, you discover several different levels on which individuals react to you as another human being to whom they can reveal themselves. You will also find different levels of the individuals' personal insight into their own problems and willingness to do something about them before God. In this respect, you have more than one kind of relationship on which to meet people on different levels of formality, informality, and combined formal and informal relationships. Your major discipline is keeping the relationship clarified and unconfused in both your own and the parishioner's mind.

These areas of action may be called *the levels of pastoral care.* Another way of describing them would be to call these levels *types of pastoral care.* I prefer to call them levels for two reasons. First, these levels tend to appear in any given relationship of pastoral care in something of the order in which they are to be described in the following pages. Therefore the character of a relationship may change perceptibly within the scope of a single hour or from one conference to another with the same person. Second, the existential psychologists have been sufficiently convincing that you can learn from them. A knowledge of the more subtle and complex areas of personality reveals that the most important forces that determine behavior are quite often out of the field of the clear level of awareness of a person. In the pastoral relationship, as it grows with time and acquaintance, "deep calleth unto deep," and "in the hidden part" people are made to know wisdom. Thus the pastoral bond is more than a mere "telling" of things by one person to another. It is the provocation of wisdom through an especial relationship. This is essentially a Hebrew concept in which a distinction is drawn between the Hebrew word that means "to tell," in the sense that one would be taught from reading a book, and another word that means "to cause to know," in the sense in which one comes to realize something by immediate, firsthand experience. It is something of what the men of the Samaritan village meant when they said, "It is no longer because of your words that we believe, for we have heard for ourselves, and we know that this is indeed the Savior of the world" (John 4:42).

Furthermore, you might use the working model of personality that is used by what has come to be known as "phenomenological psychology." These "levels of pastoral care" represent the different contexts or "frames of reference" in which a pastor encounters fellow human beings. At one time the field of relationships focuses most meaningfully in these varying identities of the minister—as a friend, comforter, priestly confessor, teacher, and counselor. These are different foci for the caring identity of the pastor in the light of the parishioner's frame of reference.[1] However, the symbolism of "levels" of pastoral care still presents to this author the most effective basis for describing the vitality of pastoral relationships, although the phenomenological approach yields what Seward Hiltner calls a "perspective" of human relationships too important to be ignored, depreciated, or left unused as a way of thinking.

Christian experience, when seen from the vantage point of levels of feeling relationships, moves from hearsay *about* Christ to the level of personal acquaintance *with* Christ and personal dependence *upon* Christ, to the level of learning *from* Christ, to the level of confession *to* Christ, to the level of healing *by* Christ, to the level of reconciliation *with* Christ, and finally achieves spiritual usefulness on the level of comradeship *alongside* Christ to witness for Christ.

You, as an "ambassador for Christ" by your own spiritual maturity, must at least be on your way to comradeship with and witnessing for Christ. As you do this and people seek your personal counsel by reason of your accurate representation of Christ, you work "on behalf of Christ." Then, you work in accord with the example of Christ and the nature of Christian experience on *five different levels of pastoral care* of people in terms of their movement toward spiritual maturity. The levels are the level of friendship, the level of comfort, the level of confession, the level of teaching, and the level of counseling and psychotherapy. On every level you are a witness to the good news of the grace of God in Christ. Your ultimate objective is the development of a coworker in the kingdom of God. You as a pastor are not primarily committed to symptom removal or even health for health's sake. You are concerned with the long-range vocation of the person and the removal of the person's impediments to genuinely caring for and ministering to other people.

THE LEVEL OF FRIENDSHIP

If you and I are worth our salt as pastors, we rely on basic friendship as the very soil of our relationship with people. However, friendship is more than merely having people's goodwill at heart in your ministry. For people whom you serve are not always friends with each other. They are at odds with each other often. Many people demand of you that if you are their friend, you *must* be their enemies' enemy. Woodrow Wilson, in a speech made on April 20, 1915, said, "The test of friendship is not more sympathy with one side or the other, but getting ready to help both sides when the struggle is over." We are indeed called to be peacemakers, ministers of reconciliation, always searching to realize that we are children of God.

If you are a Protestant pastor, you most aptly come to your people in the role of a friend. The term "brother," which many church people use for their minister, reflects the democratic friendship they have for one who is "first among equals." You mingle as a friend and neighbor with the people whom you serve. You go to wedding gatherings, all-day meetings, young people's social gatherings, and many kinds of men's and women's social clubs. However, as we have seen earlier, your people do not expect this of you as often as you think. Your being "given to hospitality" is an asset to you. It is soon sensed if you are hard to get to know and do not mingle well with people.

45

On social occasions, persons who are timid, isolated, and withdrawn can come to know you as a minister. Their confidence in you can be established so that they will later say, "It was at the 4-H cattle show when you stopped and said hello that I decided if I ever got courage to tell this to anybody, you would be the kind of person I could talk with." This establishment of rapport is the gracious making of yourself accessible to people, rather than the compulsive falling over yourself to "win friends and influence people." This latter attitude springs more from the fear of not being approved by others than it does from an easy sense of affection for people for their own sakes. Through your ministry of casual friendship, you avoid the fate of being seen *only* as a person who appears at crises. Pastors who during wars delivered telegrams advising their members that a relative had been killed or was missing in action know that the minister can be a sign of bad news. Fortunately, chaplains and other ministers do not do this now but are called in later. If you participate in the simple joys of life, you offset the perspective of a minister as a bearer of bad tidings.

The ministry of friendship is the indispensable necessity for all other deeper levels of pastoral work. It is the seedbed of most fruitful services to people. As Washington Gladden said, "To do good to all men as he has opportunity will be the impulse of the pastor's love."[2] Furthermore, a great portion of the real help that comes to people in crises is through persons whom they would term "just a good friend" and not through professional people or "full-time Christian workers." Some of the most effective pastoral care in churches has been done by laypersons who have had rich experience as parents and who are masters at the simple business of making, meriting, and keeping friends, that is, they are "given to hospitality." Someone has called this "back fence" counseling. Ways of teaching this rudiment of the Christian life should be devised through the teaching ministry of the pastor. Martin E. Marty, the eminent theologian and historian, has given you and me a *required* text for this teaching ministry in his intensive and warmly personal book *Friendship*.[3] He says that "having friends and being friends must take place in a climate of change."

However, friendly confidence with a person who comes to you for help needs to be objective and unencumbered by too much reference to mutual acquaintances and to your personal life as a pastor. For instance, a pastor was visited by a member of a nearby church. When he made a friendly reference to the pastor of that church, the woman became somewhat restless. The pastor, sensing her uneasiness, found it necessary to say, "But, of course, you know that when people come to me for a special kind of personal help I do not talk over their problems in any way with anyone else except at their request or with their permission. Also, let me ask that if you choose to talk with others about our conference, you will let me know." Promises of confidentiality work both ways, for if you choose not to talk of these matters and your pastoral counselee talks irresponsibly, you can be put into impossible ethical dilemmas.

The ministry of friendship and example may be the extent of your ministry to many people. It is the main necessity in your relationship with people of other denominations. In hospital visitation you find most valuable this "social approach" of a "hello visit" with Catholic and Jewish patients and with persons who are the responsibility of another Protestant minister. Likewise, the ministry of friendship to small children is exceptionally rewarding. Pastors give little children an example, a hero with whom to identify, and a friendship that lends security. Especially this is true in instances in which the home has been broken by death, separation, or the divorce of the parents. Children of intact and happy homes need friends older than they who are outside their family.

Whereas the objective, considerate management of a personal friendship is one of the least artificial and most effective means at the pastor's disposal of changing human character, naturally it has severe limitations. Many pastors complain that their people think of them as a hail-fellow-well-met but that they seem to avoid situations in which a private, serious conversation about the deeper issues of life can be discussed. An example of this is the rural pastor who, upon arriving at the home of parishioners for a meal, finds there a large gathering of neighbors. The host and hostess feel the need for their neighbors' presence in "entertaining" the preacher. Whereas this may turn out to be an excellent opportunity for an informal kind of *group* guidance, it does not allow for a personal conference with an individual or for developing an intimate acquaintance with a family group.

Again, you may find yourself socially identified with your people in such a way that the amount of social distance necessary for them to reach out for your care and help will be lost. Familiarity need not breed contempt, but it does represent a loss of effectiveness in your leadership when you become just "another one of the gang" and your "separateness" as a person of good is completely obscured by this "togetherness" with the people of the community. As pastor you need enough detachment that when people do come to you they will feel they have been somewhere when they get back.

This suggests the most outstanding limitation of the social level of your pastoral ministry: there are some things a person can tell only to a stranger. As one person said in conference with a pastor in a neighboring community: "I would not dare tell these things to my own pastor because he knows all the people I do. I have no doubt he would never tell a soul. I have confidence in him, but I feel that I must talk to someone who is not so close to me." Certainly a pastor needs to be able to entertain strangers.

The need for a stranger is a paradox with the need for a friend, distance and intimacy seeming to be alien to each other. Out of this paradox have grown the pastoral counseling centers that can provide distance, anonymity, and privacy that the togetherness of even the best church fellowship cannot provide.

But in spite of such limitation, your friendly pastoral access to people in the natural setting of their homes is your greatest opportunity for a careful observation of their personal needs and for a saltlike influence on their behavior.

Yet, with all these advantages of pastoral friendship, you as a pastor propose to be the friend of people who are actually enemies of one another. You are caught in the crossfire of hostile people. Inherent in your ordination is the fact that you are called to be a minister of reconciliation, with a multilateral partiality in family conflicts, vendettas between families in the church who feud with each other, and legal hassles of Christians who ignore the biblical teachings in 1 Cor. 6:1–8 in which we are taught that "to have lawsuits at all with one another is defeat for you." Being a friend means often to take your stand apart from the measly motives that can beset people who have become consumed with enmity toward one another. They dedicate their lives to the idolatry of hating, plotting, and scheming against one another. Have the good sense to bear your witness and shake the dust of the situation off your feet. You have a higher calling and more valuable uses of your time.

THE LEVEL OF COMFORT

At your best, like Jesus, you are thought of as a person "of sorrows, and acquainted with grief." Under inevitable hardships, people turn to you for spiritual fortification, emotional support, and affectionate companionship. Here Christian shepherds go with people into the "valley of the shadow of death," stand beside them in the testing times of great tragedies such as economic failures, intolerable losses of self-respect, and terrors of such calamities as war, flood, pestilence, and economic depression. People of every walk traditionally give a minister this task in life and expect the minister to fulfill a ministry of encouragement and comfort. "If you are not available when people are in trouble," said one layperson, "you need not be on hand any other time."

The different situations in which a ministry of comfort is needed are legion. *Bereaved persons* most often are in need of the supporting help of a minister. *Those who are facing death* lean heavily upon pastors and draw upon the sources of spiritual strength that the pastor offers and represents. Likewise, the pastor's approach to *persons with long-term chronic ill-*

nesses, the more serious kinds of arthritis, and the many afflictions of old age, is usually one of companionate encouragement. A supportive ministry is also a necessity in the case of *persons who are permanently handicapped,* such as blind persons, persons who have lost a limb, or those who have been paralyzed. Such losses are much like the loss of a loved person by death, and the process of mourning over the loss through which these persons go, in adjusting to their plight, is much the same process as that through which a bereaved person goes. Closely akin to bereavement is the plight of *parents of deformed or mentally deficient children,* who continually need fortification of spirit. In the same grouping of difficulties in which a supportive ministry of comfort is indicated are *those persons who suffer from acute physical pain,* which often is so intense that pain-killing drugs seem to be of little avail. The pain itself is aggravated by the straining tension with which the excited person fights to bear the suffering. The first step in relief is relaxation, which quite often comes through the efforts of a well-poised minister who does not waver in the presence of trouble and is relatively serene in the presence of fear. This is one reason why clinical pastoral education should be considered an indispensable part of every minister's education. The minister learns under supervision and under "combat conditions" what it is like to see people in acute pain, facing death, and losing the persons who are important to them. The Association for Clinical Pastoral Education, with central offices at 1549 Clairmont Road, Suite 103, Decatur, GA 30033, is an organization that coordinates, certifies, and accredits training centers all over the United States. By writing to them, you can find the training center nearest you. The facilities are abundant, the supervision is experienced and disciplined. Let me encourage you to make this a continuing part of your education.

Furthermore, *mentally depressed persons,* whose reasons for being depressed lie unrecognized in the hinterlands of their awareness, need a supportive ministry of comfort. Rational attempts at analyzing their troubles and giving them ready-made solutions quite often meet with failure, which in turn depresses such persons all the more. Most often they are in need of a physician as well as a minister, although they quite regularly go to the minister first. The possibility of suicide in such cases is rather high, and caution should be taken at every move. Recent methods of treatment make depression one of the most amenable disorders for successful recovery. The severe pain of depression *can* be healed.

Another group of persons who vitally need the ministry of comfort that you afford are the *disappointed lovers* of your parish. A smile flits across most people's minds when such persons are mentioned, but you cannot afford to let humor be your only treatment for persons who have been seriously hurt in a love affair. Efforts at patching up such situations usually are less valuable than ministry of comfort and supportive encouragement of the person who expresses such a grief to you.

More specifically, the "how" of your ministry of comfort consists of the oldest methods of personal influence that exist: *suggestion, catharsis,* and *reassurance*. These methods have been criticized by persons who have often seen them used to exploit rather than to bless human life. Nevertheless, even the worst use of an instrument does not justify the condemnation of the instrument itself but only of the ends toward which it is used. But you, by reason of your consecration and ordination, "have renounced disgraceful, underhanded ways; you refuse to practice cunning or to tamper with God's word. You openly state the truth to people in their times of stress." Hence, you are endowed with a *weight of being*.

Therefore you cannot underestimate the tremendous power of *suggestion,* which your presence itself carries even in the lives of those who actively despise the way of life in which you walk. Paul expressed it accurately when he said that "we are the aroma of Christ to God among those who are being saved and among those who are perishing. . . . Who is sufficient for these things?" (2 Cor. 2:15–16). Your pastoral presence itself spiritually fortifies you as you come alongside people in time of stress. You sit where they sit as a reminder of the presence of God.

The knowledge of this should relieve you of the compulsive necessity of "saying something" on every occasion. If you have the courage to wait and watch, you will see times when silence itself is a means of prayer during those "groanings that cannot be uttered." Especially within the fellowship of the household of the Christian faith, among those who share a common loyalty to a living Christ, "there is no speech or language, without these their voice is heard" (Ps. 19:3, marginal reading). Job aptly railed at his comforters: "Ye are all physicians of no value. Oh that ye would altogether hold your peace! And it should be your wisdom" (Job 13:4–5). If you as a minister have not learned the discipline and re-creative use of silence as a means of spiritual communication, you will draw similar reactions from those whom you seek to comfort with windy speeches and worn stereotyped "answers" to human suffering, and you are simply relieving your own anxiety by talking. You will be different, because the sheer awe that doing things differently creates in you will make all other approaches seem hollow and shallow.

Not only is your presence a spiritual fortification to your people but your capacity to bear with them in their griefs affords a *catharsis* of the spirit for them. Catharsis is something more than confession: it is a sharing of difficulty in which the weight of pain, grief, and disappointment is actually lightened. As Bacon has said, the sharing of a trouble cuts it in half, but the sharing of a joy doubles its strength. If you observe your people's expressions of deep feeling in times of bereavement, you enter an unexcelled opportunity to cooperate with the Spirit of God in the growth of the soul through grief crises. You note that at the earlier stages the bereaved person quite often *cannot* talk about the loved one but that at a later stage wants to talk and by then friends are hesitant to let the person talk about the loss. Furthermore, recent studies of stress management repeatedly emphasize "debriefing" of overstressed people who have become fatigued, distorted in their perspective, and impaired in their judgment. In your daily work with lay leaders, supportive pastoral care in regularly debriefing them will bring harmony and serenity instead of frenetic misunderstandings and poor morale. This debriefing is a form of catharsis.

Such a catharsis restores the person's perspective and helps the person to lay hold of the positive forces. Likewise, it gives the person access to the pastor and the community resources, which the pastor represents. And in many instances your actual supportive ministry will depend more upon the way Christian fellowship groups can "prop up" a dependent church member or support a "wounded comrade" than upon your minute analyses of an unchangeable situation.

Much of your time, also, will be given over to reassuring people. *Reassurance* is a primary method of comfort and is a necessary part of the pastoral ministry. A pastor says to a young college student who has an intolerable sense of inferiority because of the cultural backwardness of the family: "You are going to do an acceptable year of college work. I know you are, because your high school principal told me that you have good intelligence, and I have seen that you are willing to work." This is reassurance, and you as a pastor may find yourself saying it more than once. A reassuring letter, written in your own hand, may be read again and again. A pastor may say to a forty-one-year-old woman who has just recently given birth to a child and feels that she is not "a fit mother" and fears that the child may not be normal because of her late age for childbirth: "You have told me why you feel that you cannot go through with this. You have also told me that you would die if you had to give your baby up. You *can* carry through if you really *want* to do so; I believe in you. I want to encourage you in your struggle to be a responsible parent. I am not alone in sustaining you; many people whom you do not know yet stand ready to be your friend. You are not alone." This is reassurance, and the woman may need to talk with this pastor again and again and receive such encouragement. The ministry of reassurance involves the basic problem of low morale and the necessity for continued impartation of hope to the person. Sometimes the person's hope hangs by the single thread of your concern as a pastor yourself. If you can ward off the isolation by building a community of concerned people around the person, they and you together become a bridge over the abyss of despair.

Naturally the use of reassurance incurs many problems. First of all, you should be careful that this encouragement of people is in keeping with the facts of their own situations. Idle words said just to make them feel good are an offense. Idle encouragement given as a palliative does more harm than good. But a hardheaded optimism that nevertheless faces the facts makes you one who imparts hope and doggedly searches for fresh alternatives. Careless reassurances, on the other hand, can cause people to feel that you are minimizing their troubles and do not understand at all. Quite often this breaks the relationship completely, and they search for help elsewhere.

Again, it is easy to become trite, impersonal, and vague in the reassurances you give people. Your encouragement in these instances is not based on attention to the personal problem of the individual to whom you are talking, consideration of the way in which the person will hear what you say, or care for the essential well-being of the person and those other persons to whom they are related. Therefore ministers are likely to say the trite things to everyone regardless of the specific nature of the person's trouble. For instance, a minister was talking to one of his most substantial contributors during an illness that called for hospitalization. At the age of forty-three this man was suffering from hypertension, arteriosclerosis, and a reactive depression. He was on the verge of a divorce from his wife for having carried on a clandestine love affair for ten years, and his business was facing failure. Not knowing these facts at all, his pastor visited him for about eight minutes, at the conclusion of which he said, "You are going through the deep waters. I have had all the troubles you are going through, and I can tell you from experience that if you will just put your trust in the Bible, you will come through."

Such an approach at best missed the mark of the man's life situation. This is not to say that the pastor's words were insincere; it is to say, however, that if they were "according to knowledge," the minister had a rather lurid history!

The resource of prayer is especially helpful in the ministry of comfort. The pastor brings the assurances of the power of God through prayer. Prayer therefore should be handled as prescriptively as any powerful medication would be handled. Several guidelines are of help in determining the use of prayer in any given situation.

Appropriateness of the atmosphere is one guide. To bring formal prayer into an atmosphere of frivolity or empty gossip often is to do violence to the nature of prayer.

Brevity is a guide to the use of formal prayer. This means that every word must count and that words should be chosen to fit the need of the person to whom the pastor is ministering. This rules out the trite, worn-out phrases that are used not only by liturgical ministers but also by persons who decry "form prayer." Spontaneity in prayer is to be desired, but this is not to say that the language of prayer is not a thing that can be learned. *The Book of Common Prayer,* especially in its most recent form, has been wrought out of specific situations of need. You will find it, regardless of your denominational affiliation, an enrichment of your prayers. The best-written prayers are found in the Bible. The language of the Bible is the language of prayer. Carry great sections of the Bible in your memory for use in your prayers. (Psalms 1; 15; 23; 37; 46; 51; 79:8–9; 90; 91; 103; 139; Isa. 40:28–31; Matthew 6; John 14; Romans 8; 1 Corinthians 13; 2 Corinthians 4:15–18; Eph. 3:14–21 are good examples of the "patience and comfort of the scriptures.")

Prayer should not always be formal. You often find yourself ministering to persons in open wards in hospitals, in the crowded church corridors during the time between church school and the worship hour, and in the marketplace as you and they go about daily chores. You can pray with the person what has been called "an open-eye prayer." Instead of bowing the head and closing the eyes, you say to the person, "I want you to think of me as praying for you. When you do, remember that I will be praying that you will be strengthened with might to meet the challenge that every day gives you." Other words that are given to you in that hour will be tailored to the very pressures the person is facing. But the basic point to remember is that this kind of prayer is informal and ordinarily unobserved by other people. Similarly, prayers can be written into the text of a letter; outstanding examples of this are the letters of the apostle Paul. For example, as I write these words, I can pray for you—my reader—that you will catch my meaning even when my words are confusing to you. In doing so, I would also pray that you as my reader would be given the wisdom to push my meanings and words aside and to let the Holy Spirit be your teacher.

Relaxation is another principle of prayer. For this reason, prayer should never be "used" merely as an excuse to end a conference with a person. Often prayer will be the point at which a person moves from a social level of conversation to the deeper levels of concern. For example, a pastor was visiting a family in which the mother was seriously ill. After a brief conversation, the mother asked, as her custom was, that he read a passage of the Bible to her. This he did and led a brief prayer for God's strength to be afforded the sick woman and for the love of her family to be a medicine in itself. After the prayer, the pastor did not hurry to say goodby. Rather, he paused in silence a long while. Then the mother told him of her awareness that she was dying. The pastor had broken through to depths of communion with her of which she had "protected" her husband and children by not discussing. She did not have to face death alone. A quiet pastor was her confidant. He could not have done this had he himself been tense, in a hurry, devoid of relaxation, and terrified by death.

Finally, *prayer means more to persons if they voluntarily ask for it themselves.* You can do much to enable people to be at ease in asking for such ministry. In many cases it is taken for granted that you will pray—such as in cases of acute illness, impending death, or recent death. But these are not the rule. You can say, "There are many things a pastor can do for people, and I wonder if there is anything I can do for you?" The tone of voice inflects meaning, and the person may ask, as one woman did, "Well, I had never thought of that; what *are* the things ministers do for people?" Then that minister had an opportunity to interpret his ministry of prayer to her. It was made easy for her to say she would like him to pray.

Likewise, the use of scriptures for purposes of reassurance, comfort, and support is especially valuable. In Martin Luther's *Letters of Spiritual Counsel*,[4] there are abundant examples of this. The use of the concise, easily remembered verses of the scriptures, especially the winnowed wisdom of Psalms and Proverbs and the epigrams from the teachings of Jesus, provides an understanding for the minds of people. Their effect increases with repetition and multiplies when they are memorized. For example, Jesus said, "Sufficient unto the day are the troubles thereof. Take no thought for tomorrow." This slows down the apprehensiveness of a person whose imagination is running away. You do well to leave a passage with a person for later reading by writing it in on one of a supply of cards you carry. You may with profit prepare a set of chosen scriptures for people who have different types of difficulties, as a sort of "spiritual prescription." I have done this in my book *The Bible in Pastoral Care*. It should be emphasized that reassurance, support, and comfort are not the only purposes, or even the major purposes, of the use of scriptures. Interpretation, instruction, and historical wisdom take precedence over these purposes. However, our education as pastors so emphasizes the technical study of the scriptures that their prescriptive use for people in all manner of difficulties is neglected. (Two books will be of specific help to you in exploring the use of the scriptures in pastoral care: Donald Capps, *Biblical Approaches to Pastoral Counseling*[5] and Wayne E. Oates, *The Bible in Pastoral Care*.[6])

THE LEVEL OF CONFESSION

A pastor visited one of his parishioners at her home inasmuch as she was the victim of an incurable cancer. She was thirty-nine years of age, the mother of two grown children by her first husband, from whom she was divorced. At this time she was married to a second husband, who had also been divorced previously. On his first visit the pastor was received cordially, and the woman told him how good the Lord had been to her and how she had been given divine assurance that she would be healed. Then she asked the pastor to pray for her. His ministry was that of listening and praying. Twice a week he visited the woman. Each time she protested almost too much that everything was all right between her and God. Finally, the necessity for skilled nursing prompted the family to move her to the hospital.

At the hospital the pastor visited her regularly and was met with the same overstated assurances of God's care. The pastor listened with a sympathetic concern but without challenging the woman's conflicting feelings. One day, however, the woman said with great force that she was sure she was a saved woman and that God was going to help her get well. Then the pastor ventured a remark: "Then *everything* is all right between you and God, is it?" In a startled fashion, the woman said, "Have you been talking to someone? Do you know something that is not right between me and God?" The pastor said, "I know nothing about you except what you yourself have told me." Then the sick woman clutched at her pastor's hand and fearfully asked him to pray for her. He prayed that she might understand herself in the light of God's love and discover the peace of God that passes understanding. After a long silence he left.

Four days later the pastor returned. The woman was very sick and close to death. When he entered the room, the woman sent all her relatives away in order that she might talk in private with her pastor. Then she said, "I have sins in my life that I must talk about before I die. I have confessed them to God many times and each time he has told me to confess them before people. You are God's minister and I must tell you." Then she proceeded to reveal a crushing load of guilts connected with a series of acts that involved her close relatives and friends over a period of twenty-three years. In great remorse she sought the assurance of God's forgiveness. The pastor then brought to her the "patience and comfort of the scriptures" that assured her of God's healing redemption in Christ.

This is an example of the confessional ministry which many veteran ministers can describe. This ministry was formally institutionalized by the Catholics on a compulsory basis. Luther taught that "confession should always be voluntary and freed of the pope's tyranny. . . . There has been no law quite as oppressive as that which forced everyone to make confession." Yet he also notes that some men "do whatever they please and take advantage of their freedom, acting as if they will never need or desire to go to confession anymore." But he says that the Lord's Prayer contains a confession that "should and must take place all our lives."[7] Today, the Catholic experience of confession is far more voluntary than it is usually perceived to be by Protestants. In reaction, Protestants have neglected the importance of confessing their "faults to one another." This is one of the first functions of the Christian community. The restoration of those overtaken in faults is characteristic of Christians who have not become so sophisticated that they no longer feel the need for their own confession of sin. (See Gal. 6:1–2.) As Martin Luther said, "A man who with fear and trembling has made humble confession will receive the grace of justification and forgiveness, even though he may perhaps have done something from a hidden unbelief of which he was not aware."[8]

Protestant ministers who are near to the heart of God and sensitive to the feelings of their people still listen to the confessions of their people. A mother cries in bitter repentance of her mistakes in rearing her children. An otherwise respectable bank teller confesses a series of thefts for the first time to his pastor because he can no longer bear the guilt alone or tolerate the fear of being caught. A young man confesses the paternity of an unborn child and seeks the aid of his pastor in protecting the mother and child. A young white woman has suddenly fallen in love with a black classmate in a large university and knows that her southern parents will not understand. A husband confesses his marital infidelity and seeks to find its causes and remedy. A defense worker caught by tuberculosis confesses his money madness, which caused him to work too many hours, too many days, and brought him to his bed.

The common characteristic of all these confessions is that they are social in nature, involving many other people. But many confessions are more individualized, and the persons condemn themselves for the evil character of their private thought life. Or they may confess the practice of masturbation, as did one fourteen-year-old boy who felt that he was mentally affected by melancholia for having indulged in this practice. Of course, this was not so.

Several facts need to be considered in the practice of a confessional ministry. First, isolation is the main effect of a known transgression. The persons cannot face their community as they did before. They are "cut . . . off from the land of the living" and from the face of God. The confession is, therefore, more than a mere catharsis; it is also a socialization of an otherwise isolated experience. The person achieves a sense of togetherness with the people whose approval the person considers most worthwhile, as well as with the eternal God. As Washington Gladden has said, the load of shame and remorse can be removed if the pastor "can draw forth the rankling secret, and convince the troubled soul, *first by his own forgiveness,* that the Infinite Love is able to save to the uttermost all who trust in him."[9]

Again, you must be careful in your ministry of confession not to accept too quickly the stated problem or the confessed sin as the real one. This could be called the "A-ha reflex," in which a minister feels like saying,

"Eureka!" when a person tells of some foul deed. Especially is this true of confessions of sexual sins. These gross offenses are often merely the symptoms of deeper and more persistent ones. For instance, a young unmarried woman may confess the fact that she is pregnant, whereas her heaviest burden of guilt hovers around a burning hatred of her father, who is chairman of the official board of the church. Her sexual act is an expression of her hatred of her father and a self-destructive way of bringing shame upon him.

Another hazard to avoid in the confessional ministry is that of taking the admission of a fault too lightly and reassuring the person to the point that the person is made to feel guilty over having felt guilty. This is most common in one's ministry to children and adolescents. An adolescent may be having all manner of difficulty over some seemingly insignificant habit. The pastor may pass the whole thing off lightly—even with humor—and miss the deep feelings the person has about the behavior. This applies not only to adolescents but also to adults. For instance, a thirty-five-year-old woman, upon being asked by her pastor whether she had been to church recently, said, "No, I do not feel comfortable when I'm sitting in church." When pressed unduly for a reason, she said with great embarrassment, "I constantly fear that someone will hear my insides growl out loud." A touch of humor eased her tension. Then the pastor said, "I know that is not completely funny to you; I want you to know that I take it seriously. Would you like to talk with me more about these fears sometime? Maybe I can help you." This conversation led easily to another, and the woman confessed to feeling great remorse over having had an abortion performed several years before. Now she greatly desired children and could not have them. There was a direct connection between her fear of her "insides being noticed" in the church and her guilt over this deed.

Probably the point at which individuals most need the "disburdening" ministry of confession, as Calvin called it, is when they first enter the Christian community as adults. In some communions this will be when the young person takes Communion for the first time. In others it will be prior to Baptism and after a public profession of faith. But you will carefully create a private conference situation in which you can become acquainted with the person, learn something of the person's spiritual history, and let the person confide prayerfully in the atmosphere of trust that develops.

Another point at which confessional ministry is appropriate and often neglected is prior to marriage. Even though a couple plan to become one flesh in God, they still exist as individuals before God in their histories of sin. Some of these sins are quite independent of their chosen partner and should be confessed to God, not to a spouse. You can encourage these prayers of penitence, for if the person is left unassuaged by the forgiveness of God, it could tend to hobble the marriage relationship with fear and compulsion.

The ministry of confession is closely related to medical psychotherapy, but *there is a vital difference.* The woman to whom reference has just been made was referred to her pastor by a psychiatrist. He stated the difference this way: "Here was a woman suffering from a sense of sin about wrong deeds she had actually committed. She needed forgiveness from God, and there was very little need of my trying to turn theologian. I referred her to her pastor. The people whom a psychiatrist can help are those who are *deluded* and *think* they have committed crimes of which they are innocent, or who are hearing voices telling them the room is electrically wired in such a way as to cause them to murder, and so forth."

The confessional ministry calls for different methods of approach according to the age of the person involved and the degree of "full-grownness" of the sins the person confesses. A child needs information and guidance in the presence of ignorance, temptation, and sin. An unwitting error cannot be treated in the same way a high-handed and premeditated crime is treated. Great care must be taken in distinguishing a temptation from a sin. Many people experience more guilt over the things they are tempted to do than they do over the sins they actually commit. Also, many people are afflicted with diseases that cause them to do things against their own good judgment, and they are powerless to control their actions. In such cases it is the minister's task to heal the volition and strengthen the person's sense of personal responsibility rather than to add to the loneliness and desperation by losing patience. Quite often such persons as epileptics, acute alcoholics, sex deviants, and psychopathic thieves and liars are in need of a physician as well as a minister. They are afflicted with diseases that express their symptoms in the moral behavior as well as in the psychosomatic disequilibrium of their personalities. When starting to deal with these persons, the minister needs the compassion that Christ had for the demoniac. The communities of these persons have often ostracized them to the hinterland of isolation without the advantage of a funeral.

THE LEVEL OF TEACHING

As a personal counselor you find that some of your most effective teaching is done with individuals in a face-to-face ministry. Jesus most often appeared to his followers as a teacher. The matchless teachings that he left the world were often the outgrowth of his ministry to individuals who were drawn to him for help. As a Christian shepherd you function as an instructor of the conscious minds, the moral intentions, and the undisciplined desires of your people. On the teaching level of your personal ministry, therefore, you must know not only the content of Christian teaching and practice but also the process whereby these become a part of the spiritual tissue of the personalities of your people and the communal life of your fellowship of faith.

A person who comes to a Christian pastor for guidance in a personal difficulty usually expects that pastor to be an interpreter of the mind of Christ, "a teacher come from God." A distinct expertise is expected. You represent these realities to the person. Furthermore, you are supposed to be an authority on the teachings of the Bible and Christian history. People come to you with thorny personal problems as the base of questions as to what the Bible teaches about divorce, remarriage, adultery, the unpardonable sin, money matters, profanity, war, and a hundred other things. You are expected to know the historical context of Christian experience and to be able to use this knowledge in a way that edifies and does not tear down the person.

In addition, you are supposed to be an authority on the specific teachings and practices of your own church. A young engaged couple will come asking you to explain the difference between the teaching and practices of Catholics and Protestants, for instance, and your knowledge and attitude will have a determinative effect upon their decision. You are a clinical research person, too. If you do not know the precise facts, you can ask for time to research them. Usually you will have friends who are pastors of other denominations, priests in Catholic churches, and rabbis in synagogues. You can telephone to them while the persons are in your office. If you define your role as a teacher, build a democratic relationship of give-and-take, and provide the couple with factual information, you can exercise genuine shepherdly care for such a couple regardless of the outcome of their decision. You as a minister also find yourself the interpreter of the social attitudes of your people all the way from such matters as personal amusements that are taboo to worldwide attitudes on race prejudice, draft registration, abortion, child custody, and the need for legal counsel.

As a teacher you are caught between your stewardship of the absolute ideals of the teachings of Jesus on the one hand and the rigorism of special pressure groups in the church on the other hand. You bear a sensitive conscience in terms of your care for human persons who have failed to reach the ideals of Jesus Christ and the responsible introduction of the church in the Christian standards of human life. On such matters, an exploding body of knowledge is appearing in the literature under such topics as bioethics, medical ethics, and Christian social ethics. Even if you graduated from seminary only ten years ago, your information is out of date. Set aside some library time, consultation time, and seminar time for this kind of updating of your learning. It will enrich your teaching, preaching, and counseling.

On the teaching level of pastoral ministry, you as a Christian shepherd find a distinctive character of your work that sets you apart from professional counselors and necessitates a departure from their ideologies. This distinctive character, however, may bring you closer to the reality of people's problems, that is, *you represent both the individual's and the group's interests, and you must combine individual and group counseling procedures.* The person-minded minister knows that many personal counseling opportunities come as the result of questions stimulated in group discussions. Conversely, you must confront the "reality principle" of your group connections and those of your counselees in all personal work with individuals.

But people come to you not only for guidance on specifically religious questions but also for information on the common venture of everyday life. Parents who have not been able to have children want to know adoption procedures, problems in artificial insemination, and parent surrogating. Young people seek premarital instruction. High school graduates want to know about the college facilities available to them. Children of elderly parents want guidance concerning homes for aged people. Relatives of mentally ill persons want guidance concerning psychiatric help and legal procedures involved in institutionalization. Parents invariably want to talk over problems in child guidance with their pastor, seeking information about the simpler as well as the more complex problems in mental hygiene. The request for the recommendation of medical specialists in cases of physical illness is a very common appeal.

In all these instances and in countless others, you are expected to be a repository of information. As one young minister, after two years of pastoral work, said, "They come to me, but they do not ask me what I *thought*. They said, 'Pastor, do you *know* . . . ' " Therefore, take heed to know your Bible, your church, and your community resources. These are your equipment.

The methods of instructional guidance are varied, but in every instance these approaches must be distinguished from long lectures of moralistic exhortations filled with such phrases as, "Don't you know . . . "; "I think you ought . . . "; "Maybe you don't realize it, but . . . " *Instructional guidance is the impartation of the facts necessary for an individual to make a voluntary choice with wisdom and informed consent. Recommending the use of good books is one of the most tactful methods* to be employed here. You should take care to separate heavier volumes that you would use for your own instruction from the more brief, more plainly written books you would use for guiding other people. Likewise, you should not recommend literature before you yourself have read it. Every pastor needs a loan shelf of books and pamphlets bought with extra gifts of money received from time to time. The pastor will lose a few books this way, but they will be valuable even so. The Westminster Christian Care Books are highly specific in nature. Note the variety of their subject matter:

When Your Parents Divorce, by William V. Arnold
When the Mental Patient Comes Home, by George Bennett
Coping with Physical Disability, by Jan Cox-Gedmark
After Suicide, by John H. Hewett
The Two-Career Marriage, by G. Wade Rowatt, Jr., and Mary Jo Brock
  Rowatt
Coping with Difficult People, by Paul F. Schmidt
Pastor's Handbook, vol. 1, by Wayne E. Oates
Mid-Life Crises, by William E. Hulme
Understanding Aging Parents, by Andrew D. Lester and Judith L.
  Lester
For Grandparents: Wonders and Worries, by Myron C. Madden and Mary
  Ben Madden
Coping with Abuse in the Family, by Wesley R. Monfalcone
Parents of the Homosexual, by David K. Switzer and Shirley A. Switzer
Parents and Discipline, by Herbert Wagemaker, Jr.
Pastor's Handbook, vol. 2, by Wayne E. Oates

Supplying missing facts is another method of personal instruction. You may be listening carefully to a mission volunteer who is making educational plans, but you suddenly realize that this person is already beyond the age limit for missionaries in the area in which the person wants to serve. A member of the official board of the church may want to make a certain change in the financial policy of the church. You as the pastor supply the missing fact that the charter of the church expressly forbids it. This type of counseling is especially valuable to the religious counselor on college campuses and to people who teach in institutions of learning. "The rules" become the grooves on which much of their counseling progresses. Furthermore, outlining various alternatives and exploring their possible implications, resources, and outcomes is another method of instructional counseling. This kind of pastoral care has the advantage of appealing to the responsible, healthy dimensions of the person. This in itself amounts to treating the person with integrity, respect, and dignity. This builds the kind of confidence necessary for any more complex and profound problems the person may wish to discuss.

NOTES

1. See Donald Snygg and Arthur Combs, *Individual Behavior* (New York: Harper & Brothers, 1949).
2. Washington Gladden, *The Christian Pastor and the Working Church* (New York: Charles Scribner's Sons, 1898).

3. Martin E. Marty, *Friendship* (Niles, Ill.: Argus Communications, 1980).

4. Martin Luther, *Letters of Spiritual Counsel,* ed. and trans. Theodore Tappert. Library of Christian Classics, vol. 18 (Philadelphia: Westminster Press, 1955).

5. Donald Capps, *Biblical Approaches to Pastoral Counseling* (Philadelphia: Westminster Press, 1981).

6. Wayne E. Oates, *The Bible in Pastoral Care* (1953; Grand Rapids: Baker Book House, 1971).

7. Martin Luther, *The Large Catechism,* trans. Robert H. Fischer (Philadelphia: Muhlenberg Press, 1959), pp. 101–102.

8. Martin Luther, *Lectures on Romans,* trans. and ed. Wilhelm Pauck, Library of Christian Classics, vol. 15 (Philadelphia: Westminster Press, 1961).

9. Gladden, *The Christian Pastor and the Working Church,* p. 86 (italics added).

4

The Professional and the Charismatic

A recurrent source of tension within the ministry throughout history has been the stress generated by the need of ministers to be disciplined, educated, and appropriately certified people, on the one hand, and their need to feel that the ministry is the free gift of God, unmerited by them, and a treasure they hold in the earthen vessels of their humanity. An Amos could say that he was neither a prophet nor a son of a prophet, and yet he could initiate a prophetic movement that still is at work in the world. A Paul could say that he had been disciplined and trained in the law as a Pharisee of the Pharisees. He could also say that he received his commission as an apostle not from men but from God.

The training of ministers among Christians in seminaries was a Roman Catholic innovation. Among Protestants the theological seminary or theological school came into being because German Pietists felt that universities failed to participate in the spiritual formation of ministers and did not equip them for what they had to do practically and spiritually. The first Protestant theological seminary was founded by the Lutherans in 1690 in Riddagshausen, Germany.

In colonial America there was a shortage of certified and approved ministers. Universities such as Harvard and Princeton had the requirement of developing a trained ministry built into their charters. But a break away from universities began in America too. In the early part of the nineteenth century, seminaries began to be founded. By mid-century there were over fifty.[1]

The frontier of America moved westward, and the push of the Great Awakening raised up men to preach who had none of the benefits of formal education. A division developed among Christians over the reliability and

63

certification of such uneducated preachers. The Cumberland Presbyterians broke away, for example, from mainline Presbyterianism over this issue: "Is the ministry of the word only to be performed by the educated or is it also a gift that can be performed by the 'called' and those so gifted?" Some denominations such as the Southern Baptist straddled the issue by saying that both could perform the work of ministry and that education would not be a prerequisite to ordination. Yet they have six of the largest seminaries in the country today. Consequently, social conflict and stress is the normal state of affairs, not between the liberal and the conservative, but between the educated and the uneducated Southern Baptist ministers.

More recently, however, the tension among clergy has been intensified on a much broader canvas than the point-counterpoint arguments within denominations. This tension is between and among contending perceptions of ministry held by educated ministers, however. Is the ministry one for which persons are overeducated? Is Charles Prestwood right? He says that "nothing in the experience of the minister-in-training prepares him for the fact that the profession is essentially a menial, impotent one."[2] His "new breed" is that group of ministers who seek to renegotiate this menial impotence by developing a sense of identity as *professional* persons.

Does theological education actually produce a *functioning* professional person? Do average ministers see themselves as professional persons or do they see themselves as amateurs? Especially is this true in the function of pastoral counseling. Pastoral counseling as a discipline has developed highly supervised forms of training in clinical pastoral education. This is called "professional education for ministry." The Association for Clinical Pastoral Education, the American Association of Pastoral Counselors, and the Academy of Parish Ministers have all three opted for a conception of the minister as a professional. Other professional persons in clinical psychology, psychiatry, and social work have reminded us, however, that we have a distinctly charismatic identity to fulfill. Jerome Frank, in his book *Persuasion and Healing*,[3] Ari Kiev, in *Magic, Faith, and Healing*,[4] and Jan Ehrenwald, in his book *Psychotherapy: Myth and Method*[5] all insist that there is a charismatic quality to any effective counseling and healing. They say that the person who performs the profession must exercise belief, the power of ritual, and a sort of conservative magic if he or she is to be credible. Likewise, Paul Pruyser, in one of his articles,[6] says that the minister's intuitive response to the right of taking initiative and the perception of God's permission to convey a pastoral blessing are essential to the minister's profession. He points out the uniqueness of the minister as counselor and person of understanding as being unabashedly charismatic and filled with confidence in this calling.

Therefore my hypothesis is that both the professional and the charismatic dimensions of our identity as pastoral counselors are inherent to the task when rightly performed. In this chapter we shall explore the meaning of, first, the professional dimension of ministry; and, second, the charismatic dimension of ministry; at the same time, we shall note their paradoxical tension in relatedness.

THE PROFESSIONAL COMPETENCE
OF THE PASTORAL COUNSELOR

In spite of all the limitations and ambiguities present in the role and function of the pastor, the priest, or the rabbi, ministers nevertheless have much individual freedom to develop their work as counselors in its disciplined and professional connotations. Not only do ministers have a call to ministry but their calling implies a discipline and a sense of profession that are important to their identity as counselors.

As Daniel Jenkins says, we have been too reluctant to understand and accept the professional dimensions of the work of the minister. Enough has been said in this book about the responsibility of pastors to God, about the involvement of pastors with their churches insofar as they function as counselors, and about the distinctly commercial aspects of pastors' roles to dispel any of the more popular connotations that surround the word "professional." Nevertheless this word needs clarification in the sense that it applies to the work of the pastor as counselor. What do we mean by "professional"?

Defining a Profession

In Morris Cogan's "The Problem of Defining a Profession,"[7] one is painfully disappointed in the nebulous discussion of the ministry's ethical basis for professional identity and action. But one is genuinely helped by Cogan's own definition of a profession, in another article:

> A profession is a vocation whose practice is founded upon an understanding of the theoretical structure of some department of learning of science, and upon the abilities accompanying such understanding. This understanding and those abilities are applied to the practical affairs of man. The practices of the profession are modified by the knowledge of a generalized nature and by the accumulated wisdom and experience of mankind, which serve to correct the errors of specialism. The profession, serving the vital needs of man, considers first its ethical imperative to be altruistic service to the client.[8]

Furthermore, Cogan's summary of the literature on the topic of the sixfold criteria of Abraham Flexner in 1915 serves as an excellent guide for ministers' understanding of themselves as a disciplined as well as called servant of God: "(1) intellectual operations coupled with large individual responsibilities, (2) raw materials drawn from science and learning, (3) practical application, (4) an educationally communicable technique, (5) tendency toward self-organization and (6) increasing altruistic motivation."[9]

A study of professional competence as it is related to quackery and charlatanism has been made by William J. Goode. With a clear sense of history, he outlines the characteristics of a profession in his article "Encroachment, Charlatanism, and the Emerging Profession." He aptly observes that "in the process of institutionalization the most severe skirmishes would occur between the new profession and the occupation closest to it in substantive and clientele interest."[10] He also points to the history of some professions in which rival training organizations using different standards limit the profession's growth through internal competition. Finally, Goode identifies the historically constant factors in the emergence of a new profession: (1) The profession determines its own standards of education and training. (2) The student goes through a more far-reaching adult socialization than the learner in other occupations. (3) Professional practice is often legally reorganized by some form of licensure. (4) Licensing and admissions boards are manned by members of the profession. (5) The legislation concerned with the profession is shaped by the profession. (6) The occupation gains in income, power, and prestige ranking and can demand higher caliber students. (7) The practitioner is relatively free of lay evaluation and control. (8) The norms of practice enforced by the profession are more stringent than legal controls. (9) Members are more strongly identified and affiliated with the profession than are members of other occupations with theirs. (10) The profession is more likely to be a terminal occupation. Members do not care to leave it, and a higher proportion assert that if they had it to do over, they would again choose this type of work.

We as ministers become too moralistic when we use the word "professional" as if it were an obnoxious thing. We need to measure our own work as ministers, especially in the context of the local ministerial association, by the following standards:

In the first place, pastoral counselors are professional in the sense that they have committed all their time to the work of being pastors. Pastoral counselors have disentangled themselves from other pursuits. They thrust themselves upon all the risks involved in being dependent upon the church, the school, the hospital, the comprehensive mental health center, the board of a pastoral counseling center and the role of its ministry for their economic support and their identity as persons. This has called for singular decisiveness on their part. If they remain in the ministry and function competently, this commitment of their time thrusts upon them the responsibility of developing a clear-cut sense of purpose and identity. As Nelson Foote and Leonard Cottrell have said, "There is an inseparable relationship between identity and interpersonal competence." This particularly applies to the more distinctly professional aspects of being a minister.

In the second place, interpersonal competence is characteristic of the ministry as a profession. Nelson Foote and Leonard Cottrell aptly describe several aspects of interpersonal competence. These can be applied to the work of pastors as counselors in terms of their professional characteristics: Ministers have intelligence, which involves a breadth "perception of relationship among events," the ability to "symbolize experience" and to interpret life with "meaningful generalizations." Intelligent persons are "articulate in communication." In the Hebrew sense of Proverbs, these are the characteristics of the *'ish tebunah,* the "man of understanding." The minister is skilled in "mobilizing the resources of the environment and experience in the services of a variety of goals."[11]

Pastoral counselors have empathy, which means that professional persons can perceive situations from other people's standpoints. Thus they can anticipate and predict their behavior. Pastoral counseling requires the capacity to "take the role of the other," and "the absence of this is a sign of misunderstanding."[12] Pastoral counselors are autonomous, which means the professional persons are capable of clarifying their own conceptions of themselves. They maintain independently a "stable set of internal standards by which [*they*] act." They have "confidence in and reliance upon" themselves, and maintain "a reasonable degree of self-respect"; they have "the capacity for recognizing" that "the real threats to self" can mobilize "realistic defenses when so threatened." Pastoral counselors have judgment, which means "the ability to adjudicate among values, or to make correct decisions; the index of lack of judgment (bad judgment) is mistakes, but these are the products of an antecedent process in which skill is the important variable."[13] Referral, consultation with other people than the counselee, even acceptance of responsibility for counseling in the first place, all call for judgment.

Pastoral counselors demonstrate creativity, which means that as professionals they have "demonstrated the capacity for innovations in behavior or real reconstruction of any aspect of [*their*] environment." They have the ability to "develop fresh perspectives from which to view all accepted routines and to make novel combinations of ideas and objects and so define new goals, endowing old ones with fresh meaning and inventing means for their realization."[14] Pastoral counselors, particularly in the guidance of their counselees, are capable of inventing or improvising new roles or alternative lines of action in problematic situations and of inspiring such behavior in others. Many of their counselees are uncreative persons and continually find themselves in dilemmas and impasses. They are at their wits' end. They are shut up to a rigid adherence to one solution to their problems. A part of the professional competence of pastoral counselors is to provide the creative kind of relationships in which innovations, inventions, and the discovery of new alternatives are daily events. In short, this creativity engenders hope. When a counselee says, "There is nothing else I can do," often the very process of counseling itself is the "something else" which opens new avenues to hopeful existence.

A third characteristic of pastoral counselors as professional persons, as Seward Hiltner has said, is that they have the capacity to define and clarify their responsibilities in terms of basic principles and not just techniques or means. Similarly, this applies to the relationship of pastoral counselors and their counselees. Pastoral counselors are not simply manipulating persons toward an end of their own but are working with the persons in the development of basic principles for living. For example, the care of bereaved persons is based upon the principles of "working through" the various stages of grief. This is the principle; clinical technique grows out of it. Furthermore, marital conflict is a process of deterioration of trust, communication, and covenant. The technique of marriage counseling grows out of a detailed understanding of this process of deterioration and its arresting and reversal.

A fourth characteristic of pastoral counselors as professional persons rests on their equipment and training. The Protestant Reformation and Vatican II have shifted the emphasis from the structure of the church to that of persons equipped and trained to do the work of ministry. Pastoral counselors depend upon neither their "personage" nor the institution of the church for their professional competence as counselors. They must have submitted themselves to the disciplines and training that equip them as counselors. These disciplines include both the classical and the neo-traditional types of training in the pastoral ministry. The pastoral counseling movement in America has rightly concentrated much attention and energy upon the development of professionally valid forms of clinical pastoral education for the minister. The processes of accreditation, qualification, and authorization of the pastor as a counselor are of great importance to Protestant theological educators.

Certification of Professional Ministers

Since 1961 at least three different organizations have set about training, certifying, and unifying ministers who have had specialized training as counselors, teachers of clinical pastoral education, and functioning parish ministers.

The American Association of Pastoral Counselors has been organized and now lists a membership of 715 (about 1974) in its categories of diplomate, fellow, members, and so forth. This organization, according to Howard Clinebell, has confronted the dangers of "losing its roots and context—that is, that it will become estranged from the shepherding image of the pastor, from a religious view of existence, and from a responsible relationship with the community of faith which is the church."[15] At about the same time, I questioned the issue of specialization and asked, "How do you . . . keep [pastoral counseling] from going the way of professional evangelism as a subprofession of the ministry?" Clinebell most recently has said that we have avoided the dangers he earlier named. I think that they are still there in greater force. I agree with James Glasse when he says, "The battle will continue, but the issue is clear. If pastoral counseling develops as an autonomous specialty, it must either become a separate profession or must make clear how professional expertise in the pastoral role is related to the ministerial profession."[16]

Glasse himself has participated with Granger Westberg and others in establishing the Academy of Parish Clergy, with standards of certification based on specific amounts of study in workshops, clinics, and seminars. Every three years a member would be required to show evidence of continuing education—not as a student, but as a practicing professional as over against being an amateur. My own experience in considerable participation in such "colleague-to-colleague" on-the-job training has been that these pastors learn more rapidly, concretely, and operationally than they did when they were students. One of the main deterrents to learning among theological students is the perpetuation of their delayed adolescence in the role of student per se.

A third professional organization of ministers is the Association for Clinical Pastoral Education. The main functions of this organization are to provide clinical pastoral education for theological students and active pastors, to see to it that certified supervisors of high quality are doing the teaching, and to accredit hospitals, schools, delinquency institutions, churches, and others as adequate centers for such education. In a sense, this movement has provided some of the impetus for the development of the sense of profession in the two previous organizations.

However, all three organizations have developed a model of the equipment of the minister as a professional as opposed to being an amateur which has just now swept through theological schools in a subtle adoption of their premises in new curricula for the Doctor of Ministry degree for ministers. The ingredients of collegial, peer-group learning as over against "over-under" teacher-student learning, of *supervised* on-the-job field experience, of careful pastoral research (as distinguished from but not set over against literary-historical research) are in the designs of a considerable number of degree programs. This Doctor of Ministry degree can be a dream come true in raising the level of theological instruction to make genuine professionals and not just well-intentioned do-gooders of ministers. This can happen if adequate supervision is provided. The clinical pastoral education model has become too hidebound to the hospital setting. Clinical supervision can inform the Doctor of Ministry programs whether the clinical supervisors can and will be placed and can and will function in churches, denominational agencies, urban training centers, slum storefronts, the open marketplace, and elsewhere.

Yet the bureaucratic system of the Association for Clinical Pastoral Education has become a somewhat self-satisfied status system in its own right. The element of charisma flashes only occasionally. Anton Boisen once told me that the movement had hurried into "an early orthodoxy as to what supervision is and where it should happen." This has prevented creative experimentation, recognition of eccentric credit, and the development of a variegated and colorful array of individuality among supervisors. The next step in such a process is a reward of mediocrity for the one asset it contributes to a mass movement: conformity.

The Doctor of Ministry program offers a challenge to pastoral counselors and clinical supervisors to become involved with professors of the classical disciplines of the biblical, historical, and ethical fields. On the other hand, these professors can become involved in the actual professional lives of students they instruct.

My hope is that the American Association of Pastoral Counselors and the Association for Clinical Pastoral Education will not retreat into an ever-narrowing specialization that thrives on the middle classes only. My hope is that our members will use our skills in dealing with the deprived in institutions, to move pastors and parishioners to become involved in ministry to the downcast, the outcasts, the face-saving respectable, and the hard-nosed exploiters of the disadvantaged. The educational possibilities of the Doctor of Ministry degree are one avenue for developing a disciplined professional approach from within the churches.

However, if the American Association of Pastoral Counselors and the Association for Clinical Pastoral Education retreat into a narrower and narrower specialization of counseling and psychotherapy, we will move away from both the parish setting and the theological seminary. Then, as a separate profession, we will have to demonstrate to the Department of Health, Education and Welfare that we are indeed a viable health delivery profession. We will have to demonstrate to health insurance companies that we are authentic third-party recipients of benefits for having satisfied the health needs of people. We will have to convince companies in business and industry that we can contribute to workers' usefulness to the companies in lowering absenteeism, arresting and reversing alcohol and drug addiction, bringing greater marital harmony to workers, and increasing personnel morale. When we have accomplished this, we will be faced with the issue of our charisma—our gift of ministry as an unmerited favor of God and our identity as ministers who are distinctly *pastoral* counselors. As a pastoral counselor, I am committed to the possibility and the ambiguity of the indispensability of both a sense of profession and a sense of charisma for each other. Yet to bring them on balance with each other calls for some discernment of the elusive meaning of charisma.

MEANINGS OF CHARISMA

Charisma is a special divine gift that is conferred by God upon a believer in God as evidence of divine grace. Charisma fits persons with a dynamic for their lifework, calling, or office. At its base, charisma is God's free gift of redemption, deliverance, and affirmation in the face of our sin, bondage, and self-rejection. Such deliverance calls for thanksgiving. The life of suffering is met with the gift of grace. The gift of deliverance from suffering and bondage becomes the tool with which we participate in the deliverance of others. By means of the comfort with which we are comforted, we become a comfort to those with whom we counsel. (2 Cor. 1:3–7.)

Distortions of Charisma

Yet this general meaning of charisma is distorted by well-meaning people both in biblical times and in modern times.

Charisma as the Antithesis of Education. A considerable amount of anti-intellectualism is wrongly confused with charisma. The uneducated person may be suspicious of those persons who are "fast with the words," likely to use their education to trap, overwhelm, or intimidate the uneducated person. The suspicions of the uneducated are not without some substance in reality, but their defense is often that learned persons lack common sense, are stupid about the way life really is, and, as religious persons, do not "have the Spirit."

As one begins to edge toward the latter accusation—that educated persons lack the Spirit—one begins to see the hidden assumption about charisma emerge; that is, the uneducated are *given* wisdom, insight, ability to command the evil spirits that possess the lives of those to whom they minister. On this presupposition whole systems of folklore of the shaman, the Appalachian "granny," the Mexican-American *curandero,* and many others are built. The uneducated are often the poor, and their struggle to

71

survive is energized by the belief that the power to help, the wisdom to counsel, and the secrets of human suffering are gifts or charismata from God.

Charisma as a Particular Ritual. One of the most common distortions of charisma is to overidentify it with a particular ritual. For example, the "invitation" among churches of the revival tradition is the climax of the ceremony. Ministers who preach "stand or fall" in their own eyes and those of others as to how successful they are in getting people to make professions of faith. Such success is evidence of charisma, according to this distortion.

Another example is the experience of ecstasy in glossolalia. Persons who receive this gift are actually named "charismatic." Sophisticated authors on cultism, such as E. T. Clarke, often use the word "charismatic" to mean ecstaticism and Pentecostalism.

Another example of a specific ritual being confused with charisma is the use of healing formulas. The mere performance of these rituals—anointing, laying on of hands, and others—is often interpreted as charisma. It is possible to identify these rituals in and of themselves as charismatic, but to do so is a distortion.

The Grand Manipulator

Persons who have the capacity to overwhelm and successfully to manipulate people in large numbers are often assumed to be charismatic. These persons may have grown up in a chaotic environment in which they had to manipulate everyone and everything in order to survive. As they grew older, they became successful and no longer needed to manage, maneuver, and wheel and deal in order to survive. But by now they have come to enjoy manipulation for the sheer fun of being clever, exercising power, and overwhelming other people. Often this capacity is called charismatic when it would be more accurately called cleverness. Søren Kierkegaard drew the distinction best when he spoke of persons as having exchanged their call to be prophets for their desire to be geniuses.

Authentic Charisma

The Inherently Helpful Person. The genuinely charismatic person, in my opinion, is the therapeutic equivalent of Charles Truax and Kevin Mitchell's valuable description of "the inherently helpful person." They say that such persons may have little, some, or much training. In all instances, regardless of training, however, the inherently helpful person possesses empathy, nonpossessive warmth, and genuineness. These persons "have been rewarded for being helpful from their early formative years onward. . . .

These skills have been built upon and reflect fairly permanent personality characteristics." Truax and Mitchell say that if a person has these characteristics of accurate empathy, nonpossessive warmth, and genuineness, individuals who spend time with them "will be as helped, if not more helped, as if they were receiving formal counseling and psychotherapy from the socially sanctioned professional."[17]

Cross-cultural Communication Capacity. Charismatic persons—whether they are highly educated or not—have the capacity to move through the social class barriers that separate them from people. They can move among the aristocracy without feeling that they are owned by them or must be obeisant to them. They can move among unskilled laborers without communicating condescension. The Lord Jesus Christ was heard gladly by the common people and was unabashed by either the learned or the wealthy. In a sense, the charismatic person lives what Stephen Neill called "a genuinely human existence."

The characteristics of accurate empathy, nonpossessive warmth, and genuineness can be learned and improved with training. They improve cross-cultural communication capacity. They can be obscured and distorted when training forces an unauthentic mold upon a person, when status-anxiety short-circuits spontaneity, and when role-abrasion creates possessiveness in a power struggle over the person's approval who is being helped. As Glenn Asquith says, pastoral counselors must be able to combine "technical knowledge with personal intuition in order to relate to others in a growth-facilitating manner."[18]

Charisma as the Power of an Existential Shift. We live in a world of blending and separating mythologies. We have scientific mythologies which are more sophisticatedly called "theoretical models" or "modalities." We also have older mythologies which are held firmly and sincerely by unlearned and unsophisticated people. Much wisdom resides in these older mythologies. They have certain tenacity in the archetypal levels of being of even the most learned. In coping with scientific formulas, pastoral counselors treat by rational guidance, insight release, and reordering the memories of persons with more constructive meaning. If they are more aggressive, reality-oriented counselors, pastors use persuasion and habit-reconditioning. Only those pastors who are in touch with the deeper primitive aspects of human existence have the charisma to appeal to the older mythologies and even the magical depths of personality. Jan Ehrenwald provides an integrative approach to counseling and psychotherapy by making "proper allowance for myth and myth induced shifts in the therapeutic process."[19] The capacity to move with facility from one level of mythology—scientific and otherwise—honestly, with accurate empathy and nonmanipulative commitment to the well-being of "the other" is another way of describing charisma.

My hunch is that charisma is a gift from the point of view of one's relation to God. It is a certain raw courage to respond in a novel situation—which one has not experienced before and probably will never experience again—with a sense of divine imperative that what one is about to say or do is inherently helpful and unmistakably right. The Yiddish word *chutzpah* comes near it. One takes a plunge, says and does what the context, the moment, and the pain call for at the time. These persons unequivocally take responsibility for their acts before God. When it is done, they marvel, thank God, and are reluctant to tell anyone. Ordinarily, they go "and tell no man."

An example of this sudden shift from a rational, reflective, and scientific frame of reference to a "plunge into persuasion" is found in the following critical incident of the ministry of a highly trained pastoral counselor.

Jane was a sixteen-year-old girl committed to a treatment center for juvenile delinquents after she repeatedly ran away from home. Soon after she entered the institution, Jane was referred to the chaplain by her social worker. The social worker explained that the girl had "not gotten over her mother's death." In conversation with Jane the chaplain learned that her mother had died six years before at a state mental hospital. At that time Jane learned that she had been adopted by an aunt and that the woman who died—whom she had thought to be her mother's sister—was, in fact, her mother.

Over a period of several weeks the chaplain came to know Jane as a girl who though basically healthy, according to a psychiatric evaluation, was experiencing a morbid grief reaction. In their conversations together the chaplain and Jane explored both her fantasies and the realities of her prolonged grieving. The basic dynamic was Jane's difficulty in forgiving and reaccepting her aunt as "mother" because she was plagued by a lingering feeling of being cheated of a relationship to her real mother. Jane's idea of her real mother was more fantasy than fact.

About two o'clock one morning the chaplain received a call at home with the request that he come and talk to Jane. The report was, "She says she sees her mother." The chaplain went to the cottage where Jane was a resident and found several security men with flashlights searching the area around the cottage. The chaplain asked about the situation and was told that one of the girls said she saw someone outside the cottage. The chaplain knocked on the cottage door. The cottage parent was hesitant to let the chaplain in because she was afraid the "spirit of Jane's mother might come in." The chaplain said, "Open the door. The only spirit coming in with me is the Holy Spirit of God."

The chaplain asked the cottage parent to get the other girls to bed while he talked to Jane. Jane said that her mother was standing outside by the streetlight. The chaplain talked with Jane about what her mother's appearance meant to her. Her feeling was that her mother was only causing trouble for her. She said, weeping, "I wish she would go away and never come back." The chaplain asked if she could tell her mother how she felt. Jane said she was afraid. The chaplain asked if she would like him to tell her mother to leave. She emphatically said that she would. The chaplain opened the window, faced the streetlight, and said in a loud voice, "You have come to cause trouble—not to help. We do not want you here. As God's messenger I command you—leave and do not return."

Jane reports that her mother left that night and has not returned. The chaplain continued to see Jane on a regular basis for the next two months. She was able to complete her grief work rather quickly after this event. Two years later Jane was still doing well and renewed her relationship to her adoptive mother.

These things happen to extensively trained and highly professional persons. They do not teach these things to others because the events are nonrepetitive and cannot be reproduced by "method" or "technique" apart from a ripe timing, a serendipitous context, and an amazing amount of suffering, demonstrated competence, and hard-earned confidence from those to whom one ministers. I can record here such an instance, one that affirms Ehrenwald's "existential shift" hypothesis and my description in this paragraph. It is an event in the life of a seasoned and well-trained pastoral counselor and chaplain of a delinquency treatment center. I learned about it indirectly and persuaded him to let me record it here.

Charisma as the Stewardship of Gratitude to God. My own clearest conviction as to the meaning of charisma is that charisma is the disciplined giving of the gifts received by us from God to others who reach out to us and to whom we reach out. The psychoanalytically treated person who is released from bondage through treatment gives much of that same release to others as David Roberts did through his book *Psychotherapy and a Christian View of Man.*[20] A person who has come from a shattered home, but who by God's free gift was held together and was brought to love abounding by a charismatic teacher, in turn becomes a steward of this "good gift" from God. Charisma is then the stewardship of gratitude—gratitude to God for the comfort with which he has comforted us. The depths of gratitude become the instruments of *charis* or grace by means of which we care, counsel, empathize with, express nonpossessive warmth toward, and come through to others as being genuine.

Consequently, when counseling becomes pastoral, all the professional know-how is illumined by the charisma of gratitude and integrated into the one person without disharmony. When effective results express themselves, charismatic professionals are quite reluctant to claim credit; they are more likely to thank God, take heart, and move on to another place and person of need. They do not have time for cleverness, only for gratitude for the charismata of God.

NOTES

1. Glenn Hinson, "The Spiritual Formation of the Minister as a Person," *Review and Expositor* 70, no. 1 (1973): 79.

2. Charles Prestwood, *A New Breed of Clergy* (Grand Rapids: Wm. B. Eerdmans Publishing Co., 1972), p. 79.

3. Jerome D. Frank, *Persuasion and Healing: A Comparative Study of Psychotherapy* (Baltimore: Johns Hopkins Press, 1961).

4. Ari Kiev, ed., *Magic, Faith, and Healing: Studies in Primitive Psychiatry Today* (New York: Free Press of Glencoe, 1964).

5. Jan Ehrenwald, *Psychotherapy: Myth and Method: An Integrative Approach* (New York: Grune & Stratton, 1966).

6. Paul Pruyser, "The Master's Hand: Psychological Notes on Pastoral Blessing," in *The New Shape of Pastoral Theology,* ed. William B. Oglesby, Jr. (Nashville: Abingdon Press, 1969), pp. 364–365.

7. Morris L. Cogan, "The Problem of Defining a Profession," *Annals of the American Academy of Political and Social Science,* January 1955, pp. 105–117.

8. Morris L. Cogan, "Toward a Definition of Profession," *Harvard Educational Review* 23 (Winter 1953): 35–50.

9. Abraham Flexner, "Is Social Work a Profession?" *School and Society* 1 (June 26, 1915): p. 904.

10. William J. Goode, "Encroachment, Charlatanism, and the Emerging Profession," *American Sociological Review* 25, no. 6 (December 1960): 902–933.

11. Nelson N. Foote and Leonard S. Cottrell, *Identity and Interpersonal Competence* (Chicago: University of Chicago Press, 1955), p. 53.

12. Ibid., p. 54.

13. Ibid.

14. Ibid., pp. 55–57.

15. Howard Clinebell, "Creative Interaction Between the Generalist and the Specialist in Pastoral Counseling," *The Pastoral Counselor,* Spring 1964, pp. 3–12.

16. James E. Glasse, *Profession: Minister* (Nashville: Abingdon Press, 1968), p. 66.

17. Charles B. Truax and Kevin Mitchell, "Research on Certain Therapist Interpersonal Skills in Relation to Process and Outcome," in *Handbook of Psycho-*

therapy and Behavior Change, ed. Allen E. Bergin and Sol L. Garfield (New York: John Wiley & Sons, 1971), p. 327.

18. Glenn Asquith, "Professional Training and Charisma: Toward an Integration" (unpublished paper, 1973), p. 9.

19. Ehrenwald, *Psychotherapy,* p. vii.

20. David E. Roberts, *Psychotherapy and a Christian View of Man* (New York: Charles Scribner's Sons, 1950).

5

The Private and
the Public Ministry

Pastors as counselors are not *just* private counselors. What they do in private as counselors is always in tension with their responsibility as public figures, public speakers, persons with corporate and community responsibilities. Pastors are ordinarily employed by congregations, serve parachurch institutions, or are legally required to be answerable to ecclesiastical bodies through ordination. This latter legal requirement is made by state governments and the federal government in their employment of ministers as chaplains, for example.

A case in point is the struggle for social change that we had in the 1940s and the 1950s to wrest the appointment of chaplains from the political patronage system. A merit system appointment on the basis of professional training for the chaplaincy has, as a result of this struggle, become the prevailing mode of action in many state and federal institutions. Yet, in the late 1960s, when public protest and the use of political exposure in print and on television became the techniques of choice for social change, some chaplains felt that they should use these procedures to change things in the Establishment that they considered evil. Then they were confronted by administrators telling them that theirs were nonpolitical appointments and that this also implied that they themselves were not to engage in politics beyond casting their own secret ballot! They could not have it both ways. In such a dilemma the chaplains would have to rely on the political process apart from their own neutrality or they would have to earn their living apart from state funds and conduct their public campaigns as outsiders. This subtle ambiguity was doubly difficult for some clinical pastoral education students to see because ordinarily they were not being paid. Yet they *were*, in effect, guests of the Establishment and could be told to leave at any time.

Nevertheless individuals and small groups call upon their pastors, some of whom are chaplains in institutions, for counsel. Here the influence of pastors can be felt privately but not seen publicly. When people turn to them for any reason, they expect a measure of privacy. Therefore the private ministry of pastors to individuals and groups is set within the context of their public ministry, which in turn is nourished and/or blighted by their private ministry. They are both consciously and unconsciously directed by the heavy tension that is produced by the ambiguity between the private and the public aspects of ministry.

"I WANT A PRIVATE PASTOR"

The tension I am describing I first felt consciously in 1951. An active and loyal member of a church of another denomination came to me for counseling. She said that her pastor was a competent counselor and helpful preacher. Both she and her husband held offices in the congregational governance. I asked why it was she came to me—a total stranger—when she seemed to trust her pastor greatly. She replied that it was not a matter of trust, but that he simply could not provide the amount of privacy she needed. To involve him in her troubles would only be to complicate them as much as to talk with a member of her family. Then she said, "I want a *private* pastor." In this story rests some of the dynamics of the emergence of pastoral counseling as a subgrouping of the ministry. Some of these dynamics can be extrapolated here.

The Fear of Exposure

The woman valued her pastor's approval as a working member of his church. The fear of his disapproval and the possible disqualification of herself in the work of the church caused her to take her private burdens elsewhere. Ambiguously enough, her private problems and her public responsibilities worked at cross-purposes with each other. Consequently, she settled the tension by getting one minister to meet her private needs while continuing to rely on another minister in her durable, public needs. Yet, as a minister who keeps protesting that the private and the public ministries of a pastor cannot be separated, I myself was observing before my own eyes the two being neatly separated in the conscious thinking of a counselee who has continued to be a responsible member of her church for twenty-two years since I first saw her!

Already veteran pastors will ask, "Did you not have an ethical responsibility to advise her pastor that a member of his congregation was consulting with you?" Such a question makes me squirm. I feel that I had an ethical obligation to strengthen and not undermine her relationship to her church. This I have done and it *was* strengthened. In this sense I felt obligated to him. With the resolution of some of her stress, she told him herself after conferring with me about it. I encouraged her to tell him, and the telling strengthened our relationship to each other as fellow ministers. If she had not chosen to tell him herself, my own response to her need for a private pastor would have kept me from mentioning it to him. The fact is that he knows nothing as yet about what I heard her discuss. Neither does anyone else. Hence, the threat of exposure was removed both from her dialogue and from mine.

The Need for Confession

This woman had a burden of private loss, fear, inhibition, and anger that she needed to disburden. None of it involved anyone in her family or the extended family of her church. She was fiercely loyal to them. In Kierkegaard's fine words, her burden involved memories and decisions of "the self in relation to itself" and to God. But she needed a private pastor to be an alter ego in her soul's soliloquy and in her prayers before God. Ideally, her pastor *could* have provided this. Pragmatically, she felt otherwise. This realm of privacy in her own being was something no one, and no church, could program. She chose a private pastor to meet her need for disburdening and for spiritual direction. The private, confessional dimension of life is both traditionally and neo-traditionally an unquenchable demand of persons and also apt to be exploited and commercialized. The reactivation of an informal but deeply personal ministry of confession is perennially needed in and out of the church.

Consequently, pastoral counseling itself has absorbed much of what in highly liturgical churches is called "the confessional." Churches without a ritual of confession have been most active in the development of pastoral counseling.[1] Data confided in the confessional relationship are not given to ministers themselves. The ministers are permitted to "overhear" them as the person gives them to God. They are enablers of the person's prayers, not just the primary recipients of information. Such data therefore are now, as always, sacrosanct and told to no one by the minister. The high tradition of ministry at the distinctly confessional level is not to be shared with anyone but God. No one who has not developed a confessional-level relationship with the person has any right to know what was said. Therefore, if anyone is to tell what was said, the person who made the confession is the one to do it. Herein is where the line between the confessional and pastoral counseling—even though it is a moving line—must be drawn and redrawn. It involves the consequences of the persons themselves talking with others, not merely the pastor "breaking confidences."

The whole issue of the legal aspects of the protection of the pastor as a counselor from being used as a witness in court has been thoroughly discussed in William Harold Tremann's book *The Right to Silence.*[2] Until now this has been more of a moot issue than a repetitive problem. In nearly thirty years of pastoral work, I have been faced with the possibility of subpoena only once. With pastoral counseling vying for place as a health delivery specialty, however, this will become increasingly more real as the pastoral counselor becomes more dependent upon fees for services rendered in a contractual way, as is characteristic of other health delivery professions.

The more prevalent issues, however, in private communications with counselees are interpersonal rather than legal, covenantal rather than contractual. Persons who come to their pastor for counseling or to some other minister, as in the case above, usually are suffering from isolation and fear of rejection by others. They may or may not have done things about which they do not wish others to know. They may or may not want the fact that they have sought assistance from the pastor to be known by others. On the other hand, the pastor accepts a measure of responsibility for counselees' "stories." Just knowing some things is a heavy load to carry, especially when a pastor is responsible to the church as well as to the individual. On both sides, the pastor and counselees live under the threat of exposure. How can this threat be removed? It can best be removed by the establishment of a *covenant of communication.*

A covenant of communication is much more than a promise not to tell anything the person has said, which may or may not be a wise thing to promise. A covenant of communication consists of a mutual understanding that both the counselor and the counselee will consult with each other *before* either of them discusses their conversation with anyone else. Thus, no one is told what has been discussed without the permission of the other to do so. Thus, information will fall into at least three different categories depending upon the degree of the threat of exposure inherent with the information. First, there is *community knowledge.* The pastor receives information from the counselee that is commonly known in the community. Such information may be a matter of public record if it has appeared in the local newspapers. Or, it may be known by a considerable number of people and is therefore common information. Much that the unsuspecting pastor receives as confidential information is of just this order of knowledge. These persons may have themselves told this to many other people, each one having been told "in confidence." They probably have forgotten about these persons, and when one of them reminds these persons of it they are likely to think that the pastor has betrayed them. Consequently, it is standard clinical procedure for the pastor to find out to whom else counselees have talked about their problem.

Second, there is *privileged communication*. This is information that the pastor or counselees may pass on if the other gives the privilege of doing so. Usually this is the kind of privilege that is granted for the communication of necessary information to other professional people who may be called upon as referral sources. Sharing data with another professional person also distributes the burden of responsibility to more persons than just the pastor. Such sharing lowers the pastor's own sense of isolation and anxiety. Case conferences among professional people fall into this category of relationships in the use of information. The main feature of this is that privilege is granted only when necessity prevails. The question arises as to whether pastors' spouses should know about pastors' counseling relationships. Quite often it is necessary for spouses to know about these counseling relationships in order that they may accept their share of responsibility or in order that they may react appropriately in behalf of the counselees at times. But it is not always necessary, and when necessity does arise, the counselee should be consulted beforehand.

However, pastors need to be extremely careful how much and how quickly they accept such confidences. Persons who too quickly disburden too much may be shocked at themselves for doing so and may be reluctant to sustain the counseling relationship as a result. Also, if counselees confide in other persons, pastors then have the right to know who these persons are if the necessity arises. Pastors should at some time or other in the relationship make this clear to counselees. This is part of the reciprocal nature of the covenant of communication. If effectively established and clearly accepted, such a covenant tends to remove the threat of exposure.

Such a covenant as has just been described mutually allocates responsibility to counselors and counselees alike. But this uncovers another threat: *the threat of irresponsibility*. Talking with other people outside the counseling relationship can be done either in a responsible or in an irresponsible way. This is also true of other aspects of the relationship. For example, a pastor may have made it very clear that an effective counseling situation must be carried on in the pastor's office under discreetly private conditions. A given counselee, however, may insist upon turning every social occasion into a rehearsal of personal problems. All the while, this counselee avoids making an appointment to deal more formally with them. Furthermore, the person who comes for the interview may distort what was actually said in the interview and leave on the community impressions severely threatening to the pastor. The pastor, in turn, may be panicky at hearing the nature of the problems the person has to tell and so may make a referral before establishing a relationship deep enough for the pastor's word about the referral to be understood. These pastors may throw up their hands in helplessness and say, "There is nothing I can do to help you." On both sides of the encounter, irresponsibility can threaten the whole relationship.

The solid ground of mutually shared responsibility for dealing reciprocally with the problem must be established. The threat of irresponsibility must be faced and removed before any effective counseling actually takes place. In the event that this cannot be removed, pastors should limit their relationship to that degree of responsibility which they can effectively discharge. For example, faced with persons who refuse to discuss their problems, except as informal friends in social situations, pastors can treat them as supportive friends treat their friends but not as persons who are seriously attempting to deal responsibly with problems. Or persons, when they ask a blunt question such as, "What can I do about this?" can be told tactfully that there are persons in the community who can help them. They can be referred to other counselors. Pastors who are panicked by the stories of counselees can tell these persons what they *can* do for these persons before they tell them what they as pastors cannot do. This gives support and removes threat.

THE PROCESS OF PASTORAL COUNSELING

Once precounseling initiatives have been taken and once the "roominess" of a private counseling relationship has been established, the process of pastoral counseling is on its way. A detailed description of this process is somewhat as follows.

The Phase of Participant Understanding

The establishment of a clear covenant of communication tends to develop an atmosphere of trust and security. As William Glasser says, the first step in any kind of counseling is for the counselor and the counselee to become responsible friends. Mutual responsibility provides a basis for both counselor and counselee testing each other as persons and not as means to some ulterior ends. Now they can participate with each other with understanding and purpose as they seek to resolve whatever difficulties the counselee is facing. They focus upon these difficulties. The counselor participates in the worldview of the counselee to the limit of the counselor's vision. As Heidegger says, counselors allow the self of the counselee "to see from itself that which it shows itself, as it shows itself from itself." Counselors empty themselves of their own perspective and participate with understanding in the perspective of the counselees. They do not, for that matter, just sit and listen when what is being said is not really understood. They seek to clarify what the persons are saying in such a way that it means as nearly as possible the same thing to the counselors that it means to the counselees.

Understanding Past and Present. The self-revelations of counselees have a specific time reference. Their conversations consist largely of an alternating penetration into present difficulties punctuated by intermittent flashbacks into the past. They discuss how things have always been in times past. All the while, the present difficulties are being understood somewhat differently than before. The judgment of the present upon the past brings new interpretations to the times past, and vice versa. For example, the person is likely to say, "I used to think . . . , but now it looks different." During this phase of the dialogue, pastors actively listen to what counselees mean by what they say. The process of pastoral counseling consists in a measure of bringing the past and the present to focus realistically upon each other. This is not the abstract process of "getting facts" from counselees; rather, it is the living process of participating in the interpretation and reinterpretation that present and past bring to each other.

Conflicts of Values. The pulling power of a participant kind of listening brings to counselees' clear level of attention the excruciating conflicts in their value systems and in their feelings toward the people who represent these values in their lives. Counselees often peer through an astringent, eye-smarting spiritual smog filled with the fumes of a technological culture. These persons try to discern "between the things that differ," to sense what is vital, and to disentangle themselves from the dead weight of what is not vital. They have to make decisions as to the validity of the way of life that led them to the plight in which they find themselves. They ponder the meaning of those acts which they committed that seemed at the time to be done by others than themselves, a sort of "not me." Then they find a kinship with their own acts that enables them to confess that in deed and in truth it was they who did them. For these deeds *they* were responsible.

One little girl's mother scolded her, saying, "Mary! Only the devil could have made you push your little brother down the stairs and kick him in the face!" She replied, "The devil made me push him down the stairs, Mother. But kicking him in the face was my own idea!" If she had been a contemporary adult, she would probably have uttered some psychological truism such as, "An uncontrollable impulse got hold of me when my little brother came around, and my Mother's rejection of me made it worse." She would have learned how to interpret her own experience in such a way as to avoid responsible decisions. In other words, she could say, "It was 'not me' but my parents who did this thing." But in the process of patient and participant listening, a decisive struggle is going on as to one's own responsibilities, the things one has done which are one's own ideas. The conflict of values comes to the surface in the pastoral counseling relationship. Counselees run a hard course between a darkened, compulsive, over-scrupulous conscience on the one hand and, on the other, the temptation to use the popular distortions of psychology and religion as a means of avoiding self-encounter, personal responsibility, and mature decisions.

Self-Encounter. The acceptance of responsibility for oneself as one is involves making decisions as to the kind of person one really is. One meets oneself in the dialogue of pastoral counseling. This is true of both the counselee and the counselor. One learns of one's typical mode of life, one's characteristic ways of handling one's existence, one's own particular ways of reacting to life. The detailed patterns of self-encounter provide avenues of understanding between counselor and counselee. The point that needs to be made here is that this self-encounter is *reciprocal* at every step of the way. Counselors and counselees both bring a distinct pattern of life to the relationship. Counselors are trained persons, but their training has made them unauthentic beings if they simply "play a role," "act a part," or "pose" a certain way for effect. This is the fallacy of stereotyping one particular method of counseling as normative of all relationships. Counselors avoid real encounter with their counselees when in behalf of a given method they react in unnatural, unauthentic, or devised ways even in the counseling situation itself. This in itself is a form of masking or avoidance of encounter.

Another aspect of this needs to be emphasized. To be one's genuine self without retreat behind an assumed "pose" makes one vulnerable indeed. The vulnerability of the self involves risk in the encounter. Yet without this vulnerability, counselees do not learn to meet themselves as in deed and in fact they really are. Consequently, the process of self-encounter is more often short-circuited by focusing upon "problems," by shadowboxing with ideological positions, and by retreating behind one stereotype after another. This kind of self-avoidance can also be reciprocal in such a way that no genuine conversation ever really takes place. This kind of studied avoidance of self-encounter particularly abounds in premarital pastoral counseling. Ministers may see themselves as "friends of the family," as "functionaries of the church or state," as counselors whose task it is to participate in the processes of understanding of the meaning of marriage. The couple may see a minister only as incidental to the whole procedure, as spiritual guide and interpreter of the meaning of their marriage, or as a person who asks too many embarrassing questions. Probably no particular kind of counseling that a pastor does is fraught with as much avoidance of real self-encounter as premarital counseling.

But the decision to "face up to oneself" is in itself a turning point in the counseling relationship. This marks a "wheeling about" of direction in the processes of understanding. In doing this, persons have really taken hold of the resolving, deciding, and determining powers with which they are endowed. A definite converting of direction in their lives has set in. At the very core of our need to *solve* problems is the prior necessity that counselees *re*solve to meet themselves. Counselors can provide the atmosphere in which this can take place. They can wait patiently while it takes place. But they cannot make this resolution *for* counselees. Only the counselees can do this. A large part of the inner wisdom of counseling rests in the patience of counselors to wait this out and the skill with which they maintain the confidence of the counselees while waiting. Once counselees have resolved to encounter themselves as they really are, however, the relationship moves into a new phase called the covenant-making phase of counseling.

The Covenant-making Phase

Ludwig Binswanger and others emphasize that by nature man, as a "person-who-is-responsible-for-his-actions," chooses.[3] In other words, persons are capable of awareness of their own existence, feel responsible for their existence, and make choices as to what they are going to do with their life. On the other hand, Martin Buber and H. Richard Niebuhr speak of man as a "promise-keeping, promise-breaking being, as a man of faith."[4] One can go farther and say in these two respects that the image of God in humanity becomes vividly clear: God is a responsible God and in history has made the decision to be in Christ. God makes promises and keeps them. God makes covenants, in other words. God relates as a person to humanity within these covenants. The supreme covenant is the new covenant in Jesus Christ.

The distinct characteristic of pastoral counseling is that the covenant-making responsibility of humanity and the covenant of faith in God provide the focal center of the meaning of the counseling. The Spirit of God works within us both to will and to do God's good pleasure. A covenant within an individual or a group begins forming deep in the recesses of the unconscious. The covenant is consciously focused upon the frustration that persons are suffering. It focuses and refocuses several times before the consummatory covenant is formed. These events of concentration may be called covenants in themselves in a progression of spiritual maturity. They are the covenant of confrontation, the covenant of confession, the covenant of forgiveness and restitution, and the covenant of concern. All of them require responsible and adult decision on the part of the individual or the group.

The Covenant of Confrontation. The choice between fantasy and reality is made at the inmost recesses of a person's being. This is a painfully difficult decision because there is always just enough of reality in any fantasy to make it seem "really" real. But the dreamlike quality of this reality is such that psychological mechanisms of isolation, projection, displacement, rationalization, and, most of all, repression, must be used to make up the difference between the world in which the person as a self exists and the world that exists around the person in fact. Even apart from these more or less unconscious mechanisms, individuals and groups can deliberately and in cold blood be irresponsible and brutally unfeeling. The person (or the group) at some point takes a stand, makes a decision, and resolves to face life as it is and not as the person (or the group) would like to have it be. The person chooses not to try to recast "the sorry scheme of things" after his or her own inner design. The person faces up to life the way it is, with all its ambiguity, injustice, and frustration. This is really a covenant with oneself and with life itself. This covenant calls for courage, but the courage itself is an unmustered courage. This courage comes from the patience and understanding that the person has already received as the person has been understood by God and by the person's pastor.

But simply understanding and being understood are not ends within themselves. They lay the groundwork and provide the courage whereby the individual is encouraged to make a covenant to confront life itself as it is. The forces of resolve are counteracted by other forces of resistance. A conflict rages. But the individual covenants—as Perls, Hefferline, and Goodman put it—"to stand out of the way, to give the threat all [his] powers, and . . . to relax useless deliberateness, to let the conflict rage and destroy what must be destroyed."[5] This, put in biblical terms, is like the prodigal son "coming to himself" and choosing, whatever the cost, to face life rather than to run from it, to encounter life as it is rather than to live in a dream world of imagination, however important and treasured the imagination may be.

The Covenant of Confession. In the phase of participant understanding, the counselee may have told the pastor many personal details. But pastoral counseling is not just a matter of "getting the facts," of extracting a history, from the individual. These facts must be confronted on a deeper level of reality, and this takes time. The covenant of confrontation sets this process of "working through" into motion. Then the individual resolves to confess to God his or her own resolution to change. Until now the individual's anxiety and guilt have been directed toward first one person and then another in the individual's field of interpersonal relationships. The covenant of confrontation is followed by a resolve to relate these to God. The human idols whom the individual has both worshiped and desecrated are the sources and target of anxiety and guilt. The covenant of confession transmutes anxiety and guilt into a clearly focused sense of sin in relation to God and God alone. This refocuses the whole perspective of the counselee. The things the individual considered as heinous wrongs before appear to be trivial now. The things the individual did not consider at all become great in the person's mind. Ethical seriousness, free of "gamesmanship," makes for ethical perspective.

The vast difference between anxiety and guilt, on the one hand, and a clear sense of sin, on the other, resides in the fact that anxiety and guilt are related to one's fellow human beings and a clear sense of sin is related to God. That which our mothers, fathers, brothers, sisters, husband, or wife would consider a very grievous wrong would easily be overlooked by God. That which they would never think of would be foremost in our relationship to God, namely, our prideful unteachableness, our unwillingness to forgive, and our idolatry. The covenant of confession is in relation to God as God is known in Jesus Christ. Here is one who tells us all that we have ever done and yet accepts us, receives us, forgives us. Entry into this covenant of confession activates a deeper resolve in the counselee: a covenant of forgiveness and restitution.

The Covenant of Forgiveness and Restitution. Persons who feel they have been accepted and forgiven move to reconsider all the other relationships of their lives. Counselees who have faced their own humanity and have been accepted by God are more permissive with the persons about them. They cease to expect perfection in others and can make more room for others' personal shortcomings. Even though others have committed grievous errors, these counselees can reassess their relationship to these persons and be more forgiving toward them. The commitment to do this is a covenant of forgiveness for the wounds that one has received. This in turn reminds persons of the wounds they have inflicted in conflict with others. They are likely to discuss with the pastoral counselor at this stage the various things they can do to make restitution and to repair damages they have inflicted. This is a covenant of moral responsibility which reflects the distinctly ethical task of the pastoral counselor. One clinical note from the annals of Alcoholics Anonymous becomes relevant in most counseling relationships that reach this stage of maturity. Persons in Alcoholics Anonymous agree to make amends to those they have harmed, "except where to do so would cause more harm." Thus the covenant of forgiveness and restitution is such as to redeem and not to perpetuate the sufferings arising between people.

The Covenant of Concern. The genuinely profound changes that can and do take place in private pastoral counseling can and do issue in a new covenant of concern on the part of the person or group who has changed and been changed. This is a much more crucial stage of pastoral counseling than is true in other forms of counseling. Professional pastoral counselors who make their living through individual and group fees, for instance, have a fee-taking structure through which counselees regularly express their concern and gratitude through the fees they pay. Pastoral counselors who are supported by a church, a school, or some other institution have the resources of the church itself to which to relate persons' concern for other people and especially for themselves as persons. However, pastors may be so impressed by the superficial changes that have taken place in the reordering of their counselees' lives that they will ignore the significance of the counselees' need to express their gratitude. Their subtle adoration of counselors themselves may be the way counselees covenant to make this concern known. For example, Jesus was acutely aware of the Gadarene demoniac's gratitude when the man wanted to go with him wherever he went. Rather, Jesus sent the man back to his home village as a witness to his recovery. This was probably the most difficult task the man could have been assigned. But Jesus chose to deflect the man's adoration from himself as an individual to the community that needed him desperately, that is, to the citizens of Gadara, who were busy with the swine!

The Phase of Community Involvement

Persons who have profited from pastoral counseling still live in the same community with the pastor. The private counseling now begins to take on a public quality. Their witness to the rest of the community by whatever changes have been effected in their lives intimately bespeaks the quality and motivation of the pastor's work. On the other hand, their relationship to the community of the church becomes crucial. Persons who carried a burden of shame and who felt they were "not fit" to be in a church can now attend with a new sense of joy and participation. Persons who vowed that they would never attend church again because of wrongs done to them by some other members of the church can now, after having received the concentrated encouragement of the intensive relationships of pastoral counseling, return to church of their own accord. Persons who used the church as an atonement procedure by attending every meeting and wanting to run everything can now participate in the life of the church without so much compulsiveness.

Furthermore, the average counseling relationship refocuses in the latter phases of the interview situation. The decisions that have been made and the covenants that have been resolved must be "carried out" in daily living. The couple who were having severe marital difficulties will now begin to be concerned about their children in a way that they previously were not. The young couple who underwent more intensive counseling in their engagement period will need the resources of the church in establishing their home. Older persons who are bereaved by the loss of a spouse will need the continuing sustenance of people their own age in the church. The church provides an avenue both for expressing new concerns and for receiving the concerns of others.

In those instances where the process of counseling bogged down or the persons refused to make a decision of any kind, the pastor still has the resources of the church to draw upon in ministering to the individual. Persons may well be so irresponsible emotionally that medical and psychiatric ministries are indicated. Their very illness may be represented by their inability to make decisions and covenants. Pastors may well call upon professional medical resources, but they always do so in the name of the church.

A clear distinction has been made here between pastoral counseling and psychotherapy. The assumption concerning pastoral counseling is that it is done by the pastor of a church, a chaplain in a hospital, or a minister who teaches in a school. In this sense pastoral counseling is one function of the total role of such persons. Only occasionally do these persons do work that approximates the psychotherapeutic relationship, technically defined. Rather, they are involved in a larger public community—a church, a school, or a hospital. These institutions are integral and not incidental to the whole relationship of pastoral counseling. As has been said before, the uniqueness of pastoral counseling emerges at this very point.

Pastors and their counselees are a part of an ongoing community, and the covenant of concern that springs up within the life of the individual is tested and affirmed in their relationships in this community. The most satisfying aspect of pastoral counseling rests in the establishment of counselees and those about them in the fellowship of faith, concern, and suffering known as the church. Furthermore, the most exacting judgments of the efficacy of pastoral counseling lie in the outcome *within the community* of many so-called successes in individual conferences. Yet, if these judgments seem harsh, pastors' mistakes are also overruled in the larger wisdom of time and community. What pastors considered to be failures are later seen to be successes. But the decisive covenants made in pastoral counseling in either instance are carried out in the continuing multifaceted work of pastors.

PRIVATE COUNSELING AND PUBLIC SOCIAL ACTION

All that has been said focuses upon the private counseling relationship. The objective of such counseling, contrary to protestations of social action critics, is not the mere adjustment of people to the faulty institutions of society. As Don Browning says, effective pastoral care and counseling "acknowledges that it has a larger context which somehow or other governs its specific goals and procedures." He says that pastoral counseling techniques should "reflect and implement" the goals of the church and the larger culture of society in general.[6] Yet, as was indicated in the discussion of the institutional and personal dimensions of pastoral counseling, much that actually goes on in pastoral counseling has come to pass because both church and society are not taking responsibility for the private personal needs of the person that cannot be covered by their own rituals, routines, and over-the-counter panaceas for human suffering. In turn, much is learned in the privacy of the counseling room that gives pastors a "microscopic lab report" on the massive social injustices that need changing. Such reports make ethically and socially conscious pastoral counselors much more realistic and less sentimental about *what* social action needs to be taken and *how* to see to it that the changes are actually made.

Consequently, the phase of community involvement in pastoral counseling often turns the counseling relationship into a "coaching relationship" as counselees battle with changing a defective home situation, a set of working conditions, the interpretation of the roles of women and men, prejudice about race, specific relationships to the poor, precise injustices in the military draft, and severe damage to human life in situations such as mining, the textile industry, and migrant agricultural work. A counseling session may be a time-out from the battle for changes in these situations. Regular infusions of ego strength are needed for such social action battles. Much pastoral counseling today, for example, is with public figures who are change agents. Some pastoral counseling is with power figures who are resisting change. They are in the process of making faulty judgment decisions, or need counseling as a result of some of the threats to their lives.

Several issues arise and certain procedures are necessitated when private pastoral counseling and public social action work hand in glove together. Let me enumerate a few.

Preaching and Pastoral Counseling

The routine public appearance of the minister is as a preacher. Too many pastors are confined to this one medium, but do not need to be. Frederick W. Robertson, the English preacher of the first half of the nineteenth century, was a social activist in the early days of the labor movement. He reserved his sermons for meaty biblical exegesis in a context of worship. But for debating controversial issues he used lectures in his own church and community. Pastors today could well copy this, because much of the resistance they get from using the sermon as a tool of social change comes from the injustice people feel because they cannot interrupt these pastors to contradict *or* to reinforce what they are saying. The lecture situation provides just that opportunity. It also provides more time to develop arguments and provide detail.

The *forum* and the *panel* provide the additional force to other voices than that of the pastor as a way of shaping attitudes on social issues. A variety of positions on issues could be implemented. The hard facts of ethical and cultural pluralism in our churches, as well as in our larger community, could be made public. Thus the rigidity of our respectability "front" could be limbered up a bit.

Private pastoral counseling relationships can serve as "feedback loops," as the communication experts call them, for enabling a pastor to identify *what* issues to discuss in public and to follow up the results of pastors' public discussions. Persons who are deeply affected by such social problems will often come to a public meeting when they would never ask for private help. Massive numbers of people can begin to form a relationship of trust with their pastors through preaching, lecturing, and forums. They can then be helped on an individual, private basis in much less time. Whole families can participate together in these public experiences and then can be provided with private family therapy as a family unit.

The public discussion of issues, however, raises the problem of the specific use of counseling data from private conferences in preaching. Several things can be said about this as concrete guidelines. First, pastors should plan ahead of time for any such references and not ad-lib about their counseling experiences. This adds reflection to impulse. Second, preachers should have the person's permission in advance to make such a reference in public. The person could then participate in "the making of the sermon." I have even had people, without my asking, write down for me what they would like said. Then *their* witness is borne in their own words. At least, their permission and approval of a written version of precisely what will be said is only reasonable and right. Third, pastors should say in public only that which edifies or builds up the person; they should leave unsaid that which would embarrass, hurt, or betray the person. Many uses of case material are little more than horrible examples being held up in contempt. Other uses are expressions of frustration and anger on the part of preachers. Yet when the person's courage in the face of adversity, humor in the face of life or death, and commitment to God in spite of injustice are told, this becomes "good news," which is what preaching at its best is.

The plight of some of these persons serves as a magnifying glass for the sickness of a community as a whole, for target on social changes that need to be made, and so forth. This case material, when finely honed, becomes parables of modern man, modeled after the parables of Jesus.

Writing and Social Action. Pastors today have the medium of publication as an instrument of social change. They can gather mountains of data from personal counseling attempts to help change social conditions. For example, a mountainous set of problems recur in marriage counseling—problems precipitated by the wife taking a job. In our present inflated economy, the working wife and mother is becoming the rule rather than the exception. A broad-scale approach to the provision of adequate day care for children of parents of all stations in life is a social change that needs to be made. The problems in poverty, race, and family disorganization are all tangled together in this need. Pastors can write for the local newspaper, for the ecclesiastical newspapers, and for the publishing houses of denominations to raise the awareness of people to this need. When pastors do so they can do something specific about *one* of the objectives of women's liberation.[7]

Any topic is "open season" for writing "tracts for the times" in order to effect social change. It is one way of going on record as citizens on public issues. A reverse kind of private ministry is thus set in motion. Anonymous telephone calls, threats, and underground reactions can occur. At least, I have had it happen periodically.

The Pastor as an Organizer. Social action is so much talk unless specific changes are made in old structures and unless new structures are organized to meet new needs. The tight-knit nuclear family with fixed roles for fixed people in a fixed small-town society still meets the needs of small-town families for a haven of privacy from the extended family of the church and community where everybody knows too much about everybody else. On the other hand, the tight-knit nuclear family in a large city where the neighborhood is also nonexistent is left in isolation and with little or no life-support system. The nuclear family can be and is pulverized by economic aggrandizement of property owners, by the jungle of an impossible school system, and by the spiraling of the costs of food where there are no gardens, pigs and cattle, chickens and fish.

Therefore pastors in large cities who see this happening to family after family are inadequate pastoral counselors unless they begin to venture with groups of families to meet one another's needs for community, for concerted power to act as families in unison, and to share their unused surpluses in meeting one another's needs. Accordingly, a group of young families in the same New York apartment building formed a cooperative for purchasing at quantity and wholesale prices. Another group in the Old Cambridge Baptist Church in Old Cambridge, Massachusetts, began an experiment in cooperative ownership of property as a group of families. This takes time and energy in organizing, and unless ministers are willing to be a part of efforts to change structures more adequately to activate the love of God and neighbor, then their pastoral counseling, like their preaching, fund-raising, and membership recruitment, may be parasitic, feeding upon rather than productive of human potentials.

Private Pastoral Counseling
as a Form of Social Action

Thomas à Kempis once said that no person can safely appear abroad until they have first disciplined themselves to stay out of sight. It does not take a sophisticated person to see that some—not all—of the efforts at social action in the last decades were motivated, in part at least, by the desire for publicity, by the desire for excitement, and by the desire to destroy. When the publicity, the excitement, and the opportunity to vandalize disappeared, a considerable portion of the social activism receded. Yet the social problems remain, although their shapes may have changed. Although young men are no longer under the hammer of the draft, thanks much to social activism, the problems of children in Vietnam are still horrendous at this writing. The urban renewal movement tore down the slums, but the poor still have impossible rents and the elderly are segregated more and more.

The people who make decisions about these inequities are quite often—for other reasons—the counselees of pastors. Many pastors serve as private chaplain to powerful politicians, industrialists, and financiers. As has been nationally observed, outstanding evangelists are being pressed into public identification with political leaders. We know what these ministers do publicly; we wonder what they do privately as counselors to the heads of government. Are they captives of the publicity? Are they tools used for political purposes? Do they have any confrontations in private? The answers to these questions are not known.

Historically, the private counseling of power figures by pastors, prophets, and priests has been recorded only anecdotally. Jeremiah was sent for by Zedekiah the king. "The king questioned him secretly in his house, and said, 'Is there any word from the LORD?' Jeremiah said, 'There is.' Then he said, 'You shall be delivered into the hand of the king of Babylon'" (Jer. 37:17). Nathan also counseled with David the king concerning David's rebellion against God for having had Uriah the Hittite killed and for having taken the man's wife (2 Sam. 12:1–5). A curious commentary about the private versus the public dimensions of life appears in Nathan's words from the Lord to David: "For you did it secretly; but I will do this thing before all Israel, and before the sun." When we overidentify being prophetic with the public activities of ministers, these two quiet conversations in secret with power figures must be remembered. Sometimes the

94

quiet confrontation of a courageous personal counseling interview can effect as much social change as can much public, visible protest.

For example, the quiet visit of a pastor in a southern state, along with three of his lay church members, to the governor of the state concerning the rights of blacks in that whole state did as much to change the structures of discrimination as did much public clamor. One reason was that the three laymen were heavy contributors to the governor's campaign fund. The four of them—the laymen and the pastor together—did not have to raise their voices to convince the governor that it was to *his* advantage to withdraw a certain order. Yet no one received much publicity, not even from the governor, as to why the order was withdrawn.

My private hypothesis about the role of pastors in social action has not, to my knowledge, been researched thoroughly. And the measurable effects of the involvement of pastors in public techniques of social change have not been researched to any great extent, either. The tension between social activist critics of pastoral counseling and the general trends of the movement of pastoral counseling is a healthy one. We stand tempted to be parasitically rather than creatively involved in the established structures of church and society, particularly in the economy. We can become fat and at ease in Zion with little or no social passion or concern. Socially sensitive and ethically aware pastoral counselors, however, have a rebuttal: Our tension with the social action enthusiasts is at two points. (1) There is more than one method of social action, and our life-style is more adaptable to private methods than to public ones, although both have the same objectives. (2) Since we have seen human injustice microscopically in the counseling room, our methods of social action are geared to the pragmatic intention of actually getting results and not just to the satisfaction of having spoken about results and of having been seen trying to get results. At this last point, the sound and the fury of much social action effort is just that and it signifies nothing measurable in actual changes.

The Pastor as Politician

The question arises as to the role of pastors—both public and private—as political figures. I frankly have had a commitment as a political spirit since my days as a page in the United States Senate. The disturbing thing to me about pastors as politicians is that we tend to become politically concerned only when our own vested interests are at stake. Congregations may think it quite appropriate when pastors become concerned about the taxation of church-owned property, about Sunday closing laws, and—in many instances—about alcoholic beverage control laws. These are self-maintenance concerns. Yet when ministers become politically active about equal housing rights, equal job opportunities for women (and especially black women), about adequate treatment facilities for alcoholics, and about the confusion of four generations of late adolescents by the draft, they have begun to "mix politics and religion." The most ardent opponents that pastors tend to have are persons who are lawyers. We have worked very hard at relating ourselves as ministers to medical doctors, social workers, and psychologists. The lines between the professional politicians, most of whom are lawyers, however, is a cold war battle line as formidable as the Berlin Wall was for a whole generation of persons. Yet these professionals are by profession *counselors*-at-law. The great dividing wall of hostility to be scaled in another area of pastoral counselors is between the professional politicians and ourselves.

Pastoral counselors must recognize that in the matter of being or not being political, they have no choice. By nature, any public office, such as that of pastor, is inherently political in the classical sense of the word. The pastor's choice is between being an ethically consistent and socially effective politician and being a self-serving and/or socially ineffective politician.

The essential correspondence between pastors as counselors and pastors as politicians is that both roles call for a "weight of being." The degree of personal charisma and its attendant power of persuasion that ministers have is increased or decreased in terms of their seniority in a community and the ways in which they have stood by and cared for people in good times and bad times. When they choose to "throw their weight around" on a given issue, they must "weigh in" first. Even when they decide that they have such power, they are bound to use that power according to the historic—though not necessarily cultural—identity and function of representatives (of the right kind) of God. They cannot fritter it away on trivialities. As John Henry Newman has said, the good confessor must bypass the small things with permissiveness and wait for the emergence of the larger issues of the corporate ethical life. Wherever ministers have been effective as politicians, they have not been squeamish or careless stewards of the power they possess. Nor have they perceived it as *their* power to be used cleverly. Rather, they have used this power on a face-to-face basis; they have used it carefully, as stewards of a gift; they have perceived the power as a gift from God and not of themselves. Yet, withal, they have not permitted a covert return of pietism in which they play games about the use of power. (Such a game is played when pastors preserve their pietism by thinking of themselves euphemistically as some sort of "change agents." Thus they avoid thinking of themselves as what they are: politicians.) And, finally, ministers who are effective politicians have learned not to expect utopian success in *every* political effort: they win some, and they lose some! The crucial test of character is whether they can laugh in *both* instances or only when they win.

The ability to laugh as a politician focuses the issue of manipulation by pastors—or anyone else—as politicians. As Adlai Stevenson said upon losing the race for President, "I am too old to cry, and it hurts too bad to laugh." When he said this, he ruled out another necessary component of manipulation—deception. He was honest. On the other hand, Richard Nixon, upon losing the race for the California governorship, announced to newspaper reporters that he was through with politics. While the people were believing him, he laid plans to become President. The issue of manipulation is always at stake when pastors use power. Four conditions must prevail: a *conflict of goals* between them and their adversaries; an *intention* to cause their adversaries to do something the adversaries do not want to do; a deliberate *deception* in keeping persons from knowing all they need to know to make an informed choice; a *sense of elation, glee, and laughter* at having "outdone," "taken," or "fooled" adversaries. These are, according to Ben Bursten, the stuff of which manipulation is made.[8]

Pastors are part of a secular and religious culture that "laughs with" a considerable range of manipulators. The great contribution that the psychological disciplines of trained pastoral counselors can provide for the social action efforts of pastors in discharging their ethical responsibilities is to test their motives for social action by relieving them of their naïveté about changing structure of society and at the same time testing their lust to be clever.

Manipulation, it seems to me, is of four orders: (1) manipulation of the powerful by the powerless out of anger at injustice, in order to survive as persons; (2) manipulation as a mechanical habit formed in a situation where survival was at stake but continued in later situations where manipulation is no longer really necessary; (3) manipulation as a luxury of the clever who manipulate for the sheer delight of reinforcing their self-concept of themselves as omnipotent and all-wise (this is cleverness for cleverness' sake); and (4) manipulation as the use of old habits, learned in times of struggle for personal survival, for the purpose of protecting the helpless, providing for the desolate, and introducing the element of fairness in conflicts where the odds are uneven.

Pastors have to be wiser than the children of darkness, and as wise as serpents and as harmless as doves, because they do their work as sheep in the midst of wolves. Only in their prayers can they decide what kind of manipulators they are.

NOTES

1. See Max Thurian, *Confession,* trans. Edwin Hudson (London: SCM Press, 1958); and Eduard Thurneysen, *A Theology of Pastoral Care* (Richmond: John Knox Press, 1962).

2. William Harold Tremann, *The Right to Silence* (Richmond: John Knox Press, 1964).

3. Rollo May and others, eds., *Existence: A New Dimension in Psychiatry and Psychology* (New York: Basic Books, 1958), p. 41.

4. H. Richard Niebuhr, *Radical Monotheism and Western Culture* (New York: Harper & Brothers, 1960), p. 41.

5. Frederick S. Perls and others, *Gestalt Therapy: Excitement and Growth in the Human Personality* (New York: Julian Press, 1951), p. 359.

6. Don Browning, "Notes on the Context of Pastoral Care" (unpublished paper).

7. See Robin Morgan, ed., *Sisterhood Is Powerful: An Anthology of Writings from the Women's Liberation Movement* (New York: Random House, 1970).

8. Ben Bursten, *The Manipulator: A Psychoanalytic View* (New Haven, Conn.: Yale University Press, 1973), pp. 95ff.

6

A Pathology of Religious Leadership

Much attention has been drawn to the role of pathology in the motivation, functioning, and sense of direction of the religious leader. Underlying some of this concern is a *search for validity* of the claims religious leaders have upon the loyalty of their followers, as well as a search for the validity of the truth that they preach. Job is dramatic when he says to Zophar the Naamathite and the other "advisers" with him:

> As for you, you whitewash with lies;
> worthless physicians are you all.
> Oh that you would keep silent,
> and it would be your wisdom!
> (Job 13:4, 5)

Both the Judaic and the Christian literature of the Bible reflect awareness of and detailed concern about the sanity and soundness of mind of the leaders of Judaism and Christianity. A brief review of the experiences of Saul, for example, provides good background for the study of a pathology of contemporary leaders of religion.

In 1 Sam. 16:14ff., an "evil spirit" is said to have tormented Saul when the Spirit of the Lord departed from him. The evil spirit was also sent by the Lord. Saul's servants recommended music therapy to free him of the tormenting spirit. David, his later competitor, was a skillful musician with the lyre, "a man of valor, a man of war, prudent in speech, and a man of good presence; and the LORD . . . [was] with him." The musician was as important to the therapy as was the music. David found favor in the sight of Saul: "Saul loved him greatly" and made him his armor-bearer. Through David's music and his presence, "Saul was refreshed, and was well, and the evil spirit departed from him." The narrative speaks of *both* evil spirits *and* illness; Saul became well and free of the evil spirits.

This same Saul became troubled again, as is recorded in 1 Sam. 28:3–17. Samuel, the spiritual parent who had been Saul's guide for years, had died. Saul had previously "put the mediums and the wizards out of the land." In the face of an assault by the Philistine army, Saul resorted to prayer for guidance and then, having received no answer, turned to his dreams, to his advisers, and to prophets successively. In all these he failed. In his desperation, he himself sought out a medium, a woman at Endor. Through her he sought contact with the departed spirit of Samuel, whom the medium called "a god coming up out of the earth," to whom Saul "bowed with his face to the ground, and did obeisance." The message he received through the medium was a prophecy of his own failure as king because the Lord had "torn the kingdom out of . . . [his] hand" and given it to David. Filled with fear at the words of Samuel, Saul lost his strength from not having eaten for a day and a night. Later, having been wounded in battle, and facing capture by the enemy, he killed himself by falling upon his sword (1 Sam. 31:4).

This is one of the most complete psychosocial histories of an emotionally disturbed religious leader to be found in Judeo-Christian scriptures. It demonstrates how idolatry of the dead and a resort to magic and superstition both converged in the disabling illness and final suicide of a religious leader. Anton Boisen repeatedly said that acute emotional illnesses are a reaction to a gross sense of personal failure. The story of Saul is replete with an increasing pattern of failure. The male religious leader is likely to stay well or get sick emotionally in terms of his vocational success or failure. A religious leader comes more nearly to staking his or her whole life on the success or failure of the day's work. In this respect, *idolatry of one's role* is the most common form of sick religion among religious leaders. The resort to magic and superstition as "means of cunning" to maintain and secure one's "position" or " role" as a religious leader is the next most prevalent expression of the pathology of religious leadership.

IDEALIZATION AND OMNICOMPETENCE

This one hypothesis as to the role of pathology in the religious vocation can be stated: the investment of one's total destiny in one's power to perform a given "job" as a religious leader results in fictitious goals for life that produce a pathological religion. In turn, these fictitious goals blend with the person's illusion of omnipotence and denial of human limitations. A secondary reaction is that, moving upon the fictitious goal of one's own omnicompetence, the religion of the sick religious leader tends to deteriorate into magic, cleverness, and manipulation.

An example of this kind of pathological religious leadership is that of a case entitled "The Case of Father M.," by Herbert Holt, M.D.[1] The case is extensively presented and will be summarized here.

Father M.

Father M. is a Catholic priest studying in a secular university in order to achieve double competency in both the priesthood and a secular profession.

His Presenting Symptoms. These included a plan to dismiss all incompetent priests and to reorganize the whole Catholic priesthood. He had a labyrinthine plan for doing this. He agreed to seek psychiatric help in order to enlist the psychiatrist in his plans for reorganizing the priesthood. He was a domineering man, cynical, superior, a know-it-all who felt that humility, though theoretically a Christian virtue, would deny a man of his talent his rightful leadership role. He felt that people existed in order to fulfill his demands. Those who would make him promises and fail to keep them were hypocrites deserving of his hatred. As Dr. Holt says, his view of himself and his world "was the only reality he accepted, and he reinforced his acceptance by believing what he heard himself saying."

The History and Background. Father M. was one of a large family of children. His earliest memories were of habits of crying, soiling himself, and thinking of himself as a "great pig" and that his body was an alien "thing" to him. He had a sense of inner worthlessness occasioned by much sexual preoccupation. He had homosexual episodes with his older brothers. He defied his mother because he felt she neglected him and did not help him solve his great feelings of loneliness.

Father M.'s religious interests began when he turned into puberty. He refused to take up swimming because it was "charged with sexuality" for him. He was frightened by aggressive girls. His sexuality went to autoerotism, except for one instance when he unsuccessfully sought to seduce a girl. As a result, he was awakened to new religious commitment at a church retreat. He committed himself totally to his mother and made a habit of accompanying her each day to early mass. Religion also became a weapon for controlling the rest of the family when they sought to assert themselves against him.

His "overbearing and inconsiderate manner was the cloak in adulthood for an overpowering inner sense of unworthiness developed in childhood." In an autobiographical note, Father M. says, "I suppose if we named the central problem we would call it *my* inhumanity. It's that I think that I should be perfect; it's the guilt from not being so that punishes me when I fail. It is that which inhibits my understanding of a poem or a picture; I don't know what is going on—what emotions are being expressed—because what is expressed is foreign to my vocabulary. Although I think I should respond, I can't, because the poem elicits no real feeling. That feeling was denied long since.

"That inhumanity comes from my father. Father was authority. In my desire to please my father, to get his love, I had to please authority, and to please authority, I imitated it. So I have imitated it until it has become fairly habitual with me. I am probably as much like my father as he could make me.

"If I am to get free from this inhumanity, this superman humanity, I've got to throw off this need for authority and its approval, and free myself from the straitjacket it imposes.

"I thought for a while that I might go into the Army, without finishing school, in order to break away from my parents. But that would only put me under the rule of a greater authority, and the temptation to get approval from it would probably be too great. Instead of trying to become one of the men, I would alienate myself from them in trying to get above them."

This is one side of the religious haughtiness of Father M. However, a written message to Dr. Holt from the mother of the patient throws new light on the dynamics of his commitment to the priesthood. She wrote:

"I was very unhappy with my husband when I became pregnant with my boy. He spent very little time with me and the children, and I was very lonely. One day when my son was twelve years of age we all started to talk about what the children would become. I knew that my tender-hearted son could not cope with life outside, and so I told him that I wanted him to be a priest, but my son at that time wanted to become an architect, which would mean eight years of study. When he said so, his father flew into a rage and started to beat him in front of us all, hitting him with his fists all over his head and body, knocking out one tooth, so that he bled from his mouth. We stepped between them to avoid further injury. My husband went to his bedroom, packed a bag, and said, 'I'm leaving.' He started to leave, but my son, bleeding from his mouth, said, 'Please, Daddy, come back. Don't leave. I'll be a good boy. I'll leave and go to school.' He left next day, a pretty dejected fellow."

The pathology of religious leadership in Father M. is a poignant story of a desperate appeal for a "greater than he" who could be a "Saviour he had not found in the church or his family." He projected his denied wish, not upon God, but upon his own self-image. This grew more and more unrealistic in its idealization and omnicompetence. He idealized his own self-image on the positive side of his conscious *Eigenwelt*. However, his sadness over his mother's neglect of him and his unrepeatable woe over his father's punishment of him held him in bondage to his loneliness and rejection.

The intensely absent reality in the story of Father M. is that of any dialogical relationship to God himself. He experiences religion as a "thing" that he touches only by proxy. Forms of religion are the tools of his pathetic fantasies of power, but they are not "means of grace" whereby his self-rejection of himself as a "great pig" is nullified and replaced by an acceptance of an enjoyment of his inner life and personal space.

THE POWER ORIENTATION
OF RELIGIOUS LEADERS

Whereas the refusal to accept his humanity lay close to the heart of Father M.'s grandiosity, the honest and unabashed search for power for its own sake results differently. It evolves into a more sociopathic personality disorder.

This is seen in embryo in an intensive, in-depth study of seventeen theological students by Richard Hester. He found that five of the students felt their pastoral authority helped them to overcome "a sense of personal impotence" and to secure "personal power they would not have otherwise." Two others understood pastoral leadership and authority as a means of securing power over others. Hester says there is another, healthier alternative, and that is a *functional* rather than a *power* implementation of the leadership authority of the pastor. Six of his subjects were found to be implementing their authority as a religious leader in order to serve others rather than serve their own power needs. These students varied in their maturity within this grouping, however. One of them was absorbed in pressing technology to serve mankind by giving himself to amateur radio announcing and mastering electronic devices for "the common good." Three of these students took an immanent, humanistic view of the work of God and saw themselves "meeting human needs." Only two of these students showed a theocentric focus of their identity as a pastor. The remaining six of the group of seventeen students were suffering severe anxiety because underlying conflicts with parents, the need to be perfect, and ambivalence about being an adult kept them from a wholehearted participation in or a frank disavowal of the authority usually vested in a religious leader.

The sociopathic power orientation of the religious leader does not of itself take the leader into a hospital. Rather, his inner dividedness takes form in the groups he seeks to lead. Almost instinctively, and certainly by reason of his inconsistent and/or ambivalent parental upbringing, this person divides and conquers the groups he leads. Without forethought or plan, he effects transactions that give him a ringside seat while others fight. Occasionally this boomerangs. Those whom he has set over against each other join forces against him with the deadly purpose of hanging him from the nearest, highest yardarm or tree! Ordinarily, however, the leadership of this person only causes one minor conflict after another in the lives of those whom he purports to lead. He is known for the number of people who *leave* his church, school, or movement. Resignation is one sure way out from under the leadership of a person who divides and conquers those whom he leads. Pope John XXIII presented the antithesis of this kind of leadership as he said:

> May everyone of us be able to say: I have not dug furrows for division and distrust, I have not darkened immortal souls with suspicion or fear; I have been frank, loyal and trustful; I have looked those who do not share my ideals straight in the eye and treated them with brotherly affection in order not to impede God's great purpose.[2]

The work of Richard Hester plainly indicates that the sociopathic use of the place of religious leadership can be identified, detected, and confronted for what it is in the process of theological education. Also, John M. MacDonald suggests ways for quickly identifying the sociopathic personality. Prompt ways are needed in order to confront the sociopathic religious leader *before* he gains access to the forms of religion for the sake of the power and authority vested in them by the religious community.

MacDonald suggests that the deliberate use of vague and extensive language to answer questions is one evidence of the sociopath: he protects his real position with an abundance of vague words. Yet the sociopathic person persuades himself that he is a very truthful person because he answers other people's questions very literally. For example, when asked if he has ever applied to a theological seminary before, he will answer with a no. What he means, he convinces himself, is that he has never applied to *this* seminary before. In fact, he has applied to three and been rejected by all three. Therefore, three or four questions, not one, must be asked: (1) Has he ever applied to this seminary before? (2) Has he ever applied to any other seminary anywhere else? (3) Which seminary accepted him? (4) Which seminary rejected him and why?

MacDonald says the psychopathic (or sociopathic) person often demonstrates both paranoid and depressive reactions, especially when caught in misdemeanors or frustrated in his or her global sense of power. The sociopath, says MacDonald, undetected and allowed to go unhindered, may be found in places of high rank.[3] Obviously, the best strategy in dealing with the sociopathic person is early detection and elimination from places of religious leadership.

THE PATHOLOGY OF RELIGIOUS LEADERSHIP AS SEEN IN BREAKS WITH REALITY

Among the schizophrenic group of mental patients are found persons whose illness is focused upon a kind of religious perception that has only minimal contact with reality. The religious consciousness of these patients has been studied by Howe, Boisen, and Rokeach at different times and in different places over the last half century.

Clifford Farr and Reuel Howe

In the late 1920s and early 1930s, Clifford Farr, M.D., and the Reverend Reuel Howe made a study of the influence of religious ideas on the psychoses.[4] They noted the combined effect of both social and religious isolation, a marked factor in leadership of any kind, now spoken of as "executive loneliness." Farr and Howe extended their study to five hundred consecutive cases, 342 females and 158 males. Fourteen percent, or sixty-eight cases, "were found with definite religious content."

From the point of view of the pathology of religious leadership, several factors may be extrapolated from their work. First are the emotional breakdowns of religious leaders who are doing their work because of a desire to fulfill other people's wishes that they be religious workers rather than because of their own personal choice to do so. The following case excerpt is illustrative:

> Case 11130, female, 34, Church of the Brethren. Diagnosis: manic-depressive psychosis, mixed. The patient was brought up in a strongly religious environment to be a missionary, but she was not a very enthusiastic one. She also studied nursing. In the mission field she was considered a very efficient worker, but broke down. There had been a conflict between her own sense of inadequacy and lack of inclination for the work and the unconscious pressure of the family and the religious denomination. In her psychosis there were pronounced mood swings.[5]

A second case illustrates an interpretation of emotional illness as a call to religious leadership in its own right. A woman "claims that after

105

seeing the Lord Jesus, she was saved, and that God sent her to the hospital to save others because she had been restrained too much in the past."[6] As another patient, in interpreting her childlike behavior, told me, "I was never permitted to be a child when I was a child and now I am catching up when I can."

Farr and Howe concluded their study with a discussion by Clarence B. Farrar, who used the threefold classification of William Osler to distinguish mental patients' religious concerns. Osler said that the doctrine of immortality and other religious beliefs were accepted differently by men. One group he named the "Laodiceans," a majority, who accept a belief but their lives are uninfluenced by it. Another and smaller group he named the "Gallionians," after Gallio, "who cared for none of these things." The third group, and the smallest one, are the "Theresans," who, like St. Theresa, the Carmelite nun, are deeply religious folk "for whom the life of the spirit is the only real life."[7] Among the mentally ill, as in the general population, there are very few persons for whom the life of the spirit is the only real life.

Anton T. Boisen

Anton Boisen, however, would contend that there *are* a few persons who feel this way and that their sense of commitment should be taken seriously, even though they seem "crazy" to the Laodiceans!

Boisen calls attention to the process whereby a "deviating set of religious beliefs are translated into social organization." He says that such religious leaders as George Fox (1624–1691), the English founder of the Society of Friends, or Quakers, manifested many of the behaviors of mental patients today:

> Inventors, poets, and others who do creative work have such experiences frequently. Among men of religious genius they are of crucial importance. They figure in what is called "inspiration" or "revelation." Most religious movements are based upon faith in the divine authority of some such experience. . . . Great religious leaders . . . have had their inspirations, their revelations, their messages from the Lord. But so also do many mental patients. They too hear God talking to them and believe that they have been given a prophetic mission.[8]

Boisen then sets himself to the task of distinguishing a true prophet from a false, "and how a deviating set of beliefs are organized and tested," thus bringing about a social reform and a new social organization. One criterion he uses is the *historical continuity* of a leader like Fox with previous, tested, and approved prophets like Calvin. Continuity is *one* of the "operations of common sense." Another criterion is consistency of stabilized social effectiveness in communicating the beliefs to others. This consistency is based upon a kind of humility about the contradictions and complexities that still remain. In other words, there is an openness and a teachability in the true prophet that does not appear in the paranoid, grandiose, and persecutory attitudes of some mentally sick religious leaders. Such patients are not acutely disturbed, says Boisen, but are drifting and surrendering to self-concealment and deception.

A genuine consistency in the true prophet prompts him to test his insights and revelations "by some stream of tradition," by social criticism and acceptance, and by the social consequences they produce. Through this social process, new ideas are assimilated into social organizations.

In an extensive case history of a black patient named Mickle, Boisen discusses the concept of the patient as a religious leader in the light of his psychopathology. He concludes by saying that the "signals" or voices that Mickle got from God needed to be taken seriously as stirrings of a religious concern.

> The medieval mystics had to learn the lesson that some of the ideas which came surging into their minds could hardly come from God. They assumed that they must have come from the devil. Perhaps we of today need to learn the converse lesson, that all auditory hallucinations do not necessarily come from the devil but may represent the operations of the creative mind.[9]

Anton Boisen was my teacher. I have often heard him say that it takes more than one generation to judge whether a religious leader is crazy or not, that the mentally sick person may be in an acute fever of religious concern as he finds his real direction in life and place in the world, and that a genuine religious leader can be separated from the counterfeit by his humility or openness to instruction from others.

Søren Kierkegaard

These wise sayings are not complete, however, and Boisen would be the first to say that he too prophesies in part. An even more complete approach to distinguishing between fantasy and reality is made by Søren Kierkegaard in his book-length case study of a Danish religious leader named Adolph Peter Adler.[10]

In 1843 Adler published his *Sermons*. He said that although he had been a teacher in the State Church prior to this, the Spirit of God "commanded him to burn everything he had formerly written." He felt called by a revelation, appealed to this revelation, and began to exert authority and leadership "in the strength of the fact that he was called by a revelation." This revelation came to Adler at the age of twenty-two. As a result of Ad-

107

ler's "revelations," Bishop Mynster suspended him as a clergyman on the grounds that his mind was deranged, and in another year he deposed him. Adler was given a small pension, which gave him the leisure to continue to write books against the church. He saw himself as a John the Baptist. In an interview with Adler, Kierkegaard said to him that he could discover no new revelation in Adler's work. Then Adler told him that the book had to be read aloud in a whistling voice before its meaning would be open to him.

Kierkegaard's discussion of Adler's situation takes into account the cultural "characterlessness" of the times against which Adler was reacting. Kierkegaard says that "when an age becomes characterless it is possible that one or another individual may show symptoms of wishing to be an extraordinary."[11] However, Kierkegaard questions Adler's authenticity at two points. First, Adler expected the "established order" to join forces with him to let him be extraordinary, unusual, and different.[12] At the same time, the pathology of Adler rested not in the source of his authority in God but in his shift of his concept of his own purpose and calling in life. He made himself "presumptuously into a genius, whereas God had called him to be an apostle."[13] "The genius is what he is by reason of himself, i.e. by what he is in himself: an apostle is what he is by reason of his divine authority."[14] And, what makes this difference between the ordinary individual and the special individual is *the starting point.*[15] Then Kierkegaard describes in a short space of words the nature of the true as over against the false religious leader.

> Thus it is with the true *extraordinarius:* he is the most carefree man in comparison with the worldly man's temporal anxiety as to whether what he has to proclaim will be triumphant in the world; on the other hand he is as much in anguish as a poor sinner with a contrite heart whenever he thinks of his responsibility, whether in any way he might be mistaken; yea, for him it is as though his breathing were obstructed, so heavily weighs the weight of his responsibility upon him.[16]

Finally, Kierkegaard epitomizes the ambiguity of the religious leader who veers away from reality as it is represented in the established order of Christendom, which is essentially pagan:

> Just then when he had come nearer to being a Christian than ever before during all the time he was a Christian, just then was he deposed. . . . As a pagan he became a Christian priest, and . . . when he had undeniably come somewhat nearer to being a Christian he was deposed.[17]

Milton Rokeach

One of the most detailed studies of the pathology of religious leadership is by Milton Rokeach.[18] Over a period from July 1, 1959, to August 15, 1961,

Rokeach met with three male patients who considered themselves to be Christ. These patients were in real life named Clyde, Leon, and Joseph. They were patients at Ypsilanti State Hospital, near Ann Arbor, Michigan. At the time of the study, the hospital had 4,100 patients, 5 staff psychiatrists, and 20 resident psychiatrists. Clyde was close to seventy years of age, Joseph was about sixty, and Leon was in his late thirties. Joseph and Clyde had been in the hospital nearly twenty years and Leon had been there five years.

Each of these patients had a chronic paranoid-schizophrenic diagnosis, and this included the exalted conception of himself as the Christ and a steady resistance to entry into this delusional system to change it. Rokeach and members of the staff moved the patients into the same living quarters and developed a similar daily routine for all of them. A regular confrontation type of group session was conducted each week by Rokeach. The confrontation left Clyde and Joseph, the two older men, essentially unchanged. Leon's story changed slowly but surely as he groped with the riddle of his own identity. The most significant summary statement of Rokeach says that there was "a basic difference in the grandiose delusions of Clyde and Joseph on the one hand and Leon on the other."[19] This basic difference provided a working hypothesis for understanding and helping persons suffering from less chronic pathologies of religious vocation. Clyde and Joseph expressed the dominant theme of both vocational and sexual "*shame* over feelings of *incompetence* as a male." These are not guilt-ridden Christs, they are more preoccupied with being great than good. And the religious element is not especially prominent. These are the end result of the "power-orientation" religious leaders. They are plagued by the fear of incompetence, inadequacy, and fears of weakness *as men*. To accept their humanity would be to give in to these fears. As Rokeach says of Clyde and Joseph:

> Clyde is Christ because he needs to be "the biggest one." He is preoccupied with the carloads of money, land and women he owns. And Joseph is God, Christ and the Holy Ghost because these are the biggest personages one can be. If there were a super-God, Joseph would have been super-God.[20]

On the other hand, Leon's dominant theme is not shame over "incompetence but *guilt* about forbidden sexual and aggressive impulses. He is forever tormented with inadmissible impulses. . . . Leon is a guilt-ridden Christ who strives to be good rather than great; he is suffering not so much from a delusion of greatness as from a delusion of goodness."[21] Rokeach documents this conclusion from a minute study of each patient's developmental history. Here again the admission of human guilt would be as threatening to Leon as the admission of human weakness and lack of power would be to Clyde and Joseph.

In all three instances, however, the theological problem of salvation is that of a willingness to be a participant in the incarnation as well as an inheritor of its symbols in identification as the Christ. The real Christ was *willing* to accept his human limitations and temptations. These sick "Christs" were not. This is the issue in the development of adequate religious leaders. Can we enable them toward what Stephen Neill calls a "genuinely human existence"? Can they be encouraged early to know their real strengths and accept their real limitations? Can they very early experience forgiveness and be able to enjoy their human strengths of love and aggression rather than languish in guilt? If so, they themselves need leaders who enjoy a sense of adequacy, can provide a genuine permission to them to exercise their powers, and can give them protection as they learn to do so. For, as the pastoral epistle puts it, "God did not give us a spirit of timidity but a spirit of power and love and self-control" (2 Tim. 1:7).

"DITCHING" OF RESPONSIBILITY AND THE PATHOLOGY OF RELIGIOUS LEADERSHIP

The "three Christs" represent a psychotic break with reality as a way of handling their unbearable feelings of inadequacy and burdens of guilt. They took this route rather than a sociopathic *use* of religious leadership as a means of power and gratification. In conclusion, however, the neurotic-depressive route is taken by a larger number of people in religious work, it seems to me. In these instances, the feelings of incompetence and/or guilt are displaced into some kind of otherwise meaningless "behaviors." These acts, in turn, jettison responsibility and "get the person out" of responsibilities they can neither carry out with effectiveness nor admit with honor that they cannot or do not want to do. A list of such "odd behaviors" is as follows: A graduate student of divinity is caught making obscene telephone calls to women; just prior to his first pastorate, a minister is caught exhibiting himself sexually to young girls; a middle-aged pastor "gets out" of an executive position by taking certain money for his own use; a leading layman in a denomination gets caught embezzling funds; and others. These symptoms are what I have named "ditching" symptoms. In a depressed, self-deprecating crisis, the person ditches his high-altitude pilot's position of leadership. The behavior both gets him out of his seat of responsibility and punishes him publicly for doing so.

This handling of leadership in a pathological way is not restricted to religious leaders. Political figures have the same problem, as was evident in the case of the assistant to President Johnson who was caught in an episode of homosexual behavior.

The economy of such "ditching" symptoms is to preserve the total life of the person from literal suicide by accomplishing a professional suicide instead. It is better for a part—the prestige—of the person to be destroyed than for the whole life to end. On the other hand, a more creative alternative would be for the person to examine with psychotherapeutic assistance some of his needs for "improving his competence" and to discover more direct, courageous, and verbal ways of getting out of unrealistic and unbearable stress with honor and dignity.

With this objective, a pastor can do much to be an instrument of God's grace in enabling men and women toward a more "reasonable service" to God by anticipating crises in people's lives when they are under inordinate stress of positions of power and public service. The pastor should be able occasionally to get to people *before* they hit the panic button and jettison their responsibilities.

IN SUMMARY

This chapter has dealt with the ways in which religious leadership is a focus for the pathology of religion. Attention has been given to the ways in which idealization and omnicompetence needs distort the religious calling. The power orientation of the sociopathic religious leader has been identified in both its inception and its floration. The schizophrenic unreality of the searches for ultimate competence and ultimate goodness in human form was thoroughly discussed. The final discussion was of the flight from the responsibility of the "ditching" symptoms of "acting out" kinds of infantile behavior in religious leaders.

NOTES

1. Herbert Holt, "The Case of Father M.: A Segment of an Existential Analysis," *Journal of Existentialism* 6, no. 24 (1966): 366–395.

2. John P. Donnelly, ed., *Prayers and Devotions from Pope John XXIII* (New York: Grossett & Dunlap, 1967), p. 31.

3. John M. MacDonald, "The Prompt Diagnosis of the Psychopathic Personality," Supplement to the *American Journal of Psychiatry* 122, no. 12 (June 1966): 45–50.

4. Clifford B. Farr and Reuel Howe, "The Influence of Religious Ideas on the Etiology, Symptomatology, and Prognosis of the Psychoses," *American Journal of Psychiatry* 2 (1933): 845–865.

5. Ibid., p. 858.

6. Ibid., p. 861.

7. Ibid., p. 863. See also Harvey Cushing, *The Life of Sir William Osler* (New York: Oxford University Press, 1940), pp. 597–598, 639–641.

8. Anton T. Boisen, "The Development and Validation of Religious Faith," *Psychiatry: Journal for the Study of Interpersonal Processes* 14, no. 4 (November 1951): 455.

9. Anton T. Boisen, "Inspiration in the Light of Psychopathology," *Pastoral Psychology,* October 1960, pp. 10–18.

10. Søren Kierkegaard, *On Authority and Revelation: The Book on Adler, or a Cycle of Ethico-Religious Essays,* trans. Walter Lowrie (Princeton: Princeton University Press, 1955).

11. Ibid., p. 33.

12. Ibid.

13. Ibid., p. 24.

14. Ibid., p. 105.

15. Ibid., p. 36.

16. Ibid., p. 39.

17. Ibid.

18. Milton Rokeach, *The Three Christs of Ypsilanti: A Psychological Study* (New York: Alfred A. Knopf, 1964).

19. Ibid., p. 326.

20. Ibid., p. 327.

21. Ibid.

Part Two

CHRISTIAN LIFE
AND PERSONAL MATURITY

7

The Anxiety Reactions of the Morally Indifferent

CALLOUSNESS: A WAY OF LIFE

The anxious person is aware of a painful uneasiness of mind. He is not indifferent to his situation. He usually seeks help for his difficulty because of his self-concern if for no other reason.

The experienced pastor, however, knows that his community has a considerable number of people who act out rather than feel their anxiety. They have little awareness of any painful uneasiness of mind at all. They do not lie awake nights and worry over their sins, nor do they sit in preoccupation wondering whether they have done wrong. They do not consciously seem to care (which is a type of anxiety) that there is such a thing as the law, the rules of the game, or responsibility to others. They rarely go to anyone for help except when they are about to be caught by one authority person or another or when they are looking for someone whom they can "use" for their own purposes. They are the indifferent ones. Whatever anxiety their behavior represents may be called "the anxiety reactions of the morally indifferent."

The pastor encounters such persons indirectly more often than not. They themselves do not come to him for counseling help ordinarily. Their relatives and friends are concerned about the amount of trouble they can cause and come to the pastor for help. The concern of the relatives is quite often of an overprotective nature that sedulously relieves the person of the privilege of learning from his or her own experience. This concern is partly motivated by the family's desire to protect themselves from public embarrassment by the relative, partly by emotional needs to keep the black sheep dependent upon their directions, and partly by an ever-fleeing hope that *they* will be able to save their loved one.

For instance, the two sisters of a forty-one-year-old woman sought personal guidance in what to do about their sister. She had been a chronic alcoholic for fifteen years, had been arrested on prostitution charges twenty-three times, and had been married and divorced three times. The pastor spent over an hour simply getting the story of the number of persons to whom the sisters had been for help on behalf of their sister but was not able to discover a single situation in which the offending person had ever sought help except on occasions when she needed money or to be bailed out of jail. As one doctor described a patient of his who was similar to this person, "She needs to be in the kind of institution that does not yet exist and that has not yet been even thought of." Such persons know the difference between right and wrong, but the difference does not bother them. They handle whatever anxiety they have by narcotizing it. Their behavior has a certain smooth, mechanical character which seems to operate quite apart from any anxiety of self-control.

These persons are not always to be found among the religious portions of the population. Occasionally they are to be found in religious garb also. Sinclair Lewis, to the great discomfort of the Protestant clergy, caricatured the ministry by describing this kind of person in *Elmer Gantry*. The pampering of ministers, their tendency to make things sacred commonplace, and their lack of specific authority to outline their duties and lay down expectations of them make them susceptible to becoming presumptuous upon the very laws of the God they proclaim. They feel too often that they can get bread without working, that they can gain status in a community without observing the plain rules of fair play, and that they will be able to defy any given set of rules without penalty but always as the exception to the rule. But even with these tempting opportunities, only a few such persons actually get into the active ministry. When they do get beyond the screening procedures of the Christian fellowship, they can create an indeterminate amount of havoc in a given church fellowship, filling the newspapers with their bizarre escapades.

Church fellowship and theological education communities present mixed feelings when the necessity for dealing with such gross indifference to moral values appears in their group. Legalistic, sentimental, psychotherapeutic, and exposé techniques of treatment all come to the fore in discussions of what to do about such individuals.

Pastors also encounter similar confusion in their flock when they have to deal with scandals created by a homosexual church member, by church members who chronically steal from others, and so forth. These persons not only do these things but also teach others to do them. A doctor might say of some types of persons with this difficulty that therapy has very little to offer them. They often, but not always by any means, seem very comfortable about their problem and do not seem alarmed about the reality difficulties it presents them. They are perfectly willing to undergo treatment if it means they can hold their job, but psychiatrists may tell the pastor that they feel pretty hopeless about doing much for them inasmuch as they have so little anxiety. As one doctor described such a patient, he said, "He sits there comfortably in his chair as we talk quietly about his trouble as if it were an extraneous piece of protoplasm which he expects me to remove by surgery!"

TOWARD AN UNDERSTANDING OF THE DYNAMICS OF THE MORALLY INDIFFERENT

Some sort of working hypothesis as to the dynamics of the moral indifference of the persons described here is prerequisite to dealing with such persons. If one followed the assumptions of the psychiatrists just mentioned, one might conclude that a discussion of these persons is irrelevant to a book on anxiety in Christian experience. They, as far as appearance goes, show neither anxiety nor Christian experience. But such an attitude would be superficial indeed, even though it is the point at which both psychiatry and pastoral practice have tended to stop.

The development of the personality of morally indifferent persons often reflects moral inconsistency in the parental treatment they received. In other situations, moral indulgence is evident. In all instances, the personal histories of such individuals reveal an absence of dependable authority persons with whom they could identify and like whom they could safely become because of their deep admiration for them. The "protoplasm" of the spirit in which the conscience is grown is created and sustained in such relationships. The absence of anxiety reflects the absence of relatedness to trusted persons whose approval genuinely matters to the individual.

The concept of the development of personality set forth by Søren Kierkegaard provokes some insight into the dynamics of the morally indifferent from a developmental point of view. The first stage of the development of a spiritual selfhood, according to Kierkegaard, is the *aesthetic* stage. In this stage, a person, regardless of his chronological age, is like unto a Don Juan who is dominated by infinite passion for all women and never bothered by personal responsibility to any one. A person in this stage is absorbed only in the immediate and has no concern for past or future. His desires in the immediacy of the present moment call for infinite satisfaction with no eye to the consequences of such fulfillment. He does not reflect upon his desires, because to do so would be to knock the edge of immediacy from them. He is characterized by the young person also, says Kierkegaard. As David Swenson interprets this personality,

He has an intelligence which has compassed the world in reflection, but he lacks the experience of a decisive personal commitment to anything in life. . . . He is a possibility who has so far postponed a decisive action.[1]

This person, according to Kierkegaard, is morally dead, and this is evident the moment he opens his mouth. He cannot stand the tension of an ethical dilemma and would rather talk about something else, because he is like unto a child unto whom everything seems impossible and who defers the day of ethical choice. When confronted with such tension, he says, with Scarlett O'Hara, "I won't think about that today; I will think about that tomorrow." But tomorrow never comes, because he lives in the present. Such a person is typified in the young wife who, when caught in a clandestine love affair with another man, said, "I just can't choose between them. I love them both and want them both. I have always had everything I wanted and now at the age of twenty-five I can't seem to make any decisions about things." She was confronting divorce.

Jesus sensed this kind of searing of conscience as one of the inner conditions of which divorce was an outward result. He said for the hardness of the hearts of men and women, Moses had granted them the writs of divorcement. His own prophetic actions and teachings throw the light of his ethical concern on the situation of all morally indifferent persons.

In Jesus' teachings an ethical realism serves as a dark background for the bright light of his love, showing it up in its completeness. For him to call darkness light, bitter sweet, and bad good would have been to misrepresent reality to his followers and to have done an unloving thing to those who thrashed about in the anxiety of their self-deification. Therefore he spoke plainly to those who shut up the kingdom of heaven against men, neither entering themselves nor allowing those who would enter to go in. He roundly rebuked those who had become insensitive to the weightier matters of the law through religious professionalism. He spoke of eternal punishment for those who had lost the power to sense the needs of the stranger, the hungry, the thirsty, and the naked, and those in bondage, or to feel the brunt of oppression.

Furthermore, Jesus spoke of persons who "seeing do not see, and hearing do not hear." The context of this moral insensitivity helps one to understand Jesus' quotation from Isa. 6:9–10 in Matthew:

You shall indeed hear but never understand,
  and you shall indeed see but never perceive.
For this people's heart has grown dull,
  and their ears are heavy of hearing,
  and their eyes they have closed,

lest they should perceive with their eyes,
  and hear with their ears,
and understand with their heart,
  and turn for me to heal them.
                              (Matt. 13:14–15)

This is a passive kind of indifference and moral lassitude amounting to spiritual obtuseness. The active and aggressive kind of resistance to repentance and change of character is apparent in the teaching of Jesus about the blasphemy against the Holy Spirit:

But whoever blasphemes against the Holy Spirit never has forgiveness,
but is guilty of an eternal sin. (Mark 3:29)

The callousness to reconciliation, the refusal to confront and to become aware of the anxiety of sin and guilt, finitude and human frailty, and the need for creative change and a rebirth of the self—these were perceived to be active opposition to the Holy Spirit.

The teachings of the apostle Paul serve to deepen the understanding of the dynamics of the morally indifferent and their strange, repressed anxiety. Paul describes such a condition in Ephesians:

They are darkened in their understanding, alienated from the life of
God because of the ignorance that is in them, due to their hardness of
heart; they have become callous and have given themselves up to licen-
tiousness, greedy to practice every kind of uncleanness.
                              (Eph. 4:18–19)

Here Paul is describing the person who has lost the capacity to feel anxiety. His only anxiety is over the return of sensitivity to ethical concerns and interpersonal values. Paul registers real pessimism here about the person whose sense of moral responsibility and social feeling has become calloused, hardened over, and whose sources of tender spiritual insight have been desensitized to the point of apathy. The term for "having become callous" is translated in older translations as "being past feeling." It comes from a word that in other connections means "to cease to feel pain" and from which we also transliterate the root verb to get our word "analgesic," a kind of pain-killing preparation for rubbing sore muscles.

A figure of speech that helps to clarify further this kind of anxiety is "anesthetized" anxiety, similar to the condition of the surgical patient who has received pain-killing drugs to narcotize his sensitivity to suffering. He lives, therefore, with a braced awareness that the pain may return. This is his anxiety. Figuratively, therefore, the morally insensitive person is much like this: he lives by constantly bracing himself against the sense of moral pain. Paul speaks again of this kind of handling of anxiety in the Letter to

119

the Romans. He speaks of idolaters who have become "futile in their thinking and their senseless minds were darkened" (Rom. 1:21). In the older translations of later verses in this context, reference is made to a "reprobate mind."

Kierkegaard's idea of the infinite and omnipotent nature of the desires of such a person stands out in Paul's reference to their greediness and insatiable desires. The idea is originally that of always wanting more and more. Such lack of acceptance of limitations and avoidance of discipline repudiate the claims of others to be considered as anything other than as means toward the satisfaction of desire. Actually it becomes a hedonistic idolatry of desire, and usually the many desires of an individual war for ascendancy in this self-worship. As Paul says, they have "exchanged the truth about God for a lie and worshiped and served the creature rather than the Creator" (Rom. 1:25).

A further analysis of the dynamics of the morally indifferent appears, interestingly enough, in the concept of moral indifference in relation to repression enunciated by O. Hobart Mowrer, a contemporary research psychotherapist, in his book *Learning Theory and Personality Dynamics*. He also makes note of the overindulgence of children and adults by authority persons such as parents and teachers because of their fear that an honest interpretation of the limitations of reality living would make neurotics of their charges. Mowrer says that moral indifference is the result of such overindulgence and misrepresentation of the ethical structure of human relationships. He reinterprets the Freudian concept of repression by saying that Freud had a misleadingly limited understanding of his own concept of repression. Freud taught that anxiety is a vague and objectless apprehension that impulses of lust and hostility would "erupt back into consciousness." Mowrer criticizes and takes issue with Freud over reducing anxiety to apprehension over this kind of eruption. To the contrary, Mowrer says that repression can move also in the direction of inhibiting the moral strivings of the individual, and anxiety can be just as intense, causing the person to act out his lustful and aggressive impulses without control. He says:

> Many sources of present evidence indicate that most—perhaps all—neurotic human beings suffer, not because they are unduly inhibited as regards their biological drives, but because they have disavowed and repudiated their own moral strivings. Anxiety comes, not from repressed sexuality or pentup hatred, but from a denial and defiance of the forces of conscience.[2]

Mowrer goes on to point out that modern man is becoming increasingly *afraid of his anxieties*. He conceives of personality disorders as arising from moral rather than biological frustrations, and he challenges his fellow psychotherapists to come to grips with "the riddle of the unhinged soul," which he conceives to be primarily due to the loss of ethical concern and a desensitization to the inherent validity of the Ten Commandments even apart from their authorship. He speaks of the neurotic strategies the basic mechanisms of which are all the same: "devices for neutralizing conscience."

Professor Mowrer has moved into a more realistic direction for the solution of many psychotherapeutic problems upon which Freudian hypotheses have been long on theory and short on therapy. However, one should qualify the impression that Mowrer leaves that lustful and hostile repressions are not also sources of real anxiety reactions. He almost falls into an "either-or sandtrap" at this point. Not to make this qualification would be to overlook the express statement of Freud himself when he said that

> conflict is not resolved by helping one side [of the personality conflict between desires and prohibitions] to win the victory over the other. . . . If we were to make victory possible merely to the sensual side instead, the disregarded forces repressing sexuality would have to indemnify themselves by symptoms. . . . People who can be so easily influenced by a physician would have found their own way to that solution without this influence.[3]

THE RESPONSES
OF THE CHRISTIAN FELLOWSHIP
TO THE MORALLY INDIFFERENT

A clear word needs to be said to the effect that the term "moral indifference" as it is used here does not necessarily refer to the person who is a good moral man but never goes to church. Church attendance is important but is not the point of focus in this discussion. One may rightly ask for some more specific descriptions of the way in which morally indifferent persons react within the Christian fellowship. Such descriptions will help clarify the various responses that can be made to the needs of such persons. Two typical patterns of behavior tend to occur quite often. In both patterns a kind of hardness of heart and head appears in the interpersonal unrelatedness of the individual who is giving the trouble.

For instance, in the first place, a given individual may consistently interpret any tenderness on the part of others as weakness, stupidity, and a signal for his own exploitation. He exploits the kindness he meets in others to the fullest and uses the kind person until he no longer needs the person. Then, if the person has not already lost patience with him, blown his top, and broken his relationship to him, the apathetic exploiter ditches him and no longer has any use for him. He plays his victims for suckers and capitalizes on their permissiveness to the point of goading them to reject him. Some pastors follow this course of action with many problem persons in their community. They, by reason of their need to be do-gooders as well as their traditional role as kind persons, are often taken in by this exploitatively insensitive individual. A pastoral counselor is usually afraid of his own hostilities toward the person and tends to compensate for these feelings by appeasement policies. The person senses, however, the depths of the rejection and reacts to it in kind, becoming all the more destructive as he acts out his anxiety.

In a second instance, the hardness of heart spoken of here may appear in another form. The person may be basically threatened by tenderness. He interprets it as a sign of guilt on the part of the pastoral counselor for some real or supposed wrong he feels that the pastor is reputed to have done him. This is what the psychiatrists would call a persecutory reaction. One never forgets the jolt that he receives when he first learns that some people are frightened by closeness and affection, threatened by tenderness and concern. They may even be panicked into disruptive behavior by it. Occasionally such a persecuted personality is threatened by tenderness on the part of the pastor and other friends. He becomes irreconcilably critical of those who have been closest, most helpful, and tender toward him. He develops a "sandy spot of reality" as a basis for his complaints and pushes his hostility vengefully, harshly, uncompromisingly, and to the hurt of all who get in his way. Nothing that persons can do will set their relationship straight with him, and any attempt at clarification is distorted and becomes new timber for the feeling that all are against him.

A rather commonplace (but all the more difficult for that reason) example of this appears in the following pastoral situation:

> I first met Bill Smith four years ago when I became pastor of the church of which he is a member. At that time he was nearly thirteen and, with rare exceptions, was always at church with his mother; however, the father and the older brother never attended. During the intervening years I have pieced together the following information about the boy and his family: Bill is the youngest of four children, the two oldest ones being married. His only brother, age twenty-five and single, is the tough, hard-working son who has stayed home to help care for their two-hundred-acre farm. The father is quite antagonistic to religion but is a morally sound man. The older son, though not hostile to religion, has followed in his father's example of having little or nothing to do with church. This son and the father have been quite close to each other, but the father says Bill is weak, lazy, and will hardly work. It is reported that the mother told her husband when Bill was born, "You have raised the other boy and I will raise this one." Accordingly, she has taken Bill to church with her regularly.

Bill is popular at school, making good grades and taking a leading role in campus activities. However, he is most at home when with girls. He himself has effeminate gestures and actions, and on one occasion a girl told me, "We look upon him as being one of the girls." He hardly associates at all with boys of the church. The fact that he is the only boy in our young people's choir does not phase him in the least from regular attendance.

Approximately a year after I became his pastor, Bill made it known to me in private that he was considering entering the ministry. Later at a special church program he made a short speech and was highly complimented by members of the church. Shortly thereafter he made a public decision to do full-time Christian work. At this time Bill became most voluminous in his letter writing to me, writing at the slightest occasion concerning a party, my sermon, or a girl. Once he wrote me that his doctor had told him that he would die as a young man. Upon his returning to the church, I told him I would like to talk with him concerning the matter, but he deferred the subject "until later." He has never mentioned it again.

About this time I became aware of the fact that Bill and I were having considerable difficulty communicating in a face-to-face situation; he seemed to block, although he was able to express himself very well by letter. This problem has become increasingly apparent in the last two years. However, he is quite free in the presence of my wife, but when I join the group he "clams up."

Bill is known in the church as something of an impetuous boy who speaks his mind without much apparent forethought. For instance, on one occasion he decided that he was going to sing a solo in church the following Sunday. Since he is almost a monotone, I suggested that he wait until he could practice further on the song. However, the following week I received a letter from him informing me that I was wrong and that he was going to sing the next Sunday. Taking this as an adolescent trait, I let him sing. Then, too, there have been other instances of this type of behavior. Yet the adults of the church consider him one of the finest and most promising young men of the church.

Our real problems began one Sunday morning when I forgot and left my Bible on the pulpit. At a special program that night Bill was to read several passages from the Bible, and it appeared to me that he was using my Bible. After the service was over I forgot to see him about it. During the following week I had occasion to write him and put a P.S. on my letter stating I thought I had seen him with the Bible and would appreciate it if he would keep it until I returned. This P.S. provoked a most hostile letter from him in which he asserted that I had accused him of thievery and that he was "very mad." After a three-day cooling-off period, I wrote him stating I could see how my note could have been misunderstood and explained the whole situation, whereupon he wrote back apologizing (as he had done in the singing instance).

However, it was obvious in the ensuing months by the coldness and distance between Bill and myself that the wound had not healed. He now began a series of moves in which he tried to move counter to anything he felt I wanted to do. Prior to his explosion of temper I had asked him to preach some night, to which he had agreed and had already selected a text. The first example of his rebellion was his later refusal to preach on this night. Then he decided he would not be a preacher but rather a minister of education. Again he decided he would not attend a college that he and a group of our young people (including myself) had visited but instead would go to another one.

After our revival last year Bill wrote me that the evangelist's and my "inspiring sermons" had made it clear to him that God wanted him to preach. The following Sunday he came in tears rededicating his life. That afternoon I again approached him, but, as before, he seemed to block, except for some superficial remarks about his school work, at face-to-face communication.

At present our church is planning a week youth revival in April, and I naturally turned to Bill to serve as youth pastor since he has indicated his plan to become a minister. The day he was approached on the subject he happened to be sick at home. I noted that he became quite nervous when the subject was introduced, and presently one of our young people, Jane, who had gone with my wife and myself, broke in and asked, "Bill, is it true or not what you told me the other day?" He replied in the negative and accepted the offer to be youth pastor. Sensing something was wrong, I asked Jane, while returning, whether Bill had had a problem. She indicated that he had, but she was somewhat reluctant to talk. Therefore I did not press the issue.

That night after the services Jane apologized for being somewhat reticent in the afternoon and then told me this story: About two weeks prior to this time Bill had told her he could no longer believe as Methodists did and that he did not bow his head anymore when we prayed. He stated that he had become a member of a Catholic church in a town five miles away and that he attended early mass plus the services at our church because he feared some recrimination from our people should these things be known.

He further stated that his mother knew of this (which is highly improbable, since such information would literally crush her spirit). He also displayed some Catholic medals and stated that Catholics prayed to Mary because of their unworthiness to approach Christ directly. Jane said he told her he would not accept the youth pastor position if it was offered to him, because he was now a Catholic.

I asked Jane how widely these matters were known in the community, and she stated that nearly all the girls in their junior class knew and approximately six girls in our church were aware of this. One girl, a member of the Baptist church, had asked her a few days before whether or not it was true that the stewards of our church were calling a special meeting to "kick Bill out of the church." Therefore it seems that this matter is becoming common knowledge among the members of the community. Since our church and community is a close-knit, rural situation, this could have great repercussions.

What, then, are some of the responses that a Christian fellowship could make to such situations as these and others like them? The first response to such rebelliousness would be violent hostility, and the pastor and people alike tend to become angry with such a person. In a sense, the person is acting out the pattern of rebellion that he has always used in response to rejection. He acts out his anxiety in such a way as to *cause* others who would be kind to him to lose patience with him and reject him. In fact, he is testing the "patience quotient" of all concerned to see how much he can get by with, how far he can go.

A second response possible in this situation is to pamper and over-indulge the person. Attempts to look upon him as sick often amount to just this and turn out to be maudlin sentimentality rather than realistic understanding. In acting out his anxiety about the authority persons in the situation, the person is also counting quietly on the overindulgence of the sentimental ones. In fact, the pastor may be almost a "mothering influence" in his life.

A third response would be to represent reality to the person. This implies a balance between permitting the person to profit by his own mistakes and avoiding vindictive acts of reprisal toward him. When a person is definitely out of bounds ethically and interpersonally, those whom he has offended do him harm when, out of some sense of timidity or fear of him, they refrain from an honest expression of their sense of injustice. Professor Ross Snyder underlines this ethical structure of interpersonal relationships when he says:

> Part of the experience of love is the justice-giving demand which we experience within us and toward others. "This is not fair; this is unjust!" cannot be disregarded if man is to survive in society. For injustice is a violation of man as a human being and of the Holy in the universe.[4]

Such violations of human personality should be called to a morally insensitive person's attention in a disciplined and orderly way. The administrative organization of the home, the church, the school, the hospital, or the larger community should be set up in such a decent and orderly way that instances like this can be handled in a similar manner. Whatever aggression is expressed toward an individual should be done as a corporate responsibility of the group as a whole to which the individual is responsible rather than as the unguided hostility of an individual person, even of the pastor. This deals realistically with the problem of authority in community living. Such authority should be mobilized and expressed in a responsible way. If this is done so as to represent reality vividly and without vindictiveness to the individual, he tends to become more secure for having learned where the bounds of his habitation are. His anxiety reactions are lessened and he becomes more sensitive to the corporate fellowship to which he belongs. Mowrer indicates that this is a part of the dynamic development of healthy personality and implies a wholesome kind of aggressiveness in individual and corporate actions:

> No society can be a going concern unless there is some form of political authority. We sometimes make the mistake of thinking of aggressive behavior as being exclusively antisocial. We must remember that there is also such a thing as *prosocial* aggression, and that it is an essential element in parental discipline and in community control.[5]

But this talk of the place of aggression in dealing with morally indifferent persons will raise active questions in the minds of pastors who have become conversant with current trends in pastoral counseling. They will ask how this can be harmonized with the more permissive relationship of the typical counseling situation. Two things need to be said here. First, the pastor is not counseling, in the technical sense of the word, in dealing with morally insensitive persons. He is usually involved in some administrative or disciplinary action, which, if he is able to use his authority to create an awareness of the need for counseling, may in a real way be a precounseling situation. Ordinarily, the pastor will call for the help of some other counselor to provide the more permissive type of relationship. Second, the kind of anxiety reaction here is such that permissiveness may be interpreted as license, as a sign of weakness, and as an opportunity for exploitation of the social position of the pastoral counselor. In other words, in an uncontrolled, intimately involved pastoral situation, the amount of jeopardy to the pastor's total function is great. He may be too socially and emotionally involved in the situation to be the most helpful counselor to such an individual. If he attempts to distort the actual authority in the real social role that he does have in the life of the person, the person senses it as a sort of misrepresentation of the real situation and tends to force the pastor sooner or later to use the authority he does have.

In dealing with morally indifferent persons, the pastor cannot assume the same kind of relationship that he would have with persons who reflect even superficial concern about their life situation. A different problem exists, a different understanding is called for; and a different approach is necessary. In the terms of the psychological realities at hand, the pastor has to reevaluate his concept of counseling as being a *totally* permissive and unstructured relationship. It actually is not.

Many pastors have raised this question in a different form when they have said: "Modern counselors insist upon a 'nondirective' procedure. This throws us in conflict with our task as prophets who stand up against evil and injustice. How can we reconcile our role as a prophet with our work as a counselor if this is the whole story about counseling? This is not in keeping with the responsibility we bear to the whole church and our obligation to protect the flock from invaders." Furthermore, such pastors will quote innumerable references in the biblical account where the prophets, Jesus, and the apostles were quite forthright in what they had to say.

In dealing with his people, the Christian pastor has to combine the elements of authoritativeness with the elements of permissive love, even as he functions both as a prophet and as a counselor. In this his people find a dependable and yet free relationship with their minister that leads them to the healing of their crippling anxieties and enables them to take advantage of the power of their basic human anxieties. This is exactly what the Old Testament prophets and the New Testament apostles did. Naturally, they knew their own weakness and did not presume perfection. Nevertheless the time came when they felt called upon to speak clearly against hard hearts and to challenge the behavior of the disrupters of the community. Like these prophets, also, the pastor will need to rely upon the cleansing power of prayer at this point more than most others. For here, with inner awareness of his own weaknesses, he knows that he prophesies in part. Pastors can learn from the prophets who went into the temple of worship and purified their lips of sin before they appeared before people or individuals. They conferred with each other for wisdom and spiritual solidarity. Then they spoke in plain words of impeccable courage to the injustices and encumbrances of unreality which they saw about them. They talked to hardened hearts, fattened ears, and blinded eyes in their particular ages of anxiety when their people had become apathetic to each other's needs and to the meaning of their relationship and ultimate destiny in God.

The seeming contradictions raised by these questions draw into focus the fact that the pastoral counselor always works within the context of a specific religious community, namely, the church. What he does, he does not alone. He represents the social reality of the needs of the whole community as well as the inner reality of the overwhelming desires of the individual. Pastoral relationships, like parent-child relationships, therefore combine the tougher realism of social demand with the more tender satisfactions of personal concern for the individual. When one finds these two factors in balanced proportion in a pastor, one usually finds a pastor whose personhood unites courageous strength with secure tenderness. Such a combination of the rod and staff of a true shepherd places a pastor in the tradition of the prophets. The absence of either strength or tenderness tends to create the kind of anxiety reactions that have been discussed here. In a very real way, the Christian community is always at work balancing up these deficiencies in the way in which it deals with the anxieties of the persons to whom it ministers.

The ordering of the Christian community as it challenges and disciplines the morally indifferent usually is set in motion by its leadership, which often turns out to be the pastor. The pastor symbolizes the prophetic tension between the justice-demanding and compassion-expression character of the community. When he speaks prophetically to an offender within the community, he need not expect to be liked. He should only be concerned that he speaks for God and the Christian fellowship and not for himself. Such a pattern of relatedness on his part puts him on the spot in such a way that he can at least catch a glimpse of the loneliness of the prophets and of Jesus. The cross becomes a reality to him in such instances, because to take up such a role in society is to ask for a deeper participation in the meaning of the cross than one has known before. Therefore Jesus asks every aspiring disciple whether he is able to drink of the cup that he drank and to be baptized with the baptism wherewith he was baptized! Prophecy is more than calling fire down on people who insult the prophet. It is participation in the redemptive seriousness into which Jesus has called the prophet.

As such a prophet encounters the morally insensitive, the reality of the cross itself becomes very apparent in the interpersonal relationship if the challenged one sees it at all. The Holy Spirit sensitizes the indifferent by the combined firmness and affection of the man of God or the people of God. If it were not for the sharp contradictions of the cross, man would have remained impervious to the radical difference between destructive sinfulness and redemptive love. Once such a difference is felt, an anxiety is awakened, and "chords that were broken vibrate once more." Yet even this calls for the creative anxiety of the cross.

NOTES

1. David Swenson, *Something About Kierkegaard* (Minneapolis: Augsburg Publishing House, 1945), pp. 169–170.

2. O. Hobart Mowrer, *Learning Theory and Personality Dynamics: Selected Papers* (New York: Ronald Press Co., 1950), p. 568.

3. Sigmund Freud, *A General Introduction to Psychoanalysis* (Garden City, N.Y.: Garden City Publishing Co., 1943), pp. 375–376.

4. Ross Snyder, "Religious Living with Three and Four Year Olds," *Chicago Theological Seminary Register* 43, no. 1 (January 1953).

5. Mowrer, *Learning Theory*, p. 569.

8

The Restless and the Greedy

During World War II, I was the pastor of a church in my home city of Louisville. I was asked by a member of the church to visit one of his relatives who was a patient at a large tuberculosis sanatorium. When I arrived at the man's bedside, I found him to be a personable and talkative man of about forty years of age. I asked him how he felt about being in the hospital for such a long stay. He responded, "I am being paid back for my sin." I did not quickly move to reassure him. Rather, I asked him, "Your sin? What did you do?" Immediately he responded, "I wanted it all, Reverend." I asked, "What do you mean when you say you wanted it all?" He said, "Well, you know how scarce labor is with all the able-bodied men in the war. I got me a job at 'the powder plant' [a munitions factory in our area], and they wanted me to work all the shifts I was willing and able to work. You know the pay is the best I ever made. I wanted it all. I would work three days three shifts without sleeping. Many days I would work two shifts. I was so greedy that I broke my health down and landed in here. That was my sin. The Lord made me lie down."

We talked about his healing process and how the very conditions of healing were a form of God's forgiveness and God's instruction of him in a discipline of his desires to what is really important. What does it profit a person "to gain the whole world and forfeit his [or her] life"? (Mark 8:36).

This honest man was one of the very few persons I have ever heard confess the sin of greed or covetousness. Two stories from the ministry of Jesus present contrasting examples of how greediness requires our very lives of us and, on the other hand, how peace and serene rest of spirit *can* happen to us when we are changed by the Spirit and invitation of Jesus Christ.

The first story is that of the rich fool:

> One of the multitude said to him, "Teacher, bid my brother divide the inheritance with me." But he said to him, "Man, who made me a judge or divider over you?" And he said to them, "Take heed, and beware of all covetousness; for a man's life does not consist in the abundance of his possessions." And he told them a parable, saying, "The land of a rich man brought forth plentifully; and he thought to himself, 'What shall I do, for I have nowhere to store my crops?' And he said, 'I will do this: I will pull down my barns, and build larger ones; and there I will store all my grain and my goods. And I will say to my soul, Soul, you have ample goods laid up for many years; take your ease, eat, drink, be merry.' But God said to him, 'Fool! This night your soul is required of you; and the things you have prepared, whose will they be?' So is he who lays up treasure for himself, and is not rich toward God." (Luke 12:13–21)

Here the man's fantasy was that if he simply enlarged his investments, increased his holdings, and laid up ample goods for many years, this would bring ease. This ease would be one he would *take*, as contrasted to the promise of Jesus in Matt. 11:28 that if we take his yoke upon us, he will *give* us that same ease, that rest which we are trusting "much goods" to provide us. The very act of wrongly placing our trust can require of us our life, because greed consumes *us*. Its voracious appetite is cannibalistic.

The second story is that of Zacchaeus:

> He entered Jericho and was passing through. And there was a man named Zacchaeus; he was a chief tax collector, and rich. And he sought to see who Jesus was, but could not, on account of the crowd, because he was small of stature. So he ran on ahead and climbed up into a sycamore tree to see him, for he was to pass that way. And when Jesus came to the place, he looked up and said to him, "Zacchaeus, make haste and come down; for I must stay at your house today." So he made haste and came down, and received him joyfully. And when they saw it they all murmured, "He has gone in to be the guest of a man who is a sinner." And Zacchaeus stood and said to the Lord, "Behold, Lord, the half of my goods I give to the poor; and if I have defrauded any one of anything, I restore it fourfold." And Jesus said to him, "Today salvation has come to this house, since he also is a son of Abraham. For the Son of man came to seek and to save the lost." (Luke 19:1–10)

Zacchaeus had amassed a fortune through his despised task as a tax collector. In coming face-to-face with God in Jesus Christ, he was radically transformed in his attitude toward both his power and his possessions. When Jesus asked to be his guest at his house, Zacchaeus was overwhelmed by the calm forgiveness dramatized in this request. He received Jesus joyfully and announced, "Behold, Lord, the half of my goods I give to the poor; and if I have defrauded any one of anything, I restore it fourfold." Jesus assured him that salvation had come to him and his house. The *gift* of rest and ease of heart became his. He could be freed of the burdens of greed by sharing with the poor. He could be freed of the burden of injustices he had committed by making restitution fourfold to those whom he had wronged. His life was not required of him because of his greed; rather, it was restored to him as he found the Lord Jesus Christ at the center of his loyalties, the controlling force of his behavior.

KINDS OF GREED

Greed is not always for or about the same objects of desire. Yet it is one of the reasons most often given for not resting, for being fatigued. However, persons giving the reasons usually are unaware that greed is the source of their restlessness. "Gaining" is the verb that corresponds to the actions of greed. We struggle against poverty so hard and with enough success that the *process* of gaining money and property becomes an addictive fascination in itself. We gain prestige when we become financially successful; then the power over others associated with money makes money a means to the greed for power and control. We build a certain concept of ourselves as always being in control, "calling the shots," "naming the tune" for others to dance by, and this ego state itself must be fed more and more. Thus the maintenance of a certain image, or ego, becomes a form of greed. Even in the sphere of religious leadership, we may be so greedy for recognition and adulation that we are threatened, restless, and strained when someone else steps into our spotlight. The many-hued spectrum of greed reveals itself upon refraction to be far more than the yen for money and property. Yet we can agree with Virgil: "Curst greed of gold, what crimes thy power has caused." Whatever the *kind* of greed, all kinds have one thing in common: the appetite of greedy persons is insatiable and leaves them as restless after gaining things as they would be thirsty after drinking seawater.

LONELINESS AND GREED

A part of this restlessness is the inevitable by-product of the main mechanism of greed—inordinate, compulsive competitiveness. Competitiveness of this kind leads, not to the camaraderie of teamwork, but to isolation and loneliness. Fyodor Dostoevsky speaks of the subtle connection between greed and loneliness, restlessness and genuine security:

> All mankind in our age have split up into units, they all keep apart, each in his own groove; each one holds aloof, hides himself and hides

what he has, from the rest, and he ends by being repelled by others and repelling them. He heaps up riches by himself and thinks, "how strong I am now and how secure," and in his madness he does not understand that the more he heaps up, the more he sinks into self-destructive impotence.[1]

Dostoevsky describes vividly what Philip Slater calls our American "pursuit of loneliness." In the pursuit of affluence, prestige, and power, we paint ourselves into corners of quiet personal desperation and loneliness. We perceive others, he says, "as an impediment or a nuisance: making the highway crowded when we are rushing somewhere, cluttering and littering the beach or park or wood, pushing in front of us at the supermarket, taking the last parking place, polluting our air and water, building a highway through our house, blocking our view, and so on."[2]

Such encounters as Slater describes are filled with strain, stress, feverish hostility, and even rage. Rest, tranquillity, and renewal are the antithesis. In all our getting we have gotten neither rest nor peace.

EXCESS BAGGAGE AND FATIGUE

The end result of the day-to-day existence of greed-ridden persons is to be weighed down with and worn down by the excess baggage of things and power they have collected. Their lives become cluttered with more than they can use, more than they need or want. The mere accumulation of things, houses, land, and money becomes an energy-consuming force in its own right. In a sense, "all these things" begin to develop a life of their own. If you are such a person, they control *you* and you are not in control of your own life. Ecclesiastes 3:5 says that there is "a time to cast away stones, and a time to gather stones together." Maybe you have already gone through your time to gather stones together and it is time, as was true of Zacchaeus, to cast away stones. In Heb. 12:1 the faithful Christian is urged to "lay aside every weight, and sin which clings so closely" in order to run with perseverance the race that is set before us. This is not a race to get the most, to get it all, to get there ahead of everyone else, to have the last word, to hush everybody else. No. This is a collaborative race in fellowship with other Christians. We compete with each other only in doing honor to one another and in loving our neighbor as ourselves because we love God.

Such a perspective will help us get a fresh angle of vision on what is most important in life. Those persons whose greed makes them unhappy unless they are $100,000-a-year persons may be working sixteen hours a day, seven days a week, putting in 112 hours a week. Even at the baseline of a 50-hour week, this is working more than two shifts! Such persons are not $100,000-a-year persons but $50,000-a-year persons who work two shifts!

I have seen patients come into our hospital exhausted, depressed, and having made some very unwise decisions. In one case the patient had worked 183 days without a day off. Those were fourteen-hour to sixteen-hour days.

Similarly, I have counseled married partners both of whom worked such hours. Their relationship to each other suffered enormously. Efforts at intervening in this system of work were very difficult. Yet the concerns that brought them in for counseling were not about their relationship to each other but about the behavior of adolescent sons or daughters. I am not suggesting that we go back to the old "submission" system of the wife not working. I am suggesting that lowering the standard of living, creating more quality time together, and spending money on family events rather than on bigger houses, more clubs, more and finer automobiles, and so forth, would make better use of the resources of life. You will not rest unless you create time for rest and for peaceful communion with your family. Even if you do gradually start blocking out time for yourself with your family, at first you will be anxious and feel at a loss as to what to do with yourself. You will have to break through that wall of anxiety to rest peacefully.

THE SIMPLIFICATION OF LIFE

You have a right to rest without selling that birthright for all of the excess baggage that you are accumulating. The liberation of your life to rest in the way God created you lies within your own power if you will discipline your desires and distinguish between what you really need and *what you think other people expect you to have,* not even necessarily what you yourself genuinely want. Mencius, in the fourth century B.C., in his Oriental wisdom said, "To nourish the heart there is nothing but to make the desires few." You and I have much more time to replenish and recuperate our total beings if we learn (get someone to teach and encourage us, if necessary) to get along, as Zacchaeus did, with half the stuff we have and feel we must have in order to be a person. As Richard E. Byrd, the Antarctic explorer, said in his account of a journey, "I am learning . . . that a man can live profoundly without masses of things."

A LIVING EXAMPLE OF SIMPLIFICATION

One remarkable example has been set for older persons in the simplification of life by some young people. I know a large number of them who have simplified their lives drastically as contrasted with us as their parents. As married couples, they share in the preparation of meals. They plant and cultivate a garden. They make Christmas gifts by hand, applying arts and crafts they have learned and learned well. Out of sheer curiosity, they have learned several skills. Their clothing is appropriate but simple, casual, and comfortable. They are as likely to ride a bicycle to work as to drive a car. Increasing numbers of them, if married, are managing as a one-car instead of a two-car family. When they go on vacations their main solution of their need for housing is to camp or to stay with friends along the way. They tend to enjoy hiking, swimming, searching for food at the seaside, in streams, or in meadows and woodlands, where wild plants and berries can be found. If they do buy food, they usually prepare and cook it themselves over a camp-fire or stove.

Frankly, I admire their simplicity and the functional ways they have of making life pull their families and their friends together into a community rather than apart in isolation. As Dostoevsky says, "True security is to be found in social solidarity rather than in isolated individual effort."[3] These younger persons reflect the wisdom of our elder son, Bill, when in 1959 we moved from a smaller house with one bath into a larger one with two baths. He had been uprooted from his friendship group in "the old neighbor-hood," as he called it. He was eleven and his chums meant much to him. He said, "I would rather have two friends than two baths!"

SOME SIMPLIFICATION DISCIPLINES

Cultivating Inner Serenity Instead of "Other-Directedness." Many years ago David Riesman, with others, wrote a book entitled *The Lonely Crowd.*[4] In it he spoke of the "inner-directed," who have a heritage of a clear sense of direction in life and who live according to self-chosen goals. He contrasted such persons with the "other-directed," those whose contemporaries or peers provide their sense of direction. Other-directed persons shift direc-tion and change goals as they are swayed by the media and friends. In being exceptionally sensitive to the wishes and actions of others, they find life becoming increasingly complex. You can readily see that to be too literal about Riesman's different types of persons can become absurd. You do not want to be sensitive to doing things to please everybody with whom you come in contact. Yet you do not want to be self-centered and inconsiderate of everyone but yourself. This reduces the insight to absurdity.

This is not what Riesman, or I, would want to convey. Rather, my point is that your life becomes more simplified if you draw on the inex-haustible riches of the mind and teachings of Christ for your sense of direc-tion in life rather than on the fads, fashions, and total approval of the style setters around you. No greed is quite as subtle and yet as all-consuming as the greed for everybody's approval. A reverse form of this is the greed for everybody's *disapproval*—both are other-directed. You and I will simplify our lives, what we do, how we do it, what we buy, wear, eat, drive, and enjoy when we are guided by the inner wisdom and balance of an austerity and simplicity we draw from Jesus of Nazareth. Our lives become complex when we are consumed by our greed for being like everybody else, following the latest advertising hype, and living life in hourly awareness of being conspicuously in the spotlight of other people's expectation.

Facing Rather than Retreating from Loneliness. I have spoken, and quoted Dostoevsky, about how greed isolates. Loneliness produces restlessness. Loneliness is another thief of sleep. You may escape loneliness by fretfully working more, making more money, buying more things. In your loneliness you may assuage the pain by going on a buying spree. Then you are in debt and you punish yourself for your extravagance by working more and resting less. Overwork is one way of running from your loneliness.

To simplify your life, turn and face your loneliness for what it is. Arnold Toynbee said that he was a confessed work addict and that the source of his work addiction was his fear of loneliness.

Carl Sandburg spoke most eloquently of loneliness in an interview with Ralph McGill in 1966. He and McGill were walking about Glassy Mountain, near Sandburg's home. He said to McGill, "I often walk here to be alone. Loneliness is an essential part of a man's life and sometimes he must seek it out. I sit here and I look out at the silent hills and I say, 'Who are you, Carl? Where are you going? What about yourself, Carl?' You know, one of the biggest jobs a person has is to learn how to live with loneliness. Too many persons allow loneliness to take them over. It is necessary to have within oneself the ability to use loneliness. Time is the coin of life. You spend it. Do not let others spend it for you."

When you keep pushing more and more work into the lonely spots of your life, you are ordinarily letting others spend time for you. Do it yourself and quit running from your loneliness. The rest you get will be healing.

Learning How to Get Along Without Things. My mother was an uneducated woman who worked in cotton mills from the time she was ten until she was seventy-two. She taught herself to read, write, and count, and she learned the oral tradition her mother—my grandmother—gave her and later gave me. She lived to be ninety-one years of age. Upon our visits back home, I was always impressed by the simplicity and ingenuity with which she lived. She could have done even better at it if she had not by brute poverty been forced into a lifelong habit of borrowing money. She did this out of habit long after there was any necessity for it. Occasionally on my visits I would suggest that I buy something for her that would make life more comfortable or pleasant. She refused, saying, "I'm all right. *I'm used to doing without such things.''* She could say with the apostle Paul, "I have learned to find resources in myself whatever my circumstances. I know what it is to be brought low, and I know what it is to have plenty. I have been very thoroughly initiated into the human lot with all its ups and downs—fullness and hunger, plenty and want. I have strength for anything through him who gives me power" (Phil. 4:11b–13a, NEB).

A good sense of humor about the vanity of greed taking away our rest and churning our spirits with restlessness is an antidote to the toxic powers of greed.

This wisdom brings back to me the story of our friend Portie Tipton. My wife and I spent a night in his home as his guests. About nine o'clock in the evening, as we sat before the open fire, he suddenly said, "Dr. Oates, are you and Mrs. Oates feeling well?" We both said that we felt quite well. He said, "Well, good. I'm not going to sit up with you. I'm going to bed. I only sit up with sick people!" Then he added: "If there is anything you can see that you need, it is yours. If you can't find what you need, call us and we will help you look for it. If we don't have it, we can teach you how to get along without it." Yet for you and for me this is easier to say than to do.

We could have more time for leisure and the enrichment of life if we had someone to teach and encourage us to get along without half the stuff we think we need. But then we would have to learn how to use that leisure.

NOTES

1. Fyodor Dostoevsky, *The Brothers Karamazov,* trans. Constance Garnett (New York: New American Library, Signet Classics, 1957), p. 279.

2. Philip Slater, *The Pursuit of Loneliness: American Culture at the Breaking Point* (Boston: Beacon Press, 1970), p. 8.

3. Dostoevsky, *The Brothers Karamazov,* p. 363.

4. David Riesman and others, *The Lonely Crowd: A Study of the Changing American Character* (New Haven, Conn.: Yale University Press, 1950).

9

Grief: A Spiritual Struggle

You probably have sensed a mighty struggle with grief in yourself or in others. The purpose of this chapter is to portray the basically spiritual nature of this struggle, how it is a struggle in your relation to God and to yourself. Its further purpose is to point to sources of power for engaging in this struggle effectively and creatively.

THE STRUGGLE WITH POWERLESSNESS

Grief is not a test of "how much you can take it." The test is the loss of all strength. Something has happened over which you had *no* control. You have never been so aware of your weakness, helplessness, and powerlessness. Nor have you ever been less willing to admit it to yourself. As the psalmist says, "My heart throbs, my strength fails me; and the light of my eyes—it also has gone from me" (Ps. 38:10). Dietrich Bonhoeffer, the German pastor who was put to death by the Nazis on April 9, 1945, described this dark time as a "deliverance into Satan's hands."

> So the Christian recognizes the cunning of Satan. Suddenly doubt has been sown in his heart, suddenly everything is uncertain, what I do is meaningless, suddenly sins of long ago are alive in me as though they had happened today, and they torture and torment me, suddenly my whole heart is full of deep sorrow for myself, for the world, for God's powerlessness over me, suddenly my vexation with life will lead me to terrible sin, suddenly evil desire is wakened, and suddenly the Cross is upon me and I tremble. This is the hour of temptation, of darkness, of defenseless deliverance into Satan's hands.[1]

This is the kind of testing from which you pray to be delivered, a kind of evil from which you pray for deliverance, as Jesus taught us in the Lord's Prayer. You ask that this cup of sorrow may pass from you.

This weakness, this helplessness, this powerlessness, is one of the reasons you have trouble accepting, admitting, and facing up to the death of your loved one. It keeps you from recovering from your grief. As long as you do not *accept* the harsh reality of your loss, you *feel* as though you are in control. As one man said of the death of his son, "They tell me I must accept his death. If I do that, then he will be dead!" What he could not accept was, not that his son was dead, but that there was nothing *he* could do to change that fact. To do this is to confess one's weakness, helplessness, and powerlessness. Not to do so is to allow grief itself to become a way of life instead of recovering from it. Martin Luther, in his *Table Talk*, gave us the clue to accepting our own helpless weakness when he said:

> The Lord our God is a God of the humble and perplexed hearts, who are in need, tribulation, and danger. If we were strong, we should be proud and haughty. God shows his power in our weakness; he will not quench the glimmering flax, neither will he break in pieces the bruised reed.[2]

The apostle Paul described it this way:

> God keeps faith, and he will not allow you to be tested above your powers, but when the test comes he will at the same time provide a way out, by enabling you to sustain it. (1 Cor. 10:13, NEB)

THE SEARCH FOR MEANING

In the depths of your grief you may have been struck by the absurdity, pointlessness, and meaninglessness of the death of your beloved. Now, without that person, you feel abandoned. Sometimes you even feel angry toward him or her for dying and leaving you. You search the inscrutable face of life as it is without that loved one. You ask: "Is there any meaning at all to this death, and—now that a loved one is gone—to my life from here on?" Without some meaning, life for you either stands still or erupts into chaos in your mind. Your persistent cry of "Why?" concentrates this appeal for meaning.

You will search in vain for some "reason" that makes the death of your beloved seem fair, just, and understandable. However, God works *after the fact* of the death to bring meaning to your life. You go about your daily duties, but the inner unity of your life is a jumble of meaningless pieces. Let me tell you a parable.

When our son Bill was about five years of age, I bought him a little balsa-wood airplane. It was "powered" by a heavy rubber band. When twisted, the rubber band would unwind and turn the propeller. Thus the little plane flew well outside the house where there were no walls to hit. But one day when the weather was bad, Bill was playing in the basement with his airplane. I heard him scream with anger. I went to the basement to see what had happened to him. He had attempted to fly his plane in the basement. He was crying loudly, but all of a sudden he stopped crying and began to wipe his tears and even smile.

I asked him what had happened in his mind. He said, "I know what I will do; I will take that rubber band and make me a slingshot out of it!"

Bill is thirty-three now. He has served two tours of duty in Vietnam. He has seen the pieces, not only of real airplanes, but also of human lives. He himself has experienced pain and grief. Yet this story is a parable of his life. He has a way of grieving appropriately for a while. Then he sets about perceiving a new design, a new pattern, a new use of the pieces.

Reorganizing the pieces of your life into a useful and even humorous whole calls for a pattern to go by, a design that amounts to a fresh sense of calling and vocation in dialogue with God. The meaning will not be found in explaining how God could let someone die. The meaning will lie in those spiritual discoveries of your own calling and vocation which would not likely have happened if your loss had not punctured your superficiality. You are being pushed to the depths of human life. These depths become your deceased loved one's legacy for your own survival and hope.

YOUR CALLING AND
RECOMMITMENT TO LIFE

One thing that hinders your recovery from grief is that *for you* death has no place at all in the created order of the universe. If you are like most people, death is alien to your universe, it is something foreign to you. Intellectually you may admit that death happens to other people but emotionally you assume that it will never come near to you and your loved ones. The undercurrent of illusion that you are an exception and should be treated as such prevents you from devoting yourself to anything but an internal argument against death's intrusion into your personal world. Hence, you are tempted to make a vocation of grief, a work to which you devote full time. May God prevent you from this dead end of human existence. You have not been called to such a vocation. You "take your share of suffering for the sake of the Gospel, in the strength that comes from God . . . who brought us salvation and called us to a dedicated life . . . in Christ Jesus. . . . For he has broken the power of death and brought life and immortality to light through the Gospel" (2 Tim. 1:8–10, NEB).

139

God comforts you and me with a purpose. God equips us through our suffering to *be* a comfort to other people who are grieved. As the apostle Paul states it:

> Blessed be the God and Father of our Lord Jesus Christ, the Father of mercies and God of all comfort, who comforts us in all our affliction, so that we may be able to comfort those who are in any affliction, with the comfort with which we ourselves are comforted by God. (2 Cor. 1:3–4)

In brief, God saves us from self-centeredness and a "pity me" way of life by intensifying our awareness of our capacity to comfort other people in their suffering. You can visualize people you know who have been very helpful to you in your grief. You probably know them well enough to be aware that they themselves have had more grief than any ten people usually have. Yet they have a serenity, a quiet presence, and a healing kind of wisdom. They speak with you as veterans of grief. Your calling is to become somewhat that way yourself—a healer of broken hearts. What shape that calling takes will be determined by your unique personality and talents. Your particular grief enhances your unique gifts as a caring person.

The exercise of your calling, enabled by the power of the Spirit, takes you out of self-centeredness. It recenters your affections and loyalty. It is no act of disloyalty to your deceased loved one to begin to recommit your time, energy, and affection to new causes and new people. You may even find your perspective returning in such clarity that you can laugh. The memory of your loved one begins to turn up humorous and joyous things he or she said and did. You can—with some degree of forbearance—begin to see his or her faults and no longer hold on to an unbelievable kind of gilded saint. You may even begin to permit yourself to enjoy the freedom from responsibilities that the deceased's presence before death laid upon you. You begin to breathe more deeply. Your face ceases to be drawn and tense. You have, by God's grace, begun to live again.

NOTES

1. Dietrich Bonhoeffer, *Creation and Fall: A Theological Interpretation of Genesis 1–3,* trans. John C. Fletcher; and *Temptation,* trans. Eberhard Bethge; 2 vols. in 1 (New York: Macmillan Co., 1959), p. 99.

2. Thomas S. Kepler, ed., *The Table Talk of Martin Luther* (New York: World Publishing Co., 1952), p. 285.

10

Settling on Your Personal Ethical Code

Codes of behavior are all over the place. Persons and groups have sets of principles and rules by which they live and work. These are codes of behavior. Codes have been written down to be read by all persons since the time of the Code of Hammurabi, written by a king of Babylon who ruled from 1955 to 1913 B.C. The code with which you and I are most familiar is the Ten Commandments. The Bible is a record of many such codes, such as the Deuteronomic Code and many others. Professions today have written and revised codes for the professional responsibility of their members, outstanding among which is the code of the American Medical Association. These are all communal or corporate codes devised by groups and communities of persons.

Our primary concern here is to raise the question, What is *your* personally chosen code, based on your own experiences as a private human being? The codes of the Bible *can* and *do* become personally appropriated ways of life. The psalmist speaks of the blessedness of the person whose "delight is in the law of the LORD, and on his law he [or she] meditates day and night" (Ps. 1:2). Even so, such a person also develops individual convictions as to what hard-earned truth is from having collided with the sharp edges of daily living. This can be made more vivid by asking yourself, What do you do when you know no one is watching you and no one can find out what you are doing? In your solitude, what is your personal ethical code?

Plato dramatizes this with the story of a shepherd of Gyges, who was tending his sheep one day when an earthquake opened a gash in the earth into which the shepherd fell. At the bottom of this big ditch, the shepherd shook himself free of dirt and looked around. Much to his surprise, he found a beautiful gold ring that fit exactly. At the campfire that night, he discovered that when he turned the jewel set in the ring to the inside of his hand, the other shepherds could not see or hear him do or say anything. Later, in the village, he realized that no matter what he did he went undetected by others. He was free of the restraints that others placed on him. As a result, this man, who had previously lived an exemplary life, became an unprincipled thief, a ravager of the persons and properties of others. His previous code was built entirely on what others thought about him. When that no longer was a factor, he had no code except that of the jungle.

Immanuel Kant, the philosopher of Königsberg, East Prussia (1724–1804), raises a similar issue when he supposes (and invites you and me to suppose) that you *alone* know that wrong is on your side. You could confess it, but vanity, selfishness, and the fact that you intensely dislike the person you have wronged (who does not know what you have done) enable you to discard any notion of confession. Only your *respect for yourself* remains. This consciousness of your own personal integrity is all that you have and all that you need, says Kant, in *The Critique of Practical Reason,* to start building your own practical ethic. "When this is well established, when a man finds himself worthless and contemptible in his own eyes, then every good moral disposition can be grafted on it, because this is the best, nay, the only guard that can keep off from the mind the pressure of ignoble and corrupting motives." This calls, as we earlier saw from Kierkegaard, for turning our cleverness inward, cutting away from the vanity, the selfishness, and the malice, and building our personal ethical code on the inner core of our integrity before God. As Job said, "Let me be weighed in a just balance, and let God know my integrity!" (Job 31:6); "till I die I will not put away my integrity" (27:5b).

Maintaining your integrity in a world of sham is no small accomplishment. Doing so in a churchly world of "sweet, sweet pietism" is just as demanding also. But the confidence it gives you makes it worthwhile. It can be done, but how? Some guidelines I have tested and have seen others test may be helpful to you too. They amount to a code of personal integrity and become convictions in action. To see positive results of your own ethical actions, and to feel your integrity being strengthened, gives you both courage and confidence for facing life unafraid. Let us see what some guidelines for our code are.

GUIDELINES FOR BUILDING YOUR ETHICAL CODE

One reason you and I are chilled by the moral codes current in our day is that they major on minor morals and violate the underlying principles of behavior. As Jesus put it, they are "straining out a gnat and swallowing a camel!" (Matt. 23:24). In searching for guidelines for our ethical code, let us focus on *principles* of relationship, to God and to our neighbor. Then you can unfold the principles in hundreds of specific situations.

The Principle of Mutual Covenants

A covenant is an agreement made up of mutual promises to and from each person making the covenant. Mutuality means a two-way, give-and-take, equally responsible concern and commitment that two or more persons have to and with each other. They mutually respect, communicate with, and take one another into consideration in their actions. Mutuality generates hope in relationships both to people and to God. God's covenants with you and me are always mutual ones. God promises *and* expects. You and I are covenant-making, covenant-keeping, and covenant-breaking beings. If the promises are all on one person's shoulders, the other person is in fact either a helpless infant or being permitted to behave like one. Except in the case of a real infant, promises made on a one-sided basis run into trouble very early. When you promise like this, you expect gratitude, conformity to your wishes, and control over the other person's life. You expect these things whether you say so or not. When the other person is ungrateful, does not do as you wish, and does not allow you to control his or her life, you become unhappy, lose hope, feel betrayed, and say, "After all I have done for that person, this is the thanks I get!"

Therefore an imperative code of behavior for me is to see to it that the covenants I make, the agreements I enter, are well balanced and mutual. It is not a selfish thing to put my expectations of the other person into words, clearly and unmistakably. This is far more than a deal that says, "If I scratch your back, you must scratch mine." Reciprocity is the heart of understanding. If you do not have it built in, defined, and clear from the outset of a covenant, you have planted the seeds for later misunderstanding, conflict, and broken relationships. To see to it that your covenants are mutual, then, is to value, cherish, and protect your neighbor as well as yourself. It is ethical love, not just sentimental good intentions.

Furthermore, covenants made and not kept are sure ways of injuring, breaking, or at least bringing to crisis your relationship to the other. Promises must be made very carefully, not lightly, ill-advisedly, or indiscreetly. You know some persons who will promise anything rather than say no. They are "hail-fellow-well-met," likable Joes or Marys who sound far more accommodating than they really are. Yet you know you cannot really count on them. On the other hand, you know persons who promise little and do more. They give you a specific time by which their promise will be fulfilled. You do not have to ask them repeatedly when (and whether) they will do what they said. They are persons you can count on, and they inspire you to be that kind of person also.

The principle of carefully made and mutually kept covenants, then, can be applied in hundreds of situations, the most intense of which is marriage. Your work situation, your church relationships, and your personal friendships are others. These covenants are more than legal contracts, although they have their contractual nature also. Covenants are commitments to faithful function and ethical love, a love always balancing the mutual empathy for and response of persons to one another. The promises we make and keep endear the heart; the promises we make and break, break us apart.

The Principle of Simplicity of Speech

The capacity to speak, to use language, is a powerful source of strength and confidence. With speech we either commune with or confuse others. We reveal, hide, or distort our real selves to those around us. *Simplicity* of speech is the opposite of *duplicity* of speech. I suggest that simplicity of utterance, of the spoken word, reflects our integrity, whereas duplicity confuses others and reveals our double-mindedness. All this becomes very abstract, though, unless we have specific instances to bring it down to earth.

Take "double messages," for example. A person may say to his or her spouse, "I love you, care for you, and don't want to see you hurt, but I'm no longer able to be your husband [or wife]." A teacher says, "You will find this material easy to master, but half the class will fail the course." A father says, "Daddy loves you and wants to be with you, but I've got to go skiing this weekend and can't see you as we planned." Persons listening to this doublespeak are both confused and hurt at the same time. This is duplicity in speech. Simplicity in speech is the opposite. When you speak simply, you give *one* message. Your "yes" is "yes," and your "no" is "no." As Jesus says, "Let what you say be simply 'Yes' or 'No'; anything more than this comes from evil" (Matt. 5:37).

Again, promises made and broken with no attempt to renegotiate them are forms of doublespeak. One of the most prevalent forms of this is procrastination in getting things done that you have promised to do. Being consistently late for appointments is a variation of procrastination. People can only go by what you say you will do. When saying and doing split apart, you have doublespeak, duplicity of speech.

A basic principle of any functional ethical code is simplicity of speech. This puts you to work to get all the doublespeak duplicity out of the way you treat others and treat yourself. Character is built in this way. You become a person whose word is his or her bond, whose integrity is counted on by those around you, and an ethical love flourishes in your life. Here again, mutuality generates hope, and relationships are made durable, lasting, and trustworthy.

The Principle of Durability in Relationships

Mutual covenants lay the groundwork for relationships to persons and to God that last, that satisfy the deeper hungers you and I have for security, confidence, and hope. They are day-to-day expressions of the faith in and love for other people and for God by which we live. The apostle Paul says, "There are three things that last for ever: faith, hope, and love" (1 Cor. 13:13, NEB). Therefore I suggest that durability is a second principle of ethical decision making. This principle acts in every relationship you and I have to people and to God. When you meet someone new, you gauge nonverbally *how long* the relationship will last as you decide *how much* to invest yourself in the friendship. When you take a job, you ask, "For how long? How much tenure do I have?" When a couple gets married, the words "as long as you both shall live" raise the issue—if they do not settle it!—of the durability of the covenant. Yet, in friendship, work, and love, common sense tells you that you cannot be lastingly related to everybody you meet. Even remembering all their names is a major undertaking. How, then, can this principle work?

As I have indicated before, the principle of durability works as a guide for discerning *in whom* to invest your time, energy, and other resources. You have confidence for living by reason of your convictions. However, confidence is not just for your private consumption. It is eaten up by the passage of time if it is not invested. As you invest confidence in God and in other people, that confidence is increased in strength, value, and clarity. Yet you need a measure by which to discern the kinds of people who are trustworthy and who in turn are concerned about the lasting quality of their relationship to you. Durability is a measure for these decisions being made. Some persons are casual, superficial, and even flippant about sustaining relationships with others. They contact people for their own uses; they do not relate durably to them over time. Other people have an intuition of the Eternal in the ordinary meetings with others in the marketplace, the shops, the factories, the offices, the classrooms, the churches, the political meetings, and in the home. If they sense that you too have an eye and a heart for the Eternal in your care for other people, you "correspond," you "resonate," you "vibrate" with them.

Relationships so formed start on bases that assure they will last. They tend to form slowly. They are not instant intimacies in a short-order "use" of persons. They are steadfast in their growth over time.

As I consider friends I have known and worked with over twenty, thirty, or forty years, I know these relationships have been marked by high regard for one another, a deep sense of empathy (that works in both directions), and a fierce refusal to use and abuse each other for short-term gains. These friendships have been proven and tested over the years by crises we have suffered together. For example, my friend of forty-seven years, Henlee Barnette, the author of *Your Freedom to Be Whole*,[1] endured the Vietnam War with me. At the same time that my elder son, Bill, spent twenty months in the Naval Riverine Assault Group, one of Henlee Barnette's sons spent two tours of duty as an intelligence officer in the Air Force. His other son at the same time refused to be drafted and stayed in Sweden four years. We struggled daily in agonizing prayer together. Every fiber of our character was tested. Our faith in both humankind and in God was under fire. Yet ten years have put it behind us, and we can affirm with James 1:3 that "the testing of your faith produces steadfastness."

The principle of durability, then, could also be called "steadfastness," that is, "standing hitched together when the going gets roughest." Yet the maintenance of steadfast relationships calls for another principle or guideline for our ethical code. That is the daily discipline of face-to-faceness in human relationships and in relationship to God.

The Principle of Day-to-Day Face-to-Faceness

If you and I have lasting relationships to others, we maintain those relationships by knowing each other on a face-to-face basis. A quaint phrase from my hill-country heritage in western South Carolina says this well. People said, "I haven't laid eyes on him [or her] for too long." My grandmother would say to me when I had been away a long time, "Come here to me and let me lay eyes on you, my grandson." This tender intimacy was given a Christian meaning by Thomas Helwys in one of the Free Church confessions of 1612. He said that "the members of every church or congregation ought to know one another, that so they may perform all the duties of love to one another both to soul and body."

Yet maintaining face-to-faceness is easier said than done. People offend one another, both intentionally and unintentionally. People sin against each other with a high hand, and not just unwittingly. People get hurt. They withdraw from each other. They "never want to lay eyes on each other again." People refuse to be reconciled to each other. They live in the mistaken fantasy that human relationships *can* be ended, when in reality they can only be changed from good to bad, bad to worse, worse to impossible. Yet, with courage and conviction, persistence and patience, such relationships can be restored.

If they are kept in good health or, in the case of severe conflict, restored to well-being, then the hardest but surest way of doing so is through face-to-face meeting, renegotiation, mutual awareness, and confession of error. If you have been offended by someone, your first temptation is to say so to everyone *but* that person. Each time you tell the story, it gets exaggerated just a bit more than the last time you told it. These stories get back to the one who has offended you. He or she talks to everyone but you. There are a few people in these two sets of "everyones" who *like* to see you and the other person fight. The first casualty of this process is your face-to-face meeting with the one who has offended you.

The sayings of both Jesus and Paul give the surest guide to ethical living here. Jesus said, "If one of your fellow believers sins against you, point out the fault privately just between yourselves. If your neighbor listens to you, you have gained your neighbor" (Matt. 18:15, adapted). This is the place to start. The objective is to open the other's ears to hear you, to be heard. The apostle Paul gives an additional angle of vision: "If a man [or woman] is overtaken in any trespass, you who are spiritual should restore him [or her] in a spirit of gentleness. Look to yourself, lest you too be tempted" (Gal. 6:1). The person who fretted you may be carrying a personal burden about which you are not aware, and has certainly created a burden for you to carry. If you approach that person with a spirit of gentleness, each of you is more likely to be able to bear the other's burden.

If you adopt these instructions of Jesus and Paul as your personal code, you will, as Jesus predicted, be able to gain your neighbor [brother or sister] in many cases. Other cases fail and require that you try again and take a third reconciling person with you. This also has successes and failures, but it is worth the effort. Yet this kind of directness and face-to-faceness is a rare thing even in religious circles. We live behind masks of niceness, piety, and spiritual pride that are not easy to remove for such candor and forthrightness. Middle-class people are terrified at such face-to-faceness at first, accustomed as we are to criticizing people behind their backs and soft-soaping them to their faces. However, making this a part of your code will in the long run give you a stronger integrity and maintain other people's respect. You will not win in all instances, but you have been faithful. Stand and wait for life itself to change things. It often does.

To adopt face-to-faceness as your code is to enter the ethical sphere of life by the narrow gate where the way is hard, but it leads to life, not destruction. Wider and easier ways are everywhere.

The Principle of Greatness of Heart

The principle of face-to-faceness can become a "flamingo ethic" if it is followed to the exclusion of other principles of an adequate code of life. The flamingo is a bird native to parts of Europe and the extreme southern parts of the United States. When you drive through swamplands of Florida and Louisiana, you often see these birds in their splendid beauty, standing on *one* leg. Many ethical codes stand on one principle just like that. Face-to-faceness can take the ethical imperative of encounter to the absurd. You can "stand people down" over trivial things that could best be dealt with by ignoring or never mentioning them, or mentioning them only to your spouse or other confidant. Those trivial things are not worth the breath it takes to recount them.

To be able to do this calls for another ethical principle—that of greatness of heart, or magnanimity. This is the opposite of meanness of spirit, little-mindedness, and vengefulness. Greatness of heart, or magnanimity, is not a goody-two-shoes namby-pambiness. It is far more than a set of good feelings, real or contrived. Greatness of heart has at least three psychospiritual ingredients necessary for living productively.

First, greatness of heart consists of a *perspective* of the smallness or greatness of an event, an offense, or an issue. Large events, offenses, and issues are met firmly and courageously, but gently. Small ones are overlooked, disregarded, and ignored. They are treated with benign neglect. Even if they are noted, nothing is made of them. A greathearted perspective is fueled by the spirit of discernment whereby you, being mature, have trained your faculties to distinguish good from evil, the significant from the insignificant, the trivial from the intensely important.

Second, greatness of heart, or magnanimity, is inspired by having *convictions* in which you are confident. You are secure in your own integrity and are not thrown off balance by every petty action of others. You are guided by a North Star, your own ethical compass and sextant, and balanced by the inner gyroscope of your relationship to God. You are not blown off course by the bluster of others, nor do you drift astray by not paying attention to who you are and where you are going.

Third, greatness of heart and magnanimity are nurtured by the *sense of awe and wonder.* Immanuel Kant said, "Two things fill the mind with ever new and increasing admiration and awe, the oftener and the more steadily we reflect on them: the starry heavens above and the moral law within."

I have spoken here of only a few principles of an effective ethical code. As you reflect on the grandeur of the starry heavens above you and the moral law within you, add to my reflections your own additional principles. A growing ethical code is open-ended. It can encompass emerging principles not yet revealed to us by which we can live, courageously and with certainty, in a nuclear and hazardous world by glorifying God and enjoying God forever.

NOTE

1. Henlee Barnette, *Your Freedom to Be Whole,* Potentials: Guides for Productive Living (Philadelphia: Westminster Press, 1984).

Part Three

MINISTRY AND THE FAMILY

11

The Rights of Infants

The Fourth Gospel tells us that "to all who received him, who believed in his name, he gave power to become children of God" (John 1:12). Let us focus on the word "power" used in this Fourth Gospel passage. "Power" here does not refer to an inherent ability but to an authorization, an imparted title for a new status. The word can be translated "right." If so, we would read the passage as follows: "He gave the right to become the children of God" to those who received him and who believed in his name.

Furthermore, the word "become" does not mean merely to begin or to make a beginning but refers to having a family relationship to God. In both the writings of Paul and the Johannine words this family relationship is a gift to be received. The Pauline letters use a metaphor derived from the Roman law of adoption, and the Johannine scriptures use the Greek symbolism of regeneration, the birth from above.[1] The focus of this chapter will be on the "right" to become children of God.

The modern student of psychology must be very careful when he is interpreting the scripture. Many of the words used in the New Testament are today used in additional and different senses in contemporary psychology. For example, the word "right" in the sense of an inherent ability is not emphasized by many psychologists when speaking of children. Rather, the incompleteness, weakness, inability, and helplessness of the infant is underscored by them. Margaret Ribble says that when we observe large numbers of newborn babies "we are struck immediately by their helplessness." They breathe insecurely and irregularly. They do not adjust to cold easily. They even need help in establishing the ability to suck and feed. She says that an infant's nervous system "is incomplete and the brain is not yet ready to function in control of behavior." She points to the way in which early painters were a long time learning that a child does not even "look like a miniature man or woman." She says that "we ourselves are even more obtuse when we think of a child's mental and nervous organization as being like that of an adult but on a small scale."[2]

Yet, on the other hand, psychologists today do refer vigorously to the inalienable rights of every infant coming into the world. By the very reason that they are infants they have the right and the privilege of being treated by adults *as infants*. They are not "little adults." Ribble speaks of the maternal instinct as a gift of nature that has to do with a child's intention to live, to grow, and to become a completed person. Mothering, whether it is done by instinct or design, "is as vital to the child's development as is food." Through this process of caring the child becomes assured that he is not a thing—"a toy or an idol"—but an individual who has an innate need for a loving relationship that is met by the mother. Clues are given by Holy Writ, as well as by the sensitive insights of Dr. Ribble, concerning the unformed lives of newborn babies. Therefore I would like to use these to identify what I consider to be the basic rights to which every child that comes into the world has a privilege. These privileges are his necessities. Adults responsible for him under God are obligated to fulfill these rights.

THE RIGHT TO BE AN INFANT

I recall walking the long wards of a state hospital as a chaplain in my early ministry. One day I saw a twenty-two-year-old woman lying down in the aisle between the long rows of beds, rolling back and forth and screaming and chattering like a little child. I came near her, and she noticed my presence. I spoke to her gently and yet firmly and said, after calling her by her full name, "Tell me, what are you doing?" She replied, "I am being a little baby." I asked again, "What makes you want to be a little baby?" She replied, "They did not let me be a little baby when I was a little baby and now I am catching up on being a little baby." Every infant has a right to be an infant and not to be expected to be an adult. If we do not accord this right to an infant, sooner or later that infant will reach back and claim that right for himself or herself. We cannot put old people's heads on infant's shoulders without grotesque results. This puts the finger of judgment on our unrealistic expectations of infants. We are likely to expect them to feed themselves too soon, keep themselves dry and unsoiled too soon, and think of ourselves as failures as parents when they do not conform to these expectations.

What has been said literally about the growth of infants can be said symbolically about entrée into the Christian life. The scripture speaks of us as being "babes in Christ," "fed with milk, not solid food." The scripture both in the example of Jesus and in the exhortation of Paul as teacher takes into consideration the "readiness" of a person for certain teachings. (See 1 Cor. 3:1–4 and Heb. 5:11–6:2.) Admittedly, both of these passages to which reference has just been made are toned with an atmosphere of impatience because people are "past the time" for putting away childish things to whom these two letters are written. Nevertheless a disclaimer is entered in behalf of the spiritual infant. We are to be mature in all things, but in anger we are to be immature. Milk *is* for infants in Christ. Childlikeness is affirmed as a prerequisite for entrance into the kingdom of heaven.

Therefore, both literally and symbolically we can underscore the rights of infants to be infants. The free gift of the children of God is the right to learn the rudiments of experience with Christ in the Christian faith. Here we have a paradox, both sides of which we must live with faith, hope, and love.

THE RIGHT TO BREATHE

The scripture tells us that "the LORD God formed man of dust from the ground, and breathed into his nostrils the breath of life; and man became a living being" (Gen. 2:7). Dust was animated by the Lord God's *breath,* or "spirit," which made him into a living being, a total self. Primitive man identified life with breathing. As the psalmist says, "When thou takest away their breath, they die and return to their dust" (Ps. 104:29). However, breath and spirit are words that are used interchangeably in the Old Testament. The very next words of the psalmist are: "When thou sendest forth thy Spirit, they are created; and thou renewest the face of the ground" (v. 30). Job captures something of the same idea as follows: "The spirit of God has made me, and the breath of the Almighty gives me life" (Job 33:4).

These words must be very real to the nurse and the doctor who solicitously attend a prematurely born child and watch his every breath. The rhythm of life itself is in the breathing. We await the baby's first cry with hopes realized when this signals that the child is breathing. However, it is wrong to assume that breathing is, therefore, self-regulated and taken for granted. At birth a child must adjust to his new environment and breathe much like an astronaut or a deep-sea diver. Dr. Ribble tells us that mothering is the important fact that helps to break the deadlock between the plentiful oxygen in the air and the constant struggle of a little child for the physiological sufficiency of breathing. The brain itself takes a lion's share of the developing body's oxygen supply. The lungs must work overtime to meet the rest of the body's needs. Breathing is something that cannot be taught the child. Yet as a child learns to feed himself at the mother's breast, he is helped to breathe by her consistent personal attention. When the

153

child learns to vocalize, even the most meaningless babbling sounds, this is a signal that an inner balance of oxygen through breathing is present. The child's newfound "right to breathe" is established; he vocalizes; delight comes to both mother and child. The anxious child has "shortened breath," and, quaintly enough, one of the biblical words for "anxiety" means literally "shortened breath." The angry child "holds his breath." Even one of the signs of the depressed child is the sighs of breathing.

Once again we are moving both literally and symbolically to the nature of life itself. Crucial to our day is the right of every living being to unpolluted air to breathe. Radioactive fallout focuses the ethical struggle of mankind today. The pollution of the air we breathe removes the right to breathe and forces destruction that will "return us to dust." Therefore, whether we take the right to breathe literally or symbolically, the results are the same. Especially is this true for little babies.

THE RIGHT TO MOTHERING

The understanding love of a mother is an inalienable right of a child. Mothering is a precondition of becoming a person in one's own right. Mothering focuses in the newborn babe around two great functions: feeding and speaking. Both of these functions involve the mouth. Thus the mouth becomes the nucleus around which the trust and confidence of a newborn child is formed. As a pearl begins with a specific substance, so the personality begins with the mouth. Apart from mothering, a person perishes both literally and figuratively. William James used to say that an infant at the outset is a "big, booming, buzzing, confusion." He is not aware of himself as a *self*. His "me" is no different from the rest of the world. He is an undifferentiated self blended into the being of his mother for some time after his birth. Therefore, if he is to become a person in his own right, his mother is an imperative necessity. Her body becomes "the other." Her presence spells security. Her absence spells insecurity.

THE RIGHT TO A FATHER

A young woman, an expert in child care, was lecturing and leading a discussion with a group of theological students about the pastoral care of children. One student asked, "If mothers are so important to the care of a child, what is the place of the father in all of this?" She replied, "The father's best opportunity to care for the child is to make his wife secure in his own love for her. The mother makes the child secure. The father makes the mother secure." The anxious, fearful, bereft mother must have her resources replenished by the strength and admiration, affection and tenderness, wisdom and reassurance of a strong husband. It takes two parents to raise every child. A child has a right to a father who is *there* both to him and to the mother. A Mary can tend her child while shepherds watch in adoration. A Joseph stands between her and unkind neighbors as well as threatening Herods. This Bethlehem scene is recapitulated in every parent-child relationship. The absentee father leaves the infant desolate because the mother is deprived.

The father today, especially in the middle classes, provides much mothering, baby-sitting, caring, and tending in his own right. The taboo on tenderness in men is controverted by the presence of the helpless infant. Yet the protective and providing powers of the father are the focus of his identity as a father. Here he proves himself to be a real man. Can he protect his wife in the time of her preoccupation with and care of an infant? Can he stand by and accept full responsibility for the joys that he had in sexual relationships with the mother of his child? Every child has a right to a father who can do this.

The unchangeable element in sexual ethics can be specified here. The so-called "new moralists" miss the point when they attack Christian ethics for a sex morality confined to marriage and restricted to procreation. Those forms of Christian ethics which restrict themselves to this emphasis also miss the point. We do not hit the mark of sexual ethics until we fix our sights upon the moral principle of a man and a woman *staying by* a helpless child in a unified love that brings a child to maturity. This takes fidelity, communication, responsible love, powers of durable relationship, and plain patience. Child-rearing requires that a man and a woman lose their own lives in order that they may save themselves and the child. Here the cross of Christ is implicit in the call to parenthood. The task of the teacher is to enable the parent to accept this as the explicit commitment of the parent. This requires freedom from deception and division of commitment to each other as well as wholehearted dedication to Christ. A child has a right to such parents.

THE RIGHT TO BE WANTED

All that has been said thus far implies that the husband and wife—father and mother—have *chosen* to be parents of this child. They *wanted* this child. They *agreed* upon having this child. The child has a right to be wanted. He has a right to be brought into the world on purpose and not as the accident of a *Playboy* Philosophy of sex, within or without marriage.

This is the main theme of contemporary education and planned parenthood. A child can be unwanted by unwed parents. The fear of pregnancy is confirmed in the fact of pregnancy. But even more so, a child can be unwanted by wed parents. They may simply not like children. They may have other ambitions. They may already have too many children. They may have had painful and traumatic experiences in previous births. For many reasons they may not want children. Birth control measures are therefore ethical obligations of parents in that they widen and deepen the range of choice in becoming parents. We should, therefore, inasmuch as we possibly can, see to it that in prayerful cooperation with God the Creator, every child we bring into the world is wanted. This is the child's inalienable right. *Choosing* to be a parent assures that husband and wife from the very outset have harmonized and synchronized their wishes and long-term commitments in life. It is the precondition of the joy of childbirth and the discipline of parenthood. In this sense, marriage is a creation of God, given to us for the enjoyment of one another and of him in the creative design he has for the world. We can therefore partake of marriage with prayer and thanksgiving and thus consecrate our children to him. In doing so, we bequeath to the child his basic right to be wanted. This "wanting" is love at its heart. "Love," as Howard Rome says, "is a very light thing." In a new baby's life, "it takes a lot of love to make a pound."[3]

THE RIGHT TO A CHURCH

Every newborn infant is born into the covenant of marriage. The home becomes the center of all the rights of being an infant, of breathing, of mothering, of fathering, and of being wanted. Yet mother, father, and child cannot bear these obligations alone. All together they have the right to a larger family of mankind, which God has designed in the church of the living Christ. Here they have a hundredfold fathers, mothers, brothers, sisters, houses, land, and so forth, and a promise of eternal life. One "gushes" with an idealism that is out of touch with reality when one assumes that—unaided—the rights that have been mentioned thus far will be accorded every child that comes into the world. Death is in the world too. Sin is in the world too. Death snatches away a mother from the side of a newborn babe. War tears a father away from the side of mother and child. Slavery can shatter the rights of infants. This slavery may be like the slavery of the nineteenth century. Negro fathers were sold away from their wives and children. Industrialization snatched both mother and father—white and black—from the side of the new babe and put them to work in mills. The twentieth-century variety of slavery is just as damaging to the rights of infants though less apparent. Big business can create demands on the organization man in modern suburbia that destroy his relationship to mother and child. Slavery in any garb can shatter the rights of little children.

The intention of God is that the church fill up the empty places left by death, divorce, war, and slavery. The power of God enables the church to transcend destruction of infants' rights by man's inhumanity to man. The scripture puts it bluntly in one of its rare definitions of religion: "Religion that is pure and undefiled before God and the Father is this: to visit orphans and widows in their affliction, and to keep oneself unstained from the world" (James 1:27).

When I speak of the church here, I am not referring to the vague, nebulous, invisible sort of thing. I am referring to a specific "larger family" to which the family appropriation is "organismically" related. They know each other face-to-face. This larger community supports and sustains the father with inspiration and enthusiasm for his task of providing for and protecting his family. This church leads the father to an independent existence of his own before God and teaches him to pray. This church cheers the father in his discouragement, sustains him in his decisions, and comes to his aid in his helplessness. In the absence of the father, this church fills in the gap left by his separation from his wife and child. It does so without evil design, but with the discipline of unstained hands and uncontaminated motive. In the church's doing so, the religion of this church is made pure and undefiled before God.

The pastor of this church symbolizes both the strength of the father and the tenderness of the mother as well as the larger context of the fellowship of believers. He is a shepherd who feeds his flock as a good undershepherd of Jesus Christ. He "attends" unto little children. In the tradition of the Lord Jesus Christ, when divisions threaten the fellowship of the church, he takes unto himself the little children of the church and points to them as the ones who are being caused to stumble. He casts his lot with the little children. This is no sentimental act. It represents the hard-nosed reality of the economy of life as it is. It represents the severity as well as the goodness of God. The infant child partakes of the deposit of faith vicariously through the commitment of father and mother to God in the context of the commitment of the larger family of God, the church. Every infant has a right to such a church. Surrounding him and his older brothers and sisters are teachers like the reader of this book. These teachers bring home to the child his inalienable right in the flesh and blood of their concern and their instruction.

This rather ideal assumption of the right of an infant to the kind of church described here in no wise assumes that no other institutions, groups, and individuals than the institutional church can and do provide this kind of care for persons. I work as a part of the staff of a close-knit psychiatric unit dedicated to the care of acutely disturbed persons. This kind of care and concern appears in the seemingly secular context of this clinic. Sometimes the real community of faith appears as the church and sometimes it appears in other forms. The important thing is that it appear, not that it be haggled over as being sacred or secular.

NOTES

1. George A. Buttrick and others, eds., *The Interpreter's Bible* (Nashville: Abingdon Press, 1952), 8:471.

2. Margaret A. Ribble, *The Rights of Infants: Early Psychological Needs and Their Satisfaction,* 2nd ed. (New York: Columbia University Press, 1965), pp. 10–12.

3. Howard Rome, "Love Is a Very Light Thing," from the Broadway musical *Fanny.*

12

On Meeting Teachers and Schoolmates

The six-year-old child is young, has a measure of experience with play-mates, and yet is placed on the edge of entering a whole new world: school. He is a fully functioning self, though an inexperienced self. He has come through four stages in the organization of his personality. Erik Erikson says that the first stage has crystallized around the conviction: "I am what I am given." This is the stage of helplessness, of infancy. The second stage is one in which the self forms around the conviction: "I am what I will." This is the stage of individuality. The third stage of the expansion and clarification of the self-image may be characterized by the conviction: "I am what I can imagine I will be." Here the child works at distinguishing fantasy from reality. The fourth stage marks the child's entering school. Then the personality of the child crystallizes around the conviction: "I am what I learn." As Erikson says, "The child now wants to be shown how to get busy with something and how to be busy with others."[1]

At school the child meets other children. They are potentially competitive or cooperative beings. He also meets teachers. He is now to receive systematic instruction. Teachers are to "give it to him." But it is not as simple as that. He has more than one set of teachers. He has the classroom teacher who teaches literacy and does so by appointment, for pay, and in the structured situation of the classroom. However, there are other teachers—the mechanic at the garage, the clerk in the hardware store, the salesperson in the record shop, the librarian in the library or on the bookmobile, the old retired man down the street who has time to play with children and to teach them how to make things, and a dozen other such people. Even more than this, the child learns on the grapevine between him and other children. They teach him the ropes. These too are sources of learning. The formal, appointed teacher who is unaware of these less formal tributaries of learning simply passes his pupils in a darkness of his own making.

GREAT HAPPENINGS AT SCHOOL

Two great happenings take place when a child goes to school. First he moves away from the personal kind of authority of his parents to the impersonal: principal and teachers. On the way to school he sees an impersonal authority: the crossing policeman. In the classroom he sees the schoolteacher. On the playground he meets the recreational director. These people lay down rules and regulations, many times not interpreting their meaning to him. It is not his to ask why; it is his to do or die.

In addition to these adult authorities, there are those people who, Harry Stack Sullivan says, are "in almost every social situation: malevolent juveniles—bullies."[2]

These authorities form an imposing complex to which the child must learn to relate himself. His relationship may be complicated by the character of his parents' relationship to the larger community. In a large university town, the child of a university professor is immediately tagged. In a large political center such as the state capital or the national capital, the politician-father's name stamps the child. Furthermore, the color of his skin, the background of his parents, the cost of his clothes, and the nature of his speech tend to "pigeonhole" him.

The second great change in the life of the child is the breathtaking shifts that must take place in comparison with the way in which the child has lived at home. Sullivan calls this second change "social accommodation." The home presents, even in its grossest form, the kind of refinement in interpersonal relations that the school rarely provides. A crudeness that is almost never displayed in later life is the order of the day. Learning how to cope with bullies, how to maneuver oneself in relation to people who have come from vastly different kinds of homes, how to accept or reject the estimates that one's peers have of one—all these and a thousand other such instances provide an intensive part of the educative process. The healthy child comes to school with freedom to compare himself and his parents with other children and their parents, the teachers, and others. The unhealthy one is the compulsively bound child who looks upon all authority persons as being perfect, as persons whose words are never wrong, and as persons who are to be slavishly followed without asking questions for guidance and clarification.

In the midst of these changes, competition, cooperation, and compromise become the bases upon which the young schoolchild copes with the world around him. Learning to perform successfully in the period from the first to the sixth grade calls for "industry" and "production" as the child learns to talk, to read, and to act properly in the presence of a crowd of people not his own kin. He experiences himself as a self, but he shapes his life in such a way that his self becomes a sharpened instrument for coping with the reality of the world of which he is a part outside his home. Gordon Allport calls this the development of the self as a "rational coping agent." In this process of the development of the self as a rational coping agent several things happen that are of primary religious significance.

RELIGIOUS ISSUES IN THE
SCHOOL COMMUNITY

The religious issues in a school community are far more subtle than whether or not the teacher reads the Bible and prays or whether or not the Supreme Court of the United States thinks this is constitutional. The fundamental religious issues are far more acute, subtle, and difficult to identify. Yet their importance is so great as to make even the Supreme Court seem irrelevant.

The first religious issue is the way in which children, in their early school years particularly, *stereotype* one another. Stereotypes are simple classifications of people, necessary as a "shorthand" way of communicating. For example, we say that the lady at the desk who types is a "secretary." But this does not make all secretaries a segregated society with invariable characteristics. This is classification, not stereotyping.

For another example, in my early school years I was a child who could not afford to bring money to school to buy my lunch. I very soon saw that there were two groups of people who tended to stereotype each other—although I did not know that word at that time. I did feel stamped. I brought a sack lunch. Certain other children did not. Harry Stack Sullivan says that in his own early years he heard many things said about Jews but, did not know any Jews. His whole knowledge of Jews arose from studying the Bible. He rejoiced that he did not fix in his mind some of the grimier characteristics of Jews which other children around him had in their minds. Therefore he was freed of the bondage of stereotypes of "Jews." To the contrary, he had an intense curiosity to find out "what the devil the people who wrote the Old Testament must have been like."[3] A young woman says that when she went to grammar school she had never heard of the idea of thinking literally of a Negro. She did not stereotype them as being a fixed class of people as a result. Now she worries about her younger sister and brothers because they are going to school in a community where race prejudice against Negroes runs very high.

Teachers can aid and abet this stereotyping process. In doing so, they restrict the growing child's access to the largest family of mankind. They can make patronizing remarks about miners' children in the consolidated school or in the local church. They can pick "teacher's pets," or they can slant their sympathies toward the girls and away from the boys, a very common habit of women teachers.

The church school teacher, therefore, is well advised to be aware of the stereotyping process that goes on, not only in the weekday school but in the church school as well. When the church school teacher says that in Christ there is neither male nor female, bond nor free, Jew nor Gentile, the teacher has real data from the public school system with which to work in illustrating this fundamentally religious value.

A second religiously important problem arising in the public school era of the early years of the school life of the child is the relationship between his hearing and doing. The scripture tells us that we are to "be doers of the word, and not hearers only." Much of the formal educational process is concentrated on some supervisory person talking while some supervised person listens. This is likely to turn the most diligent listener into a spectator, or a leader into a listener. Therefore the classroom can become a prison by reducing the person's impulse to act because of the sheer oversatiation with words. Furthermore, his consciousness may be constricted in that he uses only his ears with which to learn. His other senses are not involved. But the great sacramental systems have an element of education that has been dropped out of our literacy type of education, with its heavy emphasis on words and its loss of the use of other senses than the ears. The use of incense appeals to the sense of smell. The use of the rosary appeals to the sense of touch. The use of artwork appeals to the sense of color in sight. The use of kneeling, standing, and processing and recessing utilizes the sense of touch and the exercise of muscles.

One of the most creative places in which to implement all these many rich senses of the child in learning—thereby avoiding the constriction of consciousness to hearing—is in the vacation church school. Here processions, pageants, audio-visual aids, group participation in worship, arts and crafts, and other activities are implemented. Much of the narrowing of consciousness that later on requires expansion through the use of such things as psychoanalytic free association, sodium amytal, interviews, hypnosis, and perception-expanding drugs may well have begun at the level of the earliest schooling of young people through the constriction of consciousness to unnecessarily verbal methods of teaching. The advent of television forms of education, audio-visual techniques of learning, language laboratories, and direct experience of field activity offers opportunities to avoid such constriction.

The experience of prayer itself calls for a widening of the consciousness of children and adults. Worship, especially through the use of the Sacraments or ordinances, provides a rich and abiding method of opening the range of attention and experience of elementary-age schoolchildren. The Eastern Orthodox practices include even the smallest child in the Holy Communion. This indicates a wisdom on their part from which Western Protestants could learn much, whether we adopt the particular ritual or not.

A third religiously significant experience of elementary-age children is the development of their attitudes toward their own social judgments and social handicaps. The ethical consciousness of a child as to his own worth and the worth of those around him has its most rapid growth in this era. The child who is sick at intervals and whose illness removes him from school, recurrently preventing him from taking part in physical activities, will tend to see himself as socially handicapped. The child of the town drunk (or the children of the town drunks, more accurately) may be so branded as to be "edited out" of the normal relationships of his school group. The rural child who comes to a large city to school may be nicknamed a hick. This is a day of high social mobility of parents and children. Being uprooted because of his parents' military, business, and other considerations disrupts the life of the child in his juvenile society. He becomes "the new kid" in a juvenile group.

All of this speaks to basic religious values that can be taught by the church school teacher as well as the weekday schoolteacher. For example, the sense of alienation begins here. A person is an utter stranger. He feels his complete separateness from others. The scripture advises us to be careful how we entertain strangers, because we may be entertaining angels unawares. In the very experience of the differences of race, custom, language, social class, community reputation, organic inferiorities, we may teach children—if indeed we have learned it ourselves—to see people not as strangers but as consummately interesting persons in whom we may discover fresh knowledge of God. When we see someone quite different from us, we first experience the person as an intruding stranger. But the in-group that is wholesome and ventilated will reach out toward the image of the stranger. They will form *new* ties. In doing so, they enlarge their own world and their own understanding of God. They become more secure as selves in their own right. Here we have a new view of spiritual growth. One becomes oriented in living, not just integrated as a self. The fear of others—especially those who are different—is cast out by those with courage endued by love. Perfect love casts out fear. By perfect love we mean plainly to reach out beyond one's in-group and to affirm those who are different.

Christian education calls for such extension of the horizons of the self through a careful rejection of stereotypes, an avoidance of passive substitution of listening for participating in life, and the removal of exclusiveness from the child's worldview. The end result of the learning process avoids the malignment growth of the capacity to disparage others. Disparagement is commonly thought of as snobbishness. Thus education is not education at all. It is merely the casting of artificial pearls at real swine! The nonconformist student is thought of as inferior, as not fitting in. In return, his parents feel threatened, and the teacher is disparaged as well. This process of disparagement, Sullivan says, "strikes at the very roots of that which is essentially human—the utterly vital role of interpersonal relations."[4]

THE CRISIS OF SCHOOL LIFE

Parents smite their breasts and feel totally responsible for the difficulties in living that their children experience. Such feelings were more appropriate in the era of the nineteenth century when America was predominantly rural, when the family was more a working, learning, and affectionate unit than it is today. The parent, even by law, must share the responsibility for the education and rearing of his child with the public school. The parent, by the impact of massive religious institutions, is caused to feel guilty if he does not share the religious upbringing of his child with the church. Therefore, school, church, and home cooperation sum up the shared responsibility that all three have in our complex society for the way a child turns out.

The crisis a child experiences upon entering school is a drawn issue between his sense of industry in producing things and bringing a particular job to completion on the one hand and his sense of inadequacy and inferiority in not producing things and not bringing a particular job to completion in such a way as to please his teachers. The teachers become the judges of both the parent and the child. The teachers become the ones who hand out the "goodies" of approval or the "bitter fruits" of disapproval. Both the child and his parents participate in the "goodies" and the "bitters." As Erikson says, "Family life may not have prepared . . . [the child] for school life, or school life may fail to sustain the promises of earlier stages in that nothing that he has learned to do well already seems to count one bit to the teacher."[5] Erikson notes how exciting it is to observe in the lives of gifted and inspired people "that one teacher, somewhere, was able to kindle the flame of hidden talent." In one of his letters, Thomas Wolfe describes how his relationship with one teacher brought forth the "great music" that was in him.

To Margaret Roberts

> Harvard Club
> New York
> Monday—May 30, 1927

Dear Mrs. Roberts:

. . . You say that no one *outside* my family loves me more than Margaret Roberts. Let me rather say the exact truth:—that no one *inside* my family loves me as much, and only one other person, I think, in all the world loves me as much. My book is full of ugliness and terrible pain— and I think moments of a great and soaring beauty. In it (will you forgive me?) I have told the story of one of the most beautiful people I have ever known as it touched on my own life. I am calling that person Margaret Leonard. I was without a home—a vagabond since I was seven—with two roofs and no home. I moved inward on that house of death and tumult from room to little room, as the boarders came with their dollar a day, and their constant rocking on the porch. My over-loaded heart was bursting with its packed weight of loneliness and ter-ror; I was strangling, without speech, without articulation, in my own secretions—groping like a blind sea-thing with no eyes and a thousand feelers toward light, toward life, toward beauty and order, out of that hell of chaos, greed, and cheap ugliness—and then I found you, when else I should have died, you mother of my spirit who fed me with light. Do you think that I have forgotten? Do you think I ever will? You are entombed in my flesh, you are in the pulses of my blood, the thought of you makes a great music in me—and before I come to death, I shall use the last thrust of my talent—whatever it is—to put your beauty into words.[6]

Just as easily can one find from conversations with students ways in which feelings of inferiority have been bound upon them by teachers. The child is called upon to master the complexities of a technological society. He must have know-how. But more than that, he must have a relationship in which a teacher believes in him when he has trouble believing in himself. One man speaks of his own mother as his teacher: "Mother took for granted that I could do anything the other children could do and made me believe it. Her insight and confidence in me made a lifelong difference."[7] The effective teacher works at the base of motivation that is trust formation in the student. He assumes that his students are there to learn until as individuals they prove otherwise. He does not assume that they will not work unless he makes them move like quarry slaves under the threat of external anxiety.

It is easy to find the teacher who is tyrannical and impatient with a lack of productivity and has a prissy affection for those who conform in every detail to his or her wishes. Therefore I think it is important to conclude this chapter with a careful study of the relationship between teaching and the individual's maintenance of integrity and faith in himself and others.

TEACHING, SELF-CONFIDENCE, AND THE INTEGRITY OF THE INDIVIDUAL

The teacher of today deals with his class members in the context of the intimidating complexities of a technological society. The person can be replaced and misplaced in such a society. So can the teacher. The teacher addresses himself to the person amid these complexities. His class members come from a wide spectrum of varied communities. As individuals they are usually unaware of the complexity of the society in which they live. The alert and informed teacher must be aware of these complexities. Yet this creates a communication gap between him and his students.

The teacher in the church classroom is concerned with the preparation of suitable growing conditions for the emergence of self-confidence and integrity as Christians in those whom he teaches. As a teacher, I find it to be a problem of balance to get across the communication gap between my students and myself. At one and the same time I am called to develop my students' individual integrity as persons and to maintain my own. From the difficult work of being a teacher myself, I would like to suggest a few clues for constructive thinking about the integrity of the individual in the teaching relationship. When I say "constructive thinking" I mean just that. I could join that group of professional mourners in the teaching profession or I could join that group of professional cheerleaders in the teaching profession. But I prefer to face the task of teaching and counseling individuals toward integrity by being neither a joiner, a mourner, nor a cheerleader. You and I are interested in the beams and bolts that hold children and youth together when they are under stress in a technological society. A creative combination of optimism and pessimism presents the Christian alternative of hope. Hope transcends the present circumstance and sees beyond it. With this realistic hope in mind, let me suggest four clues for both maintaining and creating the integrity of the individual in the teaching relationship.

Clue 1: The teacher who hopes to contribute to the integrity of the individuals whom he teaches is captured by a conviction that what he says and does makes a difference between life and death for some whom he teaches. This is not true of all the people whom he teaches, but it is true of some.

Here we draw a distinction between learning as retention of data and the transmission of information, on the one hand, and learning as an event in living, on the other hand. The teacher must dare to see his teaching as making a difference between life and death for some of those whom he teaches. He is not nearly so interested in the student's remembering everything that he as a teacher says as he is interested in causing something to happen in the life of the person that he cannot forget.

Anton Boisen often said that the teacher and counselor work with three different groups of persons all the time. The first group is that group of creative persons who will thrive and grow regardless of what the teacher does. The second group is composed of those persons who are so resistive, concealed from themselves, and satisfied with themselves that they drift and surrender regardless of what the teacher does. The third group is that group to whom the teacher makes the difference between living and dying, between hope and hopelessness, between purpose and purposelessness. The effective teacher is always searching for this third group. He does not ignore, lose hope, or neglect the other two groups, but he searches for the third group.

In this sense the teacher is what Holden Caulfield in J. D. Salinger's novel spoke of as a "catcher in the rye." The teacher sees himself caught up in the game of life with crowds of young children around him. He is aware of the cliffs at the edge of the abyss and sees teaching as "coming out from somewhere" to catch people on "the edge of the crazy cliffs" of life. This feeling of necessity may seem unbelievable to many people, but a real teacher understands it.

Clue 2: The teacher or writer contributes to the integrity of the individual when he sees him as a total person, as "a body" in the Old English sense of the word. Incidentally, this is the Pauline use of the word "body" too. It refers to the total person.

Seeing the student as a total person is a difficult thing to do in a technological society that has been fragmented as has ours. The average youth in school has to integrate too many roles—many of them conflicting with one another—into one person. Maintaining consistency and integrity and taking into consideration our students' many-faceted roles in life is a major issue in the student-teacher relationship.

When we look at this from the point of view of the student, we see him as a member of two families—the family into which he was born and the family which he is yet to form when he marries. We see the student, furthermore, as a member of many "joining" groups. The elementary or high school student of today is not only in church groups but in social clubs, high school classes, and extracurricular activities in his high school. In turn, he or she may be a member of other groups to which his or her parents belong. Integrating these roles, scheduling them into the dimension of time, and maintaining conflicting loyalties present a task that can tear an individual asunder. The sensitive teacher is aware of these conflicting roles. He sees his teaching as an attempt to help the individual to maintain integrity amid the conflictual demands laid upon him. This calls for coaching in the decision-making process and companionship in the heavy stresses of life.

The teaching relationship, therefore, on the part of both the student and the teacher can in effect become a process in which we learn how to keep from becoming phonies with each other. The multiple personalities of today are tragic witness to the organism's attempt to live, at different times, in terms of different sets of values and different roles. The purpose of education is to bring order out of this chaos, integrity out of this confusion, and harmony out of dissonant demands.

Clue 3: The teacher of today who is concerned with the integrity of the individual is sensitive to the problems of discontinuity—that is, the creation of something new—and the problems of continuity—that is, the conservation of what is good but old in the process of learning. In biblical terms, the good scribe brings things both new and old out of his good treasure. Much education consists of amputating the past rather than evaluating, assessing, and threshing the past for what is good. In order to maintain integrity a child must have some degree of respect and confidence in his home origins. In order to have integrity, on the other hand, a person must have some degree of freedom from his past in order that he may continue to grow and lay hold of that which is new. In the words of Robert Frost, he must have something he can look back upon with pride and something he can look forward to with hope. Erik Erikson's formula for identity is helpful here. Identity and integrity are developed through a double process—a clear sense of continuity in which we are "the same" yesterday, today, and tomorrow. At the same time, we are something different from that which we have ever been each day we live and grow. The purpose of teaching is to maintain this double perspective of the individual's integrity.

Clue 4: The teacher who is concerned with the integrity of the individual recognizes and seeks to overcome the student's distrust of and mixed feelings toward authority.

Working thinly under the surface of the minds of many of the persons whom we teach is that conception of a world as a jungle of inconsistency. Thus the child considers himself a stranger to the world. He holds out against it as an alien from the commonwealth of mankind. He holds himself back from such an inconsistent world in noncommitment.

This noncommitment is characterized by a taboo on loving impulses, inasmuch as they are seen as signs of weakness. This noncommitment is a smoldering cauldron of mixed feelings of love and hate toward people of strength and commitment. The uncommitted person suffers a radical split between confident loyalty on the one hand and trustful affection on the other hand. This split expresses itself in a beatnik negative identity of manipulation. They "plug in" into the commitment of others. But they distrustfully hold themselves back from any commitment to anyone. Such a student baits the authority person or the teacher into being punitive and then accuses him of injustice. He is double-minded, indecisive. He loses courage when confronted with the necessity for decision and choice of identity. He has the demand for production "thrown at him" in such a way that he freezes in inaction; feelings of inability "clobber" him with anxiety.

The teacher of today must come to grips with this distrust and fear of inconsistency within himself before God. It is not just a problem of the student. The jaundice of noncommitment is rather readily apparent among teachers themselves. Once the teacher has come to grips with this double-mindedness, distrust, proud inferiority, and ambivalence toward authority within himself, he comes face-to-face with what Paul Tillich has called the problem of love, power, and justice. Then he can move with some degree of clarity as he seeks to produce integrity of commitment in his students. In both the teacher and the student, that which we withhold makes us weak. As Frost says, and until we find out that it is ourselves that we are withholding, we do not discover the integrity that the teaching-learning situation has to offer both the teacher and the student. Once we discover this, we find "salvation in surrender." We stand with our students at the gates of a new life in the fullness of a consciousness that we both are and are becoming children of God.

NOTES

1. Erik H. Erikson, *Identity and the Life Cycle* (New York: International Universities Press, 1959), p. 82.

2. Harry Stack Sullivan, *The Interpersonal Theory of Psychiatry*, ed. Helen Swick Perry and Mary Ladd Gawel (New York: W. W. Norton & Co., 1953), p. 229.

3. Ibid., p. 237.

4. Ibid., p. 242.

5. Erickson, *Identity and the Life Cycle*, p. 87.

6. Elizabeth Nowell, ed., *The Letters of Thomas Wolfe* (New York: Charles Scribner's Sons, 1956), pp. 122–123.

7. Gaines S. Dobbins, *Great Teachers Make a Difference* (Nashville: Broadman Press, 1965), p. 90.

13

The Bible in the Pastoral Care of Children

Pastors are called as healers and comforters of adults whose spirits have been stunted, twisted, and maimed by inept and ill-intentioned persons who have sought to teach them the Bible. The more deeply the pastor feels this sense of mission and the more often he is pressed into the task of caring for these confused people, the more concerned he becomes about trying to prevent this from happening in the lives of those growing children of his flock who are still in the formative years of their lives.

In many instances, the adult counselees of a pastor have been alienated from the sources of religious experience by parents who used religion as a means of forcing conformity to their own wishes, however just or unjust those wishes may have been. In this way, religion was rejected by the child in order to maintain his own personal integrity. Now in adulthood, he tends to use his parents' mishandling of religion as an excuse for avoiding the discipline of a more positive search for faith. Nevertheless such adults are filled with moral wistfulness. They yearn for some new and meaningful experience *of their own.* They crave internal assurance, inner fullness, and spiritual meaning. They are lonely for a community of comrades who share meaningfully in a fellowship of belief. In a vital way they are "religious orphans," who, having been driven out from their spiritual heritage, "can't go home again" but wander spiritually as fugitives and vagabonds upon the earth.

In other instances these adults find themselves laden with the forms of their family religion but denied the power of it. They slavishly seek to conform to the teachings of parents and church (with devious motives for doing so) but develop a secret life of symptoms that they cannot understand or accept. They have been bound with "heavy burdens, hard to bear," which were laid upon their shoulders when they themselves were too young to support themselves economically or to express their emotions verbally. They have been saddled with laws for living without having been afforded the light that comes from patient explanation and tender care of inquiring minds. More than that, they have been deprived of the inspiration that came from unlimited quantities of understanding and affection. Careful study of their personal histories does not reveal either parents or pastors who have moved so much as a finger to help them carry their load.

As long as a pastor stays safely within the inner circle of the "pillars" of his church, he does not confront such adults too often. But when he gets on the outer fringe of his membership, or when he takes a post as a counselor of college students, as a chaplain in a hospital, or as a military chaplain, he begins to meet them on every hand. The misery that he confronts there causes him to inquire into the kind of use that he, his church school teachers, and especially the parents of growing children are making of the Bible in the development of healthy personalities. He concerns himself with the reasons why the Bible is a "closed book" to so many adults. He works diligently to devise ways and means of keeping its fountains open, whereby God refreshes his children on their pilgrim ways.

THE BIBLE AT THE CROSSROADS
OF THE SPIRITUAL PILGRIMAGE

In order to discover the reasons why the Bible becomes an offense to many, the pastor needs to look into the personal spiritual pilgrimages of persons who have lost their way. He needs to go back to the crossroads where the individual was misled.

A group of graduate students and I did just that in a program of clinical pastoral training at the Kentucky State Hospital in 1947. We studied the religious histories of 69 acutely mentally ill patients. We discovered that 17.2 percent of these persons were suffering from long-term moral and religious conflicts.[1] Biblical material stood prominently in the delusional pattern of these patients, and a good deal of our time was spent in a program of religious *re*-education, with the objective of maturing their religious outlook and encouraging them to disentangle their relationship to God from their morbid relationships to their parents. In about half of the cases we had a modicum of success.

Several great problems arise in the formation of a child's biblical understanding as this understanding affects his emotional growth. These problems lay the ground for later religious confusion which may necessitate pastoral counseling with the unhappy adult. Careful attention to these possibilities for trouble in the character education stages of a child's devel-

opment would effectively prevent later religious disturbances and eliminate the necessity of pastoral counseling for many people who grow up
under the close supervision of the church.

First, parents and teachers too often use the Bible as a means of
threatening and punishing a child. As a result, the child develops a fear
reaction toward the Bible. Instead of literally taking a whip and administering corporal punishment to the child, parents, and even ministers, often
take a Bible verse and "threaten and whip" with it. Both methods reveal a
spiritually threadbare parent-child relationship. A child who uses bad language is told that the Bible says he is in danger of hell-fire. A child who has
done something wrong is called in and told to sit and listen as his parent
reads the Bible to him about his wrongdoing. The Bible should *never* be
used as a fear-producing instrument for punishing little children.

Second, children are often taught goals by parents, teachers, and pastors that are mutually contradictory. Two ideals are taught and given the
sanction of infallibility "because they are in the Bible." For instance, they
are taught to honor their father and mother, and, from the same Bible, to
hate their father and mother for the gospel's sake. Likewise, they are
taught the hero-success stories of the Bible alongside the virtues of humility and noncompetitiveness. At different times, ordinarily, they get different impressions. As Gardner Murphy says, "Western culture is shot
through and through with an ambivalence that puts its mark on every
growing person: Get ahead; don't be forward. Climb to the top; don't
climb over others. Heaven helps them that help themselves; he that saveth
his life shall lose it."[2] During childhood, these paradoxes go unnoticed. But
in the normal conflicts of adolescence they become pronounced and acute
contradictions. Only the maturity that experience and careful counseling
give resolves the tensions in a higher synthesis of understanding. These
acute contradictions are regularly presented to counseling pastors by adolescence.

Third, the Bible is often taught to the child by sincere but misin-
formed church school teachers in such a way as to give him an actually
wrong attitude toward the Bible. When, on the basis of wrong information,
the child enters a class under a trained teacher, he has to unlearn the
misinformation. Devout college professors who teach the Bible to freshmen who have come to their classes from the church schools of their local
home churches are concerned about three problems that the students
present. First, the student has a bare minimum of factual information
about the Bible, even though the content method of teaching has been
used since before the child started to public school. College freshmen often are unable simply to locate the accounts of creation, the Lord's Prayer,
and the Twenty-third Psalm. Second, the student has no idea of historical

perspective in his grasp of the biblical story. Moses, for example, may be thought of as a contemporary of Jesus, and Isaiah as a close personal friend of the apostle Paul! Third, students have derived pitifully childlike misunderstandings of God from the way in which the Bible has been taught them. For example, all scriptural passages are ascribed equal validity for moral and religious living. The exhortations about remaining single, for instance, in the teachings of Paul (1 Cor. 7:25ff.) or the teachings of Jesus as to the time of his return (Matt. 24:36) are often placed on a par with their respective teachings about Christian love and the cross. Examples from the life of David are given equal sanction with those from the life of Jesus. When everything becomes of equal importance, the sense of discriminate judgment is lost and nothing tends to matter.

This indicates that the factor which Lewis J. Sherrill calls "stress and neglect" in the use of the Bible "may seriously distort the Bible in the hands of any individual or group." Ralph D. Heim, in an exhaustive study of 50,000 pieces of church school literature from a wide selection of different religious groups, further illustrates the legalistic use of the Bible. He discovered that in Christian church literature, the ten most frequently used New Testament verses taken together are used considerably less than the Ten Commandments; also, he discovered that the Commandments as a group are used with a total frequency considerably above the Beatitudes. "Perhaps there is some reason for some to say that ours is a Ten Commandments Christianity."

The overall impression one gets from a study such as that by Professor Heim is that the prophetic genius of both the Old Testament and the New Testament is considerably less in use than are the legalistic formulations of both Testaments.[3]

One of the dangers that pastors want to avoid is that of using the Bible as a means of enforcing or "retreading" their own moral convictions, which may not have biblical foundation but simply reflect community mores. An example of this is a teaching that was given to me as a child in a Sunday school to the effect that Negroes were ordained of God to be a race of servants because of the sin of Ham, the son of Noah! The pastor and lay teachers who are concerned with developing healthy personalities must of necessity pay more attention to the way in which the growing self is conditioned from within and less to the ways in which it is coerced from without. Unconscious forces are at work in the parent-child, teacher-child, pastor-child, and community-child relationship, teaching far more than the verbal exchange of words and ideas can. Children particularly are at work interpreting for themselves, and it is a fact that what they are saying to themselves is far more important than what is being said to them.

This points to a final hazard in the pastoral use of the Bible with

173

growing children and youth in their spiritual pilgrimages. Parents and pastors tend to use the Bible as a means of producing obedience and conformity rather than as a means of "opening up" significant questions and concerns within the spiritual life of the individual that will cause him to confront God *on his own*. Biblical instruction of today grew to its present state of crystallization under the shadow of a mechanistic and behavioristic psychology which is the foundation of secular education in America. The presuppositions of such a pragmatic psychology are that the teacher or the parent *always* knows or *should always* know best for the growing student; the learning process is conceived of as being a "one-way street," so to speak, and the possibility of revelation coming to the teacher from the student is not too often considered. The objective of teaching the Bible, from this point of view, then, is that of producing obedience and conformity to that which the teacher or the parent considers best.

In a real sense, the teaching of the Bible, couched in the framework of the earlier and more ancient behaviorism of the Pharisees, has fallen prey to this modern kind of mechanistic attitude. In church and home, the Bible tends to become a tool of such a consciously chosen and applied psychology. Growing persons are *manipulated* by means of the Bible instead of being introduced to it as a book that has authenticity by reason of the reality of the experience of the persons whom it describes and that, therefore, the Bible is capable of speaking for itself through the Holy Spirit in such a way that each person tends to hear it "in his own language."

However, this is not to consign to disuse the experience of personal testimony on the part of parent and pastor. Some parents and pastors, in reaction against the damage done by indoctrination, overlook growing children's needs to know what their parents' and pastors' spiritual pilgrimages have meant to them. A parent or a pastor can share those experiences in such a way that the child can know them intimately, without at the same time causing the child to feel that he has to conform to the experience of his parent or his pastor in every detail. A conformity-demanding psychology has proved most efficient at producing two types of persons: in the public school it has produced efficient robot personalities, who function without protest in a technological society without feeling and with objectivity as their reward; in the church school, it has produced efficient Pharisees, who function within an ecclesiastical tradition without rebellion and with "respectability" as their reward.

In both the scientific tradition and the ecclesiastical tradition, the psychiatrist and psychoanalyst on the one hand and the counseling pastor on the other serve as a sort of cleanup crew to care for the casualties. These casualties are those who refused or were unable to conform, and were cast out for not doing so, and those who have conformed but have, nevertheless, found their lives drab, empty, meaningless, and driven by unrequited and nameless hungers for something that eludes them constantly. In the meanwhile, they wander to and fro, not knowing who they are or where they are going, with "that one talent which is death to hide" hidden within them. The kingdom of God is denied its creative birth in the community of mankind.

THE PASTOR AS A BIBLICAL TEACHER AMONG GROWING STUDENTS

Practically every pastor who cares for his flock in their times of quiet inner desperation with such problems as have been described here is aware of the issues that I have named. However, it is a point of quiet inner desperation for us ourselves to know what to do about them. Let me venture to suggest a few points at which to begin.

It is obvious that one point at which to begin is in our preaching. Are we as pastors using the Bible as a means of coercing and cajoling, manipulating and using people from the pulpit to "get them to do what we want them to do," or "get them behind us in our plans," or "sell them this or that thing"? Preaching, like counseling, has, or should have, a strong element of sound teaching in it. By sound teaching I do not mean merely the exactness of *what* we teach but the kind of emotional frame of reference by means of which we communicate in the interpersonal relationship between us and the persons listening.

It is important, therefore, for us as pastors to begin with the psychological frame of reference from which we are operating as preachers of the Bible. The Bible itself has much to offer at this point. At least two distinct psychological approaches to personality are evident in the New Testament. One is that of the legalists, to which reference has been made repeatedly. The Pharisees were the most obvious examples of this type of psychology. They sought to control every act of every hour and at every place in the individual's life. Minute rules were set up intending to canalize human behavior completely. In Christianity another set of rules sprang up, great and small, and became what Tertullian later called "molds" for behavior. The person is overlooked as a participating perceiver in the process of discovering what is good. He may grow up to be an *obedient* person, but one untrained in discovering ethical insights for himself.

The second type of psychology of personality found within the Bible is one of the inner consciousness of selfhood in relation to a feeling of having been sent into the world for a purpose that is ever concealing and revealing itself to us. Moses, when confronted with the meaningful purpose of God, asked, "Who am I, that I should go unto Pharaoh . . . ?" The psalmist, filled with a sense of guilt (for which a purely legalistic psychology

175

has only punishment for a solution), asked that he be made to know "truth in the inward parts; and in the hidden part . . . to know wisdom." Jesus often asked himself who he was, defined again and again his purpose in the world, asked demoniacs who they were, and asked his disciples who it was that men supposed him to be.

Robert Frost states the poignant need for the personal confrontation of these questions on the part of children and adults today in his poem "The Cabin in the Clearing." Here he vividly describes the fogginess of the average American as to personal identity and clarity of selfhood. He imagines a conversation between the smoke from the cabin in the clearing and the damp mist that gathers in the early morning around the cabin. The mist says to the smoke: "I don't believe the sleepers in this house know where they are. . . . " The smoke responds with a sage kind of wisdom, saying that if the sleepers ever know *who* they are, they may know better where they are. But who they are is too much for them—or the world—to believe.[4]

Let me recommend the psychological context for preaching, pastoral care, and religious education set forth by Lewis J. Sherrill in his book *The Struggle of the Soul*. It offers a ground of meaning in which even the youngest child and oldest adult can participate. He emphasizes the need for a fresh examination of "the career of the human self . . . as it passes through certain major stages, or types of experience, during the journey from the beginning to the end of life."[5] Then he sets himself to the task of describing a biblical view of the nature of personality as being at its core the emergence of a dynamic self in the unfolding pilgrimage of a meaningful existence in relation to the purpose of God for the individual in the universe. The task of the pastor seems to be that of weaving the teaching materials of the Bible and the cherished memories of the ongoing Christian community of the church into the spiritual pilgrimages of individuals as they have to live and face life.

In brief, I have been bold enough to suggest both to myself and to my reader that the point at which to begin in relating our use of the Bible adequately to the needs of growing personalities is in *the improvement of our own attitudes* toward people and the ways in which we habitually relate ourselves and our Bible to them. Until this is set right, nothing else will come right. Naturally, this is a continual process and goes on all the while we are doing other things to use the Bible in healthy ways and to develop healthy biblical attitudes and ideas in our people.

Another rather obvious, but quite neglected, field of endeavor for the pastor can be stressed. The pastor himself should get into the actual process of the biblical instruction of his flock from the earliest stages to the latest ones in personality growth. He needs an enduring personal relationship as a basis for all his work. He cannot do this task all by himself, nor should he wash his hands of the whole affair as a task not serious enough for his attention, as one that is such dull routine that he cannot be bothered. The sardonic grin that passes over many a pastor's face when "religious education" is mentioned is partly due to unhappy experiences in some seminaries but largely due to our basic discomfort in the presence of little children and our inability to relate ourselves adequately to them.

The pastor, for instance, who sustains an enduring personal relationship to the children of his parish will covet the opportunity to participate personally in the vacation church school. He will communicate the Bible to children himself, bringing the rich store of all his years of study to the advantage of the little child and the teenager in such a way that he will not fear to hear their questions. They will learn from him to love the Bible by reason of the humanity, the simplicity, and the affectionate understanding of the man who first introduced them to it in church—their pastor.

In this particular respect the pastor of a small congregation has the advantage over the "busy" pastor of a large church. Likewise, the pastor who stays in one parish for most of his ministry has the advantage over the itinerant pastor. He can become fairly intimately acquainted with the children of his congregation and they become his guides in understanding the rest of his congregation. The pastor of a large church too often becomes alienated from the children of his church family by both his real and his imagined preoccupation. Quite often he becomes alienated from the children of whom he himself is the father. He delegates the function of teaching to others and does not participate meaningfully *himself* in the experience of the children's learning of the Bible. The teaching of the Bible, more than most other types of teaching, is an experience in interpersonal relationships between the teacher and the pupil. This interpersonal relationship is the bond of communication that transmits spiritual insight and information. The pastor cannot effectively prevent damage from being done to growing lives in their contact with biblical teaching until he has a healthy relationship to his people. But he cannot do so at all if he has no relationship at all!

In the study of the patients at Kentucky State Hospital that I have already mentioned, we were astounded to discover that in 51.5 percent of the persons studied no influence of pastoral care in biblical instruction was shown at all! And this was supposed to be in the so-called "Bible Belt" region. This was good in that harmful religious teachings did not complicate the problems of these people, but it is a rebuke to the pastors ministering near them, in that they were the men who were not on the job.

A third suggestion for the proper understanding of the most effective use of the Bible in the pastoral care of children and youth is dynamically related to the nature of a pastor's emotional frame of reference in his attitude toward the Bible and toward people. This suggestion is that the pastor needs enough flexibility and security both emotionally and intellectually to be able to stand having the Bible questioned. He needs to be more concerned with the anticipation, provocation, and acceptance of questions in children and youth than he is with the answers that he himself gives. Through his enduring relationship with many of them over long periods of time, he develops experience enough to *anticipate* the questions of youth and to provide help, both individually and in groups, on the questions they have in common and tend most often to ask. Through his interpersonal relationship with them, and through the attention he pays to their parent-child relationships, he seeks to develop an atmosphere in which children and youth feel free to articulate their deepest questions. Such a spiritual communion will find enough examples contrary to its nature in the everyday life of the children and youth actually to provoke deeper questions in their minds. As Professor Tillich has said, "the church is a surrounding reality" that "shapes the existence of a child, and slowly transforms it," so that "truly eternal questions are asked."

Then the task of the pastor is twofold: both that he accept the questions with reverence for the personality of the asking child and that he be more concerned with inspiring the confidence of the child to believe that he himself, with the pastor as a fellow seeker, is able to find the answer that meets *his* need. Paul Tillich calls this the discovery of the Bible as "the interior authorship of our own biography."

This is a very different procedure from that of "throwing answers at people's heads to questions they never ask." It is based upon the conviction that even very small children suffer despair in the realm of hidden fears and confused loyalties, and in the response to these deeper realities children show an awareness of the infinite and an unspoken knowledge of the things that matter far beyond that of their elders. It is relevant at this point to ponder the saying of Jesus that "their angels always behold the face of my Father."

The pastor's work at this point is in vain unless he has the comradeship of the parents in his task. Therefore he needs to pay exceedingly careful attention to the ways in which his suggestions about family worship in the home—its importance, its values, and its necessity—are being incorporated into the parents' treatment of their children.

Two illustrations clarify my meaning. A young woman said, "When I was in my middle teens, Dad decided we needed a family altar. (The family needed something to draw it together.) So he set a time (convenient to him)

178

and sent out the order for us to attend. He forced the shoe on the foot without using the 'shoehorn of psychology.' The toes crumpled up. In six months the plan was discontinued, never to be fully resumed. You can guess what my attitude toward prayer and Father was!"

The other illustration is that of a father who insisted that all the children in his large family should participate in the reading of the Bible and in family prayers. One son rebelled one day and said that he did not want to do so. The father told the son that as long as "he lived under the same roof with him" he would conform, particularly in family worship. When the son resisted even further, the father attempted to force him into a chair. The son balked and it turned into a fight with fists. The boy gave his father a severe beating and left the house, not to return until the time of his father's death several years later.

I have chosen these two situations to illustrate a vital factor in the transmission of biblical truth in the home. The failure in communication arises more readily from disordered interpersonal relationships than from simple ignorance about the Bible. These are merely two examples as to how the instructions from a pastor concerning the family altar can be perverted by basic family and personality disorders in the home.

All the suggestions that have been made lead the pastor back to the point at which we began: his personal counseling contact with the families and individuals in his parish. Here the work of healing and the work of prevention are going on simultaneously, as the pastor seeks to fit the eternal message of the Bible to the transient, grimy, existential necessities of everyday living. In the last-mentioned situation, the pastor does not appear anywhere on the "horizon of horror." If he had, he would have found himself seeking to understand not only the difficulties of the father, past fifty, or those of the son, in his late teens, but also the speechless terror of the silent, youngest daughter, age seven, who twenty years later told me of the agony that filled her life upon observing the whole scene! She said, "After the fight, we went on and had prayers anyway!"

I am simply suggesting in conclusion that the pastor both starts and finishes his use of the Bible in pastoral care of children in his intimate personal counseling situations. He equips himself with both the skill and the courage with which to discern what the basic questions and sufferings of his particular people are. He becomes saturated with *their* perception of things that are important. He feels *their* arrows by day and snares by night. He learns in particular what blockages hold them back from creative living. Through the interpersonal relationship, which is bound together by the Holy Spirit, the Bible speaks its message through the pastor at the level of every day's most quiet need and becomes human nature's daily food.

NOTES

1. Wayne E. Oates, "The Role of Religion in the Psychoses," *Pastoral Psychology,* May 1950.

2. Gardner Murphy, *Personality: A Biosocial Approach to Origins and Structure* (New York: Harper & Brothers, 1947), p. 579.

3. Ralph D. Heim, "The Bible in the Literature of Christian Education" (unpublished research).

4. Robert Frost, "A Cabin in the Clearing"; *The Poetry of Robert Frost* (New York: Henry Holt & Co., 1967), pp. 413–415.

5. Lewis J. Sherrill, *The Struggle of the Soul* (New York: Macmillan Co., 1951), p. 3.

14

The Nuclear Family and the Larger Family of Mankind

A dilemma is always with the pastor as a counselor. The dilemma is that of the tension between his responsibility to care for the nuclear family, on the one hand, and his prophetic and pastoral responsibility to free people from bondage to family idolatry and to give them a vision of and relationship to the larger family of mankind. By definition the nuclear family means the tight-knit relationship of father, mother, son, daughter, brother, sister, and grandparents. This might be called a "blood-kin" definition of the family. By the larger family of mankind we mean people of all races, creeds, and conditions of life both geographically and socially. The larger family of mankind includes both "Jew and Gentile, bond and free, male and female," in the larger macrocosm of humankind. One could see this as kinship by creation of all human creatures, or one could see it as Harry Stack Sullivan described it when he said that we are all more distinctly human than otherwise.

The built-in tension between the nuclear family and the larger family of mankind deeply involves the nature of religion at its best. Freud stated the three positive functions of religion in the family this way: (1) Religion, apart from pathological phenomena, lowers the importance of the family of parents and siblings. (2) Religion provides a sublimation and safe ethical mooring for one's sexual impulses. (3) Religion gives a person access to the larger family of mankind. In between the tight-knit nuclear family and the larger family of mankind is the "extended family" of the church, school, and/or neighborhood.[1]

The pastor is a counselor in the context of the church. The brunt of the stress between the nuclear family and the larger family of mankind—people of other neighborhoods, schools, and churches, people of other races, "strangers," outcasts from the nuclear family and the extended family—falls upon the church and its ministry. The pastoral counselor bears the ambiguity of encouraging the development of close affectionate ties within the nuclear family and at the same time sustaining people as they break away from the family to establish their own autonomy, as they see members of their own family reject, ostracize, or desert one another, and as the inevitable forces of illness, aging, and death break up the nuclear family. More than this, the pastoral counselor is the representative of the "larger family of mankind." He takes his stand against the idolatry of the parent-sibling family to the exclusion of people of other faiths, other races, different moral standards, different social classes and conditions that make them bachelors—male or female—widows and widowers, divorcées, and so on. Many people are alone and without a nuclear family in the present. They are often without an extended family.

To omit or overlook this source of stress in the day-to-day work of the pastoral counselor means failure to account for the large percentage of the counseling that a pastoral counselor does. The problems associated with the pull and tug among the nuclear family, the extended family, and the larger family of mankind compose from 60 to 70 percent of the cases encountered by pastoral counseling. This fact has been established in several surveys of the presenting difficulties of persons seeking pastoral counseling.

BIBLICAL PERSPECTIVES OF THE FAMILY

The Old Testament and the New Testament present contrasts of attitudes toward the family. The family is the beating heart of the Jewish faith. In the Old Testament there are nearly three hundred references to the family or the tribe, whereas the word "family" is rarely used in the New Testament. Both the parent-sibling family and the extended family of the Jewish people often became self-contained units in a hostile world. Stories such as those of Naomi and Ruth, of the flight of Jonah, and of the healing of Naaman the Syrian reflect a prophetic outreach toward the larger family of mankind who were not familially or ethnically related.

However, the main thrust of Hebrew thinking in the Old Testament was determined by the Hebrews' strong sense of destiny as God's chosen people. From among them would come, one day, the Messiah. He would be raised up as the seed of Abraham. "Every Hebrew carried that seed in his loins. It was his duty to propagate it, to beget sons and pass on the sacred torch from generation to generation. Begetting children was, therefore, a man's primary response to God. No wonder, therefore, that family life was the central focus of the Hebrew society. No wonder all Hebrew men were expected to marry and raise a family.''[2] In the absence of a clearly defined concept of personal immortality, the perpetuity of a man depended quite heavily upon the birth of children, especially sons. They bore his name. In the Hebrew conception of sexual reproduction, the womb of a woman was simply a receptacle, a vessel, an incubator, to receive the seed from a man. There was no idea of the sperm and ovum uniting to form a zygote for the beginning of human life. The man contributed the seed. The woman received it. In a mysterious way, however, direct intervention from God was necessary for "opening the womb," so that the seed of man could enter. As David Mace says: "A man's seed became his child, wherever planted. Since the woman contributed nothing of her essential self for the child she bore, but merely provided an incubator for its early growth, her role in the drama of reproduction was essentially a subsidiary one. This, rather than an inferior strength or intelligence, is probably the fundamental reason why women were considered in the ancient world to be less important than men."[3] Consequently, a man and a woman who were husband and wife were caught up together in a destiny. They and their children were bound together in the profoundly centralized unit of the family. The family and progeny became the primary value of the Hebrew man or woman. Contrary to contemporary attitudes toward the military, the family took precedence over military service. The Hebrew bridegroom was exempted from serving in the military until he had had time to get down to the business of getting his wife pregnant and seeing to it that he had children to assure that his name and line would be continued. He was given this chance before he was expected to fight in battles defending his country. The continuity of the blood-kin line and the continuity of the Hebrew race as a people took precedence over everything else.

In the life and teaching of Jesus, however, one finds considerable contrast and challenge to the basic Hebrew attitude toward family that has just been described. In Jesus' own relationship to the family, of which he was a part during his earthly pilgrimage, enough glimpses are provided the reader of the Gospels to get a consistent picture. The traditional near-idolatry of family and progeny was challenged by Jesus, and the creation story was reinterpreted.

Love, protection, and wise guidance of little children were primary in the teachings of the Gospels and of the apostle Paul. The messenger of the Lord told Zechariah that his son, John the Baptist, by his wife, Elizabeth, would "turn the hearts of the fathers to the children" (Luke 1:17). Jesus called little children unto him and blessed them. He watched as they played funeral and feigned grief, and as they piped and danced in the market-place. He likened entry into the kingdom of heaven to the birth process and to becoming as a little child. He himself became a little child. He was reverential, though not cringing, toward his parents. When he was twelve years old he demonstrated considerable independence of them. Yet he was "obedient to them." At the wedding in Cana of Galilee, Jesus and his mother were present. He was somewhat stern with her, it seems to me, when he said, "O woman, what have you to do with me? My hour has not yet come" (John 2:4). As he began his ministry, Jesus announced his mission at his home synagogue in Nazareth. He immediately ran into conflict with this extended family of which he and his parents and siblings were a part. As he continued his early ministry, his mother and his brothers came and sent for him. When told that they were outside asking for him, he said, " 'Who are my mother and my brothers?' And looking around on those who sat with him, he said, 'Here are my mother and my brothers! Whoever does the will of God is my brother, and sister, and mother' " (Mark 3:31–35). It seems to me that Jesus was putting the primacy of the larger family of the kingdom of God above the earthly family. He was lowering the importance of the earthly family and had gained access to the larger family of mankind under the sovereignty of God.

One cannot develop a one-sided interpretation of Jesus' teachings. Jesus took seriously the ambiguity of the relationship of the tight-knit nuclear family and the larger family of mankind. Yet he also upbraided the Pharisees for having taken that which would have sustained and helped their parents and for having given it to the bureaucracy of Judaism. He chided them for no longer permitting persons to do anything for their father and mother. Thus they made void the word of God through their tradition which they sought to hand on. (Mark 7:9–13.) Jesus from the cross saw both his mother and the disciple whom he loved standing near and asked her to behold her son and told the disciple to behold his mother. The disciple took Jesus' mother to his own home. These accounts show remarkable balance between affectionate ties of one's relationships to one's nuclear family and one's commitment to encompass in his affections also the larger family of mankind. They are characterized by a stern tenderness.

In summary, the Christian revolution sustained the values of the intimate funds of affection that nourish human life at its earliest beginnings in the nuclear family. At the same time, Christians challenged the idolatry of the family as the be-all and end-all of existence. Jesus said that in the resurrection there will be neither marriage nor giving in marriage (Luke 20:35). Therefore the pastoral counselor must discipline his tendency to absolutize the relative nature of the nuclear family. He works in the interfaces between the ambiguity that exists between the nuclear family, the extended family, and the larger family of mankind.

THE CHALLENGES OF PREMARITAL
PASTORAL COUNSELING

In the face of the sexual revolution of today, the overwhelming majority of people who decide to get married turn to a minister for the rituals of performing the ceremony. Therefore the opportunity for premarital counseling is prevalent in all these instances, although it may be very difficult to actualize.

Several massive social changes have occurred since about 1960 that have altered the whole context in which a pastor does premarital counseling.

First, the counterrevolution—which has been crudely nicknamed "the hippie movement"—in spite of some of its ephemeral characteristics, has left one more or less enduring impact on the interpretation of the family. The communal type of family relationship has accented one side of the ambiguity about which we are speaking in this chapter, namely, the movement beyond the nuclear and the expanded family to group relationships of men and women with each other in a larger commune.

Second, technology has advanced birth control through the use of "the pill" and more recently through the perfection of antiseptic and safe procedures for abortion. These technological advances, combined with the legalization of abortion, reduce the fear of pregnancy and resulting feminine dependency more than they have reduced the possibility of pregnancy. In reality, nevertheless, they have introduced a realism into permissive premarital sexual behavior that did not previously exist.

Third, living together prior to marriage has itself become a form of self-help in premarital preparation. Increasing numbers of persons, many of whom perceive themselves to be genuinely devout religiously, look upon premarital sexual behavior as a way to get to know each other rather than as a prize or reward for having restrained their sexual needs prior to marriage for chastity's sake. If a pastor today has a halo of self-righteousness about chastity, in both men and women, he certainly needs a good welding job to hold the halo in place if he does much serious premarital counseling today. Living together is a fact of action going on in the lives of many people who come to a minister for a wedding ceremony.

Fourth, divorce and short-term commitments to marriage itself have become twin forces in the "belief systems" of persons of all ages today. The first has become the *modus operandi* for the second. Divorce is a much more casual experience for many people than it is for ministers. Many ministers will hold private belief systems concerning divorce, but for public role performance purposes they will stay with a much more stereotyped set of beliefs. The personal stress and the institutional stress show in the pastor's life here too. Nevertheless this affects the premarital pastoral counseling of a pastor in that he is increasingly being asked to perform the weddings of persons who have been married one or more times previously. He has his options of taking a forensic-legal attitude, a teaching-reconciliation attitude, a growth-human potential attitude, or a quick laissez-faire attitude. When confronted with the variety of premarital pastoral counseling situations, he may find himself shifting from one to another of these attitudes. But shifting is a way of coping with tension arising out of the ambiguity of his commitment to the nuclear family, on the one hand, the extended family of the church, on the other hand, and both of these in relationship to the larger family of humanity.

Fifth, women's liberation and women's power movements have changed the substance of premarital counseling. These movements include responses to the changed competence of women in the economic support of themselves, the changed awareness of their identity as persons in their own right existing not by reason of relationship to a man, their own selfhood, and the increased control they have over their own bodies because of more effective contraceptives and the legalization of abortions. These responses have effectively challenged the neat packaging of roles for men and women which were previously the topic of premarital counseling. Equal opportunity work laws and the increased earning ability of women have created a movement toward feminine independence that probably is here to stay. The pastor in premarital counseling, even with relatively nonsophisticated persons, is both presented with and should present the couple with the issues raised by the increased awareness of women of themselves as persons in their own right.

SOME VARIETIES
OF PREMARITAL COUNSELING

One of the major pitfalls for pastors is the unrealistic assumption that all premarital counseling has to follow one set pattern. Since biblical times there have been varieties or alternative life-styles with reference to marriage. No monolithic pattern for premarital counseling, therefore, is clinically viable. Furthermore, under the varied "terrain conditions" of his day-to-day work, the wise pastor knows that there are many viable but different expectations for premarital pastoral counseling and care. I would identify these alternative life-styles and varieties of expectations as follows:

Old Friends and Relatives

Many of the people who come to a pastor and ask him to exercise his legal right to perform a wedding ceremony are old friends and/or relatives of his. He tends to have a much less formal relationship to these persons and a longer and more varied knowledge of them. However, the walls of personal privacy between him and them are thicker because he does not have the degree of objectivity, detachment, and anonymity that would enable a couple to reveal themselves to him most adequately. Therefore a good procedure to follow is to have the more formal kind of counseling done by a person who is not so closely related to them. The minister who performs the wedding ceremony then joins in the festivities of the occasion as a member of the family or as a friend of the family. At the very best, this kind of premarital pastoral relationship is difficult to manage, laden with anxiety, and somewhat confused. Clashing of informal and formal relationships and expectations is one of the causes of this.

"The Wedding Is the Thing"

In the highly structured, ritualized life-style of socially prominent families, "the wedding is the thing." Daughters and mothers, prospective mothers-in-law, and the circle of women friends of the bride plan for weeks and even months in an increasing crescendo of preoccupation with the wedding itself, the parties, luncheons, showers, and shopping that go with it. The groom tends to "go along" in a sort of grunting compliance. Heavy preoccupation with the social activities effectively insulates the cognitive and the emotional life of the bride and groom from any genuinely serious preparation for the more mundane, less dramatic, and deeply personal responsibilities that marriage itself will indubitably produce. Frankly, the pastor simply has to do the best he can to wedge his way into the attention of the couple with the critical issues confronting them in marriage. Counseling is better done with a couple after the fact of the wedding itself, in an early marriage-adjustment-growth group. The realities of marriage seem to hit these people harder. Life is not one long wedding party. The tragic element of this kind of situation, however, is the tendency of the feminine community to make the wedding a be-all and end-all in itself that glosses over a need for an intimate marriage, sacrifices contemplative moments of good judgment for social exhibition purposes, and exhausts both the bride and the groom to such an extent that fatigue short-circuits their relationship as husband and wife.

The "Here and Now" Wedding

A considerable number of persons who reach out to a minister for the performance of their ceremony want simply that—a wedding ceremony.

They have little conception of their need for pastoral guidance and premarital counseling. They tend to show up at the last minute. They want the pastor to perform the ceremony at that very moment. In many instances these persons are total strangers to the pastor, the church, and even the larger community. They come from other places. Several kinds of social dynamics cause this type of demand upon the pastor.

First, there are those persons who come from the lower classes of society, both rural and urban, who are not educated or affluent enough either to know about or to be able to afford the protocol, the etiquette, and the rituals of more sophisticated weddings. The engagement is not their method of announcing an intention of marriage. Rather, the technique of elopement is the method used. Elopement is practical, less expensive, and free of publicity. In many cases these persons are quite reliable and "salt of the earth" kinds of folk. Sometimes they may be literally running from disapproving parents or hurrying into a panic wedding because of pregnancy or the military draft. Or they may even be intoxicated with alcohol or on a "drug trip." The pastor can, in a relaxed interview, diagnose these.

Second, these persons may be divorced persons who are remarrying. They do not want the publicity that would go with a wedding in their own community. Occasionally one sees this in widows and widowers who likewise do not want a public wedding.

Third, a minister may discover that some very prominent persons in the political and entertainment world will use this kind of approach to their wedding in order to avoid publicity.

In all instances, the common denominator seems to be that the persons are seeking privacy, they are in a hurry, and they are usually strangers to him. Many of them have quite legitimate needs for privacy; all of them should be slowed down for a leisurely opportunity to become acquainted with the pastor as a person. In some instances, couples are likely to be in such a hurry that they do not want to be related to the pastor except as a public servant who happens to be on duty at their beck and call.

The pastor who confronts this kind of "here and now" wedding demand is fortunate if the couple will take time to talk with him in a one-interview guidance situation. My practice has always been that if they are in too big a hurry to do this, I refuse to marry them. Other pastors' practice varies. Ordinarily when couples are made to feel at home, put at ease, and treated with kindness, they tend to appreciate the minister's spending an hour or even more with them conversing about their life situation. The objectives of such an interview would be to discover who they are, where they come from, how they can be related to people in their own community for pastoral, medical, and other types of care that a newly married couple will need. They can occasionally provide the names of persons to whom the minister can write and advise that the couple are returning to the community and would appreciate their care. Such persons could be a pastor, a lay leader in a church, a physician, a business person—responsible people who could continue to be related to them as they seek to implement their plans for marriage and family.

The "After the Fact" Wedding

Some of the persons who seek a wedding ceremony have already been maritally related to each other without benefit of either a religious or a civil ceremony. In some states, common law recognizes these as authentic marriages between consenting adults. In other states, the relationship of man and woman has no legal status at all; neither do children born of the union. Such marriages have always been true of the extremely poor and the extremely wealthy. In more recent counterculture thinking, for middle-class couples, living together *is* their own do-it-yourself experiment to prepare them for marriage. Then, because of their own needs, their desire to have children, their desire to relieve the strain on their friends and relatives, they may decide to get married officially. The wedding ceremony is "after the fact" of the marital union of the couple.

I am confident that much good can be done in one-interview situations. It is a specialized kind of crisis intervention opportunity. Strategically the pastor can attempt to diagnose the situation and can seek to provide additional alternatives in the case of impulse.

Another "after the fact wedding" is the case in which the bride is already pregnant. The first thing a pastor should ask is whether or not the woman has been told by a physician that she is pregnant. Premarital pregnancies are occasionally "self-diagnosis," for example. A visit with a nearby physician could be helpful before they let their self-diagnosis push them into marriage on an impulse.

In the event that the pregnancy is a medically established fact, the pastor can converse with the couple about whether they *really* care for each other and want to do so on a permanent basis in marriage. He can explore the other alternatives they have considered or may not have thought of yet. The girl's remaining single and keeping the child is becoming more prevalent. Abortion is used by many. Abortion has been technologically perfected and is being legally sanctioned. David Mace estimates that in 1974 there will probably be 1,600,000 known legal abortions in this country. He says that as Christians this is something we are going to have to live with whether we like it or not, but as Christians we are responsible for asking and seeking a better way. The woman lawyer who pleads the case for abortion says that it should be a last-resort procedure and not the first option of irresponsible people. Abortion has been taken for granted by the rich for many years. In the minds of professional people, abortion has been a counsel of desperation to give desperate persons of the middle and lower classes a second chance. Abortion is now becoming a casual convenience for the careless and irresponsible, since it is financially feasible for the middle classes. Abortion has been the last recourse of the poor and the deprived as a defense against starvation and death of mothers who had no way of caring for their babies. The easy generalizations of propagandists on all sides of the abortion issue are usually half-truths. The dilemma of abortion, more than any other, shows the cleavage between the nuclear family and the extended family of the church and community. I find myself in agreement with Mace that Christians are under obligation to find a better way than abortion, while we exercise patience with the hard reality that it is here and is out in the open. The social issues involved in the problem of abortion cannot be neatly sidestepped in the name of a supposed counseling neutrality. Still another alternative is that of carrying the child to full term and adopting it out to another family. The pastor does not use marriage or any of these other alternatives as "advice," because these are permanent life decisions in any case. However, he can explore with the couple what *they* have thought about these alternatives. He can use delaying procedures to enable the couple to make a reflective, well thought out decision rather than an impulsive one. He might even ask them to think it over, to sleep on it, to talk it over privately. One day's time will not make any real difference.

The Leisurely Spiritual Pilgrimage

The most nearly ideal premarital pastoral counseling happens when a couple tell a pastor as much as six months to a year ahead of time about their plans to be married. He may be one of the very first persons to whom they tell their good news. They ask him to do several things: to schedule counseling sessions with them as a couple; to collaborate with them in making their wedding plans; to perform their wedding ceremony. Here a leisurely spiritual pilgrimage develops. They face each great issue of their marriage. I use the vows of the traditional wedding ceremony as a format for the several sessions (which always vary in number) that we have together. The format looks somewhat like this:

1. "To Have and to Hold"—The Communication of Tenderness and Considerateness
2. "From This Day Forward"—Freedom from the Tyranny of the Past
3. "For Better for Worse"—Celebrating and Comforting
4. "For Richer for Poorer"—Getting and Spending

5. "To Love and to Cherish"—Joint Decision Making, Give-and-Take, and Learning to Treasure Each Other
6. "Till Death Us Do Part"—The Permanence of Covenant

The pastor also can use the plans for the wedding itself to explore the relationships of the couple to their parents, to enable the couple to evaluate their feelings about close friends who will be in the wedding, to get an overview of their "larger family" in terms of whom they invite to the wedding, and to coach them in how they use their money for the wedding, the reception, the formal meals, and the honeymoon.

A whole separate volume can be written on the subject of premarital counseling. Most of what is written is out of date now. One common failing of much that is written is that it is adaptable to persons in the upper classes and overlooks the varieties of life-styles of persons who are neither highly educated nor affluent. The point of view here is to underscore some of the varieties and to encourage greater maneuverability in the attitude and technique of pastors in premarital guidance and counseling.

PASTORAL COUNSELING IN THE PROCESS OF MARRIAGE CONFLICT

Once a couple are past the wedding, tensions begin to appear between the privacy they have with each other as a couple and the demands of their parents-in-law, their social groups of peers, their interactions with the larger extended family of church and school and with the even larger community. The pastor, representing both their personal and private needs for a secure family and their larger public needs to be a part of a wide, wide world, becomes a minister of reconciliation, an interpreter, and a negotiator alongside the couple in the community.

The pastor's work as a marriage counselor is done within the shaping environment of the group life of the church. Therefore family life education groups are a necessary part of the work of the pastor as a marriage counselor. He cannot, however, with safety to the families involved, conduct such groups unless he is also ready and able to provide individual counseling to persons who have problems that cannot be dealt with in the group context. Genuine safeguards also must be set up to protect the interests and needs of persons in the church who are single, widowed, or divorced. Pronounced emphases upon the "family-centered church" tacitly exclude these persons. The church idolatrously centers on the importance of the nuclear family when this happens. The sovereignty of Christ and his concern for the larger family of mankind challenges the subtle presuppositions upon which much family-centered thinking rests.[4]

The point of concentration here is the process of conflict within marriage that leads ultimately to divorce and the specific steps a pastor can take to anticipate, stop, reverse, or set aright the process of marriage conflict. The pastor discovers that the persons who come to him for pastoral care and counseling on marriage difficulties usually do so only after their difficulties are in advanced stages of deterioration.

This suggests two basic principles of pastoral counseling which call for careful research. First, marriage conflict goes through a process that can be observed, charted, identified, and described. Second, the process itself happens within the interacting field of many persons in the family, church, and community. The couple themselves are only two among many people. The pastor is one among many people who are giving advice, counseling, and exerting influence. The process of conflict tends therefore to be conditioned by the kind and quality of communication between and among these persons.

With these two principles in mind, I spent two days a week for eighteen months working with seventy-three couples in a counseling service that I initiated. My purpose was to see what needed to be done pastorally for persons at the different stages of marital conflict and disintegration. I identified what these stages were, what characterized them, and with what understanding a pastor should be endowed as he counsels people at the varying stages of stress.

THE PROCESS OF MARRIAGE CONFLICT

Marriage conflict moves from the typical "growing pains" of marital adjustment through serious assaults upon the covenantal nature of the marriage to chronic conflict as a way of life and/or to acute conflict as a problem-solving experience. This latter problem-solving experience can result either in divorce or in personality change, based on mutual insight and understanding in the instance of creative conflict. Nowhere does the tension between the close-knit, nuclear family, the expectations and rules of the extended family of the churches, and the great forces of society as a whole surface more clearly than in the process of marriage conflict. Marital conflict can be charted as moving through at least seven definable stages:

1. The Stage of Typical Adjustmental Conflicts

Early marriage is filled with the conflicts that "are common to all marriages." If a couple do *not* have conflict over these things, one might guess that they are leaving some of their "homework" undone. One might ask whether the conflicts are actually going on and they are not aware of them. This happens very easily when the couple are enjoying the first glow of sexual freedom in marriage. But these conflicts are both tangible and intangible.

The more tangible conflicts arise over such problems as when to have the first experience of intercourse, who will accept full responsibility for birth control—the husband or the wife—and how much money will be spent on the honeymoon. The husband, for instance, can be extremely anxious about spending money staying in a hotel that has "atmosphere" and decor when a good commercial hotel is cheaper. In other words, he will be penny-wise and feeling-foolish. The nonrecurring aspect of his expenses here will not occur to him. Usually people are married only once. They are married the *first* time only once in every instance!

When a couple return home, the tangible problems take a new form. Whether or not the wife works, what will happen if she becomes pregnant, where they are going to live, and the adequacy or inadequacy of the arrangements for living quarters made prior to marriage—these are just a few of them. Whereas the fears and anxieties of courtship and engagement were relatively abstract, they become more concrete and tangible in marriage. Fatigue and preoccupation can, as a result, become the atmosphere of the first few weeks of marriage.

But the obvious tangibility of these problems should not obscure six necessary adjustments which are not so apparent. These persist from the beginning to the end of any marriage and are the hinges upon which the whole thing swings:

a. *The development of an agreed-upon schedule of work, rest, play, lovemaking, and worship.* A steady course has to be driven between being overscheduled and simply leaving the whole matter of time and schedule planning to chance. The earliest quarrels in marriage tend to center on failures to synchronize masculine and feminine uses of time. For example, the husband may sleep late in the morning and go to bed late; the wife may get up early and go to bed early. A couple like this can, conceivably, go a whole week and never talk with each other, much less have sex relations.

b. *The development of a deeper-level and mutually satisfying plan of communication.* The couple should "pause for station identification" daily, weekly, monthly, and yearly to sketch out the schedules of these blocks of time, gear them in with their overall goals and aspirations, and simply get to know each other as persons. They actually learn to talk with each other in a dramatically verbal way. Up to now they have depended upon kisses, motions of the body and hand, and the rituals of making dates and going places. But now the question is, Can they stay in the same room with each other for an evening of conversation? Do they lay plans for their lives together or do they just throw their minds out of gear and let their lives go where circumstances push them?

c. *The development of a comradely understanding as to their masculine and feminine identities, that is, what a man is "supposed to be" and what a woman is "supposed to be."* More than this, under God they should develop an understanding of why it is he made them in his image and yet created them as male and female. They thus find out what they are to *be,* and the everyday tasks of life are shaped according to this identity, their *being* man and woman. This calls for real conflict. The new confrontation in the intimacy of marriage calls for personal ability to learn from each other. The things they have "always thought" are necessarily reshaped by the greater truths about what *this* man and *this* woman conceive their function *as* man and *as* woman to be. This confrontation brings to the surface their parents' ideas about the roles of men and women. For example, the wife who works will have very different feelings about the management of money as compared with those of the mother of her husband, who never worked outside the home. Likewise, the husband, having been raised by that mother, will have different expectations of the wife from those her father had of her mother, especially if her mother worked full time and the father was an invalid. These things must be talked over and worked through. Much conflict attends the process. The major issues of the liberation of woman today are the stuff of which much conflict is made, particularly if these are the academic covers for an inherently sibling-competition relationship. Apart from such a power struggle, the issues of the liberation of woman can be a source of creative growth.

d. *The establishment of an adult-to-adult relationship to parents-in-law.* A couple bring their separate family histories to the marriage with them. Their reactions to their parents become old molds for their reactions to each other as representatives of the opposite and of the same sex. Their reactions to their siblings, if any, become patterns of conflict and cooperation, competition and collaboration for their relationship to each other. Their major task is to learn to look at these old reactions, to laugh at them, and to help each other discard them. More than this, their task is to believe in themselves and in each other enough to be assured that new patterns of reactions can be developed. Games *can* be called off, and intimacy can take their place.

e. *The growth of fellowship with other married couples and with unmarried persons.* This is especially crucial in the emphases upon "open" marriage and in the involvement of men and women—not married to each other—on the job. Women and men not married to each other often spend much more time together than they do with their spouses. When a spouse—husband or wife—expects these work relationships to be depersonalized and free of any human emotions, conflict with the mate is about to happen. They are just not this way. Here the place of work presents the "larger family" tension. These things must be talked over and worked through. Much conflict attends the process.

f. *The development of a spiritual welcome and joyous acceptance of the first child in the family*. The early, typical adjustments of the couple are consummated in the incorporation of the first child into the life of the family. The word "incorporate" is used advisedly. It literally means to "embody the child" into the life of the family as a whole. Either all other conflicts of schedule, communication, and masculine and feminine identity are faced before the coming of the child or they become forced issues when the first child comes. The element of option in adjustment is now removed. A baby with a high temperature does not ask whether the father is accustomed to going to bed early. A baby yet two months before birth does not ask whether the family can get along without the mother's paycheck. A baby who is hungry at two in the morning does not ask whether Daddy would prefer that Mother be out at a party or giving baby her full attention! In other words, the adjustment of parenthood removes fantasies of freedom from the minds of the couple. Parenthood demands that they accept responsibility of the freedom they have already exercised in creating a child. As has been said, the whole problem of whether to have children at all is an open question today in ways that it was not before.

Formerly, a pastor could assume that all couples who married took the possibility of having children as an inherent part of the decision to marry. This is no longer the case. With the population explosion, the pill, legalized abortion, and the increased independence of women, whether or not a couple will ever have children is an open question and often a source of deep conflict.

Basic changes should and must take place in the life of a married couple during the years prior to the birth of the first child. Left unattended or unmet, these conflicts will form the basis for the symptoms that emerge in the later states of conflict.

Technique and Procedures. Group counseling at this normative stage of conflicts is the optimum technique to use. A didactic springboard for discussion is usually all that is needed to get a group going, such as: "How do you plan the use of time, money, and energy so as to deepen your love for each other?" Couples need socialization with other couples who are facing the same problems in order to offset their isolation. Individual help can be given to couples who are struggling with intimate problems they do not want to share in the group. Right here the ambiguity between a nuclear family and a larger family of others is enacted in the individual and group counseling.[5]

When a couple do seek pastoral counseling during this stage of conflict, they tend to come to the interview *as a couple*. They refer to themselves as "we" and to their conflicts as "ours." The techniques of conjoint family counseling are highly useful. The objectives of counseling at later stages of conflict, when the couples are alienated and estranged from each other, point toward getting this kind of dialogue to happen.[6]

2. The Stage of a Disrupted Covenant

Attitudes and Behavior. Marriage is a covenant of trust. Legal complications occur only later after the covenant of trust has been disrupted. The second phase of marital conflict is the disruption of the covenant of trust. It may be even more serious than this: the covenant may have been defective from the beginning and only now does this become apparent. For example, a husband withholds the fact that he has a criminal record, that he must report to a parole officer, and that he cannot buy real estate because he has no rights as a citizen until he is off parole. He does not tell his wife this. She discovers it several months later when they attempt to buy a house. Or the wife does not tell the husband that she has been previously married and that she continues a clandestine relationship with her former husband upon his occasional return to town. These are *defective covenants*, that is, they were not openly arrived at and they represent matters large enough to undermine confidence in the integrity of the partner.

But ordinarily the covenant was established in something that approaches good faith, if not good faith itself. Then, because of a neglect of the problems mentioned above, the *willingness* of the partners to make the marriage work is called into question. They lose touch with each other and withdraw as selves from each other. Isolation increases and the degree of suspicion mounts in proportion to the isolation. Soon assaults are made upon each other's integrity: "I suppose you worked last night; I don't really know what you did." "It is hard for me to get through to you without yelling; I sometimes think you are just plain stupid." "Well, I would have told you what I was doing, but I knew you wouldn't believe me."

The hallmark of this stage of conflict is repeated failure of communication. The situation progressively deteriorates until the couple simply live in silence. Each partner talks about only the most superficial things and tends to go his or her separate way. Each feels that the other does not understand and does not want to understand, does not care and does not want to care. The only vestige of a covenant that remains is a mutual feeling of hopelessness: What are we going to do? Contact of selves, not communication, takes place through tears, profanity, or brutality. Occasionally violent efforts at overcoming the chasm are made by hyperactive sexual behavior between the estranged persons of the marriage. But this is not a communion of tenderness and respect. It is a hostile encounter in itself with the violent hope that passion itself will overcome the barrier of isolation.

Techniques and Procedures. At this stage of conflict the pastor ordinarily has little opportunity for counseling. He can, however, "listen" to nonverbal communication: The two people show up at church separately; they make cutting remarks on social occasions; they overabsorb themselves in work; they develop heavy involvements in work, in hobbies, and in play with members of each other's peer sex; they travel a lot but never go together; or they may begin to drink excessively. Careful note of these situations can be made.

A response that amounts to precounseling is a careful use of "bump into" contacts, casual conversation at social gatherings, and close attention to crises such as illness, bereavement, the advent of a child, or the appointment to a new job. These efforts tend to create an atmosphere of warmth and nonverbal awareness with the couple. No programmed technique or tool is very useful here. However, the pastor's own access to people at the very casual and informal levels of life—mixed liberally with personal sensitivity, effective observation powers, and much common sense—provides people with a kind of availability of help not found elsewhere.

The pastor is related also to other persons who know the couple and are concerned for a variety of motives with their marital interaction. Relatives, close friends, and neighbors who may not be close to the couple are "watchers" of their actions. Some of these people are often the first to talk with a pastor. This interacting field of relationships is the context of much pastoral counseling of married couples. The pastor walks a narrow ridge between allowing himself to be used by in-laws and friends, on the one hand, and reacting against them so much that the real assistance they can be is forfeited and/or unguided.

3. The Stage of Private Misunderstanding

Problems and Behavior. One thing characterizes the couple up to this point most significantly: the two have not verbally told anyone else of their distress. Up to this point they have kept up appearances. They have carefully covered for each other. They have even deceived for themselves and for each other. But the individual isolation, the loneliness, and the feeling of not being understood create a vacuum that must be filled.

Sometimes the distress is communicated through illness on the part of one or the other. Various organs of the body, depending upon the individual constitution, fall prey to disorders in one way or another. Stress may reactivate an old disease, such as a latent tuberculosis; it may introduce a new one in a previously healthy person; it may cause an already present one to mean more to the individual. Illness becomes the organizing center of each one's reactions.

At other times the marital distress is communicated and the vacuum of anxiety filled by behavioral reactions. Excessive spending is one form of allaying anxiety and at the same time expressing hostility. Alcohol or drugs become more useful in calming jittery nerves and giving depressed spirits a momentary lift. Contemporary advertising probes heavily into these weak spots in order to make sales and to create the illusion of security in desperately anxious persons. (Some attention to the ethical issues at stake in modern advertising needs to be given at this point as well as many others. Here is one vital point of connection between pastoral counseling and social ethics and the need for social change.)

Disease and behavior difficulties—such as alcoholism, drug addiction, excessive spending, absorption in cheap literature, and excessive soap-opera viewing—are accompanied by other symptoms of isolation. The husband may frequent prostitutes. The man or the woman may try to pick up strangers without revealing his or her identity. The man or the woman may temporarily revert to earlier homosexual pickup behavior. These behaviors are symptomatic of the private misunderstanding that has happened in the marriage itself. When, however, this loneliness and isolation become unbearable, one or both of the marital partners break away to someone in their environment with whom they feel they can talk.

Pastoral Techniques and Tools. When a couple begin to show nonverbal signs of desperation in their marriage, and the pastor is aware of their distress, he has the right to intervene with a letter, a telephone call, or a visit. If he has performed their wedding ceremony, he can act upon a covenant that pastors should regularly make with couples whom they marry, that is, that if the couple begin to have trouble, the partners will seek his counsel and guidance, and if he becomes aware that they really are in distress, he will have the privilege given by the covenant to bring the subject up with them. Such prior "credit" in the relationship is the exception rather than the rule, however. Even without this, though, the pastor has a right to visit, to inquire, and to extend himself. He may be told that this is not the time for talking with others and that the partners want to "work at it themselves." Even in this case he has gone far in raising their motivation to do just that. He can be on standby, ready for them if and when they do need him, and he can assure them of a level of privileged communication at the same time.

Referral is another tool at this stage of conflict. The couple may look on the pastor as an insider rather than an outsider. They may say he is too close to them, has been their friend for many years, and is too much like a member of their family. He should be able to discern this intuitively him-self. In this case, he can call on the resources of other counselors and sustain his most durable relationship.[7]

4. The Stage of Social Involvement

Problems and Behavior. As has been said, when the isolation and the black-out on communication become too intense, one partner or the other or both break out of the silence and talk with other people. This may be done wisely or unwisely, in a responsible or an irresponsible way. The tight-knit nuclear privacy is broken. The parental families and the larger circle of friends, work associates, and others flow in upon them. This swirling con-fusion of the family, the church, and the community as a whole is the arena of action of the pastor as a marriage counselor.

The couple may go to their parents for guidance, as they did in for-mer years. Sometimes this is not possible. Instead, they may involve a brother or a sister who has been particularly close to them. The wisdom of doing this depends entirely upon the kind of persons these people are. Are they wise? Sometimes they are; often they are not. On the other hand, the couple may choose to go to a physician, a minister, or a former teacher. Marriage counseling is a cognate function of many different kinds of pro-fessions, and all these persons should be alert to the family overtones of the kinds of problems presented to them. The happiest thing that could occur at the time of the first breakout of the isolation is that the person would go to a responsible, wisely devout, and skilled person for understanding. A faithful pastor should pray for and be committed to a more and more sensi-tive and durable relationship of trust that will enable people to come to him at a time like this. For this is the most propitious moment when a married couple can best be helped; that is, the pastor can be *the first person to whom the couple break away from the isolation of the stage of private misunder-standing.* Thus the processes of social involvement can be guided and kept at a reasonably constructive level.

But often this is not the way the movement out of isolation occurs. Too often one or the other partner talks indiscriminately to anybody whom he or she meets. A random stranger on the telephone inquiring of the husband's whereabouts in order to buy a piece of merchandise from him is met with this: "I don't know where he is. He never tells me anything. Here I sit all day with these kids, too!" Or instead of this, the husband or wife, and sometimes both of them, finds another member of the opposite sex "who understands." The other person may or may not have unalloyed mo-tives of his own. The partner may simply be looking for a little sexual plea-sure or for someone whose mate he or she can further alienate. Ordinarily, though, this may begin in an honest attempt to be helpful and only gradually become more and more involved. The third party in every instance, however, becomes a part of the problem, not the solution.

The thing we do with our more intimate personal friends when they present marital problems is to call for the help of a more detached person who can deal with them more professionally and less informally, for community gossip and extramarital involvements tend to be formed just this way. Often pastors say that we should beware of counseling with people about marriage difficulties, especially women, because we can become sexually involved too easily. One observes, however, that ministers do not get involved with counselees nearly as often as they do with their secretaries, educational directors, deacons' wives, and other persons who are associated with them in the distinctly administrative and personal aspects of their social lives. These persons come to the pastor in an uncontrolled informal relationship. The pastor thus becomes the "third person" in a marriage "triangle."

Techniques and Tools. The techniques and tools of pastoral counseling at this stage are too many, varied, and sophisticated to discuss in this brief section. Two major technical sources can be cited. *The Family Coordinator* [now *Family Relations*] is a journal devoted to the cross-disciplinary task of marriage counseling. Clifford Sager and Helen Kaplan have edited a serious work entitled *Progress in Group and Family Therapy.*[8] However, several standard operating procedures are necessary for the parish minister, especially, to use.

First, the spouses tend to seek help individually at this stage of conflict. One or the other partner does not reach out for help. Yet the pastor is responsible to both partners. It is standard operating procedure to involve the other spouse either by sending word by the one who did come, by direct contact through a bump-into meeting, a letter, a telephone call, or a formal visit, whichever tool has the least possibility of being distorted or misused. This must be done, with the permission of the partner who did come, before anything other than an initial one or two interviews can be promised wisely.

Second, if communication is extremely poor between the husband and the wife, it is better that they be seen separately in individual counseling or together in group counseling rather than together as a couple. This should continue, in my opinion, until the communication has improved enough that they can talk together without saying things in an interview to hurt each other, things they would never dare say outside the interview with a third person present.

Third, the objective of the counseling, it seems to me, at this stage is fourfold: (*a*) to provide an opportunity for the joint identification of the couple with a person whose wisdom they both respect and whose affection they both can accept in trust; (*b*) to develop an overall view of the history and the ways of relating to each other that cause them to frustrate rather than satisfy each other's needs; (*c*) to provide a *reflective* rather than an *impulsive* approach to decision making as a couple; and (*d*) to reduce the necessity for them to talk indiscriminately in the community by restricting this kind of conversation to the counseling sessions.

5. The Stage of Threats of Attempts at Separation

Problems and Attitudes. The marital conflict is further inflamed when separation is threatened or is seen as the only way out. Separation may take place on a socially acceptable plane, on a planned and legal basis, or on a chaotic and compulsive basis. Socially acceptable separations occur under the guise of changes of the husband's work. For example, the wife goes away for a long summer vacation, or the husband stays in town while she lives in the suburbs, or he may reactivate a military tour of duty. Many other stratagems may be available at the moment and may become socially acceptable foils for marital conflict.

Under professional guidance, or by reason of wisdom on each other's part, the couple may be led to plan a manifest, open, candid separation. They may do this while each of them is getting some counseling assistance. This is often done in order to prevent further infections from arising. It especially protects the children from scenes between the parents. But the objective of such separation is creative and usually aims at improving rather than dissolving the relationship. Sometimes the separation is set up on a legal basis for a cooling-off period to see whether a divorce is really what is wanted. Many dramatic changes have been observed in formal, legal separations set up as a trial period for a divorce. In fact, some state laws recognize two years' separation as the most valid ground for divorce. From a legal point of view, and from a therapeutic point of view, this is one of the wisest conditions for divorce.

But the more common kind of separation is the chaotic one, done in anger, vindictiveness, or as a means of manipulation and coercion. One person walks out and goes home to his or her parents. Another kicks the partner out the first time the spouse comes home with alcohol on his or her breath. Another becomes violently outraged by an adventure in infidelity on the part of his wife. These become lighted torches that set the whole marriage on fire. In many of these instances, processes of vindictiveness that are irreversible are set in motion. Many times the separation is neither done nor taken seriously, but becomes a repeated form of transient petulance between immature people. Often, however, the separation is only a prelude to the next phase of conflict.

Techniques and Tools. The essential tool in counseling at this stage is the refusal of the counselor to be a messenger between the partners. They are to do their own communicating. The pastor refuses to be manipulated by either of them. He encourages them to take any positive move toward conciliation that seems constructive and to avoid destructive "game" moves.

Another important tool is the weight of loneliness and its effect on changing self-perceptions. Also, extramarital involvements as a means of alleviating this loneliness come into focus for more objective appraisal.

Legal consultation, as in the case of the legal separation, can be an effective tool of counseling. Collaboration with a lawyer is often a means of informing the pastoral counselor as to legal "games" the couple might be playing.

In the case of alcohol or drug abuse in husband or wife, the trial separation has been observed to be one way of "raising the bottom" for an alcoholic or a drug user to hit, as Alcoholics Anonymous puts it.

6. The Legal Phase of Marriage Conflict

Several signals indicate that this legal phase has set in, regardless of whether separation has taken place. They are sometimes subtle and sometimes obvious signals. The subtle signal appears in the kind of demand that is laid on a pastor, for example. He is expected to "decide who is to blame." The couple present their evidence and expect him—without the help of a judge, jury, or fee to function as a lawyer—to be a judge and a divider over them. The pastor does well to refuse this role, as did Jesus in another connection when he said, "Who made me a judge or divider over you?" (see Luke 12:13ff.). The pastor not only should be alert to this but should resist being pushed into this legal role. Such problems of affixing blame, for example, cut the pastor off from the person blamed. Lawyers do not mind this, but the pastor must be related durably to both partners, not legally and punitively to one at the expense of the other. More and more, however, lawyers are looking upon themselves as counselors-at-law and charging for services of counsel apart from specific "piecework" on legal papers drawn up. In these phases of conflict such problems emerge as feelings of hopelessness and self-depreciation on both sides. Economic anxiety and insecurity flood out much rational insight. The conflict of devotions between spouse and children rages. Social pressure from both sides forces "joiners" in sympathy for this spouse or that one. Few remain objective enough to be a part of the solution rather than the problem. The end result is that many divorced persons change their whole set of friends by moving to a new environment.[9]

One of the most helpful procedures to follow at this stage is the suggestion that a legal separation be used as a trial period to test the couple's more positive feelings for each other and to test their willingness to face the realistic obstacles that divorce will later finalize. When couples get married, they really need an *engagement period* in which to test their decision to marry. When they start to dissolve their marriage, they need a *disengagement period* for similar testing of decisions before they are finally effected.

Another standard operating procedure is collaboration with the lawyer to get any advice and counsel as to how to keep from becoming a prejudicial combatant in the conflict. Also, the precise nature of child support, custody, and care is good information to have.[10]

Parents of couples this near to a marital dissolution themselves are in need of pastoral attention and grief care. They often are severely wounded by the loss of their in-laws and stand helpless to care for their own grown daughter or son.

7. The Stage of Divorce

Competent studies of divorced persons indicate that the real shock and numbness of the grief situation occurs long before the actual granting of the divorce. We should not be deceived by the seeming lack of feeling that many demonstrate in the courtroom. Nor should we be enchanted by those few miracles that do occur when partners are reconciled on the eve of the divorce decree and live happily ever after. Much that has happened has taken the marriage beyond the point of no return. Many things can yet be done, as we shall see, but not all of a sudden. People who belong together do not need to be glued together, but much has been done to separate them that is modifiable by wise pastoral care. This is not a hopeless situation, but it is a hard one.

Divorce is being viewed more and more casually. People tend not to be as upset by the experience as they were even ten years ago. However, this is deceptive. Some pastoral counselors in training will say, "She (or he) came in quite composed for the next interview after the divorce was granted. She (or he) acted as if nothing had happened." Five interviews and six weeks later, however, the same counselor often reports, for example, "She was depressed today and wept profusely over her loss and hurt." Or, even two years later, a counselee may present an unrealistic scheme for remarrying the person he had divorced.

The thing the pastor must concentrate upon at the point of the decree of divorce is the next phase into which the couple go almost immediately.

THE POST-DIVORCE
BEREAVEMENT SITUATION

More and more we are seeing pastoral care during critical incidents as a unique ministry to people in their losses. Divorce is a loss in much the same sense that death is. As has been said in connection with religious history, in a sense death is more easily assimilated than divorce. Death is clean, final, and definitive. Death cuts with a sharp knife. Divorce cuts with a dull, dirty, rusty knife. And it accentuates the poignancy of the grief. A flood of grief, characterized by much hostility and vindictiveness as well as by the tears of frustrated love and devotion, follows with a heavy depression of emotions. Loneliness and social awkwardness due to the new role and status as a divorced person complicate the process of readjustment. As one divorcé put it to me: "I feel more of a second-class citizen than any Negro in the South."

All this is compounded by the recharting of affections and the discovery of a new meaning in life apart from the previous marriage. Many divorced persons find this meaning in their work, and this is easier for professional people than for nonprofessional ones. Others find the new meaning in their children, and this is much easier for mothers than for fathers. Some find new meaning in the life of their church, but this depends upon the conditions within the church itself. Others find new meaning in completely relocating and starting over where they were not known. Pioneer areas of the country are filled with divorced persons who have "amputated the past" to the best of their ability. Even so, they are like men without a country or lost sheep of the house of Israel as far as their relationship to the churches is concerned. The majority of divorced persons find new meaning in remarriage. This has become the prevailing pattern in our society. But it puts them in opposition to the church, whose teachings hitherto allowed these people no room.

The agenda of grief-therapy groups should include the loss of persons by divorce. Such persons are not just husbands and/or wives who have lost someone by divorce. The sons and daughters of divorced parents are often similarly cut off from those whom they love and whose love they want.

PRINCIPLES OF PASTORAL COUNSELING IN THE
PROCESS OF MARRIAGE CONFLICT

The foregoing discussion of the process of marriage conflict provides the groundwork for evolving some principles of pastoral counseling at the different stages of conflict. Obviously the pastor must carefully reflect on the meaning of these different stages. Again, he must have a dynamic, developmental view of human life and the marriage relationship before this whole approach makes much rhyme or reason to him. He must learn to approach a marriage conflict situation not as a static, legal contract but as a personal covenant that is characterized by life, growth, deterioration, and so forth. This attitudinal orientation is best gained in a clinical setting where a staff of ministers discuss these problems. Reading this brief description of the stages can point one in this direction. However, the minister can compare his previous experience with what has been said here and learn much from his own experience. As he does this, he will see several principles emerging for devising specific techniques in a given situation.

The Principle of a Controlled
Counseling Relationship

In everyday speech we talk of some situations as being "well in hand" and others as being "out of control." A controlled relationship is especially needed in a marriage conflict situation. The initiative of the person *wanting* help in the marriage situation is required. This must be gained honestly and aboveboard, not covertly and surreptitiously. For example, if one partner of a marriage comes to the pastor, he or she may suggest that the pastor come by the home for a visit when the other partner is there "without that person's knowing that he knows about the trouble." This is a form of deceptiveness which should be avoided. It puts the pastor in the position of being manipulated by one partner against the other. Rather, the pastor would do much better to write, call, or visit on an aboveboard basis. Many counselors write a brief note to the other spouse. They do this with the permission of the person who did come to them. In such a note the counselor invites the other person to come by to see him. This leaves a large measure of freedom with the other spouse and at the same time clears the atmosphere of any covertness.

In addition to initiative, the pastor needs a place of discreet privacy, either in his home or in his study at the church, for conferences with the people who are having marriage difficulties. Furthermore, he needs enough time in which to do the work of counseling. For example, if the couple are demanding that he visit in the home and "settle things for them" at some late-evening hour, the pastor does well to interpret that conflict as a process of accumulated distress that will take time. Then after his visit in the home he can schedule further appointments in his office. Thus the pastor brings the whole situation under the control of his own professional relationship as to initiative and place.

But these factors are external controls as compared with the distinctly spiritual awareness of the kind of relationship the pastor has to the individual or to the couple. The role of the pastor should be clearly and mutually understood. The person should understand perfectly that the pastor is not just another *neighbor* peering into the situation, not just another *friend* trying to be nice and friendly, not just another *relative* with a vested interest and a "side" in the matter, and not just a *preacher* looking for illustrations with which to dramatize his sermons. Rather, he is a *pastor* appointed by men and called by God to minister with confidence and commitment to all concerned. This role of his should be clear, lest his motives be interpreted wrongly. Otherwise, he could be seen as a competitor for the wife's affections. The wife, on the other hand, might see him as another man that the husband has "ganged up with" against a poor, defenseless woman. Both partners may see him as a father who is supposed to spank them and send them back to play peacefully. Or, as in the case of persons at the legal phase of conflict, the pastor may be pushed into the role of judge and divider over them, to decide who is to blame and how the property should be divided. Clarity of role will facilitate communication, and the pastor must be explicit and forceful enough to make these things clear to the couple. When acute marital conflict is dealt with, passivity can be nondirectiveness, but more often it is irresponsibility.

Developing an Interprofessional Team

No matter how skilled a minister is, he cannot work effectively as a marriage counselor in isolation from other professional people. Such isolation goes hand in hand with failure. At the points of detection, diagnosis, treatment, and convalescence of his counselees, the pastor is deeply in need of colleagues such as the physician, the schoolteacher, the social worker, the lawyer, the judge, the juvenile probation officer, and the hospital official. For example, often the indications are that each couple should have a thorough medical examination. Specific medical problems have been discovered that either contributed to or caused the trouble. Early signs of mental illness can be checked by a physician as routine in such an examination. Specific medical therapies can be recommended to stabilize the situation while the counseling continues. Likewise, employers have been of vital assistance in work difficulties that aggravate the marital situation, and, in turn, pastoral assistance to the counselee has often made a better worker of the person. Public school teachers have often called stress situations to the attention of pastors and, in turn, been coached by the pastors on the needs of the children without the children ever being aware that their pastor was ministering indirectly to them through their teacher.

Identifying the Stage of Conflict

The pastor must carefully develop ways of identifying the stage at which he has found the conflict. *The kind of communication going on in the total situa-*

tion is the basis of determining the stage. For example, the couple in the typical adjustmental stage of conflict are likely to come to the pastor together. They will talk even with humor and a few tears about quarrels they have had, about their routine, their differing interpretations of the roles of men and women, their inability to talk with each other, and the like. But at the stage of serious conflict where the covenant has been threatened, they may never say anything to the pastor, although he may sense that something has gone wrong. He will see them come to different services at church for no obvious reason. They look unhappy. They may seek to depreciate each other, with humor, in a crowd or avoid the pastor, whereas they have hitherto been very open. He may hear about unusual things they have done that are not typical of their routine.

In the stage of private misunderstanding, the pastor may notice that the husband has bought a car that is just too expensive. The wife may have started dressing in a style that is out of keeping with her budget. The couple may go in over their head for a house. Or the counselor may detect the stress between the lines of a story about an illness. He may note that the couple have begun to drink or to drink more heavily.

When the couple do come to the pastor or open up to him when he goes to them, he can be assured that he has met them in the stage of social involvement. They probably talked with other people before they came to him. Therefore it is routine practice to ask, "Have you felt free to talk to anyone else?" From this point he can consult with them as to whether they *plan* to talk to anyone else. Thus he can bring some influence to bear upon regulating the communication process. Localizing the spreading conflict is a major job. On the other hand, in certain situations the counselees really should confer with someone besides us, and this is ordinarily what we mean when we speak of referral. This does not mean sending the person away from us as if he was "beyond us." It means calling in the assistance of others. As representatives of the love of God in Christ, we are confident that neither the counselees nor the people whose assistance we seek for them are ever beyond God's loving care.

Furthermore, when a couple have reached this stage they are not able to talk with each other meaningfully. Whereas in the earlier stages of conflict a pastor would see the couple together, he probably will want to schedule separate interviews with both husband and wife until the communication is clarified.

Stabilizing and Reversing the Process of Conflict

The next strategic objective of the pastor in dealing with marital conflict is to stabilize and reverse, if possible, the destructive process. For example, when an individual or a couple come to the pastor in the stage of imminent divorce, they usually are coming out of desperation. He can free the situation a bit if he tells them that if they go ahead and get a divorce, he still wants to be a pastor to them. If they expect him to accept responsibility for conferring with them toward a reconciliation, they will necessarily have to "freeze" the divorce procedures until a considerably later date. He disavows any role as a miracle worker. He uses delaying procedures to create a free situation in which responsible counseling can take place.

In this situation, the pastor may, if he has succeeded in stabilizing the process just short of divorce, attempt to reverse it to the next-earlier stage. He may suggest that the couple confer with their lawyer as to the possibility of a *legal separation* as a basis for a divorce in the future if they so choose. This will give them time to try the new identity before they finally accept it. They can use the intervening time span for further counseling. This will assure them that they have done everything possible to work things out. It will give them a greater measure of freedom from later regrets. Sentimental appeals to the "good of the children," to the "poor mother's breaking heart," and to "how it will look for Christians to be divorced" simply galvanize the rebellious into action. If the pastor uses such appeals, he may only hasten the stampede. Appeals to the couple's own self-esteem for having taken time to act wisely to seek counseling make much more sense.

When the couple come to the pastor at the stage of separation, the objective of the pastor is to keep this stage from further deterioration. But more than that, he looks back at the earlier stage and sees that his task is not to "glue these people back together" with a kiss but to assess carefully the kinds of social pressures being exerted upon them by other people. This becomes the stuff of his separate conversations with them. He knows that it only adds fuel to the fire to talk to them together. But when he talks with them separately, the hidden "deals" that have been made with "the other woman" or "the other man" emerge. The threats that have been leveled by their mothers or fathers, brothers or sisters, of "never having anything to do with them again if they do go back to that brute or that wench" appear.

When we see couples in the quiet, silent desperation of the stage of private misunderstanding, we can involve them in group discussions along with those in the earlier stages of conflict. Sometimes group work will make it easier for them to open up to the leader on a personal basis. If a particularly loaded question comes at the pastor, he can ask whether he can confer with the person for a moment after the group meeting so that he can give this more personal attention. At other times, the group work itself resolves the difficulty through straight intercommunion with other, more experienced couples. Reading helps some couples, but not nearly so many as we would think or like it to help. Simpler, briefer, nontechnical, and poetic material is of more use than the gobbledygook of much literature written by specialists in counseling. For example, one of the best self-help books on marriage was written by William Lyon Phelps, a professor of English literature![11]

When pastors find couples in the years just prior to and following the birth of the first child, they should devise family-life discussion groups for them. This is the place to do preventive work, even more than with teenagers. Here the couple find out that no marital choice is perfect and that we learn to live with the one we *did* choose, not the one the books say we *should* have chosen.

The distinctly exhortative "use" of religion in this process is not as helpful as a consistent mood and atmosphere of prayer. The pastor has chosen to place his own personal faith between the lines of his conversations rather than in them. He loves God, not because he tries, but because God loved him and he can't help loving God now that he has encountered and been encountered by the Lord Jesus Christ. If this is so, and the pastor is not fooled in it, then the counselees have already felt it in the times together with the pastor. If it is not so, then all his special pleading about religion is in vain. Many counselees have heard this from their youth up, but an authentic person of faith in Christ is new every day to them. The first principles of the faith set forth in this book provide the basis for describing the very demonic itself at work in the shattering of marriages. The pastor's job requires that he be as wise as a serpent and as harmless as a dove in the confrontation of the distortions of sin. Such is the tension he bears as he participates in the ambiguity between the security the nuclear family offers and the freedom necessary for creative function that many sense is removed in the institution of marriage.

NOTES

1. Sigmund Freud, "The History of an Infantile Neurosis," in *Standard Edition of the Complete Psychological Works of Sigmund Freud*, trans. and ed. James Strachey and others (London: Hogarth Press and Institute of Psychoanalysis, 1959), 17:114–115.

2. David R. Mace, *The Christian Response to the Sexual Revolution* (Nashville: Abingdon Press, 1970), p. 19.

3. Ibid., p. 26.

4. More detailed discussion of these problems will be found in the following resources: Clark E. Vincent, *Readings in Marriage Counseling* (Thomas Y. Crowell Co., 1957); David R. Mace, *The Christian Response to the Sexual Revolution* (Nashville: Abingdon Press, 1970); and Nathan W. Ackerman, *The Psychodynamics of Fam-*

ily Life: Diagnosis and Treatment of Family Relationships (New York: Basic Books, 1958).

5. See Howard Hovde, *The Neo-Married* (Valley Forge: Judson Press, 1968).

6. See Virginia Satir, *Conjoint Family Therapy: A Guide to Theory and Technique,* rev. ed. (Palo Alto, Calif.: Science and Behavior Books, 1967).

7. See Wayne E. Oates and Kirk H. Neely, *Where to Go for Help,* rev. and enlarged ed. (Philadelphia: Westminster Press, 1972).

8. Clifford J. Sager and Helen Kaplan, eds., *Progress in Group and Family Therapy* (New York: Brunner/Mazel, 1972).

9. See William J. Goode, *After Divorce* (Chicago: Free Press, 1956).

10. See Richard A. Gardner, *The Boys and Girls Book About Divorce* (New York: Science House, 1970).

11. William Lyon Phelps, *Marriage* (New York: E. P. Dutton & Co., 1941).

Part Four

THE WORKAHOLIC

15

The Workaholic:
It Takes One
to Catch One

Workaholism is a word that I have invented. It is not in your dictionary. It means addiction to work, the compulsion or the uncontrollable need to work incessantly. Workaholism has hidden beginnings in economic, cultural, and emotional deprivation in childhood. It becomes acute in the presence of institutional deprivation of approval and appreciation in the twenties and thirties. It also becomes aggravated in health crises and interpersonal crises of the forties and early fifties. If it is not reversed or arrested in the forties and early fifties, it becomes chronic and may lead to death in one form or another in the late fifties and/or sixties.

You ask me, "How do you know?" I answer, "I know because I was a workaholic myself."

I am not going to kid you or play games with you about it. Insofar as the printed word permits, I want to meet my readers face-to-face. These pages are a thinly disguised autobiography of a "converted" workaholic. The conversion does not change the basic personality formation of the workaholic; it only releases the power of the addiction. Once released from slavery to work, a person is enabled to recognize it in others more clearly. He never does so with pride, because he knows that the moment he becomes complacent about his own uprightness, he is about to fall into his old habits again. Therefore this chapter has a confession of a workaholic, a "working" definition of workaholism, and a description of the syndrome or collection of symptoms that identify a dyed-in-the-wool workaholic.

A CONFESSION OF A WORKAHOLIC

Most of us try to help alcoholics when we have the opportunity to do so, but we have a hard time understanding and identifying with them. When I meet an alcoholic, I am likely to respond to him as if he were a breed apart, completely different from me. Yet I learned from people who spend all their time working with alcoholics that I should face up to the fact that in some ways I was similarly addicted. I began to examine my own patterns of behavior carefully. I had to admit to myself and to those with whom I work that I have an addiction too. Although it is far more socially acceptable than alcohol or drug addiction, it is nevertheless an addiction. It is more profitable than drug addiction, let us say (unless you are a pusher as well as a user), or than alcoholism (unless you wholesale the stuff as well as drink it). Nevertheless, when it comes to being a human being, workaholism is an addiction that can be almost equally destructive.

When the truth first dawned upon me that I am a work addict, two important things happened immediately. First, I broke into laughter. The realization was too true to be anything but painfully funny. I refuse to give up this grace of laughing at myself, because it keeps the truth from knocking me down long enough for me to begin to do something about my situation. I would encourage my reader to laugh along with me and beg of him not to laugh *at* me. Because the louder he laughs the more likely he is to be a workaholic himself, rejoicing in the evil he has found in me that relieves him of the painful necessity of taking heed of his own plight. Second, I discovered a whole community of suffering among other people who either heard me talk of my addiction or read my brief article in the October 1968 issue of *Pastoral Psychology*.

Most significant in the community of suffering that I discovered were the alcoholics and the drug addicts whom I came to understand and appreciate more. I discovered I have a ground of common human frailty to stand upon *with* the alcoholic and the drug addict. I, like them, must admit that I am powerless to "kick the habit" and must ask God's help. I must "hit bottom" in desperation about the overinvolvement I have in my place of work. I had to come to terms with the problem of overcommitment. This overcommitment for me was a sort of idolatry of the job I had. It even passed itself off as a kind of religious devotion. Actually it was a false religion, an addiction to work for its own sake. Wrapped up in my own habituation to work was my self-sufficiency as a "doer" who trusts fully in my own work. Ensconced in my always-at-it work pattern was the hidden assumption that I was indispensable. The outfit for which I worked, I felt, could not really get along without me. I kept reinforcing this feeling with around-the-clock activity, as if the whole operation depended on me. This was not so. It was an illusion. I eventually admitted it.

When I did, I confessed to my limitations, finiteness, and humanity. Yet childish feelings of omnipotence fought with the confession. I as a workaholic, like an alcoholic, found that admitting my humanness called for an acceptance of my own powerlessness and helplessness. This created a feeling of need for help from others and from God. This need, in turn, was met by many people around me, most especially members of my family. The good news is that a real community was waiting, available, and responsive.

I have been astonished to see how many people begin immediately to respond with their own confessions when I spell out what I mean by workaholism. Other kinds of addicts—alcoholics, drug addicts, and others—are amazed when I admit to them my habituation to work. As I have said, I find other people who have painted themselves into impossible corners on their jobs and they become a part of the community of the addicted I have described. All of us together can sustain each other by reinforcing each other's commitment to "kick the habit" of defying the day's doing as a means of survival. For me, probably the most rewarding discovery of fresh community with persons has been among members of my own family. For years they have tried to lure me away from work to enjoy a time of effortless play with them. Now they are convinced that what they have been trying to tell me for years is finally being heard. In fact, life is more livable now both for them and for me.

A DEFINITION OF WORKAHOLISM

Naturally the word "workaholism" is a neologism, an invented word, a semihumorous word for addiction to work. Howard Clinebell says "that dependence on *overwork* (work compulsion) and dependence upon overeating (food addiction) are psychologically very similar to drug dependency."[1] When we look at classical definitions of the term "addiction" we begin to get a more serious understanding of *workaholism*. Addiction means the condition of applying habitually, of giving oneself up or over to as a constant practice, of devoting oneself or habituating oneself to something. This general dictionary definition can mean anything and everything, but a narrower use of the term is made by the World Health Organization with specific reference to alcohol addiction. Such addicts "are those excessive drinkers whose dependence upon alcohol has attained such a degree that it shows a noticeable mental disturbance or interference with their bodily and mental health, interpersonal relations, and their smooth social and economic functioning."[2] A definition of the workaholic along similar lines would say that he is a person whose need for work has become so excessive that it creates noticeable disturbances or interference with his bodily health, personal happiness, and interpersonal relations, and with his smooth social functioning.

Yet a fundamental distinction is to be made between workaholism and alcohol and drug addiction, which involves the degree to which the addiction varies from the norms of the community and culture. Our culture has a very different attitude toward the alcoholic from the one it has toward overwork. Excessive work is lauded, praised, expected, and often demanded of a person in America. In fact, one of the main criteria for determining whether a person is mentally disturbed is whether or not he or she is able to function effectively on the job. This says little or nothing about the workaholic who often is so very effective at work that he becomes isolated and at odds with his community, albeit much less obviously and more insidiously than when he "drops out of the human community" through the use of alcohol or some of the more exotic drugs. Workaholism is a much more socially approved malady than alcoholism, though both have crippling manifestations, and is more difficult to deal with.

Work, furthermore, can become the special addiction of the religious man. The monks of Cluny could say that "to work is to pray." This meant something quite different, however, from saying that work itself is the god to whom we pray, the god whom we propitiate with our bodies for the sins of our spirits, the idol who enslaves us. Addiction to work is not far from the disorder of the monasteries known as *acedia,* earlier classified by John Cassian (early fifth century A.D.) as one of the seven deadly sins. Acedia was defined by Evagrius Ponticus (fourth century A.D.) as the condition in a monk that made him fall asleep in his cell or else desert his religious work altogether. It stemmed from the fact that the religious man's work had gone beyond the point of increasing returns; he worked more and more and accomplished less and less, becoming all the while more and more bored with and anxious over his work.

Mark D. Altschule says that in contemporary life acedia has dropped out of common usage and the psychiatric concept of depression has taken its place. Erik Erikson identifies this kind of depression as a "work paralysis" in which a person has striven so hard and achieved so long that the organism rebels and refuses to produce anymore.[3] As I have said, this dark distemper of the spirit easily develops in the religious man's situation, especially in a works-oriented expression of the religious life such as is prevalent in American Christianity. For us indeed the very religion we espouse puts such a value on work that we feel more religious the more we are addicted to work! The religious group tends to extol this form of addiction. The community in general sees the work addict only from afar, in terms of what he or she gets done, expressing "oohs" and "ahs" of amazement at the workaholic's accomplishments.

A DESCRIPTION OF WORKAHOLISM

The best way to describe workaholism, or work addiction, is to discuss the developmental phases of the malady. The history of a workaholic at first is no different from that of other working people. Many people regard work as a necessary evil, a part of the human condition, and some people tend to look upon it as the special penalty laid upon us because of the disobedience of Adam and Eve in the Garden of Eden. We take very seriously the words of God to Adam and Eve: "In the sweat of your face you shall eat bread till you return to the ground" (Gen. 3:19a). Even though we give work a "holy glow," a religious halo, in our hearts we tend to look upon it as a sort of punishment; our sense of guilt is transformed into anxiety-laden work that can propitiate what we unconsciously perceive to be an angry God. In relation to our fellow men, we also quite consciously use work as a means of securing their pity—we "work ourselves to death" or "into an early grave"—and of gaining their approval; and as a means of outdoing them in competition. In these several senses, work can be vaguely described as a characteristic of the whole human race.

Thus, the first expression of workaholism is indistinguishable from honest industry in all men. We all work, as millions of men drink today: on a *social* basis. There is nothing inherently wrong with work. Everybody sooner or later gets around to it even if only in the form of exertion to avoid work! For years the average worker goes along enjoying his work, sharing his work with others, talking shop on evening social occasions, and swapping work stories with fellow workers. There is such a thing as work being play, and many people can take their work or leave it, without *having* to have it in order to be happy or to survive as a person, or without being driven to it like a quarry slave in the bondage of a compulsion to work. However, in such crowds of people there are premonitory signs of the developing workaholic.

THE EARLY OR PRODROMAL PHASE
OF WORKAHOLISM

The stream of speech of an emerging workaholic will tend to betray the true trend toward workaholism. First, at a party he (or she) will inevitably tell others how *early* he came to work or how *late* he remained. As in other disorders, this means that the next thing you hear will be how *little sleep* he has been getting. The difference here is that instead of getting worried about such an individual the community usually begins to compare him with Thomas Edison or some other genius. This person may begin by spending the hours of a regular working day drinking coffee (to counteract having lost sleep the night before), in bull sessions, and the like. Then he is forced to use the hours other people use for parties and for sleeping to catch up on work left undone during the day. If this person happens to be a housewife, she may spend several hours during the ordinary workday in long telephone conversations. Then she has to burn the midnight oil getting the day's work done. However, this is not the picture given in conversation. Instead, the person *boasts* about how early he arose or how late he stayed up or how little sleep he got.

The second symptom of early workaholism is the invidious comparisons the emerging workaholic makes between himself and other people in the *amount of work* he is able to get done in contrast to others. Everybody knows how hard he works. He is the soloist. They are the accompanying choir in singing *his* song. He boasts about "doing more than my share," "carrying more than my part of the load." I can recall almost consciously making other men uncomfortable with the amount of work I was able to accomplish. The early signs of the workaholic syndrome are loud complaints in a line organization about other people's lack of conscientiousness. Ministers are particularly liable to do this because much of our work is of an unseen, intangible, invisible kind and we cannot point to specific results. Some of the most important things we do are things about which we cannot tell anyone. We feel uneasy about not having anything "to show" at the "show and tell" moments in the marketplace, such as at the meeting of the official board. Consequently, we are likely to spend considerable time discussing how busy we are, how much we have to do, and comparing the results of our "doing" with those of men we consider less productive than ourselves. If we are ministers, this is likely to show up in our efforts to produce tangible signs of our labors—larger numbers of converts, larger increases in membership, larger budgets this year than last year, the building of larger churches. Of course, all this takes work, our work, and we never want others to forget it.

A third early telltale sign of the workaholic is the inability to say no to people who want to use his services or to limit the time he will commit to other people. The professional person expresses this by taking on more speaking engagements, more committee chairmanships, more patients, clients, or counselees, more administrative responsibilities. He does not use time limitations, case load limitations, or the definition of his job responsibilities as his limitations. He is likely to feel the economic pinch but never knows at what point to level off his budget or how to live within that line. He always feels he must have more. However, subtle ego gratification is at work as well as economic anxiety. He feels that he is the *only* one who can do his work well. When challenged about whether he is overextending himself, he is likely to say, "But if I do not do this, who will?"

The wage earner, as differentiated from the self-employed and salaried person, will "moonlight" and add more and more to his load. For example, it is not unusual to find nurses who add on extra shifts to their regular hospital schedule. These wonderful persons are liable to become

Florence Nightingales for their whole family and their in-laws as well, besides absorbing uncovered shifts in the routine of the hospital.

These attitudes are formed within the second and third decades of life when physical health and energy are at a high point. Never having known any limits on his health and energy, the person as a result tends to assume that there *are none*. The mood of omnipotence reigns. Yet, with a little attention at this stage of the game, possibly the person can be *taught* that there are limits. As one man said on the first interview of a longer-term counseling relationship, "I have always said that I will not stop until I am a $20,000 man." He worked a double shift six days a week. After the fifth interview, he remarked, "I am not a $20,000 man. I am a $10,000 man who works two shifts!" That was a beginning at least!

THE CRUCIAL PHASE OF WORKAHOLISM

The crucial phase of workaholism begins when the person's first collapse takes place. This collapse can be one that involves interpersonal relations, such as when marriage and family life run into serious trouble. A young man tries to finish his last year of college, to earn as much as his wife even when this means working on a different shift from hers, and to beat off the draft by taking a heavy Army Reserve assignment; consequently, he and his wife have serious failures of communication. Or a staff physician takes so many private patients that he is asked by his hospital colleagues to resign. Or a prestigious young pastor has so many irons in the fire that he does not realize he is out of touch with his twelve-year-old son who has started using amphetamines, marijuana, and alcohol. These are interpersonal collapses. They call for a reordering of the life. They are trouble signals that call attention to the person's pathological preoccupation with work.

The crucial phase of workaholism may also be ushered in by a physical breakdown. A young university professor has a blackout and his condition is diagnosed as a propensity to low sugar content in the blood, rendered acute by improper diet and fatigue. A young social worker suffers a severe anxiety attack with associated physical symptoms over the impossibility of meeting the obligations of his crowded schedule. Such crucial situations precipitate the necessity for at least reappraising one's life plan, for defining more specifically one's goals and the bases of one's motivation for work. A system of priorities must be developed. A new value structure must replace some old habit systems. But rarely does this happen. More often the work addict regards these crucial symptoms as something that will go away with a little rest. At the pleading of a spouse, the firm command of a doctor, and maybe a few words thrown in by a colleague who is himself a workaholic, he takes that little rest but makes no basic changes in his life.

219

CHRONIC WORKAHOLISM OR
REHABILITATION?

After a crucial collapse or two the workaholic is at a crossroad of his pilgrimage, with no signposts. The workaholic can go in one of two directions: toward chronic workaholism or toward rehabilitation. The chronic case adopts his addiction as a way of life. He continues to let all other values go—family, friendships, spiritual associations, everything. He becomes an around-the-clock man whose whole life is his work. He eats, drinks, and sleeps his job. As William H. Whyte earlier described the organization man, so it can be said of the workaholic that he is an ascetic who enjoys nothing except an occasional good meal, constant supplies of work, and a good bed to fall into from sheer exhaustion. This goes on until death. Emotional responsibilities not related to his job are relegated to other people so he can more easily fulfill his one all-consuming need for work.

If the person goes in the direction of rehabilitation, however, new ways of life and value are opened to him. He redistributes his emotional investments into many different areas of life. He ceases to put all his emotional eggs in the one basket of work.

NOTES

1. Howard Clinebell, *The Pastor and Drug Dependency* (New York: Council Press, 1968), p. 9.

2. Expert Committee on Mental Health, Alcoholism Subcommittee, 2nd Report, World Health Organization Technical Report Series, no. 48, August 1952.

3. Mark D. Altschule, "Acedia: Its Evolution from Deadly Sin to Psychiatric Syndrome," *British Journal of Psychiatry* 3 (1965): 117–119.

16

The Workaholic
on the Job

No real evaluation of the workaholic's way of life and how to change it is possible until we analyze the man actually at his job. An internal view of the workaholic in action, where he is reputed to be happiest, is necessary for a full understanding of work addiction.

MAJOR TYPES OF WORKAHOLICS

Careful observation of a business organization, a hospital staff, the military, a church organization, or a school reveals a variety of different types of workaholics. Therefore we must describe and classify these various types.

The Dyed-in-the-Wool Workaholic

This man or woman has several characteristics as you see him or her in action on the job. First, whatever kind of skill and/or profession he practices, *he is a "professional" at it.* He takes the standards of excellent performance more than seriously; these are well-nigh his total personal ethical code, if not tantamount to a religion for him. He will not touch an assignment lightly or halfway. To him there is no such thing as giving an assignment "a lick and a promise." He leaves his own professional stamp on a job if he accepts responsibility for it at all. A noncompulsive professional will be able to settle for a less than perfect result. The workaholic *has* to get 100 percent results.

Already you are beginning to see that the dyed-in-the-wool workaholic is a real *perfectionist.* He is merciless in his demands upon himself for thoroughness, mastery, and peak performance. Every operation for a workaholic physician is a dramatic, command performance. Every transaction of a businessman workaholic must be meticulously planned, force-fully accomplished, and followed up for a specific appraisal of the results. The workaholic minister is impeccable in his preparation and delivery of sermons and performs over and above pastoral service to people in dis-tress. The work-addicted salesman will feel double pride in taking care of his personal customers, accounts, and so on.

Another characteristic of this kind of work addict is his *vigorous intol-erance of incompetence* in those who work with him. His relationships with his fellow workers will be cordial, relaxed, and even warm until someone starts blundering—according to his estimate. Then the workaholic is hard, even impossible, to live with at all. He is apparently without qualms as to the consequences of telling off both high and low if he thinks they are doing a sloppy job.

This perfectionism and the corresponding intolerance create a paral-lel relationship to the peer group of the workaholic and to his superiors, or the authority structure. The peer group tends to isolate the workaholic because of his unquestioned competence which makes them feel that he is in a class to himself. Yet, when the real dirty work has to be done, they elect him to do it. They hate his guts but know that he will get the grimier jobs done. For example, he is an ideal candidate to become a union steward. He often is the unofficial and unpaid ombudsman for the organization. Be-cause of his "eccentricity credit"—that is, his earned right to be different, due to sheer accomplishment, and because of his job security and aggres-siveness—his peers say "let him do it." All of them may consider them-selves like Moses, appointed to the supreme leadership, but they think of the work addict as Aaron, who does their talking for them when the going gets rough. In these conditions lie some clues for breaking the power of work addiction.

On the other hand, the executives feel ambivalent about the worka-holic. They *need* him when a program is to be put into action. Yet they fear him. Their authority is an imputed, constituted, official authority. In the long run it has the last word. But they fear the workaholic because his authority is more personal, functional, and earned. In the day-to-day oper-ation of the plant, the company, the school, or the church, the workaholic's presence must always be taken into account in many major and minor deci-sions. A project can be adopted on paper, but it is the workaholic who must translate it into a working, day-to-day, functional reality. In most organiza-tions there is quite a collection of these workaholics. The typical adminis-trator is ambivalent toward them because they are both a blessing and a problem to him. They are a blessing because they get the job done; they are a problem because they have the prestige to buck the boss with some impunity.

A fourth characteristic of the "dyed-in-the-wool" workaholic is his *overcommitment* to the institution, business, or organization for which he works. I have often speculated that some men and women replace their fathers, mothers, or siblings with the institutions they work for. It is not by chance, for example, that a school is called *alma mater*, "our mother." This unconscious cathexis or attachment to a particular institution is the drive shaft of work addiction. I have had an opportunity to study this, since I have collaborated with a number of institutional physicians as they made decisions to change jobs. Their primary commitment was to their profession as doctors, in which they always had the option of private practice as a way of making a living. By contrast, I as a teacher have always had a keen sense of institutional commitment; and prior to the painful reappraisal of my own addiction to work, I was overcommitted to the institutions and organizations with which I was affiliated. They became the be-all and end-all of happiness to me. This led to considerable unnecessary distress, for I could not distinguish between simple loyalty and compulsive overcommitment to an institution. András Angyal is exceptionally helpful here. As a person moves from a pattern of unhealth to one of health, Angyal says, he "can gain a new life only by losing his life as a neurotic. . . . He is assailed by many doubts. . . . If I worry less and drive myself less, shall I become lethargic, lose my ambition, and end as a bum?"[1] But it takes a leap of faith to "let go." The institution is *not* a person, and its life or death does not depend on the anxiety of any one individual.

This discussion of overcommitment is clarified by comparison of the adult workaholic's situation with what Kenneth Keniston calls *un*committedness on the part of alienated youths. He studied what he called "the alienation syndrome" in a group of thirty-six Harvard students. He argues that their alienation is an extreme reaction to "dilemmas of upbringing, to social stresses, and to historical losses that affect their entire generation." One thing was certain: these youths looked upon the world of their parents' social order as a "closed room with a rat race going on in the middle. . . . They expect little in the way of personal fulfillment, growth, or creativity from their future roles in the public world." They were "cool," which "means above all detachment, lack of emotion, absence of deep commitment, not being either enthusiastic *or* rejecting of adulthood."[2]

A final characteristic of the dyed-in-the-wool workaholic is that he usually is talented to begin with and has acquired a set of highly marketable skills. He is much in demand. If he has no effective internal way of rating his priorities, he is likely to take on more and more over and above his prescribed activities. Thus he collides with himself in the face of the many demands laid upon him: he is a perfectionist but he commits himself to so many people for the use of his skills that he cannot do his job well. This results in an anxiety depression amounting to panic. His sleep is more and more curtailed by the sheer problems of scheduling and by his effort to prepare for his responsibilities when he should be sleeping. The morass of contradictory demands is too deep for him to extricate himself, and something has to be done by others to rescue him. His life has become unmanageable.

The Converted Workaholic

A second type of workaholic is the arrested or converted workaholic. He comes from the population just described. He is a "professional," but he has taken seriously the nonprofessional's way of life. The professional man is by nature a round-the-clock person. The nonprofessional is, if he is a farmer, a "sunup-to-sundown" man; if he is an industrial or white-collar nonprofessional, he is a "seven-to-three" or "nine-to-five" man. Also, these nonprofessionals guard their free time jealously. If they use some of it, they have to be paid time and a half; if they work very much overtime, they have to be paid double time.

Therefore the professional who is a converted workaholic requires exceptional pay when people make his five-day week into a seven-, eight-, or nine-day one—but he will do the extra work if paid for it. Also, for the normal day's work, he sets a hypothetical limit and stays within it. For example, it took several illnesses for my body to get the message through to my brain that I was a compulsive worker. Once it did, I decided that I would not travel past midnight, that I would not accept engagements that required my participation morning, afternoon, *and* evening in any one day and come home at a specific time.

Earlier than this, as I have described, my sons had taught me that Saturdays were ours, and I ceased to make Saturday and Sunday appointments. Today it is a regression to workaholism for me, as a professional teacher, lecturer, and writer, to take evening or weekend work assignments. I know that I have offended some of the people with whom I work in a large religious organization by confining my workday to sunup-to-sundown. If I get roped in on additional assignments, you may be sure I was napping, not looking, or at least knew better!

The converted workaholic is a person who lets "every man prove his own work," to quote the apostle Paul. He confesses his intolerance and repents. Several motives can prompt such a change: the energy required in fretting and fuming over other people's failure to function is wasted because this does not even occasionally change their behavior; the feeling of responsibility for other people's performance is unrealistic, because each person has to prove his own work and "every tub has to sit on its own bottom"; and it is sheer arrogance to assume that you and I are *the* judges of what competence is in another person.

Workaholic on the Job

As a work addict turns himself around in ways I have suggested, he begins—much to his surprise—to enjoy more approval from his peers and his superiors. They feel less intimidated by him. He senses that his *work* is not what wins their approval. If he does not work quite so much, they like him better. Strange, but true.

This suggests that the quiet strategy the converted workaholic should adopt is to defer to someone else when extra work (for which there is no extra pay) is about to be loaded upon him. If this is impossible, he can use the occasion to identify problems in the line organization that make it unwise to accept the extra work! This will mean that "the powers that be" will be, on one level, convinced that he is not as reliable as they had first thought and, on a deeper level, relieved that they are now free to choose a less threatening man for the job. If he succeeds in avoiding extra work, the work addict has only one more hurdle to get over. He has yet to go home and tell his wife that he has refused the extra work. Some wives do not see it as extra work; they see it as extra prestige! This kind of wife helps make alcoholics and/or workaholics, depending on the degree of piety in the family. Happy indeed is the man who, when he comes in and announces to his wife that he has refused a prestige assignment because it involved extra work and no extra pay, is greeted by affirmation, approval, and even a kiss.

If, despite all efforts, the extra work cannot be refused for any of the reasons above, another reason is at hand for the man whose character has changed enough to say no at all costs. He best defends himself when he goes back to the *basic satisfactions* of his job. If he is a commercial artist or an architect, he simply says, "I cannot do that because it would take me away from the drawing boards and that is where the company makes its money." If he is a salesman, he refuses to take a desk job at the maximum salary of his commissions. He says, "I can't be happy unless I am closing sales contracts." If he is a teacher, he refuses a department chairmanship because he would be distracted from giving his undivided attention to students. This has been the most valuable discovery for me. I get my basic satisfaction in classroom work, in writing, and in individual counseling of students. Other assignments tend to fret, distract, and preoccupy me. In explaining this to my colleagues, my superiors, and my family, I find understanding and appreciation from all of them. This is the single-hearted way of approaching the problem—all competitive, manipulative, and remunerative considerations laid aside. In fact, the best way of dealing with overcommitment to an institution is to limit your commitment to the main reasons that you chose to be there in the first place.

As I have said, the dyed-in-the-wool workaholic has a set of highly marketable skills. Therefore he is in great demand. If he is a converted workaholic, his problem is in limiting the extra demand that moonlighting opportunities create. The basic income and standard of living of the man and his family have much to do with this. Later, when I discuss the situational workaholic, many variables will be mentioned about this particular factor. However, I am writing on the assumption that the semi-self-employed person is being provided for at an above-subsistence level by his company, school, church, or organization. Moonlighting functions as "over-and-above" work for "over-and-above" benefits. (Often the working wife's salary is for these purposes.) A couple should therefore put a ceiling on the amount of money actually required—including compensation for inflation—to cover wants that are over and above necessities. Then the *number* and the *kind* of additional work assignments can be chosen accordingly. For example, I have decided to earn only x number of dollars by additional work assignments and take per month only that much work.

This sounds simple enough, but it is not that easy. Men and women sometimes take extra work for prestige reasons. A doctor chooses to work six months in a prestigious clinic as an expert in a particular procedure, teaching it to that staff. A professor is called as a consultant on a new project for a government agency or another nation. A minister is asked to do a national television series for his denomination. Too often these jobs pay off in honor, prestige, and publicity, with money a secondary consideration. We might conclude that it is men's egos—not overwork—that kills them!

The element of omnipotence sneaks into the workaholic's thinking. He fantasizes that *he* is the *only* person who can respond to these requests. If for any reason he turns such an opportunity down, however, he may discover that he was fifth or sixth on the list. And if he waits and observes news notices, he will certainly discover that other people followed him on the list. This should teach the work addict the lesson that came to me as good news: I could save myself a lot of additional work if I declined the opportunity and recommended another person. I learned this from an older pastor when I was visiting in his office. While I was there, the phone rang. The call was obviously from someone inviting him to take an important engagement. He declined graciously and said, "Whereas I cannot do this, I wonder if I might mention Mr. X, a new pastor in our state. I know him to be a very competent man for such an opportunity!" Go, and do likewise!

The Situational Workaholic

We come now to the person who is new on his job, is in the "starvation period" of his profession, or is at the lowest pay echelons in his organization. This man overworks out of real necessity, not for inner psychic reasons or for prestige reasons. He may have reasonable job security but large amounts of economic anxiety. It is not a part of this person's basic personality to work incessantly. As his practice becomes established or when his salary rises to a more adequate level, he corrects his course easily and lives more sensibly, letting work recede to a normal place in his value system. Nonetheless he is a candidate for compulsive work addiction. The prestige system of his organization or profession, the prestige needs of his wife, and the kind of neighborhood he lives in all serve to determine his habits. Not the least significant factor is the kind of older colleagues he has as advisers and models for his behavior. Younger men tend to pattern their standards of living, work habits, and approach to life on older professionals. Administrators of schools, hospitals, churches, and professional societies seem to be unaware of this element in their work patterns.

Sometimes the situational workaholic is a person whose job security is minimal. He may be new in a company that has periodic layoffs, and the last to come is the first to go. He may be in a trial period with his organization, such as under a three-year nontenure contract on a university faculty. In overperforming to achieve security, he is often preparing the inner ground for compulsive overwork later on.

The Pseudo-Workaholic

A fourth type of workaholic is one who has many of the characteristics of a true dyed-in-the-wool workaholic, but these are superficial. They are specific competitive accommodations to the pecking order of the organization. This person does his work in order to move from one echelon in the power structure to another. His orientation to work is not a production orientation, as in the case of the dyed-in-the-wool workaholic; his is a power orientation. He does all the right things to ensure promotion. These include having a very active social life that obligates the "right people" to reciprocate his hospitality. It involves doing favors in abundance for power figures in the organization. Thus the pattern of "I've scratched your back, now scratch mine" is set in motion. The focus of interest in choosing things to do on the job is to follow the in-group. If the in-group is thrust out of power for any reason, he shifts, without apparent embarrassment over the inconsistency, to the new in-group although their position and function on major issues is diametrically opposed. This cannot be understood unless it is seen that this man responds consistently to power and not to issues. He is opportunistic in this respect, but he can be counted on to respond this way.

The pseudo-workaholic may be spotted by the lack of perfectionism in his work. He makes many brilliant starts in what he does, but when the prestige of having made a dazzling beginning wears off, the long pull of the carry-through is odious to him. He is likely to leave one project for another very soon. The pseudo-workaholic changes jobs often. He is strictly an image man, not a performance man. Laurence Peter and Raymond Hull state it well when they say, "An ounce of image is worth a pound of performance."[3]

The real commitment of the pseudo-workaholic is to the prestige and power the organization offers *him*. He draws his name *from* the institution; he does not give his name *to* the institution. The institution is strictly a means and in no sense an end in itself. There is not attachment to or affection for the organization. In psychoanalytic jargon, the pseudo-workaholic is narcissistic. As Robert Browning said of one of his characters, this person is deeply in love with himself and probably will win the match!

The pseudo-workaholic, furthermore, moves vigorously and actively until he reaches the limits of the prestige system. Then his real character emerges. He is basically a playboy who, as Peter and Hull say, has been promoted *beyond* the level of his competence and *to* the level of his *in*competence! These men, in their painfully humorous book, lay bare the "Peter Principle" that "for each individual, for *you*, for *me*, the final promotion is from a level of competence to a level of incompetence."[4] The real work "is accomplished by those who have not yet reached their level of incompetence."[5]

I never really found a better explanation than the Peter Principle of a phenomenon I have seen monotonously in educational institutions. Assistant and associate professors carry the burden of the work of the institution (what they themselves do not pan off onto instructors, that is). As one university professor put it, "A *full* professor is one who is *gone full-time*." I have noticed the way in which full professors tend to move in four or five different directions. Some become feverishly concerned with campaigning for a position in the administration of the school. Some become totally absorbed in their hobbies—golf; raising bird dogs, game roosters, horses—to the neglect of their job. Some become full-time invalids, preoccupied with health problems. True, some focus hard on teaching. They are the real oddballs!

These are ways of saying that the pseudo-workaholic is a more populous breed than the dyed-in-the-wool workaholic.

The Escapist Posing as a Workaholic

I would not be true to the facts in describing the different types of workaholics if I did not make note of a very common phenomenon: the person who simply stays on the job—or in the place of work—rather than go home. I noticed this first when I was a page in the United States Senate and discovered there were a few senators who slept in their offices regularly! I will admit that this is extreme, but in a variety of organizations in which I have worked and in a large number of those I have observed, this species of worker exists, even if there are but few of them. A chaotic marriage is the cause for some of these situations. The marriage in which in-laws live in the home is another. I saw one case in which both sets of in-laws lived in the home. In other instances, the worker simply enjoyed the company of the people he worked with more than he did that of the people at home. For this person, work was a substitute home.

Occasionally I have seen single persons make the real mistake of expecting their job to substitute for *all* other relationships. Of course, we have a whole subculture of persons in the Roman Catholic Church who operate on this as an articulate, ordered set of values. But when it occurs without such cultural support and institutional moorings, the effects can be very frustrating, unsatisfying, and confusing.

These persons are not, ordinarily, workaholics in the sense of being compulsive workers. For them, work is an escape, and this is very different from compulsion.

SOME GUIDING PRINCIPLES ON THE JOB

It is one thing to curse the power-and-light company and another to light a candle. I think it is time to light a candle. I have done my share of the other. Some principles of health for a group of workers in a bureaucratic situation are the following:

First, a man or a woman should fear like a plague the fate of being given a new position that calls for skills in which he is not interested, for which he has not been trained, and which do not afford him basic job satisfaction. The usual reason for going into such work is not ordinarily financial. Rather, it is prestige and power. These are like salt water. Salt water does all the things fresh water does—it is wet and cool, it washes, and so on—except the one thing we need water most to do—quench thirst. Power without work satisfaction is the same: it just makes you want more.

Second, the man on the job should decide what he can best do and do it with single-minded devotion. A devout people would call this being at peace in the intention of God for our lives. Regardless of what one's image in other people's eyes may be, this should be what he strives for.

Third, health in relation to work may require that the worker reappraise his family relationships and decide that he is going to exercise leadership in his own home. An ancient Christian source suggests, for example, that the person who accepts a position of responsibility in the church must first have demonstrated effective leadership in his own home. The worker cannot continue to be intimidated by the prestige needs and money drives of his wife and children. He must lead them.

Fourth, the worker needs to begin developing a sense of humor if he does not already have one. The rollicking sense of humor with which Laurence Peter and Raymond Hull tell in a serious jest about how incompetency in an organization rises, like cream, to the top and there sours is a wholesome example of what I mean.

NOTES

1. András Angyal, *Neurosis and Treatment: A Holistic Theory*, ed. E. Hanfmann and R. M. Jones (New York: John Wiley & Sons, 1965), p. 240.

2. Kenneth Keniston, *The Uncommitted: Alienated Youth in American Society* (New York: Harcourt, Brace & World, 1965), pp. 18, 397.

3. Laurence Peter and Raymond Hull, *The Peter Principle* (New York: Bantam Books, 1969), p. 121.

4. Ibid., p. 8.

5. Ibid., p. 10.

17

The Religion
of the Workaholic

A certain kind of *devotion* seeps through every aspect of a *confirmed* workaholic's being. He is over*committed* to his work.

As you reread the above paragraph, you see the italicized words *devotion*, *confirmed*, and *committed*. Placed in an ecclesiastical context, these words can become "god talk." Work is a kind of religion to the workaholic. The plan here is to describe the religious situation of the confirmed or dyed-in-the-wool workaholic, to reflect upon the meaning of conversion as a psychological process in the life of the workaholic, and to discuss the positive faith of a person who is a converted workaholic.

THE FUTURE OF THE WORKAHOLIC

The workaholic is a person who has trouble with the future. He elides the future with the present to such an extent that he destroys the present in the process. This means to me that he pins his hopes on what he can do to ward off the specters of meaninglessness, poverty, calamity, and hopelessness that the very idea of the future represents to him. Yet the crucial factor in a healthy religion is hope—a belief in the unseen realities of the present and the future. Lack of such belief, and the associated feeling that everything must happen immediately or not at all, is the real religious problem of the workaholic. The concern of the person guiding the religious life of the workaholic, then, should be to come to grips with his pervasive feeling of futurelessness.

THE RELIGIOUS SITUATION OF THE
CONFIRMED WORKAHOLIC

A Child of His Times

The confirmed workaholic is a man of unclean lips in his worship of work, to paraphrase the prophet Isaiah, and he lives among people who are also of unclean lips. Yet he practices a highly sanctioned way of life. Some people have identified it as a Protestant malady, but close observation of Catholics and Jews indicates that they suffer from the addiction as much as do Protestants. The so-called Protestant work ethic can be summarized as follows: a universal taboo is placed on *idleness*, and *industriousness* is considered a religious ideal; *waste* is a vice, and *frugality* a virtue; complacency and failure are outlawed, and *ambition* and *success* are taken as sure signs of God's favor; the universal sign of sin is *poverty*, and the crowning sign of God's favor is *wealth*. The Hebrew Bible is filled with evidence of this way of life; the prudential ethic of the book of Proverbs is one reflection of it, and the kinds of questions the disciples asked of Jesus are another—for example, when the rich young man turned away from Jesus, the disciples asked, "Who then can be saved?" My point is that the workaholic's personal religion—quite apart from his denominational affiliation—reflects the ethic of industriousness, frugality, ambition, and success as primary virtues. To reject these is to go against the grain of his religious culture. Honoring them, he has the sanction of his religious community, which not only approves his ideals but gladly welcomes his financial contributions. That he may be idolatrous in respect to his own achievements does not even come into question.

A Victim of Success

In earlier times, success and wealth as assurances of salvation most often came at the end of a man's life span. Not many men long survived the period of reaching the top. Now, however, the life span of Americans has increased to such an extent that when workaholics achieve worldly success they generally still have ten to thirty years of life ahead of them. Where do they go from the "top"?

Success has a way of becoming a burden in a society in which there are so many pseudo-workaholics who take ambition and success seriously without taking industry and frugality to heart at all. Their only hope is to "fake it," modeling their behavior on that of the so-called heroes of the work faith, the true work addicts. But sometimes success may become such a burden to work addicts that they want out. They may misbehave in some way—revert to an old pattern of wine or women (but this time no song);

232

put their hand into the company till; or get into difficulties with the establishment and get fired.

A few more fortunate people will be like the five men described in a recent issue of *Life* magazine. All these men had achieved success—one as a salesman, one as a stockbroker, one an insurance executive, one a veterinarian, and one a policeman. They all changed their type of work to something that let them *live* as well as work. They were between the ages of thirty-five and fifty—as *Life* says, "the years of heightened susceptibility to alcohol, heart attack, worry, and divorce." They all had the enthusiastic cooperation of their wives; as one of them said, "I knew she was the kind who wasn't a prestige seeker, or I wouldn't have married her in the first place."[1]

These persons have gotten off the success treadmill. They may work as much as ever, but with a difference: they are not compelled to do so, they share their work with their families, and they are doing what they enjoy. They have renewed their lives.

Not many people make such leaps. To do so is so newsworthy that it is written up in a popular national magazine. The great majority who become victims of success stay in a field or job long after it has lost its challenge. Too often they wait for sickness or accident to make the decision for them. Many die without getting a second wind in life. The greatest tragedy is that the springs of both joy and creativity dry up in their lives. Many suffer until the age of retirement. They are obviously successful but on the defensive with the whole world. This may even be worse than death.

CHARACTERISTICS OF THE
PERSONAL RELIGION OF THE WORK ADDICT

When we dare enter the private sanctuary of the confirmed work addict's personal religion, we find an ambiguous interplay of contrasting values. It is not pure light or pure darkness. For example, the work addict is a blend of loneliness and solitude. Loneliness is the hopeless side of being by oneself; solitude is the joyful side. He may be a sporadic church attender. He may have the desire instead to go back to his work if he can be there alone, unbothered by the other employees; this is a rather common and unnoticed ritual of many people. Or he may have worked himself, as Viktor Frankl says, into stupefaction and want simply to be alone. He may be so preoccupied that he does not want to be with his family. Thus his loneliness appears.

But on the other hand, being by himself may instead produce some of his most creative times of communion with God, with nature, with himself, and all the regenerative forces of his life. His survival as a person may depend on his being alone. This is a paradox. He may choose not to go to church because he will just encounter more people and more voices there. Unlike the farmer who may have worked in comparative solitude all week, he has been in meetings, heard and delivered speeches and exhortations, and dealt with public and community problems all week. To go to church is a "rerun." He prefers a religion of solitude as one way of maintaining the integrity of his being. As Nicolas Berdyaev says, "Only when man is alone . . . does he become aware of his personality, of his originality, of his singularity and uniqueness, of his distinctness from everyone and everything else. A man may feel himself definitely more alone in the midst of his co-religionists than in the midst of men of totally different beliefs and persuasions."[2] Lord Byron expressed something of the inner world of each of us when he wrote in *Childe Harold's Pilgrimage*:

> There is a pleasure in the pathless woods,
> There is a rapture on the lonely shore,
> There is society where none intrudes,
> By the deep Sea, and music in its roar:
> I love not Man the less, but Nature more,
> From these our interviews, in which I steal
> From all I may be, or have been before,
> To mingle with the Universe, and feel
> What I can ne'er express, yet can not all conceal.

Narrowed Consciousness and Meditation

Times of solitude in the workaholic's life widen his consciousness and put him in touch with what is really important in life. But they are rare indeed, for his ordinary way of life is highly constricted. His area of consciousness is greatly narrowed. He is aware of this and has several phrases for it: he says he is in a rut; he is chained to the oars like a galley slave; he labors in the salt mines; he has his nose to the grindstone. However he describes it, he becomes anxious at the thought of what he is missing, at how short life is, and at what a hurry he is in.

In theological language, this narrowed perspective of the job as the sum total of existence is what Paul Tillich called idolatry. Something less than God is treated and valued *as if* it were God; a *limited* concern is put in the place of the unlimited and ultimate concern in life. The end result is to turn one's life over to the demonic, to become possessed—in this case, by one's job.

The work addict may be said to have a *poverty* of objects of attention. He is bound to the automatic perceptions, feelings, and centers of awareness of his job. He cannot see the whole architecture of life, because he has his eye on one brick. Nor can he *feel* anything except that it is *he* who holds that brick in place and that if he did not, the whole structure would collapse. Furthermore, he acts as if that whole structure upholds the universe. None of this is so.

Persons involved in religious institutions seem to be particularly vulnerable to this kind of idolatry. It is one thing for a minister or a religious worker to sing, "I love Thy Church, O God; her walls before thee stand . . ." It is quite another to fix one's eye upon those walls so closely that one cannot see the Lord or anything else! Such a person needs a diversionary kind of work, preferably a skilled trade that he enjoys in order to establish his separation from the church as an idol. I know a minister who is a skilled cabinetmaker. He has made beautiful furniture for his own home and sold a few pieces for fun. He *could* make his living at it. This both liberates him and reminds his church people that they do not own him. Doing this work in his leisure time, he finds that his whole perspective on his other responsibilities is widened.

Religion of Works and Productivity

Another characteristic of the religion of the confirmed workaholic is that he seeks to *merit* everything he gets. The idea of unearned acceptance and love, commonly called "grace" in theological language, is known to him only intellectually if at all.

Much has been said by theologians in the vein of Dietrich Bonhoeffer about "cheap grace," that is, a religion that salves people's conscience and lulls them into moral inattention to great social issues. Bonhoeffer had seen this during the Hitler regime. We see evidences of it in America today. Such psychotherapists as O. Hobart Mowrer argue that we have pushed the business of redemption without proper amends in good works too far. Yet the workaholic is a compulsive caricature of Bonhoeffer's and Mowrer's best intention. He does not take forgiveness from God or anyone else without paying, and paying, and paying. He is a person who *works* his way into your heart. He produces everything—on his own.

Childish Omnipotence

The reason the workaholic has a religion of work and works is that he or she thus maintains the illusion of all-powerfulness. He tries to be his own god, a trait that Sigmund Freud said is characteristic of the human race. The illusion tends to erase awareness of personal death and leaves us with the assumption that we are not only all-powerful but immortal.

Fatalism and Harsh Realism

A final characteristic of the confirmed work addict's religion is that he is a fatalist. He will, upon reading this book, say, "Yes. Much of what you say is true, but there is nothing anybody can do about it. It has always been this way and always will be." This means that he deeply feels that he has no power of decision over his own life. He is realistic to a fault. He always expects the worst and has never been disappointed; if things by chance do turn out well, it is the result of accident, luck, or winning against impossible odds. This is the sort of opinion which of course cannot be disconfirmed. Little wonder he relies upon magic—his own.

The Workaholic at Church

No discussion of the workaholic's religion is complete without an appraisal of him as a churchman. For many workaholics, the job is their church, and the actual church is a place for their wives and children, to which they themselves go only under social pressure. Once the workaholic gets there, he is preoccupied with events of the last week and plans for the next. Physically, he is present; spiritually, he is not. I recall one morning when a woman and her husband sat next to us at church. She had to punch her husband in the ribs to get him to put their offering in the plate as it passed. We all chuckled quietly together. He said, "She had to tell me to write the check before we left home. Now she has to tell me to put it in the plate." She remarked, "He was a long way from here." I said, "Your husband and I really would be at a loss without our wives when we are at church!"

On the other hand, there are some workaholics who make of church itself another form of their addiction. Each Sunday, they arise early and go to bed late. Every available moment in between is filled with an assignment of church work. The religion is another form of the compulsion.

When I was a pastor of a small church in the Bluegrass section of Kentucky, a mother of a fourteen-year-old boy brought him to me after the evening service. She said to me, "What am I going to do with Gordon? He would not come to church this afternoon. He wanted to play. He got mad. He said, 'Church, church, church! That's all I hear!' Now, Mr. Oates, what do you think of him?" The boy was terribly embarrassed. I said to him, "Gordon, I know exactly how you feel. All *I* hear is 'church,' and sometimes I get tired. And when I get real tired of church the next time, I am coming to see you, because I know you will understand." Then I turned to his mother and said, "Anybody who has never gotten tired of church just never has been to church much."

At its positive core, though, the religion of the workaholic may not be even a Sunday religion. It is an overworked weekday religion of practical good deeds to other people. He knocks himself out helping people, but unless he is converted, he does so as a means of controlling them, placing them in his debt, or at least making them feel uneasy. It is not until a basic change takes place in him that this doing good becomes less ambiguous and more relaxed, a source of pleasure.

THE PROCESS OF CONVERSION IN THE LIFE OF A WORK ADDICT

The radical self-encounter that resulted in my own right-about-face in my work habits I have referred to from time to time. When I draw it all together, I would summarize it this way. The first dawnings of awareness came to me through my sons, who insisted as little boys that I change my ways. I took them seriously, but only partly mended my ways. The second phase of self-confrontation came in a period when I was suffering from a pinched spinal nerve. Whenever I overworked, it would throw me down, at times literally. The real spiritual crisis came when my sons were old enough to have a minimum need of me and when, because of successful surgery on the third attempt, my back was made strong and well. Then I had to face the fact that I had made a fetish and idol of work, that institutional commitments were really overcommitments, that life was really meant to be enjoyed without paying for it with work, that I needed people for their own sakes and not as a means of accomplishing my work goals, and that the *now* of life is the nectar of being.

Probably what drove me to the bottom of the pit of despair was my agony over the safety of our elder son. He was a combat sailor, a machine-gunner on a small river assault boat in the Mekong Delta in Vietnam for a year. I was helpless. None of *my* actions or work could change a thing. I found myself falling back heavily on extra work to handle my anxiety. When for two months I had no work responsibility in the summer, my major defense was gone. I faced it alone before God. I realized that I could not face it alone but that I needed God's help and the help of all the other people that I could get. I learned to laugh at my work compulsions and, as Viktor Frankl terms it, to "de-reflect" them. I shifted my attention to the things I fundamentally enjoyed thinking about and doing, and I did these things. For example, when it came to accepting an extra engagement for more work, I used a new criterion—not *should* I do this, or *must* I do this? but will this be enjoyable, will it be fun, in the sense of the Westminster Catechism: "The chief end of man is to glorify God, and to enjoy him forever"? The criterion I am using now is thus not enjoying myself in the superficial sense, but enjoyment of God wherever *he is*, not was, not will be. Sam Keen put what was happening to me best: "I was coming home to the obvious. After squandering much of my time in the future and the past I was returning to my native time—the present. I had not learned how to cultivate the now, to live gracefully in the present, to love the actual, but I was no longer in exile."[3]

This is the simple unraveling of preoccupation, because being "somewhere else" is either *yesterday* or *tomorrow*, not *now*. Living in the moment means the release of much of that irritability which we feel toward someone here and now who tries to pull us out of the past or future into the present. Furthermore, it reduces our haste, because if we *are* where we intend to be, why hurry to get someplace else? And it does away with much depression, because frequently sadness arises from reliving the past or from apprehensiveness for the future.

This is all dramatically illustrated by an experience I had in the airport at Birmingham, Alabama. I had arrived at the airport late and was running wildly past other people in the concourse to get to my flight. I passed two men, who said, "Hey, mister, don't hurry." I stopped suddenly, turned about, and said, "Why?" One of them answered, "Because *we* are the pilots of your flight!" We all broke into laughter. So—if the pilot is in no hurry, why should I be?

The Psychology of the Workaholic's Conversion

Some of the ideas of Harry M. Tiebout about the psychological effects of conversion upon addiction patterns in alcoholics are useful in widening our perspective on the process in workaholics.

Tiebout describes the alcoholic as tense, depressed, aggressive or at least quietly stubborn, oppressed with feelings of inferiority and at the same time acting quite superior, perfectionistic and rigid, overpowered with a sense of loneliness, basically self-centered, defiant, living in a world apart from others. I have said that work as well as alcohol aids and abets these tendencies and when pursued compulsively will produce a similar personality profile. The process of conversion comes from the group experience of challenge by a more positive set of attitudes. Essentially both alcohol and work addictions are negations of life. The group conversion process challenges this negation by making possible a personal affirmation of life. It is a definite choice of life as opposed to death. Tiebout says that religion "too often has been identified with its dogmas and not its essence of spirituality. It is not the form religion takes; it is its function in achieving a frame of mind that is significant."[4] I would modify his statement somewhat to say that dogma is too often a screen for the things that make workaholics of men: prestige, accumulation of material goods, and the exercise of self-effort, as opposed to the satisfactions of belonging to an accepting fellowship.

THE RELIGIOUS OUTLOOK OF THE CONVERTED WORKAHOLIC

I have already given a general description of the life-style of the converted workaholic. Here I want to discuss his specific religious situation. He is not completely different, but neither will he ever be the same again.

A Forgiving Attitude

The genuinely converted workaholic is aware that his own estimate of competence is in itself incomplete. If he perceived himself as a "prophet of competence" prior to his conversion, now he knows that his prophecies are incomplete. He still values his competence highly. Yet he allows Lebensraum or spiritual territory for those around him and even actively searches for specific examples of their unique abilities. These are the topics of his conversation instead of the person's weaknesses, incompetency, and unworthiness. He becomes patient instead of intolerant.

A Sense of Irony and Humor

As the workaholic develops a new way of life, he learns how to stand off from himself and his fellow workers from time to time and laugh ironically *at* himself and humorously *with* them as they laugh at themselves. Because the converted workaholic now has a more secure, self-accepting attitude toward himself, he can jestingly say to others some fairly hard negative things about himself which they themselves half believe but do not have the courage to say. And their perception of his inner strength allows them to laugh with him. For example, any person who works as much with the mentally ill as I do is likely to be thought of by a few people as somewhat odd in his own right. I simply admit it! People enjoy it when I say it. In my previous way of life, I could not have said it humorously, and if someone else had, it would have been a high insult.

A more important observation is that this irony and humor spring from a person's new awareness that God's acceptance is freely given and not earned by the sweat of one's brow.

A Sense of Wonder and Awe

The harassed workaholic has little time or appreciation for the experience of wonder and awe. For example, it is now over a year ago that our son returned from the war. I am always filled with awe and wonder when I see him—strong, safe, well, and happy. He brought back with him a quiet devotion to the children of Vietnam. I can participate in the beauty and tragedy of these children's lives, and I am able to participate in the lives of all children. The world of nature—plants, flowers, and animals—has widened the range of my attention. I have become keenly aware again that reading is for exploration and adventure and not just for the sake of title dropping or keeping up with the academic Joneses. At the same time, I do not read as much as I did before, because I now am able to experience wonder and awe in conversation with people, and from a few television shows and some movies, and stage plays.

A De-Programming of Corporate Worship

Much effort goes into the programming of the religious behavior of people. Some of this effort is expended by unreconstructed, religion-oriented workaholics. The religion of the converted workaholic certainly is not one of disdain for the results of these people's labors and most certainly not for the people themselves. However, the converted workaholic hopes that the religionists will come face-to-face with themselves before old age and retirement force them into a corner of unmitigated disgust, despair, and hopelessness.

The hopes of the *unconverted* workaholic are almost always *deferred* hopes, religiously speaking. He thinks as Kipling did in his "L'Envoi":

> When earth's last picture is painted, and the tubes are twisted and dried,
> When the oldest colours have faded, and the youngest critic has died,
> We shall rest, and—faith, we shall need it—lie down for an aeon or two,
> Till the Master of All Good Workmen shall set us to work anew!
> . . . .
> And only the Master shall praise us, and only the Master shall blame;
> And no one shall work for money, and no one shall work for fame;
> But each for the joy of the working, and each, in his separate star,
> Shall draw the Thing as he sees It for the God of Things as They Are!

This kind of *deferred* gratification in the hereafter is a positive consolation for the scourge that work is here and now. What I wish for, however, is the de-programming of such deferred hopes. *Some* of these aspirations should be realized in the present. If churches will settle for less real estate, less "money and fame," and fewer structures of organized religion, the enjoyment of God will be more possible to more people more often.

The converted workaholic tends normally to keep his need for solitude. Going to church can nourish this need in a very positive way, for one can experience a degree of solitude and at the same time be accessible to other church members. Some people I know live and breathe as a somewhat inconspicuous part of their church. They do not try to become acquainted with everyone in the congregation. They know a few people in profound intimacy, but they do not take the activist approach to church life and worship. Some specific types of people in the church—for example, the older people, the little children, and occasionally an adolescent who has trouble belonging to the teenage "scene"—have a deep appreciation for the person who lives his life in slower motion. The converted work addict can find a quiet fellowship with these persons. Then, too, there are always a few other people whose experience with work has been similar to his. They too can provide comradeship.

The Catholic Church reveres Joseph, the father of Jesus, as a saint. They sing a hymn to him, one stanza of which is as follows:

Joseph, workmen's inspiration,
Man of faith and charity,
Make us honest, faithful, strong
With Christ's true liberty,
Make our labor and our leisure
Fruitful to eternity.

The idea of labor and leisure both being fruitful to eternal life is the highest good of the converted workaholic's faith.

The mix of work and leisure in faith is best nurtured in our accepting the fellowship of people who share our problems, can make a common confession of their plight, and join in a quest for a more sane way of living. One of the prayers I have is that this material will become a basis of communication out of which will grow groups of persons who share the dilemmas of work addiction. Being a churchman of sorts myself, I hope that churches may be one of the meeting grounds for these purposes. But I hope that they will not be the only ones. I could hope that management concerns, business establishments, schools, and universities will be places of meeting also. All of these, like the church, tend to be ghettos of a sort. I hope this material will open new ways of life and will help men and women to break out of old ones.

NOTES

1. *Life,* June 12, 1970, p. 56.

2. Nicolas Berdyaev, *Solitude and Society* (London: Geoffrey Bles: The Centenary Press, 1938), pp. 68–69, 92.

3. Sam Keen, *The Dance of Life* (New York: Harper & Row, 1970), p. 21.

4. Harry M. Tiebout, "Conversion as a Psychological Phenomenon (in the Treatment of the Alcoholic)," *Pastoral Psychology* 2, no. 13 (April 1951): 34.

Part Five

THE WORD AND THE
HOLY SPIRIT

18

The Symbolic Use
of the Bible

The Bible has an overwhelming symbolic strength. The fact that a statement is in the Bible endows that statement with a peculiar power, for weal or for woe. To the person who lives next to nature, who is relatively unsophisticated, and who has not developed a critical worldview, the Bible is even as the Ark of the Covenant: to lay unconsecrated hands upon it is to die. This symbolic significance of the Bible lives on also in the more primitive consciousness of apparently sophisticated people, who express their uneasiness by never talking about it, by allowing it to remain in the realm of the mysterious to them, or by compulsively rejecting its wisdom with an undifferentiated prejudice.

The Bible as a symbol has many uses in the counseling ministry of a pastor. He may use it as a means of identifying himself as a minister of religion to those with whom he counsels. A copy of the Bible in full sight on the minister's desk immediately identifies him as a Christian to the person who comes to his study for counsel. It has always been fascinating to me to observe a person who comes to my office as his gaze shifts half-consciously to the bookshelves and to the objects on my desk. The pictures of my family identify me as a husband and a father, the picture of Jesus and the rich young ruler identifies me as a friend of Jesus, and the Bible identifies me as one who may be able to deal with some of the person's questions about it. All these symbols do much to clarify my relationships in life to the person who seeks my help, thereby relieving me of the necessity of too much explanatory conversation.

The nonliturgical Protestant minister, who wears no special clerical garb, quite regularly finds himself at a loss as to how to identify himself to strangers when he visits them. But the stranger who sits down beside someone on a train, bus, or plane who is reading the Bible usually presumes that he is sitting by a minister. The relatively uniform appearance of most Bibles has given a clarity to its symbolism. So often is this true that the minister who is not particularly eager to appear as a "holier than thou" person as he travels is grateful for the publication of Bibles in bindings like other books. Nevertheless the stranger who sees the black leather-bound, India-paper volume knows in a deep way to whom he is speaking and who speaks to him.

The Bible can be used as a symbol to great advantage in certain difficult pastoral care situations. Examples from my own ministry are illustrative.

I was called to a local hospital at the request of a woman whom I did not know at all. The woman, according to the nurse, was deaf and was at the point of death. She wanted a minister in her last hour. I happen to belong to a denomination in which the ministers wear no distinguishing symbols of clothing. The woman could not distinguish me from a doctor, and I was not able to tell her verbally who I was because she was deaf. In order to communicate with her, I reached into my pocket and produced a small, black, gilt-edged Bible. I held it before her and began to read. She smiled a light of recognition. I prayed, folded my hands in reverence, hoping she could read lips. She faintly smiled her gratitude.

Another person whom I served as pastor over the tedious months of a chronic illness lived in a humble rural home. She had served her church and her family well and had leaned heavily upon the Bible. As her pastor, I knew the quiet symbolism of the shift of her gaze as she began to tire of conversation. She would turn her face away from me to a spot behind a little radio on her bedside table. There was a worn and much-read Bible. Her shifted gaze always told me in a tacit understanding that she wanted me to read to her. This was an unspoken liturgy of the spirit reenacted at each visit. The Bible to her was a symbol of an understood fellowship of prayer in suffering.

However, honest attention must be given here to the misuse of the Bible as a symbol. It may become little more than a fetish with which to cajole the demons that possess the spirits of men. As such it may become an instrument of the demonic, and the devil will begin to cite scripture for his own purposes.

For instance, a thirty-two-year-old man was plagued by homosexual thoughts and caught in the grip of homosexual habits. He went to his pastor with his problem, in order to get guidance, relief, and hope. His pastor gave him strong advice about how to control himself and gave him a copy of the Bible to read in the midst of his temptations. He said, "When you go to bed at night, place this Bible under your pillow, and it will drive away your evil thoughts and dreams and help you to rest." The man was at the time on the verge of a paranoid mental breakdown, and a few more days of faithful adherence to his pastor's guidance hastened his hospitalization. The point at which I interviewed the patient was in the receiving ward of a state hospital of which I was chaplain at the time. He felt at that time that God had given him up to "a reprobate mind" and that he should die. Here the Bible was used as a fetish, sincerely intended to heal; actually, however, it became a tool of the self-destructive processes already in motion in his life.

Such an example of the unwitting malpractice of ministers clearly illustrates two important clinical pastoral observations that need to be noted here. First, the pastor who carefully observes the *effects* of his use of the Bible in pastoral care situations soon begins to feel the heavy pull of authoritarianism added to his relationship by his use of it. If he is as concerned as he should be about maintaining a "permissive" relationship of relaxation, free of threat, he finds that the Bible often reduces permissiveness, creates tension, and introduces elements of threat into his pastoral context.

Why is this? It is because the Bible is nothing but a symbol of authority to many people. Culturally, the Bible is a transversal symbol of authority in the social structure of Protestantism and in the religious consciousness of Protestants. It is the minister's task to see to it that in his community the Bible is not just a symbol of authority but that it has actual meaning as well. As a symbol of authority, the Bible is both a sword and a shield for the pastor. It becomes easily an instrument whereby the minister expresses his hostility and a means of protection when he feels threatened. When the minister finds himself in an environment in which the Bible is not an agreed-upon symbol of culture and authority, as is true in a large university or on a mission field, he discovers the necessity of translating the Bible out of the realm of the authoritarian and the symbolic into the realm of the interpreted meaningfulness and the interpersonal realities that are understandable by those with whom he deals and whose suffering he seeks to relieve. It was just such a ministry that Jesus rendered when he reinterpreted the scriptures so that they gave life rather than destroyed it. The lament that Isaiah felt in his day becomes a challenge to the modern minister: "The vision of all is become unto you as the words of a book that is sealed, which men deliver to one that is learned, saying, Read this, I pray thee: and he saith, I cannot; for it is sealed: And the book is delivered to him that is not learned, saying, Read this, I pray thee: and he saith, I am not learned" (Isa. 29:11–12).

This points to the second clinical pastoral observation, that is, much of the damage done by ministers in their misuse of the Bible is caused by their own undisciplined dependence upon its symbolic use rather than their careful use of it as a teaching come from God. That was the weakness of the pastor's methodology in telling the man to trust in the Bible by putting it under his pillow. The healing power of scriptural truth lies in its appropriation by means of a deepened insight and quickened understanding, not by the fearful use of the book itself as a symbol for worship. The Bible may be misused even as a symbol of the cross, which is too often taken as a trinket to hang around the neck. Both may be little more than good-luck charms. Such a use of the cross is vastly different from being able to say, "I have been crucified with Christ."

Also, the absence of ritual among nonliturgical Protestants has resulted in their ritualistic use of "daily Bible-reading," without investing it with meaning, direction, and purpose. This feeds the obsessional trends within a personality, and great care should be used when urging people in groups to read their Bibles daily. Care should be used to follow up these exhortations with specific ways in which the Bible may be used, and as much personal supervision should be given to the reading as possible. Small-group discussions should be developed in such a way that the reading becomes a means of meeting specific personal needs, and not merely an end within itself whereby the patient atones for his guilt, allays his anxieties, and appeases the wrath of the pastor.

Examples of the misuse of the Bible as a symbol cause many persons, particularly psychologists and psychiatrists, to react negatively and to avoid its every appearance in the thought life of troubled people. Some pastors might feel that the use of the Bible with people who are hostile toward religion drives them farther from it still, and that the use of the Bible with fanatically religious persons increases their blindness.

My own answer to this is that these hostilities and prejudices need to be evaluated in the beginning and that it is better for the person to know from the beginning that he is talking to a minister if the relationship is to move honestly and smoothly. If the person feels hostile, it is better that the pastor know it as early as possible. But more than that, I feel that many people with whom we deal are so uninformed religiously that they will have little or no feeling about a Bible as a symbol. They will prefer that the pastor minister to them on a purely "horizontal" or human level. A minister needs to identify himself from the beginning by defining his relationship, to say the least, by the presence of one of the agreed-upon symbols of Protestant Christianity—the Bible—on his desk, in his waiting room, and in his living room at home.

But the main reason for such a contention is that the majority of the people to whom the pastor ministers are persons for whom the Bible has a positive, healthy, and precious meaning. It represents comfort and strength in the presence of life's typical crises—birth, baptism, marriage, parenthood, disappointment, pain, and death. They see it as a source of light and truth, as the one thing most dependable in the welter and confusion of all that they see and hear. It symbolizes security and understanding, truth and love. It symbolizes judgment for the things that they know to be wrong by any standard of wisdom they themselves would choose. Therefore they respond to the symbol and the teacher who accompanies it as an ethically well-balanced friend responds to an ethically well-balanced friend.

The pastor who is honest with himself, however, knows that some of the people who do feel deeply affectionate toward the Bible and its profound communications nevertheless present to him a distorted religious consciousness. Their use of the Bible is in keeping with the pathology of their personalities. The mentally sick person often expresses his problem in age-old symbols, and the symbols of the Bible become means whereby he desperately attempts to communicate his distress to a world of "average" conformists to a superficial reality with which he is losing, or has lost, touch. It is as if he were on an Isle of Patmos, fearful of speaking plainly lest his captors destroy him; therefore he phrases his revelations of the inner world in symbols that appear as nonsense to the outer world of threatening dictatorships. He depends upon the minister as an interpreter to discern his meaning.

Thus the symbols of the Bible become the language of the spirit between the acutely disturbed patient and the minister as the minister goes "underground" into the labyrinthine catacombs of the inner world with a mental patient who is religiously conscious and states his problem in the symbols of the Bible.[1]

The Bible is the pastor's "royal road" to the deeper levels of the personalities of his people, and particularly to those who are deeply disturbed. Traditionally the Bible has been used by ministers as a means of reassurance and comfort to people whom they visit and who come to them for counseling help. More recently, Bonnell and Dicks have stimulated a fresh appreciation of the Bible as devotional literature in pastoral care and as an instrument of religious discipline.

The use of the Bible as an instrument of diagnosis, however, needs initial attention and extended study. The question needs to be asked, "Does the biblical material in the stream of speech of an emotionally disturbed person give a pastor a 'royal road' toward understanding something of the dynamic causes of the person's distress?"

Oskar Pfister, in his book *Christianity and Fear*,[2] gives a positive, generalized answer when he says, "Tell me what you find in the Bible, and I will tell you what you are." Here the Bible is seen, not only as a record of the revelation of God to men, but as an instrument of the revelation of the personality of both the minister and the person with whom he counsels.

This concept is suggested by at least one passage in the Bible itself. In James 1:22–24, the writer says "Be doers of the word, and not hearers only, deceiving yourselves. For if any one is a hearer of the word and not a doer, he is like a man who observes his natural face in a mirror; for he observes himself and goes away and at once forgets what he was like." The implication is that the Bible is a mirror into which a person projects his own concepts of himself and which in turn reflects it back with accuracy.

The Bible, then, is to the Protestant pastor as dream symbolism and superego functions are to the psychoanalyst. The meaningful symbols and ethical realities of the Bible have dynamic connections with the forces at work in the less accessible areas of the personality of the counselee. As a fast-moving epic of human history, the Bible story itself is a psychodrama of abiding fidelity to the functional laws of personality. Likewise, the Bible as a book of pictorial illustration is to the pastor what the thematic apperception test is to the clinical psychologist. As Gardner Murphy describes this test, it is based upon the principle that the individual has specific needs that occur in response to the "press" of the environmental situation. A unified expression and need are perceived out of the individual's total background of experience and projected upon art forms in a mirrorlike fashion. The objective of the test is to get "a wide diversity of individual interpretations given."[3]

Applying this principle and objective to his use of the Bible as a means of insight into the deeper problems of people, the pastor himself is reminded of the fact that the main frustration he has faced in the use of the Bible has been that among Protestants there is such a "wide diversity of interpretations given." These interpretations may be of very little value as accurate objective exegeses of the scripture, but they are of intrinsic subjective value as reflections of what manner of person the individual is who gives the interpretations. In a word, the interpretation reflects more concerning the interpreter and his life situation than it does of the Bible itself.

Especially is this true in the case of acutely disturbed persons. The more secure and mature a person is, the more capable he is of discerning and interpreting accurately the meaning and content of the Bible. The less secure and more immature a person is, the more likely he will be to quote scripture for his own purposes. In these latter cases, the pastor (granted that he himself is secure, mature, and informed in his own relation to the Bible and also the psychodynamics of personality) can get a fairly clear-cut understanding of the life situation of the person with whom he is counseling as well as a feeling for the purposive drift of his life energies.

Three clinical examples of these facts demonstrate best the diagnostic use of the Bible.

Mrs. M. H. is a 24-year-old woman, married, with no children. She came to her pastor's attention when she complained of having committed the unpardonable sin, which she interpreted as "cursing God." She felt that she had called God a g—d— s.o.b., and that there was no forgiveness.

Later, she was admitted to a general hospital as the patient of a private psychiatrist. The psychiatrist interpreted her problem to the pastor as arising from "feelings of inadequacy in her estimate of herself as a woman, as a sexual partner, and as a social being." He diagnosed her as a severe obsessional neurotic with schizoid tendencies. The recurrent obsessive "cursing thoughts" and self-derogatory attitudes were interpreted as a sort of mental hypochondriasis.

The patient was preoccupied with scripture verses and constantly demanded interpretations of the following passages in the New Testament: "These scripture verses keep worrying me, and I cannot figure my way out: 'If you repent and then continue in sin, there is no way to repent again without crucifying Christ afresh' " (a paraphrase of Heb. 6:4–6, and 10:26–27). On the second interview, she said, "I think of myself as the wicked servant in the parable of the talents. I have taken my gifts and buried them, and I have a master who is too hard for me. I want to submit myself to him, but I just can't seem to do so fully." On the fourth interview, she repeated this parable and gave an added interpretation: "I just don't seem to be able to use myself like I want to—it's myself—I just can't seem to do so."

On a fifth interview, she asked this question: "What does that scripture mean when it says that men and women should not be married who are unequally yoked together?" (compare this paraphrase with 2 Cor. 6:14; 1 Cor. 6:6; and Deut. 22:10 for the disparity between the historical record and the projected effect).

The history detail shows that this woman was a Presbyterian before her marriage. After marriage she joined the Baptist church in her community in response to pressure from her husband and her mother-in-law. The girl felt guilty about having married and moved away from her mother, who had been a mental patient in a state hospital. She also felt quite inferior to her mother-in-law and incapable of "winning her husband's affections" away from his mother. In the intimacy of sexual relations she was frigid, and could not "use herself as she would like."

The unequalness of the life situation was accurate, and it is very probable that the apostle Paul was specifically referring to the institution of marriage. Likewise, the "buried gifts" in this instance could indicate something of the sense of ethical necessity the woman had about being an adequate marital partner. However, the master in the drama undoubtedly was the husband who had usurped the place of God in the woman's life. The idolatry of the "master" ended in dese-

251

cration—the god in the case was an s.o.b.! And the reference to idols in 2 Corinthians 6 was entirely appropriate to her.

Miss S. R., a 43-year-old woman, single, with high school education. Patient in a state hospital. Upon admission, showed general loss of interest in things about her except in that she was compelled to visit all the neighbors excessively, with no apparent reason at all and at inappropriate times. Obsessed with the idea that something was "about to happen to her sister."

In the first interview with this patient, the chaplain learned that her father had been a lay preacher and that her father had "petted her a lot." This included taking her on his lap, sleeping with her until she was "fourteen and after." The father brought another minister to "board at the home." She and the sister mentioned above both fell in love with this man, who was an older person whose first wife had died. A keen rivalry developed, and the patient's sister finally succeeded in marrying the man. The patient then went to live with the sister and her husband. The marriage between the minister and the patient's sister ended in divorce at the time of the hospitalization of the patient.

Not only did the sister defeat the patient in the case of the marriage but also the patient felt that the sister was the favorite of the mother and that some of the family money had been used to send her to college, whereas the patient did not get to go.

This history information is exceptionally significant in the light of the use that the patient made of her Bible. Being a very religiously inclined person, she laid great store by her Bible. She referred repeatedly to the fact that she loved the story of Jacob, Rachel, and Leah better than any other part of the Bible. She was asked to tell the story. The patient said, "Leah married Jacob before Rachel did, but he and Rachel were finally married anyway and it turned out right."

The sibling rivalry situation of this patient was integrally related to the affective value attached to the biblical story. The psychodramatic situation was reenacted in the interpretation.

The third patient is a 25-year-old woman, married, the mother of a five-year-old daughter. She is well oriented to time, place, and situation. She is noticeably tense and a little shy. She has an eighth-grade education, belongs to a Baptist church.

She came to the hospital because of an attempt to take the life of her child. She had entered the room while the child was sleeping, took a pair of scissors, and was standing over the child to kill her when the husband came into the room and stopped the proceedings. The patient explained that she felt called of the Lord to sacrifice the child after having heard a sermon the same evening on Abraham's sacrifice of Isaac. The minister had greatly dramatized the story.

She expressed the fear that she had perhaps committed the unpardonable sin (not necessarily in connection with the child). The child had been begotten out of wedlock; the father had to be brought home from the Army for the wedding at a rather late stage of the pregnancy. The patient was living with her parents and was the decided favorite of her father. But the father was not willing to forgive her. He sent her out of the home telling her that she was not "fit to live with the other children." She has not yet found her way back into the affection of the father. She lived with an aunt until the husband returned from overseas two years after the marriage.

The husband had selected the child as the center of his affection, leaving the patient greatly isolated. He did things for the child, forgetting his wife on almost every occasion. He seemed to have no respect or love for her.

The woman frequently says she cannot understand her own behavior since she insists, weeping, that she loves the child. She comes gradually, however, to see that she has some unbridled aggression toward the child. This aggression seems to revolve about the fact that the child has actually been the causal agent in separating her from her father's affection and from that of her husband.

The sermon on Abraham served as a precipitating point in the attempt to discharge her aggression under the guise of a sacrifice to God. Indications are that the earthly father is the god in this case, and the child becomes a sacrifice or peace offering. The patient appears to be attempting to remove the cause of the original isolation in getting rid of the child. She is out of fellowship with her god, the father, and it is of such long duration that she wonders if the unpardonable sin against him has not been committed.

The patient gradually comes to see who her god is, and takes responsibility for her aggression toward the child. She is able to make a fairly good adjustment at home.[4]

In no sense are these cases quoted in a "proof text" way. They are illustrative, however, of the integral relationship between the dynamic causes of the patients' illness and the use that they make of biblical material. These persons are acutely disturbed, and a bold connection is easily seen between their problems and their effective grasp of biblical material. Less disturbed persons would not react so obviously.

Furthermore, it is plainly evident that to argue with these patients over their interpretations would only serve to seal off insight and lucid religious thinking rather than to convince them. Again, it is obvious that the patients herein described were persons who attached great feeling to religion as such. They were not like the vast majority of people in a secular culture—biblical illiterates.

This creates the need for a further exploration of the use of the Bible in reeducation of a disturbed person. Furthermore, the diagnostic and therapeutic uses of the Bible involve equal danger as they promise help in pastoral counseling. But this is no justification for ignoring the Bible or taking away from the patients or depreciating the importance of its ideas to them.

Rather, the minister necessarily must know in comprehensiveness and detail the dramatic story, the literary structure, the historical context, the principles of exegesis, and the psychology of the Bible. Likewise, he needs the benefit of disciplined experience in a clinical counseling relationship with large numbers of people who seek his help. He must be acquainted with "living human documents" as well as with ancient manuscripts.

NOTES

1. The rest of this chapter is embodied in my article "The Diagnostic Use of the Bible," *Pastoral Psychology,* December 1950.

2. Oskar Pfister, *Christianity and Fear: A Study in History and in the Psychology and Hygiene of Religion,* trans. W. H. Johnston (New York: Macmillan Co., 1948).

3. Gardner Murphy, *Personality: A Biosocial Approach to Origins and Structure* (New York: Harper & Brothers, 1947), p. 671.

4. This third example is quoted from Myron C. Madden, "The Contribution of Søren Kierkegaard to a Christian Psychology" (unpublished thesis, Southern Baptist Theological Seminary, 1950).

19

Purposeful Suffering

In the days of his flesh, Jesus offered up prayers and supplications, with loud cries and tears, to him who was able to save him from death, and he was heard for his godly fear. Although he was a Son, he learned obedience through what he suffered; and being made perfect he became the source of eternal salvation to all who obey him, being designated by God a high priest after the order of Melchizedek.

—Heb. 5:7–10

Blessed be the God and Father of our Lord Jesus Christ, the Father of mercies and God of all comfort, who comforts us in all our affliction, so that we may be able to comfort those who are in any affliction, with the comfort with which we ourselves are comforted by God. For as we share abundantly in Christ's sufferings, so through Christ we share abundantly in comfort too.

—2 Cor. 1:3–5

When Albert Schweitzer said that the world is mysteriously full of suffering, he expressed the universally human sense of query, wonder, and mystery as to the meaning of suffering. Suffering that has meaning is bearable; in fact, it may even be entered into with joy. This was true of the suffering of the Lord Jesus Christ, "who for the joy that was set before him endured the cross." Throughout his ministry a sense of defined purpose in his travail of soul pervaded his whole pilgrimage with eternal meaning.

Yet, average, even nominal, and sometimes devout Christians search in vain for any moving purpose for the sufferings they are called upon to bear. They cannot, with all the scanning of the inscrutable darkness of their pain, find any "rhyme or reason" for it. In the presence of physical illness or handicap, they ask, "Why must I suffer this way?" When struck by grief, they ask, "Why did this have to happen to me?" They may even quite legitimately rail out against God for his mistreatment of them. More often than this, they may shrink back from the sheer size of the task of finding any meaning at all in human suffering, thereby denying themselves the revelation of God in their suffering. In numbness and apathy they live out their days. They may settle for the solution of the stoic, who simply grins and bears his pain. Or they may adopt the Oriental wisdom of Sakini in the play *The Teahouse of the August Moon*, when he said:

> Pain makes man think.
> Thought makes man wise.
> Wisdom makes life endurable.[1]

But in either event, they miss the purpose with which God in Christ endows the vocation of human suffering with his divine calling. In search of such a calling of God, the prophets and the apostles came to grips with the purpose of their suffering. Therefore, in the biblical witness, we find clear guidance as to the meaning of suffering.

SUFFERING AS OBEDIENCE

The biblical witness insists that one of the main purposes of human suffering is instruction in obedience—obedience to the fact that we are men and not God, obedience to our human limitations, obedience to the discipline of humanity from which none of us can expect to be exempt and live truthfully before God. Such was the experience of Jesus in the wilderness. Here he brought himself into subjection to the limitations of his humanity in ways that most of us seek to avoid from birth. He refused to take the shortcuts that would have given quick and easy gratification of his hungers. He, like Moses before him, chose to suffer affliction with the people of God rather "than to enjoy the fleeting pleasures of sin." He refused to subvert the purposes of the kingdom of God into a political power spectacle. He refused to seek exemption from the laws of the universe which he himself had created. As the Letter to the Hebrews puts it, "Although he was a Son, he learned obedience through what he suffered" (Heb. 5:8).

One of the marks of a spiritually mature person is his ability to learn from his own experience, to profit from the things that happen to him. He, like Jacob, wrestles at every River Jabbok until God breaks through the veil of mystery wrapped about his suffering and bestows a blessing, a revelation, upon him. His selfhood undergoes a transformation. He is borne out of the experience into the daylight of a new sense of identity under God, even though he carries with him the scars of the struggle. Without this courage to learn obedience through the things that we suffer, we come out of our pain, not with scars, but with open and running sores of infection which infect and subvert the purposes of our total being. But with such an intention to learn from suffering, we can, as the apostle Paul says, "rejoice in our sufferings, knowing that suffering produces endurance, and endurance produces character, and character produces hope, and hope does not disappoint us, because God's love has been poured into our hearts through the Holy Spirit which has been given to us" (Rom. 5:3–5).

However, one of the marks of a truly psychopathic person is his inability to learn from experience or to learn obedience by the things that he suffers. He makes the same mistakes again and again. He has little or no awareness of the kinship of his troubles one to another. He considers himself an exception to all the laws of life and society. He, strangely enough, imputes to his own cleverness the power to transcend the ordinary demands of human life. His feelings of omnipotence occasionally burst forth in his treatment of other people and he is in real trouble with his brethren. When temporarily in danger of being completely isolated, rejected, and punished, he may have a superficial surge of regret that he is as he is. However, when the immediate danger of such isolation, rejection, and punishment is gone, he makes the same mistakes again, with little or no memory of having made them the first time.

In turn, this person is a source of much suffering to other people. They pay the toll of his inability to learn from experience, to take upon himself the disciplines of life, the limitations of his own humanity, and the responsibilities of corporate existence with other people. Christians so penalized may feel themselves totally responsible for this person who refuses to learn obedience. In turn, they may completely misuse human kindness or misinterpret Christian charity. By doing so, they deprive this person of the privilege of profiting from his own mistakes, protect him from his self-incurred sufferings, and misrepresent the reality of human life to him in the process. The inalienable right of every human being is to profit by his own experience. Yet in a culture such as our own, where we overprotect one another to the point of deception, we often cheat one another out of the right to suffer from our own mistakes.

Such was the experience of Jacob, again, at Jabbok. He had deceived his father, tricked his brother, outtraded his uncle, and exploited his mother's doting love. Now he was returning to face again some of these people from whom he thought he could flee. But Jacob himself was the one person from whom he could not flee, and the eternal God chose to confront him within the labyrinthine ways of his own spirit. He thrust him into a wrestling of soul that kept him awake in struggle all night. Such anguish and suffering often accompanies that dread moment when we stand alone before God.

Both Jacob and we ourselves can thank God that no one came to Jacob's rescue and protected him from the real anxiety that became his teacher. No one hindered the noise of the struggle in the long watches of the night. No one denied him the privilege of learning from the things that he suffered. Consequently Jacob changed. Jacob was no longer the one who had "supplanted," but Israel, the one who had "striven" with God. As such, he became the namesake of the people of God. Otherwise he would simply have been a clever "operator" on the run the rest of his life.

In contemporary life, the pastoral counselor often sees mothers and fathers who, in order to keep from being embarrassed themselves, protect their children from the consequences of their wrong behavior. The pampered child of privileged parents is often denied the right of suffering the consequences of his first brush with the law. He therefore begins to assume that he can "get by with anything" and the "folks will spring him." Likewise, the alcoholic is given one "out" after another by his family until he becomes totally irresponsible through the use of alcohol. The wife removes economic responsibility from him by supporting him. The father and/or mother delivers him a lecture and pays the drunken-driving costs. But the most creative thing they all could do for him would be to let him learn from his own experience even if it embarrasses all of them to tears. Then he would have something by which to remember his mistakes. Such is the hardy realism of those who belong to Alcoholics Anonymous in their rather abrupt way of talking and dealing with their fellow alcoholics.

The purpose of less antisocial kinds of suffering is quite often instructional also. As one heart patient told me, the days before his heart attack were so filled with activity that he had forgotten how to lie down and rest. But through his illness he had been taught his limitations and "made to lie down" and depend upon the Good Shepherd to care for many of the things that he, prior to his illness, felt depended completely upon himself. God reveals himself as God in the dramatic unveiling of our humanity to us in the experiences of illness. Often this revelation is accompanied by great feelings of distance from God, because his greatness and our finiteness become awesomely contrasted with each other in the time of excruciating pain. Nevertheless the person who is able to learn obedience through what he suffers becomes all the more acutely aware of his utter dependence upon God in the revelation of the "eternal qualitative difference between God and man" which may accompany a severe illness.

SUFFERING AS STEWARDSHIP

The New Testament is most vividly clear as to the purpose of suffering, however, in those places where suffering becomes an instrument of comfort, witness, and ministry of which the sufferer is the steward. The apostle Paul makes this transparent in his conviction that God is "the Father of mercies and God of all comfort, who comforts us in all our affliction." The purpose of God's comfort, in addition to teaching us through our own sufferings, is *in order that we may become a comfort to those in any affliction.* The means of our comforting of them is our own treasure of experience as a sufferer who has been comforted of God. As Robertson says: "Paul here gives the purpose of affliction in the preacher's life, in any other Christian's life, to qualify him for ministry to others. Otherwise it will be professional and perfunctory. . . . Personal experience of God's comfort is necessary before we can pass it on to others."[2]

You have been in a particularly trying time of your life and sensed that some friend of yours understood your whole situation without your having to explain it to him or her at all. A tacit sense of having been understood, appreciated, ministered unto, and comforted comes to you from that person's direction. In almost an uncanny way you have been "met," strengthened, and given hope by the very presence of that person. The chances are strong that this person has had the same trouble as or one similar to your own. Especially is this true of bereaved persons. The person who has been comforted of God in a grief of his own is thereby equipped to become a comfort to another bereaved person in a unique way.

Here, therefore, in the above passage of the apostle Paul is found the main meaning and transforming purpose of human suffering. That very suffering and God's comfort in it become a vital stewardship to be rendered to others who are in any affliction. When Anton Boisen wandered through what he called the "wilderness" of his mental illness, he began to search for the purpose of his suffering. He found that purpose in his discovery of the suffering of his fellow patients. He dramatically laid hold of the controlling purpose of a long and useful life as a mental hospital chaplain. He became the founder of the movement for the training of ministers who would understand the struggles of mental patients as being the search for salvation and the encounter with sin. With the comfort wherewith God comforted him in his own illness, Anton Boisen became a comfort to countless thousands of other mentally ill patients through his own direct ministry and even more so through the ministry of his many students.

Jesus gave this same reassurance to the apostle Peter in advance when he predicted to him that he would be tempted and that he would crumple under the stress of temptation. But then Jesus later told Peter that when he had turned and been converted, he should in turn strengthen the other disciples. We often look upon the weaknesses of the apostle Peter without taking into consideration the fact that the Lord Jesus Christ comforted him in his temptation and denial. After he had done so, he used the bitterly achieved experience of Peter to strengthen the other disciples. The apostle Peter could rightly say with the psalmist that the bones which the Lord had broken could rejoice because God had hidden his face from his sins and blotted out all his iniquities.

But the author of the Letter to the Hebrews again gives us the supreme example in Jesus of the purpose of suffering wrought out in the stewardship of the comfort of God. He says that the Lord Jesus Christ learned obedience through what he suffered. In him we have a high priest who is able "to sympathize with our weaknesses." He is "one who in every respect has been tempted as we are, yet without sin." He, "being made perfect" through his suffering, has become "the source of eternal salvation to all who obey him." Our comfort, our salvation, our hope—all these are the purpose of the suffering of Him who calls us to participation with him in the fellowship of suffering and the ministry of the word of the comfort of God.

NOTES

1. From *The Teahouse of the August Moon*, A Play by John Patrick, Adapted from the Novel by Vern Sneider (New York: G. P. Putnam's Sons, 1952), pp. 179–180.

2. Archibald Thomas Robertson, in *Word Pictures in the New Testament*, 6 vols. (New York: Harper & Brothers, 1930–1933), 4:209.

20

The Struggle for Maturity

When I was a child, I spoke like a child, I thought like a child, I reasoned like a child; when I became a man, I gave up childish ways.

—1 Cor. 13:11

Therefore let us leave the elementary doctrine of Christ and go on to maturity, not laying again a foundation of repentance from dead works and of faith toward God, with instruction about ablutions, the laying on of hands, the resurrection of the dead, and eternal judgment.

—Heb. 6:1–2

Rather, speaking the truth in love, we are to grow up in every way into him who is the head, into Christ, from whom the whole body, joined and knit together by every joint with which it is supplied, when each part is working properly, makes bodily growth and upbuilds itself in love.

—Eph. 4:15–16

The struggle for maturity entails more suffering than do most of our momentary afflictions. Our capacity to learn from them, to discern the workings of the mind of God in stress situations, and to lay hold of the maturing resources of God's grace in these momentary situations largely depends upon our accrued maturity in Christ. The struggle for maturity is, at the heart of its meaning, the thrust of the total person in the ceaselessly changing and growing experience of relating oneself abidingly to other people and to God. The process of building mature relationships to God and to our community is another way of saying that through the divine gift of God's love we are initially enabled *to begin* to participate in the kingdom of God. God lays the foundation of the building of mature relationships to himself and others by first having loved us in Jesus Christ our Lord. He touches us in our infirmities and quickens us in our incapacities; he perceives our low estimates of ourselves and discerns the impediments of our character that hinder us from loving him and one another with abandon and wholehearted passion, unsullied by lust. Mature relationships do not come to pass by lifting ourselves by the bootstraps of self-effort. Mature relationships are activated out of the heart of God himself in that he valued us in a way we could never have valued ourselves: he so loved us that he gave himself to us.

The love of God as the beginning and end of mature relationships is set forth in the thirteenth chapter of First Corinthians. Here the perfect love of God, the necessity for mature relationships to God and to one another, and the different kinds of immaturity among growing Christians are all set forth.

First, let us look at the different kinds of immaturity among growing Christians. Second, the supreme criterion of spiritual maturity, love, as the heart of interpersonal relationships needs consideration. Finally, the practical ways in which this maturity expresses itself in interpersonal living will be given attention.

The Christian, having encountered the love of God and having entered the Christian life, is nevertheless still involved in spiritual immaturities of various kinds. The "if's" of 1 Cor. 13:1–3 depict four types of spiritual immaturity.

SPIRITUAL ARTICULATION

The first immaturity is that stage of spiritual growth which I choose to call *the articulation and explanation of the remarkable change that has occurred in one's inner being*. The early Christians, like many of us, were in many instances uneducated and unlettered persons when they entered the Christian life. They could not find words to describe their feelings. The message of the new being in Christ burned within them and sought expression in words lest it consume them with its intensity. Some of them were so overcome with its power that they could only babble like an infant. They burst forth in unknown tongues, with no language but a cry. Yet those who also had become Christians could understand through subverbal communication that which their spiritual kinsmen were trying to utter. Paul cautioned his converts, however, to work at the business of making themselves clearly understood, lest outsiders and unbelievers consider them mad. Five words with a clear understanding are more instructive than ten thousand words in a tongue (1 Cor. 14:24 and 19, respectively).

Men like Apollos were eloquent and spoke with much smoothness and power of oratory. Paul saw "cliques" of Christians go off after Apollos and was quite aware that he himself did not speak "in lofty words or wisdom" (1 Cor. 2:1). He saw that many of the Corinthian Christians had become fixated at this level of spiritual maturity and had become involved in speaking "in the tongues of men and of angels." As they became so fixated, they were more and more immature as time went on.

Even so, you and I get the impression too often that the person who can *say* his gospel most beautifully is *therefore* the most mature. We tend to judge ourselves and others by our ability to speak of the gospel.

Now speech is the lifeline of our communication with one another. It is here that counseling and healing begin: in the articulation of feeling and communication. We must therefore never cease to work at the business of devising ways of making ourselves understood to one another. Much of our irritability, our impatience, our rudeness, and our rejoicing when others go wrong comes of our plain inability to make ourselves understood to others. Our stubborn unwillingness to discipline ourselves to hear what they have to say leads to confused relationships. Rather, we are thinking up what we are going to say instead of listening to them as they talk.

However, our most profound communication is deeper than words and consists of those "groanings of the spirit which cannot be uttered." Just *telling* our troubles does not necessarily make us whole. Communication must itself grow apace with the development of our capacity to love. Even "if I speak in the tongues of men and of angels, but have not love, I am a noisy gong or a clanging cymbal." We have not matured in our love if we stop here in our growth. If many of us who are like this get together, we may develop a "tin-pan alley" religious cult.

SPIRITUAL UNDERSTANDING

The development of insight and understanding, knowledge, and the sense of mystery is a second type of immaturity. To the psychologically sophisticated, this sounds strange, because we tend to equate insight and maturity. But it is only a second way station in the pilgrimage to maturity. The more we try to communicate our experience as Christians, the more it is necessary for us to develop insight and understanding of ourselves and others. We learn how to be self-aware without being self-conscious and uneasy. We learn how to understand our own motivations and those of others without letting our understanding become a tool for our power to condemn ourselves and others. We learn how to be prophetic for the whole mind of God. We learn how to participate in the mysterious presence and ineffable knowledge of God without becoming a cultist or a spiritually arrogant individual.

Paul confronted persons among the Corinthians who had lost their balance on these important issues. He confronted the Greek philosophers who had "all knowledge" and often wanted it known. He also confronted the worshipers of the mystery cults of the day. He had to warn his followers of false prophets who had come among them. These persons permitted their systems of faith, organizations of knowledge, and particular "in-group" relationships to a few people to cut them off and isolate them from the larger Christian community. Apart from the power of love in interpersonal relationships, even knowledge itself becomes a divisive factor.

The reality of these truths is at every hand in the academic world of colleges and universities, seminaries, and divinity schools today. As Robert Frost says in his poem "A Cabin in the Clearing," we live "in the fond faith [that] accumulated fact will of itself take fire and light the world up."

Likewise, analytically oriented persons are likely to stop growing at the very point of delving for more and more subtle and occult interpretations of their own motives. Having been given the power to love, they may stop at futile speculation! If we stop in the pilgrimage of our spiritual lives at this plateau, we have not moved to the highest level of maturity in building our relationships to God and others. We must move on. This is no stopping place, only a rest along the way.

THE MOVING POWER OF FAITH

A third kind of immaturity suggested by Paul is an overdependence upon a "moving" faith, demonstrating its power. Overwhelmed by the inadequacy of our knowledge, that is, that we know in part and prophesy in part, we move upward to realize that we live by faith. We begin to "trust in the Lord with all our hearts and lean not on our own understanding." We may even tend to disparage the value of human knowledge and to decry the efforts of science. We may even discount these realities to such an extent as to set science and religion over against each other. Instead of becoming a minister of reconciliation, we may turn into an apostle of discord. Pushed by our immaturity at this point, we may feel compelled to demonstrate the power of faith, that is, that it can move mountains, help people to get well without the aid of doctors, and solve our economic distress without the necessity of work, and so on. These signs of immaturity were on hand when Paul ministered to the Corinthians, and the timelessness of his truth is obvious in that they are still to be seen in the realm of those who profess themselves to be the most powerful in faith above all others. Likewise, persons who have been in deeper analysis and psychotherapy may avoid adult decisions and impossible action by extolling the virtues of their analyst, of analysis, and of its necessity for "every living creature."

264

But even here in the demonstration of faith above all others, we can easily see that such "uses" of faith and therapy divide people from one another rather than nurture them in sustaining relationships of love. Paul, in another place (Gal. 5:6), says that faith works through love. In the thirteenth chapter of First Corinthians, he tells us that he is as nothing in spiritual apprehension and maturity as long as he uses his faith as a means of gain, that is, to demonstrate his personal prowess.

THE PERIL OF ACTIVISM

A fourth type of spiritual immaturity that we encounter on our pilgrimage toward maturity is seen in our attempts to express our faith through a vocation. Here we center down on becoming proficient in our work. We become activists who are set to a task and not to be deterred from it. This is good, but it is both our hope and our destruction. Our hope is here because it means that we have a sense of responsibility that motivates us to effective action. Our destruction is here because here lies our capacity to deceive ourselves into believing that the way to relate ourselves to God is by the sheer results of our work achievements.

We burn the candle at both ends, we "rack up" our successes, we carefully record our achievements, we remind others of our most recent honors, and we keep our right hand informed of what our left hand is doing at all times. Yet the inner gnawing of anxiety tells us that we are missing the main point of living and that we have gained nothing in reality. We have missed the power of the joy that comes to us by having taken the time to establish enduring and satisfying relationships to people and to inquire in the temple of the Lord how we may know and love him better.

Consider the person today who enters a profession and whose profession *becomes* his religion. He gives up his "body to be burned" in activistic achievement. This is his religion. He may be a doctor, a minister, a social worker, a lawyer, a psychologist, or a scientist in the physical sciences. He reaches the age of thirty-five or forty with a breathless anxiety, burned up with ambition, eaten out with tension, and fearfully apprehensive of his health. He may have the "success syndrome" of ulcers, heart pains, fatigue, confusion, and an inner sense of emptiness, meaninglessness, and boredom. He is a stranger to his family and at cross-purposes with his fellow workers, and he feels that he is in a far country, far from God.

All four of these types of immaturity are really way stations along the path toward spiritual maturity in relationship to God and others. They point in the direction of maturity only when we make the supreme criterion of maturity—*agapē*, Christian love—our aim. When we reach this realization, then speaking "in the tongues of men and of angels," developing "prophetic powers" and a moving faith, achieving knowledge and insight, and giving up our bodies to be burned in activistic competition—all these appear as childish things, and at best as ways of establishing relationships of love to God and our fellow man.

THE FULL-GROWNNESS OF LOVE

Therefore we need to arrive at an understanding of the meaning of love in terms of our maturity in relationship to God and others. In a word, without Christian love, all our other efforts at maturity thrust us into an encounter with nothingness, embroil us in futility, and make of life an empty meaninglessness that threatens our very being. We become as nothing.

Martin Buber gives a concept of interpersonal relationships in his book *I and Thou*, whereby we may think in a straight line about true maturity in relationship to God and others. Buber says that there are two kinds of relationships to God and others. The first relationship is the I-It relationship, in which we "use" God and others to achieve our own chosen ends, apart from a freehearted participation on the part of God and others in our choosing of the ends we would achieve. Such a relationship treats people as things and God as an occult power for our own manipulation. It is characterized by an *extractive* kind of relatedness whereby we "get out" of people what we want, develop hostile relationships to them, and then "no longer have any use for them." As we often say about people whom we do not like—or better, whom we cannot dominate, use, or manipulate— "we don't have a bit of *use* for them." Naturally, the very image of God within other persons rises up in rebellion at the tyranny of such exploitation, and a real break in interpersonal relationships occurs.

Prayer, which is the name we give to our interpersonal relationship to God, can be understood afresh from this point of view. Many persons relate themselves to God at one time or another in an I-It kind of prayer. God becomes a "purveyor of their own appetites," to use Robert Browning's phrase, one who caters to their own chosen ends in life, ends that have been chosen without consulting or considering his creative plan for life. A fervent desire to achieve some chosen end becomes, for all practical purposes, a god, an idol, and the eternal God and Father of our Lord Jesus Christ becomes the servant of the idol—in our own deluded way of thinking, to say the least. As such, prayer becomes a type of magic, that is, the management of infinite powers by finite persons. This is particularly true in the search for health and financial success.

Buber suggests a second kind of relationship that is radically different from the I-It relationship. He calls it the I-Thou relationship. Here we relate ourselves to God and to one another as *persons*, not as things. Persons are ends within themselves rather than means to ulterior ends. The content of the Christian meaning of love can be put into Buber's concept of the I-Thou relationship, thereby aiding in a vital discovery of the meaning of the prophetic conception of love that had its roots in Hebrew thinking. Love is the capacity to accept responsibility for others and to relate to them in terms of their essential rather than their instrumental value. People are more than sheep or cattle; they are more than mere measuring sticks for our own ego achievements; they are more than tools for us to exploit; they are essentially valuable in and of themselves as "persons for whom Christ died," as having been initially made in "the image of God."

Likewise, God is the chief end of our existence, not we the chief end of his being. We find our prayers filled with all the fullness of God when we glorify him rather than attempt to subvert him to our petty pursuits in life. Prayer becomes adoration, thanksgiving, participation in fellowship, and the transformation of our selfhood into the likeness of him more than mere petition and a childish whining after one toy of desire and another. These things are added unto us, not as the end intention, but as the "afterthought by-product" of God's already existing knowledge of our needs.

The practical outworking of such a relationship of mature love of God and others is obvious in the thinking of Paul.

We become more secure and can be freed more and more of our impatience and unkindness toward others. We can evaluate their misunderstandings of us in a new light: the light of our failure to communicate our real motives clearly and in the light of our "inhuman use of them as humans." We are not so watchful of self-comparisons, because our own status is built by their success. The necessity for arrogance and rudeness is nil in genuinely secure people who feel that they have been accepted and understood for what they are really worth: persons for whom Christ died. Such persons value one another so highly that there is no need that they build one another or themselves up through bragging and boasting. They can only rejoice in the success of others and be grieved by others' failures. The relationships of life become more enduring, and they "last on."

In the relationships of love, Jesus Christ is always breaking through in some new revelation of his love through persons' concern for one another. Mature Christians are always searching their relationships to others and testing their knowledge of God with others. They live in the constant hope that God will again make himself known to them in their breaking of bread with one another. Their speaking, their prophecy, their understanding,

267

and their faith and works are all set into a new contextual meaning of the love of God. This love, made known to them in the abiding relationship of Christ to them in the new covenant of his blood, becomes their clear channel of interpersonal relationship to one another.

21

Anger, Suffering, and the Revelation of God

Therefore, putting away falsehood, let every one speak the truth with his neighbor, for we are members one of another. Be angry but do not sin; do not let the sun go down on your anger, and give no opportunity to the devil. . . . Let all bitterness and wrath and anger and clamor and slander be put away from you, with all malice, and be kind to one another, tenderhearted, forgiving one another, as God in Christ forgave you.

—Eph. 4:25–27, 31–32

The kindling of a man's wrath both hides God from the man and reveals God to the man. This is so because we come face-to-face with ourselves in our anger in ways unknown to us in the presence of other emotions. Moses' anger waxed hot against the Egyptian slavemaster whipping the Israelites. Having fled from the punishment for his murder of the Egyptian, he had many years to contemplate his act in the lonely wilderness until he came face-to-face with God to a bush that burned and was not consumed.

Men could not hate one another if they did not deeply want to be like one another. Their love curdles into jealousy. Their hatred causes them to "breathe out threatenings and slaughters" against one another. But just at this crucial moment, men had better be careful lest some blinding and converting revelation of the eternal God in Christ thrust them into a new relationship to themselves, to God, and to their fellow man. Yet it is amazing how careful men who will not be reconciled can be at such a moment to avoid the revelations of the Eternal. These insights remain forever a closed mystery to them as their anger settles into aversion, and their aversion into a grudging, paranoid pattern of life. Thus men, as Emily Dickinson says, "erect defences against love's violence."

What, then, is the biblical witness for the Christian when he gets angry? This we must know, because the most painful sufferings we have to bear come in our conflicts with other Christians. Is there any revelation to be found in these sufferings? We cannot just be pious, sentimental, and syrupy here. We must have some clear leading. We turn to the biblical revelation for it.

ANGER AND THE PRACTICE
OF SPIRITUAL DIRECTNESS

The biblical witness reflects an understanding permissiveness about getting angry. Jesus affectionately nicknamed James and John "Boanerges," which comes from a combination of Aramaic terms meaning "tumultuous" and "thunderous anger." They were "sons of thunder." Yet, as J. B. Weatherspoon has pointed out, James later became the quiet and controlled executive of the early church, and John the tenderhearted and beloved disciple of great gentleness. These men, in their youth, though, were the ones who wanted to call down fire upon the heads of an inhospitable Samaritan village for its discourtesy to their teacher Jesus. They were like untamed stallions unbroken to the harness of the discipleship into which Christ had called them. But, as someone has said, it is easier to tame and discipline a bucking stallion than it is to put fire into a dull, dead, and spiritless dray horse! Such was the permissive and yet farseeing insight of Jesus in the selection of thunderously angry James and John.

The New Testament witness encourages and even demands the practice of directness in the expression of anger. We see this in the behavior of the leaders of the early church. For example, Paul tells us, in Gal. 2:11ff., that when Peter came to Antioch, he, Paul, "opposed him to his face, because he stood condemned. For before certain men came from James, he ate with the Gentiles; but when they came he drew back and separated himself, fearing the circumcision party. And with him the rest of the Jews acted insincerely, so that even Barnabas was carried away by their insincerity. But when I saw that they were not straightforward about the truth of the gospel, I said to Cephas before them all, 'If you, though a Jew, live like a Gentile and not like a Jew, how can you compel the Gentiles to live like Jews?'" Here Paul forthrightly expressed his displeasure in face-to-face encounter with the apostle Peter with whom he disagreed.

Another example appears in Paul's dealings with Barnabas. They had had some sort of unpleasant experience with Mark on an earlier missionary journey, and he had turned back from them. On a later journey, described in Acts 15, Barnabas "wanted to take with them John called Mark. But Paul thought best not to take with them one who had withdrawn from them in

Pamphylia, and had not gone with them to the work. And there arose a sharp contention, so that they separated from each other." We do not know all the details of these encounters. For instance, we do not know what the apostle Peter or Barnabas said; we have only one side of the account. We do know that Paul and Barnabas had other contacts that were pleasant and that Paul recognized the worth of Mark in his later years. But in both instances we have shimmeringly bright examples of Christians in the early church who had sharp disagreements and expressed their anger directly.

We get a key to the problem, however, when we read the Ephesian letter in which the author says, "Be angry but do not sin." This is not simply a matter of "loving the sinner and hating his sin," as the trite aphorism puts it. To the contrary, it is being open and transparent rather than sweetly covert and deceptive about one's feelings. We have a colloquial phrase that describes it aptly. We say that we are "leveling with" a person with whom we disagree. Otherwise, he senses the traction and withdrawal of spirit and becomes suspicious of us and we of him. This is giving place and opportunity to the devil, who enters to distort, confuse, misrepresent, and multiply discord.

QUICKNESS OF RECONCILIATION AND FORGIVENESS

The permissiveness of the New Testament writers about the expression of anger is matched by their equal insistence upon a quick eagerness for reconciliation in tenderhearted forgiveness. Popular interpreters of psychology have stressed the importance of self-expression, the way in which repressed, unrecognized, and unaccepted hostilities can damage the life impulse of a person, and the necessity of direct release of anger. Undisciplined and irresponsible persons have often justified their lack of self-discipline with such teachings. They have, as a result, taken hard-earned psychological wisdom and perverted it into a sort of "psychology of the splurged urge."

The New Testament probes this insight more deeply and couples the practice of "leveling" or "directness" with a demand for an equally necessary eagerness for reconciliation. In Ephesians, where we are encouraged to "be angry," we are in the same breath told not to let the sun go down on our anger. We are urged not to give even one night's sleep an opportunity to fester an anger into a resentment, a resentment into a settled aversion, or a settled aversion into a grudge, or a grudge into a paranoid sense of persecution.

Paul pictures this quickness of reconciliation and eagerness to forgive in terms of a childlikeness toward life. You have seen children who are playing suddenly become angry with one another. Often, before an adult can get to them to "straighten them out," they are friends again. As Paul said, "Brethren, be not children in understanding: howbeit in malice be ye children" (1 Cor. 14:20). Such was the wisdom also of Jesus when he urged that we agree with our adversary quickly, while we are in the way with him; for to fail to do so is to pay and pay and pay until we have paid the last farthing.

TENDERNESS OF HEART
AND FORGIVENESS OF OPPONENTS

Quickness of reconciliation is rooted and grounded in truth and love. We are to speak the truth directly to our brother and be eager for reconciliation. But we are to "speak the truth in love" if we are to grow up into Christ who is the head of the church. As O. T. Binkley has said, if we restricted what we have to say to those things which are spoken as truth in love, we would cut down the amount that we have to say to a tenth, but the strength of our utterance would be multiplied tenfold. We would have much less to say, and it would be far more worthwhile to hear!

Furthermore, eager reconciliation is hastened by tenderness of heart. Gentleness springs from an acute awareness of our own shortcomings, our infinite dependence upon God for forgiveness, and our deep sense of necessity for fellowship with our estranged brother, friend, and neighbor. The apostle Paul says that when we have overtaken a brother in a fault, we should restore him with a spirit of gentleness, looking to ourselves, lest we also be tempted. Our contempt for an offender is often rooted in our own struggles in temptation with the very thing we condemn in him. Whether we call this "projection," as the psychologists do, "hypocrisy," as the New Testament does, or "original sin," as the Calvinist does, we are dealing with the same streak of self-deception in human nature. Our harshness springs from our inner blindness to our own anger at ourselves.

But when the "eyes of our inner understanding are opened," we can be tenderhearted and forgiving of one another, because we have a deep sense of having been forgiven ourselves. We are not driven by our own unconscious guilts into despising another, desecrating his personality, and offering ourselves up on the altar of hatred for him. For such hatred is idolatry, an idolatry that centers our lives around a person whom we despise to the point of self-destruction, a perverted act of suicide of one kind or another.

But the Christian will not allow another man to destroy him by permitting himself to hate him. The Christian puts away falsehood and speaks directly the truth with his neighbor. He does so in love and in such a way as to edify and not to destroy his neighbor. But, more than this, he lets all bitterness and wrath and anger and slander be put away from him, along with all malice, and insists upon being kind, tenderhearted, and forgiving, as God in Christ forgave him. These are the heights of magnanimity that the forgiven Christian reaches in his handling of his anger. They are heights based upon the rock of God's forgiveness and not upon a self-sufficiency or a pride of spirit.

HATRED AND THE UNPARDONABLE SIN

Much speculation has gone into guessing about the exact character of the unpardonable sin. However, we come very near to the heart of the meaning of the unpardonable sin in our discussion of the angers and hatreds of the Christian. The simple fact remains that many Christians carry unresolved and unmet grudges in their hearts that have become the organizing center of their lives. They have dedicated themselves as if to a calling to hate some particular person, group of persons, or institutions. They are possessed by the power of hatred which they cherish, nourish, and keep alive each waking moment and fan with their dreams into deeper life each night. They are like the elder brother upon hearing the rejoicing of his father and friends over the return of the prodigal son: "he was angry and refused to go in."

We usually look in the more obscure passages of the Letter to the Hebrews for the meaning of the unpardonable sin, but at the same time we carefully avoid the plain teaching of the Sermon on the Mount in which Jesus says, "For if you forgive men their trespasses, your heavenly Father also will forgive you; but if you do not forgive men their trespasses, neither will your Father forgive your trespasses" (Matt. 6:14–15).

This is the hardness of heart that grieves the teaching of the Holy Spirit and alienates men from themselves, from one another, and from fellowship with God. This is the final test of the validity of our birth into new life in Christ. For, as 1 John 3:14 puts it, "we know that we have passed out of death into life, because we love the brethren."

The early church had much experience in dealing with anger, conflict, railings, slander, and so forth. They devised a fourfold formula for dealing with such misunderstandings, failures of communication, abortions of the new birth, and arrestings of spiritual maturity. In Matthew 18, we have a recorded teaching of Jesus that they applied to such necessities in their "life together." First, they "practiced directness," and if a brother sinned against a man, the offended person would go quietly to him and tell him his fault, a matter between themselves alone. If the offender refused to listen, a Christian brother would then go along, in order that whatever was said might be heard by another person and that by his counsel he might be able to hasten reconciliation. If this failed, they brought the matter out into public and the community as a whole sought to effect reconciliation. When this failed, they considered that the person had not even been won from among the pagans. He should be treated as a person who yet needs changing, conversion to the Christian way. In this context, Jesus is quoted as having said, "If two of you agree on earth about anything they ask, it will be done for them by my Father in heaven" (Matt. 18:19).

Unresolved conflicts with others create blockages of the prayer life and hinder the revelation of God. Deep agreement between estranged men and women looses their spiritual energies for creative achievement and spiritual discovery so great that "eye hath not seen, nor ear heard," the things that are waiting to be revealed to the Christians who will take seriously the mind of Christ.

Many times the source of anger-generating conflict lies in plain misunderstanding and failure of communication. The two persons are operating from different sets of information, and their conflict naturally results. The pooling of their knowledge quite often throws new light on their perspectives and enables them to understand each other. The Holy Spirit is always at work in the creation of a total view of any given situation, as has been said, helping people to "see life steadily and see it whole." Quick, face-to-face conference with the person against whom we are offended makes this possible.

But we do err when we assume that all misunderstanding arises from failures of communication. Many times, as in the case of the apostle Peter and the apostle Paul, fundamental disagreements do exist. Men's basic understanding of the character of the covenant of the Christian faith is not the same. In such instances, we must go back to the fundamental principles on which the disagreement turns and grasp the basic issues that transcend our personal differences, our own struggles for power, and our own security operations and defenses. Then the test of our Christian maturity is our ability to live and work with and learn from a person with whom we basically disagree. This is the supreme criterion of the mature Christian at the point of his handling his angers, hostilities, and resentments. In this balance of Christian ethics we must weigh ourselves and see if we are found wanting.

22

The Holy Spirit as Counselor

The New Testament teaching with reference to the Holy Spirit is indispensable wisdom for the practice of pastoral counseling. Especially relevant is the Revised Standard translation of the name of the Paraclete as "the Counselor." This translation of the name is certainly the proper description of the character of God as seen in both the Old and the New Testament. The eternal God strikes Paul with awe when he exclaims:

> "For who has known the mind of the Lord, or who has been his counselor?" . . . For from him and through him and to him are all things. To him be glory for ever. (Rom. 11:34, 36)

Furthermore, the Messiah in the prophecy of Isaiah is called the "Wonderful Counselor" (Isa. 9:6). This term means that the Holy Spirit brings to fresh vitality the memory of the things of Christ, thereby "bringing to light" the repentance of those who are out of touch with the truth as revealed in Christ. The Holy Spirit brings the hope of forgiveness and the redemption of the world at the same time.[1] The unity of the Trinity is apparent in the thought of God the Father as the Counselor. The Messiah is the Anointed One sent to heal the brokenhearted and to release the captives. And the Holy Spirit is the gift of the Father upon the prayer of the Son that we should never be orphans but always have the continuing counsel of the Holy Spirit.

Yet, whereas Joachim Scharfenberg and others rightly score all of us, and especially non-Barthians, for not making the Holy Spirit the theme of our pastoral theology, the only comfort we have in the face of the truth he states is that all other branches of theological inquiry are offenders with us. Henry P. Van Dusen rightly observes that most of the books concerning the

Holy Spirit are both moldy with age and filled with cries of alarm that the Holy Spirit is "the neglected stepchild of the Trinity." He entitles his work, which actually is concerned with the whole Trinitarian doctrine, *Spirit, Son and Father: The Christian Faith in the Light of the Holy Spirit,* thus giving the Holy Spirit first place in consideration.[2] Hence, I consider it highly necessary both from these competent appraisals of our neglect and from my own memories of desperation in the practice of pastoral counseling, to give more than just passing reference to the Holy Spirit as Counselor.

THE RESPONSIBILITY OF THE HOLY SPIRIT

The Holy Spirit is in truth the Counselor in every interpersonal relationship, and not we ourselves. This is the most basic affirmation concerning the Holy Spirit as Counselor. As the report of the Commission on the Ministry of the New York Academy of Sciences puts it, "The clergyman always sees God as a partner in the counseling process . . . and feels rather hesitant in attributing to his own efforts whatever success may be achieved."[3] The pastoral counselor relates himself to the Holy Spirit as Counselor in much the same way as a doctor does to life. Life itself is in reality the therapist, and the doctors are only the assistants. The Christian believes that the Holy Spirit *is* life itself. This affirms that God is sovereign in any counseling relationship. The modern pastoral counselor's rediscovery of the sovereignty of God challenges him to self-discipline. Counseling can become a clever demonstration of power for him. He may "play God" by usurping the autonomy of the individual soul before God. A pastor sometimes creates dependency relationships with people in which they lose his friendship if they do not do what he thinks is right. Or he may fear he will lose their support if he does not do what they want done. This moves very close to demanding idolatry of them or making an idol of them.

On the other hand, the spiritually secure pastor knows that the life of his counselee is actually in the hands of God, not in his hands. The Holy Spirit, not the pastor himself, is the Counselor. The processes of purpose in this life situation are deeper than his own power to probe. Consequently, he can "rest himself in these thoughts." He does not have to rush to defend God. He does not mistake his own insecurity for the precariousness of a flimsy god's position in the world. He can take people's troubles seriously without overdeveloped and overworked feelings of responsibility that keep him awake at night, worrying about all the problems people have presented to him the day before. Leslie Weatherhead describes this spirit of secure trust in God in the telling of the simplicity of the faith of an old charwoman who, during the bombing raids of London, would sit down by her cleaning buckets and go to sleep. When asked how she did it, she re-

276

plied, "The good Book tells me that the Lord fainteth not, neither is weary, and that he stayeth awake and watches over his own. So there's no use in both of us staying awake!"

THE HOLY SPIRIT AS COUNSELOR
OF THE PASTOR

This leads to the second affirmation concerning the work of the Holy Spirit as Counselor. The Holy Spirit, given the opening of a consistently culti-vated prayer life in the pastor himself, is the Strengthener and Counselor of that pastor. This applies particularly to the times in which the pastor feels inadequate, weak, and borne down by his own personal problems. The pastor encounters the overwhelming power of the evil that possesses people's lives. He contemplates the complexity of his task. He is thrust back upon the depth of the riches and wisdom and knowledge of God. He is prone to ask, "Who is sufficient for these things?" (2 Cor. 2:16). These very weaknesses and feelings of insufficiency are known by the Holy Spirit in his work in the pastor himself. As Paul puts it, "The Spirit helps us in our weakness." These weaknesses to which he refers apply to deficiencies in authority, dignity, or power, to deficiencies in strength, and even to ill-nesses of body and spirit, which plague the minister himself.

Even though H. Wheeler Robinson's *The Christian Experience of the Holy Spirit* was published in 1928, it remains one of the most dependable theological interpretations of the Holy Spirit. At the outset of the book, the author tells of his own personal experience in a serious illness in which he and his own spiritual resources had failed for lack of personal strength. He looked upon the truths of the gospel that he had preached and sought to practice as demanding "an active effort for which the physical energy was lacking." He searched his faith and that of others and found the gap in "his own conception of evangelical truth." He found it in his neglect of those conceptions of the Holy Spirit in which the New Testament is so rich.[4] The book that he was empowered to write was nourished by his redis-covery of the ministry of the Holy Spirit as he confronted his own depleted spiritual and physical energies. Such may also be said both in evaluation and remedy of the kind of spiritual dryness and destitution that comes to the pastor as he counsels with more and more people. It seems, as St. John of the Cross says, that these very aridities, rather than spiritual delights and pleasures, are a sort of necessary prelude and preparation for a more vivid knowledge of the glory of God.[5]

The pastor's main assurance at this point comes not from any perfec-tion he may imagine himself to have achieved but from the basic relation-ship he has with God. This cannot be shaken, "the Spirit himself bearing witness with our spirit that we are children of God." The Christian pastor consequently takes a positive and courageous stand in the face of the tribulations that beset him. He lays hold of every bit of counseling help he can get in his venture toward maturity. Sometimes a pastor's problems are of such a deep and wide nature that they hinder and cripple the work of God to which he has been led. Such a pastor should not be averse to getting the best medical and psychiatric help available for himself as a person. But when all is said and done, he draws the main strength of his life as a person and as a pastor from his relationship to God through the Holy Spirit. He concentrates upon and lays hold of his sufferings through the power of the love of God rather than being desecrated and laid hold of by the "spirit of slavery," to fall back into fear. He has received, instead, a spirit of sonship, of abiding relationship with God.

This personal ministry of the Holy Spirit to him becomes, therefore, the basis of his rejoicing as a counselor. He rejoices in his sufferings, "knowing that suffering produces endurance, and endurance produces character, and character produces hope, and hope does not disappoint us, *because God's love has been poured into our hearts through the Holy Spirit."* Furthermore, the very practical question as to the basis of the pastor's rejoicing over his successes as a counselor is answered also. Here again, as in the case of the Seventy upon returning with joy from their healing mission, the pastor's rejoicing is grounded in his relationship to the kingdom of heaven, not in the fact that the demons are subject to him. For if any man thinks he stands in this, let him take heed lest he fall. The Holy Spirit is at work in the life of the pastor so that his suffering helps him learn from his own mistakes. The Holy Spirit prompts him to thank God that people are brought from death unto life through his ministry by the power of the Holy Spirit as Counselor.

THE HOLY SPIRIT AND
THE ANXIETY OF COMMUNICATION

However, we need to be more specific about the work of the Holy Spirit as Counselor in the interpersonal relationship between a pastor and the individuals who "open up" their problems to him. Probably the main anxiety barrier between the pastor and his counselee is over "what to say." This is the *anxiety of communication.* Much has been said in the literature on pastoral counseling about what to say, how much to say, who should do the talking, and how things that are said can hurt or help people. Some of this writing is classified under the heading of the controversy among counselors as to how directive or nondirective they should be. These controversial discussions indicate great anxiety on the part of pastors about "what to say" in counseling.

In the specific context of the pastoral situation, the pastor especially is anxious about what to say. He knows that he may be held publicly responsible for what he says to his counselee. In the role of administrator of his church, a pastor has to deal with personal problems of church members. The problems are often thoroughly embedded and entangled in the official connections of these people with the church organizations. He therefore feels threatened as to what he says to church members. They in turn are exceedingly anxious about how much they can safely tell him.

Although the original setting of Jesus' words in Matt. 10:19–20 was that of the persecution of Christians, nevertheless the meaning is highly appropriate to the anxiety about communication of which we are thinking here:

> When they deliver you up, do not be anxious how you are to speak or what you are to say; for what you are to say will be given to you in that hour; for it is not you who speak, but the Spirit of your Father speaking through you.

The deeper a pastor goes into the inner difficulties of people, the less his ethical and spiritual perspective coincides with the popular superficialities, stereotypes, and crass ethical contradictions in the average church community. Therefore the tension of communicating the gospel at its deepest level is charged with heavy community threat for the faithful pastor. Therefore the actual context of Jesus' words is not inappropriate today, inasmuch as in some mission fields and in certain social classes and regional areas of our country today a man actually would be delivered up to the councils if he declared the "whole counsel of God" in the things he had to say.

Jesus told his disciples that he was sending them forth as sheep among the wolves. He counseled them to have a shrewdness in love that can strike the balance between sincerity and irresponsible idealism—to have the wisdom of serpents and the harmlessness of doves. He related this directly to the work of the Holy Spirit as Counselor. He told them that they should not be anxious, because the Holy Spirit would tell them in that hour what to say.

Another situation of communication anxiety exists when a pastor and his counselee struggle to understand each other clearly. The depths of feeling cannot be uttered. The power of language fails as they seek to communicate with each other. At these points, the relationship itself becomes a groping kind of prayer. This became especially real as the mother and father of a feeble-minded child came to me with the painful concern of not knowing how to pray. They said they were speechless as they sought to talk with God about the whole thing. They were filled with mingled emotions of love, fear, hostility, and mystery toward God. It is little wonder that the numbness of their grief would cause their prayers to fail for words. Their anxiety about communication brought to me anew the reality of the work of the Holy Spirit as Counselor. "For we do not know how to pray as we ought, but the Spirit himself intercedes for us with sighs too deep for words. And he who searches the hearts of men knows what is the mind of the Spirit, because the Spirit intercedes for the saints according to the will of God" (Rom. 8:26–27). This was all I could say to them; it was all I needed to say.

Alfred Korzybski, the scientific authority on communication, said that the most profound level of communication is the silent level, when language itself "plays out" and, in awestruck reverence, we can only point at what we see and feel. At this level, each person "hears in his own language," even as at Pentecost when the Holy Spirit came upon them, people of every race heard the gospel in their own language. When the anxiety of communication is converted into the hunger for reconciliation and understanding, then the work of the Holy Spirit is at the zenith of its power. The pastor in his counseling, therefore, needs to persevere in patience when people begin to misunderstand him, and at that point every effort at clarification should be exerted, because at this very point the work of the Holy Spirit is most often in evidence, relaxing the tension *between* the pastor and his counselee. Understanding comes out of confusion, and peace out of conflict. Just when the counselee is threatening to reject him most is when the pastor is at the point of learning the most himself. For the things that go on *between* a counselor and a counselee are the royal road to insight and spiritual growth.

THE HOLY SPIRIT AS TEACHER
IN COUNSELING

That last statement needs to be clarified and made more specific. This can best be done by discussing the revealing work of the Holy Spirit. The Counselor, the Holy Spirit, teaches the pastor and his counselee all things and brings to their remembrance the things that Jesus has taught. This "teaching" is informative and instructional in the case of little children who do not know the Bible and of adults who have only a smattering of the biblical content of the Christian message. But the interpretation of the scriptures and the application of the message in the light of the immediate, personal situation of a counselee are more than the repetition of a word tradition. The hearts of pastor and counselee often are like those of the two disciples on the road to Emmaus: they burn within them as the Spirit of the living God opens their eyes to the scriptures. Here the Creator Spirit is at work also in the life of those who are actually dying to an old self and being brought alive unto a new being in Christ. Old things pass away and all things become new. As one counselee described it, she felt as if she had been found half-dead and was now alive again. She spoke of the day of the discovery as her birthday and thought of herself as a new person and living unto God. She thanked her pastor for not having rushed in to do all her spiritual discovering for her. He had restrained his need to tell her what God was about to reveal to her himself. In a sense she was complimenting her pastor for not grieving the Holy Spirit as the Counselor by hindering his work. She went through many rigors of anxiety and furtive wondering as she groped toward a clear perception of the new life coming to pass within her whole being.

THE HOLY SPIRIT
AND CREATIVE INSECURITY

This person's life story suggests that not all stress and strain is bad. Some of it is the creative anxiety concomitant with any great spiritual happening. Paul called the process whereby the Holy Spirit mobilizes this anxiety toward the birth of a new life in an individual before God a "working out" of salvation. The attending anxiety he called "fear and trembling." The pastor quite often is likely to interpret peace as repose, serenity as the absence of tension, and faith as the absence of the stress of growth. This is the farthest from the New Testament teachings concerning the indwelling activity of God the Holy Spirit. When the Holy Spirit is at work within a person, peace is not repose but a tumultuous activity within. The courage of the person is mobilized for either the birth or the growth of a new self under God. Serenity is the inner security of knowing that God is in everything working "for good with those who love him, who are called according to his purpose" (Rom. 8:28).

Faith is the affirmation of the work of God through the acceptance of that inner struggle of the soul. The whole person responds in the effort to become the person that God in both his creation and redemption intends that one be. Faith involves the tearing up of old securities, such as Abraham had in Ur of the Chaldees, and going out not knowing where one goes. In fact, faith in a real sense is the courage of not knowing. Faith is a response to the call of God to a new life. Faith refuses to shrink back from the demands of growth and maturity. Faith moves out beyond the safe confines of "a known way." Louise Haskins said it best:

> I said to the man who stood at the gate of the year: "Give me a light that I may tread safely into the unknown." And he replied: "Go out into the darkness and put your hand into the hand of God. That shall be to you better than light and safer than a known way."[6]

THE HOLY SPIRIT AND
THE ANXIETY OF SEPARATION

One cannot encounter this unknownness without some newer and more eternal security than one has left behind. The threat of separation creates more anxiety than one can bear alone. A teenage boy does not leave home and seek a larger relationship to other people all by himself. He shrinks back from the homesickness, the loneliness, and the raw necessity of having to earn his own living. He hungers for a companion in his venture. A young girl does not leave her father and mother and trust her life into marriage without great trepidation if she feels that she is isolated from all those to whom she has been close until now. A fear-ridden neurotic person does not easily give up his symptoms until he has some more abiding way of coping with his imponderable anxieties. The bereaved person does not readily give up the fantasy that the loved one is not really dead until some new influx of the Spirit of the living God overwhelms the fear of loneliness. A disciple of the Lord Jesus Christ can forsake father, mother, brother, and sister for the gospel, but he cannot endure the isolation alone. What, then, is the work of the Holy Spirit as Counselor in this *anxiety of separation?*

Jesus made it very plain. He was aware of the power of loneliness himself. He reminded himself many times that he was not alone. The heavenly Father was with him. He could therefore sense the aloneness in his followers. He said to them:

> I will not leave you desolate; I will come to you. . . . If a man loves me, he will keep my word, and my Father will love him, and we will come to him and make our home with him. . . . These things I have spoken to you, while I am still with you. But the Counselor, the Holy Spirit, whom the Father will send in my name, he will teach you all things, and bring to your remembrance all that I have said to you. Peace I leave with you; my peace I give to you; not as the world gives do I give to you. Let not your hearts be troubled, neither let them be afraid. (John 14:18, 23, 25–27)

Jesus' word "desolate" is the same word from which we get our word "orphan." Christ will not leave us as orphans. The gift of the Holy Spirit is the conquest of man's loneliness and isolation. The importance of all earthly families is lowered. The Spirit of God reconstitutes the individual as a member of the family of God. The anxiety of communication is overcome by the reality of communication in the family of God. Here, God is our Father, Jesus Christ is our elder Brother, and the Holy Spirit is the life's blood of our eternally inseparable sonship with each other in fellowship with other Christians. The anxiety of loneliness is overcome by the power of the Holy Spirit. The middle walls of partition between men and God and men and men are broken down. The gathered community of Christians is always a reconstituted family of people. We are bound together by participation in the gift of the Holy Spirit.

This reality is the daily bread of the pastor's ministry to the corporate fellowship of his church. He is constantly dealing with emotionally starved, spiritually orphaned people. Their parents may well be alive, but they have deserted them, rejected them, or been otherwise unable to give them love and security. These persons are suffering from a real spiritual "vitamin deficiency." To them it is a pernicious anemia of the spirit. Psychotherapists have been known to carry these people for years as patients.[7] The main thing counselors have been able to do is to provide some of the emotional nutriment for which the person has an insatiable craving. I have seen such persons find a new life and a new meaning in the acceptance, the faithfulness, and the nonexploitative love and security which they discovered in a Christian community. Christians will find that they themselves are depleted emotionally by such persons unless the persons discover a direct personal relationship to the living God in their powerlessness to help themselves. The Alcoholics Anonymous groups are having remarkable success in dealing with fellow alcoholics this way. Instead of filling this aching, choking void with wine, the fellowship of the group fills the alcoholic with consistently firm and patient love. One wonders why some of the alcoholics who make professions of faith in our churches are not able to carry through with their confession. Maybe the people in the churches repeat the same mistakes their parents made in their treatment of them. After the alcoholic has been converted, the more conventional church member is likely to expect him to be self-sufficient in his own will power and to reject him if he falls.

The Holy Spirit inhabits and animates the church as the body of Christ. We participate in the kingdom of God in the "betweenness" of Christians in common bond with each other and as they witness to their faith to those who are not Christian. The highly personal and intense encounters of counseling provide wider openings for this breakthrough of the kingdom in the work of the Holy Spirit. Yet we need to keep in mind that the Holy Spirit does not confine his work to the church. As H. Wheeler Robinson says, "We shall be nearer the truth if we keep in mind his constant activity as Spirit in the whole extraecclesiastical world, whilst emphasizing the unique and supreme activity of his operation through the historic personality and work of Jesus Christ."[8]

Another point at which the communion of the Holy Spirit in the fellowship of the church is real to the counseling problems presented to the pastor is in his dealing with grudge-bearing personalities. Separation comes by open hostility at times. People in churches do get to the point where they do not speak to each other. This separation is a strange reversal of the anxiety of communication in that these persons are afraid of what they will say. However, this kind of spirit gnaws away at the communication of the saints. The pastor is regularly "caught in the middle" of this kind of relationship between his people. These persons too often are the main leaders of his church. This problem was encountered early in the New Testament churches, and the teachings found in Matt. 18:15–20 reflect the concern for reconciliation.

Jesus' first admonition was that one should agree with an adversary while one is still in communication with him. His second injunction was to go to the offending brother, pointing out the fault in private, lowly friendship, with no intention to humiliate. If this does not succeed, the next step is to take one or two other friends and attempt again to reconcile the matter. This occasionally clarifies communication in such a way that an understanding is established. But if not, the community of believers as a whole needs to take some kind of action, and only after this should excommunicating procedures even be considered.

The whole spirit of such a ministry is entirely dependent upon the conscious awareness of the presence of the living Christ in the attempts at reconciliation. Such gatherings together for reconciliation are doomed to failure if they are not in his name. The conscious dependence upon the Holy Spirit as Counselor in these times of broken relationship in the churches is the indispensable necessity if progress is to be made. These contextual problems are too many times forgotten, when the promise of Jesus was, "Where two or three are gathered together in my name, there am I in the midst of them."

Such a gathering of the offended with the offender in forgiveness and understanding is obviously the work of the Holy Spirit as Counselor. Many times in such situations a pastor can effectively serve as a minister of reconciliation simply by encouraging a person who has been offended by another to go to the person face-to-face and firmly but gently present his real feelings of being offended. In others, a pastor can, if the person has already attempted this, offer to serve as a third person in such a conversation, in which he tries to help clarify the basis of confused communication. Such conflicts are often based upon two things: first, confused communication, in which what was said and done was misquoted, all the facts were not known, or the persons were in too great a hurry to make their real desires understood; and second, such conflicts are based upon real disagreements in matters of principle as to how to do things. This was evident in the Jerusalem Conference reported in Acts 15.

In these instances, a pastor can work through the power of the Holy Spirit to clear up communication and to work out healthy acceptance of basic differences without a breach of fellowship. But often there comes the demonic element of conscious deception of the brethren, jealousy for power, and lust for gain. Then the pastor contends, not "against flesh and blood, but against the principalities, against the powers, against the world rulers of this present darkness, against the spiritual hosts of wickedness in the heavenly places." These are the forces that produce the kind of death-dealing relationships exemplified in Ananias and Sapphira, persons whose hearts the evil one filled to lie to the Holy Spirit. The tragedies inherent in such relationships are not confined to the New Testament. Too many modern adherents of the Christian faith go to an early grave because of the demonic possession of such "spirits of falsehood."

THE HOLY SPIRIT AND FALSE SPIRITS

False spirits, then, need to be tested. The pastor should be alert not to believe every spirit. What are the false spirits that present themselves to the pastor in his pastoral ministry and that call for the work of the Holy Spirit in testing them? Paul describes these clearly. First, he speaks of the "spirit of slavery," which causes men "to fall back into fear" (Rom. 8:15). This is slavery to the "elemental spirits of the universe" (Gal. 4:3), which take hold of a person who worships the idols of "beings that by nature are no gods" (Gal. 4:8). Herein is the dynamic connection between spirit possession and idolatry: that is, the observation of days, months, seasons, and years, the practice of rituals as a means of pride, the emphasis of one of the great doctrines of faith to the exclusion of the whole counsel of God, the placing of family loyalties above the maturing demands of the Holy Spirit, and the nursing of an old grudge to the point of idolatry—all these idolatries fill the life with possessing spirits of fear. And what Paul is saying is that these spirits did not come from God, "for God did not give us a spirit of timidity but a spirit of power and love and self-control" (2 Tim. 1:7).

The First Letter of John sharply commands the discerning of false spirits from the Spirit of God:

> Beloved, do not believe every spirit, but test the spirits to see whether they are of God; for many false prophets have gone out into the world. (1 John 4:1)

Then the writer moves into the discussion of the character of God:

> Little children, you are of God, and have overcome them; for he who is in you is greater than he who is in the world. . . . For God is love. . . . There is no fear in love, but perfect love casts out fear. . . . Keep yourselves from idols. (1 John 4:4, 8, 18; 5:21)

The Holy Spirit as Counselor is the power of love over fear, and the exorcism of spirits is essentially the casting out of fear through love. Herein are the spirits discerned from one another. Empowered by the Holy Spirit, the pastor is called to this task of discernment and becomes a "son of encouragement" because he is "filled with the Holy Spirit," even as was Barnabas.

THE HOLY SPIRIT AND THE
CONVICTION OF SIN

Finally, such discernment of spirits calls for a spiritual conviction of sin, righteousness, and judgment. Basic to all pastoral counseling is the handling of this process of conviction. The question arises again and again as to whether or not the pastor should take a condemnatory attitude toward the sin and unrighteousness of his counselee as he sees it. The impressive thing about us as pastors when we are most concerned with blasting the sinner with harshness and rough-handed condemnation is that we are usually very anxious ourselves at the time. Our own guilt fosters this anxiety. We become more concerned with asserting ourselves than with the real need of the person for confession and forgiveness. Our desire to condemn hinders our waiting to see whether the Holy Spirit is *already* at work in the heart of the person, convicting him of sin, of righteousness, and of judgment. Our anxiety and our judgmental spirit become "works of our own," which shut the doors of the kingdom to our Counselor after we have refused to enter ourselves!

If the pastor has this power to wait, he is less likely to confirm the sinner in his waywardness by adding to his need to defend himself from one more self-righteous person. This process of conviction is essentially the work of the Holy Spirit, not that of the pastor. Modern discussions of pastoral counseling insist upon a nonjudgmental attitude of accepting love. *But this does not mean that the conviction of sin does and should not take place.* Rather, it means that conviction is the inner accomplishment of the Holy Spirit, not the work of the pastor. Once the pastor takes such an attitude of judgment, he becomes intensely convicted of his own need for self-assertion. In itself, such an attitude is a form of pride as deadly as any other sin. But this conviction *in him* is also the work of the Holy Spirit. The atmosphere of the conference with the offending person then changes into a kind of worship in itself whereby *two sinful persons* confess their faults silently to God as the Holy Spirit gives them utterance at the level of relationship that is deeper than words. Then, the pastor who is self-disciplined enough to listen rejoices that even the spirits are subject to him in the power of the Holy Spirit.

One counselee writes of his counseling experience in these revealing words:

> I needed no man to sit in judgment upon me. Better than any, I knew wherein I had fallen. The pain of the load of my own knowledge of the conflict was sufficient to render conviction leading to the path of wholeness. Thus, it was in the acceptance of my own role as a counselee that I was enabled to feel the sharp awareness of my burden. Aided by the spiritual security and patient understanding of my counselor, I reached for the depths for understanding of the One who through a quiet, inner confrontation brought a source of strength to give meaning to life's suffering. I had become aware of the work of the Holy Spirit. I marveled at the Christian maturity such awareness rendered. I became conscious of the strength from within. With my counselor and this Christian dynamic, I could even face suffering with some feeling of excitement, for I had learned that only from the One source can one reap real joy, and the knowledge of this brought comfort with the mere anticipation of a further encounter leading to greater depths of spiritual maturity. Thus, it was, I needed no man to sit in judgment upon me, for who is man in the face of the Lord!

By way of summary, then, we have seen that the Holy Spirit, not the counselor himself, is the center of the burden of responsibility in the counseling relationship. He is the Counselor of the pastor himself, undergirding him with strength and guidance. The Holy Spirit is at work always in the "between situation" of the counselor-pastor and the counselee, overcoming the anxiety of communication. Again, the Holy Spirit is the teacher and instructor of the counselor and counselee in both the power of inspiration and the recovery of memory, in the healing of the truth of the past and in the solace of the hope of the future. Thus insecurity, separation, and the power of evil itself can be overcome with the creative love of God shed abroad in our hearts through the Holy Spirit. In the arena of this love we can stand to see ourselves as we really are.

NOTES

1. C. K. Barrett, "The Holy Spirit in the Fourth Gospel," *Journal of Theological Studies*, 1 (1950): 1–15.

2. Henry P. Van Dusen, *Spirit, Son and Father: The Christian Faith in the Light of the Holy Spirit* (New York: Charles Scribner's Sons, 1958).

3. "The Findings of the Commission in the Ministry," *Annals of the New York Academy of Sciences*, vol. 63, art. 3, November 7, 1955, p. 428.

4. H. Wheeler Robinson, *The Christian Experience of the Holy Spirit* (New York: Harper & Brothers, 1928), p. 4.

5. St. John of the Cross, *Dark Night of the Soul,* ed. E. Allison Peers, 3rd ed. (New York: Doubleday & Co., Doubleday Image Books, 1959), p. 80.

6. Minnie Louise Haskins, "The Gate of the Year," quoted in *Worship Resources for the Christian Year,* ed. Charles L. Wallis (New York: Harper & Brothers, 1954), p. 373.

7. See Carl R. Rogers, "A Personal Formulation of Client-centered Therapy," *Marriage and Family Living* 14, no. 4 (November 1952), p. 360.

8. Robinson, *The Christian Experience of the Holy Spirit,* p. 157.

Part Six

THE MINISTER AS COUNSELOR

23

What Makes Counseling Pastoral?

Counseling, generally speaking, is a nonmedical discipline, the aims of which are to facilitate and quicken personality growth and development, to help persons to modify life patterns with which they have become increasingly unhappy, and to provide comradeship and wisdom for persons facing the inevitable losses and disappointments in life. The counselor's task is, as the French proverb puts it, *Guérir quelquefois, soulager souvent, consoler toujours,* that is, to heal sometimes, to remedy often, to comfort always. Persons seeking counseling are usually suffering internal and interpersonal conflict. They feel the need to talk with a competent person who is not emotionally or socially involved in their lives. A counselor provides both objectivity and a reasonable degree of privacy for them, and they usually want to talk with a person who is trained and appropriately experienced. Therefore counseling is ordinarily a formal relationship between a counselor and a counselee.

By "formal" I mean that counseling is conducted within specific time limits, and at a discreet and private place. Formal counseling involves an understanding in which the counselee consciously accepts the counselor *as* counselor. Neither counselor nor counselee confuses counseling relationships with other important relationships that human beings have, such as those of friend, relative, lover, or professional colleague. Continued clarification is needed to keep confusion at a minimum. I have discussed this clarification extensively in *New Dimensions of Pastoral Care.*[1] Neither the counselor nor the counselee exploits the other for private emotional gratification. The communication between counselor and counselee, therefore, is therapeutic. The goals of healing are the reconciliation of conflicts through decision and the clarification of the purposes of life of the counselee through commitment. Furthermore, the communication in counseling is privileged: neither the counselor nor the counselee divulges his conversations to persons outside the relationship without the one first consulting the other.

The counseling relationship is focused upon the needs of the counselee. The central concern of the counselor is the quality of the relationship between the counselee and the counselor. The counseling process—however long or short in time—has a definite beginning, a midphase, and an ending. By its very nature, counseling is not the use of instant "word magic" to wave away the troubles of others. Neither is counseling the endless, lifelong supportive and emotionally nourishing process we find in a relative, a friend, or a colleague. However valuable these latter relationships may be in the everyday course of life, the counseling relationship becomes distorted if it is mistaken for these purposes.

Any preliminary definition of counseling in general tends to presuppose that the counselor has specialized training and experience. The counselor is assumed to have an institutional context for his work. As such, counseling is done by many professional persons today—guidance counselors, teachers, professors, personnel officers, military officers, lawyers, doctors, ministers, psychologists, social workers. The question with which we are concerned here is, What is it that makes the work of the pastor as a counselor unique, that is, distinctly pastoral?

THE DISTINCTIVE CHARACTERISTICS OF PASTORAL COUNSELING

One basic assumption is that something makes counseling in general specifically pastoral. This is not to say that pastoral counseling is totally different from counseling in general, but it is to say that there is an area of expertise, a body of data, and a specific historical identity as a counselor which enables the pastor to bring a fresh consciousness and unique contribution to the general field of counseling. These specifics can be detailed as follows:

The God-in-Relation-to-Persons Consciousness in Counseling

Regardless of a counselor's professional identification, social role, and body of data in which he has expertise, that person's counseling becomes *pastoral* when the counselee or the counselor focuses the relationship upon the relation of God to the process of their lives. As Daniel Day Williams puts it, God becomes the third person in the relationship. Instead of there being simply a dialogue, a *tri*alogue comes into being. Quite apart from the officialdom of therapeutic bureaucracies, *being* pastoral in one's counseling is not the private possession of paid, officially appointed priests. The reader can readily see that the point of view here is based upon the belief in the priesthood of all believers, including the counselee himself. Often, in spite of the protestations of the counselor or without his awareness of it, the counselee consciously reworks the counseling process into a God-in-relation-to-persons framework. When this happens, the counseling becomes pastoral.

On the other hand, just because an officially appointed, ecclesiastically ordained, and theologically educated pastor has the "office" of pastor, he is not exempt from the same disciplines required of counselors of other professional disciplines. The God-in-relation-to-persons frame of reference must necessarily be informed by the hard-earned factual data of other fields, such as philosophy, ethics, anthropology, psychology, medicine (especially psychiatry), and social work. Yet, for the pastor these become supporting data for the information that he uniquely brings to the counseling relationship. They become the basis for interprofessional collaboration rather than mere cooperation or amateurish competition.

This requirement came home clearly to me when I was collaborating with a private psychiatrist. Both he and I were seeing the same patient on different schedules with different objectives in mind, his psychiatric and mine pastoral. He said, "The patient is suffering from a great deal of perceptual distortion. My job as a physician is to clear up as much as I can the distortion, so that when the patient looks at God he can see God clearly. Your job is to see to it that when he looks at God he is looking at the right God and not the wrong one. That's what you are trained to do and I am not."

On another occasion a psychiatric resident asked me in a case conference, "What is it that you as a minister do in relation to a patient that I as a psychiatrist do not do?" I replied, "You have a choice as to whether you bring God into the focus of the patient's attention. I am different in that if I am introduced as a minister, I have no choice but that God tacitly or overtly becomes the focus of the relationship." The psychiatrist then asked, "Whose God becomes the focus of the relationship?" I replied, "The patient's God, not mine." The psychiatrist said, "Yes. That I know. But *who* is *your* God?" I replied that my God is the God and Father of our Lord Jesus Christ. Then she, the psychiatrist, said, "But I am a Hindu. How could you talk with me of God?" I replied that before she was a Hindu or I was a Christian we were both created by God as we later came to believe, but that as creatures, human beings, both of us are persons-in-relation-to-God as we know God. Therefore we have much we can discuss if we are open to and teachable by each other. The entry of God into our discussion made the relationship pastoral whether we had entered into God talk or not. The awareness was there.

God as Reality

The pastoral counselor's conception of what reality is differs from that of a nonpastoral counselor. The awareness of God *as* reality makes counseling pastoral. The conception of reality as mere conformity of the counselor or counselee to the least common denominator of social rectitude, conformity and acceptability, or even as the height of human wisdom in relation to the world is often what is meant by other counselors. Awareness of God is what Paul Tillich called the ultimate concern of persons. Overfixation upon proximate concerns is idolatry. The proximate concern of mental health, for example, can become an absolute value to the exclusion of everything else, and the distinctly human character of eccentricity and creativity will be missed. No one knows this better than one who has seen power-hungry staff members of a mental health center get into severe conflict with each other and begin trying to decide who is mentally sick among the staff itself. Such preoccupation is only a little less demonic than the quest of religious leaders for power through the use of varying norms of theological orthodoxy. The apostle Paul asked for a kind of militant humility when he described people who compared themselves with themselves and so proved themselves foolish. He asked for a "casting down" of "every high thing that exalteth itself against the knowledge of God."

The prophetic concern for doing justly, loving mercy, and walking humbly with God is the "stance of being" and "angle of vision" that makes counseling pastoral. Much of other kinds of counseling consists of freeing people from the moralistic minutiae of cultural habits. Pastoral counseling does not neglect this. However, pastoral counseling is concerned with the growth of a mature conscience. The role and the function of the professional minister as an ethicist *shape* the distinctly pastoral element in counseling, but they do not give it its charisma or substance. The basic data and unique tools of the pastor will not give him the sense of awe and wonder necessary to use them. Even the technical training in clinical settings now required for certification of pastoral counselors will not give the pastor the resolve and confidence to shift into a distinctly pastoral kind of counseling. To the contrary, the charisma and substance, the awe and wonder, the resolve and confidence necessary to relate to counselees as a uniquely pastoral counselor come from the counselor's own being-in-relation-to-God as an ethically serious thinker. Hence, the element of meditation, reflection, and communion with God about what is ethically serious—whether God is ever mentioned or not—pervades the pastoral counselor's personal perspective of life. To a large extent he has to shed his religious baby teeth. He can now sit still long enough to become a part of the agony of the souls of other people who are in moral confusion. He can absorb without too much fear the rebellion of the counselee against the idols others have named God. Pastoral counseling is sweaty participation with persons in their life-and-death struggle for moral integrity in relation to God. The pastoral counselor has "renounced the deeds that men hide for very shame; he neither practices cunning nor distorts the word of God; only by declaring the truth openly is he recommended [as counselor], and then it is to the common conscience of his fellowmen and in the sight of God" (2 Cor. 4:2, NEB adapted).

Conversation About Faith in God

It would be easy for my reader to hear me pleading for a lot of God chatter in the pastoral counseling relationship. It would be even easier for the reader who is in revolt against his own religious heritage and whose teeth have been set on edge against the sour religion eaten at a parent's table to understand me as some sort of God talk exponent. However, let me say that this is not the case, even though I am unabashedly forthright in speaking of God in my own counseling when the occasion calls for it. At least three things need to be said here in order to clarify the issue of pastoral conversation about faith in and fellowship with God in the counseling situation.

First, I find common cause with Dietrich Bonhoeffer's word that we need to learn to speak of God in a secular manner. Pastoral counseling can be done without a counselor's being a phony holy Joe who sounds like Carl Sandburg's "contemporary bunkshooter." There are some inherently religious words, such as hope, joy, peace, care, love, concern, life, death, and verbs such as matter. When the scent of the counselor is programmed to sniff out the presence or absence of these in people's lives he begins to take on the characteristics of a *pastoral* counselor whether or not specifically religious jargon is ever used.

Second, the plain forthright discussion of God's relationship to this person has a heuristic value. Often the mention of God provokes and draws out hostility, feelings of injustice, despair, worthlessness, and alienation. The pastoral counselor may move to deep emotional levels of the person's life in a very brief span of time. More than that, *if* the pastor is indeed interested in *being* a pastor to the person, this clearly identifies his interest and concern. It gets the process going more rapidly. Edgar Draper, a psychiatrist, has gone even farther at this point. He says that using the religious ideation of a person as a way of seeing through life's difficulties often works when standard psychiatric and psychological media of communication do not yield results.

Yet pastors can easily be "cakes half turned," burnt on one side and half cooked on the other, in the use of language about and with God. Some pastors can *only* speak in a heavily programmed "holy speech." They are unaware of how they are being heard. Other pastors are so reticent or resistive to the use of any conversation about God or with God that a need of the counselee to converse at all about his relationship to God may be unattended, at best, and totally discounted as symptomatic of "something else," at worst.

However, the pastoral counselor who sees things steady and sees them whole can be more flexible. He sees the concern of people about their relationship to God as significant in its own right. A person's ultimate concern about life and death, hope and hopelessness, the feeling of being at home in the universe or being abandoned by all, and the need to be forgiven or left with a burden of sin because of real wrongdoing are real concerns, not just covers for something else. A pastor can sense the God-in-relation-to-persons nuances in seemingly profane or even vulgar and coarse expressions of these real concerns of his counselee. A good pastor is no fool, however. He knows when he is being manipulated by persons who want to change the subject from grimy ethical responsibilities to ethereal abstractions about moot religious arguments. He resists. In the name of God, he can get down to the real issues of divine truth and say to people who would argue about *where* to worship (as with the woman of Samaria): "Go get thy husband and bring him here," or some other appropriate but earthy word that needs to be said.

The Basic Data Bank of the Expertise of the Pastoral Counselor

Morris Taggart, of the Marriage and Family Consultation Center in Houston, in the American Association of Pastoral Counseling Information Project, asks the question, "Does there exist within the profession a 'body of knowledge,' a point of view, a way of understanding human events . . . which, although found among members of other professions, is somehow represented institutionally within this particular profession?" The specific body of data of the pastoral counselor is one of the factors that makes counseling in general *pastoral* in particular. As has been said, the pastoral counselor is not exempt from the disciplines required of other effective counselors. His work as a counselor depends upon the mastery of similar sources of knowledge about human personality as does theirs. In addition to this, he has a body of data and insights of his own which he arrived at through intensive study, empirical research, and the laborious process of critical self-examination and the testing of hunches and hypotheses. In this the pastoral counselor is akin to and not exempt from demands upon the counselor of any other discipline. However, the distinctive body of data in which the pastoral counselor is expert can be identified as follows:

First, the pastoral counselor is an expert in the basic literature of his religion. The rabbi, the priest, and the minister in the Judeo-Christian traditions are experts in the Old and New Testaments, for example. The historical substratum, the guiding personalities, the stories, epics, poetry, parables, and the proverbs of these original sources are the area of his expertise. The pastoral counselor can identify cultural expressions of these teachings in the language, rituals, and behavioral compunctions of the counselee. For example, a distinguished psychologist, O. Hobart Mowrer, once said in a symposium that the Old Testament has much more to say about anxiety than does the New Testament. I challenged this on the grounds that Professor Mowrer had been reading the English Version of the New Testament, and probably the King James Version in English. In this sense, he was right. However, the Greek New Testament has a veritable pyrotechnic of insights about anxiety. I later wrote the book *Anxiety in the Christian Experience*[2] and used the several meanings of anxiety in the New Testament as chapter heads and contents. When anxious people come to the pastoral counselor, he has in his knowledge of the Old and New Testaments an institutional representation of his expertise that is a part of his body of data.

In the second place, the pastoral counselor has detailed historical and contemporary data about the variegated forms of religious culture in the lives of the counselees with whom he counsels. He understands the Oriental and European backgrounds of these religious groups. Pastoral counselors have at their fingertips resource volumes that detail the teachings, rituals, and history of these groups. They know the biblical basis of their beliefs; they know the ways in which these scriptural affirmations have been used, abused, and transmitted by particular religious groups. Pastoral counselors' training in church history is integral, therefore, to effective teamwork with other counselors. The other members of the healing team—psychologists, social workers, psychiatrists, and others—expect him to *know* this. They ask about this.

For example, a middle-class black woman was admitted to a psychiatric unit. One of the positive factors of guidance and support in her life was the Bahai religion which she espoused. The pastoral counselor on the staff was asked at the therapeutic conference to prepare a one-page description of this religious group and its beliefs for use by the whole staff. A copy was placed by the resident psychiatrist in the chart of the patient. Thus it was recognized that while the psychiatric, psychological, and social work professions themselves have contributed much ancillary data to the pastoral counselor, they in turn have a remarkable void of knowledge about the general culture of their patients and particularly their patients' religious culture. This is due to specializations in their college educations, in many instances. Pastoral counselors, by means of their own specialization, have such data. The pastoral counselor should be an expert in the data of contemporary forms of religion. As an expert, he can contribute to other professionals. His expertise in this body of data is a hard core of what makes counseling pastoral and causes many counselees to come to him rather than to other counselors.

The Specific Community Resources of the Church

First and last, the pastoral counselor represents the church—for better or for worse—in the eyes of his counselee. This makes pastoral counseling uniquely pastoral. Many of the problems that people present to a clergyman have religious overtones, even if they are not expressed. Whether or not the counselee is aware of the religious element inherent in his problem, the clergyman certainly recognizes it as such. Sometimes even a seemingly mundane problem can become attached to a larger question of the person's spiritual destiny under God and is set within the context of his religious community—past and/or present.

In the eyes of his counselee, the clergyman is the leader of the religious community. On the one hand, this gives him the privilege of taking the initiative toward people in times of need. On the other hand, it tends to prevent a clearly defined situation in which he is formally perceived as a counselor. The reason for this is that the clergyman must also function as preacher, teacher, administrator, and pastoral visitor in turn. In his own eyes, however, the clergyman sees himself always in the larger context of the pastor-parishioner relationship. As far as counseling goes, it means that he functions always as a pastoral counselor, not exclusively as a counselor. His work is distinguished always by the religious setting in which it is done. Both he and his counselee attach religious objectives, resources, and patterns of meaning to the counseling process. This is true whether or not the clergyman, depending upon the counselee and his problem, happens to choose religious terms to understand and to communicate with his counselee. The clergyman's counseling is incidental to, although inseparable from, his relationship to his total group.

In functioning as a counselor, therefore, the clergyman always does so as a representative leader of a religious community. This works out practically in several ways.

First, his responsibility to the total group limits the amount of time he can spend with any one individual, regardless of the amount of training he has as a counselor.

Second, his right to choose or select his counselees is limited.

Third, the clergyman is less free than other counselors to terminate his relationship to his counselees, inasmuch as he is enduringly related to them as communicant members of his congregation.

Fourth, the fact that a clergyman-counselor functions in the larger religious framework may be both a help and a hindrance to therapy. It would be a help to the extent that it would enable the counselee to relate readily in terms of confidence in the counselor. It would be a hindrance if the counselor were to use his position as a clergyman to dominate the counseling situation.

Finally, the pastor's leadership of a religious community puts him in touch with situations that would be considered "normal" by psychopathologists. Therefore his counseling must, as Howard Clinebell insists in his book *The People Dynamic*,[3] develop both an individual and a group "therapy for normals." Consequently much pastoral counseling is of a preventive kind, such as premarital pastoral counseling, pastoral counseling of newly-weds, of the families of the dying, of persons facing surgery, of persons planning to change jobs or retire, of parents who have problems with their sons and daughters, and of persons with marriage conflicts.

The natural setting of the community of the church, *when scientifically perceived and utilized,* becomes an organism of relationships for providing miniature life-support systems for orphaned persons of all ages and conditions of life. The uniquely pastoral dimension of counseling rests in the distinctly communal character of the pastor's counseling. Not even *group* counseling, when done by a pastor, is done in isolation from the social fabric of the larger community.

The Prophetic Context
of Pastoral Counseling

The fourth factor that makes pastoral counseling unique is the distinctly *public* character of the pastor's relationship, that is, he speaks in public and is called upon to take public stands on controversial issues. He not only counsels with persons facing divorce or contemplating remarriage; he is answerable to a community on his position or point of view about divorce and remarriage. The pastoral counselor not only counsels the mother-to-be and/or the father-to-be and/or the grandparents-to-be about an unwanted pregnancy but is called upon to discuss the ethical issues about planned parenthood, birth control, and abortion at a public level as a teacher and preacher. The counselor not only confers with draft resisters in their acute isolation but must evaluate the matters of social justice involved in the ambiguities of amnesty for draft evaders in exile. When the pastoral counselor takes a stand, whatever it may be, he is publicly responsible and "takes the rap" of public opinion and controversy.

The pastoral counselor therefore is distinctive in that the illusion of ethical neutrality enjoyed by the purely private counselor is a luxury he cannot afford. The very nature of ordination as a minister rules out the luxury of a *purely* private ministry that ignores society as a whole. This ambiguity causes tension between the private and the public responsibilities of the pastoral counselor. The tension between being a private and a public person is the soil out of which pastoral counseling has grown. The reduction of this ambiguity and tension removes the distinctly prophetic element from the counseling. It may remain good counseling, in general, but it is no longer *pastoral* counseling, in particular, when this happens. Therefore the central thrust of this book is upon the polarities of human suffering and the means of relieving them. The pastoral counselor has a prophetic responsibility to confer privately with individuals, groups, and populations. However, the counseling becomes pastoral when this privacy is not used as a sanctuary by the counselor. He speaks and writes to public audiences in behalf of the suffering people whom he serves privately. Consequently, he gets involved in social change and serves as an agent of social conscience about the broad-scale injustices in society. These injustices breed many of the problems of individuals and families, who come to the pastoral counselor. He cannot be detached from these, but must take a prophetic role in speaking for people who are helpless and oppressed, flayed and cast down like sheep without a shepherd. This makes counseling distinctly pastoral, also.

The Pastoral Counselor as an Ethicist

Another reality that makes counseling pastoral is that the counselor takes responsibility for dealing directly and frankly with ethical issues. The pastoral counselor's training equips him with technical data and conceptual frames of reference. An example of technical data involving ethical decision and responsibility is the recent discovery of the technique of amniocentesis by gynecologists and other specialists in prenatal care of mothers and their babies. This method is a technique whereby an intrauterine fluid sample can be drawn during the first trimester of a pregnancy and tests made whereby exact predictions of some birth defects can be made. The couple are faced with the option of whether to allow the child to be born badly mentally deficient or to have a therapeutic abortion. Students in clinical pastoral education in Louisville, Kentucky, are regularly involved as *pastoral* counselors with these couples. They work alongside the psychologist, the social worker, and the physician. Their concrete assignment is to deal with the ethical issues involved.

Such pastoral counselors use the case method, which consists of data collection, establishing a responsible and trustworthy relationship, and the clarification of the facts at an emotional level of acceptance rather than a purely rational computation of "the facts" to the couple. Students are faced as ethicists with either a choice or a combination of at least four conceptual approaches to the process of pastoral counseling of a couple facing such an ethical crisis. The first approach is a *forensic* one. The legal barriers and traditional biases in the couple's life must be a part of the data collection. For example, if one or both spouses is or are devout Catholics and consider any form of abortion to be against canonical law, they will have difficulty in carrying through with an abortion of this kind. If they consult only Catholic physicians, they are faced with the availability of ethical medical care. The second conceptual approach to the ethical crisis of therapeutic abortion is a *contextual* one in which the total milieu of the people involved and their investments, rights, and needs will be considered, weighed, and empathically understood in search of mercy, justice, and humility before God. The third possible conceptual frame of reference is a *situational* approach in which the dictates of love of God and neighbor are evaluated *de novo* without regard to tradition, law, or even the total context of other peripherally related people in the milieu. The fourth such frame of reference possible is a *covenantal* approach in which the kind of prior agreements, understandings, and commitments the couple have made to each other, to their other children, to other important persons, and to God are carefully assessed. For example, to commit oneself consciously to the care of a seriously retarded child involves one's commitments to one's spouse to have or not have children. If there are other children, their conception and birth was a commitment to their well-being. Does this fresh commitment contravene already established covenants? New covenants are not easily or wisely formed at the total expense of prior covenants.

Therefore, with basic technical data and a conscious use of known frames of concept in ethics, the pastoral counselor ponders with the counselee "the shape of things to come," the forms of justice and love in the here and now, and the weight of the past in the process of ethical decision and responsible ethical living.

The Power to Bless or Withhold Blessing

Withal, the ethical struggle just described is a sterile and academic process if the *pastoral* counselor does not realize that the couple look to a pastoral counselor in a unique way: they look upon him in their struggles as one who blesses or withholds a blessing. They want to know and to feel that he knows and feels that they are "all right" with God. This is what Paul Pruyser and Myron Madden call the pastoral blessing. Madden says that the power to bless is the starting of genuine self-acceptance at a point outside the self: "It must come from another self who has been able in turn to accept healing from his own brokenness. The other and outside person cannot intrude or force himself into the picture. He must be authorized or given the power by the broken one to accept and heal. . . . Just as one life comes from another life, so blessing comes from another."[4] Paul Pruyser says that this power to bless demarcates pastors' "office and functions from those of other caretakers, healers, guides, and teachers." For the pastors to relinquish or fear to use this power and refuse to think of the role of blessing in counseling is "a dear price to pay for one's own secularization!"[5]

Yet the exercise of this authority is the source of its power. It takes courage and initiative on the part of the pastor. The authenticity and truthfulness of the power lie in the communion of the pastor with God. The practice of the pastoral blessing seems to move through a threefold process: (1) *Confession.* This is the discipline of listening to the grim and often tawdry details of the person's confession of despair, loneliness, rebellion, exploitation of others, and shame over not having even achieved the minimum of his aspirations in life. This takes time, energy, careful questioning, and a disciplined childlike openness to sit still and quiet long enough to let the person "pour out his complaint before the Lord," as did Hannah with Eli. (2) *Decision making and behavior modification.* In classical religious literature this is often called penance or restitution. It is the demonstration of new behaviors that are reinforced positively and blessed with the encouragement of the pastoral counselor. (3) *Forgiveness.* This is the communication of the good news that God has forgiven the person, accepts him, and wants his fellowship and companionship. This is the forthright attempt to remove the "curse character" of the past and to affirm, bless, and consecrate the present and the future. This is the core of the power to bless— forgiveness that enables the person to forgive those who have transgressed against him. The blessed then begin to become a blessing.

This process of blessing is uniquely theological in that it takes place in the context of the God-in-relation-to-persons awareness, it is overseen by a person—a "parson"—skilled in the word of the scripture, the knowledge of religious history, the technical data and conceptual frames of reference of an ethicist, and brought alive by his daring to bring the blessing of God to the person in need. These are some of the things that make counseling pastoral.

NOTES

1. Wayne E. Oates, *New Dimensions of Pastoral Care* (Philadelphia: Fortress Press, 1970).

2. Wayne E. Oates, *Anxiety in Christian Experience* (Philadelphia: Westminster Press, 1955; Waco, Tex.: Word Books, 1971).

3. Howard Clinebell, *The People Dynamic: Changing Self and Society Through Growth Groups* (New York: Harper & Row, 1972).

4. Myron C. Madden, *The Power to Bless* (Nashville: Abingdon Press, 1970), pp. 141–142.

5. Paul Pruyser, "The Master's Hand: Psychological Notes on Pastoral Blessing," in *The New Shape of Pastoral Theology,* ed. William B. Oglesby, Jr. (Nashville: Abingdon Press, 1969), pp. 364–365.

24

Pastoral Counseling as Self-Encounter

We are indebted to Lewis J. Sherrill for synthesizing into a meaningful theological understanding the data of contemporary psychological research on what he called the "emerging dynamic self."[1] He demonstrated the pilgrimage of the self from birth to death as a venture of faith, as a struggle between the call to "cut one's way forward" in response to the redemptive love of God in Christ or to "shrink back" and thereby to lose life in an attempt to save it. Since 1951 there has been a tumultuous awakening of interest in the psychology of the self.[2] The term was used by William James to displace the term "soul"[3] and to make of the self an object of empirical study by the psychologist. Paul Tillich sought to remove the moralistic connotations from the use of the concept "self" and spoke of the self in terms of having "the courage to be," the intention to receive through faith the acceptance that God proffers to us even though we are not acceptable to ourselves. He spoke of the self as having come into conscious identity through justification by faith, the threat of meaninglessness, destruction, and condemnation having been transcended by the grace of God.

The brilliant research of Harry Stack Sullivan gave us empirical descriptions of what he called "the self-dynamism" as a person develops distinctly habitual identities as a self under threat.[4] Not until some time after their original formulation did they become influential in theological thought. Even so, the more precise formulations of Sullivan's earlier works have been unnoticed by many. Sullivan insisted that as one learns language, establishes an encounter with others, and incorporates the appraisals of others and of himself, the self-system emerges. The self consists of a composite of these evaluations and the ways in which the individual has said yes or no to them. The self encounters threat, becomes anxious, and evades, collides with, or assimilates that which threatens him.

The self can be seen developmentally, as does Earl Alfred Loomis in his book *The Self in Pilgrimage*.[5] Or the self may be seen cross-sectionally, that is, in its present struggle to maintain balance, integrity, consistency, and hope. The present task is to see the self the way the pastor has most often to deal with the individual, that is, in the living encounters of a given moment. The processes of pastoral counseling may be said to be processes of self-encounter: of the pastor with himself, of the counselee with himself, of the two with each other, and of both of them with God in Christ. A basic premise about pastoral technique of counseling, then, is this: *Our approach in a given moment is gauged by the kind of self-confrontation going on in the relationship.* We become slaves of method when we use any given approach in every situation. Yet we become victims of our own pride, caprice, and hunches when we do not have any basic principles upon which to decide the kind of approach to use in different situations.

Therefore the principle suggested here is that the kind of self-confrontation which persistently takes place in a given relationship provides the basis for decision as to the technique a pastor should implement. No one can make that decision for the pastor, nor can he long avoid it himself without either breaking, confusing, or himself becoming the victim of a given relationship. In either event, pastor and counselee both inflict and receive real hurt and damage. It takes more than just common sense, more than just a set technique, such as nondirectiveness or directiveness, to make such a decision. It takes disciplined understanding and knowledge of the identifiable self-systems that typically occur in human life as a whole and especially in the close-range relationships of pastoral counseling. These can be learned only under clinical conditions and careful supervision.

Several self-systems are encountered in pastoral work generally and pastoral counseling more specifically. These are, as Sullivan says, "reference frames for predicting what will and will not work" with a given person.

THE DETACHED SELF

Some persons refuse to take root anywhere or in relation to anyone. They studiously keep detached. They are "chiefly characterized by a lack of duration" in every interpersonal situation.[6] They expect the pastor to meet them and to serve them. Yet they avoid seemingly without effort a continuing, durable, linear, and unbroken relationship to him or to the church. They touch the pastor and the church occasionally but only in such a way as not to get involved. They refuse to make covenants, except as a means of breaking a relationship. They live through countless, fleeting, passing, and temporary relationships but never "stay put" with any one or more. The painful experiences they have with others hurt only while they are happening. They do not get bitter; they simply remain apathetic and detached.

Therefore the pastor's efforts as a counselor are doomed from the outset if he takes no initiative in setting a second, third, or fourth appointment. This person often does not show up for the second interview even when the person himself makes the appointment. But the pastor must try to establish a continuing, durable relationship with him. Many of these persons develop relationship-breaking habits, such as borrowing money, cashing bad checks, making sexual passes of one kind or another, or, in some instances, becoming problem drinkers. They do not seem to learn anything from the mistakes they make. Though these mistakes are usually petty nuisances and not large enough to get them into real trouble with the law, they nevertheless continue to make the same mistakes over and over again. They do not learn much from their own mistakes.

The detached person is intuitively skilled in manipulating and using people. He considers himself to be exceptionally clever. He usually is a quite verbal, smooth-talking, and charming person. He makes a brilliant first impression. He is usually an aesthetic person in the Kierkegaardian sense, that is, he is oblivious to the time factor in human existence. He lets his obligations move past due and simply follows the desire of the present moment without much memory or foresight.

From this we can see that the pastoral counselor must be unusually realistic if any self-confrontation is to take place *within* the detached person's selfhood. Many pastors are quite easily "taken in" by such a person on the first impression. They are exploited by him for the immediate ends the person has in mind. Then the pastors tend to lose patience with him and bawl him out for his "cussedness." A wiser procedure would be to concentrate on initiating, developing, and maintaining a kind of relationship that the person cannot by doing this, that, and the other thing break off or cause us to reject him. This means further that we shall not let our sympathy for him or those near him get the best of us to the point that we deprive him of the consequences of his behavior. He can do as he pleases for as long as he pleases, but he has to pay for it himself. Along with this goes the refusal to do anything for him which would in either our mind or his require gratitude or appreciation of him. Otherwise, he will use his seeming ingratitude as a basis for breaking his relationship to us.

Underlying the detached self's plight is his inability to trust anyone except himself. He is the victim of inconsistent treatment from those who have sought to guide him. For example, his mother may have been extremely harsh and his father extremely sentimental and overprotective, or vice versa. They probably quarreled much over him. He in turn learned to think of himself as cleverer than they were. Therefore he played each against the other and dominated the situation. His great need is for the good news of a consistent, firm, and yet kindly relationship that he cannot manipulate and that he need not fear. Rarely does he find this in the Christian community, because some sentimental person is always available and ready to be used as a "sucker" by this kind of person.

THE HANDICAPPED SELF

Jean Piaget has given us unusual insight into the effects of the body image upon the selfhood of the individual. Alfred Adler pointed out the way in which organic inferiority—real or symbolically induced by culture—has upon the self-concept of a person. The pastor meets the physically handicapped—the person with an obvious birthmark or injury, the polio victim, the cerebral palsied, the epileptic, the muscularly dystrophic. He meets the mentally retarded and their families under the impact of this difficult adjustment problem.

A great part of the pastor's task of counseling and guidance here rests in the difficult process of acceptance of reality and achievement of something more than a fatalistic understanding of the suffering. Likewise, as in the instance of the pastor who during the first month of his work in a community discovered three families with mentally retarded children, he is called upon to create groups whereby families with similar troubles can sustain one another. This pastor started a special Sunday school class for the three children and a group-counseling relationship with the parents. Here everyone involved confronted reality and set about coping with it in the fellowship of the Christian community.

More subtle, however, are those symbolic handicaps thrust upon individuals by an unregenerate community. For example, a fourteen-year-old boy is sent to his pastor's study for a conference "because he can't behave like his sister does." Or a father and mother wonder why their seventeen-year-old daughter does not have any interest in dating. Yet they have demanded that she fill the role of the boy that they wanted when she was born. They have taught her to hunt, fish, skeet-shoot, and do many other masculine things. Now they wonder why she cannot face the responsible role of a woman. She will only gradually be able to confront the feminine selfhood for which her body has been created. Even then she will fear rejection by her parents, who by implication have taught her that being a girl is a handicap.

Or the person whose skin is black may be half persuaded by his culture that this is an inferiority. The term "half persuaded" is used advisedly. He may consciously know that this is not true. But when the pressure is on "hard and heavy" he may call for concession and special advantage because he is a Negro. He may assume that all the things that have befallen him are due to his having been a Negro and *not* to any degree due to his personal refusal to see himself as he really is, and change. In this sense, the real damage of racial discrimination lies at the point of the way it relieves the Negro of responsibility as well as deprives him of his freedom. Both he and the white man share in common their "use" of each other to avoid self-confrontation. This always happens when any segment of society is culturally rejected because of supposed or real handicaps. The ghettos of the inner self will persist long past the disappearance of the ghettos of our southern and northern cities.

The handicapped person is likely to have companion and contradictory feelings of isolation and destiny. At one time his feelings of "differentness" will make him feel dreadfully alone, separated, estranged, and unworthy. At other times, they will make him feel unique, unusual, and appointed to a destiny that he must fulfill. In other words, the handicapped person lives eschatologically, either as a fated being or as a child of destiny. The pastor who knows this has the inner secret of pastoral care of the handicapped. He moves existentially in relation to the person and works directly with him in the clarification of his sense of calling and meaningful vocation. This speaks to him candidly at the point of his becoming a self-supporting and responsible citizen of the community. More than that, it communicates the assurances of the pastor that this person is treasured in God's design for human life and not merely an accident of birth awaiting the consummation of time to correct itself. Rather, in the midst of the handicap itself a calling and a vocation can be found that will give lasting meaning to life, not only for them but for others as well.

THE HOSTILE SELF

Another word for the "hostile" self is the "rejected" self. Rejections have been heaped upon each other until the person creates situations almost automatically in which he *will* be rejected. He expects to be rejected. He comes into most situations hostile. He is rejected, just as he expected.

Therefore the pastor's capacity to accept him, to be affectionately permissive without condescension, determines whether or not the relationship lasts. If this "son of thunder" can be accepted without having the injustice he feels blurred out, then the more positive and conjunctive emotions appear. Self-correction takes place rapidly, and reappraisal of the situation that triggered the hostility can take place. This person expresses his hostility "face-to-face" as Paul did with Peter at Antioch. He can be angry without letting the sun go down on his wrath. He has capacity for loyalty and deep devotion, and often becomes one of our Lord's most trusted disciples, once he has felt the warmth, tenderness, and acceptance of the love of Christ.

The pastor is often in a dire strait to give this kind of acceptance to a directly hostile person. He has not only to minister to the individual but also to cope with the effects that the person's hostility creates within the community as a whole. The pastor himself may be able to absorb much direct aggression, but many of his parishioners cannot do so. Moreover, the major emotional problem of ministers themselves, according to the detailed psychological research of Dodson, Massey, and others, is the unconsidered burden of hostility they carry. Ministers have more difficulty than other professional persons in recognizing, accepting, and expressing responsibly hostility. In fact, these hostilities many times short-circuit into sexual behavior or into depressions, or both. This makes it difficult indeed for the minister to accept hostility and aggression in others.[7] Consequently, the minister's own training should include considerable attention to the sources of his own hostilities in the rejections that he has had to absorb into his selfhood. Furthermore, the minister's training should include some deeper-level counseling for himself in order that he might lay hold of, rather than be the slave of, his own aggressive impulses.

With some training and assistance, the minister has a fresh source of wisdom for accepting and channeling the blasts of hostility and aggression that he meets day after day in his work as a pastor. Good humor and large reserves of patience will find in these encounters "teachable moments" which will make lasting disciples in the kingdom of God. The hostile person, once genuinely and openly accepted, becomes an intensely loyal and productive person. This is a subtle wisdom that Jesus repeatedly implemented in relating himself to James, John, Nathanael, and others.

THE SUSPICIOUS SELF

Contrary to the hostile self, the suspicious self does not feel as rejected as he feels *deceived*. He sees himself as being totally right at all times, and he seeks at all times to determine the total course of life about him. When things go wrong, his first impulse is to suspect foul play of those about him. Treachery is in the offing. Contrary to the hostile person, also, he does not go, vis-à-vis, to the person who has supposedly offended him. He talks in an exceptionally confidential tone to everyone *around* that person. He seeks to hurt him by isolating him, undermining his success, and detracting from any good that might reside in him.

The pastor will be drawn into this kind of ambiguous situation more often than many other persons. This kind of self-structure is common among middle-class persons, who constitute most of our churches and institutions. The pastor can effectively clarify the distrust in such a person by recommending that the individual talk face-to-face with the person against whom he is grieved. If the person has attempted this to no avail, the pastor can offer to be a third person present while the two of them talk about these matters. If both these suggestions fail to bring the inflamed relationship under control, the pastor would do well to confer with another professional person before he moves much farther.

Such consultation would bring more technical skill to bear upon the evaluation of the situation. At the same time, the pastor would thus be sharing clinical responsibility and objectifying some of his own anxieties. The indications for referral could be assessed, and the wisdom of a limited kind of pastoral counseling could be discussed. By a "limited kind of pastoral counseling," I mean a clearly defined, supportive, and ventilative kind of listening ministry. Here it is clearly understood that both the pastor and the counselee will keep the conversations confidential and not be expected to "represent" or "misrepresent" each other to the other people involved. Many times such a tightly defined relationship will create enough security that the person may after a few interviews begin to say, "Well, I really thought last fall that Mr. X was trying to get me off the deacons' board, but I suppose it had grown too big in my mind." Or a housewife will say, "I know that he has been unfaithful to me in the past, and I guess I've gotten to where I expect it of him when he hasn't really done anything wrong." This is self-confrontation. It takes place only when one *knows* that he or she is not going to lose face for having admitted a few things to be true about his own misperception of reality. Such self-confrontation involves risk; it is painful; it takes place in an atmosphere of social safety even though personal risk is being taken. The pastor's job is to create a safe situation in which real confession and confrontation of self can take place.

Once again, however, the situation of the larger community in which the minister works as a public figure as well as a private counselor complicates considerably the pastoral care of the suspicious person. Usually the multiplex and diffuse indirection of the suspicious person comes to the attention of the pastor in what is commonly called gossip. The suspicious person may inadvertently or with deliberate design say things about the pastor himself to a closer confidant of the pastor. The unerring course of events brings this "message" to the pastor. The conscious aim of the person is to hurt both the pastor and the person who is "closer" to him. The unconscious apprehension about getting too close to anyone seems to be operative in such persons, also. Therefore the pastor needs to be extremely careful about "moving in upon" such a person and trying to work out a hasty reconciliation. This only panics him further. Rather, he would do well to ponder over the matter at least overnight and probably over many nights. Sometimes the person who "brought the message" can be of assistance in working through to a clearer understanding. At others, merely an invitation sent to the person through the "bearer of evil tidings" will encourage the person to come of his own accord and announce his distress to the pastor personally. But suffice it to say that the objective in dealing with a suspiciously oriented person is to transform the indirection and suspicion into a face-to-face hostility that is in turn accepted with humility and humor and dealt with honestly and responsibly.

Yet a pathological note needs to be entered here. The suspicious person at his worst may be acutely sick, and this possibility should never be underestimated nor neglected. Consequently, professional consultation on the part of the pastor with another pastor, a fellow staff member, and a psychiatrist, if possible, is a very wise procedure to follow in serious encounters with a chronically suspicious person.

THE AMBITION-RIDDEN SELF

The society in which we live is a competitive one. American culture therefore is particularly adept at producing what Harry Stack Sullivan has called *the ambition-ridden self.* These persons are slanted toward life with what Erich Fromm calls a "marketing orientation." As Sullivan says, these people "have to use everyone. . . . If you are no good for advancing his interest, the ambition-ridden person can find someone who is."[8] This kind of personality thrives on the open leadership competition of the average Protestant church. The church itself may be to him a means of advancing his particular designs in life. In fact, the Christian ministry itself abounds with the temptations of the ambition-ridden. The upward social mobility of ministers seems to be more rapid than that of most professions, although no specific study of this particular dimension of the ministry has yet been made. The minister himself has to ask why it is he counsels with certain individuals and not with others. Do certain counselees aid and abet the minister's own particular ambitions whereas others do not? He is more likely to exploit people through counseling for competitive and ambitious reasons than for erotic motives.

On the other hand, the minister finds his counseling relationships to certain individuals within his own congregation to be almost nonexistent, although he knows that these persons desperately need such assistance. He asks himself why it is that he cannot gain access to their confidence. One reason among many is that they are ambition-ridden personalities whose very goals in life would be threatened by admitting to such a need. The minister is valued as a person if he contributes to their status, plans, or objectives. The inner pathologies of marriage difficulties, alcoholism, or obvious neurotic or psychotic behavior are hidden or revealed, faced or avoided, in relation to the ambition-ridden self in terms of the way such behavior affects the particular social, business, or professional ambitions of the individual or family.

The main characteristic of the "ambition-ridden self" is manipulativeness. He *uses* the people around him but never communicates the feeling that he really needs them as a person. He considers persons as means but not as human beings. At the inner core of his being this person is anxious and hungry but never filled. He experiences strange and persistent feelings of emptiness, loneliness, and anxiety for approval. He is hyperactive, restless, and plagued by new ideas. He is a creative, empire-building tycoon who in his own indirect way contributes much to the lives of many people. But this contribution is always a side effect, not an intention. He may, for instance, build a business that employs many people and provides work wherewith they may support their families. But this does not occur to him as a *reason* for building a corporation.

The tragedy of the ambition-ridden person is that the minister rarely gets the opportunity to counsel with him. As public figure, as preacher, and as man of influence, the pastor may be "useful" to such a person. As a counselor to whom he would impart his inner selfhood and question his own patterns of living, however, the minister is not felt by him to be useful. Yet the points at which the minister does encounter this person are crucial. He meets him amid serious illness, such as a heart attack. He confronts him when children rebel and challenge or threaten the validity of their parents' ambitions. The spouse of such an ambition-ridden person pays the emotional cost of the unattended relationships to friends and relatives, particularly the children. Sooner or later the spouse therefore may turn to the pastor for counseling assistance. Psychoanalysis in the large metropolitan centers has done much intensive therapy with the ambition-ridden, because they are often able to pay for long-term therapy. However, the specifically sociological aspects of distinctly pastoral counseling with the "successful" and the ambition-ridden need detailed research. But the very nature of this kind of person's place in the community makes it very difficult for the pastor to be objective in his research or to report his findings. The confidential aspects of this kind of counseling are extremely delicate to handle.

Beyond these situational problems, the main thing to be remembered in counseling with the ambition-ridden is to avoid being used by such a person. Frank resistance at this point is indicated. However, one should not be too optimistic that this will create changes, because if someone by resisting him is "no good for advancing his interest, the ambition-ridden person can find someone who is, with whom to enjoy whatever other satisfaction he had been having in your company."[9] In other words, he will break his relationship, if indeed such was ever genuinely established.

THE DEPENDENT SELF

Dependent persons are persistently inadequate in all sorts of situations. They borrow their selfhood from others. They are constantly in debt for their existence. They are in debt to other people who tend to be ambition-ridden selves and who, as we have seen, can relate durably only to those whom they consider inferior to themselves. These persons tend to pair off each other's "ways of life." They counterbalance each other. The dependent person may have been a very obedient child for an extremely dominating parent. However, some dependency may be culturally induced. Particularly is this true of those women who have been taught by precept and example that they should let someone else make the decisions. They will function as parents, for example, by depending absolutely and not relatively upon "expert" advice about child-rearing. Dependent men, on the one hand, will tend to seek positions in which major decisions are left entirely to other people. After World War II, we observed the need of this kind of person to reenlist in a peacetime (?) army.

An understanding of dependent selfhood gives the key to several kinds of pastoral problems. For example, a passive kind of hostility characterizes *laziness*. Sometimes the only way a person can safely express his hostility is by just not getting around to doing what others expect of him. A student can express his aggression by *not doing* what has been decided for him he must do. The profound dependency into which white Americans have thrust a whole race of people by taking their freedom of decision from them is most often expressed in their not doing or not doing well what we ordered them to do. The passive resistance of Gandhi has taken hold of the Negro race in this country and has become one of the most devastating forms of aggression.

As to techniques of counseling, we must remember that the nondirective or client-centered forms of counseling were first devised in work with college students. These students are at a remarkably dependent stage of their existence, yet are filled with the *élan vital* of life and want very much to be independent in the social and courtship spheres of life at the same time that they are dependent economically and vocationally. They are often indecisive about "what is right and wrong" and are equally indecisive about "what they want to do with their lives," "what they believe about religion," and the like. Occasionally the pastor meets college students who demand that he give them final answers about the imponderables of life. They feel that a religion that has any uncertainties in it is not defensible. They require an absolute authoritarian answer, but when it is given, they reject it as inadequate.

Yet the personal history of the dependent person reflects a poignant lack of trust in him on the part of the adults in his life. They have overseen his every move and made his major decisions for him. The pastor can take a lead from this and do otherwise. He can invest trust and confidence in the dependent personality by gradual doses of responsibility. He can wait patiently and believingly while the young person learns to use the powers that were given him before he learned to be supinely dependent upon others. This takes the nondirective approach as far as basic decisions are concerned. At the same time the evenly warm climate of acceptance and trust of which Carl Rogers speaks so definitively in his works on counseling is required.

THE DESPAIRING SELF

Desperation characterizes to a certain degree all those who seriously seek counseling help. A large measure of their personal resources for living have been depleted. They are emotionally jaded and have undergone the attrition of self-esteem even before they reach the counselor. Yet some counselees' particular mode of existence is predominately characterized by despair. The despairing person does not feel worthy of taking up the pastor's time. He laughs little if at all, breathes heavily with periodic sighs, complains of the pointlessness of his existence, has much trouble sleeping, and is likely to be contemplating making some rather drastic decisions. He may be thinking of selling out his business, of quitting his job, of giving up all his offices in the church (of which he may have too many), or of leaving his family because "they will be better off without me," or even of committing suicide. He may or may not have suffered some great loss already, such as the loss of someone by death or the loss of his business or fortune. Ordinarily, he has lived an exemplary life of conscientious community and church service. He is often from the "official family" of the church—a deacon, an elder, a steward, or a vestryman.

The religion of a despairing person is usually one of hard work and strenuous effort to get approval from both God and man. He is very scrupulous about even the smallest matters of conscience. He worries much about things that cause his friends to wish he were not quite so conscientious. Penitential literature through the ages has been filled with the descriptions of the despairing person's scrupulosity.[10] Luther went again and again to Staupitz, his confessor, to confess the same sins over and over. The Protestant minister of today meets this kind of repeated confession in the person who tells him that he has committed the unpardonable sin.

From the point of view of clinical care, the pastor does well to encourage the despairing person to consult his family physician. Ordinarily, sleep, which, as Shakespeare says, "knits up the ravell'd sleave of care," has been seriously curtailed for this person. The physician can prescribe medicine that will enable the person to sleep. He can explore other basic physiological functions that need attention. At the same time, he can assess the nature and extent of the depressed mood and the need for psychiatric help. Both he and the pastor can collaborate, with the person's permission, in deciding what steps can best be taken. Also, the family physician can share responsibility with the pastor for the outcome of the treatment.

The pastor himself has a ventilative, supportive, and sustaining ministry to perform, regardless of what kinds of other professional help may be required. The despairing person should be seen more often for shorter lengths of time. Thus he draws upon the sustenance of the minister's encouragement more often. The minister can effectively take the initiative toward a genuinely despairing person by visitation, a telephone call, or a personally written note. The despairing self will never exploit this. From the outset he will feel that the minister is using his time on an unworthy person. A dependent person would very early begin to demand it of the pastor, but not the despairing person.

Again, the despairing person has real difficulty in making decisions. He may ignore and procrastinate about smaller decisions of the day and act hastily and unwisely about major decisions of his life. The pastor can afford to be directive, in a way some psychotherapists would be reluctant to do, about minor decisions, and even give straight advice. For example, the person may be worrying unduly about taking a certain social engagement, such as attending a party with friends. He may really feel that he does not want to go but fears the disapproval of his friends if he does not. The pastor can "coach" the person on what he would say to his friends and gently agree with the basic desire of the despairing person. On the other hand, the pastor can with firmness and directness advise the person *not* to make major decisions about his work, his marriage, his property, and his attitudes toward God while he is this depressed. Very few rules of thumb can be set forth in Protestant pastoral counseling, but this one can: a person should never make a major decision while he is in the depths of despair. He should wait until his perspective of life is clear and accurate to do this, and steps toward a therapeutic program can be firmly advised.

But the main task of the pastor with the despairing person is that of collaborating concerning the person's way of life in relation to God. This person is often very religious, as we have already seen, yet his religion is a burden rather than a joy and a resource to him. He, more than most people, needs to make the transition from a religion of ethical law to one of trusting grace. He is wretched from the bondage of an inner legalism. He is a deprived person, because life has always made demands of him but has offered little in the way of nourishing support and affectionate sustenance. God is his judge, director, employer, and law, but not his Redeemer, Friend, and Comforter. The major task of the pastor is to demonstrate this "other side" of religion to the despairing person, in his very relationship, and to challenge the legalism of the despairing person with the "free grace of the Lord Jesus Christ," which accepts in love and asks only that the acceptance be received without cost.

THE APATHETIC SELF

One of the main defenses against pain is anesthetization. This may be chemical amnesia, as in the case of the surgical patient. Addiction to drugs, such as narcotics and alcohol, desensitizes the users to the reality around them. But these are obvious chemical forms of desensitization and anesthesia. The human organism has its own psychological means of raising the threshold of stimulus to pain and anxiety to the point that the person does not respond, even when heavily stimulated. These psychological means of producing apathy may be temporary defenses against massive assaults on the very existence of a person. They may be adopted as a way of life, and an "apathetic self" is the kind of person whom the pastor meets.

Apathy or numbness appears in several transitory states of life. For example, the pastor meets this numbness regularly in the recently bereaved person. The person may complain of physical sensations of coldness, or he may say that he "does not know how to feel" anymore, or he may complain that he "can't get interested" in anything anymore. Although this is exceptionally apparent in the person who is bereaved because of the loss of someone by death, it is also much in evidence in the person who has suffered a broken courtship or a divorce. Yet these states are as a rule transitory, although the person may become fixated at this point and adopt this stance toward life as a permanent way of handling threats to the self.

Another example of the apathetic existence as a transitory state is in times of great social catastrophe, such as famine, economic depression, and war. For example, the morning's paper says that an unemployed West Virginia coal miner, upon picking up his government-given food supplies, said, "Well, I don't have to worry about the gas and electric bill this week. They turned them off last week." His reaction was "not to worry." He was really concerned but could only become apathetic to that over which he had no control. Michihiko Hachiya, the Japanese physician, wrote a diary of the first three months of his medical practice in Hiroshima after the atomic bomb struck his city. He tells of his desperate struggle to keep apathy from desensitizing him to the needs of his patients.[11] Apathy seems to be an almost divine protection of the total organism against massive and overwhelming assaults upon the integrity of the self.

Apathy can become a way of life, a distinct patterning of the self in its habitual mode of existence. The pastor needs to explore very carefully the religious history of the person whose indifference seems to be a way of life. He can look for an accumulation of events that have caused the individual to conclude that it is not safe to recognize his emotions, much less to respond with them. He has been hurt, and hurt, and hurt again. He has lost out, lost out, and lost out again. He has therefore found it much safer just not to let himself think, feel, or respond with feeling. The pastor learns much more about the areas of hurt and loss by making note of the things and persons about whom he does not talk than to probe for this, that, or the other "fact" in his history.

Formal counseling itself is very threatening to the apathetic person. The occasional kind of information conversation, carefully used by the pastor, provides a more relaxed environment for the apathetic person. Also, the pastor depends very carefully upon his own relationship as the conduit of resensitizing this person's deprived emotional life. He takes great care, for instance, to be a faithful person in his appointments, promises, and follow-through of plans. If, for example, he talks with the person on occasion about some interest of his, the pastor takes care to develop that interest in later conversations. He may hand the person a book that he has found on the subject. He may recount an incident that is related to it or refer another person to him who is interested in the same subject. This may or may not be related to religious interests. The pastor is in much the same position in relating himself to the apathetic person that the physiotherapist is to the person who has lost use of a certain limb of his body. It takes time, carefully planned "exercise of interest," and a consistently faithful and nonabrasive relationship to restore the lost feeling.

Particularly is this true of apathetic persons who have lost interest in or failed to develop an interest in the Christian faith. Much that is called irreligion is apathy to that which has been presented as religion. The person is simply "left cold" by the whole interest. His religious history in itself may reveal that this is a reaction to disappointment, disillusionment, hurt, and exploitation in relation to "religious" persons, personages, and institutions. The pastor in his own way cannot restore these feelings by rational argument, by pushing group relationships too hard, or by appeals to the purely social and utilitarian advantages of the religious life. He must open

317

himself as a person with complete vulnerability to the apathetic person as a person. Through the consistent honesty and warmth of his own interest and willingness to listen, he demonstrates that the meaning of love is measured by the risks it takes in making oneself vulnerable to hurt. Strangely enough, the apathetic person is quite often acutely aware of these issues and can talk about them frankly.

THE WITHDRAWN SELF

The final pattern of selfhood to be considered here is the "withdrawn self." The hostile self, as Karen Horney says, "moves against" people. The dependent person "moves upon" other persons. The suspicious person "moves around" or circumvents persons. The ambitious self exalts himself "above" people. The apathetic person "plays dead" in the presence of other persons. The withdrawn self moves "away from" people, and his "distance machinery" works automatically and full time. Kurt Lewin calls this man's "most primitive attempt" to avoid at one and the same time both task and punishment in interpersonal relationships. He calls it "going-out-of-the-field," either bodily or psychologically.[12]

In ordinary human conversation, withdrawnness is interpreted as shyness. Carl Jung's term "introversion" has eased its way into popular speech as a description of withdrawnness, although Jung's own meaning is much richer and more diversified. The withdrawn person is a very different person from the detached self, who maintains an equal distance out of contempt for the human race. The withdrawn person both desperately wants and fears real contact with persons. He wants closeness and tenderness, understanding and love, but he fears being possessed and controlled by those from whom it comes. The withdrawn person may have previously been "smothered" by someone's sentimentality, which is a counterfeit form of love. Hence, the suspicious self and the apathetic self both have dimensions of withdrawnness in them. The withdrawn person has been both deceived and hurt, misled and exploited. As a result, the power to connect with other people has been blunted. In acute forms, this person is usually thought of as a schizoid person, and highly professional care is indicated. However, this does not mean that at the same time the pastor himself does not also have a remarkably significant ministry to perform.

From a clinical point of view, the pastor must develop a special sensitivity to emotional distance and nearness to appreciate the inner pain that a normally shy person feels. This becomes especially necessary when he is tempted to be excessively "hail fellow well met" with a withdrawn person. Another basic principle of pastoral care is that people vary widely as individuals in the tempo with which they become close to and involved with others. The pastor must therefore sense the tempo of their existence and modulate his own pace of encounter to theirs. Becoming too "pushy," demanding, or familiar with a withdrawn person is very threatening. A more matter-of-fact, less verbal, and slowly paced kind of response makes the withdrawn person feel much more secure. Frieda Fromm-Reichmann recommends a studied nonchalance with the more acutely disturbed, schizophrenic person, underscoring the painfulness of too much solicitude and warmth, especially in the earlier phases of the relationship.

The rich values within the life of the withdrawn person have much to contribute to the life of the pastor himself. The withdrawn person is usually a contemplative, nonactivistic kind of self. The activism of the life of the average church leaves little room for appreciation of this person. He often prefers to write his thoughts rather than speak them, and the pastor does well to encourage this. Next to this, the withdrawn self prefers a more leisurely telephone conversation to a face-to-face encounter. Then he does not feel "looked at" or "observed" in conversation. In the formal situation of the counseling interview, the withdrawn person is much more comfortable if the counselor looks out a window or at a portrait on the wall away from him.

The withdrawn self moves slowly in dealing with his personal difficulties in living. The pastor does well to space his interviews with him over a longer period of time with longer amounts of time between interviews. In this respect, the withdrawn person is the opposite of the despairing self, who needs shorter interviews more frequently. Much patience and unhurriedness is required. Patient work with withdrawn persons returns long-term friendships and devotions in the pastoral ministry which more than justify the use of the time.

GENERALIZATIONS CONCERNING PATTERNS OF SELF-ENCOUNTER

Several basic generalizations need to be made concerning these patterns of self-encounter. First, the pastor needs to recognize these as varieties of *religious* experience, not merely as psychological phenomena. The person relates to God in these characteristic ways also. These are modes of religious existence. The hostile person is likely to be angry at God, as is true of the rebelling "atheist." The dependent person's prayers are mostly petition and demand, rarely adoration and fellowship. The ambition-ridden person thinks of God as being "on his side" and "pulling for him" in the competitive struggle for success. The apathetic may complain about not being able to feel that his prayers are meaningful or being answered. The suspicious person may suspect that God is persecuting him in various ways. The detached person remains uncommitted in any kind of covenant with God too.

Again, this discussion of various patterns of selfhood is not a *pure* typology of personalities. All these forms of existence are participant in the life of the typical person at different times in this life. The healthy person consciously decides to deal with first one problem and then the other in one or the other of these modes of reaction. But he *does* decide and choose; he is not driven and compelled. He is flexible and can react appropriately to a given situation with the kind of response that is most meaningful to him and those persons to whom he is responsible. He is not bound and compelled to react in *one* way to all people. For example, our Lord Jesus Christ was hostile, knew how to depend upon persons like Martha, Mary, and Lazarus. He withdrew from persons like Herod. He felt the great heaviness of soul in prayer. The ethically negative kinds of response, such as ambition-riddenness and detachedness, are almost nonexistent in him but ever-present in his temptations.

These patterns of relatedness in selfhood indicate a flexibility of technique on the part of the pastor. Tender solicitude meets the despairing person's needs, whereas it may be interpreted as a sign of guilt and appeasement on the part of the suspicious person and as a sign of stupidity and weakness on the part of the detached person. The passive, nondirective approach to the dependent person draws his inner resources into focus. The same approach will be interpreted as full-scale approval of his many plans by the ambition-ridden person, who seeks simply to use the counselor for his own ends. To suggest that the pastor should use more than one method, however, is not to suggest a willy-nilly eclecticism. Basic principles of interpersonal relationships are necessary for making a clinical decision as to the approach that should be followed in any given situation. The first of these principles has been set forth here in a description of the various modes of selfhood. Yet one cannot learn them merely by reading them here. Intensive clinical supervision and staff collaboration provide a fund of experiential validation and clarification of these modes of reaction. Genuine sensitivity can best be developed in such clinical training.

But the pastor does not really sense the emotional tones of reference in these patterns of reaction unless he has seen them clearly in himself. He must encounter himself as a person before, during, and after his confrontation of his counselees. He must explore his own spiritual autobiography and draw some basic conclusions as to his own patterns of reaction. Then he begins to appreciate with greater clarity and deeper patience the problems of self-encounter in his counselees' lives.

NOTES

1. Lewis J. Sherrill, *The Struggle of the Soul* (New York: Macmillan Co., 1951).

2. See Calvin S. Hall and Gardner Lindzey, *Theories of Personality* (New York: John Wiley & Sons, 1957), pp. 467ff.

3. William James, *Principles of Psychology,* ch. 10.

4. Harry Stack Sullivan, *Conceptions of Modern Psychiatry,* William Alanson White Memorial Lectures (New York: W. W. Norton & Co., 1947).

5. Earl Alfred Loomis, *The Self in Pilgrimage* (New York: Harper & Brothers, 1960).

6. Sullivan, *Conceptions of Modern Psychiatry,* p. 37.

7. See Wayne E. Oates, ed., *The Minister's Own Mental Health* (Manhasset, N.Y.: Channel Press, 1961).

8. Sullivan, *Conceptions of Modern Psychiatry,* p. 40.

9. Ibid.

10. See John T. McNeill, *The History of the Cure of Souls* (New York: Harper & Brothers, 1952).

11. Michihiko Hachiya, *Hiroshima Diary,* ed. Warner Wells (University of North Carolina Press, 1955).

12. Kurt Lewin, *A Dynamic Theory of Personality* (New York: McGraw-Hill Book Co., 1935), p. 174.

25

The Time Element in Pastoral Counseling

The writer of Ecclesiastes tells us that

> to everything there is a season, and a time to every purpose under the heaven: a time to be born, and a time to die; a time to plant, and a time to pluck up that which is planted; a time to kill, and a time to heal; a time to break down, and a time to build up; a time to weep, and a time to laugh; a time to mourn, and a time to dance; a time to cast away stones, and a time to gather stones together; a time to embrace, and a time to refrain from embracing; a time to get, and a time to lose; a time to keep, and a time to cast away; a time to rend, and a time to sew; a time to keep silence, and a time to speak; a time to love, and a time to hate; a time of war, and a time of peace. . . . I have seen the travail, which God hath given to the sons of men to be exercised in it. He hath made everything beautiful in his time: also he hath set the world in their heart, so that no man can find out the work that God maketh from the beginning to the end. (Eccl. 3:1–8, 10–11)

In both the art and science of music, time and timing are vital. This is equally true in the art and science of pastoral counseling. In a counseling relationship, the pastor is always engaged in perceiving the work of the Eternal in his appropriate relationship to time. The pastor's awareness of the appropriateness of a given moment for decision, delay, or demand is a good gauge of his effectiveness as a pastor, and particularly as a pastoral counselor. The time factor in pastoral counseling provides a symbolic screen upon which to project an understanding of counseling and the effectiveness of the pastor as a counselor.

For instance, the ministry of some pastors consists of innumerable, superficial, brief, and passing relationships to a large number of persons.

On the other hand, other pastors are so completely unaware of time that they will spend great quantities of time with a very few individuals and allow the total "oversight of the flock of God" to go lacking. Furthermore, when a pastor is confronted with his responsibility as a counselor, the time factor is the issue upon which he tends to hang his whole case as to his responsibility for more intensive counseling with individuals. For instance, he is likely to take the attitude that "the pastor has too many other things to do" to spend more than one conversation with a troubled individual. On the other hand, in his hyperidealism, he is likely to say that "all of the administrative demands of the pastoral tasks" get in the way of what he is really called to do, namely, counsel with individuals. Thus he needs to evaluate the time factor in his total pastoral task and then to see his counseling ministry in that perspective.

THE TIME FACTOR IN THE TOTAL PASTORAL TASK

Samuel W. Blizzard describes how the minister faces basic ambiguities in performing the many roles—traditional, neo-traditional, and contemporary—that are expected of him by his people. The most troublesome roles to the minister are those in which he functions as a pastoral visitor and counselor as over against those in which he functions as an organizer and an administrator. Yet organization and administration require more than three fifths of the total workday of the pastor.[1] Blizzard notes that his "material . . . regarding the expectations of parishioners is inferred from the data that we have regarding how ministers spend their time . . . [and] it is best to stress the fact that the data that we are collecting is self-image data from the minister."[2] In other words, this is the minister's picture of himself, not an actual study of what the parishioners themselves expect of him. For instance, the parishioners say that one of the reasons why they do not bring their personal counseling problems to their pastor is that he is "too busy." This is the reason which they give him. However, in talking to chaplains, medical doctors, social workers, and others, parishioners are more likely to say they did not feel that their minister would understand or be concerned about what happens to them. Here the time factor in the total pastoral task may be used as a screen for a breakdown of communication, a lack of motivation for counseling help, or resentment at the thought that it may be needed.

Recent discussions of the minister's own mental health likewise have turned around the time factor in his pastoral relationships within his total tasks. Some persons suggest that more and more ministers are breaking down mentally because of overwork. The whole problem of the minister's own mental health is thereby reduced to the time factor in his total pastoral task. This is a severe oversimplification of his problem which obscures the more dynamic facts that we know about mental illness. More extensive study probes more deeply than this simple interpretation of the pastoral task. One rather needs to raise the question as to ministers' ability to organize their work and to use their time efficiently. They often prefer to do more tangible tasks, to "get results," and to see things happen. They, like many other professionally trained persons who have moved from the lower classes of manual labor to the middle-class professions, feel guilty if they are not "busy about many things."

Therefore, when we begin to consider the specific task of pastoral counseling as it is performed by the parish minister, we need to probe deeply the minister's conception of himself and his controlling purpose and function in life. These factors determine the way he plans and spends his time. He orders his interpersonal relationships to people accordingly. Time is the only thing that a minister has to give away. One measure of his effectiveness as a minister is his stewardship of time in his total task. One justification for teaching pastoral care and pastoral counseling in the seminaries is to enable the pastor to plan his counseling ministry in such a way as to be more effective in helping individuals and thereby to release more time for his other functions of preaching, sermon preparation, and the general administrative oversight of the flock. This necessitates his facing up to the time factor in pastoral counseling as it is related to his total task.

THE TIME FACTOR IN THE SPECIFIC FUNCTION
OF PASTORAL COUNSELING

By its very nature, pastoral counseling is defined in terms of a multiple conference relationship. It extends over a period of several weeks. Its objective is spiritual growth and the achievement of insight through a series of carefully regulated conversations between a pastor and a parishioner. In other words, pastoral counseling is a more intensive, more durable, a more highly defined, and more formal relationship between a pastor and a given individual. This "process" relationship presupposes that the deepest changes in personality occur when the revelation of God springs up within the counselee's own internal frame of reference rather than when it is projected into his consciousness by another person. The process of pastoral counseling also presupposes a "depth" view of personality. Both the deepest problems and the surest solutions of those problems spring from "the hidden parts" of man in which he is made to know wisdom, not by the pastor, but by the indwelling activity of the Holy Spirit. The atmosphere in which this takes place does not happen quickly. It comes to pass over a period of trying and testing of relationship between pastor and parishioner. This takes time. For instance, a person who is basically suspicious and has learned bitterly *not* to trust anyone does not just automatically in a moment's time start trusting people when he is told to do so. The feeling of trust does occur spontaneously in human relationships. But ordinarily it takes time to come to pass. The longer, more linear, and durable process of pastoral counseling often brings this into being. When it does so, it is no less a miracle than if it happened in a moment.

The same could be said about the experience of conversion. The first birth of man takes a normal span of time of nine months. One might grin sardonically to himself and ask what it would be like if the medical profession, in order to improve their statistics and increase the number of paying patients, decided to step up and shorten the processes of birth! This makes about as much sense as the stepping up and shortening of the process of conversion by pastors in order to increase the size of their churches and their budgets. Pastoral counseling very specifically offers a more profound kind of evangelism, one that relies more heavily upon the realities of spiritual conception and maturation within the life of man through the creative activity of the Holy Spirit.

In the light of the above definition and illustration of pastoral counseling as a process relationship, pastors then can be divided into two groups. The first group of pastors perceive counseling as giving advice. These pastors usually make time for only one very brief contact with a person about a given problem. They pride themselves on using "common sense" in their counseling. By this they really mean that all human problems are rational and can be "answered" rationally, quickly, and authoritatively. The fact of the matter is that *some* human problems are rational and can be answered quickly with "common sense." But a pastor needs a settled awareness of the deeper, irrational, contradictory, and conflicting nature of man to know when he is dealing with this kind of problem and when he is not. This first kind of pastor does not fall into the prophetic and apostolic tradition of pastoral care. Rather, he is likely to devise a set of formulas and rules of thumb whereby he "answers" problems that are presented to him. He, in the interests of time, deals quickly with problems. Much research could be done on the time element as it is related to authoritarianism. When an advice-giving pastor confronts the tempestuous and chaotic surges of deep distress of a modern Job, he is likely to answer him in much the same way as Job's counselors answered him. He depends on the magic of words. Zophar the Naamathite, Eliphaz the Temanite, and Bildad the Shuhite are still with us. They still depend upon the magic of words, posited upon the assumption that "saying it solves it." They expect this magic to relieve them of the responsibility of taking the time to hear a person out, to participate with him in his search for a deeper revelation of the helping power of God. But Jobs of our day reply in the words of the Job of the Old Testament!

> Ye are all physicians of no value. Oh that ye would altogether hold your peace! And it should be your wisdom. Hear now my reasoning, and hearken to the pleadings of my lips. . . . Hold your peace, let me alone, that I may speak, and let come on me what will. . . . Though he slay me, yet will I trust in him: but I will maintain mine own ways before him. (Job 13:4–6, 13, 15)

The ministry of reconciliation is a matter of life and death as man struggles in his mortal encounter with the eternal God. Job knew that the dread that gripped his counselors could make him afraid. The deepest encounters of the processes of pastoral counseling are threatening to the minister. His own sense of fear frightens the counselee. The neat rationalisms of the "easy answer" approach to pastoral counseling do occasionally solve the time problem for a busy pastor. But they often actually involve him in many situations in which he will waste more time than he has saved with his "pat" solutions. For instance, he is likely to become involved in long and heated discussions with people who reject his answers. Likewise, in an attempt to "settle" the person's problems "right then and there," he often will use two, three, and even four and five hours at a sitting—or standing—with one person, thereby wasting valuable time. If he had scheduled another appointment, after having asked for time in which to think about the problem, he could have done more good in less time. Five thirty-minute conversations with a person may serve him better than to talk with him three hours at one sitting. A pastor may do him triply as much good and save at least a half hour!

The second group of pastors are those who develop a disciplined use of time in multiple-interview encounters. Such a pastor encourages the person, through the processes of spiritual maturity and insight, to lay hold of and to deal with his own problem. But he is not left alone. The pastor gives him spiritual fellowship and assistance in the pilgrimage of growth. He is not alone. For a time, counseling pastors assumed that if they simply listened to a person, this in itself was what was needed and all that was needed. But more recently, pastors are discovering that their willingness to listen to people's troubles in and of itself is a symbolic way of saying things to the person that words cannot. A nonverbal kind of communication is going on. The symbolic act of scheduling a second interview, for instance, may say to the person many different things: "I am not too busy to take your problem seriously." Or it may say, "I think your problem is serious." Or it may say, "I know you came for my 'answer,' but I am treading water until I can think of one." These are just a few of the things that scheduling a second interview can mean to the person.

On the other hand, the pastor may hit resistance in the scheduling of a second interview. The person may be an extremely demanding and passively dependent individual who insists that if the pastor is the kind of person he ought to be, he could just settle the whole matter right there. A passive-aggressive person may forget to show up for the second appointment. An openly hostile person may simply "tell the pastor off" for suggesting that he needs help. In other words, a more intensive pastoral counseling is not just a matter of listening to people, although this is a very great and important part of it. The nonverbal communication going on within the context of the total relationship is in itself a healing light or a threatening irritation or both. The pastor has to listen to this with what Theodor Reik has called "the third ear."

The pastor must clearly define a mutually acceptable and mutually understood counseling relationship for what it really is. What is it? It is a process relationship of several interviews in which the pastor and the parishioner explore together the deeper ramifications and the larger and longer purposes of the parishioner's life itself. This becomes an existential encounter once it is established. A process of precounseling, however, must precede it in the uncontrolled and undefined and often confused relationships of the pastoral situation. Too much so-called nondirectiveness on the part of the pastor in this construction of a defined counseling relationship can actually break the contact, because the parishioner finds it meaningless.

This task of precounseling usually happens in the first interview. The pastor is still faced with the responsibility of knowing how to make the best use of *one hour* in pastoral interviewing. Unlike many social workers, psychologists and psychiatrists, the pastor has to do his own "intake interviewing." The first interview tends to be exploratory. Usually a third or more of the time in a first interview is required to "hear the person out" as much as that amount of time will permit. Several questions need to be asked on a first interview: (1) How long has the trouble been upon the individual? When did it start? (2) What attempts have been made to solve the difficulty, and especially to whom else has the counselee been for help? (3) How did the person decide to seek out the pastor? (4) What are the various alternatives the person has thought of as being possible solutions? If, in the process of the first interview, the pastor sees that a longer-term relationship is indicated, he may suggest this as one additional alternative and frankly explain what the process of counseling has to offer as well as what its limitations are. If the person sees and accepts the validity and wisdom of this procedure, then a second interview is more easily scheduled.

In both instances, that in which one interview is used and that in which a multiple-process relationship is initiated for pastoral counseling, the use of time symbolizes the pastor's concern and his understanding of the person. To a great extent, the establishment of such a relationship is a form of evaluation and judgment of seriousness. The relationship tends to be made or broken in the first interview. The pastor's firmness and gentleness in interpreting his limitations and his strengths to help the person make the difference. A careful management of the time relationship, then, is the pastor's mode of communicating his concern and understanding of the counselee.

Certain technical problems are involved in the use of time in pastoral counseling. For instance, one of the first questions asked is about *the length of an interview.* An interview kept within the scope of an hour tends to be most effective. The pastor may shorten it for the person who is unaccustomed to formal office situations, such as a young child, a relatively uneducated person, and a person in much physical pain. He may lengthen the interview a bit for the person who has traveled a long distance or has some other great handicap in coming for a conference. *The number of interviews* varies in terms of the basic need of the person. However, as we shall see a bit later, the social and structural limitations of the pastoral relationship prevent him from spending elaborate numbers of interviews with any one person. It may be that we shall sooner or later define pastoral counseling in terms of the situation of five to ten interviews in which we deal with more or less specific problem areas of the individual's life, such as bereavement, vocational choice, marital choice, and the making of a basic religious decision as to one's relationship to Christ. However, more and more pastors are being thrust into deeper, longer-term, and more formal types of relationships. But the more time a pastor uses in any given relationship, the more important it becomes that he shall have had intensive and extensive clinical pastoral training under careful and mature supervision. When a pastor accepts such responsibility, he obligates himself for training commensurate with the responsibility he accepts. Even a full year of clinical pastoral counseling education in and of itself is not sufficient. But when a pastor has intensive psychotherapeutic training, he soon goes beyond the point of no return in the kinds of ecclesiastical support he can secure. As yet, the church has not developed a clearly defined role, much less financial support, for the pastor as a private psychotherapist.

THE TIME FACTOR AND
THE CHANGING MEANINGS
OF THE PASTORAL SITUATION

The technical problems involved in the pastoral use of time in counseling raise some deeper issues as to *the quality and meaning* of the relationship of pastoral counseling. This changes at different phases of pastoral counseling in terms of the time encounter. A pastor's relationship, in one respect at least, derives some of its meaning, direction, and purpose from the amount of time that he is able to use with a given individual. A rough guide is somewhat as follows:

One Interview

A pastor has to be more time conscious and more directive. In a one-interview situation he depends more upon the shortcuts that his experience has taught him. He gives information; he gives support; he points out other resource people upon whom the counselee may call; he may guardedly answer questions quite directly; he may even give opinions. He should give these in an atmosphere of tentativeness. He should carefully leave the relationship "open" in the event that the person wants to come back to him. Too often pastors have confused openness and honesty with people (who are in as full a possession of their powers for living as he is) with "directiveness" in counseling. The actual fact of the matter is that the pastor does not have a counseling relationship in a one-interview situation if the way we have technically defined it here is correct.

Two to Six Interviews

Here the pastor is usually involved in short-term crisis or situational counseling. It is largely supportive and reflective, and it is intensely pastoral in nature. The immediate depths to which second- and third-interview relationships can go is amazing, especially when the counselee has been in classes that the pastor has taught or in worship services that he has conducted. The pastoral role is more significant in some areas of the country than in others. It strikes the deeper and more unconscious mechanisms of the personality more quickly and more certainly in some areas of the country than it does in others. For instance, one can detect a "New Haven bias" in the H. Richard Niebuhr report as to the degree of confusion and perplexity in people's minds as to the role of a minister. The pastor in a clearly defined religious culture quite often finds a depth-dimension in his relationship to a counselee on the second or third interview. A professional psychotherapist would need several more interviews in which to elicit such response.

Seven to Fifteen Interviews

The quality of relationship here varies also in terms of the clarity of the role of the counselor. However, if a relationship sustains this long, one is justified in saying that the pastor is involved in a more intensive kind of pastoral counseling. Deeper dynamics and mechanisms of identification, projection, transference, and so forth, tend to become active. The more aggressive and authoritarian the pastor is, the more likely these are to be set in motion. Likewise, the social situation of the pastor begins to strain a bit. The counselee is likely to want to involve him in social relationships, such as invitations to dinner, requests for a visit at his home, or ministries to members of his family who may be sick. Here the basic limitations of the ordinary pastoral relationship for a more or less professional psychotherapeutic endeavor begin to emerge. The social role of the pastor's wife is also brought into play. (This is one unique factor in the Protestant minister's task: he is usually married and his wife knows and is called upon to respond to his counselees, both men and women.) Likewise, the community as a whole begins to ask tacitly: "What is the meaning of all of this going and coming?" The pastor may assure the counselee of confidential treatment of all that he or she says to him. On the other hand, the pastor himself has no assurance of the same kind of confidential treatment from the counselee. The counselee may talk rather vividly and avidly of what goes on in the interview sessions. This in itself must be handled both strategically and tactically in such a way as to contribute to, rather than detract from, the pastor's other functions.

Eleven and Above Interviews

If the pastor has been faithful and effective up to this point in counseling, he begins to see more unconscious psychological material emerging in the counseling conferences. The counselee may begin to deal with dream material, to involve members of his own family in the drama, to make referrals to the pastor of other people with whom he is related, and to become almost a member of the pastor's family if he has been permitted to involve the pastor socially in the earlier stages of the relationship. If he decides to end the relationship, the pastor has a very definite problem as to what sort of durable relatedness he can offer the counselee in the normal interactions of community living.

THE TIME FACTOR AND THE PASTORAL USE
OF COMMUNITY RESOURCES

Obviously, the above rough guide of the shifting meaning of the pastoral counseling relationship in terms of the time factor suggests that the pastor has more than one reason for asking for the help of other community resource persons for more professional types of counseling. Therefore the time factor in pastoral counseling becomes a very real issue as an indication for referral. A referral system is indispensable for any effective, formal pastoral counseling. One of the reasons that pastors do not have time to do their pastoral ministry is that they insist on doing it all themselves. They do not evaluate the resources of their church and community for giving assistance to individuals. They have failed to build a detailed knowledge of their community as to the agencies, the professional and private practitioners, and others who could help them in their task. Pastors sometimes call long distances by telephone to ask their former teachers in pastoral care to see one of their parishioners. Occasionally the professor can suggest someone in the pastor's own city about whom the pastor did not know. In one instance, the person to whom I referred the pastor was only a few doors down the street from him!

The amount of time that most pastors can legitimately give to one individual begins to be strained when they go beyond the tenth interview. Pastors often use more interview time than this, sometimes wisely and sometimes not so wisely. However, when they do so, they defy their own limitations in dealing with a person's problems. They are likely to create undue guilt problems in their counselee, particularly if he is a more depressed kind of person. Such a person has to be reassured again and again that the pastor has the time that he really does not have! If the counselee is a passive, dependent individual, the pastor creates hostility problems for himself in that the counselee may use the time poorly and lean dependently on the pastor as a crutch. The counselee, in many instances, will feel the need to give the pastor something. He brings him gifts, offers services, and may even seek to pay for the "services." These actions are highly symbolic and may obligate the pastor in strange and embarrassing ways. On the other hand, their symbolism may often involve forms of worship of God to which the pastor is only incidental. Therefore we know that when a pastor goes beyond the tenth or eleventh interview with a person, he is moving out of a distinctly simple pastoral context and into a highly complex type of relationship. Great sensitivity and responsible maturity are imperative.

SOME THEOLOGICAL DIMENSIONS
OF THE TIME FACTOR
IN PASTORAL COUNSELING

As we plumb the depths of the time factor in pastoral counseling, the more the eternal issues of man's destiny emerge. The pastoral necessity of doing more formal types of counseling raises some fundamental theological and ecclesiastical problems. What is the purpose of the church and its ministry? What is this pastoral relationship like essentially?

Can a pastor "break" his relationship with a counselee, or is it, by its intrinsic character, a durable, eternal relationship? We have said that the pastor does not "discharge" his counselees. Instead, in terms of his purposive relationship to the church, he hopes they will become members of the lasting fellowship of the Christian community. Several observers have noted that in a few instances a pastor does a very effective job of pastoral counseling and in the process of it loses rather than gains a new member. The person may join someone else's church! On the other hand, at certain stages of pastoral counseling, the counselee may join the pastor's church as a demonstration of appreciation to him. This makes it absolutely necessary that the pastor have a synoptic and synthesized view of his theology and church polity in relation to his pastoral counseling practice. His doctrine may become a whetstone upon which the spiritual understanding of his counselee is sharpened.

Furthermore, the persistent tendency of counselees to involve the family life of the pastor indicates something definite about the intrinsic nature of the Protestant minister's role as a family man. At the same time, this presents a real conflict when the pastor begins to perceive himself in a role identity similar to that of the psychologist or the psychiatrist. These kinds of counselors are "private" in a way that the pastor is not. This same conflict is raised in terms of the traditional role of the pastor as a visitor in the home when it conflicts with the newer concept of pastoral counseling in which the person is expected by the pastor to come to see him in his study.

In such involvements, the anxiety of the pastor mounts. If he cannot break this relationship, what is the inherent meaning of his time-bound encounter with the counselee? In addition to all that has been mentioned, the counselee transfers deep feelings of love and hate to him, and he in turn develops basic feelings about the counselee. For instance, pastors quite anxiously discuss with professors in great detail the times that members of the opposite sex, and sometimes members of the same sex, begin to interpret their relationship to them as a more distinctly erotic or sexual relationship. One rarely hears a pastor discuss quite so freely his own feelings of love for his parishioners! These are feelings that he carries on in the private soliloquy of his soul at worst, and at best in the I-Thou encounter he has with God in prayer. His anxiety over these feelings may cause him to retreat from a relationship. He may break a relationship at its most crucial point and just at the time when he was on the verge of breaking out of his role as pastor or counselor and into his role as a fellow human being, a fellow sinner, a fellow child of God, one whose limitations his counselee accepts and affirms even as he has learned to accept and affirm the counselee's limitations. On the other hand, he may continue a counseling relationship past a time of redefinition because it meets his own needs.

Otto Rank says that within the therapeutic relationship there is an "end-setting" which may be used either redemptively or destructively. In his therapy, he agreed upon the limitations of time that both he and the counselee were suffering and jointly set an end to their relationship in its formal aspects. He likened this end to a death-birth in which an old restricted self died and a new and more potential self was born. The pastor does not have to set ends in his relationships quite so rigidly. Natural life has itself set ends in the great crises of human existence: birth, choice of a mate, religious conversion, the choice of a vocation, illness, old age, death—these are ends that are set within the habitation of man.

The time factor in pastoral counseling has its deepest relevance when the pastor realizes the tremendous sense of the eschatological dimension of life with which even the untutored tend to live in the face of these great crises. The processes of judgment are wrought out here, not in the petty moralisms the pastor can deliver. And we are persuaded that all of these are set within a larger context of the eschatological dimensions of the whole creation, as it groans and travails together. Hence, the high relevance of the more recent reemphasis upon man's finitude. God *has* set the bounds of our habitation, and the binding of time thrusts us into the ultimate concerns of our existence. As the Moffatt translation of Deut. 29:29 puts it, "The hidden issues of the future are with the Eternal our God, but the unfolded issues of the day are with us and our children for all time, that we may obey all the orders of this law."

No matter how much of a pastor's time a given person shall require, that person necessarily shall have reached a certain level of despair before he seeks pastoral counseling. Many times his personal defenses against the stresses of life are largely shattered. He lives from day to day in the nameless intuition "that years of life can be pressed out of him," by the catastrophes and prolonged duresses under which he lives. He senses that time has run out or is about to run out. Harold G. Wolff cites abundant clinical evidence in which such persons simply "stare out into space and die" for the lack of hope. Wolff calls it "give-up-itis," with which, in spite of our pseudo sophistication, large numbers of persons both in and out of the church suffer. The task of the pastoral counselor is so to mobilize the resources of time that eternity may break through to proclaim a "hope that does not disappoint" to those who sit in regions of despair. For, as Wolff says, "Man is capable of enduring incredible burdens and taking cruel punishment when he has self-esteem, hope, purpose, and belief in his fellows."[3]

Regardless of how much or how little time the pastor has with a given person under stress, his unique identity as a man of hope, as a son of encouragement, should remain constant. This ministry of hope is the meeting place of time and eternity in the good news of Jesus Christ.

NOTES

1. Samuel W. Blizzard, "The Minister's Dilemma," *The Christian Century,* April 25, 1956.

2. Samuel W. Blizzard, personal correspondence.

3. Harold G. Wolff, M.D., "What Hope Does for Man," *Saturday Review* 40 (January 5, 1957): 42–45.

26

The Deeper Levels
of Pastoral Care

World War II, the Korean conflict, the continuing cold war, the Vietnam War, and the turbulent social changes of the 1960s and 1970s have imprinted upon millions of civilians the expectations that a pastor shall be far more than just a friend and a comforter. Less and less do they quietly expect the pastor to be a hail-fellow-well-met who "attends all the meetings." More and more they expect the pastor to be a person who will converse in depth with them about the main meanings and excruciating meaninglessness of their lives. Consequently, this chapter is devoted to two kinds of conversations that pastors tend to have with parishioners and nonparishioners alike, either in visits with them or in their visits with the pastor: *brief pastoral dialogues, and multiple-interview pastoral counseling.*

THE LEVEL OF BRIEF PASTORAL DIALOGUE

Pastoral care is essentially spiritual conversation. Three recent volumes on pastoral counseling, in different ways, emphasize spiritual conversation as the focus of pastoral care: Wayne E. Oates, *Pastoral Counseling* (1974); John B. Cobb, Jr., *Theology and Pastoral Care* (1977); and Howard Clinebell, *Basic Types of Pastoral Counseling,* rev. ed. (1981).[1] Brief pastoral dialogue, styled along the line of the Socratic dialectic, is the most easily used technique for approaching the personal problems of an individual. This method is the commonsense approach to pastoral procedure that is most likely to do good and the least likely to do harm. It is also a preparatory approach to any longer-term counseling that needs to be done. The brief pastoral dialogue assumes that the person seeking help is of average intelligence, fairly stable emotionally, and capable of talking freely about the situation, with no unusual degree of mental blocking. Further, this dialogue assumes a strong degree of personal rapport between the individual and a pastor. It is usually appropriate with people to whom the pastor has been related over a period of time as pastor and teacher. Ordinarily there is a reasonably permanent bond of identification between the pastor and the person at hand. These are rather sweeping prerequisites for the use of such an approach. The psychologist or the psychiatrist may ask whether or not there *are* any such people living. But as pastors we deal with such people every day of our ministry, whereas these other experts do not see them professionally. We have the advantage of working with healthy as well as sick people.

The process of the brief pastoral dialogue is as follows. First, simply listen to the parishioner who comes to you in a time of decision and lays out a problem before you. Ask an occasional question in order to fill in missing facts. Here, in actuality, you yourself are a student, much as Socrates was a "student" with the youth of Athens, learning from the person at hand all the facts about the present situation confronting the person. You are "leading the person out" (in the Latin sense of the word "education").

Second, give a factual summary, a sort of recapitulation or "readback" of what the person has told you. You may initiate this by saying: "Now let me see whether or not I have really understood what you have told me." Then, upon finishing a concise statement of the situation at hand, you may say: "Do I understand you properly? Have we left anything out?" Quite often the person will say, "Yes, I failed to mention this . . . "; or, "No, I don't think you really understood what I meant . . . "; or, "I didn't mean to leave this impression, but . . . "

Third, ask the person to help you outline the alternative paths of action, and with the help of the counselee explore the end results and methods of achieving results in each one of the alternative paths of action. Usually this may be initiated by asking the question, "Now what are the things you *can* do in the situation?" After these alternatives have been carefully enumerated, each one can be discussed freely in a give-and-take manner as to obstacles preventing their realization, ways and means of accomplishment, and unique advantages inherent in each choice. Often the condition of things calls for your adding another possibility for the consideration of the individual—a possibility that the person probably has not yet seen. Many times this "other possibility" may be a careful combination of the best advantages of the other alternatives. For instance, a young woman does not know whether to stay in school or to go to work in order that she and her fiancé can marry. Finally she decides to stay in school, lighten her class load, get a part-time job, and marry. Inasmuch as both of them have only one more year, she feels they can "make it." Yet you do best simply to say: "Had you thought of doing this?" Or, "Would a good working compromise be . . . ?"

The fourth step is to appeal to the basic desire of the person. Often you may ask, "If all things were equal, now, which of these alternatives would you really want to follow—deep down inside?" Quite often an amused light comes to the person's eyes and the statement is made: "Well, I guess I did not want your advice so much as I wanted sympathy for what I have already decided to do." But on frequent occasions the answer may be: "I guess that is my big problem: I don't know what I want to do. I want to have my cake and eat it too, and I am not able to choose one thing and carry through with it." The more intense this feeling is, the more likely it is that the person is suffering from some type of anxiety state. At any rate, the "big problem" is out in the open. You are firmly established in the person's confidence, and now you may go into the deeper difficulties of the individual.

However, in the majority of the situations that confront a pastor, this brief pastoral dialogue produces a heightened degree of emotional reflectiveness, whets the sense of personal responsibility, reduces the chances of impulse decisions, and leaves the decision-making capacity of the person free and inviolate. It lends itself to one-interview situations more readily, and it is adaptable to pressurized schedules. Be sure to take two precautions in ending such a brief pastoral dialogue. First, be careful not to break the relationship by giving fixed advice. It is better to develop working hypotheses or "experiments" and try things out to see whether they will work. This is one of the main hazards of fixed advice: if the person cannot follow through with the recommendation, the person is hesitant to return to you. Of course, in some relatively rare instances, you may want this result. In the second place, you are able to make some arrangement for follow-up of the conference. Take great care not to forget about the persons who have conversed with you concerning the main issues of their life.

THE LEVEL OF PASTORAL COUNSELING AND PSYCHOTHERAPY

Not all personal encounters yield themselves to the rational approach suggested in the discussion of the brief pastoral dialogue. The Christian shepherd confronts many people who are suffering from deep inner conflicts over which they have no control. They stand in need of a minister who has psychological foundations and knowledge of psychotherapeutic skills as well as of the healing power of God. Such persons have come to the point where *they do not want to do what they want to do.* Their decision-making powers are deadlocked in a filibuster of *one* of their many selves in the congress of their soul. Unhappy people, they come to the pastor complaining that they cannot control their thoughts and actions. In the thought of Paul, they do not understand their own actions, for they do not the things they want, but do the very things they hate (Rom. 7:15).

The large majority of such persons are not "insane." They do not suffer from gross delusions of grandeur and persecution. They may live their lives in quiet desperation but are not definably depressed to the point of suicide or homicide. They do not stand in need of institutionalization and protective care. Accordingly, they are not candidates for a psychiatrist ordinarily. Usually they are not wealthy enough to afford a psychoanalyst who specializes in their kind of troubles. Rather, when they come to a pastor, they are usually people of limited means who are acutely unhappy and blocked out of the abundant life. Nevertheless they may be conscientious church members and active in the affairs of the community. Their religion, unhappily, seems to be conformed to the pattern of their unhappy way of life rather than a transforming power that renews their mind. They do not have the joy of their salvation. Yet they hopefully look to their faith in God as a promise of redemption from their inner bondage to the legalism they have mistaken for Christian faith.

In order to deal effectively with the basic religious needs that these conflict-weary persons manifest, the pastor must become acquainted with the "heart's native language" of feelings as well as with the rational precepts of theological formulations. As Nathaniel Hawthorne says:

> If he show no intrusive egotism . . . ; if he have the power, which must be born with him, to bring his mind into such affinity with his patient's that this last shall unawares have spoken what he imagines himself only to have thought; if such revelations be received without tumult, and acknowledged not so often by an uttered sympathy as by silence, an inarticulate breath, and here and there a word, to indicate that all is understood; if to these qualifications of a confidant be joined the advantages afforded by his recognized character as a physician—then, at some inevitable moment will the soul of the sufferer be dissolved, and flow forth in a dark but transparent stream, bringing all its mysteries into the daylight.[2]

Such a "feeling for the feelings" of people, a careful clinical study of people's troubles, and an equally careful reexamination of the New Testament reveal a Christian explanation of the difficulties of people: Idolatry in the sphere of values is the basic religious component in the malformations encountered in these particular neurotic processes. The person suffers, as Søren Kierkegaard said, from "inwardness with a jammed lock." They are in bondage "to the elemental spirits of the universe . . . , in bondage to beings that by nature are no gods" (Gal. 4:3, 8).

Primarily such a person is possessed by the demand of one part of the self that the rest of the self bow down in its worship. As Plato said, this type of sin is "the rising up of a part of the soul over the whole." Such individuals are not persons but many selves. They condemn themselves roundly on every hand, giving the key to their plight when they say, "I could never forgive myself . . . " Thus it is seen clearly that they are inordinate worshipers of fictitious goals in life, borrowed standards for life, fantasies of what they think themselves ideally to be. The viciousness of this idolatry lies in its self-destructiveness, its prating itself as humility, self-denial, self-rejection, and religious devotion. Their desire to become a person in their own right overshoots the mark and they aspire to become their own god.

The only answer to this plight is that the eyes of the inner understanding be opened to irresponsibility and a childish sense of omnipotence. The inner life must be opened to the ethically severe love of God. This convinces these persons that the root of their sins is in self-enchantment, that God is consistent and can be depended upon to work within them as they make and carry out decisions, and that God is "a rewarder of them that diligently seek him." Such a picture is seen in the life of the man whom Jesus asked, before he healed him, "Wilt thou be made whole?" And the surest thing that you can do for such conflict-weary persons who come to you is to put them on their own before God, to give them all the loving confidence and intelligent affection that you have time and opportunity to give. But do so on a clear covenant and disciplined basis.

But a theological orientation to the problems of such trouble-ridden people is inadequate unless it takes into account what is observably known about the processes of recovery from such states. The busy pastor needs a clear conception of *how* to go about "putting persons on their own before God and giving them all the intelligent affection that time and opportunity make possible." Every responsible pastor knows that the neurotic personalities in the church not only are unhappy themselves but cause unhappiness to others all out of proportion to their own number. We as ministers ourselves are at least as important as any other one factor in causing church splits and church failures. Therefore the minister may be forced by circumstances to ask, "What am I going to do for and about the neurotic processes in my church and in myself?"

The core of neurotic processes is anxiety and fear. Long-standing inabilities to trust people fuel impairments in the capacity to trust, commit, and bond oneself to others. This universalizes itself in the struggle of the Spirit to perceive and relate to God as a loving friend rather than as an ever-present opponent or enemy. The love of God is a perfect love. Your love and my love are impeded by fear. "Perfect love casts out fear. For fear has to do with punishment, and he who fears is not perfected in love" (1 John 4:18).

The field of counseling and psychotherapy three decades ago was thinly populated. Resources for this kind of care were few and far between. However, as of this writing, the field is becoming heavily populated. One criticism in the field leveled at pastoral counselors and psychotherapists is that we as ministers are too authoritarian and moralistic to accomplish effective results. A controlled study of this was made.

From 1956 to 1961, Seward Hiltner and Lowell G. Colston clinically contrasted the two different contexts of counseling—that of the clinical psychologist and that of the pastor. They published their findings in the book *The Context of Pastoral Counseling.* They used the term "context" for "what differentiates the pastor's counseling from that of other counselors." They concluded that "the attempt to understand and to articulate to ourselves the feelings people have about the whole context in which pastoral counseling takes place is not a nuisance but a vital instrument in the giving of help."[3] One important result of the study was that counselees felt *less* judgmentalism and authoritarianism in a church counseling service than in a psychological clinic.

The subtle conditioning factors discussed are integral parts of the context of counseling. The religious history and the characteristic modes of selfhood developed over the years of a person's life exercise a reciprocal effect on counselor and counselee. For example, pastors, psychiatrists, social workers, and psychologists seem to have equally difficult times in activating those individuals who are aggressively dependent and who insist that the counselor shall take total responsibility for their care.

For this reason and because of my own hypothesis that in the design of selfhood a particular counselee and a particular counselor reciprocally shape the responsible covenant they form and the techniques that eventuate, my position, simply stated here, is: (1) The structure of the context in which a person seeks the pastor's help—informal or formal—may be or become confused and must be continually defined, redefined, and clarified. (2) The methodology of the pastor is shaped by the patterns of self-confrontation that emerge in the relationship and that, in turn, must be sensitively appreciated, identified, and understood. (3) The religious history of the person is important to the person who is seeking a pastor's counseling, and the person should be given every opportunity to discuss it in detail. (4) The preponderant majority of pastoral counseling situations involve marriage conflict, which moves through a definable process of deterioration. This process shapes the procedures of the pastor and cannot be ignored. Therefore you as a pastor can most productively use continuing education opportunities in studying marriage and family therapy.

My hypotheses have been considerably influenced by my own specific counseling experience studies but also by the additional help of the work of Harry Stack Sullivan in his discussion of "Developmental Syndromes" in his *Conceptions of Modern Psychiatry* and his discussion of the "Detailed Enquiry" in his book *The Psychiatric Interview.*[4] These hypotheses are sufficiently clear from extensive clinical application to be good foundations for effective pastoral counseling when generously laced with common sense. However, each one is open to continuing refinement by more sophisticated and detailed research design. New generations of pastoral counselors can no longer rely upon anecdotal and "hunch" approaches to methodology. But it is sustaining to find one's previous "hunches" validated from clinical studies. More recent studies for your consideration are András Angyal, *Neurosis and Treatment: A Holistic Theory*, ed. by E. Hanfmann and R. M. Jones; and Irvin D. Yalom, *Existential Psychotherapy.*[5]

However, without *supervised* application and research the pastor cannot appreciate or understand safely such literature as has been discussed and recommended here. In actuality, the only effective means of testing the hypotheses described in these books is that of engaging in intensive clinical work under adequate supervision and in a setting where you can have a group of other professionals with whom to study in a fellowship of learning. You can get this training in theological curricula in many schools today. If you are already in a pastoral situation and cannot easily gain access to a training center during a summer, you can try to get a leave of absence or commute to the nearest center of training. In such a center of training you become a part of the healing team. Physicians, social workers, psychiatrists, nurses, and ministers are all helpfully related to the same persons in need. Furthermore, you are given close personal supervision in your individual work with people by trained theological supervisors. Here "the living human documents of flesh and blood" become the textbooks for you. The gospel comes alive to you in the face-to-face ministry to people.

Some persons ask, "How far should a pastor go in 'deeper-level counseling'?" The answer is threefold: You should go as far as your training has equipped you to accept responsibility for the outcome of your treatment. You should go as far as the uncontrolled environment in which your work will permit you to accept responsibility for the person's life. And, finally, you should go as far as the limitations of your time and social role will permit you to give yourself to the needs of the individual.

The counseling work of a minister is a dynamic and growing relationship. You do well to think of yourself as counseling in the creative processes of spiritual birth and maturation, and to think of the person before you as needing new life and spiritual maturity. *This creative process moves naturally through five phases.* The phases may take place quickly in one interview, but more often the relationship may extend over several or even a large number of conferences. This allows time for growth and reflection, during which the person has the opportunity in between interviews to deal with problems alone and in fellowship with the Holy Spirit.

The Preparatory Phase of Counseling

The more inexperienced pastor usually asks the question, "How is it that people come to their pastor for counseling help?" The veteran minister asks, "How can I get people who ask for help started off in an effective relationship for the best results in my counseling with them?" Others may ask, "How can I stimulate the need for counseling help in a person who does not yet feel either the need for help or that I am the person to give it?" All these questions indicate a *preparatory phase* in most counseling relationships. In this phase you as pastor do several things. You first discover who needs help and establish an initial contact with that person. If the person comes to you in an informal situation, you seek to construct a more formal one in which time, privacy, and quietness can be achieved. If the person must be sought out by visitation or by cultivation of friendship, you seek to stimulate the sense of need for help and to shift the initiative in the relationship in such a way that the person "stretches forth a hand" for help.

1. Discovering Persons in Need and Establishing an Initial Contact. The pastor is one of the very few persons in modern society who is still expected to visit people. In some communities even this expectation is losing its strength. But ordinarily, you as pastor have a right to visit in the homes of your community. This is one of your best means of discovering persons in need and of establishing an initial contact with them. Purposeful and patient home visitation reveals to the observant pastor, especially when visits are made in times of crises, many of the quieter and more desperate needs of individuals and families. It establishes a rapport that will be necessary to any future counseling. It gives a distinctly personal touch to your interest in people. Learn to use the pastoral visit in a disciplined, professional way. It offers you opportunities to see the individual in the context of the family and to sense the feelings of other members of the family toward that person. Home visitation presents you with a *systems analysis* of the way of life of the person which only many hours of individual counseling would ultimately reveal.

Likewise, your public ministry affords you "after meeting" conversations with persons who have private matters they wish to discuss. This is the pastoral counselor's "outlet to the sea" of human suffering. Careful, perceptive, and humanly tender preaching and teaching are avenues of exchange of feeling between a pastor and the individual who needs personal counseling.

Furthermore, a patient educating of the leadership of the church to guide persons in actual need to you as pastor rewards you with an abundance of initial contacts with such persons. This is best illustrated by a negative example. A middle-aged woman who had been married only about six years became deeply depressed and took her life by self-poisoning. One of her neighbors called the pastor immediately and asked that he make his services available to the husband of the woman in making plans for and conducting the funeral. In the telephone conversation, she said, "I have known for some time that she was thinking of doing such a thing, but I never believed she would!" If the woman had been trained to do so, she could have notified the pastor long *before* the tragedy. As it was, all she knew to do was to call him for the funeral!

Probably the most Christlike method of establishing initial contacts with persons in need is that of the pastoral "marketplace ministry." As you read the Gospels, you find only one example of a formal interview in the ministry of Jesus, the conversation with Nicodemus. The rest of his conversations were beside wells, in people's homes, along the roadside, and in or near places of worship. In the casual, informal contacts of everyday living with people—in the grocery store, at the service station, at the bank, at the garage, at social gatherings of all kinds—you as a contemporary pastor also hear the "uplifted voices" of human need. A young pastor tells of the following experience. He read in his morning paper that a man and a woman, both members of his church, were seeking a divorce. That morning he stopped, as his custom was, to get some gasoline at the man's service station. He stood reading his paper inside the man's place of business. The proprietor was posting his books, while the attendant filled the gas tank. Everything was tensely quiet until the owner looked up and snarled at the pastor: "Well, go on and say it. I know what you are going to say anyhow!" The pastor countered by saying: "I am not sure whether or not you feel that I am your friend. I don't want to say anything unless you know that my friendship belongs to you and that I care what happens to you."

The man was taken aback by this approach. Then he broke into a warm, anguished outpouring of his difficulties with his wife that had culminated in divorce proceedings. The pastor did not try to deal with it at that moment, but said, "I will be responsible with your confidence in me. Do you think you and I could get together tonight, after your station closes, and talk this over?" An appointment was made, and the more formal kind of counseling relationship had been established.

2. *Making Counseling Appointments.* This latter step suggests one of the important essentials of the preparatory phase of counseling work: you learn to be very effective in the use of an appointment system. Unless it is otherwise unavoidable, you do not attempt to deal with intimately personal problems of individuals in public places where other people can surmise and draw their own conclusions. You make appointments either to visit in the person's home or to meet in your study. Such a simplified procedure will do much toward making your time more valuable to others and to yourself. This is much wiser than setting arbitrary office hours for people to come to see you if they need help on their personal problems. It is more personal, less of an affront to the autonomy of the people of the community, and therefore less likely to create unnecessary hostility. Furthermore, your identity as a preacher, teacher, and overseer of the flock will not be obscured by arbitrarily set office hours which "strike the pose" of a formal counseling ministry which some people may resent. But more important than this, such a plan does much toward "tailoring" your relationship to the individual in such a way that you can counsel without too many personal obstructions and uncontrollable interruptions.

3. *Stimulating the Initiative of the Person Who Needs Help.* A difficult task in the preparatory phases of counseling is that of switching the initiative from yourself as pastor to the person whom you are seeking to help. This is more easily illustrated than it is defined. For instance, a young woman called her pastor, asking for an appointment *for her husband* to come and talk with him about some marital problems in which they were involved. The pastor, in the preparatory phases of the counseling relationship, said, "I will be glad to talk with *him* as to a time that is convenient for both of us. Will you have him call me about it?" The purpose of the pastor was to shift the initiative in the search for help away from the wife and onto the husband. Yet, in some instances, it might be clear that the husband's work prevented his own calling and you would feel that there was no manipulation of the husband by the wife.

Sometimes you will recognize an acute need in a person in your community but are aware that the person is hostile and resistant to any offer of help. You want to lessen the hostility and to uncover in the person a desire for your guidance. This is one of the most difficult relationships with which you deal. For example, a pastor learned that one of the members of the church had made a vow that he would never return to church after seeing his father, the senior elder of the church, with "another woman sitting in my dead mother's place," as the man himself stated.

The pastor regularly visited the man in his home, inasmuch as the man was physically ill a good portion of the time. Little mention was ever made of the fact that he did not come to church. No reference was made to the fact that the pastor knew of the conflict between him and his father, nor to the fact of his father's remarriage. The pastor "waited him out" until the man himself felt secure enough in his affections to tell him about the conflict without being asked. At this point, the man sought the pastor's guidance and became durably related to the pastor as a caring person. This relationship lasted—at differing levels of intensity—over a period of sixteen years.

Another situation in pastoral care and personal counseling that calls for a switch of initiative is that of major moral offenses among persons in the congregation. These usually first come to your attention in rumors from different persons within the community. Whispers of embezzlement, shady business dealings, sexual promiscuity, sexual perversions, and any item of the catalog that each community compiles come to the ears of the minister. Next, the person's place of authority and leadership in the church is questioned. A rift in the unity of the congregation is in the making. In smaller congregations, the whole unsavory situation can come to a crisis in a clash of personalities in the open meetings of the church. Your own leadership may become so involved that you may want to resign or be asked to resign.

Such a situation may best be handled in the rumor stage by a pastor who has a firm hand in dealing with people. The following case record shows how one pastor handled the situation:

PASTOR:

Wilhelm, I called and asked you to come by to see me for a reason. Before I tell you what I have on my mind, I want to say that my confidence in you as a person runs pretty deep and my affection for you is true and sure. Otherwise, I would not have been concerned about you. Then, too, I want to assure you that no one else knows that you are here and that all you say to me will be handled responsibly and with your full knowledge ahead of time.

You may justly tell me, when I say what I have on my mind, that I am sticking my nose into your business and have no right to do so. You will be right except in the fact that I would want you to do for me what I am trying to do for you, because I feel that you are my friend.

Now to come to the point, before you lose your patience in curiosity, let me say that I am not concerned about the truth or error of the reports that have come to me. They could be false and still do you harm. If they are false, I think you are entitled to know that these things are being said. If they are true, I think you are entitled to a sympathetic friend with whom you can talk safely about your side of the story. There are, as you well know, two sides to all such things.

The word has come to me that you have been sexually molesting some of the young boys and girls in our church. The exact situations are these: _____; _____; _____; _____. I will not tell you who told me all this, because I do not want to do all of you harm. But you can imagine for yourself, and if this is not true, you can be secure in knowing that they do not know that I am talking to you either.

What do you think about all this?

WILHELM:

Well, for a good while I have wanted to talk with you about this, but I never knew quite how to go about it. I have been doing some of those things. Not all of them, though. I came here a stranger and thought I had found a really Christian crowd that didn't do those things. I got into it, though, and found that they were not so different from myself. . . .

The conclusion of the whole history is too lengthy to report in full, but this part of the record indicates that confidence was established. The preparatory phases of such counseling can move from an authoritarian to a permissive relationship between the counselor and the counselee. However, catching in time an explosive interpersonal condition like this is not always this easy. In later stages of deterioration the situation may spread so far and so deep in the life of the church and the community that you would be forced to distribute responsibility to members of the official board and to the members of other helping professions—medicine, the law, and businesses. Making a referral to an outside uninvolved professional may be the thing to do. You may have many difficulties in dealing with such a problem in the next phases that are to be discussed, but, at least if you are as fortunate as the pastor who was mentioned in the preceding record, you have stabilized your relationship in such a way that the initiative is with the counselee more than it is with you.

The Phase of Relaxation and Development of Trust

At the outset of this discussion of the process of counseling, the problem of the place and time of the counseling ministry needs to be considered. The initiative factor has already been discussed in connection with "making the contact." You cannot afford to be careless about the place at which you meet the person. Whether the counselee is a man or a woman, in either instance you communicate your identity as a caring pastor by the place where you suggest that you meet. It is highly preferable that the person come either to your study or to your home at a time when other persons are also in the church building or at your home. This can usually be done and still allow discreet and unobserved privacy for the conversation. If this cannot be done, another time should be arranged when it will be possible. Responsible attention given to finding a place of discreet privacy, but with someone nearby, forestalls your being alone in a building with the person in the event that an emergency arises or in the event that your presence with the person would be for any reason misinterpreted either by the person with whom you are counseling or by other persons. For example, one pastor was alone in his study early one morning talking with a businessman about a personal problem, and the businessman had a heart attack. The pastor had great difficulty in handling this emergency alone.

Furthermore, you need tactfully to interpret the time situation to a person at the outset of a conversation. Thus, both you and the person will be more relaxed in the time you do have together. This avoids some of the stress and divided attention that may otherwise come at the end of the conversation. Usually an interview should be about an hour in length. It may be shortened to forty-five minutes or even to a half hour when the relationship has matured and strengthened. It may be lengthened a bit on the first interview or in the event that circumstances of distance in travel or length of time between the interviews necessitate this. Rarely should an interview continue over an hour and a half without a break. The pastoral counseling relationship does not really develop fully in hurried conditions. The amount of time the pastor, teacher, or administrator can give to one person usually begins to be strained when the more intensive phases of the relationship extend beyond a dozen interviews. However, effective pastoral counseling often comes in "rounds" of three to five interviews at a time, with months and even years elapsing between groupings of interviews.

Most persons who are suffering from emotional handicaps are discouraged, tense, suspicious, and self-conscious. In the earliest phases of your relationship to such persons, you put them at ease and disarm them of their personal mistrust of you. Likewise, you establish some meeting point of feeling with them and define clearly your own relationship to them. The success or failure of a counseling situation is often determined within the first half hour of the discussion. A "relationship of a trusted motive" must be established and the suspicions of the person relieved before progress can be made. Erik Erikson speaks of the element of trust as the foundational factor in human integrity and development. He says that in "adults the impairment of basic trust is expressed in a basic mistrust." He also perceives that the positive function of religion is to restore a sense of trust. "Whoever says he has religion must derive a faith from it which is transmitted to infants in the form of basic trust."[6]

The pastor in this phase of any relationship will therefore be sensitive to three trust-building and trust-interfering factors in the experience of the person who is being counseled:

1. The Relief of Nervous Tension. The person is often frightened at talking with you and especially about personal concerns. Breathlessness may indicate either fear of the interview situation or haste in arriving for the appointment in time. Drawn features may indicate sleeplessness, loss of appetite. Clenched fists, sweaty palms, and twisted handkerchiefs may point toward a burden of unrelieved anxiety. Rigid perching on the edge of a chair, furtive movements of the body—all these and many other signs are the tattered edges of a tense spirit showing themselves. Be alert and sensitive to the degree of tension in a counselee at all times. By the composure within yourself, the unhurriedness of your manner, and the steady certainty of your tone of voice you can communicate confidence and peacefulness to the person. Often purposely avoid talking about significant and painful matters until the person feels more at ease and under less tension. The person must be relatively free from the mental blocking that arises from emotional tension before being able to discuss difficulties profitably. This process of relaxation, by whatever legitimate means you most aptly can use, is the first prerequisite of good counseling. The small talk, superficial conversation about places and relations, a brief prayer for peace and clarity of vision, and direct suggestions such as: "Sit in this chair. I think you will be able to relax more"; "Why not pause a little while and catch your breath? You've been running"; "Lean back in your chair and take it easy"—all these point toward an easing of tension.

2. The Acceptance of Personal Antagonism. The occasion that brings many people with deep-seated emotional disturbances to a minister quite often is one of anger and resentment. A person may come to you under pressure from someone else and resent both that other person and you for being put in such a position. But occasionally the point that stimulated the person's anger may be something you yourself have done that the person did not like.

Anger is regularly denied. The word itself is taboo to many people within and outside the church. They are more likely to use the words, "I am hurt," or "frustrated," or "it's not fair." Deep wells of antagonism prevent these persons from having a relaxed relationship with you. The most common fear is that you will condemn them if you know them as they really are. They fear that you will betray them in some unknown way. But even more subtle are those antagonisms which cause persons to misinterpret and distort your words, to ascribe to you meanings that you did not reflect to them, and even to deny the truth of their own words that might be repeated back to them verbatim.

You also have the task of disarming your counselee of any antagonism toward former ministers that may be spilling over into the person's feelings toward you, the present pastor. The resentments that the person holds toward other people in the church also inhibit a friendly relationship.

By careful definition of your own relationship with and an undivided attention toward the person, you can tactfully disarm the person of much of this resistance. Sometimes this may take a whole interview; with others a "meeting point of feeling" is never established. But no smoothness of ministry can be achieved until the thermostats of the person's heart have been opened by the warmth of friendship and sustained by the strength of a basic trust. This does not mean you are doing no good for these persons. Later, in some instances they will return and thank you for not either giving in to their anger or responding in kind.

3. Mutual Acceptance of Personal Responsibility. One hazard in the establishment of rapport is that the person will shirk personal responsibility for the difficulties and shift to a complete dependence upon the pastor for a solution. Whereas some people refuse to trust a minister at all, a great many take the relationship of mutual trust as a parasitic opportunity "to pass the buck" of their troubles to the pastor. When you fail to measure up to their expectations, then you begin to get resistance from them. The genius of effective counseling is to leave the responsibility for the solution of the problem with the person who has the problem, without causing the person to feel abandoned. You provide a permissive and warmly personal atmosphere in which a counselee can objectively work through the problem to a satisfactory solution. Religiously stated, it is the careful observance of the principle of the autonomy of the individual personality before God. The counselor exercises a confident trust in the lawful working of the Holy Spirit both to will and to do for the good pleasure of God in the life of the person. Furthermore, perceive persons as they perceive themselves! Get their internal frame of reference. Exert the religious discipline of self-emptying which in itself is "good news" to your stress-ridden counselees.

From your point of view as a pastor, you take preventive measures in order that you may not become so encumbered with the difficulties of one person that you cannot minister to the many other people who come to you. It aids you in your own personal relaxation to get over the compulsive necessity of doing something about every problem that is brought to you and to accept the realism of Paul's maxim, "Each man will have to bear his own load" (Gal. 6:5). The sense in which you are fulfilling the law of Christ by bearing the other person's load with that person lies in your provision of a faithful presence of togetherness with the person. Thus the person is neither alone nor wrapped up in the self; the person is sharing the reality of the Christian community.

These three problems—the degree of tension, the degree of personal antagonism, and the degree of personal responsibility—are the issues at stake in establishing rapport with the person who comes to you with a more profound personality problem. At all stages of counseling, the degree of rapport may be strengthened or weakened in such a way as to help or hinder any further progress. No smoothness of ministry can be achieved at all, however, until the person has accepted you through the warmth of friendship and the power of genuine trust.

The Phase of Listening and Exploration

Blending into the phase of relaxation and the development of trust is the period of "talking it out." Your counselee has a story to tell, a mosaic of present events and past connotations. The person feels that life is slipping away and some real decisions need to be made. A tangled schemata of events needs to be unraveled. You listen to this intently, you create at all times an atmosphere of safety in which long-harbored events may come to light. The person socializes, often for the first time, the thoughts and feelings that have hovered in the hinterland of the consciousness, creating anxieties that could not be explained but could only be felt and responded to with blind compulsion.

1. The Ministry of Listening. The pastor at this phase of the counseling situation depends almost entirely upon the ministry of listening. Much needs to be said at this point on the use of this powerful tool of pastoral work.

The easiest way to help people is to understand them. As Lin Yutang has said, "To understand is to forgive." The easiest way to understand people is to listen to them, to hear them out. Listening creatively is an art in itself. It calls into action those other nonverbal forms of communication which are dramatically more powerful than the use of words: eye expression, bodily responses of muscle and movement to meaning, and the effect of total silence. As Theodor Reik has said, "It is important that we recognize what speech conceals and what silence reveals."[7] Listening essentially means three things.

a. It means *actually hearing what the person says,* hearing with an "evenly hovering attention." You are most susceptible to letting your attention wander from the person to whom you are listening to any one of the thousand other things that you have to think about. Preoccupation with other things is like damp rot in your counseling ministry. Shuffling papers on the desk, searching out a letter from your pocket, furtively glancing at your watch—all these are subtle ways of indicating that you are giving halfhearted attention to what is being said. Likewise, we quite often miss the mark in understanding people because we do not pay attention to seemingly insignificant details concerning their attitudes and feelings.

But it would be a mistake to assume, as Reik says, that "all observation is purely conscious. Not until we have learned to appreciate the significance of unconscious observation, reacting to the faintest impressions with the sensitiveness of a sheet of tinfoil, shall we recognize the difficulty of transforming imponderabilia into ponderabilia."[8] In this sense, listening is a sort of "free-floating attention," which "makes note of everything equally."

b. Listening means *letting the person do the talking.* Suppress the temptation to make comments and observations to the person with whom you are counseling. Don't give your own understanding of the difficulties *as soon as you yourself have seen them.* Careful restraint and attentive listening instead often reveal that the person has already thought of these things. Almost a miracle occurs to hear a person say that which it seems impossible for the person even to see, much less articulate. The counselee whom you genuinely trust to work faithfully at problems will often utter the very words *you would have* uttered, without any prompting from you.

In the sense of *letting* counselees do the talking, listening is a passive process. Here your passive listening lays hold of the "active power of silence," which "makes small talk transparent, and has a force that pulls them forward, driving them into deeper layers of their experience than they had intended." Also, it calls upon your initiative as the pastor.

Of course, the use of silence, in the sense of letting the person do the talking, depends upon the degree of trust that is present between the pastor and the person at hand. Subtle miracles can and do occur as you do this. Douglas Steere describes the process in an exquisitely written section in his book *On Listening to Another.*

> Have you ever sat with a friend when in the course of an easy and pleasant conversation the talk took a new turn and you both listened avidly to the other and to something that was emerging in your visit? You found yourselves saying things that astonished you and finally you stopped talking and there was an immense naturalness about the long silent pause that followed. In that silent interval you were possessed by what you had discovered together. If this has happened to you, you know that when you come up out of such an experience, there is a memory of rapture and a feeling in the heart of having touched holy ground.[9]

The silence of a physician of the spirit slowly changes its significance to the person with whom you are working. I was interviewing a thirty-year-old man who had always been passively dependent upon his pastors, college professors, and parents for the motivation of his behavior. The interviews consisted of many long and painful silences in between jerky, halting outbursts of insight into this infantile dependence upon others. On the fourth interview, the man said, "I have decided that I have been coming to talk with you just to get on the good side of you, just as I did with my pastor and my professors in college."

Then I said, "Have you been that eager to have my approval?" Then a long, stringent silence ensued, at the beginning of which I felt a sense of impatience at the fact that the man would not talk any further. Then I remembered that silence could uncover what speech would hide, remained silent, and felt the impulse to pray silently in the man's behalf. During the meditative silence, the man arose from his seat and walked out of the room.

Two weeks later, the man sought another conference and told me this: "During that exceedingly talkative [laughing at his own humor] interview we had the last time we were together, I made up my mind that, in order to clear my own thinking, I would just have to break my dependence on you. I felt that the only way to do this was to come in and engage you in conversation and get up and walk out and leave you. But when I came, you just sat silent. *At first I felt that your silence was an unfriendly silence, but suddenly it changed and I felt it was a friendly silence. I had the feeling that if I did leave your office, you would understand.*"

Therefore the use of a passive listening is predicated upon the "friendliness of the silence" of the pastor. This can best be approximated by facial assurances of understanding and by creating the illusion of talking by using such interjections as "Uh-huh," "Yes," "I think I see," "Did he?" Or it can be accomplished by repeating the trailing ends of sentences, such as, "You say you went from home to work that morning." This is a continual flow of encouragement from you to the person with whom you are counseling, stimulating the person's confidence to talk and making it easier for the person. If, however, you are preoccupied with trying to formulate what you yourself are going to say as soon as you find an opening, you may find the opening sooner than you think. It is much more effective to follow the lead of the most emotion-laden response of the counselee and encourage the person by reflecting these feelings back to the person to explore them more thoroughly.

c. Listening, in the third place, means *actually getting the person to talk.* In this sense, listening is an active experience on your part. Here you take some positive initiative. At this point the pastoral counselor is no longer hobbled by earlier demands for "nondirectiveness." Nevertheless you maintain person-centeredness rather than problem-centeredness, positive regard and respect for the counselee, and a steady practice of getting the person's own internal frame of reference, values, and anxieties. In the first instance, you can take the initiative in the listening by following the lead of the person and picking up the specific trailing end of the sentence that is spoken with the most feeling and strength of tone. This amounts to asking the person to talk a little bit more about the particular subject being discussed, without using those words at all.

Again, active listening calls into action your right to ask questions. This is directive listening. What the scalpel is to the surgeon, the question is to the pastoral counselor. Therefore the question is used with antiseptic motives, clean hands, and a pure heart devoid of vanity and deceptiveness. The important thing for you to remember is that you not run ahead of the sense of trust that you have with the person. You do not ask a question that the person has not given you the spiritual privilege to ask. Then, for the sake of time and because of the informal nature of much pastoral counseling, you can, with safety for all concerned, encourage the person to talk by asking well-placed questions. Here you may fill out a gap of information, you may reflect a feeling, or you may even suggest an association by the way you ask a question.

These are the three significant meanings of the listening ministry—hearing what the person says, letting the person do the talking, and actively encouraging the person to talk. They should be borne in mind as you enter upon the phase of counseling that has been called "listening and exploration." However, certain precautions as to the use of a passive or an active listening approach need to be made. Such a method may cause the pastor to spend time that should be used more valuably by a person with greater skill who could give more concentrated attention to the person. An example of this would be the case of those persons who are so acutely depressed that they become more agitated and depressed as they talk more and more to their own confusion. In fact, they may be so depressed as to be mute. An attempt on the part of the minister to explore their difficulties through a listening approach might even make things worse. Total dependence upon listening as a pastoral procedure, to the exclusion of basic knowledge and skillful evaluation of the different patterns of emotional reaction in people's lives, is ineffectual at best and dangerous at worst. For example, this approach is limited in dealing with passive-aggressive persons. In my book *Pastoral Counseling* these patterns of self-structure are dealt with in detail.

2. *The Achievement of Insight.* Your frank objective in this second phase of the ministry of counseling is that the person with whom you are dealing will achieve insight into the difficulties the person has *and* develop control over them. This is done by indirection rather than by frontal assaults on the besetting difficulties of the individual. It comes to pass through the process of listening and exploration somewhat after this manner:

Repressed memories return in the present feelings of the person. Do not think of these memories as being *past* experiences. They live actively in the present existence of the individual, who unconsciously considers them as present realities rather than as things that are in the past. For example, if a person had a sadistic, cruel parent as a child, the chances are that the parent is *still* treating the person that way. Or, the present dream life of the person reenacts the old events. As one hospital patient said upon having dreamed of her childhood, "All those people who have long been dead are now alive again in my mind." These are memories, yes, but they were buried alive, and, like Hamlet's father's uneasy spirit, find their way back into the daily affairs of the person's life. The ministry of attentive, careful, and considerate listening provides the atmosphere in which these memories and present feelings may return for the person's own reconsideration and for assimilation into the person's reasonable way of life.

You will also be alert to the *expression of ambivalent feelings* on the part of the person, or opposing feelings about the same point of concern. For example, in one context an attitude of almost worshiping the father may be expressed, and in another connection the person may mention having discovered recently that the father is dismally wrong about many things. In the presence of the contradictions, you may be prone to say, "But I thought you said you almost worshiped him!" This would give the person a trapped feeling. *Simply to reflect these feelings back to the person in a mirror fashion lets the person see the contrast, not hear it.* Whereas people see through a glass darkly, and know only in part, this is one way of moving them toward a conviction of insight that *may* eventuate in constructive actions.

This acceptance, clarification, and balancing of contradictory needs in the lives of people is vital concerning their feelings toward God. The tensions in the person between the need for aggression and the need for passivity, the need for independence and the need for dependence, the need for individuality and the need for social approval, the need for rebellion and the need for authority, constantly call for a frank conversation about God's relationship to the person. Encouraging this balance in the lives of people is a frankly accepted objective of a good pastor. In reality, these ambivalences are conflicts in the value structures coming to fresh focus in their perceptions. This struggle is an ethical struggle of the self for consistency of values.[10]

The *need for self-rejection and the need for self-acceptance* constantly tend to stalemate each other. These opposing needs usually appear in the context of the question that arises as to whether the persons at hand should express or deny themselves in the search for personal satisfaction. They may have in mind aggressive impulses and feel very guilty over losing their temper but feel that they cannot accept themselves as a weakling! Or they may realize freedom in Christ to enjoy the sexual life but do not know what to do with this freedom. Of course, such instances are illustrations of ambivalent feelings toward the self. They reflect a fear of one's own emotions and a confusion as to one's purposes in life.

Naturally the problems of self-acceptance are basically of a religious nature.[11] They suggest that the achievement of insight in the process of personal counseling may be superficial or profound, destructive or creative, temporary or permanent, depending upon the level of truly religious feeling it reaches. *The Christian pastor frankly accepts the fact that ethical values make a difference in the mental health of a person.* Discriminating judgment of such values reveals about four qualitatively different levels of insight.

a. On the *ascetic level of insight,* individuals refuse to accept the idea of even having negative feelings of aggression, passionate feelings of a sexual nature, power drives of domination, acquisitive desires for possession, and self-destructive drives because of meaninglessness. These persons live on the basis of complete repression and inner blindness to their humanity. In a word, they feel not only that they are without sin but that they are not tempted.

b. On the *fatalistic level of intellectual insight,* individuals are "sicklied o'er with the pale cast of thought," accept intellectually that they have certain problems but find more satisfaction in analyzing themselves than in attempting any changes in their way of life. Quite often they will use the opportunity for an interview as a mirror before which they can preen their symptoms. It is as though they had a filmlike image of themselves before them. Their descriptions of their difficulties become means of satisfaction rather than an unhappiness to them. Again, such persons may subtly defy the counselor to solve their problems and, when the house is swept clean, they may return a few days later with "seven other" problems to take the place of the first one.

Or these persons may take the fatalistic attitude of a stoic and become one whose "head is bloody, but unbowed," engage in heroics of their determination, and resign themselves to their fate. Such persons often mistake stoicism for Christian faith.

c. On the *sociopathic level of Machiavellian insight,* these persons see their antisocial and asocial tendencies and rejoice in the new freedom of their insight. They take their knowledge as an occasion to the flesh. They take a delinquent turn, and the people around them pay the price for this newfound "understanding" of themselves. Their insight is that of creativity gone berserk. They take advantage of society to get their own wishes, although they may use the appearance of socially acceptable standards to get their own way. This "acting out" of impulses may create havoc in the life of a church, a school, or a society as a whole.

d. On the *level of the Christian stewardship of insight,* which is the profoundest level of insight, these persons will to give up immediate pleasures for more lasting and eternal satisfactions. Impulses are used as "instruments of righteousness" unto life rather than as instruments of sin unto death. They interpret their own good in terms of social feeling for other people. They use newfound freedom as a means to liberate and understand other people. They alleviate their suffering even as theirs has been alleviated for them. This sounds the depths of Christian experience and lays hold of the need of the individual for community with other people who share in the fellowship of agreed-upon values, also. Here individuals have achieved insight not only into the nature of their own imperfections and lack of omnipotence. They also have entered into an acceptance of the imperfections and fallibilities of those about them. Temporal reality takes its proper relation to the Eternal.

The gift of such insight moves from "deep . . . unto deep" in the reality of the counseling situation. You as pastor need to be very careful not to accept the first statement of a problem as the real one. For instance, a young university student came for his first interview saying that he had begun to doubt "that God exists." Then in the third interview he said, "I have no doubt that God exists and that he is good, but I am beginning to see that my real trouble is that I am afraid my father and mother will not approve my marrying until I finish school." In the fourth interview he said, "I guess my main problem is that my mother has never wanted me to marry." In a later interview he stated, "I am going ahead with my plans to be married this summer, and I think I can help mother to take it."

The problem in this instance changed its form in the student's mind as the level of his understanding deepened. Like Job, he did not begin to lay hold of the resources of strength until he sought help for those who were at one and the same time the closest to him and his greatest vexation.

Much has been said here about the revelatory experience of insight. The qualitatively different kinds of insight I have described reflect the fact that insight for its own sake may be a waste of time and energy. It is not enough to beg the question by saying that the person simply needs more insight.

Let me go one step farther and say that insight is not always necessary for a real change of heart. Change often occurs in people from their becoming exhausted with ineffective ways of being. Change may occur when a traumatic event gives them a glimpse of death and a glaring light of deliverance. Change may come when they see their firstborn child. Change often comes when people meet, hear, and choose to follow a gifted leader. Change often takes place when individuals discover that they are no longer powerless, helpless, and in the clutch of fate.

Irvin Yalom rightly says that insight is of value only when it prompts a person to "take some stand toward change."[12] In my own words, insight must jell into convictions that involve a change of direction in life, and specific behaviors must result that coincide with the convictions. The counselee, as Ralph Waldo Emerson says, "learns to speak his latent convictions, to believe in his own thoughts, and to believe that what is true for him is true for all people." Yalom calls these "leverage-producing insights." Examples are: "Only I can change the world I have created." "There is no danger in change." "To get what I really want I must change." "I have the power to change."[13] This all sounds good except for the overtones of self-sufficiency.

Other therapists today insist that insight comes *after* the behavior has changed. Emotional response comes after a self-imposed discipline such as breaking an addiction such as obesity, being released from a phobia, or being set free of a dangerous habit such as fire-setting, exhibitionism, or child molestation. These therapists ask for an act of surrender to the person's own helplessness, participation in a group of fellow sufferers, and learning new adaptive rather than maladaptive habits. You can learn much about this from persons like William Glasser and from Halmuth H. Schaefer and Patrick L. Martin.[14]

The Phase of Reconstruction and Guidance

You are concerned not only with helping persons with their inner conflicts. Their reconstruction of purposes requires your interest in and guidance in a new way of life. God works in reorganizing personality in essentially a redemptive way. God helps a person to back the new commitments in a way of growth and consecration. Therefore you, in this fourth phase of your counseling ministry, are present when the person begins to turn a plan of action into a new freedom and a new walk of life in God. Consequently, your approach may change considerably in order that the person may be encouraged to sustain the new selfhood.

Usually you are most meaningful when you appeal to the sense of adventure and experimentation of the person with whom you are dealing at the time. Several opportunities present themselves at this stage of the relationship.

1. The Interpretation of the Life Situation. You may want to give a brief interpretation of the basic causes of the trouble or make a series of concrete suggestions. It is best that these avoid wordiness, be to the point, in simple language, and easily understood. *Usually, as in all phases of personal counseling, it is better to use the same words that the person uses and to lay hold of any figures of speech or ways of expression that the counselee has presented.* I am reminded of a member of one of my rural churches who once asked me "what to do when the plow hits a stump and a fellow swears before he can stop to save his life." Being in the midst of the preparation of a sermon on temptation, I went into a long, detailed, catacomblike explanation of how to stop swearing. The man listened with interest and attention, and when I had finished he said, "Yes, but, pastor, by the time I remember all that, I've done gone and cussed!" A few words would have been much easier to remember.

Several tested ways of interpretation are valuable. You may interpret by the kind of questions you ask, the order in which you ask them, and the tone of voice in which you speak. The interview that Jesus held at the well with the woman of Samaria is a case in point here. He interpreted her problem by asking her to go get her husband. Again, you may interpret by giving a short summary of the relationship and the different turns the conversation has taken. Another method that Jesus used constantly was that of an appeal to the experience of other people, the use of a parable, or the use of a proverb. Sometimes the parables the persons themselves use are invaluable. One person said that his life was like a wagon full of barrels which was used to haul water from the river to the church baptistry: by the time the wagon got to the church, all the water that had been in the back barrel was in the front and vice versa. He averred that his family discord had so affected his work, and vice versa, that he could not tell which was which! This is a valuable "homemade parable" for use in interpretation.

But the best way that you can interpret the life situation of a person is to encourage the person to express frankly and objectively the personal responses of affection and antipathy that the person feels toward you as counselor. This was called "relationship" counseling, devised many years ago by Jessie Taft and Otto Rank. An illustration is the young woman who, for several years, had moved from one denomination to another as she became attached to a different pastor. In bringing her difficulty to the pastor at this particular time, she finally came to the conclusion that she would unite with his church. He registered no surprise or undue elation. In the next interview the pastor was able to interpret tactfully what the changing of denominations had meant to her and to disentangle her church affiliation from too much dependence upon the minister. The pastor's interpretation of the relationship was the basis for counseling her.

2. *The Brief Pastoral Dialogue.* You as the pastor may be asked by the person to whom you are ministering to confer about a specific plan of action with reference to marriage, parental responsibilities, educational plans, or vocational readjustments. Here you may resort to the use of the brief pastoral dialogue that was suggested earlier in this chapter.

3. The Introduction to Christian Friends. At the same time, you may take on the functions of a teacher-evangelist, seeking to relate the person to the church, to fellowship groups, and to other sources of spiritual undergirding. Also, you may feel that some particular member of your church or community, such as a physician, an attorney, a business person and employer, or maybe one of the dependable members of the church, could be a meaningful friend to this person. Therefore you may introduce the person to one or more of these friends for specialized help.

4. The Selection of Appropriate Literature and Scripture Passages. At this stage of the counseling process, you may deem it advisable also to refer the person to certain literature that will be specifically applicable to reconstructing the person's outlook on life. You may find that the person knows next to nothing about the Bible and that you have the opportunity to cause the New and Old Testaments to come alive to the person in the light of the person's life situation. By and large, the persons who come to a pastor are religious illiterates and stand in need of this sort of help. You should be very careful not to hand the whole Bible to them and make some generalized and vague remark as to its healing power. You should carefully (ahead of time if possible) select the sections that give the clearest guidance to the person in terms of their educational background.

Whatever interpretation, instruction, or introduction to other people is given to the person, it should indicate a plain path of action. The person will need reassurance, spiritual support, and vital encouragement. The encouraging power of your own confidence in the person cannot be overestimated. You are wise to use down-to-earth common sense in suggesting goals as you evolve plans along with the person. These goals need to be in keeping with the abilities of the person to achieve them. All these procedures are appropriate only after you and the parishioner together have a relaxed sense of certainty that you have arrived at the real issues of the person's life situation. If you have any doubt at all that the person has not come to the core of the problem with you, or if you are confused in your own mind as to what the situation actually is, you should begin to angle for another interview. Reflection, maturation, and the opportunity for more conversation are the only things that can clarify the matter.

The Phase of Follow-up and Experimentation

Much effective counseling has gone to waste because of a failure on the part of pastors to follow up the progress of the persons with whom they have dealt. This is notoriously true of the counseling done by pastors in evangelistic meetings, religious retreats, college religious emphasis weeks, and so forth. In this final phase of personal counseling, the following issues are at stake.

1. *Overdependence.* The breaking of the continuity of regular interviews creates an emotional crisis in the life of the person in and of itself. The chances are that the person has become too dependent upon the counselor, and the interviews have become something of a sedative to soothe anxieties. The person may interpret the breaking of a series of formal interviews as a personal rejection. At this point you are made to feel more keenly the powerful charges of affection that have been transferred to you by the person. One person said to his pastor, "What will I do when you are too far away for me to find you?" The pastor interpreted the relationship in this manner: "You seem to wish that I were capable of being everywhere and probably are assuming that I am all-powerful also, as far as you are concerned. This is your attempt to deify me, but only God can be God in your life. It is God who is all-present and all-powerful, and you can talk with him anytime. We call this prayer, and I should like for you to try to develop that practice in your life." In your ministry of "follow-up," you can do nothing more effective than "tutor" in the art of prayer the people with whom you counsel. This can be done on a group basis as well as on an individual basis.

Another difficulty of an overdependent relationship between a pastor and a parishioner at the point of follow-up is that the parishioner will continue to bring each minor decision to you as the pastor for your opinion or in an attempt to sustain the former continuity. This is especially true of pastors or student counselors in a college setting. Adolescents draw a great deal of personal strength from being near a person with whom they can identify and like whom they would seek to become. They have an abundance of "free-floating" anxiety that they allay in this way when they are away from home and from those people who have naturally filled voids in their lives.

2. *Fear and Hostility.* The failure to provide room for false starts and mistakes and relapses to old patterns of behavior by holding over the person's head a perfectionistic, "sure cure" goal to be achieved may cause the person to avoid you in the event that such things should happen. Persons feel that, if one slip is made, facing you who had such high hopes for them would be too much. Later they may say that they have "let the pastor down." In a real sense they have let you displace God on this score also.

Another way of falling into the same error is by dominating the decisions of persons in such a way that the only means by which they can become persons in their own right is to rebel completely against the whole relationship with you. In the context of a pastoral community, such rebellions can take vicious turns and do more damage than can be undone in a long while. Yet a measure of real hostility—frankly and warmly accepted—may be a healthy sign of growth, even necessary for the continued autonomy of the individual. Your calling as a pastor is to be a faithful servant, not to be liked or disliked!

3. Gossip. The gossip hazard also conditions the form that a follow-up ministry may take. Parishioners may become very uneasy as they get more removed from a face-to-face relationship with you. Then they will become apprehensive lest you be irresponsible in references about them as counselees to others. Out of sheer discomfort, they may move their church membership elsewhere. Or, in the pressure of a momentary crisis, they may seek out irresponsible persons in the community and give an emotionally distorted version of some snatch of their conversation with you. Jesus, in his pastoral ministry, was continually plagued by the results of such gossip. Little wonder that he charged people to go and tell no one of their interviews! A part of the covenant of communication involves the counselee's responsible commitment to confer with the pastor if and when they plan to discuss their pastoral conversations with others.

4. Positive Follow-up. But more positively, the pastor may follow up private conferences with people by visits in their homes. You have this privilege and will often be invited into the homes of newfound friends. You may be asked to perform the wedding ceremony of the young man or woman whom you counseled prior to the marriage. These same persons will occasionally invite you to conduct a dedication service in their new home or when a baby is born to them. A young minister may ask you to preach an ordination sermon, or a young business person may want you to speak at a civic club. Although you have numerous outside contacts such as these, the majority of persons with whom you counsel will be members of your church. You will see them in church services, have them in discussion groups, and preach to them Sunday after Sunday. These contacts can enrich or impoverish your counseling ministry, depending upon your appreciation of the dynamics of group life and your sensitivity to people's feelings toward one another.

Quite often you will counsel with people whom you will not see again because they are not so closely knit with your own community. They may be people from another city who have been sent to you by someone you have helped before and who has moved away. They may be the relatives of a member of your church and are hospitalized in the city where you minister. Or they may come to you from having read something you wrote, from having heard you over the radio or on television, or from having seen you in a religious assembly. As one "person-minded" minister wrote: "I sometimes wonder how it is the word gets around about one, if he is competent to help others when they need him. But I am learning daily how much it does get around. I count it a privilege to counsel with those who come, although I am constantly amazed at my total inadequacy—but by leaning hard on the counsel of the Holy Spirit, the friend and I work out in our thinking helpful avenues through many and varied problems."

This defines the feeling of a minister who is concerned with the inner peace of people: you feel competent and full of confidence in your ministry, yet you sense your inadequacy as you confront the magnitude of human suffering. When you discover your own perennial source of dependence in the Holy Spirit and a sense of community with the person in need, helpful avenues are found.

Never become overconfident of your own skill in the use of any technique of pastoral care. If you do, you soon begin to depreciate and think irreverently of the personalities of those with whom you deal. You begin to "play on their souls," which causes them to turn on you. Shakespeare describes such careless irreverence in Hamlet's dialogue with Rosencrantz and Guildenstern, who had been sent to lure Hamlet's secret from him. Hamlet begs Guildenstern tauntingly to play upon a flute that he offers him. But Guildenstern says: "I have not the skill. . . . These cannot I command to any utterance of harmony." Then, with much vehemence, Hamlet replies:

> Why, look you now, how unworthy a thing you make of me! You would play upon me, you would seem to know my stops, you would pluck out the heart of my mystery, you would sound me from my lowest note to the top of my compass; and there is much music, excellent voice, in this little organ, yet cannot you make it speak. 'Sblood, do you think that I am easier to be play'd on than a pipe? Call me what instrument you will, though you can fret me, you cannot play upon me. (*Hamlet,* act 3, scene 2)

EXTENDED PASTORAL PSYCHOTHERAPY

At different points I have described and affirmed the specialized forms of pastoral counseling done in pastoral counseling centers which may or may not be related to a local church, an association of churches, a diocese, and so forth. Increasingly, such centers are being by economic necessity forced to solicit funds for themselves as nonprofit corporations and to complete their budgetary demands by charging fees for service to counselees. In turn, counselees ask whether the services of a pastoral counselor are covered by private insurance carriers and/or Medicare. These are called "third-party payments." Certification agencies, such as the American Association of Pastoral Counselors and the American Association for Marriage and Family Therapy, have committees and lobbying groups in Washington, D.C., to see to it that such payments are duly qualified and permitted. How the time-consuming work of the specialist pastoral psychotherapist is to be financed is as yet an inadequately answered question.

You readily see that the persons and the processes to and for which a pastoral counselor ministers are quite apart from direct answerability to the face-to-face community of Christians, although not from the reign and rule of the sovereignty of God. The inroads of secularism are ever present. Yet the critical problem is the lack of theological seriousness on the part of the churches in providing for their people's psychotherapeutic needs. The inroads of secularism are on the ground the churches leave unattended, that is, the unconsidered quiet desperation of their people. This ecclesiastical irresponsibility is the stuff that catalyzes secularism.

Yet, whether the churches come alive to their responsibilities or not, the specialized function of Christian pastors for intensive pastoral psychotherapy is growing and will continue to grow. Enterprising and gifted men and women who are called of the Lord for this work will find ways and means of doing this ministry. After many years pass and severe sacrifices of a few intrepid spirits have been made, the movement has weight, becomes popular, and many will want to climb on the bandwagon. In the meantime, if you are one of those intrepid spirits and want a guidebook for traversing the terrain over which you have to travel to become established as a disciplined and consecrated pastoral counselor whose whole discipline is in this ministry, then read the book *The Organization and Administration of Pastoral Counseling Centers,* ed. by John C. Carr, John E. Hinkle, and David M. Moss III.[15]

The most sensitive areas in the specialized practice of pastoral counseling, it seems to me, are: (1) The pastoral and theological confusion that arises out of the allure of third-party payments for the service. The person who pays the piper calls the tune. Answerability to one's ordination is primary in my value system, and the dilution or confusion of this is inherent in dependence upon third-party payments. (2) The problems of sustaining a unique theological core and content in shaping the methodologies of counseling used are inherent in the specialized function of counseling. (3) The problem of elitism exists that would make a "guild" of pastoral psychotherapists who discount the pastoral counseling done by general parish pastors. Recently some references have appeared in the literature that frankly say that the pastor of a church *cannot,* by the nature of the social context in which the pastor works, be a counselor.[16] What the authors of those references mean is that a pastor cannot be a psychoanalytically oriented psychotherapist. Yet, if you are a generalist pastor of a church, do not let this elitist stand discourage you. You have other ways of accomplishing some of the same goals a psychoanalytically oriented pastoral psychotherapist uses. The generalist pastor may effectively accomplish similar goals—some as good, some better, and some not as good—with individuals through new disciplines of systems orchestration.

Nothing we can do can ignore, safely permit us to lower our consciousness of, or make purely implicit the centrality of God's claim upon us as his ministers of reconciliation. Elitism in pastoral counseling confuses both the good theology and the good psychotherapy of the generalist pastor.

NOTES

1. Wayne E. Oates, *Pastoral Counseling* (Philadelphia: Westminster Press, 1974); John B. Cobb, Jr., *Theology and Pastoral Care* (Philadelphia: Fortress Press, 1977); and Howard Clinebell, *Basic Types of Pastoral Care and Counseling* (New York: Abingdon Press, 1984).

2. Nathaniel Hawthorne, *The Scarlet Letter* (New York: New American Library of World Literature, Signet Classics, 1959), p. 123.

3. Seward Hiltner and Lowell G. Colston, *The Context of Pastoral Counseling* (New York: Abingdon Press, 1961), p. 220.

4. Harry Stack Sullivan, *Conceptions of Modern Psychiatry*, William Alanson White Memorial Lectures (New York: W. W. Norton & Co., 1947); and idem, *The Psychiatric Interview*, ed. Helen Swick Perry and Mary Ladd Gawel (New York: W. W. Norton & Co., 1954), pp. 94–182.

5. András Angyal, *Neurosis and Treatment: A Holistic Theory*, ed. E. Hanfmann and R. M. Jones (New York: John Wiley & Sons, 1965); and Irvin D. Yalom, *Existential Psychotherapy* (New York: Basic Books, 1980).

6. Erik H. Erikson, *Identity and the Life Cycle* (New York: International Universities Press, 1959), pp. 56, 64–65.

7. Theodor Reik, *Listening with the Third Ear: The Inner Experience of a Psychoanalyst* (New York: Grove Press, 1948), p. 126.

8. Ibid., p. 142.

9. Douglas V. Steere, *On Listening to Another* (New York: Harper & Brothers, 1955), p. 1.

10. See Prescott Lecky, *Self-Consistency: A Theory of Personality*, ed. Frederick C. Thorne, 2nd ed. (New York: Island Press Co-operative, 1951).

11. Robert H. Bonthius, *Christian Paths to Self-Acceptance* (New York: King's Crown Press, 1948).

12. Yalom, *Existential Psychotherapy*, p. 339.

13. Ibid., pp. 340–341.

14. William Glasser, M.D., *Stations of the Mind: New Directions for Reality Therapy* (New York: Harper & Row, 1981); and Halmuth Schaefer and Patrick L. Martin, *Behavioral Therapy* (New York: McGraw-Hill Book Co., 1975).

15. John C. Carr, John E. Hinkle, and David M. Moss III, eds., *The Organization and Administration of Pastoral Counseling Centers* (Nashville: Abingdon Press, 1981).

16. See Richard L. Krebs, "Why Pastors Should Not Be Counselors," *Journal of Pastoral Care*, December 1980, pp. 229–233.

27

Some Indications and Contraindications for Referral for Pastoral Counseling

The various members of the psychiatric team ask what are the situations in which pastoral counseling can be useful and those situations in which pastoral counseling is not indicated. The pastoral counselor needs to be specific and precise rather than general in the prescription of pastoral counseling. This precision calls for the religious assessment of patients as to whether they are merely superficially religious or whether their religion is a profound part of their life development and purpose. The pastoral counselor needs genuine triage ability, "triage" meaning the ability to "sort out" the most pressing needs of patients from the needs that can be deferred in time. Pastoral counseling is no panacea: it is indicated in some instances and not indicated in others.

SOME INDICATIONS
FOR PASTORAL COUNSELING

Routine Pastoral Assessment

One of the most effective ways of regularizing the religious care of psychiatric patients is to establish a policy that all patients will be seen routinely for a standard religious assessment by a pastoral counselor. This assessment is *not* a psychiatric examination. A religious assessment deals specifically with the religious history, religious education, religious peak and low experiences, religious delusions, religious beliefs, knowledge about the particular sacred writing of a given group with which the patient is affiliated, the kinds of emotional and spiritual support available to the patients, and the degree of pathology in the patient's religious worldviews.

366

The following outline may be used by pastoral counselors in a facility where a routine religious assessment of all patients is done by pastoral counselors.

Date:

Patient's Name: _____ Age: _____ Sex: _____

Marital Status: _____ Parental Status: _____

Occupation: _____ Religious Affiliation: _____

Length of Religious Affiliation: _____

Changes in Religious Affiliation: _____

1. Religious Experiences, Both "Peak" and "Desolating"

2. Significant Religious Influences & Sources of Support

3. Quality and Depth of Religious Concern

    _____ None

    _____ Superficial

    _____ Compulsive Obsessional

    _____ Sociopathic and/or Manipulative

    _____ Profound and Authentic

    _____ Hostile and Alienated

4. Beliefs of Diagnostic & Therapeutic Significance

5. Pastoral Impressions & Recommendations

Obviously this procedure calls for a teaching program in which the student can both learn and provide the personnel for such evaluations and assessments. Indications *for* referral are as follow:

Bereavement

Psychiatric patients are no exception to significant personal losses by death and other means of separation, such as abandonment, divorce, and alienation. Psychiatric patients get considerable help from conversing with a pastoral counselor about the loss of someone who is very significant to them, because these desolating experiences often make them aware of God. This loss may not be "someone" but "something." For example, a person in the middle years may have lost a very significant job.

Bereavement may be *acute,* as in the case of a thirty-year-old mother whose nine-year-old son, with no premonition, simply dropped dead from a cardiovascular accident as he was walking home from school one afternoon. Bereavement may be *chronic,* as in the case of an aging man who had to sell his home and move many miles away in order to be with his only daughter and her family after the death of his wife. Bereavement may be *pathological,* as in the case of the man who, when his son was killed in an automobile accident, chose not to bury the body but to entomb it in a glass-topped casket in a room in his home. He encircled the room with all sorts of religious symbols. He sought to create a chapel there. He expected people to come there and worship. The pathological grief became blatantly psychotic when he began to develop elaborate plans for finding and killing the person who was driving the car that struck the car of his son.

A considerable portion of the training of a pastor has been in the thoroughgoing study of death and dying, of bereavement, and of the follow-up care of bereft persons. Therefore the amount of work and the nature of the problems can be shared if one refers to a pastoral counselor the patients who have either acute, chronic, or pathological grief.

Terminal Illness

Psychiatric patients quite often are suffering from additional disorders other than those of a psychotic or neurotic nature. One of the recurring disorders is that of the presence of a terminal kind of illness, such as leukemia or malignant tumors. Another disorder may be chronic alcoholism. One may find, as I did recently, a patient in whom all three of these conditions exist at the same time: terminal malignancy, alcoholism, and a bizarre psychosis. The pastoral counselor is especially equipped to care for people facing the realistic threat of death. This is not to say that a referral should be made quickly and automatically. The timing of the entry of the pastoral counselor into the therapeutic milieu of a patient is of the utmost importance. It is to say, however, that, given the right kind of timing to the particular patient's needs, pastoral counseling can be exceptionally helpful as a person moves through the critical phases of a terminal illness.

Reality-based Guilt

Some of the acts that a patient has committed are such as to cause the person to feel directly responsible to God. The patient's own perception of sin or wrongdoing is what must be considered, not the particular concepts of the pastoral counselor or the other psychiatric team members. Historically, "disburdening," or confession, has been an important part of therapy. Catharsis can result in abreaction. The pastoral counselor takes seriously the ministry of confession and intercession. For example, patients quite often suffer more of a burden of guilt over things they have not done but are tempted to do than they do over things they have actually done. Therefore the pastoral counselor can be exceptionally helpful in enabling the person to get past a feeling of self-condemnation to a feeling of injustice, anger, frustration, and the accumulated temptations that these present. Assurance of forgiveness by God is an ultimate form of acceptance.

In the confessional ministry one occasionally finds that the patient has a long-standing and chronic sense of combined grief and guilt—sin for some deed committed many years ago. For example, one may discover persons in their middle years who experienced an abortion during their late teens or early twenties. One must bear in mind that when that particular event occurred, such an act was not only felt to be sin but actually a criminal act. The compulsive obsessional preoccupation with this particular, in some cases, may be accompanied by a severe depression. The depression arises out of biochemical changes, age changes, value crises, station-in-life changes, or a plexus of these and many other changes. The depression may be cleared up, but the compulsive obsessional preoccupation with the "wrongdoing" of the past persists. Close teamwork between the psychotherapist and the pastoral counselor is intensely needed with such patients.

Patients with character disorders may present an anesthesia, a numbness, or an absence of feeling about specific wrongdoing. The psychiatrist quite often is heavily preoccupied with coping with the problems of the authentically psychotic, neurotic, and organically disordered thinking of patients. The use of his or her time with character disorders is not the primary devotion of a considerable number of psychiatrists. Similarly, pastoral counselors tend to be less challenged by the morally obtuse persons usually found in the categories of character disorders. Psychiatric theory has tended to relate aberrations of religious consciousness to schizophrenic, depressive, and neurotic types of disorder. Rarely does one find psychiatric theory focusing on religious pathology in the character disorders. Yet character disorders run rife among persons who use religion as a means of base gain, as a means of avoiding responsibility, and as a means of exploiting other people. In such instances reality-oriented pastoral counseling can be a helpful resource. However, if the pastoral counselor is timid about representing reality to the patient, it may well be that he or she is as ineffectual as anyone else. To the contrary, some patient records are extant that point to the effective role of religion and quasi-religious influences in changing behavior patterns of persons with basic character disorders. Not the least among these successful ventures is Alcoholics Anonymous and similar reality-oriented group approaches to caring for persons who have severe personality disorders.

Vocational Confusion and
Lack of Direction

Psychiatric patients struggle with a sense of "calling," the decision or the compulsion to enter religious work, to leave religious work, or to change work. Underneath this vocational confusion lies the heavy threat of the meaninglessness and purposelessness of life. Mingled with it is the often overlooked loss of curiosity and exaggerated boredom in the life of many psychiatric patients. Such persons are often helped considerably by pastoral counseling. There is a distinct "vocational heart" to the work of the effective pastoral counselor. The life and work of the minister moves on a motivation of "mission" or "call," even as does that of the other members of the therapeutic team. Pastoral counseling at its best represents a disciplined study of the work adjustment of persons, the varieties of careers of persons, and the important parameters of actualizing the "gifts," "talents," and aptitudes of a person.

In the case of psychotic persons, the sense of mission or call may be far out of touch with reality. In these instances pastoral counselors are equipped to represent the realities involved in the day-to-day work of religious leaders. For example, a patient uproots his family of four, moves his place of work to a city seven hundred miles away, and becomes absorbed completely in all-day work with a particular church and all-night work on a menial job that does not support his family. His wife in turn has to work and supply three fourths of the family budget. The children begin having all sorts of difficulties by reason of their resistance to the move. The family come into a psychiatric outpatient clinic on the assumption (a) that one of the children is mentally retarded and (b) the wife is mentally ill. These are "diagnoses" of the father. The underlying conflict of the family with the father over his religious call is a more ample explanation of the family stress than either the inability of a child in school or the understandable despair of the wife and mother. Yet the religious defenses of the father were such as to fend off any approaches of the other members of the therapeutic team. Hence, a pastoral counselor was asked to become a part of the family therapy of this particular family unit. The hope that the distinctly pastoral relationship would reduce the resistances of the father also failed.

A large range of personal struggle in terms of the vocational commitment of people appears in the care of emotionally ill pastors, priests, and other religious workers. Routinely these persons are made more productive in the treatment situation when pastoral counselors are involved either as cotherapists or parallel consultants in the process. This is a specific indication for the value of the inclusion of a pastoral counselor in a patient's therapy.

Religious Conflicts Between
Family Members

A considerable amount of alienation occurs between family members over denominational differences. Sometimes we find that one or the other person of a marital partnership will become intensely interested in a new kind of religion in an attempt to handle the insoluble stress in the family. For example, a woman may feel keenly that she as a wife does not have any personal freedom of her own. Her liberation may take the form of an interest in a religious group that is far apart from the rather routine habitual religious interest and behavior of her husband. Or, in another case, a husband may feel that he does not get the sense of warm approval, emotional support, and tender solicitude from his wife that he is due. Thus, he may become hyperactively involved in the life of the church to the neglect of all his relationships in the home. In the church, he is "somebody." In turn, he may use his religious concern as an excuse for expressing his anger covertly toward his wife for what he perceives to be her neglect of his deep needs for appreciation. Such religious overzealousness has some rather mundane and "earthy" psychological roots. The denial and defense system of such a husband or wife is sufficiently encased in religious materials that the pastoral counselor becomes a person who can "meet them on their own ground." Other members of the psychiatric team, regardless of their emotional commitment as religious persons, may be "written off" by the patient.

Biblical Interpretation

The language of the Bible is not by any means a universal language in contemporary secular culture. However, in a considerable portion of the population, biblical passages often become issues of confusion, debate, conflict, and emotional infection. In the process of treatment some psychiatric patients will repeatedly present biblical teachings on such matters as forgiveness, divorce, adultery, anger, and murder. Much of the catalog of virtues and sins that the patient has collected from a random reading of the Bible is taken out of the context of the basic meaning of the scripture. Consequently, in a culture that is dominated by Judeo-Christian teachings, persons who have been profoundly trained in the study of the whole teaching of the whole Bible on any particular subject can be of remarkable help in putting the attitudes of the patient into the right context. The pastoral counselor is a person who has had such training and equipment. In the close-at-hand operation of a psychiatric team, this responsibility for accurate and thoroughgoing interpretation of the Bible is an indication for referral to a pastoral counselor. Upon receiving such a referral, the pastoral counselor focuses forthrightly upon that teaching and deals with it in as profound and emotional a way as possible without either the pastor or the patient getting into such defenses as intellectualization, rationalization, and reaction formation.

371

Religious Support
of Psychiatric Treatment

Many patients will resist psychiatric treatment on religious grounds. For example, they may feel that it is a lack of faith to have medication for emotional problems. They may feel that to consult a psychiatrist is in and of itself a demonstration of religious weakness. They may condemn themselves and feel that if they were good Christians, they would not need psychiatric treatment. Therefore they are likely to want to "redouble their efforts" religiously in order to offset the need for psychiatric treatment.

In such instances pastoral counselors can be interpreters of psychiatric treatment as a part of the creative forces of the universe to bring wholeness and health to the person and to make him or her a more effective religious person. Similarly a considerable portion of religious teaching is focused on the idea that a person who is religious is not supposed to have any problems or sufferings. This is pure superstition. The effective pastoral counselor can work directly at challenging this particular set of ideas. He or she can teach that suffering is a characteristic of all humanity. One of the purposes of suffering is to learn from the suffering in order to be able to be instructive to others who are caught in such problems.

The need for pastoral counseling for a patient resisting psychiatric treatment is especially imperative in the case of a mental inquest patient who is being forced to take psychiatric treatment to which he or she objects on explicit religious grounds. The issue of the religious freedom of the patient is at stake. For example, there is a legal ground for such resistance and the legalities of psychiatric treatment against a patient's religious objections, especially when a patient is involuntarily committed and yet has not been adjudicated incompetent. D. S. Cohen cites a legal case in which it was ruled that such a patient may "refuse treatment on the basis of his/her First Amendment right of free exercise of religion."[1]

Post-Psychotic Convalescent Care

The point at which the pastoral counselor can be of exceptional assistance is as the patient prepares to reenter the community after a psychiatric illness. For example, psychiatric literature points to the kind of post-psychotic depression that many patients experience after having reconstituted from a schizophrenic break. Facing the task of rebuilding their lives overwhelms them. The patient often feels incapable of any form of relatedness other than being "sat with silently." It is a sort of impasse in which the patient "seems to have one purpose in mind—that of preserving the status quo."[2] It is estimated that one out of four such post-psychotic depressions occurs in schizophrenic patients. The collaboration of a pastoral counselor with the psychiatric team does two things: the psychiatric team becomes discouraged with such patients and the pastoral counselor can be a "morale officer" for the group. Also, the pastoral counselor can be a source of quiet hope for the patient.

The pastoral counselor can be a "bridge" personality, involved both in the process of treatment and in the process of rehabilitation, both in the hospital community and in the larger community of which the church is a part. Effectively working at the development of a religious support system can be a part of the collaboration of a pastoral counselor with the social worker who is also involved in the community reconstitution of the life of the patient. The pastoral counselor who has been in a given community a considerable length of time knows a "grapevine" of helpful persons. An inherently helpful person can be accurately empathetic, nonpossessively warm, and genuine in working with a convalescing psychiatric patient. The pastoral counselor who is personally acquainted with such helping persons and can relate the patient to them is in a particularly useful position in the post-psychotic care of a patient.

The Pastoral Care of the
Family of a Patient

Members of the family undergo massive confusion, shock, and conflicting emotions in their responses to the psychiatric illness of their family member. For the most healthily motivated ones of them the experience is a grief situation characterized by much helplessness and plaintive concern. The grief they bear is not easily socialized and tends to isolate them. They quite often are so omnivorous in their need for time and attention by professionals that "all hands need to be on deck" in caring for them. The pastoral counselor can be assigned the continuing care of certain family members. When patients are under the care of a private psychiatrist, the physician does not have the resources of a social work team to add to his or her own care the patient. Therefore, for practical purposes, an effective pastoral counselor focuses on the needs of the family in much the same way that a social worker would if present.

In some instances, the family may have unusually rigid religious objections, skepticism, and religiously reinforced lack of cooperation with the rest of the psychiatric team in the care of a family member. Therefore the pastoral counselor must be extremely canny and aware of the possibility of the family member "pitting" the other members of the psychiatric team against the pastoral counselor and vice versa. Thus, a given member of the family may divide the team and sabotage the whole treatment process.

Premature Psychiatric Referral

A psychiatric referral is not as easily made as even the general physician often suspects. A poorly made psychiatric referral quite often assures that the patient will not get to the psychiatrist. In the face of poorly made psychiatric referrals, quite often the pastoral counselor gets the patient on "the rebound." Regardless of the condition of the patient, the pastoral counselor may be the only professionally trained person to whom the patient will talk. Access is the essence of care in this and many other instances. There are instances when the pastoral counselor may be coached by other members of the psychiatric team as he or she carries the whole responsibility for the immediate critical needs of patients who simply will not under any circumstances go to a psychiatrist. For example, patients may have had many and negative experiences with different psychiatrists. The patients may vow that they will "cut their throat" before they will go to another psychiatrist. Therefore these patients find a pastoral counselor and begin to converse with him or her about these emotional needs. Or the pastoral counselor may visit patients who have never seen a psychiatrist. The pastoral counselor needs to take several interviews before the patients themselves come to the awareness that they really need to get medical care. Consequently, the function of the pastoral counselor becomes similar to that of the "point men" on a military patrol. The pastoral counselor is where the most danger is, that is, the open community. The rest of the team is moving carefully along behind, supporting, coaching, and advising. The pastoral counselor carries the responsibility until the patient is willing to include the rest of the team in the treatment process. Furthermore, the pastoral counselor has none of the controls of hospital walls, drugs, legal authority, and so forth. He or she works in the open community. Hazards are high.

These are simply a few of the indications for the need of pastoral counseling in the treatment situation. Now let us turn to some of the contraindications, those situations in which a patient should not be sent to a pastoral counselor or have a pastor come to the patient for consultation.

SOME CONTRAINDICATIONS FOR PASTORAL COUNSELING

Total Patient Rejection

The personal wishes of a patient not to see a pastoral counselor should be respected. A considerable number of psychiatric patients see the pastoral counselor as a "public" person. They are made extremely uncomfortable at the thought of a pastoral counselor conversing with them. They fear that their plight as a disturbed patient will become public knowledge. Other patients feel extremely uncomfortable at the idea of discussing their religious life, because these feelings are so inarticulate they cannot find words to describe them. Other patients will feel that they would like to see a pastoral counselor later but not now. The timing is off. Even other patients will perceive themselves as totally hostile to the idea of religion, religious personages, and religious organizations. They may have had too many negative encounters with the church to hazard another. Therefore they do not want to see a pastoral counselor. A considerable number of psychiatric patients have had painful rejection from previous pastors. They do not want to run that risk again. For whatever reason the patient does not want to see a pastoral counselor, my conviction is that those reasons should be respected.

"Substitute" Psychiatrist

Occasionally a patient will want to talk with a pastoral counselor as a substitute for the psychiatrist. Basic medical issues of a neurological and biochemical nature may be obvious even to the nonmedical observer. A contraindication for pastoral counseling is when a patient is seeking "to use" a pastoral counselor as a substitute for admitting the need for psychiatric treatment. The patient may also insist upon having a "Christian" psychiatrist and set this as a stipulation for any collaboration with psychiatric treatment. In this instance the psychiatrist is a "substitute pastor." Whichever way the resistance goes, it should be dealt with forthrightly and honestly as a means of developing an authentic and trustworthy therapeutic relationship. If a referral to a pastoral counselor is made when essentially a psychiatric treatment is indicated, this in itself may be a form of deception.

Rejection of Psychiatry by Other Medical Specialists

It is no secret that many physicians who are not psychiatrists reject the whole specialty. As a pastoral counselor, I have had blatantly psychotic patients referred to me for counseling by such physicians. These patients were persons whose mental status was so completely disorganized that their lives were in shambles. They were referred to me by surgeons, general practitioners, and other specialists in the medical profession who rejected psychiatry as a legitimate expression of the medical profession. I have no need at this point to delve into the intricacies of this kind of intraprofessional tension. Nevertheless such referrals to pastoral counselors in lieu of a psychiatrist are contraindicated. A pastoral counselor may, after careful assessment, use his or her own expertise as a pastoral counselor to bridge the patient's relationship to a psychiatrist who can give the specialized attention that is needed.

Therapeutic "Dilution"

Pastoral counseling is no exception to the general contraindication of more than one therapist talking to a patient when to do so is to "dilute" the patient's relationship to the therapist who is most likely to be doing the patient the most good. This therapist may be a psychiatrist, a social worker, a nurse, or the family physician. One of the common characteristics of anxiety-ridden patients is that they will flit from one counselor to another indiscriminately without regard to the particular professional competence of the person. In doing so, they will alleviate their anxiety temporarily, then break the relationship and move to another counselor. The pastoral counselor is no exception to this. A referral to a pastoral counselor that dilutes the intensity and direction of an already existing counseling relationship by another counselor is contraindicated.

Religion as a Manipulative Tool

Another contraindication for referral to a pastoral counselor is when the patient's religion is assessed by any member of the therapeutic team, and especially by the pastoral counselor, to be superficial, to be a ruse, to be a tool of manipulation in the hands of the patient. For example, such patients may use a superficial flurry of religion as a means of getting certain privileges on the ward, shortening their stay in the hospital, or making a show of "normality." Careful observation of these patients in a hospital setting by the nursing staff and the psychiatric aides has a way of providing an outside reading on the genuineness of the religious concern of the patient. When it is seen that the pastoral counselor is a tool for the manipulative patient, then judicious neglect or forthright confrontation of the patient may, after careful consultation with physicians and nurses, be indicated.

The Psychiatric Vacuum

A psychiatric vacuum is created in the lives of many psychiatric patients when there are not enough psychiatrists to meet the basic psychiatric needs of the patients in a given hospital setting. Furthermore, there may be an abundance of psychiatrists in numbers, but certain psychiatrists themselves may see no point at all in conversing in depth with their patients. When this happens, for whatever reason, a vacuum is created. When a patient is validated by three or four responsible members of the staff as "not having seen the doctor in eight days," then the pastoral counselor who is on the service may well be drawn into the vacuum created by such neglect. In essence, this kind of pastoral counseling is contraindicated because the patient is being deprived of his or her right to adequate attention by the psychiatrist in charge. This is not an uncommon phenomenon in private, well-supported psychiatric facilities. It is a widespread occurrence in state hospitals. If a psychiatrist or a psychiatric resident is too impatient, too busy, too rejecting, or too out of tune with the idea of conversing with patients, then the referral of the patient to a pastoral counselor is a ditching of responsibility rather than a responsible referral for distinctly religious care.

Social Involvement

In unique situations, a given pastoral counselor may be so socially involved with the patient and the patient's family in an ongoing, semi-family relationship that pastoral counseling by that particular pastor is contraindicated. The need for sufficient detachment from the social circle of the continuing life of the patient is just as real in pastoral counseling as it is in other types of counseling and/or psychotherapy. For example, if I as a professor have a student who is emotionally ill, it is more important that I remain an effective teacher and friend over the long pull of the person's life than it is that I do pastoral counseling. I usually see pastoral counseling under such conditions as a contraindication. Therefore I seek to enlist the assistance of someone other than myself if distinctly pastoral counseling is indicated. This keeps the relationship from becoming a confused, anxiety-ridden one.

Other contraindications of pastoral counseling could be identified, but these are the most recurrent. As has been said before, pastoral counseling is *one* of the resources for the care of psychiatric patients. It is not a panacea; nor, as is occasionally inferred, is it a pernicious influence that should be avoided in all instances. The important issue is carefully to assess the lifelong pattern of the patient. In what ways have religious experience and community been the cohesive forces in the person's life? Have they provided support when all other sources of support have failed? Such a careful assessment of the lifelong history of the patient will reveal to what extent the religious concern of the person has been a liability and a threat or an asset and a support to the integrity of the patient's functioning as a human being. On the basis of such an assessment, a "prescriptive" approach to the use of pastoral counseling can be made, rather than either thinking of it as a "patent medicine" that should be peddled over the counter indiscriminately to any and all patients at any and all times or being banned by psychiatric authority as always poisonous.

CONCLUSION

As my colleague, Conrado Weller, M.D., says, "pastoral counseling deals with belief systems." As such, it may even be thought of as one "among many psychotherapies.'' For many years I have restricted the use of the term ''psychotherapy'' to apply to that which a physician does in longer-term kinds of uncovering ''depth'' therapies. The time is here, however, when a considerable number of pastoral counselors are thoroughly educated in such depth psychotherapy. With the increased preoccupation of psychiatrists with the somatic therapies, the pastoral counselor as a psychotherapist in his or her own right is a reality at hand. Heavy caution must be observed, however, to consider the amounts of time this takes and the quality and extent of education under supervision which it implies, and the legal and financial problems involved. No shortcut to excellence is available here. Furthermore, the pastor can become a gnostic, denying the reality of the body, if he or she is not quick to seek a thorough medical examination of a counselee who is undergoing longer-term kinds of pastoral counseling. He or she does well to get an interdisciplinary assessment of the person concurrent with a pastoral counseling relationship. Personally, I am appreciative of the ways in which much that I do as a pastoral counselor corresponds with what is called psychotherapy. However, I prefer to give the name ''pastoral counseling'' to what I do. Thus, I will be sure that I am not ignorant of my true identity and source of answerability to God. Also, I feel more authentic, clear, and unpretentious about what I am doing.

NOTES

1. D. S. Cohen, ''Recent Decisions,'' *Brooklyn Law Review* 38 (1971): 211–222.

2. T. H. McGlashan, M.D., and William T. Carpenter, M.D., ''Post-Psychotic Depression in Schizophrenia,'' *Archives of General Psychiatry* 33 (February 1976): 231–239.

28

The Religious Care of the
Depressed Patient

Depression is one of the most common illnesses to which the human being is subject. "Paradoxically, it is probably the most frequently overlooked symptom, and, even when recognized, is probably the single most incorrectly treated symptom in clinical practice. Not only are the signs and symptoms of depression multiple and complex, at any given stage of the disorder, but there are many stages and different problems in different age groups."[1] The term "depression" is much overworked. It is used to describe everything from temporary states of disappointment to long-term emotional states of dejection and sadness. The term is used here to describe an outright clinical syndrome of illness. Specific clinical features of persistent sleeplessness, a loss of initiative and enjoyment in life, suicidal threat, and biochemical changes comprise the depressive syndrome. By depression as an illness we mean a syndrome of symptoms that interfere with the total life function of the person in such a way that the person is disabled. This is what is called in medical circles an "endogenous" depression. It is not within the range of normal mood changes. Mood changes occur along with other impairments of the somatic and psychosocial functions of a person's life.

PRESCIENTIFIC DESCRIPTIONS
OF DEPRESSION

Depression as an acute disorder of the total human life of persons is not new on the scene of human behavior. Many prescientific accounts are available that describe the depressed state of consciousness itself, its patterns of behavior, and the devastation that it can work in people's lives

Lengthy and accurate descriptions in detail of patterns of treatment for the disorder may also be found.

One of the earliest historical personalities in religious literature to be afflicted with depression was Saul, the king of Israel. One reads the story of this very interesting personality in First Samuel in the Old Testament. The Spirit of the Lord departed from Saul, and he began to be troubled by an evil spirit. A harpist, in the person of David, was required to charm away his deep melancholy. However, a therapeutic confusion occurred in that David himself became a competitor with Saul in the popularity and approval of the people of Israel. Saul became jealous of him and pursued him with relentless fury in bursts of vindictiveness. Apart from David, Saul and his armies became involved with the Philistines, who were invading the Israelite territory. Saul became depressed again. He began to feel sad forebodings of a fate that was awaiting him. He made a night's journey to visit a woman of Endor who was reputed to have the power of calling up even the dead. She gave him the evil news that he and his sons would perish in the battle that was approaching the next day. Saul himself was wounded. He asked his armor-bearer to finish killing him. The man refused, whereupon the depressed and defeated Saul killed himself.

Psalm 22 captures the spirit of desolation characteristic of the depressed person. This is the psalm that Jesus repeated, the opening words of which were heard by those nearby, when he was being crucified:

> My God, my God, why hast thou forsaken me?
>   Why art thou so far from helping me, from the words of my groaning?
> O my God, I cry by day, but thou dost not answer;
>   and by night, but find no rest.
> . . . .
> . . . I am a worm, and no man;
>   scorned by men, and despised by the people.
> All who see me mock at me,
>   they make mouths at me, they wag their heads;
> "He committed his cause to the LORD; let him deliver him,
>   let him rescue him, for he delights in him!"

The psalms are replete with such descriptions of depression. Such can be found in Psalm 130:

> Out of the depths I cry to thee, O LORD!
>   Lord, hear my voice!
> Let thy ears be attentive
>   to the voice of my supplications!

However, the book of Psalms is not *just* a book of depression. The whole spectrum of human emotions is described in this series of poems.

Also, the book of Psalms speaks of recovery from depression and the healing of despair in the life of prayer. For example, in Psalm 40 we read as follows:

> I waited patiently for the LORD;
>   he inclined to me and heard my cry.
> He drew me up from the desolate pit,
>   out of the miry bog,
> and set my feet upon a rock,
>   making my steps secure.
> He put a new song in my mouth,
>   a song of praise to our God.
> Many will see and fear,
>   and put their trust in the LORD.

Greek literature likewise takes careful note of depression as an illness. One of the methods most frequently used by the healing temples of Greece was that of incubation. The phenomena of sleeping visions were used in sleep temples in order to restore people to a more optimistic and joyful life. The state of sadness was distinctly perceived as a sickness that needed healing. A person would go to the grove and temple of such gods as Asclepius and Trophonius to stay in certain buildings for an appointed number of days to get in touch with "the Good Spirit" and "Good Fortune." As part of his therapy the traveler bathed in the river Hercyna, and was anointed with oil. He was then taken by the priest to fountains of water. He first had to drink the waters of "forgetfulness," that he might forget all that he had been thinking hitherto. Afterward he drank the water of Memory, which caused him to remember what happened during the stay. The traveler then engaged in worship and prayer and proceeded to the oracle on the mountain beyond the grove. Upon return from this ceremonial he visited with the oracle of Trophonius. The priest seated the pilgrim upon a chair, the chair of Memory, and asked of the traveler all he had seen or learned. After debriefing the person from the journey and gaining his information, the priest entrusted him to relatives. The relatives carried the sojourner back to the building where he had lodged before with Good Fortune and the Good Spirit, to remain until he recovered all his faculties, especially the power to laugh.[2]

This rather detailed description of one form of therapy for depression as an illness is reported with an emphasis upon the use of sleep and water. One wonders whether perhaps contemporary uses of electrosleep therapy are more efficacious than other methods in the treatment of depression for the simple reason that they re-regulate the sleep rhythm of a person's life. Interesting is the comparison also between the degree of forgetfulness and the recovery of memory that is characteristic of contemporary shock therapy.

In the early Christian era, as among the ancient Hebrews, depression was known as the "noonday sickness." Psalm 91 speaks of "the destruction that wastes at noonday." In the Christian era, after the institutionalization of the Christian religion John Cassian (early fifth century A.D.) identified what we call depression as "the spirit of acedia." He noticed the loss of initiative, the increase of helplessness, the agitation, the inability to work, the sleeplessness, and the feelings of hopelessness that we usually associate with the clinical syndrome of depression today.

Mark D. Altschule says that Petrarch shifted from thinking of acedia as a sin and understood it as what we today would call a psychiatric symptom. He spoke of it as a disease. Altschule says: "Petrarch himself manifested an important symptom that had never been mentioned in that connection: an almost voluptuous pleasure in one's own emotional suffering. Another aspect of the syndrome that he unwittingly manifested was delight in exhibitionistic self-revelation, as shown in the minutely detailed account of his own spiritual sufferings."[3]

An ancient pattern of treatment was recommended for the recovery of a person suffering from acedia. A distinct pattern of treatment, based on the apostle Paul's teachings in First and Second Thessalonians, is outlined as follows:

First, one begins with the soothing application of praise and appreciation. This is necessary to enable the depressed person's "ears to be submissive and be ready for the remedy of healing words." As this praise of the good work and achievements of the person is applied, it is generously intermixed with encouragement to continue to do as one has done in the past. There is a strong affirmation of the past pattern of life in its productivity and creativity.

Second, the depressed person is encouraged to tend to his or her own business. This is based on the assumption that a part of acedia lies in the person's feeling of inability to control the behavior of other people. In this effort to control other people's behavior, disappointment occurs and the person falls into despair. Thus, the person who accepts responsibility for doing that which is his or her "own business" is less likely to be discouraged. He or she is urged to give up trying to run other people's lives for them.

Third, the depressed person is encouraged to examine himself or herself honestly and to walk honestly in relation to other people. Thus, the person is urged to examine the accuracy of his or her perception of reality and to bring his or her thinking into keeping with things as they are and not just as they appear.

Fourth, the person is encouraged not to covet other people's goods. The ancient assessors of personality assumed that much despair arises out of the covetousness of not having achieved the things that other people have achieved. Learning to be content with that which one has was a goal of treatment. One is encouraged to prove one's own worth, to work with one's own hands, and to produce things by working with one's physical body. In fact, at one place the injunctions say that if a person will not work, neither let that person eat. In other words, if the depressed person refuses to be productive, then food deprivation is used as a form of negative reinforcement to see to it that the person does work.

And finally, the person is encouraged to cease to "gad about" among the brethren, gossiping and speaking idly of others. If indeed this pattern continues, then the community is encouraged to ignore the person and withdraw from that person. A form of "judicial neglect" is suggested.

All through these rather quaint suggestions of therapy for the depressed patient is a continuing sense of seriousness with which the suffering patient is taken by the community as a whole. This set of suggestions assumes a highly disciplined, face-to-face community of people who care specifically about what is happening to the other person. However, today, in the religious life of the average conventional religious organization, these close-knit, face-to-face communities are very, very rare. Therefore, let it be clearly understood that I am simply reporting an ancient method of therapy in the Christian community as I did the ancient method of therapy in the Greek community to indicate not only that there were accurate descriptions of the symptomatology of depression in ancient eras but also that there were formal efforts of treatment with resources that the community had at hand.

One could not review all the religious literature on depression. The above excerpts indicate something of the drift of such literature. However, one can examine the writings of Augustine, in his *Confessions*; Martin Luther, in his letters; George Fox, in his journal; John Bunyan, in his book *Grace Abounding*; Jonathan Edwards, in his *Treatise Concerning Religious Affections*; and many other historical figures. In these writings are to be found vivid descriptions of the clinical syndrome of depression. Outstanding contemporary authors such as Harry Emerson Fosdick, H. Wheeler Robinson, E. Stanley Jones, and Anton Boisen are powerful religious leaders in whose writings may be found autobiographical reports of times of depression.

More recent forms of therapy used by contemporary religious leaders are meditation, retreat centers for stress interruption, and specific emphasis upon mystical experience.

Mystical experience has been reported by Paul C. Horton in three cases of suicidal patients as being an "oceanic state" which provided the patients with a reliably soothing safeguard against their overwhelming loneliness and possible suicide. Horton recognizes as a psychiatrist the importance of a mystical state as a transitional phenomenon that, along with other therapies, will tend to offset the possibility of suicide.[4]

THEORIES OF DEPRESSION

Members of the therapeutic team, regardless of their profession, face a bewildering fragmentation of theory as to the nature and causes of depression. Similarly, the very seriousness of the disorder is interpreted from various degrees of a sense of jeopardy for the life of the patient. However, since the advent of the antidepressant drugs, there has been a remarkable revival of interest in psychiatric diagnosis emphasizing the clinical signs and symptoms in relation to the long-term life history of the patient. Dean Schuyler, M.D., presents a comprehensive review of depression in its range of emotions, its signs and symptoms, classification, theories, outcomes, and treatment options. He systematizes the research in the field with what he calls a "spectrum approach." He distinguishes between a normal depression and a clinical depression and says that in normal depression, one has "the blues" and "grief reaction." To the contrary, in the pathological depression, there is the neurotic, indecisive, depressive state and the endogenous psychotic depression.

Clinicians generally agree as to the symptomatic presentations of a depressed patient. The fragmentation and controversial thinking of the field of psychiatry has a way of becoming more confusing at the points of etiology and treatment of choice. In an overview of recent research in depression, Akiskal and McKinney seek to integrate the varieties of interpretation of the cause and care of the depressed patient's condition into ten conceptual models. The conceptual models may be subdivided into the models that are proposed by *five different schools of psychiatric treatment.*

1. The psychoanalytic schools propose four different emphases in the interpretation of depression. First, the psychoanalysts propose that depression represents *anger and aggression turned inward against one's self.* This particular conception is highly relevant for the religiously inclined patient and the religious care of that patient, in that such a heavy taboo on anger and aggression is held by so many different groups. Second, the psychoanalytic schools since Freud have made much of *object* loss as a theory of depression. This moves all the way from René Spitz's understanding of an anaclitic depression which roots back into the earliest days of a person's life when the person was abandoned to the pathological grief situation of a person who has lost someone or something and has never "worked through" the grief. This last point of view is classically set forth in Freud's article "Mourning and Melancholia." A third psychoanalytic school characterized by such persons as Erich Fromm and Karen Horney

384

would assess depression as *loss of self-esteem, poor self-image*, and so forth. A fourth set of psychoanalytic theories is that of a *negative cognitive set*. This person is characterized by hopelessness and a loss of mutuality in his or her interaction with his or her environment.

2. A second classification of theories of depression is found in the behavioral school in which Martin E. P. Seligman speaks of depression as "learned helplessness," a theory that was devised in animal experimentation. The first phase of learned helplessness is exposure to a situation that is painful, combined with the conditions that prevent a person from doing anything to put the painful situation to an end. The second phase is a "giving up" phase in which the person simply accepts passively his or her helplessness. This suggests that, even from earliest infancy, individuals may be classified as tending to express stress reactions either outwardly or inwardly, but not both. In terms of biogenic temperament, the work of Macfarlane suggests that there are "internalizing infants"—that is, those who show their difficulties by secondary gastrointestinal and other types of upsets—and that there are those other infants who are inclined to an overt expression of response in terms of action and behavior. Gardner Murphy says, "This is as good a hypothesis for a constitutional typology, though the problem will doubtless be restated many times before a really workable typology is found."[5]

In the behavioral approaches of depression, a second concept appears for which we are indebted to Joseph Wolpe. He calls this a "loss of reinforcement" view. The depression rewards the patient for losses that he or she has sustained in life.

3. A third set of theoretical models of depression has been proposed by the social psychiatrists. Social psychiatrists are not a breed apart among psychiatrists. To the contrary, they are physicians who are thoroughly trained in a broad spectrum of modalities of treatment. They consider themselves as distinct humanitarians who "as humans" maintain their respect for the dignity of the individual. They maintain awareness of the uniqueness inherent in the social situation of each patient. Ever since Freud wrote his classical work, *Civilization and Its Discontents*, the social dimension of psychiatry has been vividly present.

The social psychiatrist is likely to present a "displaced or unplaced person's" concept of depression. The patient is seen as not being able to find a place in life or, upon finding a place in life, losing it and suffering a loss of role or status. For example, the pathologically grieving widow suffers not just the loss of her husband but also the loss of her role status as a married person. She is a single person again in a "couple-oriented society." She does not have the status of being a married person. Many of the prerogatives she and her husband shared together in clubs, churches, and other associations of the community have been taken from her, and the social groups in which she moves are usually all female. She has only a minimal contact with both sexes. This role status contributes to her depression, if it does not cause it. Similar things could be said of divorced persons, some unemployed persons, persons who have finished school, and others who have finished rearing their children. They are likely to think of themselves as being "finished."

4. A fourth group of theorists are the existentialists. Such persons as Viktor Frankl, Carl Jung, and Rollo May insist that the great dynamic of depression is the loss of meaning and existence. Radical psychiatrists like R. D. Laing have built patterns of treatment that assume that mental illness is a "quest" for this meaning.

5. A final school that provides at least two models of depression is that of the biogenic school, which is at this time at an intense level of research and treatment. The biological approach to depression has been demonstrated somewhat conclusively. Martin Allen and others have studied affective illnesses in veteran twins and made a diagnostic review. They studied 15,909 pairs of twins born between 1917 and 1927, among whom both twins served in the United States Army. This large sample was screened for twin pairs in which one or both had received the diagnosis of psychosis on active duty. They found 156 twin pairs in which one or both had been diagnosed as having an affective illness. Although computer-listed comparisons between "single ovum" and "double ovum" twins were insignificant, chart review diagnoses demonstrated much more significance. A study of 25 pairs of identical twins found that both were diagnosed as depressed persons. Out of 53 "double ovum," or "nonidentical," twins, in none of the pairs were both affected by a depressive illness; only one of the pair was so affected. One raises questions about data like this: "If none of the nonidentical twins showed concordant diagnoses of depression, then how much less would it be characteristic of family members who were not twins at all?" "If identical twins present a highly elevated percentage of concordant diagnoses of depression, then is there something about identical twin genetics in and of themselves that needs studying rather than using these high percentages as criteria for judging the biogenetic possibilities of a whole population?" Furthermore, another question could be asked: "If 36.5 percent of identical twins suffer concordant depressions, then how is it that the other 63.5 percent of such twins did *not* present such concordance?"

However, the most active research in the biological approach to depression today is in the area of using drugs that have a psychological effect. Treatment hypotheses say that certain substances in the biochemistry of the body are depleted, causing the depressive episode. Groups of hormones known as "biogenic amines" are facilitators of several central nervous system functions. Elation, it is hypothesized, may be associated with an excess of such biochemicals. The British are moving on the hypothesis that other biochemicals are at a significantly high level and thus affect the person in such a way that he or she becomes depressed. Stress studies such as those of Peter Bourne, especially upon Vietnam veterans, suggest that certain steroids are out of balance, causing exhaustion, and that depression is one result that follows. Other research persons are working on the relationship between depressive illness and hyperglycemia or hypoglycemia. In the field of psychiatry today, a wide array of pharmaceutical studies seek to establish dependable hypotheses for the treatment of depression.

At the distinctly practical and clinical level, however, the treatment of depression moves toward an intensification of the importance of the diagnosis of the particular kind of depression. If the depression is an anxiety or neurotic depression, then the treatment tends to move in the direction of anxiety-controlling types of drugs. But if the depression is diagnosed as "endogenous," antidepressants are to be used (or chemically based). Thus, diagnosis cannot be written off as irrelevant today as in the years prior to 1952, when the psychologically effective drugs had not become available.

As a theologian and pastor, I emphasize that when a counselee seems depressed or is depressed, the first line of response is to ask the person to have a thorough medical examination by a doctor of internal medicine. Then I suggest that the pastor ask for consultation with that physician and collaborate as to whether or not pastoral counseling is indicated or whether additional care is needed from a psychiatrist. If the psychiatric referral can come from a conjoint assessment by a clinically trained pastor and an internist, then the patient tends to feel that he or she is more cared for and is being taken seriously. Thus the patient is more likely to accept a psychiatric referral. The patient will know that he or she has not simply been hurried off to a psychiatrist.

If indeed a psychiatric referral is necessary, it may well be that the person needs separation from his or her environment by hospitalization. The indicators of this are: (1) the degree of disability that the person is experiencing in work, interpersonal relationships, and basic sense of somatic well-being; (2) the degree to which the patient is likely to make impulsive judgment about major issues in his or her life, such as quitting a job, confessing a long list of past sins to injudiciously selected people, spending great quantities of money unwisely; (3) the degree of suicidal risk that exists in the person. One of the dangers of pastoral counseling with depressed persons is that the pastor sees many normative states of sadness and grief that "hurt" in ways similar to depression, for example, the loss of someone by death, divorce, defection, or alienation. Yet this may or may not be unreasoning, indefinable, and prolonged sadness. The person may "come through" quite well, depending upon the person's life support system, ego defenses, history of dealing with problems, and so forth.

However, a pastor may well find a person to be in a prolonged depression, have major difficulty in functioning, and unable to pull out of the state of despair. The pastor can prolong this by continuing to see the patient on pastoral counseling interviews over a long period of time when, instead, some medical intervention could alleviate the suffering much more quickly. The in-hospital treatment of a psychiatric patient by a therapeutic team that includes skilled and experienced pastoral counselors is an issue that needs attention at this point. One needs to raise the question: What are the religious dimensions of depression? Then one needs to ask: How can these dimensions be implemented in the treatment of the patient concurrent with milieu therapy, pharmacological therapy, and social work therapy that includes work at a psychotherapeutic level and at a family therapy level? It takes a smoothly working team effort. I shall attempt to answer these questions to some extent in the ensuing section.

DEPRESSION, RELIGIOUS CRISIS, AND PASTORAL STRATEGIES

Let me emphasize depression as a religious "value crisis" and identify some of the dimensions of that crisis in such a way as to reflect the fact that pastoral wisdom may be strategically helpful to persons in the religious crisis presented in many depressive illnesses.

The hallmark of effective religious therapy is interpretation and the provision of meaningful patterns of understanding of what is happening in the life of a patient. These patterns of understanding must be acceptable to the patient without too much persuasion or indoctrination on the part of the therapist. Nevertheless, clinical experience has shown that sometimes a clear-cut sentence of interpretation that provides a precise meaning or key to the plight in which the person finds himself or herself becomes lastingly useful and may mark a turning point in the person's direction toward health.

The religious crisis of many depressions presents several specific facets of these mood disorders that can be approached pastorally in definable ways somewhat as follows:

The Crisis of Nostalgia and Rumination

Nostalgia is a word that was used during the Civil War to describe depression among soldiers. To them it focused on wanting to return home. An original medical definition of nostalgia was "a severe melancholia caused by protracted absence from home, as of military personnel." In brief, it means simply looking homeward, looking backward and ruminating the way things "used to be." Nostalgia becomes a crisis in people's lives in the form of depression. Subtle development crises are often neglected in the history-taking procedures with such patients. Examples help to illustrate what is meant.

First, a fifty-eight-year-old man, a widower of ten years, became unreasonably depressed, with no particular visible precipitating event. He was a very religious person who had worked both as a tool and die operator and as a minister in his community. He was able to retain his full-time job as a tool and die operator. By reason of changes in personnel and the closing of smaller churches, the church of which he was a pastor went out of existence. He was not able to find another church. He became so depressed that he simply sat on the front porch of his son's home and "moped" and ruminated about "the way things used to be." His condition became prolonged enough that his son and daughter-in-law, parents of four little children, insisted that he get medical treatment. Upon diagnosis, he was discovered to be free of any physiological disorders, with the exception of a slightly elevated blood pressure. Yet he was extremely sad, agitated, listless, without initiative, and noncommunicative. He was somewhat hypochondriacal. He wanted medication for the slightest difficulty he felt in his body.

Upon closer scrutiny, it was discovered that this man's value system grew out of his own father's value system. His father had always believed that it was the children's God-given duty to honor their parents by caring for them after they got "too old to work." The critical issue was that the father had a religious value that prompted him to think that his creative years were over when he got his children grown. Also, he felt that his purpose in life beyond this point was to "sit and rock" and do nothing. This attitude is not an uncommon value among blue-collar people.

The staff confronted the man in psychotherapy with the fact that he had much life still left to live and that it may well be God's calling that he dedicate that life to a new chapter in his existence. The staff suggested that he could make a new contribution by continuing his work as a tool and die operator and by getting the assistance of his church people in finding an additional place for his preaching ministry. To all of this he was very resistant. He became considerably angry and his blood pressure fluctuated upward. However, he was presented with the other alternative, that if he chose his depressed state of inactivity as a chronic way of life, it would be necessary for him to be moved to a welfare type of hospital. He opposed being on welfare. He saw it as "going to the poor house." He became intensely angry. He refused any further treatment and decided to go out of the hospital against medical advice.

However, in his anger he went back to his job. He did indeed, with some assistance from the social service staff, get in touch with his church organization and find a new pastorate. He established himself as an ongoing independent person. His poignant remaining problem, however, is loneliness. The life support system of his church will, it is hoped, provide him a larger family than just his son and daughter and their children. Also, it is hoped that he will meet an eligible person to become his wife. They too might form a new home in which his loneliness can be assuaged by the pleasure of the company of a new wife, inasmuch as his first wife has been dead ten years. The "odds" on such hopes are not too good, but it has happened to other people. Maybe it can happen to him.

A second example of the crisis of nostalgia as a form of depression is found in women who have suffered the loss of their first child in stillbirth or by miscarriage or by abortion. They may have gone on into a highly productive life and been privileged to raise a normal family. Nevertheless they continue to ruminate about their "first loss."

An example of this is a forty-nine-year-old woman who had had an abortion thirty years before, at the age of nineteen. She was in an unreasonable depression. A close scrutiny of recent occurrences in her life revealed that her youngest daughter, with whom she had a close relationship, had been married just three or four months before, at the age of nineteen. This was a turning point in the patient's life and may have reactivated memories of her own youth. This mother's mind at this point was obsessed with whether or not God could forgive her for the abortion thirty years before. Both the patient's daughter and her son were apparently happily married, lived near, and were solicitous to her. Yet their words of solicitude fell with cold comfort on the mother's ears. The pastoral counseling proceeded along two lines of strong affirmation of the highly creative and productive life that the woman had lived since marrying her husband. She had apparently done a quite successful job of rearing her children. However, "the wedding over" and the "crowd having thinned out," she was faced with the necessity of reorganizing her whole routine of life. She must now reestablish her relationship with her husband in their new identity in the "empty nest" stage of family living. Yet she was exhausted by the prospects of facing these new responsibilities. Did she really want to go forward? Or did she wish to turn back and ruminate nostalgically and sentimentally over the mistakes of the past? Antidepressants were being used with this patient and she was making some progress. However, one raises the question as to how much of a compulsive obsessional type of thinking is involved in addition to the depression. How much habit remodification is going to be needed? The term "behavioral modification" does not make as much of "thought modification" as it potentially could. A few therapeutic successes I have had in the past in working with this kind of ruminative circularity of thinking are more related to thought modification built upon behavioral modification concepts than they are upon insight therapy. This is the approach that was instituted in this patient's religious care.

The Crisis of Self-Consistency

Prescott Lecky made a remarkable contribution to psychotherapy in his book *Self-Consistency*. He rejected what he termed the "hydraulic analogies" of psychoanalysis. By this he meant that human feelings such as anger and sexuality are not "fluids" whose "pressures" are created by the lack of emotional outlets, drainages, and so forth. He assumed instead that behavior is motivated by the need for the unity of one's personal values in life. He conceived of the personality as an organization of values that are felt to be consistent with one another. Behavior expresses the effort to maintain the integrity and unity of the organization.[6] Conflict arises when a value that is inconsistent with the individual's personal integrity enters the system. Such an entry may precipitate a depression, because a person cannot assimilate an experience that is contradictory to his or her values. This particular kind of depression is often thought of as a "neurotic depression." It is characterized by indecision. The person knows what he or she should do in order to maintain his or her integrity but is at a loss as to how to bring it off, or lacks the courage to do so.

An example of this kind of attempt to maintain integrity is the case of a twenty-nine-year-old black woman who was admitted to an emergency psychiatric service after having taken an overdose of sleeping pills. Upon having been resuscitated, she said that she was in one "hell of a fix." She said: "I'm trying to make my mind up. I don't know what to do." Her dilemma was that she is the mother—out of wedlock—of four children. She was living with a man with whom she did not want to have any further dealings. Her children had become attached to him and did not want to leave him. They had "sided" with him. As a result, if she left him, she would lose her relationship with her children. At least she thought she would. If she stayed with her lover, she would be subjected to a relationship in which she felt that she was treated "like dirt." Thus, in the critical dilemma, she cried for help by a minimally lethal attempt at suicide. The value conflict here between maintaining her personal integrity, on the one hand, and maintaining her relationship with her children, on the other hand, was intense. Two approaches to her dilemma were taken. The social workers instituted family therapy with the children, the lover, and the patient. Individual pastoral counseling with the patient brought to focus her own sense of self-worth, her value as a person before God, and the kinds of ideas she wanted her children to learn from her.

From a religious point of view, maintaining one's integrity means maintaining one's sense of self-respect as a person made in the image of God. In Judaism, this is an extremely important value. In Christianity, the value of being made in the image of God is the same. Added to it is the conviction of being a person in one's own right, having been redeemed by the Lord Jesus Christ as one for whom Christ died. Yet being a person of integrity calls for the capacity to make a clear-cut decision and to stay with it. A part of the religious care of the psychiatric patients suffering from an integrity crisis is that of enabling them to learn the arts of making decisions, of reinforcing good decisions they have made, and of staying with them and following through as they implement these decisions. The nineteenth-century Danish theologian Søren Kierkegaard had a remarkable analysis of this in his book *The Sickness Unto Death*. He said that despair is the sickness unto death. That despair is the sickness in the spirit. Despair assumes a triple form. First, some persons have despair at not being aware of having a self or of the necessity of having integrity. Second, others despair at not having the courage to decide or to will to be themselves, that is, to have integrity. Third, other persons despair at willing to be themselves, having decided to be themselves, and at the great burden of maintaining their integrity. The issue, therefore, of maintaining one's integrity lies at the root of much neurotic despair of depression.[7]

The Crisis of Power and Powerlessness in the Systems of Society

In some of the earliest myths, the desire to be in control and to have power in the system of which one is a part stands as one of the foremost needs of the human being, one of the most ambiguous dilemmas of the human being. The story of the temptation and sin of Adam and Eve in the garden reveals this need "to be as gods." The depression of Saul described in the earlier part of the chapter was an outgrowth of his sense of powerlessness in the system of which he was a part. Today, persons are involved in several systems out of which a considerable amount of depression ensues. These are the home, the work situation, and the political situation.

Some fertile sources of depression in the systems of society are unresolved bereavement and divorce, both of which are focused in the system of the home. A common temptation is overinvestment, or idolatry, which tends to focus heavily upon the home. Daniel Tucker, M.D., in private conversation, defined "reality" as "the least alterable facts in one's human existence." The loss of someone by death tends to be probably the least alterable fact in one's existence. Adjustment to a loss by death depends heavily upon the degree of overinvestment that one has made in the deceased loved one. However, one of the most common indications for the involvement of religious professionals in the care of a psychiatric patient is that of prolonged, pathological grief situations. The death of a spouse or a child very likely causes the depressive syndrome of bereavement where overinvestment or, to use a theological term, idolatry of the dead is evident.

A case in point is a thirty-eight-year-old woman who had lost her son three years before by death by cancer. She had him through his terminal illness for nearly a year. She said: "I simply cannot accept the fact that my son is dead. If I accept it, the fact that he is dead, then he would be dead." In speaking to me as a minister, she said: "How can God help me to accept the fact of my son's death?" She asked this question in a highly insistent manner, as if to "demand" a perfect answer to it. I told her that I felt she was having a greater problem of accepting the fact that she could not control and determine the obvious reality that her son had died three years before. I pointed out to her that one of the effects of her illness was that it dominated and controlled the rest of her family situation. She was in control over the rest of the family, even though she could not control the life and death matter of her son. There was a long silence in the conversation. I asked her to pose this issue with her psychiatrist, who had asked me to see her, and make this an item for their psychotherapy. In conferring with him, I suggested that this would be a vital issue to consider: that is, pathological grief can be a refusal to live life without being in total control. In long-term chronic cases of pathological grief, I have found the factor of personal power and control of the family system to be a driving force that maintained the depression.

The work situation is a second system in which depression becomes evident in the powerlessness of the patient. In the technological and bureaucratic structures of our society, people develop institutionalized neuroses in relation to the employment structures of which they are a part. They tend to think of their organization as the whole universe itself. They are likely to think of it as "a flat earth." If one goes beyond the edge of the organization, then annihilation is the result. Bureaucratic organizations give a person some individual satisfactions over and beyond the "uses" of those for the organization itself. The enlargement of the spiritual life and personal growth of employees is an important ingredient of effective productivity, but it is a low priority item in business, educational, and professional administrations. One obvious truth that a person can outgrow a job is rarely a topic of management planning.

William H. Whyte, Jr., has said: "Of all the organization men the true executive is the one who remains most suspicious of The Organization. If there is one thing that characterizes him, it is a fierce desire to control his own destiny and, deep down, he resents yielding that control to The Organization, no matter how velvety its grip. He does not want to be done right by, he wants to dominate, not to be dominated." In another connection, he says: "Here lies the executive neurosis. Some of the executive's tensions and frustrations are due to psychoses—his own and others'—and these are amenable to individual treatment. To a very large degree, however, the tensions of organization life are not personal aberrations to be eliminated by adjustment; they are the inevitable consequence of the collision between the old ethic and the new."[8] The whole system of healthy religious values indicates that an organization will "take care of its own." The average ethic is that the organization takes care of itself. Individuals are expendable.

For example, a leading executive enjoyed twenty-five years of effective service to his organization. When he came to age sixty-four, the policy concerning retirement was changed. Persons now could continue year after year, on the assumption of medically certified healthiness, until they were seventy. However, this man had been on the wrong side of a whole string of political issues that had arisen in the organization's relationship to the national government. He had opposed the chief executive of the organization much to the chief executive's displeasure. As a result, the chief executive terminated him at the age of sixty-five. Effective prevention of a depression was available for this man by providing a creative strategy for offsetting the sense of powerlessness he felt. This is a contradiction of the old maxim that therapy is a highly individual, idiosyncratic, endogenous matter. This prevention work was done on a macroscopic, systems-engineering basis in behalf of the well-being of an individual.

The rectifying of specific political situations of powerlessness in the development of new strategies and alternatives is integral to an adequate process of therapy. Otherwise, those responsible for psychiatric treatment fall into the errors of priesthoods of all types. One who is a member of the psychiatric team cannot be politically naive. Social ills exist that need some modification. If they cannot be changed, people will be broken. A therapist who ignores these will be much less effective. Examples of the sense of powerlessness in the depression of persons in systems of society appear in the "acting out" behavior of people who are in positions of power and who are depressed. The acting-out behavior has a way of ensuring that the patient gets the kind of therapy that he or she needs. A classical example of this is Representative Wilbur Mills in the tragic episodes that led him into a treatment situation and a recovery from depression and alcoholism. Such cases give cause to philosophize about powerlessness and powerfulness. Is the presence of unmanageable power, that is, the possession of more power than one knows what to do with, a source of depression?

Does this depression lead to inadvertencies of judgment, to malfeasances of behavior, and to dramatic conversions such as that experienced by Charles Colson and many others in the Watergate tragedy?

The Crisis of Injustice

In psychiatric services, it is almost a truism that depression is internalized anger. In psychotherapeutic sessions, patients are confronted with the possibility that they are deeply angry. This confrontation doubles the resistance of distinctly religious patients. It causes them to increase the power of their denial systems. However, statistical cross-sectional studies of depression indicate that the greater the anger score, the more likely the patient is to present a depressive syndrome of a non-endogenous type.[9]

One possible definition of anger is that it is the normal reaction of a person to injustice. Therefore a way through the resistances and denials of the distinctly religious patient as to having any "anger" is to raise the issue of injustice. Does the person feel that God has treated him or her justly or unjustly? Justice is an "okay" value for religious people. It is easy for them to discuss this. They are committed in their value systems to seeing to it that "justice is done." A considerable portion of their anger is therefore a natural reaction to injustice.

Patients will say to a therapist that they are angry, or that they may be angry with God and that they feel very, very bad about feeling this way. One of the most helpful insights that comes from a careful reading of the Old and New Testaments is that anger can be expressed openly and forthrightly in prayers to God. (See Psalms 137 and 109.) One cannot, by keeping these feelings to oneself, keep a secret from God. Nor need one feel that one is going to be destroyed if one expresses real feelings to God. Therefore a patient can be encouraged to "tell it like it is" to God with the sure certainty that God can "take it" and understand, and respond with justice and mercy and love. Such is the experience of persons like Moses, the apostle Paul, and Jesus in their expressions of anger before God.

It would not be accurate to leave the definition of anger at simply a feeling of injustice. A considerable number of persons feel angry and depressed because they have basic needs that go unmet, such as sexual desire, economic opportunity, and companionship. Frustrated as they are, they become depressed because of a lack of legitimate and affirming opportunity to express their deepest needs. In such instances, patient understanding and realistic appreciation of the poignant hungers of the person have a way of letting the person know that it is also acceptable to express these feelings to God in prayer. This comes as good news and surprising news to a great many pietistic Christians.

The Crisis of Competence

One of the real confusions that arises between members of the psychiatric treatment team when considering the religious treatment of mentally ill patients is the stereotypical assumption that the only set of values that the religious world represents today is "moral values." These values refer to self-condemnation for minor moral infractions, feeling sinful because of culturally imposed restrictions or taboos. However, the higher reaches of religious concern focus upon competency values. These values refer to the aspirations that people have, the hopes they hold, the goals they have been trying to achieve, and the expectations they have of themselves and that other people have of them in an achieving society such as ours. This set of distinctions is made forcefully and well by Milton Rokeach.[10] A person tends to feel *guilty* about having violated moral taboos. However, a great sense of *shame* comes over the person who has not achieved the goals that he or she may have set for himself or herself. Helen Merrell Lynd says that Shakespeare uses shame about nine times more often than guilt. The sense of shame contrasts, not with right doing or with approval by others, but with truth and honor in one's own eyes. The wounding of one's own self-ideal and disgrace in the eyes of oneself inhere in the feeling of shame. This shame is associated with the loss of honor and of self-respect.

Therefore it is important to consider the feelings of shame that people have when they have not demonstrated the competence they require of themselves. Depression therefore would arise out of such experiences as various kinds of impotence, particularly sexual impotence. Withdrawn persons are overwhelmed with a feeling of shame that they are not competent to attract the affection and care of other people. For example, a thirty-eight-year-old man with an I.Q. of 126 is a successful person in his chosen field of technical research. Moreover, he has such high ideals of perfection for his graduate dissertation that he is immobilized and incapable of completing the dissertation. This in turn limits his ability to succeed in his profession because of his needs for the doctor's degree as a "credential" for doing his work. He has been in and out of psychiatric hospitals for twelve years. When asked what the greatest loss he has sustained through his illness is, he replies, "The shame I feel because I have not achieved in my work as I should have." The situation can be the reverse also. Instead of the sense of failure being the cause of the shame, the depression itself may predate the testing situation and contribute to the failure of the candidate, in spite of the best efforts of conscientious committees. As Akiskal and McKinney say, "For instance, man who ascribes his depression to having lost his job may have in reality lost his job as a result of his depressive illness."[11]

The Crisis of Self-Elevation

Ancient literature reveals a perspective of depression that is rarely found in the contemporary literature of psychiatry. These sources "finger" the degree of pride and envy involved in depression. The prophet Elijah, during one of his states of depression (which seemed to alternate with states of elation as well), said to the Lord in his prayer, "I have been very jealous for the LORD, the God of hosts; for the people of Israel have forsaken thy covenant, thrown down thy altars, and slain thy prophets with the sword; and I, even I only, am left; and they seek my life, to take it away" (1 Kings 19:10). It is not uncommon, in conversing with depressed persons, to hear them remonstrate that "nobody knows the trouble I've seen" and to be told that they are unique and different in their suffering. No one could have had just the kind of suffering they have had. This theme becomes persistent enough in some patients that one gets the feeling they are proud of their plight and like to be "set apart" in uniqueness.

Similarly, depressed patients continually "suffer by comparison." They place themselves alongside other persons and compare themselves unfavorably with them to such depths and to such extent that sometimes it seems that they are envious of the other person's good fortune. This particular attitude is expressed by the psalmist in Psalm 73 when he says:

> But as for me, my feet had almost stumbled,
>   my steps had well nigh slipped.
> For I was envious of the arrogant,
>   when I saw the prosperity of the wicked.
> For they have no pangs;
>   their bodies are sound and sleek.
> They are not in trouble as other men are;
>   they are not stricken like other men.

Donald Backus, in a comparison of the "seven deadly sins scale" with the Minnesota Multiphasic Personality Inventory, discovered that in all five of the groups he tested the persons who showed high depressive elevations on the MMPI also showed similar high elevations on the seven deadly sins scale in the pride and envy categories. Whereas they also showed the same kind of correlations on the sloth scale, the sloth scale itself is almost synonymous with the depressive scale.[12] From a psychotherapeutic point of view, an exploration of these three subtle correlations would be helpful in changing the categories of thought and plowing new ground in the circularity of thinking with depressed patients. Psychotherapists find themselves stalemated with the ruminative thinking of the depressed person. Such a shift of semantics may in turn bring up the possibility that these patients would begin to think of themselves somewhat differently if they thought of themselves as being proud that they were suffering so badly. It can be used to interrupt the pattern of circular, ruminative thought.

Along with this pride in suffering is the perfectionism of the depressed person. Much of the lack of initiative of a depressed person rests, it seems to me, in the self-elevation of the person to the effect that whatever he or she does must be done perfectly or not at all. As a result, the patient falls back into sloth or inactivity or lack of initiative or physiological retardation, depending on how profound the changes in the behavior are. Once biochemical imbalances are corrected, the issues of psychotherapy and/or pastoral counseling are to make open agendas of the pride, envy, and self-elevation of the person.

The Crisis of Courage

Depressed patients will complain of a loss of faith. An initial response to this complaint is that of an intellectual discussion of "articles of faith" such as belief in God, belief in the goodness of God, belief in the existence of God. However, in the tradition of the Judeo-Christian teachings, faith is seen at its best as an expression of courage and adventure in the face of the unknown. Faith is defined in the Letter to the Hebrews as follows: "Now faith is the assurance of things hoped for, the conviction of things not seen" (Heb. 11:1). The critical issue in depression is the failure of nerve, the loss of courage. Margaret Mead has said in several places that the cross-cultural constant in all religion is that it generates hope. Erik Erikson at one time said that hope is generated by mutuality. The depression of the patient represents the collapse of the patient's sense of mutuality with things and persons about him or her. Hence, hope perishes.

In a psychiatric milieu, we are concerned about the life and death of patients. That concern heavily centers upon the possibility of suicide. Depressed patients are highly suspect as being suicidally potential. However, in our overconcentration upon suicide, we may neglect the clinical reality that depression itself may be a life setting conducive to massive physiological disorders that end in death. Gerald L. Engle, M.D., of Rochester, New York, has written an article entitled "A Life Setting Conducive to Illness."[13] He describes what he calls the giving up–giving in complex. He himself may be tempted to giving up. The staff, on the other hand, may be prone to give up on the patient. Five psychological characteristics that he identifies as being evident in the giving up–giving in complex are as follows: a feeling of giving up, experienced as helplessness or hopelessness; a depreciated image of the self; a sense of the loss of gratification from relationships of roles in life; a feeling of disruption of the sense of continuity between past, present, and future; and a reactivation of memories of earlier periods of giving up. These characteristics are easily identifiable as depressive symptoms. He describes how in both human beings and animals organisms simply die outright upon having had all the hope of a mutual relationship dashed.

The psychiatric liaison teams tend to see these phenomena more than inpatient psychiatric unit teams see them. These patients are found on medical, surgical, obstetrical, orthopedic, and other wards far more than they are found on psychiatric wards. One sees these patients in coronary care and intensive care units. The more experience one has had in the open community, quite apart from hospitals, the more reports can be produced to document the collapse of courage in the face of life's heirlooms of suffering.

For example, a couple in their middle seventies had lived a long and fruitful life together as husband and wife. The wife became psychotic and dangerous to herself and other people. She had to be placed in a nursing home temporarily. After adequate psychiatric care, she found herself in remission of the symptoms of the psychotic episode and she and her husband were able to continue to live together in the nursing home. The husband saw it as his purpose in life to "see to it" that his wife was cared for until her death. He had four heart attacks between ages seventy-five and eighty-one. He rallied from each one of them and was able to do the minimal things necessary to see to it that his wife had company and care. He continued to reiterate that his purpose in life was to care for his "sweetheart" and see to it that she was not left alone in the world.

Then came the death of his wife. Ten days passed after her death. He set his business matters in order. He called for his pastor and told him that his life's work was done. He gave thanks in prayer with the pastor for having had such a long and useful life and for having been granted the privilege of caring for his wife until her death. This was at about 4:00 in the afternoon. At 6:30 that afternoon, after having eaten his dinner, he lay down on his bed and died. One wonders, in such cases, whether or not the power of decision has anything to do with the time that a person dies, without regard to the factor of suicide.

Also, one wonders if the degree of mutuality that existed between this man and his wife was not the source of hope that kept him alive, the basis of his courage to face life. If one of the purposes of religion is the generation of mutuality and community, then the discovery and creation of new alternatives for human existence—as Elton Trueblood used to call them, alternatives to futility—seems to be the card of entry that energizes the role of prophetic religion in the therapeutic care of the depressed person.

Yet young persons, seemingly with every reason to live, nevertheless become depressed and see no reason for being. As one nineteen-year-old young man told me: "I wish there was a building in this town tall enough that I could jump off and get forgiveness for committing suicide before I hit the ground." As irrational and patently untrue is the belief that suicide is unpardonably sinful; nevertheless the belief reflects the partial truth that we are really "playing God" when we decide to suicide. We take all the matters of the whole world into our hands. We rule out God and everybody else. The belief that suicide is a sin reflects our subtle awareness that we are usurping God's place. Little wonder that so many suicidal attempts represent a spectrum of indecision on the one hand and lethality on the other. Occasionally, however, self-elevation reaches the level of intensity that Friedrich Nietzsche did when he said: "There is no God! If there were, how could I stand it if I were not he?" It was he who did commit suicide. It is as if the critical issue of suicide is to accept, not the existence of God, but the reality of our new humanness.

NOTES

1. Alfred M. Freedman, Harold I. Kaplan, Benjamin J. Sadock, *Comprehensive Textbook of Psychiatry—II*, 2nd ed. (Baltimore, Md.: Williams & Wilkins Co., 1975), 1:811.

2. Pausanias, *Description of Greece*, trans. W. H. S. Jones, Loeb Classical Library (Cambridge: Harvard University Press, n.d.), 4:349–355.

3. Mark D. Altschule, "Acedia: Its Evolution from Deadly Sin to Psychiatric Syndrome," *British Journal of Psychiatry* 3 (1965): 117–119.

4. Paul C. Horton, M.D., "The Mystical Experience as a Suicidal Preventive," *American Journal of Psychiatry* 130, no. 3 (March 1973): 294–297.

5. Gardner Murphy, *Personality: A Biosocial Approach to Origins and Structure* (New York: Harper & Brothers, 1947), p. 82.

6. Prescott Lecky, *Self-Consistency: A Theory of Personality*, ed. Frederick C. Thorne, 2nd ed. (New York: Island Press Co-operative, 1951), p. 152.

7. Søren Kierkegaard, *The Sickness Unto Death* (Princeton, N.J.: Princeton University Press, 1941), p. 17.

8. William H. Whyte, Jr., *The Organization Man* (New York: Doubleday & Co., Doubleday Anchor Books, 1957), pp. 166, 167.

9. Issy Pilowsky, M.D., and Neil T. Spence, "Hostility and Depressive Illness," *Archives of General Psychiatry* 32 (September 1975): 1154–1159.

10. Milton Rokeach, *The Nature of Human Values* (New York: Free Press, 1973), pp. 8–9.

11. Hagop S. Akiskal, M.D., and William T. McKinney, "Overview of Recent Research in Depression," *Archives of General Psychiatry* 32 (March 1975): 288.

12. Donald Backus, *The Seven Deadly Sins: Their Meaning and Measurement* (Ann Arbor, Mich.: University Microfilms, 1969), pp. 21–22.

13. Gerald L. Engle, M.D., "A Life Setting Conducive to Illness," *Annals of Internal Medicine* 69, no. 2 (1968): 293–300.

Part Seven

PITFALLS OF
RELIGIOUS LIFE

29

Idolatry and Sick Religion

The minister, by the nature of his calling, is committed to proclaiming the good news of a prophetic faith. In both the Christian and the Jewish heritages, prophetic faith is set over against their own cultural forms, which are by definition idolatrous. In other world religions, a similar obscuring of the ultimate values takes place by excessive preoccupation with the proximate, temporary things that men overvalue. The hypothesis of this chapter is that when the relative values of life take the place of the eternal and ultimate ones, a condition of idolatry exists. The person in this time and place is on the way to becoming off-center, disturbed, unbalanced, and sick at the core of his religious life.

The astute reader will readily ask: "Who is to define what is idolatry and what is the true and living God? Is this not a very relative matter?" "Are you taking a hard, party-line position that gives you the right to determine who the true and living God is and requires that everyone be in accord with this or be seen as sick religiously?" These are very legitimate questions. To answer them is possible but not easy. The questions can be approached confessionally as to who *I* think is the true and living God. The end result would be that as a Christian I *could* be heard to take a "hard party line." Or I can take the position of a psychologist of religion and ask for an empirical description of the *kind of religious sentiment* that makes for health and disease in religion. This does not require that I give specific content and character to the kind of religion a person may have. It does require a functional value judgment as to *how* the value works. I choose to follow the latter procedure. The reason for doing so is that I may speak to people of all religious persuasions and ask whether they are sick or well in their faith. Even so, I have already spoken in other places, especially in my book *Christ and Selfhood,*[1] from an unequivocally Christian point of view. Readers who wish to "positionize" me, for better or worse, can read that book against the background of what is said here. But here the distinctly phenomenological and empirical point of view is taken. What, then, are the characteristics of a religious worldview that could be characterized as laying hold of the Eternal, and what are the characteristics of an idolatrous religion?

THEOLOGICAL PERSPECTIVES

Paul Tillich has done most to make the concept of the demonic power of idolatry a negotiable concept for the modern, sophisticated reader. He says that the distinctly religious quest is concerned with the power of the New Being in that which takes the empirical form of an ultimate, not a proximate, concern. When we invest ultimate concern in that which is ultimate, we have anxiety but it is normal anxiety, which grows out of our realization of our finitude, our mortality in the face of death, and our encounter with meaninglessness in the proximate things of life. When we invest ultimate concern, however, in proximate, finite, temporal, and transitory realities, we "absolutize the finite." We give ourselves over to these proximate concerns, which become idols in our lives. As such, the idol exercises demonic power over us. It has become *the* ultimate power over us. It possesses us with a frail hand. (Illustrations for these ideas rush to my mind, but these can wait for the empirical histories of patients who have become sick in this way.) Nevertheless, the end result is pathological anxiety.[2] The person becomes "pathologically fixed to a limited self-affirmation."[3]

Tillich uses the example of the idolatrous character of utopianism, which serves to make his point very concrete in the face of the almost millennialistic social reform movements of today. He says:

> For utopianism, taken literally, is idolatrous. It gives the quality of ultimacy to something preliminary. It makes unconditional what is conditioned (a future historical situation) and at the same time disregards the always present existential estrangement and the ambiguities of life and history.[4]

Again, Tillich identifies religious nationalism as a contemporary idolatry at the same time that he defines what idolatry is:

> Idolatry is the elevation of a preliminary concern to ultimacy. Something essentially conditioned is taken as unconditional, something essentially partial is boosted into universality, and something essentially finite is given infinite significance (the best example is the contemporary idolatry of religious nationalism).[5]

Emil L. Fackenheim, a Jewish professor of philosophy at the University of Toronto, says that a particular symbol or art object is rarely thought of as a modern possibility of idolatry. However, the idolater of today is concerned with living idols that can literally hear, speak, and act. He defines modern idolatry as follows:

> The idol itself is divine. The idolatrous projection of infinite feeling upon finite object is such as to produce not a symbolic, but, rather, a literal and hence total identification of finiteness and infinitude.[6]

From a psychological point of view, one can readily discern that the mechanism of idolatrous construction is projection of both wish and fear upon an external person who hears, speaks, and acts. From our understanding of primitive religion, this can be either a living or a dead person, depending upon the sick person's attitude toward death. The ghosts of the restless dead, as in *Hamlet,* can still be operative in the spiritual distemper of the religiously sick. A disturbed and imminently suicidal Saul can consult with the departed spirit of Samuel. Even though he had "cut off the mediums and the wizards from the land" himself, Saul consulted a woman who was a medium and asked her to bring up Samuel for him (1 Sam. 28:8ff.). He did this in disguise, thereby rejecting to a great degree his role as the king. The point, in brief, is that he and Hamlet both were fixed in their loyalty upon a departed and dead hero. Yet, as Fackenheim says, their relationship was not a symbolic one but a literal and total one. They had "bet their whole lives" on what was going on between them and the departed spirits.

Insofar as I have been able to find, Islam, the religion of the Muslims, with its heavy emphasis upon monotheism, is more prone to interpret behavior in terms of idolatry than is either Hinduism or Buddhism. The Muslim likens an idolater to "the spider who buildeth her a house: But, verily, frailest of all houses surely is the house of the spider."[7] To the Muslim, idolatry is the unpardonable sin. Yet Hinduism and Buddhism alike are more syncretistic religions and permit polytheistic worship of nature, veneration of ancestors, and so forth. This "lower" type of worship for the populace rarely reaches the level of conferring ultimate significance upon the object of worship. The objects of worship do not become matters of total identification of the finite with the infinite.

PSYCHOLOGICAL ESTIMATES OF ULTIMATE AND PROXIMATE RELIGIOUS CONCERN

Several psychologists have been definitive about the mature religious sentiment, as Gordon Allport calls it. By negative reference, the sick religious concern can be pointed out. Allport speaks of religious concern in terms of *interest, outlook,* or a *system of beliefs.* This is a system of readiness that we use in coping with life. When thought and feeling are organized and directed toward some highly chosen object of value—a mother, a son, a neighborhood, a nation, or a church—"we call the system a sentiment." Then Allport defines a specifically religious sentiment by saying that it is a *"disposition, built up through experience, to respond favourably, and in certain habitual ways, to conceptual objects and principles that the individual regards as of ultimate importance in his own life, and as having to do with what he regards as permanent or central in the nature of things"* (italics his). This allows for a wide variety of religious expressions, but it gives a good inner view of how the individual with the religious sentiment feels about it.

Then Allport continues to identify the characteristics of a religious sentiment. It has a well-differentiated *capacity of self-criticism.* As Anton Boisen used to say, the mature prophet has a certain consciousness of "prophesying in part," a genuine humility. Sick religion, correspondingly, is uncritical, self-contained, and lacks any measure of humility and teachableness. In the second place, the *dynamic character* of a religious sentiment provides the main index to its health or unhealth. Immature religion is shot through with magical thinking, self-justification, and personal comfort. Mature religion is the master in the economy of life, controlling motives rather than being controlled and determined by them. The control is directed toward a goal "that is no longer determined by mere self-interest." In the third place, a mature religious sentiment is characterized by a *consistency of moral consequences of the religion itself.* The criterion of moral consistency suggests that the mature religious sentiment generates high and consistent standards of action. This speaks to the religious sociopath's situation, wherein religion becomes a *means* of immoral behavior of various kinds.[8]

The focus of this chapter on the idolatrous character of sick religion, however, is clarified best by Allport's assertion that a mature religious sentiment is a *comprehensive* sentiment. A nonidolatrous kind of religion calls for a comprehensive philosophy of life. The Hindus said that "truth is one and men call it by many names." Plato said that sin is the rising up of a part of the soul against the whole. The Hebrew prophets and the Lord Jesus Christ insisted that we cannot serve two masters but that purity of heart calls for a Lord of lords. A comprehensive faith embraces the whole order of creation. The idol is a "part-process," a restriction and constriction of the life. The negative counterpart of this comprehensive religious sentiment is what András Angyal calls the domination of the whole sphere of life by a "part-process," which thrusts the organism into a state of "bionegativity." In the illness, whether it is of a psychotic order or a behavioral disorder, the identity of the person takes on a negative character instead of a positive and constructive nature.

The previous examples of the restriction of life around the spirits of the departed dead make Allport's point of view more concrete. However, we need more precise clinical demonstration of the way in which life is constricted and controlled through the worship of something less than the Eternal. Bereavement, preoccupation with the family inheritance, and preoccupation with one role in life to the exclusion of all others provide three areas where the point of view set forth here can be demonstrated clinically.

THREE AREAS OF CONSTRICTION

Bereavement

Eric Lindemann, Willard Waller, and others have established through empirical studies the validity of interpreting grief as a process with varying but definable stages. The loss of someone by death moves through the stages of shock, numbness, a struggle with reality as over against fantasy, a time of depression and a flood of tears, a regrouping of the life with sporadic bursts of memory reactivating the previous stages momentarily, and finally a reordering of the whole life around new interests, relationships, and pursuits in life. Pathologically, the person may become arrested in the process of grief at the stage of shock, numbness, or the struggle with fantasy, or at the time of depression. The loss of someone by death can therefore be a precipitating factor in severe emotional disorders of various kinds, depending upon the life history and style of life of the person. The religious life of the person quite regularly becomes the first casualty in his life and may take on all of the symptomatology of sick religion. Various sources of data can be consulted here.

Comparative studies between a primitive religion and psychotic episodes among people in a technological society are productive of insights as to how very thin the veneer of our so-called Western civilization really is. J. H. M. Beattie offers a clinical study of the relation between belief reactions to the spirit of someone who has died and illness among the Bunyoro. He carried out these field studies in Bunyoro, Uganda, for about twenty-two months, during 1951 through 1953 and in 1955. He developed case history details on fifteen individuals whose illnesses were attributed to the ghosts of the departed dead. Of the fifteen cases, three were epilepsy, five were miscarriages, one was a sudden seizure, one was an undiagnosed fatal illness, one was leprosy, one was a painful swelling, one was an allergy to certain foods, one was ulcers on the legs, and one was a man who set fire to some property.

However, the most interesting fact about these involvements with the dead was that "in eight out of [the] fifteen cases . . . where ghostly activity was diagnosed, the original offender was not attacked directly but through his children, and in two others he was long since dead and vengeance was wreaked on his descendants."[9] The important thing for the reader to note is that bereavement is ordinarily associated in the Western mind with the death of someone, but the technical distinction I am making is that a person may be *alienated* from a living person and suffer a more profound grief reaction than if that person had died. Death is definitive and can be identified easily. A hostile separation is not so easy to grasp. For example, the Bunyoros substituted an innocent living person for a deceased individual who had offended someone. In contemporary psychotic behavior, the substitution of an innocent person for one's own offenses, for the offenses of other living persons, or for the offenses of deceased persons appears as a distortion of moral responsibility. Another example is the following:

> Mr. Daily was a twenty-one-year-old man admitted to the hospital with terrible feelings of having committed an awful and unpardonable sin that he could not identify. He was referred to the hospital from a remote rural region by an area missionary. His father was a lay preacher, and his mother a housewife. He had two sisters, one eleven and one seventeen. He felt that his father was always on his back and that he gave preference at all times to the sisters. The patient had had two years of college and had taught in a rural county school for one year. He felt much anxiety over his "call" to be a minister but daydreamed considerably about other roles in life—being a missionary bachelor, being a policeman, and so forth.
>
> There had been no previous illnesses of a psychiatric nature. The presenting symptoms at this time were sleeplessness and a strong feeling that he had sinned against God and that God was going to punish his younger sister for his sins. He was worried deeply about the safety and well-being of this sister. As he underwent treatment, both chemotherapy and electroconvulsive therapy, this fear for his younger sister's safety went away, but it returned in the form of a similar fear about the safety of the older sister. He could express his anger at God for punishing someone like his sisters, who were suffering for things he himself had done.
>
> During the course of treatment, the concerns about his sisters became less compulsive and obsessive. He could think of them in the past tense. As he did so, the focus of his anger shifted from God to a frank acceptance of negative and destructive feelings toward his father. Upon entry into the hospital he had extolled his father's great kindness to him and his perfect instruction of him in salvation from God. Upon outpatient treatment, he was able to express some of his anger toward his father, who had "restricted him too much," to use his own words.
>
> The father himself also felt that he had forced his son to lead too sheltered a life and that he had not wanted to let him be anything except his "little boy."

The conception of God in this account is a "ghostly" one. God is seen as a ghost to be feared. Also, he is seen as one who unjustly punishes someone whom we love and "gets at us" through them. Of course, the anger is really Mr. Daily's in this case, and the vengeful mood is his own toward his favored sisters. The "ghost god" is a vehicle of his own anger toward his sisters and toward his father for treating them with favoritism.

After dialogue with the patient, I met a private psychiatrist who said that within the last twenty-four hours he had met two patients. One of them had lost her mother by death about ten months previously. The other had given birth to a badly malformed child. Each said similar things of God: "God will punish you. He will get at you by hurting the person closest to you!" Here in these instances cited by the psychiatrist, grief was present in the loss of someone by death as well as alienation from someone by misunderstanding. In both instances, as in the case of the psychotic patient, Mr. Daily, and in the previous references to the Bunyoros, an innocent third party is seen to be the victim.

The overlay of Christian symbols does not remove the basically primitive character of the "ghost cult" within the ranks of somewhat educated people. The patient endows the fear of his own anger toward his parents and siblings with ultimate concern. As such, his own uncontrolled impulses are the source of his "bondage" and distress. Not until he begins to recognize his own feelings and accept limitation upon them can he begin to function effectively and happily.

No specific bereavement caused by death provided the "ghost" in the case of Mr. Daily. The bereavement was due to the breach between the patient and his father. If the father had died, the situation would be synonymous with that of the Bunyoro tribe. The young man's father was not dead. God, instead, became the ghost between father and son, working punishment on the patient by threatening his sisters. The combined erotic and hostile impulses toward the sisters made the overwhelming fear a compound of guilt and anxiety of pathological proportion. A "ghostly" conception of God took the persecutor's role.

The Japanese religions are different from modern Judeo-Christian faiths at the point of the custom of worshiping the dead. At one and the same time, the translation of a loved one into an ancestor lowers the reality of death and makes the separation anxiety less severe than in Western Christian tradition. Yamamato and his associates studied twenty widows who were the bereaved wives of traffic accident victims. Eighteen of the twenty had either Buddhist or Shinto family altars (butsudan) in their homes. Yamamato compared his and his associates' results with those of a London psychiatrist, C. M. Parkes. They discovered that the Japanese widows suffered significantly less depression, numbness and apathy, sleeplessness, and cultivation of and the actual sense of the presence of the dead than did the London group of widows. In turn, the London widows had significantly more awareness of the presence of the dead, trouble escaping reminders of the dead, and difficulty in accepting the loss of the deceased. One would ask whether or not the encouragement of ancestor reverence does not lower the psychic stress at the expense of a more realistic handling of the harsher reality of death. Yet the cultural affirmations of ancestor reverence among the Japanese might well lower the incidence of mental illness with grief as a precipitating factor.[10]

The Inheritance Syndrome

The family inheritance is another common repository of the ultimate concern of a person. In turn, the family inheritance becomes an idol constricting the life of the individual. The form and shape of this constriction often derives its power and community sanction from religious sources. Especially is this true when the life of the sick person has been religious.

The story of the rich fool, found in Luke 12:13–21 of the New Testament, exemplifies this situation. A man came to Jesus asking that he make his brother divide the family inheritance with him. Jesus refused the role of divider and judge over him. Then he told the story of the rich fool who gave himself entirely and solely to the finite task of building a bigger and bigger estate. The man's life was required of him in the process. Jesus asked, "Then whose will those things be?" It was a rhetorical question the answer to which was obvious: These things would be the sons' to argue over, to shape their lives by.

Jesus said to another man (as recorded in Luke 9:59), "Follow me." But the man said, "Lord, let me first go and bury my father." The father may or may not have been at the point of death at the time. The family fortune, a mistaken sense of loyalty to a reasonably healthy parent, and an ultimate concern for the inheritance may have bound the son against following the Lord to whom he gave lip service. Preoccupation with the family's future can become an obsession and a sick religion. The following case is significant at this point:

> A thirty-two-year-old man was the younger of two sons. The father and mother had become parents of the two sons late in life because they had wanted to become financially secure before they had children. The two sons came within two years of each other and grew to young manhood as part of the family business. The elder of the two sons became a very religious person, contrary to the pattern of the family as a whole. Under the tutelage and with the encouragement of his church, he became a missionary in a rural section of the United States, even though he had been reared in a large city. He stayed with the mission work

faithfully and was gradually promoted in his duties until he became an editor of one of his church's publications. He established himself in his own right all the way across the continental United States apart from his father's business.

The younger son tried the same method of breaking away from the family business but failed. Each time he would try to establish himself in the work of the church, he would become emotionally sick and have to return home. His reasoning was that someone had to look after his aging father as long as he lived. But when faced with the realistic job of putting up with his father's eccentricities and the demands of the family business, he would become anxiously depressed and even suicidal. Upon admission to the hospital for treatment he would say, "If I could only be a missionary like my brother, I wouldn't be sick. It is all due to my unfaithfulness to God." But underneath this, there was his quiet assurance that if he waited long enough, the inheritance would be his and he would not have to worry. As he became less depressed and expressed his hopes about life, this was the way he reassured himself. Realistic plans for him to learn a kind of work of "his own" apart from both his brother and his father ran aground upon his settled assurance that when he buried his father, his troubles would be over because the inheritance would be his. The task of therapy was to challenge and change this settled resolve of the patient at the same time that the symptoms of depression, anxiety, and suicidal indications were managed therapeutically.

The course of treatment involved intensive social-work efforts to devise a fitting kind of meaningful work in which the man could use his skills as a salesman apart from the sales organization of his father. He also needed his own identity apart from the missionary position of his brother. The pastoral counselor was in the position of collaborating with the patient to find the approval and acceptance of God for the work the patient decided he realistically should do "under God." When the clutching fingers of his devotion to the family fortune—little in fact that it was—loosened, the man became less sentimental about his father, less depressed about his own worthlessness, and more confident of his own future in a sales job for which he was both talented and fitted.

In summary, the "part-process" of preoccupation over an inheritance dominated and possessed the total life of the persons described. The inheritance takes on an ultimate significance for the person who permits it to become the total direction of his life. As subtle and somewhat nebulous as this may be, it becomes much clearer when we see the inheritance as an idolatrous construction of the individuals involved. In sentimental concern over the well-being of the father or mother whose path is presupposed if the inheritance is to be received, the person builds a reaction formation to mask his guilt at the wish for the death of the parent.

Self-Reflection

The most malignant form of religious sickness probably comes from a perfectionistic expectation of oneself as a self. The classic statement of this is Nietzsche's exclamation: "There is no God! If there were, how could I stand it if I were not he?" Caught between the necessity of his humanity and the possibility of his divinity, a person settles the tension between the two on the side of his infinitude. As Kierkegaard, who set forth this paradox most clearly in his *Sickness Unto Death,* says, a person becomes "drunk on infinitude." The following case history is illustrative:

> An eighteen-year-old girl attempted suicide at the college where she was a freshman. She was sufficiently dangerous to herself for the college authorities to advise her parents to have her hospitalized. During her hospital stay she repeatedly threatened to try suicide again.
>
> Her family history revealed a father who worked as a day laborer, a mother who served as a maid, a brother in the Armed Services, and the patient herself the youngest daughter. She was the only one of her family who went beyond the sixth grade, and her church had made her college education possible at a church-related college. Her father was hostile toward her getting so much education. Her mother silently approved it but gave little or no verbal encouragement to the strivings of the girl toward an education.
>
> The minister of the patient had been very influential in her life, convincing her that she could do excellent work and that there was no limit to her possibilities as a student. She despaired at reaching his expectations but used her assurance from him as a way of "putting down" her father. This patient vacillated between exceptional elation and unremitting despair.
>
> When I was introduced to her by a nurse, the girl's first remark to me was an elated, "What can I do for you?" She spoke of her homesickness but shifted quickly to discussing her service in a teaching project for underprivileged children. She could not get over the betrayal she felt at being shipped by her school to a hospital, and consoled herself by saying that she must now decide alone what she was to do with her life. She talked frankly about killing herself as a way of "hating my parents and the school to death." Suicide was one way of getting out from under the tyranny of her expectations of herself and at the same time of getting back at those she held responsible for her plight.
>
> One conversation pinpoints the crucial issue of her deification of her own self-expectations. In this third conversation, Miss ——— talked about what she said was "really wrong" with her. She said:
>
> "I've tried to be God and I've expected other people to be God. When I couldn't make it, nothing was worth anything. If I could not be God, I didn't want to be anything. When I was in high school I won all the honors and did not expect to do so. I was surprised, but when I got to college, I thought there was nothing I couldn't do.

Then I turned up with above-average grades but not perfect ones. This destroyed me.

"I also had a minister who I thought was a god. He could do no wrong. He was everything—savior, lover, everything—to me. Then when I didn't do as well as he expected me to, he just cut me off. He led me to believe that my intelligence was so great that I could do anything. When I didn't make it, he just cut me off."

She said: "I didn't want to be human. That is not good enough." We talked about the courage it takes to be neither less than nor more than human. It was a thorough discussion of the "importance of being human."

The crucial issue in this chapter is twofold: the true nature of the Eternal and the acceptance of the limitations of our humanity. The problem is far more than that of accepting ourselves as sinners in the face of forgiveness. The problem of the idolatry of the self is that of accepting ourselves as human—limited in power, in time, in space, in everything. When these limits are denied and rejected, whatever forms of religion we have become sick. Religion becomes a tool of our basic rejection of our human condition.

PASTORAL APPROACHES

The pastoral care of a person bound to a loyalty less than God is not one of harshness. When the finite powers an individual has trusted fail him, he is likely to become religiously sick if he has taken religion at all seriously in the first place. As a result, he is shattered along with the confidence he has placed in the idol that possesses him. A shattered person does not need further shattering. What does he need?

Comfort and Catharsis

The first prerequisite of a pastoral relationship is that of the pastor's taking the role of a comforter in the face of the disillusionment brought about by the collapse of the idol. The twenty-one-year-old young man who feared for the safety of his sisters was suffering from a collapse of his hopes that his father would *ever* come to his senses and bring some degree of encouragement to him as the firstborn, a son with a birthright that was denied him in the preoccupation of the father with the sisters. The son felt permanently denied a place of his own in the family. The objective of pastoral care of the young man was to establish a relationship in which there would be an absence of competition and to give him individual attention. This provided a comfort that was more than a superficial "cheerleader" type of words. The importance of fixed times for visits gave the patient points in

413

time to which he could look forward. The experiences of life had unhinged the patient's orientation to time, work, play, and sleep. Medication and electroconvulsive treatments were employed by the physicians to restore these. Psychotherapy was instituted by the physician after the ECT was concluded. Reeducating the parents and creating the opportunity for completing college were the tasks of the social workers. The task of the pastoral counselor was that of giving his undivided attention and comfort to the patient as these other therapies took place, plus allowing the patient opportunity to feel free to pour out his complaint to God. The infinite God was portrayed as one who can hear with affection the darkest feelings we have to express.

Thus a catharsis of the patient's feelings of disillusionment, injustice, and disappointment could be expressed. Also, he confessed that the illness itself was pleasant in that this way he could really be "Daddy's little boy" and have first place in Daddy's attention. Such confession and subsequent insight come only through disciplined listening that enables a person to speak his or her most private thoughts without fear of pastoral probing.

Confrontation of the
Constricting Powers of Idols

When patients are convalescing from an acute psychotic episode, they, like surgical patients, tend to want to "sort out" what happened to them, how they feel about the past, their treatment, and the future. At this time, *if the pastor has had an effective and faithful relationship with the patient during the episode,* he has an opportunity to philosophize with him about the nature of his primary concerns in life. The pastor runs the hazard of just replacing the idols of the past with an idolatry of himself. Both this possibility and previous constrictions on the life of the patient can be challenged and confronted. This the pastor is in a position to do during the rebuilding of the realistic confidence of a patient during convalescence.

For example, the young man who was waiting for his father's inheritance to be his was confronted very frankly with the fact that his aging father would indeed die sooner or later. Decision on the son's part now toward becoming self-sustaining in his own right could not but make for more self-confidence when the father's death did take place. Just to sit and wait for someone to die drains the present of meaning and casts a shadow on the hopes one has for the future. Encouragement of each move toward the patient's effective mastery of his own job was part of the positive reinforcement of a nonidolatrous kind of functioning. As Rudolf Dreikurs has said: *"Deficiencies are not eliminated by being emphasized.* One cannot build on weaknesses, only on strengths." The process of encouragement is more than kindness; it is constructive reinforcement of the strongest and most positive intentions of the person as a whole.[11] In Judeo-Christian values, encouragement—according to Chaplain Myron Madden—is the power to bless, to invest belief in a person in such a way that the person feels it to be genuine.

Therefore the pastoral challenge is to discover with the person the real strengths of his life and to concentrate on these, not his deficiencies. Real strengths are an individual's direct contact with his true self and with a nonidolatrous loyalty in life.

Frank Discussion of the Nature of God

The minister's primary responsibility is to know God and to speak frankly and without glibness of him. Working with the religiously sick focuses this responsibility. I recall a seminar with a group of senior psychiatric residents at an Eastern Seaboard hospital. The first question was asked by a young Hindu resident. He said, "What is it that you do in relation to a patient that a psychiatrist does not do?" I replied, "I, when I am introduced to the patient as a pastor or a minister, always represent God. The psychiatrist may occasionally do this by choice, but the minister does so of necessity when he is presented or presents himself as a minister." "But," replied the Hindu doctor, "*which* God do you represent? There are many." I replied, "The God I represent to the patient is the patient's God, and there *are* many. My first task is to discover who and of what nature is his God." The Hindu physician pressed further: "But what is *your* God like?" I replied, "My God is like Jesus of Nazareth, but this does not mean that I can assume that everyone else's God is the same as my own. These differences are the stuff of our conversation. I will learn as well as will the person with whom I converse."

Frank discussion of the nature of God is a part of the later phases of a patient's care by a minister. The beneficent restoration to a reasonable pattern of conversation is the end intention and desired result of intensive psychiatric treatment. The restoration of a rational, realistic perception is one of the healing results of psychiatric treatment. As one doctor said, "The doctor's job is to help people see straight, and the minister's job is to see to it that they are looking at the right God when they seek to be religious."

For example, the suicidal patient mentioned above, when faced with the possibility of leaving the hospital, became apprehensive about whether she would attempt suicide again. She said, "I am trapped. I don't want to return home and I don't want to stay here. Suicide seems the only way out. I wonder if God can forgive me for what I have done and am thinking about doing." When asked, "*Which* God is that?" she replied, "The Almighty God." I told her that this God could forgive her and enable her to find other alternatives for living. I explained that the god of her own need to be perfect could not be forgiving the way the Almighty God can.

In a letter she wrote after her return home, she said, "I'm finally on the road to recovery. I finally admitted to myself and others why I wanted to die—actually I did not want to die. I wanted someone to care and I needed to change some things in my life and suicide offered 'the easy way out.' "

Another patient, in speaking to a group of chaplains, said, "Go easy on how you tell us that God cares. Show us that you care and we'll decide for ourselves whether God cares on the basis of what you do!"

IN SUMMARY

This chapter has emphasized the ways in which the substitution of a limited, finite loyalty for an ultimate, comprehensive concern is for all practical purposes a false center of idolatry. This, in turn, produces a disturbed balance in the whole life. Bereavement, preoccupation over the family inheritance, and deification of the self as perfect were chosen as clinical working models for demonstrating the sickness of religion known as idolatry. Specific pastoral approaches of conflict and catharsis, confrontation, and frank discussion of the nature of the God of reality were described in some detail.

NOTES

1. Wayne E. Oates, *Christ and Selfhood* (New York: Association Press, 1961).

2. Paul Tillich, *The Courage to Be* (New Haven, Conn.: Yale University Press, 1952), pp. 40–63.

3. Ibid., p. 73.

4. Paul Tillich, *Systematic Theology* (Chicago: University of Chicago Press, 1963), 3:355.

5. Ibid., vol. 1 (1951), p. 13.

6. Emil L. Fackenheim, "Idolatry as a Modern Religious Possibility," in *The Religious Situation: 1968*, ed. Donald R. Cutler (Boston: Beacon Press, 1968), p. 275.

7. Quoted from the Koran by Edward Sell, "Images and Idols (Muslim)," in *Encyclopaedia of Religion and Ethics*, ed. James Hastings (New York: Charles Scribner's Sons, 1928), 7:150.

8. Gordon W. Allport, *The Individual and His Religion: A Psychological Interpretation* (New York: Macmillan Co., 1950), pp. 58ff.

9. J. H. M. Beattie, "The Ghost Cult in Bunyoro," in *Gods and Rituals: Readings in Religious Beliefs and Practices*, ed. John Middleton (Garden City, N.Y.: Natural History Press, 1967), pp. 259–261.

10. Joe Yamamato, M.D., and others, "Mourning in Japan," *American Journal of Psychiatry* 125, no. 12 (June 1969): 1660–1665.

11. Rudolf Dreikurs, M.D., *Psychology in the Classroom*, 2nd ed. (New York: Harper & Row, 1968), p. 97.

30

Pastoral Counseling and the Prophetic Task

In 1950 I asked a young German theological student in New York why it was that pastors on the European continent and in Great Britain had not at that time taken pastoral care and counseling as seriously as had American pastors. He replied that the troubles of Germans and Britons in postwar years were massive. The things that had happened to them as nations were catastrophic. The Germans tended to think of individual troubles as trivial. Alan Paton, in his *Cry, the Beloved Country,* said that the chieftains of South Africa were counselors in many things but that they had no counsel for the brokenness of their people.

In the mid-1960s, pastoral care and counseling have become a more regularized part of the theological curriculum in many schools. Several student generations have been graduated into active pastoral roles. Yet, intentionally or not, the work of the pastor as a counselor and as a caring person has been taught and learned as a highly individual work of pastors in purely one-to-one relationships with people. Occasionally some objecting voice puts in a plea for the pulpit work of the pastor, superficially equating this with the prophetic task of the pastor. Pastoral care cannot so easily be separated from the social context in which the counseling takes place. Nor can the quiet encounter of a private conference with an individual or a small group be so easily excluded from the work of the prophet. The private ministry of the pastor cannot be nonchalantly cut loose from his public ministry. Pastoral care itself involves the pastor in the social dilemmas of neighborhood, community, city, county, state, and nation. International situations and events that surround the pastor and his people affect the work of caring. Willingly or unwillingly, the pastor is caught in the maelstrom of human suffering that defies analysis, repudiates reason, and demands decisions.

417

My purpose, therefore, is to discuss the role and function of the pastor in the context of several contemporary social dilemmas. The present crisis of extremism, the continuing dilemma of ministering to divorced persons, the social dilemmas of the race issue, the recurrent demands for pastoral care in institutional conflict, and the major challenges to a Christian sexual ethic today are massive social dilemmas that consume much of the working day of the caring pastor. The reciprocity between the pastoral caring and the prophetic confronting of responsibilities of the contemporary minister is the core concern in this discussion.

THE PASTOR AS PROPHET

The patient application of the clinical method in pastoral care has taught us many things that illuminate the minister's responsibility to be a prophet of the living God. Clinical pastoral work recaptures neglected and omitted aspects of the biblical portraits of the prophets. It challenges easy clichés today as to what it means to be prophetic. Clinical pastoral care neither omits the responsibility of the pastor as a prophet nor leaves the stereotypes of the prophetic role unchallenged. Both the omissions and the stereotypes have to go when the pastor takes his responsibilities in pastoral care seriously and attends to their social expression in the life of the church and community.

Stereotypes of the Pastor as Prophet

Stereotype images of the pastor as a prophet must be identified. The first stereotype is that of the prophet as a tactless, loud-spoken, fist-waving authoritarian bully who browbeats people into submission to his point of view. This is often considered as "being directive." Persons who are "nondirective" and "client-centered" in their approach to pastoral care therefore shrink from such "prophecy." A second stereotype is that of the preacher who makes the pulpit his opportunity to "take a stand," to state his position heedless of the opinions and "stands" of other people. He makes these "stands" on a take-it-or-leave-it basis. Pastors who do this are identified by many people as "prophets." However, this removes responsibility from the pastor for two-way communication between the prophet and his audience. A third stereotype is that of the prophet as the "cleanser of the temple." With the knotted cords he lashes people for their wrongheadedness. The incident recorded in the scripture of the Lord Jesus Christ is used as proof text for this stereotype. It is taken out of the context of the rest of the ministry of Jesus. A fourth stereotype of the prophet is that of the modern "angry young man" who loses his job because of his convictions. He is eager to be fired. Exact parallels are drawn between this person and the prophets of the Old Testament and the "crucifixion" of Jesus. The fact that the prophets of the Old Testament were not paid employees and that the crucifixion of Jesus had nothing to do with the loss of a job in a power struggle is not made a part of the picture of the prophet. A fifth stereotype of the prophet oversimplifies issues by sharp black-and-white antitheses that leave out the ambiguities of the intermediate gray issues. This removes the element of tragedy from the genuine prophetic situation. The humanity of the prophet is omitted. That he prophesies in part is not recognized in the prophecy. A sixth stereotype of the prophet is the "face value" that is put upon his word. It is to be taken without being tested, authenticated, and tried. Yet the biblical witness never extols prophecy for prophecy's sake. True and false prophets are to be distinguished from each other. Prophecy fails. We prophesy in part. Prophecy is transcended in faith, hope, and love. Our finiteness, limitation, ambiguity, and weakness are the ground of real humility in the prophet. Confidence in God who is love puts the minister as a prophet in perspective.

Clinical pastoral approaches to the ministry challenge these stereotypes. The tactless, loud-spoken, fist-waving authoritarian bully portrays his own insecurity more than the prophetic wisdom of God. The confident and secure pastor deals with controversial situations in policy-setting sessions with his lay leadership when both he and they can set forth their points of view in dialogue. When he preaches, he extends the invitation of Isaiah to come and reason together concerning the great social dilemmas and the intentions of God in them. The pastor who understands himself refrains from equating his own methods of confrontation with Jesus' cleansing of the temple. He does not make a test case of his own job. He bears the hurt of his people with them in talking with them individually as well as collectively. He knows that a social issue is a *dilemma,* filled with ambiguity, self-deception, confusion, and contradiction. He sees himself as a minister of reconciliation. He maintains enough objectivity to see the dilemmas of his people steadily and to see them whole. He strives for enough independence of judgment to minister to people of widely varying points of view. He is not afraid of the loneliness that this ministry of reconciliation inevitably entails.

The stereotypes of prophecy are also countermanded in biblical perspectives of the prophet. Nathan did not scream to a great crowd in his prophetic confrontation of David. He spoke to him privately in a parable and applied it in a quiet voice. Jeremiah was asked for guidance by Zedekiah and apparently saw him in privacy and without authoritarian fanfare. Unlike the second stereotype, the apostle Paul rarely had a pulpit from which to preach, contending instead with people in the marketplace in vigorous two-way question-and-answer sessions. Or when he was not

419

doing this, he was teaching consecutively and deliberately to groups of inquirers, as at Ephesus. The prophets and the apostles were sometimes lashed, but they themselves seldom resorted to dramatic shows of force as the "temple cleansers" do. Unlike the angry young man of today, they could not lose their jobs, for they had not been employed in the first place! These biblical prophets wrestled and contended with themselves and with God, searching for the truth of their own message and seeking to be directed and led by God. They identified themselves with their people in bondage, and when their people were hurt, they were hurt. They were capable of empathy as well as courage, tender concern as well as stern rebuke.

Temptations of the Contemporary Pastor as a Prophet

In the presence of the confusion of stereotyped community expectations and the self-expectations of pastors as prophets, temptations abound for the pastor himself. These stereotypes "set him up" like a bowling pin for several major temptations that lurk in the glare of these stereotyped pictures of the pastor as prophet.

The Temptation to Exhibitionism. Every pastor has a streak of the ham actor in him. He tucks it away smugly enough, but it emerges when an opportunity for showmanship presents itself. The great social dilemmas tempt him to be "the hero," to show off, and to satisfy his own exhibitionistic needs. Crisis situations call the "knight on the white charger" impulse out of a pastor. He jumps on his horse and rides off madly in six directions! The need for a person to prove that he is not "chicken," that he is "brave," and to make "prophetic faces" before a crowd is not the private impulse of teenagers daring each other to steal a car in which some adult has left the keys. Social dilemmas present the same temptation to exhibitionism to the pastor and the teacher in a time of acute social crisis.

The Temptation to Publicity. Allied with the temptation to exhibitionism is the need for publicity. Mass media of communication both facilitate and impede social change in their reporting of such social dilemmas as the race conflicts of our day, the major calamities that befall masses of people, and the personal tragedies connected with such events as divorce and other socially conflictual situations. When the story gets in the papers or on the radio or on television, the problems that were simply added to each other up to that point become multiplied by each other from this time forward. The lunge for publicity does not leave the pastor untouched. The recent news accounts of a Catholic priest ministering to the dying in a hospital fire graphically express the correct stance of the Christian pastor of every persuasion in the face of the temptation to publicity. A picture showed the priest with his back to the camera as he held a burned victim in his arms. The caption beneath said simply: "My God, no! I am busy!" This was his answer to a newsman who had asked him if he had any comment to make and what his name was. One of the contributions of the medical profession to the modern practice of pastoral care has been the studious avoidance of publicity in behalf of the healing ministry. The minister of reconciliation seeks a way of transcendence of social conflict. He resists the temptation of publicity.

The Temptation to One-Way Thinking. The minister of reconciliation bases his work on both the reversal of the processes of conflict and the development of two-way communication. In order to do this, he must seek consultation, encourage negotiation between conflicting interests and intentions, and nurture the willingness to be reconciled. In his own way of life, therefore, he does not mistake deadlines, ultimatums, and ex cathedra pronouncements for the essence of prophecy. On the contrary, he *contends* with people, leaving the whole burden of breaking communication upon them. If the efforts at understanding, reason, commitment, and resolution of difficulty are to stop, the other persons will have to do the stopping. President O. T. Binkley, of Southeastern Baptist Theological Seminary, together with a prominent psychoanalyst, was on a panel discussing religion and psychoanalysis. The analyst had said that the more completely a patient recovered from his illness, the more the analyst tended to part company with religion. President Binkley said: "If there is to be a parting of the way between an effective Christian pastor and an effective psychoanalyst in the treatment of the patient, the Christian pastor will depend upon the analyst to do the parting. It is the role of the Christian pastor to stay with the analyst until *he* leaves *him!*" When psychotherapists juxtapose themselves over against the Christian faith or any other form of religion, the clergyman is faced with a dilemma, namely, that of rejecting the philosophical presuppositions of his opponent and at the same time affirming the verifiable clinical data of the psychotherapists.

The Temptation to Play God. The ultimate temptation of the pastor as a prophet is no different from any other temptation to sin. This is the temptation to take God's place. The question that Joseph asked himself and his brothers in the face of their injustices to him was: "Am I in God's place?" The social prophet, the pastor who crusades for a cause, or the pastor who works quietly out of sight behind the scenes as a minister of reconciliation should ask himself this same question every morning so that he may walk humbly and every night so that he may sleep calmly: "Am I in God's place?" Then he will resist the temptation to mistake his ability to prophesy, to crusade, to work behind the scenes for the absolute power of work, acting to settle the destinies of all men. Then he will know in part and prophesy in part. He takes the ambiguity of his cause upon himself and moves with a measure of compassion even toward his worst opponent. He remains open to negotiation, to reconciliation, to peace.

PRINCIPLES OF PROPHETIC
PASTORAL CARE

These stereotypes and temptations of the prophetic pastor are like a negative film. We are now in a position to use this negative to develop a positive print of the basic principles that should guide the pastor in exercising the prophetic ministry.

Balance Between Visibility
and Invisibility in Pastoral Practice

A careful study of parishioner expectations of pastors made by Glock and Roos revealed that parishioners tend to form their expectations of pastors on the basis of what they *see* the pastors do. The pastor as a counselor is not seen. He jeopardizes his work as a counselor unless he provides an atmosphere of privacy and trusted communication for those who seek his help. His private negotiations with leaders in a community controversy—such as a church controversy, a race conflict, a contention for the mind of a parishioner being pulled by two sets of extremists—go unseen and unpublicized by his parishioners and outsiders as well. He has, therefore, two temptations: he can play dead and do nothing in the social dilemmas of his community or he can protest that he is misunderstood and begin to advertise his "good works" as a private counselor and negotiator between controversial people. Public opinion tends to damn him in either instance.

The success of a pastor in resolving social conflicts is greatest, however, when a productive solution of the conflict is reached with little or no connection with his name or with no "credit" being given him.

The New Testament injunction about almsgiving can be transferred to the pastoral attitude toward social justice and social action:

> Beware of practicing your piety before men in order to be seen by them, for then you will have no reward from your Father who is in heaven. Thus, when you give alms, sound no trumpet before you, as the hypocrites do in the synagogues and in the streets, that they may be praised by men. Truly, I say to you, they have their reward. But when you give alms, do not let your left hand know what your right hand is

doing, so that your alms may be in secret; and your Father who sees in secret will reward you. (Matt. 6:1–4)

Keeping one's own left hand uninformed as to the activity of the right hand in social action calls for discipline on the part of the prophet himself as well as his discipline of his followers' demand that he be seen by them.

This is no new principle of the Christian life. When great social dilemmas become the domain of imperialistic extremists, Christian witnesses have been forced into anonymity. In many parts of the world today, the Christian pastor is only a stone's throw from the condition of early Christians who wrote their sign *ichthys* in the sand and utilized the elaborate symbolism of the book of Revelation as a means of subverbal communication with each other. They put more "between" the lines than "in" the lines. The Christian pastor can neither use his unseenness as a cloak for compromise nor feel too sorry for himself when other ministers who are more removed from the scene of battle complain because he does not hold daily news conferences, issue great statements, and circulate petitions. He must see himself as waging guerrilla warfare for the kingdom of God, known neither by uniform nor headline and rewarded only in secret.

The contemporary pastor's earned identity as a trained counselor, both with individuals and with small groups, particularly equips him to implement the "invisible" ministry of the Christian pastor. The effective pastor facing social dilemmas can use his role as a personal counselor, spiritual director, and small-group leader to leaven the whole social process of his community. He no longer has to depend entirely upon mass structures and public utterances to implement his prophetic vision of the City of God among men. He no longer needs whole divisions of the structures of the church to effect major social changes. The dialogue of the personal interview and the give-and-take of small-group discussion can bring more than pronouncements from the minister. It can bring insight and commitment to both the minister and the parishioner. Both develop a "tailored" understanding that deals with each other's biases and clarifies each other's purposes and positions. Neither is closed to the depersonalization and collectivization of "crowd" minds.

The personal interview and the small-group conference are certainly not the only means of effecting social change in the face of cultural dilemmas. They are the central means of pastoral care and yet the ones most likely to be neglected when any social issue—alcoholism, divorce, race, extremism, or war—becomes a celebrated "single issue" definition of human life and the mind of God. If the pastor neglects his ministry to individuals and to small groups, he may be sure that extremists will take over this function for their own purposes when a social conflict reaches fever stage.

Then he will defensively bemoan the development of a "Protestant underground" that perverts personal interviews and small-group conferences into the use of anonymous phone calls, threatening by unsigned letters, and so forth, and brainwashing all group techniques that delete the sovereignty of God and the ministry of the Holy Spirit.

Prophetic Acts and Pastoral Care

Superficial marketplace understandings of prophetic pastoral work are restricted to things the pastor *says*, pronouncements he makes, "stands" he takes, "white papers" he issues, and petitions he signs. The reverse side of this coin is the tendency of those both within and without the church to depreciate the worth of the spoken sermon. Biblical perspectives of the prophet and the apostle, however, focus not upon formal sermons, written documents, and problem-centered pronouncements but upon their acts and relationships. It is not by chance that Luke's account of the early church and the work of the apostles is not entitled "Sermons by Peter and Paul" but "The Acts of the Apostles."

In the Old Testament the symbolic acts of the prophets and the intense relationships they had to the power structures of their day were the conduit for the transmission of their identity as prophets. One among many examples may be cited. Jeremiah, in his early prophetic experience (Jer. 8:4–7), conducted a "listening-in campaign" in order to get at the root of the troubles of his people. He wanted to know why it was that when men fell, they did not get up, why when they missed the way, they did not turn around. He was concerned about their persistent desertion. Consequently, he developed the prophetic act of "listening in." He says, "I have given heed and listened" (Jer. 8:6). He was able to listen as well as to speak, and he formulated his prophetic message on the basis of hearing as well as of saying.

Another incident in Jeremiah's prophetic work illustrates the art of portraying a prophetic message in an act rather than in a speech. In Jer. 13:1–11 he says that he went and bought himself a girdle and put it on his loins, taking care not to let it go into the water. He then took the girdle and hid it in the cleft of the rock in the Euphrates River. Thus he acted out a parable. The girdle was the kind that the priests wore ceremonially. It represented Judah, the people of God. The girdle is the principal ornament of the Oriental man, worn close to his body. It represents the closeness and intimacy of the covenant of God with his people. It represents something "prized and intimate, a thing of dignity and beauty." When Jeremiah took this prized garment of high symbolic value and "buried it below the surface in the rocky water-drenched river bank," he dramatized what was happening to the religious covenant between God and his people. That which was most prized by them was saturated with a river of idolatrous influence and gradually permeated them as well. At length they were made "good for nothing."[1]

Today pastors are called upon to do prophetic things. A young Tennessee pastor, when his small city was in the throes of a race conflict over the integration of the local schools, made few if any speeches. Rather, on the morning that the tension was at its highest pitch, he made a prophetic decision to act. He went to the segregated part of town where the children who had been enrolled in school lived. He asked them for the privilege of walking to school with them. They permitted him to do so, and he walked the long fear-ridden distance with the Negro children. He was mauled and beaten by those who opposed the enrollment of Negroes in a previously all-white school. But he got his message through by a prophetic act.

Face-to-Faceness and Prophetic Behavior

A second principle of prophetic and apostolic behavior in the presence of the great social dilemmas of today is the principle of "face-to-faceness." Enemies cannot be reconciled *in absentia* without couriers. Couriers have needs of their own. Couriers can confuse rather than clarify communication. The objective of prophetic pastoral care is to produce a face-to-face, firsthand relationship and to reduce indirect, secondhand attempts to manipulate and manage people from afar. The psalmist says that the Lord prepares a table for him in the presence of his enemies. The absence of the enemy makes him more an enemy.

The estranged husband and wife come to a level of "blackout" on communication. Then go-betweens begin to do their information getting, opinion conveying, and attitude expressing for them. The pastor who falls into this work for them becomes a part of the problem rather than a part of the solution. The alienated races in a community have few lines of face-to-face communication. Their attitudes are formed on the basis of hearsay and courier-gained information. Not the least of these is information gained through newspapers. Newspapers can be divided into two groups: those which attempt to improve communication within a communication and those which exploit failures of communication and thereby magnify conflict. Occasionally the newsman rises to the level of his moral responsibility by improving communications. Occasionally ministers also do the same thing. When they do, they become prophetic, regardless of their occupational "estate." The ministry of reconciliation *intends* to get people into face-to-face conversation with each other.

This does not always mean that "sweetness and light" will ensue. Even if we use the conjoint approach to treating, the situation will itself deteriorate. If, however, an intention of removing distortions of communication, misinformation, and inadequate information can be the purpose of such face-to-face confrontations, then the basis for later, more peaceful conversations can be laid. We need go no farther than the relationship of the apostle Paul and the apostle Peter to see the sharp contention that arose over eating with Gentiles. This is recorded in Gal. 2:11–12. Paul says, "When Cephas came to Antioch I opposed him to his face, because he stood condemned." This face-to-faceness led to a higher resolution of the social conflict, a resolution that could not have taken place if Paul and Peter had relied upon what other people said to them about each other. The Jerusalem conference on the same issue of the relationship between Jews and Gentiles may have preceded the confrontation between Paul and Peter. The problem upon which they disagreed, and in which Barnabas was also implicated, had been dealt with in the conference; a "position" letter had been written by the combined group and was publicized throughout the churches (see Acts 15:22–29). I am indebted to my colleague, Dr. Harold Songer, professor of New Testament, for the following commentary on the Gal. 2:1–10 passage and other related passages:

> The theory that the letter to the Galatians was sent to the churches in South Galatia opens the possibility that the dispute described in Gal. 2:11–14 preceded the Apostolic Conference in Acts 15. On this theory, Gal. 2:1–10 may be correlated with Acts 17:27–30 rather than Acts 15. Some modern scholars hold this view. See Archibald M. Hunter, *Interpreting the New Testament, 1900–1950.*[2]
>
> Most scholars, however, hold that Gal. 2:1–10 should be correlated with Acts 15. This reconstruction of the sequence of events would make Peter's visit to Antioch subsequent to the Jerusalem Conference. See Floyd V. Filson, *A New Testament History.*[3]
>
> But even before the conference in Acts 15, the basic issue emerges in a semiofficial conference in Acts 11:1–18. In Acts 10, Peter ate with Gentiles, as he did later in Antioch. The Jerusalem Church was disturbed by Peter's conduct, but approved it. (Acts 11:1–18.) Apparently it takes more than one confrontation for some people to see the issues! Peter seems to have had two positions after Acts 15. When his status was threatened by representatives of the Jerusalem Church (Gal. 2:12), he segregated himself from Gentiles, but when he was in a context that did not challenge his loyalty to James he could integrate comfortably.
>
> It is hard to determine where Peter really stood. In Acts 10, he initiates contact with a Gentile; in Acts 15, he reminds the Jerusalem Christians of this and speaks for integration; but in Antioch a short while after this, he at first stands on one side, then on the other (Gal. 2:12).

This was not enough, though. That which had been set forth in the encyclical still had to be dealt with on the personal and pastoral level, *even among those who had been in the meeting and helped write the letter.* There was no substitute then, nor is there now, for personal and small-group working through of social dilemmas.

The early church's experience along this line was summed up in the report in Matthew 18 of the *modus operandi* of face-to-face handling of ethical issues that involve social conflict and call for confrontation. The three-step levels of pastoral and personal action are staged as follows:

> If your brother sins against you, go and tell him his fault, between you and him alone. If he listens to you, you have gained your brother. But if he does not listen, take one or two others along with you, that every word may be confirmed by the evidence of two or three witnesses. If he refuses to listen to them, tell it to the church; and if he refuses to listen even to the church, let him be to you as a Gentile and a tax collector. Truly, I say to you, whatever you bind on earth shall be bound in heaven, and whatever you loose on earth shall be loosed in heaven. (Matt. 18:15–18)

Yet this cannot be done on a simple horizontal man-to-man basis without the whole process becoming a test of courage, a test of strength, and an attempt to "prove one's manhood and prowess." This must be done with the awareness of the presence of God, in the quest for the instruction of the Holy Spirit, and with a full intention to see what it is that is in need of forgiveness. It is in the same context that the promise of Jesus is recorded:

> Again I say to you, if two of you agree on earth about anything they ask, it will be done for them by my Father in heaven. For where two or three are gathered in my name, there am I in the midst of them. (Matt. 18:19–20)

The presence of the living Christ does not exclude the possibility of real social conflict. As in personal life, social conflict may be evidence of the radical work of the Holy Spirit bringing underlying infection to a head and healing the organism of the body of Christ. Social conflict may be the Holy Spirit's challenging a community to new growth. To hold on to old ways in the presence of new demands would destroy the community itself. As such, the Holy Spirit cannot be really known in the "sweetness and light" sentimentality of pietism. Social pain, like bodily pain, may be concomitant with healing and growth. Both are destructive when allowed to become a way of life rather than a means of grace under the sovereignty of God, in the fellowship of Christ, and under the tutelage of the Holy Spirit.

In contemporary social conflicts in which a pastor is called to function prophetically, however, the *modus operandi* of the New Testament just cited is rather consistently reversed. In the first place, we have come to depend too heavily on mimeographed letters and memoranda, public ad-dresses, mass media of communication, and pronouncements of official bodies of both church and state to solve great social dilemmas. These can precede, follow, and implement personal and small-group discussion on a face-to-face basis. They cannot replace it; they can only seem to replace it. In the second place, instead of reconciliation beginning with two offended parties on a face-to-face basis, it quite often begins by one or the other or both bringing the matter before a large group and publicly calling the other a heathen of some kind. Then it moves to two or three negotiators trying to "get them together and talk things out and help them to talk themselves together." These efforts are often doomed from the outset be-cause of the hurt occasioned by the public "proclamations" and demon-strations of pseudoprophetic position taking. If the matter ever gets to the one-to-one level of both personal candor and forgiveness, then the matter may have become so infected with social repercussions that a settled aver-sion and permanent hostility is the result.

Two-Way Communication and the Pastor as a Prophet

In popular thought within the ministry, pastoral care is overidentified with "listening," and prophetic utterance is overidentified with "speaking." A further principle of pastoral care and prophetic responsibility would reject both these popular assumptions. Both are one-way forms of communica-tion. Neither is complete without the other. The pastor as a prophet who cares functions on the principle of two-way communication: dialogue, not monologue. The pastor should walk in Jeremiah's tradition of a listening-in campaign as a dialectical complement to his "utterance" ministry.

The best single treatment of this principle of pastoral care in the face of social dilemmas is Reuel Howe's book *The Miracle of Dialogue*. Howe describes the purpose of dialogical communication as over against one-way communication. He does so negatively as to what the purposes of commu-nication are *not*, and he does so positively as to what the purposes of com-munication *are*. Communication is *not* giving *our* answers to people's questions. The pastor should use his knowledge, skill, and understanding in helping people to find answers of their own through the process of creative decision making. Communication is *not* the process of getting total agreement among a group with the point of view of the communicator. Rather, the purpose of the communicator is to bring people with unique and profound differences into responsible "relation in which the unique-ness of each stands in a complementary relation to the other. And this is possible even when there is disagreement."[4]

On the contrary, the positive objectives of dialogical communication are more that of the teacher than that of the exhorter and crusader. "Communication," says Howe, "is a means by which information and meaning is conveyed and received between individuals and groups."[5] The responsibility of the pastor as a prophet, therefore, is to see to it that accurate information and a clear statement of issues are made abundantly available to the persons whom he leads. Facts and meanings fill the gap of ignorance and offset the growth of rumor and distortion. This calls for providential foresight on the part of the prophetic pastor in providing fact, experience, and meaning for those whom he leads long before opportunists, crusaders, extremists, and other forms of demagogues. A demagogue is little concerned with real communication. By definition he is "one skilled in arousing the prejudices . . . of the populace by rhetoric, sensational charges, specious arguments, catchwords, cajolery, etc.; esp., a political speaker or leader who seeks thus to make capital of social discontent and incite the populace, usually in the name of some popular cause, in order to gain political influence or office."[6]

A second positive purpose of communication is the encouragement of people in making responsible decisions "whether that decision be Yes or No in relation to the truth that is presented. . . . A decision to say No is as much a part of dialogue as a decision to say Yes."[7] Two-way communication must of necessity be an open word. Rebellion against thoroughly true propositions or social stands often produces a vehement "No!" not because the rebel is opposed to the stand but because his own freedom of decision was removed from him in a one-way monologue. A characteristic of undisciplined and false prophecy is its removal of this freedom. The rebel, on the other hand, is likely to mistake his resentment against the removal of his freedom for a violent rejection of a genuinely good proposition. The most poignant example of this is the otherwise reasonable segregationist in the South today. Not all segregationists are "otherwise reasonable," but many of them are.

A final purpose of two-way communication is "to bring back the forms of life into relation to the vitality which produced them." In my estimate, the vitality that produces life is the unadulterated covenant with which a given relationship is formed. The marriage that is threatened by separation and divorce was earlier threatened by a withdrawal of the partners from open communication with each other. This was caused still earlier by the entrée of suspicion and distrust. Underneath this was a breach of the covenant that originally produced the marriage. A church conflict follows a similar loss of touch and relation to the covenant that brought it into being. This is the conscience struggle of the churches of the South, for example, on the race issue. Many such churches were formed on the basis of a covenant that assumed without discussion the principle of segregation.

They were formed on a principle of localism and familism. Their leaders who attempt to be prophetic without going back with them to the basis of their covenant as a church, reexamining the forms of vitality that brought the church into being and doing so on the basis of two-way communication, will inevitably produce chaos. But the pastor who moves with his people on an open-ended reexamination of the nature of the church, the kind of covenant that binds it together, and the purpose of the church in the world will find a basis for the ministry of reconciliation on the social dilemma of race. However, he will be a pleasing sight neither to the irrational integrationist nor to the irrational segregationist. As one faithful pastor in the South put it, "The beatitude for the peacemaker should be revised to read: 'Blessed are the peacemakers, for they shall catch hell from both sides!' "

The Principle of Clarification

The next principle of prophetic pastoral care is the principle of clarification. Personal counseling combines the acts of listening and speaking on the part of the counselor. The counselor hears what the person is saying. He hears it together with the person in such a way that what the counselee is saying and what the counselor is hearing are mutually agreed upon by both to be the same. The counselor clarifies *with* the counselee what is being said in terms of its meaning, not just its words. The same words can mean too many different things to leave at face value the meaning of the words being used.

The pastor has this same responsibility in his work with small groups and with the congregation as a whole. In this process the question becomes more effective than the answer. In small groups and in preaching opportunities, pastors have too often let the prophetic act of "the question for clarification" go undone in behalf of the less prophetic and easier task of "giving answers" with airtight logic. The pastor who does this is indebted more to Greek rhetoric than to the Hebrew prophets and apostles. Both the Old and the New Testament give the lively interchange of vital questions between prophets and apostles on the one hand and those to whom they ministered on the other. The parable was told, the question asked, other questions asked, and the answer arrived at together. The incident—casual as could be, such as the questions of a lawyer and of a rich young man—occurred. Questions were raised in the minds of the disciples. Only then were answers given. In other incidents, already written answers in the law were given, such as those about divorce. When the disciples then asked, "Would it not be better that people do not marry?" Jesus gave his answer.

The prophetic pastor today has the responsibility of clarifying the basic issues in social dilemmas such as extremism, divorce, race, and sexual moral-

430

ity. A certain open-endedness and invitation to discussion and dialogue must give atmosphere to such clarification, however; otherwise, the element of genuine two-way communication is destroyed. Even in situations where the pastor's authority is supinely relied upon "to do whatever he thinks best," as in the case of divorce, the pastor cannot let himself be charmed by power into doing as he pleases and speaking ex cathedra. He himself may learn something new if he takes time to talk personally and in small groups with persons vitally involved and to involve people who should be more vitally related in the decision-making process. Nor can he wait until a test case appears before he clarifies the issues in social dilemmas.

However, the prophetic act of clarification and reconciliation can be interpreted by the pastor's hearers and followers as shilly-shallying between the two sides, as "not taking a stand," and as "straddling the fence" on important issues. If the pastor is a clever person and on other occasions has been guilty of manipulation, he is likely to be interpreted as being a "smooth operator" and as one who "plays both ends against the middle" to gain his own ends. In fact, these descriptions may be true, and the pastor must examine his own motives before God to assess the truth in such accusations. Without a clear covenant that defines the task of the pastor as that of a counselor amid conflict, the pastor easily becomes a Mr. Two-Positions who speaks smooth sayings to the particular persons he happens to be with at a given time. He becomes, in Bunyan's classical metaphor, "Mr. Facing-both-ways."

This can be avoided in social conflicts and dilemmas much the same way the marriage counselor avoids it with husbands and wives who are in open conflict with each other. He enters a covenant with them to be a pastor to both members of the partnership and not to "choose up sides" and "blame" one at the expense of the other. He commits himself to work at opening channels of communication between the contending sides with the objective of resolving the differences to the mutual advantage of both contenders. He refuses to be a courier or message bearer; instead, he tries to encourage openness and trust between them. He himself moves on the assumption that the "truth" is not possessed solely by either contender but that it is "between" them. No one is to blame, but everyone is responsible. Even with a covenant like this, forces of manipulation will seek to use and coerce the pastor. In massive social dilemmas, the pastor may himself be victimized and become expendable. His prophetic objective, however, is to put the whole community "on base," even if he himself is "thrown out" before he "gets to first base."

The Principle of Anticipation

The prophet in the biblical account was often the seer, and the authenticity of his work as prophet rested at times on the extent to which his capacity to foresee situations proved to be good. Consequently, the prophets of the Old Testament, for example, were exceptionally keen observers of the course of personal and social history around them. Their grasp of the totality of these events was indeed both inspired by God and enriched by their own high intelligence, an intelligence committed to God. They could anticipate the shape of things to come and acted upon the ultimate possibilities of a given situation rather than the threats and opportunities of the situation itself. They rested their lives in God's hands to vindicate their interpretation of history.

The prophetic pastor today, in both personal and public ministry, must operate on a similar principle of farsighted appreciation of the shape of things to come. If he is to deal with social dilemmas effectively, he cannot wait until the issues at hand are confused by the opportunistic needs of the extremist, the baiters, and the demagogues. One way of anticipating social dilemmas in advance is to have some contact with older, more industrialized, more urbanized, and less provincial parishes than our own. The rural pastor can study the conditions in the city pastorate, the small-city pastor can become aware of the stresses in the churches of the huge metropolitan areas, and the American pastor can learn the fate of churches in Europe. Another way of developing this farsighted perspective is by listening closely to the troubles of the broken people of our own community. Intensive acquaintance with the pathologies of individuals and groups within our home community gives empirical insight into the shape of things to come for ourselves as well. A scientific way of continuing one's education in the art of anticipation of individual, family, and social dilemmas is the disciplined study of the development of personality in relation to the cultural pattern. At this point the work of the pastor as a prophet and that of the social psychologist and political scientist merge in relevance. The discipline of the pastor in pastoral care and social ethics should have as its cutting edge of purpose the development of the capacity of the pastor to predict and anticipate the troubles of his people. He should not forever be running in the vanguard wondering what has happened, or with little awareness of responsibility for knowing, to some extent at least, what is about to happen. For as Jesus said, "When it is evening, you say, 'It will be fair weather; for the sky is red.' And in the morning, 'It will be stormy today, for the sky is red and threatening.' You know how to interpret the appearance of the sky, but you cannot interpret the signs of the times" (Matt. 16:2–4). This he said not to prophets but to both the Pharisees and the Sadducees. It is not the will of God that the sons of this world be wiser in their generation than the sons of light. The prophetic pastor does not run when no man pursues, but he has the capacity to anticipate the shape of things to come and the courage to interpret his vision of both the city of man and the City of God to men.

NOTES

1. Elmer A. Leslie, *Jeremiah* (Nashville: Abingdon Press, 1954), pp. 85–87.

2. Archibald M. Hunter, *Interpreting the New Testament, 1900–1950* (Philadelphia: Westminster Press, 1952), pp. 65–66.

3. Floyd V. Filson, *A New Testament History: The Story of the Emerging Church* (Philadelphia: Westminster Press, 1964), pp. 224–225.

4. Reuel L. Howe, *The Miracle of Dialogue* (New York: Seabury Press, 1963), p. 56.

5. Ibid.

6. *Webster's New International Dictionary of the English Language,* Second Edition, Unabridged (Springfield, Mass.: G. & C. Merriam Co., 1955), p. 694.

7. Howe, *The Miracle of Dialogue,* p. 57.

31

Religious Factors
in Mental Illness

In 1955 I published a book entitled *Religious Factors in Mental Illness*.[1] This subject needs revisiting. The issues of life and death, hope and hopelessness, meaning and meaninglessness involved in mental illness remain the same. The battleground on which these issues are fought out, however, is very different. The armaments for waging the battle have changed radically. The aftermath of the Korean War found mentally ill persons adjusting to the renewed demands of competition in the civilian pursuits of life. The quest for affluence had begun to gather momentum in America but was not at its peak speed. The psychotropic drugs had begun to take hold but had not changed the face of the hospital care of the mentally ill or made the ambulatory treatment of the mentally ill as possible as is apparent on every hand today. The religious ideation of mental patients described in my 1955 book is much more obscure to the ear of the therapist today. The pastor and the chaplain must have much better ears for it since patients are "quieted" or "elevated" chemically, even by their general physicians. Furthermore, the rapid advances in milieu and community therapy, pointing toward the outpatient treatment of the mentally ill in a variety of highly imaginative residential settings, have added to the importance of the community as a healing factor, underscored so heavily in the 1955 version of my book.

In 1967 I published a monograph in the *Internationales Jahrbuch für Religionssoziologie* in West Germany. In this monograph I sought to bring up to that date some of the salient changes in the understanding of the psychopathology of religion.

The substance of the 1955 book and of the 1967 monograph is still effectively valid. Persons of the stature of Anton Boisen and colleagues of mine who have been lifelong students of the relation between religion and psychiatry have not encouraged a revision of the book. They suggest that it stand as it is. There has been no suggestion of revision of the monograph. The purpose of this chapter, then, is this: to write a sequel to the book and the monograph. I will bring out emphases of the intervening years that update my understanding of the religious factors in mental illness and summarize the data accordingly.

Both popular folklore and scientific attempts at empirical analysis have focused attention upon the role of religion in mental illness. The empirical data that have been collected on this subject suggest some hypotheses as to the function of religion in mental disorders, both as a causative and as a curative factor. Such a study is necessary to offset some of the superstitious accretions that hasten to the mind about the relation of religion and mental illness.

RELIGION AS A FACTOR

However, problems of methodology call for a clear summary of the meaning of the thought of religion as *a factor* in life. Kurt Lewin has clarified the methodological difficulties involved in the factorial approach to any subject. The contemporary scientist is debtor both to Aristotle's philosophy and to Galileo's scientific philosophy. The Aristotelian approach to the study of phenomena isolates, describes, and categorizes various factors about the phenomena. This classification of religion as a "factor" among many "factors" in the phenomenon of mental illness is in the Aristotelian tradition of categorizing and describing. From this vantage point, this discussion of religious factors in mental illness assumes that there are other factors in mental illness than religion. We cannot reduce mental illness to one phenomenon and to one cause, although popular antagonism to religion tends to do this. Religion is only one factor in mental illness.

The Galilean approach to science, however, emphasizes the totality of things. The holistic thinker redirects attention to the dangers of overclassification. From this point of view, religion would be seen as implicit in all other factors as well as a neatly categorized factor in and of itself. The research person's scientific methodology itself has elements of reverence and awe that are compatible with the total religious mood toward life. We can "bracket out" religious factors in mental illness. The bracketing, however, is for purposes of investigation and study only, to be reintegrated later. It cannot obscure the reality of religion as an implicit if not explicit dimension of all human existence. These two perspectives—the Aristotelian and the Galilean—must be held in focus, therefore, in the study of religious factors in mental illness.[2]

With this kind of perspective, then, the following factors have been identified by a variety of research persons as *religious* factors in mental illness. A healthy faith is an expression of the total personality of an individual in his relationship to the Divine as a comprehensive and ultimate loyalty. Sick religion is the kind of religious belief or practice that makes itself a thing apart from the totality of life of the whole person. Religion becomes an "it," a compartmentalized thing to be "used" as a defense against life rather than lived as a way of life. This is what makes of it a "factor" in the Aristotelian sense.

RELIGIOUS AFFILIATION AND MENTAL ILLNESS

Gerhard Lenski defines "the religious factor" in terms of devotionalism and doctrinal orthodoxy in the affiliation of a person with a communal faith group.[3] One asks whether there is any correlation between religious affiliation and mental illness. E. Gartly Jaco studied residents of Texas who were diagnosed as being psychotic according to the classification system of the American Psychiatric Association. The patients studied were those who sought psychiatric treatment for the first time in their lives during 1951 and 1952. The following data were recorded by Jaco concerning the religious affiliation of these patients.[4]

Religious Affiliation	Psychotic Group		Total Texas Population
	Number of Cases	Percent	Percent
Protestant	7,167	79.4	70.8
Roman Catholic	1,429	15.8	28.2
Hebrew	72	0.8	1.0
Other	11	0.1	0.0
None	348	3.9	0.0
Total	9,027	100.0	100.0[b]

[b]These estimates of religious affiliation are based on recent censuses of the Texas and National Council of Churches. However, these censuses represent only 54.6 percent of the Texas population.

On the basis of these data, one could speculate as to whether mental illness does not increase as the loss of a sense of an intact, cohesive religious group increases. The group itself can compartmentalize and distort religion. Harold Fallding and others have demonstrated conclusively that alcoholism, one form of emotional disorder, increases as alcohol consumption becomes either an assuagement or a retaliation for the loss of acceptance by and secure participation in a communal group.[5]

ISOLATION AND MENTAL ILLNESS

The religious factor in life may be further defined in terms of the paradoxical tension existing between the need to be an individual and the need for community.[6] This point of view is most apparent in the contribution of Anton Boisen to the understanding of religious factors in mental illness. Briefly stated, his point of view is that the loss of fellowship with the community "whose approval one considers most worthwhile" creates a crisis of sin and salvation for an individual. He may meet this crisis in a constructive or a destructive way. In both instances, he may become emotionally ill. Mental illness is like a fever in the body: it is nature's attempt to heal the total being of the person. Boisen said that some illnesses are malignant in that the person uses concealment and defense, pride, and self-justification as a way of dealing with the threat to his life. Other mental illnesses are benign in that they are characterized by concern. The self-searching and concern take on a religious character as the person seeks to define his place and vocation in life. This kind of mental illness Boisen defined as a search for salvation. To Boisen, this search is the religious factor in mental illness. The issue at stake in the mental patient's redemption is his responsibly living as an individual in a community of faith. The illness is characterized by isolation. Healing is made possible by a discovery and acceptance of a community.[7]

This particular aspect of the religious factor in mental illness was identified by Sigmund Freud. He contrasted the obsessional neurosis with religious ritual. He defined an obsessional neurosis as a "private religion" in that the obsession is compulsive, ritualistic, and methodical. Furthermore, the obsession seeks to communicate the guilt at the same time that it assuages it. However, Freud distinguished the obsessional practice from the religious practice.[8] Religious practice is communal in character. The neurotic is isolated and individualistic. From this hypothesis Freud stated his conception by locating the universal sense of guilt in the murder of the father of the primal horde by the younger aspirants for his place.[9] Only in this highly speculative way does the father of modern psychoanalysis come to terms with the communal aspect of religion in illness and health.

IDOLATRY AS A RELIGIOUS FACTOR
IN MENTAL ILLNESS

Idolatry is a potent religious factor in mental illness. Here religion is sick at its heart. The quest for acceptance may be directed toward a constricted and limited community of faith. The most conspicuous kind of growth-limiting community is the family itself. Mental illness is related to isolation and the need for community. But, on the other hand, the community itself may be limited and constricted. Its demand for allegiance may retard, reverse, or prevent altogether the normal growth of the personality of an individual member. The person capitulates to the demands of the family or communal group. He renounces the demands of his own growth. Thereby he becomes sick.

The author studied religious groups in eastern Kentucky in the United States in relation to members of the groups who were admitted to state mental hospitals. Two major findings were evident. First, some patients became ill when they remained in the confines of a very restricted religious group made up of one, two, or three families who were interrelated to each other by marriage and the economic pursuit of farming. These in-groups were what is known in Kentucky and other American frontier states as "clans." Within these groups, a young person or a person in early or middle adulthood would tend to become sick from the accumulation of unfulfilled developmental tasks. They had omitted having close friends their own age, learning to be independent of the family structure, having the right to choose their own mate in a culture where this is the norm, and becoming economically and socially independent of their parental home. In the second place, other persons would become sick when they attempted but failed in their attempts to leave the familial religious group and become a member of another group. Thus they were isolated and caught in a religious "no-man's-land" of loneliness and misunderstanding.[10]

In both these instances, the religious factor in the illness was a bondage to the idolatry of the small, restricted, communal unit. In the eastern Kentucky hospital study, seventeen out of sixty-eight cases of psychotic disorder revealed a long-term conflict between the individual and his family that ran along religious lines.[11] The religious loyalty of the family housed the parental domination and control of the child. Religion was used as a means of maintaining control of the child. A comparative study of mission volunteers done later, however, revealed that religion was the main means of rebellion and autonomy used by these young persons. When the young person found support and protection from isolation in a new religious group, he did not become mentally sick in any psychotic sense wherein he broke away from reality. Rather, he became something of a religious "rebel," delinquent against his parents. He effected his autonomy of his parents through the use of religion. Many times after the rebellion was effected the religion was discarded.

These ideas suggest a working hypothesis concerning the role of religion in mental illness and health. The religious institution is a secondary institution to the home. Next to the home, it has, in time, first access to the developing child. Children who go to church do so before they go to kindergarten, public school, and so forth. Furthermore, the church has access to the parents at the same time, as well as to the grandparents or the great-grandparents. The cycle of the generations is or may be represented at every age level and at every generation level in the church. In other words, the church has access to the whole family constellation. Therefore the church, depending upon the leadership's understanding of familial and religious factors in mental illness, is in a remarkably strategic position to change unhealthy patterns of emotional development. Without insight and understanding on the part of the religious leadership, however, the church may contribute to unhealthy patterns of emotional development in children. Religion may become the means of domineering and even incestuous distortion of the child's life by parents who demand idolatry of their children.

From a prophylactic point of view, one could state this hypothesis of the function of religion in man's struggle for emotional stability in the following way. In the growing person, religion and its institutions encourage the tender emotions of caring for little children. Religion lowers the importance of the earthly family of the adolescent, gives the adolescent a safe mooring of ethical values for his hostilities and sensuality, and enables him to form comprehensive loyalties to the larger family of mankind. In this larger family, the smaller idolatries of life are challenged by prophetic religion. The comprehensive, ultimate loyalties and concerns of life are made clear and relevant to the individual. Such religion leads to health. Anything less than this leads to constriction of growth and emotional disorder. Furthermore, the issue of idolatrous religion is a practice of magic and superstition as religion.

Gordon Allport, professor of psychology at Harvard University, describes the mature religious sentiment as having a comprehensive character. Communism, for example, has a certain religious quality, but its sentiment is not comprehensive and does not include all of that which is permanent in life. Allport agrees with Whitehead, who said that religion deals comprehensively with "what is permanent in the nature of things."[12] Wholehearted zeal for a cause does act like a religious sentiment, but it has a pseudoreligious cast. Allport says that even from a psychological point of view such causes and secular interests "fall short of the range that characterizes a mature religious sentiment which seems never satisfied unless it is dealing with matters central to all existence."[13] From this vantage point, then, a person is immature and may become emotionally off-center and "eccentric," if not sick, when he commits himself to that which is partial and limited as an ultimate loyalty of his life. Hence Allport's definition of religion as man's "ultimate attempt to enlarge and complete his own personality by finding the supreme context in which he rightly belongs."[14]

Carl Jung developed his concept of the "complex" with this working hypothesis of the comprehensiveness of the context in which the individual rightly belongs. He defined a "complex" as "active contents of the unconscious [which] . . . have been split off from consciousness and lead a separate existence in the unconscious, being at all times ready to hinder or reinforce the conscious intentions."[15] Plato poetically described this domination of the personality by the partial, restricted, and temporary values of life as "the rising up of a part of the soul against the whole." The vital function of psychology and psychiatry today, therefore, is to challenge the petty idolatries of hearthstone gods, family fortunes, and cultural and racial mythologies that turn an individual and a culture away from health into emotional disorder and illness. In this sense, the study of psychopathology by theologians and pastors alike serves to purify their teaching and practice of that which limits and constricts the minds of their followers as surely as the primitive practice of foot-binding of Chinese children prevented the growth of their bodies.

The Protestant theologian Paul Tillich has articulated this point of view in his formulations concerning the "demonic" in human life. He views religion as that which expresses the *ultimate* concerns of man. These concerns transcend the proximate and nondurable interests of man's life as an individual. An individual may place any relative, proximate concern at the center of his existence and endow it with ultimate significance. Then that relative and proximate concern *possesses* him and has demonic force in his life. Tillich calls this the "absolutizing of the relative." The anxiety that man experiences becomes pathological and can be removed only through therapeutic means.[16] Such pathological anxiety is different from the ontological anxiety occasioned by the threats of condemnation, meaninglessness, and death that attend the existence of every individual by reason of his being human. Here again one finds an underscoring of the idolatrous or demonic aspect, or pathological conditions, as one of the religious factors in mental illness.

In the care of the sick, probably no clinical situation reveals more vividly the power of the penultimate concerns of life to produce mental illness than that of the bereaved person. We focused on this experience in the discussion of idolatry. Here one is confronted with the possibility of making the deceased an object of worship. The crisis of grief calls for the kind of mature religious sentiment that both accepts the fact of death and distinguishes love for the deceased from an ultimate loyalty to the deceased. Dietrich Bonhoeffer comments on this disrelationship between "ultimate and penultimate" concerns. He recommends that the Christian pastoral approach to the bereaved situation should be one in which we adopt a "penultimate attitude." One remains silent as a sign that he "shares in the bereaved man's helplessness in the face of such a grievous event." He says that remaining silent about the ultimate confines one deliberately in the penultimate.[17] Grief itself is a transitional despair. Time, through a process of revelation, shows the marked difference between genuine grief over the loss of a human being and idolatry of the dead. If this transition is not made, then the person becomes mentally sick.

TRUST AND DISTRUST AS RELIGIOUS FACTORS IN MENTAL ILLNESS

One large category of mentally ill persons is characterized by major difficulties in establishing durable and trusting relationships with other persons. These patients are usually spoken of either as paranoid schizophrenic or as paranoiac, according to the nature of the organization of the grandiose, persecutory, and homoerotic dimensions of the illness. These illnesses are characterized by minimal if not nonexistent personal insight and a corresponding projection of responsibility and blame on other persons, institutions, and cosmic forces. The fabric of the being of these patients seems to have been woven from threads of distrust and basic insecurity in significant relationships. From the point of view of the positive qualities of faith that characterize religion that is healthy, this factor of trust or distrust may be defined as another religious factor in mental illness.

The psychoanalyst who has been most definitive about this factor in emotional illness and health is Erik Erikson. He describes trust as the basic emotion of human life in that its formation is the first crisis of the developing infant. As a psychopathologist he could not avoid observing that innumerable people cannot afford to be without religion and that there are many whose pride in not having it reminds the psychopathologist of whistling in the dark. Erikson says that the function of religion is to restore a sense of trust in the form of faith and to give tangible form to the sense of evil that religion promises to ban. Individual trust is viewed by him as a common faith, and mistrust as a common evil. Religion must derive a faith for the individual that is "transmitted to infants in the form of basic trust." Without this basic trust, life is built upon suspicion and distrust, which may become an illness.[18]

Rev. George Bennett conducted a two-year research project in a 1,500-patient hospital for the mentally ill. Over the two-year period, he worked with ten patients intensively—five men and five women—to study the role of religion in their lives. All of these patients were predominantly suspicious, untrusting, and diagnosed as paranoid schizophrenic. None of the subjects revealed a positive relationship of love and trust between their parents; strife and tension dominated the homes of all of these patients. All of the subjects were without warm and loving mothers. No positive trusting relationship existed between the patients and their fathers. Only one of the patients had an even partially satisfying marriage. None experienced emotional satisfactions in sexual relationships. Their religion was characterized by projecting the blame for their sufferings and shortcomings on God and neighbor. Each person sought systematically to interpret himself as a very good person with special identity, special gifts, and high self-esteem.

Religious life in the hospital provided some positive benefits for these patients, nevertheless, in that they were pulled out of their isolation into a corporate experience of worship. They developed better social control over unacceptable impulses, and a narrow channel of communication with the world was opened through an indirect discussion of their feelings through conversation about their prayers. The trees of the lives of these patients, Bennett says, "had poor roots and brought forth little fruit, but the trees did stand." Bennett identifies their taproot of distrust and the absence of the supporting roots of genuine trust as a religious factor in their illness.[19]

The situation of the acute or chronic schizophrenic person is best understood under the rubric of establishing a personal space, a territory that is one's own. The overbalanced need of schizophrenics to do this is symptomatic of their having "witches messages," as the transactional analyst Robert Goulding calls them, pronounced upon them earlier in life. They were literally told not to exist, not to be, to die, to get lost, and so forth. Our discussion of the quest for one's own territory is made poignant by the succeeding stories of the Methodical Methodist, Father M., and the three "Christs" of Ypsilanti.

Irving M. Rosen, M.D., clinical director at the Cleveland Psychiatric Institute in Ohio, studied the role of religion in both the acutely and the chronically psychotic person. He challenged the assumption that strong religious interest is necessarily to be equated with mental aberration. He continued his studies further and developed a guide to the spiritual examination of the patient's religious consciousness, history, and worldview. In doing so, he did not omit examination of patients who were, so-called, unreligious. He observed that these patients usually had some sort of center to their lives, usually their mothers.

One of the most important results of applying the religious inventory to patients was the discovery of the role of reconciliation and forgiveness in the alienated and unforgiving way of life of the patient. As Rosen says, the patient "had on occasion to be encouraged to use those channels of forgiveness open to him in order to get well. With certain patients communications about anger had to be turned into the more religious terminology of reconciliation and forgiveness before their emotional lives could be tapped and opened to abreaction."[20] Rosen concluded that the sociopathic person, particularly, is aided in recovery through such spiritual confrontation and that the examination of spiritual attitude acted as a corrective for those who took reality either too lightly or too seriously. Forgiveness and reconciliation are absent from the life of the person who cannot trust. Erik Erikson calls this the acceptance of one's own life history and the people in it as "something that had to be" and for which there are no substitutes.[21] But the religious factor in the life of the paranoid schizophrenic person rests in his intention to rewrite his own life history according to his own presuppositions whether these fit reality or not.

HOPE AND HOPELESSNESS AS A RELIGIOUS FACTOR IN MENTAL ILLNESS

The manic-depressive patient's life situation reflects another religious factor in mental illness: hope and hopelessness. Margaret Mead, professor of anthropology at Columbia University, has said that hope and hoping are the most important *cross-cultural constants* that characterize religion in all cultures.[22] The religious factor in mental illness is hopelessness, and the religious factor in mental health is hope. Gabriel Marcel says that hoping does not really take place until a person is visited by calamity. A person begins hoping when he is trapped.[23] Mental illness is such a calamity. The elaborate delusional eschatologies presented by deeply disturbed patients are desperate attempts to reconstruct a hopeful and hoping way of life.

Paul Pruyser points out that the dilemma of the mentally ill is to cope with the desperation of their life situation with hoping. Reality—seen cold-bloodedly—leads neither to despair nor to hope, but to apathy. The price of sensitivity in dealing with reality with feeling is to become vulnerable to despair. Despair, however, is the paradoxical or dialectical condition of hoping. Says Pruyser, "Only against the background of 'un-hope,' or despair, is hoping possible."[24]

Psychopathology applies the "reality test" to the hoping that religion generates or fails to generate in the mental patient. Erikson says that both an individual and a religious system of belief may be so frantic in the search for a "hope-giving relationship" that they "end up lost in delusions and addictions." When a religion or an individual cuts itself loose from "living ethics," either may regress to "illusory and addictive promises or empty fantasy."[25] Erikson categorizes the various kinds of psychopathology on the basis of the factor of hope in the following ways. In *delusions*, the patient turns to a fictitious hope unrelated to reality. In *addictions*, the patient turns to an agent that supplies "intense but shortlived hope." In *depression*, the patient abandons hope altogether.[26]

Probing into the developmental sources of hope, Erikson says that "the mutuality of adult and baby is the original source of hope, the basic ingredient of all effective as well as ethical human action."[27] He gives reciprocity and mutuality a religious association as the "Golden Rule in the light of new insight."[28] In the treatment of the mentally ill—and, for that matter, in the teaching of all kinds and conditions of people—the objective is to strike that sympathetic note which produces a resonant response in the patient or the student. If a measure of mutuality can be established and a reciprocity begun, hope is engendered in both the patient and the physician, the student and the teacher.

The problem of unforgiveness and unforgivingness pinpoints the relationship of mutuality of forgiveness and forgivingness to the development of a hopeful and trusting worldview that can be called both religious and well. This dimension of the element of hope in any creative religious life contrasts with the element of hopelessness in the sick religion.

LOVE AND LOVELESSNESS
IN MENTAL ILLNESS

Another religious factor in mental illness is the deprivation of love, and the religious factor in mental health is the nutriment of love. The mutuality that engenders hope is the greater factor of love. The helpless child responds to the person who accepts responsibility for him. This acceptance of responsibility is the concretization of love. The child learns to trust those persons who demonstrate that they are dependable. Erikson defines love as the "*mutuality of devotion forever subduing the antagonisms inherent in divided function.*"[29]

The word "love" is overworked and misunderstood in the English language. The Greek language is clearer in its use of different words for love, which help clarify and summarize much that has been taught by psychotherapists about the implicitly and explicitly religious factor of love and lovelessness in mental illness and health. The Greek word *storgē* refers to family love and love of kindred. Freud pointed out that mental illness is related to the fixation of adult love at the level of the parent-child relationship. Religion may aid and abet this when it becomes a hearthstone religion with no larger or more comprehensive outlet for growth and maturity. Under stress an individual may regress to this level of maturity and thus become sick.

In the second place, the Greek language uses the word *eros* to refer to sexual love. The whole psychoanalytic movement has described the relationship of the sexual development of a person to his emotional health or disease. Early psychologists of religion such as Edwin Starbuck and William James associated religious conversion with the onset of puberty and the storm and stress of the sense of guilt about one's awakened sexual powers. More recently, Gordon Allport asserted that "to feel oneself meaningfully linked to the whole of Being is not possible before puberty."[30] Similarly, even the name of mental disorders, "dementia praecox" epitomizes early psychiatric theory that associated mental illness with the failure of growth in the years just following puberty. Leaving father and mother and cleaving to one's wife is a major personality adjustment as well as a religious command of both the Old and the New Testament.

The Greek word *philia*, in the third place, focuses upon the fraternal love of friend to friend. The developmental task of building an adequate peer group of trustworthy friends with whom one can be intimate without too much threat or suspicion is a third crisis that may turn toward illness or health. Erikson associates this with the first stage of adulthood, when the individual may move toward genuine friendship and intimacy with other people on a durable and trustworthy basis or he may move away from them into self-absorption. Expansiveness of generosity as well as of genitality is one meaning of love, he says. Such capacity is the prerequisite of productivity in creative work.[31] In early adulthood, then, the role of religion in illness and health may be measured by the power of a given community to create this fellowship among the adherents of the religious group. However, religion itself may militate against this, and, when it does, it contributes to ill health rather than health-giving relationships.

Finally, the Greek language refers to another kind of love, *agapē*, which refers to an unconditional love based on esteem. It follows the direction of the lover's free choice of the loved one for her own sake alone. It excludes the instrumental gain the relationship may afford as a direct or indirect result. *Agapē* is not only free in its choice but uncalculating in its hope of gain. Martin Buber called this kind of love an I-Thou relationship and distinguished it from an I-It relationship, in which the partners use each other for their own ends. The mentally healthy person is the one who has achieved and received a measure of ability to love in this way. As Harry Stack Sullivan defined maturity, it means to be able to love another person as much as or almost as much as oneself. The direction of mental health is to foster this kind of love. The religious factor in mental disease is the absence of this kind of love.

In addition to detailed discussion that makes clear the factors of the life of faith summarized thus far in this chapter, there is a fresh contribution to be taken from the area of preventive psychiatry. This is the stress placed upon the importance of the factors of faith, hope, and love at the great transitions of life. Apart from the functional effectiveness of religion at the great crossing points of life, men who espouse religion find it to be a salt that has lost its savor, a broken reed unsafe to rely upon with one's whole life. The word and the sacrament of religion are weighed in the balances and found adequate or wanting in these times of crisis. Again, the whole concept of spiritual territory is a new application of the concepts of behavioral science to the religious life of both sick and well persons. Furthermore, there is a point to be made regarding the pathology of religious leadership. The decisions about the wholeness or unwholesomeness of religion can rarely rise above the decisions of its most persuasive and potent leaders. They permit people to be whole insofar as they themselves have participated in wholeness. They protect people from the pathology of religion insofar as they have received this protection themselves.

NOTES

1. Wayne E. Oates, *Religious Factors in Mental Illness* (New York: Association Press, 1955).

2. Kurt Lewin, *A Dynamic Theory of Personality* (New York: McGraw-Hill Book Co., 1935), pp. 1–42.

3. Gerhard Lenski, *The Religious Factor* (New York: Doubleday & Co., 1961), pp. 23–24.

4. E. Gartly Jaco, *The Social Epidemiology of Mental Disorders* (New York: Russell Sage Foundation, 1960), p. 193.

5. Harold Fallding, "The Source and Burden of Civilization Illustrated in the Use of Alcoholism," *Quarterly Journal of Studies on Alcohol* 25, no. 4 (December 1964): 714–724.

6. Wayne E. Oates, *Religious Dimensions of Personality* (New York: Association Press, 1957), pp. 41–46.

7. Anton Boisen, *The Exploration of the Inner World* (New York: Harper & Brothers, 1952).

8. Sigmund Freud, "Obsessive Acts and Religious Practices," in *Collected Papers*, 2nd ed. (London: Hogarth Press, 1942), 2:25–35.

9. Sigmund Freud, "Totem and Taboo," in *The Basic Writings of Sigmund Freud*, trans. A. A. Brill (New York: Modern Library, 1938), pp. 807–930.

10. Oates, *Religious Factors in Mental Illness*, p. 92.

11. Ibid., p. 78.

12. Alfred North Whitehead, *Religion in the Making* (New York: Macmillan Co., 1926), p. 16.

13. Gordon W. Allport, *The Individual and His Religion: A Psychological Interpretation* (New York: Macmillan Co., 1950), p. 69.

14. Ibid., p. 78.

15. Carl G. Jung, *The Integration of the Personality* (London: Routledge & Kegan Paul, 1945), pp. 156–157.

16. Paul Tillich, *The Courage to Be* (New Haven, Conn.: Yale University Press, 1952), pp. 38–39.

17. Dietrich Bonhoeffer, *Ethics* (New York: Macmillan Co., 1955), p. 84.

18. Erik H. Erikson, *Identity and the Life Cycle* (New York: International Universities Press, 1959), pp. 64–65.

19. George Bennett, "Religious Activity and the Suspicious Person," *Journal of Pastoral Care* 18, no. 3 (Fall 1964): 140–147.

20. Irving M. Rosen, M.D., "Spiritual Attitude Examination in the Evaluation and Treatment of Psychiatric Patients," *Journal of Pastoral Care* 17, no. 2 (Summer 1963): 78.

21. Erikson, *Identity and the Life Cycle*, p. 98.

22. Statement made by Margaret Mead in a lecture at the 1959 Arden House conference of the Academy of Religion and Mental Health, Harriman, N.Y.

23. Gabriel Marcel, *Homo Viator, Prolégomènes à une métaphysique de l'espérance* (Aubier: Editions Montaigne, 1944), quoted in Paul Pruyser, "Phenomenology and Dynamics of Hoping," *Journal for the Scientific Study of Religion* 3, no. 1 (Fall 1963): 92.

24. Pruyser, "Phenomenology and Dynamics of Hoping," p. 92.

25. Erik H. Erikson, *Insight and Responsibility* (New York: W. W. Norton & Co., 1964), p. 155.

26. Ibid., p. 181.

27. Ibid., p. 231.

28. Ibid., pp. 219–243.

29. Ibid., p. 129 (italics his).

30. Gordon W. Allport, *Becoming* (New Haven, Conn.: Yale University Press, 1955), p. 94.

31. Erikson, *Identity and the Life Cycle*, p. 96.

Part Eight

STRUGGLES, JOYS, AND HOPES

32

Grieving but Staying Well

You have lost a treasured person in your life. You must take all needed wise measures not to let this loss cause you to lose your health. Your grief can itself become an illness. That is a hazard. You can avoid it. You can stay well. The tests of character by grief are unrelenting. Not all people find it in themselves to withstand the toll of grief on their health and well-being. There are those for whom grief becomes something contrary to the intention of God and the way God has created us. Instead of being a process that has its work and is done, grief becomes a way of life. In these instances, it interferes with their work, their love life, and their friendships with others. Even their relationship to God is hindered and distorted. With the help of good counsel and by the power of God in your life, you can stay well.

GRIEF AND ITS NORMAL PROCESS

Grief is a normal depression. It is healthy when one moves through a definite pattern of behaviors and states of consciousness. Generally speaking, you move through the following mental and emotional states in a time frame that varies from three or four months to two or three years.

Stage 1: Shock. The impact of the initial news of the loss leaves you in shock.

Stage 2: Numbness. In a dazed condition, you attend only to the practical necessities of the funeral, meeting those persons who would console you and interacting with relatives, especially those you have not seen recently.

451

Stage 3: The Struggle Between Fantasy and Reality. It takes time to associate things, people, events, and the delicate routines of life with the harsh reality of your loss. Great areas of your less conscious thinking continue to respond as if your loved one were still alive. During sleep, you may dream that he or she is alive. Often the dream awakens you. Then you know it is not so.

Stage 4: Acceptance of Reality. This shows itself in exhaustion, tears of helplessness, a normal time of depression. Pouring out your grief to a friend, to an intimate relative, to your pastor, to your physician, and in your prayers is a great necessity. Let yourself go in such a time as this.

Stage 5: Selective Memory. You "regroup" for living in the real world without your loved one. Yet at times something will happen. You will see someone you haven't seen since the death, or you will come across something written by the deceased or a special possession or a picture of the deceased. For a few hours, a day or two, you are "down," morose and preoccupied. You seem to go through it all again. This is a short-lived condition and you go back to a more even emotional outlook.

Stage 6: Recovery. You discover a new purpose in life and begin to recommit yourself to causes and individuals in the real world. You have done with grief work. You incorporate all that is creative about your loved one into your own way of life, but hope and joy in living return. You start "to live again," to use Catherine Marshall's phrase. You begin a new chapter in your own life.

The time span in this process varies in terms of the depth and quality of your relationship to the deceased, the kind of death he or she suffered, and the degree of willingness you have to do—and insist upon yourself doing—the grief work. Your own habitual ways of handling crises of any kind have much to do with how long you are in the process.

However, as an outside time limit, let us say that if by the end of the second anniversary of the day of your loss you are still stuck in one of the first four or five of the stages, you have cause to seek professional help from your pastor, your physician, or someone they may recommend. Your basic health is at risk. You need not forever be in bondage to your grief. Life has yet much to offer you.

GRIEF AND YOUR LIFE-SUPPORT SYSTEM

The scripture teaches you and your friends and relatives to "bear one another's burdens, and so fulfil the law of Christ" (Gal. 6:2). The law of Christ is the love of his people one for another. We are to love one another as Christ loved us and gave himself for us. In your particular grief, one of the ways of staying well is to form and maintain an effective life-support group with whom you share more than your grief. You do share your grief with them, and debrief particular intense experiences that threaten to bowl you over. However, that is not all you talk about. That is not all you do. You listen to *their* griefs as well. You celebrate positive and happy events with them, also. In fact, it may take more personal strength of character to celebrate with someone than to commiserate with that person. If you have an effective life-support system, you and they can both communicate and celebrate.

Take inventory, then, and see whether you have such a life-support system. Who are the persons that make up the system? How often do you converse with them? What do you and they talk about? Or is it that you have only one person upon whom you rely, whom you trust? Are you considerate of that one person's other responsibilities? Or do you dominate his or her life with your demands for time, attention, and affection? One way of staying well in your time of grieving is to be as considerate of those near you as you would want them to be of you. Everybody who has reached maturity has as much need of you as you have of them. One way of measuring your emotional health in your grieving is to ask: Am I overdependent on *one* person as a comforter? and, How intact is my capacity for empathy with those who seek to comfort me?

GRIEF AS A POWER LOSS

Look at your world of relationships to other persons as a system of personal power that people in the sphere use to control each other. Think of a mother and father as controlling each other and their children. Think of the death of one member as an event over which no one at the time had control—that is, no one could cause it not to happen. Grief, then, includes a loss of power, a loss of control. You berate yourself for not being more powerful. This helplessness is something you are new at feeling. Up to the time of the death, you had the situation in hand, you were in control. Now your grief itself becomes a means of controlling those members of your family who are left.

Usually this kind of reaction in the grief process is found in parents of grown sons and daughters. Most commonly, the remaining parent is mourning a deceased wife or husband. It is only natural, then, to regress to an earlier state when the parent was in complete control of the sons and daughters when they were very young. Grieving over the death of a member of the family *long past the time when you should have begun to live again* becomes a means of controlling the lives of those who remain. It keeps you in power. You become a "wailing widow (or widower)." You are lonely; you complain of fears of being alone. Yet your constant rehearsal of your grief drives people who could be companionable away from you.

This is a neurotic process that calls for therapy. If you will reserve your negative conversation for an hour or two a week of counseling with a wise and patient counselor, you will make the first strong step forward breaking out of the vicious circle I have just described. You have a right to be free from such a self-defeating way of life. You have the right to reinvest your devotions to the future and to live again.

GRIEF AND DEPRESSION

The time may be three, six, twelve months, or even years since your loved one died. One day you find yourself unexplainably sad. You cannot sleep enough to meet your day's need. You have crying spells and they are uncontrollable. Your appetites for food, recreation, and sexual relations have shut down on you. You begin to feel that life is no longer a joy and may be too much for you. In brief, you are depressed. "What has this got to do with grief?" you ask.

You may have been the person at the time of the death upon whose shoulders fell the whole load of responsibility for the business details, the emotional support of the rest of the mourners. You "held up"; you did not take time to let your own feelings loose; you were the one upon whom everyone else leaned. Besides that, you just are not the type to be very emotional about things, you think. But now, sometime later, you are depressed. Your delayed grief is catching up with you. It is time for you to face it, deal with it, and work through it.

Or perhaps the death of your loved one was totally unexpected. You may have moved through all the stages of shock, numbness, and fantasy that this is not really so. Now you are overwhelmed with depression. By nature and temperament you may have gone through episodes of depression before. Now this is another one with a different cause. You cannot pull yourself out of this one.

Whatever the causes of your depression, you may be sure of this: depression can be treated with more success than you think. If it goes untreated, it can be damaging to your whole way of life. A therapist of your choosing will help you to relive your bereavement and get a fresh perspective on it. There is a range of medications to correct your sleep disorder, to stabilize the biochemical balance of your nervous system, and to elevate your mood. Then, beginning with these new strengths, he or she will collaborate with you as you rebuild your life for the long pull of the years ahead.

BIZARRE THOUGHTS AND ACTIONS

The chances are that what I will say here applies more to someone you know than to you. Some people become psychotic with a bereavement as a precipitating, though not a causal, factor. They demonstrate bizarre, hard-to-imagine thoughts and behaviors. One man, on the night that his son was killed in an auto accident, asked the resident and chaplain in the emergency room if his son's body could be stuffed by a taxidermist so that he could keep the body in his home. He was told that this is not possible and that he was trying to do something that would be damaging to himself and other family members. He then proceeded to have his son's body embalmed and placed in a sealed casket. Instead of having the body buried, he placed it in a room in his home. He built an altar there and asked visitors to worship with him.

You immediately say, "I never heard of such a thing! That's out of this world!" You readily see how bizarre it is. However, do not fear that this kind of bizarre grief reaction is going to happen to great numbers of people. Neither should you think that the tragic death "caused" this unusual reaction. When we got a previous life history of the man, we discovered other bizarre episodes in his life, none of which were prompted by a grief situation. He had already been chronically mentally ill for a long time. Yet you can see that such patients nevertheless are grieved for their loved ones even as you and I are.

Psychiatric care is needed for such florid psychotic conditions. Especially is this true if the condition has destroyed the person's capacity to function—that is, to sleep, eat, work, and live in a reasonable degree of peace with one's family and neighbors—and if the person has been grossly hindered for as much as a year. In other words, this is not a transitory and brief state of mind. It goes on and on unless treatment is forthcoming. Furthermore, motives and threats of either suicide or vengeance to hurt or kill other people may be present. In these instances, if the person is not willing to go into a psychiatric hospital voluntarily, then legal measures may need to be taken in order to make the commitment involuntarily. This is a severe grief in its own right. If you are the relative of such a person, you have grief on top of grief. If you are that person, you need only face this crisis to see that other people are terrified by you.

INTENSIFICATION
OF PHYSICAL ILLNESSES

In your struggle to stay well in the face of your grief you may find specific bodily changes coming upon you as a result of the stress. The death of a spouse, divorce from a spouse, or the death of a child rank at the top of the scale of the most stressful events that happen to people. The multiple stressing of your life at this time may (though I hope it does not) precipitate physical disorders. Heart trouble, stomach disorders, and pain-producing disorders of other kinds are likely to be intensified. Grief, especially sudden grief, exacts its toll on the body. Yet the human body is highly intelligent in its own right. Many times it has more "sense" of its own than the person who owns it has conscious awareness and wisdom.

Therefore, confer with your physician about your habit system. Seek first how you can change your habits and thinking. Wisdom and personal discipline will be your best medicine. Do not expect a pill to take away your unhappiness and grief. It will not. If, however, you cannot sleep properly, eat properly, and work properly, then your physician's prescription will help you to function better. Stay away from medications that can be bought "over the counter" at a drugstore. They have not been tailored to fit you. They may complicate rather than facilitate your health. Prescriptions are provided only after you have been diagnosed by a physician.

Your health is important. Do not neglect it. Yet in this discussion I do not want to do much more than point to your health and urge close communication with a good physician.

YOUR SPIRITUAL WELL-BEING

Let me emphasize the importance of your filling the void of your loneliness with the companionship of the Holy Spirit. You are not alone. Be of good courage. Cultivate the presence of God. Contemplate the wisdom that we shall have no other gods before him. Your (and my) great temptation in grief is to assume that our world ended when we lost our loved one. This is not so, even though it feels that way. To be fixed and stuck in this is to worship the dead. This has been the greater idolatry throughout time. But our God is the God of the living. Worship of God alone saves us from this idolatry. As the scripture enjoins: "Keep yourselves from idols" (1 John 5:21). God has not given you a spirit of fear, but a spirit of love, power, and self-control (2 Tim. 1:7).

33

Spiritual Concerns of
the Pain Patient

Your function as a pastor in relation to the patient in pain is primarily centered in his or her relationship to God and neighbor. Alfred North Whitehead said that our relationship to God fluctuates between perceiving God as an enemy, as a void, and as a friend. Our very presence as pastors connotes all three perceptions of God to the person in pain. Instead of feeling one way consistently toward God, the patient's affective response to the very thought of God moves back and forth among all three of the perceptions of which Whitehead speaks.

Similarly, the moods that Elisabeth Kübler-Ross associates with grief—denial, anger, bargaining, depression, and acceptance—are translatable into religious affections, to use Jonathan Edwards's description of the spiritual life in his *Treatise Concerning the Religious Affections.* Consequently, pain patients look up to you as an interpreter of their distress in prayer before God and as a searcher with them of the mysteries of their relationship to God in spiritual conversation.

PAIN AND TEMPTATIONS TO INTEGRITY
BEFORE GOD

Pain is not merely the activity of nociceptors telegraphing their injured state to a person's brain. Pain is a signal that the whole organism is in trouble. Pain is a threat to the very integrity of the person as a whole, especially when the pain becomes chronic.

We see the dialogue of integrity being dramatized in Job's encounter with God. Even though both God and Satan have entered into a laboratory experiment together to test the mettle of Job, the Lord says to Satan, "He still holds fast his integrity, although you moved me against him, to destroy him without cause" (Job 2:3). Job's wife chides him after calamities have befallen him, saying, "Do you still hold fast your integrity? Curse God, and die" (Job 2:9). Job tells his counselors that "till I die I will not put away my integrity" (Job 27:5). Job prays, "Let me be weighed in a just balance, and let God know my integrity!" (Job 31:6). He refuses to be torn to pieces by his agony. He intends to keep the wholeness and completeness of his personhood in face-to-face dealings with God. He refuses to accept the assumption of his counselors that his suffering is punishment for sin, or to make a neat bargain with God for its magical removal. To the contrary, Job's expectation of God is consistency, justice, and an affirmation of his, Job's, integrity.

The integrity of people in pain is tested mightily by the persistent pain they suffer. Their own spiritual interpretation of their relationship to God, vis-à-vis their pain state, is an important issue for your conversation with them. If we look at the test of integrity of being as what is meant more profoundly by the biblical teachings about temptation, then temptation becomes something far more deeply significant than the mere transgression of minor moral codes. Temptation becomes the struggle of the whole being to stand and, having stood everything, to stand in the presence of God as one who is faithful to God and to oneself, even when adversity is heaviest. Seen from this angle of vision, what are some of the major temptations of the patient in pain?

The Temptation of Abandonment

Dietrich Bonhoeffer says, "This is the decisive factor in the temptation of the Christian, that he is abandoned, abandoned by all his powers—indeed, attacked by them—abandoned by all men, abandoned by God himself. . . . The man is alone in his temptation."[1] The private worlds of people in pain become their nemesis in the feelings of abandonment and isolation that the pain itself engenders. At the same time, self-deception enters, and pain patients hold back a portion of themselves as a private kingdom of control in relation to both God and fellow human beings in the form of pain games. This amounts to preferring the abandonment in a "to a certain extent" sort of way. Yet, as a patient continues to manipulate surrounding people through pain games, these people in turn begin to withdraw all the more. The self-deception creates the very abandonment that the isolation of the pain patient set in motion in the first place. A vicious cycle of abandonment, creating more abandonment, intensifies the temptation to isolation, forsakenness, and self-pity. Subtly the integrity of the patient is eroded.

A paradox is hidden in the feeling of abandonment. It contains in it the positive expectation of companionship and communion both with God and with one's fellow human beings. Your very presence as a pastor contradicts the abandonment the pain patient may feel. If you, a finite, erring human being, are concerned enough to do away with the distance between you and the patient, how much more can a just and loving God? This is especially true in the light of your feeling that you are not there merely on your own initiative but as a messenger, a teacher sent from God. You are there to call that person out of isolation, to establish fellowship, to participate in another's suffering. You can say as much to the patient.

The Temptation of Giving Up and Giving In

The temptation inherent in abandonment is related to a second dimension of temptation in the life of the pain patient. This is the proneness to "give up and give in" in the face of intractable and persistent pain. Those who give up and give in to pain cease to believe they can be part of their own destiny. They lose curiosity as to new ways of outwitting and coping with the pain. Their sense of wonder shrivels. Yet, within this temptation there is also a paradox. Ordinarily, the pain patient desires absolute and complete relief from pain as a unique right. Physicians and others seeking to provide help are expected to be all-competent and capable of getting perfect results. The pain patient is often unwilling to give up these unrealistic expectations. In pastoral conversation, the perfectionism of the patient can be gently but firmly challenged. If, instead of giving up and giving in totally to the pain, the patient can give up unrealistic expectations for a total cure and give in to accepting, say, a 65 percent relief, the accompanying relaxation and reduction of stress will possibly increase the 65 percent relief from pain to 75 percent.

The Temptation to Play God

However, for patients to make this kind of surrender touches the nerves of another temptation: the temptation to play god in their expectations and demands of others and the temptation to expect others to be little gods also in their perfection. Out of this temptation comes the spiritual call of patients to "join the human race": to accept their own humanity, to affirm the humanity of their physicians and other therapists, and to be more tolerant of their own and others' limitations and frailties. When this happens, their integrity in their own eyes and in relation to other people becomes more vivid. They live with more dignity and humor in the face of the frailty of the human race. In abdicating the need to be little gods themselves, they are more willing to let God be God and to shift sovereignty to God and not to themselves. As the apostle Paul put it, "We have this treasure in earthen vessels, to show that the transcendent power belongs to God and not to us. We are afflicted in every way, but not crushed; perplexed, but not driven to despair; persecuted, but not forsaken; struck down, but not destroyed" (2 Cor. 4:7–8).

The Temptation to Make Pain One's God

Paul Tillich often spoke of the demonic as the absolutizing of a relative reality. Pain very easily becomes absolute in a person's consciousness. For all practical purposes it takes the place of God as the unconditional controlling force in life. Giving up and giving in to pain in effect sets up a pain patient for this inadvertent kind of idolatry. One pain patient came to a moment of truth for himself when he said, "I will be damned to torment if I sit down and worship this constant pain. I will *not* let that happen. There has got to be a bigger center of my life than this, whether the pain goes away or not." He was rebelling against the tyranny of pain. Religious experience is not by any means always conformity; in this man's search for a "bigger center," his spiritual stance was one of rebellion.

The natural aftereffects of letting pain become one's god are legion. A person moves out of the frame of spirit to accept responsibility for management disciplines. Such disciplines call patients to accept the personal responsibility of being a part of their own therapy for pain. When a person fails to do this, he or she moves into the "blame frame," in which the whole responsibility for the management of pain is projected upon having an adequate supply of painkilling medications, upon physicians who are not obeying the patient's wishes, upon family members who complicate life by being uncooperative, and so on. Then the pain becomes a tool with which to exercise control over all these other people, manipulating them to move at one's command. In other words, a whole Pandora's box of human self-centeredness is opened when pain itself becomes the pain patient's god.

PASTORAL COMRADESHIP
IN THE STRUGGLE AGAINST TEMPTATION

Every good pastor is acquainted with the struggle with temptation. He or she may be carrying a steady amount of personal pain. This need not be part of the pastoral conversation in and of itself; the wisdom of making it so is determined by the length and depth of the acquaintance and relationship a pastor has with a given patient. In many instances, pastors who have known people over a period of years become also known by them in terms of their own personal illnesses. Even though a pastor is free of physical pain, other temptations are real to those who are honest with themselves. Thus, he or she shares with the patient a common ground of fellowship in temptation.

Hebrews sets the tone of the pastor's comradeship with the pain patient in temptation. The Good Shepherd is portrayed as one who is tempted in all points even as we are. We can approach him boldly and find grace to help in the time of need. Similarly, every good pastor can deal gently with a patient in pain or any other suffering person because he or she is beset with weakness also (Heb. 4:14–5:3).

Listening closely to what the patient says about his or her relationship to God and to those to whom the patient relates day by day reveals to the perceptive pastor what the level of temptation is that the person suffers. Carefully following the leads that the person gives enables a pastor to move the conversation from one level of frankness to another. When you measure the courage of the person to face the specifics of temptation, you encourage frank raising of the issue to the extent that the patient's confidence in you is not undermined. The substance of what has already been discussed in this chapter is, when rightly presented, good food for thought for the person to mull over and consider for acceptance. Yet, right of refusal must be given, and the element of comradeship in spiritual struggle must be maintained with genuine considerateness.

Inasmuch as the oldest, most common, and most persistent set of feelings that human beings have about pain is that it is punishment, you as a pastor are in the best position to explore these feelings with a given patient. Listening for feelings of being punished for either real or perceived wrongdoing enables you to get at the burdens about which the patient may have no one else with whom to talk. One man said to his pastor that his pain was "all because of my sin." The pastor did not hasten to reassure but simply asked, "What sin?" Then the patient reported having been greedy and frequently working at a factory job three shifts a day in order to make more and more money. Unburdening himself in a voluntary, uncoerced confession enabled this man to find forgiveness, to start reconstructing his way of life, and to take a more active part in the relief of his chronic back pain and arthritis.

The central function of a ministry of confession in the life of any person is to reconcile the person with God through the power of the presence and forgiving grace of Jesus Christ. God ceases to be perceived by the patient as the punishing enemy, the absent Lord, and becomes the present Friend who participates in a responsible way of life for controlling and healing pain.

THE SPIRITUAL TRANSCENDENCE OF PAIN

One of our functions as pastors is to encourage and instruct persons in the life and practice of prayer and contemplation. The chief end of prayer and contemplation from a Jewish or Christian point of view is adoration and worship of and conversation with God. The relief of pain is certainly one of the petitions a person can make to God. However, that relief in fact is most likely to come as a side effect of the acts of worship rather than as an end result of prayer. The very acts of worship themselves refocus the center of a person's attention; they direct energy away from pain and invest that energy in an intentional fellowship with God; they produce an awareness of the events of time in the largest possible context of the Eternal; and they restore the perspective of a person, turning his or her helplessness into a conscious comradeship with God. The acts of worship remove the sense of isolation and loneliness and replace it with a feeling of belonging to God and being in communion with God.

Pain Disciplines as a Lower Level of Prayer

In the mood and motives of prayer, the disciplines for managing pain—rest, relaxation, exercise, weight control, the responsible use of medications, avoidance of addiction to alcohol, medications, food, and work—become more than a lonely bootstrap operation of self-discipline and the "exercise of willpower." Each of these acts becomes a lower level of praying to God and bringing life into harmony with the ways God has created us. In fact, none of these disciplines is limited uniquely to people in pain. Each is an affirmation of the intention of God in creation. Each is a commitment of any person who takes seriously the way in which God has created him or her.

The systematic practice of these disciplines is a practical way of presenting the body "as a living sacrifice, holy and acceptable to God, which is your spiritual worship" (Rom. 12:1). It is the offering up of one's being to God. The body in this sense is not merely the physical substance of our humanity but rather our total personality, which is being consecrated to God in any one or all of the disciplines of relaxation, rest, exercise, the careful use of medications, and resistance to addictions to drugs, alcohol, and work. In pastoral instruction about how to pray, you can speak of these as the acting out of their prayers. This kind of choreography of pain actually does something constructive about controlling the power that pain has over people. These disciplines are motions of the whole being in prayer to God. They lift people in pain above their pain rather than letting the pain lord its power over them.

The Practice of Prayer in Assessing Priorities

Once people in pain have come to terms with their limitations and accepted the reality of pain as an ongoing process in their life, they can best be instructed to weigh and consider the particular situations that make the pain worse. What kinds of activities contribute to the amount of pain, and what kinds actually bring relief?

In many instances, chronic pain is episodic in its intensity. It comes in sieges that assault the patient from time to time. These times can be charted and identified. The stress events listed in Thomas H. Holmes's social readjustment rating scale are some of these times.[2]

By prayerful anticipation, some stress events can be avoided. Others can be spread out over greater lengths of time, rather than having too many of them descend on a person at once. Others can be interrupted with times of rest or diversion. Pastoral conversation with the patient in pain can take the form of prayerful thought about what can be done to redistribute or to avoid stresses. Direct pastoral advice and encouragement are useful, particularly when the stresses that a patient endures or faces are not the kind that involve a major life decision.

Many stresses are unnecessary and are actually invited by the stressed individual. One such stress is conflict with other people. If chronic pain patients can make the connection that being upset and angry at other people's behavior will actually increase their amount of pain, you as a pastor can encourage them to cool it when it comes to losing their tempers, getting into verbal duels with people over trivial matters, and letting other people be a "pain" to them, wherever the pain is located! This can be incorporated into a spiritual exercise of deliberately offering up the annoying situation to God in prayer and asking for serenity after the order of the prayer:

> God, grant me
> The serenity to accept the things I cannot change,
> The courage to change the things I can,
> And the wisdom to know the difference.
> (Reinhold Niebuhr, 1892–1971)

One characteristic of chronic pain patients in many instances is that they are prone to fight the system. Tilting at windmills over trivial concerns is a product of their irritability. If this can be brought into pastoral conversation as a spiritual issue for prayer for serenity, then the prayer life itself can relieve these patients of "sweating the small stuff," fretting unduly and thereby exacerbating their pain. "A closer walk with God, a calm and heavenly frame," as William Cowper put it in his hymn, is what is genuinely needed. Pastoral encouragement in this direction makes an otherwise agitated person more serene.

The establishment of priorities as to what is really important comes more easily to those who put the events and relationships in which they are involved into the context of prayer, in the perspective of the eternal God. Pain creates a scarcity of energy. Not many things use more energy than fuming over trivial matters about which little or nothing can be done. The wise conservation of energy is of major importance to the pain-ridden person. Isaiah speaks directly to the situation of the people in pain when he says:

> Have you not known? Have you not heard?
> The LORD is the everlasting God,
>   the Creator of the ends of the earth.
> He does not faint or grow weary,
>   his understanding is unsearchable.
> He gives power to the faint,
>   and to him who has no might he increases strength.
> Even youths shall faint and be weary,
>   and young men shall fall exhausted;
> but they who wait for the LORD shall renew their strength,
>   they shall mount up with wings like eagles,
> they shall run and not be weary,
> they shall walk and not faint.
>
> (Isaiah 40:28–31)

Giving Thanks for the Simple Gifts for Relief of Pain

The lot of the chronic pain patient is no different from the common lot of humankind. We become so absorbed in our personal discomforts that we neglect to use and give thanks for the simple gifts of life. Some of these are specific aids for the relief of pain. Take, for example, sunshine and other sources of warmth and heat, water (whether it is cold or warm), and things of beauty that capture the attention and renew the spirit. Using, experiencing, and offering thanks for these simplicities of life is one way of spiritually transcending pain.

From ancient times, people in pain have found their way to the sunshine as a way of relief. For a patient to walk outside on a warm, sunshiny day and feel the gift of the sun on the face, the neck, the back is to experience a relaxing of muscle tension and an easing of pain and to feel grateful. To give thanks to God for this relief is to find kinship with those who were so dependent upon the sun that they worshiped it as their god.

Likewise, people for centuries have traveled to bathe in waters that were at least temporarily helpful to their pain states. The interruption of their stresses to make journeys to these places, the company of other pilgrims, and the placebo effect of their expectations of relief all combined to help them, and the water itself was a soothing balm. Little wonder that some of these centers have become shrines of worship as well. However, the modern person in pain often concentrates too much on painkilling medications to find time to appreciate what a warm shower or tub can do to allay the power of pain. To combine this with meditation and thanksgiving for this simple gift enables a person to transcend the power of pain all the more.

Beauty has been mentioned as one of the simple gifts related to pain relief. In a cosmetic culture such as ours, ugliness and pain can easily become synonymous. Particularly is this true of older persons, who associate pain with aging and aging with ugliness. Therefore grateful concentration on the beauty of a color, a flower, a tree, a rainbow, a landscape, a work of art, or the sounds of music or silence can lift pain patients above the pain they bear. The entry of a child into the room of a pain patient who loves children is more than a distraction for that person. All these are occasions of thanksgiving.

Paul Tillich on one occasion said that the pastor and the church provide a shaping environment to give new meaning to the experiences through which people have to go. You as a pastor have it within your power to bring ultimate and transcending meaning to the life of the patient in pain by focusing the simple gifts into words of prayer.

MYSTICAL BELIEF, PRACTICE, AND THE SPIRITUAL CONQUEST OF PAIN

Earlier in this chapter the comment was made that the control of pain could well be one of the "side effects" of sincere prayer before God. This comment represents one of the convictions of persons such as ourselves who are deeply schooled in the Western Christian belief that God is to be worshiped out of devotion and adoration for God's own Lordship in all of life and not as a means of satisfying our desire for pleasure and the avoidance of pain. God participates in our humanity through the complete humanity of Jesus Christ. The teaching of some of the early church fathers of "patripassianism"—that God experiences pain—was rejected. Nevertheless this teaching has now come up for review.

Kazoh Kitamori published his *Theology of the Pain of God* in 1946. More recently, however, Jürgen Moltmann has drawn on the thinking of Elie Wiesel, the interpreter of the pain of the Jewish people in the holocaust of Nazi Germany. Moltmann perceives God as being intensely involved in the pain of his people without losing his freedom to transcend and exercise justice above and beyond the pain. God is involved in the suffering itself, which is the "situation of God as well as humankind." He quotes Elie Wiesel, himself a survivor of Auschwitz:

> The SS hanged two Jewish men and a youth in front of the whole camp.
> The men died quickly, but the death throes of the youth lasted for half

465

an hour. "Where is God? Where is he?" someone asked behind me. As the youth still hung in torment in the noose after a long time, I heard the man call again, "Where is God now?" And I heard a voice in myself answer: "Where is he? He is here. He is hanging there on the gallows."[3]

Moltmann says that for both Jew and Christian any other answer would be blasphemy. "To speak here of a God who could not suffer would make God a demon." He insists that to speak of an indifferent God would condemn us as human beings to indifference. Of the crucifixion and resurrection of Jesus, Moltmann says, "No one need dissemble and appear other than he is to perceive the fellowship of the human God with him. Rather, he can lay aside all dissembling and sham and become what he truly is in this human God. Furthermore, the crucified God is near to him in the forsakenness of every man."[4] We can add that not only is each person thereby enabled to respond to the participation of God in his or her pain, but, by the fellowship of God in Christ with those in pain, each one is endowed with a mission to reach out with empathy to others who are in pain.

The spiritual conquest of pain on Jewish and Christian bases of faith such as expressed by Wiesel and Moltmann has taken a distinctly mystical direction, whereby the suffering of the person in pain is caught up in the larger suffering of God with the whole human race and with the individual in particular. However, the influence of Eastern religions, notably Hinduism and Buddhism, is now being felt in the more recent blendings of Christian beliefs with Eastern practices of meditation.

The ability of Oriental fakirs to walk on coals of fire without being in pain is duplicated by subgroups of Christians in Greece, for example. Beginning every May 21 in Lankadas, Greece, disciplined fire walkers, clutching icons of St. Constantine and St. Helen, dance as much as twenty minutes on flaming logs. Christos Xenakis, a neurologist who has been studying these fire walkers since 1974 under the auspices of the Max Planck Institute in West Germany, searches for the secret of their incredible mastery over pain. He notes that the fire is hot enough to burn, 250–300 degrees centigrade. Their feet are not covered with thick calluses; only two out of ten even develop blisters. Xenakis feels that there must be some neurophysical explanation.[5]

The villagers say that the saints in whom they believe protect them from the pain, but they have no explanation for how this happens. The mechanism of their miracle remains a mystery to the research team. And the whole process is declared idolatrous and heretical by the bishop of the region.

Mystical beliefs demonstrably have a biochemical effect of some kind, either on the pain threshold or on the tolerance level of pain or on both. What these effects are we are only beginning to discover. Let us look at some possibilities.

HYPOTHESES FOR SPIRITUAL ANESTHESIA OF PAIN

First of all, both Hindu-Buddhist and Christian forms of mystical anesthesia are rooted in centuries of tradition, supported by the wide acceptance of a face-to-face community of believers and richly endowed with unquestioned rituals. The fire walkers in Lankadas may go back to pre-Christian times. Specific origins are traced to the thirteenth century, when the church in Kosti in eastern Thrace (now in Bulgaria) went up in flames, yet villagers who rushed in to save its icons of the saints were untouched by the fire.

Add to this remarkable tradition and community support the fact that these fire walkers are not chronic pain patients. They are deliberately exposing their feet to the noxious stimulus of fire in the presence of an emotionally inspiring audience. The stimuli are external ones, not internal, such as cancer pain, trigeminal neuralgia, or low back pain. This prompts us to ask whether we are attempting to compare essentially similar things or whether we are talking about two different kinds of pain perceived differently and experienced in radically different settings. In fire walking, the person is heroic; in chronic pain, the person is a victim. The fire walker suffers with the massive support, admiration, and affection of the community; the person in chronic pain suffers in considerable isolation and with doubtful community support or none at all.

Nevertheless the example of the fire walkers does raise dramatically the need for hypotheses to appreciate, if not to explain fully, the nature of spiritual anesthesia.

The Placebo

Previous discussion of the placebo effect affirms that what people in pain believe about surgery, medications, warm baths, exercises, and the like directly lowers their perception of pain. More recent research hypothesizes that the confident frame of mind of the patient itself releases the body's own natural opioids to raise the threshold at which pain is felt. This is yet to be demonstrated at the laboratory experimental level.

Physiological Changes in Spiritual Meditation

As Edward Thornton says in his book *Being Transformed: An Inner Way of Spiritual Growth*:

A breakthrough in research came with development of encephalographic readings (EEG). Four states of consciousness are linked with levels of EEG activity. On a scale from zero to 26 hertz (Hz) per second, the EEG measures frequency and intensity of brain wave activity.[6]

There are four stages of consciousness and levels of relaxation and centered attention: Beta (26–12 Hz), or focused attention for rational decision making; Alpha (12–8 Hz), or defocused attention, a peaceful, pleasant blankness; Theta (8–4 Hz), or reverie, a half-conscious dreamlike imagery state; and Delta (4–0 Hz), or sleeping consciousness. In the experience of pain, Alpha and Theta consciousness seem to provide the most respite from the perceptual mass of imagery that pain presents in the Beta stage of rational thought.

Spiritual anesthesia can be achieved in biofeedback, in such secular forms of meditation as Transcendental Meditation, or in distinctly Christian forms of meditation and prayer. For a Christian to repeat the words of a given scripture, the name of a biblical character or saint, or simply one word of a valued and cherished belief, such as "Grace," relaxes the whole musculature, shifts the focus of thought away from pain to a restorative rather than upsetting center, and—a side effect of the process—lowers the amount of pain. Herbert Benson, in the book *The Relaxation Response*,[7] says there are four prerequisites for this kind of relaxation: quiet environment; an object, such as the words mentioned above, or a specific symbol, such as a cross, to dwell upon; a passive attitude in which a person empties all thoughts and distractions; and a comfortable posture.

Benson frankly draws upon, but does not restrict his discussion to, the teachings of Christian mystics. He reminds us that

> to prepare for prayers of inward recollections, the true language of the heart, in which one concentrates solely upon God, one must achieve a passive attitude by dwelling upon an object. It is necessary to have 'the heart free itself and become joyous' in order to prevent thoughts from intruding. For the object upon which one concentrates, Luther suggests the words of the Lord's Prayer, the Ten Commandments, the Psalms, or a number of the sayings of Christ or Paul.[8]

Benson suggests two methods of concentration: gazing—that is, fixing one's eyes on the ground, the floor, or a symbolic object—and repeating "no" to distracting thoughts that occur.

Benson suggests practicing this discipline for twenty minutes or more at least twice a day. Whereas he does not relate this to physical pain, we can do so in our context here. What we need to ask is whether this kind of meditative relaxation turned into prayer does indeed create any specific physiological changes that raise either the threshold of pain or the tolerance level to pain, or both.

The neurons in the brain and spinal cord mediate endorphins, which integrate sensory information relating to pain and emotional responses. The field of neurobiology is moving at a fast pace to identify what the painkilling properties of these endorphins are and how they work. It is known that meditation and hypnosis increase endorphins and demonstrable EEG changes in Alpha and Theta states of relaxation. Prayer can do likewise. We know that the relaxation response and inner serenity alleviate pain and its tyranny over the consciousness of a person in pain. It is not unreasonable to move toward further research as to the direct and indirect efficacy of meditation and prayer states in the relief of pain. Already Kenneth Pelletier in the use of biofeedback has demonstrated that "an abundance of alpha activity appears to help an individual to remove himself from . . . pain and not react to it as intensely. Patients still feel the pain, but it is usually reported as a dull sensation rather than a sharp and throbbing one."[9] The mystics of the Christian faith and of Eastern religions have experienced these results for centuries. We are only now beginning to understand the mechanisms—how these things occur—so that we can repeat the results again and again for the relief of suffering people.

The Anesthesia of a Great Purpose in Life

We have already learned how soldiers at Anzio Beach were made less aware of pain from wounds by reason of their overriding purpose to return home alive. In the same way, football and basketball players caught up in the intention to win a game seem to be oblivious to pain from injuries.

Twenty-three years ago, John Bonica established the University of Washington Medical Center's Clinical Pain Service, which has become a model for pain clinics all over the country. Specialists from eight or ten different specialties combine their efforts to unravel the mysteries of pain syndromes in people who already have "suffered much under many physicians," as the Gospel of Mark (5:26) puts it.

When we learn more of this remarkable man, we discover that he himself lives and moves and has his being in a life of pain. At the age of sixty-seven, he says that only his intense involvement in his work keeps him from being "a completely disabled guy."[10]

Here is a man who, like the soldiers and athletes described earlier, is caught up in a purposeful life that lifts him above the tyranny of pain and energizes him to be of service to many other people.

One of the major contributions that you as a pastor can make to people anywhere is to inspire them to a calling and a commitment that overrules and outdistances the thousand mortal ills to which the flesh is heir. Bonica seems to have found this as a direct result of the pain he has to endure. This response to what W. O. Carver called "the glory of God in the Christian calling" is rarely mentioned as an anodyne for pain. Indeed, getting away from pain as a direct object does not do it. The pain itself becomes the life vocation. Rather, as is true of the centered worship of God, the wholehearted pursuit of God's calling seems to have as one of its side effects the assuagement, the relief, and at times the cure of pain.

We have progressed on a journey of uncharted regions for the pastor to travel. Yet we set out upon the journey through the gateway of the person's consciousness of physical pain. This gateway for you may be a new one into the spiritual existence of your people. You can become, in John Bunyan's words, "a 'Mr. or Ms.' Interpreter" and your church, your study, your home can become to pain-ridden persons a "House of the Interpreter" to guide, comfort, and even heal them of unnecessary pain and to sustain them as they bear the necessary pain in their beings. May you heal sometimes, remedy often, and comfort always in the name of our Lord Jesus Christ.

NOTES

1. Dietrich Bonhoeffer, *Creation and Fall: A Theological Interpretation of Genesis 1–3*, trans. John C. Fletcher; and *Temptation*, trans. Eberhard Bethge; 2 vols. in 1 (New York: Macmillan Co., 1959), p. 98.

2. See Thomas H. Holmes and Richard H. Rahe, "The Social Readjustment Rating Scale," *Journal of Psychosomatic Research* 11 (1967): 213–218.

3. Jürgen Moltmann, *The Crucified God* (New York: Harper & Row, 1974), pp. 273–274.

4. Ibid., pp. 276–277.

5. Nicolas Gage, "Greek Ritualists Invoking Saints Walk on Coals," *New York Times*, Sunday, June 1, 1980, sec. 1, p. 11.

6. Edward E. Thornton, *Being Transformed: An Inner Way of Spiritual Growth*, Potentials: Guides for Productive Living (Philadelphia: Westminster Press, 1984), p. 57.

7. Herbert Benson and Miriam Z. Klipper, *The Relaxation Response* (New York: Avon Books, 1976), pp. 110–111.

8. Ibid., p. 115.

9. Kenneth R. Pelletier, *Mind as Healer, Mind as Slayer: A Holistic Approach to Preventing Stress Disorders* (New York: Delacorte Press, 1977), pp. 289–290.

10. "Unlocking Pain's Secrets," *Time* 123 (24), June 11, 1984, pp. 58–66.

34

To Be Free
from Pack Thinking

At Mars Hill College, in North Carolina, one of the best friends I had was
Eugene Brissey, a fellow South Carolinian. We debated together, we had
many personal discussions of the issues of political science. We later went
from Mars Hill College to Wake Forest College and graduated in the same
class. In 1942 he went into the Navy, was wounded, and recovered enough
to become a public relations officer for Eastern Airlines. However, his
wounds finally took his life.

Brissey stands out vividly in my memory, and especially one of the
events we shared together. We belonged to the same leadership fraternity,
one that a person qualified for by achievement and not by reason of
money, political pull, or being "voted in." On one occasion the organization was considering a group protest by boycotting the classes of one particular professor because of his views on war. Brissey objected. He insisted
that each of us in our own way confront the professor one by one. As he
spoke, he said, "I don't think in packs."

His metaphor comes, as you would surmise, from the way some animals run in packs, such as wolves. I agreed with and adopted as my own the
commitment never to be enslaved to the party lines of "pack" thinkers.
This has involved me in the lifelong struggle to be free from pack thinking.
Other terms for it are bandwagon thinking, crowd psychology, and propaganda.

It would be easy and struggle-free if the resolution to resist pack
thinking were not pulled at by our necessity for community, the meeting of
minds with others, and fellowship with our own kind. This struggle is inherent in our ambivalent needs for individuality and communion. We are
caught between our need for the approval of persons who are contending

with each other and our need for independent judgment, balanced wisdom, and personal integrity.

The struggle to be free of pack thinking began when I was elected president of the Baptist Student Union at Mars Hill College. For all practical purposes, the persons in Student Union offices were the only student government the school had. As long as we were functioning on our own campus, things went smoothly. However, when we went to the Southwide student retreat at Ridgecrest that summer, we met full pressure to conform to a highly organized and carefully packaged agenda for our campus activity. I listened closely and learned what these denominational officers had to say. I had no conflict with them. I simply charted our own course the way that fit our situation.

However, a civil war was going on within me. I perceived the Christian faith to be concerned with the unique personal burdens each student brought to the college within himself or herself, the kinds of personal, family, and social problems that beset one. I did not see the projection of an organization for its own sake as a top priority. Yet this was the way the pack was going.

In the midst of this inner conflict, I began to reexamine the exact shape my destiny would take. Up to this time—the summer of 1937—I saw myself as becoming a lawyer-politician. Now all that was swept away. I had found a fresh angle of vision of my destiny in the Old and New Testaments and my experience of the Fatherhood of God and the deliverance from bondage effected by my faith in Jesus Christ. In my attempts to be a religious leader, I had found a sense of direction for my destiny under God. In the quietness of a solitary walk in the rhododendron-covered hills of North Carolina I came to a steadfast certainty both that I wanted to be a minister and that God was inviting me to be a minister. No visions, ecstasies, or loud voices accompanied the certainty. The intelligence of the eternal God worked through his creation of my own mind to bring closure to a decision to be a minister. It was not a job, a function, a role, or a part in a drama. It was something I simply started being and becoming with the full encouragement of God. The specific focus of ministry for me was the orphaned persons, the conflict-ridden ones, those with families broken as mine was, and those who were wandering without a sense of destiny. I could not see myself as concerned only with recruiting converts to a particular denomination. At once this put me into a lonely spot in relation to those around me who were so-called evangelists out to "save" the world by their efforts, zeal, and organization.

For three or four years after that I tried hard to conform to this pattern of simplistic revivalism. The more I sought to see changes take place in people's lives through these approaches, the more unreal to me they became. I found myself at variance with older leaders for whom I had much personal respect but with whose ideas and methods I deeply disagreed. Yet I was hard pressed to have anything better to offer than their stylized proselytism of masses of people. Sufficient good came in the lives of enough people to make me know that I could not just throw out the baby with the bath. Yet I could not forget the lack of genuine content and the neglect of my inner complexities at the time of my own profession of faith and baptism. I could not forget the lack of instruction preceding and the lack of follow-up after my baptism. Surely there was a better way. As it stood, I had only two things to go on: my lack of any better approach, and my certainty that this was not the way to go. It was the patent-medicine, over-the-counter remedy for everything that made me grope for freedom from this kind of pack thinking and acting. Surely there was a more prescriptive, individualized, and growth-oriented approach to the proclamation of the good news of Jesus Christ. This struggle to be free from pack thinking and a jingoistic, sales-pitch evangelism, therefore, was inherent in my experience of baptism and in my commitment to be a minister of the gospel. This struggle was destined to stay with me until this day. To me, accepting the struggle as a part of the terrain and the opposition was the only way to go.

Throughout my career this struggle has taken on an acute character at specific times and under specific circumstances. The struggle to be free of pack thinking epitomizes my experience as a college senior. In the fall of 1938, a contingent of students who graduated from Mars Hill went to Wake Forest College, then an all-male institution. We immediately met another remarkably dedicated and competent faculty. Their common commitment was to teach us to think independently and to provide us with the classical tools for doing so. Subject matter was a medium through which we were disciplined to think our own thoughts and to think God's thoughts after him. As Kepler said as he studied astronomy, "O God, I am thinking thy thoughts after thee."

Classical and Koine Greek, which I had begun studying at Mars Hill, became an intriguing passion. The clear, precise meanings of words and the dramatic syntax implementing in detail the functions of the individual psyche and interpersonal relations became a discipline that I use almost daily to this day. Latin and its kinship with Roman rule and law aided me in grasping the meaning of much of the English language. Old English and Anglo-Saxon put me into sympathy with basic English as it is known through oral tradition and not through the obfuscations of much classroom gibberish. The men who taught these languages loved their work, knew us as students at a very personal level, and could call out the best in us in a gutsy and humorous way. Yet they demanded top performance and had an inspiring way of making us feel that they personally would be alarmed, wounded, and shaken if we let them down. It mattered to them that we should achieve to the outer limits of our abilities.

English literature brought Shakespeare and Milton alive for me. While reading Tennyson's *In Memoriam,* I first detected the process of grief as the poet moved from the stage of shock, to disbelief, to fantasy, to despair, to stabbing memories, to a life of faith in the face of not knowing. Tennyson grieved for Arthur Hallam, his close friend. Pneumonia had that spring killed my roommate, Clyde Randolph, and I grieved for him. Concurrently with English literature I took my first course in marriage and family under the tutelage of Prof. Olin T. Binkley. He had just come to the faculty from the pastorate of the Chapel Hill Baptist Church. He had worked alongside the sociologist Ernest Groves in developing a college and university course on preparation for participating in marriage. This was one of the many national roots of present-day marriage and family therapy. Olin Binkley was my first counselor in *any* professional sense of the word. He counseled with me about my heritage, my charting of my academic work, my hopes for marriage and a family of my own, and about the need for pastors professionally educated to counsel with people about specific troubles they were enduring.

One of the most profound impressions Olin Binkley made upon me was his careful reviews of books he had read, the way he remembered the full bibliography, the statements of purpose, the methods of research, the central discoveries of the authors, and so on. He was a walking computer with an amazingly wide range of knowledge.

Similarly impressive to me were the thoroughness of his preparation for his classes, the deliberateness of his style of lecturing, and the atmosphere of intellectual inquiry and personal reverence that pervaded his classroom. From my identification with him as a teacher I resolved to express my ministry through the classroom and the clinic as well as through the pulpit. Olin Binkley was my mentor and teacher, my confidant and friend. He advised me to be a teacher in psychology and philosophy. He was our premarital counselor when Pauline and I married and the best man in our wedding. Later at the Southern Baptist Theological Seminary he was my teacher in Christian ethics and was a member of my doctoral committee. We taught together at the seminary and college levels. He coached me on the development of curriculum in the hitherto-undeveloped field of psychology of religion and gave me support within faculties. He has been an inspiration, an older brother in Christ, an ideal teacher after whom I modeled my work, and a steadfast friend.

When it comes to independent thinking, Olin Binkley is an artist. He coolly computes evidence, uses a minimum of verbiage, and draws conclusions on the basis of evidence that marks the path of wisdom. Pack thinking is alien to him, and his wisdom has both depth and durability.

Another powerful force in my intellectual formation was A. C. Reid, professor of psychology and philosophy at Wake Forest College. His Ph.D. from Cornell was in experimental psychology under E. B. Tichenor. However, his first love was philosophical psychology. He was steeped in the history of philosophy, especially ancient Greek philosophy. Reid taught us that "philosophy is the sincere and persistent search for truth wherever manifestations of truth may be found."

Professor Reid was a rigid disciplinarian in his classroom and a taskmaster in his advanced philosophy seminars. He demanded that we read *all* of Plato's dialogues, the psychological philosophies of Aristotle, Spinoza, Hume, Descartes, Locke, William James, John Dewey, and John B. Watson. He pointed us toward Carl Jung and ignored Freud. He is a devout Christian and has taught Sunday school for decades in the Wake Forest Baptist Church. His Christian heroes to whom he introduced us were Albert Schweitzer, Rufus Jones the Quaker mystic, and William Ernest Hocking. We were expected to evaluate our own Christian beliefs by writing serious papers on several systems of philosophy: materialism, idealism, mysticism, and pragmatism. We were expected to be able to give "a reason for the hope that was in us."

Probably the most exacting study that A. C. Reid required of me was an intensive study of epistemology, that is, theories of knowing. How does one know anything and, more than that, how does one *know* that one knows it? In other words, what are the sources of conviction, belief, certainty in life? This discipline made me reexamine all that I believed. I kept that which by specific experience I had demonstrated to be true. Never again could I take without my own scrutiny and experimentation what someone else said was so. F. H. Giddings, one of the pioneers in American sociology, put it into a sentence: "I want to know if a thing is true, or is it that everyone is simply *saying* that it is true." From this point forward I had crossed another bridge, and burnt it, and there was no turning back. I could never be a yea sayer, a pack thinker, a pawn of propaganda, a worshiper of what Bacon called the idols of the marketplace. Prayer became to me that internal action in which I sought to discern the intentions of God amid the hidden and manifest persuaders with smooth rhetoric.

Another powerful person became intensely significant to me at Wake Forest. Henlee Barnette was a classmate of mine. He and I had both gone to college after working at Cannon Towel Company in Kannapolis in 1936. I went to Mars Hill and he went straight to Wake Forest from the start. We reunited when I went to Wake Forest in 1938 as a junior. We took Greek, Latin, Shakespeare, psychology, and philosophy together. I took Milton and Tennyson; he took American literature. He had a similar cotton-mill heritage to my own, although he had worked ten years in the mills, whereas I had worked only two. He had started to work when he was thirteen. Becoming a page in the Senate had given me a temporary reprieve. He had worked at night and gone to high school during the day.

Immediately we were fellow pilgrims, and our comradeship has lasted to this very day. We work together as fellow professors at the School of Medicine of the University of Louisville. Prior to this we taught together at the Southern Baptist Theological Seminary, he in Christian ethics and I in psychology of religion and pastoral care, for over twenty-five years.

Henlee Barnette became my colleague in resisting the pack thinking that Southern Baptists, southern culture, and pseudo-intellectuals pushed our way. Neither he nor I was any more interested in the clubbiness of liberals than we were in the storm-troop tactics of fundamentalists. Yet we were eager for even-ground dialogue with both packs. Our sense of humor has been the sustaining lubricant of our friendship with each other.

This comradeship has been an intellectual quest in which we mutually informed each other about the technical inner detail of our specialties. At the same time, we have been spiritual confidants and confessors to each other, providing authentic spiritual direction to each other in times of grief, pain, illness, political adversity, and in times of celebration, achievement, and triumph. Anybody can commiserate with you. As you know, persons of great character can celebrate your successes without envy, jealousy, and greed. Henlee Barnette has that greatness of character and heart.

The weapons for dealing with pack thinking were forged, tempered, and sharpened at Wake Forest College. The full-scale battle was ahead of me. I became a veteran at this struggle to be free of pack thinking in several crucial situations.

Graduation from Wake Forest College came on May 27, 1940. We sat in bleacher seats at the stadium while heavy storm clouds with flashes of lightning gathered over us. The rumble of distant thunder was symbolic. Hitler had invaded Poland on September 1, 1939. Forty infantry divisions and fourteen panzer divisions blitzkrieged that brave but beleaguered country. By the time of our graduation, France was on the verge of defeat; the defeat was formalized on June 12, 1940. May 27 itself was a fateful day for the British against Hitler's Luftwaffe as Dunkirk harbor was put out of use. The British evacuation had already begun on May 26. By June 4, 1940, 198,000 British and 140,000 French and Belgian troops had been saved. Most of their battle equipment had to be abandoned. Of 41 destroyers, 6 were sunk and 19 were damaged.

This was the context of our graduation with the gathering storm of war around us. My work with A. C. Reid had been effective enough that I was asked to stay on as an instructor in psychology and philosophy. I would be allowed to take a pastorate if I could find the work. The pay was not enough to support even a single man. I turned to a retired professor of religion, Dr. W. R. Cullom, who was pastor of the Spring Hope Baptist Church at Spring Hope, North Carolina, about thirty-five miles from the campus.

Providentially, the rural churches at the Peachtree and Bunn communities, surrounding Spring Hope from the west and the north, were both without a pastor. Through the influence and ministry of introduction of Dr. Cullom, I was asked by these churches to be their pastor. I eagerly accepted. I began work with them in June 1940, teaching at Wake Forest during the week and serving the churches full-time in the summer and part-time in the winter.

I had never had courses in preaching, church management, and pastoral care. However, I had the continuous coaching of O. T. Binkley and W. R. Cullom. They gave me clinical supervision of my work for the two years I was pastor there. A. C. Reid gave me supervision of my teaching and his point of view as a lay Christian concerning my care of my people.

Yet the party-line thought of Southern Baptists was that the be-all and end-all of a Southern Baptist pastor was to function as an evangelist who increased the size of the church. Within this party line I set out to find *all* the people in the community. I visited everyone in the geographic reach of the churches. When I had finished visiting them, I started over again. My main reason for visiting them was to get them to come to church. If they had never professed faith in Jesus Christ, my simple appeal was that they accept him as their Savior and be baptized, and I promised to continue to follow their spiritual growth. *If they did not do this, then I continued to be interested in them as their friend and pastor.* This is where I broke with the pack thinking of Southern Baptists. I did not restrict my ministry to people who came to church. I visited tenant farmers, alcoholics, persons with sickness or grief. The dispossessed situation of blacks hit me hard as I visited. I went to the barns where people worked with tobacco, to the stores where they gathered, to the small towns on Saturday afternoons, and to cotton and tobacco markets where they sold their crops.

I continued my visitation for a third time around. Then is when I broke out of the old wineskins of pack thinking about being a pastor. I began to see and think with these people in *their* terms and not my own as a sort of salesperson for the church. I found a family who had a mongoloid child whom they kept strapped in a rocker. I found an alcoholic father who had a daughter who was pregnant out of wedlock. He never came to church, but he invited me to his home for dinner. Before he asked me to ask the blessing, he said: "Mr. Oates, we raised everything on this table ourselves, except the sugar, salt, coffee, and pepper, of course." Then I thanked God for the food and the loving hands that had raised it, cooked it, and served it. I was amazed that the daughter gave birth to her baby in the home and the child was accepted as a part of the family as a matter of love. Church members thought this was sort of "trashy," but the grandfather and grandmother of the baby did not; nor did they think the daughter was an outcast. These things puzzled me, but I continued to visit the new baby the same way I did all the others.

I saw many cancer patients for the first time in my life. They all died at home, not in hospitals. The funerals were from the homes. We had neither intensive care units nor funeral homes as we now do. People sat up all night with the corpse so the family could sleep a little. Food was brought and people visited with each other in droves. These cancer patients worked with tobacco plants, smoked or chewed tobacco. I wondered then if there was a connection.

Another family was composed of all men. There had been no daughters, only three sons. The mother had died prior to my being pastor. The father had been an active church member and a deacon prior to her death. Upon her death he dropped out of church along with all three of the sons. They did all their own cooking and cleaning—such as it was. A retarded brother of the father, uncle of the sons, lived with them. The common report of several neighbors who were very active in the church was that these men had "taken to bootlegging whiskey." The church people felt that they should be confronted about this. I asked that this matter be left to me.

I had had uncles and a brother-in-law in South Carolina who were moonshiners. I had been present when "revenuers" or officials assigned to policing the illegal manufacturing and black-marketing of alcohol caught, jailed, and fined them.

Instead of accusing these men of bootlegging, I began visiting them twice a week at different times of the day and days of the week. I told them I wanted to get to know them better and especially to know how they had lost their wife and mother. I wanted to know how they were managing to get along without her care. They made a place for me in their hearts, as Paul had asked of the Corinthians (see 2 Cor. 7:2–4, NEB). I learned about the fear of the father and sons that the retarded brother and uncle would marry a prostitute in the nearby town with whom he consorted. They thought he was too "addled in the head" to be married. He and I talked together and I discouraged the plan. He followed my advice.

But the most important effect was that these men gave up their bootlegging without my ever mentioning it to them. They began occasionally returning to church. However, the gnawing loneliness over the loss of their wife and mother was still with them when I left the area.

The most dramatic event occurred when a little six-year-old boy at vacation Bible school came to me and said: "Dr. Cheeves wants you to come to see my ma. She's sick." I went with the child to his home. The mother was in bed. She said that the doctor told her she needed someone to talk with about her troubles. He recommended me. I listened to her story of her troubles. I told her I needed to pray about her troubles and to talk with her doctor. I had prayed with her and told her not to despair; God was with us.

I conferred with the doctor and he said she was genuinely sick with stomach, intestinal, and blood pressure problems. These were aggravated by her fear of her husband, who was a heavy drinker. He encouraged me to continue to see her, to get acquainted with each of her children, and to try to understand what caused the husband to need so much booze. He urged me to listen, observe, and pray with them.

These things I did, and I was amazed to see that her health improved, her husband's sadness lifted and his drinking decreased, and her children began to laugh and play again. I stayed in touch with this family even after I left the pastoral charge there. The mother fully recovered. We all gave God thanks for his work in our lives.

Not long after this, Dr. Cheeves was called into the military. He, upon leaving, urged me to give myself to studying and teaching about the relation of the ministry and medicine. He said, "It's the wave of the future."

Pack thinking about the Christian witness focuses on the church as an institution that people serve. Salvation becomes a package of right words and phrases to say. The pastor is taught, prompted, urged, and paid to "traverse sea and land" to make proselytes (Matt. 23:15). I have no inhibition in forthrightly proclaiming the good news of God in Jesus Christ for the redemption of persons. However, I turn again and again to Jesus' own manner of resisting the package thinking of his day and pinpointing the good news of the kingdom at the site of peoples' most personal fears, burdens, complex relationships, illnesses, and loneliness.

In kaleidoscopic fashion other dramatic crises of my life have centered down upon the agony and ecstasy of the struggle to be free of pack thinking. In 1943 I entered a theological school that had a closed curriculum which *everybody* was required to fit into. The combat veterans returning from World War II brought the same demand for person-centered approaches to the pastoral ministry. Christian ethics, pastoral care, and a wide variety of electives in theology were the result.

In 1948 a whole group of young professors, of whom I was one, were added to the faculty. It was easy for the "young Turks" to become a pack. Increasingly I found myself detaching myself from the pack, much to the consternation of the young and the puzzlement of the older. This eventuated in a polarized conflict in 1958 that resulted in the resignation of twelve younger professors. I could not be a part of the pack. Neither could I be a tool of the power structure that remained.

In the 1950s and 1960s, also, we were caught in the nationwide civil rights movement. Whereas I took individual stands in specific cases for the rights of blacks, women, and handicapped persons, I have never felt at ease in lifting from these persons their own responsibilities for exerting their efforts to achieve personal freedom from exploitation.

Probably the most vivid encounters I have had with pack thinking have outstripped those in the confines of the Southern Baptist Convention. They have been in the field of clinical pastoral education and the hand-in-glove relationship our movement has with psychiatry and psychotherapy. When I entered this field in 1944, the Freudian psychoanalytic frame of reference was the going thing. I learned this approach well and had extensive psychoanalytic therapy in the course of my two years of supervised clinical pastoral education. I had a remarkably wise and thought-provoking supervisor in Rev. Ralph Bonacker, who himself had been through analysis and who had a firm grasp of Reformed and Augustinian theology. Yet when I got to Chicago and Elgin State Hospital, I found men in charge of the program who were slavishly following English and Pearson's book *Emotional Problems of Living* in a superficial way. They were in severe conflict with Anton Boisen because he resisted the bandwagon enthusiasm for popularized versions of Freud. My approach was to dig out all of the original writings of Freud himself and to do a historical and source criticism of his teachings. My doctoral committee approved this as the subject for my dissertation: "The Significance of the Work of Sigmund Freud for the Christian Faith." Many made light of it. However, my graduate committee took both the thesis and me personally very seriously and tempered my work with remarkable wisdom and perspective.

Throughout my career, the field of pastoral care has moved from one psychotherapy bandwagon to another. After Freud came Carl Rogers. Concurrent with Carl Rogers came Wilhelm Reich. Then came Harry Stack Sullivan. Then came Erik Erikson. Then came Ekstein and Wallerstein's theories on the teaching and learning of psychotherapy. Then a whole pyrotechnics of "pop" psychologies burst on the horizon: transactional analysis, integrity therapy, Gestalt therapy, encounter groups, noöthetic counseling, and others. The present concern is with systems theory.

My approach has been to read closely the primary sources of the gurus of psychotherapy and to submit them to a historical analysis of their sources and the tributaries of the influences that brought them into being. Likewise, I have studied closely the particular population of people with whom the particular guru was working while formulating his or her theory.

At no point have I accepted wholesale the teachings and methods of any of them. Nor have I been an eclectic, picking and choosing this and that from each of them.

To the contrary, I have used the criteria of Reformation and free-church theology for assessing the "trendiness" of each wave of crowd thinking. I came very near to stating fully my own personal stance about all these things in my book entitled *Protestant Pastoral Counseling*.[1] The book is still a serious challenge to the stereotyping of the ministry by psychoanalytic assumptions. It put the work of pastoral counseling in relation to the life of the Spirit, the life of the church, and the hope of the kingdom of God. It still provides my own theoretical base for pastoral counseling and psychotherapy.

Since I have been a professor in a medical school in a public university, I have seen innumerable polarizations of contending groups on crucial issues. It has been my native inclination to seek to maintain working relationships with all sides of social contentions. The truth has to be somewhere *among* these forces and no one of them has a corner on it. Life is too ambiguous and ambivalent for that. Christian love to me is the power of the Spirit of Christ working *among* people to overcome this ambiguity and ambivalence by bringing to pass a humility and reconciliation in the place of arrogance and power plays.

One might assume, since I have for eight years been a professor of psychiatry in a school of medicine, that modern clinical psychiatry has become a bandwagon for me. *Au contraire!* The chairman of the department, John Schwab, M.D., at the outset of my tenure as a full professor, said, "You are our one pastor and theologian. Do not put your own lamp under a bushel." I find that I am expected to be expert in *all* of the theological disciplines. I am accepted and respected for a steady distinctiveness. Intense debates over different treatment modalities are waged all around me by differing psychiatrists. I read intensively the published research on these controversies about the efficacy of neuroleptic medications, the amounts of medication, shock therapy, lithium therapy, short-term crisis hospitalization versus longer-term milieu therapy, and so on ad infinitum. I used a historical analytic approach to my own conclusions concerning these live issues. Here again, I find the methods of historical criticism that I first learned in the study of the Bible to be useful in maintaining independence of thought in this environment, too.

Someone reading what I have said here about the struggle to be free of pack thinking may assume that I am making a case for being a "loner," an isolated individual who is afraid to take a stand. That is one reaction of some people who resist pack thinking, that is, to pronounce a curse on all sides of controversial issues, "to shut oneself within oneself and to let the devil pipe his own." Yet that is no temptation for me. I regularly find myself in the thick of the battle among contending factions. The very discipline of pastoral counseling and psychotherapy calls for this. To the contrary, I insist on a multilateral partiality instead of a unilateral partiality. This focuses my identity as a minister of reconciliation in the name of Jesus Christ.

For example, I found myself in this position during the Vietnam War. I could readily see that we as a nation had shilly-shallied ourselves into an undeclared war that should never have been. I could identify with patriotic young men who volunteered to fight our country's war. My own son Bill was one who did so. Yet, with him, I could not repress my admiration for the Vietcong who saw themselves as fighting a civil war to unify their country in spite of a powerful outside force in the United States military effort. I could even see that Ho Chi Minh was unwittingly the instrument of God teaching us as a nation the limits of human power. I sat with all my people and wept as we blew taps on a lost cause when Saigon fell and became Ho Chi Minh City.

The person who commits himself or herself to the struggle to be free of pack thinking, propaganda, and party-line clichés does best to take a stand for justice for all and mercy for all. Yet this places him or her in the role of a reconciler, a peacemaker, a negotiator, an interlocutor. The hazard is that of being despised by all contending forces for not taking sides. There is a quantum leap of difference between taking sides and taking a stand as a minister of reconciliation. Jesus said, "Blessed are the peacemakers, for they shall be called sons of God" (Matt. 5:9). After forty-two years of this, I can say with gratitude that to know that one is a child of God is a source of peace in itself. However, my sense of sardonic or even gallows humor says, "Yes, Lord! But that is not *all* one will be called by any means!"

THE "CROWD" VS. THE "COMMUNITY": AN INVITATION TO DIALOGUE

The crowd of the popular mind is always seeking an escape from the disciplined struggle to be a person in one's own right. It is easier for you and me to fade into the woodwork or wallpaper of the prevalent opinion. But Martin Buber was right when he said that the idea of community must be guarded against all contamination by sentimentality or emotionalism. The community of struggle against pack thinking is, as Buber says, "community of tribulation, and only because of that, community of spirit; community of toil, and only because of that, community of salvation."[2]

Yet you and I have nothing to offer a community if we have no individuality of our own. A crowd is the bundling together of beings with no sense of apartness, selfhood, and uniqueness. A community is a fellowship of people of working faith who have both a clear-cut sense of individuality and a need to have fellowship with and learn from other persons who are distinct selves in their own right. Our main claim to partnership is that we bring on our own generativity to it. Otherwise we are "hangers on," with no growth apart from the nutriment that the crowd gives. To be such is a parasitic existence not worthy of you or me. Hence we can derive the maxim: Be yourself; commit yourself to the organism of the body of Christ composed of members with differing gifts, to perform the works of love to God and neighbor.

T. S. Eliot saw deeply into the struggle for individual autonomy. He saw its ambiguous nature. He said that even the lonely hermit monk praying alone in the desert prayed in the context of the body of Christ, the church. My struggle to be free of pack thinking at base is that kind of prayer. You and I do not see this struggle as an effort to be asocial. To the contrary, we commit ourselves to the fellowship of humankind through the power of the Spirit to enable us to break the bread of the body of Christ and drink the wine of the blood of Christ in gladness and singleness of heart. This is a communion and not a herding of people together under the partisan cries of this, that, or the other party line. Paul describes this struggle in his First Letter to the Corinthians. He complains that some people say, "I belong to Paul" or "I belong to Cephas." For this reason Paul baptized very few, as he told them, "lest any one should say that you were baptized in my name" (1 Cor. 1:12–17). This is the genesis of party cries, crowd thinking, pack thinking. Freedom from it is not to be found in baptizing or in various packaged sales items, all of which deny the cross of Christ of its power. It is enough to be and become according to the gospel and to convey the good news of Jesus Christ.

NOTES

1. Wayne E. Oates, *Protestant Pastoral Counseling* (Philadelphia: Westminster Press, 1962).

2. Martin Buber, in *The Way of Response,* ed. Nahum N. Glatzer (New York: Schocken Books, 1966), p. 155.

35

Rest: The Gift of God
in Christ

You and I were created with the need for rest. "The LORD is the everlasting
God, the Creator of the ends of the earth. He does not faint or grow
weary" (Isa. 40:28). Yet the creation story tells us that after God saw everything he had made, and that it was good, and after the heavens and the
earth were made, "God finished his work which he had done, and rested on
the seventh day from all his work which he had done" (Gen. 2:2). In God's
very nature and in the way God made you and me, then, rest is the gift of
life brought to us as we finish acts of creation, whether they be creative
work or creative play. Both work and play are energy consumers. They
deplete us. Renewal is necessary. Rest renews.

I recall tenderly an event in the first year of my marriage. Since I
had been a bachelor until I was twenty-five and worked full-time since I
was thirteen, work was second nature to me. Rest did not seem to be
necessary. Play was a vague entity apart from the fun of working. One
evening when I came home for dinner my wife, Pauline, gently asked me,
"Wayne, don't you ever *finish* working?" The thought had not occurred
to me.

Yet God *finished* his work and saw that it was good. He rested after
finishing the task. I doubt that this means that God created a closed-end
universe. He would always be the God who acts. Jeremiah and others speak
of God thus: "The Lord GOD of hosts has a work to do" (Jer. 50:25).
Ninian Smart speaks of "the two locations of God." Thus "God's creative
activity is not confined to his being there at the moment of creation; but he
is present at the continuous creation of the world every day and every
minute working thus in all things. . . . Inasmuch as God is a dynamic being

his presence means work, and his being present everywhere thus means that he is working everywhere."[1]

Jesus confirmed this in his ministry. Upon seeing the man blind from birth, he said, "We must work the works of him who sent me, while it is day; night comes, when no one can work" (John 9:4).

Pauline's question went to the heart of the matter: We never finish absolutely any significant work. Nevertheless we become exhausted, fatigued, and depleted. We *cease* to work. We interrupt our efforts. We begin to rest. To do so is a part of the rhythm of the creative process. For example, the heart never ceases its work, but paradoxically, in its measured rhythm, it rests half the time! Pauline has been to me that lifelong haven of rest, blessed interruption of stress, and liberator from my compulsive resistance to rest. Hence, she is a continual source of renewal to me. She keeps me in touch with God's gift of rest and renewal.

This gift of rest is bestowed on the living by a God who is the God of the living and not the dead. In three places in the scriptures rest is referred to as final, as death. In Job 3:17–19, death is referred to as the rest where the wicked cease from troubling, the weary are at rest, the prisoners are at ease together, and the slave is free from his master. If we were to translate these into goals for living and not solutions presented by death alone, then the great social justice inherent in the substance of rest would appear. The wicked would cease their troubling; the weary be at rest, prisoners at ease together, and slaves set free!

Rest as the finality of death appears again in Ecclesiasticus: "Weep less bitterly for the dead, for he has attained rest; but the life of the fool is worse than death" (Ecclus. 22:11). Also: "Death is better than a miserable life, and eternal rest than chronic sickness" (30:17).

Yet these are no biblical commendations of death as the gift of rest. On the contrary, they express the conventional wisdom that unending, unremitting, and unchangeable depletion of life is worse than death. In comparison to that, death is rest.

This laconic Jewish wisdom does not take the heights of encouragement about death that the New Testament does: Death, the last enemy to our spiritual renewal and revitalization, is to be destroyed (1 Cor. 15:26). God in Christ has given us the victory over death in his resurrection. Thanks be to God for this unspeakable gift! Through our having been crucified daily with Christ and raised to walk in newness of life, we have the resurrection as a daily reminder, metaphor, pattern of living, and manna-like gift to restore us through rest. Rest itself is the daily foretaste of the resurrection.

Even death itself, then, in the face of the resurrection, is not a *final* rest. Rest is in the harmony of an eternal rhythm of rest and creativity.

JESUS AND THE GIFT OF REST

The force that kept me working so compulsively that my bride asked if I never finished work was and—to a lesser degree—is the compulsive need to *earn* my way into the approval of God and my neighbor. Though her question was ever so gently put, it was obvious to me that Pauline did not expect this of me in order for her to love me. On the contrary, she wanted rest for me. This has always been a parable of God's acceptance of and love for me when I rest.

Jesus came teaching and preaching that the kingdom of heaven is here. His message came to a people who were weighed down by the law as it was minutely interpreted to regulate every small and large act of each day's living. The lawyers, scribes, and Pharisees enforced these rules and regulations of life. A person was in or out of the grace and approval of God, they were told (and they believed), in terms of the way he or she did or did not keep these rules. Their very religion had become an enslavement similar to their slavery in Egypt. Jesus said to the Pharisees and their lawyers:

> But woe to you Pharisees! for you tithe mint and rue and every herb, and neglect justice and the love of God; these you ought to have done, without neglecting the others. . . . Woe to you lawyers also! for you load men with burdens hard to bear, and you yourselves do not touch the burdens with one of your fingers. (Luke 11:42, 46)

In his own ministry to people carrying such burdens, Jesus said, "Come to me, all who labor and are heavy laden, and I will give you rest" (Matt. 11:28). They were to rest from the grinding load of the official religion of their land and lives. They were to be free of its weight. As Paul said, the letter of the law kills, but the Spirit gives life. Jesus invited people to follow his way of grace and love, to take his yoke upon them and to learn from him, for he was gentle and lowly in heart, and they would find rest for their lives. For his yoke was easy and his burden light (Matt. 11:29–30).

He demonstrated this in his leadership of his disciples. They traveled through Samaria. In the heat of the day, they came to a well. While the disciples went for food, Jesus, "wearied as he was with his journey, sat down beside the well" at high noon (John 4:6). The Son of God got tired! When he did, he sat down to rest! In turn he taught his disciples to do likewise. After they returned from a journey and a work on which he had sent them, they "told him all that they had done and taught. And he said to them, 'Come away by yourselves to a lonely place, and rest a while.' For many were coming and going, and they had no leisure even to eat" (Mark 6:30–31).

You know people today for whom the Christian religion has been legislated into a massive burden of rules, regulations, and laws. You yourself may be such a person. I have occasion to see many people whose religion has become a fear-laden burden. Think of those who, in spite of having lived scrupulous, exemplary lives, do not believe or feel that they are "saved." If such persons are Protestant, they are likely to attend revival after revival and make confession of faith after confession of faith. If they are Catholic, they may go from church to church all in the same day and make confession. These persons carry their religion as an exhausting burden.

Then, again, think of those people who outwardly seem just the opposite of the overly conscientious people I have just described. Inwardly, however, they see their religious memories the same way—as a grievous burden. These persons have compulsively cast aside the external restraints of their religion and have become compulsive in their sexual behavior, in their greed for money, in their use of drugs and alcohol, and in their flaunting and ridiculing of all religion. In a curiously reverse way, they are exchanging one burden for another.

Or think of those who have been through a divorce, although they have been taught by their religion that to be divorced and remarried is to live life in adultery forever. To such persons, religion has become a curse rather than a blessing, a burden rather than a renewal and rest. They live their lives with the tacit assumption that they have committed an unpardonable sin.

To all these persons and many more like them the words of Jesus are good news. "Come to me, all who labor and are heavy laden, and I will give you rest" (Matt. 11:28). He gives rest from the unyielding grip of our compulsions. He gives rest from the fear that clutches us. "For God hath not given us the spirit of fear; but of power, and of love, and of a sound mind" (2 Tim. 1:7). The perfect love of God in Christ casts out fear.

My point is that the religious lawyers of the churches of all varieties today have taken the gospel of Christ and made of it a burden of law devoid of grace and wisdom, empty of compassion. Through brainwashing procedures they have bound heavy burdens upon timid people and do not raise a finger to help anyone bear them.

You need not be intimidated any longer by these religious lawyers. Faith in Christ's invitation to rest in his way of grace, wisdom, compassion, and freeing love is the gift he extends to you.

Therefore, both in creation and by command of God in Christ, you are given the gift of rest and commanded to partake of rest as our common grace. We rest in God's approval and in Christ's instruction. Thanks be to God for the renewing gift of rest!

NOTE

1. Ninian Smart, quoted in Geoffrey Wainwright, *Doxology: The Praise of God in Worship, Doctrine, and Life* (New York: Oxford University Press, 1980), pp. 81–82.

36

Some Prizes
of the Struggle to Be Free

The struggle to be free is not a meaningless or ambiguous fight for the love of fighting. Yet I must confess that it was a long time before I could distinguish between the struggle for survival and the struggle to be free. I did not learn quickly to live serenely in the strength of the convictions given to me through the grace of God and nurtured in silence through the power and companionship of the Spirit of God. Now, however, out of the complexity of human life have emerged some vital convictions; and these are to me "prizes" of the struggle to be free. These prizes are available to everyone, and many gifted persons I know well seem to have them as native endowments. Yet who knows? They too may have won these gifts through severe struggles to be free persons in the power of the Spirit of God. You may find the prizes I name to be aspirations of your own for which any amount of struggle would be worth the effort. Let me enumerate some of the convictions and gifts that I treasure as prizes of my own struggle to be free.

THE PRIZE OF COVENANT LIVING AND RESPONSIBLE FREEDOM

The first conviction that has become a prize for me is this: To be human at its best is to make mutual covenants with other people and to keep them faithfully. A covenant is mutual. Otherwise, it is not a covenant at all. It is an effort to please, appease, obligate, or even to manipulate or be manipulated by the other person.

Earlier, I spoke of the tyranny of one-way covenants in relationship to other people. Because we are human, our freedom is a finite and necessity-bound freedom. My struggle to be free has been to push back the

489

unnecessary, externally and internally imposed constrictions of my free-dom—constrictions not set by God in the bounds of habitation. In relation to God and to man, to break such bonds was, is, and will be a categorical imperative for me.

The surest way to increase and exercise my freedom under God is to live by covenants, accept the disciplines of the covenants I make, and enjoy the exalting sense of freedom of having faithfully fulfilled these covenants. This is the way to live the life of ethical love. To resist the exploitation of one-way covenants is to live the life of justice. To go the second mile when others break their covenants with me is to live the life of forgiveness and mercy. To seek quickly the forgiveness of those with whom I have broken a covenant is to live the life of confession and restitution. The very nature of all these dimensions of covenant living is the freedom that comes out of deep reciprocity with God and our fellow persons.

We often quote the passage "The truth shall make you free." We engrave it in stone on public buildings built to last a thousand years. Yet in few instances does truth make you free, except to pose new dilemmas in which you will choose or not choose to discipline yourself to freedom. The truth of nuclear fission has not made us free; we are muscle-bound by the power it has given us. We are gripped by the "blink" we wait for in the eye of adversaries when we confront them. We haggle in the bonds of indeci-sion because we have more power than wisdom with which to handle it. We bankrupt national treasuries to keep a power that, once released, would destroy not only others but ourselves as well. The truth in this case and in many others is merely the key to a Pandora's box of restrictions of our freedom.

The unrestricted promise that the truth will make us free suggests a one-way, undisciplined covenant. Jesus never promised such freedom. To the contrary, he posed a *two-way* covenant. Notice the whole context from which this sentence is taken in John 8:31–32: "Jesus then said to the Jews who had believed in him, 'If you continue in my word, you are truly my disciples, and you will know the truth, and the truth will make you free.'" The "if" in Jesus' words embodies a commitment, an intent, a relationship, and a discipline (inseparable from "disciple"). Freedom is the fruit of the discipleship, not simply a matter of collecting true facts about the universe. Our problem is, as Robert Frost said in his poem "A Cabin in the Clear-ing," that we have lived "in the fond faith [that] accumulated fact will of itself take fire and light the world up."

My personal credo is embodied in the totality of the words of Jesus: If knowledge of facts apart from this kind of relationship and discipline—which runs through the highest wisdom of other *living* religions as well—does "light the world up," it may well be a holocaust of the whole world in nuclear stupidity, not the gentle rays of the sun, and certainly not the Light of the World from the eternal God.

THE PRIZE OF BEING A CITIZEN
OF THE UNIVERSE

Many of the struggles to be free I have described in this story of mine are struggles with the uncertainties of the institutions of our world—schools, churches, professions, and the state. When news came of the death of Leonid Brezhnev, president of the Soviet Union, I could not but be impressed with the way we as Americans and they as Soviets live without knowing each other. Yet when death strikes, the finality of it pushes us as a nation to visit them in their grief. Such visits are as eerie in their way as the space walks of the astronauts. Death and space walks remind us, if but for a short time, that the "worlds" we hasten back to are really "flat earths" to us.

One of the great prizes of the struggle to be free, especially in the context of the redemption we have in Jesus Christ, is to be liberated from the flat earths of human relationships and to become citizens of the universe. Each institution or revolution was originally established to meet a specific set of needs. The longer it survives, the more it develops a life of its own and becomes an end in itself. The institution itself becomes a world unto itself, and its members' awareness of anything *beyond* the boundaries of the institution becomes dimmer and dimmer. In effect, it becomes a "flat earth" beyond the edges of which is an abyss. Then conflicts break out because of the insulated, unventilated environment in which people rebreathe the same air, rethink the same ideas, rehash the same conflicts, and rehearse the wrongs of others.

Before intrepid explorers challenged the idea that the world was flat, certain coins of Mediterranean countries carried a picture of the Pillars of Hercules and the inscription *Ne plus ultra*—"There is nothing beyond." After the discovery that the earth is round, and that new worlds existed, the coins read: *Plus ultra*—"There is more beyond."

In the last several years I have observed the same unventilated, flat-earth thinking that I had seen earlier—and hear about now—in other denominations than my own, in other seminaries, in medical schools, in churches, in social service organizations, and in government agencies. People are a part of the "in" group or a part of the "out" group; there are those on the "enemies lists" who get nothing they want. The "fair-haired ones" get everything they want and can do no wrong. Yet the whole system is in a state of entropy because there is no reinvigoration and growth by interaction with other systems. If the system is a family shut off from the world, that family is most likely to be one in which child abuse and spouse

491

abuse take place or in which incest occurs. Whereas abuse becomes actual in the family, it becomes symbolic or metaphorical in schools, churches, and hospitals. Students, church members, and patients become incidental or nonessential while the intra-institutional entropy prevails. After all, students, church members, and patients are from "another world." They do not belong to the settlement. They are means, not ends in themselves.

The prize of discovering the galaxies of worlds beyond my own provincial "flat earths" is a treasure to me, also. Freedom from flat-earth thinking makes one a citizen of the universe. Without this freedom, much of what professionals are fond of calling "burnout" happens. According to *The Morrow Book of New Words,* burnout is "a point in time or in a missile trajectory when the combustion of fuels in the rocket engine is terminated by other than programmed cut-off."[1] The "programmed cut-off" would be the original mission. "Burnout" would be the result of the power source being cut off by something other than the original plan.

If we use this as a metaphor of what happens where there is flat-earth thinking, we would say simply that the institution has lost touch with its basic mission. A church, a hospital, a school is in the world to minister and not to be ministered unto. The ones that reach out go beyond their own pillars of Hercules to interact with the rest of the world and the rest of the worlds. There are galaxies of universes beyond our own little staked-out terra firma. To have access to the galaxies is the intention of God in Jesus Christ.

Very early in my career, Gaines Dobbins cautioned me to have many relationships, not just those in the job where I happened to be. Thus I maintained a consultantship with the School of Medicine for twenty-six years while teaching in the Baptist Seminary. I was a visiting professor at Union Theological Seminary in New York for two winters and eleven summers. I was an adjunct professor at Earlham School of Religion in Richmond, Indiana, for three years. I was a summer session teacher at Vanderbilt Divinity School and a visiting professor at Princeton Theological Seminary. Yes, there were other worlds. I dimly knew. However, it did not hit me as breathtaking good news until I joined forces with medical students, theological students, psychiatric residents, and graduate students in theology in reaching out to psychotic, suicidal, depressed, and poverty-ridden hordes of patients in our inner-city charity hospital. Then I realized that though I was only a block away from the preclinical students and a few dozen blocks away from two very fine theological schools, in fact I was as if on another planet. I was really out of that world. But God was very much present. Yet even where I was I had inherently the flat-earth possibility. I am grateful that I did not have to wait to die to be free—free at last from the company stores, plantation offices, and flat earths of this world. In one's disfranchisement from the world, freedom is the gift of God's bounty. Access to the galaxies of many systems of human kinship is a cherished prize of the struggle to be free, the intention of God for you and me from the time we were formed in our mother's womb.

THE PRIZE OF FREEDOM IN RELATION
TO POWER

Another treasure trove gained in my struggle to be free is a recently found freedom in the use of power in relation to fellow humans and to God. You may find yourself trapped in what Bonaro Overstreet used to call "over-under" relationships. You feel oppressed. You may be in what is an "out" relationship to your particular power structure. You feel ostracized. Or you may be on the "inside" of the power structure and feel an uneasy sense of false security. You feel apprehensive. To be free of oppression, ostracism, and apprehension is a prize indeed. This freedom is to be found in two relationships to power: power at the center of things and power from the periphery.

Power at the Center of Things. In his *Politics,* Aristotle wrote that "every community is established with a view to some good; for mankind always acts in order to obtain that which they think is good."[2] I assume that the place where the struggle for power occurs between members of the community is at the divergence of their opinions as to what they think is good. Therein lies the risk.

Power is creative when it is seen as the acceptance, and faithful discharge, of responsibility. Power brings the obligation for decision making in behalf of the common good. Power is transmitted in the skilled craftsman's tools that saw wood or metal; it is seen in engines that can move earth or lift a plane from the ground. Power can energize creativity and discharge responsibility to do a job. Power becomes demonic, however, when it is used to posture, pose, or set oneself apart from and over others; to embellish a public image; to form an imperial coterie of one's "palace guards."

Martin Luther applied this whole set of distinctions to the clergyperson when he said, "Every clergyman in the church . . . should first of all clearly distinguish between himself and his office." Luther's observation about clergy is similar to the comment of Harry Truman concerning the Presidency. He said that the playing of "Hail to the Chief" and the firing of a twenty-one gun salute were not for Harry Truman. They were for the Presidency. He said that the President who got the feeling they were for *him* was headed for trouble.

These reflections and interpretations give substance to my sense of freedom in the use of power, particularly by a Christian, in whatever context I work. More specifically, they apply to the use of power at the center of a church, a hospital, a school, or the state.

A Chinese proverb states my point of view: "If you have to have it, you can't have it; if you don't have to have it, it is yours." "It" can be anything in the proverb, but here I refer to "having to have" an office or position of power at the center of things as if your whole life depended upon it, as if it is your manifest destiny, right, and privilege to have this position of power. Offices in churches, schools, or the state are like bread, shelter, and clothing for a family. Such a necessity is one of the "givens" of life. However, to take the figure a step farther, this does not give the office-holder the right to lord it over the other members of the family. If you or I hold such offices, we have a responsibility to pull our share of the load and to stay out of a permanent adversary position with "the powers that be." The "lording it over" stance spawns adversarial personalities and locks us into a "siege mentality."

My own attitude to "power at the center" positions has been that I will do such work as a *necessity* for the common good, but as a burden and not as a personal pleasure. I like the salty commitment of Harry Truman: "As always, I am just trying to do the job I am supposed to do, and a lot of times in public service, that is an unusual procedure, so it causes comment."[3] As soon as possible, I would get myself out of office after my job had been accomplished. To seek, to run for, to maneuver to get such positions tends to reduce, if not destroy, the function the position calls for. It obligates you to timeservers who later try to "collect" their political debts.

National politics has a built-in adversarial system that is sometimes effective but ordinarily not. In a Christian institution, however, the adversarial system is wrong. To stay in such a position perpetually vitiates our own morale. Worse than that, it calls for attitudes and behaviors that are antithetical to the Christian witness. As we are increasingly persuaded to fight fire with fire in behaviors similar to those of our adversary, we become in the end like that which we hate. If we are to be at the center of the power system, by necessity then, I think we can best do so by seeing our position as a time-limited function (six years at the most) and not as a perpetual end in itself.

The desire to stay at the center of a power structure over a lifetime is really an outworking of our need for perpetuity, that is, to project ourselves beyond our death, to have arms that reach back from the grave and continue to shape events. This seems to be more than a subtle preoccupation of Presidents of the United States.

Power from the Periphery. Another creative way of relating to the power structure is from the periphery. Bernard Baruch, who was noted for holding park-bench consultations with government leaders in Washington, stated it best when he said that he had only a park-bench interest in administration. Paul Tillich, in his autobiographical sketch, writes: "I thought that the concept of the boundary might be a fitting symbol for the whole of my personal and intellectual development. At almost every point, I have had to stand between alternative possibilities of existence, to be completely at home in neither and to take no definitive stand against either." He speaks of being between two temperaments, between social classes, between reality and imagination, between theory and practice, between church and society, between idealism and Marxism, between a native and an alien land. And he adds: "The boundary is the best place for acquiring knowledge."[4] These are two ways of describing what I mean by the peripheral existence.

I have learned from Aldous Huxley a third interpretation of being peripherally related to power. Let me quote his words:

> It is not at the center, not from within the organization, that the saint can cure our regimented insanity; it is only from without, at the periphery. If he makes himself a part of the machine, in which the collective madness is incarnated, one or the other of two things is bound to happen. Either he remains himself, in which case the machine will use him as long as it can and, when he becomes unusable, reject or destroy him. Or he will be transformed into the likeness of the mechanism with and against which he works, and in this case we shall see Holy Inquisitions and alliances with any tyrant prepared to guarantee ecclesiastical privileges.[5]

In my present situation I live on the boundary between science and religion, the rational and the nonrational, the medical establishment and the theological establishment, the rich and the poor, the powerful and the helpless. I affect somewhat the process of theological education and that of medical education. I am vitally related to both but at the periphery of each as its boundaries come together with the boundaries of the other.

I observe closely and at first hand many conflicts of power between federal, state, county, city, and private corporate interests where large amounts of money are involved. I listen intently and with great concern to competing ideologies within medicine and within the inner workings of at least five different denominations. At times I am sought as a consultant by the military on educational, morale, and chaplaincy matters. Yet I am not responsible for the outcome of any of these matters. For example, I am influential and effective in the diagnosis, treatment, patient management, and convalescent care of many sick people. The primary responsibility for the outcome, however, is in the hands of the physician. I am glad that this is so, because I affect the process from the periphery and not from the center.

The tools of ministry of the peripheral person are friendly persuasion, "no strings attached" wisdom, and an expertise wrought out of years of experience. It could well be that the prize of living a peripheral existence comes from a long-demonstrated competence that gives integrity to seniority. It may also be that the peripherally effective person is one who has made a lifework of forming and maintaining steadfast relationships to people who have that same vocation in life. In other words, the friendly persuasiveness and influence are *not* just my prerogatives as an individual. I am only one expression of the organism, power, and weight of being of what Elton Trueblood calls "the company of the committed."

Apparently, then, the church is an organism rather than an organization of special interest groups, however worthy the interest may be. The church is a reality in which the Holy Spirit is the *center* of power. All of us are at the periphery of the sovereignty of God. His Spirit knits together the influence of many people of clean hands and pure hearts, whose souls have not been lifted up to vanity, and who have not sworn deceitfully. Good judgment, justice, and the loving-kindness of God break through.

In this sense, all of us in the family and the church can share the prize of being persons of peripheral influence. We can be spoken of in the marketplace as people who do not have any ax to grind, as "free spirits," as persons with no vested interest. As we are more formally involved somewhat away from the periphery, we may be called "consultants," although that word has of late become more and more confusing and trite. In the life of local churches, one of the most recurrent forms of the persons of peripheral power is the "interim pastor," one who does not *want* the position of permanent pastor. He or she serves as a temporary pastoral leader, worship leader, preacher, and "no strings attached" adviser to the congregation—while they look for a pastor.

You may well say that such a stance of peripheral function is possible only after long tenure in working your way up the totem pole of prestige. You may be right. But I think it comes from something more than just climbing a bureaucratic ladder. I am confident that the prize of freedom in relation to power comes from intentionally forming deep relationships to people on a face-to-face basis—"mid good report and evil report"—over however many or few years it may take. It comes from *steadfastness* of trust-based relationships when the going gets rough. It comes from "taking a stand with the pieces" in transient conflicts between people and within institutions until a true-healing takes place. This takes patience and stubbornness to stick with some very difficult situations. More than that, it takes a sense of humor that sees the absurd in most of the things people carry as grudges all their lives. At base it calls for being angry appropriately when provoked to wrath, but being quick to reconcile before the sun goes down on your wrath. Finally, it calls for being kind and tenderhearted to one another, and forgiving one another as God for Christ's sake forgave us. Just such an attitude has a humorous side effect. If your adversaries think they can get rid of you permanently, they are likely to do so. However, if they find out that they have to live with you, they are more likely to find a way of peace.

THE PRIZE OF MINISTRY TO THE "BROKEN ONES"

Many years ago, amid the wreckage of a severe institutional conflict of personalities, I was asked, "Where do you stand in all of this?" My reply was, "With the pieces." One of the prizes "of the upward call of God in Christ Jesus" (Phil. 3:14) is my privilege and yours to take a stand with the pieces of human hearts in shattered covenants, hopes, and relationships. In my own life the struggle to be free, to find an integrity of my own being in the middle of the brokenness of my family and community, has been a work of equipping myself to minister to the broken ones.

Such a ministry calls for a capacity to see through one's own tears and beyond the tears of others to find fresh new alternatives to futility. It calls for an ingenuity to find a new design and organization in the disarray of the pieces of people's lives.

Our son Bill gave me a parable for the ministry to broken lives in an event that happened to him when he was five. I brought him a little balsa-wood airplane. The propeller was driven by a long, strong rubber band which, when twisted and allowed to unwind, would turn the propeller and cause the plane to fly. Bill enjoyed this toy out of doors, but one evening he was flying it in the basement. He let it go and it smashed to pieces against the wall. He cried profusely, and I went to him from upstairs to see what was wrong. By the time I reached him, he had ceased to cry and a grin of discovery was on his face. He said, "Daddy, I smashed my plane, but I know what I can do about it. I can make me a slingshot out of that big rubber band." Human heartbreak is painful; discovery of how to rebound with a creative alternative for the pieces of broken dreams is the exercise of freedom that leads to consolation and from there to the joy of creativity.

We must "sit with" the depressed person, listen with empathy, and even give medical attention for the ravages of the depression upon his or her body. As we do these things, we find that the depressed person can see only *one* way out of his or her pain. It may be to quit a job, to break up a marriage, to "go limp" in total helplessness and be a mental patient the rest of his or her life, or, at worst, to commit suicide. All the while, the pastoral counselor, the family members, and the physician are trying to inspire the person to consider at least one or two, and maybe three, ways of putting life back together again.

Another parable comes to me from our son Bill when he was about six years old. After he was all through taking his bath one evening, he was diligently working with the drain device. I asked him what he was doing. He replied, "Daddy, I have figured out *sixteen* ways to fix this thing if it gets broken." One was not enough! He had to have fifteen more.

Getting closed up to *one* solution for a problem brings you and me to despair when that one approach fails. The capacity to generate fresh alternatives is a perennial power toward freedom within the limits of our habitation. One of the refreshing prizes of my years of struggle to be free is to engage in what Jürgen Moltmann calls "the experiment hope" with grief-stricken, brokenhearted, and depressed persons whom I encourage and inspire to figure out "sixteen ways" of repairing the damage to their lives. The psalmist expressed it best:

> Fill me with joy and gladness;
>   let the bones which thou hast broken rejoice. . . .
> The sacrifice acceptable to God is a broken spirit;
>   a broken and contrite heart, O God, thou wilt not despise.
>   (Ps. 51:8, 17)

Of all the "sixteen ways to fix this thing if it is broken," making a sacrifice of the broken spirit to God is the first move toward wholeness. The unmixed joy of being a pastor to people in this "experiment hope" offsets and neutralizes the perplexities and ambiguities that attend the task when our own tragic sense of life would otherwise overcome me. This un-mixed joy is one of the prizes of the struggle to be free.

THE PRIZE OF SHARING THE WEIGHT
OF THE TRAGIC SENSE OF LIFE

I have spent the past eight years of my life working in a large inner-city charity hospital, the central teaching hospital of the University of Louisville School of Medicine. It is a trauma emergency center; residents and medical students in their junior and senior years are the first line of service to people with "all manner of diseases." Raw green recruits they are, and they are accompanied by equally green theological students who are equally scared. The years of my own struggle to be free seem to have created for me an ambience that makes it easy for these physicians and pastors in the making to share with me the weight of their own tragic sense of life. As they fight delaying actions and often losing battles for the lives of cardiac patients and victims of collisions, gunshot wounds, suicidal overdoses, and stubbornly unresponsive psychotic deterioration of personality, I see them throw their whole energies into the battle.

When our son Charles was a third-year student at the School of Medicine where I teach, he lost a patient for whom he and his team of medical students were caring. She was a woman in her thirties, the mother of two children, and a widow. Charles and his colleagues had come to respect her very much. They went home one evening thinking she was well on the way to recovery, but that night she died suddenly. When he came to work and learned that she had suddenly died, he was overwhelmed with grief. He felt that he had not been the kind of doctor he should have been. He said, "I don't think I would want me for a physician."

I said that he was a physician in the making and should not carry the whole burden of blame. A streptococcus infection had apparently taken her life. A few days later, as I was leaving the city, I called him to tell him where I was going and said to him, "Your brother went to Vietnam and that was his hell on earth to go through. Now I guess this is your hell to go through. I'll go through it with you, too." He said, "No, Dad, I don't think we are going *through* hell. We are just getting accustomed to the heat." Then I said, "Harry Truman said that if we can't stand the heat, we should get out of the kitchen." Then Charles's humor took over. He said, "Dad, I *think* Teddy Roosevelt said that first." We laughed, and I said, "When we get the time, we will have to research that one."

The discipline of caring for others has its casualties. Yet we exercise our freedom by descending into hell with the good news of health and hope. "Hell" here is not a lightly used swear word; it is the experience of grappling with the issues of life and death. The gates of hell cannot hold out against someone who does this in the name of the crucified and risen Christ. To me, one of the prizes of my struggle to be free is to have the privilege of descending into the nethermost regions of the human spirit with my colleagues in these dire and crucial human situations. Had I not been ushered into the freedom for which Christ has set us free, I would not be able to do so.

THE PRIZE OF DREAMING WITH YOUNG PERSONS OF VISION

Finally, one of the most renewing prizes of my struggle to be free is the opportunity of dreaming dreams with young persons who have visions. I know that very early in life we can become enchanted with what someone has called "the habitual vision of greatness." I never lack for a steady stream of young persons who have a vision of what they want to become that is greater than what they are now. The level of their aspirations is attainable, but not without a struggle with those forces which would keep them from reaching their goal. And they may not be able to reach that level of aspiration without encouragement from some veteran who has not forgotten the visions of his or her own youth. They need the encouragement of someone who has to a reasonable degree fulfilled those aspirations but is not without dreams, in the still of the night, of what the struggle was like. Hence, you or I become mentors even as we were given mentors by God; we become facilitators, even as some of God's most unlikely servants ran interference for us when we struck opposition and smoothed the way for us when the going was roughest.

The most poignant aspect of the prize of dreaming with young persons is to see those whose lives have been so blighted by disease and disaster that high aspirations no longer seem to exist. What they have left is fantasies that occasionally break through into words and escape more rapidly than they appeared and do not return. I sit with and hurt with and for these too. My time is not wasted. Yet I come away filled with sadness for those with visions snuffed out, angry that their jaws have been lowered, their eyes glazed, and their bodily movements thrown into slow motion, even sometimes before they were out of their teens or far into their twenties.

These are, thank God, the exceptions and not the rule. Hope and joy come with those who have stacks of poems they have written; portfolios of art they want me to see; a song with lyrics and music blended; a plan for a book that has not been written before, insofar as we can discover; a project for starting a new kind of ministry of the gospel to a particular group of people whose sufferings have isolated them from the mainstreams of life. Here they come! No one organized their coming; no special package was prepared for the crowds like them. There is no crowd like them! Their visions are like solitaire diamonds in settings all their own.

We sit together in my office, or in my study at home, or at a lunch table in a crowded cafeteria at the hospital, or in their hospital rooms where they are patients, or at a convention where we "connect back up" after years of not seeing each other daily. I ask, "Will you catch me up on what you are into these days? What new things are you seeing?" The time flies and I forget about anything but what they are telling me. They punch my memory for associations as if it were a computer. My mind prints out past thoughts, new associations, bibliographies, and names of people who also can share their visions. Suddenly we are propelled out of the gravity of the particular world in which we started. Drawn into a new realm of being, we are orbiting to the music of the spheres of new thought. Then I return to my meditations at home after our conference is over and thank God that the prophet Joel's words, quoted by Peter at Pentecost, have come true:

> And in the last days it shall be, God declares,
> that I will pour out my Spirit upon all flesh,
> and your sons and your daughters shall prophesy,
> and your young men shall see visions,
> and your old men shall dream dreams.
>
> (Acts 2:17)

What prizes of the struggle to be free!

NOTES

1. N. H. and S. K. Mager, eds., *The Morrow Book of New Words* (New York: William Morrow & Co., 1982), p. 41.

2. Aristotle, *Politics* 1.1.

3. Harry Truman, quoted in William Hillman, *Mr. President* (New York: Farrar, Straus & Young, 1952), p. 217.

4. Paul Tillich, *On the Boundary: An Autobiographical Sketch* (New York: Charles Scribner's Sons, 1966), p. 13.

5. Aldous Huxley, *Ape and Essence* (New York: Harper & Brothers, 1948), pp. 8–9.

Epilogue

I have affirmed that to live creatively is to struggle to be free. Yet to be free lays upon you and me the responsibility and the discipline that inhere in the freedom that comes to us. To accept that responsibility and that discipline creates a zone of joy in our existence. We then fulfill the chief end of our existence, which is to glorify God and to enjoy God's love and presence. Not to accept that disciplined responsibility is to lose our own sense of integrity and our awareness of fellowship with God.

The end result of the freedom within responsible discipline is the rediscovery of a certain playfulness of being, a certain childlikeness—quite another thing than childishness. The latter has been put away in behalf of maturity. Yet that maturity, with all its awareness of finitude and limitation, has a playfulness that defies limits. As William Blake says in his *Auguries of Innocence,* the rediscovered playfulness enables you and me

> To see a world in a grain of sand
> And a heaven in a wild flower,
> Hold infinity in the palm of your hand
> And eternity in an hour.

This kind of vision seems to be a given grace of the little children like whom Jesus told us we must become if we are to enter the kingdom of heaven. I used to wonder what Robert Browning meant when he spoke of "the last of life, for which the first was made." I do not know what it meant to Browning, unless he meant for each reader to do as I am doing—supply his or her own meaning. Until recently I could not do that. Now it seems to me that the childlikeness of which Jesus spoke is a "given" in childhood but is the father of the results of a lifelong struggle to be free in adulthood. As

Erik Erikson puts it: "For the pre-senile years, with all their unavoidable *despair* and *disgust,* I have postulated the strength of a simple *integrity* which is directly perceived by children; wherefore old people and children feel an affinity for each other."[1] Hence he adjures us to avoid the unwise pretense of being wise, which he calls "sapientism."

The years of later maturity for me, then, I pray, will be years of magic laughter at the multitude of things, behaviors of other people, and tides of human politics that are beyond our control, and of canny alertness to those situations which, with a little bit of luck and a massive demonstration of Providence, we can actually do something about.

In between these extremes may we recapture something of the sense of childlikeness which Selma H. Fraiberg calls "the magic years." I was playing with our four-year-old grandson, Will, the other day. He loves to use our king-size bed as a trampoline. This time his feet were dirty, and I asked him to let me first wash his feet. Then he could jump on the bed.

I took a warm and wet washcloth and washed his feet. Then I took the cloth to the bathroom to wash the dirt out of it. When I returned, Will was gone. I assumed he had gone out of the bedroom. Hence, I went about hanging a suit up and placing some shoes in the closet.

Suddenly he jumped behind the bed where he had been hiding. I reacted with great surprise, saying, "Where on earth did you come from, and how did you get in this room?" He said: "I came through that wall right there!" I said, "Well, I don't see any hole in the wall." He said, "I know. I fixed it back just like it was and painted it this color," pointing to a special color in the wallpaper. "And," he said, "if you will touch it with your finger, you will see that it's still wet paint." I reached and touched it with my finger and looked at my finger and said, "My goodness! You're right! It *is* still wet!" At that point both of us broke into hilarious laughter together. What fun! What magic!

It may well be that the joyful meeting of children and older persons in the magic years of imagination and shared freedom is the secret that enables some older persons to take a fresh new growth and spontaneous renewal without which many others decide that life is over, fold up, and die. I am persuaded that there is a biochemistry present in our body that corresponds with the laughter my grandson and I share. Whether there is or not, I know that his and my laughter made me *want* to live for many years to come. Life seems only to have begun in the ecstasy of such an event.

NOTE

1. Erik H. Erikson, *Toys and Reasons: Stages in the Ritualization of Experience* (New York: W. W. Norton & Co., 1977), p. 112.

Index of Scripture

Index of Persons

Index of Subjects